For Betsy, my best friend

Vera —

My best

[signature]

CONTENTS

Photographs follow pages 110, 270

ACKNOWLEDGMENTS

Writing a book is never easy, and writing one in secret poses a special challenge. To avoid any possibility of leaks along the way, my publishers decided to treat this book as a covert operation.

To complete it, William Novak and I worked together by phone, by fax, and during a series of long meetings in a hotel room at Dulles International Airport. Just about every Monday, Bill would fly in with his laptop computer and book a ground-floor room with a back door opening onto the parking lot. Once he was settled, I would surreptitiously drive over to meet him. We always ordered lunch and dinner from room service, and when the waiter arrived with our meals, I hid in the bathroom. The poor guy must have concluded that this strange Mr. Novak, who always seemed to end up in the same room, was entertaining an imaginary friend.

The work was hard, but my sessions with Bill were both productive and fun. I appreciated his thoughtful attention to detail, his insightful questions, and perhaps most of all, his fine sense of humor. I'm also grateful to Linda Novak, who put up with our hectic schedule, offered many helpful suggestions, and even managed to produce a baby while her husband and I were finishing this book. Who says there are no more miracles?

Special thanks must go to Nicole Seligman, one of my lawyers at the firm of Williams & Connolly, whose help was essential.

And there were many others who helped me get this story out of the courtrooms and into the word processor.

My mother waded through old family albums and stacks of letters, and sat down with Bill and me to recall tales of my youth that I had long since forgotten—or tried to. My brothers, Jack and Tim, and our sister, Pat, pitched in with tidbits from our childhood.

Dick Bonneau, Mildred Johnson, Tom Gibbons, Bob Bowes, and Russ Robertson began contributing to this book more than thirty years ago, and helped me more than they can know.

A steadfast cadre from the Naval Academy supported me in ways too numerous to recount: Emerson Smith, Reid Olson, Bob Eisenbach, Bob Earl, and classmates Dewey Beliech, Jay Cohen, Mark Treanor, Phil Hough, and Tom Hayes.

From a long-ago war, several comrades-in-arms sought me out years later: Paul Goodwin, Bill Haskell, Richmond O'Neill, Bud Flowers, Art Vandervere, Eric Bowen, and John Rappuano. Of those who called themselves "Blue's Bastards," Wendell Thomas, Everett Whipple, Ernie Tuten, Randy Herrod, and Jim Lehnert helped me survive battles past and present.

Generals Lew Wilson, Robert Barrow, P. X. Kelley, and Tom Morgan gave new meaning to the phrase "band of brothers," as Marines like to call themselves. So, too, did Brigadier General Mike Sheridan, Lieutenant Colonel Pete Stenner, Major Gil Macklin, and Colonels Jack Holley and Larry Weeks. They were, in every sense of the phrase, *Semper Fidelis.*

When I left a quarter century of military service behind and started to hack my way into the civilian jungle, there were a handful of local guides who kept me on the path: Harry Rhodes and Bernie Swain of the Washington Speaker's Bureau; Ben Elliott, who helped me behind the scenes; Duane Ward, who got me to where I was supposed to be; and Jerry Dimenna and Dave Valinski, who kept me alive in the process.

This book could not have been finished without the help of Lieutenant General Ed Bronars and his wife, Dot, and Major General John Grinalds and his wife, Norwood. The Reverend Brian Cox helped me examine my Christian faith with clear eyes and a better understanding of how He is glorified when we persevere in adversity. And Thad Heath showed me how to live that kind of life.

I would have liked to thank David Jacobsen, Andy Messing, Ellen Garwood, and Ken deGraffenreid from my days at the NSC, and Joe Fernandez, Dewey Clarridge, George Cave, and several others from the CIA. But if I did, they would surely suffer for it.

Rich Miller and Jeb Spencer helped find and research material that no one else could locate. And Marsha Fishbaugh, my loyal secretary, made sure it all ended up in the right place.

At Williams & Connolly, Brendan Sullivan, Barry Simon, John Cline, Nicole Seligman, and Terry O'Donnell have been my staunch advocates and have become my friends. Their able assistants, Rhonda Ritchie, Brenda Lee, Lou Ann Taylor, and Betty Donahue Vannoy, have been invaluable throughout.

From the start, Rupert Murdoch had faith that we could put this book together quickly and quietly, and the HarperCollins team of Bill Shinker, Gladys Carr, Tom Miller, Jim Fox, Tracy Devine, and Jim Hornfischer helped make it happen. At Zondervan, Jim Buick, Stan Gundry, and Scott Bolinder were enormously helpful. Vincent Virga helped me dig through mountains of photographs to find just the right ones.

Most important of all were those who encouraged me every day: Betsy, and our children Tait, Stuart, Sarah, and Dornin—who gave up a lot of bedtime stories so I could write this one. Our children had some important allies in this campaign: Isabel Schmock, Margaret Esther Powell, Opal Rhodes, Isa Saliba, and Jamie Wheeler.

For their clandestine help, my thanks to Myrtle Farmosh, Ann Keene, Steve Axelrod, and especially Taren Metson.

Larry Walsh was no help at all.

CAST OF CHARACTERS

Abrams, Elliott: Assistant Secretary of State for Inter-American Affairs.

Allen, Charles E.: National Intelligence Officer for Counterterrorism, CIA.

Australian, The: Code name for Iranian official affiliated with Ghorbanifar.

Bandar, bin Sultan: Saudi prince, nephew of King Fahd and Ambassador to the United States.

Barnes, Michael: Democratic member, House of Representatives; Chairman of Subcommittee on Western Hemisphere Affairs.

Bermudez, Enrique: Military leader of the Nicaraguan resistance, Northern Front.

Boland, Edward P.: Democratic member, House of Representatives.

Buchanan, Patrick J.: Director of Communications, White House.

Buckley, William A.: CIA Station Chief in Lebanon. Buckley was seized in Beirut in 1984. He died, presumably under torture, in 1985.

Bush, George: Vice President of the United States, 1981–88.

Calero, Adolfo: A leader of the FDN (Nicaraguan Democratic Force), and Oliver North's primary contact among the Nicaraguan resistance.

Casey, William J.: Director of Central Intelligence and Director of the CIA, 1981–1987.

Cave, George: Former CIA officer who participated in negotiations with the Iranians.

Channell, Carl R. (Spitz): Founder of National Endowment for the Preservation of Liberty; fund raiser on behalf of Nicaraguan resistance.

Clark, William P.: President Reagan's National Security Adviser, 1982–83.

Clarridge, Duane (Dewey): CIA Clandestine Services Officer. Chief, Latin American Division, 1981–84; Chief, European Division, 1984-85; Chief, Counterterrorism, 1986–87.

Cline, John: Member of Oliver North's defense team.

Dutton, Robert C.: Retired Air Force colonel who worked for Richard Secord.

Fiers, Alan: Chief, Central American Task Force, CIA.

Furmark, Roy M.: Associate of Adnan Khashoggi and friend of William Casey.

Gadd, Richard: Retired Air Force lieutenant colonel who worked for Richard Secord.

Gates, Robert M.: Deputy Director of CIA, 1986.

George, Clair: Deputy Director for Operations, CIA.

Gesell, Gerhard A.: U.S. district court judge who presided at the trial of Oliver North.

Ghorbanifar, Manucher (Gorba): Iranian-born intermediary in arms sales to Iran by Israel and the United States.

Goode, William P.: Oliver North's U.S. government alias.

Grinalds, John, Major General, USMC: Oliver North's battalion commander, 1978–79.

Hakim, Albert: Iranian exile, business partner of Richard Secord.

Hall, Fawn: Oliver North's secretary.

Hall, Wilma: Robert McFarlane's secretary, Fawn Hall's mother.

Hamilton, Lee: Democratic member, House of Representatives; Chairman, House Permanent Select Committee on Intelligence.

Hasenfus, Eugene: American crewman shot down over Nicaragua on October 5, 1986.

Hussein, Saddam: Iraqi dictator.

Inouye, Daniel: Democratic senator from Hawaii.

Jacobsen, David: American hostage in Beirut, former director of American University Hospital in Beirut. On November 2, 1986, he became the third hostage released in the Iran initiative.

Jenco, Lawrence: American hostage in Beirut, Catholic priest. On July 26, 1986, he became the second American released in the Iran initiative.

Kelley, P. X., General, USMC: Commandant, United States Marine Corps, 1982–86.

Khamenei, Ali: President of Iran.

Khomeini, Ayatollah Ruhollah: Theocratic leader of Iran, 1979–89.

Kimche, David: Director General of Israeli Foreign Ministry, 1985–86.

Kirkpatrick, Jeane: United States Ambassador to the United Nations.

Kissinger, Henry: Former National Security Adviser and Secretary of State; head of President Reagan's National Bipartisan Commission on Central America, 1983.

Ledeen, Michael: Consultant to the National Security Council.

McFarlane, Robert C. (Bud): National Security Adviser, October 1983 to December 1985.

Meese, Edwin: Counselor to President Ronald Reagan, 1981–84; Attorney General of the United States, 1985–86.

Monster, The: Code name for Iranian official affiliated with Second Channel.

Moreau, Arthur, Admiral, USN: Special Assistant to the Chairman of the Joint Chiefs of Staff, 1984–85.

Mousavi, Mir Hussein: Prime Minister of Iran.

Nephew, The: Code name for the key Iranian in the Second Channel.

Nidal, Abu: Terrorist, head of Al Fatah Revolutionary Council.

Nir, Amiram: Adviser on counterterrorism to Israeli Prime Minister Shimon Peres.

O'Donnell, Terrence: Member of Oliver North's legal defense team.

Ortega, Daniel: President of Nicaragua, 1980–90.

Poindexter, John M., Vice Admiral, USN: Deputy National Security Adviser, 1983–85; National Security Adviser to President Reagan, 1986.

Qaddafi, Muammar al-: Libyan dictator.

Quintero, Raphael (Chi Chi): Former Cuban freedom fighter; former CIA officer; employee of Richard Secord, 1984–86.

Rafsanjani, Hashemi: Speaker of the Iranian Parliament.

Reagan, Ronald: President of the United States, 1981–88.

Regan, Donald T.: White House Chief of Staff, 1985–86.

Robinette, Glenn: Former CIA employee who installed security system at Oliver North's home.

Secord, Richard V., Major General, USAF (Retired): Head of contra resupply effort, 1984-86.

Seligman, Nicole: Member of Oliver North's legal defense team.

Shultz, George: Secretary of State, 1982–88.

Simon, Barry: Member of Oliver North's legal defense team.

Sullivan, Brendan: Not a potted plant.

Walsh, Lawrence: Special Prosecutor, 1986– .

Weinberger, Caspar: Secretary of Defense, 1981–88.

Weir, Rev. Benjamin: First American hostage in Beirut released as part of the Iran initiative (September 15, 1985).

UNDER FIRE

Foreword

For better or worse, most people's lives seem to turn out rather differently from what they had expected. Certainly mine has. When I first signed on with the Marine Corps in 1961, I never dreamed that I would ever serve in the upper echelons of government. And I surely never imagined that I would one day find myself at the center of a raging political controversy of historic proportions.

This book is my personal story. I will leave to others the task of producing the definitive history of Iran-contra—assuming that's even possible. The congressional investigators filled many volumes with reports and testimony, but I doubt that any one individual could possibly know the whole story. I was right in the middle of these events, and there are *still* things I don't know.

Although I refer often to "Iran-contra" in these pages, that phrase is really a misnomer. To be precise, "Iran-contra" covers two very different secret operations that were carried out by the Reagan administration in the mid-1980s. One of these was an attempt to develop an opening to the revolutionary government of Iran, an initiative that included the sale of arms to the Iranians, and a partially successful attempt to gain the release of the American hostages in Beirut. The other operation was a concerted effort to maintain American support for the Nicaraguan resistance after the United States Congress had forced the CIA to abandon the contras. These two projects were eventually linked by a financial connection, and also by the fact that several individuals, myself included, were involved in both operations.

In the chapters that follow, I portray certain episodes in my life that strike me as significant, and which surely affected my later activities at the National Security Council. I know, for example, that my experiences as a platoon commander in Vietnam colored my feelings about Central America in general and the contras in particular. And the way I was raised, and the values that were imparted to me over the years, certainly influenced my attitude about the American hostages in Beirut.

I don't ask the reader to endorse everything I did or failed to do. In the five years since I was fired, my detractors have often dramatized and exaggerated what really happened. But so have some of my supporters. While I certainly appreciate their endorsement, I am neither a saint nor a hero. I look back with pride on much of what we accomplished, but I also did things that I came to regret.

Although most of the events I describe took place within the past decade, the world began to change dramatically during the late 1980s. Most of Eastern Europe has now embraced the ideals of freedom and democracy, and Communism has shown itself to be the fatally flawed system that Ronald Reagan always insisted it was. I remember watching on television as the Berlin Wall came down. I had tears in my eyes, and Dornin, our youngest daughter, ran upstairs to say, "Mom, what's wrong with Daddy?"

Daddy was fine, of course; I was just overwhelmed by the moment. While I had known that these changes would come, I didn't really expect to witness them in my lifetime. I felt that way again in 1990, when, for the second time in eleven years, the people of Nicaragua rejected a brutal and corrupt regime. And yet again in August 1991, watching Boris Yeltsin stop a Soviet tank during the second Russian revolution.

During my five and a half years on the staff of the National Security Council, I spent much of my time working for the release of the American hostages held in Beirut. I have done some difficult things in my life, but nothing I've ever been involved with was as trying, or as painful, as this. Because of the obvious risks to the hostages and to certain individuals in other countries, most of this work was done in almost total secrecy. As I worked on this book and described some of these efforts, I prayed that by the time I was finished, all these men would be back with their families.

Those of us who served in the Reagan administration were privileged to be part of great changes. I fervently hope that these developments are permanent, and that the extraordinary events unfolding in

Eastern Europe, Central America, and what we used to call the Soviet Union will soon be visited upon places like Cuba, Iraq, Iran—and even Lebanon.

Much of this book portrays the individuals I worked with, both in and out of our government. Although I am critical of a few, most of those I am blessed to have known over the years are good and decent men and women. Like me, they were caught up in momentous events. And like me, they were sometimes less than perfect in responding to them.

Yet many of these people risked their lives and some lost them. Most can never be thanked publicly, honored for the contributions they made, or recognized for the incredible perils they faced. And though I have had to omit or change some of their names in this book, it is nonetheless a tribute to them.

O.L.N.
Narnia
September 16, 1991

1

"Relieved of His Duties"

Being fired is never a pleasant experience, which is why it's normally done behind closed doors. My own firing was handled rather differently. The room was packed, the doors were open, and millions of Americans were watching on television.

I was one of them.

On November 25, 1986, at five minutes past noon, President Ronald Reagan and Attorney General Edwin Meese marched into the crowded White House briefing room to face the press and the TV cameras. As I watched from my office in the Old Executive Office Building, the President explained that he hadn't been told the whole story of our secret arms sales to Iran, and that he had asked the Attorney General to look into the matter. He then announced that Admiral John Poindexter, his national security adviser, had resigned, and that Lieutenant Colonel Oliver North had been "relieved of his duties on the National Security Council staff."

What?

Before I could catch my breath, the President turned over the microphones to Attorney General Meese and left the room.

Then Ed Meese dropped the bomb: "In the course of the arms transfer, which involved the United States providing the arms to Israel and Israel, in turn, transferring the arms—in effect, selling the arms—

to representatives of Iran, certain monies which were received in the transaction between representatives of Israel and representatives of Iran were taken and made available to the forces in Central America who are opposing the Sandinista government there."

In plain language, some of the profits from the arms sales to Iran had gone to the Nicaraguan resistance, also known as the contras. It took a moment before the reporters figured out what Meese had said, and the White House press corps actually fell silent for a second or two. Then the barrage began.

Did the President know about this?
Meese: The President knew nothing about it until I reported it to him.
What?
Well, then, who did know?
Meese: The only person in the United States government that knew precisely about this, the only person, was Lieutenant Colonel North.
What?!
Meese: Admiral Poindexter knew that something of this nature was occurring, but he did not look into it further.... CIA Director Casey, Secretary of State Shultz, Secretary of Defense Weinberger, myself, the other members of the NSC—none of us knew.
What?!
"What Colonel North did," somebody asked—"is that a crime? Will he be prosecuted?"
Meese: We are presently looking into the legal aspects of it as to whether there's any criminality involved.
Criminality?!

For the past three weeks, ever since our Iran initiative had been exposed in *Al-Shiraa*, a Beirut magazine, the administration's strategy had been unspoken but unmistakable: *this must not become another Watergate*. Although Watergate had involved several violations of the law, most Americans believed that the most serious offense of all—and the one that eventually led to President Nixon's resignation—was not the burglary itself, but the cover-up.

And so in November 1986, somebody—probably Donald Regan, the White House chief of staff, and Nancy Reagan—decided that whatever had or hadn't happened in this case, there could not be even the hint of a cover-up. Before the news media could cause any damage, the White House itself would disclose the story.

It is a fundamental rule of politics that whoever gets his side of the story out first is usually able to set the agenda for the ensuing discussion. While the effort to realize the benefit of this "rule" was certainly true here, the administration did not reveal the "diversion" (as it soon came to be known) solely for strategic reasons. They disclosed it because three days earlier, when the Attorney General learned about it from a memo that was found in my office (and which I thought I had destroyed), he was terrified that if this story came out first in the press, like Watergate, it could lead to extraordinary political problems for President Reagan.

Like impeachment.*

The administration chose to focus almost exclusively on the "diversion," and there was certainly a lot to be gained by presenting it that way. This particular detail was so dramatic, so sexy, that it might actually—well, *divert* public attention from other, even more important aspects of the story, such as what *else* the President and his top advisers had known about and approved. And if it could be insinuated that this supposedly terrible deed was the exclusive responsibility of one mid-level staff assistant at the National Security Council (and perhaps his immediate superior, the national security adviser), and that

---

*It wasn't until my trial in 1989, when he was questioned by Brendan Sullivan, my lawyer, that Attorney General Meese revealed how seriously he had taken the possibility of impeachment:

> *Sullivan:* In fact, your assessment of the time was that unless something was done, a strong response, that the merging of those two factors [Iran and the contras] could very well cause the possible toppling of the President himself, correct?
> *Meese:* Yes.
> *Sullivan:* And there was discussion, in fact, on the days November 23rd and 24th that unless the administration, unless you and the president himself, put out to the public the facts of the use of residuals for the Freedom Fighters, unless you got it out the door first, it could possibly lead to impeachment by the Congress, correct?
> *Meese:* Yes. That was a concern, that political opponents might try that kind of tactic.
> *Judge Gesell:* And you discussed that with the President? He is asking you.
> *Meese:* I believe I discussed it with the President. I certainly discussed it with others in high-ranking positions such as the chief of staff.... I don't know whether the actual word "impeachment" was referred to, but I certainly discussed the tremendous consequences for the President personally and for the administration.

this staffer had acted on his own (however unlikely *that* might be), and that, now that you mention it, his activities might even be *criminal*—if the public and the press focused on *that*, then maybe you didn't have another Watergate on your hands after all. Especially if you insisted that the President knew nothing about it.

I immediately called my wife, but she wasn't home. As with so many other episodes in this long ordeal, Betsy learned about my firing on the car radio. I tried to get through to my mother in Albany, but her line was busy. She had seen the press conference on television, and she was trying to call me. But by then the phone lines in my office were jammed.

This was not the way it was supposed to be. I had expected to leave, and maybe even be fired—but not quite so publicly. Still, I'd had plenty of warning that my days at the National Security Council were numbered. I was, after all, deeply involved in two major, secret, and politically explosive projects, the Iran initiative and the contras, and both had begun to unravel a few weeks earlier. The secret Iran initiative was pretty much over after that report in *Al-Shiraa*, which was immediately picked up by the Western media. About a month before *that*, a plane full of supplies for the resistance fighters had been shot down over Nicaragua. Eugene Hasenfus, an American crew member, was captured by the Sandinista army, and documents were found that led to a safe house in El Salvador whose telephone records listed several American phone numbers—including mine. This only confirmed what many congressmen and journalists already knew: that while large segments of our government were explicitly prohibited from actively supporting the contras, several of us, including the President, were quietly involved in a host of other efforts to keep them alive.

Once both initiatives were exposed, it was only a matter of time before I would be forced to leave my job at the NSC. During those final days I worked harder than ever to limit the damage and to protect the lives of people who had risked so much to help us on both fronts. (Some are still at risk, which is why their names do not appear in this book.) We were also making a last-ditch effort to rescue the remaining American hostages in Beirut. One hostage, David Jacobsen, had been freed in early November as part of a deal with the Iranians; he was the third one to be released in this way, and we were desperately trying to extricate the others before the whole thing collapsed.

The contra initiative had ended even before David Jacobsen's release. Shortly after the Hasenfus shootdown, William Casey, the director of the CIA, had told me to "shut it down and clean it up." It was clear that somebody's head would have to roll, and I was prepared to be the victim. Offering me up as a *political* scapegoat was part of the plan, although Casey believed there would be others. "If it comes out," he had told me, "it will go above *you*, buddy." And when it did come out, he said, "It's not going to stop with you, either."

By the time of the press conference I was certainly prepared to leave the administration, and in some ways I actually looked forward to it. I had come to the National Security Council five and a half years earlier on what was supposed to be a two- or three-year assignment from the Marine Corps, and had ended up staying twice as long as I ever wanted or expected. I was eager to return to Camp Lejeune, North Carolina, the home of the Second Marine Division, where I would once again do what I really enjoyed and what I did best: commanding and leading young Marines. I hoped to take some leave, get to know my family again, and take them back to North Carolina to begin a new assignment. Betsy and I had talked this over at length. Of all my duty stations, Camp Lejeune was her favorite, and she looked forward to returning there as much as I did.

But now—not so fast, fella!

I had just been fired by the President on national television. If that was really necessary, I could live with it. But what was that the Attorney General had said? That there might be *criminality* involved?

Was he serious? I knew we were facing a political disaster, and that there would be political consequences. But never in my darkest nightmares did I imagine that anything I had done in the service of the President, my commander-in-chief, could lead to criminal charges.

I wasn't part of the President's inner circle, but one thing I knew: Ronald Reagan was in no danger of being impeached. For one thing, nobody wanted to go through *that* again; one such crisis in a generation was enough, thank you. For another, President Reagan was loved and trusted by a vast majority of the American people.

With a few exceptions, even his critics did not want to see him impeached. Although the President's approval rating underwent a sharp decline, the word "impeachment" was rarely spoken in public—not even by congressional Democrats. Lee Hamilton, chairman of the House Intelligence Committee, used the dreaded "I" word as part of a hypothetical response to a question on ABC's "This Week with David Brinkley." And on March 5, 1987, Congressman Henry Gonzalez introduced a resolution of impeachment in the House of Representatives, which went nowhere. But these were isolated exceptions.

In the fall of 1986, President Reagan was still so popular that he and Nancy could have invited Fidel Castro to a testimonial dinner at the White House for Ayatollah Khomeini without suffering overwhelming political damage. People would have shaken their heads, they would have wondered, but Ronald Reagan would have remained popular. If the Constitution had allowed him to seek a third term, I have no doubt that he would have run again in 1988. And, just as in 1984 against Mondale, he would have been reelected in a landslide. Iran-contra would have hurt him, certainly, but it wouldn't have been fatal.

By going public so quickly with the "diversion," the President's top advisers were essentially trading one risk for another. They could have decided to batten down the hatches and weather the storm while we made one final effort to get the hostages out. But when our government announced, in effect, that the Iranians had been overcharged for the arms they had purchased, and that Iran had been subsidizing the Nicaraguan resistance without even knowing it—what about *those* political damages? Who knew how the government leaders in Tehran, or the hostage-takers in Beirut, might react to this humiliation from Washington? Wasn't it possible that this announcement might lead to further recriminations against the hostages or other acts of violence against the United States?

President Reagan could have handled the whole thing very differently. He could have said, "The buck stops here. I knew about the diversion. I approved it because I would have done just about anything to get our hostages out of Iran, and to avoid abandoning the contras in the midst of their life-and-death struggle. It's the President's mandate to determine our foreign policy, and as your President, I accept responsibility for everything that happened on my watch."

If the President had said that, what would Congress have done?

Sure, many Democrats would have been angry, but were they any less angry when the President said he *didn't* know?

As soon as the press conference was over, everybody's favorite Watergate question began to reverberate around the nation like a battle cry: what did the President know, and when did he know it?*

There were, of course, many other questions that could have been asked—especially about our foreign policy. Was it a good idea for the United States to hold secret talks with the Iranians? And if our government really was neutral in the Iran-Iraq War, as we often claimed to be, why were we secretly supplying military intelligence to Iraq? And why, for that matter, did several top administration officials, including Secretary of State George Shultz and Secretary of Defense Caspar Weinberger (who rarely agreed on *anything*) both favor the Iraqis? Not only had Iraq started the war, but the Iraqis were more deeply involved in international terrorism than the Iranians ever hoped to be. Meanwhile, Saddam Hussein was using chemical weapons—not only against Iran, but even against his own people.

The press became so focused on the "diversion" that they neglected to ask what President Reagan had known about other critical issues: Did the President and his advisers knowingly mislead Congress with regard to aiding the contras? Did they knowingly mislead Congress and the public with regard to selling arms to the Iranians? How was the President supposed to maintain a consistent policy in Central America when Congress kept changing its mind about whether we would help the contras? And why were so many members of Congress hostile to the Nicaraguan resistance and seemingly untroubled by an aggressive Communist government in Nicaragua?

These and other questions were there for the asking, but the one about the President and the "diversion" kept bouncing back: *what did he know and when did he know it?* It just wouldn't go away, not even when the President himself said that no, he hadn't known about it, or later, during the congressional hearings, when Admiral Poindexter

*The press seemed to focus on little else. "We were all children of Watergate," wrote Lou Cannon, the veteran Washington reporter, on the subject of Iran-contra. "My editors at *The Washington Post* and most of my colleagues in the press corps were from beginning to end more tantalized by the Nixon question—what did he know and when did he know it?—than by any other issue." (Lou Cannon, *President Reagan: The Role of a Lifetime* [New York, 1991], p. 706.)

backed him up.* When the admiral maintained that he hadn't told the President about the "diversion," that lowered the temperature. But it didn't end the speculation. "No smoking gun," said the press, extending the Watergate analogy. But the American people still found it difficult to believe that the President didn't know. According to the polls, a majority believed that President Reagan *did* know.

I thought so, too.

And now, five years later, I am even more convinced: *President Reagan knew everything.*

True, he didn't learn about the "diversion" from me—at least not directly. In all my time in Washington, I never met alone with him, and the only time we talked privately on the phone was the day I was fired. John Poindexter insisted that *he* didn't tell the President either, because Poindexter wanted him to have "plausible deniability." At the hearings, Poindexter said, "I made a very deliberate decision not to ask the President, so that I could insulate him from the decision and provide some future deniability for the President if it ever leaked out."

Even if that's true, I find it hard to believe that the President didn't know.

Here's why. The contras were not the only beneficiary of the arms sales to Iran. Part of the residuals were to be used for other projects, including several counterterrorist operations and various plans involving the release of the hostages. Because these activities were so sensitive, I made sure to get explicit permission for each one. Every time one of these projects came up, whether or not the particular plan was actually carried out in the end (and not all of them were), I wrote a memo or a computer message to Admiral Poindexter outlining how the money would be used. It was always my belief that these memos were passed up the line to the President, because documents of this type generally were. In fact, it was a copy of one of these memos, from April 1986, that made the Attorney General aware of the "diversion" three days before the press conference. For all my celebrated shredding skills, I had missed that one.

I was a little surprised when Admiral Poindexter said he hadn't

*"On this whole issue," Poindexter said at the hearings, "the buck stops here with me." He added: "I made the decision. I felt that I had the authority to do it. I thought it was a good idea. I was convinced that the president would, in the end, think it was a good idea."

told the President. But is it really possible that nobody else did? Robert McFarlane, Poindexter's predecessor, had left government, but he still had unique access to the Oval Office. He could have told the President. And is it possible that Bill Casey never once mentioned the "diversion" to Ronald Reagan, his longtime friend, in one of their many private meetings? I find that unlikely.

Casey and I had discussed the "diversion" on several occasions, and he loved the idea. He praised it effusively, and called it "the ultimate covert operation," which from him was high praise indeed. He once referred to it as the ultimate irony, because Iran had been providing arms to the Sandinista government of Nicaragua. Casey would have enjoyed sharing this story with the President, and I believe he did.

It's also quite possible that the President discussed the "diversion" with one or more other high-level officials. If any of them were not aware of how the residuals from the arms sales were being used, it's only because they went out of their way not to know. A substantial amount of money—well in excess of what the U.S. government was receiving for the arms—was generated from these transactions, and intelligence material circulated to people like Cap Weinberger and Colin Powell made that clear. Even before I became involved in the operational aspects of the Iran initiative, our government made extensive efforts to gather information on Manucher Ghorbanifar and his fellow arms dealers. These very sensitive intelligence reports were distributed to a handful of cabinet-level appointees, including the Secretary of Defense, the national security adviser, the director and deputy director of the CIA, and the director of the National Security Agency. None of them could reasonably claim ignorance of the existence of residuals, although, in the end, nearly all of them tried.

President Reagan, meanwhile, was understandably devastated when, for the first time in his political career, the public didn't believe him. Don't they trust me? he asked. Do they actually think I'm a liar?

I don't believe the President was necessarily lying. I realize, of course, that in view of what I've just written this must sound like a contradiction. If the President claimed he didn't know about the "diversion," and he actually *did* know, doesn't that mean he was lying?

Not in Reagan's case. Granted, for most people, and certainly for most presidents, these two suppositions could not both be true. For Ronald Reagan, however, they weren't necessarily in conflict. For all of his achievements, this President didn't focus much on the details.

President Reagan didn't always know what he knew. I believe he was *told* about the transfer of funds to the contras, but that doesn't mean he paid attention to it or remembered it. Early in 1987, the President made clear to his own Tower Commission that he wasn't really sure *what* he recalled about the Iran initiative, or whether he had approved a November 1985 arms shipment by the Israelis. He testified that he didn't know anything about the early TOW shipments to Iran, although by the time he wrote his memoirs he apparently remembered again.

The 1989 videotape of his testimony at the Poindexter trial showed us a terribly sad portrait of an aging and confused man who appeared to recall astonishingly little about his own administration. But even in his better years, President Reagan preferred to concentrate on broad policies and values. He was never very inquisitive or curious, and he generally left the details to his subordinates. It seemed to me that he sometimes wanted to ask a question, but then didn't do so because it would have seemed to be a "stupid question," and he didn't want to appear not to know something others would think he should have known.

Admiral Poindexter has said that, hypothetically speaking, if he had discussed the "diversion" with the President, the President would have okayed it. "I was convinced," the admiral testified at the hearings, "that I understood the President's thinking on this, and that if I had taken it to him that he would have approved it."

I agree. Ronald Reagan knew of and approved a great deal of what went on with both the Iranian initiative and the private support efforts on behalf of the contras, and he received regular, detailed briefings on both topics. He met on several occasions with private donors to the resistance, and at least once, it appears, he personally solicited a foreign leader—King Fahd of Saudi Arabia—and asked him to double his contribution.* Given President Reagan's policies and directives, I have

---

*At the time, King Fahd was already supporting the contras. After his meeting with the President, he more than doubled his commitment. In all, the Saudi contribution came to thirty-two million dollars.

no doubt that he was told about the use of residuals for the contras, and that he approved it. Enthusiastically.

There is, of course, an additional possibility: that people around the President, and perhaps even President Reagan himself, were involved in an effort to protect the highest office in the land—and the man who occupied it.

In his memoirs, Ronald Reagan wrote that "we sent word to the lawyers representing Oliver North and John Poindexter, who knew what had happened, that I wanted them to tell the entire truth and do nothing to protect me." I was surprised to read that, and I asked my lawyers if they ever received such a message. They hadn't.

In fact, nobody from the administration *ever* asked me to tell the truth. The only message I heard was: exonerate the President. And I heard it from at least three different people.

At the end of January, Paul Laxalt, one of Ronald Reagan's oldest and closest political friends, called a member of my legal defense team at Williams & Connolly to say he was sending over a memo. The document, which arrived within a few days, was a legal memorandum that argued that I would not waive my Fifth Amendment rights if I chose to state publicly that the President did not know about the "diversion." My lawyers rejected this proposal out of hand.

The previous month, on December 17, I had received a visit from one of the military aides to Vice President Bush who was also a member of Bush's national security affairs staff. He and I were both military officers, and he approached me on that basis. In the presence of Brendan Sullivan, my lawyer, he suggested that I waive my Fifth Amendment rights and absolve the President of any responsibility.

Naturally, we wondered. Had this officer come on his own? Had he been sent? I still don't know.

A few days before this visit, we had heard a similar message from H. Ross Perot, the celebrated Texas entrepreneur. I knew Perot and admired him. (In the early 1970s, when I was thinking of leaving the Marines to join the corporate world, Perot had talked me out of it. And in 1981, he had helped us during the kidnapping of General James Dozier by the Red Brigades in Italy.) On December 11, he came to Williams & Connolly, where he met with Brendan. "Look," he said, "why doesn't Ollie just end this thing and explain to the FBI that the President didn't know. If he goes to jail, I'll take care of his family. And I'll be happy to give him a job when he gets out."

That's just like Ross, I thought when I heard about his offer. He thinks money can buy everything.

Six days later, Perot was back. This time he met with Brendan and me together, but the message was the same: I should forfeit my Fifth Amendment rights and make a statement that "cleared" the President.

I find it hard to believe that Ross Perot was acting on his own. But if anyone sent him, they left no fingerprints.

It's also possible that these three approaches were part of a pattern that began even earlier, with President Reagan himself. A few hours after the November 25 press conference, a White House operator tracked me down in a suburban Virginia hotel, where I had gone to avoid the press. The President wanted to talk to me about the firing. During our brief conversation, he called me a "national hero," a phrase he repeated to *Time* magazine the next day. He used it again on March 25, 1988, a year and a half after I was fired, and nine days after I was indicted: "I still think Ollie North is a hero," he said.

I knew what he meant by those words, and I was grateful for his appreciation. President Reagan was well aware that in addition to my work on the Iran initiative and on behalf of the contras, I had also been involved in a variety of antiterrorist activities. On a couple of those occasions he had even sent me letters of commendation. That's why I was so surprised to read the account of that phone call which appeared years later in Reagan's memoirs. When he referred to me as a national hero, the former President wrote, "I was thinking about his service in Vietnam."

What?!

I found that *very* hard to believe. For one thing, during my tenure at the NSC I don't believe that anyone at the White House was even aware of my Vietnam war record. For another, I don't believe the President had ever seen me in uniform until the hearings began, which means he had no idea that there were medals on my chest or what they were for. Moreover, it wasn't until well *after* I was fired that my military record was requested by the White House and delivered to Don Regan's office.

The day after the firing, the President was interviewed by Hugh Sidey of *Time* magazine. "I have to say that there is a bitter bile in my throat these days," he said. "I've never seen the sharks circling like they are now with blood in the water." But despite his bleak mood, President Reagan went out of his way to praise me. "I do not feel betrayed," he said. "Lieutenant Colonel North was involved in all our operations: the *Achille Lauro*, Libya. He has a fine record. He is a national hero."

That made it clear, I think, that the President was not referring to my war record when he called me a hero. When I read his memoirs, I was sorry to see his transparent attempt to rewrite history. It also made me wonder about something else he had said during that phone call.

That other remark was a lot more ambiguous, and in the five years that have passed since that night I have turned it over in my mind more than once. When President Reagan came on the line, I expressed my regret for what had taken place, and the fact that the Iran initiative had blown up in our faces. "I certainly hope this doesn't hurt your presidency," I told him. "I can only tell you that I did my best to serve you and our country. I never wanted anything like this to happen."

"Ollie," said the President, "you have to understand, I just didn't know."

In the heat of the moment I took him literally.

Today, looking back, I wonder why he phrased it quite that way, and whether he was implying more than I realized at the time. There were other ways he could have said it. He could have said, "Ollie, why didn't you tell me about the diversion?" Or "Ollie, believe me, I didn't know what was going on."

Instead, it was "You have to understand, I just didn't know." I now wonder whether he was alone when he made that call. Was Don Regan standing beside him? Or Nancy? Maybe what the President was *really* trying to tell me was: Look, Ollie, you and I know better, but the line we're putting out is that I didn't know, so please go along with it.

It's possible, of course, that President Reagan meant exactly what he said. On the other hand, he was almost always scripted, and he did tend to rely on those famous file cards. I don't have to stretch very hard to imagine Donald Regan giving careful thought to the language the boss should use.

*   *   *

Many of my friends and supporters believe that Ronald Reagan betrayed me. "You did everything you could for him," they say. "You knocked yourself out carrying out his policies, and you even risked your life by going to Tehran. When you were wounded, he abandoned you on the battlefield. Don't you feel betrayed?"

Sometimes I do. But I'm like a yoyo on the subject of Ronald Reagan. In terms of the difference he made in the world, I'm very glad he was President for eight years. And yet I can't ignore the fact that he could have ended years of suffering for me and my family— either by granting a presidential pardon or by shutting down the office of the special prosecutor before leaving office.

Is that betrayal? Well, it sure as hell wasn't supportive.

In November 1986, responding to pressure from both sides of the aisle in Congress, President Reagan called for the appointment of a special prosecutor. This allowed the actions that I and others had taken to support the President's policy to be treated as criminal. Meanwhile, he kept changing his story. At first, he told his own Tower Commission that he hadn't even known that the NSC staff was helping the contras. Not surprisingly, almost nobody believed him.

Later, on May 15, 1987, he was considerably more candid when he addressed a group of broadcasters and newspaper editors. "As a matter of fact," he told them, "I was very definitely involved in the decisions about support to the freedom fighters. It was my idea to begin with."

2

The Secret Within a Secret

The "diversion" did not originate with me. Frankly, I wish it had, because I'd love to take the credit. But it wasn't my idea.

The notion of using Iranian money to support the Nicaraguan resistance first came up during a January 1986 meeting in London with Manucher Ghorbanifar and Amiram Nir, the adviser on counterterrorism to Prime Minister Shimon Peres of Israel. Ghorbanifar, an expatriate Iranian, was a businessman and commodity trader who was based in Paris. During most of the Iran initiative, he was our only contact with government officials in Tehran. Gorba was a dark-eyed and hefty man who obviously enjoyed most of life's pleasures. In addition to being a gregarious, fast-talking self-promoter, he was also a world-class bullshooter, wheeler-dealer, and manipulator.

We were meeting to discuss an upcoming shipment of TOW missiles to Iran. Occasionally, these talks were held in Ghorbanifar's suite at the Churchill Hotel—a luxurious setting with thick Persian carpets on the floor and tapestries and paintings on the wall. At other times, we met at the Penta Hotel at Heathrow Airport.

During a break in one of the discussions, Gorba stood up and motioned for me to follow him into the bathroom. He must have suspected that these talks were being recorded (which they were), because he ran the water in both the sink and the bath to muffle the sound of our voices. "Ollie," he said softly, as if he were my oldest and closest friend in the world, "if we can make this deal work, there's a million dollars in it for you."

I had never been offered a bribe before, but I wasn't surprised by his offer. Everybody knew that Ghorbanifar operated in societies where *baksheesh* was common.

"That's out of the question," I snapped. "Don't bring it up again, or the whole thing is over."

But Gorba was a master salesman. If you didn't bite at his first proposal, he always had another one ready.

"Never mind," he said. "I understand. I know what you've been doing in your spare time. Maybe we can make some money available to your friends in Nicaragua."

Hmm, I thought, *now* you're talking. It was clear to me that the Israelis, with whom he was working at the time, kept Gorba generally well informed. He obviously knew, from them or some other connection, that I was involved in helping the Nicaraguan resistance. Now that Congress had cut off their support from the CIA, the contras were receiving funds from private sources, including foreign governments and several American philanthropists.

When I returned to Washington, I went to see John Poindexter in his office. "Admiral," I said, "I think we've found a way to support the Nicaraguan resistance." When I told him what Gorba had suggested, Poindexter agreed with me that this was a perfect way to have two of the President's policies work together. That evening, the admiral called me on the secure line and told me to "proceed along the lines of our discussion." And I did.

Because the "diversion" became the central focus of the Iran-contra affair, I want to explain exactly what it was—and wasn't.

I use quotation marks around "diversion" because that word usually suggests something shifty, shady, or devious—which was one reason why the "diversion" quickly became the symbol of the entire Iran-contra episode. It was inflammatory. It implied something illegal or immoral. It suggested that money was stolen. In an enormously complicated story, it was relatively easy to understand. And perhaps most important, it provided the crucial link between separate initiatives—

Iran and the contras—which had little else in common.

For all its hostility to the administration, Congress was surprisingly willing to accept the idea put forward by the White House that the "diversion" was really the key issue. The press and the public accepted it, too. But from my perspective, the transfer of funds from one project to another was not the central point. It was more like gift wrapping that fit around two separate packages: it tied everything up nicely, and made the whole parcel seem more alluring. But it wasn't nearly as significant as what was actually inside.

Despite everything that's been said or implied, the "diversion" was not illegal. You could argue that it was a bad idea—that much is certainly debatable—but despite all the allegations, the transfer of funds did not violate any laws. After five years and tens of millions of dollars spent on investigations, prosecutions, trials, and tribunals, no one involved in Iran-contra was ever tried for "diverting" anything.

Now, *if* the United States government had sold arms directly to Iran, and *if* someone in our government had decided on his own to take the money from those arms sales and send some of it to the contras instead of returning it to the Treasury, *that* would have constituted a diversion. But that's not what happened here. Our government had no direct communication with the Iranian government, and the Israelis didn't, either. The Israelis relied on third-party intermediaries to deal with Iran, and we did the same.

The "diversion" was known about and approved by American government officials who understood the need for middlemen, and who recognized that once the U.S. government had been paid, any remaining money the middlemen received belonged to them. In January 1986, President Reagan even signed a secret "Finding" that not only authorized the Iran initiative, but specifically noted this reliance on third parties in carrying out the transactions.*

American-made weapons reached Iran in two ways: from Israeli stockpiles, which we eventually replenished, and from U.S. military warehouses. In both cases, the weapons and the money moved through various private-sector American, Israeli, and Iranian intermediaries, including Richard Secord, Albert Hakim, Yakov Nimrodi, Al

---

*A Presidential Finding is a document signed by the President that explains and authorizes a particular covert action.

Schwimmer, and, of course, Ghorbanifar. These men purchased arms from the governments of Israel and the United States, and then, with the approval of those governments, sold them to the Iranians. Like all brokers, they were in this to make a profit. And part of that profit was to be sent to the contras to support their struggle against the Sandinistas.

That was the so-called diversion. To the extent that money was "diverted," it was diverted from the pockets of Ghorbanifar and the other middlemen.

They could certainly afford it. According to our intelligence reports, Gorba, and possibly others, were making tremendous profits on these deals. But not at the expense of the U.S. government. The Department of Defense established its own price for every item, and received full payment in advance. The fee for the weapons was jacked up considerably by the intermediaries who bought them, but that's another story.

Our government sells its property all the time. Take used computers, for example. A computer dealer buys a used machine at a government auction and pays the government's asking price of say, ten thousand dollars. A month later he sells that computer to a small business for thirteen thousand dollars. Does that mean there was a diversion? Does the dealer now owe the government three thousand dollars? Of course not. That's his profit, and he can do anything he likes with it.

Admittedly, a missile is very different from a computer. But the financial principle is the same.

I have already mentioned that Ghorbanifar did not exactly have the endorsement of the Better Business Bureau. Some accounts of Iran-contra have suggested that Bud McFarlane was the only one who could really see through him, and that the rest of us were naïve. Baloney. With the exception of Michael Ledeen, a consultant to the NSC, nobody trusted Gorba. Even the Israelis, who brought him to us in the first place, didn't trust him completely. As Ami Nir once told me, Gorba's loyalty had a price that had to be paid. For a long time, he was our only conduit to the Iranian government. But we also knew that he had failed three CIA polygraph exams, where he had reportedly dissembled about everything except his name and nationality.

Later, during the congressional hearings, the question came up repeatedly: how could we work with somebody like that? The answer was simple: until we could find somebody better, Gorba was our only option. Right from the start we looked for a more dependable go-between. And when we finally found one—the so-called second channel—Gorba was history.

But he did get us started, and with Gorba's help we managed to get two hostages out of Beirut. Ghorbanifar may have been corrupt, but he didn't pretend to be anything other than what he was: a wealthy merchant who was trying to make a great deal of money. And it's not as if there were other candidates with good contacts in Iran who were lining up for the job. It would have been wonderful if Mother Teresa had volunteered to approach the Iranians on our behalf, but she wasn't available.

When I first became involved in the Iran initiative, I knew next to nothing about the specialized world of arms dealers. But I now understand that by the standards of his profession, Ghorbanifar was fairly typical. I assume that's what General Dick Secord had in mind when he recalled, during the hearings, that McFarlane had once called Ghorbanifar one of the most despicable characters he had ever met. "I found that kind of an interesting comment," Secord said, "because he was far from the most despicable character *I've* ever met."

Whatever his faults, and they were legion, nobody ever said Ghorbanifar was a fool. He couldn't have missed the fact that we didn't trust him, and that we were eager to replace him as soon as we could find someone else with equally good access.

Although Gorba was the first to suggest the "diversion," I doubt that it was his own idea. Many in our intelligence agencies believed that Gorba was in the pocket of the Israelis. That doesn't necessarily mean he was exclusively theirs; it could be that he used them, just as they used him. But it was probably no coincidence that the Israelis had recently come up with their own "diversion" plan, which was very similar to what Ghorbanifar suggested.

Shortly after this whole thing had landed in my lap, the Israelis contacted me about having our government replenish their initial shipment to Iran of five hundred TOW missiles during the summer of 1985. As they understood it, McFarlane had approved their shipment and promised we would replace the missiles quickly, and at no charge. But Bud remembered it differently. He claimed he had told the Israelis that these missiles would be replaced in the course of their normal arms purchases. The Israelis, including Prime Minister Peres and Defense Minister Yitzhak Rabin, insisted they would never have agreed to *that*.

In the long, ongoing war between Iran and Iraq, with a million or more soldiers on each side, five hundred TOWs didn't amount to much more than a fart in a hurricane. But to Israel, surrounded by enemies and with limited war reserves, even the temporary loss of these missiles had serious implications for her national security.

Early in 1986, Amiram Nir arrived in Washington to keep the initiative moving, and to ensure that Israel would receive its replacement missiles as soon as possible. One option was to have the Israelis walk into the Pentagon and buy five hundred TOWs, but there was no way to do that discreetly. Then Nir came up with an intriguing possibility—in essence, the same plan that Ghorbanifar would later suggest in London, but for a different purpose. For the February shipment to Iran, the Israeli arms dealers would charge the Iranians a high-enough price to cover not only the cost of this shipment of TOWs to be sent to Iran, but also to pay the U.S. government for the cost of five hundred additional TOWs to replenish the Israelis for the shipments they had sent to Iran in the summer of 1985.

Nir's plan, then, was the antecedent of Ghorbanifar's. Assuming the idea originated with the Israelis, Gorba's version was merely a safe, arm's-length way of introducing a more attractive variation. Gorba, of course, had his own reason to offer us an incentive: if we stopped using him, he wouldn't make any money.

To this day I don't know exactly how our contacts with Iran began, because I wasn't involved at the very beginning. But by all accounts it started with the Israelis. Later, some members of the congressional committees would attempt to gloss over the Israeli role, while others, especially in the executive branch, tried to exaggerate it, or even to blame the whole thing on Israel. Both interpretations are ridiculous.

From everything I know, the Iran initiative began when David

Kimche, the director general of Israel's foreign ministry, approached Bud McFarlane in mid-1985. Like us, the Israelis had enjoyed good relations with Iran before the Ayatollah came to power, and they were eager to resume contact with the Iranians with a view toward influencing the now-hostile revolutionary government.

The Israelis also cared deeply about the outcome of the Iran-Iraq War. Although both Iran and Iraq were now sworn enemies of Israel, the Israelis recognized that Iraq was a far more dangerous threat—not only to Israel, but to the entire Middle East. Iran, by contrast, was less harmful than its rhetoric implied. For all the Ayatollah's anti-Israel talk, Iran was not part of the "Arab world" and had no recent tradition of malice toward the Israelis.

Iraq, however, was another story. Saddam Hussein had more than once sent troops to join the Arab armies allied against Israel, and the Israelis took the Iraqi threat very seriously. In 1981 Israeli planes bombed an Iraqi facility that was involved in manufacturing nuclear weapons. At the time, virtually the entire Western world condemned the Israeli raid—at least publicly.* But ten years later, in 1991, the critics were quietly grateful that Iraq's nuclear capability had been destroyed, or at least delayed, a decade earlier.

The Israelis had another motive in moving closer to Iran: they were eager to free some thirty thousand Jews who had been unable to escape from Iran when the Ayatollah came to power, and whose lives were now endangered by the militant Islamic regime. Although the Jews of Iran were not locked up and under guard like our hostages in Lebanon, they were all under the strict control of the Ministry of Internal Security, and their passports included a seal that prohibited them from traveling to "occupied Palestine." Given the level of violence against non-Islamic groups in Iran (where thousands of Baha'i adherents were imprisoned, and several hundred had been executed), the prospects for the Jews of Iran were not good. Finally, Israel was also interested in rescuing two Israeli soldiers being held in Lebanon by Shi'ite terrorists who had pledged their allegiance to the Ayatollah.

In the summer of 1985, when Kimche came to Washington, he

---

*Our own Defense and State Departments were furious because the Israeli planes were American-made, and had been provided to Israel for defensive purposes only. Secretary Weinberger rejected the Israeli argument of a "strategic defense," and urged an embargo on further arms shipments to Israel.

apparently told McFarlane that the Israelis had made contact with Iranian officials whom the Israelis believed to be moderate. Kimche suggested that if the United States wanted to join Israel in developing these contacts, this might result in the release of our hostages in Beirut. But he also warned McFarlane that these particular Iranian officials would sooner or later ask for arms, which would give them credibility with both their own military and the revolutionary guards.

McFarlane signed on and discussed the Israeli overture with the President. Exactly how President Reagan responded is not clear, and McFarlane himself has given differing accounts of their meeting at Bethesda Naval Hospital, where the President was recovering from surgery. The Israelis told me later that they had asked for and received specific assurances that the President had authorized replacements for the missiles they would be sending to Iran. According to McFarlane, the President had indeed given his approval, although Bud's version differed as to exactly how the replenishment would occur.

Nothing would surprise me more than if Bud McFarlane had moved forward on this initiative without the explicit approval of President Reagan. But despite everything that's been said, I find it inconceivable that Bud McFarlane, who was educated at the U.S. Naval Academy, would ever act without the President's permission. Yes, you take initiative, but you always check with your superiors. You'd have to be an idiot not to. And whatever our flaws, none of us involved in this were idiots.

My own operational involvement began three months later, when on the afternoon of November 17, 1985, the phone rang in my office. The caller was General Yitzhak Rabin, Israel's defense minister and the military genius behind his country's dramatic victory in the 1967 Six-Day War. I had never met him, and I wondered why he wanted to speak to me.

Rabin got right to the point. "We have a problem," he said, "and McFarlane said you could help." He then started to outline the details of an Israeli shipment of American-made HAWK missiles to Iran which had been refused landing rights at the European airfield, where it was supposed to be transferred to another plane. He asked me how soon I could be in New York.

Rabin's call had come out of the blue, and we were talking on an open line, and he was a little too explicit for my comfort. Before I agreed to anything I needed to check with McFarlane.

"We can't talk about this on this phone," I told Rabin. "Give me a few minutes and I'll call you back."

I knew the Israelis were shipping weapons to Iran, and that these shipments had led to the freeing of the Rev. Benjamin Weir, one of the American hostages in Beirut. I also knew that at that point, our own government had no operational involvement in this whole process other than to recover any of our hostages who might be released. Until now, my own role had been to monitor these transactions, and at McFarlane's instructions I had initiated a major intelligence collection operation so that we could carefully track what was going on.

I was surprised that Rabin was asking us for help, and I wasn't about to provide any without McFarlane's explicit approval. Bud was in Geneva for the President's first summit with Gorbachev, and just as I reached for the phone to track him down, a call came in on my secure line. It was McFarlane, who said, "You're about to hear from the Israeli defense minister."

"I just did," I said. "What's going on?"

"Did he tell you?"

"He tried, but we were talking on an open line."

"Listen, the Israelis are trying to ship some HAWK missiles to Iran. The whole operation is being handled by a couple of private Israeli citizens. They've run into some logistical problems. Get back to Rabin and take care of it. Just fix it. Go up to New York and see Rabin."

Over the next few days, McFarlane and I had several more conversations about this new arrangement. He gave me the go-ahead for direct U.S. involvement, and assured me that the President had approved it.

This marked a major change in the U.S. government's role in the arms sales to Iran. When McFarlane first told me that the Israelis were selling arms to the Iranians with the tacit approval of our government, he had instructed me simply to monitor these transactions—to watch and to listen. Until now, it had been a hands-off operation on our side. But we had watched carefully as the Israelis shipped 504 TOW antitank missiles to Iran in 1985, which was followed by the release of the Presbyterian missionary, Benjamin Weir, after well over a year in captivity.

As soon as Weir arrived in the U.S., McFarlane and Casey had sent me in a CIA plane to a military airfield in Virginia to deliver a personal letter from President Reagan along with a request that he cooperate with us in a debriefing. It was not a pleasant experience. Weir was openly hostile to the United States and to Israel, and despite everything he had gone through, including an entire year of solitary confinement, he clearly sympathized with his captors. Banging on the table, he let me know that he emphatically refused to provide us with any information that might result in the use of military force to rescue his fellow hostages. He showed no hostility toward the hostage-takers; all his anger was directed at us.

While I was disappointed by his attitude, I wasn't altogether surprised. Weir had been through hell. He was chained up and abused for eighteen months, and it must have seemed to him that we hadn't done anything to help. But this wasn't a case of the much-discussed Stockholm Syndrome, where hostages come to identify with their captors. Weir had lived in Lebanon for thirty-one years, and he had apparently held these views well before he was taken. But he was so hostile and uncooperative after his release that some of those who had tried to debrief him started referring to him as the Reverend Weird.*

By the time of Weir's release it was fairly clear to us that the American hostages weren't the only point of interest in the Israeli arms shipments to Iran. About a month before Rabin called me, I had come across a hint that these transactions had another dimension. In the fall of 1985, the intelligence I had been told to collect produced a report from CIA and FAA channels that a chartered transport aircraft had run into unusual problems over Turkey. We learned later that this flight had been operated by a private network in Israel, that it had carried arms to Tehran, and that arrangements had been made to allow the plane to overfly Turkey on its way back to Israel.

But apparently an air traffic controller in Iran had dropped the

*As Michael Ledeen describes it, a few days after Weir's release Ledeen asked Ghorbanifar "if it was possible for the Iranians to take Weir back, and send us a patriotic American instead." (Michael Ledeen, *Perilous Statecraft* [New York, 1988], p. 136.)

ball, and neglected to convey the message to his counterpart in Turkey. The Turkish air controller spotted the unregistered plane on his radar and immediately asked it for identification. When the pilot responded with his prearranged cover story, the Turks, being out of the loop, sent up interceptors to deal with a possible intruder. The pilot of the charter then took evasive measures and eventually declared a midair emergency over the Mediterranean. He was instructed to land in Tel Aviv, whereupon the Israelis rolled the plane into a hangar, closed the doors, and declared that the entire incident had never happened.

Our intelligence services had begun looking into it until McFarlane told me to have the investigation called off because the Israelis had things under control. We learned later that this chartered plane had not returned to Israel empty. Inside were sixty Iranian Jews. These exchanges had apparently been going on ever since the fall of the Shah: Israel was redeeming captives by sending arms.

With this background and little else, I flew to New York to meet with Rabin at the Waldorf-Astoria. I had met a number of prominent people since coming to the National Security Council, but I was genuinely excited to be meeting Rabin. Like most infantry officers, I had read about him and studied his tactics. In American military circles, Yitzhak Rabin is considered one of the great generals of all time. When he planned and executed Israel's bold air/armor/airborne strike against Egypt in 1967, Rabin had actually saved the life of his country. How many military men could say *that*?

Although he had a reputation for being cold and aloof, Rabin turned out to be far more personable and engaging than I expected. I've always considered a subordinate's perspective to be a pretty good measure of the man, and Rabin's small staff clearly revered him. He was low-keyed and direct with them, rather than arrogant. I could see that this was a man who had led other men in dangerous circumstances, and had earned their respect.

I spent about an hour with Rabin, who explained that Israel had run into major problems in trying to ship HAWK missiles to Tehran. Because of the incident over Turkey a few months earlier, the Israelis had concluded that direct flights were too dangerous. Instead, they had arranged to move the shipment through several other intermediate points, disguised and manifested as oil drilling equipment. But at the last minute they had run into problems with landing rights and other clearances.

"Can you find us an acceptable airline that can move this stuff?" Rabin asked.

"I don't know," I replied. "Why don't you send it by sea?"

"Too slow," he said. "This is all about credibility. We've got to get it there fast."

"It sounds like an operational nightmare," I said. "We just don't have those kinds of assets sitting around."

"Don't worry," said Rabin. "Our people will take care of the logistics. We just need an airline."

When I returned to Washington, I called McFarlane on the secure phone patch to Geneva, and suggested that we enlist General Dick Secord to help straighten out this mess. I picked Secord for several reasons. First, I knew that he could got the job done. Second, he was especially well connected in the places in Europe the Israelis wanted to use as waypoints for Iran because Dick was using the same locations as points of departure for supplies and arms being shipped to the contras. Third, he was an expert on fixing aviation problems. Finally, he had spent a good deal of time in Iran.

In a perfect world, I would have chosen somebody else. Although Secord was an excellent candidate, he was already absorbed in another covert operation—helping the contras—and his involvement in a second clandestine activity violated a cardinal rule of covert operations. I mentioned my concern to McFarlane, and later to Poindexter, but none of us could think of anyone who was better suited for the job. The message was clear: just take care of it, Ollie.

So I did. I called Dick, and although he was, as he put it, up to his ass in alligators, he agreed to meet with the Israelis to see what could be done.

I also called Dewey Clarridge, who was then the CIA division chief for Europe, to ask if he could help the Israelis get landing rights in various places, and if he could also recommend an airline they could charter. Clarridge checked with his staff of experts, who suggested a CIA proprietary airline.* I passed that information on to Dick, who

*A CIA proprietary is a company owned or controlled by the Agency that, as a cover for its clandestine operation, provides services like any other commercial business.

arranged for one of the proprietary's 707s to carry what was supposed to be the first of several shipments to Tehran. Shortly after arriving at the European pick-up point chosen by the Israelis, Dick concluded that the headaches, chaos, and visibility of trying to ship through this airport just weren't worth it. He promptly flew to Israel to arrange for shipments directly out of Tel Aviv.

But even so, things went from bad to worse. Only eighteen missiles were able to fit on that first plane, and when they finally arrived, the Iranians were furious. Somebody—presumably Ghorbanifar—had assured the Iranians that these missiles were capable of shooting down high-flying Soviet reconnaissance planes and Iraqi bombers. But the HAWK is a low-altitude air defense system. Moreover, some of the missiles still carried Israeli markings, which infuriated the Iranians. Because their feelings ran so high, we would later do everything possible to make it seem as if the United States had absolutely no involvement in this particular transaction.

The Iran initiative was never a screaming success, but after this unbelievably screwed-up operation, things could only improve. And they did—at least for a while.

Initially, I was brought in just to handle the logistics; the policy decisions had already been made. But while I had nothing to do with our original decision to get involved, I eventually got to the point where I had considerable input into our policy. I'm certainly willing to accept responsibility for my part in the operation, and there is no doubt that it was one of the biggest mistakes of my life.

I believe it made sense to open a dialogue with Iran. It also made sense to search for pragmatists or moderates in their government. And despite everything, I still believe there are such people in Tehran. This doesn't mean they're about to salute the American flag, but they might at least be less inclined to burn it. Moreover, the Israelis kept assuring us that some officials in Tehran had a relatively pro-Western perspective.

At the time, it seemed that selling a small amount of arms to Iran was worth the risk to try to make it all work. But to get involved in a quid pro quo arrangement of arms for hostages? This placed all of us in a moral quandary. On the one hand, human life is sacrosanct. On the other, making what people would inevitably see as concessions to terrorists was a terrible idea—especially since it violated our prohibition on arms sales to Iran. The decision to proceed was made well above my level, but I became a willing participant.

I could have resigned in protest. But I didn't do that, either, despite the fact that I had once questioned another man for a similar decision.

During 1980–81, when I spent a year at the Naval War College in Newport, Rhode Island, each of the Joint Chiefs came up to give an address. General Robert H. Barrow was the commandant of the Marine Corps, and during his presentation, he said he had been opposed to Desert One, President Carter's ill-fated mission to rescue our embassy people who were held hostage in Tehran toward the end of his presidency.

Later that evening, at a private reception for the Marines, I went up to him and asked, "General, if you were that strongly opposed to the plan, why didn't you resign?"

He replied: "I thought that by staying I could prevent other mistakes of that type."

In 1985, I found myself in a similar position, working to carry out a policy about which I had serious doubts. I certainly could have resigned, but I didn't. And while there have been days since then when I thought I should have, I also remember how it felt to sit and talk with the men whose freedom we bought, and who otherwise might still be hostages in Lebanon.

It was one thing to monitor the Israeli arms sales to Iran, but when McFarlane called me and said, "Fix it," I could have challenged him and said, "Wait a minute, what are we really talking about here? Does this make any sense? Doesn't direct American involvement in this operation violate two of our basic principles?"

But I already knew the answer, which is why I didn't ask the question. I was intimately familiar with the administration's tough policies regarding terrorists and the governments that supported them. I had personally written a number of the President's statements on the subject. Later, as the Iran initiative progressed, I had growing doubts as to whether it was a good idea. But I did nothing to bring it to a halt.

Although General Barrow did not resign over the decision to proceed with Desert One, another member of the Carter Administration did. There was a lot I didn't like about the policies of Cyrus Vance,

President Carter's Secretary of State, but I'll always respect him for acting on his convictions. When Vance objected to what Carter and Zbigniew Brzezinski were planning, he resigned—with great dignity, citing personal reasons. Only later was it revealed that he had quit in opposition and in protest, and by then it was too late for the President he had served to suffer any damage from the resignation.

For me, the most difficult aspect of the endeavor was accepting that we had established a price for a human life; five hundred TOW missiles. To this day, I find this part of our Iran initiative to be the most troubling.

But there were other problems as well. We did not adequately consider the consequences of a leak. Any premature disclosure of our dealings with Iran might not only harm the hostages, but would also damage American prestige abroad and the President's political effectiveness at home. When it *did* leak, it certainly did the latter.

And while the Iran initiative could have worked—and *did* work to some extent—there was also the danger that dealing with the kidnappers, even through intermediaries, would merely whet their appetites and encourage them to take more hostages.

Another problem was the hypocrisy of providing arms to Iran while we prohibited other nations from doing the same. There may have been good reasons for us to sell arms to Iran, reasons that were not necessarily related to the hostages, but it wasn't right for us to be doing so while we were telling the rest of the world not to.

Other countries, including France, Germany, and Italy, were willing to sell arms to *both* sides in the conflict, and to do so secretly, while denying it to the world. The difference was that they weren't screaming at everyone else not to do it.

Despite all these negatives, for me the moral issue here was still a very tough call. It's easy to condemn the trading of arms for hostages, but the State Department had achieved absolutely no success in trying to free our hostages through diplomatic channels. Given the alternatives, I'm not sure it was morally wrong to do everything in our power to free innocent Americans who were literally chained to the wall in Beirut.

Though I wasn't there when McFarlane and President Reagan first discussed the Israeli proposal to have us join their Iran initiative, Bud should have said something like this: "The Israelis are selling arms to the Iranians in order to build an alliance with any moderates they can find, and because they see Iraq as a threat, and because they'll do whatever they have to to rescue their own people. They're inviting us to get involved. This could yield some big benefits, both in terms of the Soviet threat and our hostages in Beirut, but it could also backfire. I'm inclined to go along with it, but it's dangerous, and we must be aware of the risks."

I don't know exactly what McFarlane told the President. I do know that he told me that the President had approved our involvement. "Fix it," McFarlane had said, and that's all I needed to hear. It was the kind of challenge I thrived on, and I jumped right in. I can do it, I thought. I'm a Marine. This whole deal is screwed up, but I can take care of it.

I could have followed the example of Cyrus Vance. When I found myself engaged in a process that so thoroughly compromised the anti-terrorist policies I had helped to put in place, I could have quit.

Instead, I jumped in with both feet. Which is why, in the spring of 1986, I found myself on an airplane with Bud McFarlane, heading toward Tehran.

3

Another World

I had been on covert missions before, but this one was truly dangerous. As we started our descent into Tehran, I prayed that our disguised Israeli 707 wouldn't be shot down by some trigger-happy pilot who wouldn't know what to make of this unscheduled aircraft without a flight plan, and might conceivably take us for an unmarked Iraqi bomber. Iran, after all, was a country at war.

It was May 25, 1986, a Sunday morning, and several high officials were expecting us. Or so we hoped. But when we penetrated Iranian airspace, a pair of aging F-4s flew up to check us out.

This mission was so secret that Casey had urged us not to tell our wives where we were going. Bob Earl in my office had a detailed itinerary, and he was in constant contact with us on the trip. Before I left, I told Betsy that in an emergency she should call Bob, whom we had known for years. Betsy wanted to know when I would be back, because our house was on the market and she would need my signature on a sales contract. I tried to reassure her that I wouldn't be gone too long—and added a silent prayer that this would be true.

President Reagan had authorized our trip, and so had Admiral Poindexter. There were others in our government who knew we were going, although it's been fascinating to see how many of them seem to have forgotten all about it.

Even assuming we landed safely, there were still reasons to worry. Before I left Washington, William Casey had summoned me to his office in the Old Executive Office Building, where he calmly handed me a strip of six white, triangular pills sealed in a plastic wrapper. "Take these with you," he said. "You may need them if things get bad."

It was right out of a spy novel. But for Casey, I realized, this was almost routine. He must have provided this same morbid going-away gift to dozens of men and women, not only at the CIA, but decades earlier, too. During World War II, Casey had been in charge of secret intelligence operations for the Allied forces in Europe, and I had no doubt that some of Casey's capsules had been used by brave agents in Nazi Germany and Occupied France.

The head of our little delegation was Bud McFarlane, my former boss, and a man for whom I had held considerable respect and affection. Although McFarlane had resigned as the President's national security adviser almost six months earlier, he was flying to Tehran as Ronald Reagan's personal envoy. The other members of the group were George Cave, a former CIA officer who had been stationed in Tehran before the Khomeini revolution, and who spoke fluent Farsi; Howard Teicher, my colleague on the staff of the National Security Council; Amiram Nir, who was in charge of counterterrorism for the Israeli government; and a CIA communicator. A second communicator remained in Tel Aviv: he would receive our coded messages and relay them on to Washington, where they would be deciphered both at CIA headquarters and in the White House Situation Room.

No mission from the land of the Great Satan could expect to be greeted with flowers by the immigration officials at Medrabad Airport, which is why we were traveling under phony names and false passports—courtesy of the CIA, and much to the chagrin of those who issue the real passports, who were not amused when this particular detail became known. McFarlane was Sean Devlin. George Cave, traveling as Sam O'Neill, had grown a mustache and changed his hairstyle to avoid being recognized. Nir was presented as an American named Miller, while I was John Clancy. To complete the fiction, our Israeli Air Force 707 had been repainted with the marking of Aer Lingus, the Irish airline.

It was a long trip. We couldn't fly directly from Tel Aviv to

Tehran, as this route would have taken us over Jordan, Iraq, or Saudi Arabia—not exactly friendly territory for a clandestine flight out of Israel. Instead, we took off west over the Mediterranean, then turned around, flew back over Israel and down to Eilat, and continued south along the Red Sea before eventually turning back north to Iran. There was an anxious moment or two when we overflew the Soviet fleet off the coast of Ethiopia, but they left us alone.

Even getting to Israel to begin our mission had been done covertly, and involved several stopovers and changes along the way. I had gone earlier, by way of Cyprus, while my fellow Americans made their way to Frankfurt, where they boarded a special charter for Tel Aviv. Don't ask me why, but this particular aircraft had apparently been used the previous day to haul a load of chickens. The plane was filled with chicken feathers, dust, and Lord knows what else, and my traveling companions arrived in Israel in—well, a foul mood.

Our flight to Tehran was the culmination of several previous meetings in Europe and elsewhere with both private individuals and Iranian government officials. But when we finally landed and walked into the terminal, nobody was there to greet us. A bored airport official showed us into a holding area, which George Cave recognized as the former VIP Reception Center. "They used to receive Americans here," he whispered. Whether it was congressional delegations or visiting firemen from Ohio, he added, Americans had always been welcome. This room had once been an ornate hall, with opulent Persian carpets on the floor, and huge color portraits of the Shah and his family.

Today, that was hard to imagine. Except for three or four hard chairs and a couple of unpainted wooden benches, the room was barren and stark. It reminded me of Nicaragua and other revolutionary regimes, where everything of value has disappeared long ago—either stolen by the government or ripped off by corrupt officials. Even the light bulbs were missing.

It was a scorching day, the white sun so hot you could see the heat shimmering off the roads and runways. George and I parked ourselves in front of the building in the hope that somebody would eventually appear to claim us. In the distance, a huge portrait of the Ayatollah glowered at us. A couple of young men with rifles walked back and forth, but they left us alone. After half an hour of waiting, George persuaded an immigration official to make a phone call on our behalf.

A few minutes later, we were assured that somebody was coming to meet us.

That wait at the airport was a real anticlimax after the long, tense flight. I felt especially bad for McFarlane, who was pacing back and forth like a caged lion. He clearly saw this as a deliberate snub.

I wasn't so sure. From my previous dealings with the Iranians, I saw this delay as having more to do with incompetence than politics. Maybe Ghorbanifar had told the Iranians we were coming, and his contacts knew him well enough to say, "Yeah, sure they are." Or maybe he hadn't told them anything, figuring we'd never actually show up. In any case, there was nothing to do but wait.

Medrabad had once been a busy civilian airport, but most of the action was now on the military side. We spotted a number of American F-4 Phantoms, still flying from the days of the Shah. But many more deadlined aircraft sat on the ground, including Huey helicopters in various stages of disrepair—missing engines, doors, and blades. The Iranians were cannibalizing half their fleet to keep the other half flying, and their parking aprons had been turned into parts bins. An entire fleet of C-130 cargo planes lay idle, covered with dust.

Finally, after about an hour and a half, Ghorbanifar showed up with an Iranian official whom George and I had met before and whom we called the Australian. The Australian had absolutely no government experience before the revolution, but now he was near the top of the Iranian power structure. He was harmless enough, except for his breath—which, as George put it, could have curled the hide of a rhinoceros. He certainly wasn't one of the high-ranking officials we were hoping to meet, but by then we were glad to see anyone.

Ghorbanifar, charming as ever, was full of apologies, and he presented an elaborate excuse as to how he hadn't expected us to arrive until later. McFarlane, taciturn and formal, made a little speech about how we were bringing greetings from the President of the United States, and how we hoped these talks would be productive, and so on and so forth. But he also insisted, quite properly, that we were there to meet high government officials—the implication being, Listen, we didn't come all this way to see *you*, Ghorbanifar.

Gorba, who speaks perfect English, said, "Don't worry, the Parliament's in session," as though that made everything all right. But he was clearly nervous. He looked like a man who was bluffing and had just been caught.

Ghorbanifar had assured us that we would be meeting with Hashemi Rafsanjani, the Speaker of the Iranian Parliament, who was reported by the Israelis and other intelligence services to be a "moderate." We also expected to meet President Ali Khamenei and Prime Minister Mousavi. A meeting with the Ayatollah himself was apparently out of the question, which was probably just as well. According to our intelligence reports the old man was pretty much out of it, and there were rumors that he spent much of the day sitting in front of a VCR, watching Donald Duck cartoons.

Gorba and the Australian were accompanied by about a dozen young, bearded, and armed Revolutionary Guards who had arrived in a caravan of some of the oldest run-down cars I had ever seen. It looked as if somebody had bought out a small used-car lot in a bad section of town.

"Please, out to the cars," somebody said, and we all piled into this unlikely motorcade for the half-hour drive to the hotel. It was quite a scene—men brandishing guns were hanging out the windows, and most of the cars were belching blue or black smoke from their exhaust pipes. This was a country with almost unlimited oil, but apparently nobody knew how to refine it.

On the drive into town we could see the crumbling infrastructure of Tehran, the old bridges and the broken roads. I looked around for signs of war damage, as some of the buildings at the airport had clearly been hit by the Iraqis. But from what little I saw of the city, its problems were the result of neglect rather than bombs or missiles. Nearly everyone on the street was dressed in black, and I noticed a lot of bicycles—a common sight in countries at war, where gasoline is rationed. Nir and I had brought our cameras, and nobody seemed to mind when we took pictures. Several of the guards even posed with their guns.

We drove past what had once been the Shah's giant victory arch, which was now covered with revolutionary graffiti, and past the notorious Evin Prison, where Khomeini's prison guards were busily exceeding the worst abuses of the Shah's secret police. Finally, we pulled up to the front entrance of the Tehran Hilton, which was now known as the *Istiqlal*—the Independence. An entire outer wall was riddled with bullet holes, which didn't strike me as a particularly encouraging sign; it looked like somebody had opened up on it with a fifty-caliber machine gun. Some of the windows had been blown out, but I was surprised to see that the old Hilton sign was still up.

We were given the entire top floor, where we were something between guests and captives. Don't leave the building, we were told, because "we don't want others to know of your presence, which wouldn't be good for you or for us." Everything was phrased as though it were for our benefit; the team of Rev Guards ensconced in a suite near the elevator was ostensibly there to "protect" us. From what? I wondered. Even if we were foolish enough to leave the hotel, where did they think we might go? Into downtown Tehran to foment an American-led counterrevolution?

These were presumably the finest accommodations available in all of Iran, but the water pressure was low, the lights would often dim, and the elevators worked only sporadically. Every time a new shift of guards came on, you could hear them trudging up the stairs.

And yet our hosts did what they could to be hospitable, and it was clear that they wanted these talks to succeed. Every day they sent up baskets of fresh fruit to our rooms. The fruit itself was dreadful, and wouldn't even have made it to the shelves in an American market. But this seemed to be the best they had to offer. For meals we were entirely dependent on room service, which featured a Western-style menu. You couldn't actually *order* any of these items, but at least the meals you couldn't get were in English.

We did, however, end up with some tasty Iranian dishes. Some of them practically cried out for a cold beer, especially in that heat, but under Khomeini even that was forbidden.

At mealtimes, our little delegation would gather in McFarlane's suite, where we passed notes back and forth because the rooms were undoubtedly bugged. Somebody had placed a huge bouquet of flowers in the middle of the table, and each of us, from time to time, made a point of speaking directly into it, remarking with a smile on the great beauty of Tehran, or the outstanding generosity of our hosts.

When we wanted to talk among ourselves, we stepped out on the balcony and spoke in hushed tones, looking out at a spectacular view of the mountains on one side, and the city's smoky, dusty skyline on the other. We could also talk in the communications room, where our satellite system was installed and where we had taken steps to make eavesdropping more difficult.

But we did no bugging of our own. Normally, whenever we met with the Iranians, I arranged for concealed tape recorders or other monitoring devices to record our talks. But not here. If you were caught with something like that in Tehran, you could spend the rest of your life regretting it.

Shortly after we arrived at the hotel, Nir and I walked down the hall to see if we could get things moving. Near the elevator was a room filled with Rev Guards. Their guns were stacked in the corner, and their feet were up on the furniture.

They reminded me of the Iranian "students" I had seen on television, and I wondered if any of their older brothers had been involved in the seizure of our embassy in 1979. These guys weren't friendly, but they weren't threatening, either. Several spoke English and were very proud of it. We clearly aroused their curiosity; most had never been out of the country, and they obviously didn't get to meet many Americans. If nothing else, we represented a diversion from their normal routine—and certainly an agreeable change from life at the Iraqi front.

Looking around the room, I noticed that several of the guards were playing with the matched sets of pistols we had brought along as gifts. They must have gone through our plane and emptied it. I also noticed that they were eating the cake.

In November 1986, when the world learned of our visit, it was widely reported that our payload included not only electronic parts for HAWK missiles, but also a Bible signed by President Reagan and a cake in the shape of a key—to symbolize our desire to open a new relationship with Iran. The report about the Bible was wrong. I did bring a Bible to Tehran, but it belonged to me and I always traveled with it, and I brought it home with me. Several months later, however, I did present a different Bible, inscribed by President Reagan, to another group of Iranians.

But we did bring a cake.

Because that cake has become one of the best-known details of the entire Iran-contra story, let me set the record straight. It was not in the shape of a key. Moreover, it had no real connection with our mission. When Ghorbanifar was making what he optimistically called "the arrangements" for our trip to Tehran, he had asked Nir to pick up a chocolate cake as a gift for his aging and widowed mother, who lived in Tehran. It was a touching story, although on the flight over, George and I wondered aloud whether Gorba even had a mother. But it was true that such delicacies could no longer be found in the local stores or bakeries. Tehran had become like so many other revolutionary capitals, where almost everything other than the bare necessities was exported for hard currency.

Because the cake was one of Gorba's easier requests, Nir and I had driven to a kosher bakery in Tel Aviv, where we bought a large, rectangular chocolate layer cake. When we boarded the plane, I carefully laid the cake box on the sink in the galley. Several hours into the flight, George and I got up to make some coffee. As I opened the cabinet above the sink to look for the cups, I noticed that someone had stowed the pistols on the same shelf as the dishes. Each set of pistols was packed in an elegant, lined presentation case with a handsome brass key.

Unfortunately, I had left the cake box uncovered, and when I reached up to take out the coffee cups, one of the keys fell onto the cake, making a sizable indentation. When I saw how deeply the key had fallen, I carefully rearranged it to conceal the groove, and left it there, hoping it would look like an intentional decoration. "Well, George," I said, "we can always tell Mrs. Ghorbanifar that this is the key to our hearts."

As it turned out, Ghorbanifar's gift never reached his mother. We had arrived in Tehran during Ramadan, when Moslems eat only after sundown. Apparently the Ramadan fast does not apply to hungry Revolutionary Guards and chocolate cake.

Our trip to Tehran was a symbolic show of trust, a way of saying to the Iranians, Okay, despite everything your people did to our embassy staff in 1979, and despite your anger at us for supporting the Shah, we're willing to put our bodies on the line to show that we're sincere about developing a new and better relationship between our two countries.

Beyond that, we were there for several other reasons.

One reason was William Buckley, the CIA station chief in Beirut who had been captured more than two years earlier by radical Lebanese Shi'ites. When Casey handed me those pills before I left Washington, he may well have been thinking about Buckley. I know I was. Buckley was intimately familiar with CIA operations throughout the Middle East, and from everything we knew he had been violently tortured and eventually died in captivity—after his captors had compiled a four-hundred-page transcript of his interrogation. From the moment Buckley had disappeared into the trunk of a white Renault on March 16, 1984, Casey and the entire CIA had gone to enormous lengths to get him back alive. Now, by all accounts, he was dead. But the Agency was still working to retrieve his body and a copy of his "confession"—which Casey feared had ended up in the hands of the Soviets through their connections with Palestinian terrorist groups.

We were also hoping to retrieve the American hostages in Beirut: Father Martin Jenco, director of Catholic Relief Services in Beirut; Terry Anderson, a correspondent for the Associated Press; David Jacobsen, director of the American University Hospital; and Thomas Sutherland, director of the School of Agriculture of the American University. A fifth hostage, Peter Kilburn, the former librarian at the American University in Beirut, had recently been "bought" by agents of Muammar al-Qaddafi of Libya, who had murdered Kilburn in retaliation for the recent American raid on their country.* His death was a graphic reminder that the hostages could be killed at any time, and it gave additional urgency to our mission.

We knew the Iranians had some leverage over the kidnappers in Beirut, although we didn't know how much, or exactly how that influence worked. In any case, we regarded the release of the hostages as an early goal in a much broader strategic initiative.

At least that was our intention.

But it sure didn't work out that way. While we never wanted our Iran initiative to degenerate into a straight arms-for-hostages deal, the truth is that it did.

President Reagan could never accept this, even after he left office. In his memoirs, he again pointed out that we were not dealing directly with the kidnappers themselves—the Hezballah—but were selling

---

*Edward Austin Tracy, who was released in the summer of 1991, was kidnapped after I was fired.

weapons to the Iranians in return for their intervention in Beirut. Reagan wrote that he told Secretary of State Shultz and Secretary of Defense Weinberger that it was as if one of his children had been kidnapped—which is a pretty good indication of just how strongly he felt. "I don't believe in ransom," the President recalled telling them, "because it leads to more kidnapping. But if I find out that there's somebody who has access to the kidnapper and can get my child back without doing anything for the kidnapper, I'd sure do that. And it would be perfectly fitting for me to reward that individual if he got my child back. That's not paying ransom to kidnappers."*

On a literal level he was right. But George Shultz had already warned the President that this was too subtle a distinction, and that our dealings with the Iranians would invariably be *seen* as trading arms for hostages. I was often critical of George Shultz, but on this point he was certainly right.

Throughout our dealings with the Iranians, our position with respect to the hostages went something like this: "You folks want American technology and you need our trade. You'd like us to buy your oil. You're dying to get your hands on more American arms to help you in your war against Iraq, where you're getting creamed. You also know that the Soviets would like nothing better than to roll in here, which would be a disaster for both of us.

"Well, we're willing to talk. We realize who's in charge here, and we accept that the Shah is gone forever. We can move forward—just as soon as we get over this one hurdle. We know you have some influence over the hostage-takers in Beirut, so let's get the hostage problem out of the way so we can move on to the really big issues."

Even before we had begun talking directly to the Iranians a few months earlier, Benjamin Weir had been freed. By the time we left for Tehran, we expected that the release of the other hostages was imminent. We were wrong about that. But before the Iran initiative finally collapsed at the end of 1986, two additional hostages did get out: Father Martin Jenco and David Jacobsen.

While the hostages were certainly on our minds, the *real* reason, the *big* reason we had come to Iran had to do with the broader concerns of American foreign policy. Today, of course, it sounds positively old-fashioned to speak of a Soviet threat, but in the spring of 1986

*Ronald Reagan, *An American Life* (New York, 1991), p. 512.

that danger seemed very real—especially in the Persian Gulf.

Iran had always been vulnerable to a Soviet invasion. Even before there was a Soviet Union (or an Iran, for that matter), the Russians had gazed longingly at Persia. Iran's warm-water ports, which could be used year-round, were enormously appealing to the Russians. A second enticement, which became far more important after World War II, was oil—huge quantities of it. Iran is thought to contain 10 percent of the world's known oil reserves, plus huge quantities of natural gas.

These incentives alone might have been enough to tempt the Soviets to enter a country that was just sitting there on their twelve-hundred-mile-long southern border, and would have given them access to the entire Persian Gulf. But by the mid-1980s there were two additional factors that made the Soviet threat to Iran even more menacing. One was the Iran-Iraq War, which not only weakened Iran but also strengthened the ties between Iraq and Moscow, its chief supplier. The other threat to Iran was the Soviet invasion of Afghanistan. The Russian bear was now closer than ever, which was why the Iranians were quietly transferring some of the arms we had sold them to the Afghan rebels.*

In geostrategic terms, Iran was a treasure. While we no longer had any influence there now that the Shah was gone, so far, at least, the Soviets had overtly kept their distance. But with Russian troops in Afghanistan and Soviet weapons powering the Iraqi assault on Iran, they had the place surrounded.

There was another, more subtle reason that made a relationship with Iran especially attractive to Casey. Until the fall of the Shah, Iran had been one of our key listening posts for monitoring the Soviet space, missile, and nuclear war-fighting programs. Casey was deeply concerned about restoring these lost capabilities, and he saw the Iran initiative as a possible means of rebuilding this intelligence-gathering link.

The Soviet threat was why we wanted access to Iran, and why at least some members of Iran's government were willing to deal with us. Even before I became operationally involved in this initiative, President Reagan had quietly approved efforts to create a rapprochement with Tehran. Not everybody in the administration shared the President's goal, or even knew about it, and a parallel situation prevailed

*Iran also accepted more than two million Afghani refugees, and provided more support for the Afghan rebels than any other country in the region except Pakistan.

on the Iranian side. But for all their anti-American feeling, and it was considerable, most of the Iranian leadership understood that they had far more to fear from the Soviets than they did from us.

When the Shah fell in 1979, the one group in Iran that had expected to prosper was the well-established Tudeh Communist Party. But instead of being rewarded for their opposition to the Shah, the Iranian Communists were butchered. Under Khomeini, they were reduced to conducting isolated acts of terrorism that Americans rarely heard about. We all saw footage of the American embassy being taken over, and of anti-American demonstrations in the streets, because that's what the Iranian government wanted us to see. They took a special pleasure in humiliating us. But they were equally determined to root out the Communists and fend off the Soviets.

Would Iran become a second Afghanistan? There was a time when that seemed possible, and maybe even likely. Whether the Soviets tried to subvert the Islamic revolution for their own purposes or decided to wait for it to collapse, it would not have been a great surprise to our intelligence planners if the Russians had come in. For the potential spoils of victory in Iran were far, far greater than in landlocked, resource-poor Afghanistan.

In the end, however, the Soviet invasion of Afghanistan may have been precisely what saved Iran. Here was the world's largest military power getting their butts kicked by a primitive but determined guerrilla uprising. The Afghan resistance was fragmented and ill-equipped, but there's nothing like an invasion to turn the locals against you.

In February 1989, when the Soviets finally pulled out of Afghanistan and returned home, the American media reported their retreat just as Moscow presented it—as the result of Gorbachev's goodwill. But goodwill had nothing to do with it. The Soviets left because of all the coffins coming home to Mother Russia, and because Gorbachev was desperate to save the foundering Soviet economy. He needed economic support from the West, and he knew he couldn't get it as long as his occupying army remained in Afghanistan. This was the Soviets' Vietnam, but without the protests in the streets and the nightly news reports. For Gorbachev, Afghanistan was a disaster.

It would have been even worse for the Soviets if they had gone into Iran, with its mountainous terrain and much larger population. But that's not to say they wouldn't have tried.

*   *   *

In early 1986, when we first began talking directly to the Iranians, it was by no means clear that the Soviets would be forced to leave Afghanistan. In retrospect, a *lot* of things weren't clear to us about the Middle East—things we probably should have known. Incredible as it seems, we were completely unprepared not only for the collapse of the Shah but also for the rise of the Ayatollah's theocracy and the spread of his radical Islamic fundamentalism.

I'm not one of those who blames Jimmy Carter for *every* problem we face, but the devastation of our intelligence capabilities did take place on his watch. True, the process had begun earlier, during the Ford administration, when the 1975 Senate and House committee hearings chaired by Senator Frank Church and Representative Otis Pike weakened the Agency's ability to carry out covert activities. But President Carter never really understood the need for covert action, and he was convinced that the CIA had grown too powerful. In his zeal to cut the Agency down to size, he had Stansfield Turner fire hundreds of experienced intelligence officers. Incredibly, they were dismissed through a computerized form letter!

Morale in the CIA was so low that scores of other experienced officers resigned. Carter, Vice President Walter Mondale, and Turner didn't appreciate the importance of human operatives, and tried to substitute high technology for experience and common sense. In the process, they virtually emasculated the CIA's clandestine abilities.

Although many of the consequences were not felt until the Reagan administration, President Carter became the ironic victim of his own actions. After our embassy in Tehran was overrun by the Ayatollah's young militants, we didn't have a single CIA operative on the scene who could give us the necessary information we needed to plan a successful rescue. Had President Carter been able to end the hostage crisis earlier, he might have been reelected.*

---

*In the spring of 1991, there were numerous reports of a 1980 deal between the Reagan presidential campaign and certain Iranian authorities whereby the release of our hostages in Iran would be delayed until after the election. I don't believe it, and I have yet to see an iota of evidence to suggest that anything like this ever happened. If it did, why didn't Casey or George Bush, both of whom were alleged to be engaged in this effort, ever tell me whom to deal with on the Iranian side? Surely they would have known of somebody more effective than Ghorbanifar or the Australian. Further, no Iranian ever mentioned this supposed 1980 initiative, or even hinted at it.

Now it's true that our intelligence agencies don't rely only on case officers and spies. They also make use of some truly amazing technology, some of it available nowhere else in the world. The people involved in these efforts used to say that they could detect a Cuban general coughing in his car outside Managua, or a Soviet pilot breaking wind forty thousand feet over Syria. They were exaggerating—but not by much.

But there are no machines that read the human heart, and no instruments that measure hope, ambition, or even ideology. Trying to compile useful information about another society without agents on the ground is like a doctor who treats a patient solely by consulting the charts. He can learn a lot, but unless he can also ask, "Tell me, how do you feel? Where does it hurt?"—and get real answers—there are limits on what he can accomplish.

It takes years to train agents and install them, which is why all through the Reagan years we found ourselves facing big problems in places that surprised the hell out of us. Iran. Panama. Nicaragua. Angola. Mozambique. Egypt. Somalia. Suriname. Grenada. Not to mention Cuban agents all over Central America.

If we'd had sufficient intelligence assets in these countries, they would have flooded Washington with warnings. And no matter who was running the CIA, this information would have been disseminated around the State Department, the Pentagon, the White House, Congress—until somebody said, "Wait a minute, what's going on here?"

Instead, we were shocked when the Shah was overthrown and our embassy was captured. We were devastated when our Marine barracks were bombed in Lebanon. We were dumbfounded when Sadat was gunned down, although his assassins had been planning to kill him for months. The Israelis had learned about the plot, and had issued a warning both to the Egyptians and to us, but Sadat's people were emotionally incapable of accepting that information from their former enemy. And we didn't have the assets to confirm it independently.

Our intelligence failure in Iran had another cause, too. Although the Shah enjoyed our complete support, he was terrified that the CIA had a secret plan to replace him, and he hadn't wanted the Agency to track the activities of the religious opposition. The CIA believed that if the Shah caught us looking too closely at his internal adversaries, he might conclude that we were actually supporting them. Meanwhile, intelligence analysis being done in Washington also underestimated the religious opposition in Iran, which, in turn, further decreased the incentive for the CIA to keep a close eye on it.

And so by 1985, when it came to taking the political temperature in Iran we were completely in the dark. It seemed reasonable to assume, as the Israelis believed, that some members of Iran's government were, by our standards, more rational than the Ayatollah, more moderate and pragmatic. We knew, for example, that certain Iranian officials were allowed to leave the country to deal with foreign intermediaries. And on mundane matters, such as international airline schedules, the Iranians were generally cooperative. Surely some people in their government could see that a relationship with the United States, or at least an open channel of communication, was in their best interest. But with nobody reporting to us from Tehran, we didn't know for certain whether a moderate faction even existed—let alone who might be part of it.

We were fairly certain that the Ayatollah's government was not monolithic, if only because dictators going back to the days of Julius Caesar have always tended to promote factions—usually to deter their underlings from uniting in opposition to the boss. In the case of Iran, there were persistent reports that Rafsanjani himself was relatively moderate. Surely not everyone in Khomeini's government was as fanatic as the old man, even if they all had to keep up the pretense.

Were our expectations valid, or were we the victims of our own fantasies? Even today, I can't say for sure. But I believed then, and still do, that there were at least some moderates in their government.

Despite what we didn't know, a couple of things were clear. First, it hadn't been all that long since America and Iran had been friendly. The United States had done a lot for the Shah—at least until the end, when Carter abandoned him—and despite all the hostile rhetoric emanating from the Khomeini regime, there was still a reservoir of goodwill toward America in some sectors of Iranian society, including the military. From defector reports and other intelligence sources, we knew that the radical changes at the highest levels were not totally reflected among the masses.

We also knew that the Ayatollah was very old. And despite what some of his supporters believed, we were prepared to go out on a limb and assume he was also mortal. And so the inevitable question arose: What happens when he dies? Doesn't it make sense for us to try to achieve some kind of alliance with pragmatists or moderates in the government so we'll have some leverage when a new regime takes over? And if no regime emerges, and the Ayatollah's death is followed by absolute chaos, wouldn't that be a powerful inducement for the Soviets to step in?

And wasn't it shortsighted of us to let past hostilities between our two countries be the sole determining factor in whether we would have anything to do with Iran? Germany and Japan had inflicted a thousand times more damage on us than the Iranians ever dreamed of, and they became our allies. By early 1986 we had begun warming up to the Soviets, and we were even kissing the Chinese on the cheek. We couldn't blame everybody in the Iranian government for what had happened six years earlier at the embassy. An approach to Iran was certainly politically risky, but didn't we have a lot to gain by at least making an effort?

Our first meeting in Tehran took place in McFarlane's suite at 5:00 P.M., a few hours after we arrived. Once again we were disappointed by the absence of any high-level officials from the other side. Instead of showing up with Rafsanjani or the prime minister, Gorba and the Australian trotted out a short, stocky man in his middle fifties with graying hair. Dr. No, as we referred to him, was their spokesman for Western affairs. He was higher in rank than the Australian, but he wasn't one of their top people.

He was, however, fluent in English, and very articulate, which we certainly appreciated. When Gorba was translating, you had the feeling he was making it up as he went along. You could practically see him thinking, Hmm, I can't put it quite *that* way, so let me soften it a little.

Dr. No welcomed us to Tehran, and apologized for the mix-up at the airport. He talked on for a while, and more or less told us to lower our expectations. Essentially, his message boiled down to "Please, we're trying to make this work, but I can't guarantee that the next guy through the door will be Rafsanjani. After all, we still remember the meeting in the spring of 1980 between Mehdi Barzagan, our first prime minister, and Zbigniew Brzezinski, President Carter's national security adviser. A few days later, because of that one meeting, Barzagan was deposed. Our people are interested in meeting with you, but we have to move very slowly and carefully."

When Dr. No was finished, McFarlane responded with an opening statement of his own. "We in the United States," he said, "recognize that Iran is a sovereign power. We have had some disagreements over the past eight years, but we should deal with each other on the basis of mutual respect."

Mutual respect? It sure didn't feel that way. Before the day was out McFarlane fired off a cable to Washington with a graphic assessment of the situation we were dealing with. Back in Washington, Bud was routinely mocked for his impenetrable prose and obfuscation, a circuitous dialect that was affectionately known as "McFarlanese," that was deemed evasive even by the standards of diplomacy. But this time his words were colorful, clear, and accurate. Imagine, he wrote, "what it would be like if, after nuclear attack, a surviving Tatar had become vice president, a recent grad student became secretary of state, and a bookie became the interlocutor for all discourse with foreign countries."

Bud was especially angry that the Iranians seemed completely unprepared for our visit. I was afraid this might happen, which is why I had repeatedly argued that before an American of McFarlane's stature came to Tehran, there ought to be an advance trip at the staff level to ensure that both sides were in agreement on exactly why we were coming, and what we all hoped to accomplish.

The ultimate goal, although we weren't sure it was possible, was to arrange a secret meeting between Rafsanjani and Vice President Bush, presumably on neutral ground—in Europe, the Orient, or even the Middle East. This would have let the Iranians know that we were serious not only about recovering the hostages but also about resuming some kind of relationship between our two countries. While such a meeting seemed unlikely, it would have been easier to set up than a similar meeting between Rafsanjani and George Shultz. Shultz loved being visible, and it was hard to imagine him going anywhere without the press. Bush, on the other hand, was the former head of the CIA, and he was comfortable with covert operations. As Vice President, he was the official American mourner at state funerals all over the world. As he wended his way from one funeral parlor to another, it might have been possible for him to meet discreetly with his Iranian counterpart.

It never happened, in part because Casey was strongly opposed to an advance trip. Sending McFarlane to Tehran was risky enough, he said, but for an American delegation to go over there without a high official in the group was simply too dangerous. We could all disappear, and the Iranians might claim that we never showed up. Even our own government might be forced to disavow any knowledge of our visit.

Casey may well have been right in assessing the dangers of an advance trip, but not going carried its own risks. Even with friendly governments, it's almost impossible to hold a productive diplomatic meeting without advance work. Whenever a senior American official traveled to a foreign country, we would always try to arrange in advance whom they would be meeting with, and when, and what was likely to be decided. This was part of the routine of diplomacy.

But in the case of Iran we knew very little, and much of what we *thought* we knew turned out to be wrong. Our intelligence services kept a close eye on Ghorbanifar, and most of the time we knew what he was up to. But whenever he traveled to Iran, the lights went out. When he was there, we had no idea what he was telling the Iranians, or what commitments he was making in our name.

Only after we arrived in Tehran did it become clear that Ghorbanifar hadn't prepared the necessary groundwork for these meetings, and that he had been telling different things to each side. We could also see that the Iranians didn't seem to have much respect for him, either. Well, I thought, at least we have *that* in common.

Looking back on it now, I don't believe the Iranians had really been expecting us. No wonder Ghorbanifar had looked so upset at the airport. When he finally showed up, he was almost speechless—which was highly unusual for him. When he saw us standing there—Bud, Nir, Howard, George, myself—his jaw dropped. Maybe he was shocked to see Nir, because an Israeli who came to Tehran was taking an enormous risk. But more likely it was the whole group of us that spooked him. Perhaps he had planned to go back to his contacts in the government and say, "See, I knew they weren't coming. Send me back with a better deal."

And all the while he had been telling *us*, "You must come to Tehran, and the hostages will be freed."

We should have realized that despite everything Gorba had told us, direct contact between us and the Iranians was probably the last thing in the world that he wanted. For once that happened, he would become irrelevant. By coming to Tehran, we had called his bluff.

We had been told that if we came to Tehran, the hostages would be released. Then, with that hurdle out of the way, we would move on to discuss the larger issues. But by the end of the first day we could see that nothing was going to happen quickly. To signify his displeasure, and his frustration at not meeting high-level officials, McFarlane spent the next day holed up in his suite.

Since the hostages are central to this story, it may be worth explaining why they were kidnapped in the first place. The question may seem obvious, and yet it was seldom discussed. Plain and simple, the truth is that American and other Western hostages were taken to get Americans and other Westerners out of the Middle East, and to discourage their fellow citizens from coming in. The only thing the kidnappers had against their victims was that Weir, Jenco, and the other Americans carried blue passports. The purpose of the kidnappings was to humiliate us and to instill fear into the hearts of any Americans who were thinking of traveling in the region.

It's terribly hard for Americans to accept the fact that some people just don't like us. Don't like us? They should *love* us. Look at how much we're doing to help them. We're the good guys, aren't we?

That's not how the radical fundamentalists in Beirut see it. They hate us, and everything we stand for. They despise our Judeo-Christian value system, our reverence for individual liberty, and the role America plays in the world.

President Reagan was obsessed by the hostages, and he repeatedly made it clear to all of us who worked on this issue that we should do everything possible to get them home. Many Americans shared his concern, but others felt that the hostages had been given sufficient warning to leave, and had made their own free choices. I understand that argument, and I certainly don't support the idea of a paternalistic government. But what about those brave people who stayed behind in Beirut to fulfill a humanitarian mission—and did so as Americans? David Jacobsen was the director of the American University hospital.

He was helping to save lives, and his presence was an admirable symbol of American values.

While each of us must take responsibility for his own decisions, I believe the President was right to care so deeply about the hostages. When you get right down to it, what is the American government for if not to protect the rights and the lives of individual American citizens? The same is true of Israel, which was one reason Nir had come to Tehran: he was determined to rescue two Israeli soldiers who were being held in Beirut. Nir and I had become friends, and he once cited an old Jewish proverb: he who saves a single life is as if he has saved the entire world.

I have no doubt that Ronald Reagan felt the same way, and I find it difficult to fault him for trying so hard to get the hostages home. The Iran initiative had a chance of working, and to some degree it did work. But it wasn't the only effort our government made. During this same period, our State Department undertook a wide variety of diplomatic and other initiatives to achieve the same purpose. All of them were worth trying, but none of them succeeded.

On our second day in Tehran, with McFarlane remaining in his room to show his indignation, Cave, Teicher, Nir, and I continued the meetings. In Bud's absence, I became the interim negotiator. "We're very disappointed," I told the Iranians. "President Reagan has sent over his special emissary, and with all due respect, he hasn't met anybody on his level since we arrived. This is contrary to all our expectations. It was our understanding that Mr. McFarlane would meet with Prime Minister Mousavi, or President Khamenei, or Speaker Rafsanjani."

Dr. No seemed genuinely surprised. "Who told you these things?"

"Ghorbanifar," I replied.

Dr. No just sighed. By now we couldn't avoid the fact that both sides had come to this meeting with completely different expectations. We assumed we would be meeting with high-level officials, and that the release of the hostages was only a phone call away. The Iranians didn't expect that either event would occur soon.

Moreover, they had expectations of their own. They evidently believed that if we showed up at all, we would be bringing along a shipment of HAWK antiaircraft missile parts that they had ordered and already paid for.* In fact, we had brought less than 10 percent of the total order.

The HAWK parts that the Iranians had purchased had been discreetly collected from American military warehouses by the Defense Department, and flown to Israel shortly before we arrived. The bulk of the consignment had been loaded onto a second Israeli 707 that was sitting in Tel Aviv and was prepared to take off for Tehran the moment we gave the signal.

Dr. No assured us that he was doing everything possible to get the hostages released. "We have already sent a man to Lebanon," he said. "We expect to hear from him tomorrow. Meanwhile, let us continue talking.

"But you must keep in mind," he repeated, "that not everybody in our government looks with favor on this dialogue. We must move slowly. When Brezhnev died, we sent a delegation to his funeral, and the leadership was attacked by the people for this act."

In other words, Iran is not a dictatorship. Sure, I thought, and I bet there's a bridge over in Brooklyn that you'd like to sell us.

But the Iranians were also disappointed. "We expected much more equipment than we found on your plane," Dr. No said.

I explained that we had specific orders from Washington not to send the second plane until the hostages were released.

In fact, even the parts we brought with us were supposed to remain on the plane until the Iranians had fulfilled their end of the bargain. Our pilots had been given strict instructions to stay with the aircraft the entire time—not only to guard the parts, but also to prevent saboteurs from installing listening devices, or possibly even explosives.

But on our first night in Tehran, the pilots showed up at the hotel. They were accompanied by a contingent of Rev Guards. "We know what you told us," they said, "and we didn't want to leave the plane. But see these guys? See their guns?"

*The HAWK antiaircraft system comprises sophisticated electronic detection, identification, target-acquisition, and guidance equipment, and the associated missiles that home in on enemy aircraft. It was originally sold to the Shah as a means of defending key locations in Iran. The electronic components of the system had deteriorated considerably since Khomeini had come to power, and the revolutionary government was desperate to rehabilitate it for its original purposes.

A line had been crossed and we were furious. There was a great commotion in the hallway, with everybody yelling at once and waving their hands. I hit the roof, exaggerating my genuine anger for dramatic effect. "Our pilots *must* stay with the plane," I yelled, "or else we're all leaving right now!"

Soon the air was full of apologies. "Oh, there has been a misunder*stand*ing, we're so *sorry*, we thought they'd be more *comfortable* in the hotel." The pilots were returned to the airport, but by now the plane had been stripped. While we continued meeting with the Iranians, the pilots went through it inch by inch to check for sabotage.

Back at the Hilton, the talks ground on. Even if Ghorbanifar hadn't lied to both sides, there was still an enormous culture gap that had to be bridged. "We can begin the process," Dr. No kept saying, "but you must understand, these things take time." This wasn't just rhetoric. We come from a society where things unfold quickly, and by our standards, the pace in Iran was painfully slow. It had never been fast to begin with, and now, with Khomeini in power, it was as if the entire country had slipped back into the eleventh century.

In an attempt to salvage something from this trip, I told the Iranians that at the very least we wanted to continue the dialogue. "There are those in our government, too, who would prefer that we have nothing to do with Iran. But we think it is important for our two countries to communicate. Even if we can't reach an agreement today, we must continue talking."

But even that plan sounded ambitious to our hosts. "You did a great thing by coming here," said Dr. No. "But there has been a misunderstanding. When we accepted your visit, we did not mean that a direct dialogue between our two governments would start immediately. It will take time. There are still problems to work out, but there is an old Persian saying—that patience leads to victory. We can talk, but how can we be assured that your country can keep a secret?"

I explained that we were prepared to send them a satellite communications device, similar to the one we were using to stay in touch with Washington, and that we were willing to dispatch it along with a communications team to ensure quick and secure communications between our two governments. Casey had been especially interested in this arrangement. If the Iranians agreed to it, the American technicians sent in to operate the system could serve as well-connected sources of human intelligence.

The situation looked hopeless, but I decided to give it one more try. "As soon as your government can arrange the release of the Americans being held in Beirut," I said, "we will send the second plane full of HAWK missile parts. Then, as we have already discussed, we will also sell you two radar units, and deliver them to the port of Bandar 'Abbas. After that we can talk further about your military needs. But if we leave here without overcoming the obstacles"—by which I meant freeing the hostages—"then our visit will have created new and additional obstacles."

On the third day, McFarlane joined us again. But the talks quickly went from bad to worse when Dr. No reported that he had finally heard from his emissary in Beirut. Apparently a deal was still possible, but the hostage-takers had now come up with a new and expanded list of demands. We listened incredulously as Dr. No spelled them out: Israel had to withdraw from South Lebanon *and* the Golan Heights. And Kuwait had to release the seventeen Da'wa terrorists who had been arrested for bombing embassies and other buildings in Kuwait City in 1983. We had heard that one before, perhaps because one of the prisoners in Kuwait, who had been sentenced to death, was the brother-in-law of Imad Mughniyah, the leader of the Islamic Jihad, the umbrella organization that included the Hezballah, the group responsible for the Lebanese kidnappings.

And as if these terms weren't already laughable, there was a preposterous kicker: the hostage-takers wanted us to reimburse them for their expenses! As McFarlane put it in his message back to Poindexter, "How's that for chutzpah!!!"

It wasn't easy, but we tried to remain polite. What did these people take us for? I felt like a customer in a used-car lot, where the salesman comes back and says, "Listen, I just went back and checked with the manager, and he said I could offer you a very special price. If you're willing to pay cash, we'll let you have that '85 Ford for five hundred thousand dollars."

Later that day, Dr. No reported that the hostage-takers had reduced their demands. They were no longer asking for the Israelis to withdraw from South Lebanon *and* the Golan Heights, or even to be reimbursed for expenses. Suddenly, the only remaining condition was the prisoners in Kuwait.

In other words, "I've gone back to the manager, and he agrees that the initial price was a little high. He's now willing to let the car go for only two hundred thousand—*and he'll even throw in a new set of tires.*"

McFarlane, trying valiantly to control his anger, replied that his instructions were clear: unless all the hostages were released, with no additional conditions, we were going home. "As soon as they're free," he said, "you'll have the remaining parts within ten hours. As for the Da'wa prisoners in Kuwait, there's not much we can do about that. That's between you and the Kuwaitis. But we would be willing to make every effort to persuade the Kuwaitis to be humane."

After a few more hours of haggling, we seemed to be making some progress. We even agreed on a six-point plan, which I typed up on the word processor attached to our encryption device. Assuming Dr. No could sell this plan to his higher-ups, the Iranians would arrange for the release of the hostages and of William Buckley's body on the following day. Meanwhile, we would launch the jet from Israel with the remaining spare parts. But if the hostages were not released as promised, the second plane would be instructed to turn around and go back to Israel. There were also provisions for the delivery of two radar units, and for a satellite communications system with American operators.

When the Iranians left the hotel, I took McFarlane aside and said, "If this thing is going to end up as we hope, we've got to launch that plane tonight." (The plane, laden with extra fuel, had to be airborne before the heat of the day made takeoff impossible.)

"Okay," he replied, "but don't let it pass the turnaround point." Because the flight was so long, once the plane passed a certain point it would no longer have enough fuel to turn around, and would be forced to land in Iran. There had been hours of planning with regard to that plane, and we had tried to anticipate anything that might possibly go wrong. What if the plane lost an engine? What if it had to abort over another country? What emergency radio frequency would the pilot use? With McFarlane's permission, I sent a coded message to Dick Secord, who was awaiting instructions in Tel Aviv: "Launch at 0400. If you don't hear from me again by 0800, turn it around."

Early the next morning the Iranians came back. "Give us more time," they said. "We think we can get you two hostages. We don't care what Ghorbanifar promised you. We've told you before: we have some influence, but we don't control things in Beirut. We can't just *make* things happen. We can't get all the hostages out. This is the best we can do."

This was exactly what McFarlane had feared: that the Iranians would offer a partial deal. Admiral Poindexter had foreseen this possibility several weeks earlier, and had instructed us not to consider it.*

But having participated in those long, drawn-out meetings, I no longer believed the Iranians were negotiating for a better deal. They were now making the only offer they could. The choice had come down to half a loaf or nothing at all.

I went to Bud and said, "For God's sake, we can save two of them."

But he wouldn't hear of it. "The only authority I have is all or nothing."

"Bud, I know that," I pleaded. "But at least ask." Our communications system gave us instant access to Washington, and I believe that if Bud had presented the dilemma to the admiral, Poindexter would have taken it to the President. And the President, wanting above all to save lives, would have said yes.

But McFarlane wouldn't even consider it. "Forget it," he said. "I've got my instructions, and you've got yours. They've had their chance."

We had started the conversation out on the balcony of his suite, but now we were discussing it openly and loudly in the living room. To hell with the Iranian bugs.

"I don't like this kind of dealing. It's not right," he said.

With our entire trip going down the tubes, and only a short time remaining before the second plane from Tel Aviv reached the turnaround point, I was getting emotional. "That's true, Bud, it's *not* right. But this isn't the time to get holy. Let's not kid ourselves. What

---

*Poindexter note to North, April 16, 1986: "You may go ahead and go, but I want several points made clear to them. There are not to be any parts delivered until all the hostages are free in accordance with the plan that you laid out for me before. None of this half shipment before any are released crap. It is either all or nothing.... If they really want to save their asses from the Soviets, they should get on board."

do you think we've been doing all this time? You started this process, and we've been dealing ever since."

At a level considerably above mine, President Reagan and Bud McFarlane had already decided to trade arms for hostages. And now, given the alternatives, I thought it was more important that we try to salvage the lives of two poor bastards who were chained to a wall than to try to preserve the purity of a policy that had already been violated.

Nir, too, went to Bud and made an impassioned appeal to consider the Iranian proposal. Bud threw him out, and he later chastised me for "sending" Nir. But I didn't send Nir; when Ami saw the whole thing collapsing, he was devastated.

Hearing nothing from us at the midpoint of its flight to Tehran, the second 707, with the parts aboard, dutifully returned to Israel.

A few minutes later, Bud stormed down the hall, threw open the doors, and said, "We're leaving. Pack up. We're out of here in five minutes."

McFarlane's rush to leave was so sudden that at first I thought he was bluffing. He wasn't. But the elevators weren't working, the cars weren't ready, and the Iranians were clearly panicked because the whole deal was about to go down the tubes. They tried to delay us, but Bud was too angry. "We're going home," he snapped, "even if we have to walk down the stairs and find taxis to take us to the airport."

I was sick at the idea of returning home empty-handed. Not only could we probably save two hostages, but we would have set the stage for even bigger gains. But I had given it my best shot, and now it was time to carry out my orders.

Would it have made any difference if we had stayed a few more hours, or even another day or two? I believe that two hostages would have been released, but who knows? Given the fact that they were totally unprepared for our visit, and unaware of our expectations, the Iranians had been jumping through hoops to make things work. In true American style, we wanted things done yesterday.

As we prepared to leave the hotel, they continued to plead with us. "Give us a few more hours and we'll get two of them released." CIA headquarters had already reported over our satellite link that Rafiq Dust, Iran's deputy foreign minister, had left Tehran for Damascus, as he had in previous cases when Western hostages were actually released. Later, when the French hostages came out, Rafiq Dust was again in Damascus, which would indicate that if anybody was controlling the kidnappers in Beirut, it was probably not the Iranians but the Syrians.*

Eventually the cars pulled up in front of the hotel to take us to the airport. I went in and told our communicator to send the prearranged departure message to Tel Aviv and Washington, and, once it was acknowledged, to pack up the equipment. I prayed that our precipitous departure would not mean that the waiting cars would be taking us straight to Evin Prison.

Outside the hotel, the Australian begged me to go with him, and Nir and I climbed in his car. The Australian himself drove, grinding every gear as he continued pleading with us to stay just a few more hours.

At the airport, as we climbed out of the cars and walked toward the plane, Ghorbanifar was still begging us to reconsider. The Australian actually walked up the stairway to the plane to make one last, desperate appeal, with tears in his eyes, until McFarlane said, "Close the door."

I appealed to Bud one last time before we took off. There was still time; he could have asked for guidance right there, on the runway. All he had to do was tell the communicator to open his briefcase, and in less than a minute we would have been talking to Washington. But McFarlane wouldn't budge.

The flight back to Tel Aviv was very quiet. We were all completely drained and enormously disappointed. We had come to Tehran expecting real and dramatic progress on the hostages. We even had people standing by in Beirut and Cyprus to coordinate their travel home. And now we were returning empty-handed.

But we were also immensely relieved—more so than we had expected—to be out of Tehran. On the long flight back to Tel Aviv, George mentioned that earlier that morning, back at the hotel, he too had worried that the Iranians might be so frustrated with our visit that they would prevent us from leaving. We didn't know at the time how close that possibility really was. Nine months later, the Tower Com-

---

*"The most serious problem we must address," George Cave later told the Tower Commission, "is whether the Iranians can gain control of the hostages. The French don't think they can. This could be our real problem. The Iranian side may be most willing, but unable to gain control."

mission report noted that a group of Revolutionary Guards had come to the hotel to arrest us, but that our own guards had turned them back.

We had all set aside our fears during those four days, when we were preoccupied with the meetings. It wasn't until we had cleared Iranian airspace that we admitted to ourselves that things could have ended a lot worse. "You were lucky," Casey told me later, when I gave him back the pills. "For all you knew the radicals in that government could have decided to put you up against the wall and shoot you." Now I don't believe in luck, but I do believe in Divine Providence—and the power of prayer. I'm convinced that God answered my prayer that morning, and delivered us from a very unpleasant experience. Tom Hemingway, a Marine friend of mine, has a sign over his desk: "God doesn't promise a smooth passage—just a safe landing." We made ours in Tel Aviv later that day.

When we touched down, we immediately set up our satellite communications equipment and called Washington to tell them we were safe. Nir said good-bye, and went home to his family. The rest of us flew back to Washington in a tiny Lear jet, with everybody jammed into a plane so small that we had to stop three times to refuel. When we finally landed at Dulles Airport, Bud, Howard, and I drove straight to the White House for a meeting with the President. During the Oval Office meeting I said nothing about my disagreement with McFarlane, but later I unloaded my frustrations on the admiral. To this day, I'm angry that Bud wouldn't even *ask* for permission to accept the Iranian offer for two hostages. The admiral didn't commit himself, but I'm still confident that the President would have said yes.

Just before we reported to the President, I called Betsy from my office to tell her I was back. "And not a moment too soon," she said. "I've just sold the house and you've got to sign the papers." She had told the buyer and the agent that her husband was away on a trip, and she didn't know when he would be back. It wasn't clear whether they believed her, and she had already postponed the closing twice. "This is it," she told me on the phone. "We're closing today. If you don't show up, the deal is off."

I was wiped out after that terrible flight home, and terribly disappointed, and it would have been nice to have a shower and change my clothes. But I did make it to the closing in time.

*   *   *

The previous day, as McFarlane and I had stood on the tarmac at Ben Gurion Airport in Tel Aviv, we had a moment alone to digest what had happened in Tehran. We had disagreed about the process, but we were equally disappointed at the outcome. "Well, Bud," I said, trying to cheer him up, "it's not a total loss. The one bright spot in all of this is that part of the money from these transactions is going to help the Nicaraguan resistance."

McFarlane gave me one of his inscrutable looks. He didn't ask me to elaborate.

4

Coming of Age

Whenever I tell our kids about my nearly idyllic childhood, I get the feeling that deep down, they suspect Dad is making the whole thing up. It's not that their lives are so dramatically different from mine, or that they've experienced especially hard times. Tait, Stuart, Sarah, and Dornin have all grown up with God's abundant blessings—good health, good values, and good friends. They have all been active in our church and our family Bible study groups. But they're certainly growing up in a different world than the one I used to know.

In my entire high school there were only two or three guys who drank beer or smoked cigarettes. And while we certainly talked about girls, nobody I knew actually *did* anything. My three daughters and my son have been relatively sheltered, but they all know teenagers who have had abortions, and others who have been arrested for drugs, and still others who were victims of violence, parental abuse, and even suicide.

And this was in the suburbs of Virginia.

I was born in Texas in 1943, in the midst of the war that America won for the world. I was named Oliver Laurence North, and until I was eighteen everybody called me Larry to distinguish me from my father, Oliver Clay North—who was known as Clay to distinguish him from *his* father. My father, a major in the Army, had grown up in Philadelphia. My mother, Ann Clancy, was a teacher from Oswego, New York.

When Dad returned from the war in 1945, we moved to Philmont, New York, a small mill town about thirty-five miles south of Albany where people didn't bother to lock their doors at night. It sounds corny, I know, but Philmont was the epitome of small-town America. We had it all—a baseball diamond, empty fields, trout streams, and plenty of woods where we could play capture the flag, cops and robbers, cowboys and Indians, and anything else a childhood imagination allowed. Main Street, clean and peaceful, was lined with small, locally owned businesses like Mr. Carney's hardware store. The local grocery store, an A & P, operated under the company's majestic old name—the Great Atlantic and Pacific Tea Company. We had a doctor who made house calls, and a tiny movie house where we saw black-and-white Buster Crabbe and Tarzan films and other serials on rainy Saturday afternoons.

Everyone in Philmont knew everybody else, so you couldn't get away with any savage crimes of passion—like throwing a tomato at the kid down the block—because your parents would invariably hear about it within the hour. There was no anonymity. Our graduating class at Ockawamick High School consisted of thirty-six kids, and the only reason it was that big was that the school served the entire region.

Except for my front teeth, which were blessed with a large gap, perfect for squirting water across a swimming pool, I wasn't a bad-looking kid. When I was in high school, our family dentist said, "You know, Larry, we could certainly do something about the space between your teeth, but you probably don't want to bother with that. It's not as if you're planning to be a movie star or on television, right?" I wonder what Dr. Link was thinking during the Iran-contra hearings in the summer of 1987, when millions of Americans decided that I reminded them of the "before" picture in a commercial for orthodontia.

I grew up as the oldest of four kids: My brother Jack was followed by our sister, Pat. Tim, our youngest brother, was born years later, when I was already at the Naval Academy. Jack and I were less than eighteen months apart; we were best friends, and virtually inseparable. With two older brothers, Pat had to endure a lot of teasing and a little jealousy, too, because she had her own room.

Like all the youngsters in Philmont, we pretty much had the run of the place. There was no such thing as a bad neighborhood, and we walked or rode our bikes everywhere. Bicycles were our oxygen, and we were continually tinkering with the gears and adjusting the handlebars. Mom didn't worry where you had gone after school—unless someone snitched and told her you had been speeding down Suicide Hill on Summit Street, where we'd go screaming onto Main Street. But Suicide Hill couldn't have been all *that* dangerous, it occurs to me now, because Main Street didn't even have a traffic light.

Mom used to hate it when the other mothers in our neighborhood would stand out on the porch at suppertime and yell at the top of their lungs, "*Billy! Peter! Time for dinner!*" The woman across the street had a better idea: a whistle that she blew twice when it was time to come in. My mother bought her own whistle, and our signal was three toots.

For real excitement, we'd ride over to the train tracks, about a mile or so from our house on Maple Avenue. When the railroad police weren't around, we'd sneak into the switching station shed (which was never locked), take out a few signal flares, and lay them across the track. That was the emergency signal for the engineer to stop the train. Then we'd climb up on the hill and wait for him to jam on the brakes, just to see how long it took that train to grind to a halt.

During a long summer afternoon we might hop a slow-moving freight train as it slowly chugged up the long slope heading north out of Philmont. We'd ride for a couple of miles and jump off near the house of a family we knew, but it was a long walk home so we didn't do it often. Our parents knew nothing about it, but in case my own kids are reading this, let me make one thing clear: don't even *think* of trying anything like that.

I suppose you could say that my childhood was like a Norman Rockwell painting. I had a paper route, and on Saturdays, after collecting from my customers, I went down to Palen's, the local ice cream shop, and spent my tips on a chocolate malt and a package of Nabs—cheese crackers filled with peanut butter. In warm weather we went fishing, using empty Campbell's Soup cans for worms. Dad taught us how to open the can without removing the lid; if you bent the lid just a little, you could hang the can on your belt loop. That was about as high-tech as things got in Philmont. Jack and I learned to shoot a .22 rifle before we could drive a car, and not a season went by when we didn't save up a few dollars for the mandatory hunting and fishing licenses.

Our family used to rent a small summer cottage on Copake Lake, and early in the morning we'd go out in the rowboat to catch breakfast, which consisted of two filleted sunfish over toast. At night I'd sit on the floor and listen to the radio exploits of the Lone Ranger, the Shadow, and Sergeant Preston of the Yukon and his dog, King. Every Sergeant Preston episode ended with the line, "Well, King, this case is closed," whereupon King would bark in agreement. I sat there transfixed, and vowed to become a Mountie when I grew up. It was easy to visualize what these radio heroes looked like. Years later, when I saw them on television, I was terribly disappointed by how ordinary they were.

Betsy has sometimes asked me whether my childhood was really as serene or as happy as I remember it. Maybe she's right; I do have a way of putting bad times out of my mind. I don't even recall fighting with my brother, and *all* brothers fight.

After I was more or less grown up, our family gained a new member. I was home on leave from the Naval Academy when Mom announced to the family that she was pregnant. She was well into her forties, and in those days pregnancy at that age was virtually unheard of. I thought it was wonderful. I don't remember Pat's response, but Jack was shocked: I guess he didn't believe our parents still did that kind of thing. Tim was born in 1963, when I was twenty.

It wasn't until I myself became a parent that I realized just how much my mother did for us when we were young. As a father and a husband, I can see how busy Betsy is, how her life is controlled by our kids' schedules and the countless miles of driving with a howling mob of gremlins in the back seat. Maybe you can't appreciate these things until you grow up, but I sure do now.

We may have been innocent and carefree, but we weren't totally oblivious to the outside world. My parents followed the news avidly, and I remember hearing the grown-ups talk about the Army-McCarthy hearings—never imagining, of course, that thirty-three years later I would spend six days in that very same Senate hearing room as the guest of another congressional committee.

Mom is a devout Catholic, and every Sunday our whole family went to the Sacred Heart Church. I was an altar boy, and sometimes Father Dwyer would invite me to go along with him on pastoral visits. He drove a very old Buick which had a penchant for getting stuck in the mud and the snow, and I began to suspect that the real reason he asked me to come along was to help push him out.

As an altar boy, I had to memorize the liturgy and the responsorials of the Mass—in Latin, naturally. It was a good way to start the day, and I continued going almost every morning until I graduated from the Naval Academy. Later, of course, I had to learn the Mass all over again—this time in English. I still miss the Latin Mass; I liked the idea that you could attend Mass anywhere in the world and it would always be the same. These days, although I have a much more personal relationship with my Savior, I still have fond memories of that ancient liturgy.

Nearly every Sunday after church we had a big family dinner with my maternal grandmother, who lived with us, and my paternal grandfather, who came for dinner nearly every night after my Grandmother North died in 1959. As I remember it today, the Sunday menu was always the same: roast beef, mashed potatoes, homemade gravy, green beans, and Yorkshire pudding, spiced with plenty of talk about politics and world events. My parents rarely argued, but what I remember most clearly about the Chinese attack on the islands of Quemoy and Matsu in 1958 is that my mother wanted to shut off the radio while Dad insisted on listening to the news, even during dinner. They had a similar disagreement two years later, when Francis Gary Powers was shot down in a U-2 plane over the Soviet Union. These weekly dinners were the North family version of the Sunday morning TV talk shows.

My father, who owned a wool mill, was a staunch Republican. Some people have tried to portray our family as unusually patriotic, but in small-town America during the 1950s, just about everyone believed in God, country, and motherhood. My mother had been a registered Democrat, but she eventually changed parties and later ran as a Republican for the town board.

I was very close to Dad, and although he was quiet and self-possessed, we had no trouble communicating. When I moved away from home, I wrote to him often—from the Naval Academy and from Vietnam, knowing that whatever I wanted to tell him, he'd understand.

He loved to read to us, and I grew up listening to classic children's fare: *Grimm's Fairy Tales, Treasure Island, Robin Hood,* and the collected prose and poetry of Rudyard Kipling. Our house was filled with books and newspapers. When we went off to college, Mom and Dad refused to send us any spending money unless we wrote them regularly.

Dad was far from a stereotypical military man. He had a passion for growing roses, and he loved the ballet. He'd see several performances each summer when the New York City Ballet performed in Saratoga. We weren't too far from Tanglewood, the summer home of the Boston Symphony Orchestra, and on summer afternoons we'd sit on the lawn and listen to their rehearsals. Occasionally, our parents would take us to New York. I loved the skyscrapers, but they couldn't compare to the greatest wonder of all—the Horn & Hardart Automat.

Dad was a history buff, and we must have visited every museum and battlefield on the Eastern Seaboard. His heroes were the Revolutionary War generals, and I believe we hit every revolutionary battlefield from Saratoga to Yorktown. Dad was a terrific guide, pointing out exactly where Benedict Arnold was wounded, or explaining the strategic importance of this hill or that river.

In 1969, when Jack and I were both serving in Vietnam, Dad took it upon himself to arrange a reunion for us. Without telling us, he wrote a letter to Melvin Laird, the Secretary of Defense (whom he didn't know), pointing out that both his boys were serving in Vietnam, and that it was only right that they should be able to see each other over there.

Years later, in my file, I found the Marine Corps response to his request, which simply read: "Second Lieutenant Oliver North is assigned to a Marine combat unit and is unavailable for such a visit at this time." In other words, buzz off, Dad, he's got a war to fight. But the Army was more receptive. Jack was yanked out of his unit with orders to report to Saigon, and from there to Da Nang—*and nobody told him why.* As he was being pulled out of the field, his helicopter was shot up, which is a little more excitement than you want to have on an average day, even in Vietnam. Jack wasn't hurt, but months later, when he returned home, he raised the roof with Dad.

Dad's response was classic. "Well," he said softly, "you were both over there, and you hadn't seen each other in a while, and it made your mother happy to know you'd be together."

It was hard for him to express the affection he had for his sons, but deep down, this tough guy was all heart.

Dad was always active in community affairs. He founded the local Rotary Club, and as president of the school board, he worked to centralize the schools and to provide a better education for youngsters growing up in this rural setting. These days, the phrase "community service" denotes a form of punishment, but I grew up thinking of it as a responsibility and a privilege. I didn't join the Marine Corps because my father was a military man. I signed up because he taught us all that anyone who is blessed to live in this great country ought to give something back to it. And he must have taught us well, because all three of his sons served in combat—one each in the Army, Navy, and Marines. He probably would have preferred that I join the Army, but he mentioned this only once. "I know the Marines are looking for a few good men," he said, "but remember, the Army has a whole lot more of them."

As a civilian, he wasn't one to sit on the sidelines and criticize. "If you don't like the way things are," he'd say, "don't complain about them. Work to make them better." He gave his time to a whole slew of committees, causes, and charities. He was especially generous to the Salvation Army. He used to say that during the war, the Salvation Army volunteers were always there to give a doughnut and a cup of coffee to a soldier.

For all their civic involvement, my parents also knew how to have fun. They were active in the local theater group, where Mom acted in most of the plays and Dad worked backstage with the lights and the scenery. On weekend afternoons, they'd bring us along to the rehearsals at the D.A.R. Hall.

My parents believed in discipline, and by today's standards, at least, they were fairly strict. If one of us misbehaved, we would lose a privilege, like dessert. My parents didn't believe in sending us to our rooms, because they knew we'd have too good a time with all those books, Erector sets, model airplanes, and an enormous old RCA shortwave radio.

They insisted that we live by all of the Ten Commandments, although I seem to recall a special emphasis on number five—"Honor thy father and thy mother." Heaven help the North youngster who talked back to Mom, although my brother Jack took a little longer than I did to figure that out. I can remember only one occasion when my father actually hit me: he took off his belt and let me have it for being rude to Mom.

Dad served during World War II with the Ninety-fifth Infantry Division, part of General Patton's Third Army. In 1944, just after D-Day, his unit landed in France. Dad served as an operations officer, and later on as a logistics officer, with the Third Army. He returned home with a Silver Star and a Bronze Star, but he rarely talked about the war. Once in a while an old army buddy would drop by, and the two of them would sit out on the patio or on the porch and talk about old times. Jack and I used to sit on the steps and listen in.

He kept his decorations in the bottom drawer of his dresser, and after he died, I found the blue boxes with the medals inside, along with brittle, yellowed copies of his citations. He had been decorated for heroism during the battle for Metz, a German fortress. I also found the journals from his unit, which described the fierce fighting the men had experienced. They had even liberated a Nazi concentration camp—which my father had never mentioned.

I always knew that he had been part of something historic, but he talked about the war only in general patriotic terms: the United States did this, and our unit was part of it. There were pictures of him in uniform in our family album, and that was certainly part of his identity. But the main things I learned from my father were how to be a man, and how a husband ought to love his wife. I took that first gift early, and used it in ways that pleased him. Unfortunately, it took me far too long to open the second one.

Shortly after the war, Dad and his father had started the wool processing business where Dad worked until his retirement in 1965. Then he began a second career: teaching a course in transportation at

Hudson Valley Community College in Troy. He had finally found his calling. "I will always regret making you go into the wool business," Grandfather North told my father on his deathbed, "because I can see how happy you are as a teacher."

My grandfather had come to this country from England in 1895. By the early 1920s he had become extremely successful in the textile business, with household servants and even a chauffeur to drive him around. He lost almost everything in the Depression, but he recovered. That was his lesson to me: that you can suffer a great adversity and still persevere. He didn't sit around feeling sorry for himself or waiting for some government grant. He picked himself up and started all over again.

Grandfather North was a man of great dignity, with a British accent, white hair, and a mustache. Like many English immigrants to America, he was uncomfortable with the casual nature of our society. He could never understand how Americans could be, in his terms, so "disrespectful" of their leaders as to refer to the President, for example, as "Eisenhower," rather than *President* Eisenhower. Some of that same feeling carried over to me; even today, I'm not comfortable referring to high government officials by their last names.

He was proper, punctual, and more than a little rigid. He refused to eat in a restaurant that didn't have tablecloths. Once, when my parents took him out to dinner, the waitress said, "Please keep your forks for dessert." He was horrified. "I certainly will not," he replied, and I'm sure he never entered that place again.

He and Mabel, his wife, lived on a farm in nearby Ghent. I spent many happy days there with Jack and Pat, and I still have a distinct memory of being chased by a gaggle of geese. I must have been awfully young, because the geese were as big as I was.

As we did at home, Jack and I shared a room at the farm, where we played for hours with a set of hand-painted lead toy soldiers from England which had belonged to my father when he was growing up. They were divided into British and German companies from World War I, and we used to stage mock battles on the double bed with the help of a fine set of wooden blocks. Both the soldiers and the blocks were kept in a great wooden toy chest, and although they actually belonged to my father, they weren't allowed to leave the farm. But that only made the place more special.

Because Jack and I were so close in age, and got along so well, it was almost like having a best friend living in your house. We played together constantly, and worked together, too—delivering newspapers, shoveling snow, raking leaves, or cutting the grass for families in our neighborhood.

But even though we grew up side by side, we were very different types. Jack was always more outspoken, more contentious, and more willing to argue than I was. Like a lot of younger brothers, he learned to defend himself. We had a rule in our family: if you didn't eat all your vegetables, you didn't get dessert. When that happened to Jack, he would loudly proclaim that he had spit in his dessert so that I wouldn't eat it. But that never stopped me; he was my brother.

Jack was always going to Carney's Hardware Store on Main Street to buy whoopee cushions, fake vomit, and other weapons of mischief. It was wonderful to have a brother who could always be counted on to get in trouble; I could enjoy his antics without having to pay the price.

Jack attended Niagara University, and until the day he graduated I worried that he might be the type who decided it was "fun" to go over the Falls in a barrel. Jack's willingness to seek adventure led him to the Army, where he became a paratrooper, a ranger, and a special forces officer. He served for twenty years, and now works in New England as an engineer.

In the summer of 1984, while Jack was still in the Army and I was at the NSC, Dad's emphysema took a decided turn for the worse. I was on a trip to Africa and was in Nairobi, Kenya, when the Red Cross cabled the American embassy to advise me that the end was probably near. I flew home immediately, and arrived just after Dad had come home from the hospital. He knew he was dying, and had asked to spend his final days in his own bed.

I spent the weekend at his side. He was so weak that I carried him into the bathroom and bathed him. We prayed together, and read together from the Bible: Psalms, Proverbs, Paul's Letter to the Romans, and the Gospel of John. He had been raised as an Episcopalian and had gone to church regularly, but that weekend, on his deathbed, I believe that he came to know his Savior personally. Father Robert Hart, a great old man of God from my mother's neighborhood church, came and gave Dad communion and the Last Rites.

By the next morning he had improved dramatically—so much so that I returned to Washington to file a report on my trip to Africa. The next morning, Mom called to say he had died in his sleep. The end came quickly and peacefully, and I was grateful that we'd had that last weekend together. Today, I'm glad that he didn't have to suffer through the anguish my mother has experienced during the protracted Iran-contra investigations.

I always knew that I would go to college; the only question was where I would be accepted, and what we could afford. Holy Cross and Notre Dame both said yes, but without a scholarship, so in the fall of 1961 I ended up at Brockport State near Rochester, about two hundred and fifty miles from home. The dean of students at Brockport, Dr. Harold Rakov, had gone to college with my mother. Rakov's parents were Jewish immigrants from Russia, and their son had made a success of himself through determination and hard work. When he saw that I was undecided about the future beyond a vague desire to become a teacher, he pushed me to consider either the Naval Academy or medical school. He urged me to load up on math, physics, and chemistry courses, which would be helpful at either place.

He also encouraged me to think about the Marines. Russ Robertson, our high school coach, and Bob Bowes, one of my history teachers, had already suggested the Marines when I left for college. Rakov suggested that I consider the Platoon Leader Candidate Program, which was open to college students and required two summers at the Marine Officer Candidate School in Quantico, Virginia. If you successfully completed the two summers and graduated from college, you would be commissioned as an officer and enter The Basic School as a lieutenant. There was something about men who had served in the military—Robertson, Rakov, my father—that made them seem more self-assured and a little more confident about dealing with life. I admired these men, and I wanted to follow in their footsteps. After discussing it with Russ Robertson, Dr. Rakov, and Dad, I signed up for the PLC Program during my first year at Brockport.

The moment I got to Quantico I loved the place. This was the most intense and challenging thing I had ever done, and I was surrounded by tough, hard-working, motivated men. I wasn't a bad athlete to begin with, but at Quantico I learned that I could stretch myself a lot further than I had expected. I enjoyed the discipline, but even more than that, I loved being in an environment where everybody got up in the morning headed in the same direction.

"If you don't like Quantico," Rakov had told me, "you sure won't like Annapolis. If you do like it, it will help you get in."

After that first summer, I knew I wanted to be a Marine. During my second year at Brockport, I spent the first few weeks working on my application to the Naval Academy, which was just about the biggest bureaucratic challenge I have ever encountered. I was thrilled when they accepted me.

When I arrived in Annapolis in June 1963, the first thing I did, along with about a thousand of my new classmates, was to get the shortest, fastest haircut in the history of man. How short? How fast? In about eleven seconds flat, you're practically bald. I also learned that the military's prejudice against civilians begins right there, in the barber shop. Nobody says so explicitly, but you soon come to understand that most civilians are inferior beings whom you can identity first by the length of their hair, and then by the absence of shine on their shoes, the lack of a close shave, and their generally flabby and slovenly appearance.

I have never felt comfortable with military arrogance, but I haven't been immune to it, either. "Do you want to be a *Marine*, Private Johnson," I have yelled on more than one occasion, "or would you rather be"—sneer—"a *civilian*?" It's easy to forget that your mother is a civilian, and so are your wife and your kids.

Underneath that arrogance, however, is a well-deserved pride. That swaggering, macho attitude, the confidence that comes with being part of an elite group like the Marines, that lack of patience with our civilian counterparts—these qualities were earned on battlefields all over the world.

But that pride can easily be taken too far. From the day we arrived at the Naval Academy, we were repeatedly told that we were the best, that we had been chosen from thousands of applicants, only a handful of whom were good enough to make the cut. Naturally, a lot of midshipmen believed this. Later, as a Marine instructor at Quantico, I saw hundreds of Annapolis graduates come through the rigorous Officer's Basic Course that prepares new lieutenants for command. Usually, the men from Annapolis were either among our best students or among our weakest. The worst were those who swallowed the flattery and concluded that they didn't have to work very hard.

In those days, being at Annapolis was a lot like living in a combination monastery and prison work camp. Not only were there no women around; you were insulated from the outside world and totally consumed by your day-to-day duties and the strict requirements of the Academy. This was especially true for plebes, as freshmen were known. We weren't allowed to do *anything*: watch television, listen to the radio, go out with girls, ride in a car, go into town, enjoy a beer, or even drink coffee. It was often said that the Naval Academy took away all your God-given rights and then gave them back to you, one by one, and called them privileges.

Even after you made it past your plebe year, you were still part of that insular world, where you were awakened before dawn six mornings a week by the loud clang of the bells in Bancroft Hall, the world's largest dormitory. By the time they stopped ringing, you had to be out of bed and on your feet. The entire day was controlled by bells, which marked every class, every meal, everything. You were always rushing to the next activity, because being late for anything was a reportable offense. You were constantly busy. There were many reasons why a student might choose to leave Annapolis, but boredom wasn't one of them.

One result of this busy, sheltered environment was that we didn't really know what the rest of the country was thinking. And to the extent that you're not aware of another position, it's easy to assume it doesn't count. It was at Annapolis that I came to believe that the media were exaggerating the growing antiwar sentiment among the American public as the Vietnam War heated up. The closest we ever came to witnessing such sentiments was when we marched to Memorial Stadium for athletic events. On the way to the stadium, we would pass by St. John's College. By 1967 the brigade was being treated to shouts of "Warmongers!" and the occasional egg or tomato.

We would return from Memorial Stadium informally, but we rarely encountered any problems on the way back. It was the formation itself that provoked the animosity, because it symbolized the institution. It would be several more years before antiwar protesters began to insult us as individuals.

The Academy included young men from every social and economic class, and a handful from religious and racial minorities. But even in the late 1960s there was still a fair amount of prejudice at Annapolis. Two classmates I was particularly close to at the Academy were well aware of this. Jay Martin Cohen was Jewish, and Frank Simmons was black, and both had suffered harassment, especially during their plebe years.

By June 1968, when our class graduated, most of this prejudice had melted away. You could actually see people change their attitudes and become more tolerant after a couple of years of attending the same classes and living together, elbow to elbow, twenty-four hours a day.

This was no accident. Throughout history, military organizations have been used not only for combat, but also as educational tools for the larger society. Sometimes it was blatant indoctrination. Lenin didn't create the Red Army for the sole purpose of defending Russia. He also wanted to institutionalize the revolution by immersing young people in the philosophy of Communism. They would serve for several years, and after being thoroughly indoctrinated they would then return to the larger society to indoctrinate others.

Our own military has served a parallel purpose by teaching millions of young Americans about democratic ideals and tolerance—the need to rely on somebody regardless of his color, his religion, or his background. In 1947 President Harry Truman integrated the armed forces by Executive Order. For the first time, a white soldier from Georgia would have to use the same latrine and sleep in the same room as a black soldier from Mississippi.

In 1954, when civil rights legislation became a major issue, one reason it succeeded was that there were increasing numbers of white elected officials who had served in the military alongside blacks. It has been a long, slow struggle, but without the military it would have been a lot longer. Surprisingly, President Truman has never received much credit for one of his greatest accomplishments.

But no matter what your background, to be a plebe at Annapolis was to endure a long string of harassments by the upperclassmen. Having spent two years at Brockport and a summer at Quantico, I was a little older, a little more experienced, and perhaps a bit wiser than most of my classmates, which made my plebe experience somewhat easier. The upperclassmen at Annapolis could be petty, but at Quantico I had already been harassed by real Marines. *Their* harassment at least had a purpose, whereas at Annapolis you might be sent out in the middle of the night to polish the brass balls of Bill the Goat—a big statue of a charging goat that symbolized the Navy's fighting spirit. Or you might be ordered to "bring around everything in your room that moves," which meant you had to empty your room of everything that was portable—including your roommates.

I don't mind this kind of thing during the first summer, before the academic year really begins. It helps to weed out some of the students who might crack under the tough pressure of the Academy, or later on, in combat. There's probably something to be said for learning how to endure these annoyances, because it helps you develop a kind of protective coating that serves you well in war—and even in civilian life. But I still resent the guy across the hall who would walk into my room for no reason at all and ask for fifty push-ups.

All plebes were required to memorize a set of responses to specific questions from a little book called *Reef Points*. If an upperclassman asked you, "How long have you been in the Navy?" there was only one acceptable answer: "All me bloomin' life, sir! My mother was a mermaid, my father was King Neptune. I was born on the crest of a wave and rocked in the cradle of the deep. Seaweed and barnacles are me clothes. Every tooth in me head is a marlinspike; the hair on me head is hemp. Every bone in me body is a spar, and when I spits, I spits tar! I'se hard, I is, I am, I are!"

At any given moment, a plebe might be asked to recite that day's menu, or the names of the movies playing in Annapolis, or the number of days before the Army-Navy game, or the main headlines of the *New York Times* and the *Washington Post*.

During meals you had to sit straight up on the edge of your chair without bending over or looking down. "Are your eyes on the boat?" you'd be asked, reminding you to look straight ahead.

"North, is the cow heavy?"

"No, sir!" You'd be holding a half-gallon milk carton at arm's length, and an upperclassman, wanting to know how much milk was left, would ask, "North, how's the cow?" And you'd answer: "Sir, she walks, she talks, she's full of chalk. The lacteal fluid extracted from the female of bovine species is highly prolific to the third degree!" In other words, there were about three glasses of milk left in the container.

The only relief from all of this was the prospect that our football team would win the annual Army-Navy game, which is always played on neutral ground (usually in Philadelphia) during the first weekend of December. Whenever Navy won—as we did during my plebe year—the hazing of plebes would come to an early end, and we were allowed to "carry on." We could actually talk during meals, and we no longer had to "double-time" everywhere we went.

But hazing was the least of my problems. In February of my plebe year my whole world almost came to an end when I was involved in a terrible car accident. It happened during Washington's Birthday weekend, when a group of us were driving to upstate New York to go skiing. It was midnight, and the snow was falling heavily as we approached the intersection of Route 11 and Route 15 in Horseheads, New York, not far from Corning. Everyone in the car had fallen asleep—including the driver. We had stopped for hamburgers a couple of hours earlier, but nobody had been drinking. I can still remember opening my eyes and seeing the headlights of a truck that was almost on top of us. That was just before impact.

Nobody wore seat belts back then, and the carnage was just awful. Bobby Wagner was killed outright. Tom Parker suffered major brain damage. Mike Cathey, in the so-called death seat, ended up with a broken pelvis, and a broken arm, and burns. Billy Mullens broke his back, and to this day he's paralyzed from the waist down. Compared to my companions, I was relatively unscathed: cranial injuries, crushed vertebrae in my lower spine, a broken nose, broken jaw, a broken leg, and a badly damaged knee.

I remember crawling out of the car into the cold, and hearing voices say, "Lie still, don't move." I was shivering, even after somebody covered me with a coat. The survivors were taken to Corning Hospital, where I was put in a body cast. When I complained that I had no feeling in my legs, and couldn't control my bladder or bowels, one of the doctors gently explained that I might never walk again.

Even then, I didn't realize how badly I was hurt until my parents showed up. I couldn't even talk to them, and it was painful just to breathe. I don't recall much about the Corning Hospital except that one of the nurses was named Lolly, and that we eventually recovered enough to sing to her from our beds, "Hey Lolly Lolly Lolly"—pause for a breath—"Hey Lolly Lolly Lo."

For the next few months, my life was a blur of pain and operations. After we were stabilized, we were flown to Bethesda Naval Hospital, and then transferred to the naval hospital at the Academy. It was located in the middle of the Academy cemetery, which created a real incentive to get better. By the summer I could be taken out in a wheelchair to sit in the sun.

My fondest memory of that period is that Bob Eisenbach, my best friend, came to see me every day. The workload at the Academy was grueling, and I don't know how he ever found the time. But he always showed up, even if it was only long enough to stick his head in and yell, "God, North, you really stink today!"

When I first got up after several months in bed, I couldn't even sit up—much less walk. They put me in a hydrotherapy tank to get me to move my arms and legs, and it was terrifying. I started sinking, and I thought I was about to drown. The physiotherapist, one of the cruelest—and kindest—men I've ever known, *made* me move, although my joints and muscles had begun to atrophy.

By summer I was well enough to take medical leave and go home. I had been surveyed, and was found to be medically unfit for further service. I was supposed to return to Annapolis in September—but only for medical treatment until I was well enough to be discharged.

My parents suggested that I sleep on the foldout couch in the living room so I wouldn't have to climb the stairs to my bedroom, but I refused. I had worked too hard to get into Annapolis, and I was determined to get back. Dad reinforced the handrail on the stairs, and I slowly made my way up and down. It was during these months that I came to understand the importance of persistence.

With Dad's help I filled out the mountain of paperwork that was necessary to appeal the decision to survey me out of the service. I still remember sitting on the patio that Jack and I had built with Dad, watching him trim his beloved roses when the letter arrived: my appeal was denied.

But I refused to give up, and Dad reinforced my determination to fight the decision and to return to Annapolis. He worked with me on my therapy and helped me graduate from crutches to a cane although my right leg was withered and thin. Russ Robertson, my old high school coach and a former Marine who had been badly wounded in the leg during World War II, stopped by periodically to encourage me.

The accident, the surgery, and the hospitalization taught me a lot about how much I could endure. They also taught me about the healing power of prayer. When I returned to the naval hospital, I made a habit of wheeling myself down to the chapel every day.

Being hospitalized certainly wasn't pleasant, but it wasn't all pain and suffering, either. There were a lot of us in one big ward, and we had some good times talking together and flirting with the nurses. One of my fellow patients was Roger Staubach, the celebrated quarterback of our football team, who had been injured in the Notre Dame game. Later, he went on to become a star for the Dallas Cowboys.

When the nurses left the ward, those of us confined to wheelchairs would occasionally hold jousting tournaments. With a crutch for a lance, and a garbage-can lid for a shield, you'd wheel yourself as fast as possible down the middle of the ward toward your opponent. Our ward was the scene of so much mayhem that it was probably just as well that we were already in the hospital.

I was eventually accepted back at the Academy on probation, but only if I was willing to repeat my plebe year. *Willing?* I was grateful to be there at all, and would have done almost anything to come back. I finally did—almost a year after the accident. I was determined to build up my strength, and every morning, while the rest of Bancroft Hall was still sleeping, I'd go out for a run along the seawall. By the time my classmates woke up, I was already in the shower.

I don't want to leave the impression that I was in love with the Naval Academy. It was a challenging place, but very restrictive. It's designed to give you more than you can hope to accomplish, which forces you to establish priorities. You could strive for perfection, but you never had enough time to achieve it.

Right from the start, I saw the Academy as the means to an end— a commission in the Marine Corps. Ever since that first summer at Quantico, I was determined to be a Marine. But after my accident, I knew I would have to fight especially hard to get there.

And I did—literally. Every midshipman at the Academy has to be involved in a sport during all three seasons of the academic year. Because of my injuries, football, soccer, lacrosse, and crew were now out of the question. That pretty much limited me to sailing in the fall and the spring, and boxing during the winter.

I especially liked boxing, because you're really on your own: if you lose the fight, there's no one to blame but yourself. I was far from a natural fighter, but I could take a punch, and I was in excellent shape from my morning runs. Coach Emerson Smith, a legend in boxing circles, used to tell us that boxing could be reduced to three basic rules: keep your hands up, your feet moving, and your ass off the deck.

I was a welterweight, and after two years of violating Smith's third commandment I eventually fought my way up to the brigade championships. That was a big deal at the Academy, and the entire brigade of midshipmen—close to four thousand men—showed up at Mac-Donough Hall to cheer on their favorites. My opponent that night was Jim Webb, a good fighter who went on to become Secretary of the Navy and a well-regarded novelist.

As each pair of fighters entered the ring, the band would strike up "The Look Sharp March"—better known as the famous Gillette commercial. Webb and I were about evenly matched. I had a good left, but against another lefty like Webb that wasn't much help. He was quick on his feet, so my goal was to back him into a corner to neutralize his speed advantage. It was a close fight. We both went the distance, but I beat him on points.

A year later, a medical review board had to decide whether I had recovered enough from the accident to get a commission in the Marines. I met with them and made my best case: "You people have invested thousands of dollars in training me," I said, "and I'm going to graduate with honors. I even won the brigade boxing championship. Are you seriously thinking of sending me off to be a *civilian*? I'll make a fine Marine officer if you'll only give me a chance." Emerson Smith offered to show the film of my fight against Webb as evidence of my fitness and mobility. But just in case, I also applied to the CIA.

During my final summer as a midshipman, I went off to Jump School for parachute training with the Army in Fort Benning, Georgia. When I took the physical, one of the doctors noticed that several bones in my face and nose had still not set properly from the car accident three years earlier. Not only would I have to stop boxing, but I would also require additional surgery on my nose and face if I wanted to become a Marine pilot, which was my intention at the time.

Not wanting to miss Jump School, I postponed the surgery and went off to parachute out of airplanes in Georgia. During previous summers I had gone to Survival, Escape, Resistance and Evasion School in Nevada, and Underwater Swimmers School in California. I missed a few vacations, but these programs kept me in shape and helped prepare me for the Marines.

The final year at Annapolis is normally the best. Not only can you finally see the light at the end of the tunnel, but you get to pick the service you're going into, and the location and the date for reporting to your new command. By the spring of 1968, however, Vietnam was taking a heavy toll. Our service selection happened to coincide with the Tet offensive, and more and more names and faces of dead Marines and naval officers we had gone to school with only a year or two earlier appeared on the memorial boards at the entrance to Bancroft Hall.

First classmen (seniors) were allowed to have a car and to park it on the Yard, as the campus was known. And having a car made it a lot easier to get a date. Otherwise, your date had to drive over and pick *you* up—an awkward situation for the typical American male in that macho environment.

Having a car also made it easier to see family and friends. My uncle, John Finneran, a Navy commander, and his family lived near the Academy, and I used to spend occasional weekends at their house. His daughter Kathy, my cousin, was a college student with a part-time job at Hecht's, the department store chain. Shortly after Christmas, Kathy mentioned that she thought I should meet her boss, a very attractive young lady named Betsy Stuart. Then she showed me Betsy's picture, which was all the encouragement I needed.

The next weekend, my brother Jack, who was now a second lieutenant in the Army, met me at the Finnerans'. He and Kathy encouraged me to drive to Montgomery Mall, where Betsy worked, so that I could meet her. Jack and I jumped in my green Shelby Cobra and roared off.

As we rode up the escalator at Hecht's, Betsy was talking to one of her sales clerks. When she smiled at us, I was smitten. She was tall and slender, with wide blue eyes and very long blond hair that she wore in two braids down her back. She realized immediately that this little visit had been arranged so I could check her out, and I suddenly became embarrassed by the transparency of it all. Betsy seemed to enjoy my obvious discomfort.

"Hi," I said. "I'm Kathy Finneran's cousin. You must be Betsy Stuart."

"I am. Kathy told me you might be dropping by this afternoon to do a little shopping. But this is pretty far from Annapolis. Don't they have any stores down there?"

"Yeah, well, you see, Jack—oh, this is Jack, he's my brother—you see, Jack's going to Vietnam pretty soon and we thought we would pick up a few things he might be needing."

"Of course. So you came here, to ladies' accessories."

"Well, not exactly *here*, but well, you know, we were just kind of looking around and Kathy had told us that you might be here, and it seemed like—say, have you had lunch yet?"

"Oh, yes. About three hours ago."

"Of course, sure, it's almost time for dinner. Well, we've got a lot to do, all that shopping and all, and you seem to be busy. It's been nice to meet you. Maybe I could give you a call some time?"

"If you like. Now if you'll excuse me, I have customers to attend to."

It was awful. On the way out of the store, Jack patted me on the shoulder and said, "Well, big brother, you sure have a way with girls. Do they teach that technique at the Academy, or is it something you picked up on your own? I just hope it's not genetic! But don't feel too bad about not asking for her phone number, though, because you never even bothered to give her your name."

Kathy gave me Betsy's number, and during the next few weeks I started burning up the phone lines between Annapolis and Annandale, Virginia. But Betsy was never home, and the few times she was, she always seemed to be busy on the days I suggested—usually with another date. I ended up having countless conversations with her roommate, Dana Hanshaw, who had such a sexy voice that I was ready to date *her*. But Dana kept encouraging me to try, so I continued calling. Finally, perhaps because my sheer persistence had worn her down—or possibly because another date had canceled—I got to take Betsy to dinner.

Later, some of our friends concluded that Betsy was enchanted by my uniform. Jack swears that the only reason she ever went out with me was because he was standing there when we met. Years later, Betsy told me the truth: the uniform had nothing to do with it, and neither did Jack. She was attracted to my car.

Betsy Stuart was the youngest of three sisters. She was a farm girl from western Pennsylvania, and like me, had grown up in a clean-cut, rural, common-sense small-town environment. She had already graduated from Penn State University, where she majored in retailing. Although her father, Jeb, was a direct descendant of his namesake, General Jeb Stuart, the Confederate cavalry officer, Betsy had no experience with military types. She married into a Marine Corps career with a sense of wide-eyed innocence, and even years later she still couldn't tell the difference between a corporal and a colonel.

Our first date was at an Italian restaurant that just happened to overlook the Marine Memorial in Arlington. I must have done something right, because before long we were seeing each other almost every weekend. One beautiful spring Sunday, about a month before graduation, love triumphed over duty: I spent the day with Betsy and literally forgot what time it was. By the time I returned to the Academy I was half an hour late for the evening meal formation. In many parts of this land, being fashionably late for dinner is considered almost a virtue. But not at the Naval Academy. Showing up twenty minutes late without a valid excuse is a Major Offense for which the perpetrator is put "on report." The punishments can include demerits, restriction (being grounded), and a tour of E.D. (extra duty)—which consists of the privilege of carrying your rifle around in small circles for many hours at a time. In extreme cases, being late can even lead to expulsion.

Coming into Bancroft Hall, I was greeted by a Marine captain who had just inspected my company and found me missing. I was the company commander, so my absence was hard to ignore.

"Welcome back, Mr. North. Where were you?"

"I was with my girlfriend, sir."

"Did your car break down?"

"No, sir."

"You know what this means, don't you?"

"Yes, sir."

"You're on report, Mr. North."

My punishment consisted of being restricted from that moment all the way through graduation week. It was only due to the intervention of Major Reid Olson, my company officer, that I was allowed to keep my command. Olson also arranged for me to serve as a supervisor for various social events during graduation week, which allowed me to spend a little time with Betsy.

By then, she and I had already started discussing our future. Shortly after graduation, I would be entering the Marine Officer's Basic Course at The Basic School in Quantico, Virginia. But that wasn't a major hardship, as I would still be within an hour's drive of Betsy's apartment in Annandale.

Midway through the five-month course at Quantico, which was abbreviated on account of the war, I asked Betsy to marry me. There's a tradition at the Academy that you give your future bride a miniature version of your class ring. I liked that custom, but I wanted to do it my way. One night, before taking Betsy to dinner, I presented her with a single rose on whose stem I had carefully threaded the ring. I also had her birthstone, an aquamarine, set into my own ring.

We planned the wedding for the day I graduated from Basic School, and here, too, we were following a naval service tradition. Graduation day at Annapolis is the occasion for scores of weddings at the chapel, and back in June, at the Academy, Betsy and I had been to half a dozen ceremonies in a single day.

We were married in the chapel at Quantico on November 13, 1968. My parents were there, but just barely. There had been a nasty snowstorm the previous day, and they were turned back on the New York Thruway. They ended up flying in on a chartered plane, along with my brother Tim, who was now five. Betsy's family and mine, along with our friends, practically filled the little chapel at Quantico. One guest I was especially overjoyed to see was my friend Bob Eisenbach, who had been terribly wounded in Vietnam on July 4 the previous year. Bob had been shot in the head and given up for dead. He was still in a coma when he returned home, and had undergone several brain operations. By the time Betsy and I got married, he was in a wheelchair.

Betsy wore a beautiful white gown with a veil, and I wore my dress blues. Both our maternal grandmothers made it to the wedding. As the ceremony ended, eight of my classmates formed the traditional arch of swords for the newly married couple to pass through. The

Reverend Peter John Carey, the Catholic chaplain, performed the marriage. He must have liked the idea because a few years later, he got married, too.

Those final weeks at Quantico had been a blur, with tactics, classes, and final field exercises. Within weeks, many of us would be shipping out to Flight School, Artillery School, or Armor School. But for all of us who were infantry officers, the next stop was Vietnam.

5

Combat

With thirty days of leave before my flight to Vietnam, Betsy and I started out on a leisurely cross-country drive. We had already taken a short honeymoon trip to Puerto Rico, but now we had a chance to spend some real time together before our thirteen-month separation. One of the colonels from Quantico was moving his family to San Diego, and we volunteered to drive his car to California. We planned the trip so that by the time I was due to leave for Vietnam, I could catch a flight to San Francisco and make my way to Travis Air Force Base, while Betsy would fly back to Virginia.

After dropping off our wedding gifts with Betsy's parents in Pennsylvania, we headed north to see my folks, and then west to Michigan to visit my sister and her husband. From there we drove south, planning to drive west along the old Route 66. It was only mid-November, but we soon found ourselves racing against a series of early winter storms. To avoid the snow, we abandoned our planned route and kept driving south.

We had been gone for about a week, and were pulling in to a motel in Amarillo, Texas, when a highway patrol officer drove up behind me. "Excuse me," he said, "are you Second Lieutenant North, U.S. Marines?"

"Yes, sir."

"It's a good thing we tracked you down," he said. "Patrolmen all over the state have been watching for your car. Your father gave us your plate number in the hope that we could find you and tell you to call home. He says it's urgent."

I rushed inside to a pay phone. "Bad news," said Dad. "Your orders have been modified. You're supposed to report to Travis in three days."

Three *days?* Betsy and I had been planning on another three *weeks!*

I called Marine headquarters to check. "I'm not even near an airport," I explained.

"Then you'd better get to one," they said. "You need to be on that flight."

I didn't want Betsy to drive to California alone, so we jumped back in the car and headed straight to San Diego. It was awful: she cried and I felt terrible. I knew it wasn't my fault, but I was filled with guilt about leaving her so soon. We drove in shifts, just ahead of a blizzard that seemed to be following us, and barely stopped as we raced through Texas, New Mexico, Arizona, and into California.

We arrived in San Diego just as the sun was coming up on Thanksgiving Day. I was exhausted, having driven all night with Betsy curled up beside me in the front seat. I was due at Travis that same evening.

We stopped at a Denny's for breakfast. Because of the holiday, the place was deserted. My haircut must have given me away, because the waitress came over with coffee and asked, "Are you on your way to Vietnam?"

"Yes, ma'am," I said.

"Then I guess you won't be having any Thanksgiving dinner. Let me bring you some."

Betsy drove me to the airport, where we said a long and tearful good-bye. I flew up to San Francisco and took a cab to Travis. She delivered the car and flew back to Washington. We had been married for less than three weeks.

The first thing I learned when I arrived at Travis was that for all the rush to get there, I wasn't going anywhere for a long time. There was a ton of paperwork to complete, but with thousands of men passing through each day, at least the place was organized. But it was also depressing to sit there and wait for hours in those pale green and red fiberglass chairs with nothing to do except listen to a steady stream of announcements. They blared out from a PA system that was so scratchy it could have been built by Thomas Edison himself, and obviously hadn't been updated since. "May I have your attention in the terminal, your attention in the terminal, please. Travis Air Force Base announces the departure of World Airways government contract flight Hotel Twenty-five for Da Nang, Vietnam. You are reminded to retain one copy of your orders on your person at all times. Please extinguish all cigarettes at this time. No photographs are permitted on the flight line. May I have your attention in the terminal, your attention in the terminal, please. Travis Air Force Base announces the departure..."

Finally our flight was called. As I climbed the stairs and entered the plane, I couldn't help but notice a steel plate next to the door, with a printed message that read something like this:

This aircraft is operated by the Far East Airway Corporation, which has leased it to the Inter-American Airway Consortium on a lien from the Greater East Asian Bank of Pakistan for the purpose of transporting sheep from Phnom Penh to Tehran. The company accepts no liability. This aircraft was last inspected on April 12, 1959.

Whatever the exact wording, this message didn't strike me as particularly reassuring. Nor did the chief stewardess, who had all the charm of a grizzly bear, with a physique to match. As soon as she picked up the microphone, we knew this was no ordinary flight. "Listen up," she began. "I've made this trip fourteen times, and I'm not going to take any crap from you guys, understand? Everybody reach down and check under your seat for your life jacket. There will be no smoking on this plane until I say so. There are call buttons above your seat. Don't even think about pressing them."

She was the flight attendant from hell.

"One more thing," she added. "Anyone gives me a hard time, I'm gonna tell the major."

"Oh, yeah?" somebody yelled. "What's he gonna do? Shave my head and send me to 'Nam?"

We were a high-spirited group, ready to take on the world. And none of us had any doubt that we would eventually be coming home alive.

It seemed like a week later when the pilot finally announced that we were landing: "Gentlemen, we'll be touching down in Da Nang, Vietnam, in about fifteen minutes. The local time is five minutes past noon, and the ground temperature is a hundred and two degrees. Please extinguish all cigarettes and fasten your seat belts. We've enjoyed having you with us on World Airways government contract flight Hotel Twenty-five, and we hope to see you again next year on your way home. Good-bye and good luck."

At Da Nang we were ushered into a huge, tin-roofed building that was covered with sandbags. Together with several other brand-new second lieutenants, I was assigned to the Third Marine Division. A few hours later, we boarded a muddy C-130 transport plane for the short flight north to Dong Ha, in Quang Tri province, the combat base in northern South Vietnam that was home to the Third Marine Division Headquarters. We took off into the afternoon sun, and when we reached Dong Ha the pilot dove right in, engines roaring, and came to a screeching halt. The plane hadn't even stopped rolling when the crew chief screamed, "Everybody off!"

As we ran off the ramp, somebody motioned for us to jump into a sandbagged trench beside the runway. A moment later the plane was airborne again as rocket fire came crashing down on the far side of the field.

Welcome to Vietnam.

Those of us who had disembarked from the C-130 filed into a sandbagged bunker to await pickup by our respective units.

After an hour or so, a Jeep came by for me. At least I think it was a Jeep. It was hard to tell, because the fenders were bent, the windshield was gone, and the back seat was missing.

I was feeling sorry for the Jeep until I got a look at the guy climbing out of it. He was tall and absolutely emaciated. His face was thick with stubble, his helmet cover was tattered, his flak jacket was ripped, and the heel was flapping on his boot. He was carrying a pistol, but the holster was rotted out in the bottom. His filthy uniform seemed to be welded to his body. His eyes were bloodshot, and he obviously hadn't been near a shower in weeks.

"Lieutenant North? Sorry I'm late, but the friggin' bridge was blown up and a convoy was ambushed." Taking a map from his jacket pocket, he pointed out Con Thien, the northernmost Marine combat base in Vietnam. "That's where we're headed," he said. "By the way, I guess I forgot to introduce myself. My name is Bob Bedingfield. I'm the chaplain."

If he's the chaplain, I thought, this must be one hell of a neighborhood.

Bedingfield took me to the headquarters of the Third Battalion, Third Marine Regiment, and to the supply building where I drew my gear, including ammunition and a holster for the .45 pistol I had brought with me. (The pistol was a prize from the Naval Academy for the greatest academic improvement over four years, which I always regarded as kind of a backhanded compliment.) I climbed into the back of the Jeep and sat on the fender, next to a box of hand grenades.

We joined up with a convoy and roared out of the base. Once we passed Cam Lo, the last major checkpoint, the road wasn't much more than a ditch. A mile or so outside of Con Thien, the entire convoy came to a screeching halt. Dusk was falling, and there was jungle on either side of us. Bedingfield checked his watch. "We have to wait here," he said. "It's almost time for the Hanoi Express."

Every evening at exactly six o'clock, the gunners north of the Hanoi River would fire rockets and artillery into Con Thien. You could count on it. It was as regular as the nightly news, and about as friendly. You definitely did not want to be driving in while *that* was going on.

Con Thien, our battalion's forward headquarters, had been built by the French back in the 1950s. It was originally constructed to house only a regiment, but had long since been expanded by the Marines and Navy Seabees (navy combat engineers). It looked like a huge bald circle on a hilltop, and was surrounded by miles of barbed wire, machine-gun positions, artillery and tank revetments, and thousands of mines. The original French fort had been demolished and replaced by a warren of underground bunkers which housed troop billets, operations centers, and even an aid station. Con Thien sprouted radio antennas like whiskers, and was used as a strongpoint from which we launched operations along the northern border of South Vietnam. For the next year I thought of it as home.

Con Thien was also a vital observation post. Just north of us was a defoliated swath known as the "trace"—an open strip of land about a kilometer wide, running along the DMZ and stretching from the seacoast on the east to the base of the mountains west of us. From the wooden observation towers at Con Thien, artillery and air spotters could monitor North Vietnamese Army (NVA) units heading south. Our job was to prevent their combat and supply units from crossing the seventeenth parallel into South Vietnam.

This was Marine country, commonly known as Leatherneck Square after the old slang name for Marines. (In the old days, Marines wore a high leather collar on their tunic to protect them against enemy swords.) There were probably more Marines killed and wounded on a day-to-day basis in the area surrounding Con Thien than anywhere else in Vietnam. The officers called it Leatherneck Square. The troops called it the Meatgrinder.

It wasn't until much later that I came to realize there were actually two Vietnam wars. Those of us who fought in the northern regions of South Vietnam were part of an entirely different experience than that of the great majority of American troops, who were based farther south. Our war was more straightforward: if we set up an ambush and spotted the enemy, we could be reasonably sure it *was* the enemy. We didn't have to deal with that terrible problem of Vietnamese civilians who weren't always civilians, or with Viet Cong guerrillas who would melt off into the countryside and disappear. We were fighting against NVA regulars—well-disciplined troops with reinforcements close behind—and when you were engaged with these guys, you were really engaged. Except for occasional woodcutters and the Montagnard tribes that lived in the mountains, Leatherneck Square was virtually devoid of noncombatants.*

Maybe this was why we didn't see many morale problems in Leatherneck Square. I never knew of anyone using drugs, for example.

---

*Most of the Montagnards in Northern I Corps were Bru, an aboriginelike tribe of small and primitive mountain people. Some had served as mercenaries with the French, and many of them were helpful to us, especially as intelligence gatherers. The Bru men loved to go out on patrols with us, and after one successful ambush they prepared a victory feast where the Chef's Special featured the brains of a freshly killed monkey in its original container. I didn't want to insult our hosts, but I begged off. You have to draw the line somewhere.

I'm not saying it didn't happen, especially during R & R or at the rear. But I sure didn't see any of that going on in the field, and I lived on top of those guys. Another thing I never saw was fragging, where enlisted men killed their own officers. I never even *heard* of it until I was back in the States.

The war in the north, in what was called the I Corps Tactical Zone, was fought mostly by Marines who took pride in being lean and mean. We were trained to get the job done quickly, with the lowest possible loss of life. If the Army sent out nine helicopters, we'd do the same operation with three. Because there were fewer of us, we relied extensively on air, artillery, and naval gunfire support from ships off the coast.

We were a proud bunch, with plenty of bravado. It wasn't uncommon to see a guy who had written on his flak jacket, "Yea, though I walk through the Valley of the Shadow of Death, I shall fear no Evil, because I'm the meanest mutha' in the Valley." Nobody else could criticize us, but we had no hesitation about deriding our own institution. There was a swaggering nonchalance that came up whenever a resupply was late, or some anticipated development failed to occur as planned.

Combat stimulates a special kind of profane camaraderie in the men of any unit, and my platoon was no exception. Shortly after I took command, I heard one of the squad leaders tell his men that "Blue" wanted a night ambush at a certain location. Not wanting to question the squad leader in front of his men, I asked Jim Lehnert, my radio operator, who "Blue" was.

Lehnert chuckled. "That's you, sir," he said.

"Why Blue?" I asked.

"Because that's this month's brevity code on the radio. Blue is North, Gray is South, Silver is East, Gold is West."

The name stuck, and within a few weeks the men in my platoon were calling themselves "Blue's Bastards."

When we weren't actually in combat, we were on the move, always with enormous packs on our backs. To carry something was to "hump" it, and we built up our trapezius muscles from carrying so much for so long. After a long day of humping through the thick, sharp brush, you could barely move your arms and shoulders. When it rained, which was often, the load was even heavier. Even on days where not a shot was fired you went through hell, climbing steep hills in terrible heat, or staggering through fields of razor-sharp elephant grass that cut into your elbows and knees while you carried eighty pounds of equipment on your back. We were supposed to be "light infantry," which sounded to me like somebody's sick joke.

In addition to wearing boots, a heavy steel helmet, and a flak jacket, every man carried a web belt with ammo pouches and a large, heavy pack which carried several dozen items, including an E-tool (E for entrenching), a folding shovel used to dig a fighting hole or a latrine; a folding metal can opener; a pocket knife, to cut thread, remove splinters, cut patches for the holes in your uniform, and to slice the green stuff that came in a can and was officially known as "meat." A surefire way to get a laugh was to ask some new guy to read aloud the list of ingredients on the label of one of these cans.

We also carried a hammock, an air mattress, water-purification tablets, malaria pills and flares, and heat tabs—little foil-wrapped ovals, like solid Sterno, to heat food. Plus bug juice (military-issue mosquito repellent); it smelled like death and burned your skin, but it worked. Salt tablets, because we sweated so much. A sewing kit, because your clothes got ripped, and a first-aid kit, because your body did too. A poncho and a poncho liner, because nights were chilly, even in the summer. Fifteen M-16 magazines with rounds. Six hand grenades. Three or four full canteens. A half dozen rations. One mortar round. Half a bag of plastic explosives.

Everybody carried letters from home. Most men had pocket Bibles, courtesy of Chaplain Bedingfield. Big Dan Doan, the tallest of the forty-three men in our platoon, humped a handmade machete whose blade was made from a car spring. It was heavy, but Dan was strong enough to swing it as he hacked through the brush.

Everyone carried some small personal item: cigarettes, paperback books, a lock of your girlfriend's hair, photographs, homemade cookies, extra socks. I carried laminated photographs of Betsy, my parents, my sister, and my brothers. I wore a St. Francis medal that Grandma Clancy had given me, along with a crucifix from my father, and his Hamilton watch from World War II. The watch made it all the way through Vietnam until just before the end, when the crystal was shattered by the concussions of a mortar round hitting near my hole. I also carried a strobe light to signal helicopters and air strikes at night.

Jim Lehnert, Smitty, and the other radio operators humped PRC-

25 radios with three or four extra batteries—each one the size and weight of a brick. The medical corpsmen, like Doc Conklin, carried a canvas satchel called a Unit One, filled with morphine, saline solution for treating shock, malaria tablets, battle dressings, tape, gauze pads, antibiotics, an eye kit, a breathing tube, and a large needle to poke a hole for a tracheotomy. Machine-gunners like Randy Herrod and Ernie Tuten carried a basic load plus their M-60 machine guns and ammo. M-79 grenadiers like Ev Whipple carried eighteen pounds of additional ammunition on top of the standard load.

There was no such thing as a fat Marine—not only from all that exercise, but because we didn't eat very much. We generally ate only twice a day, because if you stopped for lunch you might not be around for dinner. A guy could break out his rations on a rest break—but only if his buddy was holding his weapon at the ready. Wendell Thomas, a typical infantryman, lost eighteen pounds in a matter of weeks. I dropped down to 140.

There were four items you carried everywhere: your weapon, ammo, grenades, and hot sauce. An experienced field Marine could take a few cans of C-ration chow and turn it into something almost edible. Food was incredibly important in Vietnam, and when time allowed, some guys would spend twenty or thirty minutes preparing a little feast. It became a ritual, a small, special moment of pleasure. You'd take an onion from a care package, dice it carefully with your pocket knife, pour the liquid out of a can of beef stew, add in some cheese and onions and hot sauce and a little black pepper, and *voilà*— the frugal gourmet.

My own favorite was turkey loaf, which was one of the few items you could eat hot or cold. My idea of heaven in Vietnam was a can of turkey loaf and a warm Black Label beer. (Cold beer was unheard of.) More often, though, you'd end up with a dish known as ham and mutha's—lima beans covered in a greenish sludge that had to be heated. I don't want to get overly graphic here, so let's just say this was not high-quality meat.

Within a few weeks, the three lieutenants in the company—Rich O'Neill, Bill Haskell, and I—became very close. Before long we had all become a little too casual, in part because our resupply situation was terrible. I was carrying a Swedish submachine gun after the one I was issued was run over by a tank. I humped an NVA-issue pack, and some of my guys were even wearing NVA trousers. By January I was also sporting a fairly impressive handlebar mustache.

That all ended one afternoon when I was out on a patrol and Haskell called me on the radio. "Blue," he said, "you better get your ass back here right away."

When we returned to the camp, an officer I had never seen before was addressing the rest of my men. He was a well-built, mean-looking guy with closely cropped reddish-blond hair who didn't look like a happy camper. When I got a little closer, I noticed he was a captain. He was walking up and down, banging his helmet against his leg and delivering some sort of lecture. I walked up behind him and saluted. "Captain," I said, "Lieutenant North."

He turned around slowly, just like in the movies, and then glared at me. "Maybe you didn't notice, Lieutenant, but I was addressing my troops."

"I beg to differ, sir," I replied, "but I believe these are *my* troops."

"Come over here, Lieutenant," he said. We walked around behind the formation, where he leaned right into me and said, "My name is Goodwin. I'm the new company commander. You've got fifteen minutes to take a shower, cut your hair, and get a shave. Then get your butt over to my hooch."

"A shave?"

"The mustache goes, Lieutenant."

At first, O'Neill, Haskell, and I were dismayed that this tough-talking big shot had rolled in and taken over our happy band of warriors. But once we saw Goodwin in action, we quickly changed our minds. Within a day or two, the supplies we had been requesting for weeks suddenly materialized: new uniforms, boots, ammo, grenades, first-aid kits—the whole works. This quickly endeared Goodwin to all of us as a guy who really knew his stuff.

"He knows his stuff" was the greatest compliment you could give a guy in combat. It didn't just refer to his fighting abilities, but included his technical and logistical skills. A lot of men could fight, but Goodwin could also arrange a resupply when you needed it, bring in an air strike in the nick of time, or get a med-evac quickly for a wounded man. I learned a lot from him, and from the close attention he paid to details: how to place a claymore mine, how to maintain radio discipline, how to use every spare moment for training. Vietnam has been portrayed as an ad hoc war, but in the north, at least, the units that performed well worked their butts off. With Goodwin, you never just sat on your pack to wait for the next order.

A memory of Goodwin: We were on a routine patrol, slowly making our way up a steep mountain trail. The platoon paused for a moment, and I stood there, idly pulling leaves off a bush, and deep in thought about the wonderful letter I had just received from Betsy: the doctor had confirmed that she was pregnant.

By now Goodwin and I were close friends. He came up behind me and said, "How's it going?"

"Fine."

"What's new at home?"

"Lots," I whispered, not looking up. "Betsy's going to have a baby."

Goodwin leaned over my shoulder and said, "You can tell that from the *leaves*?"

If I seem to be focusing on the lighter side of my war experience, that may be because so much of what we did in Vietnam was an exercise in frustration. You'd take a hill and move on, and three days later you'd have to come back and fight again over the same piece of ground because there weren't enough troops to occupy it. It wasn't like World War II, where each battle had a distinct beginning and an end. This war had little sense of movement or progress: it began when your plane landed in Da Nang, and it ended when you left the country—preferably not in a body bag.

We were angry at the politicians back in Washington who set the rules, who made us risk our lives while putting up with enormous obstacles. One of our biggest frustrations was the DMZ—the so-called demilitarized zone on either side of the Ben Hai River, which marked the border between North and South Vietnam. Despite its name, the DMZ was probably the least demilitarized place in all of Vietnam. Although the area was crawling with soldiers of the North Vietnamese Army, we were allowed to fire into the DMZ only if fired upon. We were occasionally allowed to pursue the enemy inside, but this required written permission from God and several of the Apostles.

Shortly after I arrived in-country, and before Goodwin became our company commander, our unit was shipped south to An Hoa, a

Marine base west of Da Nang. Here, too, our mission was to cut off enemy supply lines, only this time in the mountains along the Laotian border. It was the same story as the DMZ. All the enemy had to do was pull back across the border, and we weren't allowed to follow them.

This operation, known as Taylor Common, took place along the edge of the Ho Chi Minh Trail. Despite its name, the Ho Chi Minh Trail was anything *but* a trail: it was actually a large and complex looping network of roads, bicycle paths, foot trails, and even highways. Even with constant bombing attacks, we were never able to destroy more than a small part of it. And regardless of the damage our planes were able to wreak, most of the men, weapons, and supplies continued moving through to the south. The enemy made good use of Soviet-supplied radar and antiaircraft weapons, and to avoid them, our planes had to fly either very high or very low—and very fast, too—all of which made most bombing missions less than accurate. There was no such thing as a surgical air strike.

It sounded so simple: if we dropped enough bombs on the Ho Chi Minh Trail, the NVA wouldn't be able to continue the war. But one thing the American public never really understood was that the North Vietnamese, with the help of their Soviet-bloc allies, had a work force of something like three hundred thousand men and women who did nothing but repair the railroad tracks, roads, and bridges that we bombed. If a dirt road was destroyed, they'd rebuild it within hours. If we hit five trucks during the night, they'd push them off the road so fifty more could drive by.

Sometimes we could actually hear the NVA trucks at night, but it was almost impossible to stop them. Even a five-hundred- or thousand-pound bomb, the most common ordnance dropped on the Ho Chi Minh Trail, makes a crater not much bigger than a double bed. It knocks down a few trees and blows the leaves off a few more, but that's about it. Ten minutes later, fifteen guys would show up with shovels to fill in the hole, and the trucks kept rolling.

During the Taylor Common operation, each action began with B-52 strikes on the area we were moving into. Then a reconnaissance team would go in to ensure that the hilltop in question was clear. Only then would our seventy-man unit rappel out of helicopters and snake down a rope with a sixty-five-pound pack on our backs.

We had two days to prepare a landing zone for the troops that followed. We'd start with a chain saw and demolitions, and as soon as we had cleared enough space we'd call in a CH-53 helicopter which brought in a small bulldozer. We'd flatten the hilltop and dig little revetments all around the edge for artillery pieces and a small communications trench. It was hard, fast work because another unit was on the way and was counting on us to finish by the time they arrived. As soon as we were done, the helicopters would come in to get us so we could move on and do the very same thing all over again on another hilltop, further west. We'd leave behind little signs reading NOW THAT YOU'RE HERE, THIS IS THE REAR—an irreverent dig at those with the easier jobs.

At first there was no sign of the enemy. Then the rains began, creating a fog as thick as the clouds. Now we had to operate without air cover or helicopter support, which meant that we soon ran low on food, ammunition, and medical supplies. At one point it got so bad that we went five days with nothing to eat except crackers, candy bars, and bamboo shoots.

On the fifth day, one of Bill Haskell's men ambushed and shot a wild boar. Despite the monsoon downpour, we managed to build a fire and cook it over a spit. But while the meat solved the hunger problem, the smell and the smoke gave away our position. And that wasn't all: several of the men, including Haskell, came down with trichinosis and were eventually evacuated.

We needed almost everything, including new uniforms; ours had been worn through at the knees and elbows. Our boots were in such bad shape that we had to use medical adhesive tape to hold them together. Going more than a few days without an airdrop of the basic necessities of life was a new and alarming situation, and it demoralized us all. John Rappuano, our commander at the time, tried his best, but there was nothing he or anyone else could do about the weather. Resupply was something we had always taken for granted, but suddenly we were on our own.

It was during this dismal period on the Taylor Common operation that Johnson got killed. I didn't actually see him get shot; that happened in the confused darkness as two listening posts clashed with an NVA probe of our little mountaintop perimeter. I heard the crack of Marine M-16s, the deeper, slower firing of NVA AK-47s, and then the louder bursts from our M-60 machine gun. In the midst of the shooting came the scream—like the cry of an animal—when Johnson was hit, followed by that blood-chilling call, "Corpsman! Corpsman up!"

It took only a few minutes for Doc to crawl forward, but it felt like forever. Then came the quiet fury as they peeled off Johnson's flak jacket and cut away his uniform. The bullets had struck him in the chest and the shoulder, and he was soaked with blood.

Using a poncho to hide the glare of his flashlight, Doc tried to stop the flow of blood and the gurgling from the sucking chest wound. He also started an IV for shock before pulling Johnson back for further treatment. Meanwhile, the enemy withdrew to the west, leaving the soaking jungle full of night sounds and blackness.

They pulled Johnson to the closest fighting hole inside the perimeter—mine. Doc was working furiously to save him, until he turned to me in total frustration and said, "Lieutenant, unless we get a med-evac in here fast, he won't make it."

As I got on the radio to call for help, it started to rain again—a steady downpour from the clouds hanging low over the treetops. Battalion called back and said the bird would try, although the weather made it doubtful. The airfield, twenty miles to the east, was completely socked in.

I crawled back into my hole, and with my back against the radio on Jim Lehnert's back, I sat with Johnson's head cradled in my lap. The chopper had to turn back even before we heard its rotor blades. The pilots did their best, flapping around in the soup for close to half an hour, but it was impossible. When they called on the radio with the bad news, I cursed them, along with the clouds, the rain, the enemy— everything. I prayed that God would spare Johnson's life.

It took him almost an hour to die. At one point he seemed to awaken, and looked up at me. He shuddered a few times, and I wrapped my poncho liner around him to keep him warm. I caressed his cheek and kept whispering to him, trying to encourage both of us: "We'll get you out, hang in there, this is your ticket home, God won't let you die." But He did.

When a man dies in your arms it makes you feel very small. Maybe doctors and pastors eventually get used to that feeling, but I find that hard to imagine. When Johnson was pressed up against me, with no breath, no heartbeat, no tears, nothing, I felt ashamed to be alive. I did what he could no longer do. I cried.

He died right in front of me, lying there in the rain. It was one of the very worst moments of my life. I almost got sick—with fear, with shock, and undoubtedly with gratitude that I had survived.

Johnson wasn't from my platoon. His listening post had been in the line of fire from our own machine guns. His team leader, confused in the darkness, had placed the listening post in the wrong location. When the enemy probed our position, Johnson was right in the path of the designated fire from our M-60 machine gun. The bullets that hit Johnson had been made in America; he was hit by friendly fire.

For the rest of my time in Vietnam, and in the Marine Corps, Private First Class Johnson served as a constant reminder to me. I used to tell my sergeants (and later on, my lieutenants and junior officers), "If you don't understand what you're supposed to do, *ask!* War is confusing enough. If you keep me informed as to what you're doing, where you're doing it, and how it's going, we can get the job done and prevent a lot of casualties."

We carried Johnson's body in a poncho, along with several wounded men who normally would have been flown right out of there, and whom we transported in litters made from ponchos and trees. It's awful to carry your wounded—awful for them, because they aren't getting proper treatment, and awful for the rest of the unit, because it slows you down terribly and makes you more vulnerable to the enemy. You get old very fast.

And yet the extraordinary thing about Vietnam was how quickly a wounded man could get medical attention—most of the time. Most Marines who were hurt were treated within minutes, and you'd have an IV in your arm even before the helicopter arrived. It wasn't uncommon for an injured man to find himself in surgery in less than half an hour, and because we all knew that, it helped morale tremendously. The doctors, corpsmen, and nurses did a heroic job in Vietnam, saving so many men who would have died, who *did* die in other wars.*

This was one area where I had enormous admiration for the North Vietnamese Army. Most of our sick or wounded were evacuat-

---

*While I was working on this book, I watched several episodes of the magnificent PBS documentary on the Civil War. I was struck by the number of soldiers on both sides who died from lack of medical attention and medical knowledge. Just about anyone who received more than a superficial wound during the Civil War was dragged off the battlefield, tossed into a wagon, and left to die.

ed within half an hour, but their soldiers were weeks away from any serious medical treatment. Inside the DMZ they had built formidable underground bunker complexes, including hospital facilities. But they weren't equipped for major surgery, and they didn't come from a medically sophisticated society to begin with.

Still, they went through hell to get their people treated. You couldn't help but admire their bravery, bringing the battle to us while knowing their casualties would not be treated for weeks, and that many of their wounded would die. Even in the shock and violence of an ambush, the NVA always made a noble effort to drag their wounded or dead off the field.

When we captured wounded enemy soldiers, they were treated in the same hospital as our troops. There were occasional incidents of abuse, when NVA prisoners were turned over to the South Vietnamese. But these were the exception, not the rule. Captured enemy troops were given a choice: they could remain in POW camps or they could join us as scouts. Many of them decided to defect.

One of our best scouts was Phu, a former NVA corporal who had been wounded and captured near Khe San in 1967. Phu spent a lot of time with my unit, and taught me a lot about our enemy. I hadn't realized, for example, that when NVA troops came across the DMZ, or crossed the border from Laos, they weren't even told they were in South Vietnam. As far as they knew, Vietnam was all one country, and we were the aggressors.

When we captured a prisoner, Phu would often begin the interrogation. We had to keep an eye on him, though, because he had a tendency to be cruel. There were some critical questions that had to be asked immediately: are you alone, or are there two hundred more NVA just over the ridge? Are there any mines in the area? Is there an ambush waiting for us?

I never witnessed any brutal treatment of prisoners, although I'm sure it happened. But to a large extent the NVA themselves made it unnecessary. They had been told such ludicrous and hideous stories about what would happen if they were captured that this alone gave them a big incentive to cooperate.

When Taylor Common ended, we were ordered back north to conduct operations to push back enemy units who were moving into

Leatherneck Square. We began an aggressive series of reconnaissance and combat patrols to keep the enemy off guard and to cut off their infiltration routes. We went out looking for trouble, and more often than not, we found it.

On one of these patrols, my platoon left Con Thien with two tanks and four M-111 armored personnel carriers that the Army had loaned to us. About five kilometers out, one of the tanks lost a tread, so I left two of the APCs and some of the men to guard it. With the other tank and the two remaining APCs, we proceeded east. Early in the afternoon we received an order to turn back due to heavy enemy movement ahead and increasingly bad weather. As we headed back, the tank was in the lead and I was riding on the back; behind us were two APCs and the rest of our troops.

Suddenly, a lone NVA soldier appeared out of nowhere and started hosing down the back of our tank with his AK-47. The men in the APC right behind us couldn't fire at him without the risk of hitting those of us on the back of the tank. I grabbed my shotgun and started shooting. Just then, dozens more of the enemy opened up with small-arms fire and rockets, hitting our tank and both APCs. I don't think they had intended to ambush us here, but once this guy started firing they all opened up. Almost instantly one of the APCs struck a mine and came to a halt.

From the back of the tank I directed the men to set up a defensive perimeter in the brush around the three armored vehicles. As I stood there directing traffic and dodging bullets, and trying to call in for help on the radio, the front of the tank was hit by an RPG. The two or three men who were with me quickly jumped off. I was reloading my shotgun when the turret swung around and batted me into the air like a baseball. I landed in the bushes, badly hurt, with the radio handset still in my hand. Unfortunately, the rest of the radio was back on the tank.

The pain was just terrible. Four of my ribs were cracked, and my left lung was filling with blood. The next thing I knew, Doc Conklin was on top of me, trying to rip off my flak jacket to find the bullet hole. I kept trying to get up, but Doc kept pushing me down. Every time I tried to talk, all I got was a mouthful of blood.

"It must be a fragment," he kept saying. But Doc didn't realize that I hadn't been hit, and I wasn't able to tell him. Besides, we were in danger of being overrun. We had rolled right into an NVA perimeter, and they were shooting us from all sides.

Somehow I had to get back to the tank to retrieve the radio. I eventually made it, and started calling in artillery and air strikes.

We established strong enough fire support to break the ambush, and after about forty minutes, the enemy withdrew. But we had suffered substantial losses. Out of fifteen men, two were killed and twelve were wounded. But under the circumstances, our guys had performed incredibly well. We had practiced drills on what to do if we were ambushed, and the men had handled themselves just as they were trained. The only thing we hadn't rehearsed was what to do when the lieutenant ends up as a deep line drive into right field.

I had lost a fair amount of blood, and was drifting in and out of consciousness. Conklin was beside himself with worry until an army helicopter came to pick me up. At the time I was more concerned about my men. I wasn't trying to be a hero, but there were other casualties and I didn't yet realize how badly I was hurt.

I was flown to the medical station at Dong Ha and taken immediately to triage, a large open area in a tin-roofed hut where doctors and corpsmen made life-and-death decisions as wounded men came off the helicopters. As I lay there on the stretcher, I could hear the doctors talking: "Take this guy to surgery, give that one morphine, don't bother with him." Suddenly I saw a familiar face: Father Jake Laboon, who had been our chaplain at Annapolis, and who used to visit me after the car accident. He was now the chaplain for the Third Marine Regiment.

"Listen up," he told me. "I want you to look real perky." Taking out a sweat-covered handkerchief, he wiped the blood off my face. When the doctor came to see me, Laboon piped up, "Looks pretty good, Doc, but I think he should be looked at right away."

"Okay, take him in."

Laboon used to kid me afterward that he saved me from being left out there to rot.

Instead of operating, the doctors inserted a needle between my lung and my rib cage, and hooked it up to a vacuum pump until the lung was working again. Then they wrapped me up and put me on drugs for a few days.

Soon I found myself in a hospital ward, lying in a bed with real sheets on it. Sheets! A pillow! There was even an air conditioner. This was an inflatable field hospital, which is a great idea unless the generator quits and the roof slowly collapses in on you like a gigantic balloon with a tiny leak. I got plenty of sleep in the hospital, and enjoyed hot water showers and real food. You can bounce back pretty quickly when you're young and eager, and I was back to the platoon a few days later. Normally they send injured men back to the rear, but my unit was on perimeter security duty at Con Thien, which wasn't too strenuous.

Les Shaeffer, who was killed in that same operation, was posthumously awarded a Bronze Star for taking over a machine-gun position after he was wounded on the lead APC. Doc Conklin was given a medal for saving several lives. Pete Rich, the tank platoon commander, was given a Bronze Star, and so was I.

There is a tendency in war to pray to God that you'll survive in the middle of the battle, and to blame Him afterward if one of your buddies didn't make it. After Shaeffer died, a lot of the men were terribly upset. Les had been a respected and extremely well-liked squad leader, and we all felt his loss. A few days after he was killed, one of our men was just lying there, staring off into space, while a couple of others were sitting on the ground with their packs up against ammo crates, talking softly and tossing pebbles in front of them.

I walked over and sat down. "What's wrong?" I said, although I already knew.

"Shaeffer. Man, there's no reason for that."

These guys had been in his squad. They had counted on each other day and night. Why him? they wanted to know. Why not some other jerk? Why anybody?

"He's in a better place now," I said.

"F--k, man, don't give me that. If there is a God, why does this happen? Just *look* at all this shit. He was wasted."

I believe in a merciful God, but I didn't have an answer. And although I know Him better today, I still don't. The only true response I could give at such a moment was to say, "I don't know. All I know is that God is ultimately in control, and that you can't let this make you lose your faith in Him."

Certainly the Scriptures helped. We often read the Twenty-third

Psalm, which is a comfort in so many terrible situations. And a passage from Psalm Ninety-one seemed especially pertinent in Vietnam. Years later it again took on special significance:

> You will not fear the terror of night,
> nor the arrow that flies by day,
> Nor the pestilence that stalks in darkness
> nor the plague that destroys at midday.
> A thousand may fall at your side,
> ten thousand at your right hand;
> but it will not come near you.

Occasionally one of the men would say, "Maybe God doesn't *want* us to be over here. Wasn't Jesus the Prince of Peace?"

If I had a Bible handy, I would open it to Matthew 8:5–13. Otherwise, I'd tell the story in my own words. A Roman centurion approaches Jesus. "My servant is dying," he says. "Can you help him?"

"Yes," says Jesus, "I'll come and heal him."

"No," says the soldier, "don't come to my house. I'm a military man, and I'm not worthy of your visit. Can't you say the word and heal him from here?"

Whereupon Jesus announces to His followers, "I have not seen such great faith in all of Israel." And the servant is healed.

"Notice what Jesus does *not* say," I would tell the men. "He doesn't tell the centurion, 'I'd really love to help, but I don't do soldiers.' He doesn't say, 'Before I heal your servant, I want you to lay down your sword and renounce Caesar.' Instead, Jesus says, 'This guy comes from the occupying army, and yet *he's* the one with faith. What's wrong with the rest of you characters?'"

Don Dulligan, another chaplain, had taught me this passage after a terrible incident west of Con Thien, where one of our engineers had tried to remove an unexploded white phosphorus mortar round from the edge of our perimeter. As he carefully picked it up, it detonated in his hands—burning the skin off the entire front of his body. It was by far the most gruesome thing I saw in Vietnam. As the medevac chopper came down to get him, he turned to us and said, "Now you all pray for me, because I'm not going to make it." He showed no bitterness or rancor—only an acceptance of death, which came, as he knew it would, later that day.

The worst battle of all was the night Captain Mike Weunch was killed. It was July, and we were on a big armored sweep west of Con Thien. The night air was chilly when Captain Goodwin sent out First Platoon to ambush the approaches to the hilltop. Third Platoon went north, while my men were ordered to establish a perimeter with the company of tanks under Captain Weunch.

A little after 0230, one of my men awakened me to report that our listening post had detected movement. I climbed up on the tank with Mike Weunch and we both looked through his starlight scope to see half a dozen NVA troops silently ascending on the north side of the draw. Those we could see were less than fifty yards away, and others were undoubtedly close behind. I had to alert my men immediately before the enemy launched its attack.

I never got the chance. Just as I turned away from Mike, an RPG round hit the tank's cupola and detonated. Mike was killed instantly and I was blown off the tank. Had I waited just one more second, I would have been a goner.

As it was, the blast threw me about ten feet, shredding the back of my flak jacket and peppering my legs, buttocks, and neck with fragments. Even my ears had little holes through them.

I blacked out. The next thing I knew, somebody was dragging me on my back. Randy Herrod, the machine-gun team leader, had climbed out of his hole and was risking his life to drag me to safety.

Despite the explosions around me, and the sky ablaze with orange and yellow tracer rounds, and the roar of the tank cannons and fifty-caliber machine guns, everything seemed to be happening at low volume. My eardrums, which had almost healed from a previous injury, were blown out again. Herrod threw me into his hole and stood over me, firing his machine gun as the NVA swept up the side of the hill behind a barrage of mortar fire and a hail of RPGs. I tried to push him off so I could get out and recover the radio. The only reason I succeeded is that Herrod left his hole again—this time to remount the M-60, which had been blown off its mount by an exploding grenade.

The air was thick with fire and smoke. Two of our tanks were burning, lighting up our position and silhouetting the infantry positions between them. With two tanks out of action, the west side of the perimeter was vulnerable. The only reason they hadn't broken through was Herrod's steady hand on the machine gun.

I climbed out of the hole and dashed to the back of the command tank. The radio was a shattered wreck, so I sprinted to the next tank and got on the infantry phone. The tank commander rotated his turret and adjusted his fire across our front, cutting down the first wave of the NVA attack.

There was a sudden lull as the tank's volley did its brutal job. The enemy fell back momentarily, regrouped, and fired another salvo of mortars and RPGs. An incoming round landed beside me and blew me into the air. For the second time in half an hour, Herrod left the protection of his fighting position, grabbed me by the remnants of my flak jacket, and again dragged me to safety.

The second NVA wave broke off under fire from Herrod's machine gun and the remaining tanks. I crawled out again, found Lehnert and a working radio, and started trying to adjust the air support that Goodwin had already summoned. Because I couldn't hear a thing, Lehnert passed the instructions to the aircraft and shouted to me as the pilots rained death from the heavens to break the third and final attack of the night.

It was over before dawn. Our line had held, but just barely. The carnage was awful. The tankers suffered our highest casualties; restricted to a fixed perimeter, they had been unable to maneuver. For the enemy it was far worse. Despite their strong initial assault, only a handful had survived. They had died in heaps from our tanks and machine guns. Before the sun rose over the battlefield, the survivors had melted away to die elsewhere, to be buried in unmarked graves, or to fight another day.

Shortly after first light, our choppers came in to evacuate the wounded and remove the dead. We stacked the weapons of the dead into nets: AK-47s and RPGs from the enemy, and M-16s from our side. These were flown out last. Then we buried the enemy dead and placed thermite grenades in the two most damaged tanks, abandoning them to the rust and the elements.

I put Randy Herrod in for a medal, and he was later awarded the Silver Star. During the attack, he had saved our entire position. Instead of hunkering down in the hole, he remounted the M-60 and spent the better part of the night repelling concerted attacks against us. He was a tall, scrawny kid from Oklahoma, a brave and natural leader who saved my life twice that night. I owed him a tremendous debt, and before the war was over I would have a chance to repay it.

Not all of Vietnam was chaos, carnage, and cries for help. There were some wonderful moments as well. One of mine occurred when we were out in East Boondock and a message came in over the radio: "Congratulations, Lt. North. You have just become the father of a seven-and-a-half-pound baby girl." Goodwin arranged for a helicopter so I could fly back to the rear and call Betsy on a MARS telephone.*

It took hours, but I finally got through. It's strange to talk to your wife in that situation, because although you've been apart for months, there's no privacy. The operators have to listen in, and I bet those guys have heard some of the deepest emotions ever expressed—and some of the raciest lines ever spoken.

Betsy was still in the hospital, because in those days new mothers were allowed to stay more than a few hours after the delivery. The conversation was a little stilted, not only because of the operators, but also because we each had to say "over" whenever we finished talking so they'd know when to stop transmitting. And every time Betsy said "over," she started laughing.

The happiest days of my tour came near the end of my year in Vietnam, during a week of R & R with Betsy in Hawaii—which was as far east as military personnel were allowed to travel. Betsy had left our baby daughter with her sister, and we must have had the highest hotel phone bill in Honolulu as she called home every day to check on little Tait, this new member of my family whom I hadn't even met. Betsy cried a couple of nights because this was her first separation from the baby. I couldn't really understand her tears. Betsy was already a mother, but I wasn't yet a father; at the time, I only barely knew what it meant to be a husband. It didn't occur to me then that Betsy had already spent far more time with Tait than she had with me.

Looking back on that fantastic week, I remember macadamia nut pancakes. Showers. Milk. Swimming. Real bread. Milkshakes. Fresh vegetables and real salads. More milk. Fresh fruit. More milkshakes.

---

*MARS (Military Affiliated Radio Station) is a network of ham operators who use their shortwave radios to broadcast messages on behalf of military personnel overseas.

The Clancy clan was a big part of growing up. Uncles John, Larry, and Joe are standing behind Mom, Gram Clancy, and Aunt Mary during World War II.

Dad was a lieutenant when this picture was taken right after the war started. By the end of the war he was a major.

Grandma and Grandpa North with the two older North boys. Grandma North is holding Jack and I'm sitting on my grandfather's lap at the farm we came to love.

Russ Robertson, standing to the left of my high school track team, was a big influence in my life. As a World War II Marine he had been badly wounded in the Pacific. His recovery was an inspiration to me after my automobile accident.

The four North kids: Tim, Pat, Jack, and me. We gave this photo to Mom and Dad for Christmas in 1965.

The 1967 Naval Academy boxing champions. Emerson Smith, the head boxing coach, at far right, was a legend at Annapolis. He's one of the finest men I've ever known. When he retired in the 1980s, I got President Reagan to send him a letter.

Major Reid Olson, my last company officer at Annapolis, taught me much of what was expected of a Marine officer.

During the summer of 1966 while I was at Annapolis, I took parachute training at Fort Benning, Georgia. This photo was taken just before our heavy equipment jump.

The Naval Academy took pictures of us in every imaginable uniform. This one was taken in summer whites just prior to my graduation in 1968.

When Betsy and I got married at Quantico, my Basic School classmates formed the traditional arch of swords as we left the chapel.

Both grandmothers made it to our wedding. Betsy's grandmother Nan (on my right) and Gram Clancy (on my left) both lived into their nineties.

Sergeant Hue was one of our Kit Carson Scouts. A former NVA soldier, he helped us find an NVA position inside the DMZ in May 1969.

Jim Lehnert, my radio man for most of my tour in Vietnam, became a dentist after the war.

The Command Group of 2d Platoon, Company K, 3d Battalion, 3d Marines. The sign says: "Welcome. Now that you're here, this is the rear. Courtesy of Blue's Bastards."

Not everything in Vietnam was terrible. Betsy sent me this photo of herself with our new daughter, taken just hours after Tait was born at Bethesda Naval Hospital. I carried it with me everywhere.

Almost everything we ate, wore, or fired arrived by helicopter. This CH-34 evacuated our wounded from a bomb crater landing zone after an operation on Mutter's Ridge.

Captain Paul Goodwin took command of Kilo Company in the spring of 1969. Here he's presenting awards to Blue's Bastards after a battle in Leatherneck Square.

Blue's Bastards conducted more than seventy successful ambushes against the North Vietnamese Army. This sun bear triggered an ambush in the middle of the night. It couldn't be confirmed as a North Vietnamese bear, so it didn't count.

Bill Haskell lost his eye in May 1969 during a terrible battle on the DMZ. We got together in 1970 for the Marine Corps Birthday Ball after he had been medically retired.

Above: Thirteen months after graduating from The Basic School, I was back as an instructor, teaching tactics to brand-new lieutenants headed for the war I had just left.

Left: Many of the classes we taught at The Basic School were held in outdoor classrooms where we could demonstrate the skills we were trying to impart.

Below: After teaching tactics at Quantico, I was sent to Okinawa to do more of the same in the Northern Training Area. Here I'm presenting an award to Doc Bell, our senior corpsman, for saving the life of a Japanese local who had been bitten by a snake.

The tour of duty at Quantico wasn't all work. Betsy and I took this Christmas photo with Tait and newborn Stuart in 1971. (William Cummings)

Betsy came to see me in Okinawa and joined me for rappeling down the face of a cliff. I used this photo to encourage reluctant Marines.

When Sarah was born in 1976, I got to be in the delivery room. We called her "Sarah Sunshine" because she smiled so much.

Below: In 1983, while I was with the National Security Council, I was assigned to work with the President's Bi-partisan Commission on Central America. Here, Lane Kirkland, head of the AFL-CIO, Robert Strauss, then chair of the Democratic Party and now our ambassador to Moscow, and Senator Pete Dominici, all members of the commission, agree on Washington's approach to the Sandinista government in Managua: hear, see, and speak no evil.

Right: Jack Kemp, then a congressman and a member of the commission, was kind enough to send this note when the commission finished its work.

Ollie —

We owe you a great debt of gratitude,

JACK KEMP
U. S. HOUSE OF REPRESENTATIVES
WASHINGTON, D. C. 20515
(202) 225-5265

Above: Henry Kissinger, head of the President's commission, wanted to meet with Daniel Ortega. Perched beneath a large photo of Sandino, Ortega put nearly everyone to sleep with his rambling soliloquy on American imperialism.

Right: At the Managua airport, the Turbas Divinas ("Divine Mobs") of Sandinista supporters turned out in a "spontaneous" demonstration to show everyone how much we were hated.

From 1978 to 1980 I served as the operations officer for Battalion Landing Team 3/8. Though we were home based at Camp Lejeune, North Carolina, we spent much of our time deployed. Here, Lieutenant Colonel John Grinalds, the battalion commander, and I present a plaque to an allied officer during one of our 1979 NATO exercises in the Mediterranean.

John Grinalds, shown here in his white dress uniform, knelt in the sand and prayed for my back to be healed. It was. John remains one of the closest friends I have on this earth.

In 1980 we packed up the family again and moved to Newport, Rhode Island, for a year at the Naval War College. It was the best year for our family during my entire career. Dornin was born just hours before this photo was taken. This time I got to participate in the delivery. In spite of this, she still likes her dad!

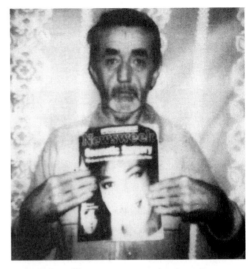

Much of my time in 1985 and 1986 was consumed by efforts to recover the American hostages in Beirut. Photos like these provided proof that they were still alive, but suffering in captivity. We never released these photos of David Jacobsen holding the *Wall Street Journal* and Bill Buckley holding a copy of *Newsweek*. Bill Casey was outraged when he saw how much Buckley had deteriorated.

Right: Two days after the Beirut terrorist attack on our Marines, President Reagan ordered U.S. military units ashore on Grenada. Five Caribbean democracies participated with us in this operation, and several of their leaders came to Washington to commend the President. Here, Eugenia Charles, the prime minister of Dominica, talks with President Reagan in the Oval Office before going out to meet the press. (The White House)

A month after the Grenada operation, my promotion to lieutenant colonel came through. Betsy and Bud McFarlane pinned on the silver oak leaves that Bud himself had once worn.

My NSC duties took me on more trips to Central America than I can count. Though many officials eventually had trouble remembering whether they had ever met me, this trip to the region with Secretary Caspar Weinberger was photographed for the record. (Don Goode)

This is the last photo of my whole family before Dad died in 1984. Tim was still in college, Pat came in from California, Jack took leave from the Army, and I made it up from Washington.

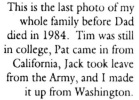

In June 1985, Jack and I commissioned our little brother Tim in the U.S. Navy. By the end of the 1980s all three brothers had been in combat in different services.

Right: In the spring of 1985, the President asked to meet with the leaders of the Nicaraguan resistance. During the meeting, Adolfo Calero presented him with a pin that read, "I'm a contra too." (The White House)

Below: On his way to Camp David one afternoon, President Reagan secretly commended this Nicaraguan Catholic priest for opposing the Communist regime in Managua. (The White House)

Bottom: Within months of this 1986 Oval Office meeting on combating terrorism, the three of us in the background—John Poindexter, me, and Don Regan—would be gone. The two men in the foreground, George Bush and Ronald Reagan, would be hounded for years by what had been set in motion in this room. (The White House)

In May 1986 Bud McFarlane went to Tehran as the President's special emissary. As this book was nearing completion, some of the photos taken on that trip were declassified. Ami Nir took this shot of me on the way to the airport at the end of our failed mission. I don't remember feeling as exhausted as I looked.

This road sign offers the Tehran government's solution to peace in the Middle East.

One of the Israeli counterterrorist agents snapped this shot as I was calling Washington to let them know we had arrived safely in Tel Aviv from Tehran. Ami Nir is standing next to Bud. We had to black out the faces of the CIA officers and the communications equipment in order to have the photo released.

MARY HIGGINS CLARK

SIMON & SCHUSTER

The Lottery Winner

ALVIRAH AND WILLY STORIES

NEW YORK · LONDON · TORONTO · SYDNEY · TOKYO · SINGAPORE

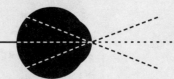

This Large Print Book carries the
Seal of Approval of N.A.V.H.

SIMON & SCHUSTER
ROCKEFELLER CENTER
1230 AVENUE OF THE AMERICAS
NEW YORK, NY 10020

DESIGNED BY EVE METZ
MANUFACTURED IN THE UNITED STATES OF AMERICA

1   3   5   7   9   10   8   6   4   2

LIBRARY OF CONGRESS CATALOGING-IN-PUBLICATION DATA
IS AVAILABLE.
ISBN 0-684-80222-8

"Death on the Cape" appeared in *Woman's Day,* July 18, 1989.
"Body in the Closet" appeared in *Woman's Day,* August 7, 1990.
"Plumbing for Willy" appeared in *Family Circle,* August 1992.
"A Clean Sweep" appeared in *Justice in Manhattan* published by
Longmeadow Press (Bill Adler Books). Copyright © October 1994 by
Mary Higgins Clark.

ACKNOWLEDGMENTS

ALVIRAH MEEHAN made her debut—if you can call it that—as a character in my novel *Weep No More, My Lady.* A cleaning woman in her late fifties, she and her plumber husband, Willy, had won forty million dollars in the New York State Lottery. Alvirah immediately decided to satisfy her long held dream of going to the Cypress Point Spa and mingling with the celebrities who frequented it.

Unfortunately for Alvirah, she was too smart, got on the track of a killer and became a victim herself. In the early drafts of *Weep No More, My Lady,* poor Alvirah did not survive to the last page.

Then my daughter Carol Higgins Clark read the manuscript and protested, "You can't do that. Alvirah is much too funny. Besides, haven't you knocked off enough people in this book?"

7

"She has to die," I said firmly.

But Carol was so persuasive that I brought Alvirah back from death's door.

I'm certainly glad I did. I count her and Willy as dear friends. They are my only continuing characters, and now I hope you enjoy reading about their adventures as much as I enjoy writing about them.

Thanks, Carol.

For my siblings-in-law and friends,

June M. Clark and in memory of Allan Clark
Ken and Irene Clark
Agnes Partel and in memory of George Partel

Dear companions of my salad days,
aren't we all still twenty-two?

Contents

The Body
in the
Closet

*I*f Alvirah had known on that July evening what was waiting for her at her fancy new apartment on Central Park South, she would never have gotten off the plane. As it was, there was absolutely no hint of foreboding in her usually keen psyche as the plane circled for a landing.

Even though she and Willy had been bitten by the travel bug after they won forty million dollars in the lottery, and had by now taken a number of exciting trips, Alvirah was always glad to get back to New York. There was something heartwarming about the view from the airplane: the skyscrapers silhouetted against the clouds, the lights of the bridges that spanned the East River.

Willy patted her hand, and Alvirah turned to him with an affectionate smile. He looked grand, she thought, in his new blue linen jacket that matched the color of his eyes. With those eyes and his thick head of white hair, Willy was a double for Tip O'Neill, no mistake about it.

Alvirah smoothed her russet-brown hair, recently tinted and styled by Dale of London. Dale had marveled to hear that Alvirah was pushing sixty. "You're funning me," he had gasped. She knew such compliments were probably hollow, but she liked to hear them anyway.

Yes, Alvirah reflected as she watched the city below, life had been grand to her and Willy. In addition to allowing them to travel at will and to buy all the creature comforts one could desire, their newfound wealth had also opened new doors of opportunity in unexpected ways, such as her involvement with one of the city's major newspapers, the *New York Globe.* It all began when a *Globe* editor talked to her and Willy after they won the lottery. Alvirah had told him that she was realizing her longtime ambition to be a guest at the elegant Cypress Point Spa, and it wasn't just the makeover she was looking forward to—it was also the chance to be mingling with all the celebrities she loved to read about.

The newspaper editor, obviously spotting in Alvirah some special talent for sniffing out news, plus the perseverance to pursue it to the end, persuaded her to take on an assignment for him. He asked her to keep her eyes open and her ears alert, with the idea in mind of writing an article about her experiences at the exclusive spa. And to further aid her in the process of gathering news and impressions, he gave her a lapel pin in the shape of a sunburst that actually contained a tiny recording device. That way she could record her impressions while they were fresh, and she might even pick up a few bits of conversation from those very people she was so anxious to meet.

The results had proved even more dramatic than either she or the editor had hoped, for at the spa she recorded someone who was in the act of trying to kill her, an attack brought on by her sleuthing into a murder that had occurred there. With the help of her detection—and the handy recording device—Alvirah had not only helped to solve a crime but had embarked on a whole new and unexpected career as occasional columnist and amateur sleuth.

Now, as she sat buckled into her seat, thinking back over her most recent trip, she fingered the sunburst pin—a more-or-less permanent fixture on any outfit she wore—and reflected on how disappointed her editor was going to be. "This trip was wonderful," she said to Willy, "but there wasn't a single adventure I could write about. The most exciting thing during the whole trip was when the Queen stopped in for tea at the Stafford Hotel, and the manager's cat attacked her corgis."

"Well I for one am glad we had a nice, calm vacation," Willy said. "I can't take much more of you almost getting killed solving crimes."

The British Airways flight attendant was walking down the aisle of the first-class cabin, checking that seat belts were fastened. "I certainly enjoyed talking with you," she told them. Willy had explained to her, as he would to almost any willing ear, that he'd been a plumber and Alvirah a cleaning woman until they won the forty-million-dollar lottery two years ago. "My goodness," the flight attendant said now to Alvirah, "I just can't *believe* you were ever a char."

In a mercifully short time after landing they were in the waiting limousine, their matching Vuitton luggage stacked in the trunk. As usual, New York in August was hot, sticky and sultry. The air-conditioning in the limo had just gone on the fritz, and Alvirah thought longingly ahead to their new apartment on Central Park South, which would be wonderfully cool. They still kept their old three-room flat in Flushing where they'd lived for forty years before the lottery changed their lives. As Willy pointed out, you never knew if someday New York would go broke and tell the lottery winners to take a flying leap for the rest of their winnings.

When the limo pulled up to the apartment building, the doorman opened the door for them. "You must be melting," Alvirah said.

"You'd think they wouldn't bother dressing you up until they finished the renovations."

The building was undergoing a total overhaul. When they had bought the apartment in the spring, the real estate agent had assured them that the refurbishing would be completed in a matter of weeks. It was clear from the scaffolding still in the lobby that he had been wildly optimistic.

At the bank of elevators they were joined by another couple, a tall, fiftyish man and a slender woman wearing a white silk evening suit and an expression that reminded Alvirah of someone who has opened a refrigerator and encountered the odor of eggs gone bad. I know them, Alvirah thought and began ruffling through her prodigious memory. He was Carlton Rumson, the legendary Broadway producer, and she was his wife, Victoria, a sometime actress who had been a Miss America runner-up some thirty years ago.

"Mr. Rumson!" With a warm smile, Alvirah reached out her hand. "I'm Alvirah Meehan. We met at the Cypress Point Spa in Pebble Beach. What a nice surprise! This is my husband, Willy. Do you live here?"

Rumson's smile came and went. "We keep an apartment here for convenience." He nodded to Willy, then grudgingly introduced his wife. The elevator door opened as Victoria Rumson acknowledged them with the flicker of an eyelid. What a cold fish, Alvirah thought, taking in the perfect but haughty profile, the pale-blond hair pulled back in a chignon. Long years of reading *People, US,* the *National Enquirer* and gossip columns had resulted in Alvirah's brain becoming the repository of an awesome amount of information about the rich and famous.

They had just stopped at the thirty-fourth floor as Alvirah remembered her Rumson tidbits. He was famous for his wandering eye, while his wife's ability to overlook his indiscretions had earned her the nickname "See-No-Evil Vicky." Obviously a perfect match, Alvirah thought.

"Mr. Rumson," Alvirah said, "Willy's nephew, Brian McCormack, is a wonderful playwright. He's just finished his second play. I'd love to have you read it."

Rumson looked annoyed. "My office is listed in the phone book," he said.

"Brian's first play is running off Broadway right now," Alvirah persisted. "One of the critics said he's a young Neil Simon."

"Come on, honey," Willy urged. "You're holding up these folks."

Unexpectedly the glacier look melted from

Victoria Rumson's face. "Darling," she said, "I've heard about Brian McCormack. Why don't you read the play here? It will only get buried in your office. Mrs. Meehan, send it by our apartment."

"That's real nice of you, Victoria," Alvirah said heartily. "You'll have it tomorrow."

As they walked from the elevator to their apartment, Willy asked, "Honey, don't you think you were being a little pushy?"

"Absolutely not," Alvirah said. "Nothing ventured, nothing gained. Anything I can do to help Brian's career is A-OK with me."

Their apartment commanded a sweeping view of Central Park. Alvirah never stepped into it without thinking that not so long ago she had considered her Thursday cleaning job, Mrs. Chester Lollop's house in Little Neck, a miniature palace. Boy, had her eyes been opened these last few years!

They'd bought the apartment completely furnished from a stockbroker who'd been indicted for insider trading. He had just had it done by an interior designer who, he assured them, was the absolute rage of Manhattan. Secretly Alvirah now had serious doubts about just what kind of rage he'd been talking about. The living room, dining room and kitchen were stark white. There were low white sofas that she had to hoist herself out of, thick white carpeting that showed every speck of dirt, white counters and cabinets and marble and appliances that reminded her of all the tubs and sinks and toilets she'd ever tried to scrub free of rust.

And tonight there was something new, a large printed sign taped to the door leading to the terrace. Alvirah crossed to the door to read it.

A building inspection has revealed that this is one of a small number of apartments in which a serious structural weakness has been found in the guardrailing and the panels of the terrace. Your terrace is safe for normal use, but do not lean on the guardrail or permit others to do so. Repairs will be completed as rapidly as possible.

After reading the notice silently, she read it aloud to Willy, then shrugged. "Well, I certainly have brains enough not to lean on any guardrail, safe or not."

Willy smiled sheepishly. He was scared

silly of heights and never set foot on the terrace. As he'd said when they bought the apartment, "You love a terrace, I love terra firma."

Willy went into the kitchen to put the kettle on. Alvirah opened the terrace door and stepped outside. The sultry air was a hot wave against her face, but she didn't care. There was something she loved about standing out here, looking across the park at the festive glow from the decorated trees around the Tavern on the Green, the ribbons of headlights of the cars and the glimpses of horse-drawn carriages in the distance.

Oh, it's good to be back! she thought again as she went inside and surveyed the living room, her expert eye observing the degree of efficiency of the weekly cleaning service that should have been in yesterday. She was surprised to see fingerprints smeared across the glass cocktail table. Automatically she reached for a handkerchief and vigorously rubbed them away. Then she noticed that the tieback on the drapery next to the terrace door was missing. Hope it didn't end up in the vacuum, she thought. At least I was a good cleaning woman. Then she remembered what the British Airways attendant had said—or a good char, whatever that is.

"Hey, Alvirah," Willy called. "Did Brian leave a note? Looks like he may have been expecting someone."

Brian, Willy's nephew, was the only child of his oldest sister, Madaline. Six of Willy's seven sisters had gone into the convent. Madaline had married in her forties and produced a change-of-life baby, Brian, who was now twenty-six years old. He had been raised in Nebraska, written plays for a repertory company out there and came to New York after Madaline's death two years ago. All of Alvirah's untapped maternal instincts were released by Brian, with his thin, intense face, unruly sandy hair and shy smile. As she often told Willy, "If I'd carried him inside me for nine months, I couldn't love him more."

When they'd left for England in June, Brian was finishing the first draft of his new play and had been glad to accept their offer of a key to the Central Park South apartment. "It's a heck of a lot easier to write there than in my place," was his grateful comment. He lived in a walk-up in the East Village, surrounded by large noisy families.

Alvirah went into the kitchen. She raised her eyebrows. A bottle of champagne, standing in a wine cooler which was now half full of water, and two champagne glasses were on a silver tray. The champagne was a gift from the broker who'd handled the apartment sale. The broker had several times informed them that that particular champagne cost a hundred dollars a bottle and was the brand the Queen of England herself enjoyed sipping.

Willy looked troubled. "That's the stuff that's so crazy expensive, isn't it? No way Brian would help himself to that without asking. There's something funny going on." Alvirah opened her mouth to reassure him, then closed it. Willy was right. There *was* something funny going on, and her antenna told her trouble was brewing.

The chimes rang. An apologetic porter was at the door with their bags. "Sorry to be so long, Mr. Meehan. Since the remodeling began, so many residents are using the service elevator that the staff has to stand in line for it." At Willy's request, he deposited the bags in the bedroom, then departed smiling, his palm closing over a five-dollar bill.

Willy and Alvirah shared a pot of tea in the kitchen. Willy kept staring at the champagne bottle. "I'm gonna call Brian," he said.

"He'll still be at the theater," Alvirah said, closed her eyes, concentrated and gave him the telephone number of the box office.

Willy dialed, listened, then hung up. "There's a recorder on," he said flatly. "Brian's play closed. They talk about how to get refunds."

"The poor kid," Alvirah said. "Try his apartment."

"Only the answering machine," he told her a moment later. "I'll leave a message for him."

Alvirah suddenly realized how weary she was. As she collected teacups she reminded herself that it was 5:00 A.M., English time, so she had a right to feel as though all her bones were aching. She put the teacups in the dishwasher, hesitated, then rinsed out the unused champagne glasses and put them in the dishwasher too. Her friend Baroness Min von Schreiber—who owned the Cypress Point Spa where Alvirah had gone to be made over after she won the lottery—had told her that expensive wines should never be left standing. With a damp sponge, she gave a vigorous rub to the unopened bottle, the silver tray and bucket and put them away. Turning the lights out behind her, she went into the bedroom.

Willy had begun to unpack. Alvirah liked the bedroom. It had been furnished for the bachelor stockbroker with a king-sized bed, a triple dresser, comfortable easy chairs, and night tables large enough to hold at the same time a stack of books, reading glasses and mineral ice for Alvirah's rheumatic knees. The decor, however, convinced her that the trendy interior designer must have been weaned on bleach. White spread. White drapes. White carpet.

The porter had left Alvirah's garment bag laid out across the bed. She unlocked it and began to remove the suits and dresses. Baroness von Schreiber was always pleading with her not to go shopping on her own. "Alvirah," Min would argue, "you are natural prey for saleswomen who have been ordered to unload the buyers' mistakes. They sense your approach even while you're still in the elevator. I'm in New York enough. You come to the spa several times a year. Wait till we're together; I will shop with you."

Alvirah wondered if Min would approve of the orange-and-pink plaid suit that the saleswoman in Harrods had raved over. Looking at it now, she was sure Min wouldn't.

Her arms filled with clothing, she opened the door of the closet, glanced down and let out a shriek. Lying on the carpeted floor between rows of Alvirah's size-10 extra-wide designer shoes, with green eyes staring up, crinkly blond hair flowing around her face, tongue slightly protruding and the missing drapery tieback around her neck, was the body of a slender young woman.

"Blessed Mother," Alvirah moaned as the clothes fell from her arms.

"What's the matter, honey?" Willy demanded, rushing to her side. "Oh my God," he breathed. "Who the hell is that?"

"It's . . . it's . . . you know. The actress. The one who had the lead in Brian's play. The one Brian is so crazy about." Alvirah squeezed her eyes shut, glad to free herself from the glazed expression on the face of the body at her feet. "Fiona Winters."

Willy's arm firmly around her, Alvirah walked to one of the low couches in the living room that made her knees feel as though they were going to meet her chin. As he dialed 911, she forced her head to clear. It doesn't take a lot of brains to know that this could look very bad for Brian, she told herself. I've got to get my thinking cap on and remember everything I can about that girl. She was so nasty to Brian. Had they had a fight?

Willy crossed the room, sat beside her and

reached for her hand. "It's going to be all right, honey," he said. "The police will be here in a few minutes."

"Call Brian again," Alvirah told him.

"Good idea." Willy dialed quickly. "Still that darn machine. I'll leave another message. Try to rest."

Alvirah nodded, closed her eyes and immediately turned her thoughts to the night last April when Brian's play had opened.

The theater had been crowded. Brian had arranged for them to have front-row-center seats, and Alvirah wore her new silver-and-black sequin dress. The play, *Falling Bridges,* was set in Nebraska and was about a family reunion. Fiona Winters played the socialite who is bored with her unsophisticated in-laws, and Alvirah had to admit she was very believable, though she liked the girl who played the second lead much better—Emmy Laker had bright-red hair, blue eyes and portrayed a funny but wistful character to perfection.

The performances brought a standing ovation, and Alvirah's heart swelled with pride when the cries of "Author! Author!" brought Brian to the stage. When he was handed a bouquet and leaned over the footlights to give it to Alvirah, she started to cry.

The opening-night party was in the up-stairs room of Gallagher's Steak House. Brian kept the seats on either side of him for Alvirah and Fiona Winters. Willy and Emmy Laker sat opposite. It didn't take Alvirah long to get the lay of the land. Brian hovered over Fiona Winters like a lovesick calf, but she kept putting him down and letting them know about her high-class background, saying things like, "The family was appalled when after Foxcroft I decided to go into the theater." She then proceeded to tell Willy and Brian, who were thoroughly enjoying sliced-steak sandwiches with Gallagher's special fries, that they were likely candidates for heart attacks. Personally, she never ate meat, she said.

She took potshots at all of us, Alvirah recalled. She asked me if I missed cleaning houses. She told me Brian should learn how to dress, and with our income she was surprised we didn't help him out. And she had really jumped on that sweet Emmy Laker when Emmy said Brian had better things to think about than his wardrobe.

On the way home Alvirah and Willy had solemnly agreed that though Brian might show a lot of maturity as a playwright, he had a lot of growing up to do if he didn't see what a shrew Fiona was. "I'd like to see him together with Emmy Laker," Willy had announced. "If he had the brains he was born with he'd know that she's crazy about him. And that Fiona has been around a lot. She must have eight years on Brian."

Alvirah was drawn back to the reality of the moment by the vigorous ringing of the front doorbell. Mother-in-heaven, she thought, that must be the police. I wish I'd had a chance to talk to Brian.

The next hours passed in a blur. As her head cleared a bit, Alvirah was able to separate the different kinds of law enforcement people who invaded the apartment. The first were the policemen in uniform. They were followed by detectives, photographers, the medical examiner. She and Willy sat together silently observing them all.

Officials from the Central Park South Towers office came too. "We hope there will be no unfortunate publicity," the resident manager said. "This is not the Trump Organization."

Their original statements had been taken by the first two cops. At 3:00 A.M., the door from the bedroom opened. "Don't look, honey," Willy said. But Alvirah could not keep her eyes away from the stretcher that two somber-faced attendants wheeled out. At least the body of Fiona Winters was covered. God rest her, Alvirah prayed, picturing again the tousled blond hair and the pouty lips. She was not a nice person, Alvirah thought, but she certainly didn't deserve to be murdered.

Someone sat down opposite them, a long-legged fortyish man who introduced himself as Detective Rooney. "I've read your articles in the *Globe,* Mrs. Meehan," he told Alvirah, "and thoroughly enjoyed them."

Willy smiled appreciatively, but Alvirah wasn't fooled. She knew Detective Rooney was buttering her up to make her confide in him. Her mind was racing, trying to figure out ways to protect Brian. Automatically she reached up and switched on the recorder in her sunburst pin. She wanted to be able to go over everything that was said later.

Detective Rooney consulted his notes. "According to your earlier statement, you've just returned from a vacation abroad and arrived here around 10:00 P.M.? You found the victim, Fiona Winters, a short time later? You recognized Miss Winters because she played the lead in your nephew Brian McCormack's play?"

Alvirah nodded. She noticed that Willy was about to speak and laid a warning hand on his arm. "That's right."

"From what I understand, you only met Miss Winters once," Detective Rooney said. "How do you suppose she ended up in your closet?"

"I have no idea," Alvirah said.

"Who had a key to this apartment?"

Again Willy's lips pursed. This time Alvirah pinched his arm. "Keys to this apartment," she said thoughtfully. "Now let me see. The One-Two-Three Cleaning service has a key. Well, they don't really *have* a key. They pick one up at the desk and leave it there when they finish. My friend Maude has a key. She came in Mother's Day weekend to go out with her son and his wife to Radio City. They have a cat and she's allergic to cats so she slept on our couch. Then Willy's sister, Sister Cordelia, has a key. Then—"

"Does your nephew, Brian McCormack, have a key, Mrs. Meehan?" Detective Rooney interrupted.

Alvirah bit her lip. "Yes, and Brian has a key."

This time Detective Rooney raised his voice slightly. "According to the concierge, Brian's been using this apartment frequently in your absence. Incidentally, although it's impossible to be totally accurate before an autopsy, the medical examiner estimates the time of death to be between 11:00 A.M. and 3:00 P.M. yesterday." Detective Rooney's tone became speculative. "It will be interesting to know where Brian was during that time frame."

They were told that before they could use the apartment, the investigating team would have to dust it for fingerprints and vacuum it for clues. "The apartment is as you found it?" Detective Rooney asked.

"Except—" Willy began.

"Except that we made a pot of tea," Alvirah interrupted. I can always tell them about the glasses and the champagne, but I can't untell them, she thought. That detective is going to find out that Brian was crazy about Fiona Winters and decide it was a crime of passion. Then he'll make everything fit that theory.

Detective Rooney closed his notebook. "I understand the management has a furnished apartment you can use tonight," he said.

Fifteen minutes later, Alvirah was in bed, gratefully hunched against an already dozing Willy. Tired as she was, it was hard to relax in a strange bed, plus her mind was reviewing all that had transpired tonight. She knew that all this could look very bad for Brian. But she also knew there had to be an explanation. Brian wouldn't help himself to that hundred-dollar bottle of champagne, and he *certainly* wouldn't kill Fiona Winters. But how did she end up in the closet?

Despite the late bedtime, Alvirah and Willy were up the next morning at 7:00 A.M. As their mutual shock over finding the body in the closet wore off, they began to worry. "No use fretting about Brian," Alvirah said with a heartiness she did not feel. "When we talk to him, I'm sure everything will be cleared up. Let's see if we can get back into our place."

They dressed quickly and hurried out. Once again Carlton Rumson was standing at the elevator. His pink complexion was sallow. Dark pouches under his eyes added ten years to his appearance. Automatically, Alvirah reached up and switched on the microphone in her pin.

"Mr. Rumson," she asked, "did you hear the terrible news about the murder in our apartment?"

Rumson pressed vigorously for the elevator. "As a matter of fact, yes. Friends in the building phoned us. Terrible for the young lady, terrible for you."

The elevator arrived. After they got in, Rumson said, "Mrs. Meehan, my wife reminded me about your nephew's play. We're leaving for Mexico tomorrow morning. I'd very much like to read it today if I may."

Alvirah's jaw dropped. "Oh, that's wonderful of your wife to keep after you about it. We'll make sure to get it up to you."

When she and Willy got out at their floor, she said, "This could be Brian's big break. Provided that—" she said, stopping in midsentence.

A policeman was on guard at the door of their apartment. Inside, every surface was smeared because the investigators had dusted for fingerprints. And seated across from Detective Rooney, looking bewildered and forlorn, was Brian. He jumped up. "Aunt Alvirah, I'm sorry. This is awful for you."

To Alvirah he looked about ten years old. His T-shirt and khaki slacks were rumpled;

had he dressed to escape a burning building he could not have looked more disheveled.

Alvirah brushed back the sandy hair that fell over Brian's forehead as Willy grasped his hand. "You OK?" Willy asked.

Brian managed a troubled smile. "I guess so."

Detective Rooney interrupted. "Brian just arrived, and I was about to inform him that he is a suspect in the death of Fiona Winters and has a right to counsel."

"Are you kidding?" Brian asked, his tone incredulous.

"I assure you, I'm not kidding." Detective Rooney pulled a paper from his breast pocket. He read Brian his Miranda rights, then handed the paper to Brian. "Please let me know if you understand its meaning."

Rooney looked at Alvirah and Willy. "Our people are through. You can stay in the apartment now. I'll take Brian's statement at headquarters."

"Brian, don't you say one word until we get you a lawyer," Willy ordered.

Brian shook his head. "Uncle Willy, I have nothing to hide. I don't need a lawyer."

Alvirah kissed Brian. "Come right back here when you're finished," she told him.

The messy condition of the apartment gave her something to do. She dispatched Willy with a long shopping list, warning him to take the service elevator to avoid reporters.

As she vacuumed and scrubbed and mopped and dusted, Alvirah realized with increasing dread that cops don't give a Miranda warning unless they have a pretty good reason for suspecting someone's guilt.

The most difficult part of her task was to vacuum the closet. It was as though she could see again the wide-open eyes of Fiona Winters staring up at her. That thought led her to another one: Obviously the poor girl hadn't been killed while she was standing in the closet, but where had she been when she was strangled?

Alvirah dropped the handle of the vacuum. She thought about those fingerprints on the cocktail table. If Fiona Winters had been sitting on the couch, maybe leaning forward a little, and her killer walked behind it, slipped the tieback around her neck and twisted it, wouldn't her hand have pulled back like that? "Saints and angels," Alvirah whispered, "I bet I destroyed evidence."

The phone rang just as she was fastening

the sunburst pin to her lapel. It was Baroness Min von Schreiber calling from the Cypress Point Spa in Pebble Beach, California. Min had just heard the news. "Whatever was that dreadful girl thinking about getting herself killed in your closet?" Min demanded.

"Buh-lieve me, Min," Alvirah said. "I don't know what she was doing here. I only met her once, the opening night of Brian's play. The cops are questioning Brian right now. I'm worried sick. They think he killed her."

"You're wrong, Alvirah," Min said. "You met Fiona Winters before then; you met her out here at the spa."

"Never," Alvirah said positively. "She was the kind who got on your nerves so much you'd never forget her."

There was a pause. "I am thinking," Min announced. "You're right. She came here another week, with someone, and they spent the weekend in the cottage. They even had their meals served there. I remember now. It was that hotshot producer she was trying to snare. Carlton Rumson. You remember him, Alvirah. You met him another time when he was here alone."

• • •

Alvirah went into the living room and out onto the terrace. Willy gets so nervous if I even step out here, she thought, and that's crazy. The only thing to be careful about is leaning on the railing.

The humidity was near saturation point. Not a leaf in the park stirred. Even so, Alvirah sighed with pleasure. How can anyone who was born in New York stay away from it for long? she wondered.

Willy brought in the newspapers with the groceries. One headline screeched MURDER ON CENTRAL PARK SOUTH; another, LOTTERY WINNER FINDS BODY. Alvirah carefully read the lurid accounts. "I didn't scream and faint," she scoffed. "Where'd they get that idea?"

"According to the *Post,* you were hanging up the fabulous new wardrobe you bought in London," Willy told her.

"Fabulous new wardrobe! The only expensive thing I bought was that orange-and-pink plaid suit—and I know Min is going to make me give it away."

There were columns of background material on Fiona Winters: The break with her socialite family when she went into acting. Her uneven career. (She'd won a Tony but was notoriously difficult to work with, which had cost her a number of plum roles.) Her break with playwright Brian McCormack when she accepted a film role and abruptly walked out of his play *Falling Bridges,* forcing it to close.

"Motive," Alvirah said flatly. "By tomorrow they'll be trying this case in the media, and Brian will be found guilty."

At 12:30 P.M. Brian returned. Alvirah took one look at his ashen face and ordered him to sit down. "I'll make a pot of tea and fix you a hamburger," she said. "You look like you're going to keel over."

"I think a shot of scotch would do a lot more good than tea," Willy observed.

Brian managed a wan smile. "I think you're right, Uncle Willy." Over the hamburgers and french fries he told them what had happened. "I swear I didn't think they'd let me go. You can tell they're sure I killed her."

"Is it OK if I turn on my recorder?" Alvirah asked. She fiddled with the sunburst pin, touching the microphone switch. "Now, tell us exactly what you told them."

Brian frowned. "Mostly about my personal relationship with Fiona. I was sick of her lousy disposition and I was falling in love with Emmy. I told them that when Fiona quit the play it was the last straw."

"But how did she get in my closet?" Alvirah asked. "You must have been the one who let her into the apartment."

"I did. I've been working here a lot. I knew you were coming back yesterday, so I cleared my stuff out the day before. Then yesterday morning Fiona phoned and said she was back in New York and would be right over to see me. By mistake I'd left my notes for the final draft of my new play here with my backup copy. I told her not to waste her time, that I was heading here to get my notes and then was going to be at the typewriter all day and wouldn't answer my door. When I arrived, I found her parked downstairs in the lobby, and rather than make a scene I let her come up."

"What did she want?" Alvirah and Willy both asked.

"Nothing much. Just the lead in *Nebraska Nights.*"

"After walking out on the other one!"

"She put on the performance of her life. Begged me to forgive her. Said she'd been a fool to leave *Falling Bridges.* Her role in the film was ending up on the cutting-room floor, and the bad publicity about dumping the play had hurt her. Wanted to know if *Nebraska Nights* was finished yet. I'm human. I bragged about it. Told her it might take time to find the right producer, but when I did it was going to be a big hit."

"Had she ever read it?" Alvirah asked.

Brian studied the tea leaves in his cup. "These don't make for much of a fortune," he commented. "She knew the story line and that there's a fantastic lead role for an actress."

"You certainly didn't promise it to her?" Alvirah exclaimed.

Brian shook his head. "Aunt Alvirah, I know she played me for a fool, but I couldn't believe she thought I was that much of a fool. She asked me to make a deal. She said she had access to one of the biggest producers on Broadway. If she could get it to him and he took it, she wanted to play Diane—I mean Beth."

"Who's that?" Willy asked.

"The name of the leading character. I changed it on the final draft last night. I told Fiona she had to be kidding, but if she could pull that off I might consider it. Then I got my notes and tried to get her out of here. She

44

refused to budge, though, saying she had an audition at Lincoln Center early in the afternoon, and since it's close by, she wanted to stay here until it was time to be there. I finally decided there probably wasn't any harm in leaving her so I could get work done. The last time I saw her was just about noon, and she was sitting on that couch."

"Did she know you had a copy of the new play here?" Alvirah asked.

"Sure. I took it out of the drawer of the table when I was getting the notes." He pointed toward the foyer. "It's in that drawer now."

Alvirah got up, walked quickly to the foyer and pulled open the drawer. As she suspected, it was empty.

Emmy Laker sat motionless in the oversized club chair in her West Side studio apartment. Ever since she had heard about Fiona's death on the seven o'clock news she'd been trying to reach Brian. Had he been arrested? Oh God, not Brian, she thought. What should I do? Despairingly she looked at the luggage in the corner of the room. Fiona's luggage.

Her bell had rung yesterday morning at

8:30. When she opened the door, Fiona had swept in. "How can you stand living in a walk-up?" she'd demanded. "Thank God some kid was making a delivery and carried these up." She'd dropped her suitcases and reached for a cigarette. "I came in on the red-eye. What a mistake to take that film job. I told the director off and he fired me. I've been trying to reach Brian. Do you know where he is?"

At the memory, rage swelled in Emmy. As though she were still across the room she could see Fiona, her blond hair tousled, her body-hugging jumpsuit showing off every inch of that perfect figure, her cat's eyes insolent and confident.

Fiona was so sure that even after the way she treated Brian she could still walk back into his life, Emmy thought, remembering all the months when she had agonized at the sight of Brian with her. Would that have happened again? Yesterday she had thought it possible.

Fiona had kept phoning Brian until she finally reached him. When she hung up, she said, "Mind if I leave my bags here? Brian's on his way to the cleaning woman's fancy pad. I'll head him off." Then she shrugged.

"He's so damn provincial, but it's amazing how many people on the West Coast know about him. I must say from what I heard about *Nebraska Nights* it has all the earmarks of a hit—and I intend to play the lead."

Emmy got up. Her body felt stiff and achy. The old window-unit air conditioner was rattling and wheezing, but the room was still hot and humid. A cool shower and a cup of coffee, she decided. Maybe that would clear her head. She wanted to see Brian. She wanted to put her arms around him. I'm not sorry Fiona's dead, she admitted, but oh, Brian, how did you expect to get away with it?

She had just dressed in a T-shirt and cotton skirt and twisted her long bright-red hair in a chignon when the buzzer downstairs rang.

When she answered, it was to hear Detective Rooney announce that he was on the way up.

"This is starting to make sense," Alvirah said. "Brian, is there anything you left out? For instance, did you put the bottle of that fit-for-a-queen champagne in the silver bucket yesterday?"

Brian looked bewildered. "Why would I do that?"

"I didn't think you would." Oh boy, what a story, Alvirah thought—Fiona didn't hang around here because she had an audition. It's my bet that the producer she mentioned to Brian was Carlton Rumson, and that she phoned him and invited him down here. That's why the glasses and champagne were out. She gave him the script and then, who knows why, they got into a fight. But how do I prove it? Alvirah paused for a moment, thinking. Then she turned to Brian. "I want you to go home and get your final version of the play. I talked to Carlton Rumson about it; he wants to see it today."

"Carlton Rumson!" Brian exclaimed. "He's just about the biggest man on Broadway, as well as one of the hardest to reach. You must be a magician!"

"I'll tell you about it later," Alvirah said. "I also happen to know that he and his wife are going away on a little trip, so let's strike while the iron is hot."

Brian glanced at the phone. "I should call Emmy. She certainly must have heard about

Fiona by now." He dialed the number, waited, then left a message: "Emmy, I need to talk to you. I'm just leaving Aunt Alvirah's and I'm on my way home." When he hung up, his tone reflected his obvious disappointment. "I guess she's out," he said.

Even when she heard Brian's voice, Emmy made no move to pick up the receiver. Detective Rooney was sitting across from her and had just asked her to describe in detail what she had done the previous day. Now he raised his eyebrows. "You could have answered the phone. I don't mind waiting."

"I'll talk to Brian later," Emmy said. Then she paused for a moment, choosing her words carefully. "Yesterday I left here about 11:00 A.M. and went jogging. I got back about 1:30 P.M. and then just stayed in the rest of the day."

"Alone?"

"Yes."

"Did you see Fiona Winters yesterday?" Emmy's eyes slid over to the corner where the luggage was piled. "I . . ." She stopped.

"Emmy, I think I should warn you that it will be in your best interest to be completely truthful." Detective Rooney consulted his notes. "Fiona Winters came in on a flight from Los Angeles, arriving at approximately 7:30 A.M. We know she took a cab to this building, and that a delivery boy who recognized her assisted her with her luggage. She told him that you would not be glad to see her because you're after her boyfriend. When Miss Winters left, you followed her. A doorman on Central Park South recognized you. You sat on a park bench across the street, watching the building, for nearly two hours, then entered it by the delivery door, which had been propped open by the painters." Detective Rooney leaned forward. His tone became confidential. "You went up to the Meehans' apartment, didn't you? Was Miss Winters already dead?"

Emmy stared at her hands. Brian always teased her about how small they were. "But strong," he'd laugh when they'd arm-wrestle. Brian. No matter what she said she would hurt him. She looked up at Detective Rooney. "I want to talk to a lawyer."

Rooney got up. "That is, of course, your privilege. I would like to remind you that if Brian murdered his ex-lover, you can become an accessory after the fact by concealing evidence. And I assure you, Emmy, you won't do him any good. We're going to get an indictment from the grand jury, no doubt about it."

When Brian reached his apartment, there was a message on the recorder from Emmy. "Call me, Brian. Please." Brian's fingers worked with frantic haste as he dialed her number.

She whispered, "Hello."

"Emmy, what's the matter? I tried you before but you were out."

"I was here. A detective came. Brian, I have to see you."

"Take a cab to my aunt's place. I'm on my way back there."

"I want to talk to you alone. It's about Fiona. She was here yesterday. I followed her over to the apartment."

Brian felt his mouth go dry. "Don't say anything else on the phone."

At 4:00 P.M., the bell rang insistently. Alvirah jumped up. "Brian forgot his key," she told Willy. "I noticed it on the foyer table."

But it was Carlton Rumson rather than Brian she found standing at the door. "Mrs. Meehan, please forgive the intrusion." With that he stepped inside.

"I mentioned to one of my assistants that I was going to look at your nephew's play. Apparently he saw a performance of his first one and thought it was very good. In fact he had urged me to see it, but it closed suddenly and I never got the chance." Rumson had walked into the living room and sat down. Nervously he drummed his fingers on the cocktail table.

"Can I get you a drink?" Willy asked. "Or maybe a beer?"

"Oh, Willy," Alvirah said. "I'm sure that Mr. Rumson only drinks fine champagne. Maybe I read that in *People.*"

"As a matter of fact, it's true, but not right now, thank you." Rumson's expression was affable enough, but Alvirah noticed that a pulse was jumping in his throat. "Where can I reach your nephew?"

"He should be here any minute. You're welcome to wait, or I'll call you the minute he gets in."

Obviously opting for the latter choice, Rumson stood and headed for the door. "I'm a fast reader. If you would send the script up, he and I could get together an hour or so later."

When Rumson left, Alvirah asked Willy, "What are you thinking?"

"That for a hotshot producer, he's some nervous wreck. I hate people tapping their fingers on tabletops. Gives me the jitters."

"Well he certainly had the jitters, and I'm not surprised." Alvirah smiled at Willy mysteriously.

Less than a minute later the bell rang again. Alvirah hurried to the door. Emmy Laker was there, wisps of red hair slipping from the chignon, sunglasses covering half her face, the T-shirt clinging to her slender body, the cotton skirt a colorful whirl. Alvirah thought that Emmy looked about sixteen.

"That man who just left," Emmy stammered. "Who was he?"

"Carlton Rumson, the producer," Alvirah said quickly. "Why?"

"Because . . ." Emmy pulled off her glasses, revealing swollen eyes.

Alvirah put firm hands on the girl's shoulders. "Emmy, what is it?"

"I don't know what to do," Emmy wailed. "I don't know what to do."

• • •

Carlton Rumson returned to his apartment. Beads of perspiration stood on his forehead. Alvirah Meehan was no dope, he warned himself. That crack about champagne hadn't been social chitchat. How much did she suspect?

Victoria was standing on the terrace, her hands lightly touching the railing. Reluctantly he joined her. "For Pete's sake, haven't you read those signs all over the place?" he demanded. "One good shove and that railing would be gone."

Victoria was wearing white slacks and a white knit sweater. Sourly, Rumson thought it was a damn shame some fashion columnist had once written that with her pale-blond beauty, Victoria Rumson should never wear anything but white. Victoria had taken that advice to heart. Her dry cleaning bills alone would have broken most men.

She turned to him calmly. "I've noticed that you always get ugly with me when you're upset. Did you happen to know that Fiona Winters was staying in this building? Or was she here perhaps at your request?"

"Vic, I haven't seen Fiona in nearly two years. If you don't believe me, too bad."

"As long as you didn't see her yesterday, darling. I understand the police are asking lots of questions. It's bound to come out that you and she were—as the columnists say— an *item.*" She paused. "Oh well, I'm sure you'll deal with it with your usual aplomb. In the meantime, have you followed up on Brian McCormack's play? I have one of my famous hunches about that, you know."

Rumson cleared his throat. "That Alvirah Meehan is going to have McCormack send me a copy this afternoon. After I've read it I'll go down and meet him."

"Let me read it too. Then I might just tag along. I'd love to see how a cleaning woman decorates." Victoria Rumson linked her arm in her husband's. "Poor darling. Why are you so nervous?"

When Brian rushed past Alvirah into the apartment, his play under his arm, he found Emmy lying on his aunt's couch, covered by a light blanket. Alvirah closed the door behind him and watched as he knelt beside Emmy and put his arms around her. "I'm going inside and let you two talk," she announced.

Willy was in the bedroom laying out

clothes. "Which jacket, honey?" He held up two sports coats.

Alvirah's forehead puckered. "You want to look nice for Pete's retirement party, but not like you're trying to show off. Wear the blue jacket and the white sports shirt."

"I still don't like to leave you tonight," Willy protested.

"You can't miss Pete's dinner," Alvirah said firmly. "And Willy, I wish you'd let me order a car and driver for you."

"Honey, we pay big bucks to garage our car here. No use wasting money."

"Well then, if you have too good a time, I want you to promise me not to drive home. Stay at the old apartment. You know how you can get when you're with the boys."

Willy smiled sheepishly. "You mean if I sing 'Danny Boy' more than twice, that's my signal."

"Exactly," Alvirah said firmly.

"Honey, I'm so bushed after the trip and with what happened last night, I'd just as soon have a few beers with Pete and come back."

"That wouldn't be nice. Pete stayed at our lottery-winning party till the morning rush started on the expressway. Now we've got to talk to those kids."

In the living room Brian and Emmy were sitting side by side, their hands clasped. "Have you two straightened things out yet?" Alvirah demanded.

"Not exactly," Brian said. "Apparently Emmy was given a rough time by Rooney when she refused to answer his questions."

Alvirah sat down. "I have to know everything he asked you."

Hesitantly Emmy told her. Her voice became calmer and her poise returned as she said, "Brian, you're going to be indicted. He's trying to make me say things that will hurt you."

"You mean you're protecting me." Brian looked astonished. "There's no need. I haven't done anything. I thought . . ."

"You thought that Emmy was in trouble," Alvirah told them. She settled with Willy on the couch opposite them. She realized that Brian and Emmy were sitting directly in front of the place on the cocktail table where the fingerprints had been smeared. The drapery was slightly to the right. To someone sitting on this couch, the tieback would have been in full view. "I'm going to tell you two something," she announced. "You each think the other might have had something to do with this—and you're both wrong. Just tell me what you know or think you know. Brian, is there anything you've held back about seeing Fiona yesterday?"

"Absolutely nothing," Brian said.

"All right. Emmy, your turn."

Emmy walked over to the window. "I love this view." She turned to Alvirah and Willy and told them about Fiona's sudden and unwelcome appearance at her apartment. "Yesterday when Fiona left my apartment to meet Brian I think I went a little crazy. He had been so involved with her, and I just couldn't stand to see that happen all over. Fiona is—was the kind of woman who can just beckon to men. I was so afraid Brian would take up with her again."

"I'd never—" Brian protested.

"Keep quiet, Brian," Alvirah ordered.

"I sat on the park bench a long time," Emmy said. "I saw Brian leave. When Fiona didn't come down I started to think maybe Brian had told her to wait. Finally I decided to have it out with her. I followed a maid through the delivery entrance and came up in the service elevator because I didn't want anyone to know I'd been here. I rang the doorbell and waited and rang it again, and then I left."

"That's all?" Brian asked. "Why were you afraid to tell that to Rooney?"

"Because when she heard Fiona was dead she thought maybe the reason she didn't answer was because you'd already killed her." Alvirah leaned forward. "Emmy, why did you ask about Carlton Rumson before? You saw him yesterday, didn't you?"

"As I came down the corridor from the rear service elevator, he was ahead of me, going to the passenger elevator. I knew he looked familiar but didn't recognize him until I saw him again just now."

Alvirah stood up. "I think we should call Mr. Rumson and ask him to come down, and I think we should call Rooney and ask him to be here too. But first, Brian, give Willy your play. He'll run it up to the Rumsons' apartment. Let's see. It's nearly 5:00 P.M. Willy, you ask Mr. Rumson to phone when he's ready to bring it back."

The intercom buzzer sounded. Willy answered it. "Rooney's here," he said. "He's looking for you, Brian."

There was no trace of warmth in the detective's manner when he entered the apartment a few minutes later. "Brian," he said without preface, "I have to ask you to come down to the station house for further questioning. You have received the Miranda warning. I remind you again that anything you say can be used against you."

"He's not going anywhere," Alvirah said firmly. "And before you leave, Detective, I've got an earful for you."

It was nearly 7:00 P.M., two hours later, when Carlton Rumson phoned. Alvirah and Willy had told Rooney about the champagne and the glasses and the fingerprints on the cocktail table and about Emmy seeing Carlton Rumson, but Alvirah could tell none of it cut much ice with the detective. He's closing his mind to everything that doesn't fit his theory about Brian, she thought.

A few minutes later, Alvirah was astonished to see both Rumsons enter her apartment. Victoria Rumson was smiling warmly. When introduced to Brian, she took both his hands and said, "You really *are* a young Neil Simon. I just read your play. Congratulations."

When Detective Rooney was introduced, Carlton Rumson's face went ashen. He stammered as he said to Brian, "I'm terribly sorry to interrupt you just now. I'll make this very brief. Your play is wonderful. I want to option it. Please have your agent contact my office tomorrow."

Victoria Rumson was standing at the terrace door. "You were so wise not to obscure this view," she told Alvirah. "My decorator put in vertical blinds, and I might as well be facing an alley."

She sure took her gracious pills this morning, Alvirah thought.

"I think we'd all better sit down," Detective Rooney suggested.

The Rumsons sat down reluctantly.

"Mr. Rumson, you knew Fiona Winters?" Rooney asked.

Alvirah began to think she had underestimated Rooney. His expression became intense as he leaned forward.

"Miss Winters appeared in several of my productions some years ago," Rumson said. He was sitting on one of the couches, next to his wife. Alvirah noticed that he glanced at her nervously.

"I'm not interested in years ago," Rooney told him. "I'm interested in yesterday. Did you see her then?"

"I did not." To Alvirah, Rumson's voice sounded strained and defensive.

"Did she phone you from this apartment?" Alvirah asked.

"Mrs. Meehan, if you don't mind, I'll conduct this questioning," the detective said.

"Show respect when you talk to my wife," Willy bristled.

Victoria Rumson patted her husband's arm. "Darling, I think you might be trying to spare my feelings. If that impossible Winters woman was badgering you again, please don't be afraid to tell exactly what she wanted."

Rumson seemed to age visibly before their eyes. When he spoke his voice was weary. "As I just told you, Fiona Winters acted in several of my productions. She—"

"She also had a private relationship with you," Alvirah interjected. "You used to take her to the Cypress Point Spa."

Rumson glared at her. "I haven't had anything to do with Fiona Winters for several years," he said. "Yes, she phoned yesterday just after noon. She told me she was here in the building and that she had a play she wanted me to read, assured me it had the earmarks of a hit and said she wanted to play the lead. I was waiting for a call from Europe and agreed to come down and see her in about an hour."

"That means she called after Brian left," Alvirah said triumphantly. "That's why the glasses and champagne were out. They were for you."

"Did you come to this apartment, Mr. Rumson?" Rooney asked.

Again Rumson hesitated.

"Darling, it's all right," Victoria Rumson said softly.

Not daring to look at Detective Rooney, Alvirah announced: "Emmy saw you in this corridor a few minutes after 1:00 P.M."

Rumson sprang to his feet. "Mrs. Meehan, I won't tolerate any more insinuations! I was afraid Fiona would keep contacting me if I didn't set her straight once and for all. I came down here and rang the bell. There was no answer. The door wasn't completely shut, so I pushed it open and called her. As long as I'd come this far I wanted to be finished with it."

"Did you enter the apartment?" Rooney asked.

"Yes. I walked through this room, poked my head in the kitchen and glanced in the bedroom. She wasn't anywhere. I assumed she'd changed her mind about seeing me, and I can assure you I was relieved. Then when I heard the news this morning all I could think of was that maybe her body was in that closet when I was here and I'd be in the middle of this." He turned to his wife. "I guess I am in the middle of it, but I swear what I've told you is true."

Victoria touched his hand. "There is no way they're going to drag you into this. What a nerve that woman had to think she should have the leading role in *Nebraska Nights.*" Victoria turned to Emmy. "Someone your age should play the role of Diane."

"She's going to," Brian said. "I just hadn't told her yet."

Rumson turned to his wife, impatiently. "Don't you mean—?"

Rooney interrupted him as he folded his notebook. "Mr. Rumson, I'll ask you to accompany me down to headquarters. Emmy, I'd like you to give a complete statement as well. Brian, we need to talk to you again, and I do strongly urge you to engage counsel."

"Now just one minute," Alvirah said indignantly. "I can tell you believe Mr. Rumson over Brian." There goes the option on the play, but this is more important, she thought. "You're going to say that Brian maybe started to leave, decided to come back and tell Fiona to clear out and then ended up killing her. I'll tell you how I think it happened. Rumson came down here and got into a fight with Fiona. He strangled her but was smart enough to take the script she was showing him."

"That is absolutely untrue," Rumson snapped.

"I don't want another word discussed here," Rooney ordered. "Emmy, Mr. Rumson, Brian—I have a car downstairs. Let's go."

When the door closed behind them, Willy put his arms around Alvirah. "Honey, I'm going to skip Pete's party. I can't leave you. You look ready to collapse."

Alvirah hugged him back. "No, you're not. I've been recording everything. I need to listen to the playback and I do that better alone. You have a good time."

The apartment felt terribly quiet after Willy left. Alvirah decided that a warm soak in the bathtub Jacuzzi might take some of the stiffness out of her body and clear her brain.

Afterward, she dressed comfortably in her favorite nightgown and Willy's striped terrycloth robe. She set the expensive cassette player her editor at the *Globe* had bought for her on the dining-room table, then took the tiny cassette out of her sunburst pin, inserted it in the recorder and pushed the playback button. She put a new cassette in the back of the pin and fastened the pin to the robe just in case she wanted to think out loud. She sat listening to her conversations with Brian, with Detective Rooney, with Emmy, with the Rumsons.

What was it about Carlton Rumson that bothered her so much? Methodically, Alvirah reviewed that first meeting with the Rumsons. He was pretty cool that night, but when we bumped into him the next morning he sure had changed his tune, she told herself, even reminded me he wanted to read the new play right away. She remembered Brian saying that nobody could get to Carlton Rumson.

That's it, she thought. He *already* knew how good the play was. He couldn't admit that he'd already read it.

The phone rang. Startled, Alvirah hurried over to pick it up. It was Emmy. "Mrs. Meehan," she whispered, "they're still questioning Brian and Mr. Rumson, but I know they think Brian's guilty."

"I just figured everything out," Alvirah said triumphantly. "How good a look at Carlton Rumson did you get when you saw him in the hall?"

"Pretty good."

"Then you could see he was carrying the script, couldn't you? I mean if he was telling the truth that he only went down to tell Fiona off, he'd never have picked up that script. But if they talked about it and he read some of it before he killed her, he'd have taken it. Emmy, I think I've solved the case."

Emmy's voice was barely audible. "Mrs. Meehan, I'm sure Carlton Rumson wasn't carrying anything when I saw him. Suppose Detective Rooney thinks to ask me that question? It's going to hurt Brian, isn't it, if I tell them that?"

"You have to tell the truth," Alvirah said sadly. "Don't worry. I still have my thinking cap on." When she hung up, she turned the cassette player on again and began to replay her tapes. She replayed her conversations with Brian several times. There was something he had told her that she was missing.

Finally she stood up, deciding that a breath of fresh air wouldn't hurt. Not that New York air is fresh, she thought as she opened the terrace door and stepped out. This time she went right to the guardrail and let her fingers rest lightly on it. If Willy were here he'd have a fit, she thought, but I'm not going to lean on it. There's just something so restful about looking out over the park. The park. I think one of the happiest memories in Mama's life was the day she had a sleigh ride through the park. She was sixteen at the time and she talked about it the rest of her life. She'd taken the ride because her girlfriend Beth asked for that for her birthday.

Beth!

Beth!

That's it! Alvirah thought. Again she could hear Brian saying that Fiona Winters wanted to play the part of Diane. Then Brian corrected himself and said, "I mean Beth." Willy had asked who that was, and Brian said it was the name of the lead in his new play, that he'd changed it in the final draft. Alvirah switched on her microphone and cleared her throat. Better get this all down, she reminded herself. It would help to have her immediate impression when she wrote the story up for the *Globe.*

"It wasn't Carlton Rumson who killed Fiona Winters," she said aloud, her voice confident. "It has to have been his wife, See-No-Evil Vicky. *She* was the one who kept after Rumson to read the play. *She* was the one who said Emmy should play Diane—she didn't know Brian had changed the name. And Rumson started to correct her, because he had read only the revised version of the play. She must have listened in when Fiona phoned him. She came here while he was waiting for his call from Europe. She didn't want Fiona to get involved with Rumson again, so she killed her, then took the script. That was the copy she read, not the final draft."

"How very clever of you, Mrs. Meehan."

The voice came from directly behind her, but before she could even blink, Alvirah felt strong hands push at the small of her back. She tried to turn as she felt her body press against the guardrail and panel. How did Victoria Rumson get in here? she wondered. Then, in a flash, she remembered that Brian's key had been on the foyer table. Victoria must have taken it.

With all her strength she tried to throw herself against her attacker, but a blow on the side of her neck stunned her. She was able to spin around so that she was facing the other woman, but the blow had been an effective one, and she sagged against the railing. Only vaguely was she aware then of a creaking, tearing sound and the feeling of her body teetering over yawning space.

Pete's retirement party was a blast. The room at the K of C in Flushing was filled with Willy's old buddies. The aromas of sausage and peppers and corned beef and cabbage mingled together enticingly. The first keg of beer had been tapped, and a beaming Pete was going from friend to friend, insisting they drink up.

But Willy could not get in the spirit of the evening. Something was bugging him, gnawing at him, telling him he should be heading home. He sipped his beer, nibbled half-heartedly at a corned-beef sandwich, congratulated Pete on his retirement, and then, without waiting for even one chorus of "Danny Boy," he slipped away and got in his car.

When he reached the apartment, the door was slightly ajar; immediately his internal panic button began to shrill a warning. "Alvirah," he called nervously. Then he saw two figures poised at the terrace railing. "Oh my God!" he moaned, then raced across the room, shouting Alvirah's name.

"Come in, honey," he pleaded. "Get back. Get away from there." Then he suddenly realized what was happening. The other woman was trying to push Alvirah through the guardrail. He took one step out onto the terrace just as a section of the railing separated and fell away behind Alvirah.

Willy took a second step toward the struggling women and then passed out.

Emmy sat in the precinct station, waiting for her statement to be typed up, heartsick with worry about Brian. She knew that Detective Rooney believed Carlton Rumson's story that he'd gone into Alvirah's apartment, thought it was empty and had left. It was obvious that Rooney had made up his mind that Brian had killed Fiona.

Why can't he see that Brian had no reason to kill her? Emmy agonized. Brian had told her that Fiona had done him a favor when she walked out on the play. That it showed him just what kind of person she was. Oh, I shouldn't have been so upset when Fiona showed up at my apartment yesterday, she thought. Brian never would have gotten involved with Fiona again, Emmy was sure of that. But when she'd tried to convince Detective Rooney of it, he'd asked, "Then if you were so sure that Brian was finished with Fiona, why did you follow her over to his aunt's apartment?"

Emmy rubbed her forehead. She had such a headache! It was impossible to believe that only a few nights ago Brian had let her read the new play and asked her advice about changing the name of the lead from Diane to Beth.

"Diane is a pretty strong name," he'd said. "I see the character as someone who comes across as vulnerable, even wistful; then as the action unfolds, we get to know just how strong she is. What do you think of calling her Beth instead of Diane?"

"I like it," she'd replied.

"That's good," Brian had said, "because you were the model for her, and I want you to be happy with the name. I'll make the change in the final draft."

Emmy sat up straight and stared ahead, no longer aware of the harsh lights in the precinct room, or even of the bustle of activity and confusion around her. *Beth . . . Diane . . .*

That's it! she thought suddenly. Tonight Victoria Rumson told me I should play the part of Diane. But the final script, the one she's supposed to have read, has the name change in it. So she must have read the copy of the play that is missing from the apartment. That means she was there with Fiona. Of course, it all fits! Perhaps Victoria Rumson's ability to overlook her husband's indiscretions had been strained to the breaking point when she had almost lost him a couple of years ago—to Fiona Winters!

Emmy jumped up and ran from the station house. She had to talk to Alvirah right away. She heard a policeman call after her but didn't answer him as she hailed a cab.

When she reached the building, she charged past a stuttering doorman and raced to the elevator. She heard Willy shouting as she came down the corridor. The door to the apartment was open. She saw Willy stumble onto the terrace and fall. Then she saw the silhouettes of two women and realized what was happening.

In a burst of speed, Emmy rushed out to the terrace. Alvirah was facing her, swaying over empty space. Her right hand was grasping the part of the railing that was still in place, but she was quickly losing her grip because Victoria Rumson was pummeling that hand with her fists.

Emmy grabbed Victoria's arms and twisted them behind her. Victoria's howl of rage and pain rose above the crash as the rest of the railing collapsed and fell. Emmy shoved her aside and managed to grasp the cord of Alvirah's robe. Alvirah was teetering. Her bedroom slippers were sliding backward off the terrace. Her body swayed as she hovered thirty-four stories over the sidewalk below. With a burst of strength, Emmy pulled her forward and they fell together over the collapsed form of the unconscious Willy.

Alvirah and Willy slept until noon. When they finally woke up, Willy insisted Alvirah stay put. He went out to the kitchen, returning fifteen minutes later with a pitcher of orange juice, a pot of tea and a piece of toast. After her second cup of tea, Alvirah regained her customary optimism. "Boy, was it good that Detective Rooney came barging in here after Emmy and caught Victoria trying to escape. And do you know what I think, Willy?"

"I never know what you think, honey," Willy said with a sigh.

"Well, I bet you one thing—that Carlton Rumson will still want to produce Brian's play. You can be sure he won't be shedding any tears over seeing Victoria going to prison."

"You're probably right," Willy conceded. "Those two certainly weren't a pair of lovebirds."

"And Willy," Alvirah concluded, "I want you to have a talk with Brian, to tell him he'd better marry that darling Emmy before somebody else snaps her up." She beamed. "I have the perfect wedding present for them, a load of white furniture."

Death
on the
Cape

*I*t was on an August afternoon shortly after they arrived at their rented cottage in the village of Dennis on Cape Cod that Alvirah Meehan noticed that there was something very odd about their next-door neighbor, a painfully thin young woman who appeared to be in her late twenties.

After Alvirah and Willy looked around their cottage a bit, remarking favorably about the four-poster maple bed, the hooked rugs, the cheery kitchen and the fresh, sea-scented breeze, they unpacked their expensive new clothes from their matching Vuitton luggage. Willy then poured an ice-cold beer for each to enjoy on the deck of the house, which overlooked Cape Cod Bay.

Willy, his rotund body eased onto a padded wicker chaise lounge, remarked that it was going to be one heck of a sunset, and thank God for a little peace. Ever since they had won forty million dollars in the New York State lottery, it seemed to Willy, Alvirah had been a walking lightning rod. First she went to the famous Cypress Point Spa in California and nearly got murdered. Then they had gone on a cruise together and—wouldn't you know—the man who sat next to them at the community table in the dining room ended up dead as a mackerel. Still, with the accumulated wisdom of his years, Willy was sure that in Cape Cod, at least, they'd have the quiet he'd been searching for. If Alvirah wrote an article for the *New York Globe* about this vacation, it would have to do with the weather and the fishing.

During his narration, Alvirah was sitting at the picnic table, a companionable few feet away from Willy's stretched-out form. She wished she'd remembered to put on a sun hat. The beautician at Sassoon's had warned her against getting sun on her hair. "It's such a lovely rust shade now, Mrs. Meehan. We don't want it to get those nasty yellow streaks, do we?"

Since recovering from the attempt on her life at the spa, Alvirah had regained all the weight she'd paid three thousand dollars to lose and was again a comfortable size somewhere between a 14 and a 16. But Willy constantly observed that when he put his arms around her, he knew he was holding a woman—not one of those half-starved zombies you see in the fashion ads Alvirah was so fond of studying.

Forty years of affectionately listening to Willy's observations had left Alvirah with the ability to hear him with one ear and close him out with the other. Now as she gazed at the tranquil cottages perched atop the grass-and-sand embankment that served as a seawall, then down below at the sparkling blue-green water and the stretch of rock-strewn beach, she had the troubled feeling that maybe Willy was right. Beautiful as the Cape was, and even though it was a place she had always longed to visit, she might not find a newsworthy story here for her editor, Charley Evans.

Two years ago Charley had sent a *New York Globe* reporter to interview the Meehans on how it felt to win forty million dollars. What would they do with it? Alvirah was a cleaning woman. Willy was a plumber. Would they continue in their jobs?

Alvirah had told the reporter in no uncertain terms that she wasn't that dumb, that the next time she picked up a broom it would be when she was dressed as a witch for a Knights of Columbus costume party. Then she had made a list of all the things she wanted to do, and first was the visit to the Cypress Point Spa—where she planned to hobnob with the celebrities she'd been reading about all her life.

That had led Charley Evans to ask her to write an article for the *Globe* about her stay at the spa. He gave her a sunburst pin that contained a microphone so that she could record her impressions of the people she spoke with and play the tape back when she wrote the article.

The thought of her pin brought an unconscious smile to Alvirah's face.

As Willy said, she'd gotten into hot water at Cypress Point. She'd picked up on what was really going on and was nearly murdered for her trouble. But it had been so exciting, and now she was great friends with everyone at the spa and could go there every year as a guest. And thanks to her help solving the murder on the ship last year, they had an invitation to take a free cruise to Alaska anytime they desired.

Cape Cod was beautiful, but Alvirah had a sneaking suspicion Willy might be right, that this might be an ordinary vacation that wouldn't make good copy for the *Globe*.

Precisely at that moment she glanced over the row of hedges on the right perimeter of their property and observed a young woman with a somber expression standing at the railing of her porch next door and staring at the bay.

It was the way her hands were gripping the railing: Tension, Alvirah thought. She's stuffed with it. It was the way the young woman turned her head, looked straight into Alvirah's eyes, then turned away again. She didn't even see me, Alvirah decided. The fifty- to sixty-foot distance between them did not prevent her from realizing that waves of pain and despair were radiating from the young woman.

Clearly it was time to see if she could help. "I think I'll just introduce myself to our neighbor," she said to Willy. "There's something up with her." She walked down the steps and strolled over to the hedge. "Hello," she said in her friendliest voice. "I saw you drive in. We've been here for two hours, so I guess that makes us the welcoming committee. I'm Alvirah Meehan."

The young woman turned, and Alvirah felt instant compassion. She looked as though she had been ill. That ghostly pallor, the soft, unused muscles of her arms and legs. "I don't mean to be rude, but I came here to be alone, not to be neighborly," she said quietly. "Excuse me, please." That probably would have been the end of it, as Alvirah later observed, except that as she spun on her heel the girl tripped over a footstool and fell heavily onto the porch. Alvirah rushed to help her up, refused to allow her to go into her cottage unaided and, feeling responsible for the accident, wrapped an ice pack around her rapidly swelling wrist. By the time she had satisfied herself that the wrist was only sprained and made her a cup of tea, Alvirah had learned that her name was Cynthia Rogers and that she was a schoolteacher from Illinois. That piece of information hit with a resounding thud on Alvirah's ears because, as she told Willy when she returned to their place an hour later, within ten minutes she'd recognized their neighbor. "The poor girl may call herself Cynthia Rogers," Alvirah confided to Willy, "but her real name is Cynthia Lathem. She was found guilty of murdering her stepfather twelve years ago. He had big bucks and was well known. All the papers carried the story. I remember it like it was yesterday."

"You remember everything like it was yesterday," Willy commented.

"That's the truth. And you know I always read about murders. Anyhow, this one happened here on Cape Cod. Cynthia swore she was innocent, and she always said there was a witness who could prove she'd been out of the house at the time of the murder, but the jury didn't believe her story. I wonder why she came back. I'll have to call the *Globe* and have Charley Evans send me the files on the case. She's probably just been released from prison. Her complexion is pure gray. Maybe"—and now Alvirah's eyes became thoughtful—"she's up here because she really is innocent and is still looking for that missing witness to prove her story!"

To Willy's dismay, Alvirah opened the top drawer of the dresser, took out her sunburst pin with the hidden microphone and began to dial her editor's direct line in New York.

That night, Willy and Alvirah ate at the Red Pheasant Inn. Alvirah wore a beige-and-blue print dress she had bought at Bergdorf Goodman but which, as she remarked to Willy, somehow didn't look much different on her than the print dress she'd bought in Alexander's just before they won the lottery. "It's my full figure," she lamented as she spread butter on a warm cranberry muffin. "My, these muffins are good. And, Willy, I'm glad that you bought that yellow linen jacket. It shows up your blue eyes, and you still have a fine head of hair."

"I feel like a two-hundred-pound canary," Willy commented, "but as long as you like it."

After dinner they went to the Cape Playhouse and thrilled to the performance of Debbie Reynolds in a new comedy being tried out for Broadway. At intermission, as they sipped ginger ale on the grass outside the theater, Alvirah told Willy how she'd always enjoyed Debbie Reynolds from the time Debbie was a kid doing musicals with Mickey Rooney, and that it was a terrible thing Eddie Fisher ditched her when they had those two small babies. "And what good did it do him?" Alvirah philosophized as the warning came to return to their seats for the second act. "He never had much luck after that. People who don't do the right thing usually don't win in the end." That comment led Alvirah to wonder whether Charley had sent the information on their neighbor by Express Mail. She was anxious to read it.

As Alvirah and Willy were enjoying Debbie Reynolds, Cynthia Lathem was at last beginning to realize that she was really free, that twelve years of prison were behind her. Twelve years ago . . . she'd been about to start her junior year at the Rhode Island School of Design when her stepfather, Stuart Richards, was found shot to death in the study of his mansion, a stately eighteenth-century captain's house in Dennis.

That afternoon Cynthia had driven past the house on her way to the cottage and pulled off the road to study it. Who was there now? she wondered. Had her stepsister Lillian sold it or had she kept it? It had been in the Richards family for three generations, but Lillian had never been sentimental. And then Cynthia had pressed her foot on the accelerator, chilled at the rush of memories of that awful night and the days that followed. The accusation. The arrest, arraignment, trial. Her early confidence. "I can absolutely prove that I left the house at eight o'clock and didn't get home till past midnight. I was on a date."

Now Cynthia shivered and wrapped the light-blue woolen robe more tightly around her slender body. She'd weighed 125 pounds when she went to prison. Her present weight, 110, was not enough for her five-foot eight-inch height. Her hair, once a dark blond, had changed in those years to a medium-brown. Drab, she thought as she brushed it. Her eyes, the same shade of hazel as her mother's, were listless and vacant. At lunch that last day, Stuart Richards had said, "You look more like your mother all the time. I should have had the brains to hang on to her."

Her mother had been married to Stuart from the time Cynthia was eight until she was twelve, the longer of his two marriages. Lillian, his only birth child, ten years older than Cynthia, had lived with her mother in New York and seldom visited the Cape.

Cynthia laid the brush on the dresser. Had it been a crazy impulse to come here? Two weeks out of prison, barely enough money to live on for six months, not knowing what she could do or would do with her life. Should she have spent so much to rent this cottage, to rent a car? Was there any point to it? What did she hope to accomplish?

A needle in a haystack, she thought. Walking into the small parlor, she reflected that compared to Stuart's mansion, this house was tiny, but after years of confinement it seemed palatial. Outside, the sea breeze was blowing the bay into churning waves. Cynthia walked out on the porch, only vaguely aware of her throbbing wrist, hugging her arms against the chill. But, oh God, to breathe fresh, clean air, to know that if she wanted to get up at dawn and walk the beach the way she had as a child, no one could stop her. The moon, three-quarters full, looking as though a wedge had been neatly sliced from it, made the bay glisten, a silvery midnight blue. But where the moon did not reach it, the water appeared dark and impenetrable.

Cynthia stared unseeingly as her mind wrenched her back to the terrible night when Stuart was murdered. Then she shook her head. No, she would not allow herself to think about that now. Not tonight. This was a time to let the peace of this place fill her soul. She would go to bed, and she'd leave the windows wide open so that the cool night wind would pour into her room, making her pull the covers closer around her, deepening her sleep.

Tomorrow morning she would wake up early and walk on the beach. She'd feel the wet sand under her feet, and she'd look for shells, just as she had when she was a child. Tomorrow. Yes, she'd give herself the morning to help bridge her reentry into the world, to regain her sense of equilibrium. And then she would begin the quest, probably hopeless, for the one person who would know that she had told the truth.

The next morning, as Alvirah prepared breakfast, Willy drove to get the morning papers.

When he returned he was also carrying a bag of still-hot blueberry muffins. "I asked around," he told a delighted Alvirah. "Everyone said to go to the Mercantile behind the post office for the best muffins on the Cape."

They ate at the picnic table on the deck. As she nibbled on her second blueberry muffin, Alvirah studied the early-morning joggers on the beach. "Look, there she is!"

"There *who* is?"

"Cynthia Lathem. She's been gone at least an hour and a half. I bet she's starving."

When Cynthia ascended the steps from the beach to her deck, she was met by a beaming Alvirah, who linked her arm in Cynthia's. "I make the best coffee and fresh-squeezed orange juice. And wait till you taste the blueberry muffins."

"I really don't want—" Cynthia tried to pull back but was propelled across the lawn. Willy jumped up to pull out a bench for her.

"How's your wrist?" he asked. "Alvirah's been real upset that you sprained it when she went over to visit."

Cynthia realized that her mounting irritation was being overcome by the genuine warmth she saw on both their faces. Willy —with his rounded cheeks, strong pleasant expression and thick mane of white hair—reminded her of Tip O'Neill. She told him that.

Willy beamed. "Fellow just remarked on that in the bakery. Only difference is that while Tip was *speaker* of the house, I was *savior* of the *out*house. I'm a retired plumber."

As Cynthia sipped the fresh orange juice and the coffee and picked at the muffin, she listened with disbelief, then awe, as Alvirah told her about winning the lottery, going to Cypress Point Spa and helping to track down a murderer, then going on an Alaskan cruise and figuring out who killed the man who sat next to her at the community table.

She accepted a second cup of coffee. "You've told me all this for a reason, haven't you?" Cynthia said. "You recognized me yesterday, didn't you?"

Alvirah's expression became serious. "Yes."

Cynthia pushed back her bench. "You've been very kind, and I think you want to help me, but the best way you can do that is to leave me alone. I have a lot of things to work out, but I have to do them myself. Thank you for breakfast."

Alvirah watched the slender young woman walk between the two cottages. "She got a little sun this morning," she observed. "Very becoming. When she fills out a little, she'll be a beautiful girl."

"You may as well plan on getting the sun too," Willy observed. "You heard her."

"Oh, forget it. Once Charley sends the files on her case I'll figure out a way to help her."

"Oh my God," Willy moaned. "I might have known. Here we go again."

"I don't know how Charley does it," Alvirah sighed approvingly an hour later. The overnight Express Mail envelope had just arrived. "It looks as though he sent every word anyone ever wrote about the case." She made a tsk-tsking sound. "Look at this picture of Cynthia at the trial. She was just a scared kid."

Methodically, Alvirah began sorting the clippings on the table; then she got out her lined pad and pen and began to make notes.

Willy was reclining on the padded chaise he had claimed for his own, deeply immersed in the sports section of the *Cape Cod Times*. "I'm just about ready to give up on the Mets getting the pennant," he commented sadly, shaking his head.

He looked up for reassurance, but it was clear that Alvirah had not heard him.

At one o'clock Willy went out again, returning this time with a quart of lobster bisque. Over lunch Alvirah filled him in on what she had learned. "In a nutshell, here are the facts: Cynthia's mother was a widow when she married Stuart Richards. Cynthia was eight at the time. They divorced four years later. Richards had one child by his first marriage, a daughter named Lillian. She was ten years older than Cynthia and lived with her mother in New York."

"Why'd Cynthia's mother divorce Richards?" Willy asked between sips of the bisque.

"From what Cynthia said on the witness stand, Richards was one of those men who always belittled women. Her mother would be dressed to go out, and he'd reduce her to tears by ridiculing what she was wearing—that kind of thing. Sounds like he just about gave her a nervous breakdown. Apparently, though, he had always been fond of Cynthia, always taking her out around her birthday and giving her presents.

"Then Cynthia's mother died, and Richards invited the young girl to visit him here at Cape Cod. Actually she wasn't so young by then—she was about to start her junior year at the Rhode Island School of Design. Her mother had been sick for a while, and there apparently wasn't much money left; she said she was planning on dropping out of school and working for a year or two. She claimed that Stuart told her that he'd always planned to leave half his money to his daughter Lillian and the other half to Dartmouth College. But he stayed so angry after Dartmouth let women in as full-time students that he changed his will. She said he told her he was leaving her the Dartmouth portion of his estate, about ten million dollars. The prosecutor got Cynthia to admit that Richards also told her she'd have to wait for him to die to get it; that it was too bad about college, but that her mother should have provided for her education."

Willy put down his spoon. "So there's your motive, huh?"

"That's what the prosecutor said, that Cynthia had wanted the money right away. Anyhow, a guy named Ned Creighton happened to drop in to visit Richards and overheard their conversation. He was a friend of Lillian's, about her age. Cynthia apparently had known him slightly from when she and her mother had lived with Richards at the Cape. So Creighton invited Cynthia to have dinner with him, and Stuart urged her to go.

"According to her testimony, she and Creighton had dinner at the Captain's Table in Hyannis, and then he suggested they go for a ride in his boat, which was anchored at a private dock. She said they were out on the Nantucket Sound when the boat broke down; nothing was working, not even the radio. They were stranded until nearly eleven, when he was finally able to get the motor going again. She apparently had only had a salad at dinner, so once they made shore she asked him to stop for a hamburger.

"She testified that Creighton wasn't very happy about having to stop on the way home, although he did finally pull in at some hamburger joint around Cotuit. Cynthia said she hadn't been on the Cape since she was a child and didn't know the area all that well, so she wasn't sure exactly where they stopped. Anyway, he told her to wait in the car, that he would go in and get the burger. All she remembered about being there was a lot of rock music blaring and seeing teenagers all over the place. But then a woman drove up and parked next to their car, and when she opened her door, it slammed into the side of Creighton's car." Alvirah handed Willy a clipping. "That woman, then, is the witness no one could find."

As Alvirah absentmindedly sipped the bisque, Willy scanned the paper. The woman had apologized profusely and had examined Ned's car for scratches. When she found none, she'd headed into the hamburger joint. According to Cynthia, the woman had been in her mid- to late-forties, chunky, with blunt-cut hair dyed an orange-red shade, and she'd been wearing a shapeless blouse and elastic-waisted polyester slacks.

The clipping went on to recount Cynthia's testimony that Creighton had returned complaining about the line for food and about kids who couldn't make up their minds when they gave an order. She said he'd been obviously edgy, so she didn't tell him at the time about the woman banging the door into his car.

On the witness stand, Cynthia had testified

that during the forty-five-minute drive back to Dennis, all of it along unfamiliar roads, Ned Creighton had hardly said a word to her. Then, once they reached Stuart Richards' house, he'd just dropped her off and driven away. When Cynthia went into the house, she'd found Stuart in his study, sprawled on the floor next to his desk, blood drenching his forehead, blood caked on his face, blood matting the carpet beside him.

Willy read more of the account: "The defendant stated that she thought Richards had had a stroke and had fallen, but that when she brushed his hair back she saw the bullet wound in his forehead, then spotted the gun lying next to him, and she telephoned the police."

"She said she thought then that he had committed suicide," Alvirah recounted. "But then she picked up the gun, of course putting her fingerprints on it. The armoire in the study was open, and she admitted that she knew Richards kept a gun in it. Then Creighton contradicted just about everything she had told the police, saying that, yes, he had taken her out to dinner, but that he had gotten her home by eight o'clock, and that all through the meal she had gone on about how she blamed Stuart Richards for her mother's illness and death, and that she intended to have it out with him when she got home. The time of death was established at about nine o'clock, which of course looked bad for her, given Creighton's contrary testimony. And even though her lawyers advertised for the woman she'd met at the burger joint, nobody came forward to verify her story."

"So do you believe Cynthia?" Willy asked. "You know an awful lot of murderers can't face the reality of what they've done and actually end up believing their own lies, or at least go through the motions of trying to confirm them. She could just be looking for this missing witness in an effort to finally convince people of her innocence, even though she's already served her time. I mean, why on earth would Ned Creighton lie about the whole thing?"

"I don't know," Alvirah said, shaking her head. "But you can be sure that somebody is lying, and I'll bet my bottom dollar that it isn't Cynthia. If I were in her boots, I'd set off to try and find out what it was that made Creighton lie, what was in it for him."

With that, Alvirah turned her attention to

the bisque, not speaking again until she had finished it off. "My, that was good. What a great vacation we're going to have, Willy. And isn't it wonderful that we took this cottage right next to Cynthia so that I'm here to help her clear her name?"

Willy's only response was the clatter of a spoon and a deep sigh.

The long and peaceful night's sleep followed by the early-morning walk had begun to clear the emotional paralysis that Cynthia had experienced from that moment twelve years earlier when she'd heard the jury pronounce the verdict: *Guilty.* Now as she showered and dressed she reflected that these past years had been a nightmare in which she had managed to survive only by freezing her emotions. She had been a model prisoner. She had kept to herself, resisting friendships. She had taken whatever jailhouse college courses were offered. She had graduated from working in the laundry and the kitchen to desk assignments in the library and assistant teaching in the art class. And after a while, when the awful reality of what had happened finally set in, she had begun to draw. The face of the woman in the parking lot. The hamburger stand. Ned's boat. Every detail she could force from her memory. When she was finished she had pictures of a hamburger place that could be found anywhere in the United States, a boat that looked like any Chris Craft of that year. The woman was a little more clearly defined but not much. It had been dark. Their encounter had lasted only seconds. But the woman was her only hope.

The prosecutor's summation at the end of the trial: "Ladies and gentlemen of the jury, Cynthia Lathem returned to the home of Stuart Richards sometime between 8:00 and 8:30 P.M. on the night of August 2, 1981. She went into her stepfather's study. That very afternoon Stuart Richards had told Cynthia he had changed his will. Ned Creighton heard that conversation, overheard Cynthia and Stuart quarreling. She needed money immediately to pay for her education and demanded he help her. That evening Vera Smith, the waitress at the Captain's Table, overheard Cynthia tell Ned that she would have to drop out of school.

"Cynthia Lathem returned to the Richards mansion that night, angry and worried. She went into that study and confronted Stuart Richards. He was a man who enjoyed upsetting the people around him. He *had* changed his will to include her, but she knew it would be just like him to change it again. And the anger she'd harbored for the way he had treated her mother, the anger that rose in her at the thought of having to leave school, at being turned out into the world virtually penniless, made her go to the armoire where she knew he kept a gun, take out that gun and fire three shots point-blank into the forehead of the man who loved her enough to make her an heiress.

"It is ironic. It is tragic. It is also murder. Cynthia begged Ned Creighton to say that she had spent the evening with him on his boat. No one saw them out on the boat. She talks about stopping at a hamburger stand. But she doesn't know where it is. She admits she never entered it. She talks about a stranger with red-orange hair to whom she spoke in a parking lot. With all the publicity this case has engendered, why didn't that woman come forward? You know the reason. Because she doesn't exist. Because like the hamburger stand and the hours spent on a boat on Nantucket Sound, she is a figment of Cynthia Lathem's imagination."

Cynthia had read the transcript of the trial so often that she had the district attorney's summation committed to memory. "But the woman did exist," Cynthia said aloud. "She does exist." For the next six months, with the little insurance money left her by her mother, she was going to try to find that woman. She might be dead by now, or moved to California, Cynthia thought as she brushed her hair and twisted it into a chignon.

The bedroom of the cottage faced the sea. Cynthia walked to the sliding door and pulled it open. On the beach below she could see couples walking with children. If she was ever to have a normal life, a husband, a child of her own, she had to clear her name.

Jeff Knight. She had met him last year when he came to do a series of television interviews with women in prison. He'd invited her to participate, and she'd flatly refused. He'd persisted, his strong intelligent face filled with concern. "Don't you understand, Cynthia, this program is going to be watched by a couple of million people in New England. The woman who saw you that night could be one of those people."

That was why she finally had agreed to go on the program, had answered his questions, told about the night Stuart died, held up the shadowy sketch of the woman she had spoken with, the sketch of the hamburger stand. And no one had come forward. From New York, Lillian issued a statement saying that the truth had been told at the trial and she would have no further comment. Ned Creighton, now the owner of the Mooncusser, a popular restaurant in Barnstable, repeated how very, very sorry he was for Cynthia.

After the program, Jeff kept coming to see her on visiting days. Only those visits had kept her from total despair when the program produced no results. He would always arrive a little rumpled looking, his wide shoulders straining at his jacket, his unsettled dark-brown hair curling on his forehead, his brown eyes intense and kind, his long legs never able to find enough room in the cramped visiting area of the prison. When he asked her to marry him after her release, she told him to forget her. He was already getting bids from the networks. He didn't need a convicted murderer in his life.

But what if I weren't a convicted murderer? Cynthia thought as she turned away from the window. She went over to the maple dresser, reached for her pocketbook and went outside to her rented car.

It was early evening before she returned to Dennis. The frustration of the wasted hours had finally brought tears to her eyes. She let them run down her cheeks unchecked. She'd driven to Cotuit, walked around the main street, inquired of the bookstore owner —who seemed to be a longtime native— about a hamburger stand that was a teenage hangout. Where would she be likely to find one? The answer, with a shrug, was, "They come and go. A developer picks up property and builds a shopping center or condominiums, and the hamburger stand is out." She'd gone to the town hall to try to find records of food-service licenses issued or renewed around that time. Two hamburger joint–type places were still in business. A third had been converted or torn down. Nothing stirred her memory. And of course she couldn't even be sure they had been in Cotuit. Ned might have been lying about that too. And how do you ask strangers if they know a middle-aged woman with orange-red hair and a chunky build who had lived or summered on the Cape and hated rock-and-roll music?

As she drove through Dennis, Cynthia impulsively ignored the turn to the cottage and again drove past the Richards home. As she was passing, a slender blond woman came down the steps of the mansion. Even from this distance she knew it was Lillian. Cynthia slowed the car to a crawl, but when Lillian looked in her direction she quickly accelerated and returned to the cottage. As she was turning the key in the lock she heard the phone ring. It rang ten times before it stopped. It had to be Jeff, and she didn't want to talk to him. A few minutes later it rang again. It was obvious that if Jeff had the number he wouldn't give up trying to reach her.

Cynthia picked up the receiver. "Hello.

"My finger is getting very tired pushing buttons," Jeff said. "Nice trick of yours, just disappearing like that."

"How did you find me?"

"It wasn't hard. I knew you'd head for the Cape like a homing pigeon, and your parole officer confirmed it."

She could see him leaning back in his chair, twirling a pencil, the seriousness in his eyes belying the lightness of his tone. "Jeff, forget about me, please. Do us both a favor."

"Negative. Cindy, I understand. But unless you can find that woman you spoke to there's no hope of proving your innocence. And believe me, honey, I tried to find her. When I did the program, I sent out investigators I never told you about. If they couldn't find her, you won't be able to. Cindy, I love you. You know you're innocent. Ned Creighton lied, but we'll never be able to prove it."

Cindy closed her eyes, knowing that what Jeff said was true.

"Cindy, give it all up. Pack your bag. Drive back here. I'll pick you up at your place at eight o'clock tonight."

Her place. The furnished room the parole officer had helped her select. *Meet my girlfriend. She just got out of prison. What did your mother do before she got married? She was in jail.*

"Good-bye, Jeff," Cynthia said. She broke the connection, left the phone off the hook and turned her back to it.

Alvirah had observed Cynthia's return but did not attempt to contact her. In the afternoon, Willy had gone out on a half-day charter boat and returned triumphantly with two bluefish. During his absence, Alvirah again studied the newspaper clippings of the Stuart Richards murder case. At Cypress Point Spa she had learned the value of airing her opinions into a recorder. That afternoon she kept her recorder busy.

"The crux of this case is why did Ned Creighton lie? He hardly knew Cynthia. Why did he set her up to take the blame for Stuart Richards' death? Stuart Richards had a lot of enemies. Ned's father at one time had business dealings with Stuart, and they'd had a falling out. But Ned was only a kid at that time. Ned was a friend of Lillian Richards. Lillian swore that she didn't know that her father was going to change his will, that she'd always known she would get half his estate and that the other half was going to Dartmouth College. She said she knew he was upset after Dartmouth decided to accept women students but didn't know he was upset enough to finally change his will and leave the Dartmouth money to Cynthia."

Alvirah turned off the recorder. It certainly must have occurred to someone that when Cynthia was found guilty of murdering her stepfather, she would lose her inheritance, and Lillian would receive everything. Lillian had married somebody from New York shortly after the trial was over. She'd been divorced three times since then. So it didn't look as though Ned and she had ever had any romance going. That left only the restaurant. Who were Ned's backers? *Motive for Ned to lie,* she thought. Who gave him the money to open his restaurant?

Willy came in from the deck, carrying the bluefish fillets he'd prepared. "Still at it?" he asked.

"Uh-huh." Alvirah picked up one of the clippings. "Orange-red hair, chunky build, in her late forties. Would you say that description might have fit me twelve years ago?"

"Now you know I would never call you chunky," Willy protested.

"I didn't say you would. I'll be right back. I want to talk to Cynthia. I saw her coming in a few minutes ago."

The next afternoon, after having packed Willy off on another charter fishing boat, Alvirah attached her sunburst pin to her new purple print dress and drove with Cynthia to the Mooncusser restaurant in Barnstable. Along the way Alvirah coached her. "Now remember, if he's there, point him out to me right away. I'll keep staring at him. He'll recognize you. He's bound to come over. You know what to say, don't you?"

"I do." Was it possible? Cynthia wondered. Would Ned believe them?

The restaurant was an impressive white colonial-style building with a long, winding driveway. Alvirah took in the building, the exquisitely landscaped property that extended to the water. "Very, very expensive," she said to Cynthia. "He didn't start this place on a shoestring."

The interior was decorated in Wedgwood blue and white. The paintings on the wall were fine ones. For twenty years—until she and Willy hit the lottery—Alvirah had cleaned every Tuesday for Mrs. Rawlings, and her house was one big museum. Mrs. Rawlings enjoyed recounting the history of each painting, how much she paid for it then and, gleefully, how much it was worth right now. Alvirah often thought that with a little practice she could probably be a tour guide at an art museum. "Observe the use of lighting, the splendid details of sunrays brightening the dust on the table." She had the Rawlings spiel down pat.

Knowing Cynthia was nervous, Alvirah tried to distract her by telling her about Mrs. Rawlings after the maître d'hôtel escorted them to a window table.

Cynthia felt a reluctant smile come to her lips as Alvirah told her that, with all her money, Mrs. Rawlings never once gave her so much as a postcard for Christmas. "Meanest, cheapest old biddy in the world, but I felt kind of sorry for her," Alvirah said. "No one else would work for her. But when my time comes, I intend to point out to the Lord that I get a lot of Rawlings points in my plus column."

"If this idea works, you get a lot of Lathem points in your plus column," Cynthia said.

"You bet I do. Now don't lose that smile. You've got to look like the cat who ate the canary. Is he here?"

"I haven't seen him yet."

"Good. When that stuffed shirt comes back with the menu, ask for him."

The maître d' was approaching them, a professional smile on his bland face. "May I offer you a beverage?"

"Yes. Two glasses of white wine, and is Mr. Creighton here?" Cynthia asked.

"I believe he's in the kitchen speaking with the chef."

"I'm an old friend," Cynthia said. "Ask him to drop by when he's free."

"Certainly."

"You could be an actress," Alvirah whispered, holding the menu in front of her face. She always felt that you had to be so careful, because someone might be able to read lips. "And I'm glad I made you buy that outfit this morning. What you had in your closet was hopeless."

Cynthia was wearing a short lemon-colored linen jacket and a black linen skirt. A splashy yellow, black and white silk scarf was dramatically tied on one shoulder. Alvirah had also escorted her to the beauty parlor. Now Cynthia's collar-length hair was blown soft and loose around her face. A light-beige foundation covered her abnormal paleness and returned color to her wide hazel eyes. "You're gorgeous," Alvirah said.

Regretfully Alvirah had undergone a different metamorphosis. She'd had her Sassoon hair color changed back to its old orange-red and cut unevenly. She'd also had the tips removed from her nails and had left them unpolished. After helping Cynthia select the yellow-and-black outfit, she'd gone to the sale rack, where for very good reasons the purple print she was wearing had been reduced to ten dollars. The fact that it was a size too small for her accentuated the bulges that Willy always explained were only nature's way of padding us for the last big fall.

When Cynthia protested the desecration of her nails and hairdo, Alvirah simply said, "Every time you talked about that woman, the missing witness, you said she was chunky, had dyed red hair and was dressed like someone who shopped from a pushcart. I've got to be believable."

"I said her outfit looked inexpensive," Cynthia corrected.

"Same thing."

Now Alvirah watched as Cynthia's smile faded. "He's coming?" she asked quickly.

Cynthia nodded

"Smile at me. Come on. Relax. Don't show him you're nervous."

Cynthia rewarded her with a warm smile and leaned her elbows lightly on the table.

A man was standing over them. Beads of perspiration were forming on his forehead. He moistened his lips. "Cynthia, how good to see you." He reached for her hand.

Alvirah studied him intently. Not bad looking in a weak kind of way. Narrow eyes almost lost in puffy flesh. He was a good twenty pounds heavier than in the pictures in the files. One of the kind who are handsome as kids and after that it's all downhill, Alvirah decided.

"Is it good to see me, Ned?" Cynthia asked, still smiling.

"That's him," Alvirah announced emphatically. "I'm absolutely sure. He was ahead of me on line in the hamburger joint. I noticed him 'cause he was sore as hell that the kids in front were hemming and hawing about what they wanted on their burgers."

"What are you talking about?" Ned Creighton demanded.

"Why don't you sit down, Ned?" Cynthia said. "I know this is your place, but I still feel as though I should entertain you. After all, you did buy me dinner one night years ago."

Good girl, Alvirah thought. "I'm absolutely sure it was you that night, even though you've put on weight," she snapped indignantly to Creighton. "It's a crying shame that because of your lies this girl had to spend twelve years of her life in prison."

The smile vanished from Cynthia's face. "Twelve years, six months and ten days," she corrected. "All my twenties, when I should have been finishing college, getting my first job, dating."

Ned Creighton's face hardened. "You're bluffing. This is a cheap trick."

The waiter arrived with two glasses of wine and placed them before Cynthia and Alvirah. "Mr. Creighton?"

Creighton glared at him. "Nothing."

"This is really a lovely place, Ned." Cynthia said quietly. "An awful lot of money must have gone into it. Where did you get it? From Lillian? My share of Stuart Richards' estate was nearly ten million dollars. How much did she give you?" She did not wait for an answer. "Ned, this woman is the witness I could never find. She remembers talking to me that night. Nobody believed me when I told them about a woman slamming her car door against the side of your car. But she remembers doing it. And she remembers seeing you very well. All her life she's kept a daily diary. That night she wrote about what happened in the parking lot."

As she kept nodding her head in agreement, Alvirah studied Ned's face. He's getting rattled, she thought, but he's not convinced. It was time for her to take over. "I left the Cape the very next day," she said. "I live in Arizona. My husband was sick, real sick. That's why we never did come back. I lost him last year." Sorry, Willy, she thought, but this is important. "Then last week I was watching television, and you know how boring television usually is in the summer. You could have knocked me over with a feather when I saw a rerun of that show about women in prison and then my own picture right there on the screen."

Cynthia reached for the envelope she had placed beside her chair. "This is the picture I drew of the woman I'd spoken to in the parking lot."

Ned Creighton reached for it.

"I'll hold it," Cynthia said.

The sketch showed a woman's face framed by an open car window. The features were shadowy and the background was dark, but the likeness to Alvirah was astonishing.

Cynthia pushed back her chair. Alvirah rose with her. "You can't give me back twelve years. I know what you're thinking. Even with this proof a jury might not believe me. They didn't believe me twelve years ago. But they might, just might, now. And I don't think you should take that chance, Ned. I think you'd better talk it over with whoever paid you to set me up that night and tell them that I want ten million dollars. That's my rightful share of Stuart's estate."

"You're crazy." Anger had driven the fear from Ned Creighton's face.

"Am I? I don't think so." Cynthia reached

into her pocket. "Here's my address and phone number. Alvirah is staying with me. Call me by seven tonight. If I don't hear from you, I'm hiring a lawyer and getting my case reopened." She threw a ten-dollar bill on the table. "That should pay for the wine. Now we're even for that dinner you bought me."

She walked rapidly from the restaurant, Alvirah a step behind her. Alvirah was aware of the buzz from diners at the other tables. They know something's up, she thought. Good.

She and Cynthia did not speak until they were in the car. Then Cynthia asked shakily, "How was I?"

"Great."

"Alvirah, it just won't work. If they check the sketch that Jeff showed on the program, they'll see all the details I added to make it look like you."

"They haven't got time to do that. Are you sure you saw your stepsister yesterday at the Richards house?"

"Absolutely."

"Then my guess is that Ned Creighton is talking to her right now."

Cynthia drove automatically, not seeing

the sunny brightness of the afternoon. "Stuart was despised by a lot of people. Why are you so sure Lillian is involved?"

Alvirah unfastened the zipper on the purple print. "This dress is so tight I swear I'm going to choke." Ruefully she ran her hand through her erratically chopped hair. "It'll take an army of Sassoons to put me back together after this. I guess I'll have to go back to Cypress Point Spa. What did you ask? Oh, Lillian. She has to be involved. Look at it this way. Your stepfather had a lot of people who hated his guts, but they wouldn't need a Ned Creighton to set you up. Lillian always knew her father was leaving half his money to Dartmouth College. Right?"

"Yes." Cynthia turned down the road that led to the cottages.

"I don't care how many people might have hated your stepfather, Lillian was the only one who *benefited* by you being set up to be found guilty of his murder. She knew Ned. Ned was trying to raise money to open a restaurant. Her father must have told her he was leaving half his fortune to you instead of Dartmouth. She always hated you. You told me that. So she makes a deal with Ned. He takes you out on his boat and pretends that it breaks down. Somebody kills Stuart Richards. Lillian had an alibi. She was in New York. She probably hired someone to kill her father. You almost spoiled everything that night by insisting on having a hamburger. And Ned didn't know you'd spoken to anyone. They must have been plenty scared that witness would show up."

"Suppose someone recognized him that night and said they'd seen him buying the burger?"

"In that case he'd have said that he went out on his boat and stopped afterward for a hamburger, and you were so desperate for an alibi you begged him to say you were with him. But no one came forward."

"It sounds so risky," Cynthia protested.

"Not risky. Simple," Alvirah corrected. "Buh-lieve me, I've studied up on this a lot. You'd be amazed in how many cases the one who commits the murder is the chief mourner at the funeral. It's a fact."

They had arrived back at the cottages. "What now?" Cynthia asked.

"Now we go to your place and wait for your stepsister to phone." Alvirah shook her head at Cynthia. "You still don't believe me. Wait and see. I'll make us a nice cup of tea. It's too bad Creighton showed up before we had lunch. That was a good menu."

They were eating tuna-salad sandwiches on the deck of Cynthia's cottage when the phone rang. "Lillian for you," Alvirah said. She followed Cynthia into the kitchen as Cynthia answered the call.

"Hello." Cynthia's voice was almost a whisper. Alvirah watched as the color drained from her face. "Hello, Lillian."

Alvirah squeezed Cynthia's arm and nodded her head vigorously.

"Yes, Lillian, I just saw Ned . . . No, I'm not joking. I don't see anything funny about this . . . Yes. I'll come over tonight. Don't bother about dinner. Your presence has a way of making my throat close. And, Lillian, I told Ned what I want. I won't change my mind."

Cynthia hung up and sank into a chair. "Alvirah, Lillian said that my accusation was ridiculous but that she knows her father could drive anyone to the point of losing control. She's smart."

"That doesn't help us clear your name. I'll give you my sunburst pin so you can record the conversation. You've got to get her to admit that you had absolutely nothing to do with the murder, that she set Ned up to trap

120

you. What time did you tell her you'd go over to her house?"

"Eight o'clock. Ned will be with her."

"Fine. Willy will go with you. He'll be on the floor in the backseat of the car. For a big man he sure can roll himself into a beach ball. He'll keep an eye on you. They certainly won't try anything in that house. It would be too risky. Next to Willy, my sunburst pin is my greatest treasure," she said. "I'll show you how to use it."

Throughout the afternoon, Alvirah coached Cynthia on what to say to her step-sister. "She's got to be the one who put up the money for the restaurant. Probably through some sham investment companies. Tell her unless she pays up, you're going to contact a top accountant you know who used to work for the government."

"She knows I don't have any money."

"She doesn't know who might have taken an interest in your case. That fellow who did the program on women in prison did, right?"

"Yes. Jeff took an interest."

Alvirah's eyes narrowed, then sparked. "Something between you and Jeff?"

"If I'm exonerated for Stuart Richards' death, yes. If I'm not, there'll never be anything between Jeff and me or anyone else and me."

At six o'clock the phone rang again. Alvirah said, "I'll answer. Let them know I'm here with you." Her booming "Hello" was followed by a warm greeting. "Jeff, we were just talking about you. Cynthia is right here. My, what a pretty girl. You should see her new outfit. She's been telling me all about you. Wait. I'll put her on."

Alvirah frankly listened in as Cynthia explained, "Alvirah rents the next cottage. She's helping me . . . No, I'm not coming back . . . Yes, there is a reason to stay here. Tonight just maybe I'll be able to get proof I wasn't guilty of Stuart's death . . . No, don't come down. I don't want to see you, Jeff, not now . . . Jeff, yes, yes, I love you . . . Yes, if I clear my name, I'll marry you."

When Cynthia hung up she was close to tears. "Alvirah, I want to have a life with him so much. You know what he just said? He quoted *The Highwayman.* He said, 'I'll come to thee by moonlight, though hell should bar the way.' "

"I like him," Alvirah said flatly. "I can read

a person from his voice on the phone. Is he coming tonight? I don't want you getting upset or being talked out of this.''

"No. He's been made anchorman for the ten o'clock news. But I bet anything he drives down tomorrow.''

"We'll see about that. The more people in this, the more chance of having Ned and Lillian smell a rat.'' Alvirah glanced out the window. "Oh, look, here comes Willy. Stars above, he caught more of those darn bluefish. They gave me heartburn, but I'd never tell him. Whenever he goes fishing I keep a package of Tums in my pocket. Oh, well.''

She opened the door and waved over a beaming Willy, who was proudly holding a line from which two limp bluefish dangled forlornly. Willy's smile vanished as he took in Alvirah's bright-red mop of unruly hair and the purple print dress that squeezed her body into rolls of flesh. "Aw, nuts,'' he said. "How come they took back the lottery money?''

At seven-thirty, after having dined on Willy's latest catch, Alvirah placed a cup of tea in front of Cynthia. "You haven't eaten a thing,'' she said. "You've got to eat to keep your brain clear. Now, have you got it all straight?"

Cynthia fingered the sunburst pin. "I think so. It seems clear."

"Remember, money had to have changed hands between those two—and I don't care how clever they were, it can be traced. If they agree to pay you, offer to come down in price if they'll give you the satisfaction of admitting the truth. Got it?"

"Got it."

At seven-fifty Cynthia drove down the winding lane with Willy on the floor of the backseat.

The brilliantly sunny day had turned into a cloudy evening. Alvirah walked through the cottage to the back deck. Wind was whipping the bay into a frenzy of waves that slammed onto the beach. The rumbling of thunder could be heard in the distance. The temperature had plummeted, and suddenly it felt more like October than August. Shivering, she debated about going next door to her own cottage and getting a sweater, then decided against it. In case anyone phoned, she wanted to be right here.

She made a second cup of tea for herself

and settled at the dinette table, her back to the door leading from the deck. Then she began writing a first draft of the article she was sure she would be sending to the *New York Globe.* "Cynthia Latham, who was 19 years old when she was sentenced to a term of twelve years in prison for a murder she did not commit, can now prove her innocence. . . ."

From behind her a voice said, "Oh, I don't think that's going to happen."

Alvirah swiveled around and stared up into the angry face of Ned Creighton.

Cynthia waited on the porch steps of the Richards mansion. Through the handsome mahogany door she could hear the faint sound of chimes. She had the incongruous thought that she still had her own key to this place, and she wondered if Lillian had changed the locks.

The door swung open. Lillian was standing in the wide hallway, light from the overhead Tiffany lamp accentuating her high cheekbones, wide blue eyes, silvery blond hair. Cynthia felt a chill race through her body. In these twelve years, Lillian had become a clone of Stuart Richards. Smaller of course. Younger, but still a feminine version of his outstanding looks. And with that same hint of cruelty around the eyes.

"Come in, Cynthia." Lillian's voice hadn't changed. Clear, well bred, but with that familiar sharp, angry undertone that had always characterized Stuart Richards' speech.

Silently, Cynthia followed Lillian down the hallway. The living room was dimly lighted. It looked very much as she remembered it. The placement of the furniture, the Oriental carpets, the painting over the fireplace—all were the same. The baronial dining room on the left still had the same unused appearance. They'd usually eaten in the small dining room off the library.

She had expected that Lillian would take her to the library. Instead, Lillian went directly back to the study where Stuart had died. Cynthia narrowed her lips, felt for the sunburst pin. Was this an attempt to intimidate her? she wondered.

Lillian sat behind the massive desk.

Cynthia thought again of the night she'd come into this room and found Stuart sprawled on the carpet beside that desk. She knew her hands were clammy. Perspiration was forming on her forehead. Outside she could hear the wind wailing as it increased in velocity.

Lillian folded her hands and looked up at Cynthia. "You might as well sit down."

Cynthia bit her lip. The rest of her life would be determined by what she said in these next minutes. "I think I'm the one who should suggest the seating arrangements," she told Lillian. "Your father did leave this house to me. When you phoned, you talked about a settlement. Don't play games now. And don't try to intimidate me. Prison took all the shyness out of me, I promise you that. Where is Ned?"

"He'll be along any minute. Cynthia, those accusations you made to him are insane. You know that."

"I thought I came here to discuss receiving my share of Stuart's estate."

"You came here because I'm sorry for you and because I want to give you a chance to go away somewhere and begin a new life. I'm prepared to set up a trust fund that will give you a monthly income. Another woman wouldn't be so generous to her father's murderer."

Cynthia stared at Lillian, taking in the contempt in her eyes, the icy calm of her demeanor. She had to break that calm. She walked over to the window and looked out. The rain was beating against the house. Claps of thunder shattered the silence in the room. "I wonder what Ned would have done to keep me out of the house that night if it had been raining like this," she said. "The weather worked out for him, didn't it? Warm and cloudy. No other boats nearby. Only that one witness, and now I've found her. Didn't Ned tell you that she positively identified him?"

"How many people would believe that anyone could recognize a stranger after nearly thirteen years? Cynthia, I don't know whom you've hired for this charade, but I'm warning you—drop it. Accept my offer, or I'll call the police and have you arrested for harassment. Don't forget it's very easy to get a criminal's parole revoked."

"A *criminal's* parole. I agree. But I'm not a criminal, and you know it." Cynthia walked over to the Jacobean armoire and pulled open the top drawer. "I knew Stuart kept a gun here. But you certainly knew too. You claimed he had never told you that he'd changed his will and was leaving the Dartmouth half of his estate to me. But you were lying. If Stuart sent for me to tell me about his will, he certainly didn't hide what he was doing from you."

"He did *not* tell me. I hadn't seen him for three months."

"You may not have *seen* him, but you spoke to him, didn't you? You could have put up with Dartmouth getting half his fortune but couldn't stand the idea of splitting his money with me. You hated me for the years I lived in this house, for the fact that he liked me, while you two always clashed. You've got that same vile temper he had."

Lillian stood up. "You don't know what you're talking about."

Cynthia slammed the drawer shut. "Oh, yes, I do. And every fact that convicted me will convict you. I had a key to this house. You had a key. There was no sign of a struggle. I don't think you sent anyone to murder him. I think you did it yourself. Stuart had a panic button on his desk. He didn't push it. He never thought his own daughter would harm him. Why did Ned just *happen* to stop by that afternoon? You knew Stuart had invited me here for the weekend. You knew that he'd encourage me to go out with Ned.

Stuart liked company and then he liked to be alone. Maybe Ned hasn't made it clear to you. That witness I found keeps a diary. She showed it to me. She's been writing in it every night since she was twenty. There was no way that entry could have been doctored. She described me. She described Ned's car. She even wrote about the noisy kids on line and how impatient everyone was with them."

I'm getting to her, Cynthia thought. Lillian's face was pale. Her throat was closing convulsively. Deliberately, Cynthia walked back to the desk so that the sunburst pin was pointed directly at Lillian. "You played it smart, didn't you?" she asked. "Ned didn't start pouring money into that restaurant until after I was safely in prison. And I'm sure that on the surface he has some respectable investors. But today the government is awfully good at getting to the source of laundered money. *Your* money, Lillian."

"You'll never prove it." But Lillian's voice had become shrill.

Oh God, if I can just get her to admit it, Cynthia thought. She grasped the edge of the desk with both hands and leaned forward. "Possibly not. But don't take the chance. Let me tell you how it feels to be fingerprinted and handcuffed. How it feels to sit next to a lawyer and hear the district attorney accuse you of murder. How it feels to study the faces of the jury. Jurors are ordinary-looking people. Old. Young. Black. White. Well dressed. Shabby. But they hold the rest of your life in their hands. And, Lillian, you won't like it. The waiting. The damning evidence that fits you much more than it ever fitted me. You don't have the temperament or the guts to go through with it."

Lillian stood up. Her face was frozen in hatred. "Bear in mind there were a lot of taxes when the estate was settled. A good lawyer could probably destroy your so-called witness, but I don't need the scandal. Yes, I'll give you your half." Then she smiled.

"You should have stayed in Arizona," Ned Creighton said to Alvirah. The gun he was holding was pointed at her chest. Alvirah sat at the dinette table, measuring her chances to escape. There were none. He had believed her story this afternoon, and now he had to kill her. Alvirah had the fleeting thought that she'd always known she would have made a wonderful actress. Should she warn Ned her husband would be home any minute? No. At the restaurant she'd told him she was a widow. How long would Willy and Cynthia be? Too long. Lillian wouldn't let Cynthia go until she was sure there was no witness alive, but maybe if Alvirah kept him talking, she'd think of something. "How much did you get for your part in the murder?" she asked.

Ned Creighton smiled, a thin sneering movement of his mouth. "Three million. Just enough to start a classy restaurant."

Alvirah mourned the fact that she had lent her sunburst pin to Cynthia. Proof. Absolute, positive proof, and she wasn't able to record it. And if anything happened to her no one would know. Mark my words, she thought. If I get out of this, I'm going to have Charley Evans get me a backup pin. Maybe that one should be silver. No, platinum.

Creighton waved his pistol. "Get up."

Alvirah pushed back the chair, leaned her hands on the table. The sugar bowl was in front of her. Did she dare throw it at him? She knew her aim was good, but a gun was faster than a sugar bowl.

"Go into the living room." As she walked around the table, Creighton reached over, grabbed her notes and the beginning of her article and stuffed them in his pocket.

There was a wooden rocking chair next to the fireplace. Creighton pointed to it. "Sit down right there."

Alvirah sat down heavily. Ned's gun was still trained on her. If she tipped the rocker forward and landed on him, could she get away from him? Creighton reached for a narrow key dangling from the mantel. Leaning over, he inserted it in a cylinder in one of the bricks and turned it. The hissing sound of gas spurted from the fireplace. He straightened up. From the matchbox on the mantel he extracted a long safety match, scratched it on the box, blew out the flame and tossed the match onto the hearth. "It's getting cold," he said. "You decided to light a fire. You turned on the gas jet. You threw in a match, but it didn't take. When you bent down to turn off the jet and start again, you lost your balance and fell. Your head struck the mantel and you lost consciousness. A terrible accident for such a nice woman. Cynthia will be very upset when she finds you."

The smell of gas was permeating the room. Alvirah tried to tilt the rocker forward. She had to take the chance of butting Creighton with her head and making him drop the gun. She was too late. A viselike grip on her shoulders. The sense of being pulled forward. Her forehead slamming against the mantel before she fell to the stone hearth. As she lost consciousness, Alvirah was aware of the sickening smell of gas filling her nostrils.

"Here's Ned now," Lillian said calmly at the sound of door chimes. "I'll let him in."

Cynthia waited. Lillian still had not admitted anything. Could she get Ned Creighton to incriminate himself? She felt like a tightrope walker on a slippery wire, trying to inch her way across a chasm. If she failed, the rest of her life wouldn't be worth living.

Creighton was following Lillian into the room. "Cynthia." His nod was impersonal, not unpleasant. He pulled up a chair beside the desk where Lillian had an open file of printouts.

"I'm just giving Cynthia an idea of how much the estate shrank after the taxes had been settled," Lillian told Creighton. "Then we'll estimate her share."

"Don't deduct whatever you paid Ned from what is rightfully mine," Cynthia said. She saw the angry look Ned shot at Lillian. "Oh, please," she snapped, "among the three of us, let's say it straight."

Lillian said coldly, "I told you that I wanted to share the estate. I know my father could drive people over the edge. I'm doing this because I'm sorry for you. Now here are the figures."

For the next fifteen minutes, Lillian pulled balance sheets out of the file. Allowing for taxes and then interest made on the remainder, your share would now be five million dollars."

"And this house," Cynthia interjected. Bewildered, she realized that with each passing moment Lillian and Ned were becoming more visibly relaxed. They were both smiling.

"Oh, not the house," Lillian protested. "There'd be too much gossip. We'll have the house appraised, and I'll pay you the value of it. Remember, Cynthia, I'm being very generous. My father toyed with people's lives. He was cruel. If you hadn't killed him, someone else would have. That's why I'm doing this."

"You're doing it because you don't want to sit in a courtroom and take the chance on being convicted of murder, that's why you're doing it." Oh God, Cynthia thought. It's no use. If I can't get her to admit it, it's all over. By tomorrow Lillian and Ned would have the chance to check on Alvirah. "You can have the house," she said. "Don't pay me for it. Just give me the satisfaction of hearing the truth. Admit that I had nothing to do with your father's murder."

Lillian glanced at Ned, then at the clock. "I think at this time we should honor that request." She began to laugh. "Cynthia, I am like my father. I enjoy toying with people. My father did phone to tell me about the change in his will. I could live with Dartmouth getting half his estate but not you. He told me you were coming up—the rest was easy. My mother was a wonderful woman. She was only too happy to verify that I was in New York with her that evening. Ned was delighted to get a great deal of money for giving you a boat ride. You're smart, Cynthia. Smarter than the district attorney's office. Smarter than that dumb lawyer you had."

Let the recorder be working, Cynthia prayed. Let it be working. "And smart enough to find a witness who could verify my story," she added.

Lillian and Ned burst into laughter. "What witness?" Ned asked.

"Get out." Lillian told her. "Get out this minute and don't come back."

● ● ●

Jeff Knight drove swiftly along Route 6, trying to read signs through the torrential rain that was slashing the windshield. Exit 8. He was coming up to it. The producer of the ten o'clock news had been unexpectedly decent. Of course there was a reason. "Go ahead. If Cynthia Lathem is on the Cape and thinks she has a lead on her stepfather's death, you've got a great story breaking."

Jeff wasn't interested in a great story. His only concern was Cynthia. Now he gripped the steering wheel with his long fingers. He had managed to get her address as well as her phone number from her parole officer. He'd spent a lot of summers on the Cape. That is why it had been so frustrating when he had tried to prove Cynthia's story about stopping at the hamburger stand and gotten nowhere. But he'd always stayed in Eastham, some fifty miles from Cotuit.

Exit 8. He turned onto Union Street, drove to Route 6A. A couple of miles more. Why did he have the sense of impending doom? If Cynthia had a real lead that could help her, she could be in danger.

He had to slam on his brakes when he reached Nobscusset Road. Another car, ignoring the stop sign, raced from Nobscusset across 6A. Damn fool, Jeff thought as he turned right, then left toward the bay. He realized that the whole area was in darkness. A power failure. He reached the dead end, turned left. The cottage had to be on this winding lane. Number six. He drove slowly, trying to read the numbers as his headlights shone on the mailboxes. Two. Four. Six.

Jeff pulled into the driveway, threw open the door and ran through the pelting rain toward the cottage. He held his finger on the bell, then realized that because of the power failure it did not work. He pounded on the door several times. There was no answer. Cynthia wasn't home.

He started to walk down the steps, then a sudden unreasoning fear made him go back, pound again on the door, then turn the knob. It twisted in his hand. He pushed the door open.

"Cynthia," he started to call, then gasped as the odor of gas rushed at him. He could hear the hissing coming from the fireplace. Rushing to turn the jet off, he tripped over the prone figure of Alvirah.

Willy moved restlessly in the backseat of Cynthia's car. She'd been in that house for more than an hour now. The guy who'd come later had been there fifteen minutes. Willy wasn't sure what to do. Alvirah really hadn't given specific instructions. She just wanted him to be around to make sure Cynthia didn't leave the house with anyone.

As he debated, he heard the screeching sound of sirens. Police cars. The sirens got closer. Astonished, Willy watched as they turned into the long driveway of the Richards estate and thundered toward him. Policemen rushed from the squad cars, raced up the steps and pounded on the door.

A moment later a sedan pulled into the driveway and stopped behind the squad cars. As Willy watched, a big fellow in a trench coat leaped out of it and took the steps to the porch two at a time. Willy climbed awkwardly out of the car and hoisted himself to his feet in the driveway.

He was in time to grab Alvirah as she staggered from the back of the sedan. Even in the dark he could see the welt on her forehead. "Honey, what happened?"

"I'll tell you later. Get me inside. I don't want to miss this."

In the study of the late Stuart Richards, Alvirah experienced her finest hour. Pointing her finger at Ned, in her most vibrant tones, she pronounced, "He held a gun to me. He turned on the gas jet. He smashed my head against the fireplace. And told me that Lillian Richards paid him three million dollars to set up Cynthia as the murderer."

Cynthia stared at her stepsister. "And unless the batteries in Alvirah's recorder are dead, I have both of them on record admitting their guilt."

The next morning, Willy fixed a late breakfast and served it on the deck. The storm had ended, and once again the sky was joyously blue. Seagulls swooped down to feast on surfacing fish. The bay was tranquil, and children were making castles in the damp sand at the water's edge.

Alvirah, not that much worse for her experience, had finished her article and phoned it in to Charley Evans. Charley had promised her the most ornate sunburst pin that money could buy, one with a microphone so sensitive it could pick up a mouse sneezing in the next room.

Now, as she munched a chocolate-covered doughnut and sipped coffee, she said,

"Oh, here comes Jeff. What a shame he had to drive back to Boston last night, but wasn't he wonderful telling the story on the news this morning, and all about how Ned Creighton is talking his head off to the cops? Buh-lieve me, Jeff will go places with the networks."

"That guy saved your life, honey," Willy said. "He's aces high with me. I can't believe I was curled up in that car like a jack-in-the-box when you had your head in a gas jet."

They watched as Jeff got out of the car and Cynthia rushed down the walk and into his arms.

Alvirah pushed her chair back. "I'll run over and say hello. It's a real treat to see how they look at each other. They're so in love."

Willy placed a gentle but firm hand on her shoulder. "Alvirah, honey," he begged, "just this once, for five minutes, mind your own business."

Plumbing for Willy

*I*f Alvirah Meehan had been able to look into a crystal ball and watch the events of the next ten days unfold, she would have grabbed Willy by the hand and raced out of the green room. Instead she sat and chatted with the other guests of the Phil Donahue show. Today the subject was not sex orgies or battered husbands but people who had messed up their lives by winning big in the lottery.

The Lottery Winners' Support Group had been contacted by the Donahue show, and now the worst-case guests had been chosen. Alvirah and Willy would be a counterpoint to the others, the interviewer told them. "Whatever she means by that," Alvirah commented to Willy after their initial interview.

For her appearance, Alvirah had had her hair freshly colored to the soft strawberry shade that softened her angular face. This morning Willy had told her that she looked exactly the same as she did when he'd first laid eyes on her at a Knights of Columbus dance more than forty years ago. Baroness Min von Schreiber had flown to New York from the Cypress Point Spa in Pebble Beach to select Alvirah's outfit for the broadcast. "Be sure to mention that the first thing you did when you won the lottery was come to the spa," she cautioned Alvirah. "Since that damn recession, business is not so brisk."

Alvirah was wearing a pale blue silk suit with a white blouse and her signature sunburst pin. She wished she'd managed to lose the twenty pounds she'd regained when she and Willy went to Spain in September, but still Alvirah knew she looked very nice. Very nice for her, that was. She had no illusions that with her slightly jutting jaw and broad frame she'd ever be tapped to compete in the Mrs. America contest.

There were two other sets of guests. Three coworkers in a pantyhose factory had shared a ten-million-dollar ticket six years ago. They'd decided their luck was so good that they should buy racehorses with their winnings and were now broke. Their future checks were owed to the banks and Uncle Sam. The other winners, a couple, had won sixteen million dollars, bought a hotel in Vermont, and were now slaving seven days a week trying to keep up with the overhead. Any leftover money was used to place classified ads trying to dump the hotel on someone else.

An assistant came to bring them into the studio.

Alvirah was used to being on television now. She knew enough to sit at a slight angle so she looked a little thinner. She didn't wear clunky jewelry that could rustle against the microphone. She kept her sentences short.

Willy, on the other hand, could never get used to being in the public eye. Even though Alvirah always assured him he was a grand-looking man, and people did say he looked like the late Tip O'Neill, he was happiest with a wrench in his hand, fixing a leaking pipe. Willy was a born plumber.

Donahue began in his usual breezy, slightly incredulous voice. "Can you believe it; after you win millions of dollars in the lottery you need a support group? Can you believe that you can be broke even though you have *big fat checks* still coming in?"

"Nah," the studio audience dutifully shrieked.

Alvirah remembered to tuck in her stomach, then reached for Willy's hand and entwined his fingers in hers. She didn't want him to look nervous on the television screen. A lot of their family and friends would be watching. Sister Cordelia, Willy's second oldest sister, had invited a whole crowd of retired nuns to the convent to see the show.

Three men observing the program with avid interest were not Donahue's usual viewers. Sammy, Clarence and Tony had just been released from the maximum security prison near Albany, where they'd been guests of the state for fifteen years for their part in the armed robbery of a Brink's truck. Unfortunately for them they never got to spend their six-hundred-thousand-dollar heist. The getaway car had blown a tire a block from the scene of the crime.

Now, having paid their debt to society, they were looking for a new way to get rich. The idea of kidnapping the relative of a lottery winner was Clarence's brainchild. That was why they were watching Donahue today from their seedy room in the shabby Lincoln Arms Hotel on Ninth Avenue and Fortieth Street. At thirty-five, Tony was ten years younger than the others. Like his brother Sammy, he was barrel chested, with powerful arms. His small eyes with hooded lids disappeared into folds of flesh. His thick dark hair was unkempt. He obeyed his brother blindly, and his brother obeyed Clarence.

Clarence was a total contrast to the others. Small, wiry, and soft-spoken, he emitted a chilling aura. With good reason people were instinctively afraid of him. Clarence had been born without a conscience, and a number of unsolved homicides would have been cleared from the books if he had talked in his sleep during his incarceration.

Sammy had never admitted to Clarence that Tony had been joyriding in the getaway car the night before the Brink's robbery and had run through a street littered with glass. Tony would not have lived to express his regret that he hadn't checked the tires.

One of the lottery winners who'd invested in the horses was whining, "There wasn't enough money in the world to feed those nags." His partners nodded vigorously.

Sammy snorted, "We're wasting our time with this. Those jerks can't rub two nickels together." He reached to turn off the set.

"Wait a minute," Clarence snapped.

Alvirah was speaking. "We weren't used to money," she explained. "I mean, we lived a nice life. We had a three-room apartment in Flushing and still keep it in case the state goes broke and tells us to take a flying leap for the rest of our checks. But I was a cleaning woman and Willy a plumber, and we had to be careful."

"Plumbers make a fortune," Donahue protested.

"Not Willy." Alvirah smiled. "He spent half his time fixing things free at rectories and convents and for people who were hard up. You know how it is. It's so expensive to get sinks and toilets and tubs working, and Willy felt that this was his way of making life easier for other people. He still does it."

"Well, surely you've had some fun with the money?" Donahue asked. "You're very well dressed."

Alvirah remembered to get in a plug for the Cypress Point Spa as she explained that, yes indeed, they had fun. They'd bought an apartment on Central Park South. They traveled a lot. They gave to charity. She wrote articles for the *New York Globe* and she'd been fortunate enough to solve some crimes along the way. She'd always wanted to be a detective. "Nevertheless," she concluded firmly, "every year since we've been winners we've saved more than half of every single check. And that money is all in the bank."

Clarence, followed by Sammy and Tony, joined in the vigorous applause of the studio audience. Clarence was smiling now, a thin, mirthless smile. "Two million bucks a year. Let's say almost half of that for taxes so that means they net a little over a million bucks a year and save half of that. They gotta have two million plus in the bank. That oughta keep us going for a while."

"We snatch her?" Tony asked, pointing at the screen.

Clarence withered him with a glance. "No, you dope. Look at the two of them. He's hanging on to her like she's a life preserver.

He'd fall apart and go running to the cops. We take him. She'll take orders and pay to get him back." He looked around. "I hope Willy enjoys staying with us."

Tony frowned. "We gotta keep him blindfolded. I don't want him picking me out of no lineup."

It was Sammy who sighed. "Tony, don't worry about it. The minute we get the money, Willy Meehan will be looking for leaks in the Hudson River."

Two weeks later, Alvirah was having her hair done at Louis Vincent, the salon around the corner from the Central Park South apartment. "Since the program was aired, I'm getting so many letters," she told Louis. "Do you know I even got one from the President? He congratulated us on our wise handling of our finances. He said we were a perfect example of liberal conservatism. I wished he'd invited us to a White House dinner. I've always wanted to go to one of those. Well, maybe someday."

"Just make sure I do your hair," Louis admonished as he gave a final touch to Alvirah's coiffure. "Are you having a manicure?"

Afterward, Alvirah knew she should have heeded the queer feeling that suggested she get back to the apartment. She would have caught Willy before he rushed into the car with those men.

As it was, when the doorman saw her half hour later, he broke into a relieved smile. "Mrs. Meehan, it must have been a mistake. Your husband was so worried."

Incredulous, Alvirah listened as José told her that Willy had come running from the elevator in tears. He'd yelled that Alvirah had had a heart attack under the dryer and had been rushed to Roosevelt Hospital.

"A guy was outside in a black Cadillac," José said. "He pulled into the driveway when I opened the door. The doctor sent his own car for Mr. Meehan."

"That sounds funny," Alvirah said slowly. "I'll get over to the hospital right away."

"I'll call a cab," the doorman told her. His phone rang. With an apologetic smile, he picked it up. "Two-eleven Central Park South." He listened, then, looking puzzled, said, "It's for you, Mrs. Meehan."

"Me?" Alvirah grabbed the phone and with a sinking heart heard a whispery voice say, "Alvirah, listen carefully. Tell the doorman

153

your husband is fine. It was all a misunderstanding. He's going to meet you later. Then go upstairs to your apartment and wait for instructions."

Willy had been kidnapped. Alvirah knew it. Oh God, she thought. "That's fine," she managed to say. "Tell Willy I'll meet him in an hour."

"You're a very smart woman, Mrs. Meehan," the voice whispered.

There was a click in her ear. Alvirah turned to José.

"Complete mistake, of course. Poor Willy." She tried to laugh. "Ah . . . ha . . . ha."

José beamed. "In Puerto Rico I never once hear about a doctor sending his car."

The apartment was on the thirty-fourth floor and had a terrace overlooking Central Park. Usually Alvirah smiled the minute she opened the door. The apartment was so pretty, and if she said so herself, she had an eye for furniture. All those years of cleaning other people's houses had been an education in interior design. They'd bought the apartment furnished—with white upholstery, white carpets, white lamps, white tables, white everything. After two months Alvirah felt like she was living inside a Clorox bottle. She gave everything to Willy's nephew and went shopping.

But today she took no comfort in the matching ivory couch and loveseat, Willy's deep comfortable chair with its own ottoman, the crimson and royal blue Oriental carpet, the black lacquered table and chairs in the dining area, the late afternoon sun that danced across the blanket of autumn leaves in the park.

What good was any of it if anything happened to Willy? With all her heart, Alvirah fiercely wished they'd never won the lottery and were back in their Flushing apartment over Orazio Romano's tailor shop. It was at this time she'd be coming home from cleaning Mrs. O'Keefe's house and joking to Willy that Mrs. O'Keefe had been vaccinated with a phonograph needle. "Willy, she never shuts up. Even shouts over the vacuum. It's a good thing she isn't too messy. I'd never get the work done."

The phone rang. Alvirah rushed to pick up the extension in the living room, then changed her mind and in stumbling haste ran into the bedroom. The recording machine was there. She pushed the Record button as she picked up the phone.

It was the same whispery voice. "Alvirah?"

"Yes. Where's Willy? Whatever you do, don't hurt him." She could hear background sounds like planes taking off. Was Willy at an airport?

"We won't hurt him as long as we get the money and as long as you don't call the cops. You didn't call them, did you?"

"No. I want to talk to Willy."

"In a minute. How much money have you got in the bank?"

"Something over two million dollars."

"You're an honest woman, Alvirah. That's just about what we figured. If you want Willy back you'd better start making some withdrawals."

"You can have it all."

There was a low chuckle. "I like you, Alvirah. Two million is fine. Take it out in cash. Don't give a hint that anything is wrong. No marked money, baby. And don't go to the cops. We'll be watching you."

The airport sounds became almost deafening. "I can't hear you," Alvirah said desperately. "And I'm not giving you one cent until I'm sure that Willy is still alive."

"Talk to him."

Moments later a sheepish voice said, "Hi, honey."

Relief, total and overwhelming, flooded Alvirah. Her ever-resourceful brain, which had been inactive since José had told her about Willy getting in the "doctor's car," resumed its normal steel-trap efficiency.

"Honey," she yelled so that his abductors could hear, "tell those guys to take good care of you. Otherwise they won't get a plugged nickel."

Willy's hands were handcuffed together. His feet were tied. He watched as the boss, Clarence, put his thumb on the handset of the phone and broke the connection. "That's quite a woman you have, Willy," Clarence said. Then Clarence turned off the machine that played simulated airport background sounds.

Willy felt like a jerk. If Alvirah had really had a heart attack, Louis would have called him from the salon. He should have known that. What a dope he was. He looked around. This was some crummy dump. When he got in the car, the guy who was hiding in the backseat put a gun in his neck. "Try to make trouble and I blow you away." The gun was jostling against his ribs when they hustled him through the lobby and up in the rickety elevator of this crummy joint. It was only a couple of blocks from the Lincoln Tunnel. The windows were closed tight, but even so, the exhaust fumes from the buses and trucks and cars were overwhelming. You could practically see them.

Willy had sized up Tony and Sammy fast. Not too much upstairs. He might be able to give them the slip somehow. But when Clarence came in, announcing that he'd warned Alvirah to let the doorman think everything was hunky-dory, Willy felt his first real fear. Clarence reminded him of Nutsy, a guy he'd known as a kid. Nutsy used to shoot his BB gun into birds' nests.

It was obvious Clarence was the boss. He called Alvirah and talked to her about the ransom. He made the decision to put Willy on the phone. "Now," Clarence said, "put him back in the closet."

"Hey, wait a minute," Willy protested. "I'm starving."

"We're gonna order hamburgers and french fries," Sammy told him as he slipped a gag over Willy's mouth. "We'll letcha eat."

Sammy trussed Willy's feet and legs in a spiral sequence of cord and knots and shoved him into the narrow closet. The door did not seal against the frame, and Willy could hear the low-toned conversation. "Two million bucks means she has to go to twenty banks. She's too smart to leave more than a hundred thou in any of them. That's how much is insured. Figuring the forms she has to fill out and the bank taking its own good time in counting the money, give her three, four days to get it."

"She'll need four," Clarence said. "We get the money by Friday night. We tell her we're gonna count it and then she can pick up Willy." He laughed. "Then we send her a map with an X mark to show where to start dredging."

Alvirah sat for hours in Willy's chair, staring unseeingly as the late afternoon sun sent slanting shadows over Central Park. The last lingering rays disappeared. She reached to turn on the lamp and got up slowly. It was no use thinking of all the good times she and Willy had had these forty years or that just this morning they were going through brochures to decide on whether to take a camel trip through India or a balloon safari in western Africa.

I'm going to get him back, she decided, her jaw jutting out a little more aggressively. The first thing she had to do was to make a cup of tea. The next was to get out all the bankbooks and lay a plan for going from one bank to another and withdrawing cash.

The banks were scattered all over Manhattan and Queens. One hundred thousand dollars deposited in each of them and, of course, accumulated interest, which they took out at the end of the year and used to start a new account. "No double-your-money schemes for us," they'd agreed. In the bank. Insured. Period. When someone had tried to talk them into buying zero-coupon bonds that paid off in ten or fifteen years, Alvirah had said, "At our age we don't buy things that pay off in ten years."

She smiled, remembering that Willy had chimed in, "And we don't buy green bananas, either."

Alvirah swallowed a giant lump in her throat as she sipped the tea and decided that tomorrow morning she'd start on Fifty-seventh Street at Chase Manhattan, go across the street to Chemical, work her way along

Park Avenue starting at Citibank and then hit Wall Street.

It was a long night lying awake wondering if Willy was okay. I'm going to make them let me talk to him every night until I get all the money, she promised herself. That way they won't hurt him till I figure something out.

At dawn she was becoming tempted to call the police. By the time she got up, at seven, she'd decided against it. These people might have a spy in the building who would report if there was a lot of activity in the apartment. She couldn't take a chance.

Willy spent the night in the closet. They loosened the ropes enough for him to stretch out a little. But they didn't give him a blanket or pillow, and his head was resting on someone's shoe. There was no way to push it aside. There was too much junk in the closet. He dozed off occasionally. He dreamed his neck was embedded on the side of Mount Rushmore, directly below the sculpture of Teddy Roosevelt's face.

• • •

The banks didn't open till nine. By eight-thirty, Alvirah, in a burst of pressure-cooker energy, had cleaned the already clean apartment. Her bankbooks were in her voluminous shoulder bag. She had dug from the closet a frankfurter-shaped plastic carryall, the one remnant on Central Park South of the days when she and Willy spent their vacations taking Greyhound tours to the Catskills.

The October morning was crisp, and Alvirah was wearing a light green suit that she'd bought when she was on one of her diets. The waistband wouldn't close, but a large safety pin solved that problem. Automatically she fastened her sunburst pin with the concealed recorder on the lapel.

It was still too early to leave. Trying to keep up the positive thinking, that everything would be hunky-dory as soon as the money was paid, Alvirah reheated the kettle and turned on the radio to *CBS Morning News.*

For once the headlines were fairly mundane. There was no big-shot Mafia guy on trial. No fatal-attraction homicide. Nobody had been arrested for inside trading.

Alvirah sipped her tea and was about to hit the Off button when the newscaster announced that as of today, New Yorkers could use the device that recorded the phone numbers from which incoming calls were made within the 212 area code.

It took a minute for her to realize what that meant. Then Alvirah jumped up and ran to the utility closet. Among the electronic devices that she and Willy delighted in taking home from Hammacher Schlemmer was the recording machine that listed numbers on incoming phone calls. They'd bought it not realizing it was useless in New York.

Dear Lord and his Blessed Mother, she prayed as she ripped the box open, pulled out the recorder and with trembling fingers substituted it for the answering machine in the bedroom. Let them be keeping Willy in New York. Let them call from wherever they're hiding him.

She remembered to record an announcement. "You have reached the home of Alvirah and Willy Meehan. At the beep please leave a message. We'll get back to you real soon." She played it back. Her voice sounded unnatural, worried, full of stress.

She forced herself to remember that she had won the drama medal in the sixth-grade play at St. Francis Xavier School in the Bronx. Be an actress, she told herself firmly.

163

She took a deep breath and began again: "Hell-lo. You have reached the home . . ."

That's more like it, she decided when she listened to the new version. Then, clutching her shoulder bag, Alvirah headed for Chase Manhattan to begin to put together Willy's ransom money.

I'm gonna go nuts, Willy thought as he tried to flex arms that somehow managed to be both numb and aching. His legs were still firmly trussed together. He'd given up on them. At eight-thirty he heard a faint rapping sound and then a door opening. Probably what passed for room service in this dump. They brought up lousy food on paper plates. At least that was the way hamburgers had been delivered last night. Even so, the thought of a cup of coffee and a piece of toast set Willy's mouth to watering.

A moment later the closet door opened. Sammy and Tony were staring down at him. Sammy held the gun while Tony loosened Willy's gag. "Didja have a good night's sleep?" Tony's unlovely smile revealed a broken eyetooth. Willy longed to have his hands free for just two minutes. They itched to give

164

Tony a matching set of eyeteeth. "Slept like a baby," he lied. He nodded in the direction of the bathroom. "How about it?"

"What?" Tony blinked, his rubbery face drooping into puzzlement.

"He needs to go to the head," Clarence said. He crossed the narrow room and bent over Willy. "See that gun?" He pointed to it. "It has a silencer. You try anything funny and it's all over. Sammy has a very nervous trigger finger. Then we'll all be mad because you gave us so much trouble. And we'll have to take it out on your wife. Get it?"

Willy was absolutely certain that Clarence meant it. Tony might be dopey, Sammy might have an itchy trigger finger, but they wouldn't do anything without getting the okay from Clarence. And Clarence was a killer. Willy tried to sound calm. "I get it."

Somehow he managed to hobble to the bathroom. After he'd finished, Tony let him splash some water in his face. Willy looked around in disgust. The tile was broken, and the room looked as though it hadn't been cleaned in years. Flecks of rust-corroded enamel covered the tub and sink. Worst of all was the constant dripping from the water tank, faucets and shower head. "Sounds like

Niagara Falls in here," Willy commented to Tony, who was standing at the door.

Tony shoved him over to where Sammy and Clarence were sitting at a rickety card table, which was piled with containers of coffee and objects that resembled abandoned Egg McMuffin cartons. Clarence nodded to the folding chair next to Sammy. "Sit there." Then he whirled. "Shut that damn door," he ordered Tony. "That stinking dripping is driving me nuts. Kept me awake half the night."

A thought came to Willy. He tried to sound casual. "I guess we'll be here a couple of days. If you pick up a few tools for me, I can fix that for you." He reached for a container. "I'm the best plumber you ever kidnapped."

Alvirah was learning that it was much easier to put money in a bank than to get it out. When she presented her withdrawal slip at Chase Manhattan, the teller's eyes bulged. Then he asked her to step over to an assistant manager's desk.

Fifteen minutes later, Alvirah was still adamantly insisting that, no, she wasn't unhappy with the service. Yes, she was sure she wanted the money in cash. Yes, she understood what a certified check was. Finally she demanded emphatically, "Is it my money or isn't it?"

"Of course. Of course." They would have to ask her to fill out some forms—government regulations for cash withdrawals of over ten thousand dollars.

Then they had to count the money. Eyes popped when Alvirah told them she wanted five hundred hundred-dollar bills and one thousand fifty-dollar bills. That took a lot of counting.

It was nearly noon when Alvirah hailed a cab to cover the three blocks to the apartment, dump the money in a dresser drawer and start out again for the Chemical Bank on Eighth Avenue.

By the end of the day she'd managed to get only three hundred thousand of the two million she needed. Then she sat in the apartment, staring at the phone. There was a way to move quicker. In the morning she'd call the rest of the banks and tell them to expect her withdrawals. Start counting now, fellows.

At six-thirty the phone rang. Alvirah grabbed it as a phone number appeared on the recording machine. A familiar number. Alvirah realized the caller was the formidable Sister Cordelia.

Willy had seven sisters. Six of them had

gone into the convent. The seventh, now deceased, was the mother of Brian, whom Alvirah and Willy loved as a son. Brian, a playwright, was in London now. Alvirah would have turned to him for help if he'd been in New York.

But she wasn't about to tell Cordelia about Willy's abduction. Cordelia would have the White House on the phone, demanding that the President dispatch the standing army to rescue her brother.

Cordelia sounded a little peeved. "Alvirah, Willy was supposed to come over this afternoon. One of the old girls we visit needs to have her toilet fixed. It's not like him to forget. Let me talk to him."

Alvirah managed a he-har-har laugh that sounded even to her ears like the canned stuff you hear on lousy television shows. "Cordelia, it must have gone out of his mind," she said. "Willy is . . . he's . . . " She had a burst of inspiration. "Willy's in Washington to testify about the cheapest way to fix plumbing in the tenements the government is restoring. You know how he can do miracles to make things work. The President read that Willy is a genius at that and sent for him."

"The President!" Cordelia's incredulous tone made Alvirah wish she'd named Senator Moynihan or maybe some congressman. I never lie, she fretted. I don't know how.

"Willy would never go to Washington without you," Cordelia snorted.

"They sent a car for him." Well, at least that's true, Alvirah thought.

She heard the "hrrump" on the other end of the line. Cordelia was nobody's fool. "Well, when he gets back, tell him to get right over here."

Two minutes later the phone rang again. This time the number that came up was not familiar. It's *them,* Alvirah thought. She realized her hand was shaking. Forcing herself to think of the sixth-grade drama medal, she reached for the receiver.

Her hello was hardy and confident.

"We hope you've been banking, Mrs. Meehan."

"Yes, I have. Put Willy on."

"You can talk to him in a minute. We want the money by Friday night."

"Friday night! It's Tuesday now. That only gives me three days. It takes a long time to get all that together."

"Just do it. Say hello to Willy."

"Hi, honey." Willy's voice sounded subdued. Then he said, "Hey, let me talk."

Alvirah heard the sound of the receiver dropping. "Okay, Alvirah," the whispery voice said. "We're not going to call you again until Friday night at seven o'clock. We'll let you talk to Willy then and we'll tell you where to meet us. Remember, any funny business and in the future you'll have to pay to have your plumbing fixed. Willy won't be around to take care of it."

The receiver clicked in her ear. Willy. Willy. Her hand still gripping the phone, Alvirah stared at the number listed on the machine: 555-7000. Should she call back? But suppose one of them answered. They'd know she was tracing them. Instead she called the *Globe.* As she expected, her editor, Charley, was still at his desk. She explained what she needed.

"Sure, I can get it for you, Alvirah. You sound kind of mysterious. Are you working on a case you can write up for us?"

"I'm not sure yet."

Ten minutes later he called back. "Hey, Alvirah, that's some dump you're looking up. It's the Lincoln Arms Hotel on Ninth Avenue, near the Lincoln Tunnel. It's one step down from a flophouse."

The Lincoln Arms Hotel. Alvirah managed to thank Charley before she slammed down the receiver and headed out the door.

Just in case she was being watched she left the apartment house through the garage and hailed a cab. She started to tell the driver to take her to the hotel, then thought better of it. Suppose one of Willy's kidnappers spotted her? Instead she had him drop her at the bus terminal. That was only a block away.

Her kerchief covering her head, her coat collar turned up, Alvirah walked past the Lincoln Arms Hotel. Dismayed, she realized it was a pretty big place. She glanced up at the windows. Was Willy behind one of them? The building looked as though it had been built before the Civil War, but it was at least ten or twelve stories high. How could she ever find him in that place? Once again she wondered if she should call the cops and then remembered again the time some wife did call and the cops were spotted at the ransom drop and the kidnappers sped away. They found the body three weeks later.

No. She couldn't risk it. She *had* to get Willy back.

Alvirah stood in the shadows at the side of the hotel and prayed to St. Jude, the saint of lost causes. And then she spotted it. A sign in the window. HELP WANTED—Room service. 4:00 to 12:00 P.M. shift. She had to get that job, but not looking like this.

Ignoring the trucks and cars and buses that were barreling toward the tunnel entrance, Alvirah dashed into the street, grabbed a cab, and rattled off the address of the apartment in Flushing. Her brain was working overtime.

The old apartment had been their home for nearly forty years and looked exactly the same as it had the day they'd won the lottery. The dark gray overstuffed velour couch and matching chair, the green-and-orange rug the lady she cleaned for on Tuesdays had been throwing out, the mahogany-veneer bedroom set that had been Willy's mother's bridal furniture.

In the closet were all the clothes she'd worn in those days. Splashy print dresses from Alexander's. Polyester slacks and sweatshirts, sneakers and high-heeled shoes purchased at outlets. In the mirror cabinet in the bathroom she found the henna rinse that made her hair the color of the rising sun on the Japanese flag.

An hour later there was no vestige left of the gentrified lottery winner. Bright red hair wisped around a face now startling with the makeup she used to love before Baroness Min taught her that less is better. Her old lipstick exactly matched her flaming hair. Her eyelids were emblazoned with purple shadow. Jeans too tight across the seat, ankles hidden by thick socks and feet stuffed into well-worn sneakers, a fleece-lined sweatshirt with the skyline of Manhattan stenciled across the front finished the transformation.

Alvirah surveyed the overall result with satisfaction. I look like someone who'd apply for a job in that crummy hotel, she decided. Reluctantly she left her sunburst pin in a drawer. It just didn't look right on the sweatshirt, and she had the backup pin Charley had given her at the other apartment if she needed it. When she pulled on her old all-weather coat she remembered to switch her money and keys to the voluminous black-and-green tote bag that she'd always carried to her cleaning jobs.

Forty minutes later she was in the Lincoln Arms Hotel. The grimy lobby contained a battered desk in front of a wall of mailboxes and four black Naugahyde chairs in advanced stages of disrepair. The stained brown carpet was pocked with gaping holes that revealed ancient linoleum flooring.

Never mind room service, they ought to look for a cleaning woman, Alvirah thought as she approached the desk.

The sallow-complexioned, bleary-eyed clerk looked up.

"Whaddaya want?"

"A job. I'm a good waitress."

Something that was more sneer than smile moved the clerk's lips. "You don't need to be good, just fast. How old are ya?"

"Fifty," Alvirah lied.

"You're fifty, I'm twelve. Go home."

"I need a job," Alvirah persisted, her heart pounding. She could feel Willy's presence. She'd have taken an oath that he was hidden somewhere in this hotel. "Give me a chance. I'll work free for three or four days. If you don't think I'm the best worker you ever had by, let's say Saturday, you can fire me."

The clerk shrugged. "So whadda I got to lose? Be here tomorrow at four sharp. Whaddaya say your name was?"

"Tessie," Alvirah said firmly. "Tessie Magink."

• • •

Wednesday morning Willy could sense the growing tension among his captors. Clarence flatly refused to allow Sammy to step outside the room. When Sammy complained, Clarence snapped, "After twelve years in a cell you shouldn't have no trouble staying put."

There was no sign of a chambermaid beating down the door to clean, but Willy decided the room probably hadn't been cleaned in a year anyhow. The three cotlike beds were lined up together, heads against the bathroom wall. A narrow dresser covered with peeling sheets of Con-Tact paper, a black-and-white television, and a round table with four chairs completed the decor.

On Tuesday night Willy had persuaded his captors to allow him to sleep on the bathroom floor. It was bigger than the closet, and, as he pointed out, if he stretched out that extra bit he would be able to walk when they exchanged him for the ransom. He did not miss the glances they exchanged at the suggestion. They had no intention of letting him go free to talk about them. That meant he had about forty-eight hours to figure out a way of being rescued from this fleabag.

At three in the morning, when he'd heard

Sammy and Tony snoring in harmony and Clarence's irritated but regular gasps, Willy had managed to sit up, get to his feet and hop over to the toilet. The rope that tethered him to the bathtub faucet allowed him just enough room to touch the lid of the water tank. With his manacled hands, he lifted it, laid it on the sink and reached into the grimy, rust-colored water of the tank. The result was that a few minutes later the dripping had become louder, more frequent and more insistent.

That was why Clarence had awakened to the distressing sound of constantly bubbling water. Willy smiled a grim, inner smile as Clarence barked, "I'm gonna go nuts. Sounds like a camel peeing."

When the room-service breakfast was being delivered, Willy was again securely tied and gagged in the closet, this time with Sammy's gun at his temple. From the hall outside the room, Willy could hear the faint croak of the obviously old man who was apparently the sole room-service employee. It was useless to even think about attracting his attention.

That afternoon, Clarence began stuffing towels around the bathroom door, but nothing could block out the sound of running water. "I'm getting one of my bad headaches," he snarled, settling down on the unmade bed. A few minutes later Tony began to whistle. Sammy shut him up immediately. Willy heard him whisper, "When Clarence gets one of his headaches, watch out."

Tony was clearly bored. His beady eyes glazed over as he sat watching television, the sound barely turned on. Willy sat next to him, tied to a chair, the gag loosened enough that he could talk through almost closed lips.

At the table, Sammy played endless games of solitaire. In late afternoon, Tony got bored with the television and snapped it off. "You got any kids?" he asked Willy.

Willy knew that if he had any hope of getting out of this dump alive, Tony would be his ticket. Trying to ignore the combination of cramps and numbness in his arms and legs, he told Tony that he and Alvirah had never been blessed with kids, but they thought of his nephew, Brian, as their own child, especially since Brian's mother— Willy's sister—had been called to her eternal reward. "I have six other sisters," he said. "They're all nuns. Cordelia is the oldest. She's sixty-eight going on twenty-one."

Tony's jaw dropped. "No foolin'. When I was a kid and kind of on the streets and picking up a few bucks separating women from their pocketbooks, if you know what I mean, I never once hit on a nun, even when they wuz heading for the supermarket, meaning they had cash. When I had a good hit I left a coupla bucks in the convent mailbox, sort of an expression of gratitude."

Willy tried to look impressed at Tony's largess.

"Will you shut up?" Clarence barked from the bed. "My head's splitting."

Willy breathed a silent prayer as he said, "You know, I could fix that leak if I just had a monkey wrench and a screwdriver."

If he could just get his hands on that tank, he thought. He could flood the joint. They couldn't very well shoot him if people were rushing in to stop the cascade of water he could loose.

Sister Cordelia knew something was wrong. Much as she loved Willy, she could not imagine the President sending for him in a private car. Something else; Alvirah was always so open you could read her like the headline of the *New York Post.* But when Cordelia tried to phone Alvirah Wednesday morning there was no answer. Then, when she did reach her at three-thirty, Alvirah sounded out of breath. She was just running out, she explained, but didn't say where. Of course Willy was fine. Why wouldn't he be? He'd be home by the weekend.

The convent was an apartment in an old building on Amsterdam Avenue and 100th Street. Sister Cordelia lived there with four elderly sisters and the one novice, twenty-seven-year-old Maeve Marie, who had been a policewoman for three years before realizing she had a vocation.

When Cordelia hung up after speaking to Alvirah she sat down heavily on a sturdy kitchen chair. "Maeve," she said, "something is wrong with Willy. I feel it in my bones."

The phone rang. It was Arturo Morales, the manager of the Flushing bank around the corner from Willy and Alvirah's old apartment.

"Sister," he began, sounding distressed, "I hate to bother you, but I'm worried."

Cordelia's heart sank as Arturo explained that Alvirah had tried to withdraw one hundred thousand dollars from the bank. They were able to give her only twenty thousand but had promised to have the rest of the cash Friday morning; she'd told them she absolutely had to have it by then.

Cordelia thanked him for the information, promised never to hint that he'd violated bank confidentiality, hung up and snapped to Maeve Marie, "Come on. We're going to see Alvirah."

Alvirah reported to the Lincoln Arms Hotel promptly at four o'clock. She'd changed her clothes in the Port Authority. Now, standing in front of the desk clerk, she felt secure in her disguise. The clerk jerked his head to indicate that she was to go down the corridor to the door marked Stay Out.

It led to the kitchen. The chef, a bony seventy-year-old who bore a startling resemblance to forties cowboy star Gabby Hayes, was preparing hamburgers. Clouds of smoke rose from the spatters of grease on the grill. He looked up. "You Tessie?"

Alvirah nodded.

"Okay. I'm Hank. Start delivering."

There were no subtleties in the room-service department. Service consisted of the kind of brown plastic tray that was found in hospital cafeterias, coarse paper napkins, plastic utensils, sample-sized packets of mustard, ketchup and relish. Hank shoveled limp hamburgers onto buns. "Pour the coffee. Don't fill the cups too much. Dish out the french fries."

Alvirah obeyed. "How many rooms in this place?" she asked as she set up trays.

"Hundred."

"That many!"

Hank grinned, revealing tobacco-stained false teeth. "Only forty rented overnight. The by-the-hour trade ain't looking for room service."

Alvirah considered. Forty wasn't too bad. She figured there had to be at least two men involved in the kidnapping. One to drive the car, one to keep Willy from bopping him. Maybe even one more to make that first phone call. She needed to watch for big orders. At least it was a start.

She began delivering with Hank's firm reminder to collect on the spot. The hamburgers went to the bar, which was inhabited by a dozen or so rough-looking guys you wouldn't want to meet on a dark night. The second order she brought to the room clerk and hotel manager, who presided over the premises from an airless room behind the desk. Their heros were on the house. Her next tray, containing cornflakes and a double boilermaker, was for a disheveled, bleary-eyed senior citizen. Alvirah was sure the cornflakes were an afterthought.

Next she was sent with a heavy tray to four men playing cards on the ninth floor. Another card-game group on the seventh floor ordered pizzas. On the eighth floor, she was met at the door by a husky guy who said, "Oh. You're new. I'll take it. When you knock on the door, don't bang. My brother's got a bad headache." Behind him Alvirah could see a man lying on a bed, a cloth over his eyes. The persistent dripping sound from the bathroom reminded her overwhelmingly of Willy. He'd have that leak fixed in no time flat. There was clearly no one else in the room, and the guy at the door looked as though he could have cleaned the contents of the tray on his own.

In the closet, Willy could just about hear the cadence of a voice that made him ache to be back with Alvirah.

• • •

There were enough room-service calls to keep her busy from six until about ten. From her own observations and from the explanations of Hank, who grew increasingly garrulous as he began to appreciate her efficiency, Alvirah got to understand the setup. There were ten floors of rooms. The first six floors all had ten rooms and were reserved for the hourly guests. The upper-floor rooms were the largest, all with baths, and tended to be rented for at least a few days.

Over a plump hamburger that she cooked for him at ten o'clock, Hank told her that everybody registered under a false name. Everybody paid cash. "Like one guy who comes in to clean out his private mailboxes. He publishes dirty magazines. 'Nother guy sets up card games. Lots of fellows come in here and get a bag on when they're supposed to be on a business trip. That kind of stuff. Nothing bad. It's sort of like a private club."

Hank's head began to droop after he'd finished the last of his third glass of beer. A few minutes later he was asleep. Quietly, Alvirah went to the table that served as a combination chopping board and desk. When she brought down the money after each order was delivered, she'd been instructed to put it in the cigar box that served as cash register. The order slip with the amount was placed in the box next to it. Hank had explained that, at midnight, room service ended and the desk clerk tallied up the money, compared it with the receipts, and put the cash in the safe, which was hidden in the bottom of the refrigerator. The order slips were then dropped into a cardboard box under the table. There was a massive jumble of them in place now.

Some would never be missed. Figuring that the top layers had to be the most recent records, Alvirah scooped up an armful and stuffed them in her voluminous handbag. She delivered three more orders to the bar between eleven and twelve. In between deliveries, unable to stand the grimy kitchen, she set about cleaning it up as a bemused Hank watched.

After a quick stop at the Port Authority to change into her good clothes, scrub the rouge and purple eye shadow from her face and wrap a turban around her flaming hair, Alvirah stepped out of a cab at quarter of one. Ramon, the night doorman, said, "Sister Cordelia was here. She asked a lot of questions about where you were."

Cordelia was no dope, Alvirah thought

with grudging admiration. A plan was forming in her mind, and Cordelia was part of it. Even before she sank her tired body into the Jacuzzi that was bubbling with Cypress Point Spa oils, Alvirah sorted out the greasy order slips. Within the hour she had narrowed the possibilities. Four rooms consistently sent for large orders. She pushed away the gnawing fear that they were all occupied by card players or some other kind of gamblers and that Willy might be in Alaska right now. Her instinct had told her the minute she set foot in the hotel that he was nearby.

It was nearly three when she got into the double bed. Tired as she was, it was impossible to get to sleep. Finally she pictured him there, settling in beside her. "Nighty-night, Willy, lovey," she said aloud, and in her head heard him saying in response, "Sleep tight, honey."

Sister Cordelia arrived at seven o'clock on Thursday morning. Alvirah was prepared for her. She'd been up half an hour and was wearing Willy's plaid bathrobe, which had the faint scent of his shaving lotion. She had a pot of coffee on the stove.

"What's up?" Cordelia asked abruptly.

Over coffee and Sara Lee crumb cake, Alvirah told her everything. "Cordelia," she concluded, "I won't tell you I'm not scared, because that would be a lie. I'm scared to death for Willy. If someone is watching this place or maybe has a delivery boy keeping an eye out, and it gets back that strange people were coming and going, they'll kill Willy. Cordelia, I swear to you, I know he's in that hotel, and I have a plan. Maeve still has her gun permit, doesn't she?"

"Yes." Sister Cordelia's piercing gray eyes bored into Alvirah's.

"And she's still friends with the guys she sent to prison, isn't she?"

"Oh sure. They all love her. You know they give Willy a hand fixing pipes whenever he needs it, and they take turns delivering meals to our shut-ins."

"That's what I need. They look like the people who hang out in that place. I want three or four of them to check into the Lincoln Arms tonight. Let them get a card game going. That happens all the time. Tomorrow night at seven o'clock, I get the call where to leave the money. They know that I won't turn it over until I talk to Willy. To keep them from carrying him out of there, I want Maeve's guys covering the exits. It's our only chance."

Cordelia stared grimly into space, then said, "Alvirah, Willy always told me to trust your sixth sense. I guess I'd better do it now."

By Thursday afternoon, Clarence's eyes were blinded with the crushing ache that was splitting his head from ear to ear. Even Tony was careful not to cross him. He didn't reach to turn on the television set but contented himself sitting next to Willy and in a hoarse whisper telling him the story of his life. He'd gotten up to age seven, the year he'd discovered how easy it was to shoplift in the candy store, when Clarence barked from the bed, "You say you can fix that damn leak?"

Willy didn't want to seem too excited, but the muscles in his throat squeezed together as he nodded vigorously.

"Whaddaya need?"

"A monkey wrench," Willy croaked through the gag. "A screwdriver. Wire."

"All right. Sammy, you heard him. Go out and get that stuff."

Sammy was playing solitaire again. "I'll send Tony."

Clarence bolted up. "I said *you.* That dopey brother of yours'll blab to the nearest guy where he's going, why he's going, who he's getting it for. Now go."

Sammy shivered at the tone, remembering how Tony had gone joyriding in the getaway car. "Sure, Clarence, sure," he said soothingly. "And listen, long as I'm out, how about I bring in some Chinese food, huh? Could taste good for a change."

Clarence's scowl faded momentarily. "Yeah, okay. Get lotsa soy sauce."

Alvirah dropped off the suitcase with her last bank pickup at twenty to four, barely time enough to rush to the Port Authority, change, and report to the job. As she trotted through the Lincoln Arms lobby she noticed a sweet-faced nun in traditional habit holding out a basket and quietly moving from one to the other occupants of the bar. Everybody threw something in. In the kitchen, Alvirah asked Hank about the nun.

"Oh her. Yeah. She spends it on the kids who live around here. Makes everybody feel good to toss her a buck or two. Kind of spiritual, you know what I mean?"

• • •

The chow mein was a welcome relief from hamburgers. After dinner, Clarence ordered Willy to go into the john and get rid of the dripping noise. Sammy accompanied him. Willy's heart sank when Sammy said, "I don't know how to fix nothing, but I know how *not* to fix it, so don't get smart."

So much for my big plan, Willy thought. Well, maybe I can stall it till I figure something out. He began by chipping at the years of accumulated rust around the base of the tank.

That night, orders were not as brisk as the night before. Alvirah suggested to Hank that she sort out all the old slips in the order box.

"Why?" Hank looked astonished. Why would anyone sort out useless slips?

Alvirah tugged at the sweatshirt she was wearing today. It said, I SPENT THE NIGHT WITH BURT REYNOLDS. Willy had bought it as a gag when they went to Reynolds' theater in Florida. She tried to look mysterious. "You never know," she whispered.

The answer seemed to satisfy Hank.

She hid the already sorted slips under the pile she dumped on the table. She knew what she was looking for. Consistent orders in quantity since Monday.

She narrowed it down to the same four rooms she'd selected from her earlier sorting.

At six o'clock it suddenly got busy. By eight-thirty she'd delivered food to three of the four suspect rooms. Two contained the ongoing card games. One was now a crap game. She had to admit that none of the players looked like kidnappers.

Room 802 did not phone for an order. Maybe the guy with the bad headache and his brother had checked out. At midnight a discouraged Alvirah was about the leave, when Hank grumbled, "Working with you is easy. The new day guy quit, and tomorrow they're gonna bring in the kid who fills in. He screws up all the orders."

Breathing a grateful prayer of thanks, Alvirah immediately volunteered to come in for the seven-to-one morning shift as well as her usual four to twelve. She reasoned that she could still rush to the banks that had promised to have the cash for her between twelve-fifteen and three.

"I'll be back at seven," she promised Hank.

"So will I," he complained. "The day cook quit too."

On the way out, Alvirah noticed some familiar faces hanging around the bar. Louie, who'd served seven years for bank robbery and had a black belt in karate; Al, who'd been a strongman for a pawnbroker and served four years for assault; Lefty, whose specialty was hot cars. She smiled inwardly. Maeve was coming through for her—these were her men.

True to their training, even though Alvirah was sure they'd seen her, neither Louie, Al, nor Lefty gave any sign of knowing her.

Willy had reduced the dripping to its original annoying level, then an irritable Clarence had shouted in for him to knock off the hammering. "Leave it where it is. I can put up with that much noise for another twenty-four hours."

And then what? Willy wondered. There was one hope. Sammy was bored with observing him fiddling around with the water tank. Tomorrow Sammy would be more careless. That night Willy insured the further need of his services by again hopping over to the water tank and adjusting the drip-drip level.

In the morning, Clarence's eyes were feverish. Tony started talking about an old girlfriend he planned to look up when they got to the hideout in Queens, and no one told him to keep his mouth shut. Meaning, Willy thought, they're not worried about me hearing them.

When breakfast was delivered, Willy, securely stashed in the closet, jumped so suddenly that the gun in Sammy's hand almost went off. This time he didn't hear just a cadence of a voice that reminded him of Alvirah. It was clearly her ringing tone asking Tony if his brother's headache was any better.

A startled Sammy hissed in Willy's ear, "You crazy or somethin'?"

Alvirah was looking for him. Willy had to help her. He had to get back into the bathroom, work on the water tank, tap the wrench to the cadence of "And the Band Played On," their song, the one the band was playing when he first asked Alvirah to dance at the K of C hall over forty years ago.

He got his chance four hours later when, at Clarence's furious command, wrench and screwdriver in hand and a jittery Sammy beside him, he resumed his task of jointly fixing and sabotaging the water tank.

He was careful not to overdo. He reasonably told a protesting Sammy that he wasn't making that much noise, and anyhow, this place would probably love to have one decent john. Scratching his four-day growth of beard, squirming in his wrinkled clothing, Willy began to send off signals three minutes apart. "Ca-sey would WALTZ with the STRAW-ber-ry BLONDE tap-tap TApppp TApppp TApppp."

Alvirah was delivering pizza to 702 when she heard it. The tapping. Oh God, she prayed, oh God. She placed the tray on the uneven tabletop. The occupant of the room, a nice-looking fellow in his thirties, was coming off a binge. He pointed up, "Wouldn't that kill you? They're renovating or something. Take your pick. Sounds like Niagara Falls or New Year's Eve up there."

It has to be 802, Alvirah decided, thinking of the guy on the bed, the doorkeeper, the open bathroom door. They must shove Willy in the closet when they order room service.

Even though she was so excited her heart was thumping through the sweatshirt that read DON'T BE A LITTERBUG, she took time to caution the drinker that booze would be his ruination.

There was a phone in the hallway by the bar. Hoping she wasn't being observed by the desk clerk, Alvirah made a hurried call to Cordelia. She finished by saying, "They'll be phoning me at seven o'clock."

At quarter of seven that night, the occupants of the bar of the Lincoln Arms Hotel were awed at the sight of six mostly elderly nuns, in traditional floor-length habit, veil, and wimple, entering the lobby. The desk clerk jumped up and made a shooing motion toward the revolving door behind them. Alvirah watched, tray in arms, as Maeve, the appointed spokesperson, stared down the desk clerk.

"We have the owner's permission to ask for donations on every floor," Maeve told him.

"You got no such thing."

Her voice dropped to a whisper. "We have Mr. ——'s permission."

194

The clerk's face paled. "You guys shut up and get out your loot," he yelled at the occupants of the bar. "These here sisters are gonna pass the hat."

"No, we're starting upstairs," Maeve told him.

Alvirah protectively brought up the rear as the bevy of nuns, led by Cordelia, entered the elevator.

They went directly to the eighth floor and clustered in the hallway where Lefty, Al and Louie were waiting. At exactly seven o'clock Alvirah knocked on the door. "Room service," she called.

"We didn't order nothin'," a voice snarled.

"Someone did, and I've got to collect," she shouted firmly.

She heard scuffling. A door slammed. The closet. They were hiding Willy. The door opened a crack. A nervous Tony instructed, "Leave the tray outside. How much?"

Alvirah kept her foot firmly in the door as the oldest nuns materialized behind her. "We're collecting for the Lord," one of them whispered.

Clarence had the phone in his hand. "What the hell's going on out there?" he shouted.

"Hey, that's no way to talk to the sisters,"

Tony protested. Reverently he stepped aside as they drifted past him into the room.

Sister Maeve brought up the rear, her hands folded in the sleeves of her habit. In an instant, she circled behind Clarence, yanked her right hand out and held a gun against his temple. In the crisp tone that had made her a superb cop, she whispered, "Freeze, or you're dead."

Tony opened his mouth to yell a warning, but it was obliterated as Lefty karated him into unconsciousness. Lefty then insured Clarence's silence with a judicious rap on the neck that made him collapse beside Tony on the floor.

Louie and Al herded the reluctant Sister Cordelia and her elderly flock into the safety of the hallway. It was time to rescue Willy. Lefty had his hand ready to strike. Sister Maeve had her gun pointed. Alvirah threw open the closet door as she bellowed, "Room service."

Sammy was standing next to Willy, his gun in Willy's neck. "Outside, all of you," he snarled. "Drop that gun, lady."

Maeve hesitated for a moment, then obeyed.

"Outside!" Sammy barked.

He's trapped and he's desperate, Alvirah thought frantically. He's going to kill my Willy. She forced herself to sound calm. "I've got a car in front of the hotel," she told him. "There's two million dollars in it. Take Willy and me with you. You can check the money, drive away and then let us out somewhere." She turned to Lefty and Maeve, "Don't try to stop us or he'll hurt Willy. Get lost all of you." She held her breath and stared at Willy's captor, willing herself to seem confident as the others left the room.

Sammy hesitated for an instant. Alvirah watched as he turned the gun to point toward the door. "It better be there, lady," he snapped. "Untie his feet."

Obediently she knelt down and yanked at the knots in the ropes binding Willy's ankles. She peeked up as she undid the last one. The gun was still pointed at the door. Alvirah remembered how she used to put her shoulder under Mrs. O'Keefe's piano and hoist it up to straighten out the carpet. One, two, three. She shot up like an arrow, her shoulder whamming into Sammy's gun hand. He pulled the trigger as he dropped the gun. The bullet released flaking paint from the drooping ceiling.

Willy threw his manacled hands around Sammy, bear-hugging him until the others rushed back into the room.

As though in a dream, Alvirah watched Lefty, Al and Louie free Willy from his handcuffs and ropes and use them to secure the abductors. She heard Maeve dial 911 and say, "This is Officer Maeve O'Reilly, I mean Sister Maeve Marie, reporting a kidnapping, attempted murder and successful apprehension of the perpetrators."

Alvirah felt Willy's arms around her. "Hi, honey," he whispered.

She was so filled with joy she couldn't speak. They gazed at each other. She took in his bloodshot eyes, stubble of beard and matted hair. He studied her garish makeup and DON'T BE A LITTERBUG sweatshirt. "Honey, you're gorgeous," Willy said fervently. "I'm sorry if I look like one of the Smith Brothers."

Alvirah rubbed her face against his. The tears of relief that were welling in her throat vanished as she began to laugh. "Oh, sweetie," she cried, "you'll always look like Tip O'Neill to me."

A
Clean
Sweep

*T*he phone rang, but Alvirah ignored it. She and Willy had only been home long enough to unpack, and already the answering machine had picked up six messages. They'd agreed that tomorrow would be time enough to catch up with the outside world.

It's nice to be home, she thought happily as she stepped out onto the terrace of their Central Park South apartment and looked down at the park, where now in late October the leaves had turned into a blazing rainbow of orange and crimson and yellow and russet.

She went back inside and settled on the couch. Willy handed her a cocktail, a Manhattan in honor of being back in the city, and carried his own to his big easy chair. He lifted his glass to her. "To us, honey."

Alvirah smiled fondly at him. "I have to say all that sightseeing does wear me out. I'm going to rest my hands and feet for at least two weeks," she said.

"Agreed," Willy nodded and then added sheepishly, "Honey, I still think riding those mules in Greece was a little much. I felt like a broken-down Hopalong Cassidy."

"Well, you *looked* like the Lone Ranger," Alvirah assured him. She paused, looking lovingly at her husband. "Willy, we've had so much fun, haven't we? If it weren't for the lottery I'd still be cleaning houses and you'd be fixing busted pipes."

And once again they sat in silent wonder, marveling over the wonderful event that had made a clean sweep of their former life. The dates of their birthdays and wedding anniversary were the numbers they'd always played, a dollar a week for ten years until the unbelievable moment when the lottery ticket with those numbers was pulled and they found themselves the sole winners of the forty-million-dollar prize.

As Alvirah said, "Willy, for us, life began at sixty, well, not quite sixty." So far among their travels, they'd been to Europe three times, to South America once, had taken the Trans-Siberian Railway from China to Russia and now had just returned from a cruise around the Greek islands.

The phone rang. Alvirah glanced at it. "Don't be tempted," Willy begged. "We need to get our breath. It's probably Cordelia, and she'll have a job for me, fixing the plumbing at the convent or something. It can wait a day."

They listened to the answering machine. It was Rhonda Alvirez, secretary of the Manhattan chapter of the Lottery Winners' Support Group. Rhonda, a founding member of the group, had won six million dollars in the lottery and been persuaded by a cousin to invest her first big check in his invention, a fast-acting drain cleaner. As it turned out, the only thing the cousin's cleaner whooshed down the drain was Rhonda's money.

That was when Rhonda started the support group, and when she read about how well Alvirah and Willy had handled their windfall, she begged them to be honorary members and regular guest lecturers.

Rhonda had already left one message. Now she got right to the point. "Alvirah, I know you're home. The limo dropped you off an hour ago. I checked with your doorman. Please pick up. This is important."

"And you think Cordelia's bad," Alvirah murmured as she obediently reached for the phone.

Willy watched her expression change to disbelief and concern and then heard her say, "Of course we'll talk to her. Tomorrow morning at ten. Here. Fine."

When she hung up she explained, "Willy, we're going to meet Nelly Monahan. From what Rhonda tells me she's a very nice woman, but much more important, she's a lottery winner who's been shafted by her ex-husband. We can't let that happen."

The next morning at nine o'clock, Nelly Monahan prepared to leave her three-room apartment in Stuyvesant Town, the East Side

204

housing development that she'd moved into over forty years ago as a twenty-two-year-old bride. Even though the rent was now ten times more than the fifty-nine dollars a month that had been the starting figure, the flat was still a terrific bargain, provided, of course, that you could spend nearly six hundred dollars a month for shelter.

But now that she was retired and living on a tiny pension and her monthly social security check, it had become painfully obvious to Nelly that she might have to give up the apartment and move in with her cousin Margaret in New Brunswick, New Jersey.

To Nelly, a dyed-in-the-wool New Yorker, the prospect of spending her final years away from the Big Apple was appalling. It had been bad enough that her husband, Tim, had walked out on her, but to give up the apartment broke her heart. And then to learn that Tim's new wife had produced that winning lottery ticket! It was just too much. That was when her neighbor suggested that Nelly call the support group, and now she had a meeting with Alvirah Meehan, who, Rhonda assured her, was a problem solver who got things done.

Nelly was a small, round, nondescript

woman with vaguely pretty features and lingering traces of brown in her gray hair, whose natural wave framed her face and softened the lines that time and hard work had etched around her eyes and mouth.

With her hesitant voice and shy smile, Nelly gave the outward appearance of being a pushover, but nothing could have been further from the truth. People who tried to take advantage of her soon learned that Nelly had a spunky streak and an implacable sense of justice.

Until her retirement at age sixty, she had worked as a bookkeeper for a small company that manufactured venetian blinds and, some years earlier, was the one who realized that the owner's nephew was bleeding the place dry. She'd persuaded her boss to make the nephew sell his house and pay back every dime he'd stolen or risk becoming a guest of the Department of Correction of New York.

And once, when a teenager tried to grab her pocketbook as he rode past her, she'd poked her umbrella into the spokes of his bicycle, causing him to go sprawling on the road with a sprained ankle. She alternately shouted for help and lectured the would-be mugger until the police came.

But these episodes paled compared to being cheated out of her nearly two-million-dollar share of the lottery money by her husband of forty years and her successor, Roxie, the new Mrs. Tim Monahan.

Nelly knew that Alvirah Meehan and her husband Willy lived in one of the fancy Central Park South buildings, so she dressed carefully for her meeting with them, selecting a brown tweed suit she'd bought on sale at A&S. She'd even gone to the extravagance of having her hair washed and set.

Promptly at 10:00 A.M. she was announced by the doorman.

At ten-thirty, Alvirah poured a second cup of coffee for their guest. For half an hour she'd deliberately kept the conversation general, talking about their shared backgrounds and changing life in the city. From her experience as an investigative columnist for the *New York Globe,* she'd learned that relaxed people tended to be better witnesses.

"Now let's get down to business," she said, touching the sunburst pin on the lapel of her jacket and turning on the recorder in it. "I'm going to be honest," she explained. "I'll be recording our conversation because sometimes when I play it back I pick up something that I missed."

Nelly's eyes sparkled. "Rhonda Alvirez told me you used that recorder to solve crimes. Well, let me tell you, I've got a crime for you, and the criminal's name is Tim Monahan."

She went on to explain, "In the forty years I was married to him, he could never hold a job because he always found a reason to file suit against his current employer. Tim spent more time in small claims court than Judge Wapner."

Nelly then enumerated the long list of defendants who had tangled with Tim, including the dry cleaner accused of putting a hole in an ancient pair of trousers, the bus company whose vehicle's sudden stop Tim said caused whiplash, the secondhand car dealer who refused to fix his car after the warranty expired, and Macy's, which was sued for a broken spring he discovered on a La-Z-Boy recliner Nelly had given him years before.

In her gentle voice she continued to tell them that Tim always considered himself a bit of a ladies' man and would gallantly rush to open doors for attractive girls while she, Nelly, walked behind him like the invisible woman. It had been especially annoying when he sang the praises of Roxie Marsh, who owned the catering outfit he worked for occasionally. Nelly had met the woman once and recognized that Roxie was the type who buttered up her help and then paid them slave wages.

She went on to explain also that while Tim drank a little too much, was a pain in the neck and looked particularly silly when he tried to act like Beau Brummell, he was nevertheless company of a sort, and after forty years she was used to him. Besides that she loved to cook and always enjoyed Tim's hearty appetite. It hadn't been perfect, but they had stuck it out.

Until they did or didn't win the lottery.

"Tell me about it," Alvirah ordered.

"We played the lottery every week, and one day I woke up feeling particularly lucky," Nelly explained earnestly. "It was the last chance to get in on the lottery for an eighteen-million-dollar pot. Tim was between jobs, and I gave him a dollar and told him to be sure to pick up a ticket when he bought his newspaper."

"And did he?" Alvirah asked quickly.

"Absolutely! When he got back, I asked him about it and he said yes, he'd bought it."

"Did you see the ticket?" Willy asked quickly.

Alvirah smiled at her husband. Willy was frowning. He seldom lost his temper, but when he did he looked and sounded remarkably like his sister Cordelia. Willy would have no use for a man who cheated his wife.

"I didn't ask to see it," Nelly explained as she swallowed the last of her coffee. "He always held the ticket in his wallet. Besides, there was no need. We always played the same numbers."

"So do we," Alvirah told her. "Our birthdays and wedding anniversary."

"Tim and I took ours from the street addresses of the houses we grew up in—1802 and 1913 Tenbroeck Avenue in the Bronx, and 405 East Fourteenth Street, the number of our building all these years. That came out to be 18-2-19-13-4-5.

"Tim didn't say one word about picking different numbers. That was on Saturday. The next Wednesday I was watching the TV when our number was pulled, and you can't imagine my shock."

"Yes I can," Alvirah told her. "I had cleaned for Mrs. O'Keefe the day we won, and let me tell you, she'd had all her grandchildren in the day before and the place was a mess. I was bone tired and soaking my feet when our numbers were pulled."

"She kicked over the pail," Willy explained. "We spent our first ten minutes as multimillionaires mopping up the living room."

"Then you do understand," Nelly sighed. She went on to explain that Tim had been out that night, working his occasional job as a bartender for Roxie the caterer. Nelly had sat up waiting for him and to celebrate had made his favorite dessert, a crème brûlée.

But when he got home, a tearful Tim handed her the ticket he was holding. It wasn't the numbers they always played. Every single one was different. "I decided to change our luck," Tim told her.

"I thought I'd have a heart attack," Nelly said. "But he felt so terrible that I ended up telling him it didn't matter, that it just wasn't to be."

"And I bet he ate the crème brûlée," Alvirah snapped.

"Every speck. He said every man should be so lucky as to have a wife like me. Then a few weeks after, he walked out on me and moved in with Roxie. He told me he'd fallen in love with her. That was a year ago. The divorce came through last month and he married Roxie three weeks ago.

"They'd announced that there were four

winners of the eighteen-million-dollar pot, and I didn't realize that one of them hadn't shown up to collect. Then last week, on the very last day before the ticket expired, Roxie, now the second Mrs. Tim Monahan, showed up at the redemption window and claimed she'd just happened to realize she had the fourth ticket, the ticket with the numbers Tim and I always played."

"Tim was working for Roxie the night your number won, and he had the ticket in his wallet?" Alvirah asked, to confirm her suspicion.

"Yes, that's the point. He had big eyes for her all along and probably showed the ticket to her."

"And she's a flirt who saw her big chance," Willy said. "That's disgusting."

"If you want to know what disgusting is, I'll show you the picture of the two of them in the *Post* saying how lucky they were that Roxie happened to find her ticket," Nelly's voice quivered into a near sob. Then she got a flinty look in her eye, and her jaw moved out an inch. "It's not justice," she said. "There's a retired lawyer, Dennis O'Shea, living down the hall from me, and I spoke to him about it. He did some research and learned that there are a couple of other cases on record where one spouse or the other pulled that scam and the court decided that the one holding the ticket is the owner. He said that it was a disgrace and a horror and a terrible shame, but legally I was out of luck."

"How did you happen to go to a meeting of the Lottery Winners' Support Group?" Alvirah asked.

"Dennis sent me. He'd read about all the people who lost all the money they made on the lottery in bad investments and thought it might help me to be around kindred souls."

Righteous wrath in her voice and a certain mulish expression around her mouth, Nelly summed up her luckless saga. "Tim moved out on me faster than you can say abracadabra, and now the two of them will live the life of Reilly while I move in with my cousin Margaret because I can't afford to stay where I am. Margaret only asked me to live with her because she likes my cooking. She talks so much I'll probably be stone deaf in a year."

"There's got to be a way to help," Alvirah decreed. "Let me put on my thinking cap. I'll call you tomorrow."

• • •

At nine o'clock the next morning, Nelly sat at the dinette table in her Stuyvesant Town apartment, enjoying a warm bagel and a cup of coffee. It may not be Central Park South, she thought, but it's a wonderful place to live. Since Tim took off, she'd made little changes in the apartment. He'd always insisted on keeping that big, ugly recliner of his right by the window, but since he'd taken it with him when he moved out, she'd rearranged the rest of the furniture the way she'd always secretly wanted and then she'd made bright new slipcovers for the couch and wing chair and bought a lovely hooked rug for next to nothing from neighbors who were moving.

Looking now at the autumn sun streaming in, and seeing how cheerful and inviting the place was, she reflected on how more and more she'd come to realize that Tim had been a lifelong drag and that she really was better off without him.

The trouble was that she couldn't make ends meet without his pitiful income, and try as she did, she couldn't find a job. Who wants to hire a sixty-two-year-old woman who can't use a computer? Answer: nobody.

Margaret had already called this morning. "Why don't you give the apartment up on the first and save a month's rent? I'm having the back bedroom painted for you."

How about the kitchen? Nelly wondered. I bet that's where you really expect me to spend my time.

It was all so hopeless. Nelly took a sip of her excellent, fresh-brewed coffee and sighed.

Then Alvirah called.

"We've got a plan," she said. "I want you to go and see Roxie and Tim and get them to admit they shafted you."

"Why would they admit it?"

"Get one of them mad enough to brag that they put one over on you. Do you think you can do that?"

"Oh, I can get Roxie's goat," Nelly said. "When they got married last month, I found a picture of Tim at Jones Beach where he looks like a beached whale and I had it framed and sent it to her. On it, I wrote, 'Congratulations and good riddance.' "

"I like you, Nelly," Alvirah chuckled. "You're a woman after my own heart. Here's the plan. One way or another you're going to make a date to see them and you're going to wear an exact copy of my sunburst pin. My editor had a couple of extras made for me."

"Alvirah, your pin looks valuable."

"It's valuable because it has the recorder in it. You're going to turn it on, get them to admit that they cheated you, and then we're going to get your lawyer friend, Dennis O'Shea, to sign a complaint to Matrimonial Court that you were cheated out of marital assets."

A faint hope stirred in Nelly's ample bosom. "Alvirah, do you really think there's a chance?"

"It's about the only chance," Alvirah said quietly.

For several minutes after getting off the phone, Nelly sat deep in thought. She remembered how a couple of years ago when Tim's mother was dying, the old woman had asked him to tell the truth: Hadn't he been the one who set the garage on fire when he was eight years old? He'd always denied it, but that day, seeing she was breathing her last, he broke down and confessed. I know how to get to him, Nelly thought as she reached for the phone.

Tim answered. When he heard her voice he sounded irritated. "Listen, Nelly, we're packing up to go to Florida for good, so what's up?"

216

Nelly crossed her fingers. "Tim, I've got bad news. I don't have more than another month." And I don't, she thought. At least not in Stuyvesant Town.

Tim sounded at least somewhat concerned. "Nelly, that's too bad. Are you sure?"

"Very sure."

"I'll pray for you."

"That's why I'm calling. I have to say I've had some pretty nasty thoughts about you in these weeks since Roxie turned in the lottery ticket."

"It was her ticket."

"I know."

"I mean I used to tell her how we played those numbers and she tried them for luck that week and I tried some other combination."

"Her numbers?"

"I forget," Tim said quickly. "Look, Nelly, I'm sorry, but we're leaving tomorrow, and the movers are coming in the morning. I've got a lot to do."

"Tim, I have to see you. I'm trying to get my soul in readiness, and I've hated you and Roxie so much I have to see you face to face and talk to you. Otherwise I'll never die in peace." More straight truth, Nelly thought.

From the background, she heard a strident voice yell, "Tim, who the hell is that?"

Tim lowered his voice and said quickly, "We're leaving on a noon plane tomorrow. Be here at ten o'clock. But Nelly, I have to tell you. I can only spare fifteen minutes."

"That's all I want, Tim," Nelly said, her voice even softer than usual. She hung up the phone and dialed Alvirah. "He's giving me fifteen minutes tomorrow morning," she said. "Alvirah, I could kill him."

"That won't do you any good," Alvirah said. "Come on over this afternoon and I'll show you how to work the pin."

The next day at nine o'clock, Nelly was about to put on her coat when the doorbell rang. It was Dennis O'Shea, the nice retired lawyer who lived down the hall in 8F. He'd moved there about six months ago. A number of times he'd fallen in step with her when they met at the elevator. He was on the small side, maybe five seven or so, with a neat, compact build, kindly eyes behind frameless glasses, and a pleasant, intelligent face.

He'd told her that his wife had died two years ago, and when he'd retired from the

Legal Aid Society at age sixty-five, he decided to sell the house in Syosset and move back to the city. He split his time now between the apartment and his cottage on Cape Cod.

Nelly could tell that, like her, Dennis had a strong sense of justice and didn't like the underdog to be pushed around. That was why she'd had the courage to ask him for advice when Roxie turned in the winning ticket.

This morning, Dennis looked worried. "Nelly," he said, "are you sure you know how to turn on that recorder?"

"Oh, sure, you just sort of run your hand over the fake diamond in the center."

"Show me."

She did.

"Say something."

"Go to hell, Tim."

"That's the spirit. Now play it back."

She snapped the cassette out of the pin and put it in the machine Alvirah had also given her and then pushed the replay button. Nothing happened.

"I guess you told your friend Alvirah Meehan about me," Dennis said. "She called a few minutes ago and explained what's going on. She said that you seemed to have trouble turning on the recorder."

Nelly felt her fingers tremble. She hadn't been able to sleep all night. Her share of the winnings was just maybe, possibly within her grasp. But if this didn't work, it was all over. She hadn't shed one tear all this year, but right now, looking at the concern on Dennis O'Shea's face, she felt her eyes fill up. "Show me what I'm doing wrong," she said.

For the next ten minutes they tried turning the recorder on and off, saying a few words, then playing it back. The trick was to snap that little switch firmly. Finally Nelly said, "I have it. Thanks, Dennis."

"My pleasure. Nelly, you get them on record saying they cheated you, and I'll have them in Matrimonial Court so fast they won't know what hit them."

"But they're moving to Florida."

"The lottery checks are issued in New York. Let me worry about that part of it."

He waited with her at the elevator. "You know what bus to take."

"It's not that far to Christopher Street. I'll walk at least one way."

• • •

Alvirah had a busy morning. At eight she started vigorously cleaning the already spotless apartment. At quarter to nine she had looked up Dennis O'Shea's phone number and called him, explaining her worry that Nelly might not have the hang of using the recorder; then she got back to polishing the polished. To Willy, it was an unmistakable sign that she was deeply concerned.

"What's eating you, honey?" he asked finally.

"I have a bad feeling," she admitted.

"You're afraid Nelly won't be able to handle the recorder?"

"I'm worried about that, and I'm worried that she may not be able to get them to say a word, and most of all I'm worried that they tell her everything and she doesn't get it on tape."

Nelly was meeting her ex-husband and Roxie at ten. At ten-thirty Alvirah sat down and stared at the phone. At ten thirty-five it rang. It was Cordelia, looking for Willy. "One of our old girls has a leak in her kitchen ceiling," Cordelia said. "The whole apartment is starting to smell mildewed. Send Willy right over."

"Later, Cordelia. We're waiting for an important message." Alvirah knew there was no getting off without explaining the problem.

"You should have told me before," Cordelia snapped. "I'll start praying."

By noon Alvirah was a total wreck. She called Dennis O'Shea again. "Any word from Nelly?"

"No. Mrs. Meehan, Nelly told me that Tim Monahan was only going to give her fifteen minutes."

"I know."

Finally, at twelve-fifteen, the phone rang. Alvirah grabbed it. "Hello."

"Alvirah."

It was Nelly. Alvirah tried to analyze the tone of her voice. Strained? No. Shocked. Yes, that's what it was. Shocked. Nelly sounded as though she was in a trance.

"What happened?" Alvirah demanded. "Did they admit it?"

"Yes."

"Did you get it on tape?"

"No."

"Oh, that's terrible. I'm so sorry."

"That's not the worst of it."

"What do you mean, Nelly?"

There was a long pause, then Nelly sighed. "Alvirah, Tim's dead. I shot him."

222

• • •

Five hours later, Alvirah and Willy posted bond after Dennis O'Shea, Nelly's self-appointed lawyer, pled her not guilty to charges of second-degree murder, first-degree manslaughter and carrying a concealed weapon. Nelly rose from her trancelike lethargy only long enough to say in a surprised voice, "But I did kill him."

They took her home. Half a Sara Lee crumb cake, neatly enveloped in plastic, was on the kitchen counter. "Tim always loved that cake," Nelly said sadly. "He looked awful today even before he died. I don't think Roxie cooked much for him."

Alvirah was feeling wretched. All this had been her big idea. Now Nelly was facing long years in prison. At her age that could mean the rest of her life. Yesterday Nelly had said that she could kill Tim. And I joked about it, Alvirah thought. I told her that wouldn't do any good. I never thought she meant it. How did she happen to have a gun?

She put on the kettle. "I think we'd better talk," she said. "But first I'll make a nice strong cup of tea for you, Nelly."

• • •

Nelly told her story in a flat, emotionless voice. "I decided to walk down to Christopher Street, to get my thoughts together, you know what I mean? I took the pin off and put it in my pocketbook. It's so pretty I was afraid I'd get mugged for it. Then on Tenth Street and Avenue B, I saw a couple of kids. They couldn't have been more than ten or eleven. Can you believe one of them was showing the other a gun?"

She stared ahead. "Let me tell you, I saw red. Those boys were not only playing hookey but treating that gun like a cap pistol. I marched up to them and told them to hand it over."

"You what?" Dennis O'Shea blinked.

"The one who wasn't holding the gun said, 'Shoot her,' but I think the other kid must've thought I was an undercover cop or something," Nelly continued. "Anyhow, he looked scared and handed it to me. I told them that kids their age should be in school and should play stickball, the way boys did when we were growing up."

Alvirah nodded. "So you had the gun with you when you went to see Tim and Roxie?"

"I couldn't take time to turn it in at the police station. Tim was only giving me fifteen minutes. As it turned out, I didn't need more than ten."

Alvirah saw that Willy was about to ask a question. She shook her head. It was obvious that Nelly was about to relive the scene in her mind. "All right, Nelly," she said softly. "What happened when you were with them?"

"I was a couple of minutes late. They're making a movie on Christopher Street, and I had to push through a lot of people who were gawking at the actors. The movers were just leaving when I got there. Roxie let me in. I don't think Tim had told her I was coming. Her mouth sort of dropped open when she saw me. The living room was empty except for Tim's old recliner, and he was camped in it, as usual. Didn't even get up like a gentleman. Then Mrs. Tim Monahan the Second, bold as brass, says to me, 'Get lost.'

"I was so nervous by then that I looked right at Tim and just blurted out everything I had rehearsed, that I only had a month left and that I wanted his forgiveness for being so angry at him, that it didn't matter about the ticket, that I was glad he had someone to take care of him. But before I died, just like his mother, I wanted to hear the truth."

"You told them that!" Willy exclaimed.

"You're smart," Alvirah breathed.

"Anyhow, Tim had a funny look on his face, like he was going to laugh, and he said that it had been bothering him from the start. That yes, he had bought the winning ticket and switched it with Roxie and he had kept it in a safe-deposit box at the bank on West Fourth Street until he took it out and gave it to Roxie to cash in last month and he was sorry for my trouble and I was a fine, generous woman."

"He admitted it just like that!" Alvirah said.

"So fast that I almost collapsed, and he was laughing when he said it. Now I'm pretty sure that he was just making fun of me. I realized I didn't have the pin on and I opened my pocketbook and started to fumble for it and Roxie yelled something about the gun and I took it out to explain and it went off and Tim went down like a load of blubber. And after that it's all vague. Roxie tried to grab the gun, and the next thing I knew I was in the police station."

She reached for her cup. "So I guess I don't have to worry about keeping this apartment or about going to my cousin's in New Brunswick. Do you think they'll send me to the same prison where they keep that woman who had her husband shot because she wanted to keep the dog when they were divorced?''

She put the cup down and slowly stood up. As Alvirah and Willy and Dennis O'Shea watched, her face crumbled. ''Oh my God,'' she said, ''how could I have shot Tim?''

Then she fainted.

The next morning, Alvirah came back from visiting Nelly in the hospital. ''They're going to keep her for a few days,'' she told Willy. ''It's just as well. The newspapers are having a field day. Take a look.'' She handed him the *Post*. The front page showed an hysterically weeping Roxie watching Tim's corpse being carried from the apartment.

''According to this, Roxie claims that Nelly just showed up and started shooting.''

''We can testify that she had made an appointment with Tim,'' Willy said, ''but Nelly did say that Roxie didn't seem to expect her.'' His forehead furrowed as he considered the situation. ''Dennis O'Shea phoned while you were out. He thinks it would be a good idea to plea-bargain.''

Alvirah flicked a piece of lint from the sleeve of her smartly tailored pantsuit. It was an outfit she usually enjoyed wearing. It was only a size 14 and she could close the button at the waist of the slacks without too much yanking. But today nothing could give her comfort. Nelly may have been cheated out of her lottery ticket, but I'm the one who gave her a ticket to prison, she thought.

"I've been thinking that if I could possibly find those kids Nelly took the gun from, it would at least prove that she didn't intend to go there with it. I made her describe them to me."

The thought of action brought a little relief. "I'd better change into some old duds so I can just hang around. That isn't a great neighborhood."

An hour later, wearing ancient jeans, a tired Mickey Mouse sweatshirt, and her sunburst pin, Alvirah took up her vigil on the corner of Avenue B and Tenth Street. The boys Nelly had described were about ten or eleven years old. One was short and thin with curly hair and brown eyes, the other was taller and heavyset. They both had duck haircuts and wore gold chains and an earring.

The odds of just running into them were

small, and after thirty minutes Alvirah began to systematically work her way through the neighborhood stores. She bought a newspaper in one, two apples in another, aspirin in the drugstore. In each place she began a conversation. It was with the shoemaker that she finally hit pay dirt.

"Sure I know those two. The little guy is big trouble. The other isn't a bad kid. They usually hang around that corner." He pointed out the window. "This morning the cops were picking up truants and taking them back to school, so I guess they won't be here till three o'clock."

Delighted with the information, Alvirah rewarded the shoemaker by purchasing an assortment of polishes, none of which she needed. As he slowly counted out change, he explained that he'd dropped and stepped on his reading glasses, but that at a distance he could see a gnat sneeze. Then, glancing past her, he exclaimed, "There are the kids you're looking for." He pointed across the street. "They musta sneaked out of school again."

Alvirah spun around. "Forget about the change," she called as she dashed out of the store.

An hour later she dejectedly related to Willy and Dennis O'Shea what had happened. "When I talked to them, they'd just seen Nelly's picture in the *Post* and recognized her. Those little skunks were on their way to the police station to report that Nelly came up to them and asked where she could buy a gun because she needed one right away and offered them a hundred bucks. They claim they didn't know where to get one but later some other kid bragged about selling one to her."

"That's a damn lie," Dennis said flatly. "Just before Nelly left her apartment yesterday morning she checked her wallet. I couldn't help but notice she didn't have more than three or four dollars in it. Why would those kids lie like that?"

"Because Nelly took their gun away," Alvirah told him, "and this is their chance to get even." She realized she did not know why Dennis had been sitting in the living room talking to Willy when she arrived home.

But when he told her the reason, she was sorry she'd asked. The autopsy was complete. One bullet had grazed Tim's forehead.

The other two had lodged in his heart, and from the angle of entry it was clear they'd been fired after he was lying on the floor. The district attorney had called Dennis to tell him the plea bargain was now first-degree aggravated manslaughter with a minimum of fifteen years in prison. Take it or leave it. "And when I spoke to him he hadn't heard from those kids," Dennis concluded.

"Does Nelly know about this yet?" Alvirah asked.

"I saw her this morning just after you left. She intends to check out of the hospital tomorrow and get her affairs in order. She said she has to pay for her crime."

"I kind of hate to bring this up," Willy offered, "but is it possible that Nelly did buy the gun and was mad enough to mean to kill Tim?"

"She pointed the gun at his heart when he was on the floor?" Alvirah exclaimed. "I can't believe it."

"I don't think she did it deliberately," O'Shea agreed. "But she did kill him. Her prints are on the gun." He got up. "I'd better call and get the plea bargain in motion. I'll see if they'll give Nelly a little time before she has to start serving her sentence."

"He likes Nelly," Willy observed when he'd let Dennis O'Shea out.

"He's the kind of man she should have been with all these years," Alvirah agreed. Suddenly she felt old and tired. I'm just a meddling fool, she thought. Once again she could hear herself advising Nelly to go see Tim. And she could also hear Nelly saying, "I could kill him."

Willy patted her hand, and she looked up at him gratefully. He was her best friend as well as the best husband in the world. Poor Nelly had put up with a guy who couldn't hold a job, who fought with everyone, who drank too much, and who was the size of a beached whale.

Why the heck did Roxie marry him?

For the ticket, of course.

That night Alvirah could not sleep. Over and over she considered every single detail, and it all added up to one thing: fifteen years in prison for Nelly Monahan. Finally, at two o'clock, she got out of bed, being careful not to disturb Willy, who was clearly in the second stage of sleep. A few minutes later, armed with a steaming pot of tea, she sat at the dining table and played back the recording she had made of the first meeting with Nelly and then her confession after they bailed her out.

She was missing something. What was it? She got up, went to the desk, got a spiral notebook and pen, returned to the table and rewound the tape. Then as she played it back, she took notes.

When he got up at seven o'clock, Willy found her poring over her notes. He knew what she was doing. He put on the kettle and settled at the table across from her. "Can't figure out what you're missing," he commented. "Let me take a look."

A half hour passed. And then Willy said, "I can't see anything. But reading about Tim's recliner makes me think of old Buster Kelly. Remember he had a recliner too. Even insisted on moving it into the nursing home with him."

"Willy, say that again."

"Buster Kelly insisted on moving his recliner—"

"Willy, that's it. Tim was sitting in his recliner when Nelly went to the apartment." Alvirah reached across the table and grabbed her notebook. "Look. Nelly says that the moving men were just pulling away when she got there. Why didn't the recliner go with

them?'' She jumped up. "Willy, don't you see? Tim had a reason for telling Nelly he'd cheated her. I bet you anything Roxie had just told him to go stuff it. She stuck with him until he handed her the lottery ticket and she turned it in. Then she didn't need him anymore.''

The more she said, the surer Alvirah was that she'd hit the nail on the head. Her voice rose in excitement as she continued. "Tim was trying to keep Nelly from claiming a share in the ticket and never thought that Roxie would double-cross him. I'll bet her telling those moving men to leave the recliner was the first notice he'd gotten that Roxie was going to dump him.''

"And by admitting to Nelly that he'd cheated her, he thought he'd get the ticket back and have half the money. It makes sense,'' Willy agreed.

"Nelly didn't kill Tim. That first bullet just grazed his forehead. Roxie didn't grab her hand to take the gun away but to aim it at Tim.''

They stared at each other. Willy's eyes shone with admiration. "Smartest redhead in the world,'' he said. "There's just one problem, honey. How are you going to prove it?''

• • •

How was she going to prove it? Alvirah made a list of where to start. She wanted to talk to the movers who had cleared out Roxie's apartment. Tim had told Nelly that he'd kept the lottery ticket in a safe-deposit box in a bank around the corner from Christopher Street. She wanted to find it and see when he took out the box and whose name was on it. Finally she wanted to talk to the superintendent of the building where Roxie and Tim had their little love nest.

Yet even as her brain busily worked away, it was with an overriding sense that she was spinning wheels. The fact remained that it would be almost impossible to prove that Roxie had guided Nelly's hand.

At nine o'clock she called Charley Evans at the *Globe,* and explained her needs. At ten he called back. Stalwart Van company had picked up the contents of Roxie and Tim's apartment, he reported. The three guys assigned to the job were working on East Fiftieth Street today. The Greenwich Savings Bank on West Fourth had a safe-deposit box in the name of Timothy Monahan. He rented it last year and closed it out three weeks ago. "They're willing to talk to you."

Alvirah wrote swiftly, said, "Charley, you're a doll," then hung up and turned to Willy. "Come on, honey."

Their first stop was at East Fiftieth Street, where the Stalwart Van movers were dismantling an apartment. They hung around the van until the three returned, struggling under the weight of a nine-foot breakfront.

Alvirah waited until they hoisted it into the cavelike back of the truck, then introduced herself. "I won't take a minute of your time, but it's important I ask a few questions." Willy opened his wallet and displayed three twenty-dollar bills.

They cheerfully explained that Tim hadn't been in the apartment when they got there. In fact, when he did come back just before ten, they could tell he wasn't expected. Roxie had yelled, "I told you to get a haircut. You look like a slob."

The burly mover chuckled. "Then he said something about having an appointment at ten that he didn't think she'd like, and she said, 'What appointment, to fix yourself a drink?' "

"We were on the way out the door and the guy yelled for us to come back and get his recliner and the wife told us to just get going," the smallest mover, the one who had carried the heaviest part of the breakfront, volunteered.

"And in court it wouldn't prove anything," Willy reminded Alvirah an hour later when they left the Greenwich Savings Bank, having confirmed that Tim Monahan rented the safe-deposit box a year ago, the morning after the disputed winning ticket was drawn, and visited it only once, the day he gave it up three weeks ago. That day he'd been accompanied by a flashy-looking woman. The clerk identified Roxie's picture. "That's the one."

"He went into the vault and gave up that safe-deposit box half an hour before they showed up at the clerk's office to turn in the ticket," Alvirah said, every inch of her throbbing with frustration.

"I know they did," Willy agreed, "but—"

"But legally it doesn't prove anything. Oh, Willy, it may not do any good, but let's try to get a look at the apartment they lived in."

They turned the corner and were treated to a crowd of spectators pressing against stanchions as they watched Tom Cruise catch up with a fleeing Demi Moore and spin her around.

"Nelly said they were filming a scene here

the other day," Alvirah commented. "Well, we've got better things to do than gawk."

She was at the door of 101 Christopher Street when a familiar voice yelled, "Aunt Alvirah."

She and Willy spun around as a thin young man with half-glasses on the end of his nose expertly made his way to them.

"Brian, as I live and breathe."

Brian was the son of Willy's deceased sister, Madaline. Now a successful playwright, to Willy and Alvirah he was the son they never had.

"I thought you were in London," Alvirah said as she hugged him.

"I thought you were in Greece. I just got back, and they wanted some additional dialogue. I wrote the screenplay for this epic." He nodded to the cameras down the street. "Look, I've got to get back over there. I'll catch you later."

An overhead camera anchored to a van was being positioned down the block. Subconsciously Alvirah made note of it as she rang the superintendent's bell at 101.

Ten minutes later she and Willy were being shown the three-bedroom apartment where the late Tim Monahan had breathed his last.

"You're in luck," the superintendent informed them. "Roxie just called yesterday to say she didn't want the apartment anymore, so nobody knows it's available. And you're the kind of tenants the management wants," he added virtuously as he thought of Alvirah's check for a thousand dollars nestled in his hip pocket.

"You mean she wasn't going to give it up when she moved to Florida?"

"No. She said it might be needed, but she'd switched it to Tim's name."

The late Tim Monahan's battered recliner caught the morning sun. The rest of the room was empty. The remains of the chalk marks on the floor the police had made to indicate where Tim's body had lain were still visible.

A shadow passed over the chair. Startled, Alvirah turned and was treated to the sight of the Mirage Films van with the camera passing outside. "That's it," she said.

The next morning, Nelly Monahan sat on a chair in her room in Lenox Hill Hospital, waiting to be discharged. On her lap she had a lined pad on which she was making notes of everything she had to do before she went to prison. A saddened Dennis O'Shea had told her that the district attorney would only let her plead guilty to a lesser offense if she would accept fifteen years in prison without the possibility of parole.

"It's only justice," she'd told him quietly. "I must pay for what I did." Then when he took her hand, she'd winced. Her wrist was sore, probably because Roxie had tried so hard to wrestle the gun from her, and there was a scrape on her index finger from where she'd scratched it trying to turn on the recorder in the pin.

Then Dennis said he thought they should go to trial and he'd represent her, but she said it wouldn't be right for her to get off. She had taken a life.

"Give up apartment," Nelly wrote now. "Turn off phone."

She looked up. A smartly dressed Alvirah was at the door. "You look nice, Alvirah," she said admiringly. "Do you know what color the prison uniforms are? It's funny. Last night I was just lying awake thinking about things like that."

"Don't worry about prison uniforms," Alvirah told her. "It ain't over till it's over. Now I'm going to take you home in a taxi, and I called Dennis and said you are *not,* repeat, *not* going near the district attorney's office or signing anything until I put my plan in action, starting with interviewing the heartbroken widow of the late Tim Monahan."

Roxie Marsh Monahan debated about what to wear for her meeting with Alvirah Meehan. It was exciting to think of having a whole article written about her in the *Globe.* She'd loved the story in the *Post* but was sorry she hadn't had her hair done Monday the way she'd planned. It had looked a little stringy in the picture of her watching Tim's body being carried out. But on the other hand, she'd been crying hysterically, so maybe it was better that her hair was going every which way. Kind of rounded out the effect.

She glanced around. The junior suite in the Omni Park Hotel was very attractive. She'd rented it the day of the shooting. The district attorney's office had asked her to stay in New York for a short time while all the facts of the case were settled. They'd told her that Nelly was undoubtedly going to cop a plea, so there wouldn't be any trial.

Roxie decided that in a way she'd miss

New York, but she loved golf and in Florida could play it every day without worrying about rattling dishes for some dreary party. Catering was hell. God, she didn't think she'd ever cook so much as a string bean for herself again.

She smiled. She'd been wrapped in a warm glow of anticipation ever since that dumb bunny Tim had handed her the ticket just as they went into the lottery office. Actually, Tim wasn't so dumb. That first night when he'd showed her the winning ticket she'd offered to hold it for him. No way, he'd told her. He wanted to make sure that they were really compatible.

She'd been stuck with having to look at that dopey face every day, listen to him snore at night, see him plopped in that shabby recliner with a beer in his hand, act happy when he slobbered all over her with clumsy kisses. She'd earned every nickel of two hundred thousand or so bucks less taxes she had coming in each year for the next twenty years.

She held up the two black suits she'd bought in Annie Sez yesterday. One had gold buttons. The other, sequin lapels. Gold buttons it would be. The sequins looked a little too festive. Roxie dressed, put on her customary bangles and turquoise rings. She knew she didn't look fifty-three. She knew that with her blond hair and snazzy figure, she was still very attractive. And now she could afford to stay that way.

It all added up to catching a really interesting guy.

Thank you, Tim Monahan. Thank you, Nelly Monahan. Incredible the way I snatched victory from the jaws of defeat, Roxie exulted. Her one blunder had been to tell Tim the truth when he saw that the movers were leaving and his recliner was still squatting in the living room. She should have bluffed it out somehow. She certainly would have kept her mouth shut if she'd known that Nelly Monahan would ring the doorbell seconds after she told Tim to jump in the lake, that he wasn't going with her. As Roxie reshaped her lips, the phone rang. Alvirah Meehan was in the lobby.

"Our angle is to talk about how the winning lottery ticket has led to such tragedy for you," Alvirah sympathized as she sat opposite Roxie a few minutes later.

Roxie dabbed at her eyes. "I'm sorry I ever found it in my makeup drawer. I came across it under a box of Q-tips and I'd just read an article about how a lot of people don't realize they have a winning ticket and never know they might have been millionaires and the number to call was listed, so I laughed and I said to Tim, 'Wouldn't it be a gasser if this was a lucky ticket?' "

Alvirah turned slightly so that the recorder in her sunburst pin wouldn't miss a word. "And what did he say?"

"Oh, that silly darling said, 'Don't waste the phone call unless it's an eight hundred number.' " Roxie squeezed tears from her eyes. "I'm sorry now I did."

"You'd rather be catering, wouldn't you?"

"Yes," Roxie sobbed. "Yes."

Alvirah never used vulgar language, but a familiar vulgarity almost escaped her lips. Instead, through gritted teeth, she managed to say, "I have just a few more questions and then our photographer wants to take some pictures."

Roxie's sobs ended abruptly. "Let me check my makeup."

Mel Levine, the top photographer from the *Globe,* had his marching orders: *Get good close-ups of her hands.*

• • •

Willy's oldest living sibling, Sister Cordelia, did not like to be left out of anything. Knowing that Alvirah was involved with Nelly Monahan, the woman who had shot her exhusband in the presence of his second wife, made Cordelia decide to pay an unannounced visit to Central Park South.

Accompanied by Sister Maeve Marie, a young policewoman turned novice, Cordelia had arrived at the apartment and was ensconced in the wing chair in the living room when Alvirah arrived home. Since the chair was upholstered in handsome crimson velvet and Cordelia still wore an ankle-length habit and short veil, Alvirah had the immediate and familiar thought that if a woman pope were ever elected, she would look like Cordelia.

"Cordelia just dropped by," Willy explained, his right eyebrow lifted. That was a signal he hadn't brought Cordelia up to date on their plans.

"I hope it's not an inconvenience, Alvirah," Sister Maeve Marie apologized. "Sister Superior felt you might need our help." Maeve had the slender, disciplined body of an athlete. Her face, dominated by wide gray eyes, was strikingly handsome. Like Willy's, her expression was saying, "Sorry, Alvirah, but you know Cordelia."

"So what's going on?" Cordelia asked, getting straight to the point.

Alvirah knew there was absolutely no other choice than to tell her the truth, the whole truth and nothing but the truth. She sank down on the couch, wishing she'd had time for a peaceful cup of tea with Willy before the visit. "We have to get Nelly off. It's my fault that she went to see Tim, and I can't let her spend the rest of her life in prison."

Cordelia nodded. "So what are you going to do about it?"

"Something you may not like. Brian wrote a screenplay for Mirage Films."

"I know that. I hope he can trust them not to put a lot of smut in it. What's that got to do with Nelly Monahan, poor soul?"

"The day of the shooting, Mirage was filming a scene right outside the building where Roxie and Tim Monahan lived. We're going to try to make Roxie believe that the camera caught her twisting Nelly's hand and pointing the gun at Tim."

"You're going to fake it?" Cordelia exploded.

"Exactly. Brian got the producer to agree

to cooperate. Mel, the *Globe* photographer, took a lot of pictures of Roxie today. Besides that, we have pictures of her when Tim's body was being carried out. We've got to find a model who in a blurry long shot resembles Roxie. We'll dress her in the same kind of striped pantsuit Roxie was wearing and do a close-up of her grabbing Nelly's hand. I still have to talk Nelly into this, but I'll manage it."

Willy gave her an encouraging nod and continued the explanation. "Cordelia, we've already put a deposit on the apartment. The only furniture in the room was Tim's recliner, and it's still there. The chalk marks where the body was lying are visible. I'll take Tim's part. I mean I'll stretch out on the floor by the re-cliner. Nelly said Tim was wearing a gray sweat suit and moccasins."

Sister Maeve Marie's eyes were snapping with excitement. "When I was a cop we called that 'testalying.' I love it."

Willy looked at Cordelia. He knew Alvirah had every intention of carrying out her scheme. Even so, it would help if Cordelia wouldn't try to throw a monkey wrench in the plans. Alvirah was worried enough about having set up the scheme that got Nelly in so much trouble. When Cordelia didn't approve of a course of action, she had an uncanny way of convincing you it was destined for failure.

Cordelia frowned momentarily, then her brow cleared. "God writes straight in crooked lines," she said. "When are we going to film?"

Alvirah felt a wave of relief. "As soon as possible. We've got to find an actress who can impersonate Roxie." As she spoke she was looking at Sister Maeve Marie. Like Roxie, Maeve was tall and had a good figure. Like Roxie, her hands were well shaped with long fingers.

"I'm very glad you two came," she said heartily.

Two days later they were ready to close the trap. In the Christopher Street apartment where Tim Monahan had gone to his Maker, Brian was directing the action.

"Uncle Willy, just lie down there. We had to erase the chalk marks, but we penciled in the outline."

Obediently Willy stretched out by the recliner.

Brian and the cameraman stepped outside, and Brian peered through the lens, then consulted the picture of the dead Tim that the editor at the *Globe* had managed to get copied by bribing an aide in the medical examiner's office.

"You don't look fat enough," Brian decreed.

"Good news," Willy mumbled.

The problem was solved when Brian took off his sweater and stuffed it under Willy's sweatshirt.

Nelly was standing in the corner. She was wearing the blue suit and print blouse she'd worn when she visited Tim and Roxie. In her purse she was carrying a gun that looked just like the one that she had taken from the boys the other day.

Only four days ago, she thought. It doesn't seem possible. She peeked over at Dennis O'Shea, who gave her an encouraging smile. Then she glanced at Sister Maeve, who looked unnervingly like Roxie. She had on a blond wig and an exact copy of the striped suit Roxie had been wearing when she became the widow Monahan. An outsized turquoise ring reached the knuckle of her index finger. Acrylic blood-red fingernails accentuated her long fingers, and wrinkles and liver spots had been painted on the backs of her hands. Just like Roxie, Nelly thought with a touch of satisfaction as she glanced down at her own smooth skin.

Sister Cordelia was watching the proceedings with her arms folded. She reminded Nelly of the nuns she'd had in parochial school.

Brian asked if she was ready. When she nodded that she was, he said, "Then go to the door, Nelly. Try to do everything just as you did it the other day."

She looked at Willy. "Then you can't be dead yet."

As he struggled to his feet, she went to the door. "Roxie let me in," she explained. "Tim was sitting in his chair. I could tell he was very upset, but I thought it was at me or maybe even because I had told him about being terminal. Anyhow, I just walked past Roxie and went over to him and just blurted out that I wanted the truth before I died . . ."

"Do it," Brian ordered. "Maeve, you go to the door."

Nelly had rehearsed the speech she made to Tim so much that it wasn't hard to stand over the recliner and deliver it again. It wasn't hard to superimpose Tim's face over Willy's. But Willy looked concerned.

"You should start smiling," she instructed. "It was very mean of you, and you shouldn't have smiled when I told you I was dying."

Oh my God, Alvirah thought. Maybe I'm barking up the wrong tree.

"But then I forgave you because right away you admitted that you'd switched the ticket." Nelly opened her purse. "And I almost fainted because I remembered I didn't have the sunburst pin on and I opened my purse and started fumbling in it like this and Roxie saw the gun." She paused. "Wait a minute. Roxie was yelling at Tim to shut up, but when she opened the door for me, she had just said something else to him."

"It's not important," Brian said quickly. "We're not doing audio."

Nelly felt as though she were watching the replay of a videotape. It was all coming back. She grabbed the pin at the bottom of her purse and, like an echo, she could hear Roxie scream about the gun.

"I let go of the pin and grabbed the gun and pulled it out and tried to show it to her. Tim jumped up. The gun went off. Tim yelled . . . what did he yell . . . 'Nelly, don't go wacko. We'll split the ticket.' Then he dove for the floor."

He dove for the floor, Alvirah thought. He didn't fall. He *dove.*

It was all clear to Nelly. She thought she'd shot him and started to faint, then felt a hand close on hers, her wrist being wrenched. That's why my wrist hurts. That's the way it happened. I'm sure of it now.

But Tim had said something else, she thought. What was it? . . . Roxie, he said something to Roxie.

She felt Sister Maeve twist her hand and point the gun down at Willy, now acting out his part on the floor. *That was when I fainted.*

She let her knees cave in and sank to the floor.

"That was very good, Nelly," Brian said. "I can't believe we did it on a first take, but I think we have it. We'll just play it back to be sure, then hope to God Roxie won't see through the trick."

Nelly sat up. She reached for her purse and dug in it for the pin, which she had failed to return to Alvirah. "I wonder," she said.

Alvirah experienced that wonderful moment when instinctively she knew something important was about to happen. "What is it, Nelly?" she asked.

"Just now it was as though I was hearing Dennis teaching me how to turn on the pin. He told me that I had to give it a hard snap with this finger." She held up the index finger of her right hand.

"And that finger has been bothering me since I was here the other day. Do you think I might have turned on the recorder just before I tried to show Roxie the gun? I never checked it. Do you think it might have picked up Tim's voice pleading for his life?"

"Saints preserve us," Cordelia breathed.

The switch of the recorder in the pin Alvirah had given Nelly was still in the On position. The battery was dead, of course, but Alvirah expertly took out the tiny cassette, switched it to her pocket machine, rewound it and pushed the playback button.

Cordelia's lips moved in silent prayer as Alvirah turned it on. The sound began immediately. A shot, Tim's voice telling Nelly not to go wacko. Nelly saying, "Oh my, oh my. Oh, I'm sorry," then a harsh voice, Roxie's voice, "Tim, you bastard."

And finally Tim's pleading, "Roxie, don't. Roxie, don't shoot me!"

Alvirah felt Willy's arm around her. "You've done it again, honey."

Two nights later, Nelly insisted on cooking the celebration dinner for the six of them: Alvirah and Willy, Sisters Cordelia and Maeve Marie, and Dennis and herself.

As a former policewoman, Maeve had insisted that, with the weight of evidence, the district attorney should be brought in on the scam, and one of his best undercover agents, posing as the cameraman who'd captured the shooting, had contacted Roxie.

When Roxie saw the videotape and heard Tim's voice pleading with her not to shoot him, she'd immediately offered the undercover agent whatever he wanted to sell it to her. Then, under his skillful questioning, she admitted everything. Now Roxie was under indictment and Nelly was vindicated and declared the rightful owner of the lottery ticket.

Dennis had brought champagne. With moist eyes, Nelly acknowledged their toast and then raised one of her own. "To all of you and to Brian. I'm sorry he has to be in

Hollywood tonight, what with the earth-quakes and everything."

"It's all so unbelievable," she said a few minutes later as she watched Dennis carve the succulent saddle of lamb she'd prepared with her own special recipe. The rest of the meal consisted of tomato-and-onion salad, mashed potatoes, crisp green beans, flaky biscuits, mint jelly, warm apple pie and cof-fee.

Nelly beamed as she accepted their com-pliments.

At nine o'clock Cordelia and Maeve got up to go. "Willy, I'll see you first thing in the morning," Cordelia ordered. "Bring your toolbox. I've got a bunch of jobs for you."

"We're ready to go, too. We'll drop you off," Willy told her.

"I'm not setting foot out of here until I help Nelly clean up," Alvirah announced firmly, then felt Willy's shoe tap hers.

She turned, following his gaze. Nelly and Dennis were smiling into each other's eyes.

"It's time to go home, honey," Willy said firmly as he put his hands on the back of her chair.

The Lottery Winner

"*A*lvirah. Come at once. I need you desperately!"

Alvirah's eyes snapped open. In a split second she emerged from a comfortable dream in which she was at a state dinner at the White House to the reality of being awakened at three in the morning by a pealing telephone, followed by the panicky voice of Baroness Min von Schreiber.

"Min, what's wrong?" she cried.

Willy grunted awake beside her. "Honey, what's the matter?" he mumbled.

Alvirah laid a soothing hand across his lips. "Sshhh." Then she repeated, "Min, what's wrong?"

Min's tragic groan rushed across the continent from the Cypress Point Spa in Pebble Beach, California, to the luxury apartment on Central Park South. "We are going to be ruined. There is a jewel thief among the guests. Mrs. Hayward's diamonds have disappeared from the wall safe in her cottage."

"Saints preserve us," Alvirah said. "What is Scott doing about it?" Scott Alshorne, the sheriff of Monterey County, had befriended Alvirah when she helped solve a murder at the spa a few years earlier.

"Oh, dear me, it's so complicated. We cannot call Scott," Min said, her voice uneven. "Nadine Hayward is hysterical. She doesn't dare admit to her husband that the insurance lapsed on the diamonds. She persuaded him to give the handling of their personal insurance policies to her son by her first marriage so he'd get the commission, and he gambled the premium check away. The insurance company would be responsible because her son was their agent, but then *he* would be prosecuted, and she can't bring herself to file a claim and have him sent to prison. So she has some wild idea of having paste copies made of the diamonds to fool her husband."

By now Alvirah was fully awake. "Having paste copies worked in "The Necklace" by de Maupassant. I wonder if Mrs. Hayward has read it."

"De MOWpassant, not de MOPpassant," Min corrected. Then she sighed heavily. "Alvirah, it is ridiculous to let anyone get away with stealing four million dollars' worth of jewelry. We can't just ignore this. Another theft could occur. You must rush here. I need you. You must take charge of identifying the culprit. As my guest, of course. And bring Willy. He could use the exercise classes. I shall assign him a personal trainer."

Fifteen hours later the limousine carrying Willy and Alvirah passed the Pebble Beach Club, then the estates lining Shore Drive. It rounded the bend, passing the tree that gave the Cypress Point Spa its name. Driving through the ornate iron gates of the spa, the car wound its way toward the main house, a rambling three-story ivory stucco mansion with pale blue shutters. Even though she was exhausted, Alvirah's eyes were snapping with anticipation.

"I love this place," she told Willy. "I hope Min gave us Tranquility. It's my favorite cottage. I remember the first time I came here. It was right after we won the lottery, and the prospect of spending a week hobnobbing with all the celebrities made me think I'd died and gone to heaven."

"I know, honey," Willy said.

"It was the beginning of finding out how the other half lives. What a lesson! Why—" Alvirah stopped suddenly, realizing she'd been about to remind Willy that when she'd helped to solve a murder at the spa, she'd almost gotten herself killed doing it.

It was obvious Willy remembered. He put his hand over hers and said, "Honey, I don't want you to get yourself in trouble worrying about somebody's lost jewelry."

"I won't. It will be fun to help out, though. It's been too quiet lately. Oh, look, there's Min."

The car had pulled up to the front door. Min came sweeping down the steps to greet them, her arms outstretched. She was wearing a blue linen dress that clung to her full but excellent figure. Her hair, not a shade different than it must have been twenty years ago, was twirled in an elaborate French twist. She was wearing pearl and gold earrings and a matching necklace; as always, she looked as though she had stepped out of a page in *Vogue.*

"And to think she's five years older than me," Alvirah muttered in awe. Behind Min, a stately Baron Helmut von Schreiber descended, his military carriage making him seem taller than his five feet seven. His perfectly trimmed goatee drifted a bit in the breeze as his welcoming smile revealed perfect teeth. Only the crinkles around his blue-gray eyes hinted that he was in his early fifties.

The chauffeur hopped out to open the door, but Min beat him to it. "You are true friends," she gushed, her arms open to embrace them. Suddenly she stopped and stared. "Alvirah, where did you buy that suit? It is well cut, but you must not wear beige. It washes you out." Then she stopped again, shaking her head this time. "Oh, but all of that will wait."

The chauffeur was directed to take the luggage to Tranquility cottage. "A maid will unpack for you," Min informed them. "We must talk."

Obediently they followed her up to her sumptuous office on the second floor of the mansion. Helmut closed the door and went over to the sideboard. "Iced tea, beer, something stronger?" he asked.

Alvirah always was tickled by the fact that absolutely no liquor was allowed on the premises of Cypress Point Spa—except in Min and Helmut's private quarters. She opted for iced tea. Willy looked pathetically grateful at the thought of a beer. Really, she thought, it had been mean to roust him out of bed in the middle of the night, but it was the only way they could make the nine o'clock flight.

Even then, they hadn't been able to get in first class, and each of them was squeezed into a middle seat, between other people. Willy's first words when they got off the plane were, "Honey, I didn't know how much I'd gotten used to the good life."

Sipping the iced tea, Alvirah got right to the point. "Min, exactly what happened? When was the robbery discovered?"

"Late yesterday afternoon. Nadine Hayward arrived on Saturday, so she'd been here three days. Her husband is staying at their condo in the Pebble Beach Club. He's in a golf tournament there. They're going on to San Francisco for a charity ball, so Nadine brought all her best jewelry and put it in the wall safe in her cottage."

"She's been here before?" Alvirah asked.

"Regularly. Ever since she married Cotter Hayward, she comes to the spa whenever he's in one of his tournaments. He's a fine amateur golfer."

Alvirah frowned. "That's what's been throwing me. There was another woman named Hayward one of the times I was here —a couple of years ago. She was Mrs. Cotter Hayward too."

"That was the first wife, Elyse. She still visits the spa, but usually not at the same time as Nadine. Even though she loathes Cotter, she was not happy about being replaced, especially since she unfortunately introduced the new wife to him."

"They fell in love under this roof," Helmut said with a sigh. "These things happen. But to complicate matters, Elyse is also a guest this week."

"Wait a minute," Alvirah said. "You mean

to tell me that Elyse and Nadine are both here?"

"That's exactly it. Naturally we have placed them at tables distant from each other in the dining room and arranged their schedules so they should never be in the same exercise classes."

"Alvirah, honey, I think you're getting off the subject," Willy suggested. "Why don't you stick to finding out about the robbery and then maybe we can go over to the cottage and catch a nap?"

"Oh, Willy, I'm sorry." Alvirah shook her head. "I'm so inconsiderate. Willy needs more sleep than I do, and he couldn't close an eye on the plane. His seat was between two kids who were playing checkers on his tray table. The parents wouldn't let them sit together because they fight so much."

"Why didn't the parents sit with them?" Min asked.

"They had their hands full with three-year-old twins, and you know how good hearted Willy is."

"The robbery," Willy prompted.

"This is what happened," Min said. "At five o'clock Nadine had gone to the salon to have her hair recombed. She got back to Repose cottage at ten minutes of six to find it torn apart. All the drawers had been rifled, her suitcases pulled out. Someone, or perhaps several people, had thoroughly searched every inch of the cottage."

"What were they looking for?" Alvirah asked.

"The jewelry, of course. You know how everyone gets dressed up for the evening. The women love to show off their gems to each other. Nadine had worn a diamond necklace and bracelet the night before. Someone was looking for those pieces but couldn't know that she also had the Hayward tiara, rings and two other bracelets with her as well." Min sighed then burst out, "Why did the stupid woman have to bring everything she owned? Surely she couldn't wear all of that to the charity ball."

Helmut patted her hand. "Minna, Minna, I cannot allow you to let your blood pressure rise. Think beautiful thoughts." He took up the story. "What is odd is that the intruder apparently stumbled onto the safe only after searching through everything else. It is hidden behind the picture of Minna and myself in the sitting room of the cottage."

"Wait a minute," Alvirah interrupted. "You

just said that you thought someone must have seen Nadine wearing the jewelry the night before. Did she leave the spa that evening?"

"No. She was at what we jokingly call the cocktail hour, then at dinner, then at the Mozart recital in the music room."

"Then the only people who would have seen her are the other guests and the staff, and every one of them would know enough to look for the safe. All the cottages have one now." Alvirah sucked in her breath and smoothed the skirt of the beige suit she had been sure would find approval in Min's eyes. I did forget that she said beige washes me out, she thought ruefully. Oh, well.

She resumed her train of thought. "That's something else. Was the safe jimmied?"

"No. Someone knew the combination Nadine had set."

"Or was a professional and knew how to find it," Willy added. "What makes you think the thief isn't a thousand miles away right now?"

Min sighed. "Our only hope is that if it was an inside job and Alvirah can track down the perpetrator, we may be able to force him or her to return the gems. All the guests are known to us. Their reputations are impeccable. There are only three new staff members, and their movements are absolutely accounted for." Min looked suddenly ten years older. "Alvirah, this is the sort of problem that can ruin us. Cotter Hayward is a very difficult man. He will not only prosecute Nadine's son, but I also wouldn't put it past him to find some reason to hold us responsible for the theft."

"When is Nadine supposed to leave for San Francisco and the charity ball?" Alvirah asked.

"On Saturday. That gives you three days to perform a miracle."

A two-hour nap and a luxurious shower revived Alvirah. Anxious for Min's approval, she settled at the dressing table and applied her makeup carefully. Not too much blush, she thought, don't go over the lip line, just a touch of eyeliner, use dark powder to soften the contour of jaw and nose. She was glad to hear Willy singing in the shower. He was feeling better as well.

On the bed she had laid out a handsome caftan that Min had selected for her during her last visit to the spa. After she slipped into it she fastened on her sunburst pin and got out her notebook. While Willy dressed, she jotted down the information Min had given her, breaking it into categories.

When she was finished, she had several immediate questions. Why was Elyse Hayward, the first Mrs. Cotter Hayward, here? Coincidence? Helmut had indicated that Elyse usually avoided being at the spa at the same time as her former friend, Nadine.

Interesting, Alvirah thought.

The three new staff members worked in the Roman Bath, which was the newest attraction at the spa. It had taken two years to complete, but was truly splendid, a replica of the one in Baden-Baden. Two of the newcomers were masseuses, the third was an attendant in the resting room. But Min had said that their movements were accounted for. Even so, Alvirah decided, I'll go to the Roman Bath and at least take a look at the three of them.

Willy appeared at the door of the sitting room. "Do I pass inspection to mingle with the swells?"

His fine head of wavy white hair framed his genial features and warm blue eyes. A handsome navy sports jacket hid the paunch that reappeared whenever they dined lavishly on a cruise. "You look splendid," Alvirah beamed.

"So do you. Hurry up, honey. I can't wait to have one of Min's fake cocktails."

The veranda was already filled with guests. Violin music from inside the mansion drifted through the open windows. As they walked up the path, Alvirah said, "Now remember, Min is going to introduce us to Nadine Hayward. Nadine knows we're here to help and that later on we're going to stop back at her cottage and get a real chance to talk to her."

Since they'd won the lottery, Alvirah had been coming to the spa at least once a year. Willy would sometimes pick her up at the end of her week and they'd go on to take a trip, but this would be his first overnight stay.

"Honey, what have I got to say to those people?" he'd ask when she'd urge him to accompany her. "The guys talk about their golf game or bat the breeze about the cutups they were in their Ivy League schools or how their companies are investing in Asia. Do I tell them that I was born in Brooklyn, went to

P.S. 38 and was a working plumber until we struck it rich in the lottery? Do you think they care that my hobby now is to trot around the world with you and, when we're in New York, to fix pipes and sinks and toilets for people who need help?"

"There isn't one of them who wouldn't die happy knowing he has two million dollars a year less taxes coming in," was Alvirah's answer. Still she admitted to herself that she *was* a little concerned that somebody might try to put Willy down with one of those sweetly chilling remarks that could cut like a knife. Anyone tried that on her and she could give as good as she got, but Willy was too kind to zing anyone.

Five minutes later she realized she needn't have worried. Willy was deep in conversation with the CEO of American Plumbing, explaining to him exactly why his biggest competitor's highly touted new line of hydro-flush toilets were totally impractical for the average home. As Alvirah watched, the CEO's expression became more and more delighted.

Tanned, tinted and handsomely dressed men and women were clustered in little groups. Alvirah chuckled over a remark she overheard one woman make to another: "Darling, you don't know me well enough yet to dislike me."

Then Min plucked at her sleeve. "Alvirah, I want you to meet Nadine Hayward."

Alvirah turned swiftly. She didn't know what she'd expected, but it wasn't this very pretty, sweet-faced, blue-eyed blonde with a peaches-and-cream complexion. She could pass for thirty and probably is in her early forties, Alvirah decided, but boy, she must be nervous. She looks as though she got dressed during a fire drill. Nadine Hayward was wearing a lime green shantung outfit with wide trousers and a waist-length jacket. It had obviously cost a fortune, but it looked all wrong. The middle button of the jacket wasn't fastened. Black pumps were a discordant note against the silvery sheen of the outfit. Nadine's dark blond hair was carelessly twisted into a chignon. A single strand of pearls was slipping under the neckline of the pale green shell.

As Alvirah watched, Nadine's expression changed to sheer panic. "Oh, my God! My husband is coming," she murmured.

"I thought you said he was attending a golf dinner at the club," Min hissed.

"He was supposed to, but . . ." Nadine's voice trailed off, and she clutched Min's arm.

Alvirah glanced at the path. A tall man was winding his way up toward the veranda. "When he heard Elyse was here he told me I wouldn't see him till Saturday," Nadine whispered through now bloodless lips.

Around them people were chatting and laughing. But Alvirah caught several sets of eyes appraising them. The tension emanating from Nadine Hayward was palpable.

"Smile," she ordered firmly. "Button your jacket . . . Fix your pearls . . . That's better."

"But he doesn't know the jewelry's missing. He'll wonder why I'm not wearing any of it," Nadine moaned.

Cotter Hayward was at the stairs. Sotto voce, Alvirah urged, "For your son's sake, you've got to fake this until I get a chance to help you out."

At the mention of her son, an expression of pain came into Nadine's eyes, then was gone. "I did a bit of acting way back," she said. Now her smile seemed genuine, and a moment later when her husband came up the steps and touched her arm, her reaction of astonished pleasure was flawless.

I don't like this guy, Alvirah thought as Hayward curtly acknowledged the introduction to her, then turned to his wife. "I imagine they'll let me stay for dinner here," he said. "I have to get back in time for the speeches, but I wanted to see you."

"You are most welcome," Min said. "Would you and Nadine prefer to have a small table to yourselves, or did you want to join her at her group table?"

"No groups, please," Hayward said dismissively.

He dyes his hair, Alvirah thought. Good job, but I can tell. Nobody in his fifties is that blond. But Cotter Hayward was a handsome man, no getting around that.

It was Min and Helmut's firm rule that their guests share tables of eight. The only exception was if a guest had a visitor and needed a chance to talk privately. In that case, never more than once a week, a table for two was available.

Tonight, Alvirah was delighted to see that Min had placed her and Willy at the group table with Elyse, the first Mrs. Cotter Hayward, who turned out to be a brittle, pencil-thin, auburn-haired fashion plate in her mid-forties. A handsome older couple from Chicago named Jennings; a stunning woman in her late thirties, Barra Snow, a model whom Alvirah instantly recognized from the Adrian Cosmetics ads; Michael Fields, an ex-congressman from New York; and Herbert Green, the plumbing CEO, were the other diners at table eight.

Alvirah managed to maneuver it so that she was only one seat away from Elyse Cotter. It quickly became obvious to her that Elyse was extremely vocal about both her former husband and her former friend. "Nadine doesn't look like Sparkle Plenty tonight," she observed caustically. "I wonder if that's a matter of choice or if Cotter has started using his favorite line about keeping the jewelry in a bank vault because he worries about a robbery. If so, it means he's met someone else and Nadine's days are numbered." Her smile was not pleasant. "I should know."

"Nadine was wearing some of the Hayward jewelry the other night," Barra Snow said. "You had dinner served in your cottage, Elyse."

Alvirah perked up her ears and switched on the recording device in her sunburst pin. Had it been just an accident that Cotter Hayward's first wife mentioned a robbery? She'd have to call Charley Evans, her editor at the *Globe,* and ask him to send her some background on all the Haywards from the newspaper morgue.

Let's see, she thought as she selected a tiny loin lamb chop from the silver platter the waitress was holding, when I was here four years ago, Elyse was still married to Cotter, so Nadine hasn't been in the picture too long. It's obvious Elyse was born with a silver spoon in her mouth, but I can tell from her voice that Nadine isn't a graduate of Miss Porter's. Wonder how she got so close to the Haywards in the first place?

"Honey, you're still holding the serving fork," Willy prodded.

At a table near the picture window overlooking the pool and gardens, Nadine and Cotter Hayward ate in almost total silence. When Cotter spoke it was usually to complain.

Then came the question Nadine dreaded. "How come you're not wearing any decent jewelry? Every other woman in this place is showing off her trophies; surely yours must be some of the finest."

Nadine managed to keep her voice even.

"I didn't think it was in the best taste to dangle them in front of Elyse. After all *she* was wearing them when she came here a few years ago."

Her fingers damp with perspiration, she watched her husband's reaction and inwardly collapsed with relief when he nodded. "I suppose you're right. Now I've got to get back. Those after-dinner speeches will be starting."

As he got up, he leaned over quickly and brushed her cheek with an impatient kiss. The way he would have kissed Elyse toward the end of their marriage, Nadine thought. Oh dear God, what am I going to do?

She watched him walk across the spacious room and then was astonished to see Elyse hurrying toward him. Even though Nadine could only see the back of his head, Cotter's body language was obvious. He stopped abruptly, went rigid, and then after Elyse spoke to him, pushed her aside and hurried out.

Nadine was sure that Elyse had reminded him that the final divorce payment was owed to her next week. Three million dollars. Cotter was infuriated at the prospect of paying it. And I'm paying for it as well, Nadine thought.

After what Elyse cost him, the prenuptial I signed will leave me penniless if he gets angry enough about the jewelry to divorce me . . .

Now what did Elyse have to say to her ex? Alvirah wondered, as she nibbled on a tiny cookie and tried to make the rainbow sherbet last. From where she was sitting she could see the expression of savage satisfaction on the divorcée's face and the angry dark red flush that colored Cotter Hayward's features.

"My, my," Barra Snow murmured with a slight smile. "I didn't know fireworks were on the menu."

"Do you know the Haywards well?" Alvirah asked casually.

"We have mutual friends and occasionally are in the same place."

Willy jumped up to hold Elyse Hayward's chair as she returned to the table, a grim smile on her face. "Well, I made his day," she said with obvious delight. "There's nothing that drives Cotter crazier than parting with money." She laughed. "His lawyers have been trying to negotiate a settlement. Instead of a final three-million-dollar payment next

week, they'd like me to accept annual install-
ments for the next twenty years. The answer
I gave them is that I didn't win a lottery, I
divorced a rich man."

That's for our benefit, Alvirah thought. "It
depends on the annual installment," she
murmured.

Herbert Green, the plumbing executive,
chuckled. "I like your wife," he told Willy.

"So do I." Willy had just finished his sherbet. "That was a great dinner, but I have to
say I'd like to top it off with a Big Mac."

Barra laughed. "I'm glad you feel like that.
My sister was awarded a McDonald franchise
in her divorce. I wasn't that lucky."

"Neither will Nadine be when Cotter tires
of her," Elyse volunteered. "Here's her settlement." She touched her thumb to the tip of
her forefinger to form a perfect circle. Her
meaning was very clear. "Nadine's a perfect
example of why we should obey the ninth
commandment."

"Thou shalt not covet thy neighbor's wife,"
Willy said.

"Or *husband.*" Elyse laughed. "Nadine's
problem is that she was unlucky enough to
get mine."

• • •

Nadine Hayward did not wait for the recital in the music room. Instead she slipped away from the dining room with the first people to leave and made her way to her cottage, which was one of the farthest from the main house.

It's Wednesday night, she thought. Saturday morning Cotter will come for me. I'll have to tell him about the robbery. He'll want to know why I didn't call the police immediately. Then I'll have to tell him that Bobby didn't pay the insurance premium to the company. And Bobby will be prosecuted.

I can't let that happen.

If only I hadn't come here four years ago and met Cotter.

It was the thought she had been trying to avoid.

As she turned off the main path to her cottage, Nadine was filled with self-loathing and regret that she had ever met Cotter. My one extravagance, she thought, coming here after Robert died, and I had to meet him.

Her first husband had been Robert Crandell, a distant cousin of Elyse's, handsome and bright and witty and loving. And a gambler. She'd married him at twenty, divorced him when Bobby was ten. It was the only way to separate herself from his debts. But they'd remained friends. More than friends. I always loved him, she thought now.

He'd been killed nearly five years ago, driving too fast on a rain-slick highway, still a gambler, still untrustworthy. But he'd left an insurance policy that was enough to take care of Bobby's college education, and it was the relief of discovering this fact, coupled with the emotional drain of his death, that impelled Nadine to treat herself to a week at Cypress Point Spa.

When she was still married to Robert, she'd occasionally met Cotter and Elyse at family events. By the time she met them again, at the spa, it was clear that they were barely speaking to each other. Three months later, Cotter phoned. "I'm in the process of a divorce," he'd announced, "because I haven't been able to stop thinking about you."

Thoughtful. Charming. Oh, how Cotter could turn on the charm. "You've never had it easy, Nadine," he said. It's time someone took care of you. I know what you went through with Robert. It's a miracle he wasn't murdered. Those bookies play rough when you welsh on debts. I bailed him out from time to time. I don't think you knew that."

He had never bailed Robert out, Nadine thought as she put the key in the door of her cottage. Cotter never bailed anyone out.

Before she could turn the key, the door opened and the frightened face of her twenty-two-year-old son stared down at her. Then Bobby threw his arms around her. "Mom, help me. What am I going to do?"

Alvirah and Willy lingered over decaf espresso with the other guests at their table, hoping to pick up more gossip, but to Alvirah's disappointment Elyse dropped the subject of her ex-husband.

"Are you attending the recital, Mrs. Meehan?" Barra Snow asked.

"We're still on New York time," Alvirah said. After Elyse's crack about the lottery, it was on the tip of her tongue to say that they were going to hit the sack, but she decided against it. "I think we'd better retire," she finished.

At a demure pace, Alvirah led Willy through the dining room; as soon as they were outside, however, she quickened her step. "Let's go," she said. "I'm dying to talk to Nadine. From what I'm learning about Cotter Hayward's attitude toward money, there's no doubt that he won't be talked out of reporting the theft to the insurance company."

When they arrived at Nadine's cottage, they were surprised to hear the murmur of voices through the open window. "I wonder if the husband came back," Alvirah whispered, but at her knock the door was opened by a handsome young man who even in the half-light she could see was the image of Nadine.

Sitting opposite them on the pale blue and white sofas in the harmoniously decorated sitting room, Willy and Alvirah waited as Nadine told Bobby that the Meehans knew all about the theft and were there to help.

It was clear to Alvirah that Bobby was desperately worried, but even so she did not like it when he tried to justify his own chicanery. "Mom, I swear to you this is the first time I ever cashed a premium check," he said, his voice shrill. "I'd made a bet. It was a sure thing."

" 'A sure thing.' " Nadine's voice broke into a near sob. "Your father's words. I heard them for the first time when I was nineteen years old. I don't want to hear them anymore."

"Mom, I was going to reinstate the policy, I swear."

"Wasn't there a notice of termination sent?" Alvirah asked.

Bobby looked away. "I knew it was coming."

"And destroyed it?" Alvirah persisted.

"Yes."

"That's also a criminal offense," she said severely.

"Bobby," Nadine cried, "I persuaded Cotter to switch the jewelry insurance to you because you'd gotten the job with Haskill. Then I persuaded him to let you live in the New York apartment."

So like his father, she thought. The repentant face, the dejected slump of the shoulders.

It was as though Bobby knew what she was thinking. "Mom, I'm not like Dad, not that way. Any time I bet before, it was with my money."

"Not always. I've covered some of your losses."

"But never a lot. Mom, if you can talk Cotter into not prosecuting, I swear, never, never again. I don't want to go to prison."

Bobby buried his face in his hands.

Nadine put her arms around him. "Bobby,"

she said. "Don't you see? I'm helpless to stop him."

Then she paused. "Or am I?"

An hour later, when Willy and Alvirah were settled in bed, Alvirah began to think aloud. "Nadine's son, Bobby, is what I would call spineless and more than a little selfish. I mean, when you think about it, his mother persuaded Cotter Hayward to switch the insurance policy on the jewelry to him so he'd get the commission, then he gambles away the premium. And my feeling is that he's more worried about the prospect of going to prison than he is about the fact that the fallout of all this might mean the end of Nadine's marriage."

"Uh-huh," Willy agreed, his tone sleepy.

"Not that I think Cotter Hayward is any prize," Alvirah continued. "He reminds me of Mr. Parker. You remember I cleaned for the Parkers on Wednesdays until they moved to Florida. I think she died. The nice ones always die, don't they, and the mean old birds hang around forever. Anyhow—picky, picky, picky! That's the way he was. And *cheap!* One day Mr. Parker yelled at his poor wife for giving away an old suit of his. He had a closet full of clothes but couldn't stand to let so much as an odd sock get away."

Willy's even breathing was his only comment.

"The only way to save Bobby Crandell from prison is to find the thief," Alvirah mused aloud. "The thing is that the night of the robbery, Nadine locked the front door of the cottage, but since Bobby said he was able to get in through the sliding glass door of the sunroom tonight, it stands to reason that anyone else could have done the same thing. Nobody really worries about locks around here."

And then a thought shot through her mind that made her gasp. How heavy a gambler was Bobby Crandell? He knew his mother had the jewelry with her. Nadine had told them that the combination she always set when she used a wall safe in a spa or hotel was the year of her birth, 1-9-5-3. Bobby probably knew that.

Alvirah pondered the notion that Bobby Crandell might have been in deep trouble because of gambling debts. Suppose his life had been threatened if he didn't produce the money he owed? Suppose he owed very big money? Suppose he decided to steal the jewelry even though he had already stolen the premium money? Maybe he was desperate enough to hope that his mother could persuade Cotter Hayward not to file a claim for the missing jewelry, she thought.

Alvirah had another question to ask herself before she fell asleep. Why did Cotter Hayward suddenly decide to have dinner with Nadine tonight?

The call came at eleven o'clock, shortly after he had retired. Still wide awake, Cotter Hayward reached for the receiver and barked a greeting.

Hayward got out of bed and dressed in chinos and a sweater. Then, as an afterthought, he made a martini. I probably shouldn't have one, he told himself sourly. But given the way his night had gone, he could certainly use it.

At quarter of twelve he left his condo on the grounds of the Pebble Beach Club and, walking in the shadows, made his way to the sixteenth hole. Standing in the wooded area off the green, he waited.

The faint snap of a twig alerted him to an approaching presence. He turned around, expectantly. Just then the clouds parted. In the instant before he died, Cotter Hayward lived a lifetime. He saw his assailant, realized that it was a golf club that was about to descend on his skull and even had time to recognize how much of a fool he had been.

At 5:45 A.M. Alvirah was dreaming that they were sailing from Southampton on the *QE2.* Then she realized that the sound she was hearing was not a ship's bell but the peal of the telephone. It was Min.

"Alvirah, please come up to the main house immediately. There is a problem."

Alvirah struggled into a pale yellow Dior sweat suit and matching sneakers, as Willy blinked sleep from his eyes. "What's the matter now?" he asked.

"I don't know yet. Oh darn if I didn't put this top on backwards."

Willy squinted in the direction of the clock. "I thought people came to this place to relax."

"Some people do. Hurry up and get dressed so you can go with me. I've got a bad feeling."

A few minutes later Alvirah's bad feeling

was compounded by the presence at the spa's main entrance of a car bearing the logo of the sheriff of Monterey County. "Scott's here," she said tersely.

Scott Alshorne was in Min's office. Min and Helmut were still in dressing gowns. Even though they both seemed distraught, Alvirah could not resist a moment of total admiration for the way the two of them could look like fashion plates even when roused from bed in the predawn hours. Min's robe was a shimmering pink satin with a lace-edged collar and delicately corded sash. Helmut's maroon knee-length silk robe was trimly handsome over matching pajamas.

Fortunately Sheriff Alshorne never changed. His teddy-bear body, his craggy and tanned face, his white, unmanageable hair and piercing eyes were still the same. He was as warm when he embraced a friend as he was implacable when he was trailing a criminal.

He hugged Alvirah and shook hands with Willy. Then, dispensing with small talk, he said, "Cotter Hayward's body was found on the grounds of the Pebble Beach Club an hour ago by a maintenance man."

"Saints preserve us," Alvirah gasped, even

290

as she thought, Which one did it, Nadine or Bobby?

"Vicious blows with a heavy object. Whoever killed him wanted to make sure he was dead." Scott looked at Alvirah appraisingly. "From what Min tells me, you're not here just to be pampered."

"Not exactly." Alvirah's mind was racing. "Does Nadine know about her husband?"

"Scott came directly here," Min said. "We will accompany him when he tells her. Helmut's medical services may be required. I only wish I knew where to reach Nadine's son so he can rush to her side."

"Bobby's—" Willy was interrupted by a warning glance from Alvirah.

The exchange was not lost on Scott Alshorne. "Do you know this Bobby?" he asked.

"We've met," Alvirah hedged, then realized it would be useless to conceal from Scott the fact that Bobby Crandell had been in Nadine's cottage at ten o'clock last night.

"Is he staying with his mother?" Scott queried.

"He was going to last night," Alvirah admitted. "Nadine is in one of the two-bedroom cottages."

Scott stood up, suddenly looming over the

others. "Alvirah, my good friend," he said, "let's get something straight. There was a major theft on these premises three days ago. I should have been notified—*immediately.* Min has given me the background, but that doesn't justify her decision to go along with Nadine Hayward and conceal the crime. What you people don't seem to understand is that we should have been collecting samples for DNA testing at the safe. Now it's too late."

He moved closer to Alvirah. "Instead of sending for me, she sent for you. Now we have not only a grand larceny theft but a first degree murder on our hands. I want any information you've picked up since you arrived here yesterday. Do I make myself clear?"

"I want to make *myself* clear too," Willy said, and his tone was icy. "Don't bully my wife."

"Oh, honey, Scott's not bullying me," Alvirah said soothingly. "It's just his version of the Miranda warning." She looked up at Scott. "I know what you're thinking—that Nadine and Bobby are the likely suspects. But I also know you're a big man and will keep an open mind. I met Cotter Hayward a few years ago when he was here with his then-wife, Elyse. They weren't exactly lovey-dovey at the time, and, believe me, from what I saw last night that lady hated him. But she had nothing to gain by killing him, or at least not as far as I know. Then again, I bet Cotter Hayward had a lot of enemies, so before you jump to conclusions, take a good look at some of the men in that golf tournament and find out which of them might have had a reason to hate him too."

Min pointed to the clock. "It is going on to six-thirty," she said nervously. "The morning walk will be starting in fifteen minutes. We must let Nadine know what has happened."

"And I think Elyse should find out, too, before the rumors start flying," Alvirah suggested. "If you'd like, I'll go to her cottage and talk to her."

"Not without me," Scott snapped, and then added with a reluctant grin, "All right, Alvirah. You can come along when we see Hayward's widow."

Min and Helmut rushed upstairs to change into jogging suits, and then the somber procession left the main house. Willy elected to go to their own cottage. "I'll only be in the way," he said.

Maids carrying breakfast trays passed

them as they walked down the winding path to Nadine's cottage. Alvirah could feel their curious stares.

As it turned out, Helmut's medical services were indeed needed. Nadine was in the sitting room when they arrived. She looked as though she had not closed her eyes all night. Alvirah noticed immediately that her robe was inside out. Must have put it on in a real hurry, she thought. Why?

Nadine's peaches-and-cream complexion went ashen when she saw them. "What's wrong? Has anything happened to Bobby?"

So that's it, Alvirah thought. Bobby's taken off and she doesn't know where he's gone. She watched as Min and Helmut stood protectively by Nadine as Scott told her that her husband had been the victim of foul play.

Nadine said nothing. Then she sighed and slumped over in a dead faint.

"If Nadine was a wreck, you should have seen Bobby," Alvirah told Willy an hour later. "He came in while Helmut was trying to revive his mother, and I guess he thought she was dead. He'd been crying, you could see that. He pushed Helmut aside and kept saying, 'Mom, it's my fault, I'm sorry. I'm sorry.'"

"Did he mean sorry about stealing the premium, or had they had an argument?" Willy asked.

"That's what I'm trying to figure out. When Nadine came to and Helmut gave her a sedative and put her to bed, Scott talked to Bobby. But all he said was that he couldn't sleep and got up to go for a jog. Then he said he didn't have another word to say until he hired a lawyer."

Willy whistled soundlessly. "That doesn't sound like an innocent man talking."

Alvirah nodded reluctantly. "You can tell he's not really a bad kid, Willy, and he certainly loves his mother, but I do think he's the kind who doesn't think things through. I mean, I hate to say it, but I could see him deciding that if Cotter Hayward were out of the way, his mother would never have to report the missing jewelry."

Willy handed her a cup of coffee. "You haven't had anything to eat. The maid left a thermos and what passes for a muffin. You need a magnifying glass to see it on the plate."

"Nine hundred calories a day, honey.

That's why people look so good when they leave here." Alvirah devoured the muffin in one bite. "But you know what was interesting? When we went to tell Elyse about her ex-husband, she went hysterical."

"I thought she couldn't stand him."

"So did I. And maybe she couldn't. But she knew that Cotter Hayward was so afraid of dying that he would never make a will. He has no children, so that means—"

". . . that Nadine may be a very wealthy widow," Willy finished. "And I guess now her son can afford to hire a good lawyer."

At twelve o'clock, Scott returned to the spa with a search warrant for Nadine's cottage. By then the media were camped outside the compound and police barricades had been erected to hold them back.

Sheriff Alshorne was besieged for a statement. He got out of his car and stood before the cameras and microphones. "The investigation is proceeding," he said. "The autopsy is presently taking place. You will be kept informed of developments."

Questions were shouted at him: "Sheriff, is it true that Mrs. Hayward's son has retained a lawyer?" "Is it true that Mrs. Hayward's jewelry was stolen a few days ago and you were not informed?" "Is it true that Mr. Hayward had a confrontation with his ex-wife last night at dinner?"

"No comment," Scott said tersely in response to each question hurled at him. He got back in his car and snapped, "Step on it," to his deputy. They were waved past the barricade and escaped onto the spa grounds. "I wonder how many of the employees will sell their inside stories to the scandal sheets," he fumed as they headed to the widow's cottage.

Nadine was dressed and, although deathly pale, she was completely composed. "I understand," she said tonelessly when Scott showed her the search warrant. "I don't know what you're looking for and I'm very sure you won't find anything incriminating, but go ahead."

"Where is your son?" Scott asked.

"I sent him over to the Roman Bath. The massage and swim treatment will be good for him."

"He does understand that he is not to leave the premises?"

"I gather you made that quite clear. Now

if you'll excuse me, I'll be in Baroness von Schreiber's office. She is helping me make arrangements for my husband's cremation when his body is released."

The search of the cottage was thorough and the results were nil. Exasperated, Scott studied the wall safe. "This is a pretty good one," he commented to a deputy. "It wasn't jimmied, so that means if it wasn't a professional safecracker, whoever took those gems had the combination."

"The son?"

"He was in his New York office Wednesday morning. The jewelry disappeared Tuesday afternoon. We're checking the red-eye flights, but of course he may not have used his own name if he was on one of them."

It was in the second bedroom, the one in which Bobby had slept, that Scott found something that he felt was significant—Nadine's pocket-sized phone directory, wedged open by the base of the telephone to the *H* page. The first five telephone numbers were listings for Cotter Hayward, his office, his boat, the New York apartment, the New Mexico ranch, the Pebble Beach condo.

"Bobby was in here last night," Scott said. "Cotter was at the Pebble Beach condo. I wonder if our friend Bobby placed a call to him and arranged a private meeting."

It was the custom of the Cypress Point Spa that luncheon was served informally at tables around the pool. Most of the guests were dressed in tank suits and robes. The ones who had completed the morning program and were planning on an afternoon of golf on the spa's newly installed nine-hole course were suitably garbed for a few hours on the links.

Alvirah had no intention of following either a beauty or exercise regime, and she'd never held a golf club. Nonetheless, she changed hastily into the dark blue tank suit and pink terry-cloth robe that were part of the standard equipment of every cottage. She had prevailed on Willy to likewise clad himself in the bathing trunks and short robe that were standard for male guests.

"We don't want to stand out," she'd urged him. "I need to get a feel of what people are saying about the murder."

She realized it probably would look tacky

to wear her sunburst pin on the robe. Even the women who looked like Christmas trees at the evening "cocktail" party wouldn't do that. Nevertheless she fastened the pin to her lapel. She turned the recording device on as they approached the pool. She didn't want to miss a word of what people would be saying about the murder.

Alvirah was surprised to see Elyse sitting at one of the tables with Barra Snow and other guests. "Come on, honey," she hissed to Willy, noting that there were still two seats available at the table.

Now appearing totally composed, Elyse had eschewed the spa-issue tank suit and robe and was wearing a striped cotton shirt, white skirt and golf shoes. "A terrible shock," she was saying to the woman who had just approached the table to speak to her. "After all, I was married to Cotter for fifteen years, and at least some of those times were happy. Thanks to him I took up golf, and for that I'll always be grateful. He was an excellent teacher. That's what really kept us together so long. I think that long after we were sick of each other we still enjoyed playing golf together."

"Are you sure you want to play this afternoon? We can get someone to fill in the four-some."

The woman who was talking to Elyse was another one of the slim, tanned, elegant types with an almost-English accent. She only looks familiar because she's a clone of half the women here, Alvirah decided after studying her a few moments.

Barra Snow answered for Elyse. "I'm certain Elyse will be better off if she plays with us. I've already asked a caddy to get her clubs from her car. She mustn't just sit and brood."

"I am not brooding," Elyse contradicted sharply. "Really, Barra, if you insist on offering sympathy, save it for Nadine. I hear that Bobby was with her last night, and I gather she wasn't expecting him. I'd love to know what kind of scrape he's in now. Nadine had to beg money from Cotter to bail him out the last time. He's going to be just like his father, that boy."

Alvirah remembered that Elyse was a distant cousin of Bobby's late father. How did she know that Nadine bailed Bobby out? she wondered. Did she hear that from Cotter? She thought about Elyse's hysterical reaction to the news of the death. Was it just because Nadine will inherit a lot of money, or was there a love/hate relationship with her ex-husband? Interesting, she decided.

The Jennings woman who had been at their table the night before hurried over. "I just heard on the television that the rumor is that Nadine's jewelry was stolen the other day. Isn't that incredible?"

"The jewelry," Elyse gasped. "The Hayward jewelry! My God, did Cotter know that? That stuff was in his family for three generations. They never gave it to the wife, you know. She was just allowed to wear it. His father was married four times, and the joke was that all four wives had their portraits done in the same pieces. They were known as the Hayward chorus line. I thought Nadine would finally be the one to keep everything. Cotter was the last of the line."

She's thrilled it's been stolen, Alvirah thought, or else she's a good actress.

A genial-looking man in the uniform of a spa caddy approached the table, a golf bag over his shoulder. "I have your clubs, Mrs. Hayward," he said, as he put the bag down, "but I think I'd better clean the sand wedge off. The sleeve is missing, and it's a bit sticky."

"That's ridiculous," Elyse snapped. "All the clubs were cleaned before they were put back in the bag."

Sticky? Alvirah's antennae began to vibrate. She jumped up and said, "I'll take a look at that, please."

She took the golf bag from the startled caddy and looked down into it. Being careful not to touch any of the clubs, she leaned over and studied the one that did not have a sleeve covering it. The curved steel head of that club was matted with dark brown stains. Even with her naked eye it was possible to see bits of skin and hair sticking to the metal.

"Somebody call Sheriff Alshorne," Alvirah said quietly. "Tell him I think I've found the murder weapon."

Two hours later, Alvirah and Willy were visited in their cottage by Sheriff Scott Alshorne.

"That was good work, Alvirah," Scott admitted somewhat grudgingly. "If that caddy had cleaned the club, valuable evidence would have been lost."

"DNA?" Alvirah asked.

Alshorne shrugged. "Maybe. We do know

that it was the murder weapon, and we know it came from the ex-wife's golf bag, which was in the trunk of her unlocked car in the parking area.''

''Meaning anyone could have taken it and replaced it,'' Willy commented.

''Anyone who knew it was there,'' Alvirah said. ''Right, Scott?''

''Yes.''

''I didn't touch that club, but it looked like it must have made a pretty nasty weapon. Am I right?''

Alvirah's forehead was furrowed, always a sign that, as she put it, she had her thinking cap on.

''Yes, it made a formidable weapon,'' Scott agreed. ''The sand wedge is the heaviest golf club.''

''I didn't know that. If I were going to bop someone on the skull with a golf club I'd have grabbed just any one of them, I think.''

''Alvirah,'' Scott said, shaking his head, ''maybe I'll just have to hire you. Yes, I've come to the same conclusion. Someone who's either a golfer or *knows* about golf chose that club for his or her encounter with Cotter Hayward last night.''

''And you're concentrating on Bobby Crandell, aren't you?''

He shrugged. "Or his mother, for all the reasons you know."

Alvirah thought about Bobby, the scared handsome young face, the attempt to justify himself by pointing out that he'd always covered his own losses until now. She figured it was closer to the truth that Nadine had always bailed him out, and he had come running to her expecting her to be able to do it again. Last night Alvirah had seen with her own eyes that he realized *this* time his mother was powerless to save him. And it was pretty obvious that Nadine would do anything rather than see her son go to prison. She'd as much as said that . . .

"It looks bad for both of them," she said slowly, "but you know something, Scott? They're both innocent. I feel it in my bones."

They were in the sitting room of the cottage. The sliding glass door was open, and a refreshing cool breeze from the Pacific had cleared the midday heat.

Running footsteps sounded from the patio outside, then suddenly Nadine was pushing open the sliding screen. "Alvirah, help me," she sobbed. "Bobby is going to confess to murdering Cotter. Stop him, please stop him." Then she saw the sheriff. "Oh my God!" she wailed.

Scott stood up. "Mrs. Hayward, I'd better go find your son and hear what he has to say. And I suggest you look into your own heart and decide why he suddenly felt the need to confess to murder."

Flanked by Scott Alshorne and two sheriff's deputies, Bobby Crandell was taken to the Monterey County police station. A few minutes later, Alvirah and Willy accompanied Nadine, as they followed in the spa limo.

Nadine was no longer sobbing. Wordless on the brief drive, when they reached the station she demanded to see the sheriff. "I have something very important to tell him," she said.

Alvirah sensed immediately what Nadine was going to do. "Nadine, I want you to get a lawyer before you say one word."

"A lawyer can't help me. No one can."

They were escorted to a waiting room, where they sat until Scott sent for them an hour later. By then Alvirah was so worried that she almost forgot to turn on the recorder in her sunburst pin.

"Where is Bobby?" Nadine demanded when they were finally escorted to Scott's office.

"He's waiting for his confession to be typed up."

"He has nothing to confess to," Nadine cried. "I—"

Scott interrupted her. "Mrs. Hayward, don't say another word until you listen to me. You've heard of the Miranda warning?"

"Yes."

Alvirah felt Willy's hand reach to comfort her as Scott read the Miranda warning to Nadine, gave it to her to read, asked her if she understood it.

"Yes, yes, and I know I'm entitled to have a lawyer."

"Very well." Scott turned to a deputy. "Get the stenographer. Alvirah, you and Willy wait outside."

"Oh no, please let them stay." Nadine was trembling.

Alvirah put an arm around her. "Let me stay with her, Scott."

Nadine's confession was straightforward. "I phoned Cotter at the condo. I told him I had to talk to him."

"What time was that?"

"I . . . I'm not sure. I was in bed. I couldn't sleep."

"What did you want to talk to him about?" Scott asked.

"I was going to tell him about the jewelry being stolen and beg him not to report it. Alvirah, you're so smart. I thought maybe, just maybe, you'd find out who took it. I *did* wear some of the pieces the other night. A number of people admired them and all those same people are here. Maybe everything is in a safe in one of the cottages."

"Did he agree to meet you?" Scott asked.

"Yes, on the golf links."

"Why not in the condo?" Alvirah asked. "You're his wife."

"He . . . he said he felt like a walk and that would make it just about halfway for the two of us. He told me exactly how to get there."

"Why did you bring a golf club?" Scott asked.

Nadine bit her lip. "Cotter could become quite violent. I was afraid that if he became enraged . . . And that's just what happened. When I told him about the theft and the premium, he was so angry. He raised his hand and tried to hit me. I backed off and raised the club and . . ." Her voice trailed off. Then she whispered, "I don't remember hitting him, but then he was lying there, and I knew he was dead."

"You put the golf club back in Elyse Hayward's car?"

"Yes. I just wanted to get rid of it."

"Why *her* car?"

"I knew she had clubs there. I'd seen her with them. On the way out of the spa, I cut through the parking lot."

Not only his forehead, but Scott's entire face appeared to be creased in thought. "You make a more credible confession than your son did," he said. "I'm sorry for you, Mrs. Hayward. You'd have done Bobby a much bigger favor letting him face the music for cashing the insurance premium check. He could have handled it. He was willing to face the gas chamber rather than let you be arrested for your husband's murder. I can tell you now that his confession didn't hold water."

Scott stood up. "When your statement is typed up and signed, you'll be formally arraigned. As of now, you are under arrest on suspicion of murder in the first degree."

Alvirah and Willy had gone to the police station with Nadine and now they returned from it with Bobby. A study in misery, he sat hunched in the car, his chin resting on his clasped hands, his eyes half closed. Alvirah's maternal instincts coursed through her entire being. He hurts so much, she thought, and he's blaming himself. Finally she spoke to him: "Bobby, you'll stay in your mother's cottage, won't you?"

"Yes, if Baroness von Schreiber allows it. My mother was only supposed to stay till Saturday."

"I know Min will have a place for you." She turned to Willy. "I think you and Bobby should stick together the rest of the day. Take him over to the gym or the pool."

She closed her lips, not wanting to promise what she couldn't deliver. But as the limo cruised along the Seventeen Mile Drive, she decided to say her piece. "Bobby, I know you didn't kill Cotter Hayward and I'm just as sure your mother didn't kill him, either. She thinks she's protecting you, just as you thought you were protecting her. Now I want the truth. What happened after Willy and I left you the other night?"

The faintest hope brightened Bobby's face. He brushed back the dark blond hair that was so like his mother's. "Mom and I were pretty wrung out. She said that she knew Cotter would start thinking about her not wearing any of the jewelry at dinner, and it might be better if she told him what had happened instead of waiting till Saturday. We both went to bed. I could hear her crying for a while, but I didn't know whether I should go to her. Then I fell asleep."

He glanced nervously at the front seat, then realized that Alvirah had pushed the button that raised the privacy glass between them and the chauffeur. "I woke up about five o'clock and looked in on Mom. She wasn't in her room. I found her address book and called Hayward's condo, but there wasn't any answer. I was scared and decided to go over there. I was afraid that she'd gone to see him and that maybe something had happened to her. I jogged over, but when I got there I saw police cars; a maintenance man told me what had happened. After that, I just kind of panicked. That's why I confessed to the murder. Because if my mother did it, she did it for me."

Alvirah looked at the young man, his face a mask of misery. "I don't believe she did it. Bobby," she said, "I told Sheriff Alshorne that there may have been other people who had a good reason to kill your stepfather. Now my job is to find out which one did it."

• • •

There was a large manila envelope waiting for Alvirah in the cottage. It was the material she had requested from Charley Evans, her editor at the *New York Globe,* volumes of newspaper and magazine clippings and stories about Cotter Hayward. Alvirah almost forgot that she had missed lunch as she began to dive into them, then she remembered the breakfast mini-muffin and realized that her looming headache was not caused by stress alone. She phoned room service.

Ten minutes later a smiling waitress appeared with a glass of spring water, a pot of herb tea and a carrot and cucumber salad, the luncheon menu of the day. Alvirah thought longingly of a nice, juicy hamburger, then remembered Barra Snow's remark about her sister getting a McDonald franchise in her divorce settlement. She half smiled, thinking that at this moment she felt as though she could eat the sister's profits in one sitting.

Alvirah found that the voluminous material on Cotter J. Hayward actually did make fascinating reading. He had been born in Darien, Connecticut, the grandson of the inventor of a circuit carrier for long-distance telephone calls who had sold his invention to AT&T for sixty million dollars.

"Huge money in those days," Alvirah thought as she made a note on her pad. That was when Cotter the first bought the jewelry for his wife. Because he was a notorious skinflint, the purchase made headlines. The jewelry was passed on to his son, Cotter the second, the playboy whose four wives each in turn got to wear it. But while the jewels may have remained intact, his lavish living and matrimonial settlements much diminished the family fortune.

Cotter the third, Nadine's late husband and Elyse's late ex-husband, seemed to be something of a chip off both blocks. There were dozens of pictures of him in his younger days, escorting film stars and debutantes. He had married Elyse when he was thirty-five, and like his grandfather, was known for his parsimony. He did his own investing and was rumored to be worth over one hundred million dollars, but no real figures were available.

He must have been a terrific golfer, Alvirah decided. Many of the pictures of him were taken on the golf course, playing with people like Jack Nicklaus and former President Ford. The older pictures showed him and Elyse, arm in arm, dressed for golfing, sometimes accepting awards together. The most recent pictures, those taken in the last three years, showed him with Nadine at social events, but there wasn't a single one of her at the golf outings.

One picture in particular caught Alvirah's eye. It showed Elyse and Barra Snow being awarded matching trophies at a charity outing at the Ridgewood Country Club in New Jersey and Cotter Hayward as chairman of the outing presenting them. That was only six weeks ago, she thought.

Cotter's smile that day seemed very genuine as he stood between the women. Elyse was smiling up at him. Love/hate, Alvirah thought. It's what Elyse felt for her ex. She read the caption under the picture and then raised her eyes. Oh my, she thought. Oh my.

Reaching for the phone she called Charley at the *Globe,* thanked him for the material he'd sent and requested him to have other material faxed as soon as possible. "I know it's eight o'clock in New York, but if you could put someone on it right away, I'll ask Min to let me have a key to the office so I can collect it tonight. Thanks a lot."

Her next job was to play back the recordings she had made at the dinner table last night, at Nadine's cottage and at lunch. As she listened, she made notes.

An exhausted Willy came in at six o'clock. "We swam, we did those exercise machines. Bobby knows all about using them. Then we had a glass of orange juice together and talked. He's a nice young fellow, honey, and knows his mother is in this situation because of him. I tell you, if somehow the real murderer can be found and Nadine gets off, Bobby Crandell won't so much as buy a lottery ticket again." Then Willy noticed the piles of clippings sorted on the table. "Any luck?"

"Not really, but I'm not sure. Anyhow, dinner should be interesting."

To Alvirah's relief, their entire table was in attendance. She'd been afraid that Elyse might decide to have dinner served in her cottage. But the first Mrs. Hayward, still icy in her composure, was elegantly dressed in a dark blue ankle-length sheath.

Barra Snow was wearing a white silk pantsuit that showed off her silver-blonde beauty. But she's not as gorgeous as her pictures in those ads, Alvirah thought—little lines were visible around Barra's eyes and mouth.

The discussion seemed to focus on Nadine's arrest. "I hope she realizes that if she's convicted, she won't collect a dime of Cotter's money," Elyse said, an unmistakable note of satisfaction in her voice.

"As you say, the ninth commandment must be obeyed," Alvirah prodded. "I mean when you think about it, if you and Mr. Hayward had patched things up four years ago . . . I guess you did that a lot didn't you? Fight and make up, fight and make up? Then *you'd* be his widow. Instead of that, he turned to Nadine. I'm sorry for you too. We all hate to lose a husband, but there's nothing the matter with being a rich widow."

"I really don't appreciate your observations, Mrs. Meehan," Elyse said sharply. "I've been made aware of your reputation as an amateur detective, but please spare me your ruminating."

Alvirah made herself look distressed. "Oh, I'm so sorry. I didn't mean to offend you." She hoped she looked properly penitent. "I'm just so sorry for Nadine. I mean, she's not a golfer. She has such fair skin, and her son told Willy that she is the world's worst athlete. She's more the artistic type, I think. Anyhow, what I mean is that it was just bad luck for everybody that Cotter and you didn't make up, wasn't it? And bad luck for her that, of all things, she carried *your* golf club when she went to meet him. I certainly hope she wasn't trying to throw suspicion on you. But then sometimes murderers get so rattled they make mistakes."

Elyse pointedly ignored Alvirah and her comments and began chatting exclusively with the Jennings couple, while Barra flirted halfheartedly with the former congressman. Over dessert, Alvirah was dismayed to hear that Elyse was leaving on Saturday.

"I just want to get a million miles away," Elyse said. "This place is totally depressing, and I never played worse golf. I *knew* I'd be lousy today."

Then Barra said, "I'm leaving too. There was a call from my agency. I have to do some retakes in New York on a photo shoot for Adrian. I'm canceling my second week here."

Alvirah found it hard not to stare at Elyse. The microphone was on, and later she'd have to listen to every word they'd said at dinner. Elyse had given something away. What was it?

The nightly entertainment was a slide show and lecture on fourteenth-century Spanish art. As people drifted into the back parlor where chairs had been placed, Alvirah asked Min for a key to her office. "I've got more faxes coming later, and I want to see them tonight."

Min's warm smile was for the benefit of observers. When she spoke, her voice was anxious. "Six guests canceled their next week's reservation. They are furious at the way the media is swarming outside the gates. Alvirah, why couldn't Nadine have killed Cotter with one of his *own* golf clubs? Why did she have to take one from these premises? Was she trying to make it look as though Elyse had committed the crime?"

"That's what's been bugging me," Alvirah replied, nodding. "I don't get it either. Why replace a club with blood all over it unless you want it to be found?"

The next morning, at Alvirah's request, Scott Alshorne came to Tranquility cottage for morning coffee. "Are you satisfied?" she asked him point-blank. "I mean totally, completely satisfied that Nadine killed her husband?"

Scott studied the contents of his cup. "Good coffee."

"You didn't answer Alvirah's question," Willy told him sternly.

Alvirah smiled to herself. She knew Willy was still a little miffed at Scott for the way he'd talked to her yesterday.

"I'm not sure I can," Scott said slowly. "Nadine has confessed. She had a motive, a very strong motive. There are two local telephone charges on the bill for her cottage. One was made on the ninth. That was Wednesday. One was made on the tenth. That was yesterday and would be consistent with her saying she called Cotter Hayward Wednesday night and Bobby saying he tried to reach Cotter early Thursday morning. So what have I got to doubt about her statement?"

"Sheriff, have you ever spread a rumor to flush out a killer?" Alvirah asked. "I mean defense attorneys in California do it all the time to protect their clients, so why not do it when it might accomplish some good?"

As he shook his head, she said persuasively, "Scott, it all has to do with the jewelry. Don't you see that? The jewelry is still missing. Let's suppose Nadine knew that Cotter Hayward was getting ready to dump her and staged a robbery so that at least she'd come

319

out of the marriage with jewelry she thought she could find a way to sell. The minute she called Bobby to report the loss and found out that he'd let the policy lapse, all she had to do was cancel the robbery. She called Bobby before she told Min about it. And let me tell you, when I met her, Nadine was frantic."

"All right, she didn't steal her own jewelry. I'll buy that."

"Are you sure Bobby was still in New York the afternoon of the theft?"

"Yes. We had his movements verified."

"Then somebody else stole that stuff, and dollars-to-doughnuts that person is the killer. Scott, go along with me on this, please."

It was a beautiful day. The morning sun beamed warm and bright over the Olympic-sized pool and the surrounding tables with their rainbow-colored umbrellas. At one of the tables a portable radio was tuned in to a local newscast, its volume on high. Riveted attention had replaced the quiet languor of guests who'd mixed a morning of exercise with facials and seaweed wraps and massages.

The voice on the radio was reporting that

there was a rumor that the sheriff had been keeping a lid on important evidence. Several clear footprints had been discovered in the wooded area near the sixteenth hole, where Cotter Hayward had been murdered. The sheriff was said to believe that they were the footprints of the killer, who apparently had been hiding and waiting for Hayward. What made this discovery especially significant was that these footprints, while clearly those of a woman, were definitely larger than the confessed killer's size, which was five and a half.

"And the shocker," the broadcaster continued, "is that the stolen jewelry was actually paste copies, which Hayward had made when he switched insurance policies. He was always concerned that Bobby Crandell would do exactly what he *did*—cash the premium check and let the policy lapse. So it looks as if whoever stole the Hayward jewelry is stuck with fool's gold."

Alvirah was not able to sit at Elyse Hayward's table this afternoon, but she did manage to capture a spot at one next to it. She switched on her recorder and turned her chair toward Elyse, then in a voice that was sure to carry, said: "That's not the whole story. You know I nose around a little, and I hear they're so sure the killer is a guest here that the sheriff is getting a court order to check the shoe sizes of all the women at the spa. If he finds a match, the judge will let him search the cottage and belongings to look for the jewelry.''

''That's illegal,'' someone protested.

''This is California,'' Alvirah reminded her. She leaned backwards as far as she dared without toppling over and was able to hear with her own ears Elyse saying very quietly, ''How like Cotter. How very like Cotter.'' Then she pushed her chair away from the table and excused herself.

Alvirah knew that a woman detective dressed as a spa maid would be following Elyse. She had another plan, however. When it was time to leave for the afternoon appointments, she quietly followed Barra Snow to her cottage, slipped around to the patio and, flattening herself against the side of the sliding glass door, peered in.

She pulled her head back as Barra looked around, then she inched forward just far enough to see Barra shove aside the portrait of Min and Helmut and dial the combination of her safe. A moment later she pulled out a plastic bag, the sparkling contents of which were heaped together.

"I thought so!" Alvirah breathed. *"I thought* so! Now Barra has to get rid of them . . ."

She stepped back. Barra's cottage, like Nadine's, was one of the farthest from the main house, a bit remote, with a wooded area behind it. Where was Barra going to try to dump the stuff? Alvirah wondered.

I was sure it was Elyse, Alvirah thought, but then when I asked Charley Evans to send me the file photos from that outing at the Ridgewood Country Club, I started seeing a different picture. In a couple of the photos, the way Cotter and Barra are looking at each other tells a lot. Then on the tape, it's so clear that Barra persuaded Elyse to go golfing yesterday. Barra was the one who sent the caddy for the clubs, knowing all along what he would find. She didn't seem to care whether Elyse was implicated, or if Nadine remained the prime suspect. Either way, no one would think her involved in the murder.

Alvirah's suspicions had been deepened when Barra had said she had to go back for a photo shoot. Alvirah knew that wasn't true. The caption under the picture referred to her as the ex-Adrian model. That's what had caught Alvirah's eye.

Plus she had made that crack about her sister getting a McDonald's franchise in her divorce settlement . . . What had Barra said? "*I* wasn't that lucky." I bet she hasn't got much money at all, Alvirah told herself.

The question remained, however, did she do the robbery on her own? And how did she know the combination of Nadine's safe.

There was only one person who could have given it to her, Alvirah realized—Cotter Hayward. Would he have stolen his own jewelry to get the insurance money to pay off that final three million to Elyse?

It was quiet inside the cottage. Barra must be going crazy trying to figure where to dump the jewelry she believes is worthless, Alvirah thought. Then her reverie was abruptly broken as something small and hard was pressed into her back, and she heard Barra Snow murmur, "You're much too clever for your own good, Mrs. Meehan."

Scott Alshorne was in a bad mood. He did not like the idea of allowing false rumors to swirl around during a murder investigation.

Therefore, it was not hard to look coldly furious when once again he got out of his car at the gates of the spa to confront the media.

"I have no comment about the alleged footprints in the vicinity of the murder scene," he said, his tone frosty. "I will not discuss the rumor that the stolen jewelry consisted of paste copies of the Hayward gems. I will actively pursue discovery of the source of any leaks from my office to the media."

And that much at least is true, he thought as he pushed his way past the microphones and cameras back to the car. The grounds of the spa had a deserted feeling. Scott knew that after luncheon was served, the serious business of beauty resumed with a vengeance. Min was always after him to take a full day of treatment as her guest. Just what I need, he thought irritably, to be wrapped in seaweed.

He went directly to Min's office where Walt Pierce, one of his deputies, Min, Helmut and Willy were awaiting him. "Where's Alvirah?" he asked.

"She should be here any minute," Willy told him evasively.

"Meaning she's up to something," Scott

said, congratulating himself that he had assigned Liz Hill, a woman deputy, to keep track of Alvirah.

He turned to Pierce. "Any reports yet?"

"Darva called in," Pierce told him. She followed Elyse Hayward to her cottage. She's got her under observation now."

"Any indication that Hayward has the jewelry?" Scott demanded.

"She went straight for the safe," Pierce informed him. "She had a bottle of gin hidden in it."

"Gin!" Min exclaimed. "It is part of our code of honor that guests will not conceal liquor in the safe. The maids are instructed to report any evidence of spirits in the cottages, but of course they do not have access to the safes."

"How can our guests lose weight if they imbibe?" Helmut sighed. "How can they retain the fresh bloom of youth?"

You manage, Willy thought.

"Darva has Elyse Hayward under surveillance with her binoculars. She says Hayward is crying and laughing and drinking. In other words, she's tying one on," Pierce continued.

"There goes Alvirah's theory," Scott said.

"If Elyse Hayward had the jewelry, she'd be trying to unload it. The last thing she'd be doing is getting drunk. Walt, what have you heard from Liz?"

"Mrs. Meehan is hiding on the patio of Barra Snow's cottage. Liz can't see the interior, just the front side opposite the patio, but so far no activity."

"How long has Liz been there?" Scott asked.

"About fifteen minutes."

The walkie-talkie Pierce was holding buzzed. He snapped it on and said, "What's up?" Then his tone changed. He looked at Min. "Deputy Hill wants to know if there's another entrance to Barra Snow's cottage."

"Yes," Min said. "That cottage has a sliding glass door from the master bedroom to the back patio."

Scott grabbed the walkie-talkie. "What's the matter?" He listened, then asked, "Are you wearing a maid's uniform? . . . All right. . . . Go up to the cottage. Make an excuse to go inside, then report back."

Willy felt the familiar sickening lurch in the pit of his stomach that always grabbed him when he began to worry about Alvirah.

A moment later the walkie-talkie buzzed

again. Deputy Hill made no attempt to speak softly, and they could all hear her. "Barra Snow and Mrs. Meehan are gone. They must have left through the back door. That's only a few feet from the woods. Snow must have opened the wall safe. The picture in front of it is pushed aside."

"We're on the way," Scott told her. "Try to pick up their trail."

Willy grabbed his arm. "Where do those woods end?"

"At the Pebble Beach Club," Min told him. "If Barra has the jewelry, she must be planning to get rid of it somewhere in those woods. It would be almost impossible to find. There are more than eighty acres, and much of it is dense and even swampy in places." Then, noting the look on Willy's face, she added hastily, "but Alvirah may simply be following her. I'm sure she is fine."

Alvirah stumbled through the thick undergrowth, prodded on by the gun in her back. The lush vegetation clawed at her ankles, and countless insects buzzed around her face. I attract mosquitoes, she thought. If there was only one mosquito in the world it would find me.

"Move faster," Barra ordered.

If I could just distract her, Alvirah thought, looking about for something to use as a club, anything with which to defend herself.

She deliberately stumbled and fell to her knees, then used the moment to catch her breath. "Where are you taking me?" she demanded, looking up at Barra Snow.

She found it difficult to reconcile this hard-eyed, thin-lipped woman with the sophisticated, amusing one she'd sat at the same table with these past few days. It was as though Barra had donned a mask. Or maybe, Alvirah thought, her other face was the mask.

"You killed Cotter Hayward, didn't you?" she asked. "You stole the jewelry?"

Snow pointed the gun at her. "Get up," she ordered. "Unless you want to die here."

Alvirah scrambled to obey. She had the presence of mind to turn on the recorder in her pin as she got to her feet. Then, hoping Barra wouldn't notice, she slid the small shoulder bag down her arm, and as she began to move, let it drop.

"That's better. Keep going."

"All right. All right." Alvirah dragged her feet, hoping to leave some trace of a trail. It was stifling in this place, with no breeze penetrating the dense foliage. She could hardly breathe. But no matter what, she needed to get a confession on record. "Tell me something," she panted. "Did you kill Cotter?"

"Alvirah, you're so smart, you must have it all figured out. Just shut up and MOVE!"

Alvirah felt the gun again, this time at the back of her head. "The way I figure it, you stole the jewelry and tried to make it look like a break-in by throwing all that stuff around. You must have really wondered why Nadine didn't report the theft."

"I'm going as fast as I can," she gasped. "Don't keep sticking that thing in my neck."

Then she continued, "The question is, why did you kill Hayward? He was meeting you on the golf course, wasn't he? My bet is that you were supposed to hand the jewelry over to him. Am I right?"

"Yes, you're right."

Fury and frustration resounded in Barra Snow's voice.

Moments later, the woods thinned suddenly, and they came upon a swampy area. Alvirah felt mud oozing beneath her feet. Directly ahead of them was a pond, all slimy water and vegetation. We have to be getting near the grounds of the Pebble Beach Club,

she thought. What does she think she's going to do now?

"I bet he gave you the combination for Nadine's safe and was going to claim the insurance money to pay off Elyse," she volunteered.

"Right on all counts," Barra said. "You can stop now."

Alvirah turned. "The thing is, why did you kill him? Was it because of the way Elyse talked about him being so cheap and Nadine being left penniless if she ever divorced him? Maybe you thought you were better off with that?" She pointed to the bag of jewelry Barra was carrying.

"Right again, Alvirah." This time Barra Snow pointed the gun at Alvirah's heart. "And when I tell them that I saw you dash past my cottage following a man who looked like one of the caddies at the Pebble Beach Club, they'll start looking for the killer here, not at the spa. And I'll be back at the spa in time for my facial.

"By the time they find you—if they find you, since that pond is deep, and the mud sucks you down like quicksand—I'll be far away from here.

"Now take these fake jewels in your

clammy little hands. I want to get rid of both them and you." As Alvirah obeyed, Barra stepped back and aimed the gun once again at Alvirah's heart.

As he ran to Barra's cottage, Scott ordered that squad cars be sent to both sides of the woods and that deputies begin the search for Barra and Alvirah. "They could have gone anywhere," he snapped. "Walt, we'll split up until more help comes. Min, you and the Baron and Willy stay out of it."

Ignoring the sheriff's command, Willy plunged into the thickets shouting for Alvirah. That woman is a killer, he said to himself, and she's getting desperate. If she knows Alvirah is following her, it's better if she realizes other people are around as well, that she can't get away with another murder.

Willy realized that the sheriff and the deputy had gone off in another direction from the one in which his instincts told him to head. Maybe I'd better veer over in the direction of the ocean, Willy thought, worried now that his instincts might be wrong. Maybe Barra Snow would try to get Alvirah down to the beach.

Then he saw it. Alvirah's pocketbook. He was sure she'd dropped it on purpose. Then he was able to make out where some grass was trampled. Yes, this *was* the right direction.

He charged ahead, reaching the clearing in time to see what was happening but not in time to stop Barra Snow.

As Barra pulled the trigger, Alvirah swerved, then felt a sharp pain coming from the vicinity of her sunburst pin. As she toppled backwards into the water, she thought, My God, I've been shot.

Willy lunged through the mud and grabbed Barra's arm just as she pointed the gun at the spot where Alvirah was starting to sink. The shot exploded into the air as he wrenched the gun from her hand, tossed it into the water, then pushing her down, leaped after it.

"I've got you, honey," he said, lifting Alvirah's head. "I've got you."

Alvirah felt a pain in her shoulder. The pin, she thought. My sunburst pin took the bullet. She had been saved by ducking—and sheer luck! Barra's aim had been thrown off by her movement, and the bullet had merely grazed the pin. She felt the pain radiating from the point of impact, but again thought in wonder, I'm all right. I know I'm all right. And I've still got the jewelry.

She managed not to faint until she had the satisfaction of seeing Scott come charging into the clearing in time to collar Barra Snow, who was struggling furiously to extract herself from the mire.

"I think the occasion calls for breaking the cardinal rule of the Cypress Point Spa," Helmut said, as a maid carrying champagne and glasses on a tray followed him into Tranquility cottage.

Alvirah's arm was in a sling. She was comfortably ensconced on a sofa in the sitting room and beaming amiably at Min, Scott, Nadine and Bobby. Willy, still pale with worry over her narrow escape, was hovering over her like a mother hen.

"I think you need rest, honey," he said for the fifteenth time in the last five hours.

"I'm fine," Alvirah said, "and forever thankful that I insisted on wearing my pin 'just in case.' Heaven knows I never thought 'just in case' would include getting shot at. The pin's pretty well destroyed, but the recording is still okay. I got Barra Snow cold." She beamed at the thought.

Scott Alshorne shook his head. Once again he found himself counting his blessings that Alvirah Meehan lived a continent away. She attracted trouble, no question about it.

He grudgingly admitted to himself, though, that Alvirah's scheme to spread the rumors about the footprints at the crime scene and the paste jewelry had certainly worked. If he hadn't gone along with it, Nadine Hayward would still be in jail, sticking to her story that she had murdered her husband—just to protect her son. And Barra Snow would be packing her bags and heading home, leaving behind a murdered man and taking with her four million dollars' worth of stolen jewelry.

He accepted a glass of champagne when offered one, and when Helmut proposed the toast to Alvirah, Scott gladly joined in acknowledging her valor. Nevertheless, with an eye to the future, he decided it was time to say his piece.

"Alvirah, my good friend, you have saved the day again. But I would implore you to realize that if a deputy had not been following you—"

"Who *you* put on my tail," Alvirah interrupted. "That was very clever of you, Scott."

"Thank you. I would like to point out that you came within an inch of losing your life today, and all because you did not simply ask for help when you followed Barra Snow."

Alvirah's attempt to look chagrined was not convincing. "I'll be honest," she said. "I was betting mostly on Elyse being the murderer. It just made sense. And let me tell you, there really *was* a love/hate relationship between her and Cotter Hayward."

"Looking back, I agree," Nadine said quietly. "Apparently one of the things that attracted Cotter to me was that I *didn't* play golf. I gather he and Elyse would get into constant screaming matches about each other's games. But after four years I think he was bored with me and missed that kind of companionship."

"Except that he was getting it from Barra, not Elyse," Scott interjected. "When Elyse Hayward learned what happened this afternoon, she admitted that she honestly thought Cotter Hayward was getting interested in being with her again. Then she sensed there was someone else in the picture, but she hadn't guessed that it was Barra."

Scott turned to Nadine. He half smiled when he saw the blissfully peaceful look on her face and the absolute happiness emanating from her son, Bobby. But then he forced himself to look stern. "Nadine, you and Bobby lied for each other. It was easy to see through Bobby's attempts to cover for you, but please realize you could have gone to the gas chamber if a judge or a jury had believed your story. Fortunately, Alvirah did not, and I had gut-level doubts about it as well."

"But you did leave your cottage after you went to bed the other night," Alvirah said. "That's why Bobby went looking for you. I never did hear where you went."

Nadine looked embarrassed. "I did make a call to Cotter, but when he answered, I was so upset I just hung up. Then I went over to the lap pool and settled into one of the beach chairs. I knew no one would see or hear me there, and I didn't want Bobby to hear me crying. I guess I was so exhausted I fell asleep."

"So *that's* why there was a blanket on one of those chairs," Min breathed. "I am glad to hear it. When it was reported to me, I did not know what to think."

"I have a point to make," Alvirah said, and

now she looked stern. "Nadine, I gather you're now a very wealthy woman. I'll say this right in front of Bobby. You won't do him any favors if you ever cover gambling debts for him."

"I agree," Bobby said. He looked at Nadine. "Mom, I don't deserve you."

Min arose. "I must get to the main house. Tonight I lecture on the need for quiet meditation as part of the overall process of achieving beauty."

This time Willy spoke up. "Min, with all due respect, thanks for your hospitality, but in the interest of achieving a little peace, we're heading back to New York in the morning. You can let someone on the waiting list know that Tranquility cottage is available."

Bye,
Baby
Bunting

*I*t was December 20th, and although later on Alvirah would call it the most awful day of her life, when it began she could not have felt more festive.

At 7:00 A.M., the phone rang with the joyous news that Joan Moore O'Brien had been delivered of her first child, a baby girl. "Her name is Marianne," Gregg O'Brien reported happily, "she weighs six pounds, two ounces and she's gorgeous."

Joan Moore had lived next door to Alvirah and Willy in Queens, and they had watched her grow up, becoming close to her and her family over the years. As Alvirah put it, "A sweeter girl never walked the face of the earth."

She and Willy had maintained their contact with Joan even after their move to Central Park South in Manhattan and had been proud to be at her wedding to Gregg O'Brien, a handsome young engineer. They regularly visited the young couple in their apartment in Tribeca and joined in celebrating Gregg's rise up the corporate ladder and Joan's promotions at the bank. They also shared the O'Briens' terrible disappointment when Joan suffered three miscarriages.

"But now, finally, praise the Lord, they have their baby," Alvirah crowed to Willy as she heaped waffles on his plate. "You know I felt in my bones that this time it was going to work out. I'd even gone ahead and bought presents for the baby, although I really have to do serious shopping this morning before we go to the hospital. After all, we are the surrogate grandparents."

Willy smiled affectionately at Alvirah, looking with love at the woman with whom he had spent the best years of his life. Her blue eyes were bright with happiness, her complexion rosy. She'd just had her hair tinted yesterday, so now it was again a soft red, and all the gray had been firmly routed. She looked warm and comfortable in the chenille robe that followed the lines of her generous body. Willy smiled; he thought she was beautiful.

"We should have had six kids," he said, "and twenty grandchildren."

"Well, Willy, the good Lord didn't send them, but now we can have fun spoiling Joan and Gregg's little girl. I mean, it's practically an obligation since Joan's folks aren't around anymore."

At three that afternoon, they were entering the crowded lobby of Empire Hospital on West Twenty-third Street.

"I can't wait to see the baby," Alvirah enthused, making her way past receptionists too busy to notice them.

"I can't wait to unload the presents," Willy commented as he strained to keep his fingers from slipping out of the handles of the heavy shopping bags he was carrying. "Why do they have to put little scraps of clothes in such big boxes anyhow?''

"Because they never heard the old saying that good things come in small packages. Oh, doesn't the lobby look cheerful? I love holiday decorations. They're so pretty.''

"I never thought of a life-sized balloon of Rudolph the Rednosed Reindeer as being pretty,'' Willy observed as they passed a card-board sleigh, complete with balloon Santa Claus and reindeer.

"Gregg said Joan is in room 1121.'' Alvirah paused for a moment. "There are the elevators.'' She hoisted one of the shopping bags she was clutching and pointed down the corridor.

"Shouldn't we get visitor's passes?'' Willy asked.

"Joan said to come right through. They really don't bother you if you look as though you know where you're going.''

They just missed an elevator and were the only people waiting when the doors of an adjacent one opened. In her haste, Alvirah almost ran into a woman who stepped out of the elevator carrying an infant. The heavy scarf that covered the woman's head fell forward, shielding her face. She was dressed in a ski jacket and slacks.

Ever maternal, Alvirah peeked down to admire the baby, who was nestled in a yellow bunting. Blue eyes opened wide, stared up at her, then closed again. A yawn enveloped the pink-and-white face, and small fists waved.

"Oh, she's gorgeous," Alvirah sighed as the woman hurried past them.

Willy was holding open the elevator door with his shoulder. "Honey, come on," he urged.

As the elevator lumbered up, stopping at every floor to take on passengers, Alvirah had the fleeting thought that in most hospitals, when a new mother and her baby were discharged, they were taken to the door in a wheelchair. Well, things change, she decided.

When they reached room 1121, Alvirah rushed in. Ignoring Joan, who was sitting up in bed, and Gregg, who was standing beside her, Alvirah hurried to the small crib against the wall. "Oh, she isn't here," she lamented.

Gregg laughed. "Marianne is having a hearing test. I can vouch that she'll pass with flying colors. When I scraped the chair against the floor this morning, she jumped in Joan's arms and started yelling."

"Well then, I guess I'd better pay some attention to the proud parents." Alvirah bent over Joan and hugged her fiercely. "I'm so happy for you," she said as tears ran down her full cheeks.

"Why do women always cry when they're happy?" Gregg asked Willy, who was trying to prop the shopping bags in the corner.

"Leaky tear ducts," Willy grunted as he grasped Gregg's hand and shook it vigorously. "I'm not going to cry, but I'm awfully happy for both of you too."

"Wait till you see her," Gregg boasted. "She's gorgeous, like her mama."

"She has your forehead and chin," Joan told him.

"And your blue eyes and porcelain complexion and—"

"Sorry folks," a voice interrupted. They all turned to see a smiling nurse standing in the door. "I've got to borrow your baby for a few minutes," she said.

"Oh, another nurse already took her. Just a few minutes ago," Gregg said.

When she saw the look of alarm on the nurse's face, Alvirah knew instantly that something was terribly wrong.

"What's the matter?" Joan asked, sitting up, leaning forward, her face turning ashen. "Where's my baby? Who has her? What's going on?"

The nurse raced out of the room, and moments later an alarm sounded throughout the hospital. An urgent voice over the loudspeaker announced, "Code Orange! Code Orange!"

Alvirah knew what the alarm meant, internal disaster. But she also knew it was too late. Her mind flashed back to the woman exiting the elevator just as they were coming up. She had been right—newborn babies and their mothers do not leave the hospital unescorted. Alvirah ran from the room to talk to security personnel, as Joan collapsed in Gregg's arms.

An hour later, at 4:00 P.M., in a small, cluttered apartment on West Ninetieth Street, seventy-eight-year-old Wanda Brown was comfortably propped up on a shabby couch and bestowing a moist-eyed smile on her granddaughter. "Such a happy surprise," she said, "a Christmas visit. You coming all the way from Pittsburgh with your new baby! You certainly have put your troubles behind you, Vonny."

"Guess I have, Grandma." The voice was monotone. Vonny's eyes, light brown and guileless, stared off into the distance.

"Such a beautiful baby. Is she good?"

"I hope so." Vonny jostled the baby in her arms.

"What's her name?"

"Vonny, just like mine."

"Oh, that's nice. When you wrote and told me you were expecting, I prayed that nothing would happen. No girl deserves to lose a baby that way, and to have it happen twice."

"I know, Grandma."

"It was better that you left the New York area, but I've missed you, Vonny. It's obvious that the stay in the hospital really helped you. Tell me about your new husband. Will he be joining you?"

"No, Grandma. He's too busy. I'll be here a few days, then go back to Pittsburgh. But please don't mention the hospital. I don't want to talk about the hospital. And don't ask questions. I hate questions."

"Vonny, I never, never said a word to anyone. You know me better than that. I've been here five years, and not a one of my neighbors knows anything about what happened. The nuns who visit me are wonderful, and I always tell them what a dear girl you are. I had mentioned that you were expecting a Christmas baby, and they've all been praying for you."

348

"That's nice, Grandma." Vonny smiled briefly. The baby in her arms began to wail. "Shut up!" she snapped as she shook it. "You *hear* me? Shut *up!*"

"Give the baby to me, Vonny," Wanda Brown pleaded. "And you go heat her bottle. Where are her clothes?"

"Somebody stole her suitcase on the bus," Vonny said sullenly. "On my way here I picked up some odds and ends at a thrift shop, but I have to get her some more stuff."

At eleven o'clock that night, sitting somberly side by side in the living room of their apartment overlooking Central Park, Willy and Alvirah watched the local CBS newscast.

The lead story was the bold kidnapping of eight-hour-old Marianne O'Brien from Empire Hospital.

Willy felt Alvirah tense as the anchorman said, "It is believed that the kidnapper was observed just prior to leaving the hospital by family friends, Willy and Alvirah Meehan, who had come to visit the proud and happy parents.

"Mrs. Meehan's description of the infant leaves little doubt that she had seen the

O'Brien baby. Unfortunately, neither she nor her husband could provide any significant details about the abductor, who apparently had disguised herself as a nurse. The O'Briens say she was about thirty years old, of medium height, with blond hair . . ."

"How come they don't talk about the yellow bunting?" Willy asked. "You noticed that especially."

"Probably because the police always hold something back so that they can tell real calls from quack calls."

Alvirah squeezed Willy's hand as she listened to the anchorman say that the heartbroken mother, Joan O'Brien, was under heavy sedation and that the hospital had announced a news conference, during which the father would broadcast a plea to the kidnapper.

Then the newsman interrupted himself in midsentence. "We're going live to Empire Hospital for a late-breaking bulletin," he said.

Alvirah leaned forward and squeezed Willy's hand again.

After a moment's pause, an on-the-scene reporter spoke from the lobby of the hospital. "Authorities here report that the uniform of a hospital attendant and a blond wig have just been found stuffed in the disposal container of a lavatory on the floor from which Baby Marianne was abducted. The lavatory is a facility reserved for hospital personnel and can be entered only by punching in a special code." The reporter paused for effect and looked intently into the camera. "Authorities now fear that this kidnapping may have been an inside job."

Or that the woman knew her way around the hospital, Alvirah thought. Maybe she had worked or was a patient there at some time. Or she could have just been visiting someone and gotten the lay of the land, watched what the nurses were doing. She was wearing a blond wig. That means we don't even know what color her hair really is. With that scarf so tight over her head, I didn't notice.

The news bite about the kidnapping ended with a doctor giving the baby's formula and the police commissioner promising compassion and help to the abductor if the baby was returned safely. Anyone with any information was asked to call a number that was flashed on the screen.

Willy pushed the remote control button and switched off the television; then he put his arm around Alvirah, who sat next to him, shaking her head. "You can't blame yourself, honey. Remember, if that woman was so desperate for a baby, she'll take care of Marianne until the police find her."

"Oh, Willy, I can't *not* blame myself. You know how my antenna just naturally goes up when something's out of whack. It's just that I was excited, so anxious to see the baby and to hug Joan and Gregg. I know there was something, something odd that registered in those seconds when I saw that woman." She shook her head again. "I just can't dig it up." Then she gasped, and her eyes brightened. "I've got it! I remember! Willy, it was the bunting, that yellow bunting. *I've seen it somewhere before!*"

Long after she and Willy went to bed, Alvirah lay awake trying to remember where she had seen the yellow bunting before yesterday and why it had made an impression on her, but for once her prodigious memory seemed to be failing her.

Ever since Joan had entered her eighth month and Alvirah had known that even if she delivered early, the baby would probably be all right, she had been shopping for it.

It was so much fun looking at everything and deciding on the kimonos and shirts and sacks and bonnets and receiving blankets. I don't think I've passed a display of baby things without window-shopping, Alvirah mused. But where did I see that bunting, or one just like it?

None of the gifts she and Willy had taken to the hospital had been opened; they had just stuck them in the closet of Joan's room. I've got to go through them and make a list of all the stores I was in, Alvirah decided.

Only after settling on this course of action was Alvirah able to relax enough to actually fall asleep. At breakfast she told Willy her plan. "The thing is, you don't see buntings the way you used to," she explained. "People just don't seem to use them much anymore. And that this one was yellow and folded back to show a deep, white satin border makes it especially unusual."

"White satin sounds expensive," Willy said. "I didn't get much of a look at that woman, but the outfit she was wearing certainly looked more thrift shop than custom made."

"You're right," Alvirah agreed. "It was a sort of run-of-the-mill dark blue nylon jacket and dark blue slacks, the kind you'd pick off a bargain rack. I just didn't pay attention to her. I was so busy trying to get a look at the baby. But you're right, a bunting with a satin border *would* be expensive."

Then her heart gave a sickening lurch. "Willy, do you think she stole the baby because she had arranged to sell it to someone else? If she did, there's no telling where they could be by now." She pushed back her chair and got up. "I can't waste time."

Despite the cardboard sleigh and the balloon figures of Santa Claus and his reindeer, the hospital lobby had lost whatever cheery atmosphere Willy and Alvirah had sensed there the day before. The corridor to the bank of elevators was now patrolled by a security guard, and no one without a visitor's pass was allowed down it.

When Alvirah gave Joan O'Brien's name, she was firmly told that no visitors would be allowed to see her. Finally she convinced the receptionist to call up to Gregg, and from him she learned that Joan had been moved from the maternity floor. "Yes, the presents are still in the closet of 1121," he said, when

Alvirah explained what she needed. "I'll meet you there."

Alvirah was stunned when she saw Gregg. He seemed to have aged ten years overnight. His eyes were bloodshot, and his face was etched with lines that creased his mouth and forehead. She was sure that any expression of sympathy would only make things worse; he knew how she felt.

"Help me open these packages," she ordered crisply. "Then I'll read the labels to see which stores the things came from, and you write the names down."

There were twelve stores in all, the gifts ranging from big items from Saks and Bloomingdale's, to hand-crocheted sweaters from a specialty shop on Madison Avenue, to small items like nightgowns and kimonos from obscure shops in Greenwich Village and the Upper West Side.

When the list was complete, Alvirah hastily stacked the purchases together and piled them into the biggest boxes. As she was closing the lid on the last one, a police officer came into the room, looking for Gregg. "There's a break in the case, Mr. O'Brien," he said. "A call came in to the hot line. Some guy claims his cousin's wife came home yesterday with a new baby she says is hers. Only thing is, she hadn't been pregnant."

A look of incredible hope came over Gregg's face. "Who is he? Where is he?"

"He said he's from Long Island and is going to call back. But there's one hitch. He thinks there ought to be a twenty-thousand-dollar reward."

"I'll guarantee it," Alvirah said flatly, even as a dark premonition told her that this was going to turn out to be a false lead.

"Vonny, the baby really needs some clothes," Wanda Brown said timidly. It was Wednesday afternoon. Vonny had been there a whole day and had only changed the baby's kimono once. "This place is drafty, and you only have one other kimono. For a baby that's two weeks old, this one is real little and mustn't get a chill."

"All my babies were small," Vonny told her as she examined the nursing bottle she was holding. "She drinks slow," she complained.

"She's falling asleep. You have to be patient. Why not let me finish feeding her and you go shopping? Where did you get the things you bought for her after her suitcase got lost?"

"The thrift shop was right down from the Port Authority. But there wasn't much left for infants, just the bunting and that." Vonny waved her hand at the kimono and shirt that were drying on the radiator. "They were getting more in. I guess I could try them again."

She got up and handed the sleeping infant to her grandmother. As an afterthought she gave her the bottle. "It's getting cold, but don't worry. And I don't want you walking around with her."

"I wouldn't try." Wanda Brown took the baby and tried not to show her shock at the icy feel of the bottle. Vonny didn't heat it at all, she thought. Then she shrank back as her granddaughter bent over her.

"Now remember, Grandma, I don't want people coming in here looking at my baby and handling it while I'm out."

"Vonny, no one ever comes here except the nuns who stop by once a week or so. You'd love them. Sister Cordelia and Sister Maeve Marie come most often. They're always making sure that people like me have enough food, and that we're not getting sick, and that the heat and the plumbing work. Only last month, Sister Cordelia sent her brother, Willy, who's a plumber, here because there was a leak under the kitchen sink that had the whole place musty. What a nice man! Sister Maeve Marie stopped in Monday, but none of them will be back again till Christmas Eve. They're bringing me a Christmas dinner basket. It's always nice, and I know there'll be enough for you too."

"The baby and I will be gone by then."

"Of course. You want to spend Christmas with your husband."

Vonny pulled on her blue ski jacket. Her dark hair was tangled on her shoulders. At the door she turned to her grandmother. "I'll pick out some nice things for her. I love my baby. I loved my other babies too." Her face twisted in pain. "It wasn't my fault."

"I know that, dear," Wanda said soothingly.

She waited a few minutes, until Vonny had been gone long enough to be out of the building, then Wanda laid the baby on the couch and tucked her frayed afghan around it. Reaching for her cane, she picked up the bottle and limped into the kitchen. A baby shouldn't drink such cold milk, she fretted.

She poured water into a small saucepan, set it on the stove, placed the bottle in it and turned on the gas. As she waited for the bottle to heat, she was troubled by the thought of Vonny and the baby on that long, cold bus ride to Pittsburgh. Then another thought struck her. On her last visit, Sister Maeve Marie had told her that the nuns were opening a thrift shop on Eighty-sixth Street. People could get clothes very cheap there, or even for nothing if they were broke. Maybe she should phone the sisters and tell them about Vonny losing the baby's suitcase. They might have some nice baby clothes on hand.

When the bottle was satisfactorily warmed, she limped back to the couch. As she fed the baby, gently rubbing her cheek to keep her from falling asleep again, Wanda pondered the pros and cons of calling Sister Maeve Marie. No, she decided, she'd wait. Maybe Vonny would have good luck and come home with some nice baby clothes. And, after all, Vonny had said she didn't want people looking at her baby. That probably even included nuns.

The baby finished four ounces of the bottle. That's not bad, Wanda thought. Then she listened intently. Was that a wheeze coming from the baby's chest? Oh, I hope she's not catching cold, she thought. She's so little, and it would break Vonny's heart if anything happened to her . . .

The television was on the blink, so Wanda turned on the radio to catch the noon news. The lead story was still about the missing O'Brien baby. The caller who claimed his cousin had the baby had phoned again and had been promised a twenty-thousand-dollar reward. Authorities were waiting for him to call back and make arrangements for the delivery of the money, at which point he would take the police to his cousin's home.

How awful, Wanda thought, as she cradled Vonny's sleeping infant. How could *anyone* steal someone else's baby?

Alvirah spent the rest of Wednesday and all of Thursday going down the list of stores where she had purchased baby clothes.

"Do you have, or did you carry a yellow bunting with a white satin border?"

The answer was always no.

Several clerks said that they didn't get many calls for buntings these days. Especially in yellow. And a white-satin border would be impractical. Wouldn't the bunting have to be cleaned?

I know it was yellow wool and white satin, Alvirah thought. It must have come from a specialty shop. Maybe I just saw it in a window? With that in mind, after she had inquired at a store where she had made a purchase, she walked around the immediate neighborhood in the hope that the window of another shop would trigger her memory.

In the late afternoon, it began to snow, light flurries accompanied by sharp, damp winds. Oh God, she thought as she headed for home, let whoever has the baby be keeping her warm and dry and fed.

The lobby of their building on Central Park South, so festively decorated for Christmas and Chanukah, seemed to mock her with its radiant warmth. When she got to the apartment, she made a cup of tea, phoned the hospital and was put through to Gregg.

"I'm with Joan," he said. "She won't let them give her any more sedation. She knows about the call and the reward. She wants to talk to you."

Alvirah thought her heart would break as she listened to Joan's whispered thanks for putting up the reward and her promise to pay back every cent.

"Forget the money," she said, trying to keep her tone light. "Just make sure Marianne's middle name is Alvirah."

"Of course. I promise," Joan said.

Alvirah added hastily, "I'm only joking, Joanie. It's no name for a baby, at least not in this day and age."

Willy came in just as she hung up the phone. "Good news?" he asked hopefully.

"I wish I thought so. Willy, if you knew your cousin's wife had someone's baby, and you'd been guaranteed the reward you asked for, why wouldn't you just say straight out where the baby is?"

"Maybe he's worried that the cousin's wife will go crazy if they take the baby from her."

"He ought to be more worried that something might happen to the baby. The reward is only if Marianne is returned safely. He knows that. Mark my words, Willy, that caller is pulling a hoax. He's trying to figure out how to get the reward and disappear."

Willy saw the misery in Alvirah's face and knew she was still blaming herself for what had happened. "I was just up with Cordelia," he said. "She phoned me right after you went out. She and the nuns are praying around the clock, and she's got all her people praying too."

Alvirah half smiled. "If I know her, she's probably saying, 'Now listen, God . . .'"

"Pretty close," Willy agreed. "Except now she's doing it while she works. Her idea of opening a thrift shop has really paid off. When I was by there yesterday, a bunch of people brought in good clothes in really nice condition."

"Well, Cordelia won't take any worn-out stuff," Alvirah said. "And she's right—just because you're down on your luck doesn't mean you have to be stuck with rags."

"And now Cordelia has a sign out asking for games and toys for kids. She's even lined up more volunteers to put Christmas wrappings on whatever people pick out for their children. She says kids should have packages to open come Christmas morning."

"Will of iron, heart of gold, that's our Cordelia," Alvirah said. Then she burst out, "Willy, I feel so helpless, so *damn* helpless. Praying is important, but I feel like I should be doing more. Doing something . . . more active. This waiting is driving me looney."

Willy put his arms around her. "Then keep busy. Go up to the thrift shop tomorrow and give Cordelia a hand. It was busy when you helped out there last week. And with only two days till Christmas, it's going to be a mob scene tomorrow."

● ● ●

On the morning of December 23rd, tension reached a fever pitch at One Police Plaza at the command center for the case that had become known among insiders as the Baby Bunting Kidnapping.

By then the entire team had come to seriously doubt the validity of the story told by the phone caller who claimed knowledge of the whereabouts of the O'Brien baby.

They had been able to keep the caller on the line long enough to trace the last two phone calls. Both of them came from the Bronx, not Long Island, and from phone booths within a few blocks of each other. Now undercover police were blanketing the vicinity of Fordham Road and the Grand Concourse, keeping the public phones under surveillance, prepared to close in on the mysterious caller.

Experts were studying December 20th security videotapes from Empire Hospital, particularly those from cameras in the lobby and the corridor to the elevators. The tape in which Alvirah and Willy could be vaguely made out revealed little of the woman carrying the infant. Only the bunting stood out,

Evaluating Leisure Services
Making Enlightened Decisions

Second Edition

by

Karla A. Henderson

and

M. Deborah Bialeschki

 Venture Publishing, Inc. • State College, Pennsylvania

Production Manager: Richard Yocum
Manuscript Editing: Michele L. Barbin
Cover Design by Echelon Design

Printing and Binding: Thomson Shore, Inc.

Library of Congress Catalogue Card Number 2001095417
ISBN 1-892132-26-5

Dedicated to Christine Z. Howe

Table of Contents

Unit One

CRITERIA: Introduction to Foundations for Evaluation

1.1 The Basic Question: What Is Evaluation? 3

1.2 Evaluation and Research: Viva la Difference 9

1.3 The Trilogy of Evaluation and Research: Criteria, Evidence, and Judgment 17

1.4 Why Evaluate? Who Cares? 23

UNIT TWO
EVIDENCE: Data Collection

UNIT THREE
EVIDENCE: Data Analysis

Unit Four

JUDGMENT: Data Reporting

List of Tables and Figures

Preface

We live in an "information" age. Professionals in any field of human services must have means to access and assess information about participants and organizations. To organize and manage leisure services, we need information about people's preferences, needs, and behaviors and the programs, administrative structures, and resources that comprise the organizations. Evaluation can provide information that will enable us to make "enlightened decisions."

Evaluation is a process that each of us uses every day. You probably made a judgment about what you liked or didn't like as you saw the cover of this book and began to thumb through these pages. Although this type of intuitive evaluation is important, this book is about systematic evaluation that focuses specifically on identifying explicit evaluation criteria, collecting evidence or data, and making judgments about the value or the worth of something.

Unfortunately, evaluation strikes terror in the hearts of many students and professionals. People are often afraid to do evaluations and afraid of what they might find. Doing evaluations does not consist of any magic formula. Further, learning to do evaluations cannot be done overnight. The more you learn about evaluation procedures, however, the easier they become. We hope to counter through this book the defeatist attitudes prevalent among students and some professionals that assessment, evaluation, and statistics are beyond their grasp. In addition, we hope to show how valuable doing evaluations can be.

This text will not make you an expert. It is intended, however, to provide an awareness and understanding of the need for evaluation research in the delivery of leisure and human services. We attempt to show how programming and management are the bases for evaluation. This book is intended to provide a basic overview and working knowledge of evaluation procedures. Knowing basic steps in evaluation research and having some familiarity with evaluation research tools can help you to begin a process of lifelong learning about evaluation and the research process in general. Each time you do an evaluation you will learn something that will be helpful for next time. Thus, this book will provide a primer that will enable you to use evaluation and become more experienced as you practice and apply the evaluation research concepts and techniques.

This textbook is designed for upper-level undergraduates, beginning graduate students, and practitioners who wish to apply evaluation research to their efforts. It is written for students, but students are defined as anyone who is in a learning situation. Many professionals find that learning makes the most sense once they are in the "real world" where they need to apply text material immediately to their situations.

This book consists of a discussion of the three main elements of evaluation divided into four logical units. The three parts are the thesis, or the "trilogy," of the evaluation process—criteria, evidence (data), and judgment. Since the evidence section is mainly oriented to techniques, strategies, and research methods, we have divided it into two units on collecting data and analyzing data. Because evaluation uses a number of conceptual ideas and specific research applications, we have organized the chapters around specific topics. Sometimes it is useful to read about a particular concept and technique and reflect upon it before moving on to the next idea. Other times you may want to turn to a particular chapter that will give information to address a specific evaluation project.

We have taken the *"USA Today"* approach to writing this text. *USA Today* uses short articles that can be read and comprehended fairly quickly. Unlike *USA Today*, we have tried not to oversimplify the ideas but we have structured chapters that will be easily read. The number of chapters in this book may seem a bit overwhelming but none of them is particularly long and we have tried to organize the reading by outlining key points and providing examples where possible.

We have also made the assumption that we are all in the recreation, park, leisure, and tourism field together. We have tried to use examples related to therapeutic recreation, youth agencies, community recreation, commercial businesses, and camping and outdoor recreation. Although not all of these examples will be directly applicable to your interest, we believe that in a field that shares the common goals of enhancing the quality of life for people through recreation and leisure, we can learn from each other. In most cases the implications of evaluation to any one area of recreation can apply to other applied areas as well.

A number of people have influenced the writing of this textbook. We are most indebted to Pat Farrell and Herberta Lundegren (Penn State University) for the model evaluation book that they wrote. We used their model in the first edition of this book and have tried to build upon their framework with the inclusion of more examples of evaluation based on qualitative data. The education we received about evaluation has largely come from our formal coursework in education and particularly adult education. Individuals who have effected those ideas greatly are Pat Boyle (University of Minnesota) and Sara Steele (University of Wisconsin—Madison). Other individuals in the field of parks, recreation, and leisure studies who have contributed to our understanding of evaluation are too numerous to mention here but are acknowledged throughout this book.

This book has evolved from the teaching of evaluation and research methods to students over the past 25 years. Although we are indebted to all students who have helped us learn about how to teach these topics, we particularly want to thank the students in recreation courses at the University of North Carolina at Chapel Hill who critiqued initials drafts of the book and have done summative evaluations that have been useful each semester since the first edition was published. We also wish to acknowledge the support of our colleagues, John Hemingway and Beth Kivel, as well as our office staff, Summer Montgomery and Meg Dawson, during the writing of this second edition. We also appreciate the assistance of our graduate students Mike Thonnerieux and Sonja Hodges. We offer a special thanks to Delaine Deal and Rhonda Mickelson for their ongoing support, and to the intuitive evaluators named Dover, Jellico, Schroeder, Lucy, and Eli.

We hope that you as students and readers will evaluate this book favorably because you set criteria that valued a readable, understandable, and useful text and that you found evidence that supported those criteria.

UNIT ONE
CRITERIA
Introduction to Foundations for Evaluation

Introduction to Criteria

Beginning a text is not easy. Because your anxiety may already be high, we dislike beginning on a theoretical note. Yet a certain framework needs to be presented to provide a foundation for evaluation. In discussing evaluation and research, we are systematic with the procedures that we outline for you. It is sometimes more tempting to start in the middle of the process than at the beginning. For example, people sometimes draft a questionnaire before they have thought about the overall design of the project or who will use the information. To explore evaluation effectively using this text, we as authors and you as readers must communicate at the same level. Therefore, we start at the beginning by providing a conceptual background about evaluation. As a reader, of course, you can start wherever you would like, but we encourage you to ground yourself in a basic understanding of evaluation and research processes *before* you begin to collect data.

Evaluating Leisure Services attempts to provide the novice student or professional with the tools to conduct evaluation research. The goal of systematic evaluation is to make reliable, valid, useful, and enlightened decisions. Of course, all of us are continually involved in a process of evaluation. How many times have you stuck your toe in a swimming pool to test its temperature before jumping in? Simplistic as it may be, dipping your toes is a form of evaluation that will lead to a judgment or a decision about whether and how to enter the water. If only formal evaluations were as easy as sticking one's toes into the water and making a decision! Unfortunately, most evaluations in leisure services are (and should be!) more systematic and complicated than this intuitive example. In this book, we provide a useful process for systematic evaluation.

This first unit sets a framework for evaluation and explores the aspects of *determining criteria*. Although not the most "action-packed" unit, it certainly is one of the most critical. One major problem with evaluations is that sometimes evaluators do not take time to plan and ascertain the appropriate criteria to use. For example, by putting your toes into the swimming pool, you determined the temperature criterion, but many other criteria could have been measured by using some other process, such as water quality or depth. Perhaps the pH level in a swimming pool is a more appropriate criterion to measure than temperature before you go swimming. Measuring the pH level with one's toes would not be appropriate if the criteria included a chemical balance check. Thus, an essential dimension of any evaluation is making sure you are collecting evidence about the appropriate criteria or research questions.

In this book we refer to the individual(s) conducting evaluations as the *evaluator(s)*. Evaluation refers to making decisions based on identified questions or criteria and supporting evidence. Evaluation research includes the processes used to collect and analyze data or evidence. Research studies are described in relationship to evaluation projects in the text, but the major focus here is on evaluation research and its use. Leisure services are the human service organizations and enterprises related to:

- parks,
- recreation,
- tourism,
- commercial recreation,
- outdoors,
- education, and
- therapeutic recreation.

Other specific terms will be defined throughout this book. In addition, we include a glossary of terms to assist you as you read the text.

In this first unit, we examine what evaluation is, its purposes, its relationship to research, and how the aspects of criteria, evidence, and judgment are defined and interrelated. We explore areas of evaluation within leisure services and the types of evaluation that might be done. Within these types we examine various approaches and models that can be applied. Further, we consider how evaluation systems, as well as evaluation projects, are designed. Finally, we address legal and ethical issues that may be encountered in conducting evaluations.

The Basic Question
What Is Evaluation?

All of us would like to live in a perfect world. We want to get all *As* because we feel our schoolwork is of the highest quality. In work situations, we want our participants to experience many benefits from recreation and leisure programs. We want staff to perform their duties enthusiastically and appropriately, budgets to reflect cost effectiveness, and people to flock to our programs. We don't want people to complain or to doubt our abilities as professionals.

In reality, however, our lives and our student or professional situations don't run perfectly all the time. We need to use the resources available to improve ourselves and to make our organizations more effective. None of us will ever be perfect, but we can use the processes and techniques of evaluation research to help us make enlightened decisions to determine the value and improve what we do.

For purposes of this text, we define evaluation as the systematic collection and analysis of data to address criteria to make judgments about the worth or improvement of something. Effective evaluation means making decisions based on identified questions and supporting evidence. Many other definitions exist that have slightly different interpretations. Generally, however, the goal of evaluation is to determine "what is" compared to "what should be."

Doing an evaluation is a bit like solving a mystery. For example, when a robbery occurs, detectives use elements of criteria, evidence or data, and judgment or decisions. The criteria would be the questions that we wish to answer: What was stolen? Who stole it? What was the motive? The evidence would include information such as statements from witnesses, an inventory of what was missing, and physical evidence such as fingerprints. Based on what they want to know and what evidence is collected, a judgment can then be made about what was stolen, who took it, and why. With those judgments, an arrest can be made and justice prevails. If they do not have enough evidence, the judgment is difficult to make. These same principles apply to evaluation.

Systematic (Formal) Evaluations

We are all continually engaged in a process of intuitive evaluation. We say things to ourselves like, "The room is too hot," or "I'm too tired to think," or "I wish I hadn't eaten so much for lunch." The evaluation we do in leisure services agencies, although it may be intuitive on an everyday basis, can be more trustworthy when it is systematically designed. A camp director told us once, "I don't use evaluations. I just watch and listen and talk to campers and staff and I find out all that I need to know." We acknowledge these important means for evaluation, but we also believe that formal systematic evaluations need to be conducted within organizations from time to time.

A systematic evaluation process takes greater effort in time and money than informal evaluations that rely on intuition or expert judgment. Systematic or formal evaluation, however, provides a rigor when outcomes are complex, decisions are important, and evidence is needed to make reliable, valid, and useful, or as we call them, "enlightened" or informed decisions.

The major purpose of evaluation is, therefore, to make decisions. We want to make the best possible decisions based on systematically gathering evidence related to a particular purpose or standard for decision making. Evaluation provides information that can lead to decisions *and* action. Through evaluation, we try to improve or show the value of various aspects of leisure services. We generate this information through the application of evaluation research methods and techniques.

Research and evaluation share common methods and a similar framework for making decisions. The differences between evaluation projects and research studies are described in more detail in the next chapter, but for now it is important to keep in mind that the methods and tools for evaluation and research are the same. Methods and tools of scientific research are used for the judgment process to make decisions more reliable, valid, and useful.

Thus, evaluation as well as research, requires the systematic use of a framework of procedures and methods that include: *criteria* (also known as hypotheses, research questions, guiding questions, working hypotheses, purposes, measures, or objectives), *evidence* or data that are collected and analyzed using standard designs and methods, and *judgment* as confirmed in conclusions and recommendations.

Criteria + Evidence + Judgment = Evaluation

Evaluation Today

We might think of evaluation today as ranging from everyday living to formal systematic studies, all of which help to assess where we are, where we want to be, and how we can reach our desired goals. Thus evaluation might entail intuitive feelings and thoughts, expert judgments, descriptive qualitative and quantitative analyses, quasi-experimental designs, or experimental designs.

Nothing is wrong with intuitive evaluation, but it is generally not enough if we want to make sure leisure services organizations are effective. Expert judgments are frequently used in our field when consultants provide information or accreditation teams visit our facilities and make recommendations. Descriptive analyses include summaries of "what is" in an organization. These descriptions provide a basis for recommended changes. Quasi-experiments and true experiments are means to measure changes that occur because of a program or intervention. Figure 1.1 provides an example of how evaluation might look as a continuum ranging from intuitive to formal systems. Each of these methods on the continuum for doing evaluations will be discussed in more detail in Unit Two.

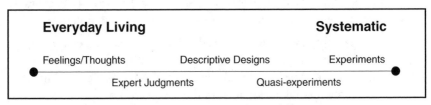

Figure 1.1 Evaluating for Effectiveness and Efficiency (or "A Continuum of Evaluation")

Developing a system for evaluation, gathering resources, and conducting periodic formal evaluations may be the basis for more efficient and effective operations, staff, and leisure programs that result in increased recreation, educational, and personal benefits for children, youth, and adults. *Effectiveness* relates to what happens or results, and *efficiency* implies how change or results happen. To focus on evaluation for improving effectiveness and efficiency in the conduct of all aspects of leisure services, several important characteristics of evaluation should be kept in mind:

1. Evaluation is a process. It consists of the three dimensions of determining criteria, collecting and analyzing evidence, and making judgments and decisions.

2. The goal of evaluation is to make decisions by ascertaining value or worth. We must be sure decisions are based on sound judgments and not just on personal biases.

3. The most common way to evaluate is to measure and judge how well objectives are met. As you will see later in this text, however, this model is only one of many ways to conduct evaluations.

4. The results of evaluation should lead to decision making about and for a specific situation or context.

5. Evaluation may be informal or formal. Systematically and formally gathered data, however, are necessary for making the best decisions within most leisure services organizations.

6. Evaluation within an organization should be ongoing with evaluation systems in place to address aspects of personnel (staff), policies (administration), places (areas and facilities), programs, and participant outcomes. Within these evaluations systems, particular evaluation projects may be undertaken.

7. Evaluation is continuous and does not necessarily occur only at the end of an event or activity. Evaluation may occur as an assessment to determine what is versus what should be, formatively to examine processes, or summatively at the end to ascertain outcomes.

8. Responsive evaluation is based on the premise that evaluation should respond to issues and concerns within an organization. Evaluation should have relevance to an organization and those people who make decisions in the organization.

9. No magic formulas for evaluation exist. Each evaluation project undertaken will be different than the last and ought to reflect the particular uniqueness of the situation of an organization.

Each of these ideas will be revisited throughout this unit and will be applied in the process of doing evaluations by using criteria, evidence, and judgment.

From Ideas to Reality

In any professional situation, you have the choice of whether you want to evaluate or not. Most of us are continually engaged in a process of intuitive evaluation about staff, programs, facilities, policies, and procedures whether we are consciously aware of it or not. Many times this intuitive evaluation is enough. Intuition is helpful, but may not be unbiased or detailed. Often colleagues, participants, or other stakeholders in an organization want some type of systematic proof that a situation exists. It may be documented information concerning the performance of a staff member, or it might be numbers that describe the average rating of satisfaction concerning a certain activity. Thus, we need to collect these data based on criteria that will provide information to make judgments about what is happening in an organization.

Now that you have studied this chapter, you should be able to:

- Write a definition for evaluation.
- Describe the importance of systematic formal evaluations.
- Identify the characteristics of evaluation for making enlightened decisions.

Evaluation and Research
Viva la Difference

This book is primarily about evaluation and the evaluation research methods used to make decisions in leisure services organizations. Anyone using this book, however, might also be interested in research projects as well. Frequently we see the words research and evaluation used together. While many similarities exist between the processes of evaluation and research, differences exist in the outcomes of each.

Evaluation is defined as the systematic collection and analysis of data to address some criteria to make judgments about the worth or improvement of something. *Research* is generally defined as systematic investigation within some field of knowledge undertaken to establish facts and principles to contribute to that body of knowledge. The goal of research is not necessarily to assist in practical decision making, but to generate facts that might be generalized to a broader knowledge base. *Evaluation research* is defined as the use of scientific principles and methods to examine something. Both evaluation and research are characterized by the use of a clearly delineated protocol in collecting, processing, and analyzing data. Evaluation, however, is a specific form of applied research that results in the application of information for decision making.

Therefore, for our purposes we emphasize that evaluation and research use the same methods but have different purposes and outcomes. The scientific method, or the way that systematic data collection is done, is not bound by purpose, so it can be applied in both evaluation projects and research studies. Evaluation projects use research methods but they do not have a method of their own. Most models of evaluation apply the basic rules of the scientific method. Since most of this book addresses evaluation issues, in this chapter we will discuss the differences between evaluation and research as well as areas of theory and literature review that are usually connected to research rather than evaluation.

Differences in Objectives or Purposes

The objectives or purposes of evaluation projects and research studies need to be discussed because they constitute one of the major differences between evaluation and research. First, research tries to prove or disprove hypotheses whereas evaluation focuses on improvement in some area related to personnel, policies, places, programs, or participant outcomes. Researchers are usually concerned with increasing understanding, satisfying an inquiring mind, or finding scientific truth. Evaluators are concerned with problem solving and decision making in a specific situation. The aim of research is new knowledge that may or may not be applicable immediately. This aim does not mean that research studies do not address problems and offer data for application, but these direct applications are not necessarily the outcome of the research study undertaken, as they would be for evaluation projects.

Second, evaluation projects compare the results with objectives to see how well the latter have been met. Research, by definition, applies scientific techniques to hypotheses testing focused on outcomes that are related to theory testing or generation. Theory is defined as an explanation of events. Evaluators usually focus at the applied level for a particular situation and usually do not get into theory questions that might be generalized beyond a specific situation. Research involves inquiry based on a desire to know something in a theoretical and generalizable sense. Thus, research is theoretically grounded whereas evaluation is problem based.

Third, evaluators are not interested in generalizing results to other situations, although sometimes that is a relevant outcome. Research by using theory and random samples should be generalizable to other situations, whereas evaluation uses specific information for making decisions about a particular situation. Similarly, in evaluation, the evaluation questions or criteria emerge from the decision maker who will use the information and not from the evaluator. In research, the hypotheses come from the researcher's interests and goals.

Fourth, evaluation projects are undertaken when we have a decision to make and we don't know the relative worth of something. Research studies are conducted to develop new knowledge. In other words, research leads to theoretical conclusions, whereas evaluation leads to decisions for solving problems. As was discussed in the previous chapter, evaluation must lead to judgment about the worth of something; the value of evaluation lies in making valid judgments that result in enlightened decision making.

Fifth, research studies are usually published because their purpose is to add to the body of knowledge; publications and presentations are the way this purpose is accomplished. Although evaluation reports are generally written and presented formally to decision makers, the information is not necessarily shared broadly. We find some exceptions when we look at the applied research in some of the major journals of the leisure services field such as *Journal of Park and Recreation Administration* and the *Therapeutic Recreation Journal*. Editors of these journals often publish evaluation studies that serve as models for research methods or provide insights for other professionals to use in their organizations.

Sharing of Common Methods

In the broadest sense, research includes elements of evaluation, and evaluation requires the use of research techniques. We frequently see separate chapters in research texts (e.g., Babbie, 1992) that focus on evaluation research. Research studies and evaluation projects, nevertheless, share common methods. If you have a good grasp of the repertoire of methods as well as data collection and analysis techniques available for evaluation, you will have a sound methodological foundation for conducting research. The use of methods may be applied differently, however, because research relies on theory as its building blocks and evaluation relies on application and decision making. Figure 1.2 shows how evaluation and research share common methods such as surveys, observations, and experiments but have different applications.

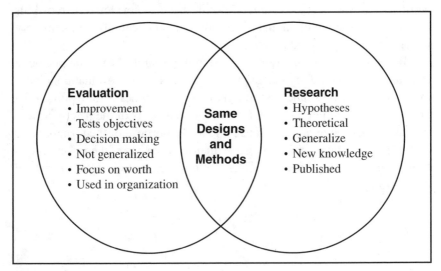

Figure 1.2 A Comparison of Evaluation and Research

A Comparison of Evaluation and Research

In some cases, either an evaluation project or a research study could be undertaken depending upon your purpose for using the data. For example, suppose you wanted to know how adolescent girls experienced a recreation activity. In an evaluation project you might develop criteria to determine how self-esteem changed as a result of participating in an activity. You could measure these changes using a pretest and posttest to see what the girls experienced. From a research study perspective you might do the same thing, but you would be interested in examining a theory such as learned helplessness as a theoretical framework for understanding the changes. The difference between evaluation and research also relates to how you explain what the changes or lack of changes mean. In the judgment phase, the evaluator would be concerned with ways to make sure that these positive changes continued to happen. The researcher would be interested in tying the findings to theory and building the body of knowledge about girls and learned helplessness further that may or may not be directly applied to a particular recreation program.

It is possible to do evaluation and research at the same time but the criteria phase will need to include theory and the judgment phase will need to include a discussion of how the body of knowledge based on a literature review can be enhanced with this information. Evaluation is generally, but not always, easier to do because it relates to addressing specific criteria for making decisions about personnel, policies, places, programs, or participants. Most people who develop evaluation skills can also develop research skills but you must keep in mind that the reasons and applications are the major differences between evaluation and research.

Remember that evaluation is not sloppy research. The same protocols and rules of methodology that apply to research apply to evaluation. Good evaluations rely on sound research methods. The process for evaluation and research is similar and even the first two aspects of the trilogy are necessary, but the major differences lie in the purpose of the research and how the evaluation or research results are used. The use of theory and literature reviews is more often associated with research studies than with evaluation projects.

A Word about Theory

The major difference between research and evaluation lies in the use of theory as an aspect of the criteria element and literature related to both criteria and judgment. Many excellent books have been written about research, theory, and leisure sciences that a student or practitioner may wish to consult. This chapter simply introduces some of the aspects of theory to consider.

Two of the major aims of research are to fit data to a theory or to generate a theory from data. Theory gives order and insight through explanations of what can be, is, or has been observed (Henderson & Zabielski, 1992). In other words, theory provides a "road map" (Tinsley, 1984). Research is sometimes criticized in the field of recreation, park, and leisure studies because it lacks theory or has poor theoretical quality. Although not all research that lacks theory may be classified as evaluative, it is generally more like the evaluation process when theory is missing from research.

Conceptual frameworks are the basis of all research regardless of whether theory is being confirmed or tested. Conceptual frameworks precede theories and describe the assumptions from which the researcher is operating. In evaluation projects, concepts are often key dimensions that also provide direction for the evaluator in understanding the relationship among variables. In evaluation, however, the focus is not necessarily on linking the concepts into a framework but using the concepts to collect data and ultimately to make decisions. Concepts are always used in evaluation projects but they are not necessarily linked into conceptual frameworks.

The use of theory ranges from theory testing and confirmation to theory development within research projects. In theory testing, a known theory is stated prior to beginning a research study. The study is then conducted to see whether or not that theory does help to explain "what is" related to the topic. In theory development, a theory is generated after the research to aid in explaining what happened. This theory emerges from the data and is frequently tied to other similar or related theories. Closely related to theory is the use of models for confirmation or development that occurs in the leisure research literature.

Theories are often associated with hypotheses in research studies. Hypotheses reflect the researcher's "guess" about what the outcomes of a research study might be. Hypotheses are like criteria in evaluation projects, and are useful because they set out goals regarding the research outcomes. These hypotheses may be stated as relationships between variables or as research questions. For example, one hypothesis stated as a relationship might be, "Organized camping programs will enhance the prosocial behavior of youth." Stated as a question, the hypothesis might be, "Do organized camping programs enhance the prosocial behavior of youth?" These hypotheses should be based on theory or evidence, should be testable, and should be brief but clear.

Frequently theory is tested and confirmed in research projects. Theory, however, might also be developed in a research project, particularly when qualitative data are collected and the researcher does not have a preconceived idea of what he or she might find. This theory, sometimes referred to as grounded theory, can then become the basis for other studies that might test it in a variety of ways.

We use a number of theories in the field of leisure research. Some of these theories are borrowed theories from other fields such as business and psychology. For example, researchers have used marginality theory to explain the lack of participation of people of color in recreation programs. Social exchange theory has been used to analyze the reasons why people choose or do not choose to become involved in advisory boards. Carrying capacity has been used to determine how much use an outdoor area can take before the resources and recreational experiences of participants are diminished. We have also developed conceptual frameworks and theory specifically related to leisure sciences. For example, travel cost models are used to examine why and how people make vacation choices. Conceptual constraints models have provided a plethora of information about why people do not participate in recreation activities to the full extent they would like. Journals such as *Leisure Sciences* and the *Journal of Leisure Research* contain numerous examples of how theory and conceptual frameworks have been applied in the field of leisure research.

Using Literature Reviews

The review of the literature involves finding other studies that are related to the planned research study. "Reviewing the literature" includes finding other sources of information in books, journals, or reports, and reading and evaluating them to see how they fit with the pending research proposal. An individual undertaking an evaluation project might also use literature to assist in conducting a project, but not necessarily. Since evaluation projects are not usually published within the scientific community, evaluation studies are often not easily accessible like research studies that are more widely published.

The review of literature undertaken for a research project is usually extensive, thorough, and aimed at trying to uncover as much as possible about what has been previous done regarding the research topic. This review is important because it provides a way to find out what others have done so the researcher can contribute beyond the existing body of knowledge by building on previous work. The literature review provides the foundation for future work if the researcher has gained insight into the meaningful results obtained by others. Doing a literature review helps to delimit the research problem, provides insight into possible methods, and uncovers the most current thinking about theories or conceptual frameworks.

With the myriad resources available in libraries and on the Internet, finding sources for the literature review should not be difficult. The difficulty lies in sifting through all the literature to critically examine what can be learned to strengthen the potential research study. The researcher must also have a means for organizing the information so the best ideas can be put together to create the foundation for the pending research project. This literature review will also provide a touchstone when the data are collected and analyzed to show how the research project contributes to what information already exists. Doing the literature review is a central task for any useful research project. A literature review may be helpful for an evaluation project but is not mandatory as it is for a research study.

Some of you reading this book may be more interested in research and theoretical applications than in evaluation. If you read this book and study Units Two and Three, as well as portions of Unit Four, you will have a solid background in research methods. If you want to do research, however, we suggest you do additional reading from texts designed specifically to address research issues and from journals that report the most recent research in our field. Doing evaluation projects does not mean that you shouldn't also know this research literature, but doing evaluation requires a different starting point and a different point of application in the end.

From Ideas to Reality

Evaluation and research are closely linked because they share common methods. As indicated previously, we find it most useful to think of research and evaluation as two separate approaches to finding answers. Regardless of whether one is doing a research study that uses theory and a literature review, or an evaluation project, the possibilities for methods such as surveys, observations, unobtrusive measures (that might include historical research), or experiments are possible. Similarly, both researchers and evaluators will need to be concerned about sampling, measurement, and analysis. The major difference compared to evaluation is the way that theory and literature reviews are used as a framework for planning and for drawing conclusions within a research study.

Now that you have studied this chapter, you should be able to:

- Describe the differences between research and evaluation.
- Explain when a research study would be desirable and when an evaluation project would be more appropriate.
- Identify the types of research that one might see in leisure studies journals.
- Describe the importance of theory and literature reviews.

The Trilogy of Evaluation and Research
Criteria, Evidence, and Judgment

As has been suggested previously, the three components that must be present for evaluation and research that lead to sound decision making are criteria, evidence (data), and judgment. If any part of this trilogy is missing, successful evaluation will not occur. In other words, we might say:

Criteria + Evidence + Judgment = Evaluation

The chapter defines this trilogy. It would be wonderful if we could offer a magic formula that showed how to use the evaluation and research trilogy for any given evaluation project, but that is not possible. Every project in every organization and setting is going to be different. An infinite number of combinations exists for linking criteria, evidence, and judgment in a project. We can, however, borrow and learn from our previous projects as well as those projects that others have undertaken. Regardless of the project, the importance of the trilogy for systematic evaluation and rigorous research lies in our ability to link and logically use the three elements of criteria, evidence, and judgment.

Criteria

Criteria refer to the standards or the ideals upon which something is being evaluated or studied. Criteria are the basic organizing framework for evaluations similar to how hypotheses or research questions are used in research. Further, criteria will determine to a great extent what method would be best to use to address the criteria. To determine criteria is to determine the purpose of an evaluation, the models that might be applied, the levels of evaluation needed, and the specific evaluation questions that will be explored. In many ways, criteria are directly tied to planning because to develop criteria is to set a framework or a road map that the evaluator will follow from the beginning to the end of a project.

All of us always have criteria in our heads, but they may not be appropriate in all situations. For example, when people disagree over how good a restaurant might be, we must be careful that the same criteria are being applied. If someone dislikes a restaurant because the servers are slow and rude, a different criterion is being applied than if the criterion is the price of the food or how it tasted. Of course when we eat at a restaurant we expect all criteria to be met or exceeded, but depending on the definition of criteria, our judgments might vary depending on what we were evaluating.

Developing criteria often appears to be the easiest aspect of the evaluation process, but in reality may be the most difficult. Depending upon the purpose of the evaluation or research project, the criteria may be very evident. For example, if a program has a set of good goals and objectives to serve as the criteria, the evaluator can then decide how best to gather evidence. If, however, you are not sure what needs to be evaluated, determining criteria may be more difficult. For any leisure services program or place, we may not be able to measure everything with any degree of depth.

One of the major pitfalls of evaluation is not stating the criteria specifically enough so that they can be measured. The evaluator must be able to articulate what is being measured. A great difference exists between determining how many people participated in a program and identifying their satisfaction with the program. Sometimes data are collected without a specific set of criteria in mind. If you are lucky, the data may answer the critical evaluation questions, but chances are they will not unless a plan was made. Sometimes we collect data believing we are addressing one set of criteria only to find out this assumption was not the case. Sometimes the evaluator has one set of criteria that she or he thinks should be measured while stakeholders (like Boards of Directors or parents) may have something else in mind. Thus, it is essential to clearly identify what questions are to be addressed or what criteria to evaluate *before* data are collected for an evaluation or research project.

Many people struggle with how to design evaluation systems, as well as specific projects, because they do not have a sense of the criteria that need to be evaluated. To skip over the step of identifying criteria (or to skip over this unit of this book) will not be useful in the long run if one is to conduct useful studies that will lead to good decision making and add to the body of knowledge. The more time spent determining what you want to evaluate, the more time will be saved later while collecting reliable and valid information and when making decisions about what the evaluation data mean.

Evidence

Evidence means data. Data are pieces of information that are collected to determine whether criteria are being met. In gathering evidence the timing, type of data, sample size and composition, and techniques for handling data must be determined.

The two major types of data are qualitative and quantitative. *Quantitative data* in the simplest form refer to numbers from measurements that result in some type of statistics. *Qualitative data* refer to words used to describe or explain what is happening. Many evaluation designs and research methods can be used to collect these two types of data ranging from the two broad categories of experimental and descriptive designs to the more specific methods related to surveys, observations, and unobtrusive measures. All of these methods will be discussed in detail in Unit Two.

The evidence relates directly back to the criteria that were established. If poor criteria were set up, designing instruments that will measure what you really want to measure will be difficult. Applying data collection and analysis techniques and using research methods are not difficult to learn. Applying them appropriately based on criteria is what requires effort.

Judgment

Judgment is the determination of the value or worth of something based on the evidence collected from the previously determined criteria. Judgment refers specifically to the conclusions and recommendations made for any evaluation or research project. Judgment is one aspect of evaluation that frequently gets left out. You can have excellent criteria and evidence laid out for an evaluation project, however, if the final step of the evaluation process is lacking, judgments in the form of conclusions and recommendations are not made about what the data mean.

Judgment is not a matter of learning a process that can be applied each time. Each set of criteria and method of gathering evidence will result in a number of possible conclusions and recommendations. Conclusions should relate back to the hypotheses, objectives, and/or criteria of the project as well as the data. Recommendations are proposed courses of action to be followed based on the criteria, evidence, and conclusions. These conclusions and recommendations must be made obvious in the form of judgments before the evaluation is complete.

Putting It All Together

The steps to evaluation and research involve more than just stating criteria, collecting evidence, and making judgments. Most evaluation projects as well as research studies use the trilogy as the framework for designing the entire process. Table 1.3 provides a summary of how the trilogy relates to the process of evaluation and research. The use of the trilogy of evaluation is a simple way to be sure that evaluation is being conceptualized appropriately. We find it a useful and straightforward way of thinking about and moving through the evaluation research process.

Table 1.3 Summary of How the Trilogy Works

Criteria
- Determining a problem and a reason for doing evaluation or research
- Examining goals and objectives (if they exist)
- Developing broad evaluation questions or a research problem statement to be addressed (for example, What are the motivations for involvement in an activity? What job related expectations should be used to evaluate a staff member?)

Evidence
- Method selection including instrument design and pretest
- Sample selection
- Actual data collection
- Data analysis (i.e., coding and interpretation)

Judgment
- Presentation of findings
- Development of conclusions
- Development of recommendations

From Ideas to Reality

Several brief examples may help to illustrate how the evaluation process works. If we wanted to examine what the outcomes for individuals participating in a particular kind of activity were, we might decide to use satisfaction as the criteria. We would then find an instrument (or develop one) to measure satisfaction with the activity. We would select an audience (or a sample) and collect evidence (data) by using that instrument. We would then analyze the data using descriptive statistics to develop conclusions and make recommendations about how satisfied people were with participation in a recreation activity.

Perhaps we were interested in determining if the riding area of a horse-back -riding program for children with disabilities was safe. We would have to determine the criteria that describes a safe riding area. Standards developed by other groups might provide the criteria to examine. By using those criteria and developing a checklist, we would observe the area where children with disabilities were riding. Based on the results we would then draw conclusions and make recommendations for how to improve the area so it will be safer for the participants.

We might be interested in whether the policy we have for refunds is appropriate. The criteria will be to determine how often the policy has been used and what the situations are surrounding its use. The data would be collected from existing records that we would examine and tabulate. On the basis of those records, we would make judgments concerning how much and how often the policy was used and possible recommendations for how it might be improved in the future.

Now that you have studied this chapter, you should be able to:

- Describe the value of using criteria, evidence, and judgment together in an evaluation project.
- Design a project showing how the trilogy of evaluation or research would be linked.

Why Evaluate? Who Cares?

The goal of evaluation is to determine the value or worth of something so that good decisions can be made. The goal of research is to get information that will contribute to the body of knowledge about a field and lead to an enhanced quality of life. Evaluative research enables us to gain information or feedback by developing criteria to be used to measure or gather data to make proactive or "enlightened" decisions.

Many reasons exist for doing evaluations and research. Each evaluation or research project conducted will likely have different purposes associated with it. Regardless of the purpose, formal systematic data collection must be done using criteria, reliable and valid evidence or data, and an open perspective for understanding phenomena and examining how programs, facilities, staff, and administrative procedures in leisure services can be improved. In other words, as Theobald (1987) suggested, an evaluator using research methods must be aware that a decision needs to be made, design the decision situation, choose from alternatives, and take action.

Some professionals are afraid of evaluation because they fear what they might find. If everything appears to be going all right, evaluation seems like more work on an already overburdened schedule just to find that everything isn't 100% right. The adage "Don't fix it if it ain't broke" comes to mind. But evaluation is not meant only for crisis situations when changes *have* to be made. When evaluation is done systematically, crisis situations can often be avoided.

The new millennium offers many opportunities for decision making. Some societal trends are making evaluation imperative. Many organizations are seeking to show that what they do really does make a difference. For example, the National Recreation and Park Association (NRPA) has undertaken a benefits-based approach to examine the positive outcomes parks and recreation brings to individuals, communities, the economy, and the environment. The approach suggests that professionals ought to identify what benefits occur because of a program, develop the program with those benefits in mind, and evaluate to see if the benefits were attained. The American Camping Association has as its slogan, "Camp does kids a world of good," and is now undertaking evaluation and research projects to ascertain that this slogan is indeed true.

Staff in many organizations need to justify how resources are being used to achieve realistic results from their programming and management efforts. Calls for good decision making and accountability are coming from participants, including clients and consumers, the professionals' desire to improve services, awareness of good management practices, recognition of society's limited fiscal and human services, and legislative mandates such as the requirements of the Americans with Disabilities Act.

In the broadest sense, professionals evaluate for several reasons: because it's compulsory and they have to evaluate, for defense and/or offense to determine the worth or lack of worth of an aspect of the organization (e.g., program, staff member, place), or to improve or validate an aspect of the organization. More specifically we believe the major purposes for evaluation can be divided into seven broad reasons:

1. To determine accountability
2. To assess or establish a baseline
3. To assess the attainment of goals and objectives
4. To ascertain outcomes and impact
5. To determine the keys to successes and failures
6. To improve and set future directions
7. To comply with external standards

These reasons are not mutually exclusive and often overlap one another a great deal. Evaluation usually does not occur for only one reason, but occurs for a combination of reasons that enable enlightened decision making. Research, as juxtaposed to evaluation, generally focuses more on theory confirmation or development that may relate to any of these broad reasons.

Accountability

Accountability, as one dimension of decision making, is often mentioned as a primary purpose of evaluation. We might think of accountability as being more reactive than proactive, although it can be used for proactive decisions. If an organization or program is not showing accountability, then a decision may be made about whether that organization or program should continue to operate.

Accountability is a relative term that describes the capability of a leisure services delivery system to justify or explain the activities and services provided. According to Connolly (1982), accountability reflects the extent to which expenditures, activities, and processes effectively and efficiently accomplish the purposes for which an organization or a program was developed. Often projects are evaluated for accountability when some external unit, such as a city manager or hospital administrator, requests the evaluation. Accountability, however, should be an ongoing concern of staff in any organization regardless of who is watching.

Accountability results in determining legitimacy. It is also applied to see if a recreation program is meeting the needs and desires of people in the community. A by-product of the evaluation is that the agency may be seen in a better light in the community, but the bottom line is that accountability should result in avoiding unnecessary expenditures of money.

Establishing a Baseline

Evaluation may be done to set a baseline. This reason for evaluation usually results in an assessment or a needs assessment depending upon the context being evaluated. An *assessment* is the gathering of data or the measurement of phenomena that is then put into an understandable form to compare results with objectives. Assessing a baseline can also provide a starting point for measuring change and a plan for future action. Community *needs assessments,* as well as clinical assessments of people with disabilities, are frequently used examples of evaluation used to establish a baseline in leisure services.

Assessing Goals and Objectives

One common reason for doing evaluation is to assess whether goals and objectives have been met. As indicated earlier, goals and objectives have been the backbone of evaluation efforts, although some approaches to evaluation don't take goals and objectives directly into account. Assessment of goals and objectives, for example, may help to determine how programs and area/facilities contribute to leisure satisfaction for individuals or how to improve the quality of life in communities.

Judgments from assessing goals and objectives result in determining if stated objectives are operating and/or whether other objectives are more appropriate. Thus, evaluation also can allow us to redefine the means for setting objectives and to determine exactly what goals our organizations ought to be setting and striving to accomplish.

Ascertaining Outcomes and Impacts

Determining the impact, effects, outcomes, and results of a program, area/facility, or administrative procedure is the bottom line of evaluation. By ascertaining the outcomes of a staff member's efforts, the expenditure of money or the changes that occur in participants as a result of a program, decisions can often be made about value and impact.

Impact evaluation asks what differences a program has made and how it has affected people both now and into the future. Outcomes are defined as the benefits or changes that occur. Outcomes and impact are not always easy to measure, but they are the essences of program planning, in particular, within leisure services organizations. If what we do in any area of leisure services does not have a positive effect on people, then it may not be worth doing whether the activity is done through therapeutic recreation, sports programming, or park planning.

Explaining Keys to Success or Failure

Some evaluations are undertaken to document processes that are used to obtain certain objectives. In other words, evaluation is undertaken to see what works and what doesn't. In addition, determining what contributes to a successful program, as well as what might create problems or failures, is useful. For example, weighing benefits against costs is one way to describe success. Other aspects of whether a program has worth relate to determining the inputs as far as staff effort, expertise, or leadership that might affect a program. This reason for evaluation allows professionals to increase the utility and probability for successful programs that they will conduct in the future, and also allows staff to share procedures and processes that might be useful with other professionals in similar situations.

Organization Improvement and Future Action

Organizational improvements related to quality control and future action are probably the most practical reasons for evaluation. Professionals evaluate staff, programs, policies, or participants to make revisions in their existing programs. In the starkest way, one might decide whether to keep programs or staff members or whether to let them go—a "go/no-go" proposition. Rationale for putting money into future programs needs to be considered. Sometimes the evaluation of staff, for example, results in promoting professional growth and education by appraising personnel quality and qualifications. The organization can also be improved by gauging public sentiment, attitudes, and awareness that provide information to enable professionals to improve and/or maintain high quality in the organization. Further, evaluation for improvement provides a way for two-way communication with participants, staff, and the public.

Improvement might be sought by appraising existing facilities and physical property as to adequacy, accessibility, safety features, attractiveness, appropriateness, availability, and utilization. The evaluator tries to seek out and eliminate any detrimental features that could create risk or prevent the best recreation experience. Evaluation for improvement might also result in replacing outmoded concepts and invalid ideas about how a leisure services program ought to be run. Summative evaluations can lay a basis for new projects and can point a professional towards how to program more effectively in the future. When we know what worked and didn't work and how people liked a particular program, it is easier to set objectives, improve programs, and implement plans in the future.

Complying with External Standards

Some organizations are required to do evaluations to comply with external standards set by the government or by some other funding agency or professional body. These evaluations often are done for other purposes that directly aid the organization, but this evaluation may be done simply to meet accreditation or licensing requirements. The current procedures done by organizations like the American Camping Association (ACA) and the National Recreation and Park Association (NRPA) use a standard evaluation whereby a camp or a recreation organization can become accredited by showing that they have complied with certain standards. The accreditation process of these organizations is meant to be a guideline for helping organizations evaluate themselves by using the external standards as a beginning point.

Many Reasons to Evaluate

As you can see, reasons for evaluation are numerous and overlapping; seldom would a professional only have one specific reason for evaluating. In fact, a problem may exist when the evaluation is so single-focused that the evaluator does not see all the possibilities for learning that can result from doing an evaluation project. For example, the initial purpose of an evaluation might be to assess goals and objectives, but the process can also highlight keys to success and expose areas that can be improved.

Evaluation experts such as Weiss (1972) have suggested some other reasons for evaluating that may not be as positive as the previous examples and may be detrimental to an organization if they are the sole reason for evaluating. Examples of these "not so good" reasons to evaluate include: to postpone decisions or avoid responsibility, to further public relations, to meet funding requirements, to justify programs, and to eliminate staff.

Sometimes professionals use evaluations to postpone decisions or to avoid responsibility. Sometimes evaluation will buy time until something else can be figured out that has no relationship to the evaluation. If a supervisor or a manager has a tough decision to make, for example, she or he might decide to evaluate in hopes that some magic solution will occur. Sometimes this happens, but usually not. Evaluation still requires that necessary third element of judgment. Ultimately the supervisor or manager will have to bite the bullet and take responsibility.

Evaluating solely for the public relations impact may not help to improve a program. It looks good to see an organization doing evaluations, but if nothing ever changes or the evaluations are not used, the public will not stay impressed for long. Related to this idea is conducting evaluations just to increase prestige within departments, in an organization, or with one's peers. Good evaluations will only increase prestige when they are appropriately used.

Evaluations done solely because of grant or funding requirements are often not as effective as those in which the stakeholders or the participants really care about how the feedback can be used for decision making. When funding sources require an evaluation, the evaluator ought to consider carefully what can be learned that may be helpful. In other words, staff should address not only the letter of the law, but also the spirit of the law. Evaluations can be helpful if we expect them to be helpful and not just another chore that has to be undertaken. A required evaluation is a wonderful opportunity to explore other reasons for evaluation that can assist in decision making.

Evaluation done only for the purpose of program justification or to eliminate staff may not be appropriate. An evaluation may result in program justification, but a great deal of bias may be built into something that has program justification as its sole purpose. Further, an evaluation may give some ideas about what needs to be done to improve an organization, but using it solely for the purpose of getting rid of people is probably not going to be beneficial to the morale of the organization or the way that employees view the value of evaluation in the long run.

Fear of Evaluation

Many professionals are afraid of evaluation for a number of reasons. Some people associate it with statistics, which is often a scary subject. If good goals and objectives have not been written, evaluations are frequently difficult to do. In other cases, people do not know how to measure the information that they would like to know. Some professionals disregard evaluations because their prior experiences didn't tell much more than they already knew. Others have done evaluations but then have not used the data so the evaluations were seen as simply a waste of time. Still others are afraid of what they might find out if they evaluate—negative results are not always easy to take. Finally, some professionals fear evaluations because they can be very time-consuming and most professionals already feel too busy. Each of these fears, however, can be countered by paying attention to planning evaluation projects based on carefully determined and appropriate reasons for undertaking them.

When *Not* to Evaluate

Although evaluation is important and can be extremely useful, Theobald (1987) suggested that a professional must also know enough about when *not* to evaluate. The first rule is to not evaluate unless you are sincere about making decisions to improve your program. Secondly, you may not want to evaluate if you know your program has serious organizational problems. The wise plan would be to try to fix those problems rather than think that evaluation is going to provide you the magic answer. Evaluation can expose problems, but is not necessarily the panacea for fixing them.

Along with these concerns, make sure that you have goals and objectives that can be measured. You do not always need to have specific objectives, but you need to be clear about what you think your program ought to be doing. If you do not have any goals and objectives, it is best to get those into written form and then do the evaluation. Usually it is not best to evaluate when something is just getting started—give the program or staff member a chance to get started or use a formative approach to make the evaluation more useful. Further, don't evaluate if you already know the outcome—it will be a waste of time, unless of course some stakeholder needs to see written documentation of the results. Finally, don't evaluate if you know the disadvantages will outweigh the advantages. If you know that an evaluation will be too time-consuming or too costly for what you will get, then don't do it or don't use that particular evaluation design.

Knowing How to Evaluate

Although many excuses are valid for not evaluating, we suspect the major reasons that evaluations are not systematically conducted are because professionals do not know how to set up an effective evaluation process, how to analyze the data, and/or how to interpret the data in useful ways to assist in making decisions.

The bottom line is that evaluations must be used for decision making. If the conclusions and recommendations are not used, the evaluation project or research study is useless. Evaluation is not necessarily a solution for solving all the problems in an organization, but the process can provide important information. We will address more specific ways to implement and use evaluation results in an organization in Chapter 4.6, but you should consider the "whys" of evaluation before you begin to evaluate any aspect of a leisure services system.

The best evaluation in the world cannot provide a definitive picture of the future, reduce the costs of goods and services, or decide the most desirable course of action. Those decisions are still up to you as a professional. You make this decision, however, based on the data you obtain from evaluations. Hopefully, as an evaluator you make good decisions because you have the best possible data collected for the most appropriate reasons just as you undertake research as a way to add to the body of knowledge to better understand human behavior and how the world works.

From Ideas to Reality

Suppose someone on your Park and Recreation Advisory Board suggests that she or he is not sure that the summer playground program is really meeting the needs of youth in your community. You believe that a systematic examination of that program may be useful to determine if the program is meeting children's needs. A number of reasons might be examined for doing this systematic evaluation: to determine if funds are being appropriately spent (accountability), to see if the goals and objectives for the program are being met, to determine if the inputs of staff and leadership are adequate to meet the program goals, to improve the program so that it better meets the needs of children, and to determine exactly what outcomes are happening to children because of the program. All of these reasons will result in determining future action concerning the program. In this situation, the reasons for undertaking the evaluation are multiple. These reasons are important to consider before an evaluation is undertaken. Further, it is important to make sure that staff, board members, and participants are in agreement concerning why an evaluation should be undertaken and how the results will be used.

Now that you have studied this chapter, you should be able to:

- List the reasons why an evaluation might be undertaken given a particular situation.
- Describe the concerns and fears that some people have regarding undertaking evaluations.
- Determine when it is best to undertake an evaluation project and when evaluation may not be to the advantage of an organization.

Developing an Evaluation System
The Five Ps of Evaluation

Every aspect of leisure services has the potential for being evaluated. As indicated earlier, some of this evaluation may be intuitive, but in other cases a systematic evaluation is needed. Whenever a new program is begun or a new staff member is hired, some plan for evaluation ought to be considered. The next two chapters introduce a discussion of the areas of evaluation in leisure services, and the systems that can be developed for evaluating within an organization.

Classifications can be used to determine broad areas of evaluation in leisure services organizations. Kraus and Allen (1987) suggested that there are program-oriented and people-oriented areas to evaluate. Lundegren and Farrell (1985) described the four major areas as personnel, program (including people), administration/policies, and areas/facilities.

For purposes of our discussion and to help you remember the areas of evaluation, we would like to discuss the five Ps of evaluation: personnel, policies, places, programs, and participant outcomes. You should realize, however, that these five areas are not discrete and tend to overlap. For example, a recreation *program* is of little use unless some kind of impact is made on a *participant*. The *policies* of an organization may affect the *program*. The nature of a *place* in terms of the area or facility will affect the job of the staff person or *personnel*. Seldom do we evaluate any one of these aspects alone without also acknowledging how they relate to one another. We will use these five Ps to describe the areas of evaluation within leisure services. This chapter will describe how we develop a system for evaluation and cover three of the five P areas: personnel, policies, and places. The next chapter will address program and participant outcomes because they are essential areas of evaluation in this new millennium.

Developing an Evaluation System

Few park and recreation departments submit themselves to a continuous and systematic program of evaluation. Those organizations that use standards for accreditation have a system in place for evaluation, but more evaluation may be needed than once every three or five years to maintain accreditation. Many organizations use evaluation for various aspects of their program like staff performance appraisal, but few organizations have a clear system for how evaluation fits into their overall organization.

Not every aspect of an organization needs to be evaluated every year. In fact, for available time and money, it may be more useful to determine what and when evaluations ought to be done. Rather than doing piecemeal evaluations, the development of a way that the entire organization or system can be evaluated over a period of time (e.g., three years) may be more beneficial. A system can enable you, as a professional, to make sure that all five Ps are covered from time to time. A system in place can enable you to make enlightened decisions concerning the entire organization. Let's examine how this system of evaluation might look.

To develop a system, you must know which of the five Ps will be evaluated and how often this process should be done. As you read further into this book, the types of evaluation that are to be done as well as the models that best serve to answer the evaluation criteria will be determined. A systematic plan might be developed by establishing goals and objectives, examining conclusions from previous evaluations, examining strategic plans or long-range plans that exist in the organization, and then setting a schedule. Figure 1.5(1) gives an example of how an evaluation system might be organized. You would determine the "what" (i.e., what area of the five Ps), the "why" (i.e., reasons for evaluation), "when" (i.e., timing related to how often and when during the year, which will be discussed in more detail later in this unit), and "who" (i.e., who will be evaluated, who will be in charge of the evaluation, and who will use this information). In developing the plan, more specifically you might want to consider the type of evaluation needed and the resources needed to carry out the evaluation such as personnel, facilities, funds, and supplies.

You cannot evaluate everything at once. To try to assess everything usually results in poor conceptualizations of projects or failure to think about the issues involved. Further, the amount of data that you would generate would be overwhelming. Those people participating in the evaluation also can become overwhelmed by the complexity and endlessness of evaluation, unless a system is established.

What	Why	When	Who
Personnel			
Policy			
Place			
Program			
Participants			

Figure 1.5(1) A System for Evaluation

Theobald (1979) offered several practical considerations as you set up the system for your organization. First, keep in mind the time and financial constraints of evaluation. On one hand, evaluation ought to be considered an investment. Quick and dirty evaluations, however, are usually not nearly as helpful as well-planned evaluation projects. On the other hand, the more money and time spent on evaluation, the less is available for program, staff, and the development and maintenance of areas and facilities.

Second, in developing a system, keep in mind that evaluations have political overtones. In determining the worth or value of something, you want to be sure that the criteria and measurement are appropriate. You also must consider the scope of evaluation and what it will cover, the size of program, duration, program input, complexity, and span of goals.

Third, to have a system in place means that you will have established appropriate reasons for evaluating based on whether staff want the information, the funding organization requires it, or you have the need to make decisions about continuing or terminating a program. The remainder of this chapter will focus on systematically evaluating the Ps of personnel, policies, and places.

Personnel

Many staff work in leisure services organizations. Some of these staff are full-time, some part-time, and some seasonal. Volunteers are also considered unpaid staff. The benefits of staff evaluation include improving job performance and providing feedback for the personal development of staff regardless of whether they are young and in paid positions of responsibility for the first time, have been a professional for thirty years, or periodically volunteer in the organization. Since evaluation is so important in the personnel process, midyear or *formative evaluations* as well as end of the year, or *summative evaluations*, are frequently used.

The formalities of personnel evaluations are up to the organization, but generally staff personnel files are kept that provide documented evidence of the performance of staff. Staff performance evaluations are generally based on a combination of the goals and objectives as found in the job descriptions and on the performance outcomes that result from doing the assigned jobs. Ideally, the evaluation should consist of an examination of the relationship between the criteria as stated in the job description and the performance of the staff member. Thus, a well-written, accurate job description is the basis for an individual staff evaluation. The staff member ought to know from the very beginning the criteria upon which she or he will be evaluated. The staff member must also receive feedback concerning the judgment that is made by the evaluator. The feedback to staff ideally occurs on an everyday informal basis, as well as during the formal process that is scheduled as part of a yearly performance appraisal.

Personnel evaluation is often called performance appraisal or performance evaluation. Most administration textbooks go into detail about this form of evaluation, but we would like to provide a bit of background so the principles of evaluation can be applied to personnel. Personnel evaluations are generally necessary for making decisions about compensation, promotion, training, and employee development. These personnel evaluations are formal, structured, systematic ways to measure an employee's job-related behavior.

Employees at all levels ought to be evaluated on at least an annual review pattern and preferably more often. This evaluation is not only a single activity, but also takes into account evaluations made throughout the year. The criteria for personnel evaluation may vary greatly depending on the organization, but usually it is best to address aspects of the job and not an individual's personality. Ideally, the job description is the criteria.

The purpose of the evaluation ought to focus on improvement and not necessarily whether to keep or fire an employee.

The procedure used in employee evaluation is to assign duties, determine criteria for evaluation based on those duties, gather information about how the employee performs, appraise the performance, provide feedback to the employee, and make decisions and adjustments about the employee's performance. These decisions may relate to letting the employee know her or his relative value in the organization; identifying people for promotion; enhancing communication among supervisors, staff, and participants; providing directions for further continuing education and on-the-job training; and helping to establish and implement career goals. As you can see, these aspects of personnel evaluation relate to how we would incorporate the trilogy of evaluation into any of the five Ps.

Glover and Glover (1981) offered four recommendations necessary for effective personnel evaluation. First, the appraisal for development or improvement purposes should be separated from appraisal for administration that results in such decisions as determining job raises. Second, the evaluation system should provide coaching" for the employees on a regular basis. Third, professionals who do the evaluating need training in how to be most effective not only in devising measurement criteria but also in how personnel evaluation is an ongoing process. Finally, the evaluation should be behavior specific concerning the job the employee performs. A concrete plan to address deficiencies should exist. No matter what data are collected, ultimately the supervisor must make decisions about the employee's behavior on the job and will need to help the employee to improve upon her or his behavior.

Data for personnel evaluations can be obtained from administrators, other employees, or participants. Table 1.5(2) (page 38) shows an example of a generic evaluation form that might be used with an employee. The supervisor would use this information in providing feedback to the employee along with other information obtained about the specific job duties that might be performed.

Policies (Administration)

Evaluation is used for a number of policies, procedures, and administrative issues. Administrative aspects that may be evaluated include the way that the organization is organized and operated. Budget analysis is another way to examine policies and administration.

A professional might do public policy and community surveys to ascertain support for a particular activity, to measure the diversity of opinions,

Table 1.5(2) Example of a Personnel Evaluation Form (source unknown)

	Outstanding	Above Average	Average	Needs Improvement	Poor
1. Demonstrates insight and vision regarding objectives and long-range plans	—	—	—	—	—
2. Possesses the physical stamina and drive to handle the rigors of the position	—	—	—	—	—
3. Demonstrates pleasant personality and good communication skills	—	—	—	—	—
4. Is consistent and fair; does not play favorites	—	—	—	—	—
5. Solves problems rationally; can come to the heart of things	—	—	—	—	—
6. Gets along well with other people	—	—	—	—	—
7. Demonstrates ability to work together as a team	—	—	—	—	—
8. Is approachable and willing to make changes	—	—	—	—	—
9. Takes personal interest in each participant	—	—	—	—	—
10. Welcomes and respects the opinions of others	—	—	—	—	—
11. Is continuously alert to new ideas	—	—	—	—	—
12. Is well-informed at all times regarding the total operation and how she or he contributes to it	—	—	—	—	—

and gain information from the public at large. Evaluations and needs assessments can allow an organization to gain a more comprehensive knowledge of the community, its people, their needs, their opinions, and special problems. Policy and administrative decisions may be made based on community dissatisfaction, perceived lack of opportunity, the need to equalize services or upgrade services, and to meet new demands.

Cost-benefit and cost-effectiveness are econometric models used as a means for evaluation in leisure services. Cost-benefit analysis is relating the costs of a program or an operation to the benefits realized from it, which are expressed in dollar figures. Benefits other than dollars are, however, often hard to quantify. Cost-effectiveness is easier because it is the ratio of costs to revenue generated. A program that generated enough income to pay the expenses would have a cost-effectiveness of 1:1. Per capita costs may be related to amount of cost per person. For example, we might have a Little League program that cost $20,000 for 150 children. The cost-effectiveness would then be $133 per child. The cost-effectiveness of one program could then be related to other programs sponsored by the organization.

Performance-based program budgets are another common administrative way that an organization evaluates how money is spent in relation to the outcomes of the programs. In this budgeting approach, the professional breaks down work or program activities into detailed subunits for the purpose of determining the specific costs of each of these units. These breakdowns are sometimes used to set the cost for a given program based on the expenditures. The information provided by the budget is useful to top administrators and to other policy boards who want to see the big picture. It also helps to think about programs in terms of unit costs. The bigger the leisure services enterprise, the more useful this budgeting approach is related to administrative evaluation.

Economic impact is a specific example of a policy/administrative area that might be measured. Economic impact relates to the amount of revenue activity generated in an area due to a particular event such as a festival or other tourist activities. For example, we might determine that for every dollar spent on tourism promotion in a community, five dollars of income might be generated from tourist spending. Economic impact also expands beyond primary initial spending to secondary spending which results in a multiplier effect in the community.

Assessments might also be useful for administrative planning. For example, Fletcher and King (1993) surveyed voters to assess how they felt about purchasing and developing recreation and park areas and facilities in the East Bay Regional Park District in California. Based on this telephone interview assessment, they learned what the people were thinking and used this information to address the policy implications that helped to guide the bond campaign. The $225-million bond measure passed.

Places (Areas and Facilities)

The level of use of leisure services, such as numbers of participants, is a common way to measure how well an organization is doing. When we evaluate places, we may examine many aspects including use, as well as safety and legal mandates. Preestablished standards are often helpful in evaluating risk management and safety concerns in the facilities, equipment, and landscape of an organization. Routine checks of facilities and equipment in the form of "walk-thrus," as well as scheduled maintenance procedures and the keeping of maintenance logs, can serve as a formal system of evaluation.

Master plans done for long-range planning are a form of assessment and evaluation. In these plans, one might examine the distribution of areas and facilities. Table 1.5(3) shows an example of such a checklist that might be used for evaluating what exists or does not exist in a community. *Carrying capacity,* defined as the amount of use an area can take before recreation experiences become diminished, is another example of evaluation applied to places.

A frequent way of evaluating places is through the application of standards. Many examples of standards exist in parks and recreation. The

---

Table 1.5(3) Example of a Neighborhood Evaluation Checklist for Facilities for the State of Pennsylvania (adapted from Lundegren & Farrell, 1985, p. 191)

Recommended Component	Yes	No
1. Turf for field sports	___	___
2. Multipurpose, hard surface, all-weather court area	___	___
3. Space for recreational sports	___	___
4. Individual and dual sports	___	___
5. Water Facility—Outdoor pool	___	___
6. Winter Activity Area	___	___
a. Ice area	___	___
b. Sledding slope	___	___
7. Outdoor education area	___	___
8. Natural area for nonmotorized travel	___	___
9. Communication space for dance, drama, music	___	___
10. Building	___	___
a. Multipurpose meeting rooms	___	___
b. Assembly area	___	___
c. Specialized activity area	___	___
d. Physical recreation area	___	___

American Camping Association, for example, offers standards for camping that relate to property risks and safety equipment as well as standards that relate to personnel and program. The Joint Commission on Accreditation of Healthcare Organizations (JCAHO) has standards for hospitals. A set of standards for evaluation of public park and recreation departments (Council for the Accreditation of Parks and Recreation Programs) exists with standards that relate to aspects of facilities/areas as well as programs.

One of the newest and most exciting tools available to use in evaluating places as well as other aspects of leisure services is the use of Geographical Information Systems (GIS). The GIS technique integrates spatial and demographic information (Wicks, Backman, Allen & Van Blaricom, 1993). GIS is being used for numerous applications including such examples as land information systems, urban planning, land-use mapping and facilities management, environmental impact assessment, wildlife and park management, identifying socioeconomic demographics, and geographic survey and mapping. GIS consists of census information combined with resource data that enable a professional to pictorially display an element such as the distribution of people around a park. Based on that mapping, decisions can then be made about new landscape designs or where activity areas might best be placed. GIS also allows for an analysis of demographic characteristics in an area. For example, a map could indicate locations of community centers and the concentrations of racial groups that exist in a city based on data obtained from census information. This technology goes far beyond maps and site analysis for use in planning and policymaking. It also has immediate applications for marketing strategies. In addition, GIS is not only useful for evaluation of places and facilities, but also has implications for information about assessing the needs for programs, as we will discuss further in the next chapter. Regardless of whether you are a land-use planner, a parks and recreation director, or a therapeutic recreation specialist working with older adults, GIS applications will likely become a part of your evaluation process. Figure 1.5(4) on page 42 shows an example of a GIS map.

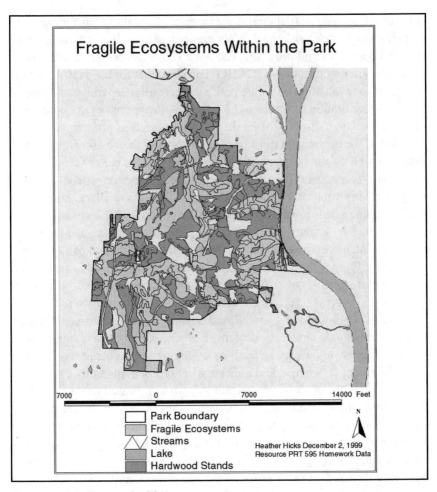

Figure 1.5(4) Example of a GIS Map

From Ideas to Reality

Many aspects of organizations can be evaluated. An evaluator, however, must be able to make decisions about what can be feasibly and systematically evaluated at any given time. This chapter has provided some examples of the variety of aspects related to the five Ps that might be evaluated in leisure services organizations. Not everything can be evaluated at once, but over time and with thoughtful planning, a system of evaluation will then develop. For example, many organizations have good staff evaluation systems in place that simply will need to be maintained. The professional might then focus on determining if places are being adequately evaluated. These current ideas taken in conjunction with the areas of program and participants that will be discussed in the next chapter can provide a basis for a sound evaluation system within any community or organization.

Now that you have studied this chapter, you should be able to:

- Describe three of the five Ps related to personnel, policies, and places and what components of each might be evaluated.
- Make a plan to determine what aspects of the five Ps might be evaluated in an organization over a five-year period.

Evaluating Programs and Participants

Probably the most common association with evaluation that most leisure services professionals have relates to program evaluation. The impact of program evaluation is most often assessed regarding participant outcomes, although program may also have influences that can be measured relative to community, environmental, and economic impact. The benefits-based movement in leisure services received a great deal of attention in the 1990s and this way of thinking about programs and participants has influence on programs for the future.

This chapter describes the remaining two Ps, program evaluation and participant outcomes, within the framework of the benefits-based movement. First we describe the benefits-based approach, and then show how program and participant outcome evaluation fits within this emerging movement.

Benefits-based Movement

The notion of benefits of recreation is not a new idea. Since the beginning of the organized recreation movement in the late 1800s, volunteers and professionals have extolled the values, importance, and benefits of recreation and associated areas, such as camping and youth development. In the mid-1990s, however, the National Recreation and Park Association (NRPA) defined the "benefits movement" and sought to make it the basis for what parks and recreation organizations do.

The benefits movement focuses on the individual, environmental, community, and economic benefits that occur because of recreation programs in a community. The premise is that recreation agencies must develop effective programs and services that influence the quality of life for citizens. Awareness of the benefits is the beginning. The creative implementation of programs and management decisions for recreation to make a difference is key. NRPA has developed training components to help leisure services professionals see how benefits can be enhanced in an organization. These three areas of training include awareness, programming, and management. The slogan of these NRPA materials is "The benefits are endless..."

A benefit has been defined as anything that is good for a person or thing. A benefit might also relate to a desired condition that is maintained or changed. A benefit also equals an outcome or end result. NRPA has identified four areas of benefits. *Individual benefits* include improving health and wellness, building self-esteem, providing alternatives to self-destructive behavior, reducing stress, and providing opportunities for living a more balanced life. *Community benefits* include building stronger families, reducing loneliness and alienation, enhancing community spirit, reducing crime, and promoting ethnic and cultural harmony. *Economic benefits* are associated with attracting business relocation and expansion, contributing to healthy and productive work forces, attracting tourism, and enhancing real estate values. *Environmental benefits* might include protecting natural resources and open space areas, enhancing air and water quality, reducing congestion, and providing and protecting wildlife habitat. All of these areas would likely be included in evaluations to determine if, in fact, leisure services are providing benefits for citizens.

Efforts to spread the word about benefits is only beginning. It is a useful approach to ensure that the efforts of leisure services providers do make a difference in people's lives. Determining the influence that leisure services programs want to have on individuals, the community, the economy, and/or the environment is the first step in this process. Documenting this difference is the vital role that evaluation can play.

Program

One of the chief ways that leisure services organizations provide benefits is through programs. Programs, however, are not just a bunch of planned activities. A benefits-based approach to programming suggests that activities must be designed and implemented to meet certain outcomes that address specific community needs. Evaluation of programs is a means to determine whether those activities have been successful.

Evaluation is seen as one of the prime components of a program system when it is examined along with the phases of assessment, objectives, and implementation, and revision. Evaluation, however, may not only occur at the end of a program but also may occur throughout it and/or even at the beginning. Thus, as Howe and Carpenter (1985) illustrated in Figure 1.6(1) that evaluation may occur at all stages of the program. Evaluating programs at all stages of their development may be important to assure that the desired results are being obtained.

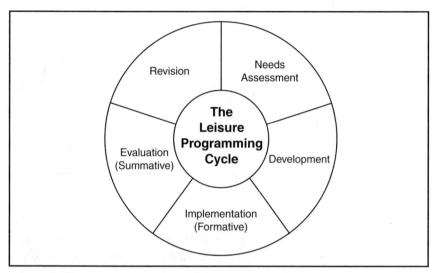

Figure 1.6(1) The Relationship between Program and Evaluation (adapted from Howe & Carpenter, 1985)

Many possibilities exist for developing program evaluations. An examination of levels of program evaluation adapted from the work of Bennett (1982) may be useful in further understanding program evaluation. See Figure 1.6(2) on page 48. Seven levels of program evaluation are suggested. The first four relate to how the organization designs a program and how participants respond. The last three levels relate to outcomes that are generally related to the benefits discussed previously.

1. Inputs—Resources available and expended such as money, paid staff and volunteer time, facilities, and equipment.

2. Activities—The strategies, techniques, and types of undertakings and organizational processes that are used including publicity, actual activities, and the delivery of program.

3. People involvement—The output usually measured in terms of volume of activity pertaining to statistics and demographics describing the number of people, characteristics of people, frequency, and intensity of involvement.

4. Reactions—Responses from the participants including degree of interest, like or dislike for activities, satisfaction, expectations, appeal, and opinions.

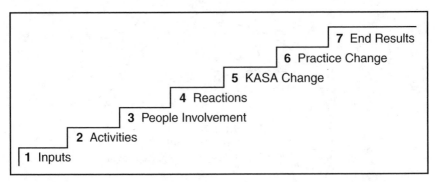

Figure 1.6(2) Levels of Program Evaluation

5. KASA outcomes include the benefits and changes for individuals or populations during or after participating in program activities. These may relate to knowledge, attitudes, skills, or aspirations.

> *K*nowledge—awareness, understanding, problem-solving ability
>
> *A*ttitudes—feelings, change of interest, ideas, beliefs
>
> *S*kills—verbal or physical abilities, new skills, improved performance, abilities
>
> *A*spirations—desires, courses of action, new decisions

6. Practice change outcomes—Adoption and application of knowledge, attitudes, skills, or aspirations to leisure or lifestyle.

7. Long-term impact on quality of life outcomes—Social, economic, environmental, and individual consequences, how people are helped, hindered, or harmed as a result of this program.

This illustration of the levels of programming shows how many different aspects might be evaluated in a program. Leisure services professionals are frequently interested in how well they are designing and implementing programs and this information can be evaluated in the first four steps of this model. For an organization to function efficiently and effectively, these aspects must be considered. The benefits-based approach, however, would suggest that the significance of leisure services programs depends upon the outcomes associated with KASA, practicing change, and impact on quality of life. Many of the outcomes are measured as individual change, which will be discussed in more detail later. The important point to note is that the evaluator must be aware of what exactly she or he is measuring when a program evaluation is undertaken.

One of the challenges in program evaluation is to make sure that you are not trying to evaluate too many criteria at once. The seven levels identified provide a framework for making decisions about what aspects of a program may be most important to evaluate. Most program evaluations do not measure, or often cannot measure, all seven levels. The evaluator must determine what the most important aspects are to evaluate, and then design measurement instruments and evaluation projects to get at those.

Two examples of program evaluation forms are illustrated in Tables 1.6(3) and 1.6(4). Table 1.6(3) is an example for evaluating camper reactions (level 4), and Table 1.6(4) on page 50 shows how to measure inputs (level 1).

Scoring:				
Awesome! = 5	Good = 4	Fair = 3	Yawn = 2	Boring = 1

Activity	Score	Activity	Score
Archery	_____	Soccer	_____
Battlefield Tour	_____	Camp Fires	_____
Crafts	_____	Bible Classes	_____
Canoeing	_____	Swimming	_____
Cycling	_____	Nature	_____
Hiking	_____	Physical Fitness	_____
Sports	_____	Music	_____
Basketball	_____	Meals	_____
Softball	_____		

Figure 1.6(3) Camper Program Evaluation (source unknown)

Participant Outcomes

The goal of leisure services programs and organizations is to produce benefits seen as positive end results or outcomes that result from involvement in recreation. Participant outcomes have emerged as a central area for evaluation. Some organizations refer to proof of these outcomes as impact research. As noted above, outcomes can refer to KASA, practice, or quality of life outcomes. Participant outcomes include what individuals know, think, can do, and how they behave or change. Although the goal of recreation is

Table 1.6(4) Example of Parks and Recreation Department Program Evaluation (adapted from Durham Parks and Recreation)

How Well Are We Serving You?

Please take a minute to compete this brief questionnaire and return it directly to our staff. We value your participation and want to serve you better. Thank you.

Location _____ Date _____

Activity _____

Please check Yes or No: **YES**   **NO**

1. Was the staff courteous?   _____   _____
2. Was the facility clean and attractive?   _____   _____
3. Was the activity well-organized?   _____   _____
4. Was the area in a good state of repair?   _____   _____
5. Did the activity start on time?   _____   _____
6. Did you feel safe and comfortable at
   the facility?   _____   _____
7. Would you return to this facility for
   another activity?   _____   _____
8. Was the activity interesting?   _____   _____

9. Overall, how would you rate this activity (please check one)?

   _____ Excellent   _____ Good   _____ Fair   _____ Poor

10. What other activity or activities would you like us to provide?

11. How did you hear about our classes/programs? Check all that apply.
    ____ Mailed brochure   ____ Yellow pages   ____ TV
    ____ Picked up brochure   ____ Flyer/poster   ____ Newspaper
    ____ Friend   ____ Radio   ____ Referral
    ____ Called P&R office   ____ Called facility   ____ Other

to satisfy the participant in terms of her or his wants or interests, we also hope that involvement in leisure services addresses a human need that improves an individual's life.

We use the term participant throughout this book to refer to the people who receive leisure services. In applied cases, these participants might have other names such as consumers, clients, patients, guests, tourists, or

campers; no matter what they are called, they all share common characteristics related to what recreation experiences may mean. The common goal
of all recreation and human service programs is to make life better and more
rewarding for people. For example, we may be interested in evaluating the
acquisition of a certain skill level or the improvement in attitudes toward
recreation or towards oneself. Self-constructs including such aspects as self-
confidence and self-esteem are frequently assessed in participant outcome
research. For example, Table 1.6(5) provides an example of some questions
asked in a recent national Girl Scout study (Girl Scouts USA, 2000).

Table 1.6(5) Sample of Self Questions Asked in a National Girl Scout Study (selected
items adapted from Girl Scouts USA, 2000)

DAL = Disagree a lot; D = Disagree; A = Agree; AAL = Agree a lot;
DU = Don't understand

It's OK that I'm good at doing some things, but not good at doing other things.	DAL D A AAL DU
I know what I'm good at.	DAL D A AAL DU
I feel comfortable talking about my feelings with some people.	DAL D A AAL DU
I will let someone know if I'm afraid to do something.	DAL D A AAL DU
When I feel happy about something, I usually tell other people.	DAL D A AAL DU
My friends usually think my ideas are good.	DAL D A AAL DU
If I try hard, I can learn anything.	DAL D A AAL DU
I have good ideas.	DAL D A AAL DU

The value of measuring participant outcomes lies in assuring that the
inputs and activities undertaken by leisure services agencies really are making a difference. Therefore, accountability is important in measuring participant outcomes particularly from a benefits-based approach. This information,
however, also results in improved services so that the outcomes are likely to
occur over and over again. We must keep in mind that instruments designed
to measure program effectiveness should not be used to make judgments
about participant outcomes. Although well-designed programs ought to lead
to positive changes in people, the two issues are separate.

To do effective participant outcome measuring, several steps must be employed. First, the outcomes you want to measure (i.e., the criteria) must be determined. Then you must determine what data are needed to measure the outcomes. Data must be collected and analyzed and compared to the intended outcomes. Finally, you need to use your findings in the form of conclusions and recommendations. For example, if we wanted to know if a midnight basketball program reduces the youth crime rate in a community, we would determine the desired outcome to be a reduced crime rate, measure the crime rate *before* the program started, again periodically *during* the program, and then make judgments about the value or worth of the program in relation to the outcome of reduced crime. We recognize that other good things might happen to individuals as a result of the midnight basketball program, but in this use of participant outcomes we would focus on determining specific goals that could be measured.

Different populations may need to be examined using different tools if participant outcome evaluation is to be effective (Sengstock & Hwalek, 1999). For example, evaluating programs for children and youth may be more difficult than for adults. Youth may have a shorter attention span than adults. Measurement is also complicated by the rapid developmental stages that youth undergo. Therefore, changes in aspects such as social skills may not be the result of a recreation program as much as it might be the maturation of a child. Instruments must also be age appropriate for children. Evaluators must be concerned that evaluation is diversity sensitive. For example, youth for whom English is not their first language may understand the wording of instruments differently and, therefore, may not interpret and score in the same way as native speakers of English. People with disabilities are another group that may interpret instruments differently than the evaluator intended if their needs are not considered. As we will discuss in Unit Two, pilot testing is a way to address some of these potential problems.

Outcomes evaluation is not nearly as easy to do as evaluating inputs, activities, and reactions. There are no magic formulas. Yet, it is an area that must be addressed.

Five Ps Summary

Developing an evaluation system will not be easy. As you work through this book, however, certain aspects of how the five Ps can be systematically analyzed within any organization over a period of time should become evident. Table 1.6(6) summarizes a number of examples of ways that the five Ps might be used in leisure services organization evaluations.

Table 1.6(6) Summary of the Components of the Five Ps of Evaluation

Personnel
- Performance appraisal
- Assess training needs
- Provide feedback for improvement

Policies
- Accountability of budget
- Cost-benefit analysis
- Cost-effectiveness analysis
- Equitable provision of services

Place
- Safety concerns
- Master planning
- Adequate facilities

Program
- Effective leadership
- Promotion of program
- Did participants gain anything
- Risk management

Participants
- Motivations/Satisfaction
- Changes in attitudes as outcomes
- Changes in knowledge as outcomes
- Changes in skills and abilities as outcomes
- Carryover into other situations
- How individuals interact
- Demographic characteristics

From Ideas to Reality

Leisure services offer many potential benefits. The benefits are often measured through program and participant outcome evaluations. Program evaluation is a large area and the evaluator might want to focus on particular programs during different years and the myriad of benefits that might occur. When evaluating participant outcomes, you might want to examine an outcome such as skill development in a particular area. The possibilities are endless and the evaluator must use a system to determine the most important aspects to evaluate given the time, money, and expertise that may exist within an organization. All of the five Ps are important and all can be evaluated in a variety of ways, but the undertakings must be carefully considered so that appropriate and useful evaluations are conducted that can document the services provided and improve on programs for the future.

Now that you have studied this chapter, you should be able to:

- Describe the benefits-based movement.
- Determine when to use the levels of program evaluation.
- Discuss the value of measuring participant outcomes.
- Give examples of each of the five Ps of evaluation.

Timing of Evaluation

The five Ps of leisure services (i.e., personnel, policies, places, programs, participants) can be evaluated in different sequences and ways. For our discussion about evaluation, we will examine the timing related to three areas—assessment, formative, and summative evaluations.

Timing conveys a temporal or time sequence. It may be done at the beginning (assessment), during the process of a program or over the course of a year (formative) or at the end of the program or year (summative). These three approaches can be illustrated through a classroom example. Some professors may want to know how much students know about a particular topic at the beginning of a semester. They may give a quiz or exam on the first day of class to assess the knowledge level or attitudes that students have about a subject. Many professors are required to give final exams, which are summative evaluations. They tell the instructor what happened at the end of the course, but at that point, little can be done to change the learning or lack of learning that occurred. For this reason, many instructors give midterm exams that might be thought of as formative evaluations. When these midterms are given, the instructor then has the opportunity to immediately improve upon the class if the learning has not occurred as planned. Three different timings of the evaluations or exams result in differing outcomes for those people who are using the exam evaluations. Assessment, formative, or summative evaluations may occur within any of the five Ps. These three ways of doing evaluations are based on criteria that must be determined before an evaluation project is undertaken.

Although not completely congruent, we might say that assessment always examines some type of need and is the foundation for further *planning*, formative utilizes an examination of the *process*, and summative measures the *product* referred to as outcomes, impacts, effectiveness, and/or overall efficiency. Thus, the criteria developed for an evaluation project will depend on its timing and whether the use of the evaluation will be for planning, improving the process, or measuring the product.

Assessment and Planning

Assessment is a process of determining and specifying what a program, a facility, a staff member, a participant's behavior, or administrative procedure is. In community recreation programs, we often conduct needs assessments. These assessments identify the differences between "what is" and "what should be." The needs assessment often results in a process of prioritizing results to use in planning programs, places, policies, or the use of personnel. Therapeutic recreation specialists use assessment as the initial evaluation necessary to plan intervention strategies and serve as a baseline for measuring client outcomes (Stumbo, 1991).

The assessment serves as a set of outcomes or judgments that focus on gaps between current aspects of the five Ps and desired results; assessments provide the direction for reducing those gaps. Assessments may determine answers to such questions as:

- What is the socioeconomic profile of a community?
- What are unmet needs?
- What forms of recreation services are needed?

Needs are complex and often hard to understand, so an assessment evaluation can help to address such aspects as the context of need, denial of need, and/or how needs can be used in program planning.

Assessment evaluation assumes that you want to find out where to begin. Where to begin applies to whether you are assessing a participant, the resources available in a community, or the needs for training a new staff member. To collect data for a needs assessment, for example, a plan must be devised. The plan usually includes defining what it is you want to know, developing a plan of action, generating goals, collecting data about "what is," analyzing data for discrepancies between "what is" and "what should be," and then developing a plan of action for the desired intervention or for the programs to be initiated. The assessment is based on determining criteria, collecting evidence, and making judgments about where any of the five Ps of your organization is now, where to go in the future, and how to get there. Table 1.7(1) shows an example of a popular needs assessment and evaluation approach being used in communities and organizations across the United States. The Search Institute (1996) has identified 40 assets considered to be the building blocks for development for young people so they can grow up healthy, caring, and responsible. As an assessment tool, a community might examine how some of these assets are or are not being addressed within an organization of community.

The only time you do not need to conduct an assessment is when you are sure of the goals and objectives for your organization, program, clients or staff, and when that information is complete, correct, valid, and useful. An assessment may be done internally or externally depending on the particular situation.

Table 1.7 (1) Samples from 40 Developmental Assets Identified by Search Institute (1996)

Support
1. *Family support:* Family life provides high levels of love and support.
3. *Other adult relationships:* Young person receives support from three or more nonparent adults.

Empowerment
7. *Community values youth:* Young person perceives that adults in the community value youth.
8. *Youth as resources:* Young people are given useful roles in the community.

Constructive Use of Time
17. *Creative activities:* Young person spends three or more hours per week in lessons or practice in music, theater, or other arts.
18. *Youth programs:* Young person spends three or more hours per week in sports, clubs, or organizations at school and/or in community organizations.
19. *Religious community:* Young person spends one or more hours per week in activities in a religious institution.
20. *Time at home:* Young person is out with friends "with nothing special to do" two or fewer nights per week.

Social Competencies
32. *Planning and decision making:* Young person knows how to plan ahead and make choices.
33. *Interpersonal competence:* Young person has empathy, sensitivity, and friendship skills.

Positive Identity
39. *Sense of purpose:* Young person reports that "my life has a purpose."
40. *Positive view of personal future:* Young person is optimistic about her or his personal future.

Formative and Process Evaluation

Formative and summative evaluations may not be measuring different aspects of leisure services, but the timing is such that the results often are used in different ways. In general, formative evaluation is concerned more with organizational objectives such as efficiency and effectiveness, while summative evaluation is concerned with the overall performance objectives and outcomes.

When we are interested in examining the processes associated with an organization, we often use formative evaluation. *Formative evaluation* is defined as the systematic examination of steps in the development and implementation of a program, organizational structure, policy, or staff person. Formative evaluation occurs while a program or administrative procedure is in progress and is used to examine the process as it is occurring within the organization. Feedback is provided early so that revisions can be made and weaknesses pointed out while there is still time to correct them. The value of formative evaluation lies in the changes that can be made while a staff member is working, when a budget is being used, or when a program is going on. Examples of process evaluation questions that might be asked are: Is the program attracting a sufficient number? How are staff contacting participants? Are some media methods working better than others? Are the participants making progress toward their individual goals?

An example of how formative evaluation might be embodied could relate to university teaching. An instructor could do a formative evaluation at the midterm of the semester to determine how a class is going. She or he might ask such questions as: What is the instructor doing that is contributing to your learning? What are you doing that is contributing to your learning? What could the instructor do to improve your learning? What could you do to improve your learning? From those data, the instructor might make changes to enhance the learning process. Similarly, the use of this type of formative evaluation might result in students evaluating their behavior and making changes as well. This formative evaluation allows for changes to be made midway rather than waiting for a summative evaluation at the end of the semester that will not benefit the students who are currently taking a class.

Evaluation using standards of practice developed by professional organizations is another good example of formative evaluation. For example, in therapeutic recreation, the concept of quality assurance (QA) is frequently cited. This concept pertains to providing quality healthcare and determining what constitutes quality care within therapeutic recreation (Riley & Wright, 1990). QA is a mechanism employed to systematically monitor and evaluate the appropriateness and quality indicators of patient care activities. This system uses written criteria that directly contain structure, outcome, indicator, and process measures that can be evaluated formatively to aid in ongoing patient care.

Another example of a formative process might refer to the concept of quality of service (MacKay & Crompton, 1990). Professionals in tourism and other areas of recreation have a growing interest in service quality. The intent is to use any number of methods to examine how services are provided. Tangibles are measured such as *physical facilities*, *equipment*, *appearance of personnel*, *reliability* including the ability to perform the promised service dependably and accurately, *responsiveness* defined as the willingness to help users and provide prompt attention, *assurance* which indicates courteous and knowledgeable employees who convey trust and confidence, and *empathy* that includes offering caring and individualized attention to users. By comparing what customers expect and what they experience, an organization can make formative changes to provide better services for present, as well as future, participants.

Another common formative evaluation is done with seasonal staff. In this process, staff is evaluated after the first two weeks or midway through a summer to see how they are doing. At this point in time, changes can be made in duties or needed training can be provided to address whatever potential problems are uncovered. Rather than waiting until the end of the season to give a staff member an evaluation, the formative evaluation allows one to receive feedback that can be used to improve or to change immediately.

Summative and Product Evaluation

When most people think of evaluation they tend to think of the final evaluation, the evaluation that occurs at the end of something that measures the outcomes or the end results. A grade at the end of the semester or the bonus and/or pay raise at the end of the year are examples of how a summative evaluation might be applied. Summative evaluation uses an overall examination of impact and effectiveness that is completed at the end of a program or the end of the year. A decision to continue or discontinue the aspect evaluated is imminent although the material gained in a summative evaluation can be applied to subsequent programs. Formative evaluation can occur within any stage of organization process whereas summative only occurs at the end. Summative evaluation particularly is important for accountability purposes, but should not be used exclusively for that purpose.

A common form of summative evaluation is outcome or impact evaluation that ascertains if a program produced the intended effects. The evaluator is interested in determining the net effects of a program, policy, or place. The results are comparative in that you examine what happened based on where an organization began. For example, experimental designs often are used for the purpose of summative evaluation. A pretest is given before a program and a posttest after it is over to determine the impact and change that was a result of a program. In another example, the bottom line of impact analysis relates to a comparison of what did happen after implementing the program with what would have happened had the program not been implemented (Mohr, 1988)

Iso-Ahola (1982) described one illustration of summative evaluation. He suggested that intrinsic leisure motivation should be the main concern of evaluation. If leisure is a state of mind, then we ought to evaluate those aspects in participants such as an outcome goal of leisure satisfaction. He defined leisure satisfaction as having feelings of freedom and control and suggested measures whereby we could determine how leisure helps people receive a degree of balance in their lives, promotes social interaction, and gives feedback about their competence. Different people prefer different leisure activities/programs for different intrinsic rewards at different times. Rossman (1982) suggested that the notion of leisure satisfaction is best measured by investigating underlying satisfaction dimensions rather than a single, all-encompassing measure of "overall satisfaction." Table 1.7(2) shows examples of some of the impacts that could be measured through a summative evaluation.

Summative evaluation, however, becomes a complicated aspect when one starts to evaluate what really happened to people. Halle, Boyer, and Ashton-Shaeffer (1991) suggested two types of impact criteria that ought to be examined: experimental and therapeutic. Experimental criteria implies that a program causes a desired effect or has a definite outcome. We also need to consider, however, the therapeutic criterion that refers to the importance and meaning of the change produced. In other words, does a particular leisure program make a difference in people's lives? Halle and colleagues (1991) did a study of ten ambulatory students with moderate intellectual disabilities participating in aerobic exercise paired with fourteen exercise buddies. They collected data on weight, percent body fat, graded exercise, and the frequency and quality of social interaction between

---

Table 1.7 (2) Examples of Measures of Leisure Satisfaction (adapted from Rossman, 1982)

Achievement
- I learned more about the activity.
- It was a new and different experience.
- My skills and ability developed.
- I became better at it.

Family Escape
- I was able to be away from my family for a while.

Environment
- The area was physically attractive.
- The freshness and cleanliness of the area.
- I liked the open space.
- The pleasing design of the facility.

Risk
- I liked the risks involved.
- I liked the chance for danger.

Autonomy
- I was in control of things that happened.
- It gave me a chance to be on my own.

Physical Fitness
- I enjoyed the exercise.
- It keeps me physically fit.

Social Enjoyment
- I enjoyed the companionship.

---

those individuals with and without disabilities. They found that the social value of the program was just as important as any physical change that had occurred in fitness levels. Thus, summative impact was broader than just an experimental design.

Summative evaluation may be measured related to different levels of program evaluation (as we discussed in the previous chapter) as well as timing. For example, we might look at changes immediately after a program or examine what is occurring six months later or ten years later. Similarly, outcomes may be specific to a situation or may influence an individual to change her or his quality of life. Summative evaluation can become complex as we seek to determine what criteria or levels of evidence ought to be measured.

Efficiency, another aspect of summative evaluation, relates to inputs and activities in terms of numbers and costs to organizations. We are often concerned with examining costs in comparison to benefits. Were funds spent for intended purposes? Did a program achieve its success at a reasonable cost? Can dollar values be assigned to outcomes? Efficiency assessments, including cost-benefit and cost-effectiveness, provide a frame of reference for relating costs to program results. Inputs and outputs are measured in numerical terms. To calculate efficiency, you must look at costs to and benefit for whom. Further, costs and benefits may refer to individuals, program sponsors, or the society at large. These are all examples of summative evaluations.

We need to use a proper amount of caution in determining summative economic benefits. Not all benefits can be converted to monetary terms. Cost-benefit and cost-effectiveness often are viewed more conceptually than they are technically because the required technical procedures of converting benefits to dollar amounts may be beyond expertise and resources of most evaluators. Political and moral controversies also exist about whether you can put value on some outcomes. For example, what is the value of a child's life if she or he is given swimming lessons so that someday she or he will not drown? These dilemmas about dollar figures may obscure the relevancy of evaluations if one gets too caught up in the numbers. Measuring benefits, however, as a form of summative evaluation is a useful and popular activity as evidenced by the use of the benefits-based management approach now undertaken by the USDA Forest Service (Driver, Brown & Peterson, 1991).

Efficiency evaluation might also relate to the concept of a program audit, an accountability term to refer to the process of quantifying the amount of services rendered and the identity of program participants. Program audits provide a year-end descriptive summary of what happened within an organization during a given year.

From Ideas to Reality

As indicated previously, timing can relate to all aspects of evaluation. Assessment involves getting potential baseline information about available inputs, what needs and interests people have, current involvement, attitudes and reactions to leisure or a particular situation, and an assessment of what knowledge, skills, aspirations, and attitudes now exist. A formative evaluation would be concerned with various aspects of efficiency as leisure services are delivered. The summative evaluation would be concerned with outcomes or effectiveness. Clearly the timing of evaluations will be closely linked to the reasons for conducting an evaluation project.

All aspects of timing evaluations are needed within organizations but not all personnel, policies, places, programs, or participants need to be evaluated within each timing sequence. Decisions will need to be made concerning the most appropriate timing to be used for a particular evaluation system and project. Sometimes in the case of personnel, you may be doing assessments, formative, or summative evaluations whereas in other situations such as evaluating safety procedures on a camping trip, only formative evaluation might be used. As an evaluator you will need to decide when and how evaluations are most appropriate and most useful to aid you in making the most enlightened decisions.

Now that you have studied this chapter, you should be able to:

- Describe the differences between formative, summative, and assessment evaluations.
- List some possible applications for each of the timing types of evaluation.

Five Models for Evaluation

When we examine the evaluation literature and try to make sense of the process of evaluation, we can become easily overwhelmed. Numerous models for evaluation provide a framework for conceptualizing and planning evaluation projects. No one model is specific to leisure services, however, because professionals in our field have borrowed heavily from education evaluation principles as well as from business management and operations.

This lack of specific models for leisure services creates both problems and opportunities. It is a problem in that we have many choices that have to be made based on the models designed in other fields. On the other hand, it is an opportunity in that we can choose the best model for the specific criteria that we want to measure for one of the five Ps.

In determining how various aspects of leisure services might be evaluated, we discuss five models that may provide helpful frameworks. Intuitive judgment is a pseudomodel with the other four systematic models being: professional judgment, goal-attainment, goal-free, and systems approaches. No one model of evaluation will work everywhere and every time. Further, for an evaluation project, more than one model might work. The evaluator, therefore, must choose the best model for the situation. We simply cannot apply a standardized model across organizations or even across the five Ps within leisure organizations. The value and applicability of any of these models lie in diversity and adaptability, not in uniformity and rigidity (Patton, 1978). All of these models have some relation to one another and offer a framework for organizing evaluation systems and planning projects.

A Pseudomodel: Intuitive Judgment

A traditional component of evaluation is gut-level judgment. After you have conducted some type of program, you have a sense of whether or not it went well. With the development of the scientific method applied to evaluation, however, more systematic models have evolved beyond these intuitive feelings.

The pseudomodel, intuitive judgment, has importance but is not necessarily a systematic approach. This form of evaluation relates to the day-to-day observations that we make that provide information for decision making. For example, if staff sensed that potential participants had not heard about a special event to be held even though a promotional plan had been implemented, something would need to be done. Even without a systematic evaluation, changes could be made immediately to better promote the event. Many changes and improvements occur in our organizations based primarily on intuitive judgment and experience. Personal and collective reflection within an organization is important. The intuitive judgment model is useful, but reliable and valid evaluations that use systematic approaches to determine criteria, collect evidence, and make enlightened decisions are also necessary. We acknowledge the value of gut-level evaluations, but they should not be the only means of evaluation if leisure services are to be accountable and based on a commitment to improvement.

Professional Judgment

Evaluation by professional judgment or expert opinion is commonly used in leisure services. It often relates to two common approaches that might be used: hiring an external evaluator or using a set of external standards. Even if an external evaluator is hired, she or he may use one of the other models to obtain information in addition to his or her expert judgment.

Howe (1980) talked about evaluation by professional judgment as being like an art criticism model where someone other than the artist critiques the artwork. Using the professional judgment of an external person may be a good idea when a high degree of objectivity is required, money is available, and an expert is available. The pros and cons of using a consultant or an external evaluator are discussed in more depth in Chapter 1.10.

A more common way that professional judgment is used is in evaluation by standards—generally through some type of accreditation process. Essentially, *evaluation by standards* involves a critical review by an individual or individuals who are experts because they have had training in judging established predetermined minimum criteria.

A standard is a statement of desirable practice or a level of performance for a given situation. Standards are indirect measurements of effectiveness. People evaluating by using standards assume that if stated desirable practices are followed, the program will be effective. These judgments about standards enable evaluation by comparison through ascertaining what is actually happening within an organization compared with what the accepted standard of desirability is. They are *not* maximum goals but instead are minimal goals and should be used as a guide, but not necessarily a quality rating.

Standards change and must be reviewed regularly and revised as conditions change. Standards ought to reflect the needs of the patients, clients, participants, or campers in the specific area being served, must be reasonably attainable, and must be acceptable and useable to the leisure services professional. Standards are based on sound principles and the best information available about practice. They should stand the test of time, although they also should be revised to reflect changing societal conditions.

The process used for evaluation by standards is generally to have an organization (e.g., hospital, public recreation department, a camp) do a self-evaluation, make changes and improvements to comply with the minimum expectations or guidelines established by the accrediting body, and have trained outside experts confirm that particular situations exist that meet the standards. The process of evaluation by standards is well-known in the recreation field. Many professionals are aware of van der Smissen's *Evaluation and Self-Study of Public Recreation and Park Agencies* (1978). An example of a standard from this publication is the use of a population ratio method like ten acres of parkland per one thousand people in a community.

The American Camping Association has *Accreditation Standards for Day and Resident Camps* (1998). Table 1.8(1) on page 68 shows some examples from the camping accreditation process. The National Recreation and Park Association and the American Association for Leisure and Recreation have been accrediting recreation and leisure curricula in universities for the past fifteen years. Quality assurance standards within therapeutic recreation are related to the Commission on Accreditation of Rehabilitation Facilities (CARF) and the Joint Commission on Accreditation of Healthcare Organizations (JCAHO).

The standards used for accreditation are usually *criterion referenced*. That is, evaluations are based on some standard level of performance. They also may assess whether standard objectives have been met. Criterion-referenced evaluation is not compared to any other organization but simply is used as a standard for measurement. In the case of the above examples, the standards usually exist in a checklist to which the evaluator responds yes/no, or fully met/partially met/not met. In some situations such as the NRPA/AALR accreditation of universities, qualitative comments are made for standards that are not met to indicate where a problem exists and how it might be corrected.

Norm-referenced standards might also be applied in some situations. These measures tell the relative position of a person or thing in reference to

---

Table 1.8(1) Sample of Standards (adapted from *Accreditation Standards for Camp Programs and Services*, 1998, p. 143)

PA-32 Watercraft Activity Orientation
DNA if watercraft activities are not provided.
Do procedures specify that all persons using watercraft be provided the following training prior to use:
    1. Boarding and debarking, trimming, and movement on the craft,
    2. The use of life jackets, and
    3. Self-rescue in case of capsize or swamping?   **YES   NO**

Interpretation: This standard applies to the use of all watercraft including sailboats, rowboats, canoes, sailboards, rafts, and motorized boats. Training in self-rescue may include an actual "tip test" for appropriate craft, where conditions permit.
Compliance Demonstration: Director/staff description of training procedures; visitor observation of randomly selected watercraft activities.

PA-33 Aquatic Sites
Does the camp implement procedures for use of public pools or natural bodies of water that require:
    A. The following conditions be met:
        1. Campers and staff are oriented to rules and boundaries,
        2. Trained staff assess water and weather conditions to identify hazards and determine appropriate activities,
        3. Camper access is limited, as appropriate,
        4. Facility and equipment appear to be in good repair? YES   NO
    B. Rescue equipment is readily available and in good repair?
                                  YES   NO

Interpretation: Rules, boundaries, schedules, responsibilities, communication, and other safety issues should be reviewed with all persons prior to participation. Trained personnel must evaluate possible hazards in pools and other bodies of water and limit access and activities as necessary. Such hazards include waves, riptides, currents, lightning, and winds.
Compliance Demonstration: Director/staff of areas used and procedures in use; visitor observation of aquatic activities when possible.

---

another person or thing, using the same measuring tool. Persons compared to a norm of performance such as physical fitness tests would show the sif an individual were in the top quartile, she or he would be among the top 25% of those who took a particular test. The meaning of the score lies in the comparison to others. Professional judgment is used in these measures to determine the meaning of the rank of one person in relation to others.

Although evaluating by professional judgment is an important means of evaluation for recreation and leisure agencies, several precautions should be noted. Although a great deal can be learned from professional judgment about the administrative procedures, places, and programs, the model is less useful for people dimensions such as measuring personnel performance or participant impacts. According to Howe (1980), the implied association of standards to performance is a problem; high scores on standards do not necessarily reflect high quality or effectiveness. Another criticism of the professional judgment model related to standards is that the standards often become the maximum rather than the minimum guidelines. Lastly, evaluation by standards assumes that all recreation and leisure programs operate in the same context when this may not be the case at all. We must be careful that the use of standards does not result in homogenized programs that are the same everywhere regardless of the context and resources of an organization.

Goal-attainment Model

The goal-attainment model, also known as evaluation or management by objectives, is the backbone of educational evaluation applied to recreation and leisure programs. Goal-attainment is a preordinate model because preestablished goals and objectives are used to measure outcomes. The model works best when goals are discrete and/or objectives are measurable. Within this model, an evaluator can measure broad goals or specific objectives. Generally a focus on specific objectives when using the model is easiest and best. The current focus on benefits-based programming underlines the need to determine what benefits one wishes to address, and then to measure to see if those benefits are attained. The benefits are stated in the form of goals and objectives.

A goal is a clear general statement about where the organization and its programs are going related to the purpose or mission. Goals may be expressed in broad terms or may be readily quantifiable and measurable in objective terms, which are usually then called objectives. Objectives may be defined as written or expressed intentions about intended outcomes. Goal-attainment evaluation is based on measuring the congruence between performance and objectives. For this model to work, you must have well-written objectives and good criteria. Writing objectives may not always be the most fun activity, but they are necessary if the goal-attainment model is to be applied. Goal-attainment can be used in any area of recreation and applied to any system. It may also be used in assessment, formative, or summative evaluations. Therapeutic recreation specialists, for example, have used the model effectively in setting goals and objectives during the assessment phase of treatment (Touchstone, 1984).

· The prerequisite for using the goal-attainment model of evaluation is to have appropriate and measurable goals and objectives. This process requires the setting of goals at the outset, preferably before a program is begun, before an employee begins work, or before an administrative procedure or policy is implemented. Goals and objectives can be set prior to beginning the actual evaluation, although this timing is not as desirable as prior to the beginning of delivering services.

Objectives, then, are specific operational statements related to the desired goals and accomplishments of the organization, staff, participant or program. Many objectives may exist for an organization depending on who is setting them. Objectives may be written for participants as well as for staff and for the organization. Objectives are the criteria when using the goal-attainment model. Thus, determining the appropriate measurement of objectives is critical.

For purposes of this discussion on the goal-attainment model, we will refer to outcome and organizational objectives. Outcomes and behaviors are often described synonymously. Organizational objectives address the process that will be used to achieve the goals of the organization. For example, an organizational objective might be to recruit, train, and supervise ten volunteers to assist with the youth athletic program. Another organizational objective might be for a staff member to obtain a good or better rating on 75% of the evaluations completed by a tennis class.

Objectives are descriptions of the performance you want participants or staff to be able to exhibit when they have achieved the stated objectives. For example, an outcome objective might be that a participant would pass half of the skills in the swimming test. An organizational objective for a staff member might be that she or he would oversee the publishing of a program brochure three times each year.

Although writing objectives has probably been covered elsewhere in your college degree program, a quick review of how to write these objectives may be helpful. The essential components include describing a task, who will do it, identifying the action that should be taken and the conditions, and stating the criteria for an acceptable minimal level of performance for the task (Lundegren & Farrell, 1985). In writing these objectives, consider using strong verbs, stating only one purpose or aim per objective, specifying a single end product or result, and specifying the expected time for achievement. Examples of action verbs that might be used in writing objectives include: to enjoy, to assume responsibility, to engage in, to accept responsibility, to examine, to identify characteristics, to change, to develop, to define, to prepare, to compile, to visualize, or to understand.

Within the behavior objectives, several domains have been identified:

1. Cognitive (i.e., thinking, knowledge)
2. Affective (i.e., feeling, attitudes)
3. Psychomotor (i.e., movement, acting)
4. Social (i.e., how people relate to each other)

When writing objectives for a participant or a program, you need to keep in mind the area where you want to see change in performance or behavior. As indicated previously, these objectives then become the criteria for evaluation. Objectives are often written for KASA (i.e., knowledge, attitudes, skills, aspirations) as were identified in the program evaluation found in Chapter 1.6. In measuring the outcomes or benefits of a program, objectives often provide the foundation for collecting data and making judgments about the success of a program.

In summary, the goal-attainment model is a useful model for leisure services professionals. It requires well-written and measurable goals and objectives. One of the cautions is to make sure that you don't get so focused on evaluating the goals that you ignore other evidence that suggests good things came out of an organization, a program, or a staff member's work. Measuring objectives does not mean you cannot measure unplanned objectives; the goal-attainment model must be kept flexible enough to accommodate unplanned measurement. The information received may result in more appropriate goals and objectives written for evaluation next time.

Goal-free (Black Box) Model

A model of evaluation that is receiving more support in the field of recreation and leisure services is referred to as goal-free or the black box model (Scriven, 1967). The model has been around for a long time, but its value is only beginning to be realized. The basis of the model is the examination of an organization, group of participants, or program irrespective of the goals. In other words, the intent of goal-free evaluation is to discover and judge actual effects, outcomes, or impacts without considering what the effects were supposed to be. The evaluator begins with no preordained idea about what to find. The broad goal of the evaluation is to find out what is happening. The value lies in discovering descriptions or explanations that may have unintended side effects. Scriven argues that if the main objective of an evaluation is to assess the worth of outcomes, you should not make any distinction at all between those outcomes that were intended as opposed to those that were not.

You must realize that to be completely goal free is impossible because an evaluation always involves some type of question or comparison. Further, the evaluator must select only certain information out of the total information pool that she or he could collect. Data are collected in relation to recognized concerns or guiding questions. Otherwise you might be collecting data forever. Often results emerge, however, from the issues identified by participants, citizens, or staff. The proponents of the model argue that the evaluator should be free to choose the range of issues to use for an evaluation and should be able to recognize concerns and issues as they arise.

The data collected in the goal-free model may be either qualitative or quantitative, although the model lends itself best to qualitative approaches, as you will see when we discuss data collection methods. In the goal-free model, the evaluator will usually talk to people, identify program elements, overview the program, discover purposes and concerns, conceptualize issues and problems, identify qualitative and/or quantitative data that needs to be collected, select methods and techniques to use including the possibility of case studies, collect the data, match data and the issues of audiences, and prepare and deliver the report. The evaluator is a detective, in a way, as she or he tries to identify the important relationships and outcomes that exist within an organization or a program. Unlike the goal-attainment model, however, the evaluator does not start out with a specific plan for what criteria will be measured.

The goal-free evaluator uses logical analysis and observation as well as any other needed data collection methods. The drawback to this model of evaluation is that it may be very time-consuming and some outcomes may be difficult to measure. The results, however, can be helpful in understanding in depth aspects of the five Ps of evaluation in leisure services.

Systems Approach

The systems approach, as an important model of evaluation, is commonly used in understanding how a program or place contributes to the overall mission of a leisure services organization. This model is process-oriented and does not use objectives. The model is used to establish a working understanding of an organization that is capable of achieving end products such as the provision of leisure services. The focus is on determining the degree to which an organization realizes its goals under a given set of conditions. The type and timing of data collected depends on the structure of the system or the organization.

The systems approach is often used in management planning and has specific designs that are developed. Examples include Program Evaluation and Review Technique (PERT), Critical Path Method (CPM), Program Planning and Budgeting System (PPBS), Management by Objectives (MBO), and Total Performance Measurement (TPM). Data related to inputs, process, and outputs result in feedback used for decision making. If you were to develop an evaluation system for a recreation, park, or leisure services organization, you would likely use a systems approach in determining how evaluating the five Ps fit into the overall operation of an organization. Fiscal evaluations also are frequently used within a systems context.

Within leisure services organizations, program planning is often based on a systems approach with evaluation being just one part of it. The strategy and goals are the inputs, the program design and implementation are the process, and the evaluation yields outcomes and provides a means for feedback. Planning, delivery, and evaluation are related to one another. An evaluator can examine how an organization is operating to determine how effective it is. Within the systems approach model, an entire organization or just components of it can be examined. An evaluation through the systems approach results in the determination of outcomes as well as an assessment of the processes used by an organization. The model assumes that different decisions require different types of information inputs. Decisions are based on continuation, modification, or termination of the program or staff or whatever is being measured.

• • • • •

These five models provide a way to frame evaluation. They offer a context for assumptions for determining how to set criteria and collect data. They are applied in varying degrees when conducting evaluation projects. In undertaking an evaluation project, it is essential to set the stage by determining which model best sets the framework for the evaluation. Table 1.8(2) on page 74 provides a summary of the strengths and weaknesses of each of the models. If experts and standards exist, professional judgment might be best. If goals and measurable objectives exist for a program, evaluating by using those goals and objectives as the foundation will be best. If one is interested in finding out what is happening without comparing to established goals, the goal-free approach may be superior. If the evaluator is examining one component of a leisure services organization in relation to the inputs, processes, outputs, and outcomes, then a systems approach will enable her or him to choose the elements to examine in relation to the broad mission of the organization. The evaluation model chosen will depend upon the purposes of the evaluation and the situation that currently exists.

Table 1.8(2) Summary of the Strengths and Weaknesses of Evaluation Models

Model	Strengths	Weaknesses
Intuitive	• Relatively easy • Day-to-day analysis	• Not scientific • Lacks reliability
Professional Judgment	• Uses expert opinions • Standards-based • Easy for organization • Less time required	• Must have expert • Expensive • Standards must be valid
Goal-attainment	• Most commonly used • Uses preestablished goals and objectives • Objectivity	• Need good goals and objectives • Requires measurement instruments • Too much focus on goals possible
Goal-free	• Allows for qualitative data • Examines actual effects • Uses logical analysis • Allows depth analysis	• Goal-free impossible • Possible bias • Time-consuming • Evaluator driven
Systems Approach	• Process-oriented • Useful in management • Integrates elements of an organization	• May be too broad-based • Complicated to use • Can't evaluate everything

From Ideas to Reality

Choosing evaluation models is not the most exciting task that an evaluator undertakes yet it is important to consider from which model you are operating so that appropriate decisions can be made about criteria and methods. The five models outlined here might be used for any of the five Ps. Further, depending upon how your organization is set up, any one of the models might be applied to a particular situation. For example, say you wanted to find out if your older adult program was contributing to the life satisfaction of the individuals who participated. You could use the intuitive judgment model and informally observe the older adults to draw conclusions. You might invite in external evaluators (professional judgment) to help you determine the contribution that your program is making to the lives of older adults. You could use the goals and objectives set for the program (goal-attainment) as the basis for collecting data to determine how the program affects life satisfaction. Or you might use a goal-free approach and do in-depth interviews to find out how the older adult programs affect the individuals who participate. The exact model is not as important as the framework that you decide to use for your evaluation. The models simply provide a roadmap for making decisions about how an actual project might best be conducted by helping you determine criteria and ways to collect data.

Now that you have studied this chapter, you should be able to:

- Describe the differences between the five models for evaluation.
- Choose an appropriate model given a particular situation that requires evaluation.

Designing Evaluation Projects and Research Studies
Doing What You Gotta Do

No data for an evaluation project or research study should be collected until a solid plan has been carefully identified. Once you have determined what to include in your organization's evaluation system you can then plan specific evaluation projects. Once you know what burning questions you want to answer for a research study, you can begin to design the proposal. Planning a project includes choosing a model to guide you, determining the timing of evaluation and the area (five Ps) within leisure services that you will evaluate, and then selecting specific methods to use. A research proposal requires the initiation of a literature review, the identification of the role of theory, and design and methods selections. In this chapter, we examine how to design an evaluation project as well as how to develop a research proposal. Both tasks share some commonalities, but each also has uniqueness.

Sometimes the design for a project, such as a performance appraisal of staff development, is a tool that will be used over and over again. Other times, each individual evaluation project or research study will be designed anew. Generally, small scale, highly focused, and manageable studies are more useful than large, broad evaluations. Sometimes more complex projects will be necessary and cutting a major project or study into manageable portions may be needed to complete it successfully. Regardless of the magnitude of the undertaking, keeping the project focused and on target is essential.

A design for evaluation or research is a plan for allocating resources of time and energy. The design must be carefully considered for each project depending on the specific context of the evaluation situation. You have many choices. Various constraints, however, are associated with every plan and you must do the best you can given the financial, time, and human resources constraints that may exist. In addition, for any evaluation or research endeavor, many designs may be proposed, but no single plan is necessarily going to be perfect. Thus, you will have to make decisions about what is likely to be the best approach.

Taking time to plan is important in any project or study. Careful planning saves time in the long run and can result in better research and evaluation. You will need enough lead-time to plan the entire process for evaluation or research before you begin to collect data.

Developing Plans for a Specific Evaluation Project

We have found planning guidelines to be a most useful framework in developing individual evaluation projects. In general, when planning an evaluation project you will be examining several basic questions:

- *Why* (e.g., For what reason or purpose is this evaluation project being done? Is it worth the effort? What use will the results have?);
- *What* (e.g., Which of the aspects of personnel, policies, places, programs, or participants will be evaluated? What issues need to be addressed? What criteria are to be measured?);
- *Who* (e.g., Who wants the information and in what form? Who will actually conduct the evaluation? Who is the sample to ask for information?);
- *When* (e.g., timelines and timing);
- *Where* (e.g., sample size and composition); and
- *How* (e.g., How to collect and analyze data, methods, techniques, ethics? How will the final report with be presented? What resources are needed?).

These questions resemble what was asked in setting up an evaluation system, but in the evaluation project design you will get more specific about how a project will actually be conducted from the beginning to the end. The design of the actual project is the "nitty gritty" of evaluation.

Theoretically, you will consider the *why, what, who, when, where* and *how* together but in practicality, each will build upon the others. Smith (1989) suggested that we must avoid two types of errors in the initial planning: measuring something that does not exist, and measuring something that is of no interest to management and policymakers. Thus, the first three steps of determining *why, what,* and *who* are essential.

The *why* of doing evaluations has been discussed extensively in Chapter 1.4, but the evaluator must always keep in mind the purpose of the project to stay focused and on track. The why has implications for *what* and *who*.

The *who* often refers to the stakeholders or who wants the information. Stakeholders are those individuals who are personally involved in the organization, who derive income from the organization, whose future status or career might be affected by the quality of the organization, and/or who are the clients or potential recipients of the organization's services. Arranging a meeting of the stakeholders for a proposed evaluation project is often useful before you begin. Staff is usually more involved in the organization than either sponsors or clients, so they need to have input about how an evaluation will be conducted. Many aspects of the evaluation plan such as the type of evaluation, the availability of resources, and the reasons for evaluating can be determined early in the project by talking to stakeholders. Further, clarifications should be made specific about *why* a project is being undertaken and *what* the project is.

A second part of the *who* question is to determine who has the needed information. In some cases, documents may already exist that can help to address the evaluation criteria. Existing research or evaluation literature may be used as well as organizational records. You may want to find out what has been done elsewhere if possible, and "borrow" or adapt their approach and/or instruments whenever possible and appropriate.

A third part of *who* is to determine who will be in charge of the evaluation. Although one person may do an evaluation project, a team approach is often desirable. The more people involved in an evaluation project, the more likely they are to have ideas that can help to make the evaluation recommendations useable when completed. You may want to use a citizen advisory committee, for example, depending on the type of project undertaken.

What relates to the model to be used and the criteria to be measured. Is it possible to measure the criteria desired? Do the resources exist to do an appropriate evaluation project? Are the level of evaluation and the timing of the evaluation consistent with what the stakeholders want and need? These answers represent a critical aspect in developing the evaluation plan because now is the point that an initial decision should be made about whether to attempt a particular evaluation project or not. If the goal-attainment model is to provide the framework, for example, you must be certain that measurable goals and objectives exist or can be written. At this point in time, you will also determine which model is going to be best to use.

When refers to the timing and timelines. Should the evaluation be assessment, summative, or formative? If the evaluation is summative, when is the best time to collect information: immediately or after several weeks have passed after a program? How long will the project take to complete? When are the results of the evaluation needed? When is the best time during the program or the year to do the evaluation? To some extent, these answers will depend on the criteria being used. You must be realistic about how long a project may take to complete. Keep in mind that it takes time for proper pretesting of instruments, training of data collectors, getting related material from other books and journals, analyzing the data to draw conclusions and make recommendations, and writing the report. It is possible, but very unlikely, that someone could do a survey in two to three weeks if it is brief and done on a telephone. A survey of several hundred or a few thousand, however, may take a few months or more than a year to complete. Also think about the unintended consequences that might be encountered such as an inadequate sample size that could slow down the data collection. All of these issues will be discussed further in Unit Two, but the conscientious evaluator will consider the possible problems in the planning phase to try to prevent them from happening when the evaluation is actually implemented.

Where the evaluation is conducted will depend upon the leisure services area being examined, the sample to be used, and the timing. The particular aspect of the five Ps will also determine the *where*. Usually the *where* question is not difficult to answer once the other components of the planning have been carefully considered.

The final task is to determine *how* to do a project. *How* relates primarily to data collection and analysis. Such decisions include sampling, research design, data collection administration, choice of statistics, and how the findings will be reported. Once the preceding questions are answered, these *how* questions will likely fall into place, although decisions about *how* will still need to be made. The problem with some evaluations is that we decide we are going to use a particular technique, like mailed questionnaires, before we determine any of the other aspects of designing the evaluation project plan. The *how* aspect of the plan, however, has to be realistic because one must also assess the resources available for the project. The evaluator must be careful to avoid "data addiction." That is, you should plan to collect only the data that are needed, not everything that would be interesting to ask. If criteria are appropriately delimited, data addiction should not be a problem. The *how* also includes considering costs such as:

- Staff time for planning
- Labor and material costs for pretesting
- Copying costs
- Supervisory costs for interviewer hiring, training, and supervising staff or use of volunteers

- Labor and expense costs of checking a certain percentage
- Cost of preparing codes and mailing
- Labor and material costs for coding and entering data
- Cost of cleaning the data if mistakes are made in entering it
- Computer programming or software costs
- Computer time
- Labor time and material costs for analysis and report preparation
- Telephone charges, postage, photocopying/printing

A good evaluation is not always inexpensive, although some projects are more economical than others. The costs will obviously increase with the complexity of the project and amount of analysis needed.

After these *why, what, who, when, where,* and *how* decisions are considered, a brief proposal or written plan will be useful to make sure that all people involved in your organization agree with what will be done in the evaluation project. Sometimes when you see things written down on paper, possible mistakes or problems are easier to see. The following planning framework outline (Table 1.9, p. 82) is offered as an example and a model that can be used in doing evaluation project planning.

Several other items might be considered in designing an evaluation project. First of all, baseline data about a program, participant, staff member, or place may be needed before the data collection begins. You may want to know the current state of affairs that existed up to the present time. This information might provide a standard of comparison against which the outcomes of the evaluation are measured.

Second, evaluators also need to be aware of their agendas and biases for any evaluation study as well as those of the stakeholders or audience. Possible conflicts should be discussed ahead of time and negotiated. The goals of the project should be agreed upon and the possibility of unexpected consequences, such as what happens if undesirable effects are found, should be anticipated. All parties in the evaluation should be aware of how the evaluation is to be conducted and how the data will be presented.

Finally, usefulness for enlightened decision making is the primarily focus of evaluation. As Patton (1978) suggested, evaluations are not a panacea for problems. For an evaluation project to be used, criteria must be addressed to answer questions for decision makers. Avoid questions that decision-makers do not want answered. Avoid questions that already have known answers. Unless a lack of knowledge and information is a part of the problem, evaluation research will not help an organization. If the problem

Table 1.9 Example Evaluation Project Planning Framework (adapted from the work of students: Ginna Millard, Sara Shope, and Amy Bryan)

Agency: University of North Carolina Hospitals (Pediatric Play Room)

Why?

Background: Problems exist trying to keep track of the toys, videos, and other resources that are available to use and check out in the Pediatric Play Room

Purpose: To describe the process (success and failures) in the present system, set a baseline, and to provide for organizational improvement in the future

Cost-effectiveness: The administration of the project can be done by volunteer undergraduate students who will provide a report to the CTRS responsible for the playroom

What?

Model: Goal-free.

Criteria: What are the problems? What policies currently exist? How are they enforced? How willing are staff and volunteers to enforce policies?

Data Type: A combination of qualitative (field observations) and quantitative data (questionnaires to staff and volunteers who supervise the play room)

Who?

Who Wants the Information: Director of Therapeutic Recreation Services at UNC Hospitals and CTRS in charge of playroom

Who Will Do the Project: Undergraduate TR students in an evaluation class

Who Will Provide Data: The evaluators will observe the playroom and survey all individuals who have responsibilities for supervising the playroom

When?

Timing: Formative evaluation

Time lines: March (observation) and April (surveys and analysis) 1994

Where?

Sample Size and Composition: Random sample of observations during various hours that the playroom is open; a population sample will be done of supervisors in the playroom

How?

Method(s) to Use: Field observations and quantitative questionnaires

Time and Money Resources Needed: Time to plan, conduct, and write report is volunteer time from students; supplies for printing from hospital budget=$10; computer analysis free

Special Considerations: Gaining cooperation of supervisors in the play room

---

Note: More detail will be added to each of these as the specific plans for data collection are solidified.

is a disorganized organization, one should organize it rather than try to evaluate it. Further as Hudson (1988) suggested concerning community needs assessments, evaluation projects must be comprehensive, customized, versatile, flexible, and efficient. They take a commitment of time and resources and often have limitations. They must be designed, however, to provide the greatest potential to get useful information for making the best possible decisions.

Developing a Research Proposal

Many of the principles that apply to designing an evaluation project plan also pertain to a research proposal. The aspects of criteria in the form of theory testing or development along with the use of a literature review are coupled with data collection and analysis issues that result in some kind of conclusions that add to the body of knowledge. The research proposal should include as much detail as possible. This plan is important to clarify thinking and give focus and direction to the work. The value of a research plan, just like the evaluation plan, is to state one's ideas so that others might react to them and improve upon them. Planning may prevent serious flaws in implementing a study.

Most research proposals include the following sections:

- Introduction
- Statement of the theory or hypotheses
- Initial review of the literature
- Description of proposed sample
- Methods and techniques to use in carrying out the study
- Plans for how data analysis will be done

The *general introduction* identifies the area being studied and how it will contribute to the body of knowledge that already exists. The need for the study and the statement of the problem being addressed is generally included in this introduction.

The statement of the *theory and/or hypotheses* gives a framework for the study. This framework tells the reader what is being addressed and the possible questions or relationships that are to be examined. Theory is the foundation for any research study being undertaken. For studies that focus on generating theory, the guiding research questions serve as the framework for this part of the research design.

In a proposal, an initial *review of literature* should be described. More may be added to the literature review as the study is undertaken, but the researcher needs to determine what literature currently exists and what methods have been employed to address these topics in the past. The most important and recent literature is usually included in this brief review.

The researcher will also want to identify the *sample* to be used and how it will be selected. This description will include the characteristics of participants in the study as well as the number needed. Sampling procedures and rationale would be determined as well as the source of the data to be collected.

The *methods and techniques* for data collection in carrying out the project will need to be identified. This aspect is also referred to as the research design. The methods and techniques should be consistent with the theory or hypotheses that are used.

Related to the procedures of data collection is a plan for *data analysis*. The analysis may have impacts on the number of participants needed as well as the way the instruments are used or designed. The analysis must also result in being able to answer the hypotheses and research questions that are generated.

A research proposal is generally longer than an evaluation plan, but both are critical to designing studies that will address the questions that need to be answered for decision making or for contributing to the body of knowledge in a field such as leisure services.

From Ideas to Reality

Planning evaluation projects and research studies beyond the idea stage is often not the most exciting endeavor. Some evaluators and researchers, particularly when they are novices, have a tendency to want to begin to collect data and later work out the "bugs" of a study. We encourage you to consider drafting an outline for each phase of your evaluation or research study before you begin to collect data. It will set a course for you that can provide direction as you move through the undertaking. As you can see by the examples given in this chapter, the plan or proposal does not need to be elaborate at this stage, but it at least can give you a path to follow. It may be modified slightly as the project or study develops but a plan at least provides a foundation upon which to begin to build. Once you have more information about the methods such as questionnaires or observations, and techniques such as sampling and analysis, you can develop a more sophisticated plan to follow as you complete your evaluation project or research study and write the final report.

Now that you have studied this chapter, you should be able to:

- Write an evaluation project plan including the why, who, what, when, where, and how.
- Describe the elements of a research proposal.
- Determine the considerations that should be made in planning any type of evaluation project or research study.
- Analyze whether an evaluation plan is feasible and has the potential for producing usable results.

Competencies and the Art of Evaluation

Most leisure services professionals are pretty good intuitive evaluators, but education, training, and practical experience are necessary to become confident and competent at systematic formal evaluation. As indicated in the preface, reading this book is not necessarily going to make you an expert evaluator. That learning will take years of experience. You do, however, need to have some basic skills and background to conduct and evaluate your own projects and improve upon your abilities.

A critical aspect of learning is that when we acquire knowledge about a few things, we often find out about all the things that we *don't* know. We have learned as professors over the years that sometimes the value of a college education is not in what you learn, but how a person comes to appreciate what she or he doesn't know. Thus, one important aspect of developing competencies for evaluation in leisure services is to learn the limitations of one's own skills, as well as the limitations of what evaluation can do for an organization.

Sometimes understanding how to evaluate evaluations or to critique research is just as important as being able to actually conduct studies. Some organizations rely on external evaluators. Other organizations use only internal evaluators who are professionals within the organization and have job responsibilities that include evaluation. Therapeutic recreation specialists, for example, spend a great deal of their time doing individual assessments and evaluation for their clients. Whether you are actually the internal professional who conducts the evaluation, or whether you use the information obtained from an external evaluator, you still need to know the terminology and the components that must be considered in the evaluation process.

Internal versus External Evaluations

The ideal situation for a leisure services organization is to have both internal and external evaluations conducted appropriately within the evaluation system. The decision whether to use internal or external evaluators may depend on a variety of factors. Table 1.10 provides a summary of the advantages and disadvantages of internal or external evaluators.

Table 1.10 Advantages and Disadvantages of External and Internal Evaluators		
	Advantages	**Disadvantages**
Internal	• Knows the organization • Accessible to colleagues • Realistic recommendations • Can make changes	• Pressure to have positive results • Difficult to criticize • May lack training
External	• More objectivity • Competence • Experience • More resources • Less pressure to compromise • Lower costs	• Threat to employees • Must get to know organization • May disrupt organization • May impose values • Expensive

Certainly many advantages exist with using internal evaluators. The professional who is a member of the organization ought to know a lot about the organization. Less time will be needed for the evaluator to become familiar with the ins and outs and the intricacies of the organization. An internal evaluator will also be more accessible to colleagues and will likely not be as obtrusive as an external evaluator. Once the evaluation is complete, the internal evaluator may be in a better position to make changes and to use the results of the evaluation for decision making. When internal evaluators are used, they receive their regular salary so the costs would likely be lower. Further, because the internal evaluator knows the organization, realistic recommendations that can enhance the efficiency and effectiveness of the organization might be more easily offered.

Obvious advantages also exist to using an external evaluator. These individuals, often called consultants, may have more objectivity due to the remoteness they have to the situation and the freedom from responsibility for the organization or the services. Their objectivity is also based on a professional commitment to the field and not the individual organization. Further, they have credibility based on their professional experience and competency. With more experience, they may have access to a greater variety of methods and techniques. They may also know more about how other organizations address some of their evaluation concerns. They may have resources such as sample measurement instruments or computer programs for data analysis that may not be available to internal evaluators in an organization. Since external evaluators have less investment in a program, they may feel less pressure to make compromises in their recommendations. In addition, if staff conflicts are a problem in an organization, outside evaluators may be able to mediate them better than someone who is involved within the organization. Their objectivity will likely be unencumbered by knowledge of personal issues and conflicts. A further advantage is that they may have data from other organizations that would make for comparative evaluations.

A downside exists to using only internal or external evaluators. The internal evaluator may feel pressure to have positive results or her or his job, or the jobs of colleagues, may change. It is generally easier for an internal evaluator to focus on strengths rather than weaknesses. An internal evaluator may find difficulty in criticizing certain aspects of a program. Further, an internal evaluator that does not have extensive training in evaluation may not be as competent as someone who has evaluation as a specialty.

The external evaluator may also have disadvantages. This outside individual may be seen as a threat to employees; staff will be on their best behavior so the organization may not appear as it really is. The external evaluator must spend a great deal of time just getting to know an organization and may miss some of the nuances that go on within a particular organization. The outside evaluator may take valuable time away from staff or may disrupt the normal functioning of an organization. As is true in any situation, the external evaluator may impose her or his value system on an organization that may not hold the same values. Further, to hire an external evaluator often is expensive and many leisure services agencies do not have those kinds of resources.

Decisions will have to be made about who is the best person to conduct an evaluation. Some decisions are obvious. For example, one's immediate supervisor usually conducts personnel evaluations and bringing someone from the outside would not make sense. On the other hand, when standards are applied through an accreditation process, external reviewers are required. Some programs may be evaluated easily "in-house" whereas hiring someone to conduct a more thorough evaluation may be useful every once in awhile. We would hope that all recreation majors would be good internal evaluators and would also possess some of the skills to be external evaluators too. The development of these skills, however, takes education and practice. Just as important is knowing when you see a well-done evaluation that is useful to an individual or an organization. Doing, as well as consuming, evaluations are both important.

Developing Competencies

Regardless of who conducts the evaluation, every recreation, park, tourism, and leisure services professional ought to have some training in systematic evaluation that can be used in an organization. The more individuals who have evaluation training, the better off the organization will be. Even if an external evaluator is hired, the professionals in the organization have to know how to formulate criteria for the project and will need to determine the reliability and validity of the judgments made by external evaluators.

In hiring an external reviewer or conducting an evaluation with organizational staff, several specific competencies ought to be required:

1. The individual conducting the evaluation should have some knowledge about the topical area being evaluated. If the adult sports league is being evaluated, for example, the evaluator ought to know something about recreation programming for adults and about sports programming. In addition the basic terminology of evaluation should be understood.

2. An evaluator ought to know something about designing evaluation systems, developing planning frameworks for individual projects, and writing goals and objectives. Knowing why and what to evaluate are necessary prerequisites for writing different types of objectives. The evaluator must be able to judge how measurement can be conducted in relation to these goals and objectives.

3. The evaluator ought to know all the possible evaluation research methods. She or he should know how to determine the best way to collect data, how to choose a sample, and the appropriate techniques for analysis.

4. The evaluator should be able to interpret the data and relate those results to the criteria. An understanding of the trilogy of evaluation and how the parts fit together are essential.

5. The evaluator should know what to look for in analyzing both qualitative and quantitative data using the most appropriate strategies or statistics. As you will see later, evaluators may be partial to qualitative or quantitative data. These preferences, however, do not preclude knowing the basic assumptions about each type of data so that sound evaluation judgments can be made.

6. An evaluator must understand how to use evaluation results in decision making regardless of what area of the five Ps are being

evaluated. This competency will involve knowing how to organize, write, and present evaluation reports so that the information can be communicated effectively to those individuals (e.g., staff, Board or Commission members, parents) who want and/or need the information.

7. An evaluator needs to be able to address the political, legal, and ethical issues that may be encountered during an evaluation. Certain legal and ethical concerns must be addressed as well as how evaluators can be politically responsive to those users of the evaluation information. More detail will be given about these issues in Chapter 1.11.

8. Although most of the above competencies relate to conceptual and technical skills, certain personal skills are an additional aspect needed to be a successful evaluator. Personal qualities are necessary such as an interest in improving personnel, policies, places, programs and/or participant outcomes. The evaluator must be worthy of trust of his or her colleagues as well as of the administrators and the decision makers of organizations. She or he must be as objective as possible, although one's personal biases cannot help but enter into any undertaking. The effective evaluator must be able to see and respond to sensitive issues and situations as they relate to the uniqueness of organizations.

When one begins to examine the competencies needed to conduct evaluation projects, they may appear to be a bit overwhelming. These competencies are not that rigorous if the evaluator sees evaluation as a system of linking criteria, evidence, and judgment. Conducting evaluation or using evaluation information need not be anything to fear. The best way to learn is to "just do it" and the only way to get started is to begin. Some aspects of evaluation are technical, but not so difficult that they can't be used by an enthusiastic and committed leisure services professional.

From Ideas to Reality

As indicated earlier, to become a good evaluator requires a combination of education, training, and practical experience. All leisure services professionals ought to have a basic background in evaluation that will enable them to do projects and judge the merit of evaluation projects done by others. No magic formulas exist to learn how to be a competent evaluator but by learning the basics and trying them out, evaluating your own work, and practicing, you can become effective and successful as an evaluator.

Whether to use internal or external evaluations is a decision left up to an organization. Both have advantages and disadvantages. Many times organizations do not have the funding necessary to hire outside consultants so they rely on internal evaluators. In some situations, it is better to go outside the organization regarding some types of criteria that may need to be measured. The professional will need to determine when it is most appropriate to do internal or external evaluations and how that relates to the entire evaluation system.

Now that you have studied this chapter, you should be able to:

- Describe the advantages and disadvantages of using internal versus external evaluators.
- Determine when it is best to hire an outside evaluator or use an internal evaluator.
- List the competencies needed to become a successful evaluator.

Political, Legal, Ethical, and Moral Issues
Doing the Right Thing

Most research and evaluation books include a chapter or a section on legal and ethical issues toward the end of the text. You may not have enough information about data collection at this point to fully comprehend this chapter placed toward the beginning, but we believe that the political, legal, ethical, and moral questions surrounding evaluations and research ought to be put in the forefront. Chances are you will not be forced to address many of these issues negatively if you have carefully considered the design of your project. On the other hand, you will likely have to make some decisions about planning a project or study based on some of these concerns.

Regardless of the project, the bottom line is to consider how you will treat subjects and organizations with dignity. You will hopefully not have many political, legal, ethical, and moral issues to address in your work, but it is important to consider these issues. If you are honest with yourself and the people with whom you work, you will probably have few problems. Treating people with dignity is easy to articulate but often hard to implement into practice because of the many issues that may arise when conducting evaluation projects and research studies.

Political Issues

Politics deals with practical wisdom related to the beliefs and biases that individuals and groups hold. Evaluation systems and projects can be political in that they may support or refute the views that people hold. The simple fact that people are involved in evaluation projects makes them political.

Politics encompasses personal contacts, value-laden definitions, controversial recommendations, subtle pressures to please, and advocacy for certain results or outcomes. According to Patton (1978), to be innocent of politics in evaluation is to become a pawn. Value orientations and the collection of empirical (observable) data make evaluation projects, as well as research studies, political whether we like it or not. The fact that criteria, evidence, and judgment are used makes them political. Further, politics affects the utilization process. By their nature, evaluations are political when the information is used to "manipulate" other people even though the manipulation may be positive.

As an evaluator or a researcher, be aware of several considerations that can make the evaluation process less political. First, you must understand an organization well before a project is undertaken. This suggestion means understanding the strengths and the limitations of an organization. Second, before claiming any conclusions about the evaluation or research, you must provide evidence. Thus, the judgments must be directly linked to the criteria and the evidence. Sometimes generalizations and recommendations are easy to make without paying attention to the data. Evaluators and researchers, however, must be careful not to go beyond the actual findings in drawing conclusions. Third, the purpose of the evaluation must be made clear to all involved *before* it is undertaken. That purpose must also be kept clear throughout the process.

The only way that evaluation and research studies are not political is if they are not used, but even nonuse may make a political statement. Not understanding the political ramifications may be a reason why evaluations do not get used. What a waste of time however, if the recommendations from a project are never even considered. If we acknowledge that evaluations and research are often political, then we can use those politics to our advantage and not resist or ignore them.

Legal Issues

In the vast majority of evaluation projects and research studies, you will probably encounter no legal concerns. If you were collecting information about an illegal behavior and its cessation due to a recreation program, however, you might run into legal issues. For example, if someone admits to you during an evaluation interview that they are drinking at the recreation center, are you obliged to turn them in? The answer is probably "no," but you might be careful that you do not associate any names directly with your data in the event that some legality must be addressed.

Ethical Issues

Ethics have to do with what is right and wrong and how you conform to the standards of a given profession. Certain "rules" must be considered when doing evaluation projects and research studies. Ethics involve primarily being as open as possible about a project within the constraints of privacy. This statement means that people (i.e., participants or personnel) have the right to know that they or their programs are being examined. In addition, they also have some right to privacy and confidentiality concerning the information that they wish to divulge.

As an evaluator, you have ethical obligations to the people with whom you work. First of all, you must be careful not to promise too much from an evaluation, but should be realistic about an evaluation project's value and limitations. The evaluator must assure loyalties to the profession and to the public above the program evaluated.

Privacy is a second ethical issue. Evaluators and researchers also have the responsibility to assure anonymity and confidentiality (if it is needed) in the evaluation. Anonymity means that no one, including the people collecting the data, will know the names of the participants in a project, such as the individuals who complete a survey. Confidentiality says that the evaluator or researcher will know who participated, but no one else will. Some projects do not require this assurance, but others may require confidentiality or anonymity. For example, you may want to use only code numbers to identity respondents instead of people's names. Those codes must be kept separate from questionnaires and the codes should be destroyed once all data are tabulated so even the evaluator does not know who provided information. The evaluator may also want to present statistics by broad enough categories that no one can figure out how a particular individual might have responded. You should realize that people answer differently sometimes depending if their name goes on the survey. Sometimes the person's name makes a difference and you will want to use it, but that person *must* give you permission to do so.

Coercion is a third ethical concern in some evaluation projects. People should never be forced into participation unless involvement is a necessary prerequisite. For example, staff evaluations are required in most organizations. A staff member knows when she or he takes a job that a performance evaluation is required, so the person should not feel any coercion. In other evaluation and research situations, however, participation should be optional. As evaluators, we need to make a project interesting and important enough that people *want* to participate.

Related to coercion is the fourth area of written consent. Written informed consent is not necessarily required in most evaluation projects, but evaluators need to be aware of its potential use. Most research studies do require institutional review board approval and the use of informed consent. Written consent is a way to assure anonymity or confidentially to individuals by having them sign a form indicating that they are aware of how data will be collected and used. For some types of extensive evaluation involving children in particular, informed consent may need to be obtained from parents or guardians as well as from children.

A fifth ethical question raised in evaluation relates to how someone may be harmed by evaluation or research. If any harm is possible as a result of an evaluation, you should make sure that the harm does not occur. This ethical concern refers to physical or psychological harm in doing an evaluation or in *not* getting a treatment. For example, if we want to find out if some new activity in therapeutic recreation really works, we may design an experiment where half of the clients will get the treatment and half will not. In this situation, we have to ask what possible harm could be incurred to the group not getting the treatment. After considering the possible negative physical and psychological effects, the ideal experimental design may not be possible in some cases, if harm would be caused. Most recreation professionals will not be in situations where these concerns of possible harm will arise, but one must always be aware of them.

A final ethical aspect that might be considered relates to how much participants have the right to know about the results of a project. We believe that they have the right to know the results of an evaluation project. Sharing results with participants as well as other professionals is the best way to assure that good evaluation and programs are developed. You may want to offer to send the results to participants or have a meeting to explain what you learned from an evaluation project. Sometimes this procedure is referred to as *debriefing*, but it need not be that formal. People, however, who have been involved in giving you information, should have access to that information.

Moral Issues

Moral issues are closely related to ethical issues. We will address them separately, however, as they relate to what the evaluator might do that could be construed as right or wrong in conducting a study. Moral concerns relate to biases and mistakes that might be unintentionally made in conducting an evaluation project that may affect the outcome of the project. For example, the choice of an inappropriate or inadequate sample may affect the outcomes of a study. If we wanted to know how effective a program was we might need to survey program drop-outs as well as those individuals who completed the program. If the evaluator is aware of a concern such as this and does nothing to compensate for it, that person has acted in a morally inappropriate manner.

Cultural and procedural biases may also cause evaluation problems. The careless collection of data by using an inappropriate instrument for the respondents or poorly written questions are moral concerns. As an evaluator, you must be honest about your skills and either get help or do an evaluation project that is appropriate to your competence and skill level.

Allowing bias, prejudice, preconceived perceptions, or friendship to influence the evaluation outcomes, or being a patsy to the stakeholders, are further moral issues to avoid. The evaluator must also be careful not to be predisposed to any particular outcome.

When the evaluator actually gets to the judgment phase and writes the report, several aspects must be considered. For example, not publishing negative results is a problem as is discounting some findings or not letting all the information out. All the details of the study need to be reported including procedures that may not have gone particularly well. The possibilities of negative results should be discussed and addressed ahead of time with the stakeholders of an evaluation to avoid moral conflicts and embarrassment arising from the evaluation situation.

Taking too long to get results out also has moral implications. Since evaluation is oriented toward problem solving and enlightened decision making, most people need that information just as soon as possible. Although not morally wrong, an evaluator has a responsibility to get an evaluation project completed in a timely manner.

Morally the evaluator or researcher is bound to do the best possible evaluation. Thus, shortcuts must be avoided. Improper sampling procedures and the use of a convenience sample rather than a probability sample may not be appropriate and may affect the results of a study. Further, procedures need to be pretested to assure that they are appropriate.

Quality control must be instituted throughout the project. The evaluator must also be able to address the possibility of, what are called in research, Type I and Type II errors. *Type I errors* are false positive errors, or finding that a program really makes a difference when it does not. These errors may be compared to *Type II errors,* false negatives that assume a program makes no beneficial difference when it really does. In evaluation, Type I errors are more likely, but you have to consider the possibility of both and what they mean from a moral perspective.

Avoiding Problems in Evaluation and Research

Posavac and Carey (1992) have offered several key ideas to consider in addressing political, legal, ethical, and moral issues in evaluation. First, humility won't hurt. You must realize what can and cannot be done, be able to admit your limitations, and adjust. Second, evaluation is not easy and it is not a "slam-bang" proposition. Patience is necessary and impatience may lead to disappointment and problems. Planning is essential to avoid pitfalls. Third, the evaluator must focus on practical questions and feasible issues. The evaluation questions must be well-focused and the criteria clearly defined. Get other staff to support you and make sure they know what is going on and are able to monitor the quality of your project as well. Finally, adopt a self-evaluation orientation in your work. You as the evaluator are ultimately the one who knows whether you have made the appropriate moral, political, ethical, and legal decisions. You must be the one to continually monitor yourself to do the right thing.

From Ideas to Reality

One of the safeguards that you may need to address is obtaining consent to do your evaluation or research study. Many institutions like hospitals, schools, camps, and residential facilities have formal procedures that ensure the safety and privacy of their participants. In these situations, you may be required to submit your plan or proposal with the ways that you will address the issues described in this chapter. This proposal may require formal approval by the organization. Until you gain the support and approval, you will not be able to begin your evaluation project or research study.

Political, legal, ethical, and moral issues will be different in each study. Hopefully none of these will be a problem for you, but they are always a possibility. If you are honest with yourself, your colleagues, and the individuals associated with any aspect of the evaluation project, you will probably not face major dilemmas. If you do run into problems, it is best to face them squarely and try to adjust to overcome them. Covering up problems or deceiving people in any way is likely not the way to find success in conducting evaluations.

Now that you have studied this chapter, you should be able to:

- Identify possible political, legal, ethical, and moral dilemmas that you might face in doing an evaluation.
- Avoid possible problems by being honest with all involved in an evaluation project.

UNIT TWO
EVIDENCE: Data Collection

Introduction to Evidence

Now you should have a firm background in the way that criteria are identified and/or developed and how people plan evaluation and research projects. After the criteria are determined, the evaluator can begin to examine possible ways to gather evidence, usually referred to as *data collection methods*. Once the methods are determined, you can develop procedures and strategies for obtaining that data. The possible methods, techniques, and tools used for gathering evidence for evaluation projects are the same as those used in research studies. The ways that these methods are applied and the use of theory determine the differences between evaluation and research.

Unit Two explores the differences between quantitative and qualitative data. In addition, we examine the options available for methods. We discuss the actual procedures used in developing questionnaires, conducting interviews, designing experiments, and doing observations. Further, we examine the specific application of some types of evaluation tools used in recreation and leisure services. Sampling, triangulation, and determining the trustworthiness of data will be discussed. These applications will tie to the second phase of evidence, data analysis, described in Unit Three. Evidence relates to both data collection and data analysis, but considering them separately may be less overwhelming.

In this unit, we move into the technical part known as the "how-tos" of doing evaluations. Methods have particular rules, guidelines, and protocols associated with them that we will explain. We hope this unit provides you with the tools needed to address most of the evaluation questions and criteria that you will encounter as a recreation, park, and leisure services professional. We also believe these second and third units give a sound background that can be used in any research project or evaluation study.

Qualitative and Quantitative Data
Choices to Make

We mentioned qualitative and quantitative data as we talked about designing evaluation and research projects. Before making methods decisions, you must understand the differences and the similarities between qualitative and quantitative data used for evaluation and research as well as how these data might be used. In simplest terms, quantitative data are based on collecting and using numerical calculations or statistics. Qualitative data refer to the use of words for data collection and result in patterns ascertained through analyses.

Some individuals are purists who believe that evaluation or research can best be done using only qualitative or only quantitative data. We believe that different situations may call for a particular type of data. We also believe it is possible to collect and use both qualitative and quantitative data in a single evaluation project if the criteria are such that this combination would be helpful. In this chapter we describe both types of data and why they might be used either separately or together in collecting evaluation evidence.

Worldviews and Data

The differences between worldviews and data used in evaluation or research are important to clarify. Worldviews, also called paradigms, represent broad assumptions we might articulate about how projects ought to be done. Data are the evidence. Methods are the tools for data collection.

Because people see the world from different worldviews, different methods of inquiry are typically used. Patton (1980a) described how paradigms are linked to methods such that allegiance to a paradigm is usually the major, but not the only reason, for making methods decisions. For example, if one's theory of evaluation is more closely related to wanting to gather facts more than gaining a broad understanding, one will usually favor those research methods that are linked to a quantitative data. Further, qualitative and quantitative data are pure types and the real world choices usually vary. The use of methods will typify more closely the attributes of one of the paradigms. Methods will depend on measurement options including kinds of data, evaluation design opportunities, personal involvement, and analysis possibilities such as inductive analysis (i.e., moving from specific to general) versus deductive analysis (i.e., moving from general to specific).

Most of the models of evaluation imply a *positivist worldview* that purports facts and truth can be found; this view is most often associated with the scientific method and generally results in quantitative data. For example, the goal-attainment evaluation model is usually closely related to the positivist paradigm. Positivist approaches to data usually result in the use of statistics to make decisions or to develop theory. Because evaluation requires that judgments be made, however, all quantitative data are always going to call for a certain amount of interpretation.

A second paradigm, the *interpretive paradigm*, suggests that not one answer, but many truths may exist within any evaluation project or research study. The goal-free model is often used in this case to collect qualitative data to gain a broad understanding of a problem or question. An interpretive approach to a project assumes that the realities of a program are multiple, and that different perceptions, descriptions and interpretations can be found in the same program when data are collected. For example, programs sometimes have outcomes broader than initially intended. In an evaluation of an exercise program for older adults, the gains made in cardiovascular fitness might be secondary compared to the positive social experience that older adults experienced as a result of this organized walking program.

Evaluation Data Types

We do not wish to debate whether one approach to data collection, qualitative or quantitative, is better than the other approach. One approach may be better given a particular evaluation situation and the criteria that are to be measured, but you must make that determination. Much has been written about qualitative and quantitative data in the past several years, but a discussion of which one is better is not useful as each has its place in research studies and evaluation projects. How to use the data is a more important question.

We also want to emphasize that no such thing as a qualitative and quantitative *method* exists. You can do an interview and collect either type of data, quantitative data or qualitative data, depending upon the design of the interview and the types of questions asked. The same is true of observations and even questionnaires. The nature of the data provides the framework for whether a project is qualitative or quantitative, not the methods that are used.

Either of the two types of data may be collected depending on the questions asked and the way the data are collected. The simplest distinction between the two types of data is to suggest that quantitative data use numbers or easily convert words to numbers such as 1 = yes and 2 = no. Qualitative data use words almost exclusively. The meanings of these differences, however, are more complicated than this simple explanation would imply.

Qualitative data allow individuals to describe experiences in their own words. Open-ended questions that allow for elaboration on the part of the respondent result in qualitative data. These data are usually highly useful in providing an in-depth understanding about issues that may be impossible to acquire through quantitative procedures related to scales or yes/no questions. Ellis and Williams (1987) suggested that questions about outcomes and change across time, the context within which change occurs, and the nature of the causes or conditions associated with outcomes are being asked in evaluation projects. Questions about the context in which change occurs and the use of goal-free models of evaluation make qualitative data useful. Rather than provide a list of preestablished responses to questions about a particular activity or program, the evaluator using qualitative data elicits responses in the actual words of the participants.

Depending upon the criteria being measured, either or both quantitative and qualitative data may be useful in measuring any of the five Ps. Further, although qualitative data may seem most useful in evaluating recreation programs, they may be used in any area of leisure service evaluation. You will need to determine how best to collect the data to assist in decision making.

Describing Differences in Data

A number of contrasts can be made between evaluation projects that rely on collecting quantitative or qualitative data. Table 2.1(1) on page 106 gives an example of some of those differences, but it is also useful to explain them.

Quantitative data usually follow standard procedures of rigor related to instruments used and statistical data analysis. Quantitative data are deductive in that particular evaluation questions serve as the start and data are reduced to measure those questions. Quantitative data are often the result of a goal-attainment or systems-oriented model with verification as the purpose. The instruments used for data collection in quantitative are paper-and-pencil tests or surveys. Preordinate designs are used. *Preordinate* refers to having

---

Table 2.1(1)   Making Choices about Quantitative and Qualitative Data (adapted from Henderson, 1991)

Quantitative	Qualitative
• Rigor in techniques	• Relevance of techniques
• Reductionist stance	• Expansionist stance
• Verification purpose	• Discovery
• Paper/Physical instrument	• Inquirer as instrument
• Systems or goal-attainment usually	• Goal-free model
• Experimental setting	• Natural setting
• Stable treatment of data	• Variable data treatment
• Variables as analytic unit	• Patterns as analysis
• Fixed methods	• Dynamic methods
• Product-oriented	• Process-oriented
• Reliability-based	• Validity-based
• Uniformity	• Diversity
• Deductive	• Inductive
• Results in facts	• Results in understanding
• Preordinate designs	• Emerging designs

---

a specific plan laid out ahead of time concerning the data to be collected. Once the data collection begins, nothing changes with the preordinate design. The treatment of quantitative data is stable with specific statistical procedures. Variables or analytic units are used in analyzing quantitative data. Statistics are used to determine averages and relationships among variables. Quantitative data are generally highly controlled, such as in experimental designs. Fixed procedures and specific rules for data collection and analysis are common in collecting quantitative data.

Qualitative data, on the other hand, are concerned with the relevance to the context or the situation. Qualitative data are often goal-free and concerned with discovery. Qualitative data are expansionist as we try to understand all the causes or reasons for something. The logic of generalization for qualitative data is to examine individual cases to determine a number of conclusions that fit the data. The inquirer or the evaluator is the instrument in the qualitative data collection as she or he interprets the meaning of the words and tries to find patterns. Data collection and design are likely to emerge together as data are uncovered in projects using qualitative data. In an emerging design, the evaluator may follow ideas that flow from the data such that the questions and answers about a project are occurring simultaneously. Dynamic and evolving procedures are used to collect these data.

In general, quantitative data usually measure the most common results of an intervention or a program, while qualitative data are used to describe what was done. In other words, quantitative data tend to be more focused on the products of an evaluation whereas qualitative data more often reflect the process. Reliability is paramount in quantitative data and validity is more important for qualitative data. Finally, quantitative data are quantifiable and concerned with facts, whereas qualitative data provide a means for understanding phenomena within their context.

Choosing Qualitative and/or Quantitative Data

One approach to data collection is not superior to another. The dominance of quantitative data, however, sometimes has severely limited the evaluation questions asked and the way that criteria are applied within evaluation projects in recreation, park, leisure, and tourism organizations.

Different situations and criteria may require different types of methods. Table 2.1(2) on page 108 provides a checklist that may be useful in determining what type of data to collect. If, for example, we want to know how many people with and without disabilities attended a program, counting them generates quantitative data and statistical procedures may be appropriate. If we want to understand whether the attitudes of people without disabilities have changed due to a recreation program offered, and what the interaction is between people with and without disabilities, then some form of qualitative data, such as interviews or observations, might better allow the evaluator to obtain that information.

Qualitative data, however, have not been without critics (Patton, 1978). For example, qualitative data are often considered too subjective. Objectivity is traditionally thought to be the essence of the scientific method. Some people think that to be subjective means to be biased, unreliable, and nonrational. Subjectivity implies opinion rather than fact, intuition rather than logic, impression rather than confirmation. The scientific community tries to control subjectivity particularly with an emphasis on reliability. Subjectivity, however, may never be completely possible and qualitative data enables evaluators to acknowledge how opinion, intuition, and impression cannot be divorced from understanding just how evaluation works.

This dichotomy between qualitative and quantitative data, however, is false. Quantitative data can be subjective and qualitative data can be objective. Subjectivity also refers to getting close to and involved with the data; it allows researchers to take into account their own insights and behavior

(Patton, 1978). Subjectivity involves applying critical intelligence to important problems.

The evaluator or researcher who knows the advantages and disadvantages of qualitative and quantitative data is best equipped to do their projects. Making decisions about what data to collect and how to collect it is not easy. You must look at the criteria and determine which type of data or combination is most appropriate.

Table 2.1(2) Checklist for Considering Qualitative or Quantitative Data (adapted from Patton, 1980a)

	Yes	No

Is the evaluator interested in individualized outcomes?

Is the evaluator interested in examining the process of evaluation and the context in which it occurs?

Is detailed in-depth information needed in order to understand the phenomenon being evaluated?

Is the focus on quality and the meaning of the experiences being studied?

Does the evaluator desire to get close to the participants/staff and immersed in their experiences?

Do no measuring devices exist that will provide reliable and valid data for the project?

Is the evaluation question likely to change depending upon how the data emerge?

Is it possible that the answer to the evaluation question may yield unexpected results?

Does the evaluator wish to get personally involved in the evaluation?

Does the evaluator have a philosophical and methodological bias toward goal-free and qualitative data?

If the answer is *yes* to any of these questions, the evaluator ought to at least consider the collection of qualitative data as a possible way to approach the evaluation or research question being addressed.

Using Qualitative and Quantitative Data Together

Qualitative and quantitative data can be used together and may compliment each other. In Chapter 2.14 we address triangulation and the use of more than one method or data set. Purists say you cannot mix qualitative and quantitative data, but many evaluators agree that in some projects this mixing may be necessary and important. The pursuit of good evaluation should transcend personal preferences for numbers or words. Further, the evaluator must recognize that quantitative data may become qualitative when explanations are needed for unexpected results. Qualitative data can become more quantitative as evaluation criteria become more focused and specific within a particular project.

From Ideas to Reality

Choosing the type of data that you will use depends upon a combination of determining the criteria that need to be measured and your personal preference. One type of data is no better than the other if the data provide the answers to your evaluation or research questions. A combination of the two may also be appropriate in some situations. Decisions about data will need to be carefully considered by the evaluator as a project is planned.

Now that you've studied this chapter, you should be able to:

- Describe the differences between qualitative and quantitative data.
- Describe general differences between the interpretive and positivist paradigms.
- Explain the link between paradigm, methods, and data type.
- State why one type of data might be preferable to another given a particular evaluation project.
- Make a decision, given evaluation criteria and a particular situation, about which type of data or combination of data is best to collect.

Choosing Designs and Methods
The Big Picture

If we were to try to classify the types of evaluation designs used in recreation and leisure services, we might classify them into two broad categories: experimental designs and descriptive designs. Within those two designs we could construct a continuum, as was done in Figure 1.1 (p. 5), that ranges from the most sophisticated double-blind experiment on one end, to an intuitive judgment on the other end, with quasi-experimental, empirical descriptive studies, and expert judgments in the middle. Within the descriptive studies we would see the possibilities of collecting quantitative or qualitative data; experimental designs are concerned almost exclusively with quantitative data.

Some texts refer to experimental versus nonexperimental as the two major categories of evaluation or research design. This dichotomy puts more focus on the value of "experimental" by referring to its opposite as "non." Thus, we will refer to experimental and descriptive designs to highlight the value of both. *Descriptive designs* include all empirically focused projects that are conducted in real-world situations. This description might also be appropriate for true experiments, but they have the difference of having an associated control group that descriptive evaluation projects seldom have.

Experimental designs are empirical investigative techniques employed to assure control so that the evaluator or researcher can feel confident that the results of the experiment conducted represent the true situation (Lundegren & Farrell, 1985). Experimental studies or projects that focus on a randomized sample and a controlled setting are probably the classic example of evaluation, but these designs are not commonly used in leisure services. Within the category of experimental designs falls true randomized experiments and quasi-experiments that are discussed in more detail in Chapter 2.11

True experimental designs require that an independent variable be controlled and manipulated. When we refer to quasi-experimental methods we mean research designs that are "seemingly" experimental but do not have all the qualities of true experimental designs, and that are more closely related to descriptive than experimental approaches. Many important variables like skill development, aptitudes, integrity, and characteristics of recreation leaders, however, cannot be controlled and manipulated within experimental designs. Further in the evaluation of personnel, places, and policies, true experimental designs are frequently impossible to apply so we use quasi-experimental and descriptive approaches.

As suggested, descriptive designs are more commonly used in recreation, park, leisure and tourism organizations. They do not require matching or comparison, but are concerned with gathering empirical data. Empirical data are data that you can observe or see. Empirical data may be qualitative or quantitative, and are logical and practical.

The purpose of descriptive designs is to determine existing conditions. The descriptive studies might include quasi-experimental designs, group surveys, needs assessments, and interpretive explanatory projects. The major methods that are employed are surveys, observations, and unobtrusive measures. These designs can be further divided to include specific methods such as questionnaires and interviews (including focus groups) as tools comprising the survey method, checklists and field observation tools used as observation methods, and document analysis and nonresearcher contact tools within unobtrusive measures.

An evaluator or researcher will need to determine how to make method choices based on the two broad categories of experiments and descriptive designs. You will further need to choose specific techniques to use depending upon whether surveys, observations, unobtrusive measures, or experimental designs are chosen. Each of the major evaluation methods will be discussed in more detail later in this unit, but Table 2.2 is provided for comparing the possible broad methods that might be chosen. In the use of all methods, the relationship between the criteria, data, and judgment will be considered together in making a method selection. Ethical considerations also must be taken into account with each method that is chosen.

Table 2.2 The Advantages and Disadvantages of Selected Designs and Methods

Experimental Designs

Method	*Advantages*	*Disadvantages*
True Experiments	• Assures control • Randomized sample • Pretest used • Represents what happened • Generalizable	• Manipulation required • Lab setting sometimes best • Control may be difficult • Sample sometimes difficult • People feel like guinea pigs
Quasi-experiments	• Some qualities of experiments • Control some outside variables • May be appropriate to situation	• Nonrandomized • Threats to validity

Descriptive Designs

Method	*Advantages*	*Disadvantages*
Surveys	• Most commonly used • Generally inexpensive and easy • May allow face-to-face encounter • Determine existing conditions • Discovery of quan/qual relationships • Useful for validity checks, triangulation • Uses methods protocols and statistics • Perspectives from participant	• May be obtrusive and reactive • Dependent on instrument • Misinterpretation possible • Requires skill and training • Requires respondent cooperation • Evaluator effects • Highly dependent on evaluator's abilities
Observations	• Face-to-face encounter or not • Large amounts of data obtained quickly • Low/High interaction with respondents • Can allow for emerging data • Wide range of data possible • Many possibilities for sample • Discovery of possible relationships • Useful in triangulation • Data on nonverbal, unconscious, and communication behaviors	• Missed data such as attitudes • Misinterpretation possible • Lack of respondent's words • Success depends on evaluator • Bias by evaluator possible • Possible observer effects on those observed
Unobtrusive	• Data often easy to analyze • Wide range of types of data • Usually efficient to administer • Often easily quantifiable • Good for nonverbal behavior • Measuring devices may exist • Provides for flexibility • Good for documenting major events • Often uses natural setting	• Possible misinterpretations • May be expensive • Depends on evaluation model • Dependent on evaluator's investigative ability • Minimal interaction

From Ideas to Reality

Having design options presents both opportunities as well as challenges for an evaluator. The advantages are that there is no one best way to do any project and the creativity of the evaluator can be exercised in developing evaluation projects. On the other hand, the options can also seem a bit daunting and overwhelming. As you get more experience and practice in doing evaluation projects, the options will make more sense and the best choices will become easier to make. Keep in mind that usually more than one way exists to do a project and you will need to choose the best design based upon the project and the resources available to you.

Now that you have studied this chapter, you should be able to:

- Describe what constitutes an experimental design and a descriptive design
- Specify the methods most often associated with each design
- List some of the advantages and disadvantages of each of the methods that might be used to collect data

Trustworthiness
The Zen of Data Collection

A great evaluation or research project idea can have wonderful criteria and research questions, but if the tools you use aren't appropriate, your project may be doomed to failure. You should always be concerned that data collected for any project are trustworthy, or of high quality. Evaluators and researchers want to make sure that measurement instruments possess characteristics of reliability and validity. Thus, trustworthiness is a foundational aspect of data collection. If a data collection instrument fails to do what it is supposed to do, everything else fails in an evaluation or research project.

Error can exist in any measurement device. To be completely reliable or valid would mean there are no sources of error—a feat that is next to impossible. Our goal then is to try to minimize the errors as much as possible. We will examine three areas of trustworthiness as they relate to aspects of data collection for any type of design or method: reliability, validity, and usability. *Reliability* is concerned with the replicatability, consistency, and dependability of scientific findings. *Validity* addresses meaning and meaningfulness of data, or "Does the instrument do what it should?" related to credibility and transferability. *Usability* refers to collecting data efficiently and finding meaningfulness and application for the results.

Reliability

Reliability, also known as dependability, relates to whether a measure consistently conveys the same meaning to readers; it addresses the degree of stability or consistency that a scale yields. A test is reliable to the extent that retesting results in virtually the same scores. In other words, a reliable measure of behavior will perform in the future the way it did in the past.

In collecting qualitative data, we refer to dependability as meaning something similar to reliability. To be dependable, the evaluator must keep a record of how data were collected. This process is sometimes referred to as an audit trail. To audit means to examine. Reliability is strengthened when similar results would occur if the same process or procedure were followed. Dependability "depends" on documenting exactly how data were collected and how conclusions were drawn. This audit process will become clearer when in-depth interviews and field observations are discussed later in this unit.

For some quantitative instruments, a reliability correlation or coefficient is given as a statistic that tells just how likely the instrument is to measure consistently. Correlation refers to the similarity between two sets of scores for one person. In other words, when the score for one test remains in the same relative position on the retest, the reliability will be high. Test-retest is one way to measure the stability with a comparison between the two test administrations.

The reliability coefficient ranges from 0 to 1.00 with the scores closest to 1.00 being the best because they indicate the test has less error variance. The level that one is willing to accept depends on the nature of the evaluation being done. Most instruments that have a reliability coefficient greater than 0.40 may be used with some confidence, although an evaluator would rather have coefficients higher than 0.60. The higher the reliability, the more consistently the instrument measures what it is supposed to measure. Reliability coefficients may be obtained by measuring consistency through correlation statistics, by giving alternative forms (i.e., rearranging the item order) of the same instrument, or by test-retest procedures.

Interrater reliability is another term that the evaluator may wish to address if more than one person is making observations. Interrater reliability is a measure of the consistency from rater to rater rather than from time to time. Comparing the ratings generated by two or more observers who have observed the same event or behavior produces the reliability coefficient. The two are compared by correlation. High correlations indicate a high amount of agreement. Observer training and a clear delineation of the behaviors being rated can improve this interrater reliability. The higher the correlation is (i.e., generally over 0.80), the more dependable the observations. With a low interrater reliability, too much error may be associated with an observation.

Without reliability or dependability, a measurement instrument's usefulness is in doubt. As we discuss questionnaire development in the next chapter, you will note a number of ways that reliability can be improved. For example, items that do not communicate effectively should be eliminated. Items should be clear, unambiguous, and appropriate in length and difficulty. To improve reliability, one can lengthen the test although extreme lengthening may produce a fatigue or boredom effect. Further, suppose we wanted to know what was good about a particular recreation program. A questionnaire with only one item would be highly unreliable. A participant might have liked a lot of aspects of a program but not have liked the one aspect that you asked in the questionnaire. A one-item test is subject to a number of chance factors and therefore is not usually reliable. The bottom line is that to improve reliability, an evaluator has to try to reduce as much error as possible.

Validity

As defined in the introduction to this chapter, validity concerns whether or not the instrument measures what it is supposed to measure. Other synonyms for validity might be accuracy, authenticity, genuineness, and soundness. In other words, the respondent must understand the question the way that the evaluator asked it, and must provide the information in a manner that is consistent with the criteria or purpose the evaluator had established. Validity refers to the results of the measurement, and not the test or questionnaire itself. An instrument is valid only if it is appropriate for the group and the evaluation criteria being measured.

Reliability is necessary for validity to occur. Data, however, can be reliable without being valid. People can be consistent in their responses, but an instrument can be measuring the wrong information. Therefore, if an instrument is not valid, it doesn't make any difference how reliable it is. If we wanted to know the changes in attitude about art that result from a crafts program, but ask participants their reactions to the instructor's teaching techniques, we may get reliable responses but the measurement is not valid for the issues we are analyzing. Figure 2.3(1) on page 118 shows how validity and reliability might be pictured.

Several types of validity are frequently mentioned in evaluation research. Validity may refer broadly to internal and external validity depending upon how it is applied. *Internal validity* is how well the instrument measures what it is supposed to measure for a particular evaluation project. It also shows whether a difference exists in any given comparisons. Lincoln and Guba (1985) referred to credibility in qualitative approach as the equivalent to internal validity. One type of internal validity is known as concurrent or criterion-related validity, which simply asks whether the scores on a particular instrument correlate with scores on another existing test.

The most important type of internal validity for evaluation is content validity. *Content validity* reflects the contents or the theoretical expectations

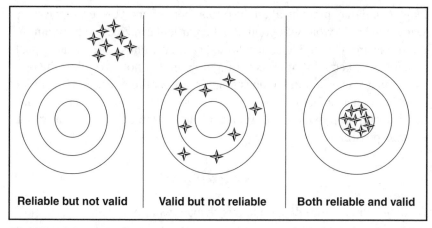

Figure 2.3(1)   Illustration of Reliability and Validity

that one wishes to measure with an evaluation project. Subjective judgment, sometimes called face validity, is often used regarding whether the instrument measures the content intended. The evaluator must define the content and establish its relevance. Further, levels of evidence discussed in Chapter 1.6 play heavily into content validity. For example, you may think you are measuring how attitudes change toward a particular activity when you are really measuring satisfaction with the process. Content validity requires a careful analysis of what you want to measure and how the items you select and the data you collect actually contribute to that measurement. You must make sure the instrument you select or develop and the data collected do in fact measure the criteria you have identified.

External validity refers to how well the measures can be generalized to other situations. External validity is also called transferability in qualitative data collection. Predictive validity is associated with external validity and is used to examine the way an instrument can predict some behavior. A common example of predictive validity is the fact that the high performance on SAT tests usually predicts success in college.

Validity must be a concern early in the use or development of any evaluation instrument. As an evaluator you will be responsible for content validity, but frequently others can be involved in the process to confirm that validity exists. For example, expert panels may be used to confirm content or face validity. Experts are asked to judge the instrument's ability to measure the desired content. Or it might be desirable to involve colleagues or a supervisor to examine the instrument. Those individuals can be asked if what you say you are evaluating is really coming across in the way the instrument is constructed.

The more adequate the planning time in designing an evaluation project, the more likely reliable and valid measures can be used. To improve reliability or validity, don't rush into developing an instrument. Take time to make the instrument clear and write it at an appropriate reading level for those respondents who will be using it. Items need to relate to constructs, enough items to measure the constructs must be presented, and no identifiable pattern or response should be evident. Further, the evaluator needs to keep in mind that you can't necessarily use the same instrument for every evaluation situation. Some instruments work better with some groups than do others. The evaluator must develop the reliability and validity of an instrument in a particular setting for the specific audience that is using the instrument.

In collecting qualitative data, credibility can be improved by prolonged engagement in interviews or observations, persistent observation, and/or by using more than one data source or method. One can also pay attention to negative cases (i.e., cases that are not like the others) as well as use member checks (e.g., go back and talk to people) to see if the way you interpreted the interview data or observation is the way the participants intended. Transferability can be enhanced by using examples from the data and by using *thick description*. Qualitative evaluators use thick description to mean using the direct quotes and words of respondents about what happened or how they felt in a given situation.

Usability

Usability relates closely to reliability and validity, but has particular significance for evaluation and research. If the instrument cannot be effectively administered and if the data collected are not used, the project is a waste of time. For example, although an instrument might be highly reliable and valid, if data collection cannot be efficiently managed, the measurement tool may be of little use to an evaluator or a researcher.

Several issues must be considered in assessing the usability and quality of data. The administration of an instrument can affect reliability and validity. An instrument should be easy to administer whether as a self-administered test or as one given by a tester. The time required should be reasonable for the situation and for the population being studied. The instrument should be easy to score and should be able to be interpreted. Directions should be consistent. Providing a good atmosphere for testing is necessary. Dunn (1987) used the example of not giving program satisfaction surveys in a pool where people don't have a dry place to write. You need to always ask yourself if the evaluation procedure is appropriate for the setting and be aware of the subject's situation and attitudes when administering any test or questionnaire. Further, the costs should not exceed the potential benefits that might come from using a selected measurement instrument.

Usability also relates to qualitative data, but it is assumed that these data would not be collected unless they are usable in some manner. Competent evaluators who have training in qualitative methods are needed. One becomes best at collecting qualitative data by practice. Further, to assure data are usable the qualitative evaluator must devote adequate time to the data collection and analysis. As one looks for a range of responses and attempts to explain the variance between individuals or situations, a time commitment is necessary. Finally, triangulation may make an evaluation project more useful if data come from more than one method or source. Table 2.3(2) provides a summary of some suggested ways to improve the trustworthiness of your evaluation and research projects. After reading subsequent chapters, you may want to review this table again.

Trustworthiness is essential to the collection of data. Data are only as good as the means used to collect them. To have a trustworthy evaluation project, the evaluator attempts to eliminate error as much as possible. This error may be from respondents, the investigator, or the sampling procedures. For example, the respondent may feel the guinea pig effect whereby she or he is aware of being tested. She or he may also demonstrate other kinds of

Table 2.3(2) How to Improve Trustworthiness of Data Collected

	Quantitative	Qualitative
Reliability	• Well-written items • Lengthen the test • Pilot test/Planning • Clear directions • Appropriate to group	• Use audit trail
Validity	• Subjective evaluation • Predictive • Choose appropriate model • Pilot test/Planning and level of evidence • Clear directions	• Prolonged engagement • Use range of cases • Use examples • Thick description • Effect of evaluator described
Usability	• Easily administered • Reasonable time required • Easy to score/Interpret • Appropriate cost • Explain link between criteria and data collected	• Competent evaluator • Time commitment • Triangulation • Explain all variance

behavior such as hostility, or indifference that would also affect the results of some measurement instruments. Further, sometimes participants are aware of the social desirability associated with some instrument and will respond the way they think society would. Some of these errors are difficult to avoid, but an evaluator must be aware that they can exist and try to minimize them if the evaluation project is to be useful. If the data are not reliable and valid, they will have little benefit for the evaluation project.

From Ideas to Reality

Unless the evaluator can "count on" the data and the design, an evaluation project may not be helpful. Reliability, validity, and usability are the keys to conducting good evaluations. In this chapter we have presented a number of ways to make evaluation projects trustworthy. You will need to refer to these suggestions continuously while conducting an evaluation project to make sure that you are on the right track. No magic formulas exist but the suggested strategies will help to assure that you are doing the trustworthiest undertaking possible.

Now that you have studied this chapter, you should be able to:

- Describe the factors considered in determining whether an instrument used in an evaluation project or research study is reliable and valid.
- Design or select an instrument that has high reliability and validity.
- Explain how the selection of criteria is related to validity.
- Assess evaluation or research instruments to ascertain that they are reliable, valid, and usable.

Measurement Instruments
Choosing the Right Ones

Once the criteria to be examined are determined and a research design has been selected, you will need a measuring device. To collect qualitative data, the evaluator or researcher is most often the instrument used. The relationship between qualitative data and the evaluator will be discussed later in this unit.

For most quantitative studies, however, a paper-and-pencil instrument, questionnaire, or test of some type is developed. If a reliable and valid instrument already exists that you can use, you will save yourself time and effort by using that instrument. Unfortunately, not many instruments exist in leisure services that have been standardized and tested for reliability and validity. Further, evaluators must look at their particular situations to decide what type of instrument can best measure the criteria desired. Thus, you must be able to do two things well:

1. Evaluate existing instruments to see if they are reliable, valid, and usable.

2. Develop instruments that are reliable, valid, and usable to address evaluation criteria specific to a situation.

When we talk about measurement instruments, we are referring to tests, checklists, or questionnaires that might be developed. Some measurements might refer to observation checklists, while others will refer to attitude or performance measures. When a set of questions is written specifically for an evaluation project with the assumption that respondents will answer honestly, the instrument is commonly called a questionnaire rather than a test. Instruments may be used to collect qualitative or quantitative data, but measurement instruments usually refer to quantitative surveys and observations.

Tests

Tests usually include standardized ways of asking for information. Tests have additional features such as scores and inferences from scores. They usually involve some questions about the respondent's ability and/or willingness to answer accurately, honestly, or completely.

Tests given to individuals are usually divided into four areas: ability, achievement, attitude, and personality tests. Ability tests measure what a person is capable of doing. Achievement tests show what a person has learned. Attitude tests attempt to measure some opinions or beliefs of the test taker about an object, person, or event; they refer to some internal state of mind or set of beliefs that is stable over time. Personality tests refer to most anything else that relates to characteristics of an individual.

Locating Existing Instruments

Assessment instruments are abundant in the field of leisure services, as many communities have conducted needs assessments and therapeutic recreation specialists use a number of assessment instruments in their work. Fewer "already developed" instruments exist for formative and summative evaluations.

Several resources exist for finding already existing instruments. In the field of therapeutic recreation, several researchers have compiled lists of such instruments (burlingame & Blaschko, 1997). The *Mental Measurements Yearbook* (Impara & Plake, 1998) is available in most libraries and tells about various personality and achievement instruments including their reliability and validity. Table 2.4 shows an example of some of the information that would be found in this *Yearbook*.

Often we borrow instruments from other professionals to use in various recreation settings. Borrowing from another department or another organization may save time because you don't have to develop your own instrument, but the evaluator must be careful to assure that the instrument is really a reliable and valid measurement.

Standardized Measurements

Most students are familiar with standardized tests such as the Scholastic Aptitude Test (SAT) or the Graduate Record Exam (GRE). A standardized test is one that has been previously used for a relatively large group of

Table 2.4(1) Example of Material Found in a Standardized Test Summary (adapted from *Mental Measurements Yearbook*)

Torrance Tests of Creative Thinking. Grades K through graduate school; 1966–84; TTCT; 2 forms; 2 tests; norms-technical manual ('74, 80 pages); scoring worksheet ('66, 1 page) for each test; 1983 price data: $12 per 20 sets of tests, 20 scoring worksheets, and 1 manual; $5.70 per norms-technical manual; $6.50 per specimen set; scoring service, $2.25 or less per booklet; E. Paul Torrance; Scholastic Testing Service, Inc.

a) Verbal test. Test booklet title is Thinking Creatively with Words; 3 scores: fluency, flexibility, originality; individual in grades K–3; Forms A, B, ('66, 15 pages); directions manual ('74, 49–50 pages) for each form; $20 per examiner's kit of reusable toys and pictures; $3.40 per directions manual; 45(60) minutes.

b) Figural test. Test booklet title is Thinking Creatively with Pictures; 4 scores: fluency, flexibility, originality, elaboration; Forms A ('66, 8 pages), B ('66, 7 pages); Form A directions manual ('66, 43 pages, minor revisions 1972), Form B directions manual ('74, 43 pages); streamlined scoring workbook figural A ('84, 39 pages); streamlined manual figural A and B ('84, 74 pages); $3.40 per directions manual; $3.40 per streamlined scoring manual; 30(45) minutes.

subjects. Many standardized test results have provided information about the answers or scores to expect from similar subjects. These standardized tests usually come with elaborate and complete instructions about how to administer the test so that your results are comparable to results from other testers. You can be sure that major question design problems have been resolved as these tests have been improved and standardized.

If you want to compare the results you obtained from using a standardized test, however, the tests must be given exactly as the instructions suggest. You can"t even give additional explanations. The standardized test may be reliable and valid in general, however as was discussed in the previous chapter, it must be valid for the particular audience involved and evaluation criteria that you are using. To develop your own standardized tests is difficult, complicated, and goes beyond what we can discuss in this book. If available and appropriate, however, you may use standardized tests developed by others. Personality tests such as the Tennessee Self-Concept Scale, for example, might be used if you were interested in determining if self-concept changed as a result of participating in a summer camp program.

Making Instrument Choices

Dunn (1989) has suggested some guidelines for using published assessment evaluation procedures that might also include standardized tests. She noted that locally developed assessments may be good, but the confidence may not be as high in them as in previously published tests. All standardized instruments have specific instructions that tell you time limits, oral instructions, preliminary demonstrations, ways of handling inquiries, and other details for the testing situation. They also may have norms or averages established from previous testing done. The instrument chosen should provide evidence of validity and should have been validated on a representative sample of sufficient size. The relationship of subscores to total scores should be evident. Further, information about reliability should be provided. The manual and test materials should be complete and have appropriate quality. The assessment should be relevant to the participants served by the agency and finally, the instrument should be relevant to the decisions made based on evaluation or assessment results.

Dunn (1989) further indicated that an assessment or evaluation instrument should be revalidated when any changes are made in procedures, materials, or when it is used for a purpose or with a population group for which it has not been validated. The instrument should be selected and used by qualified individuals and should be used in the intended way. The published instrument might be combined with other tests, but it should maintain its integrity. The administration and scoring should follow standardized procedures. During the administration, care should be taken in providing a comfortable environment with minimal distractions. The administrator of the instrument also must be aware of the importance and effect of rapport with respondents. Additionally, the security of materials must be protected if confidentiality is guaranteed. Specific test results should not be released without the informed consent of the test-taker. Data regarding patients' assessment in therapeutic recreation, for example, should be kept in a designated, usually locked, file.

Many advantages can be found in choosing existing instruments rather than developing your own measures. As you can tell from this discussion, however, many considerations must be weighed thoughtfully in choosing instruments. In summary, you as an evaluator or researcher might want to ask several questions about any instrument being examined as illustrated in Table 2.4(2).

Table 2.4(2) Checklist for Considering an Instrument

	Yes	No
Do measures exist for reliability and validity?	☐	☐
Does the instrument measure the factors or traits desired to be measured?	☐	☐
Is the instrument appropriate for the participants who will be completing it?	☐	☐
Is the instrument reasonable in time and cost to administer?	☐	☐
Are the directions clear, concise, and unambiguous?	☐	☐
Is the instrument easy to score or are specific directions for how to do scoring included?	☐	☐
Does it provide the best way to measure the data that we wish to measure?	☐	☐

If the answer is *no* to any of these questions, then perhaps you should look for another instrument or consider developing your own.

From Ideas to Reality

In quantitative studies, you will generally choose or develop instruments to collect empirical data. Using existing instruments often saves time but you must be sure they are reliable and valid for the group with whom you wish to use them. Before undertaking evaluation or research data collection, ascertain if any existing instruments might be available. If they are reliable, valid, and useable for your criteria, then use them.

Now that you have studied this chapter, you should be able to:

- Determine the aspects to consider in evaluating and choosing an existing instrument.
- Describe the advantages and disadvantages of using standardized tests.

Developing Your Own Measurement Instruments

Developing your own instrument for an evaluation project or research study may be appropriate rather than using something that already exists. Developing good measurement instruments and surveys is an art that requires care and practice. Fortunately, many guidelines exist to help you develop good instruments. These guidelines can be applied to the development of checklists, survey questionnaires, or test items. Several basic steps are consistent in the development of any questionnaire or test:

1. Define the problem;
2. Determine the contents including criteria to be evaluated and broad questions;
3. Identify and categorize the respondents;
4. Develop items, structure, and format;
5. Write directions; and
6. Ensure response.

This chapter focuses on determining the contents of surveys, developing items and structures, and designing formats and directions. We divide the development of instruments into several components: types of questions (determining the contents), question structures and wording tips (developing items), and instrument design (formats and directions). Sampling and identifying respondents are covered in Chapter 2.6, and how to ensure responses will be addressed in Chapter 2.7.

First, however, a word about the overall development of survey instruments. To develop a questionnaire, you must know what you want to find out or what criteria are to be evaluated. Orthner, Smith, and Wright (1986) gave us an excellent example of a process used for developing a needs assessment survey for the Navy. Figure 2.5(1) on page 130 shows the process used to develop a measurement instrument for the Navy. Although most of the evaluation projects you undertake may not require such an elaborate plan,

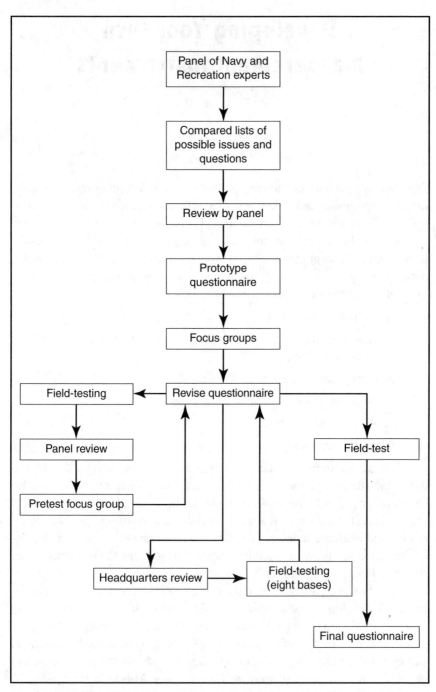

Figure 2.5(1) Navy Model of Instrument Development (adapted from Orthner, Smith & Wright, 1986)

the diagram is helpful in understanding how a problem is defined and how a questionnaire is refined.

Orthner, Smith, and Wright (1986) first got a panel of Navy and recreation experts together and asked them to examine and review a list of possible issues and questions. From this procedure, prototype questionnaires were developed. The items were then revised, the questionnaire tested in a real situation, revisions to the questionnaire were made, a panel once again reviewed it, the questionnaire was pilot tested in a focus group and revised again, presented to headquarters for review, field-tested on eight bases, revised, field-tested for a final time, and the final questionnaire was then completed.

It is *not* necessary to go through all of those stages unless the survey is going to be standardized and/or completed by thousands of people. Several parts of this model, however, are particularly important to consider. First, you must make sure you know what it is you want to find out and that this information may be obtained from some source whether it is participants, colleagues, or organizational leaders. Second, you will need to go through several revisions of the questionnaire. Even people who have been designing questionnaires for years cannot write a perfect questionnaire the first time. Third, you will need to pilot test the questionnaire with a small sample to make sure that it is doing what you want it to do. Fourth, even after you use the questionnaire, some flaws (hopefully, all minor) may be discovered that you can correct if the questionnaire is administered again.

Ask only necessary questions. Sometimes evaluators think that they can ask many questions and then determine later on what information to use in the evaluation report. This endeavor is a waste of paper and a waste of the respondents' time. Know exactly what criteria are being measured at the start, and then develop questions to get that information.

Contents of Questionnaires

Questionnaires are used as a common survey technique. The questions asked for any survey will have great variability depending on the nature of the evaluation or research project, the design used, and the criteria measured. Specific questions may be addressed followed with peripheral questions to get in-depth information.

A result of designing good instruments is that people will respond honestly. Questions may be asked in the time frame of past, present, or future. For most recreation, park, and leisure service organizations, questions are likely to address one or all of these five areas: experience/behavior, opinion/values (i.e., needs and interests), feelings (i.e., emotional responses), knowledge/facts, and background/demographics. The questions may be open-ended or close-ended, although most of the discussion in this chapter will be based on writing objective, close-ended questions. No matter what type, good questions should be neutral, singular, and clear.

Let's talk about the information that you want to obtain from a questionnaire. The questions are going to pertain to the level of evidence you are addressing. For example, if you wish to determine the reactions that individuals had to a particular recreation activity, you would likely use opinion/value or feelings types of questions. On the other hand, if you wanted to find out what people learned as a result of an activity, you might ask questions about knowledge or facts.

In a single questionnaire, you might ask several different content questions and you might ask them in different time frames. You must be clear however, as to what criteria you are trying to measure. If you want to know what people will do in the future, you must be sure to write questions that pertain to the future. Let's look at a few examples of possible questions to address these five categories:

Experience/Behavior Questions—What a person does or has done. For example:

Past: How many times did you swim in the XYZ pool in 2001?

Present: What program are you registering for at the community recreation center today?

Future: On the average, how many times do you anticipate any member of your family swimming at the XYZ pool during the coming summer?

Opinion/Value/Attitude Questions—Cognitive and interpretive processes held by the individual. For example:

Past: What did you like about last year's volleyball league?

Present: When you call the recreation office, are the receptionists usually: very helpful, helpful, or unhelpful?

Future: Would you support the development of both a recreational and a competitive volleyball league?

Feeling Questions—Emotional responses (past or present) of people to their experiences. For example:

Past: Did the trip make you feel happy?

Present: How does volunteering with this youth group make you feel?

Knowledge Questions—What factual information the respondent has, usually at the present time. For example:

Present: What is your target heartbeat during aerobics classes?

Present: How many fouls does a basketball player get before she or he fouls out?

Background/Demographic Questions—*Present* personal characteristics. For example:

Past: In what state were you born?

Present: How old are you?

Question Structures

A number of structures can be used in question design. The structures used will depend to some extent on the content and criteria that you wish to address and the statistical techniques you want to use. Writing good questions and using the best structure takes practice.

Three major structures and the scales that can be used with each include:

1. Open-ended questions

2. Close-ended quantitative questions with ordered (forced) choices and unordered response choices

3. Partially close-ended questions

Open-ended Questions

Open-ended questions are directed with no preformed answers. The respondent supplies her or his own answer(s) with no restrictions on the content of the response. In paper-and-pencil tests, respondents often use lists or short essay responses. Responses to verbal open-ended questions often result in the respondent providing anecdotes and examples.

Open-ended questions are most often used when a variety of information is needed and the evaluator is unsure of possible responses. In this way, open-ended structures also provide diagnostic information. These structures are used to collect qualitative data and to develop specific questionnaires from broad information. As you develop questionnaires, you will have to ask yourself if all the information is currently available so that categories of responses can be written in advance, or whether open-ended questions will provide responses not currently known. Open-ended questions are easy to ask, but tallying the results is not always as easy, as you will see when we discuss qualitative analysis in Chapter 3.7.

The advantages of open-ended structures are evident when the population characteristics are not known and when the evaluator does not wish to overlook any possible answers to a question. From initial open-ended questions, it is possible to draft more specific close-ended questions, especially if the open-ended structure is used as the first step in developing a more quantitatively oriented questionnaire. A further advantage to open-ended structures is that the answers are less influenced by the evaluator writing the question; a wide variety of responses which include many that are unique to an individual's situation can be elicited. Open-ended structures can help to introduce new topics or allow respondents to summarize what is on their minds. These structures can provide valuable background for interpreting evaluation results and can add "richness" to the data because of the potential for depth of response.

The disadvantages of open-ended responses include a lack of uniform responses that may not be easy to tabulate. Further, this structure is affected by a respondent's verbal ability and written communication skills. The data obtained are sometimes more useful when the respondents have a higher educational level. When using open-ended questions, problems of definition and vocabulary may occur and fewer questions can be asked. Open-ended questions typically take longer to complete and people may not take as much time with them if they require lengthy writing responses. In addition, problems with coding or organizing the data for interpretation may emerge and some responses may be irrelevant based on the criteria the evaluator established.

An evaluator who is writing open-ended questions must be careful to be asking genuinely open-ended questions. A question such as "Did you enjoy playing in the soccer league?" may appear to be an open-ended inquiry when, in fact, it is potentially a close-ended "yes/no" response. A useful open-ended question to get at this information might be: "What was it about the soccer league that you enjoyed?" Sometimes evaluators ask a question such as "Did you enjoy playing in the soccer league?" and then follow with a "Why or why not?" The use of why can sometimes be threatening since the respondent assumes there ought to be a definitive answer. The best open-ended questions are those that the respondent feels competent and comfortable in answering.

In summary, open-ended structures are easy to write and are usually straightforward. The evaluator, however, must also be prepared for the volume and variability of information that may be provided by respondents.

Close-ended Questions

In close-ended quantitative questions, specific responses are provided for the respondents to select. These responses may be of two types depending on the nature of the question: (1) ordered with a forced choice or (2) unordered. Close-ended structures that use ordered responses include Likert scales, semantic differential scales, rankings, and self-assessments. Unordered close-ended questions are typically used as multiple-choice checklists and are unique to the specific evaluation criteria being measured.

Several concerns must be kept in mind in developing close-ended forced choice question items. First of all, response categories should not overlap. The answer categories should be mutually exclusive so the answer falls into one category only. For example, if you ask someone her or his age and give choices, make sure the categories are listed as "19 or younger, 20–29, 30–39" and *not* "younger than 19, 19–29, 29–39." Second, the responses should be exhaustive and cover the gamut of possible answers. Third, the responses also must be appropriate to the questions asked and consistent in focusing on the same dimension being measured. Finally, remember that the same question may be asked in many ways using a variety of close-ended choices. The evaluator has to choose what is going to be best.

The advantages of close-ended responses are that they are uniform and can be easily coded for data entry and analysis in a computer. If you want a quick analysis, then close-ended question structures are the easiest to administer and analyze. For example, if you asked, "Overall how satisfied were you with the organization of the crafts fair?" you might provide forced ordered choices of, "4 = very satisfied, 3 = satisfied, 2 = dissatisfied, 1 = very dissatisfied." Tallying the results to find out the percentage of people satisfied or the mean or average score for this question would be fairly easy to do.

The disadvantages of close-ended structures occur if you do not provide the most appropriate choices for response. If the real responses are missing from the list of choices, you will get only partially valid answers or no answers at all. In the example concerning satisfaction with the organization of the crafts fair, an individual might have been satisfied with some aspects but not all aspects. A disadvantage to the close-ended response is that she or he does not have an opportunity to explain anything about the response.

As indicated, two types of close-ended questions exist: unordered close-ended responses and ordered forced choices (commonly called *scaling devices*). Close-ended questions with unordered responses are structures used with items that have no particular value associated with them in the statistical analysis. You may want to know as many possibilities for a question or the one best answer. For example you could ask someone to choose the best thing about an aerobics program or you could ask her or him to check all of the items that apply. An example of an unordered response would be the following question:

> What did you like best about the aerobics class? Check one item.
> _____Becoming more physically fit
> _____Getting out of the house or away from your job for a while
> _____Meeting other people
> _____Having fun
> _____Moving to the music

As indicated above, this same question could be asked in another unordered form by allowing individuals to check all of the items that applied about what they liked about an aerobics class.

Yes/No questions or true/false questions are another form of unordered close-ended question structures. These responses are appropriate to use and easy to write. The evaluator, however, must keep in mind the limited amount of information that may be obtained from yes/no questions. Some people can clearly answer yes or no for a given situation particularly related to knowledge or experience/behavior questions. Many times, however, yes/no responses require qualification. In using close-ended yes/no questions, the evaluator must consider the information that may not be evident in these responses.

Scaling is the major form of ordered close-ended questions used for measuring participation rates, attitudes, and opinions. An example would be, "How often do you compete in a road race?" A scaling technique would be to use the ordered responses: "a=never, b=once a year, c=3–4 times a year, d=monthly, e=weekly, or f=twice or more a week." Descriptive terms, or word anchors, should be used at each point on the scale so the respondent knows what the letters mean. In other words, the respondent must be clear about what the ordered responses mean. Common forms of other scaling devices include Likert scales, semantic differentials, rankings, and self-assessments.

Likert Scales
Likert scales, named for Rensis Likert who developed this summative scale, are a particular kind of close-ended question structure that uses a scaling system. Likert scales are most often used for attitude measurement. Usually both negative and positive statements are used with four to six responses related to strongly agree, agree, disagree, or strongly disagree. These scale names are referred to as *response anchors*. Some people will make a three-to-seven item response scale and include a middle option of neutral

or no opinion. We have found it works better to use an even number of items so respondents are forced to "take a stand." Some respondents may see "no opinion" as the "easy way out" and evaluators generally want to force people to choose one response or another. Without a neutral option, however, respondents might skip a question, which may result in unreliable data. As an evaluator, you will need to decide the best way to design a Likert scale for a project.

A Likert scale usually has a matrix type of design with statements on the left half and anchored responses on the right half. Each response is then scored in some way, usually with the most positive response receiving the highest point value. In a four-point scale, anything with a mean or average of 2.5 and above is usually considered positive; below that score would be negative. The Likert scale is easy to construct, has moderate reliability, explores attitudes, involves simple computations, and is easy to score. Table 2.5 (2) shows an example of a Likert Scale.

Table 2.5(2) Example of a Likert Scale Used to Measure Satisfaction with a Campground

	Strongly Agree	Agree	Disagree	Strongly Disagree
1. The entrance to the campground was attractive.	SA	A	D	SD
2. Staff were friendly and courteous.	SA	A	D	SD
3. The campsites were large enough.	SA	A	D	SD
4. The distance between campsites was appropriate.	SA	A	D	SD
5. Restrooms and showers were clean.	SA	A	D	SD

Semantic Differentials

Semantic differentials, as another scaling structure for close-ended questions, include a list of bipolar adjectives written in linear fashion (see Table 2.5(3), p. 138). Semantic differentials are often used to assess attitudes and responses and are assigned numbers as done with Likert scales. The items to be measured are selected and then bipolar adjective pairs are chosen to anchor both ends of the scales. These words should be as near to opposite as possible (e.g., good and bad), and may or may not necessarily be the same words (e.g., familiar and unfamiliar). Points should be anchored with numbers on the scales between the two points so that scoring averages can be calculated later. In the listing down a page, the items should be put in opposite directions so not all the positive attributes are on one side of the scale. Semantic differentials are particularly good scales for examining the past and present attitudes and opinions about a particular phenomenon.

Table 2.5(3) Example of Semantic Differentials for Evaluating a Youth Leader

Please indicate your perception of the leadership ability of your youth leader. Check where you believe she or he falls on the scale.

Dedicated	___	___	___	___	___	___	Could Care Less
	6	5	4	3	2	1	
Enthusiastic	___	___	___	___	___	___	Very Low Key
	6	5	4	3	2	1	
Organized	___	___	___	___	___	___	Disorganized
	6	5	4	3	2	1	
Strict	___	___	___	___	___	___	Lenient
	6	5	4	3	2	1	
Always Late	___	___	___	___	___	___	On Time
	6	5	4	3	2	1	

Ranking

Ranking is another form of a forced close-ended structure that is used to get a sense of how individuals might evaluate certain items. Where items fall on a ranking scale does not indicate good or bad, but simply an attempt to look at the relative meaning of one item to another. These ranking scales are simple to use for descriptive data, but require less commonly used statistical techniques. The biggest problem ranking has is with validity. Too many items to rank are confusing to the respondent. Usually ten or eleven items is the maximum number you will want to use. If you have more items to rank than that, you might want to divide your scale into two questions.

One of the major disadvantages to ranking as a question structure is that the directions often confuse respondents. You need to be clear and thorough in your directions so the individual knows exactly what to do. Be sure to say how you want the items ranked such as suggesting that a 1 is the *best* and 2 is next best and so on. The ranking is often useful but you have to realize that it is difficult to say much about what the rankings mean. For example, in Table 2.5(4), you do not know for sure whether the camper liked any of the activities. Further, she or he may have liked them all and may have seen little difference among the ten items.

Table 2.5(4) Example of Ranking Question about Camp Activities

Rank the following ten activities from what you like the best to what you liked the least. That is, choose the activity that you liked best and give it a 1. Choose the second best activity and give it a 2. Continue through all the activities until each has a number from 1 to 10. The number 10 ranked activity will be your least favorite.

_____ horseback riding
_____ swimming lessons
_____ free swimming
_____ evening programs
_____ free time in the afternoon
_____ arts and crafts
_____ overnight campout
_____ mealtimes
_____ cabin activities
_____ afternoon rest period

Self-Assessments

A further example of an ordered close-ended structure is called a self-assessment. It is not uncommon in everyday language for someone to ask you, "On a scale of 1–10, how would you rate XYZ?" In the self-assessment structure, a respondent is asked to describe where she or he would be located on a scale, usually scored as 1 through 10. For example, you might ask a question such as "After taking this class, based on a 1–10 scale with 1 being lowest and 10 being highest, how would you rate your knowledge of the rules of tennis?" The response may be a ladder where the respondent places an "X" to show the position of the response; or may be a mark on a line with "1" on the left, the numbers written consecutively and "10" on the right; or you might simply ask the respondent to write down a number in a space after the question.

Partially Close-ended Questions

A final type of close-ended question structure is called *partially close-ended*. These questions provide some responses, but also leave room for people to write in their own answers or additional information. To assure that the response categories are exhaustive, "other" is sometimes included as an item response. Care should be taken to allow enough room to write what "other" means and that the respondent knows that "other" replies are acceptable.

An example of a partially close-ended question is:

How did you hear about the Sunday hike at the Nature Center?
_____Announcement on the radio
_____Flyer at the recreation department
_____From a friend
_____Other (please explain)_____

Partially close-ended questions often provide important information, but the evaluator is better off to try to anticipate the most common responses rather than letting the respondents do all the thinking. Although partially close-ended responses may improve the validity of a question, reliability problems can exist. The evaluator must make sure she or he is as informed as possible in developing any type of close-ended question.

Wording Issues

Writing questions seems fairly easy at first, but mistakes often are made. Many of these mistakes could be avoided by paying careful attention to the wording of each and every question. Here are some considerations to think about:

1. **Use only one idea per question**. Make sure the question is straightforward and that you are asking an individual to respond to one construct or idea.

2. **Clear, brief, and simple are the rules for good question writing**. Make questions as simple to answer as possible. You may want to begin with a major question and then break it down into several additional questions, but the respondent must always know how to proceed. Two or three simple questions are better than one complex one.

3. **Avoid leading questions that suggest that you want a particular kind of response**.

4. **Avoid asking people to make estimates**. Try to force them to answer as honestly as possible to assure reliability.

5. **Think about trying to formulate a question from the respondent's viewpoint**. Use words that are familiar to the respondent.

6. **Avoid advanced language and technical jargon that is familiar to you but that the respondent may not understand**. Avoid the use of acronyms (e.g., abbreviations such as ADA that may be common for you, but meaningless to the general public). As leisure

service professionals we use many words such as programming, multiple use, and therapy that may be misunderstood by the public. People are reluctant to admit they don't understand words, and this attitude may affect the validity of measurement instruments.

7. **Be clear about what is being asked**. Don't say "Should the P&R Department be more active with environmental education?" Respondents may misunderstand the question because they do not know the words or what "more active" means. Every question should have a time frame. Phrases such as "more active" should be explained by saying what is already occurring.

8. **Avoid negative questions that may confuse the reader**. For example, don't say "Why would you not want the bond issue to be defeated?"

9. **Avoid the use of "iffy" words like often or seldom**. These words may mean different things to different people, so they need to be defined if used.

10. **Do a pilot study**. Examine every comment made in the pilot concerning wording. Don't take anything for granted about a questionnaire and work to keep the wording as simple as possible.

11. **State the alternatives precisely**. "Should the government put more money into recreation or not?" is a poorly worded question. Make clear what you are asking. Put options into the question if you are asking for options or else explain what those options are going to be. For example, a good question might be, "The current greens fee for 18 holes of golf is $20. Should the greens fee at the public golf course be higher, lower, or remain the same?" People, unfortunately, will often tend to choose the middle of the road if they are unsure about a response.

12. **Some questions may require several stages to get adequate information**. These staged questions require several questions to assure a valid answer. Shafer and Moeller (1987) suggest, for example, that a complex question might require up to five questions: first determine awareness by a free-answer question concerning knowledge, next develop uninfluenced attitudes on the subject with another open-ended question, record specific attitudes through multiple choice, then find out the reasons through another open-ended question, and finally determine the intensity with a multiple-choice question. An example of this process can be seen in Table 2.5(5) on page 142.

Table 2.5(5) Example of a Question Asked in Stages

1. Have you visited Rivers Bend County Park?
   _____ Yes (go to question 2)
   _____ No (go to next section)

2. What did you like about Rivers Bend County Park? _____

3. How satisfied were you with your visit to Rivers Bend Park?
   _____ very satisfied
   _____ satisfied
   _____ somewhat satisfied
   _____ dissatisfied
   _____ very dissatisfied

4. What do you look for when you visit a County Park? _____

5. How likely are you to visit Rivers Bend County Park in 2002?
   _____ very likely
   _____ somewhat likely
   _____ not likely

Formats and Instrument Design

Clearly worded questions and an aesthetically pleasing instrument will often invite a respondent to complete a survey. Too often, no more time is given to the layout of a questionnaire than to creating a grocery list. General appearance, however, may be critical to the success of a survey; all instrument developers should be concerned with overall effects and a motivational design. Simple graphics are often important, as is the amount of white space on the page. At first glance, a potential respondent will form an opinion about the importance, difficulty, and length of a questionnaire. From this first impression, she or he is likely to decide whether or not to complete the questionnaire.

The sequencing of the questions is important. Always begin with questions that have a direct relevance to the purpose of the evaluation. These questions may also provide a context for determining attitudes and knowledge. Choosing the very first question should be done carefully. Although demographic questions may be easy to answer, they are seldom directly related to the purpose of the evaluation. Save the demographic questions until last. If a respondent doesn't get to them you will still have the important information collected at the beginning. Put questions of less importance later in the questionnaire. Controversial items should be grouped with less controversial ones. If you think you may not get a response for something because it is really controversial, put it at the end of the questionnaire. The evaluator may start with general questions and proceed to more specific or may begin specific and proceed to more general questions. The choice depends upon the nature of the evaluation criteria.

Group the questions together according to content. Use the same types of question structures together as much as possible if content is appropriate. It is easier to fill out an instrument when similar question structures are grouped. Also, build ties between the questions. If you have different content being collected in the instrument, you may want to head sections such as: (a) attitudes, (b) participation, and (c) background (demographics). This format may help divide a long questionnaire into manageable sections and allow the respondent to move through the questionnaire easier.

You want to design the instrument layout so that respondents don't get confused and/or miss an item. It usually helps to maximize white space on the questionnaire so that an individual does not feel overwhelmed with questions. Design staged questions or questions that require the respondent to "go to" another item with easy to follow directions. For example, if answering yes leads to another question, make sure the individual knows where to go in the questionnaire to answer the next question. Similarly, if no means that you skip questions, make that clear as well. Some questionnaires use exclusively verbal instructions, such as "If NO, then skip to Question 10. If YES then go to the next question." Some questionnaires make use of heavy lines and directional arrows that indicate where to go next. Whichever technique is used, establishing a vertical flow through the instrument is essential to motivating a respondent to continue to the end.

Several other formatting issues might be considered. It is often useful to use lower case letters for questions, upper case letters for answers. An individual could also design a questionnaire using different sizes of fonts or by using bolded, underlined, or italics to show the differences between directions, questions, and responses. Using numbers to identify answer categories rather than boxes to check or letters to circle will be easier later in the coding of responses into numbers that can be entered into the computer. Try to make sure the responses to a question fit all on one page or else move the whole question to the next page. In the case that a series of Likert responses are used that move onto another page, put the scaling anchors at the top of the next page so that the respondent does not get confused about how to answer the questions. Layout should include enough space in-between questions and consistent spacing. Table 2.5(6) on page 144 shows an example of a possible questionnaire layout. This example comes from Dillman (1978), who presents excellent information about mail and telephone surveys.

Table 2.5(6) Example of Questionnaire Layout for Demographic Questions

Q1. What is the number of children you have in each age group?
(If none, write "0")

_____ Under Five Years
_____ 5–13 Years
_____ 14–18 Years
_____ 19–24 Years
_____ 25 Years and Over

Q2. What is your present age? _____Years

Q3. Do you own (or are you buying) your own home? (Circle number)

1. No
2. Yes

Q4. What is your present job status? (Circle number)

1. Employed
2. Unemployed/Between jobs
3. Retired
4. Full-time Homemaker

Q5. What was your approximate net family income from all sources, before taxes, in 2001? (Circle number)

1. Less Than $19,999
2. $20,000 to 29,999
3. $30,000 to 39,999
4. $40,000 to 49,999
5. $50,000 to 59,999
6. $60,000 to 69,999
7. $70,000 to 79,999
8. $80,000 to 89,999
9. Over $90,000

Q6. Which is the highest level of education that you have completed?
(Circle number)

1. Completed Grade School
2. Some High School
3. Completed High School/GED
4. Some College
5. Completed College (Specify Major _____)
6. Some Graduate Work
7. A Graduate Degree (Specify Degree and Major_____)

The way that the questionnaire is put together physically is important. Colored paper is often more interesting than plain white. A subdued color, such as yellow or light blue, is usually good for most instruments. The more professional an instrument looks, the better people will respond. Using a booklet with saddle stitching is desirable for lengthy surveys, although it is also more expensive. The front page should include the title of the questionnaire, some type of graphic (optional, but interesting), the time of year it is being administered (e.g., Fall 2002), any needed directions, and the information (name, title, and address) of the sponsor or evaluator who is conducting the project. The back cover may include a "thank you" and allow space for individuals to write further comments.

Whatever you do, make sure the instrument looks professional and that there are *no* typographical mistakes or anything else that might raise questions about the credibility of the instrument or the evaluator. Also, make sure the items can be easily read. Smaller print allows one to get more on a page, but may be difficult to read for some people.

The length of an instrument is important to consider also. Instruments should be long enough to get the needed information, but not too long. Shorter questionnaires reduce fatigue and are more likely to be completed. You may get a higher response rate with a two-page rather than a six-page questionnaire. On the other hand, a well-designed six pager is better than a poorly designed one pager. Let people know about how long it will take to complete an instrument so they can plan their time. As stated before, the better the layout and design, the easier the questionnaire will be to complete and the more likely you will get a high response rate.

Clear directions throughout the instrument are essential, but are often overlooked. Tell people if you want them to check a response or circle numbers. Tell them if you want the *best* response or more than one. Give complete directions, especially if you have a series of questions. Explain the directions for each scale each time it is encountered in a questionnaire. Most instruments have an introduction that tells the respondent what to do and how to do it. The instructions should be clear, concise, and adequate to explain what is expected, but you may need to remind respondents as they proceed if the questionnaire is lengthy.

From Ideas to Reality

This chapter is full of ideas regarding developing instruments. Developing your own instrument can be a lot of fun but it also can be time-consuming as you can see by the myriad of details that you need to address. Any instrument that is developed should be just as reliable, valid, and usable as any preexisting instrument chosen. The instruments must also be practical and simple—easy to use, easy to understand, and easy to summarize. Whether you use existing instruments or develop your own is up to you. As usual, the criteria that are set likely will determine the choice that you make.

Now that you have studied this chapter, you should be able to:

- State the basic procedures used to design questionnaires.

- Write questions representing the five question types using past, present, and future tenses where appropriate.

- Describe the differences between open-ended, close-ended, and partially close-ended question structures.

- Evaluate the difference between a well-worded and formatted questionnaire and one that is not.

- Develop a questionnaire to measure criteria that uses different content types and questionnaire structures.

Choosing a Sample

No matter how great the criteria or how reliable the instrument, an appropriate sample must be selected. Sampling procedures vary depending upon the methods used and the resources that are available. Sometimes an evaluator may not select a sample, but may use the entire population. For example, if we wanted to find out the attitudes toward a pottery class that had ten people in it, we would likely survey the entire population of ten people in that class. Similarly, if we were evaluating staff performance, we would evaluate all staff and not just a select few. Other times, however, evaluators will choose a smaller group from a large population.

Population refers to all the people who might comprise a particular group. For example, when talking about the population of a city we refer to all the people that reside there. When we talk about the population of intramural sports participants we are referring to all who played during a given period of time. Many times, however, we do not have the ability and the resources to have all individuals, the entire population, participate in an evaluation project so we have to select the sample carefully. A sample should represent the population so the results of the results of the evaluation can be generalized to the total population.

Sampling can be divided into three categories: probability, nonprobability, and theoretical sampling. Probability refers to everyone within a population having the same potential of being selected as part of a sample. Nonprobability samples are selected in a way that not everyone has an equal chance and the likelihood of selecting any one member from a population is unknown. Theoretical sampling is used primarily with qualitative data and refers to sampling until the evaluator reaches a point of data saturation. Saturation is reached when no new data are emerging. Each of these categories will be discussed in greater detail in this chapter.

Keys to Appropriate Sampling

Several key points should be emphasized regarding sampling. First, do not confuse size of sample with representativeness. The sample size required for a survey will depend on the reliability needed, which in turn depends on how the results will be used. A large (several thousand people) sample is not necessarily better than several hundred and often does not make economical sense. On the other hand, too few responses is also problematic if the response rate is low. No simple rule for sample size can be applied to all evaluations. A moderate sample size is sufficient for most needs. For example, national polls usually use samples of 1,500, which is appropriate for a representative sample of a country with over 270 million people. A properly selected sample of only 1,500 individuals can reflect various characteristics of the total population with a small margin of error.

Second, you can select the sample size in various ways. Table 2.6(1) shows an example of the sample size needed for various populations. For example, if you had 500 campers, you would need to randomly select a sample size of at least 217 people. You can also calculate the approximate sample size by using statistical procedures, but we will not get into that detail in this text. (For more information about calculating sample sizes see a statistics text.) Generally the statistical dividing line between large and small samples is 30 people. Further, data are usually considered fragile if you get less than 60–70% of a sample to respond.

Third, methods of sampling are grounded in statistical theory and theories of probability. The sample used depends on the objective and scope of the method used including the overall budget, the method of data collection, the subject matter, and the characteristics of the respondents needed.

Fourth, the relevant population must be clearly identified. From there, a sample can be selected based upon the method used and the data desired. In other words, you must decide whether you will sample participants, parents, staff members, or board members depending upon the program that you wish to evaluate.

Fifth, in sampling, we seek to survey as few people as necessary to get an accurate probability representation. Crompton (1985) used the example of having a barrel with 10,000 red and white marbles from which you take 400. According to probability, the proportion of red and white marbles would be the same as if you took 400 from a barrel of 100,000 marbles.

Sampling Errors

Sources of errors must be addressed related to sampling and nonsampling. Sampling error is the difference between the characteristics of a sample and the characteristics of the population from which the sample was selected (Babbie, 1992). The larger the difference, the larger the error. If you have a

Table 2.6(1) Table for Determining Sample Size (adapted from Krejcie & Morgan, 1970)

Population	Sample	Population	Sample	Population	Sample
10	10	220	140	1,200	291
15	14	230	144	1,300	297
20	19	240	148	1,400	302
25	24	250	152	1,500	306
30	28	260	155	1,600	310
35	32	270	159	1,700	313
40	36	280	162	1,800	317
45	40	290	165	1,900	320
50	44	300	169	2,000	322
55	48	320	175	2,200	327
60	52	340	181	2,400	331
65	56	360	186	2,600	335
70	59	380	191	2,800	338
75	63	400	196	3,000	341
80	66	420	201	3,500	346
85	70	440	205	4,000	351
90	73	460	210	4,500	354
95	76	480	214	5,000	357
100	80	500	217	6,000	361
110	86	550	226	7,000	364
120	92	600	234	8,000	367
130	97	650	242	9,000	368
140	103	700	248	10,000	370
150	108	750	254	15,000	375
160	113	800	260	20,000	377
170	118	850	265	30,000	379
180	123	900	269	40,000	380
190	127	950	274	50,000	381
200	132	1,000	278	75,000	382
210	136	1,100	285	100,000	384

sampling error of ±4 points it means that if 50 percent of the sample say they did something, then the true percentage would be between 46% and 54%. The smaller the error range, the more accurate the survey. We can allow error in sampling for evaluation projects, but we must be careful about how much we allow. If you want to look at subgroups within a sample, you will have to draw a larger sample. Good survey practice includes calculating sampling errors, when possible, so that you know the percentage points above or below an item. The formula for the calculation of the *standard error*, a measure of sampling error, is:

$$S_{error} = \pm \sqrt{\frac{P_1 \times P_2 \times \ldots \times P_x}{n}}$$ **Standard Error**

where S_{error}:   Standard error
  P_1:   Population parameter 1
  P_2:   Population parameter 2
  P_x: Last population parameter
  n: Number of cases

The standard error is the square root of the population parameters (P_1, P_2) multiplied together and divided by the number of cases (n). P_1 and P_2 are the population parameters or the percentage of agreement with a particular item. These population parameters are calculated by subtracting the percentage from 1. If we knew, for example, that 60% of the participants were satisfied with a program and 40% were not and we had a total of thirty participants, the standard error would be 0.089 or rounded off 9%. Thus we would conclude that the true approval rate lies somewhere between 51% and 69%. Also keep in mind that the standard error is a function of sample size. As the sample size increases, the standard error decreases. In the sample above, if we had 60 participants, the standard error would be 6% so the actual approval rate would be somewhere between 54% and 66%.

A second type of error is called *nonsampling error*. Nonsampling errors have no simple and direct method of estimating. Nonsampling errors concern the biases that may exist due to who answers a questionnaire or participated in an evaluation project compared to those people who did not. Errors also may be created by biases. These biases come from sampling operations, noninterviews, participants not understanding the ideas being measured, lack of knowledge of respondents, concealment of the truth, loaded questions, processing errors, and interviewer errors. For example, according to Rossman (1982), a nonsampling error might occur in giving out evaluations during the latter part of a program when dropouts and absentees would not get included. The dropouts are probably dissatisfied, but you don't know that so reliability could be a significant problem. Therefore, to avoid nonsampling error, you need to sample all registered people, not just those in attendance. Only then can you be sure that high satisfaction was not the result of poor sampling because the dissatisfied people left an activity. The evaluator controls as much nonsampling error as possible by designing good evaluation projects and using appropriate methods and measures.

Sampling Theory

Probability sampling theory suggests that all units must have a known, nonzero chance of being included in the sample, and sample design must be explained in sufficient detail to permit calculation of sampling errors. When these guidelines are followed, you can draw inferences from the sample to the appropriate population. The types of samples range from simple random samples to highly complex sample procedures. Quantitative data collection usually involves probability or nonprobability samples, which will be discussed first. Evaluators collecting qualitative data are more likely to use theoretical sampling. Table 2.6(2) gives a summary of the types of sampling that an evaluator might choose.

Table 2.6(2) Sampling Types That May Be Used

Probability
    Simple random sampling
    Stratified random sampling
    Systematic sampling
    Cluster sampling
 	
Nonprobability
    Purposive sampling
    Convenience sampling
    Quota sampling
    Expert sampling
    Snowball
 	
Theoretical

Probability Sampling

Every unit or person who makes up a population has a chance of being selected in probability sampling. *Random sampling* is the most common type of probability sampling and is superior over nonprobability sampling. Mills, Um, McWilliams, and Hodgson (1987) examined the importance of random sampling when conducting visitor surveys. They used haphazard or convenience samples (nonprobability) and a random sample from the same visitor population. By comparing the data from probability and nonprobability samples they concluded that random sampling provided the most reliable data.

If you do a good job in selecting a random sample, the sample will resemble the population in demographics and background. You can select the sample using the table of random numbers or literally put all numbers or names from a population into a hat and draw out the number of individuals needed.

Selecting from a table of random numbers may be the most unbiased and useful tool to use in random sampling. The basis of the number configurations on the table is completely arbitrary. Hudson (1988) gave a good example of how to select random numbers for use in an evaluation project. If you had a known population of 1,500 people and you were going to select 306 people you would first number each of the people from 1–1,500. You then determine the number of digits you will need to select. Since 1,500 has four digits, you will use four digits. Turn to the table of random numbers found in the back of this textbook (Appendix A, p. 363). Notice several rows and columns of five-digit numbers. You can decide to select a five-digit number, but use only the first four numbers. Deciding where to start is a matter of choice. Most people close their eyes and point a finger. This assures that no biases existed in choosing the number. From that starting point move either across or up and down, however you choose, but do it consistently. Ignore any number outside the range of 1,500 and go to the next. Keep on with the procedure until you have selected 306 different numbers out of the 1,500 with which you started.

A *stratified random sample* is used when proportionate representation is sought. It might be based on age, sex, or activity involvement. For example, an evaluator might want the number of African Americans surveyed in the evaluation project to represent the number of African Americans in the population. Or, you might want to stratify a sample so that a proportionate number of boys and girls are observed. If we knew the population consisted of 70% male and 30% female, we would randomly draw 70% of the sample from the list of boys and 30% from the list of girls. Stratified random sampling requires that we draw samples from separate lists. Thus, you have to be able to know what strata you want and the proportion of each stratum in the population.

Systematic sampling determines a rationalization for some kind of routine sample. It is somewhat easier to do than simple random sampling and individuals have a somewhat similar probability of being chosen. All selections are determined by the first selection and then you choose every "n^{th}" one after that. If you knew there were 2,000 members of an organization and you had enough money to sample 200, you might go through and pick every tenth name on the organizational list until you had 200 names drawn. An important point is to choose a random starting point by taking a number from the table of random numbers or by closing your eyes and pointing to a random spot on the list. Systematic sampling is less cumbersome than some other sampling strategies, but not everyone has quite the same chance of being chosen after the first person is selected. The technique, however, is still considered a form of random sampling.

Cluster sampling subdivides a population into groups or units rather than individuals such as geographic areas, city blocks, or recreation centers. These subgroup units would be listed and the evaluator would then choose subgroup units randomly and collect data from the people within those groups. This method is a time saver, but you must be sure that the units or groups are somewhat homogeneous. For example, if a community had ten recreation centers but you only had resources to collect data from four of those centers, you could put the names in a hat and randomly draw out the first four center names as a way to do a cluster sample.

Nonprobability Sampling

Using probability samples is most desirable but not always possible in all evaluation or research projects. Nonprobability sampling includes the procedures used when the sample is not drawn by chance from a population. We do not know the probability of selecting a single individual so we have to "assume" that potential respondents have an equal and independent chance of being selected. Biases may occur and caution is suggested in making generalizations to the broader population, although evaluators frequently do generalize. Several types of nonprobability sampling might be rationalized in an evaluation project.

Purposive sampling is arbitrarily selecting a sample because you believe evidence supports that the sample represents the total population. In using this sampling process, you will need to be able to justify clearly why you believe a particular sample is representative. Purposive sampling also may be used for not only deciding what people to observe and interview, but also which activities to observe, what locations, and what time periods. For example, we might want to sample first-year university students' attitudes toward building a new student recreation center, so we select students from classes in English composition because we believe they represent all first-year students.

Convenience sampling, or incidental sampling, refers to a sample that happens to be available for an evaluation project. This haphazard sampling technique has very weak generalizability and external validity. Convenience sampling is generally not recommended, although there may be some justification for it if no other sampling techniques are possible or affordable. Convenience sampling is easy because the audience is captive and available, and may be representative but you don't know that for sure. You are taking a chance in drawing conclusions for a larger population. If we wanted to survey students on a college campus, a convenience sample would be to pass out questionnaires to the courses that the evaluator was teaching or to which he or she had easy access.

Quota sampling is based on dividing the population into subgroups and drawing a sample to fulfill a specific quota. For example, you may wish to survey an equal number of men and women even though that may not represent the population of an aerobics program. In quota sampling, you would simply choose an equal number of males and females until you reach the number that you wanted. For example, if the evaluator wanted to get the opinion of the public, she or he might go to a mall and give a questionnaire to the first "*x*" number of people that pass by a given area. The problem in quota sampling is that the evaluator does not know if the people chosen represent the population. Further, once the quota is reached, no one else has a chance of being selected. A bias may exist toward individuals who are willing to cooperate with such a sampling procedure. Quota sampling is not a bad strategy, but one can never be fully sure that error does not exist.

Expert sampling, or judgment sampling, is a process where people are chosen on the basis of an informed opinion that they are representative of the population. This best-guess form of sampling is similar to purposive sampling but is based on a good deal of prior knowledge. Case studies are frequently selected on the basis of expert judgment as well as Delphi studies.

One might also get a sample by using the *snowball approach.* The evaluator gets people she or he knows to recommend others to be the sample for a project. The researcher may ask friends, go to an agency and ask for suggestions, or advertise for volunteers just to get the process started. The initial respondents are asked to recommend others who might get involved. For example, if an evaluator wanted to know the constraints to why people with disabilities did not participate in community recreation programs, she or he might contact several individuals with disabilities to survey and then ask them to recommend others whom they know who might be willing to participate. Obviously a bias exists in this form of sampling, but if one does not know the makeup of an entire population, a sample can be obtained in this way.

Theoretical Sampling

A third form of sampling frequently used in collecting qualitative data is different than either probability or nonprobability samples. Theoretical sampling does not focus on numbers of respondents, but the contribution each person makes to address the evaluation or research purposes. Theoretical sampling includes the selection of informants through the stages of the interview or field observation process (Glaser & Strauss, 1967). The evaluator makes decisions on who and how many to sample as information begins to unfold and as it becomes apparent that certain views are or are not being represented.

Theoretical sampling, in the context of collecting qualitative data, means deciding what group of people you want to study. Further, it involves realizing that you cannot observe everything so you can only address certain aspects related to people, settings, events, and social processes. In other words, the evaluator using interviews and/or qualitative observations is not concerned about adequate numbers or random selection, but is trying to present a working picture of the broader social structure from which the data are drawn. Within qualitative approaches, the evaluator is interested in sampling so that the observations made or data collected are representative of the more general class of phenomena. The evaluator is also interested in whether the observations or interviews made are representative of all the possible observations or interviews that could have been conducted.

The exact number or type of informants is not specified ahead of time in theoretical sampling, although the evaluator may have some sense of what those numbers might be. In some cases, the evaluator may need to spend more time in the field or interview more people than was originally proposed to get data that are trustworthy. In other cases, the data may be grounded more easily and quickly than was initially planned. After the first few cases, you may select the sample purposely to get a number of perspectives. Toward the end of data collection, the researcher will focus more on interpretation and verification of data with the respondents. The more variability in responses or observations one uncovers, the more sampling the evaluator will need to do.

Samples used for qualitative evaluations are usually small and purposive. About ten to twenty people is the usual number. *Saturation* is reached with simultaneous data gathering and analysis; it occurs when the evaluator realizes that the data collected are repetitive and no additional information is being uncovered. In any sampling done to collect qualitative data, you should consider how each respondent or situation contributes to an understanding of the evaluation criteria that have been established.

Other Aspects of Sampling

Several other sampling strategies are frequently used in evaluation projects. One example is *random-digit dialing* as a random phone sampling method. According to Dillman (1978), random-digit dialing is based on identifying all working telephone exchanges for an area, generating the last four numbers from a table of random numbers, and calling. The nonworking numbers reached are discarded and the interview is administered to numbers reached. A lot of wasted effort results in this process because of missing phone numbers, but it is a way to get a representative sample from a population.

Another form of sampling for the telephone is sampling from telephone directories. You might use random numbers to locate a starting page and then use another random number to locate a name on the page. It is convenient while still allowing for randomness.

No matter how hard we try, we will unlikely get a sample that perfectly represents the population. We can use an entire population, which is often done in smaller evaluation projects and then you don't have to worry about sampling. We do, however, have to be concerned about both sampling and nonsampling error.

From Ideas to Reality

Sampling is an important aspect of evaluation projects. Sometimes we do not need to be overly concerned about sampling because we use an entire population, but other times it is important if our projects are to be trustworthy. The possibilities for sampling described in this chapter should provide a basis for the sample decisions you will need to undertake in your projects. If you follow the suggestions, you should be able to choose an appropriate sample and justify why it is appropriate given a particular situation.

Now that you have studied this chapter, you should be able to:

- Describe the differences between probability, nonprobability, and theoretical sampling.
- Draw a sample from a population using one of the strategies for probability sampling.
- Calculate the standard error of measurement and explain what it means.
- Use the Table of Random Numbers to draw a sample.
- Determine the appropriate sample size based on the population and the data that will be collected.

Surveys
The Winner of the Popularity Contest

The most common type of descriptive design found in the evaluation of rec-reation and leisure program services and in the examination of participant outcomes is the survey. Surveys are used frequently in leisure research. Surveys are generally easy to administer and can provide information from the participant's perspective related to most aspects of a program including reactions, KASA (i.e., knowledge, attitudes, skills, aspirations) changes, practice changes, and even end results. People are familiar with participating in surveys. Further, many professionals are more accustomed to surveys than observations or unobtrusive methods. Because surveys are so popu-lar, however, does not mean that they should be used automatically. In this chapter, we explore the advantages and disadvantages of the various survey techniques.

Surveys refer to all types of self-administered questionnaires as well as phone, personal, e-mail, and group interviews. Survey methods are designed to get information from individuals. They may include open-ended or close-ended instruments used to collect qualitative or quantitative data. The choice of the specific technique will depend upon the criteria to be measured, the sample selected, the expertise of the evaluator or researcher, the needs of the organization, and the availability of time and other resources. Choosing the best method is essential for any project and surveys are often the best.

No survey technique is perfect for every situation, although idealistically we are always striving to find perfect methods for specific situations. Many times we have to settle for "good-enough" approaches to data collection. It is essential, however, that we carefully consider the options for collecting data from surveys and then make the best possible choices. Sometimes we can collect data with more than one method, referred to as triangulation, but more often the researcher has to make choices.

Response rate is an issue that must be considered in administering any kind of survey. The rate refers to the percentage of surveys returned based on the number that are distributed. For example, if you gave out 25 ques-tionnaires in a class and got 25 back, you would have a 100% response rate.

If you gave out 25 and only got 20 back, it would be an 80% response rate. Crompton and Tian-Cole (1999) examined what might be an acceptable and achievable response rate for mailed questionnaires sent about recreation. They found that 70% was a reasonable expectation among special interest groups (e.g., parents of youth in sports programs), 60% would be desirable from professional groups (e.g., staff and volunteers), and 55% estimated from general interest groups (e.g., individual participants in any recreation program). You are always hoping for 100% response rate but that is not generally possible. The response rate, however, can be greatly improved by some of the suggestions in this book including making the survey the appropriate length, using incentives (if possible), and targeting the sample you will use.

Each of the survey methods has particular strengths and weaknesses. These strengths and weaknesses are summarized in Table 2.7 (pp. 164–165) and discussed throughout this chapter. Self-administered questionnaires and interviews are the two major survey approaches used. Both require the development of questions for respondents to answer. Within these approaches, we may choose from among several techniques for gathering data: mailed questionnaires, drop-off/pickup questionnaires, group administered questionnaires, call-ahead-and-mail questionnaires, e-mail questionnaires and Internet surveys, telephone interviews, personal interviews, or group interviews (also known as focus groups). The technique used will depend on the evidence needed to measure the evaluation criteria or research questions.

Self-Administered (Written or Paper-and-Pencil) Questionnaires

Self-administered questionnaires can be done by mail, drop-off/pickup, group administrations, call-ahead-and-mail, or on the Internet. The advantage of these written questionnaires lies in the ease of presenting questions that may require visual aids. Questions that are long and may require more complex responses, such as stage questions (i.e., questions that require several items to get a response) can be done more easily with self-administered questionnaires. You can also ask a battery of similar questions without tiring the respondent. A high degree of anonymity is found in self-administered questionnaires assuming no identifying information is requested. The respondent also does not have to have a face-to-face encounter with the evaluator.

Disadvantages, however, exist with self-administered questionnaires. First of all, careful questionnaire wording and layout is needed because the evaluator has no chance to clarify the questions being asked. Second, long open-ended questions usually do not work well in self-administered questionnaires, as people do not like to write long responses. A personal interview is a better approach if you want detailed information. Finally, good reading skills are required to do self-administered questionnaires. All questionnaires should be directed at the appropriate age of the respondents. In general, a fifth grade reading level is suitable for most adults. In areas with high ethnic diversity, multilanguage questionnaires may be needed.

Mailed Questionnaires

Advantages exist for mailed self-administered questionnaires. The cost is relatively low and data can be collected with minimal staff and facilities. A mailed survey can provide access to geographically dispersed samples and samples that might be difficult to reach in other ways. With self-administered questionnaires, the respondents typically have time to give thoughtful answers and/or look up information.

Written, mailed questionnaires are obviously easy to administer. Anonymity or confidentiality can be assured in this method even if code numbers are used to keep track of questionnaire returns. With mailed questionnaires, one has access to high and low income groups, although a certain level of education is usually necessary to be able to respond to the questions. Weather does not impact the response rate and one can include a range of questions. The technique of mailed questionnaires is particularly good for larger samples (over 100 cases). One can be confident with the results especially with a 50% return rate or better. The standardized instructions should result in objective responses if the directions are clear and the questions are well-worded.

Disadvantages of mailed questionnaires lie in possible nonsampling biases. The possibility of a low response rate exists. It is possible to miss some homeless people if they do not have mailing addresses or some people who may not be able to read or understand English. Further, you can't determine how an individual perceives the questions, and whether the person you intended is filling out the questionnaire. With a mailed questionnaire, you as the evaluator have limited ability to pursue answers deeply. Questionnaires often require "accurate memory" which is not always possible. Mailed questionnaires are sometimes an ineffective way to get cooperation because you have no personal contact. In addition, the mailed questionnaire technique also takes time to collect data. Sending out a questionnaire, allowing several days to respond, and mailing the questionnaire back takes time.

You must be sure to have current mailing addresses and recognize that people without postal addresses will not be included in the survey. Mailed questionnaires are seldom used with the general public because names are not available and response rate is low. It is possible, however, to obtain or purchase mailing lists from local government tax rolls, utility companies, and telephone companies although these lists will also have limitations. If you wanted to collect data from a community or a neighborhood, you might be interested in obtaining these kinds of lists of names. Mailing companies exist that will charge you to purchase lists based on the population and sample that you want to contact.

On the other hand, mailed questionnaires are usually highly useful for particular groups that have a vested interest in an activity. For example, if we wanted to know what Girl Scout leaders thought of the training they received, a short mailed questionnaire might be a good way to receive feedback with the likelihood of a fairly high return rate. Presumably Girl Scout leaders would have a vested interest in making sure that training was done well.

In doing any kind of mailed questionnaire, an evaluator or researcher must be concerned about *nonsampling error*, also known as nonresponse bias. In other words, it is likely that those who do not respond to a survey may be different from those who respond. As is discussed in the chapters on sampling and administering questionnaires, the evaluator must do as much as possible to assure that a high response rate is obtained and that nonrespondents are not different from those who respond.

Drop-off/Pickup Questionnaires

Dropping off one day and picking up questionnaires at a later date has some advantages beyond what has already been discussed related to self-administered questionnaires. With a drop-off/pickup technique, you can explain the study and answer questions when the questionnaire is dropped off. If someone is unable to do the questionnaire, they can say so. Thus, the return rate is likely to be higher than with mailed questionnaires. Having time with the questionnaire also provides the individual with the opportunity to give thoughtful answers.

Some disadvantages exist in the drop-off/pickup method. Frequently the costs are as high as personal interviews because field staff and travel money are required to do this legwork. Getting access to sites may also be a problem, as is making arrangements to get the questionnaires picked up.

Group Administrations

Group administrations of paper-and-pencil tests have advantages in getting a high cooperation rate. This group administration process is similar to what a teacher does in the classroom when she or he gives a test. Each respondent is given a questionnaire and can take as long as needed. The evaluator also has the chance to explain and answer questions about the survey. Frequently the cost for this technique is low.

Disadvantages of group administrations include the possibility of only collecting a small number of surveys because of the logistics of getting people together in groups. If people already exist in a group, however, logistics and numbers generally are not a problem.

Call-and-mail Method

Another method for self-administered questionnaires is to call people to enlist their cooperation and then send them a questionnaire. Once people make a commitment to you over the phone, they are more likely to complete the survey. This technique usually has a relatively high response rate. The evaluator can also answer any questions about the evaluation initially over the phone. Additional expense of staff time is added in phone calls, but this cost may be offset with the assurance that questionnaires are not wasted on people who do not want to return them.

Internet Questionnaires

A new area of collecting survey data is emerging in the form of Internet data collection. Two types of surveys currently exist: e-mail surveys and HTML surveys. By the time you read this book, there will likely be more options. A number of businesses have developed that bill themselves as "online market research experts." It is possible that you as an evaluator could do these types of questionnaires on your own. Using the Internet and doing web evaluation may provide a greater diversity of the sample without the need for constant monitoring. Generally the costs can be kept low. Disadvantages to web evaluation, however, include some loss of control and the possibilities of subject fraud including people doing a survey more than once. Issues of privacy and confidentiality may appear more difficult to maintain. In addition, since not everyone has access to the Internet, you may have an upper to middle class bias built in if the Internet is used. Respondents to Internet surveys tend to be males more likely than female and are more likely to be Caucasian (Mehta & Sivadas, 1995). All ages, however, seem to be involved in using the Internet.

Table 2.7a Advantages and Disadvantages of Survey Techniques

Technique
• Advantages	*• Disadvantages*

Self-administered

• Ease of presenting questions	• Requires careful wording
• Longer, stage questions can be used	• No chance to clarify misunderstandings
• High degree of anonymity	• Reading skills required
	• Not good for open-ended questions

Mailed Questionnaire

• Low cost	• Low response rate possible
• Minimal staff/facilities required	• Is right person filling it out
• Widely dispersed samples	• No personal contact
• Time for respondent to respond	• Nonresponse bias
• Easy to administer	• Can't pursue deep answers
• Anonymous and confidential	
• Weather not a factor	
• Good for vested interest groups	

Drop-off/Pickup—*Same as Mailed Questionnaire plus:*

• Can explain person-to-person	• Costly for staff time and travel
• High response rate	• Access may be a problem
	• Safety of staff

Group Administered

• High cooperation rates	• Logistics of getting people together
• Low cost	
• Personal contact	

Call-Ahead-and-Mail

• Usually higher response rate	• More costly with phone calls
• Personal contact	
• Time/money not wasted on nonresponses	

Internet

• Fast response and data collection	• No population lists available
• Good and easy follow-up	• Restricted to people with access
• Cost savings	• Must use a computer
• User convenience	• Browser incompatibility problems
• Wide geographic coverage	• Respondents are traceable
• No interview bias	• Possibility of multiple submissions
• Flexible use	

Table 2.7b Advantages and Disadvantages of Survey Techniques

Technique • *Advantages*	• *Disadvantages*
Interviews	
• Ability to probe	• Time and personnel requirement
• Establish and maintain rapport	• Trained interviewers needed
• Questions can be clarified	• Simple questions asked
• Low literacy rates can do well	• Usually smaller sample size
• Unplanned information possible	
• Interviewer can be adaptable	
Telephone	
• Lower costs than personal	• Sampling limitations for those
• Random-digit dialing sampling	without phone
possible	• People can hang up
• Broad geographic area covered	• Visual aids can't be used
• Data can be collected quickly	• Sometimes superficial
• Control over data collection	• Timing is important
• Possibility of callbacks	
• Rapport but not face-to-face	
Personal	
• Elicit cooperation	• Costly
• Probing and follow-up used	• Requires highly trained interviewers
• Other observations to use	• Long data collection period
• Establish rapport	• Some populations not accessible
• Longer interviews	• Small geographic area
• High response rate	• Possible interviewer bias
• Spontaneous reactions	
Group Interviews	
• Fast to conduct	• Logistics of getting people together
• Same as personal	• Leader must work to get all opinions

E-mail is a viable tool because it is low cost, quick, and reasonably easy. E-mail surveys are also one of the least intrusive ways to collect information. If you have e-mail lists, you can put together a questionnaire, following the tenets of good design, and ask individuals to complete it and return to you. According to The Research Spectrum (2001), e-mail surveys are good because most people check their e-mail when they have time to respond and therefore, may be more likely to respond at their convenience and that raises cooperation rates. In addition, respondents can be more objective when they type in their own responses without any interviewer influence. Some of the disadvantages of this e-mail technique are that you cannot control the parameters of the responses, you have limited multimedia capabilities, and isolating addresses of small localities unless you create your own e-mail directory. Also, many people consider receiving unsolicited e-mail about as appealing as calls from telemarketers, and won't even open message from anyone they don't recognize.

HTML surveys are a good tool for taking a paper-and-pencil survey online. In this format, an individual goes to a website to do a survey and "sends" it when completed. These surveys are generally low cost, quick, can incorporate graphics, and are visually appealing. Some of the disadvantages lie in the need to think about technical aspects such as the browser compatibility, duplicate responses, and whether it is completed online or downloaded. The use of HTML may be limited by the evaluator's ability and the limitations of HTML code. Further, the sampling process may be not as clear with this technique.

Interviews

Interviews may be divided into three categories: telephone interviews, individual personal interviews, and group interviews. The general advantages of interviews include the evaluator's ability to probe to a greater depth, the opportunity to establish and maintain rapport, and the possibility of clarifying questions. People with lower literacy levels can often do well with interviews, although the more articulate an individual is the more information will be obtained. The evaluator may also get unplanned or serendipitous information and may gain insight into the true feelings of respondents. The evaluator can encourage respondents to answer questions and can be somewhat flexible and adaptable to the situation.

Weaknesses of interviews, in general, include the great amount of time and personnel that are usually needed. Trained interviewers are usually required and interview biases are always a concern. Although interviews may be quantitative, the questions need to be simpler than self-administered questionnaires because respondents will have to listen rather than read. Open-ended questions provide rich information but may be more difficult to analyze than close-ended questions. In addition, interviews usually result in a smaller sample size.

Telephone Interviewing

Telephone interviewing has a number of advantages. The costs are lower compared to personal interviews and moderate compared to mailed questionnaires. Sampling processes like random digit dialing can be used. The evaluator has access to certain populations in a broad geographic area. Further, the potential exists for a short data collection period. A smaller staff is needed compared to personal interviews, but more people are generally needed than for doing a mailed questionnaire. The evaluator has a little more control over the data collected in an interview because the interviewer can explain questions if needed. It is often easier to get sensitive data over the phone because individuals do not have to see you in person. A telephone conversation sometimes seems more anonymous. You are likely to get a better sample because of the personal contact and possibility of callbacks. In some cases letters are sent ahead of time to inform respondents that they will be receiving a call in the next week. In some telephone surveys, an initial call is made to ascertain cooperation and to set up an appointment for a more convenient time.

Disadvantages of telephone interviews include sampling limitations, particularly for those people without telephones or with unlisted numbers. Since phone interviews rely on verbal communication, response alternatives are limited with the impossibility of visual aids and visual observations. For example, you would not be able to ask people to rank more than three or four items in a phone interview. Some superficiality may result because you can't probe as deeply with phone interviews. Without prior contact, telephone interviews are less appropriate for personal or sensitive questions. One must consider timing if the calls are to be successful. In addition, telephone marketing is so overused these days that people often are not excited about spending time with someone they don't know on the phone, and will hang up.

Personal Interviewing

Personal interviews with individuals are a frequent form of survey data collection. The data collected may be quantitative or qualitative. These interviews may be brief encounters such as someone in a shopping mall stopping to ask people four or five close-ended questions about the mall, or personal interviewing can be done with in-depth oral histories or case studies that may last an hour or more.

Personal interviewing is an effective way to enlist cooperation. Most people like to be asked to state their opinions. If someone does not want to be involved, they will say so immediately. Accurate responses to complex issues are possible in personal interviews because the interviewer can probe and ask the interviewer to provide examples. In addition to the words, you can also get additional data through observations and visual cues. Rapport and confidence building is easier when you are face-to-face with another individual. In addition, longer interviews can often be undertaken. The success of interviews, however, often depends on the interviewer's ability to get information. Personal interviews usually result in a high response rate and allow the evaluator to control the process to address the purposes of the evaluation project.

Disadvantages of personal interviewing include the cost and the need for trained interviewers who live near the interviewees. Unless you have a great deal of money, your sample size will likely be small. Further, data collection may take a longer period of time. Some populations may not be accessible for personal interviews, such as people in high crime areas or elite people. Logistics must be taken into account, as it is difficult to interview over a large geographic area. The interviewer could provide bias if she or he is not well trained.

Group Interviewing

Group interviews, commonly referred to today as *focus groups*, have advantages because they are faster to do even though logistics exist in getting people together. They often result in speedier results and can be relatively low in cost. Focus groups allow the moderator to probe and can be high in face validity. Krueger (1988) summarized the advantages of the focus group by stating they are socially oriented evaluation procedures that allow the interviewer to probe and can use fairly large samples if several small groups are combined in data analysis. The limitations of focus groups are that there is less control in a group interview, the interviewer must be carefully trained, groups may vary considerably, groups may be difficult to assemble, and the discussion must be in an environment conducive to conversation. As we will discuss in Unit Three, analyzing qualitative data obtained from group interviews may be difficult.

Focus groups can also be conducted over the Internet. This technique allows for an immediate, permanent, and secure record of responses. These can be developed in the form of real-time chat groups, or ongoing groups. The real-time chat group can be set up to allow several users to engage in a discussion with moderator control. An ongoing group will provide respondents time to post responses and enable post follow-up questions.

Some of the same disadvantages exist with both group interviews and personal interviews. The focus group interviewer must be skilled at getting people to talk, and directing the group interview so that all individuals feel free to state their ideas and not sucumb to peer pressure or conform.

From Ideas to Reality

The survey technique you choose will depend upon the object of study and the use of the evaluation. Many survey possibilities exist. The use of the right technique coupled with a good questionnaire or interview schedule will contribute to the success of survey methods. If you follow these suggestions for making decisions, you should be able to conduct the best possible survey evaluation project.

Now that you have studied this chapter, you should be able to:

- Describe why surveys are the most common method used in recreation, park, tourism, and leisure.
- Explain the advantages and disadvantages of self-administered and interview surveys.
- Choose the appropriate survey technique based upon the criteria and resources that are available to you for a given evaluation project.
- Outline the procedures to follow given a particular survey project.

Surveys
Administering Questionnaires, Telephone Interviews, and Internet Evaluations

When using a survey, one must consider the best way to administer it. This chapter identifies some of the procedures to be followed in administering questionnaires, conducting interviews, and completing web-based evaluations. We assume that the criteria are well-established for a project and that you have selected or developed a reliable, valid, and useable instrument.

Pilot Testing

All evaluators and researchers should pilot test their instruments with a sample similar to the one that will be doing the actual evaluation. Usually the pilot test is done to see if any problems exist with the instrument or the sample. This recommendation was discussed to some extent in the chapter on choosing and developing instruments but we cannot emphasize the importance of pilot testing enough. Changes may need to be made in the instrument after the pilot is completed or you may use the data obtained in the pilot test to develop plans for sampling or for data analysis.

A pilot test usually consists of going to a small sample (5–10 people) that is similar to the individuals who will ultimately receive the survey. The evaluator will give the survey exactly as it will be administered and note the responses from the sample. In addition, people taking the pilot might be asked if all the items on the questionnaire were clear and understandable. Some problems may be evident to you as you assess the way that people responded to the questions. As indicated previously, you must pay attention to the information you get in the pilot as it can give you a great deal of information to consider before you actually begin to collect data.

Some people also use the pilot to test the reliability, validity, and usability of an instrument. The pilot test will determine if, in fact, an instrument can be successfully administered over the phone or whether another method would be better. If a standardized test is used, a pilot test may not be necessary, but doing one may help to assure that the instrument is valid for its intended use.

Implementing Mailed Questionnaires

In conducting mailed questionnaires, several aspects need to be considered including cover letters, mailing procedures, and follow-ups.

Cover Letters

A questionnaire should never be mailed without some explanation of the evaluation project or research study. This description is usually done with a cover letter. The letter should contain a clear, brief, yet adequate statement of the purpose and value of the survey. If possible, the letter should be personally addressed to the respondent. With computer mail merge programs, we easily can address the individual by name who is receiving the questionnaire. The cover letter should engage the potential respondent in a constructive and appealing way and should provide good reason why the respondent should take time to complete the questionnaire. The respondent's professional or public responsibility, intellectual curiosity, or personal worth are typical response appeals. The tone should be one that is inviting and not authoritarian.

The cover letter should indicate a reasonable but firm return date. Usually people need two to three weeks to respond. Make sure a deadline is given or you may still receive questionnaires for months after you have completed your project. An offer to send the respondent a report of findings is an ethical responsibility. Make this offer only, however, if you are committed to making sure that a summary is sent. The use of letterhead, signature, and organizational endorsements lend prestige and official status to the cover letter.

The cover letter should guarantee anonymity or confidentiality and explain carefully how the data will be used. The evaluator should sign the letter individually, if at all possible. It is often best to avoid using words like questionnaire and study, as these terms sometimes are not perceived as positively as are words like project and survey. Figure 2.8(1) shows a sample cover letter that might provide a prototype to follow when designing your own letter.

Department of Recreation and Leisure Studies
CB #3185 Evergreen House
University of North Carolina at Chapel Hill
Chapel Hill, NC 27599-3185

February 1, 2002

Dear (name):

Summer staff salaries are an issue each of us will address shortly. For some time, many camp directors have wondered how their summer camp staff salaries compared to other positions in the same region and in comparable camp settings. Baseline data about summer camp staff salaries may be useful information for the camping movement in general, as well as for specific camps.

Your camp has been randomly selected for participation in this project. We are asking only a small percentage of accredited agency, religiously affiliated, and independent day and resident camps across the United States to complete and return this short questionnaire. Therefore, your participation is *extremely important.*

You may be assured of confidentiality. The questionnaire has an identification code number for mailing purposes only. This coding is done so that we may check your camp's name off our mailing list when your questionnaire is returned.

The results of this survey will be made available to the American Camping Association and will be distributed at the next ACA Conference in Denver. You can receive a copy of the results in mid-February if you send us a self-addressed stamped envelope along with your completed questionnaire.

To get the results tabulated by April, it is necessary to have the data as soon as possible. We are asking that you please return the questionnaire by February 18. Since ACA is doing this study on a small budget, you can contribute further to the organization by putting your own stamp on the return addressed envelope enclosed.

We appreciate your assistance. We believe we are undertaking a valuable and useful project. If you have any questions, please call us at 919–962–1222. Thank you again.

Sincerely,

(names)
(titles)

Figure 2.8(1) Sample of a Cover Letter

Mailing

Depending on the number of questionnaires to be sent, one may use bulk mail or first class. First class is faster, but more expensive. Bulk rate may take up to two weeks for delivery, but is less expensive. If an address is wrong, first-class letters will be returned to the sender but this is not the case for bulk mail. Therefore, with bulk mail you do not know if a percentage of your nonresponse was due to people not receiving the questionnaires, or due to respondents not taking the time to complete the questionnaire.

The higher your response rate, the more confidence you can have that your survey represents the views of the sample. Dillman (1978) suggested having a goal of getting a 100% response rate. To get a higher response, you can do such things as enclose a self-addressed, stamped envelope. A business reply envelope will also work. Business reply envelopes are usually more financially desirable, because you are only charged postage for the questionnaires returned. Response rates are generally higher if it is as easy as possible for someone to return a questionnaire. Some evaluations may use self-mailers in which the respondent simply folds the questionnaire, staples or tapes it, and puts it in a postal box. You will need to decide the best way, but keep the return mailing as easy as possible for the respondent.

Although 100% is a possible goal, for most mailed surveys you should realistically expect at least a 50–70% response rate. The shorter the questionnaire, the better the response rate. If the response is lower than 50%, you may have nonrespondent bias resulting in problems with validity. Response rate is calculated by dividing the actual number of responses returned by the number in the sample size minus those individuals who were not reachable (such as questionnaires returned due to incorrect addresses or no forwarding address), and then multiplying by 100. The fraction should be as close to 100% as possible. For example, if we had 80 names on a list that received questionnaires and 48 of them returned the questionnaire and three letters were undeliverable, we would have a response rate of: 48/(80–3) x 100= 62%

$$Response\ Rate = \frac{N_r}{N-N_u}\ x\ 100$$ **Response Rate**

where N_r = number returned N = sample size
N_u = number unreachable

A low response rate does more damage than a small sample size since no valid way exists of scientifically inferring the characteristics of the population represented by nonrespondents. People likely not to respond often have little or no interest in the topic, are low income and blue collar workers who tend to express themselves less frequently in written form, and citizens with little formal education (Michigan State University, 1976).

Sometimes you can provide incentives such as a small amount of money, gift certificates or coupons, pencils, newspaper clippings, gifts (e.g., a small memento), or a promise of a copy of the results to encourage people to respond. Providing incentives adds additional expense to the survey, but may be important in some situations. We know of one health club that offered two free guest passes to any member who returned a completed evaluation questionnaire. The best thing to do, however, to assure a high response rate is to convince people of the value of their input on a mailed questionnaire.

Many evaluators use a code number system to keep track of who and how many people return questionnaires. This code is accomplished by giving each respondent a number associated with her or his name and address. This number is then written somewhere on the questionnaire. In the cover letter, you should explain what the number means. When the questionnaire is returned, the name can be crossed off the list so that no additional money is wasted on follow-up reminders, and the individual does not have to deal with, what then becomes, junk mail. Destroying the list of names and numbers after the data are coded and tabulated also assures the respondent of anonymity.

Follow-up contacts should also be conducted to obtain a higher response rate. Dillman (1978) suggested that a reminder postcard be sent to individuals who have not returned questionnaires after the first ten days or so. It is just a friendly reminder. A second follow-up letter should be sent several days after the initial due date. It should include a second cover letter with much of the same information as in the first, including a plea to "please complete the questionnaire by" a new due date. This follow-up letter might suggest that the evaluator hopes the questionnaire is in the mail, while also reaffirming the value of the evaluation project. Another questionnaire and a self-addressed, stamped envelope should be included with the second follow-up letter. A final contact in the form of another postcard should be mailed about ten days after the second letter is sent to anyone who has not returned the questionnaire. If you still have not received a good response rate, a telephone call to nonrespondents might be initiated to either ask them to return the questionnaire or, if possible, complete the questionnaire over the phone.

For some evaluation studies, you may want to determine nonresponse bias. In other words, are those people who didn't respond different than those who did? You can call to get demographic data or check if late respondents are different demographically than early respondents to your survey. If you get a high response rate (high is usually 50–70%), determining nonresponse bias is probably not necessary.

Administration to Groups

The administration of surveys to groups mainly requires getting people together to give them an evaluation instrument. You may need to provide them with a writing utensil and a place that is conducive to filling out the instrument. Clear directions should be given about the purpose of the survey and what to do once it is completed. The response rate is much higher when people are required to complete a questionnaire on the spot, although sometimes people do not want to take the time if the questionnaire looks long.

Sometimes it may be necessary to allow people to take the questionnaire with them. In that case, you may want to use a code procedure similar to what was done with the mailed questionnaire so that you can send out postcards or make phone calls as reminders to those who do not return their questionnaire. If people are asked to return a questionnaire, make sure they know where and when. In some situations, mailing may be easier than a drop-off. Provide a self-addressed, stamped envelope along with the questionnaire when you distribute it.

Telephone Interviews

Telephone interviews may be conducted by sending a preliminary letter or by simply calling the interviewee on the spot. Forewarning is usually helpful if the individual needs time to consider the topic and it alleviates the suspicion that a call may not be legitimate. The advance letter, similar to the cover letter, is written with the details about the project and when the phone call is going to occur.

Timing is often critical for telephone interviewing. The best time to catch people at home is between 6:00–9:00 p.m. This time slot is not always the most convenient time to get people to do interviews, however. Most telephone interviews are not completed during the first contact. Often several calls are required to get someone and to set up an appropriate time for the interview if it requires more than a couple minutes on the phone.

You may call from a predetermined list, use a random sample from a directory, or do random-digit dialing. When making the call, the first thing to do is to confirm that the phone number is correct or that the appropriate residence has been reached. If a particular person is wanted in the household, the person should be requested. The interviewer should then state to the desired respondent who she or he is and why a phone survey is being conducted. A brief description of the evaluation project should be given (two or three sentences). You might also want to tell how her or his number was obtained and/or remind them that a letter was sent previously. You should tell the individual how long the interview will take and ask if now is a convenient time. If it is not, try to schedule another time that would be more convenient. Remember that you are interested in getting as high a response rate as possible, so do all that you can to get the interview completed. If someone hangs up on you, they are considered a nonrespondent or no return. As discussed previously, we want the return rate to be as close to 100% as possible.

Proceed through the survey on the phone as quickly as possible, but make sure you allow the individual enough time to respond. If you are tape-recording the conversation, be sure to inform the individual of the recording. If not, mark your responses to the questionnaire accurately or enter them into the computer appropriately. Many telephone interviewers now use computers that immediately enter the data and, depending upon the response, will move the interviewer to the next appropriate question. Table 2.8(2) (pp. 178–179) shows an example of a telephone interview schedule.

Interviewers doing telephone interviews will need to be thoroughly trained. Sometimes you can get volunteers to do phone interviews, but often you will need to hire people. Regardless of whether paid or volunteer, the interviewers must be knowledgeable about the process and how to conduct the interview. Interviewers must also learn to read the questions exactly as they appear. They must understand the telephone system and must know how to respond to questions. It is usually best if all interviewers operate from a central location for ease of supervision. One of the best ways to train interviewers is during the pilot test so they can practice their responses before you collect the real data.

The big difference between telephone interviews and mailed questionnaires is the need to have a third person between the evaluator and the respondent. Thus, much effort goes toward making sure the interviewer is adequately prepared.

Internet Surveys

As indicated in the previous chapter, Internet surveys can either be done via e-mail or HTML. The process of developing a questionnaire is the same as with other methods. You must also determine how to get the sample you will need. With the growing popularity of the Internet, online surveys will

Table 2.8(2)a Sample Telephone Interview for Recreation Trails Survey

Q1. As we said, this survey is about the use of any designated recreational trails in Wisconsin. By this we mean any trail in Wisconsin that is marked and maintained specifically for recreational activities. Did you use any of these trails at all in 2001?

    1. yes (Go to Q2)   2. no (Go to 1a)   7. don't know   9. NA

                                                 (skip to Q 46)

Q1a. Is it very likely, likely, unlikely, or very unlikely that you will be a user of Wisconsin trails five years from now?
    1. very likely   2. likely   3. unlikely   4. very unlikely
    7. don't know   9. NA

Q1b. Have you heard of these trails, or didn't you ever know they exist?
    1. heard (Go to 1c)   2. didn't know they exist (skip to Q46)
    7. don't know (skip to Q46)   9. NA (skip to Q46)

Q1c. Was there anything that kept you from using these trails in 2001 if you had wanted?
    1. Yes (skip to Q33)   2. No (skip to Q46)
    7. don't know (skip to Q46)   9. NA (skip to Q46)

Q2. During 2001, about how many times did you use a designated recreational trail in Wisconsin for any of the activities I'll name?

    First: for backpacking? (ENTER "0" IF NONE) #:____

Q3. …hiking without backpacks? #:____

Q4. …biking? #:____

Q5. …horseback riding? #:____

Q6. …cross-country skiing? #:____

Q7. …snowmobiling? #:____

Q8. …driving or riding motorcycles or off-road vehicles? #:____

Q9. …canoe trails? #:____

Q10. What other activities, if any, did you use the trails for in 2001, and about how many times did you do each one?
    0. none
    (a) _____ #:____
    (b) _____ #:____

Interviewer: If "0" to Qs 2–10, return to Q1. If not, proceed to Q11.

Table 2.8(2)b Sample Telephone Interview for Recreation Trails Survey (continued)

Q11. In 2001, did you tend to use these trails more on weekdays or on weekends?
1. weekdays   2. weekends   3. no difference
7. don't know   9. NA

Q12. How many different designated recreational trails in Wisconsin did you use last year?
#:____

Q13. In 2001, did you use any nationally operated trails in Wisconsin?
1. yes   2. no   7. don't know   9. NA

Q14. …any state-operated trails?   1. yes   2. no   7. don't know   9. NA

Q15. …county-operated trials?   1. yes   2. no   7. don't know   9. NA

Q16. …city-operated trails?   1. yes   2. no   7. don't know   9. NA

Q17. …privately -operated trails?   1. yes   2. no   7. don't know   9. NA

Q18. Do you usually use these trails with a friend, or with a relative, or do you usually go alone?
1. friend   2. relative   3. alone   4. all of the above
7. don't know   9. NA

Q19. When you used any of these trails, was it usually on outings sponsored by a club or organization?
1. yes   2. no   7. don't know   9. NA

Q20. Do any members of your household use designated recreational trails in Wisconsin that you do not use?
1. yes   2. no   3. single-person household
7. don't know   9. NA

---

likely become more commonplace and many ways will be found to conduct them (Dommeyer & Moriarty, 2000).

You will likely send a "cover letter" preceding the survey instrument by either mail or e-mail. The respondent will need to know answers to the same issues as described in the mailed cover letter: purpose and value of the study, how the sample was selected, and a deadline for transmitting the response back. The deadline can be shorter (e.g., a week) since returning will include responding and hitting a send button. With the use of the Internet, you will need to establish how anonymity or confidentiality will be guaranteed. You can indicate that the results of the survey will be posted on the web on a certain date as one way to provide an incentive.

The simplest method is to send the questions in an e-mail. The respondent can hit the reply button and include the original message in the text. The respondent can then type their responses underneath each question. This technique is probably the easiest to use, but it limits the evaluator's ability to formulate sophisticated questions since the text is usually "flat" with no color or bold words. Although some e-mail clients interpret simple HTML code to stylize text and embed graphics in messages, problems can arise between clients and make such efforts unreadable to some potential respondents.

Another approach is to send the questionnaire as a text file attachment that the respondent has to download. Once the questions are answered, the respondent can save their responses in the file and send it back. This technique obviously has some drawbacks because of the multiple steps involved. It also assumes that the respondent has the ability to do all the steps, has the software to interpret the downloaded file, and that their word processor can read the document.

A third way to conduct an online survey is to send an e-mail with an attachment that contains a survey program. In other words, the respondent downloads this file and executes it in a format that looks just like a survey that might be sent in the mail. A "submit" button allows the respondent to reply without attaching a file. This approach requires some sophisticated programming expertise, is more costly, and can run into crossplatform incompatibility.

The fourth technique is to use web-based surveys (HTML). In this technique, the respondent is sent an e-mail and asked to go to a web site to complete the survey, usually with a link to the web site somewhere in the message. This method allows for elaborately designed questionnaires and the software is often automatically programmed to follow skip patterns, collect data and provide ongoing summaries of the data. This method may be a more expensive option than some others, but the ease of replying may be worth the investment of time and money.

Some of the advantages and disadvantages of Internet surveys were discussed in the previous chapter. This new way of data collection offers a great deal of promise but time will tell how effective it is. It currently appears that the response rate to Internet surveys is lower than other survey techniques (Dommeyer & Moriarty, 2000). The effectiveness may improve as people become more proficient at designing these surveys, targeting e-mail addresses or developing in-house databases of local e-mail addresses, and as respondents feel more secure about responding and being assured confidentiality. If the opportunity exists and the population one wishes to evaluate or research is available, Internet surveys may be a useful tool.

From Ideas to Reality

Survey administration is a necessary step in data collection. This aspect of the evaluation or research project is not difficult to do but the tips provided should help to make sure that the process goes smoothly. A pilot test is almost always a useful undertaking even though it often takes time. Any kind of good research is challenging enough so you will want to do everything to try to make sure that data can be efficiently and effectively collected whether you are using paper and pencil questionnaires, telephone surveys, or Internet surveys. Basic principles of administration apply to all types of surveys.

Now that you have studied this chapter, you should be able to:

- Conduct a pilot test for a survey evaluation study that you would like to undertake.

- Describe the steps in implementing a mailed questionnaire so that you will get the highest possible return rate.

- Write a cover letter.

- Determine the steps that need to be followed to complete successful telephone interviews.

Surveys
Personal and Group Interviewing

The purpose of interviewing is to find out what is in and on someone's mind. It allows us to enter into another person's perspective. We assume that the perspective is meaningful, knowable, and able to be expressed. Interviewing may be done over the telephone or face-to-face. Interviews may be done individually or in groups. The questions asked may collect quantitative or qualitative data, although personal interviews often have been used to collect qualitative data. In-depth interviews are usually used to collect detailed and comprehensive qualitative data and to understand the meanings behind an interviewee's words.

The value of interviewing is in finding out those perspectives of an individual that we cannot directly observe. For example, we cannot observe feelings, thoughts, and intentions. We cannot observe behavior that took place at some previous point in time. We cannot observe how people organize their world and the meanings they attach to what goes on in the world. We have to ask people questions about these things.

Interviewers sometimes feel they are imposing on people. Handled appropriately, however, what could be more flattering to an individual than to be asked to talk about her or his views about various issues? Most people like to talk about themselves and the interviewer should encourage them to talk. Nevertheless, as in all survey situations, the interviewee is giving a gift of time and emotion so the interviewee should be respected for that contribution as well.

Approaches to Interviewing

Four approaches, according to Patton (1980b), may be used in conducting interviews whether they are done one-on-one or in a group situation. The first, *structured close-ended interviews*, has already been discussed in the Chapter 2.5 on developing instruments. In this first approach, an interview schedule is developed ahead of time and the interviewer simply asks the quantitative questions as they appear on the preestablished questionnaire. As indicated previously, telephone interviews typically use this approach where the respondent is provided with a series of close-ended responses from which to choose.

The remaining three basic approaches are open-ended and are used to collect qualitative data. The three approaches require different types of preparation, conceptualization, and instrumentation:

1. the standardized open-ended interview (structured)

2. the general interview guide approach (semi-structured)

3. the informal conversational interview (unstructured)

In the structured approach, the interviewer must follow verbatim what the questions are. The *standardized open-ended* interview consists of a set of questions carefully worded and arranged with the intention of taking each respondent through the same sequence and asking each respondent the same questions in the same way. Flexibility in probing is limited. Sometimes you can only interview each participant once for a limited period of time. The questions are written in advance *exactly* how they are to be asked. Each question is carefully worded with the probing written into the questions. These questions are also asked to try to get as much information as possible. Therefore, wording is often used such as: "Tell me what you think about XYZ" or "What examples show how the recreation leader did a good job?"

The standardized open-ended technique minimizes interviewer effects by asking the same questions. Interviewer judgment does not enter into the interview and data organization is relatively easy to do. Three good reasons to use this approach are:

1. the exact instrument used is available for inspection;

2. variation among interviewers can be minimized; and

3. the interview is highly focused so interviewee time can be carefully used.

In general, this approach minimizes issues of legitimacy and credibility. The weaknesses are that the interviewer is generally not permitted to pursue topics or issues that were not anticipated when the interview schedule was written. Individual differences and circumstances might be reduced using this structured interview.

The semi-structured or *interview guide* approach allows freedom to probe and to ask questions in whatever order seems appropriate. In the general interview guide a set of issues is outlined and explored with each respondent. The questions are prepared to make sure the same information is obtained from a number of people by covering the same material. The issues, however, are not necessarily covered in a particular order and the actual wording of each question is not deter mined ahead of time. The interview guide serves as a basic checklist during the interview. The interviewer must adopt the wording and sequence of questions in the context of the interview.

The interview guide provides topics or subject areas so the interviewer is free to explore, probe, and ask questions that will clarify and illuminate that particular subject. The interviewer can remain free to build a conversation within a particular subject area and to establish a conversational style. The guide allows the interviewer to take as much time as needed to cover all the aspects of the guide. Interviewees can provide more or less detail depending on their interests and the follow-up probes done by the interviewer. Other topics may emerge during the course of the conversation and the interviewer must decide whether or not to pursue those additional ideas. Interview guides are especially useful for focus group interviews. Groups differ from one another and an interview guide enables the interviewer to get participants to talk.

Unstructured approaches are also referred to as *informal conversational* interviews. They have no preestablished questions but result from a conversation. In this informal approach, spontaneous generation in the natural flow of interaction results so the respondent may not realize she or he is being interviewed.

The strength of unstructured interviews is that they allow the interviewer to be highly responsive to individual differences and situational changes. The technique, however, requires a greater amount of time and conversational skill to collect systematic information. The interviewer must be able to interact easily with people in a variety of settings, generate rapid insights, formulate questions quickly and smoothly, and guard against asking questions that impose interpretations on the situation by the structure of the questions. In the unstructured approach, the evaluator gets great quantities of data that will result in much time devoted to data organization and data analysis. Table 2.9 (p. 186) provides a summary of the strengths of these four interview approaches.

Table 2.9 Variations in Interview Approaches (adapted from Patton, 1980b)

Type of Interview Characteristics	Strengths	Weaknesses
1. Closed Quantitative Questions and response categories are determined in advance. Responses are fixed; respondent chooses from among these fixed responses.	Data analysis is simple; responses can be directly compared and easily aggregated; can ask many questions in a short time.	Respondents must fit their experiences and feelings into researcher's categories; may be perceived as impersonal, irrelevant, and mechanistic; limited response choices.
2. Standardized Open-ended The exact wording and sequence of questions are determined in advance. Same basic questions in same order.	Respondents answer the same questions; increased comparability of results. Reduced interviewer effects and bias when several individuals and interviewers are used. Permits decision makers to see and review the instrumentation used in the evaluation. Facilitates organization and analysis of the data.	Little flexibility in relating the interview to particular circumstances; Wording may constrain and limit naturalness and relevance of Q&As.
3. Interview Guide Topics and issues to be covered are specified in advance. Outline form. Interviewer decides sequence and wording of questions in interview. Interview is conversational and situational.	The outline increases the comprehensiveness of the data; systematic data for each respondent. Logical gaps in data can be closed.	Important and salient topics may be omitted. Comparability of responses is reduced.
4. Informal Conversational Questions emerge from the immediate context and are asked in the natural course; no predetermination of question topics or wording.	Increases the salience and relevance of questions the interview is built on and emerge from observations; interview matched to individuals and circumstances.	Different information collected from different people with different questions. Less systematic. Data organization is difficult.

Content of Interviews

Similar to any type of instrument development, one must determine and develop the content of interview questions. You must decide what questions to ask, how to sequence questions, how much detail to solicit, how long to make the interview, and how to word the actual questions. In developing questions for any survey, the evaluator may address the past, present, or future and may ask about behaviors, attitudes, knowledge, feelings, and/or background. Examples of these question types were described in Chapter 2.6.

In conducting structured and semistructured interviews, the sequencing of questions is important although no fixed rules exist. An evaluator usually starts with fairly noncontroversial questions to get the interviewee talking. Asking questions about behaviors, activities, and experiences are usually a good place to begin. Then you can ask about interpretations, opinions, and feelings. Questions about the present are usually easier to answer than questions about the past or the future.

Asking open-ended questions is an art just like asking close-ended questions. You need to make the questions neutral, singular, and clear. Try to avoid "why questions" because they presume a cause-and-effect. Many possibilities are evident in why questions; use words other than why to get at specific philosophical, economic, outcome, or personality factors you wish to explore. Instead of "Why did you join?" you might say: "What is it about the program that attracted you to it?" or "What is it about your personality that attracts you to this activity?" Why questions are often difficult to analyze with any comparability unless they are made more specific.

Collecting qualitative data through personal interviews requires that the interviewer use probes and follow-ups to deepen responses and to get detailed information. As an interviewer you may want to think about probes, such as who, what, where, how and when, as you listen to someone describe their experiences. These follow-up questions can prompt the interviewee to elaborate and give more detail. Such nonverbal signs as head nodding may also elicit more information. Probes and listening responses are seldom written into an interview schedule, but a successful interviewer knows how to use them appropriately.

The general conduct of any individual or group interview will require that both the interviewer and interviewee see themselves engaged in two-way conversation. The interviewee must be willing to talk. The interviewer must ask for the desired information, explain why it is important, and let the interviewee know how the interview is progressing. Further, the interviewer must maintain control of the interview. Encouragement should be given, but you may also want to stop an interviewee if she or he takes an irrelevant tangent. It is disrespectful to let someone go on about something that isn't appropriate for the particular evaluation project or research study. It wastes everybody's time. In qualitative data collection through interviewing, however, you sometimes do not know how relevant someone's tangent might be to better understand a phenomenon.

Setting Up the Interview

Contact should be made with interviewees by mail, e-mail, or phone. The time, place, and other logistics of the interview should also be described and discussed. Usually an in-depth personal interview will take one-half to two hours; a place should be scheduled where privacy is possible. Enough time and the proper place can greatly affect the nature of the interview. Let the interviewee know whether or not the conversation will be taped when you first contact him or her. The evaluator must be clear about the evaluation intentions and assure confidentiality to the respondents. You will probably want to explain the general topics that will be covered in the interview and offer the interviewee an opportunity to receive a copy of the abstract or the final report.

Recording the Data

Recording the data will depend upon the interview approach used. In a close-ended quantitative interview, the interviewer can mark a response sheet much as would be done if a questionnaire were self-administered. For any of the other three approaches, the primary raw data are quotations so the interviewer must try to capture the actual words said. Data interpretation and analysis involve making sense of what people have said, looking for patterns, putting together what is said in one place with what is said in another place, and comparing what different respondents have said. Since this process is necessary for analysis, you must record what is said as fully and fairly as possible during the personal interview.

A tape recorder is indispensable for in-depth personal or group interviewing. The use of tape recordings frees the interviewer to concentrate on interviewing, improves the fullness and quality of responses, avoids interviewer selective listening bias, and allows the evaluator to check up on an interviewer's technique. Most research suggests that tape recording does not increase resistance, decrease rapport, or alter people's responses (Weiss, 1975). If a tape recorder cannot be used to get verbatim responses, then the interviewer must take thorough notes. Taking verbatim notes is extremely difficult. Not only does the tape recorder increase accuracy, but it also allows the interviewer to give the interviewee full attention during the interview.

When using a tape recorder, the interviewee must know why it is being used and how the tapes will be handled. Further, the interviewer ought to jot notes in case of a mechanical problem; these notes will also help to supplement the transcription. Notes help formulate new questions and help organize information on the tape. In tape recording, use high-quality tapes, lapel mikes (if possible), and always carry a back-up tape recorder. You may want to make a back-up tape if you will not get a chance to transcribe a tape immediately. Be sure to label the tapes and protect them so that they do not become damaged. Remember, when using qualitative data, the words are the data and you do not want to lose any of them. If you lose your data, you have no evaluation or research project.

Making a full transcription of all tape-recorded interviews as soon as possible after an interview is highly desirable. Transcribing tapes, however, is time-consuming. The ratio of transcribing to tape time is 5:1. It takes at least five hours to transcribe one hour of tape. Transcribing can be costly as well, but you must consider its usefulness and how the benefits may outweigh the costs. If resources are not available for transcribing, you can work back-and-forth between tape and notes, although in the long run this working back-and-forth may be more time-consuming than doing the transcribing.

Notes-on-Notes

As soon as an interview is complete, it is important that you make notes about the interview. List proper names and any unfamiliar terminology that may have been encountered; make notes about anything observed that had relevance to the interview like where the interview occurred, who was present, how the interviewee reacted, observations about the interviewer's role, and any additional information that might be important. You should also make notes-on-notes about how you felt the interview went. To do a good job of personal or group interviewing, you should spend time after the interview going over and reflecting on what occurred.

Depending upon the nature of the interview, particularly if it is qualitative, you may want to follow-up for a second interview with an individual. Therefore, you will want to keep in touch with the people initially interviewed through a thank-you note or some communication. When you do the initial interview, you may want to see if that person would be willing to do a second interview if needed.

Training and Supervising Interviewers

The comments in the first part of this chapter have assumed that the evaluator will be conducting the interview. You or other staff may be able to conduct interviews, and sometimes interviews ought to be done by outside (volunteer or paid) people. Often organization staffs are too busy to do data collection. On the other hand, they know the participants well, and sometimes you have no choice but to use them due to financial constraints. Hiring interviewers is costly and time-consuming, but may be a viable option if staff is not available.

Regardless of who does the interviews, they must have some training. Hiring or using interviewers who have experience is best, but experienced interviewers may not be easy to find. If experienced interviewers cannot be hired, extensive training must be conducted. In hiring or choosing interviewers, sometimes peoples' attitudes may make a greater difference than their actual skills. Middle-age women are often the least threatening to interviewees and it is often useful to try to match race if possible. The research on race matching as well as sex and age, however, has been inconsistent. Indigenous interviewers may be good in establishing rapport, but may not always have the best interview skills unless they have extensive training.

The purpose of training is two-fold: to explain the details and objectives of the study and to familiarize individuals with the interview schedule and allow them to practice. Several key ideas might be emphasized in interviewer training. First the interviewer must learn to recognize and control any subtle or pervasive bias and become as neutral as possible. The interviewer should be told to always carry identification about the project so that any safety concerns on the part of interviewees can be allayed. The interviewer should not dress to any extreme (rich or poor) but should look neat, conservative, and casual. The interviewer should show interest and concern without seeming to spy on respondents. In general, however, the interviewer is only as good as the training she or he gets.

Problems Associated with Interviewing

In conducting interviews, certain problems may be encountered. One problem relates to the influence of social desirability on validity. For example, people will often overreport participation because they think they should. Income is the exception to desirability; people often underreport it. To avoid issues of social desirability, the interviewer should show complete acceptance of answers and reassure the interviewee that answers are confidential.

Providing opportunities to explain rather than just answer yes/no may also encourage a respondent to answer honestly. An individual is more likely to give an honest answer if she or he understands the questions being asked. The language used in any personal interview must also be considered. A respondent has the opportunity to ask for clarification if she or he doesn't understand a question, but using the wrong language or unknown jargon may result in problems in communication. People are sometimes reluctant to admit they don't understand. In interviewing we must also be concerned with different cultural perspectives. As interviewers we must recognize that language and speech patterns may result in data different than initially expected. Being able to understand leisure interests and behavior through different cultural experiences, however, may be an essential value of using in-depth interviews in evaluation.

Some controversy surrounds the paying of respondents or offering them other types of incentives. On the positive side, some evaluators say the answers are better, the interview is put in a commercial light, and the payment or valued incentive reflects the value of the time and energy spent giving information. Those who are against paying respondents say that it increases the cost of a project. Further, respondents may come to expect to be paid and a bad precedent may be set for other evaluators or researchers. Other opponents feel paying respondents may affect the validity because people will respond in more socially desirable ways. Many times evaluators do not have money available to paid interviewees, so payment is not an issue. Other times it may be a possibility to consider.

Interviewing is not always done with individuals who are educated, middle-class, and articulate. To get information about a diversity of people who may want or use recreation services, a variety of people ought to be interviewed. Malik, Ashton-Shaeffer, and Kleiber (1991) have described some of the aspects to consider in interviewing people with mental retardation, for example. They believe interviewing can be successful and helpful because it deobjectifies a person and allows the evaluator to get more information that couldn't be obtained some other way. Designing questions so that the individuals with mental retardation have the ability to understand and can accurately convey facts and opinions are important. They suggest that considering the time, place, length of interview, and interviewer rapport can enhance an interview session. An interview should be conducted where the fewest distractions exist; usually 30 minutes is an appropriate length of time. For many people with mental retardation, yes/no and either/or questions are easiest to answer.

Every evaluator should seek to minimize the degree of interview error in the evaluation project. Because of authority relationships, direction of desirability of response, and the nature of the subject matter, response accuracy is always suspect. Interview error may occur due to the predisposition of respondents such as whether they are suspicious, hostile, indifferent, unmotivated, lacking information, lacking insight, or have limited language. Error may also be due to the predispositions of the interviewer who may be uncomfortable with the people interviewed, shy, ill at ease, unable to establish rapport, lacking in an understanding of the language, or who may have stereotyped expectations. The procedures of the project are, however, under the evaluator's control and the evaluator must try to reduce as much error as possible

Specific Examples

Not only do leisure service professionals use interviews of the general public or participants such as through community needs assessments or formative evaluations, but there also may be some special clinical applications of interviews. Ferguson (1983), for example, has described the components of a Therapeutic Recreation Assessment interview technique. The purpose of the assessment interview is to gather information for inferring the leisure needs of the client. An interview usually involves assessing client readiness for treatment, assessing client rationality and appropriateness, identifying leisure behavior patterns, gaining insight into personal leisure values, determining relationships between client and family, ascertaining personal strengths and assets of the client, determining needed lifestyle adjustments, analyzing available leisure systems, and examining economic factors.

Clinical interviewing techniques are not the focus of this book, but they relate to evaluation interviewing in general. Clinical techniques apply to any interview session, but they are particularly useful for purposes of the assessment interview. Ferguson (1983) suggested it is best to use open-ended and not yes/no questions, make questions short and specific, don't use "why" (i.e., use "how" instead because it is less threatening), ask one question at a time, give the client time to think, ask questions that address the purpose of assessment, show empathy, use client's first name, and clarify mixed messages. This advice is good as a summary for *any* interview situation.

Staff performance appraisals are another example of regular interviews conducted each year. A supervisor can apply the principles of interviewing as she or he interacts with an employee by establishing rapport and communicating in a two-way conversation.

Group Interviews

Leisure service professionals may want to consider the use of meetings or group gatherings to collect data from individuals. Ewert (1990) suggested the possibilities of decision making through public participation by using open public meetings, meetings for specific users, advisory committees, and focus groups. According to Krueger (1988), a focus group includes people who possess certain characteristics and who provide qualitative data through a focused discussion. Focus group interviews are used more frequently today than ever before and offer possibilities for evaluators to consider. The value of group interviews lies in the ability to stimulate new ideas among participants by allowing spontaneity and candor.

Group interviews with five to ten respondents can often save time and money. In a group interview, interviewees can direct thoughts to each other and not just the interviewer. The evaluator can also directly observe group process. The group interview can serve as a useful scouting device for other situations and is especially good for groups who have some common denominator, such as people who live in the same geographic location or who share the same activity interest. Another use of a group interview is to test an evaluator's interpretation of evaluation findings from a survey or to establish the questions to be asked for a more quantitatively oriented questionnaire.

In conducting a focus group interview, the evaluator will first need to arrange to get people to attend a gathering. Sometimes a group already exists that can be used; at other times you may need to form and assemble a group. Focus groups run by commercial organizations sometimes provide a complimentary meal and may offer a stipend for being involved, but a monetary incentive is not always the case. Individuals need to know in advance the purpose of the group interview and the parameters including time commitment, remuneration, or whatever compensation will be given. As the evaluation planner, you will need to make a list of the administrative and logistic aspects necessary to conduct the group interviews or focus group.

In preparing for group interviews, the purpose of the forum/meeting (also known as the *criteria*) should be clearly established. Based on the purpose, an agenda will be developed. Focus groups might be pilot tested just like questionnaires, although pilot test data might be part of the data collected since each focus group is done slightly different. Prepare the questions to ask just as you would any guided or standardized interview schedule. As is true in any aspect of interviewing, quality answers are directly related to quality questions. These questions are similar to a structured open-ended interview in that they should be carefully prepared, presented within a context, and logically focused. Everyone should have consistent and sufficient background information. You also will need to have the session videotaped or audiotaped, and will need to make plans for transcribing and analyzing the data.

In conducting the focus group interview, Krueger (1988) suggested that the interviewer must hone her or his moderating skills. The interviewer must be familiar with group process as well as with the topic that is being examined. It is often best to have two moderators so one person can direct the conversation while the second person takes notes and handles logistical issues. Having nametags or name cards is useful if a group does not know one another. The beginning of the focus group is crucial, as the right amount of formality and informality must be established. The introduction might consist of a welcome, an overview of the topic, and a brief discussion of the ground rules. Ground rules might include such aspects as speaking one at a time, guaranteeing confidentiality, asking for negative as well as positive comments, and a statement about whether and when breaks will be taken. The first question is usually something that will help the group get acquainted. During the focus group, the interviewer will want to make sure the conversation flows and everyone gets involved. She or he should use pauses and probes. At the end of the focus group, the interviewer should thank the participants and summarize briefly what the main points were that emerged during the discussion to assure that they are accurate.

Another variation of a group interview used in leisure services is community forums. Citizen advisory groups can reflect the interests of the community for needs assessments and evaluation. Public meetings and workshops can be used to solicit citizen input, facilitate a two-way dialogue, and share ideas and emotions. Workshops can get people into small groups to identify needs. In these situations, people come together to address particular issues that may reflect assessment, formative, or summative evaluation. The participants in community forums are often self-selected rather than chosen, which could indicate some sampling biases. The disadvantage to community forums is that these meetings may not represent the entire community. An evaluator must be careful in drawing broad conclusions from only specific individuals. The advantages of community forums are, however, the open access, low cost, and good ideas that may be generated. In these forums, audiotape or videotape recordings may not be used. Extensive notes taken by several people often provide the best type of data. These data will need to be qualitatively analyzed just as data are from other individual and group interviews.

From Ideas to Reality

Many options exist for doing face-to-face interviewing. Individual and group interviews are useful as a way to get into "people's heads." To use interviews effectively, you must appreciate their value and train people adequately in how they can best be used. We have found interviewing to be an interesting and useful way to conduct evaluation and research projects. You may not feel the same way but we encourage you to try interviewing if it seems appropriate for the evaluation or research project that you want to undertake. Focus groups appear to be offering great possibilities for recreation evaluation and research.

Now that you have studied this chapter, you should be able to:

- Identify the four approaches that can be used to organize interviews.
- Develop an interview schedule using one of the four approaches, including the determination of question content, sequencing, and possible follow-ups and probes.
- Conduct a meeting to train interviewers about the skills that they will need to be effective as interviewers.
- Design a project that could make use of focus group interviews.
- Identify possible problems that might occur when using interviewing methods.
- Implement a procedure for collecting interview data.

Observations
"On a Clear Day You Can See Forever"

Observation methods are available to leisure service professionals for evaluation and research projects, although they are not used as frequently as surveys. Evaluation by judgment through accreditation and standards programs, and checklists such as maintenance checklists are common examples of observations. Researchers can also use observation. For this chapter, we examine observations by addressing checklists, professional judgments, and fieldwork or participant observation. All methods share a commonality in using observational techniques, although they may be applied differently.

Becoming a good observer requires practice. Many of us take observation for granted or do not realize the extent to which we have learned to be selective in what we observe. To be a good evaluator, one has to watch, listen, concentrate, and interpret data apart from gathering it. Just as most of us were not blessed inherently with the ability to do math without being taught and given chances to practice our mathematical and analytical abilities, evaluators have to learn observational techniques and practice them to become good.

Roles of Observers

The most common roles of observation include a range from outside observer to full participant. The roles can also range from unknown to known. Figure 2.10(1) (p. 198) illustrates these continua. Depending upon the placement on each continuum, the evaluation outcomes may be influenced.

A nonreactive or outside observer might remove herself or himself completely from involvement with the group observed. An example of nonreactive observation might be someone analyzing the way the leisure behavior of women is portrayed on television by watching the shows or viewing videotapes of television programs. Outside observers usually try to be as invisible as possible and seek to elicit very little reaction to the

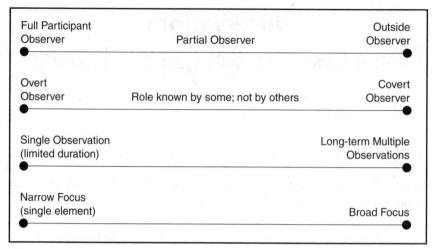

Figure 2.10(1) Dimensions of Approaches to Observation

evaluator from the individuals being observed. The full participant or participant observer, on the other hand, is completely involved in an activity, and observing is not her or his only role. A danger with the participant observer role is the possibility of becoming highly involved as a participant and losing objectivity or losing concentration on the events occurring. As indicated, it is also possible to be a partial observer, which would combine aspects of full participant and outside observer roles.

An unknown (covert) observer is not identifiable by the participants whereas the known (overt) observer has identified her or his role. The covert observer becomes a group member and, in essence, is posing as an "undercover agent." The overt observer is an outsider who makes her or his intentions clear. The known evaluator does not try to pass as anything but identified and recognized. Being in a situation where some participants know they are being observed and others do not is also possible within these continua.

Similarly, the role of the observer may range from single observations to long-term multiple observations and from a narrow focus to broad foci (Patton, 1980b). If a goal-attainment model is being used for evaluation and the data being collected are quantitative, a single selected observation using a narrow focus may be appropriate. On the other hand, if the goal-free model is being used and the researcher is not sure what may result from an observation, long-term multiple observations may be used with an initial broad focus. These observations may become narrower as time progresses. As on any continua, variations of these ranges may exist depending upon the particular evaluation criteria being measured.

No one observation role is best. Each role has value in certain situations. The evaluator or researcher may want to keep in mind the possible ethical problems discussed in Chapter 1.11 that addressed covert observation including invasion of privacy and what may happen to the evaluation project if one is "found out." Therefore, different situations with specific evaluation criteria will require both ethical and methodological considerations.

Regardless of the roles played by observers, the basic procedure followed in any observation is the following:

1. Choose a behavior or situation to observe

2. Decide on mode for recording observations and collecting data (quantitative or qualitative)

3. Determine sampling strategies

4. Train observers or practice in the situation

5. Analyze data

6. Evaluate observation instrument

Quantitative Observations

Many therapeutic recreation professionals believe that systematic observation instruments are needed to reliably assess behaviors (Stumbo, 1983). The systematic observations usually include a checklist or a standardized form with units of analysis identified. The more structured an observation, the more likely analysis will involve scoring and statistical analysis (Denzin, 1978).

The most common quantitative observations use checklists and similar recording scales. These checklists are measurement instruments that the evaluator completes, not the person(s) being evaluated. Evaluators using checklists assume that a priori (i.e., before the observation) factors can be identified. The design of these instruments, thus, must follow the same design principles as addressed previously when we talked about developing questionnaire instruments. The criteria measured must be determined followed by the development of measurement scales.

Checklists are a technique for recording whether a characteristic is present or absent and/or whether an action is taken or not. Often a yes/no response is used, but several checklist formats might be considered. Rating scales are used to indicate the degree of a characteristic or action. Other similar methods include frequency counts, ranking scales, and duration recordings. These techniques may be useful, for example, in observing activities done during recreation instruction, in therapeutic recreation settings, or for the recording of specific behaviors in the outdoors.

Just as one may ask questions about a number of aspects of people's lives, you can also observe many aspects of their lives. Several possibilities might be considered for quantitative observations. You might measure the affective or emotional component of what people do. How many times did they smile or act out? The cognitive observations examine intellectual components and thought processes. How does an individual work through a situation? Procedures and routines might be observed. For example, you might observe in what ways a lifeguard describes and enforces the safety rules at a pool. Often in recreation settings we observe physical environments such as space and equipment. For example, we do playground inspections or adventure course equipment inspections. Psychomotor aspects might be observed such as posture, position in relation to others, types of movement, and facial expressions. Sociological structure relates to who is talking to whom, the roles that people take on in a group, and the numbers and types of people interacting. Finally, we might observe the activities in which people are engaged.

Different coding units are also used in observation. Sometimes you will simply be counting and will use frequencies or percentages. Other times you will be using rating systems that are predetermined and defined. These systems might be scales that determine amounts or judgments of quality such as poor, fair, good or hierarchical ratings such as not at all, seldom, occasionally, constantly. No matter what unit, you must clearly define what each of these words mean if they are used in a checklist system.

Strategies to Obtain Quantitative Observation Information

Several checklist strategies may be used to obtain quantitative observational material. The first is *interval sampling* whereby a series of brief intervals are observed and the evaluator notes what was observed. The interval sampling may be systematic as in doing a recorded safety check of a swimming pool, based on a preestablished list of criteria, every day or may be used as a running account of what happened sequentially during a prescribed period of time. The running account might be a rough estimate of frequency and duration. In interval sampling, the evaluator records for a brief period of time some particular task—like when a child plays with a particular toy. Both the relative frequency and the duration of behavior are reported. The rate of behavior needs to be low enough to count, and you need to be able to determine the size of intervals and mark whether a behavior occurs.

A second strategy uses *frequency counts, event recordings,* or *tally methods.* The frequencies are converted to percentages. In this strategy, one counts the number of discrete events of a certain class of behavior as they transpire during a given time (e.g., minute, hour, day, week). The behavior needs to be clearly defined. This strategy is useful when determining behaviors or seeing what more than one individual is doing. An example includes counting the number of complete and incomplete tasks performed by a client in a therapeutic recreation program. You also might record the number of times a behavior is done appropriately or inappropriately. Frequency counts are relatively easy to do. In some situations, you could use a wrist golf-stroke counter or grocery store counter to keep track of how many times a particular behavior is happening or you could put tally marks on a paper.

Observing duration is another quantitative observation strategy. *Duration* refers to the length of time spent in a particular behavior or how long a behavior occurs. As in other situations, the behavior must be readily observable. The duration is then converted into percentages. For example one might determine the popularity of a piece of playground equipment by how long children use it. A stopwatch or other timing device would need to be used in this observation. This strategy is time-consuming and one needs to pay constant attention.

A related strategy is *latency recording* where the time elapsed between a cue and the response is measured. For example, one might measure the time between telling a child to put away toys and when she or he actually begins the process. A stopwatch is used in measuring latency time.

Checklists might also be done using a *rating system.* For example, if we were observing an instructor in a swimming class, we might have a list of criteria that we would indicate whether the individual had performed in an excellent, very good, average, fair, or poor way. In using any type of rating system, the meanings of the words such as "excellent" or "poor" must be clearly defined so that reliability exists in the ratings. Checklists are a common system used in personnel management.

Time sampling or *spot-checking* involves recording behavior at a particular point in time. In this strategy, the observation occurs periodically at predetermined time intervals. The evaluator specifies in advance the timing, number of observations, and type of observation within a particular context. These observations are usually done in equal intervals with a recording of the number of times something occurs. This spot-checking may include ascertaining the total number of participants using a picnic area at different times of the week, for example. You could not observe picnicking all the time, but a systematic time sampling could give you valuable information.

Quantitative Observation Tips

For sophisticated quantitative observation systems, rigorous training periods for observers are needed. Observation systems with few categories require less training, are easy to learn, and result in greater interobserver reliability. Most quantitative observation systems used in leisure services fall between these two extremes.

The evaluator or researcher needs to be concerned about several aspects of doing observations or in supervising others who may be doing quantitative observations. First, behaviors to be observed must be defined carefully. Since few standardized procedures exist for observations, the evaluator will often need to develop the measurement instruments carefully and pilot test them in the situation where they will be used. Second, the interaction between the observer and the participants must be noted. Are there any reactive effects? How did behavior change because of the observer? Did the observer impose consciously or unconsciously any of her or his biases on the events so the meaning became different? Were any self-fulfilling prophecies coming true? Did the observer overidentify with the participants or a faction of them? Third, reliable measures are needed. Thus, the observer will need to be sufficiently trained, use an instrument with clearly defined and nonoverlapping categories, and use a small manageable number of categories that can be sufficiently observed.

Interobserver reliability is also a concern. Do all observers see the same things? If observations are to be useful, they must be reliable. The formula for reliability is number of agreements (between two observers) divided by number of observations (including agreements and disagreements) multiplied by 100, which equals the percentage of agreement:

$$\frac{\text{Agreements}}{\text{Observations}} \times 100 = \% \text{ of Agreements} \qquad \textbf{Interobserver Reliability}$$

For example if two observers agreed on 24 items and disagreed on five, we would divide 24 by 29, then multiply by 100 giving a result of 83%. This result should be as close to 100% as possible. Observers should be trained until they can reach a high agreement—defined as anything over 90%.

Professional Judgment

Professional judgment is the direct observation and evaluation by an expert or someone familiar with a particular program. Professional judgments are based on intuitively evaluating the quality of something based on formal and/or informal criteria.

Some evaluation procedures use professional judgment in conjunction with preestablished criteria. In other cases, experts may be invited into a situation to observe and use their expertise as the criteria. The advantages of using professional judgment observations are the ease of implementation and immediacy of judgment. Precautions are urged, however, when having outsiders rather than staff evaluate a program. A value exists in having several judges, making sure the professionals clearly understand the criteria, and providing some training about the factors to consider and their relative importance for a particular situation (Weiss, 1972).

The accreditation processes used in various areas of recreation are examples of professional judgment observation. In cases of accreditation, certain standards are established ahead of time and are then observed. The experts answer questions or write a report concerning their responses.

In therapeutic recreation, a peer program review process has been used successfully in some organizations (Coyne & Turpel, 1984). The peer program review is a method of program evaluation that utilizes established professional standards. The process facilitates making these standards a pattern of practice. Two techniques encouraged within this system are program observation and case review. Therapeutic recreation practitioners who ask peers to observe and evaluate what they are doing initiate the process. In addition, within other therapeutic recreation agencies, professional judgments are made in the form of internal service audits that give therapeutic recreation specialists information about how their record keeping is done.

Staff/personnel reviews are further examples of professional judgment. In performance appraisals or staff reviews, the supervisor is the professional judge. Other data besides the supervisor's expertise may be collected, but frequently it is up to the supervisor to take all input and use her or his professional judgment to make an evaluation. This process of staff evaluation works best when clear performance criteria have been set through the job description, the supervisor knows the organization well, and when the supervisor's personal biases do not enter into the evaluation.

Qualitative Observations

Advantages exist in using qualitative observations, also referred to as *field observations*. These techniques may be used to collect anecdotal material and critical incidents that may not be recorded elsewhere. They might also be done when an individual is a participant observer. They are in-depth and the evaluator is able to examine the background and meanings of what may be happening in a program or organization. Flexibility exists regarding what to observe and what data to collect.

Qualitative observations are only unscientific when improper techniques are used. All of us are involved in observational activities in our lives, but qualitative observations must be systematically collected and analyzed. Observation techniques are a highly valid and reliable form of data collection. To do qualitative observations, however, requires a highly trained individual or group of individuals that will expend much time and energy in field observations.

Doing qualitative observations is time-consuming any may introduce bias. Including quantitative observations along with using multiple observers, however, can reduce this bias. A further disadvantage may be that single conclusions should not be drawn, but multiple explanations, conclusions, and descriptions for a phenomenon are usually the result of qualitative observations.

Qualitative observations may be done in two ways. One method is to keep an account of anecdotal records and critical incidents. *Anecdotal records* are factual descriptions of meaningful incidents and events and/or detailed accounts or running logs, often referred to as progress notes. To use these for evaluation, the interpretation is kept separate from factual description. *Critical incidents* refer to unusual situations that occur that are recorded and described in detail. In analyzing critical incidents, one also attempts to describe the antecedents, behaviors, and consequences.

Field observations occur when the evaluator goes into a "natural" or "normal" situation, such as a playground or a staff meeting, to serve as a participant observer. Data are recorded in the form of field notes and conclusions are then drawn about what is occurring based on volumes of descriptive notes. The process of field observation involves defining the purpose, populations, samples, and units of analysis to be included, just as is true with any other method of evaluation. The data are analyzed to draw conclusions. The field observation techniques often are combined with other techniques such as interviews, case studies, or document analyses.

Prior to beginning a field observation project, the evaluator would need to become acquainted with the site or program, assume a role as known or unknown, and prepare an initial broad focus checklist of things to observe. As you begin to collect data through taking extensive notes, themes will develop. In the interpretation process, these themes will be tested, refined, reinterpreted, expanded, and discarded, and new data will be observed until final conclusions have been reached. This process will be discussed in more detail in Unit Three.

Notetaking

Data are collected in field observations by recording information through notetaking by the evaluator(s). The evaluator is, thus, the data collection instrument. Since the notes are the data, they are central to qualitative observations. Even in a complete participant role, the evaluator must write down notes as often and as completely as possible. The less time between an observation and recording it through notes, the more accurate the data will be. The notes are taken within the context of what is observed and will depend upon the criteria being evaluated. Often information like weather, the people present, your mental state, start and finish, location, changes in environment, and formal roles observed are important to note.

The field observer should be careful to separate facts from interpretation when taking notes. The observer should be particularly careful to identify whether the idea recorded is a fact, quote, or interpretation. The evaluator as observer must indicate what she or he knew happened as well as what she or he thought happened. Just as you cannot observe everything, you cannot record everything, so the evaluator must practice recording the most important observations. Table 2.10(2) (p. 206) shows an example of notetaking. In addition, Henderson (1991) offered several considerations in notetaking:

- Record your notes as soon as possible after making your observation.

- Write, type, or word process the notes in detail. The notes should include a running description of events, people, things heard and overheard, conversations among people, conversations with people, and incidents that occur.

- Make copies of the notes as soon as possible. If something happens to your notes, you have lost your data.

- Indicate on the notes whose language was being used. Who exactly said what? Did you? Did someone else? Include verbatim quotes, if appropriate, and always use concrete description with specific detail.

Table 2.10(2) Sample Notes from Observations of Leisure Education Class

Facts	Interpretations
March 25, 1991 The CTRS meets with Richard in the 7th class meeting: CTRS is slouched in the chair at the table with her arms folded across her chest waiting. Richard walks up, smiles and fumbles as he pulls the chair out to sit down. He sits forward in the seat with his hands holding up his head. CTRS continues to look at him as he wiggles in the chair. She begins with "How are you?" He mumbles, "Fine." She says, "You look a little tired." He shrugs his shoulders. She waits a moment and then begins. She is still sitting with her arms crossed. "What did you do this weekend?" "Nothing," Richard replies. Silence for about five seconds. "Were you bored?" she asks. He shrugs his shoulders again. The CTRS pauses and then points to the decision-making board that has four words written on it: GOAL, OPTIONS, IF/THEN, DECISION. She says, "We are going to talk more about these today. Let's try to talk about leisure. What is your goal for leisure?"	Instructor looks tired Both look tired I wonder if people know when they are bored I'm not sure what she is asking

- Leave wide margins on the notepaper so you can write ideas in or note additional interpretations if they occur to you. Start new paragraphs often so the note sheets can be easily read.

- The length of field notes will differ considerably. A rule of thumb might be several single-spaced pages for each hour of observation.

- It is possible to talk your field notes into a tape recorder and then have someone else transcribe them. If this seems appropriate, the evaluator will need to review the transcriptions as soon as possible.

- Do not be afraid to record notes about what you do not understand. Something may not make sense at one time, but it will possibly become clearer later. Record your notes at will and do not be afraid of making mistakes.

- Continually monitor yourself as a data gatherer. Tiredness, emotional reactions, relationship with others, energy level, use of discrete observations, and technical problems may all affect the data collection and these manifestations should be noted.

- The length of time spent in notetaking will depend on the evaluation questions being asked.

- And finally, remember, "If it is not written down, it never happened" (Taylor & Bogdan, 1984, p. 52).

Tips on Qualitative Observation

In observation, the evaluator must be a reliable and valid measurer. As an effective observer, you must be trained to notice events and actions that are relevant to your perceptions as well as those that contradict your perceptions. Field observations take enormous amounts of energy to look beyond your ordinary day-to-day observations to apply the rigor of scientific evaluation and interpretation.

Part of good observation is learning what to observe. Everything cannot be observed, and even if you could, total sensory overload would occur. Therefore, observation becomes more focused as the evaluator continues with her or his work on a particular evaluation or research project. Ultimately, the observations should result in a written report that will allow the reader to actually enter the situation and understand what was happening based on detailed descriptions of the observer.

At the observation site, it will be necessary to establish a role. You may choose to be a full participant, an outside observer, or something in between such as a staff member or a volunteer. The role may affect your ability to gain acceptance within a group so the role should be carefully chosen. In some cases, you may be a staff member already who wants to use field observations to collect evaluation data. It is possible for you to adopt this observer role, but you must be aware of the possible biases that you bring to the situation. No matter what role is used, as an observer one must be explicitly aware of the situation being observed, use a wide-angle lens, take the insider/outsider perspective, be introspective yourself, and keep good notes of both your objective and subjective feelings.

Establishing rapport in the field site will be an important early aspect of the field research. Taylor and Bogdan (1984) offered several tips for establishing social interaction including:

- remaining passive in the first few days,

- putting people at ease however you can such as doing favors or helping out,

- collecting data as secondary to getting to know people,

- acting naive,

- paying attention to people's routines,
- explaining who you are,
- explaining what will be done with the data,
- trying to figure out what being at the right place at the right time means,
- beginning with small amounts of time and then increasing the time at the site, and
- keeping your overt note-taking to a minimum initially and adjusting to more visible notetaking as you and the participants feel comfortable later.

Above all, the field observer doing an evaluation should act interested and the people being observed will see that she or he is serious about them and the project being undertaken.

Qualitative observation is an ongoing process of data collection and analysis. An evaluator may begin a project with some general criteria in mind, but these criteria may change and become redefined as you observe and interact with people. In other words, you will develop new insights and new ways of obtaining information as you discover new data. The qualitative observation process is one that will evolve over time. In addition, your skills as an observer will improve over a period of time.

Field evaluation requires a high level of concentration to pay attention to what is happening. If the evaluator cannot take notes immediately, concentration is required to imprint the notes in mental photography. The observer must look for key words in people's remarks, concentrate on the first and last remarks of each conversation because those are generally the most important, and be able to play back the observation or conversation easily in the mind.

A final, but not unimportant, aspect of field evaluation research is the utilization of key informants. Respondents are people you observe or who answer questions with no particular rapport having been established. Key informants, on the other hand, are people who provide more in-depth information about what is occurring because the evaluator has established trust with them. This information is data that must be recorded in the form of notes similar to the notes that might be collected during an interview. Information is usually obtained from key informants by either formal or informal interviews. One way to regard these informants is as "evaluation collaborators." The value of key informants is in helping the evaluator ascertain if people "say what they mean and mean what they say." Some

informants may have general information about the past and their perceptions of the present, others may be representative of a group of people,
and others may serve as observers when you are not there to observe in
person. Relationships with key informants will help the evaluator develop
a deeper understanding of the setting being evaluated.

Sometimes observers will run into hostile respondents. You need to be
friendly, but not pushy. You may want to employ some additional investigative skills to determine why the lack of cooperation is occurring. The
data collector will often have to talk to people that she or he dislikes or
distrusts. For an effective evaluation or research project to be conducted,
you must observe and talk to all types of people within the setting, and
not just to the people that you like or that are friendly.

From Ideas to Reality

In all cases, someone using observations is looking for accurate, reliable, valid data. A reliable observation is one that is not biased by idiosyncrasies of the observer, the subject, or constraints of time and place. These observations may be quantitative or qualitative depending on the preexisting knowledge, expertise, and resources of the evaluator or researcher. Observations are not always the easiest methods to use, but they can provide information that will be helpful in determining what is actually happening in a particular situation.

Now that you have studied this chapter, you should be able to:

- Describe the differences between qualitative and quantitative observations.
- Choose the appropriate roles that an observer will take given a particular project.
- Develop a quantitative checklist using two or more of the strategies described.
- Explain to an administrator the value of using professional judgments as a means for evaluation within an organization.
- Take descriptive notes within a field observation setting.
- Critique whether a field observation project has been undertaken appropriately.

Unobtrusive Methods

A number of years ago, Webb, Campbell, Schwartz, and Sechrest (1966) suggested that maybe too much emphasis has been placed on survey methods such as interviews and questionnaires. That observation is still true today. Perhaps evaluators and researchers ought to consider methods that may not be as obtrusive or that may not infringe on people's time and privacy. Unobtrusive methods may complement methodological weaknesses in surveys, such as people's socially desirable responses and the tendency to survey people who are accessible, cooperative, literate, and verbose.

Unobtrusive, sometimes called *nonreactive*, methods refer to observing, recording, and analyzing human behavior in a situation where interaction with people generally does not occur and people are unaware that their behavior is being observed. Some aspects of observations and unobtrusive methods may overlap, but they are different methods. Unobtrusive methods do not require the cooperation of individuals as is generally needed in some way with quantitative or qualitative observations. Unobtrusive measures are often used to provide supplementary data for evaluation projects or they may be used on their own. As in other methods, either quantitative or qualitative data may be collected.

These unobtrusive methods are sometimes called *odd ball* because they are unlike what is done in traditional evaluation and research projects. Their value lies in being able to address some criteria that one could not easily measure by asking or observing people directly. These methods counter the notion of dependence on language for obtaining information.

In unobtrusive methods, the anonymity of people is almost certain. Usually some activity such as watching the behavior of individuals in a public park or tracing activity such as by counting the types of vandalism that occur in a park, is observed. The data generally consist of physical evidence, archives, or unobtrusive and covert observations. The unobtrusive measures may be systematically identified and analyzed in an evaluation project or they may be found accidentally when other survey or observation data are being collected. Examples of unobtrusive measures that may be used to obtain data about people's behavior include observations of body language and other nonverbal behavior, short cuts or worn grass in a park indicating where people walk most frequently, types of graffiti and where it is likely to be found, noting the stations that car radios are tuned to in a parking lot to ascertain station popularity, the number of beer and soda cans in household garbage, litter frequency and type along a highway, and rental records for a business.

Sometimes these unobtrusive methods require detective-like tactics. Similarly, they offer clues to what people are doing. Some of the strengths of unobtrusive methods are the face validity, the simplicity and directness, the inconspicuous and noninterventional nature, the nonreactivity, the easy combination with other methods, the stability over time, and the independence from language (Guba & Lincoln, 1981). In evaluations of policies and administrative procedures, for example, evaluators may rely solely on records and archives.

Problems exist in using unobtrusive methods, however, because they are heavily inferential, information often comes in bits and pieces, and the situations cannot be easily controlled. Unobtrusive methods alone do not tell how people see and experience their activities. Additionally, if subjects are aware in some way that they are being observed, their actions may be distorted and confounded. Hardware such as hidden cameras, gauges, and one-way mirrors may be used for data collection although some ethical problems exist in using these devices if people can be identified and their privacy is invaded. Further, unobtrusive studies may also have associated biases unless appropriate random sampling procedures are used.

The three ways to collect data unobtrusively include physical evidence, archives, and covert observation. Each will be discussed and applied to evaluation in leisure services.

Physical Evidence

Physical evidence, or traces from past behavior, is one way to do unobtrusive evaluations. These data may be collected quantitatively or qualitatively. For example, physical evidence might include the wear on vinyl tiles in a museum as a measure of the popularity of certain exhibits (e.g., measured quantitatively in millimeters of wear or qualitatively in terms of visual scuffing). Another example would be to measure and categorize the food that is thrown away at camp to determine popularity of certain food items (e.g., tally the most common items by using a checklist). Although the number and types of books checked out (quantitative data) of a library would be an example of archival document data, the wear and tear on the books to show what was actually read would be an example of a qualitative assessment of physical evidence. One could put a "Cal-trac device" or a pedometer on an individual to measure activity level and calorie expenditure as another example of quantitative physical evidence data.

The advantage of physical evidence data is the lack of conspicuousness. A major drawback to the method, however, is that one gets little information about the nature of the population that is doing whatever is being measured. For this reason, physical evidence *alone* is not necessarily the best method to use for evaluation. It may be useful as data in combination with other evaluation methods.

Archives

Archives include written materials that can provide a past or present historical perspective for the review of patterns. Documents and records are often used to supply data for content analysis. Records are used to keep track of events and serve as official chronicles. They are generally used for trend analysis and integration. Examples of records might be sales records (quantitative data) or minutes of a meeting (qualitative data). Documents may be personal, institutional, or public, and often provide a historical context for an evaluation project. These documents may be letters and diaries, brochures, or newspaper articles. They may be running records or may be episodic. If the data are portrayed as numbers, they are generally considered quantitative and can be organized in that manner with statistical analyses. If the data are in the form of words such as copies of past brochures, the data will need to be analyzed qualitatively if one is interested in determining changes or trends.

Archives are generally inexpensive to access, easy to sample, and provide specific population restrictions. A great advantage in using archives is cost savings because data collection is not needed. Sometimes it is difficult, however, for external evaluators to get access to some types of records. In addition, records are sometimes incomplete, out-of-date, and/or inaccurate. Another problem is that often records were not collected for the same reason as the evaluator wants to use them. Further, limitations may lie in the selective deposit of certain documents or archives and how well they survive over time.

Despite possible limitations in using archives, previously collected data are often helpful to an evaluator. Records that tell information such as density of population, population distribution, age distribution, sex distribution, racial composition, education level, occupation type, per-capita income, family income, housing type, housing age, employment rate, birth rate, expenditure patterns, and crime rate and type are examples of archival records. You may want to use city maps and photos, school records, church records, real estate records, building permits, libraries, state and federal organization records, radio and television stations, public utility records, chamber of commerce data, health and welfare records, actuarial records, large scale social studies, voting records, weather and traffic reports, public records such as gas use or water use, sales records, institutional records, personal documents such as collections, newspaper records, tax assessments, information from scouting groups and other youth-serving agencies, business and professional groups, financial institutions, planning agencies, data from state organizations and the National Recreation and Park Association (i.e., operating and capital expenditures, amount of recreation acreage, number of full-time and part-time staff, and populations served). Good sources of archives are city planning departments, Visitor and Convention Bureaus, and Councils of Social Agencies. As described earlier, Geographical Information Systems (GIS) is a new area that provides huge quantities of unobtrusive data that an evaluator might want to use.

Within leisure services organizations, several sources of archives might be interesting. These include financial reports, attendance rosters, trip reports, annual reports made to the recreation commission or board, and old evaluation reports. We frequently use previous records to do various evaluation procedures such as cost-benefit and cost-effectiveness analysis. Program records and agency files are useful if good data have been kept. Inappropriate data for evaluation purposes, incomplete data, or changes in procedures may be problems in using leisure service agency archives. With the widespread use of computer systems, evaluation from agency records ought to become easier in the future. One secondary outcome in working with archives is that the evaluator learns to develop better record-keeping procedures to help an agency with evaluations in the future.

Unobtrusive and Covert Observations

Covert observations are a form of unobtrusive data collection that one must handle carefully. In the chapter on observations, we did not discuss covert observations as particularly useful. In some situations, however, they might be helpful.

Unobtrusive and/or covert observations may occur in a variety of ways. One must be careful in using this technique of data collection because it can infringe on people's privacy. People do not like to be watched if they do not know they are being observed. People need to give their informed consent. Contrived observation such as what is done with hidden cameras and "bugging" should be avoided, but once in a while these obser-vation techniques can be justified. Unobtrusive observation involves the data collector being unknown and passive. These observations are often used to measure physical behavior through audiovisual analysis.

Physical signs may be used in a group to examine such simple aspects as expressive movement including facial expressions, finger and hand move-ments, rituals of athletes, physical location like proximity to the leader, seating, personal space, clothing, how people sit, or how people stand. These observations might also be used to analyze language behavior like the subject of conversations and with whom they occur. These data might be quantitative if they are collected in the form of a checklist or they may be qualitative if they are observations gathered in the form of notes. The values of unobtrusive observations are that no role taking is associated, measuring these activities doesn't cause change in behavior, interviewer effects are not an issue, and data are collected first hand.

Observation in public places is one type of unobtrusive method used in studying recreation, parks, tourism, and leisure settings. In this unobtrusive method, an evaluator uses observation and casual conversation. Observa-tion in public places is sometimes hard to do but a researcher can get a sense of such aspects as exterior physical signs (e.g., clothes, bumper stickers, li-cense plates), expressive movement, physical location of types of activity, conversational sampling, and time duration in particular activities. The data could be recorded and analyzed like other forms of qualitative observations or quantitative checklists.

Observations can also be recorded using tapes, films, and photos. Audio-visual aids allow the evaluator to examine a phenomenon a number of times. Audiovisual analysis can be divided into several categories. One category may refer to an analysis of media. This technique is essentially a content analysis of pictures, graphics, or words. A second category includes audio-visual analyses that may refer to using photos and media to collect data, which can be replayed for analysis. For example, time-lapse photography may give information about patterns of movement in a park. After the pho-tography is done, evaluators can use the data for analysis. A third variation of this category is to make a tape or film and then show it to people to get their reactions. This strategy has been used in park planning where pictures of outdoor areas are taken and shown to people. They are asked to describe their reactions to what is pleasing and not pleasing about particular places.

The method of using audiovisual devices to collect and analyze data has pros and cons. Sometimes the use of audio or visual recordings presents a way to get better samples if an evaluator cannot observe everything at one time. On the other hand, there is a problem with not being able to observe everything even when cameras or recording devices are being used. Most evaluators have found that initially people may be bothered by a video camera or tape recorder, but they forget the presence of these devices after a few minutes. It appears, in general, that the use of audiovisual equipment does not affect the data that may be collected. As in the other techniques, data collection and analysis using audiovisual devices may be quantitative or qualitative depending on how the evaluation project is designed.

The most sophisticated data are *ratio data*. Ratio data have a true zero point as well as all of the ordering and distancing properties of interval data. Height is an example of ratio data because a six-foot tall adult is truly twice as tall as a three-foot tall child.

Let's review these four types of data. Assume you had following variables such as age, job title, income, number of visits to a facility, race/ethnicity, and IQ scores. To some extent the way that you ask questions will determine what level of data that you have. For example, you could ask someone how old she or he is and the response would usually be ratio data such as 21 years old. On the other hand, you could ask how old and then provide a close-ended ordered response such as: 17 or younger, 18–29, 30–39, 40–49, and 50 years or older. In this case, the level of data is nominal. Generally however, age is considered ratio data as is income (they have a zero starting point), unless you are describing income categories such as low income or middle income, which are nominal data. Job title is usually nominal as is race/ethnicity. According to the definitions, the number of visits to a facility is ratio data. IQ scores are ratio data.

Evaluators must be aware of the different levels of measurement for data because each statistical procedure requires a specific level. For example, if you wanted to explore the relationship between two types of information that were categorical (nominal level data) such as sex and job title, a chi-square analysis would be appropriate. If data were interval or ratio level data such as in comparing self-esteem scores and age, then a Pearson correlation analysis might be the best choice.

Describing Variables

In preparing to analyze data, you will need to define the variables. For example, each separate item on a questionnaire is a variable that in turn, may become an element that can be analyzed. The initial selection of variables for an evaluation is made when evaluation criteria are selected and the items for a survey are drafted into questions for the respondents to answer, or when an observation checklist is developed. These variables might include demographic information such as age and sex, behavioral aspects such as the type of recreation program in which they participate and frequency of participation, or attitudes such as program satisfaction and the importance of facility amenities.

Variables can be divided into *dependent variables* (ones that can be influenced), and *independent variables* (ones that can exert influence). For

From Ideas to Reality

Unobtrusive evaluation methods are not commonly used in leisure services projects but there is no reason why they cannot be. Some of the value of unobtrusive techniques lies in not having to approach people to gather data. They have great value in analyzing history and changes over time if one were to examine, for example, how the budget has increased or the changes in the number of participants in a particular activity over a period of time. Less is known about the potential for these methods than for other more commonly used methods but they are no less reliable, valid, and useful. They also represent data, especially in the form of physical evidence or archives that already exist within an organization. Unobtrusive techniques offer some possibilities that you may want to consider as you undertake particular projects. These techniques might also be particularly useful when triangulated with surveys or observations.

Now that you have studied this chapter, you should be able to:

- Identify when unobtrusive methods might be used in a project.
- Describe the differences between physical evidence, archives, and unobtrusive observations.
- Give examples of the uses of physical evidence, archival data, and unobtrusive observations.

Experimental Designs

The two major classifications of evaluation and research designs are experimental and descriptive, as introduced in Chapter 2.2. Within experimental designs we have true experiments and quasi-experimental designs. Quasi-experimental designs may be more descriptive than experimental, as you will see in this chapter. True experimental and quasi-experimental designs, however, share some characteristics from a methodological perspective. Preexperimental designs are almost solely descriptive but we talk about them as another possibility that may provide some information that can be considered when you want to do something like an experimental design.

When attempting to show that a summative evaluation is really the result of an intervention, experimental methods are often used. For example, if we wanted to know if participation in a summer camp program resulted in increased self-esteem among young people, we would measure self-esteem scores before and after the camp session and compare those scores to before and after scores from young people who did not go to camp during that same period of time. Experiments may be done using people as well as things. For example, you might be interested in what type of grass grows best in a playground area. You might plant half the area with one type and half the area with another. Through various observations during the summer and at the end, you might determine which grass was greenest or held up the best in this particular situation. The type of experiment used would depend on the criteria you wish to examine and the resources that might be available.

Many types of experiments exist, but true experiments use a randomized sample with a control group. Quasi-experimental evaluation methods, a "cousin" of experimental designs but more characteristic of descriptive procedures, do not necessarily control for randomized sample, control group, or use pretests. True experimental procedures are more valid if participants are "blind" about the group in which they are participating. That is, they know they are a part of an experiment, but they do not know to which group they have been assigned (e.g., experimental or control). In leisure service situations, however, individuals seldom are blind to the experiment.

Thus, the purpose of the experimental design in its purest form is to control as many of the factors as possible to minimize any outside effect that might account for change due to some intervention. In this way, the evaluator as well as anyone using the results can be assured that the results of the experiment represent what really happened. Experimental designs provide a way to measure the outcomes or impact of a program and/or what happened to individuals as a result of a particular intervention.

The Characteristics of Experimental Designs

According to research textbooks, experimental designs range from "true" methods such as the pretest-posttest control group, to single group methods that are essentially equivalent to one-group surveys or tests. For purposes of our discussion of experimental and quasi-experimental methods, we only focus on examples that use some type of comparison and/or pretest. To begin, however, we discuss why experimental and control groups and randomization are important.

An experimental group includes the individuals that receive some kind of intervention, such as participating in a recreation program. A control group is a similar group of individuals, with characteristics like the experimental group, who do not receive the same treatment. If an experimental group was children 8–10 years old who went to camp, the control group would be children 8–10 years old who did not go to camp during the time the experiment was being done.

When no control group is used, several threats to the results concerning internal validity (i.e., whether the procedure really measured what it said it measured) may occur. The first threat is maturation or whether a change might be due simply to a group maturing. For example, given a particular age group, basketball skills might improve naturally with practice regardless of what kind of instruction is given. Related to this threat is that history or time passing may change people's abilities or knowledge. The effects of taking a test upon the scores of a second test may be a validity threat if a participant remembers how she or he answered the first time. Changes in the measuring instruments or changes in the observers or scoring can also pose a validity problem in conducting evaluations. The Hawthorne effect can be described as the result of people improving just because they get attention. The Hawthorne effect is mitigated by using a control group. Sometimes no changes are seen in a group because of what is known as *statistical regression*. This phenomenon occurs when groups have high scores, also known as the *ceiling effect*. On a second testing, the scores tend to move back toward the mean because they were so high initially.

To *randomize* means to assign people to groups by chance. Randomization is important because selecting or choosing experimental and control units with different characteristics may affect the results. The mortality or differential loss of respondents must also be considered. Addressing the selection-maturation interaction, which is the different maturation of members of experimental and control groups, is a further value of using randomization in experimental designs. According to experts Campbell and Stanley (1963), randomization controls against many threats to the validity of the findings. Random assignment is highly desirable, although sometimes difficult and often uncommon in many parks and recreation evaluation projects and research studies.

The major problem with using experimental designs is that controlled experiments are often impossible in real settings. Extra people may not exist who can serve as controls. Your professional obligations require that no one be denied services. Further, control group members may get angry if they don't get their choice about recreation services. These true experimental designs are difficult because the program must be held constant and formative evaluation isn't desirable in experimental designs. In using experiments in real life and not just in laboratories, a concern exists that evaluators often try to control too much and the recreation activity may become stale. Despite these problems, experimental designs may still be a possible way to conduct useful evaluation projects.

Using True Experimental Designs

Traditionally in research and evaluation books, certain symbols are used to indicate the procedure used:

E = group receiving the experimental treatment
C = control group receiving no treatment
R = randomized sample
O = observation or testing done usually followed by a number
X = treatment

For example, if you wanted to know if the skill level and knowledge of a group of children improved as a result of Saturday morning basketball instruction, you could set up an experiment whereby the children were assigned to two groups—one for instruction and one for free play. We could give a pretest on skills and then randomly divide the group in two with a similar skill level in each group. One group could be given instruction

Symbol Key

E = group receiving the experimental treatment

C = control group receiving no treatment

R = randomized sample

O = observation or testing done usually followed by a number

X = treatment

for six weeks while the other group engaged in free play. At the end of the period, we could test the skill levels of both groups again and compare the differences between the pretest and posttest for each group. This *true experimental* method would look like this:

R   E   O1   X   O2
R   C   O1   O2

As is true in many cases in recreation, we may want to make sure that the control group does not miss an opportunity, so we might allow the group that did not receive instruction to get six weeks of instruction after the experiment is completed. This procedure will assure that no ethical issues are being violated in doing harm to a group because the members of one group did not receive a program or treatment. In this case the design would look like:

R   E   O1   X   O2
R   C   O1   O2   X

The only possible problem with this pretest-posttest control group method is that the initial testing might have some effect on the results, but it is virtually impossible to control for those effects unless you eliminate the pretest.

Other True Experiments

The Solomon Four-group Design

The Solomon four-group design is another example of a true experimental method. The configuration looks like this:

R   E   O1   X   O2
R   C   O1   O2
R   E   X   O
R   C   O

In the Solomon four-group design, four random groups are used. Two of those groups receive an observation or pretest at the beginning. One of those two groups then receives a treatment along with one of the other groups that was not pretested. At the conclusion of the treatment or the program, all four groups receive a posttest. This true experimental method assures that the pretest does not influence the results of the treatment of the posttest.

Posttest-only Control Group

The posttest-only control group method does not have the problem of a possible interaction of having had a pretest. It resembles this configuration:

R   E   X   O
R   C   O

Two groups are randomly selected and one receives a treatment. Both groups are then given a posttest to see if the treatment made any difference between the groups. The only problem with this method is that you cannot be sure that you started out with similar groups although the randomization ought to ensure that a similar baseline occurred.

Quasi-experimental Designs

Quasi-experimental methods do not satisfy the strict requirements of the experiment. Campbell and Stanley (1963) have legitimized quasi-experimental methods as possibilities to be used in any number of settings. The best methods control relevant outside effects and lead to valid inferences about the effects of the program or treatment. Quasi-experimental methods, unfortunately, leave one or several threats to validity uncontrolled. These methods include the following examples:

Time-series

In the time-series method, observations are taken several times before a treatment is applied and then, additional observations are used. The configuration looks like this:

E   O   O   O   O   X   O   O   O   O

One of the problems of the method is the inability to control for the effects of history between measurements. Because a control group is not used, you would have to use this format in different situations to generalize the results more broadly. An example of a control group time-series is new playground equipment at a park. To conduct this time-series quasi-experiment, you would take several visitor counts at a park. The new equipment would be installed and then you continue taking the counts at the park (Ellis & Witt, 1982). You would see if participation increased in the park compared to what it was before the new equipment was installed.

Symbol Key
E = group receiving the experimental treatment
C = control group receiving no treatment
R = randomized sample
O = observation or testing done usually followed by a number
X = treatment

Equivalent Time Samples

The equivalent time sample is an extension of the time-series method by alternating treatment and measurement. It looks like this:

E   XO   XO   XO   XO

The procedure is useful when the effects of the treatment are anticipated to be short-term. An example of its use might be in measuring how reality therapy could be used for patients with Alzheimer's disease in a therapeutic recreation program. You would do the therapy and make an observation and then do the therapy again and observe to see if repetition resulted in behavior changes. The disadvantage of this method is the inability to generalize the findings to other subjects in other settings.

Nonequivalent Control Group

The nonequivalent control group method has the same structure as the standard pretest-posttest control group with the exception that no random assignment of subjects to groups is made. This method assumes a random assignment. Often prearranged groups are used. For example, if you wanted to compare the gains in aerobic capacity made between people in a class taking step aerobics and a regular aerobics class, you could use the two groups that exist rather than randomly assigning them. The configuration looks like this:

E   O   X   O
C   O   O

Preexperimental Designs

Preexperimental methods are more descriptive than experimental methods, but they share some characteristics with true and quasi-experimental designs. The evaluator has to be careful, however, in referring to them as experimental methods because they result in descriptive, rather than predictive or cause-and-effect, outcomes.

One-group Pretest-Posttest

Although more a preexperimental or survey-oriented method than a quasi-experimental procedure, we will discuss the possibility of a one-group pretest-posttest design briefly because it does have possibilities in evaluation. It looks like this:

$$E \quad O \quad X \quad O$$

The advantage is the comparison between pre and post performances by the same subjects. The drawback is that no control group or randomization occurs. The subjects would be tested for knowledge, attitude, or skill level before a treatment or program begins and then again after it is over. The disadvantage is the inability to accurately determine whether the differences from beginning to end are due to the treatment or some other variables.

Static Group Comparison

The static group comparison is not technically experimental, but it has the comparison aspects of experiments in that a treatment is applied to one group of subjects. Testing or observation is then done on two groups, the one receiving treatment and another that had nothing. The method looks like this:

$$E \quad X \quad O$$
$$C \qquad O$$

The value of this preexperiment is that it can provide comparisons to evaluate a group after it is completed. The problem is the equivalence of the groups is unknown from the beginning because randomization is not used.

One-shot Case Study

A third common type of preexperimental method is referred to as the one-shot case study where a treatment is given and an observation is made. The configuration is basically this:

$$(R) \quad E \quad X \quad O$$

This framework is used often in survey designs where no control group is needed. In the one-shot case study, the sample may or may not be randomized.

Making Experimental Design Decisions

As indicated previously, a number of objections exist to experimental designs. Some people feel funny about being "guinea pigs" and some professionals do not wish to perpetuate that idea by using experimental designs for recreation evaluation or research. In addition, great time and effort is involved in planning experimental projects. The values of using experiments and quasi-experimental procedures, however, cannot be discounted in doing summative evaluations and in assessing goal attainment.

They are particularly good in assessing participant changes in behavior, skills, knowledge, or attitudes.

Experiments might be considered when a new program is introduced, when stakes are high, when there is controversy about program effectiveness, and when change or the value of something needs to be shown. Ultimately, experiments are best used to determine whether or not a program caused any personal or social change. Prediction and cause and effect are the most important outcomes of experimental designs.

Regardless of how an experiment is used, several criteria must be considered. Adequate control must be guaranteed so the evaluator can be assured that the results were due to a treatment and not to something else. In the field of leisure studies, the results must apply to the real world. Comparisons are essential. Further, the measurement instruments must be sound. Thus, when you do experiments you will either have to choose existing instruments or develop instruments for measuring the pretest and posttest information. This information has been discussed in some detail in previous chapters. Finally, the experimental methods employed in leisure services evaluation need to be kept simple. Figure 2.12 shows a flow chart that may be useful in deciding whether to use experimental designs.

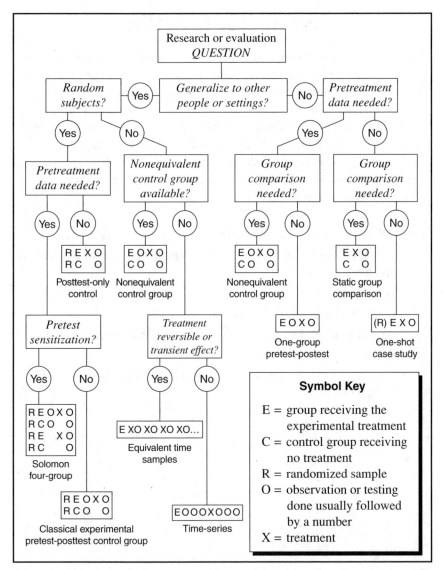

Figure 2.12 Decision Matrix for Experimental Designs (adapted from Okey, Shrum & Yeany, 1977)

From Ideas to Reality

Experiments are commonly discussed in the scientific literature and have been a respected way that research and evaluation have been undertaken. These methods, however, are not always as easy to administer as are descriptive methods such as surveys and observations. Nevertheless, experiments have much to offer leisure service evaluators. They may be the most appropriate methods to use if we want to determine whether changes actually occur as a result of the programs and interventions that we conduct. Experimental designs are worth considering as options for particular kinds of evaluation situations.

Now that you have studied this chapter, you should be able to:

- Explain the differences between true experiments, quasi-experiments, and preexperiments.

- Describe why randomization and control groups are important in evaluation and research projects.

- Analyze the advantages and disadvantages that are associated with using experimental designs.

- Conduct a simple experiment using one of the methods described in the chapter.

Specific Applications to Evaluation

We have discussed descriptive and experimental designs and the broad methods categories of surveys, observations, and unobtrusive measure. We will now examine some common applications of techniques used in evaluating leisure service organizations. Each of these techniques can be used to measure aspects of the five Ps (i.e., personnel, policies, places, programs, participants) and can be applied to assessment, formative, and summative evaluations. The steps of determining criteria, selecting methods and samples for data collection and analysis, and using the information to make judgments apply to all of these techniques. We will address importance-performance, case studies, single-subject designs, economic analysis, consensus techniques, sociometry, and several other miscellaneous evaluation techniques.

Importance-Performance

A technique that has been popular in recent years is the use of importance-performance (I-P) survey questionnaires to measure program effectiveness. I-P surveys are based on the notion that evaluation must be obtained from the consumer (Guadagnolo, 1985). Rossman (1982) found that knowing the importance of a program is essential and that people were sometimes satisfied with performance aspects of programs that they did not indicate were important to them.

The I-P technique uses a measurement instrument to quantify customer satisfaction with performance by combining importance with satisfaction. Several steps are involved in the process. First, one must determine attributes (criteria) to measure. These attributes can be discerned through literature review, focus group interviews, and/or the use of managerial or professional judgment. Second, one must develop two sets of questions asking how important an attribute or amenity is to a participant and how satisfied the participant is with the organization's performance regarding that attribute or amenity. Third, data are collected. Fourth, the responses to those two sets of questions are then matched and the means or medians plotted against one another on a two-way dimensional grid where importance is represented by one axis and performance and/or satisfaction are represented by the other. The respondents' perceptions are then translated into management action through a facilitated interpretation. Figure 2.13(1) shows an example of an I-P grid.

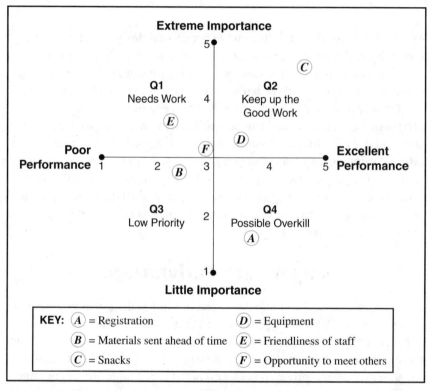

Figure 2.13(1) Example of an Importance-Performance Scale

Elements in quadrant 1 (Q1) are perceived as high on importance but low on performance and they represent areas requiring managerial attention (i.e., concentrate here). Q2 is perceived as high on both importance and performance. The status of performance should be maintained (i.e., keep up the good work). Q3 is perceived as low importance but high on performance suggesting overcommitment of resources in these areas (i.e., possible overkill). Q4 is perceived as low on both importance and performance, which represent those attributes or amenities of low managerial priority.

Several examples exist in the parks and recreation research literature about using I-P. Siegenthaler (1994) was interested in developing and maintaining quality programs for older adults and wanted to find out what this population thought was important. She identified program features important to participants in the Austin Parks and Recreation Senior Programs and how well participants felt the agency was performing. Hollenhorst, Olson, and Fortney (1992) used I-P to examine the importance of various attributes of the West Virginia state park cabin experience and to determine visitor satisfaction with these attributes. They examined factors like cleanliness, furniture, reservation systems, appliances, location, kitchenware, linens, bathtub showers, fireplaces, open porch, deck, cathedral ceilings, and telephones. They found that the cabin design and construction didn't need to change. Visitors valued basic comforts, rustic and simple character, seclusion, natural surroundings, and access to water-based recreation. Guadagnolo (1985) used the I-P with the Pittsburgh Citiparks Department 10K race. He used the instrument to examine such aspects as preregistration, packet pickup, awards, layout of course, challenge of course, running surfaces, restrooms, starting procedures, crowd control, traffic control, split times given, water stations, first aid stations, medical care, temperature, adjacent parking, and time of day. He then segmented the runners on certain issues of satisfaction and examined these by groups including males and females and repeat vs. first-time runners. Bartlett and Einert (1992) evaluated the design features of a newly constructed adult softball complex and found the most acceptable features were the night lighting, perimeter fencing, grassed outfields, and restrooms. They focused on user perceptions as a means for planning designs. Havitz, Twynam, and DeLorenzo (1991) applied I-P to staff evaluations. They found that the same things used to attract customers might be used to attract staff (referred to as internal marketing). Such items as attending training seminars and conferences, conducting training seminars for staff and volunteers, answering the phone (phone etiquette), responding to complaints from the public, giving tours to the public, handling funds and cash, monitoring inventories, initiating requisition requests, and preparing reports were measured. These authors suggested that I-P helped to provide a clear outline for collecting and interpreting data, was tangible and easy-to-do, and allowed for gathering input from a number of employees.

Several tips must be kept in mind when using the I-P. First, determine the attributes to measure carefully. Be sure to separate importance from performance items on the questionnaire. Finally, as is true for any evaluation, the evaluator must interpret what the data mean after they have been analyzed.

Case Studies

Case studies are used to gather information about individuals, groups, places, or policies (in communities, organizations, or institutions). Case studies may be the ultimate form of triangulation in that they require multiple methods and data sources such as surveys, observations, and unobtrusive data. Case studies are not as "easy" to do as many people think; many aspects must be considered in doing an evaluation case study project.

According to Howe and Keller (1988), a case study is an intensive investigation of a particular unit; an analytical description or construction of a group as they are observed over a given period of time; or the in-depth study of the background, current status, or interactions of a given unit which might be an individual, social group, institution, or community. Case studies are particularly good if an evaluator is examining one situation and doesn't wish to compare it to another situation, individual, or group. Case studies are both specific and broad as they capture many variables and include descriptions of history and context. They are often longitudinal because they tell a story that covers a period of time, and usually qualitative because they often use prose and literary technique.

The purpose of the case study is to measure how and why something occurs. In a case study, you are not necessarily concerned about generalizing the results to other situations, although case studies often give insight to other situations. You might choose a unique case or a critical case to evaluate. Further, you may collect qualitative and/or quantitative data. You might do a single case study or you might do several case studies in combination. If multiple cases are used, a similar system and logic should be used in data collection for each. The important aspect in designing a case study evaluation is to determine the unit to be examined whether it is an individual, event, or small group.

Case study techniques are frequently used in therapeutic recreation to analyze a particular client situation. For example, a Case History Review approach has been used in the *Therapeutic Recreation Journal* to provide a basis for examining aspects of therapeutic recreation. Practicing therapeutic recreation specialists write about particular cases and include an assessment, goals and objectives, program planning, implementation, and evaluation as it pertains to a particular person in a situation. The intent of these case studies is to show how the therapeutic recreation process works through treatment.

According to the procedures used for any type of evaluation, the evaluator will need to do the following:

1. Identify the focus of the investigation
2. Outline what needs to be studied
3. Select appropriate measurement tools
4. Develop a plan to collect the data considering effectiveness, efficiency, budget and time frame
5. Collate all the data
6. Interpret the data
7. Make recommendations from the study

For case studies, many methods previously discussed might be used to gather relevant data.

Data collected for case studies will vary depending on the situation. Data included might be observations, interviews, parent interviews and other individuals' interviews, review of documents, archival records, clinical or organizational record, life history profiles, diaries, and reports. Often longitudinal information in the form of unobtrusive data is collected to provide a historical context. In addition, a multidisciplinary assessment (i.e., using psychological, social, economic, and other information) of the participant, group, or organization is done with an emphasis on precise descriptions. These data are then assembled, organized, and condensed. The analysis for case study data consists of examining, categorizing, tabulating, and recombining evidence, just as is done in other forms of qualitative data collection. Similarly, case studies use patternmaking, explanation building, and are conducted over a period of time.

Writing the case study report is ongoing and occurs during the entire process of doing the case study. A final case study narrative is presented which provides a readable, descriptive picture of the unit (e.g., person, group, organization, or program) that was examined. It should make accessible to the reader all the information necessary to understand the person or program. A case study may be presented either chronologically or thematically. As a case study is read, you should get a sense that all aspects of a situation have been addressed. The final product should show the patterns that developed, explain what happened, and show information over a period of time. The boundaries of the case study should be clear with alternative perspectives offered along with evidence to support the conclusions that are made. The report should combine descriptive, analytic, interpretive, and evaluative perspectives into the report.

Doing good case studies requires several competencies. The evaluator must be able to ask questions that address the criteria being examined, be a good listener, be adaptive and flexible, be able to put together ideas, and be unbiased. As indicated above, using multiple sources helps in this process. Taking good notes, just as in field observation, is essential. All data sources need to be pulled together in a systematic order. According to Yin (1984), it is essential that multiple sources of evidence are used, a case study database is created, and that one maintains a chain of evidence concerning the data that are collected.

Case studies have sometimes been criticized for their lack of rigor and lack of generalization and comparisons. Sometimes they appear to be "easy" to do, but generally they require great time and effort. Exemplary case studies are significant, complete, consider alternative perspectives, display sufficient evidence, and engage the reader in an understanding of the case being studied. Case studies may be applied or generalized across settings if a congruity exists between the case and where it will be used. The case study report must be written in such a way that people can see how their situation may or may not be like the case being described. The purpose of case studies is to allow the evaluator to learn the intricate details of how something is working, rather than to generalize to other situations.

Single-subject Techniques

A single-subject technique allows you to evaluate the effect of interventions on an individual participant or client. Single-subject techniques use an application of time-series experimental methods with subjects being their own control. Multiple and repeated assessments are used to measure intervention and its effects on an individual. Both qualitative and quantitative information can be collected.

The single-subject technique is similar to the case study except only one person or a very small number of people are used as the sample for the evaluation. For example, suppose you wanted to know if a particular recreation technique worked with children who had autism. You might observe the behavior of that child for a period of time to establish a baseline, observe the child during the time the recreation technique is being used, and then observe again as follow-up after the treatment is over. This approach done on individuals would show what happened and might enable us to know why some recreation techniques were more effective for some individuals and not for others. According to Datillo (1988a; 1988b) the single-subject technique offers a way to make informed decisions about the quality of a recreation program and provides a context for understanding behavior dynamics. The technique allows the evaluator to learn the details of how treatment is working for an individual rather than averaging the effects across a number of cases.

The focus of single-subject evaluation is on an individual; a series of measurements or observations occur over a period of time to determine how an individual may be changing as a result of a particular recreation program or as in therapeutic recreation, a particular treatment plan or intervention. Figure 2.13(2) shows an example of the way a single-subject data plot might look. The procedure used is to measure a behavior for an individual before treatment, apply a treatment, and withdraw the treatment and measure. This establishes a baseline (A). Over a period of time the treatment will be given and reinforced and then additional measures are taken (B). Subsequently after a treatment period is over, follow-up measures (C) will be used to see if and how long the behavior continues.

A single-subject technique will often address the rate and level of attainment of objectives, program strengths and weaknesses, standards of individual performance, validity of innovations and trends, and cost-benefits. The technique does not lack precision and sensitivity. As in other situations, however, the results of single-subject analysis can be compromised by

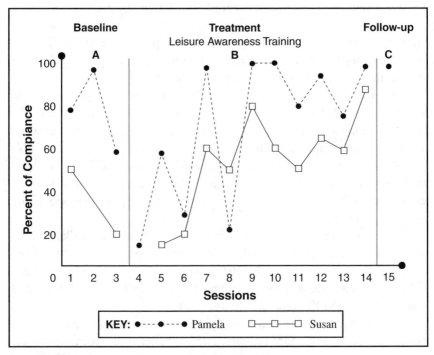

Figure 2.13(2) Example of a Plot for the Single-subject Technique

inadequate assessment tools, measurement procedures, or observation techniques (Dattilo, 1988a). Although most of the studies using the single-subject technique in therapeutic recreation have used quantitative data, qualitative data could also be used. The value of single-subject evaluation techniques lies in using patterns identified in baseline and intervention conditions to determine how intervention affects an individual.

Economic Analysis Techniques

The policy/administrative application of evaluation often includes a focus on techniques for economic evaluation. Economic impact and cost-benefit analyses are commonly used unobtrusive techniques and require a great deal more explanation if they are to be applied to park, recreation, tourism, and leisure services organizations. A brief description of some econometric techniques, however, may be useful.

Economic impact evaluations might be done to measure the role of a special event on the local economy. These data are often difficult to gather and expensive to analyze, although standard questionnaire development and analysis can be applied. Economic impact studies attempt to determine both the direct and indirect financial benefits of an activity by gathering expenditure data. For example, if we wanted to measure the economic impact of a sporting event, we would get expenditure data from a sample of visitors and then extrapolate to an entire group. A multiplier is used, which refers to the fact that money spent can be spent again and again. An increase in spending will create an indirect effect greater than the original expenditures. A multiplier of 2.0 is a conservative multiplier to use. For every dollar of income spent, two dollars circulate through a community. For example, if someone pays to stay in a hotel, the hotel owner will then pay her or his housekeeping staff who will then go out and buy groceries. The grocer will have money to pay his employees who will then spend their money on clothes for their children and so on. Therefore, the initial money spent will continue to multiply.

Economic impact can be measured along with other data like visitor satisfaction. One can find examples of economic impact studies in the *Journal of Park and Recreation Administration* such as those done by Gitleson, Guadagnolo, and Moore (1988), Loomis (1990), Yardley, MacDonald, and Clarke (1990) and Kanters and Botkin (1992).

Little consensus exists concerning the best way to analyze costs and benefits. Costs are not hard to determine but benefits are difficult to measure in either economic or noneconomic terms. In cost-benefit analysis, the evaluator has to determine the benefits in monetary terms. In cost-effectiveness one looks at the cost in relation to some type of outcomes that may not be economic. Henderson (1988) has given an example of how cost-effectiveness might be determined in relation to volunteers (see Table 2.13(3), p. 238). The cost-effectiveness evaluation technique provides additional information from an economic view; however, it does not suffice for evaluating other aspects of volunteers and volunteer programs. You can do a similar analysis with other leisure service programs to determine how much they cost. One must be careful, however, not to make decisions about programs based solely on costs. Some programs that cost more also have many more benefits that are difficult to measure.

A criticism of cost-benefits approaches is that it is hard to put a price on psychological benefits and the value of lives. The appropriate units of analysis are often difficult to determine. However, the problems associated with economic analysis should not prevent an evaluator from considering the possibilities in examining policy/administrative aspects of an organization.

Consensus Techniques

The nominal group technique and the Delphi technique are examples of consensus strategies that can be used for evaluation. They may be done using questionnaires or group interviews. The Air Force, for example, used the nominal group technique (NGT) to assess future directions (Lankford & DeGraaf, 1992). The NGT is a means to identify issues, opportunities, and ways to reach potential participants. This collective decision-making technique can be used for strategic planning, policy development, and goal formation. More structured than brainstorming, the evaluator can obtain consensus on ideas and strategies.

Delbecq, Van de Ven and Gustafson (1975) outlined a six-step process for NGT:

1. Introduce topic and explain
2. Participants write down responses on card
3. All responses are listed
4. Items are clarified
5. Individuals voting on the issues identified
6. Votes are tabulated

You can go through this process twice to get additional information and you can assign value to the tabulated votes.

Table 2.13(3) Cost-effectiveness Analysis Worksheet (adapted from Henderson, 1988)

A. COSTS

1. Direct

    a. coordinator's salary $ _____

    b. recordkeeping/secretarial   _____

    c. recognition materials   _____

    d. expenses—mileage, meals, etc.   _____

    e. printed materials   _____

    f. office supplies   _____

    g. insurance   _____

    h. other   _____

    TOTAL DIRECT $ _____

2. Indirect

    a. overhead   _____

    b. other staff   _____

    c. equipment   _____

    d. other   _____

    TOTAL INDIRECT $_____

                        TOTAL COSTS $_____ *(A)*

B. OUTPUTS

Activity = # of volunteers (B) x # of hours (C) x rate/hr = $ _____(D)

  a. _____   _____ x _____ x _____ = _____

  b. _____   _____ x _____ x _____ = _____

  c. _____   _____ x _____ x _____ = _____

  d. _____   _____ x _____ x _____ = _____

  e. _____   _____ x _____ x _____ = _____

  f. _____   _____ x _____ x _____ = _____

                                  $

     Total (B)   *Total (C)*   *Total (D)*

C. COST-EFFECTIVENESS ANALYSIS

Output (D) divided by Cost (A) = 1: ____ ratio

For every $ spent, $x of service are provided

D. OTHER CALCULATIONS

Cost (A) ÷ # of volunteers (B) = Cost per volunteer

Cost (A) ÷ # of clients served = Cost per client

Cost (A) ÷ # of hours volunteered (C) = Cost per service hour

The consensus method most often used is the Delphi technique. Although the data in a Delphi study are often analyzed quantitatively, they are collected initially using a qualitative process. The Delphi technique is frequently used to establish goals, determine strategies, predict problems, access group preferences, and project needs. Weatherman and Swenson (1974) suggested that the critical characteristics of the Delphi technique are that it relies on the informed judgment of knowledgeable panels concerning a topic that has little reliable objective data. The technique is done anonymously with controlled feedback given to produce a group response.

The first step involved in the technique is to select a panel of "experts" for the topic being addressed. The number of individuals is not as important as the quality of the panel. An open-ended questionnaire is then sent to the panel. The responses to that questionnaire are grouped and tabulated; a second questionnaire is sent asking people to rate, on a Likert scale, the importance of all the initial responses received. The second questionnaire is tabulated and a final questionnaire is sent to obtain further ratings and rankings to move toward as much consensus as possible. The final product of the Delphi generally looks like a ranking of the most important issues that the panel uncovers. Anderson and Schneider (1993) used the Delphi process to identify important innovations from recreation management in from 1973–1993 and rated their relative importance for meeting specific management goals. Anderson and Schneider concluded that the most important implication of their study was how complex innovations in the field of natural resource management are becoming.

Sociometry

Sociometrics survey and analyze how groups operate by asking how people "get along" with each other. Sociograms are a tool used to identify how members of a subgroup interact and how they function. The sociogram illustrates choices made in a group by plotting them on a matrix. According to Lundegren and Farrell (1985), one merely asks "Name three people with whom you would most like to work as a partner for the xyz group?" You could ask any question such as: "With whom do you like to play?" (for children), "With whom would you like to go to lunch?" (for adults), or "Who is most supportive of you in the work environment?" This technique is not designed for large groups. It works best with groups of fewer than twenty.

The evaluator then sets up a matrix with each person across the top and down the side. The choices are tallied. You could analyze between sex choices if you wanted or any other category that seems appropriate. Figure 2.13(4) shows an example of a sociogram analysis. Four concentric circles are drawn representing the level of choice with the highest in the center. Circles are labeled and entered on to the diagram. Arrows are drawn for each individual to the symbol of the person chosen. If the choice is reciprocated, a double-headed arrow for mutual choice is used. The process tells you who is most chosen and also shows the isolates. It also tells where pairs are and shows simple choices as well as mutual choices. This technique might be useful for analyzing group cohesiveness or how a group can function better.

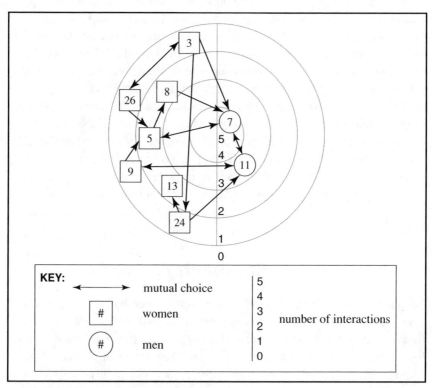

Figure 2.13(4) Example of a Sociogram Analysis

Miscellaneous Evaluation Techniques

A number of other techniques have been described in the recreation and leisure services literature that might be of interest to evaluators. They provide further examples to consider and will be described briefly. We encourage you to check these references if you want more details about any of the techniques..

Program Planning

O'Sullivan (1988) has written about a nine-cell strategy of program planning and unobtrusive evaluation. This approach examines different programs and assesses them by industry attractiveness (external) and business strength (internal), which she refers to as program potential and organizational capability. The program potential includes the market size, market growth rate, profit margin, competition, cyclicality, seasonality, and scale economies. The organizational capabilities include the market share, price competitiveness, program quality, knowledge of participant, and sale effectiveness. One can ascertain these ratings by gathering professional staff together and having them numerically rate each category, assign points, average the items, and give a rating to each activity. You also might weight the items within the group. If you think product quality is three times more important than market share, you would calculate in that way. Once all activities have been categorized, they are plugged into the cells with either program as high, medium, or low and organizational capacity as strong, average, or weak. See Figure 2.13(5), p. 242. For the three "go" categories, you can allocate resources. In the black categories, you can eliminate programs. You will need to think carefully about grays. The value of the nine-cell approach is that it allows you to evaluate several programs by comparing them to each other.

Report Cards

Report cards are a questionnaire technique that can be used to focus on indicators of satisfaction. They use items and ask people to rank them as A=excellent, B=better than average, C=average, D=below average, E=poor. When used in a park, one might ask about first impression, helpfulness of staff, cleanliness of restrooms, information at park, attractiveness at park, safety and security, cleanliness of ground, ease of access, hours or operation, control of pets, and overall satisfaction. You can then use GPA averages to rank services: 4.00–3.80=A, 3.79–3.67=A–, 3.66–3.33=B+, 3.32–3.00=B, 2.99–2.67=B–, 2.66–2.33=C+. You could look at these

Figure 2.13(5) O'Sullivan's Nine-cell Planning Screen (adapted from O'Sullivan, 1988)

grades over a period of time or compare one facility to another. It is usually best to include qualitative summaries with both the letter grades and the numbers.

Service Quality

Service quality is a concept measured frequently according to Wright, Duray, and Goodale (1992) and MacKay and Crompton (1990). The premise of service quality evaluation is that consumers are more demanding and an increased competition for customers exists. Five quality dimensions of expectations and perceptions are measured in this survey approach including tangibles, reliability, responsiveness, assurance, and empathy. The expectations are measured with a statement such as "tell us the degree to which you think an excellent recreation center should have the following features." A seven-point Likert scale anchored from "not at all essential" to "absolutely essential" is used. The perception part asks individuals to "tell us the degree to which you feel Center X has the features described in each statement." A seven-point Likert scale of "strongly agree" to "strongly disagree" is used. Features include such aspects as prompt repairs to facilities and equipment, clean and sanitary shower and locker rooms, good quality healthy food at snack bar, staff interested in patrons, and accurate class descriptions (Wright, Duray & Goodale, 1992). A service quality score is obtained by subtracting the mean expectation rating from the mean performance rating. Negative results indicate where a "service gap" exists. Zero implied met expectations. In using this approach, adaptations can be made in the item pool for a particular service. Similar to importance-performance, this method is proving to be useful to evaluators in all areas of leisure service management.

From Ideas to Reality

This chapter has shown examples of how specific approaches using the methods described previously can be applied to evaluation in leisure services. We can learn a great deal from seeing how others have applied methods and developed instruments. In addition to considering some of these possible applications, we encourage you to read journals like the *Journal of Park and Recreation Administration* and *Therapeutic Recreation Journal* to see what techniques others have used in evaluation projects and research studies.

Now that you have studied this chapter, you should be able to:

- Describe how these evaluation techniques might be applied to a specific situation.

- Analyze the possible strengths and weaknesses of any technique that might be applied to collecting data for evaluation.

Triangulation

As you have seen, a variety of methods choices and sampling possibilities exist for doing evaluation projects and research studies. The use of more than one method, more than one source of data, or more than one evaluator often strengthens a project. The use of more than one method, source of data, or evaluator is referred to as triangulation. It may be economical to use only one method, source of data, or evaluator, but the possibility for more reliable and valid results obtained from triangulation ought to be considered. If you think about the old adage "Two heads are better than one," you have a rationale for considering the use of triangulation.

Triangulated Methods

Since no one method is perfect, using more than one method (method triangulation), may give additional information to an evaluator or researcher. Howe and Keller (1988) suggested that triangulated program evaluation is kindred to the case study. Triangulation is often useful when what is being evaluated is easy to identify (e.g., an in-service training program), where the subjects are clustered in settings that have definite boundaries in time and location, and when it is desired to know why and how well a program works and how it or similar future programs might be improved. Two uses of triangulated methods are frequently used: within-method triangulation and between-method triangulation. These approaches are also sometimes referred to as mixed methods.

Within method triangulation includes the collection of both qualitative and quantitative data using the same method. Issues of complementariness of qualitative or quantitative are sometimes debated, but you must keep in mind that methods themselves are neither qualitative nor quantitative as was discussed in Chapter 2.1. Depending on how a method is used will result in either, or both, qualitative and quantitative data. Some evaluators feel that combining qualitative and quantitative data is difficult to do from a purist view, but it is not uncommon. For example, you can use survey questions that may be both close-ended (quantitative) and open-ended (qualitative).

Different data are received depending on the use of open-ended or close-ended questions.

Between-method triangulation is the use of two or more methods to measure the same phenomena. This form of triangulation strengthens the validity of the overall findings. *Congruence* relates to similarity, consistency, or convergence of results obtained from two or more methods, whereas *complementariness* refers to one set of results enriching, expanding upon, clarifying, or illustrating the other. An independent assessment of the same phenomena should result in complementary results. For example, you might observe an event and also interview a selected group of people that were in attendance at that event. Or you might use participation records from unobtrusive document analysis and then survey a sample of participants to determine their satisfaction with an activity.

Greene and McClintock (1985) suggested that between methods triangulation could be differentiated along two dimensions: (1) the degree of independence of the methods used for data collection, and (2) the degree to which the implementation of both methods is sequential versus concurrent. The evaluator will need to decide which approach is going to be the best: to have one method follow another or to use two methods at the same time. Evaluators often use qualitative approaches such as focus groups to get information that will then allow them to develop quantitative questionnaires. In addition, sometimes quantitative data are collected and then interviews are used to understand the meaning behind some of the numbers. Nothing is wrong with combining qualitative and quantitative data in these ways and the combination may make for a deeper and more useful project. Howe and Keller (1988) provided a description of how qualitative and quantitative data might be used together (see Table 2.14).

The biggest problem with using mixed methods in leisure services is that few good examples and guidelines exist. Nevertheless, triangulated methods are becoming more common. The evaluator or researcher, however, can make a case for triangulated methods by examining the congruence, as well as the complementariness, of the methods used. Further, triangulated methods can reduce threats to internal and external validity. The problem with mixed methods is that it often takes more time and money to implement two methods than one. Also, in using any method, it must be done rigorously in terms of the development of the evaluation or research project. In other words, using two poorly implemented methods does not make for one good method (i.e., two wrongs don't make a right). The evaluator must be aware of the strengths and weaknesses of methods and the resulting data when multiple methods are used.

Table 2.14 Summary of Benefits from Triangulating Methods (adapted from Howe & Keller, 1988)

Contributions of Qualitative Data to Quantitative Data

Design

Qualitative data can enrich quantitative data by improving:

1. The sampling framework by exploratory interviews and observations to confirm or rationalize the framework.
2. The overall study design by prioritizing information needs and posing the right questions.

Data Collection

Qualitative data collection can enrich quantitative data collection by improving:

1. The instrument package by exploratory interviews and observations.
2. Instrument administration and interpretation by pretesting for validity, reliability, and utility.

Data Analysis

Qualitative data analysis can enrich quantitative data analyses by providing:

1. A conceptual framework to guide the analysis developed from multiple data sources to guide instrumentation, data collection procedures, and analysis.
2. Verification of quantitative findings in areas where methods yield an overlap of information.
3. Item construction for questionnaires, which can be generated from initial observational data.
4. Case study illustrations of statistically derived models.
5. Clarification of quantitative findings by comparing them with field notes covering the same topics.

Contributions of Quantitative Data to Qualitative Data

Design

Quantitative data can enrich qualitative data by identifying:

1. Representative cases, to serve the goal of generalizability.
2. Unrepresentative cases, to refine models and theories.

Data Collection

Quantitative data collection can enrich qualitative data collection by providing:

1. Leads for later interviews and observations probing specific areas.
2. Correction of the "elite" bias or "gatekeeper" effect of a highly articulate and engaged informant.

Data Analysis

Quantitative methods can contribute to the understanding of qualitative analysis by:

1. Correcting the tendency to observe all aspects of a situation as congruent.
2. Verifying qualitative interpretations by statistical analysis.
3. Casting new light on field observations by yielding unanticipated findings.

Triangulated Sources of Data

Different participants (sources of data) can provide insight about a topic or issue. An evaluation project often can benefit from more than one data source. For example, if you were interested in the changes that occurred in campers as a result of going to a four-week summer camp, you might talk to campers, but you also might interview their counselors and parents. You would be getting data from different sources that address the same evaluation criteria.

Another way to triangulate sources is to get data from different periods of time. For example, before a program begins, you might ask in-depth interview questions about expectations. While the program is going on, you might interview the same people again. After the program is over you might ask if those expectations were fulfilled. The sources of data would be dependent on the timing of the data collection.

You might also use the decision makers for an evaluation project as one important additional source of data. For example, you might interview the Board of Directors of an organization as a source of additional data for making decisions. Unobtrusive data such as participation statistics could be combined with newly collected questionnaire data. Other sources of data might be program records, program participants, staff delivering programs, family members and other significant relationships to participants, observations made by evaluator, and/or community-level indices. The potential sources of data are numerous for most evaluation projects. These data can be triangulated to provide complementary information.

Triangulation Using Multiple Data Collectors

Triangulated perspectives can also be obtained from multiple evaluators. If more than one person is interpreting results, developing instruments, or doing interviews, it is likely that more information will be uncovered. "Two heads are better than one" really applies here. Many times evaluation projects are done as a team effort and this teamwork provides the potential for the highest quality because of the variety of perspectives that can be incorporated into a final product. Multiple evaluators, however, must be able to communicate with one another and clarify exactly what the criteria are and how data are to be collected and analyzed.

Cautions in Using Triangulation

Regardless of what form of triangulation is used, you must report the design and results for all triangulated aspects. It is unethical to try a couple different methods and then only take the data from the one that works the best. If you choose more than one method or more than one data source, you must report them in your final evaluation.

Triangulation does not guarantee overcoming all biases. Be careful to not only proliferate methods, sources, or evaluators, but also to see how they can be integrated. You can compound the error in a poorly designed project that lacks specific criteria if you add more methods or more sources. Problems also arise when data are in conflict due to triangulation. You have to acknowledge that possible situation and try to interpret what is meant by the discrepancies that you may uncover. You are also ethically obligated to report incongruence and inconsistencies and explain them to the best of your ability. Often different data are the result of the methods used. The evaluator needs to have a good grasp of all the methods and techniques that might be available so she or he can make the best possible choices.

From Ideas to Reality

Triangulation can add to the validity of an evaluation, but it can also be expensive in terms of time and money. Most evaluation projects involve limited budgets, short time frames, and political constraints. It is better to use one good method, source of data, or evaluator than a series of poorly implemented methods or sources. If possible, however, triangulated methods, sources, and evaluators can often enhance the reliability, validity, and usability of an evaluation project.

Now that you have studied this chapter, you should be able to:

- Define triangulation.
- Give examples of how triangulation might be used between methods and within methods.
- Identify possible sources for data triangulation.
- Describe the problems that may be encountered when triangulating in an evaluation project or research study.

UNIT THREE
EVIDENCE: Data Analysis

Introduction to Data Analysis

Once data are collected, the data analysis begins. The exception to this rule is in qualitative interviews and field observations where the data analyses occur simultaneously with the data collection. Regardless, analysis is a part of the evaluation research process where "evidence" must be carefully considered. In Unit Three, we will continue the discussion of evidence, but we will specifically address what to do with data and how to manage it so judgments can be made about its meanings for evaluation or research purposes.

Data analysis scares many people because they associate it with statistics. In fact, when some people think of evaluation or research, they think about statistics immediately. The math anxiety that some people experience has resulted in a fear of doing projects. We do not suggest that statistics are easy to comprehend, but neither are they that complex. Understanding a few basic principles allows you to logically select the appropriate statistics for your analysis.

In this unit we discuss measurement, organization and coding data, descriptive statistics, qualitative analysis, and relationships among variables. Data analysis is an exciting aspect of evaluation and research because it helps us understand what our data mean. We will also talk about how computers make statistical analyses easy in our high-tech society. As the old adage goes, however, "garbage in, garbage out." You, as an evaluator or researcher, must know how to get a computer to give you the appropriate statistics that will be useful in drawing conclusions and making recommendations.

We also discuss how to analyze qualitative data. Because qualitative data are not mathematical, some people assume that these types of data are easy to analyze. Qualitative analysis is different, but not necessarily easier, than quantitative analysis. When you have completed this unit, you will have a good working knowledge of data analyses that use common statistical procedures and typical qualitative data strategies.

Data According to Measurement

Two kinds of numeric data exist in the world: continuous and discrete. You can imagine continuous data as data that can be measured along a continuum and can take on endless possibilities of intermediate values (Lundegren & Farrell, 1985). Examples of continuous data would be weight (e.g., a woman weighs 59.6 kg or 131.12 pounds), time (1:45:36 as a time for completing a half marathon), and temperature (5.3°C or 41.6°F). Values are considered to be approximate because even though the technology applied to measuring instruments might be sophisticated, we can never be exact.

The other kind of data is called discrete data. These data are noncontinuous and finite. There can be no "in-between" numbers as in continuous data. For example, the number of mountain bikers using a trail on the weekend is a discrete number (i.e., 152 bikers, not 152.75). With discrete data, we can count "things" that result in an exact number.

Levels of Data Measurement

During the evaluation process, different types of data are collected. In many instances these data are words, observations, or numbers. Measurement is the process of turning the words and observations into numbers that can then be used in statistical analyses. An evaluator must be able to distinguish the level of measurement obtained to make the right choices for statistical procedures. For example, data that are nominal or categorical, like biological sex, will be treated differently than continuous data such as from a test score. These levels of data measurement can be divided into four distinct groups: nominal, ordinal, interval, and ratio.

Nominal data, or categorical data, are the "lowest" typology because no assumption is made about relationships between values. Each value defines a distinct category with no overlap and serves to label or name a particular group. An example of nominal data might be the biological sex of an individual (e.g., 1 = female and 2 = male). The numeric values attached to the nominal data are merely identifiers that allow the responses to be counted for later analysis. Other examples of nominal data are items such as birth state, political party affiliation, or a yes/no response.

Ordinal data are more sophisticated data that have some implied rank or order to the categories according to some criterion. An example of ordinal data might be whether one placed or ranked first, second, third, or tenth in a road race. Each category has a position that is higher or lower than another, but you do not know how much higher or lower. Although the data are ranked or rated, no distance is measured. Both ranking and rating scales use ordinal data. Ratings generally define points on a scale and any number of people may be assigned a given point. In rankings, the individuals form a kind of scale with each person having a place in the ordering. Therefore, in rankings the individuals form the scale while in ratings, the scale preexists. An example of ordinal data used in a rating would be the classification of employees as leaders, supervisors, or administrators (e.g., Recreation Leader I, Recreation Leader II) with the ordering based upon responsibility or skills. Another example of ranked data could be the high school grade rankings of students (e.g., first in class, eighth in class). Although these data are discrete and categorical, they differ from nominal data because they have an order.

More precision is needed when you want to add scores or calculate averages. Unlike ordinal data where the distance between categories is not equal, data are needed that have equal intervals. *Interval data* result when the ordered categories have meaningful predictable size differences or distance between values. The interval scale, however, does not have an inherently determined zero point. This type of data allows you to study differences between items, but not their proportionate magnitudes. An example of interval data would be temperature. The difference between 40°F and 41°F is the same as between 80°F and 81°F but 80°F is not twice as hot as 40°F because 0°F by definition is not equal to the absence of heat. Those of us who have lived in the north know that below zero days are realities; there is no point at which you can say this temperature is as cold as it can get. Therefore, no inherent zero point exists.

You may be wondering where Likert scales fit. The definitive answer is, "It depends." Philosophically, many statistical purists believe that Likert scales can only be treated as ordinal data, because they are discrete and categorical data that provide a type of rating scale. Other statisticians believe that these scales can legitimately be viewed as interval data because the ordered categories have implied meaningful size differences. As you will see later in the discussion on statistical procedures, defining the data as ordinal limits the analyses to less powerful statistics. Many researchers and evaluators will choose to treat Likert scale data as interval data and use a wide variety of statistical calculations.

example, if you were interested in how frequently men and women in your town participated in open swimming at the community center, the frequency of swimming may be *dependent* on the sex of the individual (independent variable) completing the questionnaire. Thus, variables like sex, age, and ethnicity are usually independent variables while variables like participation rates, scale scores, and rating scales are often dependent variables.

Several other examples can help us recognize dependent and independent variables. If you wanted to examine the differences between salaries of park and recreation professionals and city size you would conclude that salaries would be the dependent variable and city size would be independent. Determining the relationship between cognitive function and age would mean that cognitive functioning would be dependent and age independent. In this case, cognitive functioning would be dependent upon age but age would not change regardless of functioning. A final example might be a question about whether juvenile crime rates change after implementation of an after-school program. In this situation, crime rates would be the dependent variable and participation in the program would be independent. Participation or not would result in an increase or decrease in crime rates.

Types of Analyses

Three types of analyses can be conducted using quantitative data. These analyses hinge on whether you want to examine the characteristics of just one variable, two variables, or more than two variables.

Univariate analysis is the examination of the distribution of cases on only one variable. This type of analysis includes the frequency distribution (i.e., the percentage and values) of a particular variable as well as appropriate measures of central tendency (i.e., mean, median, mode). These analyses are generally used for descriptive purposes. For example, you may want to know the numbers and percentages of individuals from different ethnic groups that completed a survey about your community center programs. A univariate analysis would tell how many people and the percentage of the total that represented these groups. Another example of a univariate analysis is the scores on a midterm exam. We could calculate the mean, median, mode, standard deviation, and range on the test scores as univariate data.

Bivariate analysis is the simultaneous evaluation of two variables. Usually one is independent and the other is dependent. This type of analysis is descriptive but allows you to compare subgroups. For example, you can now compare the frequency of participation in community center programs (i.e., dependent variable) by individuals of different ethnic groups, such as

African Americans, Latino/Latina, European Americans, and Asian Americans (i.e., independent variable). For example, bivariate statistics can tell you if African Americans participate more than Latino/Latinas.

The third type of analysis, *multivariate analysis*, is just like bivariate except that this analysis uses two or more independent variables and one dependent variable. For example, the frequency of participation could be analyzed by sex and ethnicity; in other words, you could tell if participation rates were different for men and women from different ethnic groups who participated in your community center programs. Both bivariate and multivariate analyses are used to explain and compare subgroups.

From Ideas to Reality

Types of analysis options are important. As you will see, a multitude of statistical procedures exist for your use. You will need to determine the type and level of data measurement generated by your evaluation, select independent and dependent variables, and make the appropriate statistical choices for the analysis that will best address your evaluation or research questions. These decisions are not always easy to make but if you have a solid understanding of the data that you are collecting, the analysis process will be easier to conduct and understand.

Now that you have studied this chapter, you should be able to:

- Identify the differences between the levels of data measurement.
- Choose the independent and dependent variables that might be used in a statistical analysis.
- Determine whether a univariate, bivariate, or multivariate data analysis would be most appropriate.

Getting Your Data Together
Organizing and Coding Quantitative Data

A critical step in data analysis involves how the information in the form of variables from a measurement instrument is organized and coded. The easiest way to think about data organization is to imagine each questionnaire as a case or observation that has a set of variables with values. Each case has only one response for each variable. The case, usually the individual who completes the questionnaire or a specific observation, becomes the basic unit upon which measurements are taken. A case could also be a larger unit such as a parks and recreation department, a time period such as the month in which measurements were taken, or a special event.

Once the pilot study is done, the evaluator decides how to systematically organize and record information. As soon as the data are collected, the analysis begins. Data should be recorded in as much original detail as possible. Specific information can always be recoded into larger groups later in the analysis process. For example, age as a value for each case could be recorded as the respondent's actual age and grouped later into age categories; however, if age is originally recorded as two values that encompass individuals 54 and younger and individuals 55 and older, only these two age categories can *ever* be used in your analyses. By reducing the number of values for a variable, you also have eliminated the possibility of getting more specific statistics such as the average age of your respondents. You can always combine values later, but you cannot expand them beyond the values recorded from the original measurement data.

The data from a variable is assigned numbers, called *values*, to represent the responses. This process is known as *coding*. When only numbers are used, the system is *numeric coding*. For example, instead of entering "agree" or "disagree" into the computer, the evaluator could code an agree response as a "1" and a disagree response as a "2." When using computers for analysis purposes, this numeric coding makes the process of getting from verbal responses to statistical answers easier.

Since a coding system is often arbitrary, creating a code book is helpful. The code book is like a road map. It tells the evaluator, and anyone else who might be using the data for statistical procedures, how the data are coded. For a very short and simple questionnaire, the code book may not be necessary but it is usually a helpful tool for the evaluator to create. Most code books are easy to put together. Code books can be created at any stage in the evaluation project, but we suggest you construct your code book before you begin to analyze your data. Working through your coding decisions will help you anticipate the various types and levels of data. Coding shows the levels of data you have. As you will see in subsequent sections of this unit, levels of data will affect your choice of statistics.

Usually the code book will include the variable name, the value labels for each variable, and the corresponding question from the questionnaire. If the data are to be entered into a computer for statistical analysis, the code book can also include additional information such as the location of the data for each case. Table 3.2(1) is an example of questions from a survey that will generate data and Table 3.2(2) is the corresponding code book.

Table 3.2(1) Sample Survey Questions

1. Do you feel that women have as many opportunities to advance in the recreation field as men?
   ___ Yes   ___ No   ___ Don't know

2. Please indicate the extent to which you agree or disagree with these statements as they apply to the Park and Recreation field.

	Strongly Disagree	Disagree	Neither	Agree	Strongly Agree
a. Women are often excluded from informal male networks.	1	2	3	4	5
b. There is unconscious discrimination based on gender.	1	2	3	4	5
c. Women tend to work in areas that are not promotable.	1	2	3	4	5
d. Women are less committed to their careers because of family obligations.	1	2	3	4	5

3. What is your age? _____ years

Table 3.2(2) Example of a Code Book

Variable Label	Variable Name	Value Label	Questionnaire #
Opportu	Same opportunities	1= Yes 2= No 3= Don't know	#1
Exclude	Excluded from networks	1= Strongly disagree 2= Disagree 3= Neither 4= Agree 5= Strongly agree	#2a
Discrim	Unconscious discrimination	(same as #2a)	#2b
Promote	Areas not promotable	(same as #2a)	#2c
Commit	Women less committed	(same as #2a)	#2d
Age	Age	21–99	#3

Figure 3.2(3) shows how this same information would appear when coded and the numeric values needed for computer analysis with statistical programs like SPSS (Statistical Package for the Social Sciences) or spreadsheets like Microsoft Excel. Each row of information entered is usually the equivalent to one respondent's survey answers. The values of each variable appear in sequential columns in exactly the same order as the code book. The evaluation data are then saved as a specific data file that becomes the basis for statistical procedures.

Just a word about coding missing data. Almost every evaluator will run into a situation where some data are missing or where the respondent did

SPSS Data Editor Screen

(CASE)	OPPORTU	EXCLUDE	UNCONSC	NONPROM	LESSCOM	AGE
1	1	2	4	2	1	26
2	2	5	4	1	1	44
3	1	3	2	1	1	32
4...	...	...	...	...	...	...

continue to enter data until you run out of cases

Figure 3.2(3) Example of Data Screen for Code Book

not understand the directions, so they ended up with inappropriate responses. Perhaps the respondent filling out the questionnaire did not want to answer a particular question or maybe decided that two programs needed to be ranked as number one priorities. Rather than throw out the entire questionnaire just because some information is missing or incorrectly indicated, you can devise a system for handling missing data. You may select a particular code to represent your missing information, or if you are using a computerized statistical package, a predetermined code may exist in the program.

Let's look at an example of how to deal with missing data. Assume you are entering data from your survey, and your code book is set up to enter the age in years as indicated by the respondent. However, the person did not answer the age question so you have no age data to enter. In SPSS, you would enter nothing in the column for age for that one individual, but the program would insert a period because that is what the SPSS system uses to indicate missing data. Anytime you see a period in a column while working in SPSS, you know the computer will skip that observation in any calculation using that variable. So if we wanted the average age of our 100 respondents, the average is only going to be based on 99 observations because of our one missing answer. Not all statistical packages have the same coding schemes for missing data, but they all have a way to handle missing information when computing statistics. Be sure to take the time to find out what the program generally uses as the default for missing data.

Another fairly common coding dilemma is how to code information when your respondent did not answer the survey as directed. For example, you may have asked respondents to select just one answer, but they chose two. You could consider that variable as having missing data, or you could make yourself a coding rule such as if the person chooses more than one answer, you will always take the first answer selected or perhaps the one with the most conservative answer. The main point is that you need to be consistent with your missing data and the way you code inappropriate answers. If you are not careful, your statistics may be incorrectly calculated or biased because of your lack of attention to missing or conflicting information.

From Ideas to Reality

This chapter offers some basic and practical techniques for getting data from a questionnaire into numeric forms to be used in computer data analysis. The procedures are specific and must be followed carefully if analysis is to be properly conducted. During this phase of the evaluation project or research study, you will need to carefully consider the analyses that you want to do and be concerned with accurately coding and entering the data. Once your data are coded, you will need to double check to make sure they were coded correctly and what to do with missing data is considered.

Now that you have studied this chapter, you should be able to:

- Identify values as they relate to variables within a questionnaire.
- Code data with as much specificity as measured.
- Given any questionnaire, write a code book for it.
- Be ready to enter data into a data file in the appropriate format.
- Decide how to handle missing data.

Descriptive Statistics
Options and Choices

After you have coded your quantitative data, you are ready to find the answers to the evaluation criteria or the research questions you initially established. Some answers will be fairly straightforward. For example, univariate statistics such as adding up totals for overall participation rates or figuring percentages of people who participated in different programs are easy with descriptive statistics like frequencies and percentages. Sometimes you want to know more complex answers, however, such as: "Are there differences in the satisfaction levels of participants based on their age?" or "Is there any relationship between geographic location of participants and the activities in which they participate?" These types of questions require more sophisticated bivariate and multivariate statistical analyses. To make appropriate choices about which statistics to use, you need to know your options and how to make appropriate choices about the options.

The Basics of Descriptive Statistics

Descriptive statistics are exactly as the name implies; they describe and summarize characteristics of your data (Hudson, 1988). These descriptive statistics are univariate and include frequency counts, individual and cumulative percentages, measures of central tendency, and variations in data characteristics.

Frequency Counts and Percentages

Most evaluators are interested in the actual number of responses they generate for a question. For example, let's say you were interested in the ages of the adolescents that participated in the teen outdoor adventure program. Since one of the questions on the questionnaire instrument asked for age, we can get an actual frequency count of participants who are thirteen, fourteen, fifteen, and so on. See Table 3.3(1) on page 266.

Table 3.3(1) Age of Participants in the Teen Adventure Program

Age	Frequency	Percent	Cumulative Percent
13 years old	15	12%	12%
14 years old	24	20%	32%
15 years old	28	23%	55%
16 years old	35	28%	83%
17 years old	21	17%	100%
N=123			

You may also want to know what percentage of the total group of respondents was comprised of thirteen year olds. Individual percentages will provide this information. We also can take percentage use a step further with cumulative percentages. These percentages are added together as we move from group to group. As illustrated in Table 3.3(1), over half of the participants were between the ages of thirteen and fifteen years old. Also note on the table that N is the total number of respondents for a particular question. When discussing any aspect of univariate statistics, the number of people being described should be noted.

Central Tendency

Measures of central tendency (i.e., mode, median, and mean) are useful for describing the variable under consideration. The *mode* is the most frequently occurring value and is usually indicated by "M." The mode can be used for any level of data but is not generally the preferred measure for interval or ordinal data. For these levels of data, the mode tends to ignore too much other important information. An example of the mode would be the results from asking people to check the month in which they participated the most in community center programs. If the evaluator had coded the answer from 1–12 to correspond with the months, and the analysis indicated that July received the highest number of positive responses, then M=7. In the example illustrated by Table 3.3(1), the mode is sixteen years old.

The *median* is the value above and below which one half of the observations fall. Statisticians use "m" to indicate median. For ordinal data, the median is a good measure of central tendency since it uses ranking information. The median would be incorrect to use for nominal data, however, since ranking is not possible. In the example, we could rank the ages of the 123 teenagers, and the 62nd observation would be the age where exactly half of the respondents were above and half below. For this example, m=15 years. If the same size had been 124 (an even number sample), we would have to take the halfway point between the 62nd and 63rd observation. In this age example, our median would still be 15 since the 62nd and 63rd observation were both 15.

The third type of central tendency measure is the *mean* ($\overline{X}$=sample mean), also known as the average. The mean is used with interval and ratio data. The mean is the sum of all the values of the observations on that variable divided by the number of observations:

$$\overline{X} = \frac{\Sigma(x)}{N}$$ **Mean**

where $\overline{X}$ = mean Σ = sum of

       x = sample variable   N = total number sampled

In the age example in Table 3.3(1), the average age is 15.19 years. Finding means for nominal data is usually inappropriate and useless.

Several points about measures of central tendency should also be considered. First, these three measures (M, m, $\overline{X}$) need not be the same; in fact, they would not be the same except in a perfect normal distribution. If the distribution is symmetric, however, the mean, median, and mode are usually close in value. Secondly, the means are greatly affected by outliers while the median is not. An outlier is a score that is on the extreme end of a scale. A good example of the effect of an outlier can be found in salary information. Often the average salary may be quite a bit higher than the median because the outliers who earn high salaries bring the average up. Thus, the employer might point to the average salary as a way of suggesting that salaries are at an adequate level while the employees may use the median to illustrate that the midpoint salary levels are considerably lower than what management may be implying the mean indicates.

Variations in Data Characteristics

Measures of Dispersion (How Spread Out Are My Data?)

Two distributions can have the same mean for central tendency and yet be quite dissimilar. For example, two basketball teams could have their members shoot 20 free throws each. Team A could make 0, 1, 10, 14, and 20. Team B members could make 8, 8, 9, 10, and 10 free throws. Although the mean is 9 for both teams, the teams are obviously dissimilar.

One of the easiest calculations of dissimilarity, or dispersion, is the *range*. The range is the difference between the maximum and minimum observed values. Therefore the range for Team A is 20 and the range for Team B is 2. The range is sensitive to extremes, which is useful with ordinal data, but does not take into account the distribution of observations within the range.

Variance is a dispersion measure of variation that is based on all observations and describes the extent to which scores differ from each other (Struening & Guttentag, 1975). In other words, variance tells you how far the scores differ from one another. Many times the amount that the observed scores vary from each other is critical for understanding your sample. In our basketball example, the coach of Team A might work on free throw shooting differently than the coach of Team B. The variance (represented as s^2=variance) is obtained by summing the squared differences from the mean for all observations and then dividing by the number of observations minus 1.

$$s^2 = \frac{\sum (X - \bar{X})}{(n-1)}$$ **Variance**

where s^2 = variance X = observation
$\bar{X}$ = sample mean (average) $\sum$ = sum of
n = number of observations

If all of the observations are identical (that is, no variation), then variance is equal to 0. When looking at the distribution curve, the more spread out, the greater the variance. For the basketball team example, the variance for Team A=73 while the variance for Team B=1.

The most familiar measure of dispersion is the *standard deviation*. It is the average of the degree that scores deviate from the mean and has a special relationship to the normal distribution, as you will see in the following discussion on normal distribution. One of the reasons the evaluator pays attention to the standard deviation (represented by SD) is to gain some idea about how scores are dispersed around the mean (Lundegren & Farrell, 1985). The more the scores cluster around the mean, the more you can conclude that everyone is performing at about the same level or is answering questions similarly on an instrument. You derive the standard deviation by taking the square root of the variance. This measure is expressed in the same units of measurement as the observations while the variance is in the units squared. Thus, standard deviation is a clearer way to think of variability. In the basketball team example, the standard deviation for Team A would be 8.5, or 8.5 free throws and the SD = 1 for Team B.

The Distribution Curve (How Do My Data Look?)

The observations of most variables seem to cluster around the middle of the distribution, and the frequency of observations seems to decrease as you move away from the central concentration. This type of distribution is often called "bell-shaped" or a normal distribution. In society, characteristics such as height, weight, and blood pressure are thought to be approximately normal. Theoretically, if you plotted every person's weight, for example, the results would look like a bell-shaped curve.

The *normal distribution* is the most important theoretical distribution in statistics and serves as a reference point for describing the forms of distributions of quantitative data (Norusis, 1983). Let's say you ask for the weights of the people enrolled in a wellness program at your community center. By plotting the weights of your participants (or calculating them statistically), you can determine if your group is "normal." In other words, does your data fit the bell-shaped distribution?

The normal distribution is symmetric with the three measures of central tendency (i.e., mean, $\overline{X}$; median, m; and mode, M) theoretically coinciding at the center with gradually diminishing numbers toward the extremes (Lundegren & Farrell, 1985). In the normal distribution, we would expect to find 68% of the observations falling within approximately one standard deviation of the mean and 95% of all the observations falling within about two standard deviations of the mean. See Figure 3.3(2). If an observation

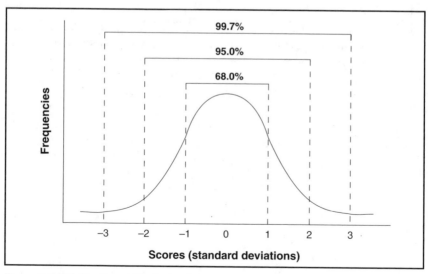

Figure 3.3(2) The Normal Distribution Curve

is outside the area covered by two standard deviations, you may want to consider that observation so unusual that it would not fit what is "normally" expected.

Other Measures Associated with Distributions

Skewness is a measure used when the distribution is not symmetric, and has a "tail." If the "tail" is toward the larger values, then the distribution is considered to be positively skewed. If the "tail" is toward the smaller values, it is considered to be negatively skewed. If we were to measure the attitudes of parents toward a youth baseball league and found most of the responses were toward positive values, we would conclude that the responses were positively skewed. In either case, this information would indicate that the distribution of the sample was not normal, because fewer scores are on one side of the mean. Figure 3.3(3) shows examples of a skewed distribution. The issues of central tendency and distribution will be the basis for more advanced statistical procedures discussed later in this book.

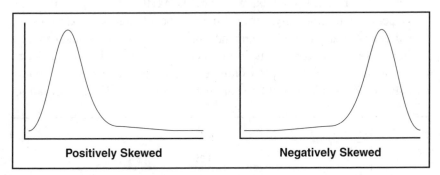

Figure 3.3(3) Positively and Negatively Skewed Distributions

From Ideas to Reality

Descriptive statistics are the most basic statistics that you will use. Many times they are used first in your analysis to describe the characteristics of the data and the general responses that have been received in a questionnaire. They are helpful for what the name means, to describe the information that you have. From these descriptive statistics, many other possibilities exist for data analysis.

Now that you have studied this chapter, you should be able to:

- Explain the most common types of descriptive statistics.
- Calculate and interpret the meaning of frequencies, percentages, mean, median, mode, standard deviation, range, and variance by hand or by using a computer.
- Explain the meaning of normal distribution.

The Word on Statistical Significance

As you use univariate, bivariate, or multivariate procedures to address evaluation criteria or research questions, you will likely want to know how much faith you ought to have that the differences or relationships are important. While a discussion of probability theory is beyond the scope of this text, a general understanding of statistical significance is important. *Statistical significance* refers to the unlikeliness that relationships observed in a sample could be attributed to chance alone. In other words, when we determine statistical significance we want to be as sure as possible that, indeed, a true relationship exists among variables.

Before you begin quantitative analysis, you must decide upon a level at which you are willing to say, "If my finding exceeds this level, then I am going to consider the findings different from what I would expect due to chance." In the social sciences, statistical significance, by convention, is generally set at probability $(p) < .05$. In the simplest terms, p(probability), of less than .05 means that 95 times out of 100 you would expect to get the same results and only five times out of 100 the result might be due purely to chance. For example, say you wanted to see if a difference existed between women's and men's participation rates in free swim at the community center. You select the appropriate statistical test and if your results indicate $p < .05$, then you accept that the women and men differ significantly from each other in participation rates. You will have to examine the means of each group to determine whether it is males or females who participate more or less.

There is a caution, however. Tests of significance are based on probability, so $p < .05$ is really saying that if you repeated this test 100 times, in only five times out of the 100 trials would you be wrong in thinking that the groups were different, when in actuality they were the same. In some fields like medical research, this error rate would be too great, so these researchers may set a significance level of $p < .001$. Thus, a medical researcher who was evaluating a new drug that resulted in statistically significant difference between the experimental and the control group would be assured that his or her finding was due to chance only one time out of 1,000. Most of us would rather except the odds that one out of 1,000 times something might not work than 1 out of 100 times.

At this point you may be asking yourself, "But what if I do get a wrong answer purely due to chance?" Let's say you are interested in the effect of play in the hospital on the recovery rate of children receiving tonsillectomies. You find through the analysis of your data that the recovery rates of children involved in play were faster and differed significantly at the .05 level from the children who were not in these play sessions. Given the evidence so far, group membership seems to make a difference. Maybe in reality your finding was due to chance and little real difference existed; you have made an unintentional error by assuming that the play opportunity made a difference in recovery as indicated by your statistics. The risk you take in making this type of error, called Type I error, is the same as the level of significance (Salkind, 1991). A significance level of $p < .05$ means that there is a 5% chance that you will say the groups are different when in actuality, they are the same, thus committing a Type I error. If you are using evaluation to determine whether to keep or eliminate a program, you must be careful that you consider a Type I error possibility so inappropriate decisions are reduced.

Another form of error is called Type II error. This error results when the data suggest that the groups are the same (no significant difference), but in actuality they are different. Ideally, you want to minimize both types of error, but Type II error is not as easy to control as Type I. In Type I situations, you as the evaluator select the significance level that you are willing to accept. Type II errors are not directly controlled but can be decreased by increasing the sample size. In other words, as you increase the sample size, you are also increasing the likelihood that the sample characteristics will more closely match or be representative of the population in a normal distribution. Therefore, you are reducing the likelihood of Type II error (thinking the groups are the same when they aren't).

If you try to reduce the Type II error rate by increasing the sample size, you must be careful because statistical significance can also be influenced by sample size (Babbie, 1992). For example, a large sample has the power to make everything seem statistically significant and in reality, little substantive differences may exist. Conversely, an extremely small sample may not show differences that do exist between groups. This weakness points out the importance of always determining whether or not the statistical difference is *meaningful*.

Meaningfulness is often as important as statistical significance. For example, you may ask all visitors to your parks during the summer to rate on a seven-point Likert scale their satisfaction with the available facilities. Your sample size at the end of the summer is over 15,000 visitors. Your statistical test may indicate that statistical significance exists between tent campers and RV users at the $p < .05$ level, but upon closer examination of the data, you find that the means only differ by three tenths of a point. This example is a good case to illustrate the need to use your judgment when determining how meaningful differences really are. In this case, a tenth of a point difference on a seven-point scale is probably really not important enough to justify facility changes. Sometimes, statistical procedures exist that will help you determine meaningfulness of difference, but often the evaluator is the one who makes a final determination.

A word of caution is in order here regarding sample size, statistical significance, and meaningfulness. You might have a small sample (e.g., ten people) and find no statistical significance on a variable, but large differences exist between the means. You cannot assume any meaningfulness because if the data do not have a p value that is significant, you do not know that the difference is not due to chance. Meaningfulness only relates to data that are statistically significant, not to data that are not.

Lastly, you do not always need to find statistical significance for a result to be important. Sometimes, not finding a difference is extremely useful. For example, if you know from previous research that adolescent girls generally have lower self-concepts based on self-esteem measures than their male counterparts. You decide to explore this idea in your teen adventure club that has been established to help teens build self-esteem and experience leadership opportunities. As a part of the summative evaluation you find that the girls' self-esteem is high and no different than the scores of the boys. The result is important and useful because it suggests that perhaps the content of the teen program is contributing to the development of self-esteem among both girls and boys.

Statistical significance is an important concept for you to understand, regardless of what statistics you use. For the evaluator, statistical significance is often used as a screening device for making subsequent conclusions and recommendations.

From Ideas to Reality

Statistical significance is one of the most helpful concepts that you will use when doing quantitative data analysis. The probability value (p) tells you whether or not a statistically significant difference exists between variables. Keep in mind, however, that the meaningfulness is also important. In addition to using what the statistics tell us, we must always examine our variables to see if the differences discovered are meaningful, useful, and important.

Now that you have studied this chapter, you should be able to:

- Define what statistical significance means.
- Describe the difference between Type I and Type II errors.
- Apply probability statistics to making conclusions about evaluation and research.

Inferential Statistics
The Plot Thickens

We have been talking about ways to calculate and describe characteristics about data. Descriptive statistics tell us information about the distribution of our data, how varied the data are, and the shape of the data. We are also interested in information related to our data parameters. In other words, we want to know if we have relationships, associations, or differences within our data and whether statistical significance exists. Inferential statistics help us make these determinations and allow us to generalize the results to a larger population. We provide background about parametric and nonparametric statistics and then show basic inferential statistics that examine associations among variables and tests of differences between groups.

Parametric and Nonparametric Statistics

In the world of statistics, distinctions are made in the types of analyses that can be used by the evaluator based on distribution assumptions and the levels of measurement data. For example, *parametric statistics* are based on the assumption of normal distribution and randomized sampling that results in interval or ratio data. The statistical tests usually determine significance of difference or relationships. These parametric statistical tests commonly include *t* tests, Pearson product-moment correlations, and analyses of variance (ANOVA).

Nonparametric statistics are known as distribution-free tests because they are not based on the assumptions of the normal probability curve. Nonparametric statistics do not specify conditions about parameters of the population but assume randomization and are usually applied to nominal and ordinal data. Several nonparametric tests do exist for interval data, however, when the sample size is small and the assumption of normal distribution would be violated. The most common forms of nonparametric tests are chi-square analysis, Sign test, Mann-Whitney U test, the Wilcoxon matched-pairs signed ranks test, Kruskal-Wallis test, Friedman analysis of variance test, and the Spearman rank-order correlation coefficient. These nonparametric tests are generally less powerful tests than the corresponding parametric tests. Table 3.5(1) provides parametric and nonparametric equivalent tests used for data analysis. The following sections will discuss these types of tests and the appropriate parametric and nonparametric choices.

Table 3.5(1) Parametric and Nonparametric Tests for Data Analysis (adapted from Loftus and Loftus, 1982)

Data	Purpose of Test	Parametric	Nonparametric
Single sample	To determine if an association exists between two nominal variables	—	Chi-square
Single sample	To determine if sample mean or median differs from some hypothetical value	Matched t-test	Sign test
Two samples, between subjects	To determine if the populations of two independent samples have the same means or median	Independent t-test	Mann-Whitney U test
Two conditions, within subjects	To determine if the populations of two samples have the same mean or median ranks test	Independent t-test	Sign test or Wilcoxon signed
More than two conditions, between subjects	To determine if the populations of more than two independent samples have the same mean or median	One-way ANOVA	Kruskal-Wallis
More than two conditions, within subjects	To determine if the populations or more than two samples have the same mean or median	Repeated measures ANOVA	Friedman ANOVA
Set of items with two measures on each item	To determine if the two measures are associated	Pearson correlation	Spearman

Associations among Variables

Chi-square (Crosstabs)

One of the most common statistical tests of association is the chi-square test. For this test to be used, data must be discrete and at nominal or ordinal levels. During the process of the analysis, the frequency data are arranged in tables that compare the observed distribution (your data) with the expected distributions (what you would expect to find if no difference existed among the values of a given variable or variables). In most computerized statistical packages, this chi-square procedure is called "crosstabs" or "tables." This statistical procedure is relatively easy to hand calculate as well. The basic chi-square formula is:

$$X^2 = \sum \frac{(O - E)^2}{E}$$

Chi-Square (Cross Tabs)

where X^2 = chi-square   O = observed
         $\sum$ = sum of   E = expected

Spearman and Pearson Correlations

Sometimes we want to determine relationships between scores. As an evaluator, you have to determine whether the data are appropriate for parametric or nonparametric procedures. Remember, this determination is based upon the level of data and sample size. If the sample is small or if the data are ordinal (rank-order) data, then the most appropriate choice is the nonparametric Spearman rank order correlation statistic. If the data are thought to be interval and normally distributed, then the basic test for linear (straight line) relationships is the parametric Pearson product-moment correlation technique.

The correlation results for Spearman or Pearson correlations can fall between +1 and –1. For the parametric Pearson or nonparametric Spearman the data are interpreted in the same way even though a different statistical procedure is used. You might think of the data as sitting on a matrix with an x-axis and y-axis. A positive correlation of +1 ($r = 1.0$) would mean that the slope of the line would be at 45 degrees upward. A negative correlation of –1 ($r = -1$) would be at 45 degrees downward. See Figure 3.5(2), page 280. No correlation at all would be $r = 0$ with a horizontal line. The correlation approaching +1 means that as one score increases, the other score increases and is said to be positively correlated. A correlation approaching

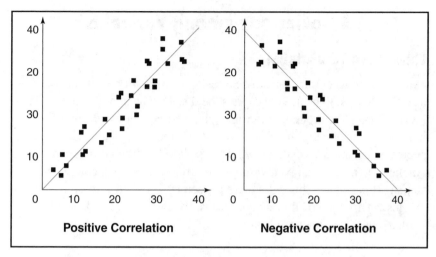

Figure 3.5(2) Examples of Correlation Relationships

–1 means that as one score increases, the other decreases, so is negatively correlated. A correlation of 0 means no linear relationship exists. In other words, a perfect positive correlation of 1 occurs only if the values of the x and y scores are identical, and a perfect negative correlation of –1 only if the values of x are the exact reverse of the values of y (Hale, 1990).

For example, if we found that the correlation between age and number of times someone swam at a community pool was $r=-.63$, we could conclude that older individuals were less likely than younger people to swim at a community pool. Or suppose we wanted to see if a relationship existed between body image scores of adolescent girls and self-esteem scores. If we found $r=.89$, then we would say a positive relationship was found (i.e., as positive body image scores increased, so did positive self-esteem scores). If $r=-.89$, then we would show a negative relationship, (i.e., as body image scores increased, self-esteem scores decreased). If $r=.10$, we would say little to no relationship was evident between body image and self-esteem scores. If the score was $r=.34$ you might say a weak positive relationship exists between body image and self-esteem scores. Anything above $r=.4$ or below $r=-.4$ might be considered a moderate relationship between two variables. Of course, the closer the correlation is to $r=+1$ or –1, the stronger the relationship.

Correlations can also be used for determining reliability as was discussed in Chapter 2.3 on trustworthiness. Let's say that we administered a questionnaire about nutrition habits for the adults in an aerobics class for the purpose of establishing reliability of the instrument. A week later we gave them the same test over. All of the individuals were ranked based upon the scores for each test, then compared through the Spearman procedure. If we found a result of $r = .94$, we would feel comfortable with the correlation referred to as the reliability coefficient of the instrument because this finding would indicate that the respondents' scores were consistent from test to retest. If $r = .36$, then we would believe the instrument to have weak reliability because the scores differed from the first test to the retest.

Two cautions should be noted in relation to correlations. First, you cannot assume that a correlation implies causation. These correlations should be used only to summarize the strength of a relationship. In the above example where $r = .89$, we can't say that improved body image causes increased self-esteem, because many other variables could be exerting an influence. We can however, say that as body image increases, so does self-esteem and vice versa. Correlations point to the fact that there is some relationship between two variables whether it is negative, nonexistent, or positive. Second, most statistical analyses of correlations also include a probability (p value). A correlation might be statistically significant as shown in the probability statistics, but the reliability value (-1 to $+1$) gives much more information. The p value suggests that a relationship exists but one must examine the correlation statistic to determine the direction and strength of the relationship.

Tests of Differences between and among Groups

Sometimes, you may want to evaluate by comparing two or more groups through some type of bivariate or multivariate procedure. Again, it will be necessary to know the types of data you have (i.e., continuous or discrete), the levels of measurement data (i.e., nominal, ordinal, interval, ratio), and the dependent and independent variables of interest to analyze.

In parametric analyses, the statistical process for determining difference is usually accomplished by comparing the means of the groups. The most common parametric tests of differences between means are the t tests and analysis of variance (ANOVA). In nonparametric analyses, you are usually checking the differences in rankings of your groups. For nonparametrics, the most common statistical procedures for testing differences are the Mann-Whitney U test, the Sign test, the Wilcoxon signed ranks test, Kruskal-Wallis, and the Friedman analysis of variance. While these parametric and nonparametric tests can be calculated by hand, they are fairly complicated and a bit tedious, so most evaluators rely on computerized statistical programs. Therefore, each test will be described in this section, but no hand calculations will be provided. For individuals interested in the manual calculations, any good statistics book will provide the formulas and necessary steps.

Parametric Choices for Determining Differences

T tests

Two types of *t* tests are available to the evaluator: the two-sample or *independent t test* and the *matched pairs* or *dependent t test*. The *independent t test*, also called the two-sample *t* test, is used to test the differences between the means of two groups. The result of the analysis is reported as a *t* value. It is important to remember that the two groups are mutually exclusive and not related to each other. For example, you may want to know if youth coaches who attended a workshop performed better on some aspect of teaching than those coaches who didn't attend. In this case, the teaching score is the dependent variable and the two groups of coaches (i.e., attendees and nonattendees) is the independent variable. If the *t* statistic that results from the *t* test has a probability $< .05$, then we know the two groups are different. We would examine the means for each group (those who attended as one group and those who did not) and determine which set of coaches had the higher teaching scores.

The *dependent t test*, often called the *matched-pairs t test*, is used to show how a group differs during two points in time. The matched *t* test is used if the two samples are related. This test is used if the same group was tested twice or when the two separate groups are matched on some variable. For example, in the above situation where you were offering a coaching clinic, it may be that you would want to see if participants learned anything at the clinic. You would test a construct such as knowledge of the game before the workshop and then again after the training to see if any difference existed in knowledge gained by the coaches that attended the clinic. The same coaches would fill out the questionnaire as a pretest and a posttest. If a statistical difference of $p < .05$ occurs, you can assume that the workshop made a difference in the knowledge level of the coaches. If the *t* test was not significant ($p > .05$), you could assume that the clinic made little difference in the knowledge level of coaches before and after the clinic.

Analysis of Variance (ANOVA)

Analysis of variance is used to determine differences among means when there are more than two groups examined. It is the same concept as the independent *t* tests except you have more than two groups. If there is only one independent variable (usually nominal or ordinal level data) consisting of more than two values, then the procedure is called a one-way ANOVA. If there are two independent variables, you would use a two-way ANOVA. The dependent variable is the measured variable and is usually interval or ratio level data. Both one-way and two-way ANOVAs are used to determine if three or more sample means are different from one another (Hale, 1990). Analysis of variance results are reported as an F statistic. For example, a therapeutic recreation specialist may want to know if inappropriate behaviors of psychiatric patients are affected by the type of therapy used (e.g., behavior modification, group counseling, or nondirective). In this example, the measured levels of inappropriate behavior would be the dependent variable while the independent variable would be type of therapy that is divided into three groups. If you found a statistically significant difference in the behavior of the patients ($p < .05$), you would examine the means for the three groups and determine which therapy was best. Additional statistical *post hoc* tests, such as Bonferroni or Scheffes, may be used with ANOVA to ascertain which groups differ from one another.

Other types of parametric statistical tests are available for more complex analysis purposes. The *t* tests and ANOVA described here are the most frequently used parametric statistics by beginning evaluators.

Nonparametric Choices for Determining Differences

For any of the common parametric statistics, a parallel nonparametric statistic exists in most cases. The use of these statistics depends on the level of measurement data and the sample as is shown in Table 3.5(1) (p. 278). The most common nonparametric statistics include the chi square, Mann-Whitney *U* test, Sign test, Wilcoxon signed ranks test, Kruskal-Wallis, and Friedman analysis of variance.

Mann-Whitney *U* Test

The Mann-Whitney *U* test is used to test for differences in rankings on some variable between two independent groups when the data are not scaled in intervals (Lundegren & Farrell, 1985). For example, you may want to analyze self-concept scores of high fit and low fit women who participated in a weight-training fitness program. You administer a nominal scale form where respondents rank characteristics as "like me" or "not like me." Thus, this test will let you determine the effects of this program on your participants by comparing the two groups and their self-concept scores. This test is equivalent to the independent *t* test.

The Sign Test

The Sign test is used when the independent variable is categorical and consists of two levels. The dependent variable is assumed to be continuous but can't be measured on a continuous scale, so a categorical scale is substituted (Hale, 1990). This test becomes the nonparametric equivalent to the dependent or matched *t* test. The Sign test is only appropriate if the dependent variable is binary (i.e., takes only two different values). Suppose you want to know if switching from wood to fiber daggerboards on your Sunfish sailboats increases the likelihood of winning regattas. The Sign test will let you test this question by comparing the two daggerboards as the independent variable and the number of races won as the dependent variable.

Wilcoxon Signed Ranks Test

The Wilcoxon test is also a nonparametric alternative to the *t* test and is used when the dependent variable has more than two values that are ranked. Positions in a race are a good example of this type of dependent variable. As in the Sign test, the independent variable is categorical and has two levels. For example, you might wish to know if a difference exists between runners belonging to a running club and those that do not compared to their finish positions in a road race. The results of this analysis indicate the difference in ranks on the dependent variable (finish position) between the two related groups (two types of runners).

Kruskal-Wallis Test

The Kruskal-Wallis test is the nonparametric equivalent to the one-way ANOVA. It is used when you have an independent variable with two or more values that you wish to compare to a dependent variable. You use this statistic to see if more than two independent groups have the same mean or median. Since this procedure is a nonparametric test, you would use the statistic when your sample size is small or you are not sure of the distribution. An example of an application would be to compare the attitudes of counselors at a camp (dependent variable) toward three different salary payment plans: weekly, twice a summer, or end of the summer (independent variable).

Friedman Analysis of Variance

The Friedman Analysis of Variance test is used for repeated measures analysis when you measure a subject two or more times. You must have a categorical independent variable with more than two values and a rank-order dependent variable that is measured more than twice (Hale, 1990). This test is the nonparametric equivalent to repeated measures of analysis of variance (two-way ANOVA). An example of a situation when you might use this statistical procedure would be if you had ranked data from multiple judges. For example, suppose you were experimenting with four new turf grasses on your four soccer fields. You ask your five maintenance workers to rank the grasses on all four fields for durability. You could analyze these results with the Friedman's procedure.

Making Decisions about Statistics

The decision model for choosing the appropriate type of statistical procedure is found in Figure 3.5(3) (p. 286). This model provides a logical progression of questions about your parametric and nonparametric data that will help you in your selection of appropriate statistics. Many other forms of statistical measures are possible, but the ones described here will provide you with the most common forms used in evaluations.

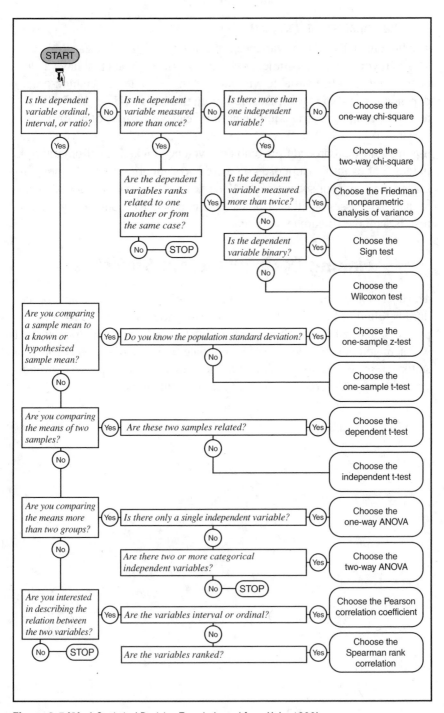

Figure 3.5(3) A Statistical Decision Tree (adapted from Hale, 1990)

From Ideas to Reality

This chapter initially may seem complex and full of terms not familiar to you. We realize that statistics are often confusing and overwhelming to some people, but as you begin to understand what they mean, they can be extremely helpful. We acknowledge that one short chapter will not make you an expert on these statistics, but we hope this chapter will at least show you some of the ways that we can gain valuable information by examining the relationships between and among variables. The more that you use statistical procedures, the more you will understand them. Thank goodness we have computers these days to save time and effort. Computers, however, do not absolve us from knowing which statistics to use to show associations or differences within our data. If you want more information than is offered in this short chapter, you may want to consult one of the many statistics books that exist.

Now that you have studied this chapter, you should be able to:

- Explain when parametric and nonparametric statistics should be used.
- Given a situation with the levels of measurement data known, choose the correct statistical procedure to use.
- Use the decision model for choosing appropriate statistical procedures to make decisions about a statistical problem.

Using Computers for Analyses

As you saw in the description of inferential statistics, some calculations can be complex. As computers have become an integral part in the lives of recreation and leisure service professionals, the options for computerized data analyses have become quite common. As an evaluator or researcher, you likely will be faced with the question, "How can I best use my computer to help with my data analysis?" Most of you will likely meet your needs with the popular general public software that is standard or easily purchased with most personal computers. Some of you may also have access to specialized software designed specifically for statistical or qualitative analyses for your organization. Regardless of the type of software, you will likely be expected to know how to use basic applications for your evaluation and research projects.

Many agencies and virtually all universities have statistical software packages available. Computer technology has changed so quickly that most professionals today have available to them on their desktop or in their hand-held devices the computing power that was available only to the most elite computer-based industries a few years ago. The memory needed to do advanced statistical analysis on large data sets is usually not an issue these days. Professionals can use software to do many evaluation and research-related tasks such as statistical analyses, data entry and processing, graphics, qualitative analyses, and telecommunications. Most of the time, you will use commercially available programs that are widely used by evaluators and researchers from around the country or world; other times, your agency may have acquire specialized software written specifically for your organization. In either case, you will have to learn how to use the software program unless your organization has a computer specialist who can run the analyses for you. Even if someone else does your analyses, you must be able to interpret the results and assure that the appropriate statistics were used.

Learning the statistical packages will require some investment of time on your part. Commercially available statistical programs such as the Statistical Packages for the Social Sciences (SPSS) have a fairly detailed set of procedures used to run the statistical package. Although you can try to learn about these procedures by reading the manuals, it is usually easier to attend a workshop that will give you hands-on experience that will help you acquire the basics.

The advantages to using commercially available statistical programs, however, are often worth the investment of time and energy to learn. You can do virtually any type of statistical analysis and most of them have built-in help features that provide advice on everything from the correct statistics to run to troubleshooting for possible errors. Many statistical software companies also have online help desks that you can contact through e-mail, browser-based chat, or phone for personalized help with more complex problems. Most programs have built-in graphic and report options that allow you to present your results in interesting, professional formats. As a beginning evaluator or researcher, these statistical packages allow you a great deal of flexibility and sophistication in your analyses. Even if you are doing only descriptive statistics, these computer programs will allow you to work easily with large data sets and use almost an infinite number of variables and values. These packages also enable you to convert data directly into figures and tables.

Some of you may not have access to specific statistical packages like SPSS. In these cases you probably do have access to more generic spreadsheet software such as Microsoft Excel or Lotus 1-2-3 for your personal computer that will allow you to conduct statistical analyses as well. Spreadsheet programs, while smaller and a bit less sophisticated than specialized statistical packages, still allow you to do most analyses needed to complete your evaluation and research projects. Most beginning evaluators and researchers conduct basic descriptive and inferential statistics for their analyses. Spreadsheets provide these basic statistics in fairly easy-to-learn procedures with good documentation to help you if problems arise.

For illustrative purposes, we used the interactive version of SPSS and, in a few spots, a spreadsheet in the following overview about computerized statistical packages. It is not within the scope of this book to teach the use of a specific statistical package like SPSS or Excel, but most packages for personal computers are not difficult to learn and use. If you know the variables that you wish to analyze and the way to enter data, almost any statistical package will allow you to do the descriptive and inferential calculations that have been discussed in the previous chapters.

An Example of SPSS Program

SPSS has several formats for use but the one we are using in this section is an interactive statistics and graphics package that can compute descriptive and inferential statistics. The SPSS graphics allow the visualization of one-dimensional and two-dimensional data. SPSS can handle almost unlimited numbers of cases (respondents) and variables. Spreadsheet programs may have more limitations about the numbers of cases and variables. You need to check your specific program for its parameters.

SPSS, as well as most spreadsheets, has several windows for performing the basic commands. For example in SPSS, the Variables window allows you to enter and modify your data, the Data window displays your data, and the Output window allows you to see the results of your requested statistical analysis. The program also has a series of menus that allow the user to edit data and create, change, or delete variables. You can analyze data through a variety of statistical procedures and get help if needed. SPSS can also accommodate imported files such as those data files you construct through Excel. This easy exchange in files is useful to evaluators and researchers, who might initially enter data through their spreadsheet for some basic calculations, then transfer the data for further, more sophisticated analyses to SPSS.

SPSS offers a broad range of statistical procedures through the Analyze menu. The option called "Descriptive statistics" provides an array of frequencies, descriptive statistics, and even a crosstabs option. "Compare means" provides independent and paired t tests as well as one-way ANOVAs. "Correlate" computes the Pearson correlation coefficients, "Regression" computes simple and multiple regression models, and "Scale" will provide a reliability analysis. SPSS also provides selected nonparametric statistics through "Nonparametric tests" that include chi-square, two independent samples tests (Mann-Whitney U), two related samples tests (Wilcoxon and Sign), and K-related samples (Friedman).

As previously mentioned, SPSS also has graphing capabilities. The Graphs menu provides a choice of selections including bar, line, area, and pie graphs. You may also select plots such as box plots and scatterplots. Several other graphing options exist for more complex data.

For all of these procedures, you control the location of your statistical output. For example, while doing your initial analyses, you will likely direct the results to your screen. At the end of your computing session, you may want to save a copy of the analyses to a file on a floppy disk or on a hard drive. You may also want a paper copy of your final results, so you can direct your output to your printer. In some cases, you may even want to create new data files based upon the results of your analyses. Further, the output produced from SPSS and other spreadsheets is easy to copy and paste directly into a word processing program like Microsoft Word when it comes time to write your evaluation or research report.

To get the most from data, every evaluator and researcher analyzing quantitative data will need to use a computer. You can learn how to run the program by reading the documentation, completing the interactive tutorial, and practicing with sample data. Learning to use a computer is a lot like learning a foreign language—the more you practice, the better you become. You can start out slowly using descriptive statistics and then move to more sophisticated analyses as you become more comfortable with the computer and data analysis.

Interpreting Statistics

Each computer program you use will give you a slightly different output as far as how data analyses will look. We will provide several general examples of how you can interpret data.

Descriptive Statistics

In most computer programs the descriptive statistics will include a list of the frequencies reported for the values of the variables, the mean, median, number of cases, standard deviation, standard error, skewness, and the sum. Most people understand these statistics fairly easily and you will usually just want to choose those statistics that are most meaningful to discuss. For example, Table 3.6(1) shows data runs from an evaluation of a Student Recreation Center (SRC). A five-point Likert scale was used to ascertain attitudes toward select aspects of the center such as entertainment (e.g., TV, music) while working out, extra equipment (e.g., towels, lockers), staff friendliness, type of equipment, and hours of operation. Each item was rated on a five-point Likert scale with 1 = terrible and 5 = outstanding. Table 3.6(1) is the output from SPSS "Descriptives" that provides statistical information including the range, mean, variance and standard deviation for these items. These descriptive statistics tell you that the respondents thought these aspects of the SRC were on average fair to very good. The example of a frequency table for entertainment provides additional detail regarding the percentage of distribution on each value. In this example, over 83% of the respondents thought the entertainment was fair to very good while only 9.3% thought it was terrible or poor. This table also illustrates the use of *percent* (based on

Table 3.6(1) Examples of SPSS Descriptive Statistics

Descriptive Statistics

	N	Range	Minimum	Maximum	Mean		Std.	Variance
	Statistic	Statistic	Statistic	Statistic	Statistic	Std. Error	Statistic	Statistic
ENTERTAI	43	4.00	1.00	5.00	3.4186	.1341	.8792	.773
EXTRA	44	3.00	2.00	5.00	3.2727	.1189	.7884	.622
STAFF	43	4.00	1.00	5.00	3.7907	.1270	.8326	.693
EQUIP	44	3.00	2.00	5.00	3.8864	.1309	.8685	.754
HOURS	44	3.00	2.00	5.00	4.0909	.1118	.7414	.550

Example of Frequency Table for One Variable

ENTERTAI		Frequency	Percent	Valid Percent	Cumulative Percent
Valid	terrible	2	4.5	4.7	4.7
	poor	2	4.5	4.7	9.3
	fair	18	40.9	41.9	51.2
	very good	18	40.9	41.9	93.0
	outstanding	3	6.8	7.0	100.0
	Total	43	97.7	100.0	
Missing	System	1	2.3	·	
Total		44			

all respondents including those who did not answer the question) and *valid percent* (based only the respondents who answered the question).

Correlations

The correlation usually shows the relationship between two interval variables. You will generally receive an *r* score to indicate correlation. Often if you correlate more than two variables you will get a matrix with a number of *r* scores so that each variable is compared to every other variable. As indicated earlier, correlations range from −1 to +1 so you will look at a score and interpret two aspects: whether it is a positive or negative correlation and the strength of that association (arbitrarily termed as weak or strong). The *p* value or "Sig.(2-tailed)," as in all analyses, indicates the probability of the finding. For example, if the correlation between how much an individual enjoyed working out and the perception of the quality of the instructors had a Pearson correlation (sometimes called an *r* value) of .394, you could conclude that a weak to medium positive relationship existed between enjoyment and instructors (see Table 3.6(2), p. 292). As the quality of the instructor also increased, the level of enjoyment increased. If the result had been $r = -.89$, you would conclude that as enjoyment increased, the quality of the instructors decreased. In the case illustrated in Table 3.6(2), significances is .034, so would say that the finding was statistically significant and that a moderate positive relationship exists between the two variables.

Table 3.6 (2) Correlations between Enjoyment and Quality Instructors

Descriptive Statistics

	Mean	Std. Deviation	N
ENJOYMNT	4.7586	.9124	29
QUALINST	4.4138	.9826	29

Correlations

		ENJOYMNT	QUALINST
ENJOYMNT	Pearson correlation	1.000	.394*
	Sig. (2-tailed)	.	.034
	N	29	29
QUALINST	Pearson correlation	.394*	1.000
	Sig. (2-tailed)	.034	.
	N	29	29

*Correlation is significant at the .05 level Sig.(2-tailed).

T tests

If we want to compare the means of two groups, we do an independent *t* test. The statistic that the computer will generate is a *t* statistic as well as a *p* (probability) statistic. We examine the *p* statistic to see if it is above or below our statistical significance standard set. For example, if the $p = .23$ and our standard was set at .05, we would conclude that no statistical significant difference existed between the means of two variables. If however, we were measuring the results of a basketball rules test taken by boys and girls after attending a one-day basketball clinic, we might find that the difference between the two means was significant at .008. In that case, we conclude that a statistical difference existed between the two means. In most computer printouts, the means and standard deviations for both groups are given along with the *t* and *p* values. You will need to look at the means to determine the location of any significant differences.

Table 3.6(3) shows a *t* test comparing opinions about the atmosphere of the Student Recreation Center compared to the gender of the respondents. The males' mean response was 3.00 with a standard deviation of .45 and the females had a 3.03 mean with a standard deviation of .78. The next piece of information to check is the Levene's Test for Equality of Variances to determine if the results indicate the two groups have equal variance. If the significance standard was preset at .05 and was not exceeded, then you look at the *t* test results for "equal variance assumed." In our example, Levene's test was .053, so we look at equal variance *t* test results ($p=.901$). This result indicates we have no statistically significant differences between women and men on their perceptions about the atmosphere of the SRC. If Levene's had been less than .05, we would have looked at "equal variance not assumed" ($p=.873$). It is important to remember to look at Levene's results because some analyses will show very different results in the *t* tests based on the assumption of variance. You can also see that the mean score between the males and the females were very similar, which further confirms that no differences existed. Had the results been statistically significant, we would turn to the means to see where the difference existed.

Table 3.6 (3) *T* test for Overall Atmosphere Compared by Sex

Independent Samples Test

| | | Levine's Test for Equality of Variances | | t-test for Equality of Means | | | | | | |
		F	Sig.	t	df	Sig.(2-tailed)	Mean Difference	Std. Error Difference	95% confidence interval of the difference Lower	Upper
ATMOSPH	Equal variance assumed	3.985	.053	-.125	41	.901	3.125E-02	.2500	-.5360	.4735
	Equal variance not assumed			-.162	31.025	.873	3.125E-02	.1931	-.4252	.3627

Group Statistics

SEX		N	Mean	Std. Deviation	Std. Error Mean
ATMOSPH	male	11	3.0000	.4472	.1348
	female	32	3.0313	.7822	.1383

Analysis of Variance

Analysis of variance (ANOVA) works the same way that independent *t* tests do except that you are interested in determining the differences in means between three or more groups. The statistics given on a print out are the sum of squares, mean-squares, *F* ratio, and a *p* value. The *F* ratio is the actual ANOVA statistic but the bottom line is the *p* value. You look to the *p* (or

"Sig." column) value to see whether it is above or below the standard set, which is usually .05. If the *p* value is above, no statistically significant differences occur among the means. If the *p* value is below .05, a difference exists somewhere among the means. As in *t* tests you will need to examine the means and standard deviations of the three or more variables to determine where the difference lies. Most statistical programs provide a list of the means for each group. In other cases you may have to run descriptive statistics to get the means for each group. You will need to know the means if you want to interpret which of the groups is different from the others. Sometimes when "eyeballing" the means it is difficult to determine which group(s) differ the most from the others. We recommend that you run a *post hoc* analysis, for example a Scheffes or Bonferelli analysis, to statistically help you determine the groups that significantly differ from the others. In SPSS, varied *post hoc* choices exist for this purpose. Table 3.6(4) shows an example of one-way comparing the quality of the workout at the Student Recreation Center to whether students were first-year/sophomore, junior/senior, or in graduate school. The significance level was .212 so we conclude that no statistically significant differences existed between the year in school and the quality of the workout at the Student Recreation Center.

Chi-square Statistics

These nonparametric statistics may also be found as *Crosstabs* or *Tables* in different statistical packages. When you run these types of analyses, you

Table 3.6(4) One-way Analysis of Quality of Workout by Year in School

Descriptive Statistics

QUALITY	N	Mean	Std. Deviation	Std. Error	95% confidence Interval for Mean Lower	Upper	Minimum	Maximum
FIRST/SOPH	18	3.3889	.5016	.1182	3.1394	3.6383	3.00	4.00
JR/SR	18	3.1111	.5830	.1374	2.8212	3.4010	2.00	4.00
GRADUATE	8	3.0000	.7559	.2673	2.3680	3.6320	2.00	4.00
Total	44	3.2045	.5937	.951E-02	3.0240	3.3851	2.00	4.00

ANOVA

QUALITY	Sum of squares	df	Mean square	F	Sig.
Between groups	1.104	2	.552	1.610	.212
Within groups	14.056	41	.343		
Total	15.159	43			

will generally get a variety of statistics. The statistic that you are most concerned with is the chi-square statistic and the p statistic. As in the other cases, you will see what the p value is and then you can compare it to the standard you have set. Most computer programs that run chi-square will give you a warning if more than 25% of the cells in the computed tables have less than five responses in them. When this occurs, the results are suspect. In chi-square analysis, you will have to eyeball your data to determine where the difference exists if you find a statistically significant difference. Since a matrix is provided that shows the number of responses in each cell, you can usually figure out where the difference exists fairly easily.

Table 3.6(5) shows a two-by-two table using a chi-square statistic to show relationship between students participation in cardiovascular activities and their biological sex. The chi-square statistic was .201 ($p=.654$) so there

Table 3.6(5) Crosstabs for Cardiovascular Workout and Sex

Crosstab

			SEX male	female	Total
CARDIO	yes	Count	7	21	28
		% within CARDIO	25.0	75.0	100.0
		% within SEX	58.3	65.6	63.6
		% of Total	15.9	47.7	63.6
	no	Count	5	11	16
		% within CARDIO	31.3	68.8	100.0
		% within SEX	41.7	34.4	36.4
		% of Total	11.4	25.0	36.4
Total		Count	12	32	44
		% within CARDIO	27.3	72.7	100.0
		% within SEX	100.0	100.0	100.0
		% of Total	27.3	72.7	100.0

Chi-square Tests

	Value	df	Asymp. Sig. (2-sided)	Exact Sig. (2-sided)	Exact Sig. (1-sided)
Pearson Chi-square	.201[b]	1	.654		
Continuity Correction[a]	.009	1	.924		
Likelihood Ratio	.198	1	.656		
Fisher's Exact Test				.732	.456
Linear-by-linear Association	.196	1	.658		
N of Valid Cases					

(a) Computed only for a 2x2 table
(b) One cell (25.0%) has expected count less than five. The minimum expected count is 4.36.

was no relationship between cardiovascular activities and the person's sex. Women were as likely as men to do a cardiovascular workout. The table is also useful in getting a picture of the specific details of the analysis. For example, the count shows seven men and 21 women did cardiovascular workouts. For all cardiovascular workouts, 25% were done by men and 75% were done by women. However, the actual number of men in the study ($n = 12$) was substantially fewer than women ($n = 32$), so the table helps look at proportions. In another example from this table, you find 58.3% of all men and 65.6% of all women did cardiovascular workouts. Even though the actual counted numbers looked like there might be differences between men and women, this percentage demonstrates why our analysis showed no significant relationships in our testing.

• • • • •

Although the data generated from statistical analysis can be rather daunting, the more you work with it, the easier it becomes to interpret and understand your results. Do not hesitate to find someone who understands statistics to help you interpret what you find out. Using inferential statistics that computer programs supply can contribute greatly to making decisions about the organizations in which we work.

Computer Use with Qualitative Data

The computer can be an effective tool for managing and analyzing qualitative data. While a computer is not mandatory for doing qualitative analysis, they can be extremely helpful to a researcher or evaluator. The computer can help cut down on fatigue, save time, reduce the tedium of clerical tasks like cutting and pasting quotes from transcripts, and can allow the evaluator to have more time for data interpretation (Henderson, 1991). Computers can be used for qualitative data collected from in-depth interviews, focus groups, unobtrusive data, or notes from fieldwork. Just as with the mushrooming possibilities for using computers to help analyze quantitative data with myriad statistical programs, researchers and evaluators have many possibilities for "computer help" when working with qualitative data. Technology is changing so rapidly that what we write today will likely be "dated" by the time you read this text. We want, however, to raise some current general options that should still be considered when working with qualitative data.

One of the drawbacks to qualitative data has been the process of going from the spoken words from an interview or focus group to transcriptions that serve as the hard data to be analyzed. This process usually involves tediously transcribing tapes. With the advent of inexpensive voice recognition software, this process can be done much easier and cheaper than the old way of hiring someone to listen and type a word-for-word tape transcription. With voice recognition, you can dictate your interview data into your computer and have the text simultaneously transcribed into text that is then usable by many software programs such as word processors or more specific analysis programs.

A number of good software packages exist to help with the analysis and interpretation of qualitative data. Some of the most popular current programs include NUD*IST, Ethnograph, Nvivo, and Atlas. All of these programs prepare a data file based upon the transcribed data. If you are considering purchasing one of these software programs, you will want to explore carefully the options each software package offers.

We will use NUD*IST as an example of some of the specific aspects you may want to consider from a qualitative data analysis program. NUD*IST helps users:

- Manage and search the text of multiple documents (e.g., interview notes)
- Manage and explore coded ideas about the data
- Search multiple files for coded concepts
- Generate reports including basic statistical summaries
- Index (code) text units
- Link ideas and construct theories
- Test theories about the data. (NUD*IST, 1997)

While most evaluators and researchers in recreation and leisure services are concerned with qualitative textual data, NUD*IST can also handle nontextual data such as maps and photographs. NUD*IST does more than provide a coding system for documents. This program helps us shape our understanding of the data, form and test theories, and reorganize and reshape all aspects of our analysis system.

Just as the statistical packages use varied windows for different functions, NUD*IST has editable windows for different parts of the project and the analysis. Your qualitative data are set up in two parallel databases called the document system and the index system. These systems help you keep track of all your text files, organize your codes, and keep track of how they are indexed in your text. Both of these systems become very important in the analysis functions because they allow you to construct new theories about the relationships in your data and test your theories by exploring the links with your data.

Other Uses for the Computer in Evaluation

Rapid technological developments produce many advancements that will help the researcher and evaluator. Telecommunications provides us access within seconds to the most updated resource materials that used to be difficult and time-consuming to acquire. Word processing and desktop publishing can help produce professional and commercial quality questionnaires as well as final reports for an evaluation. Hand-held computers can be easily taken to a site where interviewers can ask participants survey questions, enter the responses (often with a stylus rather than a keyboard) into a formatted data file to download (often through a wireless connection) for analysis. Information can be beamed between computers, and if hard connections exist, these systems of fiber optics are so quick that they may seem instantaneous. As the public becomes even more technologically oriented, we may collect data from our constituents through their cable connections in their homes to computer stations found in our parks, community centers, or libraries. As researchers and evaluators with similar interests, we may become part of "teams" spread across the country who collect and share data with almost limitless possibilities for data collection, varied interpretations, and applications to theory and practice.

During the next few years, other discoveries certainly will be produced that will be helpful to an evaluator or researcher. As competent evaluators you will want to continue to read about changing technology, attend workshops at professional meetings, and talk with colleagues who have discovered new uses for computers and technological advances. Computers have become an important part of leisure services evaluation and research. The challenge may come in trying to maximize all of the possibilities that will make your evaluation projects easier!

From Ideas to Reality

This chapter provided a broad overview of the possibilities of using technology such as computer packages in evaluation and research. We do not know what potential software packages you will have available for conducting your data analyses in the future, so it is not useful to teach any particular approach. Most packages, however, use similar formats and if you understand how data are coded, entered, and interpreted, you should be able to read the documentation that comes with the program and figure out how to run particular analyses. Once these runs are completed, the easy part is looking to see whether statistical significance exists and what the results mean. For many people, doing the data analysis is the fun part after much time has been spent collecting, coding, and entering data.

Now that you have studied this chapter, you should be able to:

- Describe the options available for using computers in evaluation and research projects.
- Use basic statistical or qualitative data options available within a software package that will meet the needs of your evaluation project or research study.
- Explain how to interpret whether an analysis is statistically significant and meaningful.

Qualitative Data Analysis and Interpretation

In projects and studies that use qualitative data, we are *not* necessarily concerned with a singular conclusion, but with perspectives or patterns. In qualitative data analysis and interpretation the evaluator or researcher tries to uncover perspectives that will help understand the criteria being explored in an evaluation or research project. Further, doing qualitative analysis is a time-consuming task as the evaluator reads over notes or transcriptions, organizes the data, looks for patterns, checks emergent themes back-and-forth with the data, validates data sources, and makes linkages. This work is the heart of qualitative analysis and interpretation.

As was described earlier, in-depth interviews and qualitative observations are the most common ways to obtain qualitative data. An evaluator or researcher might also ask open-ended questions on a questionnaire that would result in qualitative data. It is particularly important that open-ended questions are asked in such a way that a yes/no answer is not possible. One of the difficulties with collecting qualitative data, however, is that it is easy to get overwhelmed with the amount of text generated. Too much data results in data management problems. Qualitative data can be coded, but not in the same sense as quantitative data. Coding is used as a way to organize qualitative data into brief word descriptions. Further, since the qualitative data are not reduced to numbers as in quantitative analysis, the interpretation of what the data mean is the evaluator's responsibility. Thus, the evaluator becomes personally involved in the analysis.

Analysis is the process of bringing order to qualitative data and organizing words into patterns, categories, and basic descriptive units. It can be likened to what we do with quantitative data in terms of coding and actually running statistics. Interpretation involves attaching meanings and significance to the analysis, explaining descriptive patterns, and looking for relationships and linkages within the data. In statistics, it is like determining if statistical significance exists and what it means.

According to Patton (1980b), an interesting and readable evaluation report provides sufficient description to allow the reader to understand the analysis, and sufficient analysis to allow the reader to understand the description. Analysis comes from focusing on the criteria raised at the beginning of a project and then describing how the data evolved into perspectives and conclusions. Qualitative data are often used for formative evaluations but may also be used for summative evaluations and assessments.

Qualitative analyses provide descriptions of what actually happened using word pictures and word summaries. The aim is to get both "outer" and "inner" perspectives. The inner perspective is the actual words. The outer perspective is the interpretation of what the words mean. Making sense of the words, however, and not having conclusions that appear to be the evaluator's opinions require a rigorous analysis process. When done properly, qualitative data analysis is just as systematic as any quantitative analysis.

Organizing for Qualitative Analysis

No magic formulas exist for how to do qualitative analysis. In general, however, the data must be organized into some manageable form, referred to as data reduction. Data reduction involves the process of organizing data and developing possible categories for analysis. As soon as field notes are taken or tapes are transcribed, data reduction begins. Additional written procedures are generally used to summarize some of the raw data. This data management requires judgment calls and decision rules that each evaluator will develop in summarizing and resummarizing the data.

Qualitative Coding

The evaluator using qualitative data must consider how to organize data so that one can return to it quickly without having to read through reams of material. Coding is probably one of the most difficult aspects of analyzing qualitative data. Much reading and rereading of data are necessary to become completely familiar with the data. After the reading, coding can be done by reducing the words to numbers, short phrases, or to short descriptions. Evaluators are cautioned about coding to numbers because often the richness of words can be lost when number coding occurs. Descriptive word codes may be more useful.

The coding for qualitative data may be descriptive, interpretive, or explanatory. These codes are likely to change over time as more data are collected. One way to start the data analysis process is to code the data descriptively according to the evaluation questions or criteria that were originally conceptualized. Codes can then be revised as new ideas emerge and are revised. If possible, it may be useful to have two evaluators code the raw data to assure greater reliability. Coding may be done line-by-line but is usually done in chunks. It may be quite general at first and then more focused later. The coding also will help the evaluator or researcher become familiar with the nature of the data that are being discovered and may help in focusing future interviews or observations for broader or deeper information.

Write-ups

Field notes and transcripts can be converted into write-ups, and memos (i.e., notes on notes). The write-up indicates the most important content of a study at a particular time. These write-ups provide a way to organize thoughts and will evolve over time. Memos or "notes on notes" are short summaries about data from the evaluator's perspective, and can also be used to highlight possible patterns and clarifications of concepts. You also might want to include memos addressing personal emotional reactions as well as any methodological difficulties that might have occurred during data collection. These memos may be gut reactions to what is going on, inferences about the quality of the data, new connections made, notes about what to address later, elaborations, or clarifications. Written material should be dated, titled, and anchored to particular places in the field notes or transcripts. The memos require the researcher to think rather than to just collect data and ideas.

Other Organizing Strategies

A filing system can also be developed for organizing data. This system may be developed on the computer for coding chunks of data or by actually physically cutting and pasting notes and putting these edited pages into file folders. Guba and Lincoln (1981) suggested a technique of using note cards to sort ideas into look alike piles that could be used to organize data. Qualitative computer packages, as discussed previously, are more commonly used today with large amounts of data. The use of note cards or chunks of data organized on the computer allows one to visually examine the grouped data and to begin to visualize how data may be categorized. The computer can help a great deal in organizing data, but it is still the individual who must make decisions about the way the data are organized and ultimately put together.

Displaying the Data

Once the data have been organized, you may then want to develop ways to display it further. Data display is the organized assembly of information that permits the drawing of conclusions and the presentation of the respondents' words. Data displays are not required but they may be helpful as you begin to make sense of the coded data. A number of ways exist to display data as a means for organizing for data interpretation. Each evaluator will find that certain display strategies work well and others do not, depending on the situation. In each case, no matter what kind of visual techniques are used to display data, the evaluator will have to make judgments about what data are or are not important.

A matrix based on words and phrases may also be used after data are coded. A matrix can easily be viewed and compared to other matrices. Usually the evaluator will develop categories for the matrix and then fill in the matrix with words or examples from the notes/transcripts that describe the categories. A matrix may be used to outline specific examples that fit particular themes or it may be used for compiling the number of responses to particular analysis categories. A number of matrices for a set of data can be developed. Some people prefer to build a matrix on a huge sheet of paper with 15–20 variables (although 5–6 is usually more manageable). For example, if we wanted to examine what activities adults said they enjoyed most, we might make a three-by-three matrix with the age groups young adult, middle age, and older adult across the top and then categories of leisure, home, and paid work down the side. See Table 3.7(1). We would display our data by indicating within the cells, what specific types of activities were described *or* perhaps what the benefits were to these adults according to their age groups.

Visual maps may be used to show the interrelationships that make up behavior. Diagrams are often helpful in organizing ideas and themes as well as patterns and configurations of interaction. You should also make notes about how you, as the evaluator, moved from one idea to another and how you refined the data displays. Conceptual maps, which may be likened to a flow chart, tie patterns together with arrows and directional lines. See Figure 3.7(2). Visual maps may be useful in stimulating thinking and may be useful to evaluators who like to see analyses visually. For example, if we were examining how people get information about available recreation opportunities in a community, we might make a diagram showing how the different ways are linked or not linked to one another.

These suggestions for displaying data are tools to be used in interpreting data. Data reduction and display are not the end products, but are techniques to assist the evaluator or researcher. The reduction techniques are a means to the ultimate ends of providing a rich description and explanation of the meaning of the evaluation data.

Age/Activity	Young Adult	Middle Age	Older Adult
Leisure	• Volleyball • Socializing • Aerobics • Drinking	• Arts and crafts • Walking • Eating out • Vacations with family	• Seeing grandchildren • Walking • Going to senior center • Senior Games
Home	• Cleaning • Talking on phone • Internet	• Cooking/Cleaning • Childcare	• Looking after grandchildren • Cooking
Paid Work	• Busy • Committed • Important	• Balancing work and leisure • Perfection not needed	• Volunteering important • Part-time work as leisure

Figure 3.7 (1) Matrix of Comments about Age and Activity

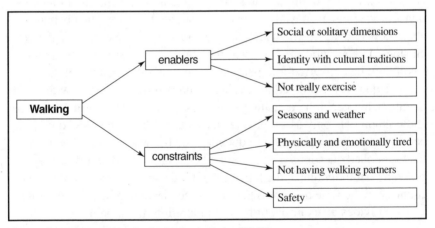

Figure 3.7 (2) Visual Map for Qualitative Analysis of Walking

Techniques for Data Analysis

Once the data are organized, a number of techniques may be applied to qualitative analysis. For purposes of evaluation research, we will discuss two major techniques for developing themes or patterns: enumeration and constant comparison. Content analysis will also be discussed as a category of constant comparison. Enumeration refers to the counting of items that are similar. Constant comparison of patterns and themes is a summary of the major ideas that emerge. Content analysis refers to examining the meanings of communication and is similar to constant comparison except that it is usually used with written materials.

In any type of qualitative data analysis, the evaluator is attempting to account for all ideas that are presented, not just the most popular ideas. Evaluators interested in using qualitative data attempt to explain all the variance. We are interested in the outliers as well as what the majority says or does. In other words, the focus is on interpreting conclusions including pointing out contradictions that exist in the data. Further, the effort of uncovering patterns, themes, and categories is a creative process that requires carefully considered interpretations about what is significant and meaningful in the data.

Enumeration

Enumerative strategies often supplement descriptive data. In this technique the evaluator codes qualitative data and counts it. One may be interested in the number of times certain behaviors occur or the duration of behaviors. Numbers are used in this case to show the intensity and amount of interaction. These numbers may also help the researcher to be analytically honest about how much agreement and disagreement existed about particular conclusions. In enumeration, however, the numbers are only numbers and should not be converted into percentages or any other statistical data.

In a qualitative project, the evaluator may do some analysis with enumeration, but generally a qualitative evaluator will rely primarily on words and use numbers only as supplementary material. In open-ended questionnaires, however, numbers are frequently used because they are comparable to close-ended questions. For example, you might ask what it was about a program that individuals liked the best, provide an enumeration of number counts, and then use the words to explain the meaning of the results. Table 3.7(3) provides an example of how enumeration might be used.

Constant Comparison

Constant comparison is a popular systematic analysis technique for recording, coding and analyzing qualitative data. The process of constant comparison includes reading through all data, developing major themes or key conclusions, reading the data again to see that it all fits within the themes, adjusting the themes, and reading again to confirm that the interpretation is valid. See Table 3.7(4) (p. 310) for an example of the first part of this process. Obviously, data analysis takes time. The technique also may mean going to others (e.g., colleagues or respondents) to have them confirm that they see similar themes uncovered or that interpretations are correct.

The goal of constant comparison is to maximize credibility through the comparison of groups and data. It involves comparisons among data,

---

Table 3.7 (3) Example of Enumeration Coding and Analysis

Background about Data: An evaluation was done in a southern university eight months after a Four-day Workweek was mandated as a measure to try to save energy costs. A questionnaire using both close-ended and open-ended questions was sent to a random sample of faculty and staff who worked at the university. These are some of the responses to a question about attitudes toward the Four-day Workweek and how they might be coded using a simple enumeration process of indicating whether the attitude is positive, negative, or neutral.

I don't have the physical stamina to hold up to a ten-hour day.   (code=negative)
There are inconveniences such as trying to cram too much into four days.
                                                                          (code=negative)
What is gained on the "off" day does not compensate for the stress on
the other four days.   (code=negative)
It causes hardships at home with trying to take care of kids when they
aren't in school early in the morning and in the afternoon.   (code=negative)
It's great. It would be hard to adjust to going back.   (code=positive)
I can be home on Fridays with my 4-year-old son and I like it a lot.   (code=positive)
I am able to spend time on Fridays with friends, relatives, and I enjoy
doing these things.   (code=positive)
I don't feel I'm getting as much done during the week as I did before.   (code=negative)
It's not good for morale because it squeezes too many expectations
into too little time.   (code=negative)
The week goes by quickly and it gives me a chance to catch up on my
personal projects on Friday.   (code=positive)
It makes sense.   (code=positive)
I like it a lot but my older colleagues are not coping very well with it. (code=neutral)

Total = 6 negative, 5 positive, 1 neutral, 12 total.

The data would be reported as numbers to show the relative amount of agreement concerning how the data were coded. Percentages should not be used as they may be confusing to the reader who is accustomed to seeing percentages related to quantitative statistics.

---

data sets, documents, and different groups sampled. Different "slices of data" can also be compared. For example, one might triangulate surveys, observations, and anecdotal records and analyze how the results compare to one another. The constant comparison technique is inductive like other forms of qualitative analysis, which means the patterns and themes emerge from the data rather than being imposed prior to data collection.

Four stages comprise the constant comparison process:

1. Reduce, code, and display the major themes or patterns that emerge.

2. Integrate the categories and compare them to one another and to the themes.

3. Delimit and refine the themes.

Table 3.7(4) Example of Doing Constant Comparison

These are some of the same responses to a question about attitudes toward the Four-day Workweek and how they might be coded using an initial constant comparison approach.

I don't have the physical stamina to hold up to a ten-hour day.   (code: tired)

There are inconveniences such as trying to cram too much into four days.   (code: inconveniences, not identified)

What is gained on the "off" day does not compensate for the stress on the other four days.   (code: stress)

It causes hardships at home with trying to take care of kids when they aren't in school early in the morning and in the afternoon.   (code=inconveniences with children)

It's great. It would be hard to adjust to going back.   (code: like, but no reason)

I can be home on Fridays with my 4-year-old son and I like it a lot.   (code: time to spend with people)

I am able to spend time on Fridays with friends, relatives, and I enjoy doing these things.   (code: time to be with people)

I don't feel I'm getting as much done during the week as I did before.   (code: time problems)

It's not good for morale because it squeezes too many expectations into too little time.   (code: time problems)

The week goes by quickly and it gives me a chance to catch up on my personal projects on Friday.   (code: personal time)

It makes sense.   (code: logic)

I like it a lot but my older colleagues are not coping very well with it.   (code: concern for others)

This is a preliminary coding. You would go through all the data and work with it until you saw themes emerging. For example, time is both a negative and a positive factor concerning the attitudes toward the Four-day Workweek. It opens time up for some people on the weekends but the time also creates stress and a feeling of lack of production in some people.

---

4. Provide examples from the data that show how the themes were derived.

First the researcher takes "pieces" of data and organizes them by identifying, reducing, coding, and displaying categories of data. If an interview guide or standardized interview guide is used, the initial stage might comprise organizing the responses based on the questions.

The second stage is to integrate the categories and their properties by comparing them to one another and checking them back to the data. In the case of the interview guide, data may appear as a response to one question that really fits better into another theme. Therefore, the evaluator must reorganize the responses according to themes. In this stage, the evaluator might also uncover and describe subthemes.

In the third stage, the categories are delimited and refined, if necessary, to further focus a story about the data and how it fits together with *a priori* or emerging evaluation criteria. The evaluator wants to make sure that no other themes or categories might be included or that any important data are being excluded. If new themes are discovered, then the researcher must go back through the data, compare them to the new categories, and go through the analysis process once again. The evaluator must also consider the wide variety of data that might exist.

The final stage involves going back to the original data and pulling out quotes, phrases, or anecdotes that support the themes. If these data are not included, the reader does not know if the project has been appropriately analyzed.

The constant comparison method causes one to look continually for diversity. It allows the assurance of accurate evidence, establishes generality of a fact, specifies concepts, verifies theory, or generates theory. According to Glaser and Strauss (1967), constant comparison does not generate a perfect theory or perfect conclusions, but rather perspectives and conclusions relevant to the context in which the data were observed or recorded.

Content analysis is a form of constant comparison commonly used to analyze documents, records, transcribed conversations, letters, or any document in a textual form. It is a process for making inferences by systematically identifying characteristics of messages. It may be done in words, phrases, sentences, paragraphs, sections, chapters, pictures, books, or any relevant context. Content analysis and its many forms relate to a process of ascertaining meanings about a written phenomena being studied. In this sense, the strategy is more analytic than oriented toward data collection. Like unobtrusive techniques, this method may be used with a project that stands alone or may be used in triangulation with other data analysis strategies. Field evaluators frequently use document analysis as a form of content analysis to obtain historical information about a setting or situation being evaluated.

Making Interpretations

Drawing conclusions to make interpretations about qualitative data occurs throughout the evaluation process. It is usually but not always an interactive, cyclical process that is ongoing as data are collected and organized. As you are reading data to organize it for enumeration or constant comparison, you are continually reexamining the data. You will be looking for *negative evidence* which means you will be trying to make sure everything fits your categories. If not all the data fit the themes or categories, you will either have to explain contradictions or make new categories.

As stressed throughout this chapter, you will also be looking for multiple sources of evidence to draw conclusions. Sample systematically and widely and try to avoid becoming too attached to initial themes and patterns. An important strategy concerning data analysis is, therefore, not to stop the analysis process too soon before you are sure you have interpreted the data as well as you can. Although an evaluator often is focusing on the end product, you must make sure that you do not reach the end too soon or become locked too quickly into a pattern of analysis that misses other possible meanings. The emergent nature of qualitative data must be allowed to happen. Documenting your feelings throughout the data collection and analysis process is useful as your attitudes and feelings may give insights about the data and its context.

The complete qualitative data analysis process generally includes the simultaneous techniques of collecting, coding and organizing, analyzing, and interpreting data in its context. As indicated earlier, interpretation involves attaching meaning and significance to the data. With the voluminous amount of data collected in qualitative projects, beginning the analysis during data collection helps to organize the data and make it less overwhelming. Data analysis and the development of interpretations should, therefore, begin as soon as possible after data collection.

Another key strategy to emphasize is that interpretations in qualitative projects come from being intimately familiar with the data. Therefore, one of the important tasks the evaluator does is to read the data over and over. The interpretation of meanings is not a task that can be assigned to someone else like one might hire someone to enter data into a computer or to run the statistics and give the evaluator the printout. Only through interaction with the data will you become familiar enough to see the emerging patterns and themes.

When all data are collected and analyzed, however, you will need to draw conclusions and make recommendations based on your interpretation of the results of the evaluation or research project. During the final stage of data analysis you will also double-check what data you will use to support or exemplify your findings. The data will be used to illustrate how your conclusions were drawn. Two important aspects will be evident in the conclusions. You will be using examples of *emic*, noted as ideas expressed by the respondents, as well as *etic*, which are data expressed in the evaluator's language. As you begin to do interpretations, you will make statements, called *thick description* (Geertz, 1983), based on both the emic and etic that is uncovered in the analysis. Table 3.7(5) shows an example of a write-up that might be used. You will note that the evaluator made an interpretation and used the respondents' words to illustrate the point.

The evaluator or researcher using qualitative data will actually use quotes and anecdotes to tell the story from the data. These descriptions and quotations are essential and should not be trivial or mundane. You will want to use a balance of description with the analysis and interpretation. The interpretations from qualitative data can be fairly lengthy but you should try to condense them to hit upon the important points. The summaries that you write let the reader know what happened during the organization, what it was like from the participant's view, and how the events were experienced. The description will depend to a great extent on the evaluation criteria being addressed. In making interpretations, however, you must acknowledge that a fine line exists between description and causes. We can describe the causes, but we can't always say the direct relationship that might exist among variables or themes. The application of this caveat will depend to a great extent on the nature of the data analyzed.

Table 3.7(5) Sample of a Few Lines of a Qualitative Evaluation Write-up

The women with disabilities interviewed in this project defined leisure as free time or having time do the things they wanted to do. They also talked about "having fun," "relaxing," "doing nothing," and "doing things at your own will and pace" as their definitions of leisure. A general distinction was made between recreation and leisure as indicated by the 41-year old married woman with chronic fatigue syndrome:

> To me, recreation is doing something physical. Playing softball with
> your child or riding a bike or something along that line. And leisure
> can be just doing something quietly like reading a book or even playing
> a game, but something that's quiet. So to me that's the difference.

Among the examples of leisure and recreation activities that the women with disabilities said they enjoyed doing were: dancing, eating out, shopping, painting pictures, writing poetry, gardening, listening to music, sewing, swimming, photography, walking, church activities, watching TV, and playing games. No single activity or even group of activities was common for all women with disabilities who were interviewed. Overall the women interviewed suggested that solitary and more passive activities were done at home, while going into public places to participate in more active recreation generally required some type of assistance or companionship....

From Ideas to Reality

This last section of this chapter has addressed the judgment part of the trilogy related to evaluation and research. As indicated throughout this text, however, it is difficult to separate the processes involved with analyzing qualitative data into distinct steps. Thus, we have described data collection, data analysis and drawing interpretations that lead to conclusions or recommendations as going hand in hand. You should have all the information you need from this chapter to work with the qualitative data that you might collect. You will find, however, that handling qualitative data effectively requires practice. You can learn best by actually working with such data.

Now that you have studied this chapter, you should be able to:

- Describe the options that are available for analyzing qualitative data.
- Explain the value of being as familiar as possible with data.
- Given a block of qualitative data, analyze it using the enumeration and the constant comparison techniques.

Unit Four
JUDGMENT: Data Reporting

Introduction to Judgment

An evaluation project isn't over until the judgment is made. Similarly, a research study is not done until the question of "so what?" is answered. The intensive work part of evaluation or research is set once you determine your criteria and get evidence through data collection and analysis. But the third part of the trilogy, the judgment phase, is often the real thinking part. You have to try to make sense of the findings that you have analyzed. By its very definition, evaluation requires that you determine the worth or make judgments. Research requires that you try to find answers. Thus, if you do not make judgments, an undertaking may have little value.

In Unit Four we discuss how to report the evaluations by developing conclusions and recommendations. We also talk about using visuals to display data and how to write and present evaluation reports and research data. We focus on the most important part of all evaluations—their use. Finally, evaluation systems and projects as well as research publications also need to be evaluated so we discuss some of the common problems that occur in conducting projects and how you can do a self-assessment of your own work.

When you have completed this last unit of this textbook, you should be fairly familiar with how evaluation projects and research studies are supposed to work. You will not be an expert, but you will have a working knowledge of how to proceed with an evaluation or research project and how to justify the use of evaluations within an organization.

Using Visuals for Displaying Data

One of the most important steps in the evaluation or research process is the transmittal of the information that you have gathered to people who will use it in decision making. Sometimes this process is simplified through the visual representation of the data findings in tables and graphs. These visuals are usually incorporated into reports and presentations but also offer a way to organize the findings so that judgments through conclusions and recommendations can be made.

The old adage "a picture is worth a thousand words" is true in evaluation, especially when handling complex quantitative data. A good rule of thumb is to use a visual when you find yourself visualizing something as you write or if you have several sets of numbers to compare (Robinson, 1985). You should know not only when to use visuals, but the best type to use, such as drawings, charts, tables, graphs, or photos.

When designing effective visuals, consider several general points. The visual should be appropriate to the audience and as simple as possible. No matter how "glitzy" you make your visuals, they will be totally useless unless the reader or audience understands them. Each part of the visual should be clearly labeled and visually pleasing with neat spacing, plenty of white space, and an easy-to-read typeface.

Further, the visuals and the text should work together to provide integral documentation and support for the findings you discuss in the narrative part of your report. You should always refer to a table in the appropriate place in the text. For example, if you included a table showing the participation in various recreation centers based on race, you might show this in two ways. You might say, "As seen in Table 1, some recreation centers are predominated by a single racial group" or you might say, "Some recreation centers are predominated by a single racial group (see Table 1)." The following sections will address specific information about making tables and figures.

Tables

Tables are the most common form of visual used for showing data. One of the primary advantages to tables is that the "number clutter" in the text can be drastically reduced. For example, instead of reading a tedious list of means used to compare two groups of participants, these data can be displayed in a table. A second advantage is that comparisons are shown more clearly in tables than with words. Tables also allow you to display data in a concise form. Do not include tables, however, if all the information on a table can be more easily included in the narrative. Tables supplement the text, but should not duplicate it.

Always refer to the specific table number in the text and place the full table as close as possible after its reference in the text. If the table does not follow immediately after it is referenced, place it as soon as you can on the next full page. Try not to divide a table between two pages unless it is too long. A table that covers more than a page, however, may be better placed in the appendix rather than in the body of the report.

Most publication manuals provide guidelines for the specific information and format of tables. For example, the *Publication Manual of the American Psychological Association, Fourth Edition* (1994) has explicit instructions for authors on the correct format to be used with tables. Several general guidelines for tables should be kept in mind:

1. Put table number (in Arabic numbers) and title at the top of the table.

2. The title should be as descriptive as possible but not overly wordy.

3. Indicate on the table itself (either at the bottom or with the title) the source of the data if it is not directly from your evaluation data.

4. Include units of measure in the headings or entries to avoid confusion.

5. Arrange data that are to be directly compared in vertical columns.

6. Arrange data in logical order, preferably by the most important characteristic.

7. Align on the decimal point columns of numbers representing the same units of measure. Numbers rounded off to the nearest whole, tenth or one-hundredth are easier to read than long decimal numbers.

8. If independent/dependent variables are to be presented, independent variables should be in the row and dependent variables should be in the columns.

9. Use notes in the form of superscript letters if you need to explain anything further. You can put a superscript letter next to a heading and then explain its meaning under the table. Asterisks (*) are usually used on tables to note statistical significance.

10. For tables that have data cases, always include the number of respondents at the bottom of the table by indicating N=(the number).

Tables are usually quantitative but can be used with qualitative data or examples of written material. Sometimes a table with words or phrases can help a reader understand a concept more easily than reading through paragraphs of information. Whether qualitative or quantitative data are displayed, you should be able to see the significance of a table at a glance. It is usually best to use lines to separate tables and to separate related information within tables. A number of examples of tables, as well as figures, that follow the APA format can be found throughout this book. An example of a qualitative table is included in Table 4.1(1) on page 320.

Figures

Any type of illustration other than a table is usually called a figure. A figure can be a chart, graph, photograph, drawing, or some other graphic depiction. Just as with tables, you must carefully consider how to use a figure. A well-prepared figure can show a great deal of information. Figures do take time, however, to produce. Like tables, you must make sure that a figure supplements the text and does not simply duplicate it. Further, you need to consider what type of figure ought to be included and how elaborate it ought to be. The figure should convey essential facts, be easily read, be easily understood, and be carefully prepared. Several guidelines that pertain to tables also pertain to figures:

1. Put figure number (in Arabic numbers) and title at the bottom of the figure.

2. Indicate on the figure itself (either at the bottom or with the title) the source of the data if it is not directly from your evaluation data.

3. Use notes in the form of superscript letters if you need to explain anything further. You can put a superscript letter next to a heading and then explain its meaning under the figure.

4. For figures that have data cases, always include the number of respondents at the bottom of the table by indicating $N=$(the number).

Table 4.1(1) Focus Group Themes: Barriers and Supports to Physical Activity (adapted from Sharpe, Greaney, Henderson, Royce, Neff & Ainsworth, 2001)

Themes	Dimensions	Illustrative Examples & Comments
What does physical activity mean?	Structured physical activity	• Aerobics, weightlifting, StairMaster, swimming, exercising at the senior center • Mall walking • Basketball, baseball, golfing, softball, volleyball, tennis • Horseback riding • Boating and water skiing • Martial arts • Bicycle riding, hiking, fishing, hunting and processing the game, roller skating, swimming in home pool, line dancing • Go-cart racing
	Unstructured physical activity	• "I don't like bending over and touching my toes 20 times. I do not find that fulfilling. But bending over to pull a weed I don't mind doing it. So, I find I have to think of ways, things to do so I will be active, things that are productive." • Vacuuming • Washing windows • Climbing stairs • Mowing and competing with neighbors to see who has the best lawn • Washing the car and restoring autos • Shopping (of all kinds) • Leisurely walking—with dog, to get mail • "Keeping up with the kids and grandkids." • "Playing soccer with my son and taking him to basketball practice. Running back-and-fourth for everything from my mother to my husband, son, daughter all day." • Coaching children's athletic teams • Dancing in the living room
	Occupational activity	• "Some people get exercise from working in the factories."

Graphs are a popular way to display visual data. Graphs show data in pictorial form, but also have the advantage of showing relationships. The most commonly used figures are line graphs, bar graphs (also called column graphs), and pie graphs or charts.

Line Graphs

Line graphs are the most useful for showing trends in relationships between two variables; generally the shape of the curve is more important than the precise value of any given point. The following guidelines suggested by Robinson (1985) are useful when constructing line graphs:

1. Use a full grid only if you must for precision (hash marks on the axes usually work best).

2. Label both axes in direction of increase with the independent variable on the horizontal axis and the dependent variable on the vertical axis.

3. Avoid using a legend or key if possible; label the curve directly.

4. Adjust scale for ease of reading. If the graph is too big when zero is used at the intersection of the vertical and horizontal axis, you can use a double slash mark to show that numbers were skipped for a large interval on either of the axes.

5. Make data curves easy to identify.

Figure 4.1(2) shows an example of a basic line graph.

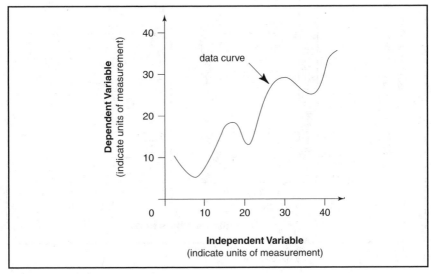

Figure 4.1 (2) Example of a Basic Line Graph

Bar Graphs

Bar graphs, and a variation called histographs, are used to show quantitative relationships. Technically speaking, if the bars are vertical, they may be called column graphs; if they are horizontal, they are usually called bar graphs. An example of data appropriate for a bar graph would be the number of participants in six different recreation programs in one year. Robinson (1985) has suggested the following guidelines for bar graphs:

1. Be sure to make it easy to distinguish the bars by using width or shading,
2. Label the graph clearly.
3. Choose between vertical or horizontal bars logically. For example, use vertical bars for quantities we think of vertically (e.g., temperature), and horizontal bars for ones we think of horizontally (e.g., distance).

Figure 4.1(3) provides an example of a generic bar graph.

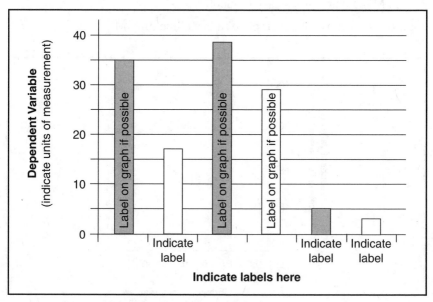

Figure 4.1 (3) Example of a Generic Bar Graph

Pie Graphs

Pie graphs or pie charts are useful for showing the relative proportions to the whole. They are sometimes called 100% graphs because they show how 100% of something is distributed. Expenditures for budgets are often shown pictorially in pie charts. Sometimes the precise quantities are difficult to see when displayed as a pie graph so it is best to use five or fewer categories. Shading or using color also makes the graphs easier to understand. The following suggestions are useful when constructing pie graphs (Robinson, 1985):

1. Arrange the segments clockwise in order of size with the largest at 12 o'clock.

2. Place labels within the segments if possible.

3. Avoid making the reader rotate the page.

4. Include percent for each segment, if space permits.

Figure 4.1(4) shows an example of a generic pie chart.

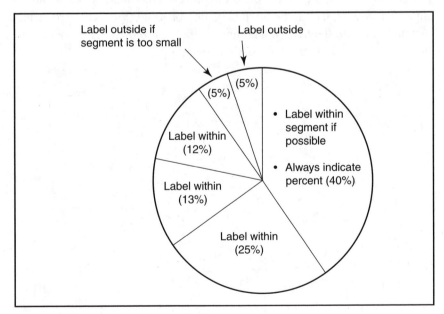

Figure 4.1(4) Example of a Generic Pie Graph

Other Types of Figures

Graphs are the major type of figures that you will likely use in your evaluation and research reports, but you might also consider drawings or pictures depending upon the topic that is being addressed. The "rules" for these types of figures are the same as for other figures and tables. They must be necessary, simple, and easy to read. They should be labeled appropriately and should be keyed to the text. All figures should be numbered consecutively. You should also consider how well drawings and photographs will reproduce if more than one copy of a report is needed.

Further Considerations

For any of these graphics, remember that the actual construction of a visual may be enhanced through the use of computer graphics programs. Programs such as PowerPoint allow you flexibility in designing your visuals. Statistical packages such as SPSS also offer graphics possibilities. The finished product from computers can be high in professional quality. We would suggest, however, that no matter how your tables and figures are produced, manually or with the help of a computer, that you remember to make them simple, uncluttered, and easily understood.

From Ideas to Reality

Some people find the development of tables to be interesting work especially when the data have been collected and analyzed. Graphics offer an opportunity for the evaluator or researcher to be creative with many possibilities existing for how you might visually portray ideas and data. As people read a report, some will find that the tables and figures are the most interesting part of the report because they allow the reader to make interpretations about the data. Whatever the case, you should consider the possibility of using tables and figures when they are appropriate in an evaluation report. They can add greatly to the readability of the findings section of an evaluation project.

Now that you have studied this chapter, you should be able to:

- Explain the differences between different types of graphics.
- Prepare an appropriate graphic given data results.
- Evaluate a well-presented graphic from one that is not done well.

Developing Conclusions and Recommendations
The Grand Finale

Drawing conclusions is ongoing throughout an evaluation project or research study, but a point comes when the conclusions and recommendations must be finalized and written. For qualitative data, the process of analysis is the process of drawing conclusions. For quantitative data, however, statistics and probabilities are only numbers until the evaluator interprets them in the form of conclusions.

Evaluation does not occur if judgments are not made. Similarly, research data are worthless unless they provide conclusions to help us understand a body of knowledge better. The evaluator's responsibility is to base judgments on the data that are available. Judgment occurs in the form of conclusions and recommendations. Although some conclusions may result in self-evident recommendations, the good evaluator will explain the recommendations that evolve from conclusions. Sometimes recommendations are made to keep the program, policy, or whatever is being evaluated the same, while other times they result in specific suggestions about improvement, change, or even termination. Whatever the case, the evaluator needs to have confidence in what is being concluded and offered as recommendations.

How easy or how difficult conclusions and recommendations are to write will depend to a great extent on the type of project and the desires of the stakeholders in the evaluation process. Mobily and Iso-Ahola (1980) suggested that as the amount of data available increases, so do the number of alternatives that can be addressed in conclusions and recommendations. This statement, however, assumes that the data are reliable and valid. If you have followed the appropriate procedures for data collection and analysis, the trustworthiness of your conclusions and recommendations should not be a problem. The criteria established and the evidence collected should result in a framework for developing conclusions and offering the best course of action.

The Relationship between Findings/Results and Conclusions/Recommendations

You will need to organize your data to discuss your findings. Developing visual presentations is a good way to organize the data but you will also need to discuss them in a narrative form in the report. By using the narrative and various visuals, you will tell the story. You will report statistics and tell p values in the findings. You will show qualitative data by actually using quotes and anecdotes to interpret the results. In other words, findings or results are the data summaries portrayed either through narrative and tables/figures if the data are quantitative, or are the etic summaries of descriptive and anecdotal material from qualitative data. From the findings, then, it will be necessary to communicate the bottom line including essentially what the overall conclusions are and what action needs to be taken to address those conclusions.

Writing Conclusions

Conclusions follow directly from the findings and are used to summarize what has been learned as a result of the evaluation project or research study. The conclusions should relate *directly* to the criteria or objectives of the project. In a report, which will be discussed in more detail in Chapter 4.4, the conclusions section follows immediately after the findings or results section. No new evidence or findings are presented in the conclusions that have not been presented previously.

Several aspects should be considered when writing conclusions. Some of the important qualities: conciseness, accuracy, relevancy, and reflection of the purposes and findings. Smith (1989) suggested several key points to keep in mind. First of all, be sure to make conclusions. You should not expect the reader to have to make judgments based on the findings in an evaluation project or research study. Conclusions are an essential part of the evaluation research process. It is also useful to involve others in an organization when writing conclusions so that they understand what the data say and why conclusions were drawn. Others may also be helpful in providing additional ways to interpret the data.

Second, present conclusions with the best possible justification for why they were made. Draw conclusions from evidence and make recommendations from conclusions, but do not overextend either. No conclusion should ever exist that does not have explicit data as the basis for it. Although often difficult, try to keep personal biases out of the conclusions. The conclusions should be a summary of what the findings mean that have already been presented.

Finally, keep in mind that conclusions are not difficult to make if the criteria are clear, the evaluation questions are explicitly stated, and the data are reliable and valid. If the study has not been adequately designed, conclusions are difficult to make in actuality and may raise ethical issues.

Making Recommendations

Recommendations are the proposed courses of action to be followed based on the conclusions. Recommendations in evaluation projects relate to what needs to be done. Recommendations in research project often include how the data might be applied in practice or how the research should be done differently next time. The recommendations and conclusions should be closely linked such that the recommendations appear as an inevitable outcome of the conclusions. They are the finale to the project and follow from the study's findings and conclusions. Many evaluators often stop short of making recommendations even though the purpose of evaluations is to determine the worth or value of something so that action can be taken. Although the findings should speak for themselves, a good evaluator will need to interpret the data and make specific judgments in the form of recommendations.

Several aspects should be kept in mind when writing recommendations, particularly for an evaluation project. Recommendations must relate directly to the criteria and the conclusions. Don't stray off to tangentially related topics in developing recommendations. Keep in mind the purpose of the project. Judgments should be made based on the best information available even though sometimes this information is not perfect. Indeterminacy always exists in any evaluation project, but as the evaluator you simply have to acknowledge anything that might be less than ideal for a given situation. People are continually making judgments anyway, so you might as well state them formally as recommendations so that they are less likely to be misunderstood. Not to make a recommendation or a judgment is to make the suggestion that everything is fine concerning whatever aspect of an organization you're evaluating.

Some people have a hard time differentiating between conclusions and recommendations. Conclusions state an interpretation of the findings whereas recommendations are specific tactical proposals for action that eliminate, replace, or augment current actions to steer a program, personnel, policy, place, or participant into preferred directions. Recommendations may provide examples, call for further evaluation and more information, suggest an allocation of resources, advocate offering the same services to others, propose reordered priorities or changes in policy or program, or may rank program strengths or deficiencies according to their importance or seriousness. As you can see, recommendations may take a number of directions. Table 4.2 shows an example of conclusions and recommendations resulting from conducting an evaluation project.

The evaluator, as well as the user or stakeholders, should keep in mind that recommendations are not surefire prescriptions for success (Sadler, 1984). They are suggestions based on what the evaluator saw in conducting the evaluation project. The use of recommendations is another issue that must be considered by those who have the power to make changes, and this use will be discussed further in Chapter 4.5. Not all recommendations can be addressed, but stakeholders should at least know the possibilities for changes that are offered through recommendations.

Table 4.2 Example of Conclusions and Recommendations (material adapted from a class evaluation report by Lara Pietrafesa, Kim Boyette, and Tonya Bryan)

This project was an evaluation of satisfaction with the Student Recreation Center Aerobics Program at the University of North Carolina at Chapel Hill. Data were collected using the triangulated methods of questionnaires to participants, interviews with instructors, and observations of randomly selected classes.

Conclusions:
1. Participants and instructors were generally satisfied with the aerobics program as indicated by the high marks given to the facilities and equipment.
2. Participants had high satisfaction with the instruction and the total workouts that they were able to achieve.
3. Instructors were satisfied with the management of the classes and the teaching schedules that they were assigned.
4. Concerns were expressed by both participants and instructors concerning the large class sizes, the number of classes offered, and the scheduling of the classes.

Recommendations:
1. The Student Recreation Center should continue to maintain the high quality of the facilities and equipment and the communication that exists between management and the instructors.
2. More classes need to be offered at different times during the day. No classes are offered in midafternoon or after 8:30 p.m. so these times might be appropriate to consider as new class times. Offering more classes should cut down on the classes that are presently overcrowded and might make the offerings more convenient to student schedules.

The evaluator might wish to consider who should be involved in making recommendations. It is generally best to involve others who will be affected by possible recommendations. If the evaluator, for example, talks to program staff that may know parts of an organization better than herself or himself, these staff may be most helpful. If staff is involved at every step of the evaluation and especially in drawing up recommendations, then they are more likely to become invested and use the evaluation results.

In making recommendations, the evaluator should also consider the organization's willingness or ability to make changes. Recommendations that are impossible to carry out because of insufficient resources may cast doubt on the ability of the evaluator to do her or his job. If you only have hunches about possibilities for changes, make sure you say those ideas are hunches rather than presenting them as specific recommendations. In other words, the recommendations should be realistic and practical for implementation possibilities. For research studies, recommendations may be made for practice, but they also may be made regarding further research needed.

The end result is that that conclusions and recommendations offer judgments about gathering more data, making a change, raising an issue, leaving things as they are, contributing to the body of knowledge, or a combination of these possibilities. In making recommendations, the evaluator must have confidence that the evaluation project or research study was done well and that judgments are based on sound data.

From Ideas to Reality

Writing conclusions and recommendations is the final process in interpreting the data and making judgments within an evaluation project or research study. These conclusions and recommendations are usually brief, concise, and to the point. When you have reached the point of writing conclusions and recommendations and are able to address the criteria that you have been using throughout the project, you have reached the bottom line of the evaluation. Sometimes conclusions and recommendations are easy to write; other times you will have to work to figure out what your findings or results mean. If you have done a good job of planning the project and collecting data, the conclusions and recommendations should become obvious once the data are analyzed.

Now that you have studied this chapter, you should be able to:

- Describe the differences between conclusions and recommendations.
- Write conclusions and the subsequent recommendations from project findings.

Report Writing
Saving a Paper Trail

Evaluation projects ought to result in written reports. Research studies ought to result in a written report at the very least, and hopefully in publication in a research journal. A situation might occur when you would conduct a project and you, or a very small group of people, would be using the results directly, so a report would not be written. Most of the time, however, you will want to have written material as a record of what you did and what you learned. Without something written, in time you will have a hard time remembering what was done and the recommendations that were made. Even regular activities like staff evaluations should have a summary written that can be placed in an individual's personnel file. This chapter describes what goes into an evaluation report and to provide a brief summary of how a research publication may differ.

The evaluation report may range from a full report to a *Reader's Digest* condensed version. The report length and type will depend upon the agency, the extent of the project, and how the information will be shared. The extent of the report needs to be negotiated between the evaluator and agency at the beginning of the project. Regardless of the extent or nature of the report, as an evaluator you will want to strive for technical detail and excellence. As Hudson (1988) suggested, reports should be comprehensive, organized, and clearly written. Regardless of the temporal, financial, and physical resources, you should not shortcut the preparation of the final report.

The report should provide a clear picture of the evaluation process and answer the questions or criteria posed. It should tell who, what, when, why, where, and how—just as you did when you planned the project. In the final report, however, these responses should be precise and concise. And, of course, the report must contain judgments in the form of conclusions and recommendations. The formal report consists of several components that will be discussed in detail: cover; executive summary (abstract); table of contents; the body of the report (i.e., introduction, methods, findings, conclusions, and recommendations); and appendices.

Cover

The cover is not necessarily the most important aspect from the evaluator's standpoint, but it is the first thing that the evaluation report reader will see. The cover should be designed with thought because it gives the first impression. It need not be fancy, but should include the title of the evaluation project, who was evaluated, names of evaluators, for whom the report was prepared, dates of the evaluation, and date of the report.

Depending on the relationship of the evaluator to the agency, the report might be sent under a cover letter or a cover letter might be one of the first pages. The cover letter states that the report is completed and offers any other general information that ought to be considered by the agency or the reader.

Executive Summary (Abstract)

Evaluation reports typically include an executive summary, sometimes simply called a summary or an abstract. The summary almost always appears before the main text. It includes a statement of the purpose, how the project was conducted, and the main conclusions and recommendations. The summary usually comprises about a page, or less than 500 words, with the most important points of the entire project described. Most people will read the executive summary and then decide whether to read the rest of the report. In other cases, the summary may be the only part read as some people will simply not have time to read an entire report.

The executive summary is written in nontechnical terms to be accessible to a wide audience. In many cases, the full evaluation report will not be distributed widely within an organization, but the executive summary might be shared with a number of people who can then get the full report if they want further details.

Even though the executive summary goes first, it must be written carefully *after* the rest of the report is written. Nothing should appear in the executive summary that is not carefully described in the main part of the report. The executive summary is the condensed version of the most important aspects of the report. Table 4.3(1) shows an example of a well-done executive summary.

Table 4.3(1) Example of an Executive Summary (adapted from the work evaluation project of students Cathy Mitchell, Tonya Sampson, and Charlene Hardin)

The Qualifying Tournament at the University of North Carolina at Chapel Hill (UNC-CH) for the Intramural Big Four Tournament was the focus of this evaluation. The purpose of the evaluation was to improve the qualifying tournament at UNC-CH with a specific focus on determining the reason for low participation and analyzing the currently used methods of advertising. Three methods were used for data collection: captains of teams that participated in the qualifying tournament received a questionnaire during the tournament, captains of regular season teams that did not participate received a telephone interview, and the directors of the intramural programs at the Big Four universities involved (Wake Forest, Duke, North Carolina State University, and University of North Carolina-Chapel Hill) were personally interviewed. Two major conclusions were drawn. First, the majority of regular season captains did not know about the qualifying tournament or they would have considered participating. Second, very little advertising was done at UNC-CH to inform potential participants of the qualifying tournament. The evaluators recommend that the following methods of advertising be considered in the future: use the student newspaper to make announcements, put banners around campus, send flyers to residence halls and fraternities/sororities as well as post them on campus, and set up a table in the "pit" to provide information to interested persons. The evaluators also suggest that the organizers of the Big Four Tournament consider automatically sending regular season champions for each activity to the tournament. In the event that a team or individual cannot attend, then a qualifying tournament should be held.

Table of Contents

Depending on the length of the report, you may or may not need a table of contents. Often this list of topic areas of the evaluation is helpful to the reader in finding a particular topic. If a number of subheadings are used, these should be listed in the table of contents and indented appropriately to show their levels. If a number of tables and figures are used, the evaluator may want to list the tables and figures by title and page number immediately following the table of contents as was done for this textbook. The table of contents, like the executive summary, cannot be completed until the main body of the report is written even though it is placed at the beginning of the report.

Introduction

The introduction is the first of the four sections that are typically included in the body of the evaluation report. Each of these sections should begin with a brief introduction about the project and what will be covered in that section. In any of the sections, subheadings should be used liberally as they help the reader to follow the report. Subheadings, however, are not meant as crutches and should not preclude the writer using transition sentences between subheading topics.

The introduction to the main report sets the scene and provides a context, tells the purpose of the project evaluation, and describes the characteristics of the agency or the units being evaluated. Depending on the criteria, the introduction might refer to an organizational chart to show information about the organization and may explicate the purpose or mission of the organization. Program goals and objectives might be presented as well as a bit of history if the reader is unfamiliar with the background of an organization.

The introduction also describes the design procedures, including the evaluation model used, the timing, and a justification for why a study was undertaken. The evaluator should describe any limitations and restrictions that were imposed or encountered in doing the project. Also state the evaluation process briefly and provide a general time line.

The specific criteria that were examined and the evaluation questions that you addressed are the most important aspects of the introduction. If these questions are made specific at the beginning, the conclusions can be addressed as answers later in the report and the reader will be able to understand why the evaluation project was undertaken.

Methods

The methods section contains details about the procedures used for data collection and analysis, the development or selection of instruments, and the details of sampling including composition, size, and time periods. The methods should relate directly to the criteria identified. The connections between the method(s) chosen and the evaluation questions should be evident. Any examples of questionnaires, checklists, or interview schedules should be put into the appendix with a note in the narrative saying, for example, "Appendix A is an example of the questionnaire used."

Any limitations or problems that existed in data collection or analysis should be noted in the methods section. The methods should be specific enough that if someone wanted to do a similar evaluation project, they could read the methods section and replicate the project. The strengths and weaknesses of methods used should also be justified and noted briefly.

Findings

The findings section is where the results are presented. In most reports, this section is the longest section. The findings may include qualitative or quantitative analyses. If triangulated methods or data sources are used, all results from the methods or sources should be mentioned in this section.

A description of the respondents usually is presented first in the findings section of a program evaluation. This information provides the reader with background about who comprised the sample. Organizing this section in relation to the specific criteria or the evaluation questions raised is useful. In the case of a goal-free evaluation, the findings section should provide a structure for organizing the results that will evolve as data are collected. The use of tables and figures, described in Chapter 4.1, are also helpful in presenting the findings. In addition, the analysis of patterns, themes, tendencies, trends, and categories should be made clear in this section. All the data should be presented here that are relevant to the project. No additional data should be introduced outside of this section.

Conclusions and Recommendations

The conclusions and the recommendations are the final sections of the body of the report and should naturally link to the criteria identified and the findings. The conclusions will show the relationships of the findings to the evaluation criteria. The recommendations address the strengths and weaknesses of the findings about the area being evaluated and propose courses for action. Possible and/or desired recommendations for change or improvement should be stated along with possible suggestions for future evaluations. A summary of how to write conclusions and recommendations was presented in Chapter 4.2.

Appendices

The appendices of an evaluation report will include any material that is too detailed or technical to be considered in the regular report. Information that might be in the appendices include organizational charts, instruments, instructions given to subjects, human subject approval forms, tables of data if too large for the findings section, and copies of correspondence. Few people ever read appendices, but they will look at them if any questions arise, so this information needs to be included.

Sometimes additional information is included in an appendix such as the cost of a project or a detailed summary of evaluation procedures. Do not, however, include anything in the appendices that has not been referred to in the text. The text should indicate why and where each appendix exists. Similarly, the appendices should be given page numbers and are often labeled with A, B, C and so on to enable the reader to find them easily and reduce potential confusion with the Arabic numerals from tables and figures.

Table 4.3(2) gives a summary outline of the order that information should appear in an evaluation report.

Table 4.3(2) Outline for a Written Report
Cover
Cover Letter (optional)
Executive Summary
Table of Contents including Appendices
List of Figures/ Tables (optional)
Introduction
Purpose
Setting
Models/Design/Theoretical framework
Criteria Measured
Methods
Procedure
Sampling
Statistics or Analysis Used
Findings
Results of Analysis
Tables and Figures
Conclusions
Recommendations
Appendices

General Observations about Evaluation Report Writing

The evaluation project report should be readable and free of academic jargon. You may know a lot about evaluation, methods, and statistics, but your audience may not. Therefore, you should make the report as simple and as straightforward as possible with explanations as needed. The data in an evaluation project should do the impressing, not a fancy writing style. Don't write to impress—write to communicate.

People write in different ways. Some people find a detailed outline to be helpful. Others like to start with lead sentences or like to develop tables and figures first. Some people like to write the findings first and then fill in the other parts. It doesn't matter where you start writing a report. You just have to end up with a final product that tells the evaluation story.

For some people, writing the report is a delightful experience once all the other hard work is done. Other people will struggle with writing. As stated before, the better the criteria and data collection and analysis, the easier the report will be to write. Writing, however, requires a fair amount of effort. You will likely have to write several drafts before the report is complete. Some people find it helpful to write for awhile and then set the report aside and come back to it in a couple of days with fresh eyes. Writing is a personal experience so you have to decide what is best for you. Be sure, however, to give yourself adequate time to write the report as it is not easy to organize and complete at the last minute.

Keep in mind that you can't include everything in the evaluation report. You will have to think carefully about what to address and what data you will supply. A fine line exists between too little and too much data in an evaluation report, but you will need to try to find that compromise. Having others in an organization look at the report before it is finalized to get their reactions to the information that is included may be useful. It is paramount, however, to keep your criteria in front of you as you write so you don't wander into unnecessary tangents.

Sometimes rather than writing a full report, you may want to use a summary sheet for a particular project. The executive summary may be a basis for this summary, but you may want to go into a bit more detail concerning the conclusions that you draw.

If a short summary is used instead of a full report, it should include the name of activity/event, place of activity/event, participants (characteristics and number), strengths of program, weaknesses of program, and recommended changes. A series of these short reports would provide a good paper trail that may help in planning future evaluation projects.

It is beyond the scope of this book to describe how to write a research report. Guidelines for particular journals are usually included in those journals or are available from the journal's website. A research article includes the same four dimensions of the evaluation report—introduction, methods, findings, and conclusions. In addition, it generally includes a literature review and a section at the end that describes the recommendations for application of the conclusions and recommendations for future research. The other "rules" for good writing generally apply to writing research articles for publication, although these articles may be more detailed than most evaluation reports. The focus on the connections between theory as criteria for research, the data collection and analysis, and the results and conclusions are similar regardless of whether an evaluation project or research study is undertaken.

From Ideas to Reality

The final report is the composite of all your work on an evaluation project or research study, so you want to make it readable and usable. As outlined in this chapter, standard components are usually found in an evaluation report but you can be creative within that report as long as the information is communicated clearly. In writing a research article, the writing style and organization should fit the guidelines of the journal where the article will be sent. Before beginning any project, determine what the final report will resemble, and then work on the components of the report as you move along. Writing the evaluation report or research article can be exciting and fun because it is the tangible evidence that documents all the hard work that you have done on a study.

Now that you have studied this chapter, you should be able to:

- Outline the components that comprise an evaluation report or a research article.
- Given a report, write an executive summary from the report.
- Assemble a report or article as a result of having developed criteria, collected data, and interpreted the findings.

Oral Presentations
Telling the Tale

Along with a written report for an evaluation project, sometimes an oral report or presentation is also given. In the long run, the oral report may be the most effective way to get the information to people. Many people will not take the time to read an entire written report but they will listen to a presentation. Sometimes presentations of research reports are also given. The same principles that apply to any good evaluation oral report or presentation also apply to a research presentation.

The oral report will vary greatly and may be long or short, formal or informal, and addressed to technical or general audiences. Many of the same principles of the written report pertain to oral presentations regarding the format. A written or oral report will have an introduction, methods, findings, and conclusions and recommendations sections. Many times in an oral report, however, you will not have much time so you must be selective with the material that you present.

Several basic principles should govern any type of oral presentation. First, present your material in terms of your purpose and audience. Second, make important points stand out. Third, state the points as simply as you can.

As you begin to develop the oral presentation you will need to ask questions. What sort of people will make up the audience? What will be their primary concerns? Should you focus on the whole picture or just a portion of it? Keep in mind that for most people, listening carefully is harder than reading carefully. As a listener, if you miss a point in a speech, you can't go back to it as you could if you were reading. Therefore, as a speaker you must be careful to catch and hold the audience. You must try to make the report interesting and easy to follow.

In writing a report, you can write an executive summary for the non-technical audience, but in a speech you can't give a two-part speech and ask some people not to listen to portions of the presentation. Thus, you have to carefully consider what you will discuss and keep the presentation at the general audience level. You have to figure out the target audience and write the presentation aimed at them. How much do they know now? How technically sophisticated are they about the content of the evaluation as well as evaluation procedures? What will they do with the information given to them?

Most speeches either inform or persuade. In an evaluation report, you are presenting a summary with recommendations so you are attempting to both inform and persuade. You are, in a sense, selling your ideas. You want to present the material carefully, honestly, and as truthfully as you analyzed it. If you believe in the trustworthiness of your evaluation project, it will be difficult to present the material any other way.

Planning the Oral Presentation

You need to know if the audience will have the report in front of them or whether they will have read it previously. You will need to think about what two or three questions would be uppermost in their minds. What do they most want to know? From this information, you can begin to prepare the presentation by writing an outline. Like the written report, an oral report is a matter of selecting and organizing information on the basis of the purpose of the project and your analysis of the audience. Keep in mind that you have to think of your time limits. The presentation speech needs to have a beginning, middle, and end. In the presentation, you should always tell the audience what you are going to tell them, tell them, and then tell them what you told them.

Time limits are important. For every minute a speaker runs over her or his allotted time, the more hostile the audience often gets. People talk too long for two reasons: they haven't planned their presentation and/or they haven't practiced and don't realize how long it takes to cover a point. Good organization is even more important in an oral report than a written one. You will not be able to cover everything. Plan the presentation, however, so you can shorten it if needed, or go into more detail if time allows.

You will also need to choose a mode of delivery. Speaking from memory is not recommended. Speaking from the actual written report can result in not talking to the audience. Speaking from notes is the best way to assure a conversation with the audience. Also, always keep in mind that your audience is listening, not reading.

The introduction, which includes your purpose and process (methods), sets the stage. Most audiences will listen carefully for sixty seconds at the beginning of a talk. Then they decide what to do next. If the topic and/or presentation are interesting, they will continue to "tune in." The bottom line is that you have to get their attention.

The body has the substance of your talk and usually includes a brief description of the procedures used and some of the major evaluation findings. The conclusion of the presentation will include your conclusions and recommendations or "calls for action."

In making the oral presentation, keep it simple. Concentrate on the overall picture and stick to the basics. Just as you would use subheadings, use verbal cues to make clear to the audience the pattern of what you say. Use words like "for example" and highlight your conclusions and/or recommendations with number indicators like first, second, and third. It is usually best to limit the use of math and numbers in a speech or else explain what it is you are doing. Visual aids such as slides and transparencies can also help you get your message across.

Using Visual Aids

Think about how visual aids might be helpful. In a short presentation, however, don't try to use too many. For fifteen minutes three to six visual aids would be enough. Make sure the audience can easily see the aids.

You may want to use flip charts which are portable, require no special equipment, do not require a dark room, and allow for spontaneity. Flip charts, however, are usually not good for large audiences because they cannot be seen easily in the back of a room.

A chalkboard can be used spontaneously, but writing takes time and attention away from the time you have to present. Slides are permanent, portable, and versatile and can include photos, graphs, and/or charts. Slides, however, take advanced preparation, require a darkened room, and can provide a distraction when the room is darkened.

Overhead transparencies or PowerPoint presentations are commonly used and can be effective with large audiences. They are, however, easy to abuse and must be simple with *big* print. On PowerPoint presentations, the resolution must be such that it is easy to read what is on the screen. The use of too many "bells and whistles" can be entertaining but can detract from the important content of your presentation. You must remember to coordinate your visuals with your speech.

Handouts are useful for detailed or complex material, especially statistical examples. They can also be used to cover content you may not be able to get across in a speech. Only distribute handouts ahead of time if you are going to use them in your speech, otherwise the audience will read them while they are being handed out instead of listening to you. If handouts are a backup, give them out at the end of the presentation. Use different colored paper if you have several handouts for people to examine during your presentation to make them easier to refer to (e.g., Take a look at the pie chart on the blue paper.).

Props can be effective attention-getters but they must be large enough to be seen by the whole audience. Passing an item around is not a good substitute for a large prop.

Make visual aids big, simple, and clear so their meaning can be grasped quickly. When people are looking at the visual aid, they are not listening to you. Try to keep distraction from visual aids to a minimum by practicing with the aids. Practice using them when practicing your speech. Try to get the audience to shift its attention naturally. Be sure the audience can see the aids. Point to and emphasize major aspects on the screen or overhead. And of course, know how to operate any equipment you plan to use.

Giving the Presentation

The delivery of an oral presentation takes practice. Do not expect to do it perfectly the first time. Learn from your mistakes. With competence comes a feeling of being in control of the situation. When you feel in control, you will feel more comfortable in the situation. Practice ahead of time, preferably to someone else or videotape it, but at least practice out loud. Evaluate the presentation and work to improve it. Don't practice until the speech sounds canned, but do go over it two or three times.

When giving the actual presentation, dress appropriately for the setting. Avoid anything flamboyant or extreme that would distract your audience. The four most common voice errors made are talking too softly, too fast, without expression, or using vocalized pauses (e.g., uh, ok, now, you know, I mean). Practice avoiding these errors. Also, use your eyes to connect with the audience—they will tell you how the presentation is going. Maintaining frequent eye contact is essential to a good speech.

Ninety percent of the audience's perception of how good your presentation is will be determined by the attitude you project. You need to project an attitude of competence and confidence. Remember that you are the expert on this topic. Show interest in the evaluation project. Treat the audience with respect and courtesy and they will respond in kind. Watch your time limits—use a watch.

After a presentation, time is usually allowed for questions. In answering questions, repeat the question so all can hear. This repeating of the question will also give you a moment to gather your thoughts. If you don't know the answer, say so. Unexpected questions often offer interesting perspectives.

Don't get into a long argument with one member of the audience. Other people will get bored. Invite that person to talk further with you afterward.

Presenting an oral report after an evaluation project is the frosting on the cake. After all the work you have done, you will want to share your results with an interested audience. It will be up to you, however, to make sure that your presentation is as interesting as your project conclusions.

From Ideas to Reality

It isn't possible to include a videotape along with this book to show an example of a good presentation, but most of us have had numerous experiences with listening to presentations. The advice suggested in this chapter is useful to consider, but it is also important to draw on our own personal experience about what we have liked and not liked about other presentations. We can learn a great deal by observing others and adopting the strengths of their modes of communication. The prerequisite for a good presentation, however, will always be having something important to say as a result of the hard work that was put into developing the criteria, evidence, and judgment for an evaluation project or research study.

Now that you have studied this chapter, you should be able to:

- Give a presentation that describes the results of an evaluation project.
- Evaluate another presentation in terms of its strengths and weaknesses.
- Choose visuals that will be appropriate for the presentation that you are giving.

Using Evaluations for Decision Making

The best evaluation or research criteria and data collection will be useless unless the conclusions and recommendations are applied in some way for decision making or to contribute to the body of knowledge. The purpose of any evaluation research is to get information for action. Depending whether you are an internal or external evaluator, you may have a different stake in what action occurs. Nevertheless, if an evaluation is to be done as more than just an application of research methods, it needs to be used. As an evaluator, you can use several strategies to make sure that the evaluation is used. These strategies are not just done at the end of the project, but must be considered throughout the project.

Several authors (Chenery & Russell, 1987; Guba & Lincoln, 1989; Patton, 1978) have discussed the value of utilization-focused evaluation. Patton (1978) described the active-reactive-adaptive approach to evaluation that starts by keying the decision makers and information users, and then determining what relevant evaluation questions should be asked or what criteria should be examined. When offering suggestions for changes in an organization, those people (e.g., staff, participants) directly affected by the changes should be consulted and should be involved in making recommendations. This involvement is not always possible, but should be considered.

The recommendations you propose are a starting point for action. This action can be applied to any of the five Ps. You can always suggest several types of actions: evaluate some more, change something, take no further action, or terminate something. An agency also has the prerogative to ignore the recommendations, but hopefully this does not occur unless the benefits and consequences of the recommendations have been carefully considered. For any evaluation project, the potential exists for implementing findings, considering the findings for implementation, implementing changes, or accepting the findings but taking no action. Is an evaluation project successful if recommendations are:

- Implemented in total?
- Implemented in part?

- Considered, but rejected?
- Not implemented, but other changes made?
- Not implemented, but other nonrelated changes made?
- Not implemented and no changes made?
- Not implemented and evaluation findings challenged or rejected?

No specific answers exist to these questions, but an evaluator must consider what they imply. According to Farrell and Lundegren (1987), evaluators may experience some resistance to recommendations if the organization is more fixated on survival rather than change. Some organizations don't want to rock the boat, have hidden political issues, ingrained staff conventions, and/or staff with inadequate skills and competencies to make necessary changes. An evaluator can do little about some of these factors except know that they exist and try to design the evaluation project keeping those considerations in mind.

In general, a successful evaluation might be defined in many ways. Utilization might be defined as serious consideration of the results in making decisions whether the actual recommendations are actually instituted. Utilization also occurs when the results are actually applied to a situation. As an evaluator who has spent much time and effort working on an evaluation project, you would hope that at least some of your recommendations are used and/or implemented.

Conducting Projects to Influence Their Use

Theobald (1979) says evaluations run two major risks: (1) a technical failure in research design, and (2) political barriers in terms of how a study will be received. This textbook has been about designing technically appropriate and trustworthy evaluations. Sometimes recommendations are not used because the evaluation project is done poorly and the findings do not seem trustworthy.

Addressing potential political barriers is often more difficult to do. Potential users of evaluations should be identified early and you should find out what they want to get from a project. Administrators need to be informed and involved in the process because these individuals generally will be responsible for providing resources for implementing the recommendations. The prompt completion and early release of results is often another way to encourage use.

As an evaluator you should not undertake an evaluation project if you are sure the results will have no effect on decisions, or if you believe an organization is not interested in change. Don't undertake an evaluation project unless a high probability of producing valid, precise, and applicable information exists, and the results can be made conceptually clear to program administrators, managers, and practitioners. Otherwise, an evaluation project is a waste of time and resources.

Although writing reports has already been discussed at length, the use of an evaluation may be dependent on how a report is written. Effective methods of presenting findings and dissemination of information using clarity and attractiveness, clear recommendations, summary sheets, and evaluators who are strong advocates of the recommendations will be essential. The report, however, can be written in a variety of styles. For example, a research study was done by Brown, Braskamp, and Newman (1978) where they developed four reports that they called jargon-loaded objective, jargon-loaded subjective, jargon-free objective, and jargon-free subjective. Jargon referred to words that conveyed a concept to a professional audience. Objective included local and national survey results and said "75% said..." Subjective used phrases like "I believe, I think." After reading the four reports, teachers and school administrators were asked to indicate how much they agreed with the recommendations. The authors concluded from this research study that the style of report did affect the audience. Jargon-loaded were perceived as more technical. The jargon-free subjective was the easiest to read. The style, however, did not affect the acceptance or believability of the recommendations.

Encouraging Evaluation Utilization

Once the evaluation project is completed and reported, several plans might be offered to communicate the recommendations both inside and outside the organization. First, it may help to call a staff meeting and discuss the recommendations and their implications. Meeting with individual staff to discuss the results may also be useful and appropriate.

Secondly, participants might be consulted. Sometimes the program participants can make sure that their recommendations are considered, as can colleagues and coworkers who understand the importance of conducting the evaluation.

Third, the organization's decision makers will need to reevaluate their goals and objectives to see if they are realistic in light of the evaluation recommendations. The Board of Directors or Recreation Commission may be the appropriate people to involve. Once possible recommendations to address are determined, then a list of priorities must be set and a timeline for making changes developed. Often more recommendations are made than can be handled at any one time. Some of the less expensive and less complex items can be addressed immediately, while others may take more planning. Budgets and other resources may also need to be tied to the plans.

Fourth, the evaluator must not expect that *all* recommendations for change can be made. Sometimes it is a matter of priority or identifying the relative importance of different recommendations. Time lag may also result with recommendations. Some take a few weeks or months to implement while others may take years. Sometimes we must impress upon people the value of moving slowly toward some kinds of change. Further, sometimes the recommendations may result in greater change or more changes than an organization actually wants. Thus, in making recommendations that have the potential for use, the evaluator may find it is better to suggest only a few moderate changes rather than extensive recommendations.

Fifth, keep in mind that in some situations the conclusions from a project may be negative. It is important to carefully consider what the negative evaluations mean. One of the problems with some evaluation methods, like experiments, is they don't tell why something happened. The evaluator must carefully examine what results mean before offering recommendations to terminate a program. The same is true with evaluations that show no difference occurred or show mixed results. As was discussed earlier, no difference may not be sufficient reason to eliminate a program, but it may mean that the recommendation is for further evaluation using a different method. If the results of an evaluation are unclear, you may want to do further evaluation.

Finally, additional suggestions to encourage the implementation of evaluation recommendations include encouraging positive attitudes about evaluations in staff and decision makers. The focus of evaluations should be on what they tell us that can improve the delivery of leisure services, rather than just a summary of good news/bad news. Evaluators will need to help people see the connections between findings of evaluations and what is going on in an organization. Helping staff and decision makers develop positive attitudes about evaluation, however, should not occur only at the end of the project, but throughout the design, data collection, and judgment phases.

From Ideas to Reality

The most likely way that evaluations will be used is if a trustworthy evaluation has been done and if the evaluator has drawn specific conclusions and recommendations that can be feasibly implemented. Evaluations are sometimes not used because the evaluator is afraid to go out on a limb and draw conclusions or make unpopular recommendations. In this case, a gap exists between evaluation findings and clear courses for future action. The implications of making changes, however, are not always obvious. If the evaluator does not make judgments in the form of conclusions and recommendations, decision makers in agencies may not realize the ways that evaluations can help them improve. We have offered a number of ways to think about how evaluations can be used, but we must emphasize that utilization is a process that has its origins when a project is first designed. You will need to set the stage for using the recommendations from an evaluation project at the very beginning and then strive to conduct the best project and communicate the results as effectively as possible.

Now that you have studied this chapter, you should be able to:

- Explain the value of involving potential users in all phases of the evaluation process.
- Describe the ways that recommendations might be used in an organization.

Evaluating Projects and Studies
Pitfalls and Problems

The process of evaluating an evaluation system or project is ongoing. Now that we have covered the major topics of criteria, collecting and analyzing data (evidence), and judgment related to conducting evaluation projects and research studies, a few words of summary about how to evaluate evaluation systems, individual evaluation projects, and research studies may be appropriate. For any undertaking, a professional should always consider what she or he did well and what could have been improved. In this final chapter we will offer some notes on what to consider in evaluating evaluation and research—your own or someone else's. We will also identify several common pitfalls that can get in people's ways in doing evaluations. This summary will likely sound familiar as most of these points have been addressed elsewhere in the text, but we would like to try to pull together the underlying themes one last time.

The Process of Evaluation and Research

Evaluating or researching is not always easy, especially when approached in a formal, systematic way. You must be confident that an evaluation system or project can make a difference in an organization and that research can contribute to the body of knowledge. Many people are fearful of evaluations, so you must make sure that receptivity to what you are doing exists. Some people are afraid of criticism and evaluation has the potential for offering criticism—hopefully in a constructive way. Some people have little faith in evaluations because they have been through them before and they did little good or the recommendations were never carried out.

Further, political pressures exist. Fears and biases can affect an evaluation project and the evaluator ought to know that they may exist. You should make sure that you are in agreement with the stakeholders and decision makers about what is to be evaluated. For example, if the Park and Recreation Commission thinks that the youth basketball program ought to be evaluated and as Athletic Director, you think the entire youth sports program needs to be examined, you will have to do some negotiation concerning what the evaluation will entail. If you are not aware of the political pressures, you may become discouraged during the course of the evaluation process. All of these skepticisms need to be taken into account in evaluating the success of an evaluation project.

An individual needs to go into an evaluation project or research study with all good intentions and with her or his mind open. Each undertaking will be different so you can't use the same old method or the same instrument in every case. Organizations that have good objectives or standards to follow will likely be able to do evaluations easier than those organizations that do not. Where objectives do not exist, you will have to write your own or rely on other models. The evaluator will also need to work with resource and time constraints. Sometimes nothing can be done about time and money constraints, but in some cases doing no evaluation is better than doing one that is poorly designed, that collects too limited data, or even collects the wrong data. Even though determining criteria, using models, and determining types of data are not very exciting, these design steps are crucial in setting up a good evaluation.

For a project or study to be successful, you must select good methods and measurement tools. Sometimes it is difficult to measure some evaluation criteria. You must be aware of this possibility in undertaking an evaluation project and not promise more than you can deliver. A lack of assessment tools exists in leisure services; in many cases, you will have to develop instruments to address the criteria for particular projects. Developing instruments is not a bad situation, but it will take an additional amount of effort. A lack of standardized instruments exists in the field of leisure services because most professionals have not been particularly oriented toward measurement and statistics. We do not suggest that you have to use sophisticated statistics in evaluation projects, but you do need to know what statistics are appropriate given particular situations and how to be sure that instruments are reliable and valid.

Gremlins to Avoid

In conducting an evaluation project, potential problems will always exist. Table 4.6 provides some guidelines to assist in developing evaluation systems as well as individual evaluation projects. The evaluator can also be aware of some of the downfalls or gremlins that commonly occur in doing evaluations:

- Make sure you have the skills and knowledge necessary to do the type of evaluation needed. If not, get help or get someone else to do the evaluation.
- Be clear about the purpose of the evaluation. Make sure stakeholders are clear about those purposes as well.
- From an administrative point of view, make sure the expense of an evaluation in terms of time and effort is comparable to the value received from doing the evaluation. This cost-benefit may be difficult to measure, but this concept should be kept in mind.

Table 4.6 Guidelines for Evaluation Systems, Evaluation Projects, and Research Studies

Type	Guidelines
Evaluation Systems	• Make data appropriate to criteria • Rebut evaluation fears • Get receptivity within the organization • Use both external and internal evaluators • Institute a systematic process • Be aware of political pressures • Counter possible measurement problems
Evaluation Projects	• Conclusions and recommendations should reflect data • Determine evaluation criteria carefully • Checking trustworthiness of instruments • Collect data carefully • Have a clear evaluation purpose • Develop the necessary competencies to be an evaluator • Write a clear, concise evaluation report • Make the evaluation project timely and on time • Use sound instrument design • Select an appropriate sample • Use statistics and data analysis properly
Research Studies	• Use sound theory • Thoroughly review the literature • Make research questions or hypotheses clear • Collect and analyze data carefully and appropriately • Tie the theory to data findings • Determine the "so what?" of the study • Provide recommendations for application and future research

- For an evaluation system in an organization, consider how both internal and external evaluators can be used from time to time. Using only one or the other has some drawbacks. In setting up a system, consider how you might use both.

- Remember that evaluation does not only occur at the end of something (summative), but may occur as an assessment or as a formative evaluation as well.

- Try not to allow bias, prejudice, preconceived perceptions, or friendship influence the evaluation outcomes. Further, do not let the whims of the administration prevent you from doing the type of evaluation that you think needs to be done.

- Make sure you go into an evaluation understanding thoroughly the organization and its limitations. This suggestion may pertain more if you are an external evaluator, but it should be considered in all situations and contexts.

- Select and use evaluation research methods and measurement instruments that are specifically related to the criteria. To avoid this gremlin you must spend time at the *beginning* of a project carefully planning what you will do.

- In conducting evaluation projects, think about the logical timing of the project. Keep in mind when it can best be done within an agency and when people involved are most likely to be receptive to data collection as well as the reporting of conclusions and recommendations.

- Continually think about how the criteria, evidence, and judgment phases of the project fit together. Each succeeding component should be a natural outgrowth of what has gone before.

- Collect data carefully. Careless collection of data results when the wrong instrument and/or poorly written questions that are inappropriate for the respondents are used.

- A well-written questionnaire is necessary to avoid pitfalls related to reliability and validity. In addition, consider the reading level of the audience when preparing a questionnaire so you do not bias the sample toward higher educated groups.

- When doing any evaluation using quantitative data, keep in mind issues related to randomization, maturation, and history.

- Consider sample selection carefully so that you are not biased. In addition, think carefully how you will motivate people to participate.

Before you begin to collect data think about the size of the sample, who it represents, and the desired response rate.

- When doing evaluation be aware of the possibility of the Hawthorne effect, whereby people will act different just because they are glad you are paying attention to them.

- Data analysis should be considered before a project is begun. The statistics or qualitative analysis to be used need to be determined early on.

- In using statistics where you will address statistical significance, you must be able to determine how much difference makes a difference. Small differences may be statistically significant with a large population, but they may not be meaningful. As an evaluator, you must be able to decide what the statistics mean.

- Make conclusions and recommendations based only on the data that you collect from the project. Do not claim more than you have evidence to support.

- Make sure you address all the results from an evaluation, not just those aspects that are positive. You may have to handle negative results carefully, but you also have an ethical responsibility to make sure they are addressed. Be careful that you don't discount any findings.

- Be open to finding unexpected results as you conduct an evaluation project. The real value of some evaluation projects is what you learn that you didn't expect.

- Write a concise, complete, well-planned evaluation report. Unless you are able to communicate the results of a study, the project will do little good. This report also requires that you write specific recommendations.

- Get results disseminated as soon as possible after an evaluation project is completed. Nothing kills the enthusiasm for an evaluation like having it drag on for months or even years.

Thoughts about Research Studies

Many of the same principles apply for evaluating research studies as for evaluation projects. The audience for research studies is often broader than for evaluation projects. Further, other researchers often are most interested in the body of knowledge, although practitioners certainly will be interested in applied research studies as well.

When a research study is submitted to publication, it is usually sent to a juried journal. To be *juried* means that peers (usually other researchers) review the work and comment about its relevance, rigor, and presentation style. Different journals will have different guidelines but generally the evaluation criteria for such articles includes significance and contribution, content and rigor, and writing style. The paper must make a contribution to the literature and the development of a body of knowledge. The data must be collected and analyzed appropriately so the reader sees the trustworthiness of what she or he reads. In addition, the paper needs to be written in a manner that is understandable and according to the publication's guidelines (e.g., *American Psychological Association (APA) Stylebook*). A researcher writing the results for publication in a juried journal should read the guidelines of the journal and follow them carefully. Some topics are better suited for some journals than others.

Articles for publications are generally submitted to an editor with several copies included. The editor will send the paper to an Associate Editor who has expertise in the topic of the article. This Associate Editor will generally ask one to three other individuals to review the paper and make an evaluation. This process may take two to three months. A decision to accept, accept with minor revisions, resubmit with major revisions, or reject is generally made. Writers are encouraged to resubmit if that is an option, paying close attention to the recommendations made. It is the leisure services professional's obligation to make sure that she or he contributes to the body of knowledge and this is best done through good research and efforts to get that research published.

Problems and pitfalls will occur in all projects and studies but they are worth considering as you embark on doing usable evaluations and that will result in enlightened decision making. Successful evaluation projects and research studies will require careful planning and hard work, but the rewards and benefits will be there for those professionals who understand the value of evaluation and research in all areas of leisure services.

From Ideas to Reality

Many topics have been covered in this textbook. As we discussed early in the book, you will not become an expert simply by reading this book. If you take any single chapter discussed here you could probably find numerous books and articles written about that given topic. To become an expert will require much deeper study and further assistance on all these topics. This book was designed to give you a foundation and a beginning point for exploring and applying evaluation processes further. If you heed some of the suggestions offered in this chapter and throughout this book, you should be able to make evaluation not just an idea in your professional life, but also a reality. As indicated in the very beginning, becoming a good evaluator requires education, training, practice, and a healthy dose of common sense. We hope that we have provided you with some education and training. The practice and common sense is up to you. Best wishes.

Now that you have studied this chapter, you should be able to:

- Summarize how to avoid problems in conducting an evaluation project or research study.
- Evaluate your own studies as well as those of others to make sure they are trustworthy.

Appendix A

Table of Random Numbers

```
10480 15011 01536 02011 81647 91646 69179 14194 62590 36207 20969 99570 91292 90700
22368 46573 25595 58393 30995 89198 27982 53402 93965 34095 52666 19174 39615 99505
24130 48360 22527 97265 76393 64809 15179 24830 49340 32081 30680 19655 63348 58629
42167 93093 06243 61680 07853 16376 39440 53537 71341 57004 00849 74917 97758 16379
37570 39975 18137 16656 06121 91782 60468 81305 49684 60672 14110 06927 01263 54613

77921 06907 11008 42751 27756 53498 18602 70659 90655 15053 21916 81825 44394 42880
99562 72905 56420 69994 98872 31016 71194 18738 44013 48840 63213 21069 10634 12952
96301 91977 05463 07972 18876 20922 94595 56869 69014 60045 18425 84903 42508 32307
89579 14342 63661 10281 17453 18103 57740 84378 25331 12566 58678 44947 05585 56941
85475 36857 53342 53988 53060 59533 38867 62300 08158 17983 16439 11458 18593 64952

28918 69578 88231 33276 70997 79936 56865 05859 90106 31595 01547 85590 91610 78188
63553 40961 48265 03427 49626 69445 18663 72695 52180 20847 12234 90511 33703 90322
09429 93969 52636 92737 88974 33488 36320 17617 30015 08272 84115 27156 30613 74952
10365 61129 87529 85689 48237 52267 67689 93394 01511 26358 85104 20285 29975 89868
07119 97336 71048 08178 77233 13916 47564 81056 97735 85977 29372 74461 28551 90707

51085 12765 51821 51259 77452 16308 60756 92144 49442 53900 70960 63990 75601 40719
02368 21382 52404 60268 89398 19885 55322 44819 01188 65255 64835 44919 05944 55157
01011 54092 33362 94904 31273 04146 18594 29852 71585 85030 51132 01915 92747 64951
52162 53916 46369 58586 23216 14513 83149 98736 23495 63250 93738 17752 35156 35749
07056 97628 33787 09998 42698 06691 76988 13602 51851 46104 89916 19509 25625 58104

48663 91245 85828 14346 09172 30168 90229 04734 59193 22178 30421 61666 99904 32812
54164 58492 22421 74103 47070 25306 76468 26384 58151 06646 21524 15227 96909 44592
32639 32363 05597 24200 13363 38005 94342 28728 35806 06912 17012 64161 18296 22851
29334 27001 87637 87308 58731 00256 45834 15398 46557 41135 10367 07684 36188 18510
02488 33062 28834 07351 19731 92420 60952 61280 50001 67658 32586 86679 50720 94953

81525 72295 04839 96423 24878 82651 66566 14778 76797 14780 13300 87074 79666 95725
29676 20591 68086 26432 46901 20829 89768 81536 86645 12659 92259 57102 80428 25280
00742 57392 39064 66432 84683 40027 32832 61362 98947 96067 64760 64584 96096 98253
05366 04213 25669 26422 44407 44048 37937 63904 45766 66134 75470 66520 34693 90449
91921 26418 64117 94305 26766 25940 39972 22209 71500 64568 91402 42416 07844 69618

00582 04711 87917 77341 42206 35126 74087 99547 81817 42607 43808 76655 62028 76630
00725 69884 62797 56170 86324 88072 76222 36086 84637 93161 76038 65855 77919 88006
69011 65795 95876 55293 18988 27354 26585 08615 40801 59920 29841 80150 12777 48501
25976 57948 29888 88604 67917 48708 18912 82271 65424 69774 33611 54262 85963 03547
09763 83473 73577 12908 30883 18317 28290 35797 05998 41688 34952 37888 38917 88050

91567 42595 27958 30134 04024 86385 29880 99730 55536 84855 29080 09250 79656 73211
17955 56349 90999 49127 20044 59931 06115 20542 18059 02008 73708 83517 36103 42791
46503 18584 18845 49618 02304 51038 20655 58727 28168 15475 56942 53389 20562 87338
92157 89634 94824 78171 84610 82834 09922 25417 44137 48413 25555 21246 35509 20468
14577 62765 35605 81263 39667 47358 56873 56307 61607 49518 89656 20103 77490 18062

98427 07523 33362 64270 01638 92477 66969 98420 04880 45585 46565 04102 46880 45709
34914 63976 88720 82765 34476 17032 87589 40836 32427 70002 70663 88863 77775 69348
70060 28277 39475 46473 23219 53416 94970 25832 69975 94884 19661 72828 00102 66794
53976 54914 06990 67245 68350 82948 11398 42878 80287 88267 47363 46634 06541 97809
76072 29515 40980 07391 58745 25774 22987 80059 39911 96189 41151 14222 60697 59583
```

5 Ps: the components that might be evaluated within a leisure services organization (i.e., personnel, policies, places, programs and participants.)

a priori: the determination ahead of time of processes or procedures.

ability tests: tests to measure what an individual is capable of doing.

abstract (also called *executive summary*): the overview of 200–300 words that says what has been found in a project; placed before the body of a written report.

accountability: a relative term that describes the capability of a leisure service delivery system to justify or explain the activities and services it provides.

accreditation: the process of assuring that an organization has met specific standards set by a professional or an accrediting body.

achievement tests: tests to show what an individual has learned.

American Camping Association (ACA): the organization that sets standards for organized camping in the United States.

American Psychological Association (APA): an organization that provides guidance among many aspects about psychological research and guidelines for writing reports.

analysis of variance (ANOVA): parametric statistic used to measure the differences between three or more group means.

anonymity: when no one knows the identity of the participants.

ANOVA: see *analysis of variance*

appendices: the supportive material included with an evaluation report that includes more information about the sample, instrument, and analyses.

archives: historical records or documents.

assessment: the examination of some type of need that provides the foundation for further planning.

attitude tests: tests that measure the opinions or beliefs of the test taker about an object, person, or event; questions usually pertain to some internal state of mind or set of beliefs that are stable over time.

audit trail: the process of documenting how data were collected and analyzed in a qualitative study.

between-methods triangulation: the use of two or more methods to measure the same phenomena.

bivariate: the examination of the relationship of two variables.

black box model (also called *goal-free model*): a type of evaluation that examines something irrespective of goals and objectives.

body: the major part of an evaluation report that includes the introduction, methods, findings, and conclusions/recommendations.

case study: an intensive investigation of a unit that might be an individual, a group, or an organization.

case: the individual who participates in a survey.

central tendency: the measures of mean, median, and mode.

chi-square: a nonparametric statistical analysis of two categorical variables.

close-ended questions: questions asked that provide specific options for answers.

code book: the written information that indicates how coding was done.

code numbers: the numbers used to identify individuals for purposes of keeping track of who responded and who did not respond to a survey.

code sheet: a compilation of all of the data and records for the cases examined in a study.

coding: the numeric assignment of a value to a variable.

Commission on Accreditation of Rehabilitation Facilities (CARF): the national accrediting body for rehabilitation programs.

competencies: the abilities one has to undertake a task.

conclusions: a summary of the major points learned in an evaluation project.

concurrent validity (also called *criterion-related validity*): a form of internal reliability that asks whether the scores on a particular instrument correlate with scores on another instrument.

confidentiality: the identity of the participants is known by the evaluator, but she or he does not share that information.

consensus: overall agreement.

constant comparison: a systematic method for recording, coding, and analyzing qualitative data that includes comparisons among cases, groups, and themes; used to reduce data.

content analysis: a process used for analyzing documents, records, transcribed conversations, letters, or anything in a textual format.

content validity: the contents of the theoretical expectations that one wishes to measure.

continuous data: data that can be measured along a continuum and have an infinite number of possible values.

control group: the group in an experimental design that does not receive an intervention or a treatment.

conversational guide (also called *unstructured interview*): an interview form in which no questions are predetermined but they emerge as the interviewer and interviewee begin to converse.

correlation: measurement of association.

cost-benefit analysis: relating the costs of a program or an operation to the benefits realized as expressed in dollar figures.

cost-effectiveness analysis: a ratio of the costs of a program or service to the revenue generated.

cover: the physical paper that surrounds an evaluation report and gives the information including the title of the report, evaluator(s), organization for whom it was prepared, who was evaluated, for whom the report was prepared, dates of the evaluation, and dates of the report.

cover sheet: the letter sent with a questionnaire or a final report to explain what the enclosure is about.

covert: when something is hidden or not known.

credibility: a quality measure of the internal validity or how well something measures what it is supposed to measure.

criteria: the standards or the ideals upon which something is being evaluated.

criterion-referenced evaluations: measurement based on a level of performance.

criterion-related validity (also called *concurrent validity*): a form of internal reliability that asks whether the scores on a particular instrument correlate with scores on another instrument.

data display: a form of data reduction where information is assembled to aid in interpreting themes that emerge from qualitative data.

data display: the presentation of qualitative data so that it can be analyzed.

data reduction: the process of examining data to analyze it.

data reduction: the process of organizing data to interpret themes that emerge from qualitative data.

debriefing: the process of discussing and informing participants of the results of a project.

deductive analysis: examining something by going from broad ideas to specific applications.

Delphi studies: a technique that seeks to draw conclusions based on the consensus established from experts about a particular topic.

demographics: characteristics of an individual (e.g., age, sex, income, race).

dependability (also called *reliability* or *stability*): the consistency of an instrument to measure the same results time after time.

dependent variable: the variable that is assumed to have been caused by another variable (usually the independent variable).

descriptive designs: investigative methods used to gather factual data.

descriptive statistics: mathematical measures used to characterize data.

discrete data: noncontinuous finite numbers that have no in-between measurements.

econometrics: any process that involves an analysis of how economic aspects affect an organization.

economic impact: the amount of revenue activity generated in an area due to particular events such as a festival or tourist trades.

effectiveness: the end results (e.g., the impact on individuals).

efficiency: the relationship between inputs and outputs.

emic: ideas expressed by the respondents that are shown as quotes or anecdotes.

empirical data: data that can be observed.

enlightened decision-making: using systematic evaluations to make the best and most informed decisions concerning the value or worth of a leisure services delivery system.

enumeration: a qualitative data analysis procedure that counts the number of occurrences.

ethics: the philosophical basis for determining right and wrong.

etic: interpretations of the researcher concerning how respondents expressed their ideas.

evaluation: the systematic collection and analysis of data to address some criteria to make judgments about the worth or improvement of something; making decisions based on identified criteria and supporting evidence.

evaluation process: the steps undertaken in doing an evaluation project that include broadly the establishment of criteria, the collection of data, and the judgment of the results.

evaluation project: the specific study undertaken to determine the worth or value of some aspect of the five Ps.

evaluation report: the written or oral report that summarizes the evaluation project.

evaluation research: the process used to collect and analyze data or evidence.

evaluation system: a process for determining and addressing the evaluation needs of an organization related to the five Ps.

evaluator: the individual or individuals conducting the evaluation; may be a student, professional, or an outside consultant.

evidence: the data that are collected and analyzed in an evaluation project.

executive summary (also called *abstract*): the overview of 200–300 words that says what has been found in a project; placed before the body of a written report.

experimental designs: investigative methods used to assure control in the collection of data.

expert judgment: the use of professionals who have expertise or training to enable them to make educated judgments.

external evaluator: someone who evaluates from the outside and is not a employed regularly by the organization.

external validity: how well the results of a measurement can be generalized to similar situations.

face validity: whether an instrument measures the contents it is supposed to measure.

five Ps: the components that might be evaluated within a leisure services organization (i.e., personnel, policies, places, programs and participants.)

focus groups: a type of group interview where individuals within a group are asked to respond and discuss particular criteria or issues.

follow-up contact: a second or third encounter with an individual, usually in the form of a phone call, postcard or letter, to request that they respond to a survey.

follow-up questions (similar to *probes*): questions asked during a interview to try to encourage people to give additional information.

formal evaluation: the systematic evaluation undertaken where specific criteria are set, data are collected, and judgments made.

formative evaluation: the systematic examination of the steps in the development and implementation of some aspect of the five Ps; usually related to some aspect of the process that occurs during an activity.

frequency counts: the number of times a behavior occurs.

Friedman's analysis of variance: a nonparametric test used for repeated measures.

full participant: an individual who participates fully in a group, either overtly or covertly, while using observation as a method of evaluation.

goal-attainment model: a type of evaluation where preestablished goals and objectives are used to measure outcomes.

goal-free model (also called *black box model*): a type of evaluation that examines something irrespective of goals and objectives.

goal: general statement about an organization and its programs that reflects the organization's purpose or mission statement.

Hawthorne effect: a term used to describe how the presence of evaluators may affect responses of those being evaluated.

hypothesis: the questions or hunches, based on theory, that are derived concerning the possible outcomes of a research project.

impact evaluation: another term for program evaluation that refers to whether or not interventions produced the intended effects.

importance-performance: a research technique that is used to quantify customer satisfaction by combining measures of importance with satisfaction.

independent variable: a variable who values are given and which may affect another variable.

in-depth interviews: personal interviews that cover a range of topics in which the interviewee is asked to talk.

inductive analysis: examining something by going from specific examples to broad ideas.

inferential statistics: measures used to compare variables, or to predict future behavior.

informal evaluation: intuitive, unstructured approaches to making decisions.

informed consent: a person's permission to participate in a project.

inputs: the resources available and expended in an organization.

internal evaluator: someone who evaluates some aspect of the five Ps from within the organization.

internal validity: how well an instrument measures what it is supposed to measure for a particular project.

interobserver reliability (also called *interrater reliability*): a measure of the consistency of agreement from rater to rater.

interpretation: the process of analyzing data to determine what they mean.

interpretive paradigm: a worldview that suggests the world can be seen from multiple perspectives and truths.

interrater reliability (also called *interobserver reliability*): a measure of the consistency of agreement from rater to rater.

interval data: data put into ordered categories that have meaningful size differences.

interval sampling: choosing predesignated periods of time for doing sampling.

interview guide (also called *semistructured interview*): a list of the topics to be covered in an interview; they include no particular sequence or specific wording, but are all covered at some point in the interview.

interview schedule: the list of questions asked in an interview.

interviewer bias: the potential prejudice, inadvertent leading, or unconscious judgment that may exist in conducting an interview.

intuition: the internal sense that one has about something.

intuitive judgment: a pseudomodel of evaluation that allows an individual to evaluate based on gut-level feelings about some aspect of the five Ps.

Joint Commission on Accreditation of Healthcare Organizations (JCAHO): the organization that sets standards of evaluation and accreditation for hospitals.

judgment: the determination of the value or worth of something based on the evidence collected from previously determined criteria; the outcome of data collection.

juried: peer reviews done to ascertain the rigor and value of a research article.

KASA: a level of program evaluation that includes the measurement of knowledge, attitudes, skills, and aspirations.

key informants: people who provide more in-depth information that regular respondents.

Kruskal-Wallis: a nonparametric test used to examine the differences in means between two or more groups.

latency recording: a measure of the time elapsed between a cue and when a behavior occurs.

leisure programming cycle: the process of conducting needs assessments, setting objectives, planning programs, implementing programs, evaluation, and making revisions.

leisure services delivery system: human service organizations and enterprises that provide recreation, leisure, and/or educational services to improve the quality of life of individuals within the society; may be therapeutic, private, not-for-profit, public, or commercial organizations.

Likert scales: a particular kind of close-ended question that uses a scaling system that usually ranges from "strongly disagree" to "strongly agree."

Mann-Whitney *U* test: a nonparametric statistic used to determine differences in rankings on a variable.

mean: the mathematical average of a variable; abbreviated as $\overline{X}$ or M.

measurement instrument: the tools, usually in the form of a survey, used to gather data.

measurement: the collection of information or the gathering of data, usually quantitative.

median: a descriptive statistic of the point at which half the scores lie above and half lie below; abbreviated as m or Mdn.

methods: the established procedures used to collect data.

missing data: information not reported by an individual on a questionnaire; the missing data may be due to an oversight or because the individual did not want to answer a question.

mode: the most common response to a variable; also abbreviated as M.

multiplier: a number used in econometric studies to show the potential that a dollar has to be spent and respent in a community.

multivariate: the examination of the relationship of more than two variables.

National Recreation and Park Association (NRPA): the professional association of individuals employed in leisure services delivery systems.

negative evidence: qualitative data that is opposite or contradictory to the major points that are being uncovered.

nominal data: categorical data that define a distinct group.

nominal group technique (NGT): a collective decision-making technique used to do assessments and strategic planning.

nonparametric: statistics based on assumptions of a nonnormal distribution commonly used with smaller sample sizes.

nonprobability sampling: the sampling strategy used to select people in some way that is not based on an equal potential for being selected.

nonreactive: unobtrusive observation by not interacting with people.

nonrespondents: those individuals who are asked but fail to respond to a survey.

nonresponse bias: the error that might exist in a survey because some people responded and those that did not might be different.

nonsampling error: the biases that exist due to who responds to a survey.

norm-referenced evaluations: measurement based on the relative position of a person or things in relation to each other using the same measuring tool.

normal distribution: the way that scores occur.

open-ended questions: questions asked that do not provide options for answers.

oral histories: in-depth interviews conducted that explore the entire life of an individual.

ordered responses: responses to a question that have a logical order associated with the way that the responses are listed.

ordinal data: data that is ranked and shows how each measure relates to another measure.

outcomes: the results, impacts, or effects of something.

outlier: responses that occur way outside the normal distribution.

overt: when something is known.

paper-and-pencil tests: measurements that are provided for an individual to administer to herself or himself.

paradigm: a worldview that describes how one thinks about evaluation.

parametric: statistics based on the assumption of normal distribution and randomized groups.

partially close-ended questions: questions asked that provide fixed responses, but allow the respondent to add her or his additional responses if the given ones are not appropriate.

participants: the individuals who receive the services in a leisure service delivery system; may be clients, consumers, players, or anyone otherwise involved in programs and activities in communities, organizations, or in institutions.

Pearson's correlation: a parametric statistic used to measure the relationship between two variables.

peer program review: a process used in therapeutic recreation where professionals review and evaluate one another's programs.

people involvement: the number and characteristics of individuals who participate in a program.

performance appraisal (also called *personnel evaluation*): the evaluation of staff.

personality tests: tests that relate to a variety of characteristics of an individual.

personnel evaluation (also called *performance appraisal*): the evaluation of staff.

personnel: all staff that work for pay or without pay within a leisure service organization.

physical evidence: traces from the past that provide information (e.g., floor wear).

pilot study: a "practice run" for an instrument or a project that gives the evaluator preliminary information about measurement instruments, sampling procedures, or method administration issues.

politics: the personal and collective beliefs that exist.

population: all the people who might comprise a delineated group.

positivist worldview (also called *positivism*): a worldview that suggests facts and truths can be found and articulated.

posttest: the measurement given to an individual or group after some intervention is done.

practice change: the personal or organizational adoption and application of new ideas.

predictive validity: the ability of an instrument to predict some behavior.

preordinate: preestablishsed goals and objectives are used to measure outcomes.

pretest: the measurement given to an individual or group before an intervention is done.

probability sampling: the sampling strategy that allows everyone within a group to have an equal opportunity of being selected.

probes: the questions asked in interviews to encourage people to give additional information; these include questions like: "Can you give me an example?" "Can you tell me more?" or "How did you feel?"

professional judgment: a model of evaluation using expert opinions to determine the worth or value of a program.

program audit: an accountability term used to quantify the amount of services rendered and the identity of program participants.

program: all of the activities, instruction, competitions, and events that are planned by a leisure services organization.

qualitative: data that appear in the form of words.

quality assurance (QA): the process used in healthcare organizations, as well as other organizations, to assure that certain standards are being met.

quality control: assuring that the highest standards of practice are maintained.

quantitative: data that appear in the form of numbers.

quasi-experiments: those methods that do not meet the strict requirements of an experiment; experiments include using random samples, control groups, and pretesting.

random-digit dialing: a sampling method used for phone interviews where prefixes and numbers are randomly dialed to contact respondents for a study.

randomization: the process of assigning people randomly to groups when an experimental design is used.

range: the difference between the highest and lowest scores.

rapport: establishing a trusting relationships between two individuals or between an individual and a group.

ratio data: the most sophisticated level of data in which a true zero point is calculated.

reactions: the degrees of interest, likes and dislikes, satisfaction, motivation, appeal, and perceived benefits that people attribute to a program.

recode: to change a code by collapsing or reducing data.

recommendations: the proposed courses of action to be followed based upon the conclusions drawn.

record: the listing of all the information from an individual or a case.

reliability correlation (also called *reliability coefficient*): a statistic that tells how likely an instrument is to measure evidence consistently.

reliability (also called *dependability* or *stability*): the determination of whether a measure consistently conveys the same meaning.

research: the systematic collection of data to answer a question or hypothesis.

response rate (also called *return rate*): the percentage of responses to a survey based upon the actual number returned divided by the number sent.

responsive evaluation (also called *utilization-focus evaluation*): the active approach to evaluation that starts by finding out what the key decision makers expect from an evaluation, and then determining how to conduct the evaluation.

return rate (also called *response rate*): the percentage of responses to a survey based upon the actual number returned divided by the number sent.

sample: a representation of a total population.

sampling error: the amount of statistical error that might exist because you can't always sample correctly.

sampling: the process of drawing a representative selection of respondents from the population.

scientific method: the formal process used in research whereby research questions or hypotheses are generated, data collected, and results related back to original questions or hypotheses.

self-check: the process of examining oneself in relation to making evaluation decisions.

semantic differentials: a particular kind of close-ended question that includes a list of bipolar adjectives from which the respondent chooses.

semistructured interview (also called an *interview guide*): a list of the topics to be covered in an interview; they include no particular sequence or specific wording, but are all covered at some point in the interview.

service quality: a technique used to measure the dimensions of consumer expectations and perceptions.

Sign test: a nonparametric statistic used to determine differences when the data are categorical.

single-subject technique: a way to evaluate the effect of interventions on an individual participant or client.

skewness: a measure of the symmetry of a distribution.

snowball sampling: using an initial sample of people, and then asking those individuals to suggest others who might fit the criteria for the sample.

social desirability: the possibility that a respondent may answer a questionnaire based on what she or he perceives to be the socially acceptable answer or the "right" answer.

sociometrics: a technique used to analyze how individuals within groups relate to one another.

Spearman correlation: a nonparametric statistic used to measure the relationship between two variables.

SPSS (also called the Statistical Package for the Social Sciences): a commonly used computer program that can be used for statistical analysis.

spreadsheet: a computer worksheet that uses matrices to list data.

stability (also called *dependability* or *reliability*): the consistency of an instrument to measure the same results time after time.

staged questions: questions asked in such a way that one must respond to a question to know which question to answer next.

standard deviation: the measure of dispersion or how closely data group around a mean.

standardized interview (also called a *structured interview*): an interview form that includes the exact wording and sequencing of questions as they are asked to each individual participating in a study or project.

standardized tests: tests designed and modified by a process that results in specified instructions for administration and interpreting the results.

standards: predetermined criteria used to evaluate how an organization functions.

statistical packages: software developed to assist in statistical analysis.

statistical significance: the unlikeliness that differences between groups are a result of chance.

structured interview (also called a *standardized interview*): an interview form that includes the exact wording and sequencing of questions as they are asked to each individual participating in a study or project.

summative evaluation: the systematic examination of the impact and effectiveness of a program; it usually occurs at the end of something.

surveys: the category of methods that asks people directly about some criteria; surveys may be done using questionnaires or interviews.

systems approach: a model of evaluation that focuses on determining whether an organization is successful under a given set of conditions; commonly used to understand how a program or place contributes to the overall mission of a leisure services organization.

t **tests**: parametric statistic used to measure the difference between two group means.

theoretical sampling: a sampling strategy used to collect qualitative data where people are interviewed or observed based on the data gathered until a saturation point is reached when no further new data are being uncovered.

theory: a systematic structure for giving order and insight to what has been observed.

thick description: a way of writing qualitative data that includes both the evaluator's and the respondent's perspective.

time sampling: spot checking based on a plan for doing behavioral observations.

transferability: the qualitative equivalent to external validity or how well the results of a measurement can be generalized to other situations.

triangulation: collecting data for an evaluation project by using more than one method, source of data, or evaluator.

trilogy: three of something; the focus of evaluation is on criteria, evidence, and judgment.

trustworthiness: the quality of the data collected that assures that errors do not exist; this term usually refers to qualitative data but may be appropriate for quantitative as well.

Type I error: a belief that two groups are different when in fact they are the same.

Type II error: a belief that two groups are the same when in fact they are different

univariate: the examination of the distribution of cases based on only one variable.

unobtrusive methods: observing, recording, and analyzing human behavior in a situation where interaction with people generally does not occur, and where people are unaware that their behavior is being observed or recorded.

unordered responses: responses that have no specific order related to the way they are portrayed.

unstructured interview (also called *conversational guide*): an interview form in which questions are not predetermined, but they emerge as the interviewer and interviewee begin to converse.

usability: how easy an instrument is to administer and analyze.

utilization-focused evaluation (also called *responsive evaluation*): the active approach to evaluation that starts by finding out what the key decision makers expect from an evaluation and then determining how to conduct the evaluation.

validity: the determination of whether a measure does what it says it does; the meaning and meaningfulness of the data.

variable: logical groupings of characteristics.

variance: a dispersion measure that describes the extent to which scores differ from one another.

visual maps: a method for graphically showing the relationship of concepts in qualitative analysis.

Wilcoxon: a nonparametric test used to determine the relationship when the dependent variable has more than two values ranked.

within-method triangulation: the collection of both qualitative and quantitative data using the same method.

worldview (also referred to as *paradigm*): the philosophies of how individuals each view the world.

References

American Camping Association. (1998). *Accreditation standards for camp programs and services*. Martinsville, IN: Author.

American Psychological Association. (1994). *Publication manual of the American Psychological Association* (4th ed.). Washington, DC: Author.

Anderson, D. H. and Schneider, I.E. (1993). Using the Delphi process to identify significant recreation research-based innovations. *Journal of Park and Recreation Administration, 11*(1), 25–36.

Babbie, E. (1992) *The practice of social research* (5th ed.). Belmont, CA: Wadsworth Publishing Co.

Bartlett, P. and Einert, A. E. (1992). Analysis of the design function of an adult softball complex in a new public recreation park. *Journal of Park and Recreation Administration, 10*(1), 71–81.

Bennett, C. F. (1982). *Reflective appraisal of program (RAP): An approach to studying clientele-perceived results of Cooperative Extension programs.* Ithaca, NY: Cornell University.

Brown, R. D., Braskamp, L. A., and Newman, D. L. (1978). Evaluator credibility as a function of report style: Do jargon and data make a difference? *Evaluation Quarterly, 2*(2), 331–341.

burlingame, j. and Blaschko, T. M. (1997). *Assessment tools for recreational therapy* (2nd ed.) Ravensdale, WA: Idyll Arbor.

Campbell, D. and Stanley, J. (1963). *Experimental and quasi-experimental designs for research*. Chicago, IL: Rand McNally.

Chenery, M. F. and Russell, R. V. (1987). Responsive evaluation: An application of naturalistic inquiry to recreation evaluation. *Journal of Park and Recreation Administration, 5*(4), 30–38.

Connolly, P. (1982). Evaluation's critical role in agency accountability. *Parks & Recreation, 17*(2), 34–36.

Coyne, P. A. and Turpel, L. T. (1984). Peer program review: A model for implementation of standards. *Therapeutic Recreation Journal, 23*(2), 7–13.

Crompton, J. L. (1985.). *Needs assessment: Taking the pulse of the public recreation client*. College Station, TX: Texas A&M University.

Crompton, J. L. and Tian-Cole, S. (1999). What response rate can be expected from questionnaire surveys that address park and recreation issues? *Journal of Park and Recreation Administration, 17*(2), 60–72.

Datillo, J. (1988a, March). *Single-subject methodology.* Paper presented to the 1988 SPRE Institute on Research at Sarasota Springs, NY.

Dattilo, J. (1988b). Assessing music preferences of persons with severe disabilities. *Therapeutic Recreation Journal, 22*(2), 12–23.

Delbecq, A., Van de Ven, A., and Gustafson, D. H. (1975). *Group techniques for program planning: A guide to nominal group and Delphi processes.* Glenview, IL: Scott Foresman.

Denzin, N. K. (1978). *The research act. A theoretical introduction to sociological methods* (2nd ed.). New York, NY: McGraw-Hill.

Dillman, D. A. (1978). *Mail and telephone surveys: The total design method.* New York, NY: John Wiley & Sons.

Dommeyer, C. J. and Moriarty, E. (2000). Comparing two forms of an e-mail survey: Embedded vs. attached. *International Journal of Market Research, 42*(1), 39–50.

Driver, B. L., Brown, P. J., and Peterson, G. L. (Eds.) (1991). *Benefits of leisure.* State College, PA: Venture Publishing, Inc.

Dunn, J. K. (1987). Establishing reliability and validity in evaluation instruments. *Journal of Park and Recreation Administration, 5*(4), 61–70.

Dunn, J. K. (1989). Guidelines for using published assessment procedures. *Therapeutic Recreation Journal, 23*(2), 59–69.

Ellis, G. D. and Williams, D. R. (1987). The impending renaissance in leisure service evaluation. *Journal of Park and Recreation Administration, 5*(4), 17–29.

Ellis, G. D. and Witt, P. A. (1982). Evaluation by design. *Parks & Recreation, 17*(2), 40–43.

Ewert, A. (1990). Decision-making techniques for establishing research agendas in park and recreation systems. *Journal of Park and Recreation Administration, 8*(2), 1–13.

Farrell, P. and Lundegren, H. N. (1987). Designing and objectives-oriented evaluation and translating results into action. *Journal of Park and Recreation Administration, 5*(4), 84–93.

Ferguson, D. D. (1983). Assessment interviewing techniques: A useful tool in developing individual program plans. *Therapeutic Recreation Journal, 17*(2), 16–22.

Fletcher, J. E. and King, M. (1993). Use of voter surveys to plan bond campaigns for parks and recreation. *Journal of Park and Recreation Administration, 11*(2), 17–27.

Geertz, C. (1983). Thick description: Toward an interpretive theory of culture. In R. M. Emerson (Ed.). *Contemporary field research* (pp. 37–59). Boston, MA: Little, Brown.

Girl Scouts of the USA. (2000). *Tool kit for measuring outcomes of Girl Scout resident camp.* New York, NY: GSUSA.

Gitelson, R. F., Guadagnolo, F., and Moore, R. (1988). Economic impact analysis of a community-sponsored ten kilometer road race. *Journal of Park and Recreation Administration, 6*(4), 9–17.

Glaser, B. G. and Strauss, A. L. (1967). *The discovering of grounded theory: Strategies for qualitative research.* Hawthorne, NY: Aldine.

Glover, R. B and Glover, J. (1981). Appraising performance—Some alternatives to the sandwich approach. *Parks & Recreation, 16*(11), 27–28.

Greene, J. and McClintock, C. (1985). Triangulation in evaluation. *Evaluation Review, 9*(5), 523–545.

Guadagnolo, F. (1985). The importance-performance analysis: A evaluation and marketing tool. *Journal of Park and Recreation Administration, 3*(2), 13–22.

Guba, E. G. and Lincoln, Y. S. (1981). *Effective evaluation.* San Francisco, CA: Jossey-Bass.

Guba, E. G. and Lincoln, Y. S. (1989). *Fourth generation evaluation.* Thousand Oaks, CA: Sage.

Hale, R. (1990). *MYSTAT: Statistical applications.* Cambridge, MA: Course Technology, Inc.

Halle, J. W., Boyer, T. E., and Ashton-Shaeffer, C. (1991). Social validation as a program evaluation measure. *Therapeutic Recreation Journal, 25*(3), 29–43.

Havitz, M. E., Twynam, G. D., and DeLorenzo, J. M. (1991). Importance-performance analysis as a staff evaluation tool. *Journal of Park and Recreation Administration, 9*(1), 43–54.

Henderson, K. A. (1988). Are volunteers worth their weight in gold? *Parks & Recreation, 23*(11), 40–43.

Henderson, K. A. (1991). *Dimensions of choice: A qualitative approach to recreation, parks, and leisure research.* State College, PA: Venture Publishing, Inc.

Henderson, K. A. and Zabielski, D. (1992, February). *Theory application and development in recreation, parks, and leisure research: An examination of the literature from 1981–1990.* Paper presented to the Southeast Recreation Research Conference, Asheville, NC.

Hollenhorst, S., Olson, D., and Fortney, R. (1992). Use of importance-performance analysis to evaluate state park cabins: The case of the West Virginia State Park System. *Journal of Park and Recreation Administration, 10*(1), 1–11.

Howe, C. Z. (1980). Models of evaluating public recreation programs: What the literature shows. *Leisure Today/Journal of Physical Education and Recreation, 50*(10), 36–38.

Howe, C. Z. and Carpenter, G. M. (1985) *Programming leisure experiences: A cyclical approach.* Englewood Cliffs, NJ: Prentice-Hall.

Howe, C. Z. and Keller, M. J. (1988). The use of triangulation as an evaluation technique: Illustrations from regional symposia in therapeutic recreation. *Therapeutic Recreation Journal, 22*(1), 36–45.

Hudson, S. (1988). *How to conduct community needs assessment surveys in public parks and recreation.* Columbus, OH: Publishing Horizons, Inc.

Impara, J. C. and Plake, B. C. (Eds.) (1998). *The thirteenth mental measurements yearbook.* Lincoln, NE: Buros Institute.

Iso-Ahola, S. (1982). Intrinsic motivation—An overlooked basis for evaluation. *Parks & Recreation, 17*(2), 32–33, 58.

Kanters, M. A. and Botkin, M. R. (1992). The economic impact of public leisure services in Illinois. *Journal of Park and Recreation Administration, 10*(3), 1–16.

Kraus, R. and Allen, L. (1987). *Research and evaluation in recreation, parks, and leisure studies.* Columbus, OH: Publishing Horizons.

Krejcie, R. V. and Morgan, D. W. (1970). Determining sample size for research activities. *Educational and Psychological Measurement, 30*, 607–610.

Krueger, R. A. (1988). *Focus groups.* Thousand Oaks, CA: Sage.

Lankford, S. and DeGraaf, D. (1992). Strengths, weaknesses, opportunities, and threats in morale, welfare, and recreation organizations: Challenges of the 1990s. *Journal of Park and Recreation Administration, 10*(1), 31–45.

Lincoln, Y. S. and Guba, E. G. (1985). *Naturalistic inquiry.* Thousand Oaks, CA: Sage.

Loftus, G. R. and Loftus, E. F. (1982). *Essence of statistics.* Monterey, CA: Brooks/Cole Publishing Co.

Loomis, J. B. (1990). Estimating the economic activity and value from public parks and outdoor recreation areas in California. *Journal of Park and Recreation Administration, 7*(1), 56–65.

Lundegren, H. M. and Farrell, P. (1985). *Evaluation for leisure service managers.* Philadelphia, PA: Saunders College Publishing.

MacKay, K. J. and Crompton, J. L. (1990). Measuring the quality of recreation services. *Journal of Park and Recreation Administration, 8*(3), 47–56.

Malik, P. B., Ashton-Shaeffer, C., and Kleiber, D. A. (1991). Interviewing young adults with mental retardation: A seldom used research method. *Therapeutic Recreation Journal, 25*(1), 60–73.

Mehta, R. and Sivadas, E. (1995). Comparing response rates and response content in mail versus electronic mail surveys. *Journal of the Marketing Research Society, 37*(4), 429–437.

Michigan State University. (1976). *Survey research for community recreation services.* Research Report 291. East Lansing, MI: Michigan State University Agricultural Experiment Station.

Mills, A. S., Um, S., McWilliams, E. G., and Hodgson, R. W. (1987). The importance of random sampling when conducting visitor surveys. *Journal of Park and Recreation Administration*, 5(2), 47–56.

Mobily, K. and Iso-Ahola, S. (1980). Mastery evaluation techniques for the undergraduate major. *Leisure Today/Journal of Physical Education and Recreation*, 50(10), 39–40.

Mohr, L. B. (1988). *Impact analysis for program evaluation*. Chicago, IL: The Dorsey Press.

Norusis, M. J. (1983). *Introductory statistics guide*. Chicago, IL: SPSS, Inc.

NUD*IST. (1997). QSR NUD*IST 4 User Guide. Thousand Oaks, CA: Sage.

Okey, J. R., Shrum, J. W., and Yeany, R. H. (1977, Fall). A flowchart for selecting research and evaluation designs. *CEDR Quarterly*, pp. 16–21.

Orthner, D. K., Smith, S., and Wright, D. (1986). Measuring program needs. *Evaluation and Program Planning*, 9, 199–207.

O'Sullivan, E. L. (1988). Formulating strategic program decisions utilizing the nine-cell approach. *Journal of Park and Recreation Administration*, 6(2), 25–33.

Patton, M. Q. (1978). *Utilization-focused evaluation*. Thousand Oaks, CA: Sage.

Patton, M. Q. (1980a). Making methods choices. *Evaluation and Program Planning*, 3, 219–228.

Patton, M. Q. (1980b). *Qualitative evaluation methods*. Thousand Oaks, CA: Sage.

Posavac, E. J. and Carey, R. G. (1992). *Program evaluation: Methods and case studies*. Englewood Cliffs, NJ: Prentice Hall.

The Research Spectrum. (2001). Available: http//:www.researchspectrum.com

Riley, B. and Wright, S. (1990). Establishing quality assurance monitors for the evaluation of therapeutic recreation service. *Therapeutic Recreation Journal*, 24(2), 25–39.

Robinson, P. A. (1985) *Fundamentals of technical writing*. Boston, MA: Houghton Mifflin.

Rossman, J. R. (1982). Evaluate programs by measuring participant satisfactions. *Parks & Recreation*, 17(6), 33–35.

Sadler, D. R. (1984). Evaluation and the logic of recommendations. *Evaluation Review*, 8(2), 261–268.

Salkind, N. J. (1991). *Exploring research*. New York, NY: Macmillan Publishing Co.

Scriven, M. (1967). The methodology of evaluation. In R. W. Tyler, R. M. Gagne, and M. Scriven, *Perspectives of curriculum evaluation*, (pp. 39–83). Chicago, IL: Rand McNally.

Search Institute. (1996). Developmental assets. Available: http//:www.search-institute.org

Sengstock, M. C. and Hwalek, M. (1999). Issues to be considered in evaluating programs for children and youth. *New Designs in Youth Development, 15*(2), 8–11.

Shafer, R. L. and Moeller, G. (1987). Know how to word your questionnaire. *Parks & Recreation, 22*(10), 48–52.

Sharpe, O., Greaney, M., Henderson, K., Royce, S., Neff, L., and Ainsworth, B. (2001). Conceptualizations of physical activity: A focus group study. Unpublished paper.

Siegenthaler, K. L. (1994). Importance-performance analysis: Application to senior programs evaluation. *Journal of Park and Recreation Administration, 12*(3), 57–70.

Smith, M. F. (1989). *Evaluability assessment: A practical approach.* Boston, MA: Kiuwer Academic Publishers.

Struening, E. L. and Guttentag, M. (1975). *Handbook of evaluation research.* Thousand Oaks, CA: Sage.

Stumbo, N. J. (1983). Systematic observation as a research tool for assessing client behavior. *Therapeutic Recreation Journal, 17*(4), 53–63.

Stumbo, N. J. (1991). Selected assessment resources: A review of instruments and references. *Annual in Therapeutic Recreation, 2,* 8–24.

Taylor, S. J. and Bogdan, R. (1984). *Introduction to qualitative research methods: The search for meaning* (2nd ed.). New York, NY: John Wiley & Sons.

Theobald, W. (1979). *Evaluation of recreation and park programs.* New York, NY: John Wiley & Sons.

Theobald, W. (1987). Historical antecedents of evaluation in leisure programs and services. *Journal of Park and Recreation Administration, 5*(4), 1–9.

Tinsley, H. E. A. (1984). Limitations, explanations, aspirations: A confession of fallibility and a promise to strive for perfection. *Journal of Leisure Research, 16*(2), 93–98.

Touchstone, W. A. (1984). A personalized approach to goal planning and evaluation in clinical settings. *Therapeutic Recreation Journal, 18*(2), 25–31.

van der Smissen, B. (1978). *Evaluation and self-study of public recreation and park agencies.* Arlington, VA: National Recreation and Park Association.

Weatherman, R. and Swenson, K. (1974). Delphi techniques. In S. H. Hedley and J. R. Yates (Eds.), *Futurism in education* (pp. 97–114). Berkeley, CA: McCutcheon Publishing Co.

Webb, E. J., Campbell, D. T., Schwartz, R. D., and Sechrest, L. (1966). *Unobtrusive measures: Nonreactive research in the social sciences.* Chicago, IL: Rand McNally.

Weiss, C. H. (1972). *Evaluation research.* Englewood Cliffs, NJ: Prentice-Hall.

Weiss, C. H. (1975). Interviewing in evaluation research. In E. L. Struening and M. Guttentag (Eds.), *Handbook of evaluation research*. Thousand Oaks, CA: Sage.

Wicks, B. E., Backman, K. F., Allen, J., and Van Blaricom, D. (1993). Geographic Information Systems (GIS): A tool for marketing, managing, and planning municipal park systems. *Journal of Park and Recreation Administration, 11*(1), 9–23.

Wright, B. A., Duray, N., and Goodale, T. L. (1992). Assessing perceptions of recreation center service quality: An application of recent advancements in service quality research. *Journal of Park and Recreation Administration, 10*(3), 33–47.

Yardley, J. K., MacDonald, J. H., and Clarke, B. D. (1990). The economic impact of a small, short-term recreation event on a local community. *Journal of Park and Recreation Administration, 8*(4), 71–82.

Yin, R. K. (1984). *Case study research: Design and methods*. Thousand Oaks, CA: Sage.

Other Books by Venture

Great Special Events and Activities
by Annie Morton, Angie Prosser, and
Sue Spangler

Group Games & Activity Leadership
by Kenneth J. Bulik

*Hands on! Children's Activities for Fairs,
Festivals, and Special Events*
by Karen L. Ramey

*Inclusive Leisure Services: Responding to
the Rights of People With Disabilities*
by John Dattilo

*Internships in Recreation and Leisure Ser-
vices: A Practical Guide for Students,
Second Edition*
by Edward E. Seagle, Jr., Ralph W. Smith,
and Lola M. Dalton

*Interpretation of Cultural and Natural
Resources*
by Douglas M. Knudson, Ted T. Cable,
and Larry Beck

Intervention Activities for At-Risk Youth
by Norma J. Stumbo

*Introduction to Recreation and Leisure
Services, 8th Edition*
by H. Douglas Sessoms and Karla A.
Henderson

*Introduction to Writing Goals and Objec-
tives: A Manual for Recreation Therapy
Students and Entry-Level Professionals*
by Suzanne Melcher

*Leadership and Administration of Outdoor
Pursuits, Second Edition*
by Phyllis Ford and James Blanchard

*Leadership in Leisure Services: Making a
Difference, Second Edition*
by Debra J. Jordan

*Leisure and Leisure Services in the 21st
Century*
by Geoffrey Godbey

*The Leisure Diagnostic Battery: Users
Manual and Sample Forms*
by Peter A. Witt and Gary Ellis

*Leisure Education: A Manual of Activities
and Resources, Second Edition*
by Norma J. Stumbo and Steven R. Thompson

*Leisure Education II: More Activities and
Resources, Second Edition*
by Norma J. Stumbo

*Leisure Education III: More Goal-Oriented
Activities*
by Norma J. Stumbo

*Leisure Education IV: Activities for
Individuals with Substance Addictions*
by Norma J. Stumbo

*Leisure Education Program Planning: A
Systematic Approach, Second Edition*
by John Dattilo

Leisure Education Specific Programs
by John Dattilo

*Leisure in Your Life: An Exploration, Fifth
Edition*
by Geoffrey Godbey

*Leisure Services in Canada: An Introduction,
Second Edition*
by Mark S. Searle and Russell E.
Brayley

*Leisure Studies: Prospects for the Twenty-
First Century*
edited by Edgar L. Jackson and Thomas
L. Burton

*The Lifestory Re-Play Circle: A Manual of
Activities and Techniques*
by Rosilyn Wilder

*Models of Change in Municipal Parks and
Recreation: A Book of Innovative Case
Studies*
edited by Mark E. Havitz

*More Than a Game: A New Focus on Senior
Activity Services*
by Brenda Corbett

*Nature and the Human Spirit: Toward an
Expanded Land Management Ethic*
edited by B. L. Driver, Daniel Dustin,
Tony Baltic, Gary Elsner, and George
Peterson

*Outdoor Recreation Management: Theory
and Application, Third Edition*
by Alan Jubenville and Ben Twight

Planning Parks for People, Second Edition
by John Hultsman, Richard L. Cottrell,
and Wendy Z. Hultsman

The Process of Recreation Programming Theory and Technique, Third Edition
by Patricia Farrell and Herberta M. Lundegren

Programming for Parks, Recreation, and Leisure Services: A Servant Leadership Approach
by Donald G. DeGraaf, Debra J. Jordan, and Kathy H. DeGraaf

Protocols for Recreation Therapy Programs
edited by Jill Kelland, along with the Recreation Therapy Staff at Alberta Hospital Edmonton

Quality Management: Applications for Therapeutic Recreation
edited by Bob Riley

A Recovery Workbook: The Road Back from Substance Abuse
by April K. Neal and Michael J. Taleff

Recreation and Leisure: Issues in an Era of Change, Third Edition
edited by Thomas Goodale and Peter A. Witt

Recreation Economic Decisions: Comparing Benefits and Costs, Second Edition
by John B. Loomis and Richard G. Walsh

Recreation for Older Adults: Individual and Group Activities
by Judith A. Elliott and Jerold E. Elliott

Recreation Programming and Activities for Older Adults
by Jerold E. Elliott and Judith A. Sorg-Elliott

Reference Manual for Writing Rehabilitation Therapy Treatment Plans
by Penny Hogberg and Mary Johnson

Research in Therapeutic Recreation: Concepts and Methods
edited by Marjorie J. Malkin and Christine Z. Howe

Simple Expressions: Creative and Therapeutic Arts for the Elderly in Long-Term Care Facilities
by Vicki Parsons

A Social History of Leisure Since 1600
by Gary Cross

A Social Psychology of Leisure
by Roger C. Mannell and Douglas A. Kleiber

Steps to Successful Programming: A Student Handbook to Accompany Programming for Parks, Recreation, and Leisure Services
by Donald G. DeGraaf, Debra J. Jordan, and Kathy H. DeGraaf

Stretch Your Mind and Body: Tai Chi as an Adaptive Activity
by Duane A. Crider and William R. Klinger

Therapeutic Activity Intervention with the Elderly: Foundations & Practices
by Barbara A. Hawkins, Marti E. May, and Nancy Brattain Rogers

Therapeutic Recreation: Cases and Exercises, Second Edition
by Barbara C. Wilhite and M. Jean Keller

Therapeutic Recreation in the Nursing Home
by Linda Buettner and Shelley L. Martin

Therapeutic Recreation Protocol for Treatment of Substance Addictions
by Rozanne W. Faulkner

Tourism and Society: A Guide to Problems and Issues
by Robert W. Wyllie

A Training Manual for Americans with Disabilities Act Compliance in Parks and Recreation Settings
by Carol Stensrud

Venture Publishing, Inc.
1999 Cato Avenue
State College, PA 16801
phone: 814–234–4561
fax: 814–234–1651

because of the wide satin border. There was still intense debate over releasing details about the yellow bunting. Of course, every police officer in New York had a description of it, but as one detective argued, "Let the kidnapper hear that bunting described, and it will show up in a trash can. At least this way there's a chance the abductor might put it on the baby when she takes her outdoors, and that one of us might spot her."

The informant had been due to call again at ten o'clock on the 23rd. As Joan and Gregg O'Brien clung to each other awaiting word, ten o'clock came and went. Eleven o'clock. Then twelve, and still no call.

At three the expected call finally came in. The caller had changed his mind. "I saw all those cops laying for me," he snarled. "You'll never see that kid again. Let my cousin's wife keep her."

He's lying. Everyone at the command post agreed on that. He was a phony right from the start.

Or was he? Had they botched the exchange? A few minutes later, the media were carrying frantic pleas. Call back. Reestablish contact. No questions asked. If you're wanted for a crime, you're promised leniency. Marianne's parents are on the verge of nervous breakdowns. Have pity on them.

The baby clothes Vonny had brought back from the thrift shop near the Port Authority were much too big for the tiny infant. "They were just about cleaned out," she had said angrily. It was after the noon feeding, and she was trying to pin an undershirt at the shoulders to keep it from sliding down the baby's arms. "Hold still!" she snapped at the infant.

"Here, let me do that," her grandmother said nervously. "Vonny, why don't you go down to the deli and pick up a nice hot coffee and a bagel. You didn't eat anything for breakfast, and you always love a toasted bagel."

"Maybe I will."

As soon as the door closed behind her granddaughter, Wanda limped to the phone and dialed the apartment ten blocks away where Sister Cordelia and Sister Maeve Marie lived with four other nuns. They jokingly called the apartment their miniconvent.

One of the elderly sisters answered. Cordelia and Maeve Marie were at the thrift shop, she told Wanda. They were getting some wonderful donations and sorting them as fast as possible. Oh, yes, Maeve Marie was saying they had a good supply of baby clothes. "You just send your granddaughter over and let her take what she needs."

But when Vonny came back with her coffee and bagel, Wanda could tell that her mood was even blacker than before, so she did not dare to talk about the thrift shop to her. She knew Vonny would guess that she had discussed her and the baby with someone.

Maybe tomorrow she'll be her sweet self again, Wanda thought, then sighed. She'd been sleeping on the couch since Vonny arrived, and the broken springs intensified the chronic arthritis pain that made getting around so hard. Nonetheless, she'd gladly given up her bed to Vonny, although she worried about her sleeping in the same bed as the baby. Suppose she rolled over on her the way she had with the first one six years ago, Wanda thought. Wanda would never forget that terrible night at Empire Hospital when they said the baby was gone. Or suppose she had one of her dizzy spells and fainted while she was bathing the baby, and the baby drowned. That had happened to the second one in Pittsburgh. It's a shame she had a third baby so soon after getting out of the psychiatric hospital there, Wanda thought. I just don't think she's ready to take care of an infant yet.

Alvirah found that in one way it helped to be busy, to be working with her hands and around people. In another way, though, it was incredibly hard to sort and fold baby and toddler snowsuits and overalls and T-shirts and sweaters, all of them gaily decorated with pictures of Mickey Mouse and Barney the Dinosaur and Cinderella and the Little Mermaid. It brought home with crushing, numbing pain the realization that Gregg and Joan might never see Marianne wear outfits like these.

"I'll work with the adult clothes," Alvirah told Cordelia after an hour of sorting baby items.

Sister Cordelia's steely gray eyes softened. "Alvirah, why don't you have a little trust in God and pray instead of blaming yourself all the time?"

"I'll try." Tears stung the back of her eyes

as Alvirah headed for the table where women's clothes had been stacked. Cordelia's right. Dear Lord, she thought, I'm no good as a detective this time. It's up to You now.

Alvirah usually enjoyed chatting with people. There was no one she did not find interesting in one way or another. But today she stayed at the sorting tables, efficiently matching skirts and jackets that had been separated, sorting items by size and placing them on the appropriate counters. Still, it gave her heart a lift to see people come in and hear them exclaim over the attractive clothing.

As she was putting teenage skirts and tops on a size 6 table, a woman exclaimed, "Everything looks so fresh. You'd think they were brand-new! My daughter will be thrilled. I didn't think I could afford to get her a pretty outfit for the holidays, but these are so reasonable. You'd think this one came right from Fifth Avenue!"

"Yes, you would."

Alvirah stayed until the shop closed at eight o'clock. Willy had been right—being at the shop, keeping busy, had helped. Yet she couldn't shake the feeling that she was missing something. And that "something" was nagging, nagging at her all the way home.

Willy had dinner waiting, but Alvirah found she had little appetite and could hardly swallow even a few bites of the stuffed pork chops that were his specialty.

"Honey, you're going to get sick," he fussed. "Maybe it wasn't a good idea for you to go to the shop today."

"No, it helped, it really did. And, Willy, you should have heard those people talk about the clothes they were selecting. One woman picked out an outfit for her daughter and said that it could have come right from Fifth Avenue, that it looked brand-new."

Alvirah laid down her fork. "Oh my God," she said. "That's it!"

"What do you mean?"

"Willy, I was in the thrift shop last week. *That's where I saw the bunting.* I'm sure of it. I was working with the men's clothes at the time, but one of the volunteers was matching baby clothes, and she held it up when she folded it." Alvirah jumped up, all trace of lethargy gone. "Willy, the kidnapper must have been in Cordelia's thrift shop. I've got to call the police hot line."

• • •

Christmas Eve dawned with heavy clouds gathering ominously overhead. Weather forecasters warned that by evening as many as six inches of snow would fall. A white Christmas was guaranteed.

For Alvirah it had been a long and intensely worrisome night. The Baby Bunting Kidnapping squad had agreed to meet her at the thrift shop at 8:00 A.M., when it was scheduled to open, but her call last night to Cordelia had brought disheartening news. Last week they'd sent some of their donated clothing, including baby apparel, to several other outlets sponsored by the convent. Two were in the Bronx. Another was near the Port Authority, in midtown Manhattan. Until they could round up all the volunteers and then get them to try and remember what had been shipped where, Alvirah couldn't be sure if the bunting had been sold at the Eighty-sixth Street shop or at one of the other locations.

"I'll have as many of my volunteers as I can reach at the shop in the morning," Cordelia had promised. "Let's hope that one of them remembers what happened to the bunting. And keep praying, Alvirah. You're already getting answers."

Alvirah had discussed the troublesome situation with Willy throughout the sleepless hours. "If we find out the bunting went to the Bronx, then there's a strong possibility that the caller was for real and does know where Marianne is being kept. On the other hand, if it went to the shop near the Port Authority, that woman may have just stolen the baby and gotten on a bus to God knows where."

By 6:00 A.M., Alvirah was certain she had put in the longest night of her life.

"I'm gonna go back today, Grandma," Vonny announced as she returned to the apartment at eight o'clock that morning, carrying a bag that contained two coffees and two bagels.

She was in a good mood. Wanda could see that. Just bringing the second coffee and bagel for her grandmother proved it. Vonny could be so sweet, Wanda thought. She had yelled at the baby once during the night but then had come out from the bedroom and heated a bottle for her. So she was settling down.

Wanda decided to take a chance on upsetting Vonny by protesting. "But the weather report isn't good, and on Christmas Eve, so many people are traveling."

Vonny smiled briefly. "I know they are, but I like that. I like to travel when there are a lot of people around."

Wanda took another chance. "Vonny, I didn't say anything before. You were so disappointed that the thrift shop downtown didn't have much baby stuff. But you know, there's a thrift shop right in the neighborhood that my friends the nuns run." She decided a small fib wouldn't hurt. "When Sister visited me the other day she said that they had wonderful clothes for children and babies. Why don't you just pick up some things before you leave? The baby has a little cold, and you've got to be sure she doesn't get a chill on the trip."

"Maybe I will. What time do you expect those nuns with the Christmas basket to come by?"

"Not before three."

"I'm getting a two o'clock bus."

She doesn't want to meet Sister, Wanda thought. Vonny always was a loner.

By 9:00 A.M., the investigators had interviewed all the volunteers Sister Cordelia had managed to gather at the thrift shop, and most important, they'd talked to one who distinctly remembered that the box with the yellow bunting had been sent to the outlet near the Port Authority.

"The worst possible luck," one of the detectives admitted to Alvirah. "If it had been sold here, we might be able to hope the abductor is in the neighborhood. If it had been sent to the Bronx, there'd still be hope that the caller was for real and not just an extortionist trying to latch on to reward money. We'll try to find out who sold the bunting, but even if we do succeed in getting a better description of the woman, my guess is that she and the baby aren't in New York anymore."

"I agree," Alvirah said quietly. "But I'm going to keep hoping anyway. And praying. Has anyone talked to Gregg this morning?"

"The inspector did. There was talk of O'Brien's wife going home today, but her doctor nixed it. She's so depressed, he's afraid of what might happen if she's not under observation at least until after tomorrow. Christmas is going to be one awful day for Joan O'Brien."

"But Gregg will be with her."

"That poor guy's so exhausted, the doctor said he could fall asleep standing up." The

374

detective nodded as he received a signal from the lieutenant. "We're on our way downtown now. We'll keep you posted, Mrs. Meehan. And thank you."

I'm going to go too, Alvirah decided, then realized Cordelia was bearing down on her.

"Alvirah, I hate to do this to you, but won't you please stay until noon? I really need the help."

"Sure, Cordelia. What do you want me to do?"

"Sort the baby clothes. They're such a jumble again. A lot of the sizes got mixed up last night. Some people are just so inconsiderate."

Cordelia hesitated, then said, "Alvirah, after you called last night, we were talking about the missing baby and everything, and Sister Bernadette said something that I've been wondering about ever since. She said that someone called and asked if we had baby clothes in the thrift shop. The caller said her granddaughter was visiting with her new baby and that her suitcase with the baby's clothes had been stolen."

"Did the caller give her name?" Alvirah asked.

"No. Sister Bernadette is sure she recog-

nized the voice but she can't put a face to it."
Then Cordelia shrugged. "Are we all grasping at straws?"

Somehow for the next hour Alvirah managed to keep a smile on her face as she sorted and matched and stacked the baby apparel. The hardest moment came when at the bottom of the leftover pile she found a tiny yellow wool jacket with narrow white satin ruching on the hood. It reminded her of the bunting.

Then her eyes widened. Was it possible, she wondered? Could this jacket *belong* with the bunting? It must. In fact, she was sure of it! The same fine quality wool, the satin ruching. It must have been separated from the bunting and not been included in the shipment that went to the outlet near the Port Authority. She would turn it over to the police. At least that way they'd know the exact color and texture of the bunting.

"Can I see that, please?"

Alvirah turned. A woman of about thirty stood at her elbow. She was wearing a nondescript ski jacket and jeans. Her dark hair had a wide white streak down the center.

Alvirah felt a sickening lurch in her stomach. The woman was the right size, the right age. And no wonder she had worn a blond wig and a scarf. Anyone would notice that bizarre hair. She would be easy to spot and to remember.

The woman looked at her curiously. "You got a problem?"

Silently, Alvirah handed the jacket to the woman. She did not want to say anything. She didn't want the woman to pay attention to her, perhaps to recognize her. But then as suddenly as she had reached for it, the woman tossed the jacket down and hurried to the door.

Oh God, it *is* her, Alvirah thought. And she recognized me. Not waiting to get her coat, she rushed to the door, but in her haste she tripped over the pull-toy a toddler was dragging, and fell. "Wait!" she called.

Hands reached to pick her up. The mother of the toddler tried to apologize. Alvirah brushed past them and hurried onto the street. By the time she got to the sidewalk, the woman was halfway down the block.

"Wait!" Alvirah shouted again.

The woman glanced over her shoulder and began to run.

Passersby looked at Alvirah curiously as

she pushed her way through the crowded streets. Unheedful of the chill wind and the snow that was starting to fall, she ran, keeping the woman in sight, hoping to see a cop.

The woman abruptly turned left on Eighty-first Street. Alvirah caught up with her when she stopped at a car that was parked in front of the Museum of Natural History.

The driver of the car jumped out. "What's the matter, Dorine?"

"Eddie, this woman is crazy. She's following me."

The man hurried around the car and confronted Alvirah, who was panting for breath. "What's your problem?" he demanded.

Alvirah glanced into the backseat of the vehicle. A toddler and an infant were strapped in child seats. The infant had a mass of dark hair. "I *was* following you," she gasped to the young woman, "but I see I've made a mistake. I'm sorry. When you picked up that little jacket, I thought you might be someone else. Then when you threw it down, I was sure you'd recognized me."

"I put it down 'cause I could tell it's too small for my kid," she said, nodding toward the baby in the infant seat. "As for you, I never laid eyes on you, and the look you gave me, I thought you were nuts." Then she smiled broadly. "Hey, listen, it's okay. It's Christmas Eve. Everybody gets a little unstrung, right?"

Alvirah slowly retraced her steps to the thrift shop. I'm chilled to the bone, she thought. I'll phone the police and let them pick up the jacket and I'll go home.

When she reached the thrift shop, she fended off questions the other volunteers threw at her. "It was nothing. I thought I knew that woman." Then she headed for the table where she'd left the little yellow jacket. It was gone.

Oh no! she thought. Tara, a teenage volunteer, was working nearby. "Tara, did you notice someone pick up an infant-sized yellow wool hooded jacket?" Alvirah asked her.

"Yeah, just about three minutes ago. I'd helped her pick out some other stuff, clothes and blankets and sheets, then she spotted the jacket and was real pleased. She said that the other day she'd found the rest of the outfit in a different thrift shop. I guess it went with leggings or something. Wasn't that lucky?"

Alvirah thought her knees would buckle. "What did the woman look like?"

Tara shrugged. "Oh, I don't know. Dark

hair. About your height. Late twenties or so. She had on a dark gray, no a dark blue ski jacket. If you ask me, she should have looked at the racks of women's clothes while she was at it."

But Alvirah was no longer listening. For an instant she thought about taking the time to call for help, but she knew that every second was vital. She grabbed the teenager by the hand. "Come with me."

"Hey, I'm supposed to—"

"I said, come!"

As they rushed out the door, Cordelia was emerging from the back room. "Alvirah!" she shouted. "What's wrong?"

Alvirah took an instant to reply. "Send for the police. The kidnapper was here a few minutes ago."

Columbus Avenue was crowded with shoppers. Alvirah looked around hopelessly and stopped. "You said the woman had taken other things. What did she carry them in?"

"Two of our big white shopping bags."

"If the bags are heavy, she won't be able to move too fast," Alvirah said, more to herself than to the girl.

Tara seemed to suddenly understand what had triggered Alvirah's reaction. "Mrs. Meehan, do you think the jacket went with the yellow bunting the cops were questioning us about? The bags were so heavy that I asked that woman how far she had to go and she said, not too far, just up to Ninetieth Street and over a few blocks."

Alvirah wanted to kiss Tara. Instead, she snapped, "Now listen hard. You go back inside and tell all this to Sister Cordelia. Tell her to have the cops blanket the area between here and Ninetieth Street. Tell her we're closing in on Baby Bunting!"

The early morning's pleasant mood that Wanda Brown had found so endearing in her granddaughter did not last. The baby had started fussing after her ten o'clock bottle and would not be soothed. Wanda didn't dare raise the subject of more baby clothes again.

Vonny grumbled and cursed and finally, to escape the infant's wails, headed for the thrift shop. Now, as she hauled the heavy shopping bags through the snowy streets back to her grandmother's apartment, the seven blocks from Eighty-sixth to Ninetieth and West End started to feel like miles.

As she trudged angrily along, her nerves

felt raw and stretched. "Damn kid," she said aloud. "Damn pest, just like the others."

The baby was still screaming when she got back. Wanda, looking frayed and weary, held it in her arms, rocking it gently.

"What's the matter with her now?" Vonny snapped.

"I don't think she feels well, Vonny," Wanda said apologetically. "I think she's a little feverish. I don't think you should take her out today. I think it would be a mistake."

Without acknowledging Wanda's remarks, Vonny crossed to her grandmother and looked at the baby. *"Shut up!"* she yelled.

Wanda felt her throat go dry. Vonny had that look, that angry scowl, that stubborn, blank expression in her eyes. Wanda had seen it before, knew how dangerous it could be. Still, she had to tell her. "Vonny, dear, Sister Maeve Marie phoned after you left. She's coming in a few minutes with the Christmas basket. They started delivering them early because the weather's turning bad."

Vonny's eyebrows molded together to form a single, angry black slash across her forehead. "Did you ask her to come early, Grandma?"

"No, dear." Wanda patted the baby's back. "Ssh . . . Oh, Vonny, her chest is getting raspy."

"She'll be fine when I get to Pittsburgh." Vonny stomped into the other room with the shopping bags, then returned immediately. "I don't want to talk to that nun, or to show my baby to her. Give her to me. I'll bring her into the bedroom until that nun is gone."

Alvirah hurried uptown, her eyes constantly roving back and forth as she passed the intersections. Along the way she stopped passersby to ask if they'd seen a woman in a dark blue ski jacket carrying two white shopping bags.

At Eighty-sixth and Broadway she lucked out. A news vendor said he had seen a woman of that description zigzag across the street. "She went toward West End," he said.

At Eighty-eighth and West End Avenue, an old man pulling a shopping cart claimed a woman with white shopping bags had passed him. He said he remembered because she had set her bags down for a minute. "She was mumbling to herself and swearing," he said disapprovingly. "Some holiday spirit."

The first squad cars arrived as Alvirah reached Eighty-ninth Street. Tara had obviously given an excellent account of what had happened. "We're going to canvas this whole area," a sergeant told her crisply. "If necessary, we'll make a house-to-house search. Why don't you go home, Mrs. Meehan?"

"I can't," Alvirah said.

The sergeant looked at her with compassion. "You're going to get pneumonia. At least sit in the squad car and stay warm. Let us take over from here."

It was at that moment that Sister Maeve Marie came up the block, carrying a heavy basket. Her short veil fluttered in the wind. Like Sister Cordelia, she chose to wear an ankle-length habit. When she saw Alvirah talking to the cop, her expression became startled. Moving as rapidly as she could, she hurried over. A former police officer herself, she knew the sergeant. "Hello, Tom," she said, then asked, "Alvirah, what's wrong?"

When she heard, she exclaimed, "The baby's kidnapper is in the neighborhood? God be praised!" Immediately the cop in her took over. "Tom, have you sealed off the neighborhood?"

"That's what we're doing just now, Maeve. We'll be going from door to door in every building, making inquiries. But please try to persuade Mrs. Meehan to wait in the car. She looks like she's going to keel over."

"Alvirah won't keel over," Maeve said briskly as other squad cars screeched into the block. "Alvirah, help me deliver the baskets. Two of us can move faster. Some of our people will be more likely to talk to us than to the cops. The van is parked at the corner." She looked at the sergeant. "Illegally parked."

It was something to do. It was action. And Alvirah knew that Maeve was right. For fear of repercussions, old and sick people often didn't want to get involved by cooperating with the police, even when they might know something critical. "Let's go," she said.

"I have four deliveries on this block," Maeve told her.

The first basket went to an elderly couple who had not been outdoors since Thanksgiving. Their neighbor did their shopping for them. Alvirah rang that neighbor's bell.

When she came to the door, she talked freely. "No," she said, "I'm in and out all the time and I'm one to gab with people, and nobody mentioned a new baby in this building." Nor had she seen anybody carrying a baby in a yellow bunting in the neighborhood.

The second delivery, three buildings away, was to a ninety-year-old woman and her seventy-year-old daughter. When Maeve introduced Alvirah, they knew all about her. Willy had replaced their toilet. "What a wonderful man," they told her. Unfortunately, they knew nothing about a baby.

At the third house, a woman with three small children had packages under the tree. "All of them from the thrift shop," she confided in a whisper. "The kids are dying to see what's in them."

But she too knew nothing about a woman with dark hair who had a new baby.

"This is it," Maeve told Alvirah as they shared carrying the last basket. "Wanda Brown is the nicest old woman. She's pretty crippled with arthritis and doesn't have any relatives except a granddaughter who lives somewhere in Pennsylvania. She doesn't talk about her much, but apparently the poor girl's experienced a lot of tragedy. She had two babies that died as infants."

They were about to enter the building at

the corner of West End and Ninetieth Street. Down the block they could see policemen going from house to house. Then Alvirah and Maeve stared at each other. "Maeve, are you thinking what I'm thinking?" Alvirah demanded.

"Sister Bernadette's call from someone asking about the thrift shop because her granddaughter had a new baby and no clothes for it. Oh, dear God, Alvirah, I'll get Tom."

Some raw instinct made Alvirah pull her back. "No! Let's get into that apartment now."

Vonny stood at the window watching the police activity below. The baby was lying on the bed, its cries reduced to tired whimpers. Then she saw a nun and another woman heading for the entrance ten floors below. Between them, they were carrying a basket.

Vonny went out to the living room. "I think your Christmas basket is coming, Grandma," she said flatly. "Remember, not one word about me and the baby."

Wanda smiled timidly. "Whatever you want, dear."

Vonny went back into the bedroom. The baby was asleep. Lucky for you, she thought.

"It's a three-room apartment," Maeve whispered as she rang the bell and called, "It's me, Wanda, Sister Maeve Marie."

Alvirah nodded. Every ounce of her being was vibrating. Please, dear Lord. *Please!*

The bell, a loud and raucous sound, echoed through the apartment. In the bedroom, the startled infant jumped and began to wail. An angry Vonny grabbed a sock, bent over the bed and scooped up the baby.

Wanda Brown made her painful way to the door. Smiling nervously, she greeted Sister Maeve. "Oh, you're too good," she sighed.

"Mrs. Meehan is helping me deliver the baskets," Maeve told her.

Alvirah brushed past the older woman, carrying the basket of food into the apartment. Her eyes raced over the small foyer and the cluttered living room. But there was no one else there. She could see into the kitchen. Pots were stacked on the stove, dishes piled on the table. But she could see nothing to indicate the presence of a baby.

The bedroom door was ajar, and through

the narrow crack she could make out the unmade bed and two sides of the narrow room. It had to be empty.

She scrutinized the living room. There was nothing here to indicate the presence of a baby, either.

"Wanda," Maeve was asking, "were you the one who called about your granddaughter needing clothes for her baby? Sister Bernadette thought she recognized your voice."

Wanda paled. Vonny was up to her old tricks, hiding behind half-opened doors and listening. She'd be furious. And Vonny in one of her rages . . .

"Oh, no," Wanda said, her voice quavering. "Why would I do that? I haven't seen Vonny in nearly five years. She lives in Pittsburgh."

Alvirah knew that the look of intense disappointment in Maeve's eyes was mirrored in her own.

"Well, enjoy Christmas," Maeve said. "We'll leave the basket on the kitchen table. The turkey is still warm, but be sure to refrigerate it after you've had dinner."

Alvirah's sense of urgency was overwhelming. Her premonition that the baby was in danger seemed stronger than ever. She wanted to get out of that apartment, to keep looking for her. She hurried across the room with the basket, carrying it into the kitchen. Then, as she turned, the sleeve of her sweater caught the door handle of the refrigerator, and the door swung open. She was about to close it when her eyes fastened on a half-empty baby bottle on the top shelf.

"You did make that call!" Alvirah yelled at Wanda as she burst back into the living room. "Your granddaughter is here. Where is she? What did she do with Marianne?"

Wanda's terrified glance at the bedroom was enough to give Alvirah the answer she needed. With Maeve on her heels, she charged toward the door.

Vonny stepped out from behind it. She was holding the baby at arm's length in front of her. The infant's mouth was gagged with an old sock and her eyes were bulging. "You want her," Vonny screamed. "Here, take her!"

Alvirah had just enough time in that split second to raise her arms, pluck the infant from midair and cradle it to her breast. An instant later, Maeve had yanked the gag from around Marianne's mouth, and the blessed wail of an angry infant filled the apartment.

The ambulance raced down Ninth Avenue, its siren blasting as it rushed toward Empire Hospital. The medic in charge was bending over Marianne, who, securely strapped on the stretcher, was staring up at him.

"She's a tough little bird," he said happily. "Other than a slight cold, I'd say she seems to be in remarkably good shape, considering the adventure she's been through."

Alvirah was sitting beside the stretcher, her eyes firmly fixed on the baby. Sister Maeve Marie was seated next to her, wreathed in smiles.

Alvirah still could not believe that it was over, that Marianne was safe. Her hands still tingled with the impact of catching the baby, of feeling that little heart fluttering beneath her fingertips.

Everything that had happened after that point was still something of a blur. She remembered snatches of things—Vonny running to her grandmother, crying that she didn't mean to hurt the baby, that she never meant to hurt any of her babies; Maeve hanging out the window and yelling to the cops below; the cops rushing into the apartment; the crowds of people and the cameras and reporters that materialized on the street in the few minutes it took the ambulance to appear. It was a jumble of images, like a crazy, dizzying, wonderful, happy dream.

The ambulance pulled into the driveway of the hospital, and as soon as it had stopped, the doors were thrown open by waiting attendants. As hands reached in to take the baby, Maeve stood and said firmly, "There's only one person who should hand that baby back to its mother, and that is Alvirah Meehan."

Less than a minute later, as cameras clicked and onlookers cheered, Alvirah strode triumphantly into the lobby of Empire Hospital, holding Marianne, now snugly wrapped in the yellow bunting. Minutes later she laid her small charge in the yearning arms of a radiantly happy Joan O'Brien.

"It certainly didn't take you long to bounce back," Willy observed as he and Alvirah walked home arm in arm along Fifth Avenue from St. Patrick's Cathedral. They had just attended Christmas morning Mass, which seemed especially joyous this year.

"Isn't that the truth," Alvirah responded, shaking her head. "Oh, Willy, I've never had a better Christmas. At Mass I prayed for that girl, Vonny. I know she's sick and needs help, and she deserves to get it. But let me tell you, my throat closed at the thought of putting in a good word for that skunk who called with all those false messages. But then I decided that since the cops had tracked him down, and I know he'll pay for what he did, I'd go ahead and mention him."

She looked around. "Isn't New York beautiful with the snow on the ground and the store windows all decorated? Tomorrow morning I'm going shopping again for Marianne—after, of course, I write a report on the Baby Bunting Case for the *Globe*. But today . . ." Alvirah smiled. "Today I just want to savor the miracle."

"That Marianne is okay?"

"That she's okay because of the way everything happened. I realized she was in that apartment only because my sleeve happened to catch on the handle of the refrigerator door, and that handle happened to be loose. That's the miracle, Willy. If that handle hadn't been so loose, if that door hadn't opened so easily, if I hadn't seen that baby bottle . . ."

Willy laughed. "Honey, be sure to mention that to Cordelia at dinner tonight. When I fixed the leak in Wanda Brown's kitchen last month, I noticed that handle was loose and promised to come back and fix it. And only last week Cordelia was bugging me about it, asking when I was going to get back there. But then you kept me so busy shopping and carrying packages, I just never got a chance." He paused. "I see what you mean. A miracle."

AUTHOR'S NOTE

MARY HIGGINS CLARK, born and raised in New York, is of Irish descent and constantly draws on her Irish background to create the characters in her books. "This was never more true than in the case of Alvirah and Willy," she says.

"Alvirah and Willy had worked all their lives—she as a cleaning woman and he as a plumber. Never having had children of their own, they lavished their affection on family members, friends and the needy. A couple who lived next door when I was growing up in the Bronx were my inspiration for Alvirah and Willy," she recalls.

"Their names were Annie and Charlie Potters. Charlie, whom Annie always referred to as 'my Charlie,' was a big, good-looking Irish cop. Annie had dyed red hair, a jutting jaw and a warm heart. What Annie couldn't wear she carried, and she'd sail out bedecked from head to toe in mismatched outfits, sure she was stepping out of the pages of *Vogue.* Annie and Charlie were wonderful neighbors, and I hope I have caught something of their essence in Alvirah and Willy.

"Winning the lottery changed the way Alvirah and Willy lived. But it never changed Alvirah and Willy's innate wisdom about what really matters in life."

In the fall of 1986, the two secret initiatives I had worked so hard on came apart within weeks of each other. This bumper sticker (*above, left*) was part of the Reagan administration's effort to build support for the Nicaraguan resistance. By the end of October the whole world knew Ilopango military airbase in El Salvador was a secret operating and maintenance base for the Nicaraguan resistance resupply effort.

Bob Dutton, a retired Air Force colonel, was brought in to help run the Nicaraguan resistance air resupply effort. Like most of the people involved, he didn't lack courage. To get a firsthand feel for how difficult the missions over Nicaragua were, he flew several himself and introduced a new set of procedures.

Circus Maximus. The Iran-contra congressional hearings in the summer of 1987 took on the aura of a Roman amphitheater. (AP)

Starting in November 1986, *Newsweek, Time,* and nearly every newspaper across the land made the Iran-contra affair the centerpiece of their reporting for months. (*Newsweek*, June 20, 1987, Arnie Sachs/Sygma)

Dry socks. Sleeping in a real bed. Newspapers! A radio. More milk. Shoes instead of boots. No uniforms. Clean clothes. More milk. No mosquitoes. More milk.

Somebody told me later that the weather in Hawaii was awful, but I didn't even notice. We walked on the beach and drove to see a volcano, but mostly we spent hours just sitting quietly together and talking, sharing memories all the way from our tearful and premature farewell in San Diego until our reunion that very week. I read through a big pile of letters from everybody in my family, and looked at stacks of pictures of Tait. It finally began to dawn on me me that I was a father. I had received a few baby pictures in the mail, but Betsy arrived with hundreds more, and she brought them to life with her stories. She also brought a picture of my pal Bob Eisenbach, still recovering from his war wounds and wearing a football helmet to protect his head. He was sitting in a wheelchair, in his bathrobe—and holding my little girl.

It was a glorious time, with no phone calls to return, no errands to run, and no plans except being together and trying to catch up on each other's lives from the past few months. But oh, what a tearful parting. It was one thing to go off to war having never seen combat. But to return to the war, having seen men die in front of you—*that* was hard.

Normally, all communication between home and Vietnam came through the mail, which was why we lived and died for letters and packages. The great occasions in the field were when a resupply mission brought in not only food and ammo, but those red and yellow mail sacks. Mail was our link to home, and we treasured it.

I used to read each letter at least five times, and that wasn't unusual. You'd break out a letter and read it again at the oddest times, trying to squeeze out an extra drop of information or affection. Even if the news wasn't all good, at least the mail gave you something to focus on aside from your wet boots. A letter might be filled with the most trivial, mundane details, and your mother, your wife, or your brother might apologize for having nothing "interesting" to say, but they couldn't imagine how wonderful it was to receive a letter, any letter, and to know that somebody back home was thinking of you and wanted you back.

Letters were so vital to the morale of the troops that if any of our guys weren't receiving mail, I'd notify the chaplain. When a guy got hit and you went through his gear for inventory, it wasn't unusual to come across a huge wad of forty or fifty letters.

A care package was always welcome. Betsy used to send M&M candies; I don't recall having any special fondness for them before Vietnam, but I have loved them ever since. Homemade cookies were a great treat, along with birthday cakes. Occasionally, these cakes even arrived in one piece, but regardless of their condition, they disappeared instantly.

Sending letters was almost as important as receiving them. Not that we needed any encouragement, but it was a good feeling to write FREE where the stamp would normally go and know that your letter was on its way. We usually wrote home in the late afternoon, after digging in for the night. I wrote many a letter with my poncho pulled over my head, especially if the mail bird was coming early in the morning. Often the paper was so wet you had to write very lightly, so it wouldn't tear. If you didn't have paper you used the back of a C-ration carton.

Our letters home were filled with plans for after the war, which was a way of focusing beyond our immediate concerns, such as whether the resupply would arrive in time, or whether we'd be ambushed, or whether we'd stay alive until tomorrow. I wrote often to Betsy and my parents, although I didn't tell Betsy about my various injuries because I didn't want her to worry. That was a serious mistake, and I still haven't heard the end of it.

We used to refer to home as "the world," as in "He's gone back to the world." It was as if we were living on a different planet, and I suppose we were. My unit was in Vietnam during the 1969 moon landing, and while we certainly heard the news, I didn't get around to seeing the television pictures until ten years later, during a visit to the Air and Space Museum in Washington.

It's funny, the things you remember. I don't think of myself as a complainer, or as being especially susceptible to fear. And I've already noted my marvelous ability to recall the good parts of life and blot out the bad. But in writing this book, I looked through some of the letters I sent home to my parents from Vietnam in 1968 and 1969, and a few of the lines jumped out at me:

- "Last night I spent six hours just waiting for the firing to stop. Of course it was our own counter-battery fire—outgoing! Who was the new Lt. with a red face?"
- "I don't really know how much more of the John Wayne stuff I can take. This tour has just about done it."
- "Most of all, I wish the politicians would get off their fat, soft posteriors and come through with something one way or the other to clear this mess up."
- "Don't worry. I have not yet begun to write."
- "I am writing this on an ambush out west of Con Thien. Rather strange in a way, to be sitting out here in the weeds, waiting for Charlie to come along so that we can kill him, and writing to my father while I'm waiting."
- "I sent Betsy a letter explaining this whole operation. The only thing I didn't say is how much of a mess this whole thing really is. We've had two killed and five wounded to date—one guy that got it was right next to me. I never even got scratched."
- "Last night we had two killed when we went out with special forces. It's sickening because they are such good boys and there is so damned little else that can be done."
- "Believe me, I pray every day. Not just for myself, but for getting these Marines home safe."
- "We haven't had any mail for almost two weeks and I think I can understand how Betsy and you all must feel when the letters are sparse in the other direction."
- "I'm glad to be leaving. Not just because it is an escape from the hell of war—but an escape from the particular hell of *this* war. An escape from the indecision of fighting an enemy that is allowed a safe harbor from the power of *our* storm. An escape from the haunted looks of men who have seen their friends and brothers die because they were collectively hamstrung by political gestures and spineless decision-makers. Oh, but it's been a swell war! A grand and glorious reversal of that war almost two hundred years ago when we lost all the battles but won the war, for here we've won all the battles but lost the war."
- "What's all this fuss now? They're half a world away. Let 'em help themselves. And anyway, we only gave our word and 37,000 lives."

* * *

The scariest part of combat is to be under "incoming," when you're being hit with indirect fire: artillery, rockets, or mortars. With a mortar, the first thing you hear is the distant sound of something popping in a hollow tube, which means you'd better dive for cover in a hurry. Then, *shhhh-boom!* The time between that first sound and that *shhhh-boom* feels like the longest moment of your life. All you can do is wait to see where it hits—and pray that it doesn't find you as you crouch deeper in your hole and pull the helmet tightly over your head, trying to make yourself as small as possible while you're screaming into the radio for return fire.

That is fear. And that's why we wore two sets of dog tags: one around our necks, the other laced into a boot. That way, if your head got separated from your body, you could be identified from your foot. If your foot was missing, well, hopefully your head was still attached. But there were plenty of times when a body could not be identified in the field, and had to wait until the lads in the morgue matched the remains with the medical and dental records.

Commanders had their own fears: you could never be sure that you weren't inadvertently leading your men into a trap or an ambush. We were hunting the enemy, but they were also hunting us, and you never forgot that every maneuver or patrol might be the last for any number of your men. The very worst thing that could happen to a lieutenant in Vietnam was that all his men could be killed and he would be left alive.

I dealt with my fears through my faith. Trusting in God doesn't mean you take foolish risks; every time somebody shot at me, I ducked. And you've got to have a healthy respect for the consequences of being hit by a bullet, or blown up by artillery. But there's also a lot of truth to the old saying that there are no atheists in foxholes. As a group, Marines are an irreverent lot. And yet there's a real spiritual depth to many of them—and not only when the bombs are falling.

I urged my men to attend chapel services, although most of them didn't need much encouragement. And I developed a lot of respect for the chaplains who worked with us. They would give the Last Rites to a dying Marine, or provide solace for the man who had just lost his best friend and who was desperate to find some meaning amid all the tears, blood, and chaos. And they were the ones who had to answer that most difficult of all questions: if there's a God, how can He let this happen?

One of my tasks as a leader was to help the men separate the legitimate fears from the trivial ones. One night a radio call came in from a squad leader on an ambush. "I've got movement," he said.

"You know what to do," I whispered. A moment later, like clockwork, we heard the rifles, the claymore mines, the machine guns, and the illumination round. Then a long silence. Finally, from way down in the valley, a voice rang out: "Oh, *shit*! Call the lieutenant."

They had killed a bear, and the new battalion commander made them bring it back. He said he wanted proof, but the men all believed that he wanted to make a fur coat for his wife. They were so angry after lugging the animal back to base that they gutted the bear and buried its entrails next to his bunker, about an inch deep. The stench was awful.

What I'm proudest of from Vietnam are not the decorations for heroism, but the fact that I led seventy ambushes and that most of my men came home alive. "I have one goal here," I'd tell the troops, "and that's to get the job done and get you guys back home safely."

The key to good military leadership is to make the men feel like they're working *with* you rather than for you. Instead of sitting back and issuing orders, you've got to know every one of their jobs at least as well as they do. No matter how charismatic you might be, nobody in uniform will follow you unless they're convinced that you know what you're talking about. Each member of your platoon has to believe that if he does what you tell him, he will survive an otherwise unsurvivable experience.

To improve the odds, I became a stickler for detail and discipline. I made my men get frequent haircuts so they'd have a better chance of spotting leeches, slugs, ticks, and wounds. I insisted they brush their teeth, because you didn't want a guy lost for three days because of dental problems. They washed their socks once a month, whether they needed to or not. When we came to a stream, we'd set up security so everybody could bathe; the men were in enough danger without the additional risk of illness. The next best thing to heaven was to get back to Con Thien, where somebody had set up a primitive shower which consisted of a hose coming out of a fifty-five-gallon drum. After thirty seconds you'd feel like a new man.

I insisted that my men wear their helmets and flak jackets on all operations and keep them at arm's reach even back in base. Some commanders felt that the troops could move more easily without this heavy armor, and while that was certainly true, some of those men died. My own life was saved several times by my flak jacket when grenades, RPGs, and mortars exploded nearby. In my platoon you even had to sleep with your helmet and flak jacket on. It was hot, it was sweaty, and you stank. But you also lived.

Each man had to carry his gear packed exactly the same way: mortar rounds on top, canteens in the same place on the belt, grenades in the same pocket. I inspected the troops before each patrol and every ambush, and if I saw anything extraneous in a guy's pocket, out it came. A guy who stood out for any reason could end up as a target for snipers.

No chin strap? Get a new helmet. Grenades on your belt? Not in this platoon. Just came off an operation? Clean your rifle. Rest stop? One man cleans his weapon while his partner stands watch.

Training was continual. We'd go back to a fire base, and instead of resting, we'd practice combat formations or ambush drills. Americans are not a patient people, and it takes extraordinary discipline to lie perfectly still on the ground for hours while staying alert. There were times that the enemy was so close that I told the men to be sure they covered up the luminous dials on their watches. It didn't matter if they had been up all night: I was always running drills.

Sometimes I went too far. There were times when I demanded too high a standard from men who couldn't always live up to it. Sometimes I pushed my men too hard, and made them walk a little farther and dig a little deeper and carry a little more than was necessary. And there were times when I was too controlling, when I drove my men crazy by insisting there was a right and a wrong way to do *everything*. "If you took a leak," one guy complained, "North would critique the way you held yourself." He was exaggerating, but not by much.

I was blessed with the ability to motivate people, and I spent countless hours counseling, cajoling, and convincing—talking to the men in twos and threes, and sometimes one at a time—not because they were shirking, but because I was asking so much. The greatest compliment I ever received came after a firefight, when one of the Marines turned to Goodwin and said, "Captain, you should have seen my lieutenant. He was magnificent." It wasn't the word "magnificent" that meant so much. It's what he called me—not "the lieutenant," or "Blue," or "Lieutenant North," but "*my* lieutenant." That was probably the kindest thing anyone ever said about me.

I was warm and supportive when a man was hurt or in trouble, but I could also be a nasty s.o.b. if he screwed up. Jones might have worked twenty hours that day, but if he was supposed to be guarding our position at 0200, he had damn well better be awake. If I came across a man who was asleep in his hole, I'd stand right behind him, undo my chin strap, and bang my helmet against his. That usually did the trick. "You should be real glad I'm not an NVA soldier," I'd tell him when he stopped trembling, "because I would have cut your throat."

If I didn't witness it personally, I might confront the man privately the next day and say, "Smedley, I understand you fell asleep last night. If you do that again, somebody might drop a hand grenade in your hole, and I'll have to send a letter to your mother. Or somebody might drop a hand grenade in Jackson's hole, and it will be your fault, and you're the guy who's going to write that letter to Jackson's mother."

The company gunnery sergeant had a slightly different approach. If he found a man who was sleeping on the perimeter, he would pee into his foxhole.

Whereupon the guy would wake up and say, "Hey, what are you doing?"

This was what the gunny was waiting for. "You awake, Smedley?"

"Yeah."

"So tell me, Smedley, would a guy who's awake let another guy piss on him?"

"I guess not."

"That's right," the gunny would say. "So either I didn't piss on you, or else you were sleeping. If you were, I'll have you court-martialed, and you'll spend six months in the brig. Now, then, did I piss on you?"

"I guess not, Gunny."

Of all my memories of Vietnam, there was one incident that remains as vivid as anything I have ever experienced.

It was after a successful ambush, where we killed three enemy soldiers. We always searched the bodies quickly, grabbing weapons and radios, looking for documents, and collecting the enemy I.D. tags so the Red Cross could notify their families. Then we'd get the hell out of there.

This time one of my men yelled, "Hey Blue, we've got an officer." He could tell by the man's insignia, and by the fact that he'd carried a pistol. I inspected the body myself. Officers were more likely to carry documents, and I wanted to be sure we found everything.

He had been a young, dark-haired, good-looking guy, probably around my own age. The Soviet-made pistol was still in his hand. He had taken a burst of fire in the chest, which killed him instantly. In addition to documents, he was carrying a whole slew of letters wrapped in plastic, just like we did. Later that day, after I had called in a report on the ambush and everybody dug in for the night, I looked through his pack.

Among other things, I found a map and a notebook with names of men in his unit. During my final semester at Annapolis I had taken an optional course in Vietnamese, and my roommate at The Basic School was a Vietnamese Marine lieutenant. I could read the language well enough to see that the dead NVA soldier had also been a lieutenant. There were letters from his wife and his parents, along with a photo of him in his dress uniform and a big smile, posing with his wife and two little kids. He also carried a book of little drawings he had evidently been making for them. There were no scenes of combat, only pictures of mountains, birds, and trees, and little poems he had written to go with them.

It occurred to me—and how could it not?—that had things gone just a little differently a few hours ago, he would have been going through the items in my pack, looking at pictures of Betsy and our little baby. He became real to me at that moment, as it struck me that his family would never see him again, and would probably never even know the circumstances of his death.

I have thought about him a few times since, and while I don't recall crying that day, I still find it hard to tell this story without a lump in my throat. Whenever one of our men was killed, the troops would say he got "wasted." What an appropriate word. There are some deep truths embodied in the slang and jargon of war, and that's certainly one of them.

I was tempted to keep some of the materials from his pack, and then decided no, it was better to make sure it all got back to his wife. I wrote up a report on what happened, adding a few more details than usual in the hope that when it was filed with the Red Cross, his family might eventually learn that he died bravely and quickly, without pain or suffering. I slowly replaced all of his personal material in the pack, including a letter he had started writing to his family, describing how much he missed them. I could have written that letter myself.

I have always wondered about the kind of man who glorifies combat, or who could even consider going to war for money, or adventure. The bravest military men I've known have all hated war, and it was a great general who uttered that famous remark—that war is hell. War changes you forever, and I can't believe that anyone who's ever been to one is eager to go again.

6

A New Life

After Vietnam I returned to Quantico as a tactics instructor at The Basic School, where I had been a student just over a year earlier. I was now preparing young lieutenants who would soon be on their way to Vietnam to lead platoons of their own, just as I had. My specialty was patrolling and counterinsurgency tactics for small infantry units—everything from rifle squad combat formations to platoon-sized ambushes.

We would start the course with a few classroom sessions, using slides, films, and a blackboard to explain the theory and dynamics of the operations. To stress the importance of surprise in battle, we instructors would occasionally charge into a classroom without warning, firing blanks from an M-16. This was intended as a graphic reminder that in the war these men would soon be fighting, they and their troops could find themselves under fire at any moment.

After the introductory classroom work, we moved outside for field demonstrations. Some of the training areas at Quantico were remarkably similar to the terrain in Vietnam, which enabled us to replicate authentic battlefield conditions. As the students observed from the bleachers, we would organize a group of enlisted Marines into the appropriate formations for combat, reconnaissance, or ambush patrols. Then we'd take the students on demonstration exercises and walk them through these same maneuvers. We concluded with several days of field training, where we tested the men in a variety of skills. It was hard work, but this was the one place a lieutenant could screw up without getting anyone hurt or killed.

My goal was to turn every mistake into a constructive learning experience. Whenever possible, I'd begin with a positive comment: "You did a good job on that operations order. You deployed your troops well, and your use of supporting arms was excellent."

When it came time to point out the errors, I changed the focus slightly by shifting from the active voice to the passive: "Overall, Jones, you did an excellent job. But during the final objective, the first squad was deployed too far to the left. The base of fire for the machine guns should have been moved farther to the flank." The lesson I wanted the men to remember was not that Jones screwed up, but that the base of fire should have been shifted.

This technique of personalizing the praise while maintaining a certain distance around the criticism was something I had learned from my father, who spoke this way not only with the workers at his wool factory, but also with his children at the dining room table. Later on, when he became a college instructor, he continued this practice. "You took care of the first section perfectly," he would tell a student. "But this is how we should handle the ending." "We"—as if the whole class could have made that same mistake.

I loved teaching, and I enjoyed getting to know the students. There were instructors at Quantico who really knew their stuff, but never bothered to learn the names of the men in their classes. I still can't understand that. The military is full of wonderful leaders, but it also has its share of brusque, impersonal automatons. (And so, I have learned since, does business and government.) I served under some of these types, and they rarely inspired me to do my best.

There's so much that a teacher or a coach can accomplish with just a little personal effort. At the end of a long day, before I went home to my family, I'd sometimes walk through the Bachelor Officers' Quarters just to say hello. "Hi, there, Smedley, how'd it go, today?" People respond to an instructor who cares about them. If a student feels you know him personally, or is aware that you took the trouble to learn his name, he'll usually try a little harder and perform a little better. Granted, I was teaching under ideal circumstances. These guys were all highly motivated and talented volunteers, and it was a joy to work with them.

Because nearly all our students were headed for Vietnam, we kept a close eye on the latest developments in the war. If a new weapon was introduced or a new tactic was tried, we knew about it within days from reading "after action" and "incident" reports from the war. I had been back at Quantico only about three months when I read a particularly gruesome account of a Marine corporal who had been charged with murder in the deaths of sixteen Vietnamese civilians in a village near Da Nang. When I read the defendant's name I practically fainted: the alleged killer was Randy Herrod, the machine-gunner who had saved my life in Vietnam.

As if Herrod wasn't in enough trouble, this incident took place shortly after the infamous My Lai massacre was revealed, with its devastating effect on the public's perception of the U.S. military. The killing of innocent civilians was terrible, but what really infuriated the American public was that several Army officers were accused of having covered up the killings for over a year and a half until the event was exposed in the press. The facts in Randy Herrod's case were in dispute, but with My Lai still fresh in the public mind, the Marine Corps lost no time in making it public.

I couldn't believe Randy was guilty. For one thing, I had trained him better than that. For another, only a coward would murder unarmed civilians, and Randy Herrod was certainly no coward. He had proved that time and again in my platoon, and twice during a single battle he had risked his life to drag me to safety.

But even if Herrod had acted wrongly, which I doubted, I still wanted to help him. Randy Herrod had saved my life, and you don't forget something like that.

In a letter to Gene Stipe, Herrod's defense attorney, I explained that I had been Randy's platoon commander in Vietnam, and that I knew him to be a brave and responsible Marine. If Stipe and his colleagues thought it might help, I added, I would be willing to return to Vietnam to testify at Herrod's trial.

Stipe contacted me the following week to accept my offer. Some of my fellow instructors were less than delighted that I was going to abandon them in the middle of a particularly busy training period.

Not only would I be going against the Marine Corps hierarchy, at least implicitly, but these guys would have to take over my teaching assignments. The commanding officer of the Basic School called me down and pointedly asked why this trip was so important. "Okay," he said when I explained the situation. "If you're convinced it's the right thing to do, I'll authorize it." (I needed his permission because military personnel could not return to Vietnam on their own.)

Betsy wasn't exactly thrilled, either. For one thing, she was now pregnant with our second child. For another, the prospect of her husband returning to the war at his own expense, and using his leave time to do it—all this did not strike her as a particularly brilliant course of action. We had been married a year and a half, and I had already spent two-thirds of that time in Vietnam.

When I returned to Vietnam in August 1970, I found that Herrod's situation was even worse than I expected. The My Lai incident had traumatized the entire military, and the word was out all over the base that there would be no cover-up in this case. (This wouldn't be the last time in my life when those around me were motivated less by the facts of the case than by the threatening memory of a previous cover-up.)

A number of the officers I met thought I was crazy. "What? You actually returned to 'Nam on permissive orders?" When I explained that I had flown over to testify at the trial of Private Herrod (he had already been demoted from corporal), the hostility was palpable. One evening I conducted an informal survey among some of the officers, and nearly every man told me the same thing—that Randy Herrod didn't stand a chance. A few days later, I was shocked when Herrod's defense counsel cited my unscientific opinion poll as evidence that a fair trial was not possible. But as I would eventually discover for myself, a good defense lawyer will do everything within the law to protect his client.

Other than what I had learned about courts-martial at The Basic School, I had no experience with legal procedures. But I spent hours in a sweltering hut overlooking Da Nang harbor, discussing Herrod's case with his lawyers. I urged them to object to anyone assigned to the court (the military equivalent of a jury) who wasn't a combat officer or NCO, because only men who had served in combat could appreciate the pressures that Herrod must have been under. In the end, every member of that court was a decorated combat Marine.

Inevitably, there were differing accounts of what had actually transpired on the night of February 19, 1970. According to Herrod, he had been leading a small ambush patrol into the village of Sonthang in the southern part of the First Corps Tactical Zone, which was known to be a Vietcong supply area. When the enemy opened fire with an M-60 machine gun, he ordered his men to shoot back. Several civilians were caught in the cross fire, and others were shot when they appeared to be reaching for weapons.

In my testimony, I explained that the charges of murder against Herrod were totally inconsistent with the qualities I had seen less than a year earlier. I also pointed out that he had been trained in a different war. We saw very few civilians in the northern part of the First Corps Tactical Zone, where the rule of thumb was: it's either us or the NVA, and if it moves in the killing zone of an ambush—*shoot!* In a night ambush, nobody asked questions. But I also recalled an incident on a daylight patrol where Herrod had ordered his machine-gun team not to fire because he wasn't 100 percent sure that what they saw was actually the enemy.

I explained how Herrod had demonstrated his courage again and again, and I described the battle for which he had been awarded the Silver Star. It takes forever for an award to be processed in the Marine Corps, and Herrod's had only just come in. It was now being held up further, pending the outcome of the trial.

When my testimony was finished, I flew back to California. When I landed in San Francisco, I learned that Randy Herrod had been acquitted.

By now a large segment of the American public had turned against the war. We could feel the hostility whenever we left the base at Quantico, and the resentment was particularly strong in and around Washington. It got to the point where the C.O. of The Basic School issued an order that officers going off base should no longer wear their uniforms. Over at Marine headquarters in Arlington, they were now wearing civilian clothes to work.

But even without uniforms, young Marines and other military men were easy to identify: their age, their build, their haircut, and their posture all made them conspicuous during an era when so many of their contemporaries wore long hair and colorful clothes. My students would occasionally tell me of being spit on in Washington, and especially in Georgetown. They used to drive there on weekends in the hope of getting a date, but the antiwar sentiment at most of the local colleges was so strong that many of these guys couldn't even get to talk to a woman. I felt bad for them. I was only a few years older than they were, and while there was plenty of antiwar sentiment when I graduated from Annapolis, it had increased exponentially between 1968 and the early 1970s.

In March 1971, the reputation of the American military took a direct hit when Lieutenant William Calley was convicted of the My Lai murders. From the reaction in some circles, you'd have thought this sort of thing was almost routine in Vietnam, rather than an aberration. At Quantico, West Point, Annapolis, and every other military school in the country, instructors spent hours discussing the proper treatment of civilians in a war zone. I can remember being asked about the Calley incident in class, and telling my students that if the stories we heard were true, Calley deserved the harshest sentence that could be meted out.

In the summer of 1971, Seymour Hersh, the reporter who first broke the My Lai story, came out with a book about the incident in which he suggested that war crimes were commonplace in Vietnam. After Hersh appeared on William F. Buckley's "Firing Line," three of us who taught at Quantico—John Bender, Don Carpenter, and I—wrote a letter to Mr. Buckley, expressing our outrage at Hersh's insinuations.

Not only did Buckley write back, but he invited us to appear on "Firing Line," to discuss the issue. We showed his letter to Col. Bill Davis, our commanding officer, who took it to the commanding general at the base, who took it to Marine headquarters, who said, "Okay, why not?"

We taped the show at American University in Washington. I was struck by Buckley's posture: he slouched so badly that I thought he was about to fall off his chair. I have never been nervous about speaking in public, and the prospect of appearing on any other television show would not have bothered me. But to be interviewed by William F. Buckley was more than a little intimidating. Should I bring along a dictionary? Not having gone to Yale, I was not incontrovertibly certain that I would comprehend the copious elongated locutions he was inclined to approbate. In the end, I managed to understand most of Buckley's vocabulary and all of his questions.

On the air, the three of us explained that it would be a terrible injustice if everyone who served in Vietnam came home under suspicion of being a "war criminal." We were not there to defend William Calley, or to suggest that war crimes had never occurred. But all three of us had served in Vietnam, in different units and diverse areas, and none of us had even heard about anything like this until we came home. In fact, the vast majority of American units went out of their way to avoid harming civilians, even to the point of endangering their own men.

We taped the show in front of a live audience, and while their questions were tough, only a few were hostile. It was a highly satisfying experience: we had been able to present a different view of our servicemen in the war, and had helped to defend the honor of the military.

Two years later, I came very close to leaving the Marine Corps. I had originally joined up with the intention of becoming a pilot, but at Quantico in 1968 I had opted for the infantry so that I could serve in Vietnam before the war was over. (Little did I imagine how long the conflict would last.) By the time I applied again to Flight School, in 1973, the war was winding down and the maximum age for new pilots had been lowered by two years. Now that I was too old to realize this particular dream, I started looking around for other opportunities.

I applied for a job with EDS, the Texas-based company headed by Ross Perot. EDS had a wonderful reputation, and people said it was the closest you could come to a military environment within the private sector. After submitting my resignation request from the Corps, I received a call from Colonel Dick Schulze, my old battalion commander from Vietnam who was now the aide to the Secretary of the Navy. "We hate to lose you," he said, "but I understand you're interested in EDS. Ross Perot is coming in next week to have lunch with the Secretary, and I'd like you to join us."

I remember being pleased that Schulze wasn't trying to pressure me to remain in the Corps. Or so I thought.

At lunch, Dick Schulze sat with a quiet smile as Perot gave me a thirty-minute lecture on why I should remain in the Marines. He threw in everything: the value of serving your country, patriotism, mom, apple pie, the works. I found him enormously compelling. He would have made a terrific recruiter.

When he was finished, Perot turned to me and said, "Well, what are you going to do?"

By then I was feeling pretty selfish for wanting to leave. "I guess I'm staying," I said.

"Good," he said. "If that's the way you feel—" And here Perot turned to Schulze, who handed him my letter of resignation. Perot gave it to me and said, "Why don't you just tear this up?" Schulze had set up this meeting to keep me in the Marines, and it worked like a charm.

When I look back on my career in the Marines, one of the accomplishments I'm proudest of had nothing to do with combat. In the mid-1970s, when I was working at Marine headquarters, I played a major role in helping to do away with "dependent restricted" tours. This program, in which Marines used to leave their families for an entire year to serve in units in the Western Pacific, had started after World War II as a means of ensuring that Marine units overseas were always ready to deploy. Thirty years later, it was still an integral part of the Corps. Men in other services were allowed to bring their wives and families on extended overseas tours, but Marines were supposed to be tougher than anyone else, and combat-ready. We also had the highest divorce rate in the military.

Over the course of his career, a professional Marine could end up with as many as four or five of these tours, any one of which could wreck his marriage. That's why Marine wives, who had to hold the families together, deserved their own medals. But thousands of marriages *were* ruined, and many men, including some of our finest and most caring officers, left the Corps because of these tours.

My marriage to Betsy survived my dependent-restricted one-year stay in Okinawa—but just barely.

In 1971 I had been promoted to captain, and in late 1973 I was put in charge of the Northern Training Area on Okinawa. I soon had reason to be grateful to Ross Perot, because I couldn't have been happier in my work. In addition to the challenge and the responsibility that I craved, I now had the chance to do all the exciting things the

Marine Corps depicts in its recruiting commercials—and without getting killed in the process. We conducted mountain-warfare training, ran jungle-warfare tactics, taught amphibious nighttime raids in rubber boats launched from ships and submarines, rappeled from helicopters, and parachuted with Army and Marine reconnaissance units. We taught survival skills to pilots and air crews, ate snakes and other jungle delights just to impress the new arrivals, and had an absolutely glorious time. It was exhausting and occasionally dangerous, but it was also the most fun I ever had as a Marine. Most of the time I was too busy to think about how much I missed home.

Our mission was to train the combat units on Okinawa in the various warfare skills they would be needing to fight in the jungles of Asia. Although American troops were being withdrawn from Vietnam, our task was to train those who might be called upon to go back in, or worse yet, to conduct evacuations.

The Northern Training Area was a sixty-square-mile tract of rugged, mountainous terrain at the remote northern end of the island, more than thirty miles by dirt roads from any other base. My small, virtually autonomous training detachment lived at a tiny base camp of Quonset huts and primitive shelters in a clearing hacked out of the jungle. All communication was by radio. Everything about the place was sporadic—electricity, supply and mail deliveries, and even time off. Training continued around the clock, seven days a week, so the only breathing space was when there was no unit aboard. Even then, most of the day was taken up repairing rubber boats, climbing lines, and safety gear.

My staff consisted of former drill instructors. Everyone in the unit was handpicked, and all the lieutenants on Okinawa were men I had trained at The Basic School. Our austere and challenging facilities were practically inaccessible except by helicopter, and we were the toughest guys on the block. There were few complaints about the long hours or the spartan conditions because we were doing the things Marines signed up to do in the first place.

By the late summer, things were running so smoothly that I was able to take some leave. I actually had a chance to fly home and see my family, but like a jerk, I didn't even consider it. Instead, I encouraged Betsy to come to Okinawa so we could spend some time on the island followed by a few days in Tokyo.

Betsy arrived in Okinawa just ahead of a major Pacific typhoon, which meant that we had to postpone and shorten the trip to Tokyo while I returned to the NTA to supervise damage repair from the storm. She came with me, and watched from a distance as we taught the men how to rappel out of a helicopter and down the side of a mountain—a procedure that involves suspending your life on a length of nylon line seven-sixteenths of an inch thick. It was always interesting to see how a tough Marine could be reduced to a quivering mass of jelly by the mere prospect of dangling a hundred and twenty feet in the air by nothing more than that thread.

My staff included some of the most talented NCOs in the entire Marine Corps, all of whom were terribly proud of the fact that they were surviving in this remote place, braving the wild boars and the poisonous Habu snakes, scaling mountains and jumping out of helicopters and persevering in the wilderness.

Until this *woman* showed up.

Somehow, one of the lieutenants convinced Betsy to try rappeling. Without letting her see how high she was, two of the instructors helped her tie in and started her over the cliff, talking her through the procedure. As she stepped over the side, she looked down for the first time. Her voice was remarkably calm. "I don't want to be doing this," she said. It was then that Lieutenant Vince Norako explained that once you began, the only way to go was down.

To provide some encouragement, I tied on the cliff next to her and slid down beside her. This wasn't the ideal time for conversation, but Betsy wondered aloud if I could possibly understand why the mother of two small children, a woman who hadn't seen her husband in months, might not think of this as the perfect vacation. Besides, how could I be so sure that she was going to make it alive to the bottom of the cliff?

I gave Betsy the same answer I had given to so many Marines who had wondered the very same thing: "Trust in the Lord and use good equipment."

When it was over, Betsy said she had found my comment less than convincing, coming, as it did, just as she was wondering exactly how high she would bounce if she slipped off that rope and plunged to her death. I had obviously been gone too long, because I was about to ask her if she wanted to try it again. Instead, I assured her that even one such descent was a real accomplishment. But for years afterwards, Betsy continued to bring it up, saying, "I can't believe you would let me do something like that."

Fortunately, one of my fellow instructors had taken a picture of Betsy rappeling down that cliff. From then on, whenever a trainee faltered, I would pull out that photograph and show it to him, saying, "Well, if this *woman* can do it, you probably can, too."

When we finally got to Tokyo, we were the guests of a close childhood friend of Betsy's mother. I had looked forward to this trip, and had imagined it would be a lot like that marvelous week of R&R in Hawaii, just the two of us hidden from the world. We stayed at the Sanno Hotel, the former headquarters of General Douglas MacArthur during the military occupation of Japan after the war. It was now a military billeting facility, but any hope of conjugal bliss and relaxation was completely sabotaged by our hostess—a sweet and well-meaning old lady who turned out to be tougher than most of the Marines I had left behind on Okinawa. Every morning at dawn she showed up to take us sightseeing until midnight, which turned our brief vacation into an endurance contest. Betsy had traveled halfway around the world, and we hadn't done much more than say hello.

Throughout Betsy's visit I was preoccupied by the rapidly deteriorating situation in Southeast Asia. It was becoming increasingly apparent that unless the United States intervened, as we had promised to do, the Republic of Vietnam would cease to exist. Back on Okinawa we reoriented our training to focus more on evacuation operations, survival skills, escape and evasion, and the like. By this time, all Marine combat units had been pulled out of Vietnam, along with the bulk of American troops. By the fall of 1974, the Third Marine Division was making preparations in case we were sent back in.

I was given orders to select a team of men from the NTA detachment who would train with the Army's Special Forces. Although my own tour of duty was winding down, I included myself on the roster. I was eager to see my family again, but I was also obsessed with developments in Vietnam. Entire Vietnamese units were being overrun, and the Armed Forces Radio Network news was full of foreboding. American citizens and advisers were already being evacuated from Saigon.

It was against that background that a call came in from Lieutenant Colonel Chuck Hester on the other end of the island. Hester was about to take command of First Battalion, Fourth Marines—the next air-alert unit—the first to go if the Third Division sent units back to Vietnam. He was looking for additional company commanders, and he asked if I was interested.

"Sure," I said. "When do you want me?"

"Get down here as soon as you can," he said.

A couple of days later I said good-bye to my men in the Northern Training Area, and reported to Camp Hansen in the central part of Okinawa. I was now the commanding officer of Company A, First Battalion, Fourth Marines.

As soon as I arrived, I sat down and wrote a letter to Betsy. I explained that I had just taken over a rifle company, and that our battalion would soon be on air alert, ready for instant deployment to Vietnam (or Cambodia, or Laos) at any moment. Although my tour of duty was about to expire, I wrote that I didn't think it was right for these Marines to take on a new commander who would abandon them when they were facing the imminent prospect of combat.

A year earlier, I had left for Okinawa just two weeks before Christmas. And now I was telling Betsy that I wouldn't be home this Christmas, either. She was normally a faithful correspondent, but it took much longer than usual before I received an answer to my letter. When it finally came, it read something like this:

> Dear Larry,
> I now realize that the Marine Corps is obviously more important to you than I am—or our children. You've made that very clear over the years, and I shouldn't have taken so long to see it. Stay over there and do whatever it is you need to do, and don't forget to keep in touch with the children. But I've had enough. I want a divorce. Here's the name of my attorney.

The worst part about receiving Betsy's letter was that I more or less accepted it. I believed that what I was doing really *was* more important than my family. I was worrying about the two hundred and ten Marines whose lives I was responsible for, not to mention the fate of the free world. Betsy would just have to wait.

I kept myself so busy during those weeks that I barely thought about her. And when I did, my reaction was always the same: this will keep until I get back; I'll take care of it later.

In early December I came down with a very bad case of bronchitis. I was out in the field one night with my company, acting as the aggressor force for a major field exercise. Chuck Hester was there as an evaluator, and he turned to me and said, "What's the matter with you?"

"Me? Nothing. I'm fine."

"The hell you are. You're sick and you're exhausted. What's your rotation date?"

"I was supposed to leave next week, but I put in my extension request."

"What about your family? What do they have to say about all this?"

My eyes filled with tears. I couldn't speak.

"Go home, Ollie. It's not worth it. You care about these guys, and I appreciate that, but nobody else does. The politicians in Washington have thrown away the lives of so many young men. They don't care if your family gets ruined, or your kids grow up without you. The war is over anyway; it's only a question of when the shooting stops. Your giving your life over there won't change a thing. Go home to your family."

In my heart I knew he was right, but I still wasn't ready to admit it. I finally decided to take his advice and return to the States—after two old friends and former classmates, Pete Stenner and Bob Earl, ganged up on me one night and told me what a dope I was. They convinced me to withdraw my request to extend, and I left Okinawa a few days later.

By the time the plane landed in Los Angeles I was really sick. I was already on antibiotics, but I was still coughing up blood. There was also blood in my urine.

When I called Betsy from the airport, I could hear the chill in her voice. "I meant what I wrote in that letter," she said. "I'm sorry, but I can't live like this anymore. If you want to see the kids, call my lawyer."

I was furious. I had just returned from a year in Okinawa, training hard to save lives (or so I thought), while she was enjoying life in the safety of our nice house in Virginia. Meanwhile, the government of Vietnam and the South Vietnamese Army were collapsing. Everything I had fought for and worked for was coming apart. And now she expected me to walk away from my Marines. Okay, I had. But it didn't make any difference. I accused her of being ungrateful, unrealistic, and unilateral, but she wouldn't budge.

"If that's the way you want it, fine," I said. "It doesn't bother me."

And then I said the stupidest thing of all: "I don't care."

"I know," said Betsy. "That's the whole point. *You don't care.* That's why it's over."

I flew to Washington, still sick, and feeling very sorry for myself. Christmas was only a few days away, and I couldn't even visit my wife and kids. Tait was now five, and Stuart was four, and neither of them really knew who I was. The truth is that even before Okinawa I didn't spend much time with them. I left for work early in the morning before they got up, and came home late, when they were already asleep. I hadn't been around much on weekends, either.

I called Betsy's lawyer and ended up speaking to his secretary. "He left for the holidays," she told me. "Why don't you call back in January, and we'll try to work out some way for you to stop by and see the kids. By the way, who's *your* attorney?"

That's when it really hit me that Betsy was serious.

I moved into the BOQ (Bachelor Officers' Quarters), the only temporary officers' billeting available in the Quantico area. With Christmas approaching, the place was emptying out and becoming even more desolate than usual. There was a TV in my room, and when I turned on the evening news that first night, it was all about the impending fall of South Vietnam. Marines, *my* Marines, were being readied and deployed for evacuation operations up and down the coast of Southeast Asia. Within days, Colonel Chuck Hester and the battalion I had just left behind deployed to rescue the American crew of the *Mayaguez*, a freighter hijacked off the coast of Cambodia. Instead of being with them, I was sitting alone in Virginia with what appeared to be an unsalvageable marriage and two children whom I couldn't even see on Christmas.

The weather outside was damp and cold, and I felt the same way.

When I had decided to leave Okinawa, I had convinced myself that I would be able to make everything all right with Betsy as soon as I got home. But she didn't even want to see me.

This was devastating. Until now, I had never failed at anything. Everything I had ever set out to do I had been able to accomplish by dint of hard work and persistence. At least that's what I thought. What a fool I had been to give up command of a rifle company in order to come home to—nothing.

I was hurt, angry, and confused. Physically, I was in miserable shape with a terrible cough that wouldn't go away, no desire to eat, and for the first time in my life, an inability to sleep. For years I had exercised hard every single day, but now I could barely drag myself out of bed. Today, I can look back on that period and recognize the full-blown symptoms of depression. Back then, I wouldn't have admitted it even if I had recognized it. *Real* men didn't have that kind of problem—and I knew I was a real man.

A day or two later I decided to drive to Maryland to visit Bill Haskell, my old friend from Vietnam, who was now a CPA. Driving north on Route 95, the interstate highway right outside the base at Quantico, I was overwhelmed by the greatest sense of despair I've ever felt. Betsy and I had driven back and forth on this highway scores of times when we were dating. The day we were married we drove up this road to begin our new life together. Now I was driving alone to see an old friend and talk about old times.

As I raced up the highway, another coughing spasm struck and I nearly went off the road. I pulled off to the side and stopped the car to pull myself together. The fresh air from the open window allowed me to stop coughing long enough to catch my breath. I had to do something for this cough! I turned the car around and drove back to Quantico, where I headed straight for the dispensary.

There, sitting in the waiting room, was Colonel Dick Schulze, my old battalion commander from Vietnam and the man who had introduced me to Ross Perot. Dick had just been promoted to brigadier general, and he was there for his promotion physical. He greeted me with a bear hug, and then stepped back to look me over. "Blue? You look terrible," he said. "What's the matter?"

I was in tears. This made twice in one month, and I wasn't a guy who cried often. And certainly not about anything personal.

When the door opened to the doctor's inner office, Schulze grabbed me by the shoulders and vectored me right in. "Before you look at me," he told the doctor, "check this guy out."

After giving me a complete exam, the doctor said, "You're a wreck. You've probably got parasites, you're anemic, and you have fluid in one of your lungs. I'm putting you in the hospital today."

"Not today," I said. "I just got back, and I've got a million things to take care of."

"They'll all keep, Captain. Besides, from what you've told me, there's nobody waiting for you, anyway."

That same afternoon, Schulze drove me up to Bethesda Naval Hospital and stayed with me while I was admitted. Dick Schulze was one of those great military leaders who can get personally involved with their men. With his deep, sad, blue eyes, he looked like Abraham Lincoln without the beard. Everybody who dealt with him came to love him. He was the kind of guy who could take a young Marine who went bad, bust him two ranks, fine him six months' pay, confine him for a month in the brig, and the kid would almost be grateful. How could such a gentle man be successful in such a violent business? I realize that this goes against the popular image of the military, but the best leaders I have known were all men of kindness and compassion.

I spent the next few days lying in bed, trying to read every book I could find. But I couldn't concentrate; I'd put the book down after five minutes, with no memory of what I had read. I have never watched much television, but I did then—even in the *daytime*, which would have been truly alarming if I had been able to pay attention. The only thing I could focus on was news from Vietnam and Cambodia, and all of it was bad. Other than the news, nothing seemed to matter except feeling sorry for myself. I tried desperately to avoid thinking about Betsy or the kids, although Christmas was growing closer by the minute.

And yet I refused to admit that I was depressed. I knew I was angry at Betsy, and I was convinced that all of this was her fault. On top of that, the war I had fought in and trained for, and trained so many others to fight, was ending all wrong. I was in trouble, but I didn't know it.

When Schulze came back to see me a few days later, we went into the solarium, a sun-filled room dotted with green vinyl couches. "I've been talking to the doctors," he said. "You don't have pneumonia, or liver disease, or anything like that. But you're still sick. You've got this terrible cough, there's blood in your urine, and you don't seem to be getting better. They tell me you're agitated and irritable. Frankly, it sounds to them like you don't care about much of anything anymore. And you certainly don't care about getting any better. They think that you'd benefit from psychiatric help."

I like to see myself as calm and in control, but when Dick Schulze said those words, I blew up at him—which was totally out of character. I must have looked ridiculous as I sat there, yelling at him, *"I'm fine. There's nothing wrong with me! I am very calm! I don't need that kind of help!"*

All I wanted was to get out of there. A decade earlier I had spent eleven months in hospitals after my car accident, which was enough to last me a lifetime. I hated hospitals, from the moment they woke you up at four in the morning to make sure you were asleep to the time they came in at night to wake you for your sleeping pill.

"Listen," he said. "In combat, I've seen you take the worst kinds of pressures that can be put on a man. But this is different. You trusted me in battle when the situation was far more dangerous than this, and you've got to trust me now. I feel strongly that you need psychiatric care, and so do the doctors. But it won't happen unless you agree to it."

This was humiliating. Me, in a psychiatrist's care? Psychiatrists were for crazy people. Maybe I had a couple of problems, but even if I did, I could solve them myself. I certainly didn't need the help of a shrink.

Schulze and I had been to hell and back together. I loved the man. How could he say this to me?

"Don't decide yet," he said. "Take a couple of hours and think it over. I'll come back later. You know I wouldn't be suggesting this unless I thought it was the right thing to do."

In the midst of my anger and frustration, I began to realize that maybe Schulze was right. Maybe the treatment I needed couldn't be found in antibiotics.

When Schulze returned, I said, "Okay, I've decided to do it." After all, it was a place to be for Christmas.

"I figured you would," he said. "I've already made the arrangements."

He returned to visit me every one of the eleven days I was there.

Now this was something *really* new. I don't know what I expected: drugs, electroshock therapy, straitjackets, padded cells. But there was none of that. Instead, I was put on a regimen of "milieu therapy"— hours of group discussions and one-on-one sessions with a battery of doctors. I hated it. It was humiliating even to be there. I kept looking around and asking myself, *Who are these people, and why am I here?* (This was the same question I would ask myself in 1987, at the Iran-contra hearings.)

The doctors asked if I felt guilty about not being back with my unit. They asked me what seemed like thousands of probing psychiatric questions: Do you hate your father? Your mother? How do you feel about your wife? Your children? The Marine Corps? Your friends? Et cetera, et cetera, et cetera.

Looking back, I'm sure that my answers reflected my deep-seated sense that this was none of their business, and I recall being hostile and sarcastic. That was a mistake. These people were trying to help, and they *did* help.

During the group therapy sessions I was overwhelmed by some of the stories I heard. Many of the men described bouts of heavy drinking and acts of violence in their homes. I had never even seen a man strike a woman in anger, and I was shocked as some of my fellow patients recalled how their mothers had been abused or how they themselves had been violent to their own wives or children. No wonder these guys have problems, I thought. I've got nothing to match this. My father was always home for dinner. My parents loved each other. How weak I must be if I'm being bothered by something as trivial as my marriage falling apart.

And so I concluded that my own problems weren't so serious, which I was all too inclined to believe anyway. I was too full of pride and ego to admit that anything serious was really wrong and that I needed help. I had accepted that idea on a superficial level by agreeing to stay in the hospital, but I didn't really believe it.

When one of the doctors suggested that Betsy and I might want to see a marriage counselor, I just laughed. (Just about every suggestion the psychiatrists offered was phrased in terms of "might." Coming from over ten years of a military environment, full of black and white rules and certainties, I found it hard to accept the idea that life was a series of options.) Besides, marriage counseling didn't seem to be a realistic option. Even if Betsy accepted the idea (which didn't seem likely at the time), I didn't like it. If we had a problem, we'd work it out ourselves.

What a jackass I was.

Finally, one of the younger doctors got through to me by being kind, blunt, and persistent. "You've told me so often that you don't care, but I think you do. You care very much about what happens to your wife and your kids. You don't really want this divorce, do you?"

"I already told you, I don't care. Neither does she."

"How can you be so sure? Have you ever tried counseling? Have you tried working it out?"

"She's not interested. I told you that. She told me to call her lawyer."

"Maybe she's not interested because you two are so angry at each other that you can't even discuss it. Why don't I call her?"

"No, I won't go crawling back. I refuse to beg. Besides, I don't have to stay here. I can leave at any time."

"Yes, but where would you go?"

"Back to work. I've got my orders."

"You can leave at any time, but I don't think you're ready. You've still got a lot of anger and bitterness to work out."

He was very skilled, and he badgered me without mercy. But I liked him, and that made all the difference. Eventually, when he brought up marriage counseling for the third or fourth time, I relented and agreed to his calling Betsy. I wasn't ready to accept any responsibility for what had happened, but at least I knew I was angry.

"I've got a couple of things to tell *her*," I said.

"You won't be telling her anything," he said. "Not yet. First I'm going to talk to her."

After meeting with Betsy, he came back to see me. "Let me tell you what I learned," he said. "You've always been a faithful husband. And you've been a wonderful father—when you're around. You'll do anything for the kids and for her. You've worked hard to provide for them on a Marine salary. It broke Betsy's heart that the Marine Corps was more important than she was."

When I heard this, I was too moved to speak.

"I think you're ready to leave," he said. "General Schulze knows a chaplain at Quantico who's an excellent marriage counselor. I'll put you on outpatient status, and I'd like you to call in every day and tell me how you're doing."

I was grateful for what I had learned at Bethesda, but I was even more grateful to be out of there. It had been less than two weeks, but it seemed like much longer. And I guess I showed my ambivalence by the silly things I said on the telephone when I checked in every day. "Hi. I'm calling from Mexico where I've just robbed a bank. Just kidding."

There was a lot I hadn't liked about the psychiatrists at Bethesda, including what seemed like a strong push to get the patients to blame their problems on other people—and especially our parents. To me this seemed like a way of avoiding responsibility. Another thing I didn't care for was the way some of the therapists played out a psychiatric version of good cop/bad cop. The hospitalization was helpful, but not as effective as the marriage counseling would become. But for me it was a crucial first step, and I shudder to think what would have become of my life if I hadn't been there.

During my stay at Bethesda, I had concluded that whatever problem I had stemmed from Vietnam. I felt angry and betrayed over the many lives that were wasted over there while our political leaders kept putting restraints on how we could respond. I still feel that way, but today I understand that this wasn't the singular cause of my depression. My hospitalization forced me to think about things that I had always been able to avoid—like the real nature of my relationship with Betsy. In the past I was too busy being the tough guy to see into my own heart. But now I knew what I had denied in Okinawa and in the weeks after my return—that I loved her, and that I wanted her back, and that the prospect of losing her was the basis of my depression. The doctors at Bethesda had helped me realize that I could, indeed, survive without her. But now I wanted to survive *with* her.

When I left Bethesda, it was by no means clear that Betsy and I would be able to get back together. Nor did I know what effect my hospitalization was going to have on my career as a Marine. Nobody ever stood up and announced that a Marine couldn't seek psychiatric help. But it was understood that a "successful" officer has never experienced emotional problems.

The Marine Corps was not unique in clinging to this prejudice. There is a deeply ingrained belief in our society that if you've ever suffered from depression or any other kind of emotional illness, you're never really cured. I hate to think how many people suffer from emotional ailments and don't know what to do about it, or are too afraid or embarrassed to seek help. It's not hard to get someone to a doctor for pneumonia or a broken arm, but it can be enormously difficult to get that same person to seek help for emotional distress.

Until recently, the prevailing wisdom in many institutions, and especially in the military and in government, was that anyone who has had psychiatric help, or marriage counseling, or who has overcome an addiction, is automatically suspect. It wasn't until the 1980s that a Marine could check himself into a hospital for an alcohol problem and, after treatment, return to his unit.

As a result of my own experience, I became far more attentive to signs of emotional problems in other people, and over the years I advised a number of young Marines to seek treatment or to at least talk to counselors. In the military it's often the chaplains who assume this role; a young soldier, sailor, airman, or Marine can often unload on a chaplain in a way that would be impossible with his commanding officer. And a well-trained chaplain can also offer something special to a troubled person—an awareness of God's power and love.

That certainly helped me. While I was still at Bethesda, I began to visit the small hospital chapel to ask God for His help directly, as in "Please, God, help me to get out of here, and help me save our marriage." By the time Betsy and I finished marriage counseling, I more fully understood how powerful prayer could be in healing—whether it's broken bodies, minds, or marriages.

By the time I checked out of the hospital, Betsy and I had, over the phone, set up a joint appointment with Larry Boyette, a Navy captain and one of the chaplains at Quantico. I arrived early for our first appointment, and as I sat in the waiting room, I picked up a book that was lying there called *Dare to Discipline*, by James Dobson, a professor of pediatrics at the University of Southern California School of Medicine. I didn't yet know Dobson's name, and from the title of his book I probably assumed it had something to do with the Marine Corps. It was, instead, a book of advice for parents, as I learned when I opened it to a random page and started reading: "I hope to give my daughter a small gold key on her tenth birthday," Dobson had written. "It will be attached to a chain to be worn around her neck, and will represent the key to her heart. Perhaps she'll give that key to one man only—the one man who'll share her love for the rest of her life."

Those words hit me like a bolt of lightning. I, too, had a daughter at home, although I hadn't seen her in a very long time. If this counseling didn't work out, if this *marriage* didn't work out, what kind of gift would I be able to give my own daughter, whom I barely knew, when she turned ten? What kind of example was I providing her about the kind of man she should seek as a mate? How could I ever do something as beautiful as this James Dobson had done, and had written about in that book? And for the third time in this whole ordeal, I cried.

Betsy still hadn't arrived when Chaplain Larry Boyette opened the door, and I ended up attending most of that first session without her. She had been even more reluctant to come than I was, perhaps because Boyette wore a uniform and had been recommended by General Schulze, which meant that he came from my world. When she did show up, she was on her guard. "I'll come a few times," she told Boyette, "but I hope you won't be bringing in any of this God stuff." Some chaplains might have taken offense, but Larry just leaned back and said, "You don't have to worry about that, Betsy. He's already here."

The counseling eventually helped us, but it took a long time before things got better. In one of our early sessions, Betsy blurted out that the only reason she had bothered to show up at all was because she felt sorry for me. That *really* got to me.

After several weeks of counseling, I moved back home. Betsy and I were each seeing Larry separately as well. (My appointments were on Monday evenings; heaven forbid I should miss an hour of work at Marine headquarters!) I still remember the session where I told Larry I was living with Betsy again. I expected to be congratulated, but he wasn't impressed, and I was disappointed by his reaction. But he knew how much work still lay ahead, and he wasn't especially interested in superficial changes.

On Friday afternoons, Betsy and I would see Larry together. Then we'd spend an hour or two together, sometimes doing errands, or shopping, or just going out for coffee.

I was beginning to understand that my wife was a helpmate, and that a helpmate isn't there to take orders, but to help you carry the load. We both had to learn how to talk to each other clearly but without hostility, and how to express ourselves directly, as in: "It really hurts me when I call the office and I don't get a call back." Don't tell her how *she* feels, Larry would say, tell her how *you* feel. Don't tell each other what you're doing wrong; instead, be clear about what you want and what you need. Instead of "You didn't take out the garbage," try, "I need help with the garbage," or, "I really appreciate it when you take out the garbage."

It wasn't just the long separations that led to so many divorces in the Marine Corps. It was also the striking contrast between military culture and the requirements of a marriage. As a Marine officer, I was used to giving orders and telling other people what to do. But a marriage is a partnership, not a platoon, and being a father is entirely different from being a commander.

Moreover, Betsy had changed enormously during my year in Vietnam, and again while I was in Okinawa. I returned from Vietnam saying, in effect, "I'm back, and here's how we're going to do things." But Betsy had been living without me for a year, being mother, father, and keeping house and home together while working part-time as an executive assistant at a translation service.

So many military spouses go through that same experience. In the case of the wives, while their husbands are away for long periods of time, they have to take care of everything—not only the kids, but the house, the mortgage, the car, the finances, and all the rest. When the men come back, ready to reassert themselves in their traditional roles, they discover that everything is different, and that their wives have grown stronger and more independent. In our case, all of this took place against the backdrop of enormous changes in the roles and relationships of men and women—changes so profound they permeated even the military.

Another thing I came to understand was that in addition to the two of us, there was a third entity—the relationship itself—that had to be nurtured. I started spending more time at home, and although my tendency is to fall back on old work habits, Betsy became more tolerant, and the time we spent apart was no longer as great a source of tension between us.

I began to see Betsy not only as my wife, but as my friend, too. I had never thought of a woman as a potential friend before. When I was growing up, my friends were exclusively male. Girls were people you dated, and held the door for, and occasionally even kissed.

Larry Boyette spoke often about responsibility, and how I couldn't fulfill my commitment to Betsy and my children if I wasn't around—either because I was determined to be SuperMarine or because we were divorced. He spoke of our children, Tait and Stuart, as being gifts, on loan from God. And he helped us understand that when you really need help, there is only one place you can always, always, find it—from Him who made us all.

The recovery process took time. It began the moment I turned around on Interstate 95 on that bleak December day, and it required the help of several people. There were ups and downs along the way, but by the time Saigon fell at the end of April, I was able to watch it on television with Betsy. I cried unashamedly, and Betsy had her arm around me. She understood.

With the amazing grace of God and plenty of hard work, we gradually put our marriage back together again. Now, I'm certainly not advocating that marriage repairs need to start with psychiatric treatment. But in our case, if I hadn't ended up in the hospital and gone from there to marriage counseling, I doubt that our marriage would have survived. We might have patched things up temporarily, but we wouldn't have reached a real resolution.

As I worked to repair my relationship with Betsy, there was one more relationship left to work on, although I didn't realize it at the time. And here, too, my growth was helped along by a man in uniform.

When I left Bethesda I was assigned to work in the Manpower Department of Marine headquarters in Arlington, Virginia. It was my first—and, I hoped, my last—desk job as a Marine, but for a career officer these assignments are unavoidable. There was little, however, that made a tour at the Marine headquarters attractive. The building is an old warehouse across the street from Arlington Cemetery, and old hands would point out the window and tell newcomers like me, "See those graves? They're reserved for action officers who miss their deadlines."

It was during this assignment that I worked on replacing individual dependent-restricted assignments with a new system called the unit deployment plan. Instead of sending individual Marines overseas for twelve or thirteen months (or eighteen months in the case of bachelors), we started sending entire units for six months at a time. The tours were shorter, morale was higher, unit integrity was far better, and a lot more marriages survived. A year later, I was actually awarded a medal for my work on this project; I hadn't even known you could get a medal for administrative work.

It was at Marine headquarters that I met a man who would lead me to change my life. Major John Grinalds worked at a desk across a partition from mine. Highly decorated from his two tours of duty in Vietnam, he was a graduate of West Point who went on to become a Rhodes Scholar and White House Fellow, and to earn a Harvard M.B.A. He was enormously respected in the office: whenever there was an important decision to be made, people would ask, "What does Grinalds think about this?"

He was also in terrific physical shape, which wasn't true of everyone at headquarters. There were a number of chubby Marines floating around in 1975, probably because of the commandant, who was known affectionately as "Fat Bob" Cushman. The standing joke was that the physical fitness test consisted of three laps around old Bob.

John Grinalds was on the fast track. While we were at headquarters, John was deep-selected—selected early—for lieutenant colonel. (Around the same time, I was deep-selected for major.) But this wasn't the only thing that made John Grinalds different from other officers. Instead of the training and administration manuals that most officers kept on their desks, John kept a Bible, and from time to time I would see him reading it. He was known to be a "born-again" Christian—a term I didn't really understand at the time. But he was never one to wear his faith on his sleeve. Even after we had come to know each other fairly well at headquarters, about the most he ever told me about his personal belief was to point to his Bible and say, "You might want to know a little more about this."

In 1978, when John was named to become a battalion commander in the Second Marine Division, based at Camp Lejeune, he asked if I wanted to come along as his operations officer. I was delighted with the prospect, but before Betsy and I moved the family to North Carolina, we drove down there so she could see what I hoped would be our new home. We left Virginia on a Friday afternoon, and pulled into Jacksonville, the town outside the sprawling base at Camp Lejeune, around midnight. Betsy had fallen asleep, and when she opened her eyes and looked around she almost died. "Tell me it's only a nightmare," she said, for Jacksonville in 1978 was like the towns outside most large military bases. The main street was lined with seedy bars, strip joints, pawn shops, fast-food joints and used-car lots—each with its own flashing neon sign. It looked like a poor man's Times Square. It's better today, but back then it was a shocking, garish, and depressing sight, made all the more so by its contrast with the nearby base.

When we drove through the sentry post onto Camp Lejeune, the difference was simply amazing. The base was beautiful and immaculately maintained, with miles of forests which double as training areas for the twenty-five thousand Marines assigned there. Betsy also discovered one of the military's best-kept secrets: Camp Lejeune has a world-class recreational beach. We spent the weekend there, looked at where our new quarters would be, and returned to Virginia to sell our house, pack up our belongings, and move to North Carolina.

It was very hard to move from our house in Stafford, and not just because of all the "stuff" we had accumulated by then. (On my first military move, from Annapolis to Quantico in 1968, everything I owned fit in the back of my car. Now, ten years and three children later, we needed a forty-foot moving van.) This house was also the setting for so many memories as well. This was the first home we owned, and we had watched it being built. It was the scene of our near-divorce, and the rebuilding of our marriage. We brought our little Sarah home to this house from the Quantico base hospital where she had been born. Here, Tait and Stuart had built fast friendships with neighboring children. We had laughed, loved, and cried together in that house, and leaving it was wrenching for all of us.

As the operations officer of the Third Battalion, Eighth Marines, I was responsible for the training and the preparation of a two-thousand-man unit as it prepared to deploy to the Mediterranean—or, if necessary, the Middle East or even the Pacific. One of the great joys of this job was that I could see the early results of the new policy I had worked to implement at headquarters: because Marine units were now kept together longer, there was a speedy decline in what we called personnel turbulence, and a visible improvement in both proficiency and morale.

One morning, about two weeks before we were due to leave for our six-month deployment to the Mediterranean, I jumped off the back of an armored amphibious vehicle and reinjured my back, exactly where I had broken it during the car accident in 1964. This had happened once before, during a parachute accident in 1973 which had landed me in the hospital for a week, followed by another week or so of bed rest, the only time since Vietnam that I missed a day of duty. Now I was lying on the ground, writhing in pain, and wondering how I was ever going to recover in time to ship out to the Mediterranean with my unit.

This was not a routine deployment: we were about to become the Landing Force for the Sixth Fleet—one of the most critical assignments in the Marine Corps. As I lay there, I didn't even want to contemplate sitting in traction while the battalion that I had trained with for months deployed without me.

Someone ran off to find the battalion commander and a corpsman. Grinalds got there first. He helped me up to a sitting position, and knelt down beside me. Placing his hands on my legs, he said, "I'm going to pray for you."

This wasn't exactly the kind of help I had in mind. I'm lying here in agony and he wants to *pray?* This guy must be nuts.

Then John Grinalds called out in prayer: "Lord Jesus Christ, You are the Great Physician. Heal this man."

Suddenly the pain disappeared. Slowly, the feeling came back in my legs. I didn't know what to say beyond a muttered "Thank you."

"Don't thank me," said Grinalds. "Thank your Lord and Savior. *He* is the Great Physician. You have to turn to *Him.*"

Sometimes, if you're too thick to get the message any other way, God has to hit you over the head with a two-by-four. He'd certainly sent me the message before, but I wasn't paying attention. In the car accident in 1964, everyone I was with was either killed or terribly injured. Yet I was not only able to recover, but to win a boxing championship at Annapolis, and to graduate, and to get a commission in the Marines. When the doctors told me I might never walk again, I refused to believe them. I took a lot of pride in my recovery, and with all my persistence and hard work, I wanted to believe I had done it on my own.

Later, in Vietnam, there were times when nearly everybody around me was either killed or grievously wounded, and I escaped relatively unscathed. There were times when I was painfully hurt, but was able to recover quickly and return to duty.

After the war, when I received two early promotions in the Marine Corps, I wrote it off to being a good officer. When the Lord blessed us with our first two children, I didn't see His hand in it. When my life was coming apart, and I was sitting in the chaplain's office at Quantico, there were any number of books or magazines I could have picked up in the waiting room. *Time* and *Reader's Digest* were right there, but I started reading a book by Jim Dobson. Betsy already had a copy in our house, but I didn't even know it was there. And I had no idea that Jim Dobson, the founder of an organization called Focus on the Family, would later become an important person in my life.

What struck me so powerfully about John Grinalds's prayer and his strong admonition in the sand at Camp Lejeune that morning was that for so long I'd had it all wrong. I had been taking credit for all the things I had been able to do over the years, but I didn't deserve it, any of it. The message He had been sending was *put your faith in Me*. Not in yourself, not in others, not in the things of this earth, *but in Me*.

The profound faith of John Grinalds had a powerful effect on me. It made me realize that I was a little like the military radios I was so familiar with. They have two modes: transmit and receive, and they work on many different frequencies.

But I had been too busy transmitting to receive. I had transmitted a lot of prayers over the years, but I hadn't stopped long enough to acknowledge that my messages had been received and that *He* was answering. I came to see that He had been sending a message back: trust in *Me*. And more. "I don't do these things to glorify you," He had been telling me. "I do them that others will glorify Me. You must become an instrument by which others come to understand that. You can't take credit for healing yourself. Everything that happens to you happens because of My grace.

"If you have succeeded, give Me the credit. If you prevail in adversity, bear witness to My power. Let others see My hand in your life that they might come to know Me. And by the way, get to know Me a little better in the process. I am the God of the Universe, but I'm also your personal Savior."

I was profoundly humbled by this understanding. I now knew what others meant when they described John Grinalds as being "born again." Over the months to come, this understanding led me to a much deeper relationship with my Maker.

I had been raised to know who my Lord and Savior was. I knew *about* Him, but I didn't know Him personally. It was like reading about some important world figure, seeing him on television, reading things he had written and said, but never actually meeting him. That, to me, is the clearest way I know of explaining how that relationship has changed. Today, I've met Him and I know Him personally.

Later that month, after we'd deployed, I sat with John and our chaplain, Bruce Jayne, as they led Bible studies on Sunday evenings in the ship's wardroom. While we were at sea, I managed to read the entire Bible from cover to cover, and by the time we returned from the Mediterranean, I felt comfortable in leading a few Bible studies myself. For me, John Grinalds's extraordinary expression of faith was the first step in a long walk. By the time I was fired in November 1986, I knew that with God's help, I could withstand any pressure. In the months that followed my firing, I suffered a number of disappointments. Terrible things were said about me in public. People I had thought of as close associates, colleagues, and even friends became sources for absurd and ugly newspaper articles, media stories, and accusations.

And yet I never felt alone, and never doubted that the outcome would be positive. And while I didn't need a reminder, I got one anyway. On July 7, 1987, on the very first morning of my testimony before the Joint Congressional Committee, an elderly woman whom I had never seen before broke out from the crowd of reporters and onlookers and through the throng of security guards, and handed me a little card. During those days my lawyers wouldn't allow me to read anything except specific materials relating to the inquisition, and Brendan Sullivan, my lawyer, snatched the card from my hand even before I looked at it.

By the time we walked into the hearing room, I had forgotten all about it. But just before we sat down, Brendan put the card on the microphone stand in front of me. Every time we stood up to leave during a recess, Brendan picked it up and took it with him, and every time we returned, he put it back. The reporters who crowded around us tried to get a glimpse of what was on the card, but Sullivan wouldn't let them.

Imprinted on the card was a biblical verse:

They that wait upon the Lord
shall renew their strength;
They shall mount up with wings as eagles.
They shall run and not be weary.
They shall walk, but not faint.
—Isaiah 40:31

As I went through an extraordinary experience with the whole country looking on, that card was in front of me the whole time.

7

Byzantium on the Potomac

All my life I have struggled to strike the right balance between my work and my family. Mostly, I failed. But there was one year when I got it right.

In 1980, after two years in the Second Division and two six-month deployments to the Mediterranean from Camp Lejeune, I was one of about twenty Marine officers selected to spend the 1980–81 academic year in the Command and Staff course at the Naval War College in Newport, Rhode Island. This was easily the best family tour of my Marine Corps career. The classes were stimulating, the setting was idyllic, and the hours were civilized: classes ran from eight-thirty to three, and I was home for dinner every night.

I probably spent more time with my family during that one year than in the rest of the 1980s combined. We went skiing in winter, and toured Boston and a good bit of New England in the spring and fall. Betsy and I even got to see a couple of shows in New York. Whenever the weather was decent, we went sailing. I had learned to sail at Annapolis on Chesapeake Bay, where the bottom was so soft you could run aground without even knowing it. But Narragansett Bay, off Newport, is full of rocks, and I must have hit every one of them.

There were five of us when we moved to Newport, and six when we left. As I look back on the birth of our children, it's almost as if I had been acting out some broad sociological trend of the deepening involvement of fathers. I was in Vietnam when Tait was born in 1969, and I didn't even see her until months later. In 1970, when Stuart appeared, I was reading a book in the hospital waiting room. The door opened, and a nurse came out. "Congratulations," she said. "You have a healthy baby boy. You can see him through the window at the end of the hall, and you can see your wife [unspoken but implied message: *that poor woman whose terrible suffering is all your fault*] tomorrow."

In 1976, when Betsy was pregnant with Sarah, we enrolled in a Lamaze class at the clinic in Quantico. Betsy went into labor during a family dinner at McDonald's, and we rushed to the hospital just in time. When Dornin came along in the spring of 1981, Betsy and I were in a hospital room in Newport when everything seemed to happen at once. I yelled for help, and a male nurse came running in. By the time the doctor showed up, our third daughter was already in my arms.

When our year in Newport was up, I had hoped to return to the Fleet Marine Forces—preferably back at the Second Marine Division at Camp Lejeune. But the Marine Corps had other plans. One afternoon in early February, I was pulled out of class and told to report to Washington for a series of interviews that might lead to my next assignment—as a staff member at the National Security Council. I didn't even know the NSC was an option, and when I learned that it was, I made clear to everybody that I wasn't interested. I didn't want another desk job, and I *certainly* didn't want one in Washington.

But in the military you go where you're sent. One of my interviews was with General Robert Barrow, commandant of the Marine Corps. Barrow, tall and thin as a rail, stared at me from across the desk where he stood with his hands behind his back. "Majuh," he said in his long Louisiana drawl, "Ah understand that you'd prefer not to go to the National Security Council."

"Sir," I replied, "I'll go where I'm sent, of course, but I'd rather return to the fleet."

"Brotha' North," he said, "'tisn't like you to whine. Carry out yo' orders."

Although I had groused like hell about being sent to the NSC, I did appreciate the compliment. Whenever the Marine Corps picks you to go "outside the service"—whether it's to the Joint Chiefs of Staff, the CIA, the White House, embassy duty, or anywhere else where you're serving in the presence of other services, or among civilians, it's considered an honor. This is especially true in Washington, because that's where the major decisions on roles, missions, and budget are made; issues that affect the entire Marine Corps. Later, I was told that another reason I was selected was that John Lehman, Secretary of the Navy, had liked a paper I wrote at the War College in which I argued that there was still an important role for battleships in modern warfare.

Even so, I had no business being assigned to the NSC. And I ended up there for a relatively trivial reason. Ronald Reagan had been elected, in part, because he promised to shrink the size of the federal government. His advisers soon discovered that one of the easiest ways for the White House to reduce overhead was to replace political appointees on the government payroll with military officers detailed from the Army, Navy, Air Force, and Marines. Because our salaries were paid by our respective branches of the armed services, we were a source of cheap labor.

I was over my head at the NSC, and I knew it. The problem wasn't my military background, because there were military officers at the White House who certainly belonged there. But most of them had advanced degrees in foreign studies or political science, while the bulk of my experience was in military units and combat training. I was well-versed in battlefield tactics and intelligence, and I certainly believed in the goals and policies that President Reagan had articulated in the 1980 campaign—especially his promises to rebuild America's military and to restore a sense of confidence to our economy. His views matched my own: smaller government, an emphasis on entrepreneurship, and a strong America.

But none of that was especially helpful when it came to dealing with Congress, the State Department, or the other gargantuan bureaucracies in Washington. And just because in previous assignments you had worn a uniform to work didn't mean you were familiar with the inner workings of the Pentagon.

I started out as a gofer, working on the reams of paperwork that were necessary to get congressional approval for the sale of Airborne

Warning and Control System planes (AWACs) to Saudi Arabia—the same planes that were used so successfully in our war with Iraq in 1991. Because I was unprepared and inexperienced, the only way to keep up, whether the subject was AWACs, terrorism, Iran, or Central America, was to read like crazy and to get my hands on every possible bit of information—books, articles, monographs, intelligence reports, and whatever else I could find. I spent just about every night and weekend studying, and talking to people from the State Department and the CIA who could teach me the things I needed to know. I was in the office by seven each morning, skimming through newspapers and poring over intelligence cables and State Department reports. I worked like a dog, right up until the day I was fired.

The National Security Council had been established in 1947, during the Truman administration, "to advise the President on all matters relating to national security." It was intended as a cabinet-level coordinating body, a bridge between the President's political goals and various implementing arms of the government, including the departments of State, Defense, Commerce, Treasury, and Justice, as well as the CIA. The NSC's mandate is to synchronize the work of the various federal bureaucracies with the President's national security objectives.

It sounds simple enough, but in practice it's enormously complicated. For unlike the larger, entrenched agencies in Washington, the staff of the National Security Council pretty much comes and goes with each new administration. For that reason, and because of its relatively small size (a few dozen staff members and a budget of four million dollars when I arrived), the NSC staff is generally close to the political sentiments and views of the President. In this respect it differs markedly from the larger agencies, like State, the Pentagon, and the CIA. These organizations are far too big and cumbersome to reflect serious political shifts within a short period of time—particularly when the shift is as dramatic as the one between a liberal Democratic President and his conservative Republican successor. The permanent bureaucracies of government tend to change slowly, and are attuned to a longer-term mentality. They don't have much respect for political appointees—a perspective I came to understand a little more clearly the day I heard a mid-level State Department official dismiss the cabinet as "the Christmas help."

This attitude is especially common at the State Department. There has always been some friction between the State Department and the NSC, but these tensions tend to be particularly pronounced during a conservative Republican administration, probably because most conservatives avoid government work in favor of the private sector. The State Department tends to attract idealistic and well-meaning liberals, and, like the other bureaucracies of Washington, is composed mostly of Democrats, with a handful of liberal Republicans. This was true even during the Reagan administration.

While that certainly wasn't the only reason Alexander Haig didn't last very long as President Reagan's first Secretary of State, it wasn't irrelevant, either. "I found no great enthusiasm in the Department of State for the Reagan administration," Haig noted in his memoirs. I noticed the same thing. But that was okay, because the feeling was mutual.

Although the State Department exists as an instrument to carry out foreign policy, it has evolved into an institution of foreign *relations*. This difference is more significant than it sounds. State Department officials who deal with a particular country often seem more concerned with that country's perception of us than with our policy toward them. Later, when I became involved in implementing the administration's counterterrorism policies, working with the State Department was often a nightmare: if we had a problem with country X or country Y, the first instinct over at State was not to convey our real views, but to avoid offending the other side.

I found a discernible corporate culture at the State Department, where many of the officials subscribed to an almost unconscious set of values, although they were never discussed or spelled out. Part of it was a tendency to assume that in just about every conflict between the United States and the Third World, the Third Worlders were right and the U.S. was wrong. The unspoken but pervasive rule was that we had been so shameful in our past treatment of these countries that we always owed them the benefit of the doubt. There was a standing joke that what we really needed at the State Department was an American embassy—to represent the views of the American people.

There was certainly a State Department perspective on Israel. Again, nobody ever said so aloud, but it seemed to me that many officials at State were automatically opposed to whatever it was the Israelis favored. There were times, of course, when the White House, too, disagreed with particular Israeli policies, and certainly the Israelis were not pleased about those AWACs going to Saudi Arabia.

But within the State Department there seemed to be a constituency that actually relished any antagonism that could be fostered between us and the Israelis. Some of this came from a long-standing and barely hidden pro-Arab tilt at State, which I'm hardly the first to notice.* Another large chunk, I believe, is the result of an ingrained streak of anti-Semitism in our government. Many mid-level government officials—and not only at the State Department—are the sons and grandsons of the great elite American families, where a genteel, discreet anti-Jewish prejudice was often taken for granted.

In early 1983, an adviser to a senior government official sent me a weird magazine clipping about an Israeli conspiracy to dominate the world—and suggested that I might want to look into it. When I went to see him, he showed me the publication where the article had appeared; it was put out by Lyndon LaRouche and his followers.

While this incident was certainly not typical of our government as a whole, I noticed a distinct anti-Israeli bias in some circles. This sentiment had been growing since the 1973 Arab-Israeli War, after which many Americans (including some conservatives) blamed Israel for the Arab oil embargo, and the devastation that followed in our economy. This hostility grew more pronounced in 1981, when Israeli planes destroyed Iraq's nuclear facility—which *really* infuriated the State Department. It wasn't until early 1991, when the Israelis were repeatedly attacked by Iraqi SCUD missiles during Operation Desert Storm and did not retaliate, that Israel once again enjoyed widespread support in Washington. Unfortunately, it took a situation where Israel was once again a victim to bring about this change.

This bias did not seem to be shared by President Reagan or Vice President Bush, but Caspar Weinberger was another story. Weinberger seemed to go out of his way to oppose Israel on any issue and to blame the Israelis for every problem in the Middle East. In our planning for counterterrorist operations, he apparently feared that if we went after Palestinian terrorists, we would offend and alienate Arab

*In his recently published memoirs, Clark Clifford recalls "a group of Mideast experts in the State Department who were widely regarded as anti-Semitic." Clifford was referring to 1948, but things change slowly in Washington. (Clark Clifford with Richard Holbrooke, *Counselor to the President* [New York, 1991], p. 5.)

governments—particularly if we acted in cooperation with the Israelis.

Weinberger's anti-Israel tilt was an underlying current in almost every Mideast issue. Some people explained it by pointing to his years with the Bechtel Corporation, the San Francisco engineering firm with contracts in many Arab countries. Others believed it was more complicated, and had to do with his sensitivity about his own Jewish ancestry.

For all our proximity to the President and his senior advisers, the NSC, too, was a bureaucracy, and much of our work was routine and tedious. Every time the United States conducted a military exercise or deployment in the vicinity of the Soviet Union or its allies, we would prepare a paper summarizing the activity which outlined how the Soviets responded to our last exercise, and what we might expect this time. If an American destroyer sailed into the Black Sea, this required a memorandum. We wrote countless letters on behalf of the President, and memoranda to the national security adviser, the secretaries of State and Defense, foreign heads of state, and the Congress on every conceivable matter affecting our national security. An average day consisted of a long stream of phone calls, two or three hundred pages of reading, a dozen or so pages of writing, and a minimum of three or four meetings—beginning with the morning staff meeting at seven-thirty.

In the summer of 1981, when I first came to work at the NSC, I was struck by how old-fashioned the place was. The Marine headquarters in Arlington was widely perceived to be light-years behind the rest of the military, but it seemed almost space-aged compared to our creaky offices in the Old Executive Office Building. The OEOB had been built just after the Civil War, and was said to be the largest solid granite structure in the world. It had been designed in the French Renaissance style, but while the outer façade is beautiful and ornate, some of the offices were downright dangerous. One of my colleagues was sitting at his desk when a two-hundred-pound block of plaster fell from the eighteen-foot ceiling and landed on his desk, just missing his chair.

Some people swore that the electrical wiring in the OEOB had been installed before the invention of electricity. The lighting was positively medieval, and the heating system was so antiquated that some staff members would bring in their own portable heaters, which often led to some blown fuses in the neighborhood.

And this was, at least technically, the White House! The State Department had the latest telecommunications equipment, but we barely had secure telephones. Initially, the NSC secretaries all left at four-thirty, and to get a secretary to work overtime you actually had to submit a memorandum—assuming, of course, that anyone was still around to type it. Half of our furniture was broken, and the drapes looked like they had been hung by Dolley Madison the year before the British burned the city in the War of 1812.

The other government agencies loved the fact that the NSC was so antiquated and therefore ineffectual. For years, the State Department, the Pentagon, and the CIA were the only ones with instant communication links to American installations and armed forces around the world. But when Judge William P. Clark came in as national security adviser in early 1982, he had Tom Reed and Admiral Poindexter design a major upgrade of our facilities, putting the NSC on an equal footing with the larger agencies.

Unknowingly, and certainly unintentionally, I played a role in the early departure of Richard Allen, Judge Clark's predecessor. When I arrived at the NSC, I was assigned an office* on the third floor of the OEOB that I was to share with two army lieutenant colonels: Dick Childress and Alan Myer. We were also given a safe to keep classified documents. The first time we opened it, we were amazed to find several watches, a couple of gift-wrapped bottles of liquor, and an envelope containing ten one-hundred-dollar bills. I had heard about government perks, but this was ridiculous.

I reported our discovery to Jerry Jennings, the NSC Security Officer, who dutifully informed the FBI. The FBI determined that the contents of the safe had belonged to Richard Allen, the national security adviser. Unbeknownst to me, Allen had used this same office during the transition period between the election and the inauguration, and apparently the money and the watches were gifts from Japanese journalists who wanted to arrange an interview with Nancy Reagan. Although Allen was later cleared of any wrongdoing, the press had a field day, and he was soon replaced by Bill Clark.

Clark came in amid his own storm of controversy. The press attacked him for his lack of knowledge about foreign affairs, and made

---

*According to the local lore, this had been Henry Kissinger's old office.

much of the fact that during his earlier confirmation hearings for Deputy Secretary of State, he had been unable to recall the names of the leaders of Zimbabwe or South Africa. Bill Clark was a man of considerable modesty who didn't pretend to be a foreign policy expert. But he was very close to Ronald Reagan, and he understood what the President wanted and how to achieve it.

Judge Clark was tall, thin, and soft-spoken; Mike Ledeen, a consultant to the NSC, once described him as the Jimmy Stewart of the Reagan administration. Maybe so, but Bill Clark was a lot smarter than people gave him credit for. He passed the California bar exam without ever graduating from law school. He eventually became a respected justice on the California Supreme Court, but when Ronald Reagan became President, Clark left a perfectly good lifetime appointment to come to Washington to serve a man he greatly admired.

With his cowboy hat and his boots, the judge cut an unusual figure in Washington. He kept a low profile, and insisted on walking to work from his apartment near Foggy Bottom. He hated any signs of pretension, but I was finally able to convince him that in light of the terrorism threat, he ought to consider a more secure form of transportation. With the help of Ed Hickey, head of the White House Military Office, I persuaded him that a driver and an armed guard were good ideas.

Back in the 1970s, when I worked at Marine headquarters, Betsy and I would occasionally drive into Washington to catch a show, or to take the kids to one of the city's magnificent memorials and museums. But my job at the NSC marked the first time I had ever worked in the District, and for a military man making his first foray into the civilian world there was a lot to get used to.

The reverse was also true, as very few White House staffers had any idea of what the military was all about. They were pretty sure that the Navy had something to do with ships, that the Air Force flew some planes, and that the Army was somewhere off in Europe, holding back the red tide at the Iron Curtain. But the Marines were a complete mystery, except that whatever it was that we actually did was thought to involve an extraordinary degree of violence.

In the military, of course, we wore our rank on our uniforms. At the White House, everybody wore business suits to work. At first I

concluded that rank didn't make much difference in civilian life—
which is roughly equivalent to the naïve assumption that people living
under Communism have no interest in money or material objects. I
soon discovered that rank and status were terribly important in government, except that in Washington such things were designated not
on your uniform but through a series of perks. If you were really powerful, you had an office in the West Wing of the White House. The
next level down was an office in the Old Executive Office Building,
but facing the White House. If you were a drone like I was, you were
lucky to have a window at all. I had one, which provided a truly
breathtaking view of a dark blue dumpster.

Status was also conferred by your telephone style, and I soon
learned that military officers at the NSC had created their own special
rank—the telephone colonel. Nine times out of ten, Lieutenant-
Colonel Smith's secretary would answer his phone by saying,
"Colonel Smith's office," thereby giving her boss an instant promotion. Not wanting to lie, but also not wanting to burden my secretaries with three unnecessary syllables, I instructed them to answer the
phone by saying, simply, "NSC." When I answered my own phone, I
said, "Ollie North."

Now that I was part of the upper atmosphere of government, I
had to learn a new form of telephone etiquette. When my secretary
called someone on my behalf, she had to remember to put me on the
line before he picked up. In Washington, as I soon learned, talking to
a "mere" secretary is considered demeaning to the deputy assistant to
the under-assistant to the deputy assistant secretary. The junior official
always defers to the senior one by coming on the line first, the reason
being, presumably, that the senior official's time is more valuable. So
you had to know whether the Deputy Secretary of X was higher than
the Under Secretary of Y, and woe unto you if you got it wrong,
because people took these things *very* seriously. We were all given a
protocol list which explained the various levels of appointments in the
administration, and most people kept it taped to the slide shelf on
their desk so they could refer to it when the phone rang.

Once you got through to the person you were trying to reach,
your problems had only begun. For now you had to try to accomplish
something in the peculiar language of Washington, where almost
nobody communicated directly and to the point. Only on rare occa-

sions, for example, would anyone actually admit, flat out, that he or his agency was "opposed" to a particular plan or proposal. Instead, he would say "we don't concur." If he knew he was going to get steam-rolled but still wanted to register his displeasure, he would "interpose no objection." You could live with this, but the phrase you really wanted to hear, and rarely did, was "we concur." In other words, even though this wasn't our idea, we're willing to go along with it.

The OEOB was considered part of the "White House Complex," and for security reasons we were all given either a blue White House staff pass, or a red OEOB pass, which most people hung around their necks on a chain.* I kept my badge in my pocket, but I noticed that many of my colleagues wore theirs all over town, as if to announce: "I'm important. I work at the White House."

The White House staff badge was certainly a biggie, but the real status symbol was a parking pass for West Executive Avenue, next to the West Wing of the White House. After that, just about the only honor you could aspire to was to be appointed Secretary of State. But then, of course, you wouldn't need a parking pass at all, because you'd be driven to work.

We junior dogs parked along the lower half of the Ellipse, about half a mile away, and even there you needed a special White House parking pass that you hung on your rearview mirror. But this was a mixed blessing, because you'd sometimes find that somebody had decided to express his First Amendment rights by letting the air out of your tires, or even smashing your windshield. My colleague, Alfonso Sapia-Bosch, left the office very late one night and came back half an hour later, claiming that his Volkswagen was missing. "Come on," I said, "you forgot where you parked it. How could it be stolen? That area is guarded by the Secret Service, the Metropolitan Police, and the Park Police. Look again. I'm sure you'll find it."

Al's car turned up a few days later. In Pennsylvania.

There were fewer parking spaces than passes, so you got to work early and didn't dare move your car once you arrived. This, in turn, led to another perk—the use of a White House car and driver. This

---

*I was never able to figure out the criteria for who got which pass. My badge was blue, but why? Was it based on height? Weight? Astrological sign? I still wonder.

one was normally above my level, but Ed Hickey, the head of the White House Military Office that ran the White House Motor Pool, was a former Marine, and he put me on the access list. I used these cars to attend meetings in other parts of the city, or to get out to Andrews Air Force Base to catch a plane.

There was a tremendous infatuation with perks. Were you invited to a state dinner? (I never was.) Did you fly with the President on Air Force One? I did twice, and that was enough, thank you. At the time, Air Force One was an old and noisy 707 that dated from the Kennedy administration. But everybody who flew on it, or on Air Force Two, received a certificate testifying that he or she had really *been there*. These souvenirs were greatly valued.

So, too, were photographs of oneself shaking hands with the President or Vice President, along with letters or notes from high-level officials. Most of the staff plastered their office walls with these mementos. The walls of my office were decorated with pictures of my family, drawings done by my kids, maps of Central America and the Middle East, and several posters. One of the posters depicted a Nicaraguan freedom fighter and said, "For 53 Cents a Day You Can Feed a Contra." Another was a photograph of a female commando leader from the Nicaraguan resistance, holding a machine gun. It said, in big letters, THIS MUTHA' WEARS COMBAT BOOTS. A third poster was a fake movie advertisement for a film called *The Return of Walter Mondale*, which promised to be "more boring than ever!" There was one photograph of me with the President hanging in my office. Fawn had lifted it from the west wing of the White House.

I also displayed a handful of souvenirs that were a little unusual: a canteen cup that had been shot off my hip in Vietnam, an FLMN neckerchief with a hammer and sickle that had been found on a Communist guerrilla in El Salvador, a fur hat with a red star from the Chinese People's Liberation Army, a Cuban military helmet with a bullet hole through the side—a gift from Jonas Savimbi in Angola, and a Cuban officer's belt buckle from Grenada.

Another custom that surprised me about government life was the extent to which the entire city of Washington seemed to shut down for lunch every day. At noon the traffic was almost as bad as during the morning rush hour. I rarely ate lunch, and often used that time to go for a run, or to work out in the Secret Service gym—another of Ed Hickey's favors. When I did go out to lunch, it was usually at the McDonald's at Seventeenth and Pennsylvania.

I burned out several secretaries before I hired Fawn Hall. They were perfectly competent, but my hectic pace, late hours, and all too frequent weekends took their toll. My third secretary was so exhausted at the end of the day that I often had to drive her home, and when she left, there were several applicants for the job. My requirements were simple: I was looking for someone who could type like a banshee and didn't mind working overtime.

When Fawn came in for her job interview, she had been working in the office of the chief of naval operations. She struck me as articulate and efficient, and she was willing to work overtime. Her mother, Wilma Hall, was Bud McFarlane's secretary, but one thing that impressed me about Fawn was that she didn't try to use that connection to get the job.

And no, I didn't ask her if she knew how to operate a shredder.

And yes, I did notice that she was attractive.

It certainly wasn't Fawn's fault that she became famous around the same time as Donna Rice and Jessica Hahn. The media coverage implied that these women were all pretty much alike, which was terribly unfair to Fawn. She understood the prejudice she was up against, which was why her opening statement at the congressional hearings included a line that read, simply, "I CAN TYPE."*

She certainly could. "Just talk," she'd say, and about six seconds after I was finished, the memo would be completed, and in the right format. Fawn was one reason I was so productive. She was terrific at keeping my hectic schedule straight. She always knew how long a meeting would take, and even how much time it would take to get there and back. She was great on the phone, and was adept at protecting me from conversations that weren't really necessary.

Maybe these qualities are inherited, because Fawn's mother was the consummate executive assistant. Gregarious, outgoing, bright, and cheerful, Wilma Hall was Bud McFarlane's alter ego. She had first

---

*"My hours were long and arduous," she said in her testimony, "but I found my job to be most fulfilling. I was a dedicated and loyal secretary, and performed my duties in an exemplary manner." I'll vouch for that.

met Bud when he was a White House Fellow, and over the years she had worked for several national security advisers, including Kissinger. In every case, but especially with McFarlane, she helped optimize her boss's effectiveness.

Fawn Hall wasn't much older than my own daughter Tait. Like many young people, she had enormous energy, and even after a twelve-hour day she could go on to one of her occasional modeling jobs.

After Fawn started working for me, I noticed that some of the men who had previously dealt with me only by telephone were now stopping by the office. One of them was Arturo Cruz, Jr., a handsome young man and a real charmer whose father had been induced to join the leadership of the Nicaraguan resistance. Arturito, as the son was known, began showing up fairly often, and he would always stop in the outer office to chat with Fawn. I didn't realize how close they had actually become until I received a report from the CIA that Fawn had been seen with Arturito in Miami.

I called her in and said, "Listen, you've got to make a decision. This guy is a foreign national. He used to be a Sandinista adviser. We think we can trust him, but he also had a relationship with Cuban intelligence, the DGI. You have the highest security clearances in the land, and your association with him offers the potential for compromise. You'll have to make a choice between this man and your job. If you really love him, just give me two weeks notice, marry him, and have lots of kids."

Fawn was embarrassed that I had to speak to her about it, and I felt awkward for intruding in her personal life. But several weeks later, when I received another call, this time from the FBI, I had to speak to her again. Fawn eventually broke off with Arturito, whereupon I introduced her to Major Gil Macklin, a young Marine who had once worked for me. Everything seemed to be going great for them until he was sent to Okinawa—and I've already explained what *that* can do to a relationship.

In the months after I was fired, there were all kinds of stories and rumors about the "cowboy colonel" and his blond secretary, and the office they supposedly shared in the White House basement. Innuendos were even raised during the hearings. These kinds of stories, invariably based on anonymous sources, are routine in Washington, but in my case there seemed to be no limits. According to one account, I used Iran-contra money to buy Fawn Hall her red Fiero sports car, and to pay for an island in the South Pacific to which the two of us were planning to flee.

That story set me off like a rocket, and I stormed in to see Edward Bennett Williams. Ed, who had founded the law firm that represented me, was a grand old man of the law and a strong believer in "no comment" when it came to the news media.

"That does it," I said. "I know you don't like clients to respond to the press, but this thing has to be answered. My wife will see it, and so will our friends. And what about our kids?"

"Sit down, Ollie," he said. "You're getting to be like a dog chasing fleas. You're not going to get rid of the fleas until you take a flea bath, and son, you'll be taking a couple of them. You also have to understand that the people telling these stories actually believe they're true."

I was dumbfounded. "How can you say that?" I asked.

"Listen," he said, "if the people writing these stories and spreading these rumors had the chance to abuse their position, steal millions of dollars, and have an affair with a beautiful secretary, they would have done it. So they have to believe *you* did. Otherwise they couldn't face themselves in the morning."

My first major assignment at the NSC came out of the blue. One autumn afternoon, shortly after the Senate voted to supply AWACs to Saudi Arabia, several boxes of paperwork were delivered to my office along with a memo from Admiral Poindexter, asking me to look through all of this material and to brief him on it the following week. I'm still not entirely sure why it ended up on my desk, but I started reading through the various papers and documents, which turned out to be fascinating—and highly classified.

During the final year of the Carter administration, the President had been trying to conclude a major disarmament agreement with the Soviets. Zbigniew Brzezinski, his national security adviser, had convened a group of scientists and former senior government officials to consider various scenarios of war and peace, including what would happen in the event of a Soviet nuclear attack on the United States. One result would be enormous bursts of electromagnetic energy which could immediately disable our electronic communications equipment. If that happened, the scientists wanted to know, how could we ensure that the President could continue to lead the country and assert his role as Commander-in-Chief if he couldn't communicate with either the citizens or the military? We knew that the Soviet Union had made plans for its leadership to survive a nuclear war by having them whisked off to a network of secret tunnels under Moscow. But what would *our* leadership do?

I put together a summary of the papers, and was summoned to the Oval Office to brief the national security adviser and the President. (This was the first time I briefed President Reagan.) My recommendation was that the work of the "Wise Men's Group," as this outside team of advisers was known, was so important that the group ought to be reactivated. Judge Clark asked me to take charge of this effort, and for the next year and a half I did little else but work on this undertaking, which we called The Project.

As the de facto administrator of The Project, I arranged meetings of the Wise Men, wrote up the minutes, and brought back their ideas for implementation. Initially The Project was headed by Tom Reed, a former Secretary of the Air Force and a confidant of Judge Clark.

During these meetings, I sat there in awe as this incredibly brilliant collection of people discussed electromagnetic pulses and other scientific topics about which I knew next to nothing. I had taken engineering courses at Annapolis, and had completed a course in nuclear weaponry in the Marine Corps. But there were terms thrown around in that room that I'd never even heard before.

As a result of the work done by the Wise Men, a permanent government-wide working group was formed to address a number of difficult questions pertaining to a possible nuclear attack. Suppose, for example, that the President does not survive the attack, the Vice President has been killed in his helicopter, and the Speaker of the House has collapsed and died of a heart attack. Suppose further that the highest-ranking member of the cabinet who is alive and accounted for is the Secretary of the Treasury, who had gone out to Wisconsin to give a speech. The rest of our government, the American people, and particularly the military must be informed that the Secretary is now the constitutional President, but it's still too dangerous to announce his exact location. In the absence of normal channels of communication, how does the new President assert his authority? How does he stop the war, or continue it, or take whatever other actions may be necessary?

Years later, as the Iran-contra hearings began, a particularly bombastic and outrageous article appeared in the *Miami Herald* and several other newspapers, claiming that during my years at the NSC I had been involved in drawing up plans "to suspend the Constitution in the event of [a] national crisis such as nuclear war." This story was not only wrong, but offensive. The whole point of The Project was to protect our constitutional system even under the worst imaginable conditions.

During my work on The Project, I wrote several directives which President Reagan signed, authorizing further steps to be taken to ensure that our government could not be rendered impotent by enemy action or an extraordinary disaster. This was also where I came to know Vice President Bush. As the first in line to succeed the President, he took an active interest in this program. I briefed him often, and he asked detailed and penetrating questions about how things worked, and how they could be improved. It was obvious that his interest was more than a formality.

And because The Project also involved the Congress—both on matters of succession, and for funding—I also briefed two of the Reagan administration's strongest political adversaries: Speaker Tip O'Neill and Congressman Ed Boland.

Even at the NSC, only a handful of people were aware of The Project. But for me it was enormously satisfying. The Project enabled our government to safely conduct arms-reduction talks with the Soviets, secure in the knowledge that the United States would never be decapitated.

In 1983 I was given another fascinating opportunity. When the Kissinger Commission was established to study the situation in Central America, Judge Clark asked me to serve as the NSC liaison. As part of its work, the commission invited each of the three living former presidents to appear before it and present his views on the deteriorating situation in the region. It was my job to make sure they all had access to the appropriate classified information.

I soon discovered how different each of these men really was. We began with President Carter, who didn't want to be briefed and showed no interest in the documents we were prepared to send him. "Don't bother," he told me on the phone. "I have my own sources." When he appeared before the commission, he brought along close to forty pages of notes, which he delivered in a familiar monotone. Within about twenty minutes, several members of the commission appeared to be snoozing. Even the Democrats were clenching their teeth, trying to suppress a yawn.

President Carter's analysis consisted of an extended diatribe against the administration's policies in Central America. Despite his suspicions about the Sandinistas, he had obviously never envisioned that the United States would support a covert war against them. And no wonder. In his meetings at Camp David with Menachem Begin and Anwar Sadat, he had succeeded in one of the most difficult negotiations ever. It was hard to blame him for believing that Nicaragua's problems could and should be resolved in similar fashion.

President Ford, by contrast, was delighted to be briefed, and together with another staff member I flew out to Colorado to bring him back in a White House jet. We briefed him during the flight to Washington, and President Ford's presentation more or less matched the administration's view.

President Nixon was an altogether different story. About two weeks before his appearance, I began talking on the phone with him and an aide. He'd plow through the material I sent in a day or two. Then he'd call me to say, "Okay, now send me the current analysis of the economic conditions between Colombia and the Rio Grande—trade, employment, refugees, everything." I would put together a package and shoot it up to him by White House courier. Later that same day, he would call again: "Have you got anything else? That second paper you sent me wasn't deep enough."

"I'm sorry to hear that, sir." (I neglected to mention that I had written that paper myself.)

"Well, don't give me that pablum. Send me a more detailed analysis."

President Nixon had an insatiable appetite for information, and his questions were always incisive. When he appeared before the commission, he took off his watch and set it down on the podium. "I have exactly an hour and a half," he said. "I'll talk for forty-five minutes, and then take questions for another forty-five before Major North takes me back to the airport." Then, without a single note or index card, he proceeded to review all of Central and South America from the Rio Grande down to Tierra del Fuego. He knew every head of state, every political movement, and every economic trend. Without missing a beat, he spoke for *exactly* forty-five minutes, and then answered questions. His performance was absolutely dazzling.

While President Nixon was talking, I looked over at Kissinger, who was grinning like a Cheshire cat. Maybe we have it backward, I thought. Maybe Kissinger was really Nixon's student. That day, at least, it seemed that the real mastermind behind the foreign policy of the Nixon administration was Richard Nixon himself.

I missed a lot of family dinners during my years at the NSC, but in spite of the incredible hours and far too many weekends in the office, our family managed to sneak away for a few camping trips and short vacations in North Carolina, Virginia, and Maryland. In 1986 I took the whole gang to Costa Rica, where I had planned to meet with several of the contra leaders, and with Joe Fernandez, the CIA station chief, whom I had come to know in Washington before he was posted to Costa Rica. We visited Ambassador Lew Tambs and stayed with the Fernandez family. Over a weekend, our two broods—with a combined total of eleven kids—all went to a beach house on the Pacific coast, just south of the secret airfield that Dick Secord had built at Santa Elena.

I rarely worked on Sunday mornings, and unless I was away, our family normally attended church together. But I've had an easier time loading up an entire battalion on ships than getting the six of us into one car and arriving at church on time. Stuart and I would usually end up sitting around and waiting for the girls, and he'd use the opportunity to tease me: "Way to go, Dad. Let's hear it for that ironclad military discipline."

All through my years at the NSC, our family was part of a weekly Bible-study group. This was something we had started during our year in Newport, where we normally began each session with children's Bible stories and songs. Then one of us would take all the kids over to a neighboring house while the rest of the parents studied together. We took turns leading the sessions, and we'd prepare for that evening's topic by reading various biblical commentaries, looking up the appropriate scriptural references, and integrating them with our own interpretations.

One of my favorite study sessions was on the marriage relationship as described in the fifth chapter of Ephesians, which includes the well-known verse, "Wives, submit to your husbands as to the Lord. For the husband is the head of the wife as Christ is the head of the church...."

A lot of men use that verse to justify an authoritarian, male-dominated household, but that's not what the verse says to me. It compares the husband's role to that of Jesus, and His style was to lead with love. I think the real message of this verse is directed not to the wife at all—but to her husband.*

Because Stuart is my only son, I've probably spent more time with him than with my daughters. We have hiked along the Appalachian Trail, paddled canoes on the Shenandoah and Potomac, and scaled a few heights in Yosemite. During that idyllic year in Newport, I even had time to coach his soccer team.

Our three girls are consumed with horses—an interest that began at the base stables when we were living at Quantico. Horses are completely foreign to my experience, and I've learned that I'm not the only father in that situation. At horse events, the dads are the ones leaning on the fence with their hearts in their throats as their offspring take thousand-pound animals over fences and jumps. From talking to these other dads, I've learned that their involvement, too, is limited to two specific tasks: mucking out the stables, and driving our daughters and their horses to and from these events—"but slowly, please, Daddy." It's gotten to the point where several of us show up in T-shirts that read, "They ride, I provide."

Today, when I think back on my job at the NSC, all I can see is the work. But there were some perks, too. We got to bring the kids to the Easter Egg roll on the White House lawn, and to the White House staff Christmas party, where they got to see the President and the First Lady. And occasionally, Betsy and I were given free tickets to the Kennedy Center. When foreign diplomats come to town, a member of the White House staff generally escorts them to the Kennedy Center, where the entire party sits in the President's box. Sometimes

*Moreover, the previous verse (5:21) reads, "Submit to one another out of reverence for Christ," which makes it clear that submission goes in both directions.

these tickets went to Bud McFarlane, and every few months, Wilma Hall, his secretary, would call and ask if Betsy and I were free to go as escorts. This invariably happened at the last moment, but we jumped at the chance whenever we could.

Now we're not talking here about Margaret Thatcher or Mikhail Gorbachev; the most socially desirable visitors were quickly snapped up by higher-ranking officials. By the time it got down to my level, these events invariably involved emissaries from countries nobody else was interested in—nations at the lower end of the alphabet, or with hyphenated names, or governments whose major industry consists of issuing colorful postage stamps.

Betsy and I would greet our guests in a little anteroom just behind the presidential box. As the host and hostess, we'd get there early enough to unlock the telephone, and to ensure that the little refrigerator was stocked with small bottles of California champagne from the White House Mess. These bottles were emblazoned with the White House seal, and most of our guests took them home as souvenirs.

I joke about it now, but Betsy and I got to see some terrific shows, and we met some fascinating people from countries we had barely heard of. (I would always do a little research on these places so as not to appear *totally* ignorant.) Before the curtain, the audience would often look up toward the box, wondering who was occupying it that night. Just before the show began, there would be an announcement: "Ladies and gentlemen, viewing from the President's box tonight is Ambassador Zlygbat and his wife, Eirwox, from the dictatorship of Epidermos."

But these intersections of work and family were all too rare. As far as my kids were concerned, I might have been working on another planet.

"How come you're never home, Dad?"

"Because I've got a lot of work to do, honey."

Poor Daddy. How smart could he be if it takes him *that* long to finish his work?

But while I couldn't talk to my kids about the details of the job, we did discuss the general issues of American policy. Tait and Stuart were both in high school, and I visited each of their classes to talk and show slides about the situation in Central America.

Betsy knew the general outline of what I was working on, but not the details. She was aware that I used to travel to Central America on NSC work and that the administration was backing the Nicaraguan resistance, but she didn't know what country I was going to, or why. During some of the busiest times she even met me at the airport with a couple of clean shirts. And while she knew in a broad sense that I was working on the hostages, she didn't know who I was meeting with, or that I had gone to Tehran. It wasn't until the congressional hearings in 1987 that Betsy learned exactly how I had been spending my time. When it was all over, she turned to me and said, "I'm glad I came. Now I know where you were all those nights."

8

Close-up

During my five and a half years at the White House, I had a fairly close-up view of several high officials in the Reagan administration.

I don't pretend to know Ronald Reagan well, and I have to admit that my negative feelings about him are the direct result of what has happened to me since I left the White House in 1986. Before I was fired, I was with him at scores of meetings during my five and a half years at the NSC, which was certainly enough to get a good sense of the man.

The first thing I noticed is that he worked a lot harder than people gave him credit for. While he undoubtedly knew how to enjoy life, it was equally clear that he plowed through a huge amount of paperwork and attended innumerable meetings. I also found him to be a far more involved President than he was portrayed in the media, and while I don't know whether that was true across the board, it was definitely the case in the areas I worked in—counterterrorism, the hostages, and the Nicaraguan resistance.

He was a great storyteller, and in my experiences the anecdotes he told were generally relevant to the issue at hand—or to the atmosphere in the room. Sometimes he'd come up with a reminiscence to defuse tension and make the participants in the meeting feel more at ease. And sometimes he used humor to build a consensus between Democrats and Republicans.

He could also laugh at himself. Although he was the leader of the most powerful country on earth, and was reelected by an overwhelming mandate, he still had an aw, shucks attitude that endeared him to people. Part of it was an act, of course, but underneath the act he was still amiable and unassuming.

He was the same way with visiting dignitaries. In October 1983, in the midst of the Grenada operation, the President hosted a series of meetings with the leaders of the Caribbean island nations that had participated with us in the rescue mission. One of these visitors was Prime Minister Compton of Turks and Caicos, a small former British dependency, who showed up with his very attractive wife. The meeting in the Oval Office was all business—until the end, when she interrupted the good-byes to say she had brought a message from her people: "Mr. President, our people think that you are very brave to do what you have done in Grenada. They say that you have"—and here she thrust out her cupped hands, palms up, and groped for the right word—"big balls."

In this formal setting, the scene of countless historic moments, you could just about hear the strains of barely suppressed laughter as the President's senior advisers strove to choke back their natural response. As for the President, he just smiled, blushed a little, and lowered his head. "Well," he said in his inimitable manner, "well..."

I have already discussed my personal disappointment in Ronald Reagan. Politically, my regret is that instead of strengthening the office of the presidency, he actually weakened it. He just wasn't forceful enough when it came to fighting for the constitutional prerogatives of the Executive Branch. He could have opposed the appointment of a special prosecutor, and he could have challenged the War Powers Resolution when he decided to use military force in both Grenada and Libya. Instead, the President acquiesced by calling in the congressional leadership and informing them of his intentions. The War Powers Resolution, which was passed in 1973 over President Nixon's veto, greatly expanded the power of Congress at the expense of the presidency. Once you give away that authority, it's almost impossible to get it back.*

The same thing happened with the Boland Amendments, which severely restricted American support for the Nicaraguan resistance. When Congress started to obstruct the President's authority to carry out our foreign policy, he should have stood up to them and announced, "If you send me a bill that includes that amendment, I just won't sign it. It's unconstitutional. If necessary, the government will come to a screeching halt until you send me a bill I *can* sign."

Future presidents may well be constrained by an imperial Congress because Ronald Reagan, one of the most popular presidents in American history, did not reclaim the original powers of his office.

My attitude toward President Reagan was also affected by disclosures that have come out since we both left Washington.

As the whole world knows by now, both the President and the First Lady consulted astrologers. For the life of me, I can't understand how a man who purports to be a Christian can believe in that malarkey. I am aware that millions of Americans say they believe in the God of the Universe *and* in the stars. But the idea that a man could get up in the morning and let an interpretation of the great sidereal movement guide his day is simply beyond my understanding.

Ultimately, however, I think of Ronald Reagan in terms of my four children and their future, which is why I can't stay angry at him. I remember what the world was like in 1980. The man whom Ronald Reagan defeated in that election liked to tell us that our best days were behind us. President Carter believed that the only hope for America lay in more and bigger government, and that we had to start scaling back our expectations. He left us with a failing economy, an emasculated defense, and a sagging spirit.

Then Ronald Reagan came along and showed us another way, and the American people responded to him as a revolutionary of the right. People living under Communism saw it, too. They regarded Ronald

---

*No President has ever signed a bill restricting constitutional presidential authority to deploy military forces. But every President since Gerald Ford has complied with the provisions of the War Powers Resolution before committing American troops. Ronald Reagan was the first President popular enough to challenge the Congress on what many scholars believe is an unconstitutional restriction on the presidency. Unfortunately, he failed to do so.

Reagan almost as a spiritual figure who inspired them to reject the system they had known and hated all their lives.

The world we live in today is a far better place than it was in 1980. *Time* magazine gave the credit to Mikhail Gorbachev, their "man of the decade." But it was Ronald Reagan who transformed the world in the 1980s. It was he who made the changes under Gorbachev possible—and even necessary. If Karl Marx provided the stimulus for the first Russian Revolution in 1917, it was Ronald Reagan who inspired the second in 1991. And it was he who revitalized America's power and its economy, and led the whole world a few steps closer to freedom and prosperity. For the better future he offered my children, I will always be grateful.

Unfortunately, Reagan's policies were not always shared by the people around him. Some of his priorities, such as helping the contras and reducing the size of our government, could not be accomplished by one man. And several of his top advisers, like Richard Wirthlin and Mike Deaver, seemed to be more interested in Reagan's popularity than in his programs or policies.

Some people maintain that Ronald Reagan's finest speech was his 1964 television address for Barry Goldwater. That one certainly changed Reagan's life, but as far as I'm concerned, his greatest moment as a communicator did not occur in the United States at all, but in the Soviet Union, of all places. On May 31, 1988, he stood beneath a gigantic bust of Lenin and spoke to the students at Moscow State University about the real meaning of liberty. "Freedom is the right to question and change the established way of doing things," he told them. "It is the continuing revolution of the marketplace. It is the understanding that allows us to recognize shortcomings and seek solutions. It is the right to put forth an idea, scoffed at by the experts, and watch it catch fire among the people. It is the right to dream—to follow your dream or stick to your conscience, even if you're the only one in a sea of doubters."

The greatness of Reagan wasn't just that he gave that speech, which was written for him by Josh Gilder. It was that he had made it possible for that speech to be given in the first place. As far as I'm concerned, that marked his finest moment.

The tragedy of Ronald Reagan is that he will not be remembered for that speech in Moscow. Instead, what lives on in the public mind and on the airwaves is the President's pathetic videotaped deposition at John Poindexter's trial in 1990. Ronald Reagan deserves an honored place in the history of the world, but millions of people will always think of him as a confused and muddled old man. I always assumed that Ronald Reagan had good attorneys, but I just can't understand why they allowed him to make that tape.*

I had relatively little direct contact with Secretary of State Shultz and Secretary of Defense Weinberger, but like everyone else in the national security community, I couldn't help being aware of the persistent, continual squabbling between them. Part of their rivalry was institutional: in every administration the Defense Department tends to be more suspicious of the Soviet Union, for example, while the State Department, by its very nature, is more inclined toward compromise and reconciliation. But this conflict was personal, and the hostility between Shultz and Weinberger inevitably spilled down into the bureaucracies, and undermined relations between lower-level officials at both State and Defense.

I used to see them in action during meetings of the National Security Planning Group in the White House Situation Room. Whenever Shultz spoke, Weinberger would slouch down in his chair and close his eyes. When Shultz was finished, Weinberger would usually speak up in disagreement. Sometimes—especially with regard to Central America—he'd talk as if Shultz had never spoken.

They fought constantly—in front of the President, in meetings, and through their public statements. Sometimes you had the feeling that one of them took a more extreme position just to annoy the other guy. Their quarrels were so frequent, and so out of keeping with their position, that I sometimes wondered whether Weinberger and Shultz had something to gain by creating the impression that they didn't get along.

They had apparently been at each other's throats for years—ever since 1970, when Weinberger worked for Shultz in Nixon's Office of Management and the Budget. According to the local lore, their con-

---

*One of the most astonishing statements in the deposition was Reagan's testimony that "to this day, I don't have any information or knowledge that...there was a diversion.... I, to this day, do not recall ever hearing that there was a diversion."

flict had continued at Bechtel, where Shultz was president and Weinberger was general counsel.

It was also reflected in their very different personalities. Shultz was certainly the more interesting of the two. In public, he always tried to portray himself as the cautious, behind-the-scenes conciliator, struggling hard to stay out of the limelight. But he struck me as just the opposite: a man who loved the attention of the media and wanted to be seen as being in charge of foreign policy. In private meetings he was contentious, especially with Weinberger and Casey, and he frequently contradicted them in meetings with the President.

He also struck me as the more ambitious of the two. Later, in preparing for my trial, I learned that Shultz had confided to one of his aides that he hoped to use the Iran-contra fiasco as an opportunity to become national security adviser while maintaining his position as Secretary of State. Whenever I think of him, I'm reminded of that marvelous title of John Dean's book on Watergate: *Blind Ambition*.

Weinberger, on the other hand, was clearly uneasy in front of the media, where he would often stutter and stammer his way through a press conference. He was far more effective when he held forth in the Situation Room, where his perspectives were clear and concise. He knew that in order for the United States to have credibility, we had to have military strength. Shultz, however, didn't seem to care deeply about any particular foreign policy issue—so long as he got to negotiate it.

Shultz's lack of a clear philosophy was most evident when it came to dealing with the Soviets, where he turned into Mr. Nonconfrontation Man. He didn't want to confront them over their arms deliveries to Nicaragua, and it was common knowledge that his State Department was willing to sacrifice the Strategic Defense Initiative in order to conclude a new arms treaty with the Soviets.

Just about the only thing that Shultz and Weinberger seemed to agree on was that they were both strongly opposed to our dealings with Iran. They said so loudly and often—mostly after the fact. Their opposition was real enough, but in Shultz's case, especially, I believe he made sure to cover all his bases. If the Iran initiative failed, he could credibly claim he had opposed it. After I was fired, Shultz insisted that the State Department be placed in charge of further contact with the Iranians. If they succeeded, he would be able to share in the credit.

During the firestorm of publicity on Iran-contra, the story came out that Shultz had threatened to resign in protest over the arms-for-hostages policy. I don't believe it. I'm confident that if the Secretary of State had walked into the Oval Office and said, flat out, "Either this Iran business stops or I'm leaving," the entire initiative would have been stopped dead in its tracks. As much as President Reagan cared about the hostages, after Alexander Haig left, the President simply couldn't afford to lose a second Secretary of State—especially one whose personal relationship with Foreign Minister Eduard Shevardnadze mirrored Reagan's own rapport with Gorbachev. For in the final analysis, everything else in the foreign policy arena was seen as secondary to the main issue, which was U.S.-Soviet relations.

Had Shultz and Weinberger been as strongly opposed to the Iran initiative as they later claimed, it would never have continued. Secretary Weinberger simply could have forbidden the shipment of U.S. military equipment from our stockpiles. And consider the impact if both men had gone in together to see the President and said, "Hey, boss, we finally found something to agree on. Either this thing stops or we're both out of here." Instead, as pragmatic politicians, they kept their options open.

Although his major battles were with Weinberger, Shultz was no great fan of Bill Casey either. The feeling was mutual. Casey believed that Shultz had his own private agenda, and regarded him as working for the benefit of all Shultzkind.

"Shultz thinks every problem can be negotiated," Casey once told me. "And the longer he negotiates, the more powerful he becomes. If Shultz had his way, no problem would ever be solved. All we'd do is keep negotiating."

Casey wasn't merely being sarcastic. He sincerely believed he had real solutions to problems, while Shultz was content just to talk about them.

They sparred frequently—especially over Nicaragua, where Shultz favored a multilateral negotiating process while Casey was a passionate supporter of the armed resistance. It wasn't that Casey couldn't accept a negotiated end to the conflict, or that he believed that a purely military solution was likely. But he was convinced that the pressure of the Nicaraguan resistance was essential for negotiations to succeed, and he turned out to be right. It was military pressure which eventually forced the Sandinistas to accept open elections, which led to the defeat of Daniel Ortega in 1990.

The Casey-Shultz conflict was considerably more dignified than the Shultz-Weinberger rivalry, and was more along the lines of the traditional tensions between secretaries of state and national security advisers. While Shultz's view of the world was hard to discern, Casey had already formulated what later became known as the Reagan Doctrine, which encouraged active American support for anti-Communist movements around the world. Afghanistan, Nicaragua, and Angola became its most vivid manifestations, but Casey wasn't merely anti-Communist; he was enthusiastically pro-democracy. One of his greatest frustrations was that few Americans seemed to know that many new democracies around the world had emerged (or in some cases, reemerged) during the Reagan years, including Argentina, Brazil, Ecuador, El Salvador, Grenada, Venezuela, Colombia, Honduras, Guatemala, the Philippines, and South Korea.

Casey felt strongly about the need to redress the perception around the world that the United States was an unreliable ally and a fair-weather friend. He understood why this image was so widespread, and he would cite the consequences for those who had been gullible enough to take America at its word: from the Bay of Pigs to Vietnam, Cambodia, and Laos, to the Shah, and to Latin American leaders who had believed President Carter when he assured them that the Sandinistas would be better for them than the Somoza regime. In short, he was determined to restore our credibility.

I admired Casey enormously, and I came to know him well. After his death in the spring of 1987, the nature of our association became the subject of intense speculation. According to some reports, I was like a son to him, while others swore that I barely knew the man.

Our relationship was close, and yet it wasn't especially personal. We often spoke on the secure telephone, and we met regularly at one of his offices, or occasionally at his house in Northwest Washington. He had three offices that I knew of, but knowing Casey, there may well have been others.

I admired him, and he knew it. But I was never Casey's protégé, and I don't believe he saw me as the son he never had. We were not buddies. He never picked up the phone to say, "Come on over and let's have drinks tonight." Casey had friends, but I didn't count myself among them.

And yet we were more than colleagues. He was somebody I could turn to and say, "What's going on here?" I could talk to him about wanting to return to the Marines, and I often asked him for advice. He gave it eagerly: "Here's who you should be dealing with on Nicaragua. But stay away from so-and-so; he's no good."

I knew nothing about covert operations when I came to the NSC, but Casey taught me a great deal. In 1984, when McFarlane told me that one of our allies was about to contribute significant funds to support the Nicaraguan resistance (only later did I learn it was Saudi Arabia), and instructed me to set up a procedure by which the money could be delivered, it was Casey who told me what to do. Later, people seemed to assume that a Marine infantry officer somehow just *knew* how to set up an overseas bank account to receive wire transfers, but I didn't have a clue. To me, a bank was a place where they gave you a toaster when you opened a new checking account, and where you applied for a mortgage. I had never even heard of a wire transfer, and I certainly didn't know how to arrange one. But Casey, among other things, was a financial genius. He had been chairman of the Securities and Exchange Commission during the Nixon years, and before that he had actually invented the concept of the tax shelter—and even gave it its name.

Casey's habitual mumbling obscured the fact that he was incredibly bright and knowledgeable. He was trained as a lawyer, and had apparently been a good one, as he often reminded people. He saw himself, justifiably, as an intellectual, and he gravitated toward people who were interested in big ideas and in painting a broad panorama. He had an especially good rapport with Jeane Kirkpatrick, and on two separate occasions—first, when Judge Clark left as national security adviser, and again when McFarlane resigned—he lobbied hard for Jeane to take over that job. Although both Casey and Weinberger supported her, her appointment was blocked on both occasions by George Shultz. I believe that the reason Shultz didn't want Jeane Kirkpatrick to be any closer than the U.N. was that he felt threatened both by her formidable intelligence and her strong anti-Communism.

I got to know her fairly well when I worked with the Kissinger

Commission on Central America. She had been Bill Clark's first choice as a commission member, and she clearly knew more about what was going on in the region than anybody else in that group. It wasn't just book learning; she had been to the area, and she knew many of the leaders personally. Her obvious grasp of the issues and the personalities made other members of the commission—even Kissinger—uncomfortable. She was sometimes acerbic when she explained the folly of a particular proposal or idea, and those who didn't appreciate her found this grating. I thought she was terrific, and I could see why Casey admired her.

Casey's mind was always processing new data. He was relentlessly curious, and he often broke into a machine-gun burst of questions: Why? What makes you believe that? What's the proof? How do you know?

I often had the feeling that his mumbling was at least partly an act, because when he wanted to speak clearly, Casey rarely had trouble being understood. And he was actually easier to understand on the phone, which struck me as odd. In some of the high-level meetings I attended, it seemed as if Casey was mumbling to force other cabinet members to lean forward to listen to him. He didn't speak loudly, but he had a way of commanding attention. Caspar Weinberger, who often appeared to sleep during these meetings (a result, people said, of his arthritis medication), always woke up for Casey.

And Washington's most notorious mumbler certainly knew how to work a crowd. I was sometimes sent out to address new intelligence officers at CIA training centers, and I was always surprised by how many of them said they decided to apply to the CIA after hearing Casey give a speech at their college or university. Casey loved young people for their energy and enthusiasm, and it showed.

The one word he could never pronounce was the name of the country that was always on his mind. He called it Nica-wog-wa, and at meetings people would go out of their way to try to get him to say it. Some congressional Democrats joked that they would never vote to undermine the government of any country that the director of Central Intelligence couldn't pronounce. And yet Bill Casey spoke several foreign languages and paid attention to detail. Was he putting us on?

He was always reading. I was with him on a flight to Panama when I saw him start in on the paperback edition of *Modern Times*, by the British author Paul Johnson. This tome is nothing less than a history of the world from the end of World War I to the 1980s, and it runs to over eight hundred pages. I was sitting behind him, across the aisle, and as we landed he turned around and said, "Have you read this? It's really good." Then he tossed it to me.

Modern Times is one of the best books I've ever read, but you have to pay attention. It took me weeks to plow though it, but Casey had devoured it during a single flight.

At Mayknoll, his family home on the Long Island shore, books were stacked up from floor to ceiling. Wherever he traveled, he told his advance team to find two things: a Catholic church and a good bookstore. He was always buying more books—and giving them away. "Have you read this yet?" he'd say. "This guy knows what he's talking about."

One book that influenced him enormously was *The Terror Network*, by Claire Sterling, a free-lance American journalist living in Italy. Sterling described an international terrorist fraternity, a collection of groups who received extensive support from the Soviets and their Eastern European allies. "The KGB's role was not a matter of guesswork," she wrote, "but documented fact." And she excoriated Western governments for refusing to acknowledge this fact in the face of overwhelming evidence.

Casey was highly impressed with Sterling's work, and concluded that she had great sources. But his praise for Claire Sterling was not shared by Washington's intellectual elite. When *The Terror Network* was published, the critics dismissed it as right-wing propaganda. But only a few years later, when Communism began to crumble all over Europe, Sterling's allegations and Casey's convictions were vindicated again and again—mostly by the guilty parties themselves.*

---

*In East Germany, for example, the interior minister revealed that his government had allowed PLO operatives to use their nation as an operations base, and had knowingly given refuge to Carlos, one of the world's most notorious terrorists. The authorities in East Berlin admitted that they had not interfered when a Libyan-Palestinian terror group planned the bombing of a disco in West Berlin that killed two American servicemen and wounded over two hundred people in April 1986.

The Hungarian Interior Ministry revealed in 1990 that his country, too, had given sanctuary to Carlos and thirty-five of his men. The Czechs had provided training and explosives to terrorist groups, while Yugoslavia was a major base of operations for Abu Nidal, the master terrorist who was responsible for the massacres at the Rome and Vienna airports. In short, most of Sterling's charges turned out to be true.

Casey somehow found the time to write several books of his own, including one on Allied espionage in World War II (about which he obviously knew a great deal) and another on early American history. He carried a yellow legal tablet everywhere, and would scrawl in pencil in huge script, using up three or four lines at a time.

He had remarkable energy, and even in his seventies he routinely put in a twelve-hour day. He realized he wouldn't live forever, and he was determined to accomplish everything in the time he had. Despite his age and a grueling schedule, I never once recall him dozing off, not even on airplanes. An assistant would always be getting him something to work on—another file to look over, another book to read. When his plane returned to Andrews Air Force Base, his exhausted aides would drive home, desperate for sleep. Casey would head right back to the office.

This hectic pace led to a certain gruffness, and with Bill Casey there were never a lot of pleases and thank-yous. If, during a meal, he could finish some paperwork, read a book, or interview somebody (or ideally, all three at once), so much the better. Somebody once said that when Bill ate, he dripped. It isn't polite to disparage other people's table manners, but in Casey's case there weren't any. If he invited you to lunch, you rarely had the chance to enjoy it: he would gobble down a few mouthfuls while he gave out advice and fired questions. Throughout the meal he would be playing with his tie, and would occasionally use the back of it as a napkin.

He was always fidgeting, his hands constantly in motion. Usually he'd be playing with a paper clip—bending it or poking the straight end between his teeth. After a while he would appear to nod off, like a crocodile sunning himself. One eye would be closed, and the other would be open just a little. Then, just when you thought the other eye was closing—*snap!* Those jaws would go into action and suddenly the air would crackle with questions. Why do you think that? How do you know? What are your sources?

He was a more sociable man than he appeared, and despite his prodigious work habits there was room in his life for golf and other enjoyments. He liked to hold forth at parties, and he got a kick out of tossing out ideas—sometimes just to see what kind of reaction he'd get.

He was usually amenable to a good laugh—even at his own

expense. When a severe hurricane damaged his Florida beachfront home, I sent him a note of apology, ostensibly from something called the CIA Weather Control Office. The storm was supposed to have hit Cuba, I explained, but the weather control satellite had veered off target at the last minute.

Casey liked to joke about members of Congress, and he was well aware of their private peccadilloes. Although the world's most impressive intelligence resources were at his command, when it came to the private lives of senators and congressmen, he relied on an even more impressive network—the Washington rumor mill.

He loathed what Congress had become, and believed that the sport of preference on Capitol Hill was exposing covert operations. He hated testifying before the congressional oversight committees, where he was expected to reveal the intimate details of a covert operation merely to satisfy what he called their "prurient interests." In the belief that members of Congress couldn't be trusted to keep secrets, he told them as little as possible.

He died in the spring of 1987, at the beginning of the congressional hearings. I wanted to be at the funeral, but by then my presence would have been embarrassing for the President, who was also planning to attend. The night before the funeral, at the suggestion of Sophia, his widow, I flew up to New York with another of his close colleagues, and we had a drink at Bill Casey's wake on Long Island.* While we were there, one of Bill's relatives told me that during his final days, Bill had looked up at her from his bed and said, "He'll never get away with it." I've always wondered if he meant the President.

Bud McFarlane is a mystery to me, a real enigma—and ultimately a disappointment. But it wasn't always that way. He sought me out soon after he arrived at the NSC, perhaps because he saw in me some of his own past—the young Marine who had served in Vietnam, and

---

*The day of Casey's wake, I had been held in contempt for resisting a grand jury subpoena on the grounds that the special prosecutor had no constitutional legitimacy. The judge had ordered me jailed as soon as I returned from Long Island. While I was in New York, my attorneys successfully prevented my incarceration until the case could be heard by the Court of Appeals.

who later found himself as a major assigned to the White House. We grew to be close, and remained close even after he resigned. At his farewell party in December 1985, he hugged me and cried on my shoulder. There were tears in my eyes, too.

Although Bud was only six years older than I, he seemed to belong to another generation. Maybe it was his gray hair, or his long experience in Washington that gave him that older demeanor. Or perhaps it was because he had first come to the NSC back in 1973, when the Vietnam War was still going on.

There were many late nights when I would be working in the Sit Room, preparing paperwork for a meeting the next day, or for the President's morning briefing. Bud would often stop by to say good night, or to give me what Marines call a "howgoesit?"

Sometimes he would call my office at eight or nine in the evening. "You got a few minutes?"

"Sure, I'll be right over."

Some incident had occurred in the world that needed to be written up, or there was an intelligence report he wanted to show me.

Although nobody ever described McFarlane as the life of the party, he wasn't quite as stiff and reserved in private as he appeared to be in public. He would tell the occasional joke, and he did a terrific imitation of Henry Kissinger. We had a professional relationship, but he was a boss in whose presence I could lean back in my chair and say, "Lord, isn't this a mess!"

He was kind to me beyond the call of duty. In November 1983, when I was promoted from major to lieutenant colonel, Bud decided to turn it into an event. "Wear your uniform tomorrow," he told me. "This calls for a promotion ceremony, and we're going to have one." Without telling me, he had asked Wilma, his secretary, to arrange for Betsy and our children to be there.

"Come on, Bud," I told him. "I'm pretty busy, and besides, it's not necessary."

"Don't give me that. And I don't care what you have scheduled. Just be there."

The ceremony was held in the ornate Indian Treaty Room at the OEOB, and Bud administered the oath, reciting it from memory. Ron Hall, Wilma's husband, took pictures.

This turned out to be my fifth and final promotion. I still remember the first one, when I was commissioned as a second lieutenant upon graduation from Annapolis. And I remember this last time, when Bud presided. It was a warm and generous act, and I was moved that he thought to include my family, especially since they sacrificed so much while I was at the NSC. In keeping with a great old tradition of the Corps, Bud, after administering the oath, pinned one of his own oak leaves on my epaulet. Betsy pinned on the other, and she kissed me. Bud shook my hand.

Although Bud and I are very different types, there are some similarities in our backgrounds. Like me, Bud was a graduate of the Naval Academy, where he had taken his commission in the Marine Corps, and he, too, rose to the rank of lieutenant colonel. We had both served in Vietnam, although he had been there a few years earlier, and had participated in the earliest landings of American troops at Da Nang. And we both remembered all too well that the American military withdrawal from Vietnam was based on what turned out to be a false assumption: that the United States would continue to support the South Vietnamese even after our troops were gone.

The similarity of these events to the Nicaraguan situation was hard to ignore, and we both felt strongly that the tragedy of Vietnam should not be repeated in Central America. As Bud once put it, "The people who went through Vietnam came away with the profound sense that a government must never give its word to people who may stand to lose their lives, and then break faith."

Unlike me, Bud had come to his current job with considerable experience in both government and foreign policy. He had been a military aide to Henry Kissinger in 1973, and when Kissinger became Secretary of State, Bud remained at the NSC under Brent Scowcroft. Later, after retiring from the Marines, Bud joined the staff of the Senate Armed Services Committee under the tutelage of Senator John Tower.

After Reagan was elected, Bud's career really took off. When Al Haig became Secretary of State, he brought McFarlane to the State Department. Bud had been one of the leaders of the administration's push to get Congress to approve the sale of AWACs aircraft to Saudi

Arabia, which was when I first met him. Shortly afterward, when Bill Clark replaced Richard Allen as national security adviser, Bud came over from State as Judge Clark's top deputy. In 1983, when Clark left to become Secretary of the Interior, the President named McFarlane as national security adviser.

While other candidates had been suggested, most people thought McFarlane was a good choice. Bud had earned a fine reputation as a bright and talented man who worked hard and got the job done. He was also known to have excellent relations with the Congress, a highly prized asset in the Reagan administration.

I respected and admired him. Some people came to see Bud as too ambitious, but he was so adept at covering his ego that I didn't even notice that side of him. He occasionally admitted to a desire to become Secretary of State, but I believe that his aspirations went even further. I think he wanted to be President.

And yet I never had the impression, as some observers have suggested, that McFarlane was trying to outdo Henry Kissinger, his old mentor. On the other hand, I have no doubt that Bud was influenced by Kissinger, and that he hoped to emulate some of Dr. K's accomplishments. Kissinger had been applauded around the world for making a secret trip to China and creating an historic opening to that country during the Nixon years. I believe that Bud saw our trip to Iran as his chance to accomplish something similarly impressive.

But Bud McFarlane was no Kissinger. From my contact with Kissinger, who headed the President's Commission on Central America, I could see immediately that he was a man of enormous self-confidence. When Kissinger was insulted in a meeting with the Sandinista leadership in Managua, he was strong enough not to let it bother him.

Bud McFarlane was less secure. He once stormed out of a meeting in Honduras because of a minor mistake in translation that he perceived as a slight. There was an element of this in all of Bud's trips: I'm Robert McFarlane, the emissary of the President of the United States, and I'm not going to be pushed around by any tinhorn official. This attitude surfaced several times in Tehran, when Bud perceived diplomatic insults in what was merely incompetence.

Unlike Kissinger, who was a strategic thinker, Bud was primarily a synthesizer of other people's views. Some of us on his staff would encourage Bud to stand up to Weinberger or Shultz, but his natural inclination was to avoid confrontation. He looked for a way to work with everybody. He wanted people to like him, and most of us did.

He was reserved—almost to the point of being mysterious. He kept his own counsel, and preferred to meet with staff officers individually on issues of substance. The regular morning meetings in the Sit Room and the weekly meetings of the entire NSC staff were usually perfunctory events. Rarely did we have meetings—as I had expected when I first came to the NSC—where a group of us would sit around and discuss the wisdom of various options.

McFarlane was well aware that he was never really "one of the boys," which put him at a real disadvantage within the President's inner circle. The rest of the President's top advisers were either wealthy, self-made men or gregarious locker-room buddies; one or two, like Don Regan and Bill Casey, were both. Bud mentioned on several occasions that Ronald Reagan preferred the company of these affluent, outgoing guys over the reserved Washington types like himself. That was true, although it shouldn't have come as a surprise after Bud's many years in government. Like most politicians, Ronald Reagan disliked government bureaucrats, and McFarlane's great frustration was that he was usually perceived as just that.

And perceptions are everything in Washington. Some foreign policy officials, like Kissinger, Brzezinski, and Kirkpatrick, were valued as intellectuals or academic experts. Others, like Al Haig and John Poindexter, were respected as military officers. Then there were the self-made types, like George Shultz, Jim Baker, and Bill Casey. A fourth group of inner-circle advisers consisted of the king's own friends, like Bill Clark, Ed Meese, and Mike Deaver.

McFarlane didn't fit into any of these categories, and it must have rankled him terribly to be relegated instead to the ranks of the despised but essential bureaucrats. He deserved better. He was both a Marine and a scholar, and had probably written a good deal of what Kissinger was credited with. Many of Ronald Reagan's positions on the big foreign policy issues of the day—arms control, Soviet-American relations, and the Middle East—had emanated from McFarlane's pen.

But while McFarlane was a good writer, in person he often came across as pretentious—assuming you could understand what he was saying. Everyone made fun of his language, which was oblique and indirect even by Washington standards. Some people thought he was putting on airs and deliberately trying to be incomprehensible. Perhaps the most famous example of McFarlanese occurred when he testified under oath before the House Foreign Affairs Committee on December 8, 1986. In response to a question about third-country support for the Nicaraguan resistance, McFarlane replied, "The concrete character of that is beyond my ken."*

I still don't know why Bud resigned. He said he was leaving to spend more time with his family, but nobody in Washington believed *that*, probably because almost nobody in Washington does spend much time with his family. (And I, alas, was no exception.) In addition to the constant feuding between Shultz and Weinberger, Bud had numerous run-ins with Don Regan, who generally made life miserable for him. Some people thought that Bud was leaving his job in order to run for Congress or the Senate. His father had been a Democratic congressman from Texas, and Bud had grown up in Washington and was at home inside the Beltway. But I don't think he seriously entertained that possibility.

Well after he resigned as national security adviser, Bud continued to wield considerable influence over the course of American foreign policy. Although he no longer worked at the White House, he still had a secure White House phone system and PROFS† terminal in his home, both of which were maintained by the White House Communications Agency and protected by a security system installed by the Secret Service. And he kept his blue White House pass, which allowed him to come and go whenever he pleased.

After he left, we stayed in touch through the PROFS and the secure telephone. He continued to be interested in what I was doing, both to assist the contras and to pursue the Iran initiative, and at the time, he clearly approved of both projects. In the spring of 1986 he even proposed that I join him in his new position at the Center for Strategic and

---

*This statement was one reason that Bud pled guilty to a charge of withholding information from Congress.
†Professional Office System, an IBM electronic mail network.

International Studies, a conservative think tank in Washington.*

On February 8, 1987, just prior to his third meeting with the Tower Commission, Bud McFarlane took an overdose of Valium in an apparent suicide attempt. He was found unconscious, and was rushed by ambulance to Bethesda Naval Hospital. "I thought I had failed the country," he said later.

I heard about it on the radio, and I was shocked. By then I had learned to check with my lawyers before taking any action, and they asked me not to visit him in the hospital. They did, however, permit me to write him a letter. In it, I told Bud that I, too, had once suffered despair but had come to know that God never allows us to be burdened with more than we can bear—as long as we stick with Him. Having spent most of the previous five years with Bud, I thought I could offer him some hope for the future.

He had so much to lose, and he lost it all. Iran-contra was his undoing, and his apparent suicide attempt undid him further. When I left the White House, I had expected that of all the people who might have defended me from the absurd allegation that I had been off on my own, Bud was the most likely to step forward and say, "That's ridiculous. Ollie always told me what he was doing, and I always told him to go ahead." I hoped that Admiral Poindexter, too, would say that, and he did. But from Bud I expected it.

But the Bud McFarlane who testified at the hearings, and again at my trial, was a different man from the one I thought I knew. Ironically, backup copies of thousands of computer messages that McFarlane, Poindexter, and I had written to one another were discovered just before Bud was taken to the hospital. According to one theory, this discovery precipitated his overdose of Valium. But although the PROFS notes and scores of memos taken from my office by the Iran-contra investigators provided documented evidence that he had approved of my activities, Bud continued to maintain that he knew

---

*PROFS message, McFarlane to North, March 11, 1986: "Frankly, I would expect the heat from the Hill to become immense on you by summer. Consequently, it strikes me as wise that you leave the White House. At the same time, there will be no one to do all (or even a small part of what) you have done. And if it isn't done, virtually all of the investment of the past five years will go down the drain. How's this for a self-serving scenario: 1. North leaves the White House in May and takes 30 days leave. 2. July 1, North is assigned as a fellow at the CSIS and (lo and behold) is assigned to McFarlane's office. 3. McFarlane/North continue to work the Iran account as well as to build other clandestine capabilities so much in demand here and there."

very little about what I had been doing for the resistance.

And that's what he claimed at the hearings. But a year later, when he appeared as a prosecution witness at my trial, the full nature of his approval for my involvement with the contras was exposed during the cross-examination by Brendan Sullivan. Bud's statements were so muddled and incoherent that the judge called the lawyers up to the bench. "This man has told so many stories since he has been on direct [examination]," said the judge, "that there isn't any way to know what he believes or what he knows. He is an intensely unreliable witness in almost every respect of his testimony."*

Naturally, I felt betrayed by Bud's version of events. But even more than that, I felt sorry for him.

When McFarlane resigned as national security adviser, Admiral John Poindexter took over. I liked him then, and I like him now. He brings to mind a scene in a movie I once saw, where a British sergeant major and his men are attacked by a tribe of Zulu warriors. As the air is filled with spears and arrows and the defensive line begins to waver, the sergeant major calmly tucks his baton under his arm and walks along the trench line. Showing no hint of anxiety and not a trace of fear, he circulates among the troops saying, "Steady lads, steady now."

That's how I think of John Poindexter—steady. Those of us from military backgrounds tend to judge others by whether or not we would want to have that person next to us during a firefight. John Poindexter is just the man I would want at my side when the shells are coming in.

Poindexter, too, had attended the Naval Academy, and it was well known (although he never mentioned it) that he had graduated first in his class of nine hundred. He was also the midshipman brigade commander—an appointment of extraordinary honor, and a tribute to his leadership ability. (The only other man I know of who was awarded both such distinctions was Douglas MacArthur, at West Point.) Poindexter went on to earn a doctorate in nuclear physics from Cal Tech. From 1976 to 1978 he served as executive assistant to the Chief of Naval Operations, and was promoted to rear admiral

---

*"I'm not at all sure that it's intentional on his part," Judge Gesell added. "I'm not at all sure he isn't a victim, a physical victim, of what he has been going through. But the fact of the matter is, he is not a reliable witness."

in 1980. A year later, he came to the White House as a military assistant to Richard Allen. In 1983 he became Bud McFarlane's deputy, and little more than two years later was appointed national security adviser.

When McFarlane recommended Poindexter for the job, he informed President Reagan that the admiral had already been offered the prestigious job of commander of the Sixth Fleet. The President approved Bud's memorandum recommending Poindexter's appointment as national security adviser, and added an eerily prescient notation in his own handwriting: "I hope this doesn't hurt his future career."

Contrary to popular myth, John Poindexter was more than an aloof, balding, pipe-smoking automaton. He was also capable of brief forays into anger or humor, although he didn't remain long in either place. More than any man I've ever known, the admiral kept his feelings to himself. He actually made McFarlane seem colorful.

Some people found him almost unbearably taciturn. Certainly he was reserved and formal. Even in private, he always referred to President Reagan as "the President." I was never at his home, but I knew that his wife, Linda, had been ordained an Episcopal priest, and that they had five fine boys, four of whom were in the Navy. By his standards, we were on a first-name basis: he called me Ollie, and I called him Admiral.

He would use his pipe as a way to mull over a thought before he spoke. I can see him now, measuring the competing views of his staff officers as he filled the pipe with tobacco. When it was finally lit, he'd send up a thick cloud of smoke—a signal that he was about to weigh in with his decision.

When you came to him in busy situations, he gave you only as much time as it took to clean the pipe, fill it, and light it. If you hadn't stated the gist of the problem and offered a recommendation by the time the smoke appeared, you might as well go back to your office to think things through in greater depth.

He was a tireless worker and a classic introvert—reserved, thoughtful, and careful. Later, at the hearings, he described himself as a "very low-profile person." That was an understatement. As he put it, "I don't feel that I need a lot of acknowledgment in order to get any sort of psychic income." That's true. John Poindexter was a man with no hidden agenda. He simply wanted to serve wherever he was sent.

He hated politics. Unlike McFarlane, who had excellent connections on Capitol Hill, the admiral seemed to have no friends in Congress, and certainly none in the media. He was reclusive, which was unusual in high government circles, where most people clamor to be visible. There were days when he took all three meals in his office. He was once asked why he ate breakfast and lunch at his desk, but moved over to a table in the corner for dinner. His reply was classic: "Because variety is the spice of life." He meant it, too.

Next to his family, his great love was technology. Once, during a trip to Central America, he asked me what my hobbies had been when I was a kid. I told him that I used to build and fly model airplanes, which was how I had learned the virtue of patience. Then I asked him about his hobbies—assuming he had any. The conventional wisdom around the NSC was that other than going to church and spending time with his family, John Poindexter did nothing but work.

He thought for a moment, and then distantly allowed as to how, in his "off-duty" hours, he had built several televisions and personal computers.

I was impressed. "You build them all from kits?"

"No," he replied. "I build them from scratch. It's more fun that way."

I should have known. Back in 1982, when Poindexter was a military assistant to Judge Clark, he had initiated a massive upgrade of our telecommunications capabilities. One part of this project was the installation of PROFS, which ran on a mainframe computer that was installed and maintained for the NSC by the White House Communications Agency. When you keyed into the system by typing in your password—and you had better have gotten it right the first time—a warning message would appear on the screen to remind you the system was classified. It was also protected against electronic emissions that could conceivably be read from outside the building.

The PROFS system was a godsend, for it saved us countless hours that would otherwise be taken up with meetings and phone calls. It also meant that if Fawn Hall had already left for the evening and I wanted to draft a memorandum for the State Department, I would compose the memo and transmit it directly to her terminal. The next morning, when she came in, it would be waiting for her to convert into the appropriate format and print on letterhead stationery.

But the PROFS went far beyond convenience. It also reduced the amount of paper floating around the NSC, most of which was highly sensitive and classified. Less paper, in turn, meant less risk of a security breach.

For many of us, the PROFS terminals became a free and uninhibited means of communication, just like a secure telephone. Not only was it private and easy to use, but nobody, apparently not even the admiral, suspected that the messages were permanent. We were all under the impression that once we deleted a PROFS message, it disappeared forever. It turned out, however, that the "delete" button wasn't as powerful as we believed. Our correspondence might be gone from our screens, but it was hardly forgotten. The computer kept it in its memory.

Early in 1987, during the Tower Commission's investigation, a young military technician with the White House Communications Agency suspected that copies of our PROFS messages might still be retrieved from backup tapes and the main computer. He turned out to be right. My lawyers were overjoyed at this discovery. I had described my many written exchanges with McFarlane and Poindexter, but until now the lawyers were missing what lawyers really crave—documentary evidence. The PROFS notes, along with my office files that turned up shortly before my trial, verified my claim that what I had done was known and approved by my superiors. Even so, I never imagined that the White House would allow so much of this highly classified material to be published.

Unlike McFarlane, who had extensive experience in foreign affairs, John Poindexter came to the job without much background in the upper echelons of government. And yet he made a vital contribution to our national security, although few people are aware of it. Poindexter accompanied the President to the Reykjavik summit in October 1986, where President Reagan was on the verge of capitulating on the Strategic Defense Initiative in order to achieve a breakthrough in arms-control talks with the Soviets. John Poindexter was far too modest to say so, but to my knowledge he was the only high-level American official at the summit who held firm in the face of enormous pressure from Congress, the State Department, the media, and many in the scientific community, all of whom thought that SDI should be negotiable.

The Soviets were more realistic. They understood that their technology was light-years behind ours, and that they couldn't afford even to try to catch up. Because John Poindexter convinced the President that SDI was not negotiable, the summit appeared to be a failure. But it was shortly after the Reykjavik summit that the Soviets agreed to withdraw their intermediate-range missiles from Europe, pull out of Afghanistan, and enter into serious negotiations on limiting nuclear weapons. Even if John Poindexter had accomplished nothing else in his tenure as national security adviser, he deserves America's gratitude for that alone.

He served his country loyally and well, and what was his reward? Three concurrent six-month sentences. It made me sick when I heard the verdict, and sicker still when I heard about the sentence. He never should have been charged to begin with. Breaking the law was the furthest thing from his mind.

I'm not the only one who feels that way about him. As I travel around this country, people are always coming up to ask, "How's the admiral?" They respect him, and they have a great deal of compassion for a man who served his boss, did his job, and was then punished by politicians who were out to get the President. What happened to John Poindexter was an outrage.

9

"We Bag the Bums"

There were only two occasions when I saw President Reagan get really angry, and they both had to do with Beirut. The first time was on October 23, 1983, just after the terrorist bombing of our Marine barracks at the Beirut airport. The President was in Georgia on a weekend golf trip, and when the news came in he flew back immediately. He was in a white rage as he walked into the Sit Room, but he was also as alert and as purposeful as I'd ever seen him. "We'll make them pay," he said, and he clearly meant it.

The second time was in June 1985, during the hijacking of TWA flight 847 between Athens and Rome. The hijackers flew to Beirut, where they killed Robert Stethem, an American Navy diver, and dumped his body on the runway. For seventeen days there was live coverage of the hijacking, with those unforgettable pictures of the American pilot peering out of his cockpit window while a terrorist with a mad grin held a gun to his temple. The terrorists wanted us to look impotent, and they certainly succeeded.

During the crisis, the President convened several meetings of his National Security Planning Group (NSPG) in the Situation Room. As we were leaving one such meeting, Bill Casey said to McFarlane, "I've got something to show you. Can we talk?" When we got to McFarlane's office I turned to leave, but Casey said, "If you don't mind, I think Ollie should see this." Bud nodded, and Casey handed McFarlane a sheet of paper on which he had outlined plans for a new CIA antiterrorism unit. "I've talked to Cap about this," he said. "He'll support it if you do."

McFarlane read the proposal and handed it to me saying, "Do up a new NSDD and a Finding to cover this." I ended up writing three separate National Security Decision Directives for the President to sign. One created a task force chaired by Vice President Bush to develop new ideas. The second outlined new security measures for U.S.-operated aircraft and domestic airport security. The third document formalized an improved structure for dealing with the terrorist threat, and officially sanctioned a secret entity with a mandate to coordinate our government's response to international terrorism—preemptively if possible, reactively if necessary. I became its first chairman, which made me the de facto counterterrorism coordinator.

Despite my deep involvement with the contras and on the Iran initiative, I actually spent more hours working on counterterrorism than on anything else. My appointment was never made public, but whenever a terrorist event took place—and minor incidents occurred far more often than the media reported—I was the guy who got the call.

The Task Force was established as an offshoot of the Terrorist Incident Working Group (TIWG), a government-wide committee formed in 1983. But for a variety of reasons, the TIWG just hadn't worked.

Among other things, it was simply too large to be effective. "It takes far too long to get nothing accomplished," said Admiral Art Moreau, the representative from the Joint Chiefs of Staff, before he stopped attending. The very size of the TIWG created an obstacle to confidentiality. The representatives from the CIA, the FBI, and the Pentagon often sat at these meetings like mummies, unwilling to discuss classified details about their counterterrorism capabilities for fear the information would leak.

But the biggest obstacle to an effective response was that terrorism was seen as an "international" problem, which therefore required foreign policy "expertise." For that reason, all TIWG meetings were chaired and hosted by the State Department. But a committee chaired *at* State and *by* State was inevitably regarded by the other agencies as being *for* State. And the State Department was itself so large that practically every major terrorist event touched off an internal bureaucratic battle over exactly which bureau at State would have the honor of sabotaging an effective response. After one Palestinian terrorist attack in which Americans, Europeans, and Israelis were killed, a dispute raged for hours as to which bureau—European, Middle East, or Counterterrorism—would chair the meeting and then draft a message or prepare a press statement.

Whenever terrorists attacked an American embassy, the typical TIWG response was to build a higher wall around the complex and review the security procedures. Going after the perpetrators was rarely even considered.

The TIWG continued to exist after the Task Force came into being, but operational responses to terrorist threats or attacks were now coordinated by this small group, which met at the White House. My associates on the Task Force included Noel Koch (and later Richard Armitage) from Defense, Dewey Clarridge and Charlie Allen from the CIA, Buck Revell and Wayne Gilbert from the FBI, Bob Oakley from State, and Art Moreau (and later General Jack Moellering) from the Joint Chiefs of Staff. These were highly placed men with excellent access to the heads of their respective agencies. They were cool under pressure, and they knew how to move quickly. If a proposal was absurd, they'd say so. But if it was imaginative or bold, they wouldn't block it merely because of "NIH" syndrome—Not Invented Here, the recurring disease of Washington's bureaucracies.

The members of the Task Force were all linked by secure phone lines, fax machines, and a computer network. While the Task Force was designed to be action-oriented, much of our work was devoted to planning. One of our first projects was to start building an all-source classified data base that could be used in a crisis. This data base included information essential to resolving terrorist incidents around the world. The idea was to have this information available to those who needed it at a moment's notice.

Although the data base itself was classified, much of the information it contained was derived from open sources. But one of its more sensitive areas was a detailed description of what kinds of information could, and could not, be revealed to specific countries.

Rod McDaniel, a Navy captain who later became executive secretary of the NSC, was given the thankless task of building these data bases and coordinating the effort with the appropriate agencies of our government. His small, supersecret team worked out of a highly secure, restricted space directly below my office, and was linked to it by scores of cables drilled through the floor. McDaniel's group was still engaged in the monumental process of collecting and updating this information when I was fired in 1986.

Except for times of crisis, which had their own momentum, the Task Force normally met three or four times a month to discuss ongoing covert initiatives aimed at frustrating terrorists before they could strike. At Buck Revell's urging, we drafted, and the TIWG supported, new legislation that extended the authority of the Justice Department to apprehend international terrorists who harmed Americans or American property overseas. But operations of this kind took time. One of them, initiated in mid-1986, was aimed at capturing Fawaz Younis, a Palestinian hijacker who had come to my attention through the Drug Enforcement Agency during our hostage recovery efforts. The Task Force coordinated a remarkably effective effort among the alphabet soup of government agencies—the DEA, the CIA, and the FBI—and Younis was eventually captured. Ironically, he was tried in Washington in the same courthouse and at the same time as I was.

By no stretch of the imagination were we always successful. But on several occasions we succeeded in our ultimate goal of preventing a terrorist attack before it occurred. And sometimes we were able to engineer an effective resolution to an ongoing event.

The most famous of these, and certainly one of the most successful, followed the hijacking of an Italian cruise ship, the *Achille Lauro*.

It began on October 7, 1985, a Monday, and my forty-second birthday. The ship, which had left its home port of Genoa four days earlier, had dropped off most of its passengers that morning in the Egyptian city of Alexandria, where they began a bus tour of the Pyramids. They were to board the ship again that night in Port Said, and from there they would sail on to Israel.

The *Achille Lauro* was thirty miles from Port Said when it was taken over by four Palestinian terrorists who had come on board with false passports. It had been twenty-five years since a cruise ship was last hijacked, and like most ships, the *Achille Lauro* had no security procedures, not even a metal detector. As a result, the terrorists had been able to bring aboard all the tools they needed: weapons, ammunition, and hand grenades.

We learned later that they hadn't actually intended to hijack the ship. Originally, the terrorists had planned to carry out an attack on land when the *Achille Lauro* docked at the Israeli port of Ashdod. But when one of the ship's stewards found them cleaning their weapons in a cabin, the terrorists panicked. They rushed into the ship's dining room and rounded up about a hundred passengers. They then demanded the release of fifty Palestinian terrorists in Israeli jails.

The following day, off the coast of Syria, they murdered Leon Klinghoffer, a retired American citizen who had suffered a stroke and was confined to a wheelchair. They announced his death to the Syrians over the radio, and threatened to start killing other passengers unless their demands were met.

I had just arrived at my office that Monday morning when I was called by the Senior Watch officer in the Situation Room. He had received a "heads up" from CIA headquarters, but no hard intelligence. "Something is going on with an Italian cruise ship somewhere in the Med," he told me. "They're sending a mayday. It could be terrorists. I'll get back to you as soon as I hear more."

I immediately called Charlie Allen, the CIA's expert on terrorism. Charlie knew the name of the ship, and told me it had been seized with some Americans aboard. We both did what by now had become routine during terrorist events: we turned on CNN. The admiral called after seeing the first alert: "Why don't you get your group together and come up with some recommendations?" I quickly typed up a computer message for the Task Force members, calling them to a meeting in the Sit Room later that morning.

At the meeting, we immediately agreed that the President should authorize the dispatch of a JSOC (Joint Special Operations Command) team to the Mediterranean. In addition to a highly mobile headquarters element, JSOC also has several special ops teams. These small, highly trained military units use the latest equipment and just about every possible type of technology. They have the ability to get to the scene of action by almost any conceivable means, and are ready to deploy to a trouble spot at a moment's notice.

Recommending that the President deploy JSOC forces was not something we did lightly. It meant that the United States was about to commit American military forces to possible hostile action. But it was essential to start planning for a possible military operation in case the hijacking could not be resolved peacefully. As more and more information arrived, the group began to explore a wide range of options, including some that were right out of James Bond stories and others that were somewhat less preposterous.

The main challenge facing JSOC was how to board the ship and subdue the terrorists without hurting the hostages. After several conversations between Admiral Art Moreau and General Carl Stiner, the JSOC commander, it was agreed that we should position a special ops team near the scene so that it could quickly move to the ship. By noon on that first day, we knew the terrorists were heavily armed. And while the ship's captain had reported only four of them, he might have been saying that with a gun to his head. There could also be additional terrorists on board who hadn't yet shown themselves.

The uncertainty about the size of the terrorist force on the ship delayed the JSOC deployment. They could accomplish this mission in a number of interesting ways, but they wanted to make sure that they took with them everything they might possibly need. Once they took off, they would be ten to twelve hours from their U.S. base.

You might have thought that by this time, with all the terrorist incidents that had occurred during the 1980s, the United States would have had several counterterrorist units stationed overseas and ready to strike. Incredibly, we didn't.

In the Task Force, we had done everything we could to make that happen, but we hadn't succeeded. The State Department didn't want us to position counterterrorist units overseas covertly, because this could anger our allies when they eventually learned about it. The CIA and the Joint Chiefs didn't want us to do it openly—not only for security reasons, but also because the host governments might not approve of a particular mission.

And so nothing happened. Despite the obvious need to move quickly in an emergency, we never succeeded in getting the upper echelons at State and Defense to agree to this crucial preparation for a crisis *before* it occurred. I used to wonder: how many dead Americans will it take before we do something?

The Israelis had time and again offered to make their own bases available for such prepositioning, but Cap Weinberger wouldn't hear of it. And the State Department was totally uncooperative—although Shultz was usually the first to complain when we didn't have forces on the scene. The Air Force had hundreds of transport planes, but the Pentagon refused to leave two of them sitting on a runway unless a crisis was already in progress. But by then, of course, the whole world can see what you're up to. The press gathers at the end of the runway at Pope Air Force Base in North Carolina, just waiting for the planes to take off.

At midnight on Monday, the special ops team finally took off for the Mediterranean. Meanwhile, the job of the Task Force was to look for other solutions. Working out of the Crisis Management Center at the OEOB, we drafted a flurry of cables to our embassies in Egypt, Syria, Italy, Algeria, Greece, and even the Soviet Union. It was my job to draft cables from Robert McFarlane to his British counterpart.

The biggest challenge in drafting these messages wasn't putting the words on paper; it was coordinating those words within the U.S. government—where it seemed that practically everybody had a "need to know" and a comment. By comparison, my later dealings with the Iranians were relatively easy. The Iranians we met with didn't always tell the truth, but at least their numbers were limited.

By Tuesday afternoon, the *Achille Lauro* was approaching Tartus, Syria, where the terrorists requested political asylum. We drafted several urgent cables for State to send on to our embassy in Syria. The U.S. ambassador was instructed to immediately ask the Syrian government, in the strongest possible terms, to deny the terrorists' requests.

It was during this Syrian standoff that Leon Klinghoffer was killed. We later learned that the terrorists shot him in the head and ordered two crew members to dump his body and his wheelchair into the ocean. But all we knew at the time was what the hijackers told the Syrians over the ship's radio. They bragged about murdering an American, and threatened to kill additional passengers unless they were granted asylum. Although we had no way of knowing for sure that the terrorists' claim was true, we were all stunned as we read the reports of the murder and the threat to kill more of their seaborne hostages. Art Moreau went into the Situation Room Watch Officers' area, picked up the handset to the satellite radio, and had a long conversation with General Stiner, who was now on the ground at an allied base in the Mediterranean. Moreau signed off by saying, "We've got to get those bastards."

The Syrians refused to give in to the hijackers' demands—not from any lack of sympathy for the terrorists, but because by now the whole world was watching. We also suspected that President Assad relished the opportunity to undermine Yasir Arafat. And we were fairly sure that despite Arafat's fervent denials, he was up to his ears in this event.

When the Syrians turned them down, the terrorists ordered the ship's captain to return to Egypt. Night had fallen, and the weather in the eastern Med was rapidly deteriorating. As the storm intensified, we lost track of the ship. Until now, our intelligence agencies had been tracking the *Achille Lauro* by satellite, Navy aircraft, and the ship's own navigation reports. For a while, the captain had continued his normal practice of announcing his exact location during his calls to the ship's home office. But when the terrorists caught on, they quickly put a stop to it.

Despite our advanced technology, it is extremely difficult to pinpoint a single vessel among many in a big ocean, especially in bad weather. If you're forced to rely on ships and aircraft for surveillance, there's a risk that the terrorists might notice, and could retaliate by killing passengers. After several anxious hours and long discussions with the CIA and other agencies, I called Major General Uri Simhoni, the military attaché at the Israeli embassy in Washington. Back in June, we had worked together on the hijacking of TWA flight 847, and we trusted each other. I gave Simhoni the last reported position we had for the *Achille Lauro*, and asked if his people could help. About a half an hour later, he called me back with the ship's exact location. From his prompt response, I surmised that the Israelis had been following the ship ever since the hijacking began. Israel's ability to gather human intelligence in the Middle East was widely respected, but even our own government often underestimated their technical abilities.

We spent a long, sleepless night in the Situation Room, watching and waiting as the ship sailed back to Egypt. Early Wednesday morning we lost the ship again. Once again, Simhoni put us back on track.

Meanwhile, looking through the intelligence traffic, Charlie Allen noticed that Abul Abbas, the head of the Palestine Liberation Front and a member of the PLO executive committee, had suddenly been granted diplomatic clearance into Egypt. Charlie, who had been working nonstop in the Crisis Management Center and the Sit Room since Monday, had returned to his office for a change of clothes and a brief rest. He called us on the speakerphone and pointed out that Abbas was a key Arafat lieutenant with a history of brutal but poorly executed attacks on Israeli citizens. "Let's watch this guy," he said. "I wouldn't be surprised if he planned the whole thing."

As soon as Abbas arrived in Egypt, he began to play the role of a neutral peacemaker dispatched by Arafat to help "resolve" the hijacking. But when the *Achille Lauro* came within radio range of Alexandria, and Abbas started "negotiating" with the terrorists, they greeted him with the words, "Commander, we are happy to hear your voice." That's when we knew Charlie was right.

But what we didn't know was that Arafat and Abbas had struck a deal with Egyptian president Hosni Mubarak. Over the ship's radio, Abbas explained to the terrorists that if they surrendered to the Egyptians they would be given safe passage out of the country. Early Wednesday evening, a tugboat sailed out of the harbor to bring the terrorists ashore. When they heard about this, Art Moreau and the JSOC planners were both relieved and disappointed. Earlier that day, the President had approved the plan to put the special ops team aboard the ship that night.

Shortly after the *Achille Lauro* arrived off Alexandria, Nick Veliotes, our ambassador in Cairo, boarded the ship. With the help of the Egyptians, the terrorists had fled just prior to his arrival. Veliotes's first words on the ship-to-shore radio came just after he had learned from the traumatized passengers and crew about the brutal murder of Leon Klinghoffer: "You tell the foreign ministry that we demand that they prosecute these sons of bitches!"

Ambassadors don't normally talk this way, and to the exhausted handful of us in the Task Force, these words came as a shock. But they were also a refreshing breath of air in the diplomatic fog.

With the murder of an American citizen confirmed, we sent a series of messages to the Egyptians—both to their embassy in Washington, and through our diplomats in Cairo—asking them to turn over the hijackers. Together with Jim Stark, a Navy captain on the NSC staff, I drafted a strongly worded personal message from President Reagan to President Mubarak, asking that the Egyptians turn the terrorists over to us—or at least to the Italians. Following the usual procedures, the document went from the NSC staff to McFarlane. Then, with clearance from State, it went to the President and on to Mubarak.

But with the hijackers safely ashore, the Egyptian government suddenly clammed up. Veliotes was unable to deliver the message to the Egyptian foreign minister, who was conferring with Mubarak and the defense minister.

By now I was thoroughly exhausted, and on Wednesday night I drove home for the first time since the hijacking began. The passengers were out of danger, and we had reason to hope that Egypt might even allow the terrorists to be extradited to the United States and put on trial for their crimes. This had never happened before, which was why Buck Revell had wanted the new anti-terrorist legislation extending the reach of the FBI. But now it was up to the diplomats. Our part was over—or so we thought.

Early Thursday morning, after a few hours' sleep, I returned to the White House. For the first time in days, the Crisis Management Center was quiet and empty. The room was littered with empty coffee cups and cigarette butts—signs of intense activity and fatigue. With a cup of coffee in my hand, I went down to the Sit Room to look through the overnight cables before the morning staff meeting. There, in the stack, was a cable that indicated the Egyptian government had let the four terrorists leave Egypt. There was also a cable reporting Mubarak's public statement about their departure. "I don't know where they went," he had said. "Possibly to Tunis. When we accepted their surrender, we hadn't known about the murder."

I was stunned to read that the terrorists had left Egypt. Mubarak might not have known for sure about the murder of Leon Klinghoffer when he cut the deal with the PLO, but he certainly knew about it by the time he let the terrorists go. And President Reagan had practically begged him to hold them.

From the Sit Room, I called Simhoni's office at the Israeli

embassy. Uri wasn't in yet, so I told one of his colleagues that the hijackers had left Egypt.

"I saw that, too," he said, "but I don't believe it, and you shouldn't either."

"What do you mean?" I asked.

"They're still there."

"How do you know?"

"Believe me, we know."

I called Charlie Allen. He couldn't confirm whether the terrorists were still in Egypt, but he hadn't seen any evidence to indicate they had left.

Just before the morning staff meeting, I told McFarlane what I had learned from Simhoni's colleague.

"He could be right," Bud said. "Check it out with all our sources."

When the morning staff meeting ended, I was back on the phone to the Israeli embassy. Simhoni was in. "Uri," I said, "where are the four thugs?"

"Still in Egypt," he replied.

"Please keep an eye on them," I said, although they were undoubtedly doing that anyway.

Jim Stark was standing next to me when I hung up. "They're still there, aren't they?" he said.

I nodded. "Why don't you call around and see what else you can find out?"

A few minutes later, Jim brought in additional confirmation that the terrorists were still in Egypt. He had also learned that the Egyptians were planning to fly them out of the country that night, and by now it was already late afternoon in Egypt. Jim called Art Moreau and Charlie Allen while I ran upstairs to grab McFarlane. Bud was about to leave for a trip to Chicago with the President, who was scheduled to give a speech on tax reform. I found him just as he was leaving to board the helicopter for the trip to Andrews. Admiral Poindexter was with him.

"Our friends say the terrorists are still in Egypt," I said, half out of breath from running up the stairs. "We've confirmed it. They're flying out tonight. Do you remember Yamamoto?"

Admiral Isoroku Yamamoto was the man who had led Japan's attack on Pearl Harbor. During World War II, after our intelligence had uncovered his flight plans to visit a naval base in the Solomon Islands, we ambushed his plane and destroyed it in the air. The idea that we might try something similar had just occurred to me.

"We can't just shoot them down, Ollie," said Poindexter.

"No," I said, "but we can intercept them and force them down at a friendly base, transfer them to one of our planes, and fly them back here for trial."

"It's a possibility," said Bud, as he ran off to board Marine One on the White House lawn. "Work out the details," he called back. "Call me in Chicago."

Over the next few hours, Jim Stark and I were on the phone continually—with the Israelis, the Pentagon, and our own intelligence services. With remarkable speed, Art Moreau began to pull together a plan for the Navy to intercept the hijackers. Meanwhile, we had only a few hours to learn exactly when, where and how they were leaving Egypt.

By mid-morning in Washington, we knew that the Egyptians had prepared a commercial airliner to fly the terrorists to Tunis that night. Once again the Israelis came through, providing us with the takeoff time, the tail number of the EgyptAir 737, the air base (Al Maza, outside of Cairo), and the information that a false flight plan would be filed for Algiers.

While Jim worked with Admiral Moreau, who was in touch with the Sixth Fleet through the Joint Chiefs' Communications Center, I drafted a message for President Reagan to send to President Habib Bourguiba of Tunisia, asking him to deny landing rights if the plane came to Tunis. Similar messages were drafted for Athens and Beirut, and the Sit Room readied all three for transmission after the Egyptian plane was airborne.

In the Mediterranean, Sixth Fleet ops officers, working directly with Admiral Moreau, had already come up with a plan for the intercept. Meanwhile, the Israelis called with dramatic news: Abul Abbas, the mastermind of this whole event, was flying out of Egypt with the terrorists!

Poindexter called Bud McFarlane in Chicago, and found him with the President at a Sara Lee bakery plant in Deerfield, Illinois. Bud had already briefed the President on Moreau's plan: F-14 Tomcats from the U.S.S. *Saratoga*, backed up by E-2C surveillance/command and control planes, would intercept the terrorists' plane and force it down either at Akrotiri, the British base on Cyprus, or at Sigonella, a joint Italian-NATO base in Sicily.

"The President likes it," McFarlane said. "Keep working on it."

Stark and I were euphoric. Although there were still many details to work out, at least we had a chance.

In approving the plan, the President had made clear that no innocent people could be hurt. The rules of engagement had to be airtight. But what if the Egyptian pilot refused to obey the instructions to land at Sigonella? Shooting down the plane wasn't an option. Even if the terrorists didn't deserve to live, there was a pilot, a copilot, and possibly a flight attendant on board. Innocent people should not have to die in order for the terrorists to be punished.

Somehow we had to make the pilot believe he had no choice but to land at Sigonella. And so one of the rules of engagement that Moreau developed allowed the Tomcats to fire warning shots across the nose of the Egyptian plane.

Stark and I were utterly amazed that Moreau was able to get the intercept plan through the Pentagon without Caspar Weinberger's coming unglued. We learned later that Weinberger had objected, and had tried to talk the President out of the operation on the grounds that it would harm our relations with Egypt. But the President wasn't buying it.

Nothing happens in government without paperwork, and at Admiral Moreau's request, Jim and I quickly prepared a directive for the President to sign. This document, which was faxed to Air Force One, ordered the intercept of the EgyptAir flight and outlined the rules of engagement that Moreau had drafted. President Reagan was flying back to Washington, and as soon as he signed it, he called Secretary Weinberger and told him he had ordered the intercept. Weinberger, who was en route from Ottawa to his summer house in Maine, called Admiral Crowe at the Pentagon and confirmed the order.

As the Navy jets scrambled off the darkened flight deck of the *Saratoga*, Moreau, Poindexter, Stark, and I began working out the final details. Our Special Ops forces, already in the air and headed for home, were diverted to Sigonella. We hadn't yet informed the Italian government of our plans for fear that the information would leak, but we would soon need permission to land. With Simhoni's help we had worked out a backup plan: if Sigonella couldn't be used, the plane would be diverted to an Israeli military base.

The EgyptAir plane took off at 11:15 P.M. Cairo time. By midnight it was just south of Crete, where the F-14s were waiting in an ambush. With their lights off and their cockpits dark, the four Tomcats throttled back to follow the Egyptian airliner. About a hundred miles behind them sat Commander Ron Sims (a pseudonym) in his E-2C Tracker. When it was time to make radio contact with the Egyptian plane, Sims would do the talking.

As Sims listened in, the Egyptian pilot requested landing rights in Tunis. Permission was denied. He tried Athens—same answer. With no place to land, the pilot, unaware that he was now flanked by two F-14s, requested permission to return to Cairo.

That's when Sims made contact with him. "EgyptAir 2843. This is Tigertail 603, over."

There was no answer. Sims repeated the message three more times before he received a reply: "Tigertail 603. EgyptAir 2843. Go ahead."

"EgyptAir 2843. Tigertail 603. Be advised you're being escorted by two F-14s. You are to land immediately—immediately—at Sigonella, Sicily. Over."

The Egyptian pilot must have been astounded. "Say again. Who is calling?"

"Roger. This is Tigertail 603. I advise you are directed to land immediately, proceed immediately to Sigonella, Sicily. You are being escorted by two U. S. Navy interceptor aircraft. Vector 280 for Sigonella, Sicily. Over."

The pilot tried to radio Cairo for instructions. But Art Moreau and the Sixth Fleet planners had anticipated this, and had directed Sims's plane to jam him up and down the radio frequency spectrum. Now the only communication the pilot had was with Sims.

"You are to turn immediately to 280," Sims repeated. "Head 280 immediately."

The two F-14s turned on their lights and flew close enough to peer into the cabin. They dipped their wings in the aviation symbol for "follow me." And to show they meant business, they blasted the EgyptAir plane with their afterburners.

The pilot got the message. "Turning right, heading 280," he

reported, and followed through. The poor guy must have been scared witless. "I'm saying you are too close! I'm following your orders. Don't be too close! Please!"

"Okay, we'll move away a little bit." Sims spoke as if he himself were flying one of the F-14s, rather than trailing them miles behind in the slower E-2C. By now the four original Tomcats had been airborne for hours and were running low on fuel. On another frequency, Sims requested new planes to replace them.

There was quite a parade heading for Sicily: in addition to the Egyptian plane, the four replacement Tomcats, and Sims's Tracker, there were also a couple of C-141s carrying General Stiner and the special ops unit. Once the EgyptAir plane was on the ground, our plan was to remove the hijackers and Abul Abbas, transfer them all to one of Stiner's C-141s, and continue on to the United States.

It was finally time to get permission to land in Sicily. Everything else was in place, and Poindexter, Stark, Moreau, and I were elated that it all seemed to be working. But now that we had to notify Prime Minister Craxi in Italy, our embassy in Rome was unable to locate him. An officer at our Rome embassy finally found him, but no one from the State Department could get through.

I remembered that Michael Ledeen and Craxi were old friends. Frantically, I called Mike at home. "We need your help," I said. Violating all kinds of security precautions, I quickly brought him up to speed. "You've got to get hold of Craxi," I said. "Otherwise those planes can't land."

Ledeen asked the White House switchboard to put him through to the Hotel Raphael, where Craxi lived. One of the prime minister's aides picked up the phone.

"He's not here," Ledeen was told.

"You'd better find him," Ledeen said in Italian. "I'm calling from the White House, and lives are at stake. If anyone dies because you won't put me through, tomorrow morning your picture is going to be on the front page of every newspaper in the world."

Unlike all the rest of our government agencies, Mike knew the right button to push. Prime Minister Craxi was on the line in less than a minute.

"Why Sicily?" Craxi wanted to know.

"Well," said Ledeen, thinking fast and taking quite a risk, "No other place in the world offers such a combination of beautiful weather, history, tradition, and magnificent cuisine. "

Craxi laughed and said he would arrange it. But it wasn't that simple. Connections between Rome and the base on Sicily were less than efficient, and Craxi's order was late getting through. The Italian air traffic controllers didn't give permission for the planes to land until the Navy aircraft declared a midair emergency. Then, in quick succession, the Egyptian 737 and the American C-141s touched down on the airfield. The Egyptian plane, still buttoned up and with one engine still running, was quickly surrounded by General Stiner's special ops unit.

At first the pilot refused to open the doors or even turn off the engine. Then General Stiner had a portable stairway brought over. Stiner, one of the braver men on this planet, laid down his weapon, climbed up the stairway, and opened the door.

He was met by an Egyptian commando officer who pointed his submachine gun straight at the general.

"I don't want you," Stiner said. "I want *them*."

After a few moments of hesitation, the commando lowered his weapon. Down the stairway came the four terrorists, together with their ringleader, Abul Abbas.

This is where the story should have ended, but events rarely turn out exactly as planned.

While Stiner's men were surrounding the plane, they, in turn, were surrounded by a team of Carabinieri—the Italian national police—who now demanded custody of Abul Abbas and his terrorists. From the Sit Room, we listened in on a live, running account of the events at Sigonella, including the confrontation between Stiner's men and the Italian police. Reluctantly, Admiral Poindexter made the only possible decision—that we couldn't risk a shootout with the Italians.

Over the course of the next few hours, the Craxi government assured us that the terrorists in their custody would be brought to trial. We, of course, wanted them to be extradited to the United States, and we continued pressing that point. The White House sent Craxi a strongly worded message, reminding him of the extradition treaty between the United States and Italy, which spelled out that a suspected terrorist could be held for up to forty-five days while evidence was collected against him.

*   *   *

The *Achille Lauro* incident ended in a tremendous anticlimax. In order to put the four terrorists on trial, the Italians needed evidence of their crimes. For the past three days, the Task Force had worked this operation from the seat of its pants. It had succeeded brilliantly, and we were exhausted. But the legal battle had only begun.

Attorney General Meese and a deputy from the FBI came down to the Sit Room to help us prepare the necessary paperwork for a warrant to be drawn up. The Justice Department had to show a federal judge that there was enough evidence against the terrorists to present a reasonable case. But most of the evidence consisted of extremely sensitive intelligence that had been gathered by our own agencies as well as the Israelis. The Israelis were willing to help us in a variety of practical ways, but they weren't willing to expose their sources and methods—and neither were we.

But with the help of the Israelis, we were able to collect enough evidence to take before a judge. It was during the process of building this evidence for extraditing the terrorists that I had extensive contact with Amiram Nir, Prime Minister Peres's coordinator for counterterrrorism. Over the next fourteen months, I would get to know Nir much better.

Not everyone was as euphoric about the outcome as we were in the Task Force. George Shultz was angry about the damage that had been done to our relations with Egypt and Italy. Despite his pique, the State Department was helpful in the extradition work, and by early the next morning we had the paperwork in order. Although the situation required haste, we took care to abide by both the letter and spirit of Italian and American law.

But we didn't succeed. In the end, the four terrorists were tried and convicted in Italy. Although the state prosecutor bravely asked for life sentences, the terrorists got off with terms of twenty to thirty years. Yussef Molqi, who admitted to killing Leon Klinghoffer, was so grateful for the lenient judgment that he called out in the courtroom, "Long live Italian justice, long live Palestine."

And what about Abul Abbas? Incredibly, the Italians actually helped him escape! After bringing the five men to Rome, they separated him from the others, dressed him in a pilot's uniform, and put him on a plane to Yugoslavia. We immediately prepared extradition papers and had them served in Belgrade, but by then the battle had been lost. Yugoslavia had diplomatic relations with the PLO, and Abbas was protected under diplomatic immunity. (No, I'm not making this up.) In the days that followed, we tracked him as he fled from Belgrade to Baghdad, where he became a permanent guest of that great human rights advocate Saddam Hussein. As far as I know, he's still there.

Not that there was any doubt, but the trial made clear to the world that Abul Abbas had indeed planned the entire operation. He and three of his lieutenants were tried and sentenced in absentia to life terms.

But the big fish got away. Compared to Abul Abbas, the four terrorists who had carried out the hijacking and the murder were just two-bit trigger men. We knew we'd never make a dent in the worldwide terrorist threat simply by capturing a few foot soldiers. We had to get the ringleaders.

It was infuriating to lose Abbas. Despite the brilliant success of this dramatic operation, we were unable to convince the Italians to let us have the main criminal—or even to prosecute him themselves. The Italians knew full well that Abbas was the mastermind of the entire operation, but they apparently wanted the rest of the world to believe that he just *happened* to be on that unscheduled EgyptAir flight.

It was an enormous betrayal, but in retrospect it isn't all that surprising. The Italians, like the Egyptians, lacked the resolve to fight terrorism, because they feared the consequences of capturing and trying the terrorist leaders. Although we could never confirm it, I believe that both governments had made commitments to the PLO that Abbas would be released. That way, the operation couldn't be linked directly to Arafat.

Five years later, Abul Abbas surfaced again. In the spring of 1990 he planned an operation in which Palestinian commandos would land on a Tel Aviv beach and start shooting everyone they saw. The terrorists who intended to carry out this act were captured by the Israelis, and no civilians were hurt.

In March 1991, there was more news about the *Achille Lauro* terrorists. Abdulrahim Khaled, one of Abul Abbas's lieutenants, was arrested in Greece in connection with a planned terrorist event in Athens. Khaled was originally on the *Achille Lauro*, but he apparently left the ship in Alexandria just before his comrades seized it. When his true identity was revealed, the Italian government asked Greece to turn him over.

Although we were bitterly disappointed about losing Abul Abbas, the American people were jubilant when the intercept was reported. "WE BAG THE BUMS," wrote the New York *Daily News* in a banner headline. In an amusing footnote to the whole event, I was in Pat Buchanan's office, working with him on the President's announcement that the terrorists had been captured, when a call came in from Niles Latham, an editor at the *New York Post*. "We need a great headline," Niles said. "We'd like to use 'YOU CAN RUN BUT YOU CAN'T HIDE.' If you can get the President to use it, we'll put the whole line in quotes."

It was a little unusual for a journalist to suggest language for the President, but Pat and I had to acknowledge that this was a much better conclusion for the President's remarks than the ending we had written. The President used the new line, and the reaction was terrific. Niles has been telling that story for years; maybe now people will believe him.

A lot of people have given me the credit for our success in the *Achille Lauro* affair. I'm proud to have been part of it, but the praise belongs to the Navy flight planners and pilots, and a host of others. Bud McFarlane should be acknowledged for authorizing the planning for the capture, and getting the President to override Weinberger's objections. But the bulk of the credit should go to Art Moreau. He hated the Washington bureaucracy, but he was a master at cutting through it. A few months later, he was named commander of NATO's naval forces in the Mediterranean. As soon as he arrived he was targeted by the Red Brigades and several Palestinian terrorist groups. He and his wife spent that year under heavy guard. Art Moreau died of a heart attack the following year without ever being recognized for the enormous contribution he had made to the fight against terrorism.

As the old saying has it, no good deed goes unpunished. Angry voices were raised in Egypt, where Mubarak was attacked both by moderates, who thought he should have apprehended the terrorists, and by Muslim fundamentalists who were convinced he had tipped us off and enabled the capture to succeed. In Italy, Prime Minister

Craxi's coalition suffered the fate of so many previous Italian governments: it collapsed.

With all of this diplomatic fallout, our Secretary of State must have felt a fair amount of pressure. One afternoon, shortly after the fall of Craxi's coalition, George Shultz was leaving McFarlane's office as I was coming in. He looked up, glared at me, and muttered, "So here's the man who brought down the Italian government."

"Good afternoon, Mr. Secretary," I replied with a smile.

On Capitol Hill, there were others who objected. Senator Dave Durenberger, the ranking Republican on the Senate Intelligence Committee, was apparently upset that the President had supposedly violated the War Powers Resolution! Other members were outraged that we didn't consult with them before committing our Special Ops units. If we had, we'd *still* be looking for the killers of Leon Klinghoffer.

But these were exceptions. All over America, the response was overwhelmingly positive. The cooperation had been marvelous—among various branches of government, our intelligence services, and between us and the Israelis.

As successful as it was, the *Achille Lauro* episode did not end the problem of terrorism. Libya, the prime sponsor of international terrorist activity, showed no inclination to stop. On the contrary: when other supporters of terrorism closed down their training camps, Qaddafi moved in to fill the gap.

In late December 1985, Qaddafi was linked to Abu Nidal's deadly terrorist attacks at the Rome and Vienna airports. Over the winter, we watched as Qaddafi planned other terrorist events aimed at the United States. Within the administration, there was a growing sentiment in favor of a military response against Libya.

On March 28, 1986, Qaddafi made a statement calling on "all Arab people" to attack anything connected to the United States, "be it an interest, goods, ship, plane, or a person." Around the same time, our intelligence sources picked up instructions from Tripoli to various Libyan People's Bureaus—the Libyan equivalent of an embassy—to prepare for action. We didn't know what target they had in mind, but these were the same kinds of instructions that had been given to Libyan offices abroad prior to Libya's 1984 killing of anti-Qaddafi protesters in London.

A few days later, on April 5, 1986, a bomb went off at La Belle discotheque in West Berlin, a popular gathering place for off-duty American servicemen. Although we had compelling proof of Libyan complicity, there was no way to disclose the evidence without revealing sensitive details of our intelligence-gathering operations. Critics of the administration charged that we were inventing the Libyan role, but several years later, after the Berlin Wall came down, the East Germans admitted what we had claimed all along: that the orders for the bombing had come from Tripoli.

On April 14, American planes responded by bombing terrorist-related targets in Libya. As with the *Achille Lauro* incident, the Task Force coordinated the various bureaucratic requirements for the raid. But, because this action was going to be significantly more prolonged in its planning, the chair shifted from Bud to Don Fortier, by then deputy national security adviser. The strike was one of several possible responses we had considered against Libya. But it wasn't our first choice. Unfortunately, our "allies" were unwilling to support us in other measures against Qaddafi.

The action against Libya was essential in our fight against terrorism, but it wasn't undertaken lightly. There were numerous discussions about the bombing targets, and we made every effort to avoid killing innocent people. But we also knew that civilian casualties were probably unavoidable. A surgical strike is a nice concept, and while it may be achievable under test conditions when nobody is shooting at you, it rarely works as well when the air is full of antiaircraft fire. When a pilot is dodging antiaircraft missiles at six hundred miles per hour, pinpoint accuracy is an illusion.

In the old days, the United States would have found a way to assassinate Qaddafi. But despite what Seymour Hersh and other journalists have claimed, killing him was never part of our plan. On the other hand, we certainly made no attempt to protect him from our bombs. By law, we couldn't specifically target him. But if Qaddafi happened to be in the vicinity of the Azziziyah Barracks in downtown Tripoli when the bombs started to fall, nobody would have shed any tears.

While no single military strike can end the problem of terrorism, our bombing raid on Libya destroyed Qaddafi's command post and communications center. But its greatest effect seemed to have been psychological. Qaddafi immediately went into hiding in the desert, and for over a year he initiated no terrorist action of any kind. While he is still in no danger of winning the Nobel Peace Prize, it appears that the bombing raid on Tripoli taught him a lesson.

10

The Contras

I rarely met a contra I didn't like. And I never met one at all until 1983, when I was introduced to Juan. Like many members of the Nicaraguan resistance, Juan was a former Sandinista officer who had fought for years against the hated Somoza regime. This is the story he told me of how he joined the resistance.

In July 1980, on the first anniversary of the day the Sandinistas came to power, an enormous victory parade was held in Managua. In honor of the occasion, the old cathedral and the square around it were draped in red and black, the Sandinista colors. An enormous poster of a hammer and sickle was flanked by huge portraits of Marx, Lenin, Castro, and Augusto Cesar Sandino, the legendary guerrilla leader who had fought against the U.S. Marines in the late 1920s and early 1930s.

Juan was marching in the parade along with his men, and he was shocked by what he saw. After all, the Sandinistas had always denied they were Communists. He turned to his commanding officer and asked, *"¿Qué es éste?"* ("What's all this?")

"Es verdad" ("It's the truth"), said the officer.

"No por mío" ("Not for me"), Juan replied.

That night, Juan and eleven men from his unit started walking north to Honduras to join the resistance.

He was one of thousands who became what the Sandinistas called *contrarevolucionarios*—counterrevolutionaries—or contras. The resistance never liked that term, because it implied that they wanted to restore the old Somoza regime. In fact, most of the contras had supported the revolution against Somozoa. They just weren't willing to live in the totalitarian society that the Sandinistas were building.

But the name stuck—one of many public relations victories for the Sandinistas. The administration preferred to call them freedom fighters, but "contras" was so widely known that even their supporters came to use that word.

To this day, I still hear it said that the contras were a creation of the CIA. Not true. And they certainly weren't created by me, or Dick Secord, or Dewey Clarridge. To the extent that anyone "created" the contras, it was the Sandinistas.

When the Sandinistas came to power, it was with the support of the United States. The Carter administration was so intent on getting rid of the brutal Somoza regime—which was certainly a worthy goal—that nobody wanted to look too closely at how that was being done, who was doing it, or where it might lead.

The Sandinistas came to power with grand declarations of freedom and democracy. They promised a society marked by free enterprise, free elections, a free press, freedom of religion—and just about everything else the United States wanted to hear. In return, our government became their main source of support. During the first few months of the new regime, we sent Nicaragua thirty-nine million dollars in emergency food aid—a considerable sum for a country of three million people. Just stay out of El Salvador, we told them, and we'll keep those dollars flowing. In 1980 our contribution to Nicaragua was raised to seventy-five million dollars.

But as soon as they came to power, the Sandinistas began breaking their promises. Within months, anyone who wasn't a "scientific socialist" was driven out of the leadership. We know today that the Sandinistas had no intention of creating a free society—and every intention of trying to overthrow the governments of El Salvador and Honduras.

In the face of irrefutable evidence, President Carter came to have second thoughts about the Sandinistas. In the final weeks of his presidency he suspended all U.S. aid to Nicaragua and resumed support for the government of El Salvador, which was now fighting for its life.

By the time I became involved in Central American issues, I was shocked at how long it had taken us to recognize the Sandinistas' true colors. In July 1980, at their first-anniversary celebration, the guests of Nicaragua's new regime had included Fidel Castro and Yasir Arafat, and delegations from such freedom-loving states as Vietnam, North Korea, and East Germany. Meanwhile, the glowing promises of freedom had turned to dust.

Instead, the Sandinistas began organizing Nicaragua along the same lines as Cuba. President Daniel Ortega even named his younger brother Umberto as defense minister, just as Castro had done with his own brother, Raul. And like the Cubans, the Sandinistas began searching for opportunities to export what they themselves called a "revolution without frontiers."

Before long, they had replaced Somoza's dictatorship of the right with their own dictatorship of the left. They seized radio and TV stations. They herded farmers into state-run farms. They created an elaborate system of block wardens—or neighborhood spies. They censored *La Prensa*, the country's largest newspaper, and shut down the Catholic radio station. They fought against the Church, and forbade broadcasts of the Mass on radio or television. They established a secret police force and began confiscating private property. They killed, jailed, and exiled their political opponents. They started a nationwide conscription, drafted children into their youth movements, and sent the "elite" off for indoctrination in the Soviet Union, Cuba, East Germany, and Bulgaria.

And like their mentors in other Communist dictatorships, the new rulers of Nicaragua set themselves up in the finest houses, which they stocked with the best French wine and Russian caviar. It's a cliché, but that doesn't make it any less true: even the most ardent capitalist would be hard-pressed to match the material appetites and amenities of a privileged Communist. On my first trip to Managua, one of the regime's few remaining internal political opponents passed on a joke that became popular when Tomás Borge, the son of a peasant family, was named interior minister. Like many of his fellow Sandinistas, Borge had appropriated the enormous mansion of a former Somoza official. When his mother came to visit, he proudly showed her around: the swimming pool, the huge kitchens, the visitor's suite, the fountains, the patio, the splendid gardens, the maids, the butlers, and all the rest.

Halfway through the tour, she turned to her son in tears.

"*¿Mama,*" he said, "*qué pasa?*"

"Oh, Tomás," she replied. "It's so beautiful! But tell me—what will happen to all this when the revolution comes?"

When Ronald Reagan became President in 1981, he offered the Sandinistas one last chance to withdraw their support for the rebels in El Salvador and to make the promised democratic reforms at home. The Sandinistas didn't even blink. By now they were supported by a long list of governments: Cuba, the Soviet Union, the Communist bloc in Eastern Europe, Iran, and even France. And let's not forget Libya. During the Ortega years, the Libyans gave Nicaragua several *hundred* million dollars in economic assistance, not to mention technical support, weapons, and military assistance.

In March 1981, President Reagan authorized the CIA to begin supporting the growing army of Nicaraguan rebels, mostly in Honduras, who were opposed to the Sandinista regime. Congress provided funding to enable these fighters to interdict weapons and supplies on their way from Nicaragua to the FMLN guerrillas in El Salvador.

In the summer of 1981, Casey appointed Duane Clarridge, an experienced clandestine service officer and former CIA station chief, to be the CIA's link to the resistance. Officially, Clarridge's new title was head of the Agency's Latin American Division.

"I told Casey that sounded fine," Dewey told me later. "Then I got out my atlas to see what countries we were talking about."

Dewey Clarridge was a master spy who had been almost everywhere and done nearly everything. His experience in the clandestine service was so extensive that it was rumored that his résumé consisted of his name—followed by three blank pages. He had a great sense of style, and was known around Washington as an elegant dresser. One of the few times I saw Dewey get really angry was when a reporter described him in print as having shown up at a congressional hearing in a polyester suit. You'd have thought he had been called a Communist.

Clarridge and Casey had a lot in common, including an unmistakable lack of affection for the Congress. But unlike most people who had to testify on Capitol Hill, Dewey didn't even try to hide his attitude. I was with him on several occasions when senators, congressmen, and staffers asked inane questions based on farfetched newspaper stories about what the CIA was allegedly up to.

Washington is a city of rituals, and the ritual response is to say, "Thank you for the question, Senator. I'm not aware of any indication of that, but I can assure you, sir, that I will look into it closely as soon as I return to my office. I will be sure to give you a full report by tomorrow morning. You can be confident that we at the CIA share your concern about that article."

Dewey Clarridge's answers were more succinct: "That's absolute bullshit."

In the summer of 1981, Bill Casey asked Dewey to come up with some recommendations about Central America. "We can try to interdict the Nicaraguan arms shipments to El Salvador," Dewey said. "But we won't be able to cut it off completely. If the resistance can create a backfire to keep the Sandinistas busy, that will make it harder for them to concentrate on El Salvador. In other words, we've got to take the war to Nicaragua."

When Casey heard that, he knew he'd found his man.

At the time, the fledgling anti-Sandinista resistance movement along the Honduran-Nicaraguan border was being supported by a small group of Argentine officers and senior enlisted men. The Argentine military had just fought a particularly brutal war against the Montoneros, a Communist insurgency. Some of the rebels had taken refuge in Nicaragua, which had already become a kind of World's Fair for terrorists from all over the planet: the Red Brigades from Italy, M-19 from Colombia, the Baader-Meinhoff Gang from Germany, Libyans, Chinchoneros from Honduras, the *Sendero Luminoso* (Shining Path) from Peru, the IRA, and several factions from the PLO. One of the first reports I ever read about Nicaragua described a firefight between two rival Palestinian terrorist groups.

Casey met with General Leopoldo Galtieri, head of the military junta that ruled Argentina, and suggested that the United States join in supporting the anti-Communist guerrilla activity. Galtieri was delighted. But he was wary of America's reputation for abandoning its friends, and he gave Casey a prescient warning: "Don't get involved in this unless you're prepared to see it all the way through."

A month later, President Reagan signed a top-secret Finding that authorized the CIA to begin helping the rebels directly. In 1982, primarily because of the war in the Falklands, Argentina withdrew its support. From then on the Nicaraguan resistance was in the hands of the CIA.

Even so, nobody in our government was under any illusions about the Nicaraguan resistance. After all, the Sandinista military was larger than all the other armies in Central America put together. And the Soviets were equipping them with tanks, attack helicopters, long-range artillery, armored personnel carriers, and sophisticated communications equipment.

Later, as the resistance grew, the administration's goals for the resistance grew with it—to the point where we believed they could exert enough pressure on Managua to bring about a democratic outcome. And in the end, that's exactly what happened.

My own involvement with Central America began in the spring of 1982, when Roger Fontaine, who headed the Latin America section of the NSC, asked me to provide a military perspective for an NSC policy paper on Central America. Bill Clark liked the results, and he asked me to start attending a Saturday morning study group on Central America. These informal meetings were held at the CIA, and were hosted by Bill Casey in his conference room on the seventh floor of the Agency's headquarters. Jeane Kirkpatrick used to attend, along with Dewey Clarridge, Fred Ikle, General Paul Gorman, Tom Enders from the State Department, and several others. I knew little about Central America when I arrived at the NSC, but I had been reading like crazy and paying close attention to the speeches and writings of Jeane Kirkpatrick and others. The more I learned, the more reason I saw for our involvement.

I wasn't shy, and at the Saturday meetings I started asking questions and making occasional comments. Some of my ideas must have had merit, because I was soon invited to other meetings and events, including seminars at various CIA sites on the training of anti-Communist resistance movements.

Early in 1983, when Pope John Paul II was scheduled to visit Central America, I was asked to serve as a liaison from our government and to provide information on potential death threats. The Pope was not harmed in Nicaragua, but when he addressed a crowd in Managua, a "spontaneous" demonstration drowned him out. For the Sandinistas, this turned out to be a domestic and international public relations disaster.

Events like the Sandinistas' treatment of the Pope convinced Casey, Kirkpatrick, Clark, and Weinberger that the situation in Central America required more from the United States than mere containment. It was clear to them that the Soviets and the Cubans were using Nicaragua as a secure base for the attack on their next target: El Salvador.

It was also apparent that a strategy of using an indigenous resistance movement to reverse the Communist gains in Nicaragua was going to take time. In the interim, El Salvador was in jeopardy of succumbing. Judge Clark had me prepare several position papers and legislative requests in support of increased American military presence in the region—especially El Salvador.

At the time, El Salvador was squeezed between the Communist guerrillas on the left and brutal death squads on the right. Under the guise of anti-Communism, the death squads terrorized the entire country—murdering nuns, teachers, labor organizers, political opponents, and thousands of other civilians. Some officials, both in Washington and in San Salvador, preferred to sweep this problem under the rug, and tried to dismiss reports of the death squads as Communist propaganda. But a lot of it was real.

I made several trips to El Salvador, and in the summer of 1983 I wrote a paper about the death squads. From talking with our ambassador, our military liaison personnel, and with CIA people who knew the area, it was clear there were numerous allegations that the murders were connected to a leader of the right-wing Republican National Alliance Party, also known as ARENA. Back in Washington, I met with those who were lobbying the Congress on behalf of El Salvador. "Stay away from this guy and his cronies," I'd tell them. "Don't try to whitewash the problem. The death squads are real, and they must be stopped. Yes, we have to support the fight against Communism, but our ultimate goal isn't just to prevent Central America from going Communist—it's to help these countries become real democracies."

I made the same point in briefings to congressmen and senators, and to their staffs. Most of them were open to the evidence, although two or three congressional staffers advised their principals that I was soft on Communism. I've been called a lot of things, but that was a first.

On Capitol Hill, the prevailing view was that the way to combat the death squads was to withdraw the American military presence in El Salvador—which consisted of only fifty-five advisers. I disagreed. I have always resented the view that the American military contributes to an atmosphere of violence and repression. Are American soldiers known for engaging in criminal acts against the civilians of other countries? Is the United States so full of human rights abuses that our soldiers are a menace to other countries?

In places like El Salvador, American military advisers are a moderating influence. There are ways to defeat a Communist insurgency without killing innocent people, but the Salvadoran military was lacking in both discipline and experience. At the time, this was an army that was used to doing only two things: marching in parades on national holidays, and organizing palace coups. My son's Boy Scout troop had been on more camp-outs than some of these guys.

The administration's opponents in Congress argued that we shouldn't be training the Salvadoran military because it was so undisciplined. But one reason it *was* so undisciplined was that we weren't allowed to train them.

In December 1983, I was assigned to be the NSC representative on a trip to El Salvador by Vice President Bush. It was clear that unless something was done to stop the death squads and to guarantee the long-promised transition to democratic rule, U.S. military aid to El Salvador would soon be terminated.

The Vice President was given the unenviable job of delivering this message, and along with Tony Motley, the new Assistant Secretary of State for Inter-American Affairs, I was tagged to accompany him. From Andrews we flew straight down to Argentina for the inauguration of Raul Alfonsin, Argentina's democratically elected president. Then we headed north, to Central America. During the flight, Tony and I typed up the talking points for the Vice President's scheduled meeting with President Alvaro Magaña in El Salvador, and we briefed the Vice President on the situation there.

On the way to El Salvador we stopped in Panama, where Mr. Bush held a brief airport meeting with President de la Espriella and General Manuel Noriega. The Vice President reminded Noriega that he had just returned from a democratic transition in Argentina and urged that same thing had to happen in Panama.

Noriega sat there like a sphinx. In retrospect, it was clear that he didn't get the message.

I had met with Noriega before, and I would meet him several times more. Whenever I accompanied a high-level visitor to the region, whether it was Casey, Weinberger, or another senior official, we would invariably stop in Panama for a meeting with Noriega. The message from our side was always the same: democracy must prevail.

I once met with him in London after an intermediary told us that Noriega wanted to help the Nicaraguan resistance. But that meeting went nowhere. We were looking for tangible support for the contras, while he was more interested in things like bribery and murder. Sitting in the lobby of a London hotel, I admonished him that despite our antipathy to the Sandinista leadership, we could not get involved in assassinations. But if he were willing to help train contra units, provide logistical support, and even use his assets to destroy Sandinista targets in Managua, we would certainly compensate him for his efforts.

In arranging for this meeting, the intermediary had emphasized that Noriega wanted our help in "cleaning up his image." But I was blunt with him. There were reports that he was involved in drug trafficking and murder, and had ties to Cuban front companies operating in Panama. This had to stop. The best thing he could do, I told him, was to step back and allow a real democracy to emerge in his country. But he didn't listen to me, or to anyone else with that same message.

For me, one of the ugliest aspects of the whole Iran-contra affair was the way my meetings with Noriega were described in some quarters as though the two of us had some kind of alliance. We didn't. Noriega was probably the single most despicable human being I ever had to deal with. After a meeting with him, you just wanted to go home and take a shower.

After the meeting with Noriega, the Vice President's plane flew directly to San Salvador, where we landed right after a rainstorm. The air was oppressively hot, and the humidity felt like 150 percent. We stood at attention, dripping with sweat, as the band played what seemed like all two hundred verses of the Salvadoran national anthem. Then it was off to the President's residence, where the meeting rooms were right out of a movie—dark and cool, with high ceilings and slow-turning fans.

At his initial meeting with Vice President Bush, President Magaña asked if Vice President Bush would object to giving President Reagan's message on human rights directly to the Salvadoran field commanders.

The Vice President agreed.

During a break, everyone except the two leaders went upstairs, where we guzzled down glass after glass of Coca-Cola with lemon. Meanwhile, the Vice President met alone with Magaña. This was vintage Bush: long before he became President, he had a knack for developing a personal, effective working relationship with foreign leaders.

As the two men talked in the conference room, we could hear a commotion in the hallway below. I was standing beside Admiral Dan Murphy, the Vice President's chief of staff, when the head of the Secret Service detail came running upstairs. "The commanders are here," he said. "And they are *armed*. We can't let them go in with guns."

The Secret Service agent was right to be worried. Latin America wasn't the most stable place on earth, and the Vice President of the United States was about to have an unscheduled meeting with about thirty armed field commanders. It was possible that some of these guys had connections to the death squads, and that they wouldn't be too happy with the message that Bush was about to deliver.

It got so noisy outside the conference room that the Vice President came out. "What's the problem?" he asked. "We're trying to talk in here."

"These guys have guns," said Murphy. "It would be dangerous for this meeting to take place."

"Look," said Bush. "This meeting is absolutely necessary. President Magaña wants to hold it, and we're going to do it the way they've asked."

The Vice President spoke bluntly, without notes and without any diplomatic cushioning. He made it clear that if El Salvador had any interest in receiving additional American aid, the death squads had to stop and the murders of American nuns and labor leaders had to be solved. Although it was very tense in that room as Bush delivered his message, he came across as calm, strong, and determined. Some of the commanders who met with him that day were angry and defensive. They felt humiliated that a senior American official was telling them what was wrong in their own country. This was not what they had expected to hear. The Grenada operation had occurred a few weeks earlier, and some of these guys hoped that American troops would be sent to help them fight the guerrillas, or their Sandinista sponsors. But Bush's message was very different: unless you clean up your act, it's all over.

Later, during the 1988 presidential campaign, when George Bush was called a wimp, I would look back on this moment. I know a wimp when I see one, and George Bush was no wimp.

The effect of the Bush visit to El Salvador was mixed. Though death squad activity did not stop completely, the State Department was able to begin an important judicial reform program to train and protect judges, prosecutors and investigators. Investigations were opened into a number of previous murders. And, perhaps most important, the elections were held as planned. Over 80 percent of the population voted, and Napoleon Duarte became El Salvador's democratically elected president.

Although I began working on Central American issues in 1982, my involvement increased dramatically the following year when Bill Clark asked me to serve as the NSC liaison on the Kissinger Commission.* He obviously respected my abilities, but one reason I was picked was that NSC staff members were not exactly standing in line to work on Central America. This was a no-win issue, because the government was deeply divided as to how to help the nations of Central America

*In addition to Dr. Kissinger, who chaired it, the members included Jeane Kirkpatrick; Jim Wright, the democratic congressman from Texas and future Speaker of the House; Pete Domenici, Republican senator from Arizona; Michael Barnes, Democratic member from Maryland; Republican congressman Jack Kemp; John Silber, president of Boston University; William Walsh, head of Project Hope; Bill Clements, former (and future) governor of Texas; Robert Strauss, Democrat-at-large; retired Supreme Court Justice Potter Stewart; and several others.

move toward democracy. Amidst all the turmoil and infighting, by 1983 only one thing was clear and steadfast: Ronald Reagan's support for the Nicaraguan resistance.

Henry Kissinger headed the presidential commission on Central America, and my initial encounter with him was downright embarrassing. At one of the commission's first meetings, which was held at the NSC, I was asked to deliver a briefing on anti-Communist resistance movements around the world. I often used slides to enhance a briefing, and in preparing for this one I must have picked up a slide carousel that wasn't completely empty.

As the slides were projected behind me, I cheerfully began my presentation without bothering to look over my shoulder at the screen. Everything went smoothly until a familiar voice with thick German accent boomed out from the back of the darkened room.

"Major North," said the voice. "I vas unavare of anti-Soviet resistance movements in Norvay."

I slowly turned around to face the screen, which indeed showed a huge color map of Norway.

"Oops. Sorry, sir, wrong slide."

I was apparently forgiven, because when the Kissinger Commission traveled to Central America and Mexico, I went with them and helped arrange meetings with opposition groups. One of our stops was Managua, which by then was a very depressing place. After forty years of plunder by the Somozas, a terrible earthquake, and four years of Sandinista "economics," Nicaragua had become the second poorest country in the Western Hemisphere. Only Haiti was worse.

Our meetings with the Sandinistas were a complete waste of time. They would expound for hours on their grievances against us, and we would ask them embarrassing questions about human rights, freedom, and their support for the guerrillas in neighboring El Salvador and Honduras. We were clearly talking past each other, and we couldn't even agree to disagree.

During one of these sessions, Miguel d'Escoto, Nicaragua's foreign minister and a former Catholic priest, harangued us at length about the many heinous crimes the United States had committed against Nicaragua and the rest of the Third World. He had just said something about Nicaragua's being a peace-loving country—I don't recall exactly what, because I had stopped paying attention—when Senator Pete Domenici, who was sitting next to Kissinger, jumped to his feet with such energy that his chair fell over. Pete virtually exploded.

"You lying s.o.b.!" Pete yelled, which immediately woke up several members of the commission. "When you came to see me in 1978, you were wearing your collar. You said you were a persecuted priest. I took you to meet my colleagues, and you swore to us that you and your buddies only wanted to get rid of Somoza. We helped you, and *now* look at what you've done. You're arresting your opponents. You're threatening your neighbors. You're building up an enormous army. You're nothing but a damned hypocrite! You lied then, and you're lying now!" D'Escoto went white. As he sat there with his hand on his chest, he seemed to be on the verge of a heart attack. It wasn't until Pete stormed out of the room that d'Escoto began to regain his color.

Sitting just behind d'Escoto and not even batting an eyelash during Pete's tirade was the infamous Nora Astorga. She was a household name in Nicaragua, and a heroine among the Sandinistas for her role in killing one of Somoza's top generals. She had lured him into her bedroom, where he was ambushed and brutally murdered by Sandinista guerrillas. According to the story, after slitting his throat, they cut off his genitals and stuffed them into his mouth. She had actually been proposed as ambassador to the United States, but the Reagan administration had refused to accept her credentials. This became the subject of some nervous laughter among a couple of the Sandinistas' supporters in the Senate, with whom Nora Astorga was said to be on very close terms.

This was the same woman who later became the Sandinistas' human rights advocate at the United Nations.

We also met with Danny Boy himself, who unrolled his own litany of complaints about the evils of American imperialism. Ortega struck me as a dull and humorless little clerk, hunched over his papers. As he droned on from his prepared text, it was hard to imagine him as a former guerrilla leader. He reminded me of the joke about the man with "negative charisma": when this guy enters the room, it feels like three people just left.

But he sure knew how to work a crowd. When his followers were out in force, leading the chants—*"Ortega, Ortega, Ortega"*—he became a different man: proud, self-confident, and fully in charge.

Although the Reagan administration had the right approach with regard to Nicaragua, we did a lousy job of selling it. In view of the President's rock-hard commitment to the contras, why couldn't the Great Communicator rally the public to join him?

For one thing, not everybody in the administration shared the President's views. George Shultz believed the problem could be solved through negotiation. Richard Wirthlin, the White House pollster, saw Nicaragua as a no-win issue, and encouraged the President's advisers to leave it alone. With the exception of Casey and Clark, most of the President's inner circle viewed the contras as a political liability, as indeed they were. Others just didn't believe Nicaragua was a serious threat—despite the fact that the Soviets were pumping in two and a half billion dollars in military aid.

Over at the State Department, there were those who couldn't entirely give up their earlier sympathy for the Sandinistas. They refused to admit that the Sandinistas were Communists, and continued to insist, long after the evidence was in, that the new rulers of Nicaragua were merely democratic socialists and land reformers. They felt that almost any government in Nicaragua was preferable to the ruthless and corrupt regime that the Sandinistas had overthrown. And they were right: almost any government was. But not this one.

American voters had little interest in Nicaragua, especially when they were told repeatedly by the news media that the contras consisted of thugs, drug dealers, and former members of Somoza's National Guard. Besides, Central America was seen as far away, unstable, and dangerous. One survey showed that 38 percent of the American public believed that Nicaragua was in the same part of the world as Vietnam.

And for many Americans it was. President Bush was correct when he declared, following the war with Iraq in early 1991, that the Vietnam syndrome had finally ended. The specter of Vietnam was so powerful during the Reagan years that many people—including some in the administration—believed that any help we gave the Nicaraguan resistance would only bring us closer to sending our troops into a protracted jungle war.

Opponents of the resistance preyed on this fear, and brought up Vietnam at every opportunity. We have no business interfering in other countries, they said. Nicaragua has a population of three million, so how could it possibly be a threat to the United States? Even a minimal amount of support to the contras is dangerous. Remember— *this was how we got started in Vietnam.*

Those were scary words, but they just weren't true. On the contrary: supporting the contras was the best possible guarantee *against* our ever having to send American troops to Central America. Alfonso Robelo, one of the resistance leaders, said it best when he met with President Reagan at the White House. "All we want is your support," he told the President. "This is our country we're fighting for, and we're willing to shed our own blood to get it back."

Most of the contras never wanted us to send troops, and nobody in the administration who had the President's ear ever had that in mind.* But there were some right-wingers who cynically suggested that it might be best if we let the Sandinistas prevail so that the left could be blamed for "losing Central America." Then we would send in the Marines.

On the left, there were those who came to a similar conclusion through a different route: we shouldn't help the contras, they don't deserve it, and if things get bad enough down there we can always send in the Marines.

No matter which side it came from, I was horrified by this attitude. Send in the Marines? I was a Marine, and this sounded crazy to me. Sure—if war is the only alternative, send me. I'm good at it. But as long as Nicaraguans themselves were willing to risk their lives by taking on the Sandinistas, and all they wanted from us were the resources to do it, wasn't that a far better option?

Today, when support for Marxism is confined to a handful of poverty-stricken countries and certain American college professors, it's difficult to understand the popularity of the Sandinistas among American opin-

---

*Neither did President Reagan, despite the belief among many congressional Democrats that he was continually looking for a pretext to invade Nicaragua. At a news conference in February 1982, the President was asked about the possibility of sending American troops to Central America. He replied: "Maybe if they dropped a bomb on the White House, I might get mad."

ion leaders. But in some circles the equation was simple: if the United States government opposed the Sandinistas, then the Sandinistas must be the good guys. Moreover, the Sandinistas were revolutionaries. They appeared to be idealistic. Some had been imprisoned by the Somoza regime and had been treated terribly. Many were good-looking, and most of them were young. They had glamour and sex appeal. On their visits to the United States, Sandinista officials, and especially Ortega, were the darlings of the Hollywood and New York jet sets. *El Presidente* liked to go on shopping sprees along Rodeo Drive and Fifth Avenue, buying up that great staple of revolutions everywhere—designer sunglasses.

With few exceptions, the Sandinistas received unusually gentle treatment in the American press. Very few reporters took the trouble to examine the truth behind their claims, especially their allegations of human rights violations by the contras. Certainly there were some, as there are in any war. But the Sandinistas frequently circulated outright fabrications, and reporters who were normally skeptical would report these stories as if they were true.

The public relations effort on behalf of the resistance could have been far more successful if the contras had produced a charismatic leader (ideally, with a beard or a mustache) who could have effectively symbolized their struggle as an anti-Communist Ho Chi Minh, or Fidel, or Che. The resistance offered up several candidates who were brave fighters and fine leaders, but none of them could command a large following. One possibility was Mike Lima. He was a fierce combat leader who had been wounded half a dozen times. Mike was young and handsome, and with the help of a friendly reporter in Honduras, we were able to set up a press conference for him.

The first question was harmless enough: "When did you join the resistance?"

"Well," said Mike, "when I was at the National Guard Academy..."

CUT! Mike Lima had been fighting the Sandinistas for five years, but that was the end of his brief media career.

The most persistent rap against the contras was that they consisted of former members of Somoza's National Guard. In the early years of the resistance, there was some truth to that claim. When the Somoza regime collapsed, somewhere between a thousand and fifteen hundred

Guardsmen escaped to Honduras, where they formed a government in exile that nobody recognized. This group became the formative nucleus of the resistance, and was quietly supported by Argentina.

Certainly there were some bad men in the National Guard—just as bad as the dictator they supported. But not all of them fit that profile. There were also young officers in the Guard, including some who graduated from West Point and other American military academies, who cared about democracy and believed in it.

Besides, former Guardsmen were only one segment of the resistance. By early 1983, there were around ten thousand contras, which meant that the Guard consisted of no more than 15 percent of the total. They were easily outnumbered by disenchanted Sandinistas—like Juan, who brought his entire unit to Honduras to fight against his former colleagues. Most of the contras were young *campesinos*, simple farmers who had fled from Communism and wanted land and freedom for themselves and their families. By the end of 1984 they had become the largest peasant army in Latin America since the Mexican revolution.

The American public may have been apathetic about Nicaragua and the contras, but it was a hot issue in Congress all through the Reagan years. This was especially true in the House of Representatives, where the Democrats formed a strong majority—and held some strange views on the funding of anti-Communist resistance movements. The farther away the insurgency, the more willing Congress was to fund it. It was relatively easy to get support for resistance forces in places like Cambodia and especially Afghanistan, which were halfway around the globe. Angola was a little closer, and therefore more problematic. Central America, right next door, was nearly impossible.

In the fall of 1983, after lengthy and acrimonious debate, Congress narrowly approved an allocation of twenty-four million dollars for the CIA to spend on the Nicaraguan resistance. But this money didn't go as far as we had expected. Much of it went to the CIA itself, for salaries, travel and living expenses for their trainers, logistics personnel, technicians, communicators, and other employees who were involved with the resistance.

Meanwhile, the contra base camps along the Honduran border were being overwhelmed with volunteers—far beyond the CIA's fondest hopes. And these volunteers rarely came alone. Often they showed up with their entire extended families: a wife, three kids, a couple of grandparents, an uncle, and two cousins. All of them had to be fed, clothed, and cared for, which meant that a lot of money went for food, shelter, clothing, blankets, medicine, baby formula, and training. That didn't leave as much as we'd hoped for guns and ammunition.

So early in 1984, the administration went back to Congress for an additional appropriation.

It was around this time that Dewey Clarridge came up with his plan to mine the harbors of Nicaragua. The contras had already hit several Sandinista bridges, warehouses, oil facilities, and power stations, but they hadn't yet matched the damage done to Nicaragua's economy by the Sandinistas' own policies. Dewey's mandate was to increase the pressure on the Sandinistas—particularly their state-controlled economic infrastructure. But so many volunteers had joined up that he was quickly running out of money for the insurgency.

Mining the harbors was Dewey's way of getting more bang for the buck. The idea came to him late one night while he was reading about the Russo-Japanese War of 1904–1905. The Japanese had enjoyed great success in mining some of the Russian harbors, and Dewey proposed that the CIA could do the same with Nicaragua. Except that instead of a real mining campaign, which would lead to foreign and civilian casualties, Dewey suggested using "firecracker mines," which created a loud explosion but caused little damage. Our hope was that Lloyd's of London and other insurers would stop insuring ships that were bound for Nicaragua, which would make it difficult for the Sandinistas to receive oil and other supplies necessary to keep their enormous army in the field.

Casey loved the idea, and so did the President. Even George Shultz went along. Bill Casey and Dewey Clarridge went up to Congress to meet with the relevant committees, where they mentioned the mining plan as part of their review of covert operations in Nicaragua.

In terms of damaging the Nicaraguan economy, the mining program was only a limited success. But the political damage in Washington was enormous. When details of the mining were revealed in the *Wall Street Journal*, all hell broke loose in Congress. Normally, when the President signs a Finding authorizing a covert operation, the congressional intelligence committees are briefed on it in detail within a matter of days. But most committee members swore they knew nothing about the mining. Their memories were so selective that even Senator Patrick Leahy of Vermont, no friend of the resistance, rebuked his colleagues for their deceit. One classified report to the intelligence committees had spelled it out in plain English: "Magnetic mines have been placed in the Pacific harbor of El Bluff, as well as the oil terminal at Puerto Sandino."

It got so bad that Bill Casey actually went up to the Hill to apologize to the members of the Senate Intelligence Committee. He must have gagged on his words, but he would have done anything to protect the CIA. "You shouldn't be here to apologize to us," said Senator Jake Garn of Utah. "We should be apologizing to you for pretending we weren't briefed." When Casey left the room, Garn exploded at his colleagues—using such colorful language that it raised a few eyebrows when word got back to his constituents in Salt Lake City.

The mining led to a spate of hearings. When Tony Motley was called before the House Intelligence Committee to answer questions about the mining, the congressmen jumped all over him. "This is terrible," one of them said. "We're involved in illegal, covert actions, and we're killing innocent sailors from other countries."

"Just a minute," Tony replied. "Let me put this thing in context. Fewer people were killed by these mines than died at Chappaquiddick."

Maybe that's why Tony didn't last too long in the job. As good as he was, you can't talk like that and stay very long at the State Department.

For many in Congress, the mining of the harbors was the last straw. Instead of providing additional money for the resistance, the House of Representatives gave us a new Boland Amendment.

In all, there were five separate so-called Boland Amendments passed by the House between 1982 and 1986. These became an annual rite of summer in Washington: the cherry blossoms would come out, the administration would ask for more funding for the resistance, and Congress would respond with another Boland Amendment.

The Boland Amendments were named for Edward Boland, chairman of the House Intelligence Committee, who proposed them. Although each of the amendments was different, all of them were restrictions on the use of appropriated funds, and were therefore attached to large appropriations bills. None of the Boland Amendments was by any stretch of the imagination a criminal statute, and none of them included any civil or criminal penalties. And despite what some Democrats—and even Bud McFarlane—claimed later, none of them applied to the President, or to his staff at the National Security Council.*

Shortly before Boland One came into being, several members of Congress had tried to ban aid to the contras from *every* branch of the government, including the White House and the National Security Council. This amendment, proposed by then-Congressman Tom Harkin, an Iowa Democrat, would have prohibited any government agency from "carrying out military activities in or against Nicaragua." This was very different from the language of any of the Boland Amendments, and especially from Boland One.

The administration hit the roof when it heard about Harkin's proposal. It was obviously unconstitutional, because Congress has no right to limit the President's authority to carry out foreign policy. The President let it be known that if Congress approved the Harkin Amendment, which was unlikely anyway, he would promptly veto it. It was then that Congressman Boland offered his own amendment *as*

---

*The first Boland Amendment (or Boland One, as it came to be known), covered the period from December 1982 to December 1983, and outlawed the use of funds by the CIA or the Department of Defense for the purpose of "overthrowing the Government of Nicaragua."

Boland Two (which covered the period from December 1983 to October 1984) specified that no more than $24 million could be spent "by the CIA, the Department of Defense, and any other agency or entity of the United States involved in intelligence activities" to support military operations in Nicaragua.

Boland Three (which covered the period from October 1984 to December 1985) was the most restrictive. It specified that "no appropriations or funds made available" to the CIA, Defense Department, "or any other agency or entity of the United States involved in intelligence activities" could be spent to support "directly or indirectly, military or paramilitary operations in Nicaragua by any nation, group, organization, movement or individual."

Boland Four (covering the period from August 1985 through March 1986) outlined the same restrictions on military assistance, but allowed $27 million in "humanitarian aid, communications support, [and] intelligence sharing."

Boland Five, which ran to October 1986, allowed the Nicaraguan resistance to receive a very specific and limited amount of CIA support, and authorized the State Department to solicit humanitarian aid for the resistance from other countries.

a compromise. Boland himself called the Harkin Amendment "not necessary," and "a bad precedent."

Later, there would be an enormous controversy as to the exact meaning and scope of the various Boland Amendments. I don't pretend to be a legal authority, but common sense tells me that if a Congress that was known to be deeply divided on this issue nevertheless voted for Boland One *by a margin of 411 to zero,* there's no way on earth that this amendment could have been understood as forbidding all aid to the contras.

Not that everybody was happy with Boland One. It was criticized in the Senate—not by supporters of the contras, but by Senator Christopher Dodd. He complained that it gave a "green light" to continued support of the resistance—and indeed it did.

The mining operations in Nicaragua left us with Boland Three, which forced the CIA to withdraw all of its support for the resistance. If the Reagan administration was going to continue funding the contras, we would have to find another way.

11

Body and Soul

When Congress cut off the CIA's support for the contras, a lot of people expected the resistance to wither on the vine and disappear. But President Reagan had no intention of abandoning the contras, and he made that clear in both word and deed. He compared them to the Founding Fathers and the French Resistance. He met with their leaders at the White House. "I'm a contra, too," he announced. As he later wrote in his memoirs, "I wanted the contras maintained as a force, to the fullest extent that was legal, until I could convince Congress to appropriate new funds for the freedom fighters."

Within the administration, there was no doubt that the resistance would continue to be supported. The only question was how.

Even before the spring of 1984, when congressionally appropriated funds for the resistance began to run out, there were serious discussions within the administration, and even on Capitol Hill, about asking foreign governments to help support the contras. Later on, this approach would be referred to contemptuously as "tin-cup diplomacy." But Casey, McFarlane, and others saw it as a logical way to broaden the anti-Communist coalition. The Reagan Doctrine, after all, went beyond mere "containment." It also meant enlisting the help of our allies—not only against Communism itself, but against the entire

Communist empire. This was already being done in Afghanistan, where several other governments had quietly joined us in supporting the rebels. Casey believed the Nicaraguan resistance deserved a similar effort.

Back in the fall of 1983, McFarlane had asked me to draw up a list of countries that might conceivably be approached. My nominations included the United Kingdom, West Germany, Taiwan, Singapore, Saudi Arabia, and Israel. But when I gave the list to Bud, he pointed out that we had to rule out Israel, as well as any other nation that received American aid. If a country we were helping then turned around and sent money to the contras, it would look as if we were simply laundering our foreign aid.* Besides, although almost nobody knew about it, Israel was already helping the contras in a very different way.

Operation Tipped Kettle had been Casey's idea. In 1982 and 1983, the Israelis had captured vast quantities of PLO arms in Lebanon. Much of it was Soviet-bloc weaponry that was intended for a guerrilla army, and the Israelis had little use for it. But if these arms could somehow be passed on to the contras, it would be a godsend.

The Pentagon sent a team of experts to Israel to examine the captured supplies and to make the appropriate arrangements. Twice—in May 1983, and again the following year—the Israelis shipped hundreds of tons of PLO weapons to Department of Defense warehouses. From there, most of the weapons were transferred to the CIA and distributed not only to the contras, but to anti-Communist resistance movements in other countries as well.

Operation Tipped Kettle came off without a hitch or a leak. One reason it succeeded so brilliantly was that the man in charge of the Pentagon team really knew what he was doing. He was a major general in the Air Force with extensive experience in covert operations. His name was Richard Secord.

After McFarlane asked me to draw up a list of potential supporters, I heard little more about the idea until the following spring. But Bud must have been discussing it with Bill Casey, because in late March

---

*I learned later that McFarlane had asked my colleague Howard Teicher to approach the Israelis to help. They declined.

1984, Casey sent him an EYES ONLY memo telling Bud that he, Casey, was "in full agreement" that McFarlane should "explore funding alternatives with the Israelis and perhaps others."

It wasn't long after he received the Casey memo that Bud made a rare visit to my office. As I rose to greet him, he came in and quietly closed the door. Sitting on a chair next to the coffee table across from my desk, Bud said, "I want you to have the resistance open up an offshore bank account so that a foreign contributor can make deposits directly into it."

Naturally, I wondered who that foreign contributor might be. But McFarlane clearly didn't want to tell me, and I knew better than to ask. He knew I would be going to Casey for advice on how to set this up, and I assumed he didn't want to put the CIA director in an awkward position. Casey was continually being called up to Capitol Hill to answer questions, and life was a lot easier if he didn't know those kinds of answers.

I walked down the hall to Casey's office in Room 345 of the OEOB.

"I've been told to have the resistance set up an offshore account," I told him, "and I could use some help."

Casey leaned back on his chair. He was chewing on a yellow wooden pencil. "Is it the Saudis?" he asked.

"I don't know."

"Come on, don't bullshit me. It's the Saudis, right?"

"Honestly, I don't know."

Casey smiled. "Well, it must be. How much are we talking about?"

"I don't know that either."

He peered at me skeptically over his glasses. Then he picked up the secure phone and asked for a number. When somebody picked up at the other end, Casey asked, "If a third party wanted to help our friends down south, who can we trust to handle the money?"

When Casey hung up the phone, he looked at me and said, "Calero's your man."

Adolfo Calero was a prominent figure in the resistance, and we had already met a couple of times.

"Go see Calero," Casey said. "He should set up an offshore account if he doesn't have one already. The money shouldn't come all at once. Have it arrive in regular payments, every month. That will give us more control."

Casey got up and motioned for me to join him over in the sitting area. Then he held school.

"Here's what to do," he began.

I took out a notebook.

"Put that away," he said. "If you have to write everything down, you don't belong in this business. The money should go directly from a foreign account into Calero's offshore account. It shouldn't come into this country at all. Do it with a wire transfer."

"What, exactly, is a wire transfer?"

Casey sighed before explaining. He had spent most of his life in the financial world, and had even served as chairman of the SEC. Asking Bill Casey about a wire transfer was a little like going up to Einstein and saying, "Excuse me, Professor, but what is a square root?"

"Why does it have to be an offshore account?" I asked.

"Two reasons," he replied. First, he explained, all Nicaraguan bank accounts in the United States had been frozen. Second, the Treasury Department monitors large transfers of funds in and out of American banks. Someone was bound to notice these transactions and start asking questions.

It wasn't until months later that I learned that Casey was right about Saudi Arabia. On the afternoon of June 25, 1984, the President and his top national security aides met in the Situation Room to discuss ways to keep the resistance alive. Casey spoke in favor of soliciting contributions from other countries. Shultz opposed it, but suggested that the Attorney General look into whether it was legal. Ed Meese agreed to check with the Justice Department. Everyone agreed that the matter had to be handled with great discretion. "If such a story gets out," President Reagan said as the meeting ended, "we'll all be hanging by our thumbs in front of the White House until we find out who did it."*

Shultz didn't know it at the time, and neither did I, but the President had already authorized McFarlane to see Prince Bandar bin Sultan, the Saudi ambassador to Washington, to ask for a contribution

---

*From the declassified minutes of the National Security Planning Group meeting, June 25, 1984, p. 14.

from his government. The first deposit, in the amount of one million dollars, arrived in early July, and over the next seven months the Saudis continued helping the contras at the rate of a million dollars a month. While this wasn't enough to cover all that an army needed, it did help buy food, clothing, weapons, and ammunition.

It was enough, in other words, to do what the President had told McFarlane he had wanted done—to hold the resistance together "body and soul" until Congress could be persuaded to change its mind and allow the CIA back in.

In February 1985, King Fahd of Saudi Arabia arrived in Washington on a state visit. During his meetings with the President at the White House, he agreed to provide additional funds to the resistance. I wasn't there, but Bud McFarlane said later that he gave the President a note card on the matter. Knowing how President Reagan felt about the resistance, I never doubted that he'd be willing to ask King Fahd outright for another donation.

Later, there were those who concluded that the Saudis' generosity came in return for an expedited delivery of Stinger antiaircraft missiles that was being held up by Congress. While the missiles may have figured into it, this explanation ignores the honest-to-God affection that the Saudis, like many of our allies, had for President Reagan. They truly liked him, and they also liked what he stood for—especially after four years of Jimmy Carter. If Ronald Reagan cared about supporting the contras, they were happy to help.

In addition, the Saudis have always been strongly anti-Communist. They knew what it meant to have a Communist presence in the neighborhood, which is why they were already supporting the Afghan resistance to the tune of *hundreds* of millions of dollars.

Armed with McFarlane's instructions and Casey's advice, I flew down to Tegucigalpa, the capital of Honduras, to meet with Adolfo Calero.

Calero, who looked like a silver-haired bear, was easily the most visible leader in the resistance. He had a law degree, and had been a successful businessman in Managua, where he had run Coca-Cola's operations. He had a special rapport with Americans, and had even gone to college in the United States. After graduating from Notre Dame, he returned to Nicaragua committed to both free enterprise and American-style democracy. His political views got him in trouble with the Somoza regime, and he was jailed more than once. But when the Sandinistas came to power, Calero's public opposition to Somoza didn't stop the new government from seizing his property and sending him into exile.

I thought Space Mountain at Disney World was a pretty good ride until I flew into Tegucigalpa. The airport's only runway is stretched between a mountain on one end and the edge of a cliff on the other. In order to land, the pilot has to fly in over the mountain; then he makes a sudden, deep dive, pulling up just as he hits the runway. He practically has to stand on the brakes until they smoke. You find yourself praying that the plane will be able to stop before it drops off the cliff and into the ravine—which is littered with the wrecks of planes that didn't stop in time.

I had pretty much stopped shaking by the time I got to the contras' safe house, which was located in one of the city's residential neighborhoods. About a dozen senior people from the resistance were waiting for me, including Enrique Bermudez, who was wearing his fatigues. From the way they greeted me, it was clear that even a visit from a relatively junior White House official meant a lot to them. In addition to the standard contra fare of black beans and rice, Adolfo proudly served chicken, which he had barbecued on the back porch.

Most of the table talk centered on recent cross-border operations by the Sandinistas, and on the inevitable topic that marked almost every discussion about the contras—the deplorable conditions in the camps. When the meal was over, I spoke to the group with the help of a translator and delivered the message that McFarlane had instructed me to communicate: "Our goals and yours are the same. Like you, we want to see a democratic Nicaragua. Although the Congress has cut off the CIA, President Reagan wants you to know that we will find a way to help you. I can promise you that you will not be abandoned."

We finished dinner around ten. When most of the others had left, Calero motioned for me to step out on the porch. He tried not to show his disappointment, but it was clear that he felt let down.

"Colonel," he said, "I was led to believe that you would be bringing us something more than promises."

"I am," I said. "But I couldn't talk about it in front of the others. There is a benefactor."

"Who is it?"

"I can't say. I've been told to tell you to set up an offshore bank account. I'll need the account number, a telex code, and a wire transfer address."

"How much will be deposited?"

"A million dollars a month."

Adolfo was silent for a moment, and I wasn't sure whether he was pleased by this figure or disappointed. Finally he said, "Yes, that will help."

"You can't let anybody know that I am involved in this," I said. "And we'll also need careful records of how the money is spent."

We talked on for a while. As I was leaving, Adolfo said, "We appreciate this help. I'll come up soon with the information you want. Some day, I'd like to thank President Reagan in person."

I spent that night at the ambassador's residence and flew back to Washington the next morning.

Calero came to town about a week later. McFarlane was nervous that somebody would learn about our arrangement, so instead of having Adolfo come to the White House, we met in a town house overlooking Lafayette Park. Without referring to notes, Calero gave me the information I asked for: The account was in the name of Esther Morales, a member of the resistance directorate. The number was 541–48 at the Miami branch of BAC (Banco America Central) International Bank in the Cayman Islands. As I jotted down the details, I noticed that Adolfo was smiling. He must have been amused that this American who was supposed to be an expert in covert operations had to put it all in writing.

Calero returned to his hotel, and I went back to my office, where I typed the information on an index card for McFarlane. Then I called Bud to let him know I had the information he was waiting for. "As long as Adolfo's in town," I said, "would you like to meet him?"

"Sure. But not here."

"Why don't I pick you up in the Military Office station wagon? You two can talk in the back."

(I could have used my own car, but it was parked on the Ellipse, half a mile away. Besides, I didn't want to surrender a parking space unless it was absolutely necessary.)

I arranged to pick up McFarlane on West Executive Avenue, and then turned right on Pennsylvania, where Calero was waiting in front of the Treasury. While I took them on an impromptu tour of the city's monuments, Bud and Adolfo talked in the back. Bud seemed to get a real kick out of meeting this way. This wasn't exactly high adventure, but it must have been a welcome break from the endless mundane meetings and paperwork he had to deal with. He reminded Adolfo that the monthly payments from the anonymous benefactor were meant as a bridge to tide over the resistance until Congress once again changed its mind and resumed funding the contras. He mentioned the need for regular accounting and stressed the importance of secrecy. No one at the CIA or the State Department, or anywhere else in the U.S. government, was to know the details of this arrangement.

When the Saudi money began to arrive, Calero used it to buy weapons and supplies for the resistance. He often called me for advice, which inaugurated a deepening level of confidence and contact between us. As time went on, we conferred about almost every aspect of the resistance movement—from where the contras could buy surface-to-air missiles to the need for more obstetricians in the base camps.

One afternoon, Casey called me from his office at the Intelligence Community Staff Building on F Street.

"Can you come over and see me right now?"

I threw on my coat, ran over to F Street, and took the creaky old elevator to Casey's office. This old building, with its high ceilings and peeling paint, was a relic from another era. Every time I entered it I was reminded of the dingy, cramped offices in London where George Smiley and his colleagues worked in the novels of John le Carré.

Casey was alone in his office. When I sat down, he said, "You're talking too much."

"What do you mean?"

"On the phone. How often are you talking to your pal in Honduras? Three, four times a week?"

"Something like that."

"All in the clear, right?"

"Yes."

"Well, it's got to stop," he said. I already knew that both U.S. and foreign intelligence services spent most of their time watching each other. Casey emphasized that these telephone calls made it too easy for the Soviets to listen in on my conversations with Calero.

He handed me a small black book. "Have you ever used one of these before?"

I opened it. Inside was a series of little pockets.

"No. How does it work?"

He shook his head, as if to say, Do I have to explain *everything?*

"It's a code book," he said. "You get one, he gets one. You change the code numbers on a set pattern. Now you can talk to each other without giving away the store."

It was a simple, do-it-yourself encoding/decoding device. All you had to do was enter the relevant words—Honduras, Nicaragua, guns, ammo, medicine, planes, whatever—and then line them up with the code numbers in the book, which could be changed every day. It was low-tech but effective. Even if somebody was listening in, he'd have virtually no idea what you were talking about.

These black books, a variation of a "onetime pad," were the first of several efforts on Casey's part to improve the security of our contacts with the resistance. Later, when more people were involved, he called me in again. "What are you doing about security?" he asked. "Your COMSEC [communications security] stinks."

Casey was concerned about the Soviets' ability to monitor telephone calls from their listening post in Lourdes, Cuba. What had begun as a simple link between Adolfo and me soon involved over a dozen people on at least two continents. Adolfo and I were still using the original code books, but that didn't protect the rest of the group. Casey suggested the Phillips PX-1000, a European-made encryption device, but when that turned out to be inadequate, he recommended a brand-new American-made device manufactured by TRW, called the KL-43. I didn't even know these incredible machines existed until Casey had a few of them sent to my office.

The KL-43 resembled what later became known as a laptop computer, except that it came equipped with an encryption chip. You'd type in your message, which would appear on the tiny screen in plain English. After reviewing what you had written, you'd push the "encode" button on the keyboard, whereupon everything on the screen would turn to gibberish. Then you'd call the person to whom you intended to send it. After confirming that you were both using the same code, you'd put your telephone receiver in the modem. At the sound of the beep, you would push "transmit," and another beep would sound, locking both machines into sync. Within seconds, the recipient received the encoded message. For added security, he would hang up the phone before decoding the text with the push of a button.

In open conversation we referred to these machines as typewriters. Once a month, an intelligence officer would deliver a new cassette of codes, which looked like a tape dispenser. Every day you'd tear out another code, enter it into the machine, and burn the previous day's code strip. Even if a KL-43 fell into the wrong hands, there was little risk; the code would be obsolete within hours.

The KL-43, which came with its own little printer, was completely portable. I rarely left home without it.

The code books and secure communications equipment may have helped keep the Soviets and the Cubans from knowing the details of what I was doing to support the resistance, but it didn't keep the secret from spreading within our own government. Over time, the circle of knowledge inevitably expanded beyond Casey, McFarlane, Poindexter, and the President.

In part this was because of the Restricted Interagency Group, or RIG, which acted as a "compartmented" coordinating body for U.S. diplomatic, military, and covert activities throughout Central America— and especially for the actions we took to deal with the growing threat posed by the Sandinistas. The RIG, which was chaired by the Assistant Secretary of State for Inter-American Affairs, reviewed and cleared scores of covert operations proposed by the CIA, including the mining of key harbors, attacks on strategic targets inside Nicaragua, and measures to improve the support the contras received from the neighboring governments.

The process functioned reasonably well until late in 1984, when the RIG was caught up in the Washington game of musical chairs. By the middle of 1985, Tony Motley had been succeeded as chairman by Elliott Abrams, and the CIA's Dewey Clarridge was replaced by Alan Fiers. Eventually, Admiral Art Moreau from the Joint Chiefs of Staff was replaced by General John Moellering. Throughout this period, I remained as the RIG's NSC representative.

Like their predecessors before them, Abrams and Fiers became key players in the administration's effort to sustain the resistance. They were both enthusiastic about the need to keep military pressure on the

Sandinista regime, and both men had access to their respective bosses, Shultz and Casey. We met frequently, traveled together to the region, and talked almost daily on the phone.

Elliott Abrams became the front man for the resistance, speaking out forcefully and articulately to Congress, in the media, and within the administration. Fiers, although less visible, was also very helpful. Inevitably, both men came to know more and more about what I was doing to support the resistance, in part because they had separate and accurate reporting channels from Central America. I came to count on them as allies in the struggle, and they were, at least until I was fired.

The personnel changes in the RIG also meant increased exposure for the various actions that the RIG reviewed. In all, there must have been well over a hundred people in our government (including State, Defense, CIA, the White House, and Congress) who knew at least some of what was being done to support the Nicaraguan resistance. As the CIA phased out its involvement and I became the focal point for the resistance, we tried to tighten that circle. But it could never be closed completely.

By 1986 a number of individuals, both in and out of government, were actively seeking me out to provide help, offer advice, ask questions, or request that I provide specific assistance to one or another of the resistance factions. Senator Jesse Helms urged me to do more for Eden Pastora and his group. Congressman Dave McCurdy prodded me to arrange for additional deliveries to the Atlantic Coast Indians. Bernie Aronsen, who replaced Elliott Abrams as Assistant Secretary of State for Latin America, suggested several new leaders for the resistance. Don Gregg, Vice President Bush's national security adviser, suggested Felix Rodriguez as a good contact in El Salvador. For a covert operation, there sure were a lot of people who knew about it— at least until the great plague of amnesia that hit Washington in the fall of 1986.

It soon became apparent to everyone that simply replacing the CIA's funding wouldn't be enough to sustain the resistance. For one thing, the initial Saudi contribution was quite modest. For another, the CIA had provided the resistance with far more than money. They had also found the weapons, bought them, and delivered them, and had provided training, communications, intelligence, command and control, and various other administrative services.

Critics of the resistance have argued that when the CIA pulled out, the contras should have been able to manage these tasks on their own. Ideally, that's true. But the CIA had never been particularly eager for the contras or any other resistance movement to learn these skills. For it was precisely by providing various support services that the Agency was able to maintain control and encourage a certain amount of unity among competing factions within the same general movement. As one clandestine services officer told me in Honduras, "I taught them everything they know. But I didn't teach them everything *I* know."

With the CIA out of the game, the contras had to learn how to run their own show. But for now they needed people who knew how to do these various jobs. In most aspects of life, OJT—on-the-job training—is a great way to learn. In war, however, it's a great way to get killed.

It wasn't until the CIA started pulling out that both the contras and their supporters in Washington came to appreciate just how much the Agency had been doing. The CIA had provided everything from standard propaganda techniques like running a radio station and dropping leaflets to far more delicate tasks, such as providing liaison between the resistance and the governments of neighboring countries. These governments were willing to help, but only if they could do so discreetly. They, too, were threatened by the Sandinistas, and they insisted on deniability.

As the CIA began to withdraw, Calero and other resistance leaders began calling on me for everything from intelligence and communications support to weapons and liaison with neighboring governments. It wasn't hard for the contras to buy most of their nonmilitary requirements, such as food, clothing, and some medicines. But without the CIA, they didn't have the necessary contacts to purchase Soviet-bloc weapons and ammunition. In a guerrilla war, it's always better if the insurgents use the same weapons as the government they're fighting. Anything else creates logistical problems, and prevents the guerrillas from effectively using and integrating whatever weapons and ammunition they manage to capture.

As the summer of 1984 came to an end, I felt like I was straddling a canyon. On one side was the resistance, always expanding, always needing more. On the other was the CIA, which was steadily withdrawing its support. The canyon was growing wider by the day. Unless I had help, and soon, I was going to fall in.

But Casey could see what was happening, and he asked me to come out to Langley on a Saturday morning to discuss the state of the resistance. He was wearing his golf clothes, and he looked a little incongruous in his bright yellow sweater.

I described the long list of problems that were developing in the wake of the CIA's withdrawal. "Money alone isn't enough," I said.

He nodded. "I know. And it'll only get worse in October, when all our people will be gone. You need somebody who can help you out."

He leaned back and looked up, as though the answer was written on the ceiling. Whenever he did this, it was all I could do to restrain myself from looking up there with him.

"Do you know Dick Secord?" he asked.

"The Air Force general? I know who he is. I talked to him a couple of times during the AWACs project."

"That's the guy," said Casey. "He's got the right experience for this sort of thing. He knows the right people, he gets things done, and he keeps his mouth shut. Why don't you call him?"

At the time, practically all I knew about Secord was that he had been a major general in the Air Force, a Deputy Assistant Secretary of Defense, and a key player in getting the AWACs package through Congress. In fact, he had a much wider reputation than I realized. He was known as an expert in unconventional warfare and a master of covert operations.

In the early 1960s, Dick Secord had been a key player in the CIA's secret war in Laos. People said he had ice water in his veins, and having later read one of his citations for bravery, I can easily picture him leading a squadron of aircraft through enemy flak without breaking out in a sweat.

Later on, all kinds of people came forward to allege that Dick Secord was unsavory and nefarious, and that despite his high position in the Department of Defense, he was somehow "shadowy." But I sure didn't hear any of that at the time. Not only did Casey recommend him, but Bud McFarlane was more than happy to have him involved.

As I recall, the only person who raised any objection to Secord at the time was Clair George, Casey's deputy director for operations.

"What are you using *him* for?" he asked me.

"Because he was recommended by the director," I replied. Objection overruled.

Later on, the press raised Secord's previous association with the notorious Edwin Wilson, a renegade CIA officer who was jailed for selling arms to Qaddafi. But Secord had never been charged with any wrongdoing, and Casey, who yielded to nobody in his hatred for Qaddafi, did not seem troubled by any of this. But as I would eventually learn for myself, once you're under suspicion, evidence has nothing to do with it. If you're in the government and someone thinks you're guilty, you can kiss your job good-bye.

Dick had retired in the spring of 1983, leaving in disgust over the derailment of what had been a brilliant career. Albert Hakim, a businessman who had known Secord when Dick served in Iran, brought him into Hakim's trading company—Stanford Technology Trading Group International.

When I first met with Secord and asked him to become involved with the resistance, he wasn't especially eager. When he finally agreed, he made it clear that the only way he could help was if he set aside his other business activities. Casey, McFarlane, Secord, and I all agreed that he would be compensated from the proceeds of his activities. He had many contacts, and to the extent that he called upon them to help the contras, they, too, would have to be paid.

Let me be absolutely explicit on this point: by the time we involved Dick Secord in helping the contras, he was a businessman. He came in on that basis. While he genuinely believed in the cause of the Nicaraguan resistance, he was not coming to us, or to them, as a volunteer. Everybody understood that he would be making a profit.

I didn't know how much money Dick Secord made—if any—and I still don't. But I do know this: everything he was asked to do, he did. In retrospect, Secord and I should have agreed then and there on a set fee for his work. We never discussed exactly what fair and just compensation would entail—an omission that eventually led to major problems for both of us.

When Iran-contra erupted, critics of the operation pointed to this administrative failure as one of my major shortcomings. And it was. If the CIA had still been running the show, and Dick Secord had come in, they would have set him up with accountants, lawyers, communicators—a whole support staff. We didn't have this kind of help, and given the restrictions of time, secrecy, and budget, and the desperate needs of the contras, the choice I faced was between helping the contras imperfectly or not helping them at all. To me, the answer was obvious.*

Perhaps I should have gone to McFarlane and said, "Look, either I get five or six people to help me, or we'll have to stop. God simply did not put enough hours in the day for me to do everything necessary to supervise this."

But I was a junior staff officer, and the circle was supposed to be small, and nobody was eager to create a bureaucratic structure that would be dismantled when the Congress turned the CIA money back on. Besides, I loved the work, even if it was a little overwhelming. I was constantly on the phone—with McFarlane, Secord, Casey, and Calero and other contra leaders, as well as the State Department, our ambassadors in Central America, and our friends around the world. All this was in addition to the counterterrorism projects with the Task Force, and, starting in November 1985, the Iran initiative.

I had some reservations about the Iran initiative, as I have explained. But I had absolutely no qualms about doing all I could to sustain our commitment to the Nicaraguan resistance.

After Dick Secord agreed to help the resistance, he sent Raphael "Chi Chi" Quintero, a former Cuban freedom fighter who had once worked for the CIA, down to Honduras to meet with the resistance leaders. Quintero visited the contra camps, wrote up a detailed analysis of what the guerrillas needed, and provided a report back to Secord.

As Dick's involvement grew, he started hiring more people. In addition to Quintero, he brought aboard several men with whom he had worked in Southeast Asia: Tom Clines, Richard Gadd, and Bob

---

*There were times when I was simply overwhelmed by all that had to be done. On June 10, 1986, I sent a PROFS message to Admiral Poindexter in which I expressed my frustration that I couldn't possibly accomplish all that the CIA had done for the resistance: "An extraordinary amount of good has been done, and money truly is not the thing which is most needed at this point. What we most need is to get the CIA reengaged in this effort so that it can be better engaged than it now is by one slightly confused Marine Lt. Colonel."

Dutton, along with pilots, air crews, logisticians, and maintenance technicians for airdrops into Nicaragua.

Following the CIA's standard practice for a far-flung covert operation, Secord and his people set up shell corporations in Portugal, Switzerland, Panama, and elsewhere. Using the money that went from the Saudis to Calero, they bought weapons, planes, ammunition, and just about everything else the resistance needed. They hired pilots, leased and bought planes, paid foreign agents, and built warehouses and even a runway—all of this in several different countries.

Much of this activity was simply an attempt to replicate what the CIA had been doing since 1981. Some of it was frustrating and wasteful, because the CIA had already created an infrastructure that Dick and his people weren't allowed to use. Several warehouses and other facilities in the region were just sitting there, gathering dust. But because of the Boland Amendment, everything the CIA had built up to help the resistance had to be done all over again. Working within the private sector, but with only a fraction of the Agency's resources, Secord and his team tried to create a mirror image of the CIA's earlier support.

Obviously, they couldn't do it all. One job they couldn't handle was the liaison and coordination that was necessary with government officials in neighboring countries. That task became mine. In order to base Secord's "private benefactor" planes at the Salvadoran Air Force Base at Ilopango, I met with President Duarte and received his personal permission. I had similar meetings with other leaders in the region.

Ilopango was a risky place to conduct such operations because American officials were always coming in and out of the base, while the resistance support aircraft, warehouses, and maintenance facilities were just sitting there, in plain view. Later, when the congressional inquiries began, the collective amnesia was amazing. Suddenly, almost nobody could remember that the resistance airplanes had been based at Ilopango. American officials throughout the region somehow forgot that I had been there often, and had even stayed in some of their homes and met there with resistance leaders.

Lewis Tambs was an exception. He and I had known each other at the NSC, and we stayed in touch when he served as the American ambassador to Colombia. After he was threatened with assassination, he was reassigned to Costa Rica. Even before he moved to San Jose we had talked about the need for a southern front against the Sandinistas.

Lew Tambs believed in the resistance, and he also believed in the power of prayer. He insisted that Joe Fernandez, the CIA station chief, notify him of every resupply mission. Every night there was an aircraft on a run over Nicaragua, Lew Tambs would light a votive candle at a little shrine in the embassy for the success of the mission and the safety of the crew. And with one exception, his prayers were answered.

Over time, Dick Secord was called upon to do more and more—both by me and by the resistance. When contra leaders came to me with their requests, I often put them in touch with Dick, who made purchases from arms dealers all over the world. By 1986 his operation had a small air force delivering supplies, a ship called the *Erria* to make overseas pickups, a construction company building a secret runway in Costa Rica, warehouses in El Salvador and Honduras, and communications and maintenance facilities around the region. Without Dick Secord, the resistance would have ceased to exist.

Dick wasn't the only retired general who helped the resistance. General John Singlaub came to me several times and asked what he could do for the contras.* When I described some of the problems they were having, Singlaub contacted a European arms broker and obtained several thousand Polish AK-47 assault rifles and ammunition. The price was terrific, much lower than what Secord was charging, but Casey was furious at the amount of "noise" that the sale generated. For Casey, control and discretion were more important than price, and at Casey's direction, my active involvement with General Singlaub came to an end.

Throughout this period, I kept reporting to McFarlane to make

---

*John K. Singlaub was a retired army major general, a short, tough-talking hero from both World War II and Korea. He had been the commanding general of U.S. Forces in Korea until President Carter decided to withdraw our troops. Singlaub made a statement in congressional hearings saying, without quite using these words, that the President's plan was just about the stupidest idea he had ever heard. President Carter didn't think it was so stupid, and although Carter later changed his mind, Singlaub decided to retire. In 1984, when Congress pulled the plug on the contras, Singlaub was furious. He felt so strongly about maintaining our commitment to the resistance that he volunteered to do whatever he could to make sure they were not abandoned.

sure he was comfortable with both my own expanded mission and with Secord's increasingly prominent involvement in providing arms and services to the resistance. On several occasions he made it clear that both he and the President were more than satisfied with the results.

The hardest part of supplying the contras wasn't buying the weapons, but delivering them to the resistance forces inside Nicaragua. After the CIA pulled out, the entire contra "air force" consisted of half a dozen aging, rundown transport planes flown by former National Guard pilots. They had neither the training nor the equipment to make nighttime drops, which are absolutely essential in this kind of war. Although this was Secord's area of expertise, it wasn't a problem that could be fixed overnight.

The people and the planes that Dick Secord brought in were the same kind he had used years earlier in Laos. Many old C-7s and C-123s were still around, collecting dust in desert boneyards. But it took months to find the necessary parts and to get the planes—and the pilots—back into shape. Everything took longer and cost more than we expected, but I wasn't about to second-guess a renowned Air Force general with Secord's experience.

Looking back on it now, however, it certainly looks as if the air-support team that Dick assembled was still fighting the last war. Moreover, they were trying to do so without the extensive infrastructure that the CIA had provided in Laos—and not even Dick Secord could replicate that.

Invariably, there were problems. During a flight to El Salvador, one of the C-7s developed engine trouble. As it lost altitude, the crew started pushing out anything that wasn't alive. It must have been a hell of a sight, with suitcases, boxes, and even a refrigerator tumbling out of the sky. The plane made an emergency landing on a road—and then sat there for days until somebody came out to fix it. Nobody was hurt, but this little episode became widely known among the small circle of people who were involved in supporting the resistance, and was the subject of considerable laughter. It was a textbook case in how not to run a covert operation.

To be fair to Dick, the team he assembled flew many dangerous missions over Nicaragua, and made numerous airdrops to resistance units. It's easy to dwell on the problems, but if I had to do it all over again, Secord is still the man I'd call.

Airdrops are inherently difficult, especially at night. If you were dropping eight bundles, you'd consider yourself fortunate if six were recovered. The supply plane would fly in ever-widening circles as the pilot looked for bonfires on the ground. But if the ground was wet, or the plane was half a mile off, the drop might never occur. The contras didn't have the kind of sophisticated electronic equipment that would make this process easier, and the airdrops didn't always go smoothly.

Before Secord came in, all of this had been handled by the CIA. But even they had screwed up a few times. To the bewilderment of the contras, one drop had consisted of nothing but sanitary napkins. Fortunately, the resistance was able to use them as battle dressings.

This brings to mind a story I heard years later from a CIA official who had convened a strategy meeting in Florida with some of the resistance leadership. The Agency had booked a hotel suite in Coral Gables, which had been paid for in cash. When everybody was assembled, the group decided to order lunch from room service. One of the CIA officers picked up the phone and called down to the kitchen. "What's that?" he said. "No room service? *What?* Because we're CIA? You're kidding me, right?"

By now every man in the room was on his feet, scooping documents into briefcases and heading for the door.

"Wait a minute," the officer called out. "Come back! They just told me that CIA stands for 'cash in advance.'"

Militarily, the biggest challenge the contras had to face occurred when the Soviets introduced HIND helicopters into the region. These devastating attack helicopters were armed with gun pods, rockets, and infrared sensors that could detect movement on the ground. The Soviets used them in Afghanistan, too, where the rebels referred to them as flying tanks.

A normal helicopter is vulnerable to small-arms fire from the ground, but the armor-covered HINDs were virtually indestructible. We developed a variety of plans to deal with them. We even printed up handbills, which were circulated all over Nicaragua, offering a reward of a million dollars to anyone who would fly one to Panama, where the CIA and the Pentagon could take it apart and have a good look.

One response to the HINDs was suggested by a brave, former British SAS officer who had provided several discreet services to Her Majesty's government. After looking into the problem, he concluded that the best solution was to attack these helicopters on the ground.

We finally agreed on a plan to attack the military air facility where the helicopters were assembled. But this was an extremely complicated arrangement, and we never did work out all the details. Sending in a group of commandos to do the job wouldn't have been all that difficult, but getting them out again was another story.

As the Soviets delivered more of these attack helicopters to Nicaragua, the resistance implored us to help them with portable surface-to-air missiles. There were three possibilities: American-made Stinger, or Red-Eye missiles; British Blowpipes; and Soviet-bloc SA-7s. American missiles were politically impossible. Besides, the Sandinistas might retaliate by providing Soviet antiaircraft missiles to the rebels in El Salvador. After a futile effort to obtain Blowpipes, we finally settled on the SA-7s which we bought from China—of all places.

Officially the missiles would be shipped from China to Guatemala, and I flew down to Guatemala to make the arrangements. (In order for the Chinese to have deniability, Guatemala had to issue end-user certificates for the missiles.) Back in Washington, I met with a Chinese military officer assigned to their embassy to encourage their cooperation. Before our meeting, I made sure that the FBI was aware that our discussion was sanctioned by the national security adviser. The last thing I needed was for anyone on our side to wonder if the Chinese were trying to recruit me as a spy.

The Chinese officer was a short, gray-haired man who, according to our records, had fought against the U.S. Marines in the Korean War. Only now, instead of meeting as adversaries on a frozen hilltop overlooking the Chosen Reservoir, we enjoyed a fine lunch at the exclusive Cosmos Club in downtown Washington. Most of the conversation centered on "Soviet hegemonistic designs" on the Third World—one of the few subjects we could agree on.

Oddly enough, the Sandinista government had never bothered to establish diplomatic relations with China. Despite all their revolutionary rhetoric, they maintained the old Somoza government's connection to Taiwan. While there may have been some intricate explanation behind it all, I suspect it had less to do with politics or ideology than with simple bureaucratic ineptitude.

On the surface, it was certainly odd for us to be asking a Communist government to help us in supporting an anti-Communist resistance movement. But for the Chinese, this was another way to stick it to the Soviets. The sale of the missiles served two of their interests at once: better relations with the United States, and worse relations with the Soviet Union. They certainly weren't doing it for the money, which in this case was fairly trivial.

The shipment of missiles took so long to arrive in Guatemala that Calero started referring to it as "the slow boat from China." Like many covert operations that go on too long, this one began to generate reports in CIA cable traffic. Several reports specifically referred to Dick Secord's role in the delivery. So many cables were coming in that Casey ordered his stations to stop reporting on this shipment.

When the boxes containing the missiles and their firing mechanisms finally reached the military port of San Jose, Chi Chi Quintero was there to receive them. The twenty-truck convoy rolled through Guatemala, protected by an army contingent, complete with helicopters, to guard against an ambush by Salvadoran guerrillas. After all, how would it look if a shipment from a Communist country ended up in Communist hands?

But like so many other aspects of supporting the resistance, what should have been the easiest part became the most difficult. When the shipment finally reached Honduras, where the Honduran army was supposed to deliver it to the resistance, they diverted the missiles to a military base and refused to release them.

This was just another example of the terrible bind that the struggle over Nicaragua had created for the Honduran government. Emotionally and philosophically, they supported the contras. But they were also terribly afraid of antagonizing the Sandinistas, who crossed the border at will to strike at the resistance. Whenever this happened, Honduran civilians ended up getting killed. And so officially, as far as the Honduran government was concerned, the contras in Honduras did not exist.

Because Honduran support was so critical to the resistance, I had several meetings over the years with President Roberto Suazo Cordoba. Suazo was a popular politician who was widely revered for his medical work in the Honduran back country and his strong opposition to Communism. He was an enormous fellow, who seemed to gain weight before your very eyes—in spite of the fact that he was also a physician, who presumably understood the risks of obesity. He was a man of prodigious appetites who reportedly didn't hesitate to indulge them. I can still picture him in his huge sombrero, sitting on the veranda with his feet up and his hands stretched over his ample stomach.

When the Chinese missiles arrived in their country, the Honduran military was dumbfounded. "For years we've been begging you for surface-to-air missiles," they said. "The whole world knows you're providing them to the Afghan resistance. Now you're sending them to the contras. Why don't you have any for us?"

This shipment of ammunition and weapons had come halfway around the globe, but now it was being held up just a short drive from the contra camps along the border. We needed action—and quickly. I wrote a memo to McFarlane, urging that President Reagan call President Suazo in Honduras to ask him to release the shipment at once.

President Reagan made the call that very afternoon, and I monitored their conversation from the Sit Room. The weapons and ammunition were released that same day for delivery to the contras.

The Hondurans exacted a price for allowing the contras to remain in their country, and in 1985 the Reagan administration agreed on several incentives: the prompt release of thirty-five million dollars in economic support funds, and an expedited delivery of military assistance, including trucks, boots, radios, and weapons. We also agreed to supplement our CIA Honduran programs.

In 1989, when some of these details were documented at my trial, there were various claims and counterclaims as to whether there had been any quid pro quos for the Honduran help. There is no doubt about that. Prior to a meeting that President Reagan had with President Suazo on May 21, 1985, a routine NSC "meeting memo" for the President included the following paragraph:

"In your meeting it will be important to reiterate to Suazo the importance we attach to his continued cooperation in enabling the FDN [the contras] to remain a viable element of pressure on the Sandinistas. Without making the linkage too explicit, it would be useful to remind Suazo that in return for our help—in the form of security assurances as well as aid—we do expect cooperation in pursuit of our mutual objectives. In this regard, you could underline the seriousness of our security commitment, *which the Hondurans seem to regard as the main quid pro quo for cooperating with the FDN.*" (Italics added.)

Later, at my trial, the story of American efforts to entice Honduran assistance to the contras became a key element in my defense. Following public disclosure of the Iran-contra operation, I had been described repeatedly as a loose cannon who acted pretty much alone. While I certainly got things done, reports of my "power" were greatly exaggerated. Obviously, there was no way that I could have helped get those missiles all the way from China to the Nicaraguan resistance without both the knowledge and the extensive help of senior officials in the United States government. At one point, when the Chinese were dragging their heels on the missile delivery, General John Vessey, Jr., chairman of the Joint Chiefs of Staff, was asked to "encourage" them to speed it up, which he did. The story of the Chinese missiles, together with the extensive documentation that exists on this and other efforts by the administration to help the contras, was more than enough to destroy the myth that I was a lone, unsupervised cowboy, off on my own.

Despite the enormous workload, my efforts on behalf of the contras were extremely satisfying. My original project was by now well under way and I had begun counting the months until I could leave the NSC and return to the Marines. But when I began working with the resistance, I started feeling productive again. Whether it was watching Secord find the right Soviet-bloc weapons for the resistance forces, or arranging for medical supplies to be delivered to the contra camps, the feeling of actually accomplishing something was enormously gratifying. At last I was doing something more useful than pushing paper from one side of my desk to the other.

There was, however, a heavy price to pay. Although I spent almost all my free time with my family, there wasn't that much of it to begin with. At home, the phone would ring at all hours of the night. Sometimes it was the White House calling about a terrorist attack. Occasionally, Adolfo or Dick Secord or one of my contacts in Central America would call to discuss an operational problem. Or it might be

Ami Nir in Israel, who could never seem to remember that Tel Aviv and Virginia were located in different time zones. Ami was a captain in a reserve armor unit, and one night, during a particularly sensitive negotiation with the Iranians, he actually called me from his tank. He simply drove up to a telephone pole, hooked up to the line, and placed the call.

When I first came to the NSC our telephone was on Betsy's side of the bed, but as these nocturnal interruptions increased she put her foot down. "I know you *like* sleeping on that side," she said, "but if your friends are going to be calling you in the middle of the night, you'll have to answer it yourself." And so, after fifteen years of marriage, I started sleeping on the other side of the bed. It sounds trivial, but that little change took me months to get used to.

12

Image Problems

My enduring memory of the contra base camps is the savory smell of wood smoke. Fires were burning constantly—not only for cooking, but for warmth, too, especially on chilly mornings in the mountains. Yamales, Las Vegas, Las Trojes, Bocay, Cifuentes, Las Manos, El Paraíso, Rus Rus, Aguacate—I visited the camps on several occasions to learn for myself what was going on there, and what the people needed. Looking back, it was probably these visits that motivated me to put so much energy into supporting the resistance. You couldn't help but be moved by the plight of these people, who had left their homes, their modest farms, and the land they were born on to make the long trek north to Honduras.

During the day, the camps were a hub of activity. As the men trained for incursions back into Nicaragua, the women washed clothes in the river, collected wood for the fire, and carried water from the purification system. They also prepared the meals—black beans and rice in the morning, and then, for variety, rice and black beans at night. The dining area was often no more than an open pavilion with a plastic sheet overhead to keep out the rain. By the end of the day, everyone was exhausted from the spartan labor of survival.

When times were good, the soldiers had boots. For everyone else, it was bare feet, sneakers, or sandals. The fighting men wore whatever would pass for a uniform: it wasn't unusual to come across a formation that included Honduran army fatigues, Guatemalan khakis, U.S. Army–type camouflage outfits, and even Cuban army clothes, captured from a warehouse in Nicaragua. Some of the best uniforms were dark-blue work suits that Calero had ordered from Sears—right out of the catalogue.

Many of the camp residents wore clothes donated by American philanthropic organizations, and I would see kids wearing the most incongruous T-shirts: Alcatraz Prison, Minnesota Twins, Esprit, Harvard University, even "Kiss me, I'm Irish."

No matter how often I visited the camps, the resistance fighters were always younger than I expected. At Yamales, the largest of the camps, I met a dark-eyed ten-year-old named Tomás who had arrived at the camp with his teenage brother. Their parents were described as "missing"—probably detained, or worse, by the Nicaraguan authorities. Tomás had a child's eagerness for what his older brother was doing, and when he insisted that he, too, wanted to fight the Sandinistas, the officers allowed him to tag along with his brother during the training. He was quite a sight with his heavy AK-47, which was almost as big as he was.

When his brother's unit left the camp and went back into Nicaragua, Tomás had to be restrained from going with them. He was crushed: the only real connection he had left in the world was leaving, and Tomás knew that his brother might never return. That night, Tomás ran away from the camp. They found him in the morning, safe—but still furious that his brother had gone off without him.

In one respect, however, Tomás was fortunate. At least he and his brother were fighting on the same side. As in any civil war, there were families in Nicaragua where brothers were actually shooting each other.

The White House and the State Department's Office of Public Diplomacy did what they could to make Americans aware of the conditions in the camps, but it was never easy. In 1991, when the Kurds starting fleeing Iraq, I was reminded all over again of what the contra camps were like. Americans are a generous people. We send relief to earthquake victims and refugees all over the globe. But the contras, most of whom were refugees from Sandinista oppression, were largely ignored.

The ignorance among Washington's decision-makers included an almost willful denial of the true size of the resistance movement. From a handful of former Guardsmen in 1980, the resistance had grown steadily. By the time U.S. government funds were running out in the spring of 1984, there were thousands of fighters spread out in half a dozen camps along the Nicaraguan-Honduran border. By then, a small southern front of the resistance had sprung up along the Nicaraguan–Costa Rican border.

In most guerrilla wars, if ten men go out on an operation, they consider themselves fortunate if nine come back. With the contras, a group of ten would disappear into Nicaragua, and two months later they'd return with a net gain of two or more men. They didn't have to work very hard to round up volunteers; when a contra unit moved into an area, disenchanted Nicaraguans would almost invariably seek it out and join.

But while actual numbers might have been in dispute, there was no question that the resistance was still conducting major operations deep inside Nicaragua—without any apparent support. Naturally, the survival of the resistance after the Boland cutoffs led many people to wonder where the support was coming from. The Saudi funding, which started in 1984, was a well-kept secret, as was a gift of two million dollars that General Singlaub solicited from the government of Taiwan.*

The invisible support for the resistance solved the most pressing problem: survival. The people in the camps were hungry, but they weren't starving. The guerrilla army needed more arms and better weapons, but at least they had rifles and some ammunition. The contra "air force" was a joke, but at least there were planes.

---

*Later on, the resistance received a third foreign contribution, although this one never actually reached the contras. In the summer of 1986, after being approached by the State Department, the Sultan of Brunei (whose full name was Haji Hassanal Bolkiah Mu'izzaddin Waddaulah) gave ten million dollars to the resistance. In a rare mistake, Fawn Hall accidentally reversed two digits while typing the account number of Lake Resources in Geneva: the money went to account number 368-430-22-1 instead of 386-430-22-1, and never reached its intended destination. By then, however, the resistance had two additional sources of income: private money raised by the National Endowment for the Preservation of Liberty (NEPL), which was headed by Spitz Channell, a conservative activist; and the "secret within a secret"—profits from the sale of arms to Iran.

On Capitol Hill and in the press, the question kept coming up: who was paying for all of this? There was a lot of speculation about third-party support, and reports of donations coming in from Israel, South Africa, and elsewhere. There were also rumors that the Saudis were involved, as indeed they were.

Some people, who disliked the contras to begin with, concluded that the resistance was being supported by the drug trade. "They're not getting any help that we can see," people said. "They've got to be running drugs."

We heard these stories, too, and we continually probed these allegations and their origins and acted on them as best we could. When the CIA believed that two associates of Eden Pastora, the colorful but erratic southern front commander, had ties to the drug trade, word was put out to have nothing more to do with them. Aside from that, however, we found no evidence of any drug connection. There was enough animosity among the various contra factions that if drugs *had* been involved, somebody would have blown the whistle.

Bill Casey believed that the drug rumors constituted a classic case of disinformation. He was convinced that these stories originated in Cuba and circulated from Havana and Mexico City to Capitol Hill, where they were eagerly spread by opponents of the resistance. There was irrefutable evidence that the Cubans themselves were involved in the drug trade, and what better way to deal with the issue than to focus attention on the other guys?

The Sandinistas, too, were involved with drugs. In 1984 I helped coordinate an elaborate interagency sting operation which involved a convicted drug dealer named Barry Seal. In return for a reduced sentence, Seal agreed to help the DEA. Part of his mission involved flying from Colombia to Nicaragua in a special plane that was equipped with hidden cameras and microphones. In April he flew to an airfield north of Managua, where he was met by Federico Vaughan, an aide to Tomás Borge, Nicaragua's interior minister. Vaughan helped Seal load seven hundred and fifty kilos of cocaine—an operation that was documented by a series of vivid black-and-white photographs. In July, Seal returned to Nicaragua. He again met with Vaughan, who agreed to set up a cocaine processing center in Nicaragua.

Based on various intelligence sources, we believed that the Sandinistas were setting up a program to process Colombian cocaine in

Nicaragua and ship it to drug dealers in the United States. The Sandinista regime was going to help by providing security, personnel, airfields, and transportation support.

We had hoped to use Seal to run this operation long enough to capture Pablo Escobar, the infamous Colombian drug lord (who later surrendered to Colombian authorities after being assured that he wouldn't be extradited to the United States), as well as any Sandinistas who might be working with him. But this plan had to be terminated when a story about the operation and Sandinista involvement with Colombian drug dealers appeared in the *Washington Times*. The operation was immediately shut down.

Barry Seal then became a government witness against the drug dealers who had received his shipments. But he refused to accept the federal protection available to a witness in these circumstances. In February 1986, he was ambushed outside a halfway house in Louisiana, and he died in a hail of bullets. The three-man hit team was caught, convicted, and sentenced to life without parole. The C-123 transport plane that Seal had flown on his covert missions to Nicaragua was later purchased by General Secord, who used it to help the contras. Stripped of its surveillance equipment, this was the same plane that was shot down by the Sandinistas in October 1986, with Eugene Hasenfus on board.

No matter how hard we tried to disprove the rumors about the contras and drugs, the stories never really went away. Some are circulating to this day, despite the fact that all of us involved with the contras did everything we could to identify any possible violators.

Very little in my life has angered me as much as the allegations that I or anyone else involved with the resistance had a drug connection. I hate to put it in these terms, but since December 1986, the office of the special prosecutor has spent tens of millions of dollars investigating us—and me in particular. If there was even a grain of truth to these stories, it surely would have come out.

As part of the effort to unify the Nicaraguan resistance, Casey asked me to bring together the various factions in a single umbrella organization. Adolfo came up with the name: the United Nicaraguan Opposition—UNO. (Fortunately, the Spanish version yielded the same initials.)

To help UNO become a reality, Casey wanted Dick Secord's role expanded. Until now, Secord had simply served as a foreign purchaser of arms, ammo, and military matériel that the resistance was unable to purchase locally. Casey wanted Secord to become the sole provider of supplies to all the factions, not just Calero's FDN. In retrospect, we probably should have gone this route from the start, rather than putting the whole burden on Adolfo. It would have made it easier to implement the unity effort, and it would have prevented Adolfo from becoming the target for wild rumors.

During an all-night meeting in Miami with Adolfo, Enrique Bermudez, Dick, and others, we agreed on the need to encourage the departure of some thirty or forty American soldiers of fortune, whose increasingly conspicuous presence was unacceptable to the Honduran government. We also discussed the need to end the involvement of several Central American arms dealers who were selling weapons to the contras. Although their prices were generally good, and occasionally *very* good, most of these dealers had unsavory reputations, and one of them was suspected by the CIA of having been involved in the transfer of restricted American technology to the Soviets.

From now on, Secord would be the only source of arms. "Tell the resistance to stop dealing with these other guys," Casey had told me. "They have enough problems. I gave you the name of a reliable man. Use him."

And so Dick Secord emerged with a greatly enhanced role. He was now charged not only with the purchase of weapons, but with the entire resupply effort. Later on, congressional investigators and the press referred to this operation as "the Enterprise"; we knew it as Project Democracy. It consisted of airplanes, a ship, warehouses, flight crews—the works. The financial side of the operation was run from a master account called Lake Resources, a shell corporation in Geneva that was controlled by Dick Secord and Albert Hakim. When private money was raised for the contras, this was where it was sent.

As a result of that meeting, Secord created an airlift operation that could deliver supplies to resistance units deep inside Nicaragua, regardless of which faction they were from.

When I wasn't traveling in connection with the contras, or the Iran initiative, or counterterrorism projects, I gave a number of briefings about Central America. These talks, which were essentially narrated slide shows, were normally held in Room 450 of the OEOB, where the audiences ranged from a small handful of people to several hundred, and usually consisted of church groups or grassroots political organizations.

I would reveal as much as I was allowed to say about the Soviet and Communist bloc involvement in Central America. I described how the Soviets and their Cuban and bloc allies intended to create turmoil in the Caribbean basin to divert our attention and resources away from NATO, and from various Third World trouble spots. I pointed out that the Soviets were outspending us by a ratio of four to one *in our own hemisphere.*

Early in the presentation, I showed a series of slides in which we tracked the movement of a single weapon, a rocket-propelled grenade launcher that was manufactured in China. During the Vietnam War, the Chinese had sent it to Hanoi, where it was stamped by the North Vietnamese Army inventory control system. The weapon was subsequently captured by American forces in Vietnam, and left behind when we abandoned Vietnam in the spring of 1975. The grenade launcher was once again in Vietnamese hands. From Vietnam it went to Cuba, and from Cuba to a warehouse in Grenada, and from Grenada to the Sandinistas in Nicaragua—who passed it on to the insurgents in El Salvador. The Chinese grenade launcher was subsequently captured by the Salvadoran Army, which was how it ended up in our hands.

Sophisticated Americans used to snicker at any reference to an international Communist conspiracy. But documents found in Grenada, as well as our own intelligence reports, made clear that many weapons, like this RPG launcher, had definitely been around the bloc.

In these briefings, I would also describe the 1983 Grenada rescue operation. Here was a tiny island in the middle of the Caribbean where we discovered enough guns to arm every man, woman and child three times over. We also found an enormous archive of documents that was brought back to Washington to be analyzed. It offered the first detailed case study of a Soviet takeover of another country that we had ever seen. One of the experts assigned to study these documents was Michael Ledeen, which was how I met him.

Among other things, the Grenada documents revealed a massive indoctrination program for the island's population. Selected individuals from Grenada were sent to study and train all over the Soviet empire: Moscow, East Berlin, Ho Chi Minh City, Prague, Sofia, Havana. Could anybody honestly argue that there was no evidence of an international Communist connection?

The Grenada documents also included an item that McFarlane would not allow me to mention—not because it was classified (it wasn't), but because Bud didn't want to risk antagonizing the Congress. The document in question was a letter from a top aide of Congressman Ron Dellums of California to Prime Minister Maurice Bishop of Grenada. (Bishop was a protégé of Castro who was assassinated in 1983 by an even more extreme group, which precipitated our rescue operation.) "He really admires you as a person," Dellums's aide wrote to Bishop, "and even more so as a leader. Believe me, he doesn't make that statement often about anyone. The only other person that I know of that he expresses such admiration for is Fidel."

In 1991, Congressman Dellums was named to the House Intelligence Committee.

This wasn't the only information that I couldn't use in these briefings. We also had evidence of disturbing connections between other U.S. government employees and leaders in the Central American Communist movement. One such individual was a senior staffer for a powerful member of Congress. Casey had reliable information that this man was providing advice to the Sandinistas—coaching them, in effect, on how to improve their standing with Congress. But Bud wouldn't let Casey confront anyone on the Hill with this information, and he told me not to mention it in my briefings.

Finally, my briefings would include an explanation of why the Sandinistas posed a threat—not just to Central America but to the United States as well. Staff members at the NSC are paid to think about contingencies, and I would spell out what was admittedly a worst-case scenario. If the Communist regime in Managua succeeded in exporting its "revolution without frontiers," the entire region could turn into one mass migration of people fleeing north.

Historically, when Communists take over a country, almost anybody who can flee does. It happened in Cuba, in Vietnam, in Cambodia, and again in Afghanistan, where more than 25 percent of the population had fled to Pakistan, India, and Iran. The same thing was

The Iranians we met with knew so little about the U.S. government that I had to bring a photo with me to show them who the players on our side were. I took this picture of an Oval Office meeting with me to Tehran, showing, from left to right, Bud McFarlane, me, David Chew (assistant to Don Regan), Bob Sims (Bud's press spokesman), Admiral John Poindexter, President Reagan, and Don Regan. (The White House)

This Oval Office meeting with Vice President Bush, Admiral Poindexter, Don Fortier (the deputy national security adviser), Don Regan, me, John Whitehead (deputy secretary of state), and Elliott Abrams was to discuss a mission to Central America that Abrams and I went on in the spring of 1986 to reassure our neighbors about our commitment to the Nicaraguan resistance. (The White House)

At their joint White House press conference on November 25, 1986, Ed Meese and the President announced that Admiral Poindexter had been "reassigned." As I watched from my office, the nation was told that I had been relieved of my duties. In other words, *fired*! (Bob Daugherty/Associated Press)

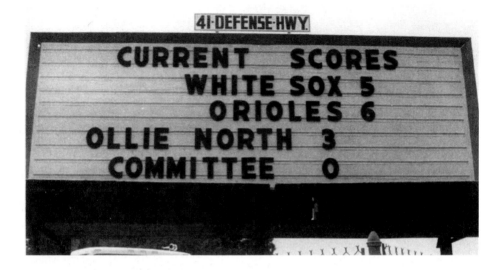

People from all over America wanted to show how they felt about what was going on in Washington. This photo was sent after the third day of televised hearings.

All the visibility changed things dramatically for our family. When Brendan, Barry Simon, and I took our sons to see an Orioles game, we had to bring along security agents. (Kevin Allen/Impact Images)

Between the hearings in the summer of 1987 and my indictment by the special prosecutor the following spring, we had a brief respite from all the controversy. The Sullivan and North kids gathered with their dads across the Severn River from my alma mater for a picnic. (Tait, our oldest, missed the party.)

Brendan trusted two old sea dogs, Admiral Poindexter and me, to pilot his sailboat around Chesapeake Bay on a summer weekend. Both of us are wearing appropriate "nautical attire"—white shorts, navy blue shirts, and suntans.

In the aftermath of all the controversy and visibility, someone demonstrated the viability of the free enterprise system by making a postcard showing my boyhood home in Philmont, New York. The caption on the back reads: "Ollie North's boyhood home is located on a typical quiet, tree-lined Columbia County street. Ollie was well liked by all who knew him, was competitive and a good kid. If you happen to run into someone who knows him, be prepared to spend a little time listening." (Joe Connors)

WITH A FEW NOTABLE EXCEPTIONS, NO ONE CAN TRANSFER YOUR MONEY ROUND THE WORLD MORE EFFICIENTLY THAN US.

After the hearings, numerous groups and organizations used my name and face to raise funds, claiming that a check to them would somehow help me. Sometimes it was even true—if my attorneys could catch them. In other cases, there was outright commercial exploitation—some of which, like this full-page ad in a British newspaper, was enough to make you laugh.

When he was campaigning for President, the press speculated that George Bush was a wimp. If he was, I never saw it. It took personal courage for him to invite Admiral Poindexter, me, and our wives to his home for this Christmas party in 1986. (The White House)

The day I retired from the Corps in 1988, everyone in my office at the Marine headquarters posed for one last photo.

Above: Much of the last five years has been like this white-water raft ride that Betsy, Stuart, Sarah, Dornin, and I took in Colorado in 1990 when we were on a retreat with the Officers' Christian Fellowship. It reminds me of the caption a Marine friend has on a photo in his office: "God doesn't promise you a smooth passage —just a safe delivery."

With the help of retired Marine Lieutenant General Ed Bronars, I organized a grassroots educational and charitable organization called Freedom Alliance. For Christmas 1990 we sent out more than 120,000 Christmas packages to soldiers, sailors, airmen, and Marines deployed in the Persian Gulf for Operation Desert Shield and Desert Storm. The gift packs were assembled in this sheltered workshop by workers with handicaps.

Betsy and I at the 1994 Army Navy Game at Veterans Stadium in Philadelphia, Pennsylvania. This is an annual event of Freedom Alliance, founded by Oliver North in 1990.

Betsy North, President George W. Bush, First Lady Laura Bush and me at a White House Christmas Party 2001.

now going on in Nicaragua, the only country in Latin America whose population was actually declining. Four hundred thousand people— over 10 percent of the population—had already left for Honduras, Costa Rica, Guatemala, and Panama. Some made it as far as Mexico, and a few walked and hitchhiked all the way to Texas and Florida.

If the Sandinistas succeeded, I explained, and Communism took hold in the region, the tide of people heading north would be over-whelming. It was conceivable that millions of refugees would arrive at our borders, hoping to get in. What would it cost to provide food, clothing, housing, and medical treatment for five or ten million immi-grants?

Later on, I was accused of using these briefings as fund raisers. I did give similar presentations to wealthy members of the National Endowment for the Preservation of Liberty (NEPL), a nonprofit foundation in support of President Reagan's agenda that was headed by Carl "Spitz" Channell, a veteran conservative political activist. But I was careful never to ask for a contribution, and I always left the room before Spitz brought up the matter of money. McFarlane had told me not to ask for contributions, so I didn't. (I assumed that as a government employee, I simply wasn't allowed to solicit funds from private citizens. I learned later that this wasn't true.)

There were times when people just walked in and volunteered their help. One summer afternoon, Joseph Coors, the beer company executive, was sitting with his old friend Bill Casey in Casey's OEOB office, and he asked Bill how he could help the Nicaraguan resistance. "The guy to see is Oliver North," Casey told him. "His office is just down the hall."

Coors is a tall, self-effacing man who certainly didn't fit my image of what a multimillionaire would look like. When he asked what vari-ous amounts of money would buy for the resistance, I described the Maule M-7 airplane, a little four-seater that was used mostly by bush pilots and oil workers. Secord had already bought two of them, and used them for both med-evacs and resupply. The Maule was a STOL (short takeoff and landing) single-engine aircraft that didn't even require a landing strip. All you really needed was a straight stretch of dirt road.

A couple of days later, Joe Coors sent a check for $65,000. Dick

Secord used it to buy another Maule, and for the rest of the war it flew with a Coors label on its tail.

Project Democracy became the operator of a seven-plane air force, consisting of three Maules, two C-123s, and two C-7s. Later, during the investigations, one of the few questions that nobody ever asked was what happened to those planes. It wasn't until much later that I learned the answer. After the Hasenfus incident, when Casey told us to shut down the whole contra supply operation, all the pilots, maintenance men, and mechanics whom Dick Secord had hired returned home on commercial flights, leaving the planes and equipment behind.

Later, in an effort to tidy up the loose ends from Project Democracy, the CIA undertook an extraordinary operation. First they had the little air force flown to a remote airfield. Then an enormous crater was dug with bulldozers. The planes were pushed into the pit, covered with explosives, and blown up. The remaining wreckage was saturated with fuel and then cremated. The fire burned for days.

When the smoke finally cleared, the charred remains were buried. It was probably the only time an air force had ever been given a funeral. One might call it the ultimate cover-up.

Around the end of 1984, I had gone to see Casey about the overall problem of funding a growing number of resistance activities. He recommended that I set up an "operational" account that would be run out of my office. He gave me a ledger, an accountant's notebook with a spiral binding, and told me to keep meticulous records of all the money I received from Calero (and later, from Secord), and all my disbursements on behalf of the resistance. "Keep good books," he said. "You've got to be able to answer for every penny."

I did as I was told. I kept careful records, including the serial number on each of the traveler's checks. I kept the ledger in my office safe, along with the cash and the checks. Some of the money went for emergencies, like the time Eden Pastora showed up broke and presented me with a bill for his five-day stay at the Four Seasons, one of the most expensive hotels in Washington, or the morning I was called by a member of Congress, who told me that several members of the Nicaraguan Indian resistance were in town and couldn't pay their hotel bills. Rob Owen, Jonathan Miller, and I had to go out to nearby banks and stores to cash traveler's checks for the Indians. Rob met them at the corner of Seventeenth and Pennsylvania and handed them the money.*

Fawn Hall cashed some checks, too. And once, on a weekend, when the banks were closed, she asked me for a loan of sixty dollars. I gave her three twenty-dollar traveler's checks, and she repaid the account the following Monday.

Around this same time, McFarlane was getting nervous about all the traveling I was doing. Many of my trips were covert, and Bud didn't want any record of them at the NSC. Besides, I was traveling so often that I was using up most of the NSC travel budget. The CIA maintains operational accounts for just these purposes, but the NSC has no such funds. McFarlane, and later, Poindexter, authorized the use of the Calero operational account for trips I took to both Central America and Europe, and to support hostage rescue efforts, an activity for which I also had Calero's approval.

Sometimes, when I was short of traveler's checks, I would use my own money to travel. The next time checks came in from Calero, I'd reimburse myself—just as I reimbursed resistance leaders for their hotel bills. That's why some of the checks were cashed at Giant Food, a local supermarket, and other stores near our house. Another check was made out to a store called Parklane Hosiery, which became the subject of great titillation during the hearings until Betsy reminded me that this was where we bought leotards for our daughters.

In all, over $100,000 in traveler's checks passed through the operational account. Like almost everything else about my work for both the contras and the hostages, the operational account was kept secret.

We certainly could have done more to hurt the Sandinistas economically. Despite the fact that they were virtually in a state of war against their neighbors, the State Department was opposed to any economic restrictions that went much beyond a cutback in the coffee quota. As they saw it, a serious economic embargo would result in hardships for the Nicaraguan people. While that was certainly true, some of us, including Casey, Weinberger, and Ray Burghardt at the NSC, believed that with a well-mounted propaganda campaign, we

---

*During the hearings, Jonathan Miller was working at the White House. When his name came up as one of the people who had cashed traveler's checks, he was immediately fired, and ordered to leave the premises within the hour.

would be able to demonstrate to the people of Nicaragua that their economic problems were the fault of their own government's policies.

The debate raged on within the administration, where everybody knew that if the President exercised his authority and imposed an embargo, this would infuriate Congress. Finally, Don Fortier, the number-three man at the NSC, urged Ray Burghardt and me to sit down and draft an Executive Order for the President's signature freezing all of Nicaragua's assets and implementing a full-scale economic embargo. With McFarlane's blessing, we sent copies to State, Defense, the CIA, Justice, Commerce, and the Treasury. Each agency was asked to concur quickly, because the draft Executive Order was being sent on to the President that same night. The other agencies either "concurred" or "interposed no objection," but we heard nothing at all from State. Late that evening, in one of the rare occasions when he was willing to confront the State Department openly, McFarlane sent the draft executive order to the President at Camp David. The President signed it the next morning, and the embargo began.

But for some supporters of the resistance, this didn't go far enough. They just couldn't understand why we still had diplomatic relations with Nicaragua. They blamed the State Department, but this was one time when State was not guilty. While the boys at Foggy Bottom were certainly horrified at the prospect of reducing our diplomatic presence anywhere on the planet, in this case they were right. True, the Nicaraguan embassy in Washington had its share of spies, and yes, its officials met regularly with congressional opponents of contra aid. But on balance, it was still to our advantage to maintain a presence in Managua. In addition to serving as an important symbol of liberty, our embassy was a vital source of reliable information.

It was also well protected. Although the U.S. embassy in Managua was often the target of angry demonstrations against the United States, these protests were tightly controlled by the authorities. In fact, Nicaragua was the one country in all of Central America where our diplomats didn't really need bodyguards. If the American ambassador so much as tripped on the curb, three Sandinistas would be there to catch him before he hit the ground. Certainly our embassy was a lot safer than the one in El Salvador, which was periodically hit by rockets, or our embassies in Honduras or Costa Rica, which were occasionally fired on with mortars and machine guns. The Sandinistas were careful not to provide us with any reason to take direct action against them.

One plan we discussed, but never implemented, was the possibility of establishing a Nicaraguan government in exile. During World War II, several countries, including France, Poland, and Yugoslavia, had established "free governments" in Britain. And in 1990, after Kuwait was invaded by Iraq, the Kuwaiti leadership set up a government-in-exile in Saudi Arabia.

In the case of Nicaragua, however, there were some fairly big obstacles. Unlike World War II, or Kuwait in 1990, there was no surviving head of state who could lead such a government. And what country in Central America would be willing to serve as the host? "Terrific idea," said Nicaragua's neighbors. "But please, not in our backyard. Say, why don't you try down the street and ask Costa Rica?"

These countries had good reason to be afraid. With the large and powerful Sandinista army so close, it would have taken an enormous dose of testosterone for any nation in the region to allow an official resistance presence within its borders.

Another possible site for a government-in-exile was Miami, which was both safe and convenient. But politically, Miami was a terrible idea. If the Free Government of Nicaragua were based in Florida, the rest of the world would regard it as nothing more than a pawn of the United States.

If it wasn't feasible to establish a government-in-exile, another possibility was to do essentially the same thing—inside Nicaragua, on a section of land that the resistance would seize. We actually looked into the possibility of having the contras capture one or two of the islands along the Atlantic Coast, or perhaps the northeast corner of Nicaragua, which included the port of Puerto Cabezas, where the Sandinistas were vulnerable. President Suazo in Honduras thought this was a fine idea—assuming that the new government was recognized and immediately supported by the United States. In El Salvador, President Duarte told me the same thing.

I even wrote a paper on how such a plan might work, and the idea was discussed at the Restricted Interagency Group. McFarlane thought it was worth pursuing, but here again there were numerous obstacles. Would any other countries recognize and support the new government? For that matter, could we be absolutely sure that the

United States would? And who would head this new entity? Naturally, each of the three leaders of the United Nicaraguan Opposition saw himself as the ideal candidate. Was it really possible for them to share the spotlight?

Militarily, it could have worked. If the contra forces had taken over a section of northeast Nicaragua, it would have been difficult for the Sandinistas to dislodge them. The risk was that such a step might bring in the Cubans, which in turn would lead to the sending of American forces. That would have been serious indeed—although after Grenada, it was unlikely that the Cubans were looking forward to another military encounter with American troops.

Another idea that didn't quite materialize came up in February 1985. The CIA alerted me to a Nicaraguan arms ship, the *Monimbo*, which for years had been wending its way around the Soviet bloc, picking up artillery, surface-to-air missiles, mines, ammunition, and other weapons for the Sandinistas. The ship was loaded with military supplies that could have been enormously helpful to the resistance, and I sent McFarlane a memo proposing several means by which the *Monimbo* might be intercepted, including seizing it on the high seas and removing its cargo. If that wasn't possible, perhaps there was some other way to prevent these arms from reaching the Sandinistas.

I received permission from Poindexter to see if we could prevent the *Monimbo* from reaching its intended destination. Poindexter even put his response in writing: "We need to take action to make sure [the] ship does not arrive in Nicaragua," he noted at the bottom of my memo.

In the end, it did not prove possible to seize the ship. But oddly enough, the *Monimbo* ran aground off the coast of Nicaragua, where its cargo was thoroughly ruined by seawater.

13

The Second Channel

When the McFarlane delegation returned from Tehran in the spring of 1986, one thing was certain: Ghorbanifar had to go. Although he had been helpful in opening up the connection to the Iranians, and had played a major role in the rescue of two hostages, Gorba had also given us plenty of evidence—more than he knew—that he couldn't be trusted. As soon as the Tehran meetings began, it was obvious that he had been overstating to each side what the other was willing to do. Now it was more important than ever that we find a replacement.

It was Albert Hakim, Dick Secord's partner, who made the connection to the man who replaced Ghorbanifar and became known as the Second Channel. Hakim and Secord are one of the all-time great odd couples. Whereas Dick is a gruff, cold, aggressive, straight-to-the-point military man, Albert is a warm and fuzzy, courteous and courtly Iranian Jew who fled Iran shortly before Khomeini took over. They had met in Tehran during the mid-1970s, when Secord was stationed there as head of the U.S. Air Force programs.

My first encounter with Albert occurred under somewhat ridiculous circumstances. In February 1986, Secord and I were in Frankfurt for a two-day meeting with Ghorbanifar and the Iranian government official known as the Australian, who later played a major role in our Tehran meetings. These talks, at the airport Sheraton Hotel, were the first direct contact in years between American and Iranian representatives.

The meeting had been convened fairly quickly, and the CIA officer who was with us couldn't speak Farsi. Nor could the Agency come up with a Farsi-speaking translator on such short notice. Gorba could have handled the job, but we had already spent enough time with him to realize that we couldn't rely on him in this role. It was Secord who suggested that we bring in his partner, Albert Hakim. (Secord himself spoke Farsi, but not fluently enough to be the translator.)

When Ghorbanifar learned that Hakim would be translating, he was outraged. "We know who he is," Gorba said. "Hakim is an enemy of the state. He opposed the revolution, and we cannot accept him."

Hakim was our only choice. But what if Gorba recognized him? And what if the Australian did? We hadn't yet met the Australian, and we weren't even sure exactly who he was. This was one of the great frustrations in dealing with the Iranians. With virtually every other nation in the world, you could pretty well assume that one of today's junior men would emerge as tomorrow's leader. When Gorbachev came to power in the Soviet Union, the whole world was surprised. But at least he had been part of the political establishment.

Iran was different. Khomeini's revolution resulted in a government without a history, and a regime led by men with no political background. Assuming the Australian really was a high government official, as Gorba had insisted, it was possible that in an earlier incarnation he was Hakim's barber, or his car mechanic. In fact, he turned out to be a former tailor—although not Hakim's.

Albert's version of how we solved this problem is simply irresistible:

And so I'm sitting there and said to the group, "I certainly would remember Ghorbanifar. There is no reason that he would not remember me. So how do you want me to go into this meeting?"

So they turned to the CIA official and said, "Do you have somebody that can disguise Albert?" And the guy said, "By the time I go through the bureaucracy it will be the end of the meeting."

So Oliver North turned around to me and said, "I've heard from

Richard [Secord] that you're very resourceful. Why don't you go and disguise yourself?"

I said, "Thanks."

So I left the hotel, came down to the concierge, and said "I need to buy a gift for my father and I want to get a wig for him. Where is the best place to go?"

So a lady is looking at me, gave me a couple of addresses, recommended one. I got a cab. I went to the place and the lady started to go through all kinds of salesmanship to sell me the best wig and if I wanted to swim, I didn't want to swim, and I'm sitting there knowing that the meeting is going to start very soon and I cannot—"Lady, let's get on with it, I don't give a damn, just give me a wig."

So she goes and brings me a number of wigs to select from. This has that advantage, this one this. Finally, to make a long story short, I said, "This is beautiful, just let's try it on." And so we tried it on and I looked at myself, I said, "Oh, this is not good enough." I said, "I don't like the style of this. Do you have a barber?" They sent me to the basement. There was another lady. I said, "I would like my hairdo in this form." We managed to shape it in such a way that it doesn't look like me.

And I normally don't wear eyeglasses, but I have a pair of folding eyeglasses that I carry in my briefcase. I put that on and walked into the room and those three guys were just shocked, amazed. They didn't think that there was a chance for Ghorbanifar to know who I was.*

He certainly had *me* fooled. Hakim is nearly bald, and if I hadn't been expecting the disguise I would never have recognized him. At the meeting, we introduced him to the Iranians as Ibrahim Ibrahimian, a Farsi-speaking Turk of Armenian descent. They didn't have a clue as to his real identity. Later, I was asked whether Albert did a good job as our translator. I think he did—but then, how would I know?

Months later, following our trip to Tehran, two of Hakim's business associates put him in touch with one of Speaker Hashemi Rafsanjani's many nephews in Tehran. The Nephew, as we called this young man, became the so-called Second Channel who eventually replaced Ghorbanifar.

*Deposition of Albert Hakim in Appendix B of the *Report of the Congressional Committees Investigating the Iran-Contra Affair*, B-13, pp. 591–92.

In late August, 1986, the Nephew flew to Brussels to meet Secord and Hakim. Dick called me right afterward, and for the first time in months he sounded enthusiastic about the Iran initiative. He was convinced that we had finally broken out of a web of duplicity. He was also impressed with the Nephew, in part because the Nephew had been candid in acknowledging that Iran did not really control the Hezballah hostage-takers in Beirut. Those of us who had gone to Tehran had already heard this, but Dick saw it as a positive sign.

Back in Washington, the conventional wisdom was that the Iranians *did* control the hostage-takers. Ghorbanifar certainly encouraged us to think so, and at first, I too had believed this. But the more intelligence reports I read, the more I began to believe that the link between the two groups was less a matter of control than of influence, especially on financial and religious matters. Although the question is still open, this wasn't a simple case of a division commander in Tehran sending orders to his officers in Beirut.

Months before the Second Channel came along, Gorba had told us that some of the money from the earlier arms deals had gone to pay off Hezballah officials in Lebanon. The Nephew said the same thing and added that while the Iranians couldn't actually order the release of the hostages, they had been able to bribe the Hezballah leaders to gain the freedom of both Weir and Jenco. Unlike Gorba, the Nephew conceded that his contacts could *not* arrange what we really wanted, which was to get all the remaining hostages released together.

In just about every respect, the Nephew was a pleasant and welcome contrast to Ghorbanifar. Whereas Gorba was a fat cat who lived in Paris, the Nephew was a family man living in war-torn Iran with a brand-new baby. While he wasn't part of the government, he apparently had good connections. He had fought with the Rev Guards in the war against Iraq, and he struck both Secord and me as someone who wanted to improve his country's situation and to give his children a better and more peaceful life. In short, he was idealistic—a quality I had certainly never observed in Ghorbanifar.

And while Gorba never hid the fact that he was in it for the money (although he certainly tried to hide how much he was making), the Nephew didn't appear to have a financial motive. That, at least, was my impression; it's entirely possible that Hakim had warned him not to mention money in my presence. Albert knew that what I cared about was freeing the hostages and trying to achieve an opening with Iran. While Albert was certainly willing to work toward those ends, he was primarily a businessman who saw the initiative as an opportunity to make money.

It didn't take long for Gorba to discover that we were trying to open a second line of communication with Iran that would exclude him. Not surprisingly, he was furious. By this time, his incessant wheeling and dealing had apparently caught up with him. He had been dealing with the French, trying to deal with the British, and hoping to deal with the Irish—all of whom had hostages in Beirut. He was also angry that we still hadn't delivered the second shipment from our May visit to Tehran. Gorba maintained that he'd had to finance this one himself, and was therefore in debt. As he described it, he'd had to raise the money in short-term loans from various sources while he was simultaneously working any number of deals with other governments, ranging from soybeans to oil wells. He said he owed money to several parties, including Adnan Khashoggi, the flamboyant Saudi businessman.

While we waited to see if the Second Channel would work out, Charlie Allen from the CIA remained in touch with Ghorbanifar. Charlie had already called to warn me that if we dropped Gorba without either delivering what he had paid for or at least reimbursing him to the tune of four or five million dollars, we ran the risk of having Gorba expose the entire initiative. In other words, we should make sure to buy him out before dropping him.

Charlie was right, and we should have taken his warnings more seriously. But the trouble with someone like Ghorbanifar is that you're never really prepared for when he might be giving it to you straight. In retrospect, two of Ghorbanifar's statements turned out to be all too accurate. He had warned us that if he wasn't handled properly, the whole Iran initiative would come crashing down. He had also promised us that as long as he was involved, there wouldn't be any more kidnappings.

We should have paid more attention to that one. Soon after Dick made contact with the Second Channel, two more American hostages were seized in Beirut: Frank Reed, an educator, and Joseph Ciccipio, the comptroller at the American University in Beirut. I was sick. Throughout the Iran initiative, our worst fear was that the Hezballah would send around a videotape of the hostages being executed. Our second worst fear was that additional hostages would be taken—and now that fear had been realized. While the Iranians couldn't necessarily get all the hostages released, until now they had at least been able to discourage further seizures.

The two new kidnappings led to a number of meetings in Washington, where we seriously considered shutting the whole thing down. But while there was a risk in continuing, there was also a risk in stopping. We decided to go ahead.

I suspected that at least one of these new kidnappings had been orchestrated by the Australian's faction. He and his cronies must been furious when they learned of the Second Channel, which presumably left them on the sidelines, and they surely knew that the Nephew had been authorized to leave Iran to meet with us. Later the Nephew confirmed my suspicions.

Shortly after Secord returned from his first meeting with the Nephew, we invited the young Iranian to Washington to meet with George Cave, Secord, Hakim, and myself. This was a quick way to determine whether the Second Channel was real: if the Iranians let this guy visit the land of the Great Satan, they probably meant business. Besides, we had already been to Tehran, and we weren't all that eager to go back.

On September 19, 1986, the Nephew arrived at Dulles Airport with two escorts. One was Hakim's business contact who had made the introduction, and the other was the Nephew's keeper, a combination of bodyguard and commissar. Unlike the Communist world, where the commissars reported to their political bosses, the Iranian keepers answer to the religious authorities.

When the Iranians landed, they were met by officials who had been sent by the CIA, and who sped them through customs and immigration and delivered them to their hotel. The previous day, I had run around Washington getting the necessary authorizations to conduct surveillance on them while they were here. These things are not done casually. Surveillance on foreign nationals in the United States requires very senior level approval, the request for which had to be submitted with the signatures of four government officials or their principal deputies: the head of the FBI, the director of the CIA, the Attorney General, and the national security adviser. After collecting the necessary signatures, I had a courier deliver the request for final approval.

Throughout the time they were here, the surveillance was maintained—just as the Iranians had undoubtedly done for *our* visit to Tehran. One good turn deserves another.

I liked the Nephew as soon as I met him. He was a cheerful and friendly guy who had obviously put on a little weight since his time on the Basra front. He had lost several friends in the conflict with Iraq, and he seemed to be truly disgusted by what the war was doing to his country.

Despite the fact that Gorba had always shown up with fine Iranian caviar, the talks with the Second Channel were far more pleasant than our meetings with Gorba's group—if only because we didn't have to sit through hours of revolutionary diatribe. For the most part, however, the issues were not new. The actors had changed, but the script was the same.

Unfortunately, the Second Channel didn't move any faster than the First Channel. These meetings, too, lasted for hours at a stretch, and continued (at intervals) over a period of months. Our negotiations with both groups of Iranians were so interminable and frustrating that I actually developed some empathy for employees of the State Department.

Later, people who read or heard about the Iran initiative couldn't quite understand why it took us so long to accomplish so little. It's a good question, and there are several answers.

First, our goals were extremely ambitious: not only to recover the hostages, which was difficult enough, but also to reopen a relationship with a closed and hostile society. Second, there were years of acrimony and layers of distrust that had to be overcome. Third, everything had to be done through translators. Fourth, the Iranians have a different concept of time than we do, and life moves much more slowly in their world. Finally, it's clear, at least in retrospect, that there was an enormous gap between what each side wanted and what was actually possible. They wanted us simply to turn on the spigot of American aid; we wanted them to snap their fingers and get the hostages released. Neither feat was possible for either side.

During the Nephew's three-day visit to Washington, we met both in my office at the OEOB, and at Secord's in suburban Virginia. As always, we spent a lot of time discussing the hostages. I explained yet again that the hostage problem had to be resolved before there could be normal relations between our countries, that this was a hurdle to be overcome before we moved on to bigger issues.

At the same time, I didn't want the hostages to seem overly important. "We want them out," I said, "but let me put this problem in perspective. Fifty-two thousand Americans die each year in highway accidents. Well over a hundred thousand die of lung cancer. In a country of our size, five hostages are not very many. But the American people would be outraged if President Reagan helped Iran without first resolving this obstacle."

In reality, the hostages were on my mind more than ever. By the time we made contact with the Second Channel, I had been to any number of meetings with the hostage families. (The hostage problem fell under the rubric of counterterrorism, and McFarlane had asked me to meet with the families of the men who were held in Beirut.) A few family members, like Peggy Say, the sister of Terry Anderson, and Eric and Paul Jacobsen, the sons of David Jacobsen, came to my office regularly.

These visits would increase whenever there was news of any kind about the hostages. From time to time, the hostage-takers in Beirut would release a videotape or a letter from the hostages in an effort to put more pressure on our government. I can't speak for the rest of the administration, but they sure worked on me.

On one occasion, David Jacobsen's sons brought me a letter from their father that the captors had allowed to be smuggled out. Despite the deplorable conditions and the terrible uncertainty he was enduring, Jacobsen's letter was full of love for his family and concern for his welfare. Long before I finished reading it, my eyes had filled with tears. The hostage-takers also sent out occasional photographs of their prisoners, who were usually portrayed holding a contemporary periodical to show that they were still alive. These photos reached us from various sources, but we never made them public unless they had already been released to the press. The successive photos of Terry Anderson, Ben Weir, Father Jenco, and David Jacobsen were graphic illustrations of the effects of stress, poor diet, lack of sunlight, and the general debilitation caused by their confinement. For me, these pictures always provided additional incentive to push on, no matter how exhausted or disillusioned I might have been.

When the family members met with me and other government officials, they were understandably angry and impatient, and they demanded answers. "What have you heard? What are you doing to get them out?" They were dying to know what we were up to, but I couldn't reveal anything. They were convinced that our government wasn't doing enough, and I couldn't tell them otherwise. Despite everything I knew, part of me agreed with them.

And yet our government was actually doing a great deal, far more than we could ever make public. There were many unsung heroes in this effort: officers of the CIA, DEA, and our embassy staff in Beirut had all risked their lives in efforts to recover the hostages. None of this could be revealed to the long-suffering families, and the Iranian initiative, too, was a well-kept secret. Meanwhile, both the State Department and the White House were quietly working through a variety of other channels to gain access to the hostage holders.

Poindexter and I had several meetings with foreign diplomats both in Washington and in Europe to seek their help in the name of the President. We traveled to France and England to try to determine whether there might be other approaches that could work. Our government had several other diplomatic initiatives under way, any one of which could have become that rare long shot that actually paid off. At least four other heads of state were actively and energetically trying to help, and so were the Vatican and the Anglican Church. Although none of these approaches succeeded, they were all time-consuming and emotionally exhausting.

For the most part, these foreign governments were acting in their own self-interest. Governments are made up of people, and generally behave like people. Favors are expected to be reciprocated: If Harry lends me his lawnmower today, I shouldn't be surprised if he wants to borrow my pickup truck next Saturday. If our government asks for another country's help on the hostages, nobody is shocked when they ask us for our vote in the U.N., or some military hardware, or even a new economic aid package. These terms are rarely articulated up front, and they're generally negotiable. But eventually the chits are called in.

The Nephew appeared to be well briefed on what had transpired with the First Channel, and he arrived in Washington with a long list of military hardware that Iran wanted to buy. But guns weren't the only items on his agenda. He wanted medical equipment and supplies for Iranian soldiers and civilians who had been wounded in the war. He was also desperate for chemical decontamination equipment for the Basra front, where the Iraqis were using chemical warfare weapons. And, just like the First Channel, he asked for our help in freeing the seventeen Da'wa prisoners in Kuwait.

Another topic on our agenda was Ghorbanifar, who was complaining that he was in debt to the tune of millions of dollars, sometimes he said as much as fifteen, sometimes as little as four. He said he couldn't even afford the interest payments. Although we believed that the figures were inflated, we urged the Nephew to keep him quiet by paying him off. Presumably, we weren't the only ones who wanted to keep Gorba happy; the Iranians, too, had a lot to lose if the initiative became public. But when it did, they certainly made the most of it.

During one of our Washington meetings, the Nephew brought up a new topic: getting rid of Saddam Hussein. I regret that there wasn't more willingness within our government to take that one seriously. I said flat out that we couldn't make any commitments about Saddam, but he brought it up again the next day. "The Arab nations can do it," he said, "and the United States can use its influence to make that happen."

In subsequent meetings, I assured the Nephew that the United States recognized that Saddam was the real problem in the region. "President Reagan told me that he thinks Saddam is a shit," I said. Albert Hakim, who was translating, couldn't bring himself to render that line into Farsi. "Go ahead," I told Albert. "That's the President's word, not mine."

Unfortunately, everything I told the Nephew about our attitude toward Saddam Hussein was a lie. I say "unfortunately" not because I lied to the Iranians, which I did whenever I thought it would help, but because our government's attitude toward Saddam Hussein should have been more along the lines I described.

Despite our loud declarations of neutrality in the Iran-Iraq conflict, our government was quietly siding with Iraq. It wasn't just a diplomatic tilt, either; we took affirmative steps to ensure that Iraq would not lose this war it had started. Operation Staunch was a major U.S. diplomatic effort to stem the flow of weapons to Iran, and with the obvious exception of the secret Iran initiative, it was quite effective. Iraq, however, continued to receive a steady supply of arms from the Soviets, the French, the Chinese, and anyone else who wanted a piece of the action. The Kuwaitis helped Saddam pay for what he bought in the international arms bazaar—an act of generosity they would later regret.

When Operation Staunch proved insufficient, President Reagan authorized our intelligence services to pass military information to the Iraqis. And even after the war was over, our pro-Iraq tilt continued. In the summer of 1990, just days before the invasion of Kuwait, the State Department was still trying to convince Congress to grant financial credits and other aid to Iraq.

The American tilt toward Iraq and antipathy toward Iran were two of the few things that Shultz and Weinberger ever agreed on. "We wouldn't want to see" an Iranian victory, George Shultz told a news magazine in 1984, and so "we have been deliberately working to improve our relationship with Iraq.... We have been cooperating with the Iraqis to a certain extent."*

While that was certainly true, it was also an understatement. Back in 1982, Shultz had instructed the State Department's Near East Bureau and our embassy in Baghdad to offer "incentives" if Saddam renounced terrorism. Eager to obtain American computer technology and other embargoed machinery, Saddam informed the State Department that he had "expelled" Abu Nidal. In fact, Abu Nidal and his henchmen had simply departed to work for a higher bidder—Muammar al-Qaddafi. Despite the objection of the State Department's own Office for Combating Terrorism, and several of us at the NSC, State's Near East Bureau prevailed and Iraq was removed from the list of states sponsoring terrorism.

Weinberger showed similar leanings. Toward the end of his tenure at the Pentagon, he told a network television interviewer that he

*U.S. News & World Report, March 12, 1984.

looked forward to a "totally different kind of government" in Iran, and called the Khomeini regime "irrational" and "fanatical."*

What disturbs me about the positions of Shultz and Weinberger is not that they were necessarily wrong about Iran, but that they were so *totally* wrong about Iraq.

"I felt strongly then and do to this day," Weinberger wrote in his memoirs, "that the conduct of the kind Iran exhibited during the seizure of our embassy completely disqualified it from any civilized intercourse with other nations."†

It's funny, but I don't recall Weinberger saying anything like that about Yasir Arafat, or Saddam Hussein. And yet it was Iraq that had started the war by invading Iran. And it was Saddam Hussein who was using chemical weapons against his own people, and who "accidentally" fired an Exocet missile into the U.S.S. *Stark,* and who, despite his disclaimers to the contrary, continued to provide a haven to some of the world's most notorious terrorists.

I certainly don't excuse the Iranian seizure of our embassy in 1979. But every new administration in Washington brings with it the memory of the worst catastrophes that affected its predecessors. Weinberger and Shultz were so obsessed with how Iran had humiliated us under Carter that they ignored the sins of Iraq, which were less visible, but in many ways, far worse.

As this book goes to press, the United States is making a similar mistake by cozying up to Syria. Hafez al-Assad is cut from the same bolt of cloth as Saddam Hussein. He, too, is a brutal leader with dangerous delusions of grandeur who imagines himself as a modern-day Saladin. This is another "friendship" that may well come back to haunt us.

In one of our early meetings, the Nephew came up with a startling and dramatic proposition to free the hostages: he would learn, and then pass on to us, the details of exactly where in Beirut they were being held. We, in turn, would be free to mount a rescue operation to free them. While I thought the idea had possibilities, the dangers were immense. I remembered Desert One, when President Carter's attempt

---

*On "This Week with David Brinkley," September 27, 1987.
†Caspar Weinberger, *Fighting for Peace* (New York, 1990), p. 354.

to rescue our hostages in Tehran had turned to dust and ended in death.

Secord was more optimistic. "Think about it, Ollie," he said. "They're giving us a gift. Imagine what a successful hostage raid would signal to the world. If we could get some collateral intelligence, Beirut is a beautiful place for something like this. It's perfect for helicopters at night."

I dutifully circulated the proposal to the Task Force, but it was met with a decided lack of enthusiasm. Even General Carl Stiner, the hero of the *Achille Lauro* operation, said, "Forget it, Ollie, it's a no-go." I'm not necessarily averse to taking risks, but on this one I agreed with Stiner.

Both Casey and Poindexter told me to keep the idea alive with the Second Channel, if only to see what would come of it. But I knew that a raid was extremely unlikely. Nobody wanted our rescuers to get caught in a trap, and there was no sure way to eliminate that threat.

Then Nir came up with an intriguing variation. If the United States didn't want to take this risk, maybe the Israelis could. Nir even suggested an insurance plan. To "facilitate" the Israeli rescue, which would include the two missing Israeli soldiers, Nir would arrange for Israeli intelligence agents to grab the Nephew, together with any other Iranian officials who might be wandering around Europe. To guard against the possibility of a double cross, they would all be held until the rescue was completed.

"Now you're talking," said Casey. And no wonder: if anything went wrong, the Israelis would take the blame. But the idea of an armed raid into Beirut never got past the talking stage, and it was probably just as well. The Nephew was too nice a fellow to throw into a dungeon. Besides, none of us could be sure just how much affection his uncle Rafsanjani had for him, anyway.

At several points during his visit to Washington, the Nephew asked for a brief intermission so he could pray. He hadn't brought his prayer rug, so one of my colleagues offered his multicolored gym towel. All this praying led me to make several references to Abraham, the biblical father of three great religions: Judaism, Christianity, and Islam. I also stressed that President Reagan was a man of God, but I apparently pushed the religious comments a little too far.

At one point, the Nephew's keeper took Secord aside to complain about me. "General," he said, "what's with this guy? We just *left* a country full of mullahs. And what do I find here but another lousy mullah!"

Someone in the delegation must have been looking forward to his brief escape from the strict religious environment of Tehran, because that night, when the Iranians returned to their hotel, there was a concerted effort to scare up a little female companionship from local escort services. Someone ended up making dozens of tries, not only because the hotel was well out of the city, but also because the Iranians could barely speak enough English to order room service—let alone ladies of the evening. These efforts went for naught, and our visitor spent the night alone.

The next night I took the Nephew on a tour of the White House, with Albert Hakim as our translator. Later, people wondered how I could possibly bring a secret Iranian contact into the White House, as if this somehow compromised national security. But it wasn't all that different from taking my cousins from Oswego, or visiting firemen from Oshkosh, or old classmates from Annapolis. I had taken dozens of visitors through the White House—including my parents, my brothers, my sister, my kids, and even the cousin of the secretary who worked down the hall. In the evening, especially when the President was out of town, such tours were actually encouraged, and the West Wing was always bustling with staff members showing people around. As for secrecy, I simply wasn't important enough for anyone to wonder whom I was with.

Foreign visitors were part of the atmosphere. At the request of a CIA colleague, I once took a group of Afghan resistance fighters on a White House tour, although I don't think they had the slightest idea where they were. After hours, and on weekends, when the President and First Lady were at Camp David, there were visiting pooh-bahs wandering through the White House from every planet in the solar system.

The Nephew brought along his camera, and he asked Albert and me to take a few pictures of him in the White House—presumably to show the folks back home that junior had made it to the top. That night, I took him through the West Wing—the Press Room, the Cabinet Room, and up to the doorway of the Oval Office, which is always guarded by a Secret Service agent and is closed off with a rope whenever the President isn't there. But what I really wanted to show him was President Theodore Roosevelt's Nobel Prize, which is displayed, appropriately enough, in the Roosevelt Room. "This is the Nobel Peace Prize," I explained. "It's the first one ever awarded to an American. It was given to President Roosevelt for his success in ending the war between Russia and Japan in 1905. Although that war had no direct impact on the United States, and took place thousands of miles from here, President Roosevelt brought the leaders of these two countries to Portsmouth, New Hampshire, where they negotiated an end to the fighting.

"President Reagan feels the same way about the war your country is fighting with Iraq," I added. "He wants to do whatever he can to bring peace."

Before the Nephew left Washington, he asked if the United States could issue some kind of public signal that would prove to his contacts in Tehran that he had indeed been meeting with high-level Americans. Obviously, I couldn't get President Reagan or Secretary Shultz to stand up and say anything nice about Iran. What we needed was an American statement that would satisfy the Iranians, but which nobody in our country would even notice.

Once again, history provided an answer. I recalled that during World War II, the Free French government in London used to broadcast coded messages to the French Resistance in their occupied homeland by inserting previously agreed-upon phrases in routine radio broadcasts. I wondered if we could arrange something analogous through the Voice of America. Perhaps the United States could thank Iran for its help in resolving the recent hijacking of a Pan Am plane. (The Iranian "help" had consisted of not allowing the plane to land in Tehran, but even that was appreciated.) The Nephew and I agreed on the wording, and he wrote it down. With the permission of Admiral Poindexter, I asked the Voice of America if they would include our brief insert in an upcoming Farsi-language editorial, and they agreed. Shortly after the Nephew returned home, the phrase was used in our broadcasts.

As soon as the Nephew left Washington, I sent a summary of our talks to Admiral Poindexter. He responded with an enthusiastic PROFS message to Bud McFarlane at home. "Your trip to Tehran paid off," the admiral wrote. "You did get through to the top. They are playing our line back to us. They are worried about the Soviets, Afghanistan, and their economy. They realize hostages are an obstacle to any productive relationship with us. They want to remove the obstacle.... If this comes off, may ask you to do second round after hostages are back. Keep your fingers crossed."

The following day, October 4, McFarlane responded in kind: "If you think it would be of any value, I might be able to take a couple of months off and work on the problem," he wrote. "No guarantees and no need for any sponsorship (except for airfares and hotels) but I might be able to turn something up. Think about it."

McFarlane claimed later that after our May 1986 trip to Tehran he had wanted nothing more to do with the Iran initiative. But in the fall of 1986, he evidently still shared our belief that a strategic opening to Iran was both important and possible. Admiral Poindexter was suggesting a "second round"—meaning another trip to Tehran—*after* the release of the hostages. Cynics may scoff, but our goals with Iran went well beyond the hostage problem.

The optimistic sentiments expressed by McFarlane and Poindexter were apparently felt in Tehran as well. After hearing the VOA broadcast, the Iranians agreed to have the Nephew meet us again, three weeks later, in Frankfurt.

As always, this meant that we had to arrange for the meetings to be recorded. Because it wasn't always possible to have the hotel rooms where we met wired in advance, I often ended up doing the job myself. In addition to the KL-43 encoding device, I normally traveled with two machines that had been provided by the Agency: an audio recorder that was hidden in a briefcase, and a tiny video camera concealed in a gym bag. (Both recorders utilized special long-lasting batteries and tapes.)

I tried to make sure that all our meetings were taped. After all, I often promised the Iranians far more than we were prepared to deliver, and I told them things that clearly were not true. I wanted my superiors and anyone else with a need to know to be aware of exactly what each side had said. Secord urged me to run my tape recorder even when the room was already bugged. "Just in case," he would say. I didn't share his worries, but I went along with his request. Just in case.

Shortly after the Iranian initiative began, Casey had told me to get an alias identity to provide an added layer of security. I had been issued a black diplomatic passport, but he was concerned that my name was becoming too well known, and that an alias would provide deniability in the event that my missions were detected. I was issued a standard blue passport with my photograph, in the name of William P. Goode. I was now a businessman.

To authenticate Mr. Goode's identity, I was provided with appropriate "pocket litter"—business cards, receipts, and credit cards. While the credit cards couldn't be used to charge anything, the business cards were slightly more functional: the phone number listed on them was supposed to ring somewhere in the bowels of Washington, where it would be answered by somebody who would verify that Mr. Goode was indeed who he claimed to be.

Like me, Mr. Goode worked for the NSC. But whereas my NSC stood for the National Security Council, his NSC was a private business known as the National Security *Company*. When anyone asked, Mr. Goode explained that he sold a line of security equipment to companies in Europe which required special machinery to protect their secret work on the Strategic Defense Initiative. That would explain the two recording devices.

My only regret is that William Goode never bothered to sign up in a frequent-flyer program. When I think of the places he could have taken his wife and family, assuming he ever had the time...

Each time I left Dulles, I carried the two hidden recorders and my KL-43 secure communications device. To my surprise, the concealed recorders would pass right through the security X-ray machines without a flicker of concern on the part of the guards. I had my cover story all prepared, but nobody asked.

Except once. And then all the pocket litter and false identity papers and even my cover story still weren't enough for the skeptical authorities at London's Heathrow Airport. When I landed overseas, I was normally met by an embassy official who would clear me through customs. But this flight had arrived early. Passing through customs, I was stopped by the ever-vigilant and humorless British customs officials, who asked me to explain, and then demonstrate, all the electronic equipment I had with me—and that I was supposedly offering for sale. George Cave, who had gone through in another line, waited for me a few yards away, trying in vain to suppress his glee as I tried to talk my way out of this one.

The customs officials were fascinated by all this unusual equipment. I believe they knew very well that I was an American government official trying to pass as a businessman, but they insisted on hearing my entire cover story—several times. Why was I there? With whom would I be meeting? What were these toys I had brought along, and how did they work? Exactly what is the National Security Company? What other equipment does your company make?

It was awful. I had carefully memorized my story, but I soon had sweat rings from my armpits down to my belt loops. I felt like I was onstage as part of an improvisational theater troupe where the rest of the cast had been working together for years. Although Mr. Goode's performance did not quite live up to his name, after about twenty minutes of fun our man from the embassy finally showed up, and they let me go. George and I flew on to Frankfurt, where we were met by somebody from our embassy in Bonn in plenty of time to alleviate the need for another song-and-dance routine from the inexperienced (but not altogether untalented) Mr. Goode.

In Frankfurt, the Nephew showed up with a new keeper, whom Cave and I had already met in Tehran. Although we weren't able to confirm it, we believed he was an intelligence officer with the Rev Guards. But here again, we never learned exactly who he was or where in the power structure he fit in.

But one thing was clear: the new keeper was obviously more important than the guy who had accompanied the Nephew to Washington. He was also a lot less friendly. Because of his gaunt, severe appearance, and the intense, scowling way he looked at us, Secord and I referred to him as the Monster. Hakim called him the Engine, because he also seemed able to make things happen and keep them moving.

Prior to the Frankfurt meeting, the Nephew had told us he would be bringing along a Koran, a gift for President Reagan. To reciprocate, I brought an elegant, leather-bound Bible for Speaker Rafsanjani. I had thought it would be appropriate if, in addition to signing the Bible, the President would also write out a suitable biblical verse in his own hand. Recognizing the Khomeini government's prejudice not only toward Israel but also toward Jews, I chose a passage from the New Testament. With the help of a concordance, I turned to Galatians, which includes several references to Abraham as the progenitor of three different faiths. I selected Galatians 3:8, which reads: "And the Scripture, foreseeing that God would justify the Gentiles by faith, preached the gospel beforehand to Abraham, saying, 'All the nations shall be blessed in you.'" I asked Admiral Poindexter to have President Reagan inscribe the Bible with this verse and his signature, and it was done.

When I presented the Bible to the Iranians, I said that President Reagan had authorized me to tell them that the United States accepted their revolution. Throughout our discussions with the Iranians, it seemed terribly important for them to hear that. We had already made it clear in Tehran, and I thought it would have been obvious from the fact that ever since Khomeini had come to power, the United States and Iran had been negotiating at the International Court of Justice in the Hague about the disposition of Iran's frozen assets. But these men hadn't spent many years in government, and perhaps they felt insecure in their new identities. Whatever the reason, they needed to hear of our acceptance again and again.

The Nephew never did bring that Koran he had told me about. But at our next meeting he offered me a gorgeous, deep red Persian carpet that must have measured at least ten feet by fifteen. "I would like you to have this," he said. "I believe you are sincere, and that you want to help your country. I know that as a military man, you could never afford something like this."

He was certainly right about that. But there was no way I could accept his gift, and I tried to explain that as politely as I could.

Later on I asked George Cave, "How on earth was he able to bring that huge rug out of Tehran?"

"It probably came out years ago," George replied. Shortly after the revolution, he explained, the new government of Iran had removed an enormous quantity of valuables—carpets, gold, silverware, paintings, and even chandeliers—from the Shah's palaces in Iran, and shipped them to warehouses in Frankfurt. Periodically, the Iranians would sell off some goods to raise hard currency.

By the end of the first day in Frankfurt, it looked like the Second Channel might lead to some real movement on the hostages. But what I didn't know was that thousands of miles away, the entire contra initiative had just come crashing down. Literally.

I didn't learn about this until we broke for dinner, when I went to my room and turned on CNN—just in time to see a disheveled-looking American being paraded past the wreckage of a C-123 transport plane. His hands were tied behind his back, and he was guarded by a Sandinista soldier. Looking straight at the camera, the American said: "My name is Eugene Hasenfus. I come from Marinette, Wisconsin."

My heart stopped. I didn't recognize the name, but I certainly knew what this meant.

I immediately called my office, where Bob Earl responded with a KL-43 message that he'd already drafted. Bob confirmed everything CNN was saying, and gave additional details. This flight, as I already knew, was part of Project Democracy's aerial resupply to the resistance deep inside Nicaragua. Three other men on that plane had been killed, including Buzz Sawyer, whom I had come to know and admire, and Bill Cooper, the chief pilot, whom I had met. I did not know the third man, who was a young communicator and logistician from the resistance. Hasenfus was the "kicker," the crewman who rigged the parachutes on the payloads and literally kicked them out of the plane during an airdrop. Like the other two Americans, he had been recruited by Secord's team.

Their plane had taken off from Ilopango, El Salvador, and was carrying a full load of supplies for the resistance: rifles, grenade launchers, medicine, and boots. At 12:45 in the afternoon, it was hit by a Sandinista antiaircraft missile and had exploded in flames. Hasenfus was the only one with a parachute, and as he floated to the ground, he watched the plane crash and burn. It must have been a terrible experience, and I can't blame him for talking. When he was captured a few hours later, the poor bastard must have thought it was all over.

The Hasenfus episode gave the Sandinistas what they'd been hoping for: concrete proof that American mercenaries had been flying over Nicaragua. They had been claiming for months that American planes were dropping bombs on their country, and while they were wrong about the bombs, the rest of it was true.

I immediately left Frankfurt to return to Washington. Dick left, too, to deal with the firestorm. Cave, who was under orders from

Langley not to carry on discussions with the Iranians without me, flew back to the States. That left only Albert to stay behind with the Iranians, which was a big mistake.

We left Albert behind not to negotiate, but to stay with the Second Channel and hold the fort until I returned. When I left Frankfurt, I naïvely expected to return in a couple of days. But I had no idea what awaited me in Washington, and it turned out to be three weeks before I came back.

Meanwhile, Albert continued the negotiations. During the next day or two, he made concessions that the rest of us would never have agreed to. Among other things, he promised the Iranians that we would approach the government of Kuwait and urge them to release some of the Da'wa prisoners. He also agreed to sell five hundred more TOW missiles to Iran—at a considerable discount from previous prices.

When Nir learned about that, he was beside himself. "It makes us look terrible," he said, referring to his own government. "And where does it leave Ghorbanifar?"

Nobody was pleased with Hakim's negotiation. But it wasn't such a big deal at the time, and none of us could imagine just how unhappy it would make Congress nine months later, during the hearings. Although I didn't like the so-called Hakim Accords, I went along with them because I would have promised the Iranians just about anything to free more hostages. "You want the next ride on the space shuttle? It's yours, baby."

Later, in the midst of all the inquisitions, I was asked whether I had any qualms about lying to the Iranians. The answer is no. My only reservation was that one of my lies might be discovered, and that the hostages would pay the price. I lied to them not because they were Iranians, but because lives were at stake.*

As soon as I returned from Frankfurt, Casey asked me to come out to his office in Langley for a long, serious talk. The administration was denying any link to the Hasenfus flight, but sooner or later the real story was going to come out. "It's over," Casey said, referring to Project Democracy. "Shut it down and clean it up. Bring everybody home. We're going back in."

*In the Bible, in the second chapter of Joshua, Rahab lies to the authorities in order to save the lives of the two Israelite spies. I don't recall reading about her trial.

Fortunately for the contras, Congress had finally approved the allocation of one hundred million dollars for the CIA to resume helping the resistance, and soon the money would begin to flow. The Hasenfus flight went down less than two weeks before the CIA began resuming its support for the resistance.

But Nicaragua wasn't the only thing on Casey's mind. He also described a disturbing conversation he'd had with an old friend named Roy Furmark. Furmark, who was said to be a business partner of Adnan Khashoggi, told Casey that Ghorbanifar was deeply in debt to Khashoggi and two Canadian investors. Gorba had threatened to go public with both the Iran initiative and the "diversion" unless he recovered his losses. But Ghorbanifar was only part of the problem. Casey was also unhappy to hear that Furmark, an outsider, had detailed knowledge about Lake Resources, the use of the residuals, and my own involvement in all of this.

Casey's admonition to "clean it up" meant more than just bringing back the pilots and others who had worked for Secord. Between the Hasenfus problem and Furmark, we were facing the strong possibility of the imminent exposure of all our operations, including the hostage recovery effort. My office was littered with files and documents that, if exposed, would jeopardize the lives of people we had worked with in Nicaragua, Europe, and Iran. Among other things, I had detailed financial statements from Adolfo showing how the Saudi money was spent—which included sensitive payments to individuals still inside Nicaragua. If there were leaks, these people would be in real danger.

And so I began to shred more than the routine excess paperwork from the office. A paper shredder is an essential piece of equipment in any office that deals with classified material. These papers can't be disposed of in the regular trash; they must be destroyed to protect legitimate secrets. Casey's warning got my attention. Although I normally shredded every day, during my final weeks at the NSC I shredded more than ever.

It wasn't a matter of staying late at the office and shredding documents into the wee hours, although at the very end I did that, too. I tried to destroy all documents that mentioned the "diversion," or the names of people who might conceivably be at risk. I also destroyed the ledger that Casey had given me the previous year, in which I had kept records of all the money and traveler's checks flowing in and out of my office. The ledger, too, was filled with names of individuals and organizations whose public exposure would have been a disaster.

It took three weeks before the Frankfurt meeting with the Second Channel was resumed. We met again on October 29, this time in Mainz, a university town outside of Frankfurt. I arrived in an optimistic mood: although the contra project had come unraveled at the end, at least we had been able to keep the resistance together until the CIA could get back in the game. And now the Second Channel seemed to be leading somewhere: we seemed close to a deal that would result in another hostage release in Beirut.

But the Nephew and the Monster arrived in Mainz with alarming news. Pamphlets were being circulated in mosques in Tehran and Qum which disclosed both the arms sales and the McFarlane trip to Tehran. Although several of the key details about the trip were wrong, we were horrified to learn that any news of that visit was being discussed openly.

According to the Nephew, the pamphlets had been distributed by a rival faction in the government which wanted to stop the initiative. But the source hardly mattered. No matter where the pamphlets had come from, we were now living on borrowed time. We figured it might take as long as a month for the stories circulating in Tehran to be picked up in the United States. In fact, it took about a week.

I immediately sent a KL-43 message to Admiral Poindexter, telling him the news and recommending that we press on and do everything possible to get out more hostages before the Iran initiative met the same end as Project Democracy. In his reply, the Admiral okayed what would be our final transaction.

It was later alleged that my frantic attempts in late October and early November to get the remaining hostages released were related to the upcoming midterm elections. There *was* a connection, but it wasn't what it seemed. Nobody in Washington ever told me to get the hostages out by Election Day. Had this been a presidential election, a timely release of the hostages might have had some effect. But the outcome of these races, for the House, the Senate, and for governor, wouldn't have been changed in the slightest by a hostage release.

The Iranians saw it differently. They assumed, with some justification, that the seizure of hostages from our embassy in Tehran had led to the defeat of President Carter in 1980, and they thought that our hostages in Lebanon were similarly important to this campaign. I knew better, but because of Hasenfus and the pamphlets, I didn't want to set them straight. If anything was going to develop, it had to happen soon. I went along with their premise, and insisted that we had to get the hostages out before Election Day, November 4.

"We've got to move quickly," I told them. "If the Democrats win big on Tuesday, we won't be able to send you any more shipments."

It could have been the elections that finally made them move. It could have been the pamphlets. Perhaps it would have happened anyway. But before we left Mainz, the Nephew promised us that by the end of the week, in return for five hundred TOWs, two or three hostages would be released in Beirut.

I passed on the good news to John Poindexter, who directed me to go to Cyprus to make the necessary arrangements with our embassy. I then flew back to Washington—losing Bill Goode's luggage in the process (but, thankfully, not the KL-43 and the recorders)—to await word from the Iranians.

On Friday afternoon, I heard from Hakim that a hostage release was imminent. When Charlie Allen at the CIA confirmed that at least one hostage would be released on Sunday, I immediately flew to London, where, as William Goode, I boarded a British Air flight to Cyprus.

I couldn't fly directly to Beirut. The Beirut airport is in West Beirut, the Moslem section of the city, and just about the only Westerners who end up there have been hijacked from somewhere else. My plan was to fly into Cyprus and then make the rest of the trip in a U.S. Army helicopter. And while a long overwater helicopter flight into a city full of gunfire was not my idea of a good time, it was still safer than flying into the Beirut airport.

On Saturday night, when I landed at Larnaca Airport in Cyprus, the place was teeming. I looked around for Harry, my contact from the CIA, but there was no sign of him. I was standing in line to get change for a phone call when I finally noticed Harry standing near the exit. He nodded, and I followed him out to the car.

Harry was already in the vehicle when I came out. "Hurry up!" he yelled. "Get in!" I looked up to see three men running toward me. They were all carrying something, but I couldn't tell what it was. I ran for the car. I stood there, trying to open the right rear door at the same time that the driver was trying to unlock it for me. For a long moment or two the door was stuck as both of us kept fumbling with it. When it finally opened, I tumbled in as the driver hit the gas.

As we pulled away, I looked back at the men who had been coming toward me. They weren't a hit team after all. They were a film crew, and their camera was still running.

Later that night, Harry turned on a local news broadcast. To my horror, I saw myself falling into the car like a scared rabbit. Harry had his face in his hands. "I can't believe it," he said. "They've just identified you as being from the CIA. They said you're working on the hostage release."

I immediately wrote up a detailed account of the incident and sent it to Admiral Poindexter on the KL-43. To this day, I still don't know how the film crew knew I was coming in. We learned later that they were associated with a PLO news organization. There had been rumors in Beirut about an imminent hostage release, and Harry and I assumed that the camera crew had simply been waiting at the airport. But that still didn't explain why they had focused on me. Had they tailed Harry's car? Or was there a security leak in our communications?

Late that night, I called John Kelly, our ambassador in Beirut, to tell him that we expected a hostage release the following day, although we still didn't know who it would be—or how many. I asked him to arrange for a pickup and a quick medical check, and not to tell anyone—not even the State Department. Those were Poindexter's instructions.

I spent that night on Harry's couch. Early Sunday morning, I spoke to Ami Nir in Tel Aviv. He, too, had seen the film of my little dance recital at the Cyprus airport. "Nice going, North," he said. "Real nice."

That morning, I got the word from Bob Dutton, Secord's man, who was in Beirut, that David Jacobsen had just been released.

The Second Channel really worked!

"Keep a lid on it," I told Dutton. "Keep it quiet." If Jacobsen's release was announced too early, it could prevent the other hostage we expected from getting out.

I spent that day pacing in a room at the Golden Bay Hotel outside

Larnaca as Chi Chi Quintero and I waited for additional good news. It never came. As the hours passed, it became increasingly clear that it was Jacobsen—and only Jacobsen.

Talk about mixed feelings! I was elated and depressed at the same time. I returned to the embassy and called the admiral to tell him what had happened.

"Okay," said Poindexter. "Go get him."

Early Monday morning, before dawn, I boarded a U.S. Army helicopter for the flight to Beirut. It was cold, damp and windy at the airfield, and I could see we were in for a rough trip. But I didn't know the half of it. We tried to avoid several line squalls blowing in from the west, but it was impossible to dodge them all. The weather was so bad that the two helicopters couldn't see each other, and the "chase" bird had to turn back to avoid a possible collision. Our pilot, a young Army warrant officer, took a compass fix in the general direction of Beirut, which was somewhere off in the distance, beneath the clouds.

We landed at the provisional embassy compound in the hills above East Beirut. Fortunately, there was no gunfire to welcome us, although in Beirut that was always a possibility. When we touched down, the security team rushed us off the Landing Zone—a scene vaguely reminiscent of Vietnam. Once we were safely inside, I was introduced to the man we had worked so hard to recover.

David Jacobsen was skinny and pale, but he looked to be in reasonably good health. He was, to say the least, enormously grateful to be free. As the helicopter was being refueled, he told me how he had been released the day before. At about nine in the morning, his guards had driven him through the pockmarked streets of West Beirut to the old American embassy, which we had abandoned in 1983 after a car bomb destroyed the building. I apologized for keeping him waiting an extra day, and explained that we had been anticipating the release of another hostage. He brushed it aside. He couldn't stop praising the convoy of volunteers from the embassy who had driven into West Beirut, risking their lives to pick him up.

The small sitting room was crowded with men who had prayed along with Jacobsen for this moment: Ambassador John Kelly, who held the least-wanted post in the entire diplomatic corps; the Deputy Chief of Mission, who had led the convoy of cars to recover Jacobsen; Bob Dutton, who had flown to Beirut a couple of days earlier; and

Terry Waite, the special envoy of the Archbishop of Canterbury. Terry had risked his life to gain the release of all the hostages, but not long afterward, in January 1987, he too would become a hostage.

As soon as the helicopter was ready, we climbed aboard. David was dying to talk, but it was simply too noisy. He settled for writing a note in which he made clear that despite everything that had happened to him, his sense of humor was still intact. "Is it true," he wrote, "that the in-flight movie will be *Bedtime for Bonzo?*"

The flight back to Larnaca was not much smoother than the flight into Beirut, although at least we were flying in daylight. When we landed, Jacobsen was greeted by an official American delegation. Having already been spotted by one news team, I remained in the helicopter as Jacobsen, Waite, and our ambassador to Cyprus met with the press. As soon as the cameras were turned around to cover the press conference, I got out and boarded the waiting Lear jet that Secord had leased. In a few minutes we would be taking off for Wiesbaden, West Germany, where Jacobsen would be debriefed and checked over by the doctors. His two sons would be meeting him there, and he couldn't wait to see them.

I could hear Jacobsen's press conference from the plane. When David described how he had taken comfort in the words of Psalm Twenty-seven, I opened my Bible and looked it up. I was wearing a baseball cap, and I took it off and wrote a passage from that psalm on the bill: "I will see the goodness of the Lord in the land of the living." As soon as David came on board, I gave him the cap.

On the flight to Wiesbaden, we finally had a chance to talk. The poor guy was so starved for human discourse that the words just poured out of him. While he was angry at those who had taken him, he was even more grateful to be free. He also accepted the fact that he couldn't know all the details that led to his release.

He told me the whole story, which he repeated again, more than once, in Wiesbaden. On May 28, 1985, he had been kidnapped and shoved into a small, hidden compartment under the floor of a van. He thought he was about to be killed. Instead, his captors brought him to a cold basement, where he was chained to the floor and blindfolded.

Over the next year and a half, David was moved to several different locations. These were no ordinary prisons: there were many times when his guards wouldn't even let him use the bathroom. At one point they forced him to make a videotape, and then beat him severely when an American network anchorman speculated that David might be using the opportunity to send coded messages. (He wasn't.) On several occasions his captors told him he was about to be released. It was painful to learn that one of those times had coincided with our May visit to Tehran.

He told me he survived the ordeal through his faith. They let him have a Bible, where he found great comfort in the patient message of Ecclesiastes, and in Psalm Twenty-seven, whose opening line is "The Lord is my light and my salvation. Whom shall I fear?"

He also described some of the mental exercises that helped pass the time and keep him sane. In his imagination, he drove slowly down the main street of Huntington Beach, California, his hometown. He recalled every store, every cross street. He spent hours thinking about his past, including his brief tenure as director of Beirut's American University Medical Center.

Later in his captivity, he was held in a room with other American hostages. They prayed together, talked, and argued, too, as they often took out their anger and frustration on each other. There were also moments of levity, like the day they composed a handy phrase book for travelers in Lebanon:

Fekr cabul cardan davat paeh gush divar. I am delighted to accept your kind invitation to lie down on the floor with my arms above my head and my legs apart.

Auto arraregh davateman mano sespaheh-hast. Thank you. It is exceptionally kind of you to allow me to travel in the trunk of your Mercedes. It is so much nicer than other trunks I have been in.

In sharp contrast to Benjamin Weir, Jacobsen was eager to share every bit of information he could recall that might conceivably help us know more about the hostages. He was terribly disappointed when I told him that Weir had refused to answer our questions. He angrily pointed out that he and the other hostages had been kept in the same location for twenty-nine days after Weir was released. He was anxious about the fate of the remaining hostages, and was determined to say nothing to the press that might possibly add to their danger.

On November 7, three days after the midterm elections, David

Jacobsen arrived at the White House to meet with President Reagan. I brought him into the Oval Office for what became a very emotional meeting for both of them. The President wanted to know firsthand what the experience had been like, and David described his confinement in vivid detail. It was incredibly moving and satisfying to see these two men talking together after all this time. Weir and Jenco had also met with the President, but it just wasn't the same.

When President Reagan took Jacobsen out to the Rose Garden for a photo opportunity, the press was in an uproar. The story of McFarlane's trip to Tehran had just been reported in the United States after appearing in *Al-Shiraa*, a Beirut magazine. But even so, the way they went after Jacobsen was unbelievable. Although he had just been through a long and terrible experience, the reporters were shouting at both him and the President, demanding answers to their questions. I stayed behind in the Oval Office, watching from the window as the assault began: "How did you get him out, Mr. President? What truth is there to these stories out of Lebanon?"

One reporter asked, "Why not dispel the speculation by telling us exactly what happened, sir?"

"Because," the President replied, "it has to happen again and again and again until we have them all back."

The whole scene infuriated Jacobsen. He knew all too well that this speculation could cause the terrorists to harm the hostages, and he pleaded with the press to show restraint. When a reporter asked a particularly delicate question about the details of his release, Jacobsen let him have it: "Irresponsible speculation like your question nearly resulted in my death," he said. "You have endangered the lives of hostages remaining in Lebanon. I don't want that to happen and I don't think you want that on your conscience. So in the name of God, would you please just be responsible and back off?"

I have no doubt that David was speaking for the President, too. He was certainly speaking for me.

When the two of them returned to the Oval Office, Jacobsen was incredulous. "They really don't care, do they?" he said to the President.

President Reagan gave one of his famous headshakes. "Well—" he began. Then he stopped himself.

I know how I would have finished that sentence.

*   *   *

David was so angry at the press that I recommended that we leave via the ground-floor portal to the West Wing, and that we stop by my office long enough to let the press corps filter out through the northwest gate. I had an ulterior motive: I wanted to introduce him to some of my coworkers who had done so much to gain his release. Bob Earl, Craig Coy, Fawn Hall, and Barbara Brown had all worked long hours for months, and here, at last, was a hostage who genuinely appreciated their efforts. It was a joyous experience for us all.

Later that afternoon, the admiral and I talked about the possibility of continuing the initiative. Although Rafsanjani had confirmed the details of McFarlane's visit to Iran, and had even added some new distortions of his own, the Nephew made it clear that he wanted to meet again. I left for Geneva the next morning.

While I was angry at the Nephew for not delivering what he had promised, I was still hopeful that we could work something out.

"What happened?" I asked him.

"Please," he said. "We did the best we could. You know that we don't control these people. We offered to tell you where the hostages are being kept."

"So tell us."

He never did.

"Get them out now," I pleaded with him.

"We'll do everything we can," he said.

I have no idea whether he was telling the truth.

The meeting ended inconclusively, with promises on both sides. But nothing came of it, and I returned to Washington to face the music. I never saw the Nephew again.

In December, several weeks *after* I was fired, there was one last meeting in Frankfurt between American negotiators and the Second Channel. Charles Dunbar, a State Department official, and George Cave represented the United States. The Monster represented Iran, but the Nephew didn't show. When the Monster brought up the Hakim Accords, Dunbar replied that the United States was no longer interested in selling arms to the Iranians.

The Iran initiative was finally over.

14

Endgame

When I returned on November 11 from the final meeting with the Second Channel, Washington was in an uproar. The wreckage from the Hasenfus shoot-down had spread well beyond the immediate problems of trying to recover the bodies of the downed airmen, paying their death benefits, and negotiating the release of Hasenfus himself. On Capitol Hill, the Democratic leadership was howling for political blood. In El Salvador, inquisitive reporters—possibly, as Bill Casey believed, with help from the Cuban intelligence service—had been provided with phone records that linked the house in San Salvador where the air crews lived to the CIA station in Costa Rica, my office in the OEOB, and Secord's office in Virginia.

Meanwhile, both the FBI and the Customs Service were investigating Southern Air Transport, the Miami-based company that handled the maintenance on the planes belonging to Project Democracy. Years earlier, Southern Air had been a CIA proprietary, and it still provided contract services to several U.S. government agencies—and to Dick Secord's operation. Now questions had been raised as to whether Southern Air had been shipping weapons from the United States to the contras, as some in the media had claimed. While they hadn't done that, they had transported TOW missiles from U.S. Army depots to Tel Aviv, where they were transferred to Israeli planes and sent on to Iran. We were hoping to stop this connection from being exposed.

And that wasn't the half of it. By mid-November the press was full of stories, leaks and speculations, not only about the contras, but about the Iran initiative, too. My name was starting to show up a little too often, and I knew I was in trouble when the ABC evening news named me "Person of the Week." I missed the original broadcast, but Dornin, our youngest daughter, who was five, told me about it with great excitement. "Daddy, I saw you on television. You were the week of the man!"

Sarah, who was ten, and old enough to read the newspapers, was similarly confused. After seeing a reference to the religious tensions in Lebanon, she said, "Dad, what's the difference between the Sunis and the Shitties?"

The disclosures in *Al-Shiraa* about the meetings in Tehran became even more interesting when Rafsanjani himself held a press conference in Tehran to discuss the McFarlane visit. He confirmed that an American delegation had indeed arrived in Iran, but his account of the trip was as colorful as a Persian carpet.

As Rafsanjani described it, McFarlane and four other Americans had flown to Tehran illegally, disguised as members of an airline crew. The five of us were then supposedly locked up in a hotel while the Ayatollah was consulted on what should be done with us. "Iman Khomeini instructed us not to talk with the Americans and not to accept their gifts," Rafsanjani said, adding that these gifts included a cake that was decorated with a key, to symbolize the new opening to Iran. Unfortunately, he said, the cake was eaten by the security "boys." Rafsanjani also displayed the Bible inscribed by President Reagan that I had given to the Nephew in Frankfurt just a month earlier, claiming that this, too, had been brought to Tehran by our little group. The visit ended, he said, when the American intruders were expelled from Iran by the Revolutionary Guards.

Other than the fact that the security guards really did eat the cake, virtually nothing else in Rafsanjani's announcement was true. Yet some of the details he cited are still accepted as the conventional wisdom about our trip to Tehran.

Back in Washington, the administration did its best to put a more positive spin on the McFarlane visit. Several high-level officials provided both on- and off-the-record interviews with key members of the press, and at Admiral Poindexter's request, I did, too. On November 13, following a speech by President Reagan, Bud McFarlane appeared on ABC's "Nightline" with Ted Koppel. In sharp contrast to Rafsanjani's version, Bud explained that the Tehran trip had consisted of "four days of talks that went reasonably well." He added, "We were received hospitably and treated with the normal practice that surrounds meetings like this."

"Did you bring in a cake?" Koppel asked.

"I didn't have anything to do with a cake," McFarlane replied.

True. The cake was for Gorba's mother. It's possible that Bud didn't even know about it.

"Bible?"

"No Bible."

"Pistols?"

"I don't operate that way, Ted."

Bud may have forgotten about the pistols, but the rest of his account was generally accurate. I think it's sad that the American press was more willing to believe Rafsanjani than the President's former national security adviser. But for once I couldn't really blame them. From the President on down, the administration was putting out so many versions of the Iran initiative that nobody knew what was coming next. And in case things weren't confusing enough, just a week after Rafsanjani's disclosures, Iran's ambassador to the United Nations came out and backed President Reagan's position by denying that his country had been involved in *any* arrangement with the United States to trade arms for hostages.

Meanwhile, Secretary Shultz took it upon himself to denounce the Iran initiative during an appearance on "Face the Nation." This was hardly the time to break ranks with the President, and some of Shultz's cabinet colleagues were outraged. Rumors were flying that Shultz was about to resign, and that his job would be given to one of the Baker boys—probably James, but maybe even Howard. Things got so bad that Larry Speakes, the White House press secretary, felt compelled to go out and assure the press corps that the President didn't want Shultz to resign.

Weinberger, who had also opposed the initiative, at least had the decency to say nothing. But Cap was in an awkward position, because it was his own Pentagon that had shipped the weapons and sold them to the CIA for the explicit purpose of having the Agency sell them again, through private channels, to Tehran.

Casey was furious, and thought Shultz was being disloyal to the President. A few days after Shultz appeared on television, Casey sent a personal letter to President Reagan recommending that Shultz be fired and replaced by Jeane Kirkpatrick. "Dear Mr. President," he wrote. "On Friday I spent over five hours discussing and answering questions for the House and Senate Intelligence Committees on *our* effort to develop a relationship with important elements in Iran.... The public pouting of George Shultz and the failure of the State Department to support what we did inflated the uproar on this matter. If we all stand together and speak out I believe we can put this behind us quickly.

"Mr. President," Casey concluded, "you need a new pitcher."

But Shultz had no intention of leaving the game. In fact, as I learned while preparing for my trial, the Secretary of State was hoping to play two positions at once: he wanted to replace John Poindexter as national security adviser while continuing to serve as Secretary of State.

On November 13, President Reagan had gone on television to give his version of events. In the wake of all the leaks and unattributed sources, he promised to tell the whole story. "You are going to hear the facts from a White House source," he promised. "And you know my name."

He continued: "The charge has been made that the United States has shipped weapons to Iran as ransom payment for the release of American hostages in Lebanon; that the United States undercut its allies and secretly violated American policy against trafficking with terrorists.

"Those charges are utterly false. The United States has not made concessions to those who hold our people captive in Lebanon, and we will not. The United States has not swapped boatloads or planeloads of American weapons for the return of American hostages, and we will not.

"We did not—repeat, did not—trade weapons or anything else for hostages, nor will we."

As I explained earlier, President Reagan wasn't exactly lying, but he wasn't telling the truth, either. He believed what he said, and he *still* thinks we didn't trade arms for hostages. After all, he reasoned, the people we were dealing with were Iranians, not the hostage holders themselves. Technically, he was correct.

In his speech, the President insisted that the arms we shipped to Iran could have fit in a single cargo plane. He took a lot of heat for that remark, but it wasn't wrong. Before the speech, Admiral Poindexter had asked me to determine whether what we had shipped would, in fact, have fit into a single plane. I called the Pentagon to check on the size and the weight of two thousand TOWs, plus the electronic parts, and I calculated that yes, they would have fit in a C-5A, the largest cargo plane in our Air Force. Regardless of how it was portrayed, this was not an enormous quantity of arms.

Hindsight is always easy. But I still wonder how events would have turned out if, having decided to put aside the ongoing rescue efforts and address the nation, President Reagan had made a somewhat different speech that evening—which might have gone something like this:

My fellow Americans: The charge has been made that the United States has shipped weapons to Iran as ransom payment for the release of American hostages in Lebanon. Let me tell you what we did—and why.

In an effort to open a relationship with the revolutionary government of Iran, we sold two thousand TOW missiles and some electronic parts to Tehran. We had reason to believe there were moderate, or pragmatic, individuals in the government of Iran who were not hostile to the United States. In an effort to reach these people, we worked secretly through two different channels. We also worked to free the American hostages in Lebanon, and three of them were in fact released.

Two members of my cabinet were opposed to this initiative, but they were willing to see it through. All of us understood that this was a very high-risk venture, but we believed it was a risk worth taking.

As you now know, our effort to open a relationship with the current government in Iran did not succeed. Tonight, I call upon the government of Iran to begin an open dialogue with the United States—a dialogue that could lead to a better relationship between our two countries, and, possibly, an end to the fruitless war between Iran and Iraq.

We know that the government of Iran has some influence over those who hold the American and other Western hostages in Beirut. I call upon Iran to use its influence so that the hostages are released.

In other words, President Reagan could have tried to make a virtue out of a necessity.

Although it was true as far as it went, even this speech would not have revealed the whole story. It would have made no mention of the "diversion," for example, or of the American role in the 1985 HAWK shipments from Israel to Iran. It's possible that this speech might have revealed enough to contain the damage and make a constructive difference, but not necessarily. As things turned out, nothing we did during those days made much difference at all. We only made things worse.

Shortly after the *Al-Shiraa* revelations, Admiral Poindexter asked for a chronology of the Iran initiative. He assigned the task to my office, and gave instructions to work with the CIA, the Pentagon, and anybody else who could help in preparing it.

Because my own operational involvement in the Iran initiative had not begun until I heard from Rabin in November 1985, I relied on Michael Ledeen, Bud McFarlane, and Ami Nir for some of the earlier details. Invariably, people remember things differently, and there were several discrepancies in their recollections that had to be talked through and synthesized. The chronology started out as two pages, but it soon expanded into twenty.

On Tuesday, November 18, at about eight in the evening, Bud McFarlane came to my office to "lend a hand" in reworking a draft of the President's opening remarks for the press conference scheduled for the following night. In a PROFS message to Admiral Poindexter, he proposed several changes in the text, including a denial that the United States had approved of any shipments to Iran before the January 1986 Finding. When he had finished working on the President's remarks, Bud turned to the chronology and made these same changes on my draft.

By now, President Reagan, Admiral Poindexter, and Don Regan had met with various congressional delegations to discuss the Iran initiative, and all of them had studiously avoided any mention of our involvement in the 1985 shipments. On November 12, when President Reagan and his senior foreign policy advisers met with the congressional leadership at the White House, the President pointedly omitted any reference to his okay for the Israeli TOW shipments in the summer of 1985 or to his December 1985 Finding retroactively authorizing the Iranian initiative activities. And although the senior government officials who were present knew about it, no one mentioned our involvement in the November 1985 HAWK shipment.

From then on, the President and his senior advisers were committed to this version of events. In his speech to the nation from the Oval Office on November 13, the President made no mention of U.S. government approval for or involvement in these early shipments.

By the time McFarlane sat down at my computer to type his rendition of the 1985 events, his account coincided with the President's. In his description of the HAWK shipment from Israel to Iran, Bud totally altered the facts about the delivery and our role in facilitating it, and made it appear that we didn't even know about it at the time.

To this day I don't know McFarlane's reasons for these changes. I have mine, and at the time, that was enough; we knew from our intelligence and from meetings with the Iranians that the HAWK shipment of November 1985 had infuriated the Iranians. They had been led to expect a long-range system that could shoot down high-altitude Soviet and Iraqi aircraft. But HAWK is a low-altitude, relatively close-in, antiaircraft system. To make matters worse, there was the awkward problem of the Israeli markings on several of the missiles when they arrived in Iran.

When the Iranians had confronted us with these problems, we had assured them that we'd had nothing to do with that particular shipment. With the agreement of the Israelis, we presented ourselves as the good guys. "Deal with us from now on," we said. "You can return those HAWKs, and we'll help you get what you need."

Now, in November 1986, I still didn't want us to reveal our connection with that 1985 shipment. I was concerned that if the United States was perceived as having played any role in that transaction, the hostage-takers in Beirut might take out their anger on the hostages. As David Jacobsen had told me earlier in the month, that sort of thing really *did* happen. We also worried that additional hostages might be seized. That had happened when we switched from the First to the Second Channel, which had apparently infuriated somebody in the Iranian government.

We were also concerned that any revelation of our role in the 1985 shipment could harm the Nephew. He might end up being targeted as the fall guy in Tehran, especially if it was revealed that even the most recent shipments to his country had gone through Israel. Although by that time I fully expected to lose my job at the NSC, at least I had a career in the Marine Corps to look forward to. The Nephew might find himself in a more difficult situation. In Iran, after all, the word "firing" was often followed by the word "squad."

There was still another reason for not disclosing the American role in the 1985 shipment from Israel. The original Presidential Finding which Reagan had signed in December 1985, authorizing the covert shipment of arms to Iran, had been worded in such a way as to make the Iran initiative sound like nothing more than arms for hostages:

Scope: Hostage Rescue—Middle East.

Description: The provision of assistance by the Central Intelligence Agency to private parties in their attempt to obtain the release of Americans held hostage in the Middle East. Such assistance is to include the provision of transportation, communication, and other necessary support. As part of these efforts certain foreign materiel and munitions may be provided to the Government of Iran which is taking steps to facilitate the release of the American hostages.

Any disclosure of this Finding would have been enormously embarrassing for the administration, especially since the President had insisted in his speech, and continued to insist, that the Iran initiative was *not* about arms for hostages.

On the afternoon of November 21, John Poindexter and I sat in his office and discussed the problem. In January 1986, the President had signed a second Finding, which made clear that the Iran initiative was much broader than simply arms for hostages. This second Finding spelled out the President's goals: to create an opening to Iran, to help bring about an end to the Iran-Iraq war, *and* to recover the hostages. The admiral believed that the poorly worded first Finding had been effectively superseded by the second Finding.

If that first Finding was ever revealed, the President would be humiliated. The admiral asked Paul Thompson, his lawyer, to bring in the signed original 1985 Finding. Admiral Poindexter then tore it in half and placed it on the coffee table. This was one of the charges on which the admiral was later indicted and convicted.

In changing the chronology and in destroying the superseded Finding, Bud and the admiral had taken steps to preserve lives and to protect the President. But there were other matters, too, that we didn't want anyone to know about. No version of the chronologies mentioned the secret within a secret. We were trying to avoid the political explosion that such a revelation would entail—and we were certainly right about *that*. We also knew that the Iranians would be furious if this story came out. They had been taken to the cleaners, and charged enough for the weapons to fund the Nicaraguan resistance and other projects as well. If it was revealed that these funds were used to support the contras, the Iranians might well go ballistic. After all, they had been supporting the Sandinistas. While the government of Iran had no great sympathy for Communism, they apparently believed that the Sandinistas qualified for that old Middle Eastern proverb: the enemy of my enemy is my friend.

Meanwhile, back in my office on the night of November 18: When McFarlane finished making the changes in the President's press statement and the chronologies, he pushed himself from my computer terminal. As he stood up, he said, "What did you do about that stuff from the NSA?" He was referring to a PROFS message he had sent me a few days earlier, in which he had stated his hope that certain National Security Agency intelligence files on the Iran initiative had been purged. Bud, it seemed, believed history could be rewritten by deletions and alterations. When I explained that these files were in various government agencies, and probably could not be recovered, he changed the subject. "Did you ever take care of that other stuff—way back then?"

"Other stuff?"

"What did you do with *that*?" He gestured toward my computer. There, taped to the monitor, was a list of six NSC document control numbers that Bud had written out and given to me more than a year earlier. The numbers referred to memos I had written to Bud back in 1984 and 1985, seeking his approval for some of my efforts in support of the Nicaraguan resistance. In the fall of 1985, Bud had directed me to change these memos, removing any reference to my support activities and his knowledge of them. But I still hadn't done it.

In the summer of 1985, after a number of stories had appeared in the press about secret support for the Nicaraguan resistance, two prominent members of Congress started asking questions about the NSC's involvement in the resistance. Congressman Michael Barnes, chairman of the Western Hemisphere Subcommittee of the House Foreign Affairs Committee, was a leading opponent of the President's policies in Central America. Congressman Lee Hamilton, chairman of the House Intelligence Committee, was less vocal than Barnes, but he too was opposed to military aid for the resistance.

After the news stories appeared, both Barnes and Hamilton wrote letters to McFarlane, asking whether the NSC had indeed been supporting the resistance. The letter from Barnes specifically asked about press reports of contact between me and the contra leaders.

There are two ways to protect a secret when you're asked about it directly. One is simply not to answer. The other is to lie.

I preferred the former, and I argued with Bud that we shouldn't answer these letters. As I saw it, this was precisely the kind of situation that executive privilege was invented for. After all, the Executive Branch is not compelled to answer every question that Congress asks.

Bud disagreed. He said he had talked to the President about it, and that my approach was too confrontational. McFarlane refused to accept my input. Instead, Bud invoked his own form of executive privilege. He lied. In letters* to Barnes, Hamilton, and others—and in meetings with still other congressmen—he flatly denied that the NSC in general, and Oliver North in particular, were involved in these activities: "Dear Mr. Chairman," he wrote to Barnes,

I can state with deep personal conviction that at no time did I or any member of the National Security Council staff violate the letter or spirit of the law. At no time did we encourage military activities. We did not solicit funds or other support for military or paramilitary activities, either from Americans or third parties.

At the hearings, Bud would describe responses such as this as "too categorical." That's putting it mildly.

On September 30, 1985, Barnes again wrote to McFarlane. This

*Because of these letters, McFarlane pled guilty to withholding information from Congress.

time he specifically asked to see NSC documents. I again argued that we should simply tell Barnes that we weren't going to answer his questions. I even went up to the law library on the top floor of the OEOB to research the history of executive privilege. When I returned to my office I drafted a letter for Bud to send:

These internal documents are the appropriate purview of the Executive Branch, which must abide by its commitments to other governments not to compromise sensitive information. The Executive Branch cannot delegate this responsibility to the Congress and maintain its credibility with those entrusted to govern in other countries. The right of the Executive to maintain confidentiality of information important to the conduct of our foreign policies must be sustained.

This principle dates back to the time of our first President, wherein he refused to lay before the House of Representatives the instructions, correspondence, and documents relating to the negotiations of what came to be known as the Jay Treaty. This long-standing principle has been consistently upheld by the Supreme Court in a number of cases, including the *United States* versus *Curtiss-Wright Export Corporation.**

Whether simply to placate me, or to get a second opinion from a real lawyer, Bud forwarded my letter to Fred Fielding, the White House counsel, for his comments. But Fielding, too, preferred not to confront Congress, and as far as I know, the letter was never passed on to the President—the only person who could actually invoke executive privilege.

McFarlane knew that Barnes and his allies were not going to stop their fishing expeditions, and he was worried that Congress would somehow succeed in getting its hands on our documents. When the first letters had arrived from Barnes and Hamilton, an NSC security officer had gathered our permanent record files dealing with aid to the contras and delivered them to Bud's office. Now, months later, Barnes was demanding to see them. Apparently confident that Barnes wouldn't summon the energy to do any of the hard work himself, Bud invited Barnes down to his office. With the pile of memos sitting in plain view, he invited Barnes to review them on the spot. Barnes refused, and asked for copies to be sent to his staff for their review. That was out of the question. We had serious concerns about a mem-

*The Curtiss-Wright case was decided in 1936, when the Supreme Court upheld the right of the President to prohibit the shipment of arms to Bolivia and Panama.

ber of Barnes's staff who was close to the Sandinistas, and McFarlane had no intention of allowing these papers out of his office.

After Barnes renewed his request to see documents, Bud called me in. "Ollie," he said, "some of these need to be fixed." Bud explained that the memos, all of which I had sent to him, were inconsistent with what he had said and written to Congress, and that they were "problematical." He handed me a piece of paper on which he had written the numbers of six NSC documents.* He also cited several other documents whose numbers I wrote down on the back of that same piece of paper. In "fixing" them, Bud said, I should remove all references to my operational role, and make the memos consistent with what he had said and written to Congress.

If these memos ended up on Capitol Hill, the resistance would be finished. Any hope of restoring CIA funding for the contras would evaporate and sensitive operations would be jeopardized. We knew that Congress had two ways of dealing with something they didn't like. They could legislate against it—and with the Boland Amendments they had already gone about as far in that direction as they could. Or, in the case of a secret operation, they could leak it. Still, I didn't understand why McFarlane had selected only certain memos, when I had written *dozens* of memos that were equally "problematical."

"Just take care of it," McFarlane said, showing me a document he had already changed. "And from now on, no more memos with this kind of detail. And no more PROFS notes about it, either."

Now, I'm not normally a procrastinator. But until Bud came to my office on November 18, 1986, I still hadn't gotten around to revising these papers. With so many other NSC memos that revealed similar information, I just didn't see the point. But that Tuesday night, when Bud brought it up again, I dutifully started changing the memos to make them appear more benign. Specifically, I removed references to my operational role, and to McFarlane's knowledge of it— just as he told me to.

But it was too late. I was still working on these papers when I was

*One of these memos described my meeting in Washington with a Communist Chinese official in our effort to obtain antiaircraft missiles for the Nicaraguan resistance. Another outlined my proposals to take action against the *Monimbo*, the Sandinista arms ship. The rest dealt with specific resistance activities and operations, and the support we were providing for them.

fired. Later, they were published for the whole world to see, which was an odd way of shutting down a covert operation.

It wasn't until 1989, during my trial, that I finally understood why Bud had selected these particular documents. Whether or not there were other memos in the same category, Bud knew that these six documents all revealed his detailed awareness and approval of my activities, and perhaps, to his way of thinking, the President's as well.

By November 1986, it was far too late to hide *my* role. By then, ambassadors, military officials, CIA officers, members of Congress, and scores of individuals in foreign governments all knew what I had been doing. But that night, when McFarlane told me again to change those memos, I did.

This was the third time in the space of a year and a half that the NSC in general, and I in particular, had become the focus of attention. The first spate of press reports, in the summer of 1985, had prompted congressional inquiries and McFarlane's subsequent letters to Barnes, Hamilton, and others, leading to Bud's directive that I change the six memos.

The third, and by far the most serious, was the current imbroglio.

But there had also been a second go-round with the press and Congress in the summer of 1986, a few months after Bud had resigned. Following another spate of news stories about the NSC and the contras, the House of Representatives took the highly unusual step of drafting a Resolution of Inquiry, specifically directing the President to tell Congress what Lieutenant Colonel Oliver L. North had been doing on behalf of the resistance. To my knowledge, this was the only proposed resolution in the history of the United States that directed the Commander-in-Chief to do anything about a lieutenant colonel.

The Resolution of Inquiry was offered on the House floor by Representative Ron Coleman of Texas. But word quickly spread that the real originator was his congressional colleague Michael Barnes, who was evidently trying a little covert operation of his own.

Like all proposed legislation, this draft resolution was submitted to the White House legislative affairs office for comment. They, in turn, passed it on to the NSC legislative office. When Ron Sable, senior director of legislative affairs at the NSC, told me he wasn't sure what the administration was going to do about the resolution, I was livid. I went to the admiral and said, "I certainly *hope* we're going to oppose it! And since I'm the one who's named, you ought to let me write the response."

"Come on, Ollie," the admiral replied. "I know what you'll say. The whole world knows how you feel about this. You'll just want to cite executive privilege and tell them to go to hell."

That was certainly true.

"Well, that's not going to work," he said. "If we start throwing up roadblocks, that will only make things more difficult." As it turned out, the admiral was right. At the time, we didn't know that one of the congressional staffers had written a memo explaining that the Resolution of Inquiry was designed solely to embarrass the administration by forcing the President to invoke executive privilege. But we didn't learn this until three years later, during preparations for my trial.

After several days of bureaucratic wrangling, Sable's office drafted letters for the admiral's signature, telling the appropriate committee chairmen that the administration opposed the Resolution of Inquiry. Unfortunately, Sable also wrote that the admiral was standing by McFarlane's 1985 responses to Barnes and Hamilton. For signing these letters, which included the references to McFarlane's earlier correspondence, the admiral was later indicted and eventually convicted. This was another first: McFarlane sends two letters to Congress, and two other men are indicted for what's in *his* letters. The ways of justice can be very strange.

Congress was less than satisfied with the admiral's letters. In July 1986, Congressman Hamilton called the admiral. "We need to talk to North about this Resolution of Inquiry," he said.

"No, you don't," said Poindexter. "The White House isn't in the business of sending its staff up there to testify, and we're not going to start now."

But Hamilton insisted it all could be handled much more casually. Instead of appearing before a congressional committee, I could simply sit down with some of the members of his intelligence committee and answer their questions during an "informal off-the-record" meeting in the White House Sit Room.

Calling it a meeting instead of a committee appearance and moving it over to our turf certainly made it more palatable. So did the fact that, as I understood it by the time we met the Resolution of Inquiry was dead anyway, because the House Armed Services Committee had voted it down. But I still didn't think it was a good idea, and I said so to the admiral. We both knew that there was a great deal of information that I couldn't reveal, including the Saudi donation to the resistance, my role in the delivery of military supplies, and, of course, the fact that by then, the Ayatollah was unwittingly helping us to fund the resistance.

"You can take care of it," the admiral said.

The Sit Room meeting took place early on the morning of August 6, 1986. The President was in California, and the admiral had taken some well-deserved leave. Congress usually isn't around during August, either, but unfortunately for me, several members of the intelligence committee were in town and attended the meeting along with two of their staffers.

Some of the congressmen had never been to the Sit Room before, and I could see them looking around in astonishment, just as I had when I first arrived at the NSC. Entering the Sit Room for the first time, I had expected to find something ultramodern and high-tech, like the situation rooms depicted in movies, and I was disappointed that this place seemed so ordinary. For a moment it had actually occurred to me that maybe this wasn't the Sit Room after all. Maybe *this* room was nothing more than a gigantic elevator, and when somebody pushed a hidden button on the wall, it would lower us down to the *real* Sit Room, in the seventh sub-basement, hundreds of feet underground. If that's what the congressmen expected, they were disappointed.

I, too, was disappointed that morning. I had been hoping that the committee members who supported the contras would be able to steer the conversation away from the really tough questions. I was wrong.

Somebody asked if I had ever given military advice to the Nicaraguan resistance.

My answer was something like, "Look. Enrique Bermudez is a colonel. I'm a lieutenant colonel. It's inconceivable to think that a couple of military guys sitting down to talk about a war they both feel strongly about won't also talk about military things. But do I give him military advice on day-to-day operations? Even if I thought I could, we both know that you can't run this war from Washington. The war is being fought and planned right down there in the region."

At best, this was a nonanswer. It was meant to be evasive, and it was. While it was true that this war, like all guerrilla wars, was being planned and fought at the small-unit level, that wasn't the whole truth. In fact, I had given the resistance all kinds of advice.

That morning, in the Sit Room, I tried to avoid telling outright lies. But I certainly wasn't telling the truth. I knew that full and truthful answers would have destroyed the Nicaraguan resistance. And some of the congressmen knew that, too.

By the time this meeting was held, the House and the Senate had each appropriated one hundred million dollars in covert CIA military support for the resistance. We all knew that it was just a matter of time before Speaker O'Neill would have to "conference," or reconcile, the two bills, and nobody in the administration—least of all me—wanted to rock that boat. The admiral and I also wanted to avoid the kind of political firestorm that would hit us with full force less than four months later.

Despite my anxieties, the Sit Room meeting was surprisingly cordial—perhaps because I wasn't the only one there who knew I was avoiding direct answers to their questions. I had already given numerous briefings about the resistance to several of these men and to dozens of their congressional colleagues. Many of them had been to the region, visited the camps, met with resistance leaders, and seen the close quarters at Ilopango Air Force Base, where the resistance planes were stationed. For years, they had been asking CIA briefers about the sources of contra support, and they had all seemingly accepted the Agency's claims of ignorance. One of the committee members, Dave McCurdy of Oklahoma, had even called me late one night to ask that supplies be provided to the Atlantic Coast Indians. I had done as he asked. I was certain that McCurdy didn't want me to talk about that, and I didn't.

I look back on that meeting today knowing that what I did was wrong. I didn't give straight answers to the questions I was asked. When the admiral sent me a PROFS note a day or two after the meeting, he wrote, simply, "Well done." But I didn't feel that way then, and I don't now.

I know the difference between right and wrong, and I can tell good from bad. But I also know that the more difficult decisions come when we have to choose between good and better. The toughest calls of all are those we have to make between bad and worse. That was the choice I was faced with on August 6 in the Sit Room. Later, I was indicted for lying to Congress during that meeting. Although I admitted what I had done openly in the hearings, and again during my trial, I was not convicted.

Maybe that's because in two hundred years of sparring between the Executive Branch and Congress over the control of foreign policy, no one else has ever been charged with such a "crime." Until special prosecutors came along, these kinds of informal, unsworn exchanges between the Executive and the Congress had always been treated as part of the political process. Regardless of whether it was morally right or wrong—and I knew it was wrong—I certainly never imagined that anything I was doing was a crime.

Looking back on it today, it's clear to me that the best thing I could have done was not to have gone to that meeting at all. I should have said, "Admiral, I can't do it. You and I both know what these guys are going to ask, and we also know that I can't answer those questions without destroying the resistance."

But I didn't say that to the admiral, and I don't blame him for what happened.

After McFarlane left my office on that Tuesday evening in November, I had less than a week left at the NSC. I didn't know it at the time, but I could sure see where things were headed. I began to expedite the process I had started in October of "cleaning things up," and every evening that week I went through more of my personal files. It took days to go through the scores of individual files from which I pulled a memo here, a letter there, and various notes that could put people at risk. The documents that I removed from my files included the names, addresses, and phone numbers, and in some cases account numbers, of people who had worked with our government in both the hostage initiative and the contra support project. In a number of cases they were people who had received money from me in support of these efforts.

These were people who had trusted us in general, and me in particular, to keep their names and identities secret. I shredded these papers, along with letters and reports that I had received from them, detailing what was going on in a particular operation or event. Despite all the jokes and accusations, the amount I actually shredded was far, far less than people imagined. Most of the "shredding" time was spent looking through my files.

Later on, the investigators asked whether the "risks" I had spoken of included political risk. And I can't deny that I also tried to find documents like the "diversion" memo that would not only endanger lives, but also put the President at risk. But there wasn't a wholesale effort to destroy everything. I knew that even if I wanted to, I couldn't change the record.

Within weeks, those who survived the blowup of late November, 1986, started a wholesale declassification and exposure of the files in my office. As the Tower Commission, the congressional panels, and the special prosecutors pressed their inquisitions, nearly everything in my office was laid open for anyone to read. I watched in horror as a top-secret presidential Finding was reproduced in dozens of American newspapers. Publishing the text of classified documents was bad enough, but in the case of the Finding, and numerous other documents, it wasn't just the text. These were photocopies, which revealed the *format* of these documents—allowing the KGB or any other adversary to know exactly what a classified presidential document looked like. From now on, anyone could create an authentic-looking presidential Finding, and could use it as "proof" that the U.S. government was involved in some alleged misdeed or another.

As the week wore on, press speculation about what had been shipped to Iran, how it had gotten there, and why it had been sent became even wilder. On several occasions, Ami Nir and I talked and confirmed that both governments, as we had previously agreed, were going to stick with "no comment" when we were asked about U.S.-Israeli cooperation in the Iran initiative. Nir reaffirmed that the U.S. role in the 1985 HAWK shipment should be "protected" because of possible harm to the hostages in Beirut. Understandably, he was still concerned about the two Israeli soldiers.

On Thursday afternoon, November 20, several of us sat with Bill Casey in the admiral's office to discuss his upcoming testimony on the Iran initiative. His staff at the CIA had been preparing various drafts of what he would say. But as usual, Casey, who had been on a secret visit to Central America until that morning, insisted on preparing his own testimony.

After the meeting in the admiral's office, Casey and I walked back to the OEOB together. As we stepped up the ramp that led into the building, he said to me, "It's over. You know that, don't you?"

I nodded. When we got to his office, we talked for a few minutes about the testimony he would be giving the next day on the Iran initiative. As I started to leave, he said, "It's going to be okay down there."

I gave him a puzzled look.

"You know, Nicawogwa. You did a good job. We're back in. But you kept them going."

Although I saw him briefly later that week, this turned out to be the last real conversation we ever had.

On Friday, November 21, both Casey and the admiral met with members of the congressional intelligence committees. The admiral, meeting with a handful of legislators at the White House, apparently stuck with the cover story that the administration had adopted over the preceding weeks: that the United States had not learned of the 1985 HAWK missile shipment from Israel to Iran until January 1986. Casey, giving testimony on Capitol Hill, claimed that the CIA hadn't learned until sometime in 1986 that their proprietary airline had transported HAWK missiles from Israel to Iran. Neither statement was true.

What *was* true were several references that Casey volunteered about me in his testimony. Although this hearing was about the Iran initiative, Casey pointedly suggested three different times that *the committee might be fascinated to know what Oliver North had been doing operationally to help the Nicaraguan resistance.* By bringing this up, Casey was doing what he and I had already discussed: he was ready to throw me out of the boat in the hope that the rest of the administration would stay afloat. But at the time, the committee wasn't interested in this particular diversion.

Because of all the conflicting stories, the President asked Ed Meese to "pull the facts together" and produce a coherent account of what had happened, and when, in the Iran initiative. Admiral Poindexter told me about the Meese mission on Friday afternoon. He mentioned that Don Regan wanted this information by Monday afternoon, and that some of "Ed's guys" would be coming by on Saturday. Could I come into the office to give them a hand?

I assured him I would.

When I arrived at my office on Saturday, two men from Meese's office—William Reynolds and John Richardson—were already there, looking through the red file folders that Bob Earl and I had left out for them. I showed them how to work the copy machine, and they continued reading through documents and copying some of them. I went to work: taking and making phone calls, reading cables, and generally taking care of business. On several occasions I got up and shredded some of the papers I was finished with. Later on, the press accused Meese's aides of incompetence (or worse) for allowing me to use the shredder while they were there. That's unfair. Shredding was a standard part of our office routine. Besides, this wasn't a raid, and I hadn't been accused of anything. They were working on their projects; I was working on mine.

Shortly before two o'clock, Reynolds and Richardson left for lunch, where they met with Ed Meese and Charles Cooper, another of Meese's aides, at the Old Ebbitt Grill on Fifteenth Street. I went upstairs to the admiral's office, where I found Poindexter and Casey having lunch. When I mentioned that two members of Meese's staff were going through my files, Casey said, "That's not so bad. We've got congressional staffers all over the place, poking into things that are none of their business."

Richardson and Reynolds returned to my office around three-forty-five. I assumed they wanted to ask me some questions, but no, they said, they were only there to review documents. Although I didn't know it then, I would be seeing them again the following afternoon, when I went to meet with Ed Meese.

I arrived at Meese's office in the Justice Department shortly after two o'clock on Sunday. Reynolds, Cooper, and Richardson were with him. Ed opened the meeting by asking me to try to recall everything that had happened on the Iran initiative. "Don't worry about trying to protect the President or anyone else," he said. "Just tell me the story."

This may sound strange in view of what happened at this meeting, but the tone of our discussion was friendly and casual. I had known Ed for more than five years. I first met him in connection with the sensitive project at the start of my tour. We worked together on counterterrorism and in several other areas. He personally detailed two

DEA agents to help me with hostage recovery efforts, and when I had to arrange for wiretaps and FBI surveillance of foreigners, he was one of the officials I had to call.

I didn't expect this meeting to be especially dramatic. I thought we were still trying to put the best possible face on what happened— to reveal enough to satisfy Congress and the press, but not so much as to endanger the hostages.

About an hour into the meeting, Meese said, "Is there anything else that can jump up and bite the President on the ass?"

"Not that I can think of," I replied.

"How about this?" he said, handing me a nine-page document. It was an April 1986 memorandum from me to Admiral Poindexter, which detailed a planned arms shipment to Iran and included a specific mention of twelve million dollars in residuals from the arms sale that would go to the Nicaraguan resistance.*

Oh, shit, I thought.

This was precisely the kind of document I had shredded. Or so I thought.

"Where did this come from?" I asked.

"That's not important," said Meese. "Did this happen?"

"No, that particular shipment never took place," I said. This was true, but the next question was inevitable.

"Well, did anything *like* this ever take place?"

I paused. This was the secret within a secret that was never supposed to be revealed. But there was no way I was going to lie to Ed Meese. After what seemed like an eternity, I said, "Yes."

Nobody screamed. The earth didn't shake. The walls didn't come crashing down. Nobody fell out of his chair. Nobody said, "Get out the handcuffs! This man has violated the Boland Amendment!"

---

*The critical part of the memo read as follows:

"$2 million will be used to purchase replacement TOWs for the original 508 sold by Israel to Iran for the release of Benjamin Weir. This is the only way that we have found to meet our commitment to replenish those stocks.

"$12 million will be used to purchase critically needed supplies for the Nicaraguan Democratic Resistance Forces. This material is essential to cover shortages in resistance inventories resulting from their current offensives and Sandinista counterattacks and to 'bridge' the period between now and when Congressionally-approved lethal assistance (beyond the $25 million in 'defensive' arms) can be delivered."

Ed Meese was certainly *interested*, but there was no hint in his reaction of what was to come just two days later, at the November 25 press conference.

"Was there a cover memo?" I asked. A cover memo would have indicated whether this particular document had been forwarded to the President—and I still didn't know where this memo had been found.

"No," said Reynolds. "There was no cover memo."

"Should we have found a cover memo?" said Meese.

"Not necessarily," I said. "I was just wondering."

Meese and his assistants asked a number of other questions. Had I ever discussed this arrangement with President Reagan? No, I said, but if anyone had, it would have been Admiral Poindexter.

The meeting ended shortly before six o'clock, when Meese left to pick up his wife at the airport. As he was leaving, I expressed my concern about the safety of the hostages. "I certainly hope this won't be made public," I said.

Famous last words.

After the meeting, I drove to the White House to find Admiral Poindexter. He wasn't in his office, or at home, either. The Sit Room watch officer told me he was at RFK Stadium, where the Dallas Cowboys were playing the Washington Redskins. "Do you want us to beep him?" he asked.

"That's all right," I said. "It can wait." I thought I'd let him get home before I gave him the bad news.

When I finally reached the admiral, at home that evening, I told him that Ed Meese and his people had shown me a memo from April which was explicit about the "diversion."

The admiral was silent for what seemed like a long time. "Well," he finally said, "what did you tell them?"

"I told them the truth," I replied. "I explained that this particular transaction hadn't occurred, but that other transactions had."

Another long silence. "You did the right thing," said the admiral.

I stayed in my office very late that night. I knew it wouldn't be long now, and I had stacks of material to straighten out before I left.

I also took the time to redraft a farewell letter that I had previously prepared for Admiral Poindexter:

There is that old line about you can't fire me, I quit. But I do want to make it official so that you know I sincerely meant what I said to you over the course of these last several difficult weeks. I'm prepared to depart at the time you and the President decide it to be in the best interests of the Presidency and the country.

I am honored to have served the President, you and your predecessors these past five and a half years. I only regret that I could not have done so better. My prayer is that the President is not further damaged by what has transpired and that the hostages will not be harmed as a consequence of what we now do. Finally, I remain convinced that what we tried to accomplish was worth the risk. We nearly succeeded. Hopefully when the political fratricide is finished there will be others in a moment of calm reflection who will agree.

Warmest regards, Semper Fidelis, Oliver North

I sent that letter on Monday. By Tuesday I was gone.

15

Lights, Cameras…

I have always been an early riser. The morning after I was fired, I left the house, as usual, at six o'clock, and held the front door open so that Max, our Labrador retriever, could go out for his morning ritual. It was still dark, and at first I didn't notice anything out of the ordinary. But as soon as I closed the door behind me, all hell broke loose: klieg lights lit up the yard, cameras flashed, and dozens of reporters started shouting to me from the fence along the road in front of our house.

Max was not amused. He's a tough-*looking* dog, but he's actually a wimp. He didn't even object when Dornin climbed on his back and rode him like a horse. But Max has one great talent: a ferocious bark that belies his basic cowardice.

And that morning, as soon as those lights came on, Max let loose. The press panicked. "Run for it, Bob! It's an attack dog!" Light stands came crashing down, car doors slammed, and reporters scrambled for their cars. Poor Max just stood there, quivering in fear with his tail between his legs—but barking like crazy.

But when they really want to, journalists learn fast, and it didn't take them long to break the code on Max. He was a pushover for a 7-Eleven doughnut, and over the next few months that dog must have gained about twenty pounds. But for those first couple of mornings after the firing, there was only very brief footage of Oliver North leaving his house.

From November 26, 1986, until after the hearings the following July, the press was at our house every morning at five o'clock. They came on Sunday. They showed up on Thanksgiving. They were even there on Christmas.

Christmas! That really shocked me. With four children, we get up early on Christmas morning. First we take pictures of the kids sitting on the stairs. Then we sing "Silent Night." After the kids open their Christmas stockings, we all go into the kitchen, where Daddy makes blueberry pancakes. When breakfast is over, we gather around the tree to hand out the presents. That's when I noticed that Dornin, our five-year-old, was missing.

Just then the front door opened, and in walked Dornin with an empty tray.

"Where were you?" I asked. "It's time for the presents."

"I went outside to give the 'porters some Christmas cookies," Dornin said.

"I thought I told you never to talk to them," I said.

"But Daddy," she said. "It's Christmas, and they were cold."

Only months later, when I looked back on this incident, did it occur to me that Dornin's Christmas spirit was a lot better than mine. I realized that those reporters and cameramen had been sent there by their editors and producers. I'm sure it wasn't their choice to spend Christmas morning standing outside our house. At least I hope not.

But even today, nearly five years later, I can't quite get over the fact that the press showed up on Christmas morning. They also came on Easter and on Passover. The only morning they missed was New Year's Day. Was *that* their religious holiday?

Thanks to these daily visitors, I must have been the most photographed commuter in America. Anyone with a television must have thought I *lived* in my car. Soon Johnny Carson was doing routines where he put on a uniform and answered questions through a car window:

Reporter: "Colonel North, sir, is it true that you secretly sold arms to Iran and used the money to help the Nicaraguan resistance?"
Carson (looking up at his questioner): "Say, did you know you had a very long hair growing in your left nostril?"

By then, of course, I was no longer driving to the White House. The night I was fired, I received a call from General P. X. Kelley, commandant of the Marine Corps. "You've been reassigned," he said. "Put on your uniform and report to headquarters tomorrow morning."

General Kelley posted me to the Plans and Policies division at headquarters, and I appreciated his vote of confidence. He could have assigned me to some far less visible job, or even asked me to resign. Instead, he had me working right down the hall from him. I offered to leave the service, but he wouldn't hear of it. "Come in tomorrow," he said. "If anyone doesn't like it he can talk to me."

Late that night, I got out my uniform and dusted it off. I had rarely worn it at the NSC, probably no more than half a dozen times in five and a half years. At one point, somebody at the White House had decided that every Wednesday, all the military people on the White House staff should wear their uniforms. This lasted about a month, until some of the civilians started looking around and muttering, "My God, there are so *many* of them!" And there were. It wasn't long before we were back in civvies.

That first morning after I was fired, the reporters chased me all the way to Marine headquarters in Arlington, following me in vans, cars, and motorcycles. Every morning thereafter, the press was waiting as I left the house.

They descended on us like a plague of locusts, intent on devouring our privacy and scouring the neighborhood for tidbits of information about our family. We couldn't go to the store, or to church, or the gas station without being watched. We couldn't get the newspaper, fetch the mail, wash the car, or mow the lawn without being observed, filmed, videotaped, photographed, tape-recorded, or written about. They followed me to work, to the dump, to the baby-sitter's house. They chased our children to the bus stop and pumped them with questions. When Betsy and I started driving them ourselves, they interviewed the neighbors' children. When my pickup had a flat tire on the way back from the dump one Saturday, they stopped and jumped out of their "chase car"—not to help me change the tire, but to film me doing it.

We soon developed a morning routine. I'd get into my car, and as I drove out to the road, a flock of reporters and photographers would be standing there, blocking the driveway. I'd wave them aside with a smile. They'd shake their heads. I'd slowly ease forward, always keeping in mind the admonition of Brendan Sullivan, my lawyer: "Whatever you do, don't run them over."

They'd signal for me to roll down the window—my ticket out of the driveway. As soon as I did, they'd start shouting questions: "Colonel North! What do you have to say about reports in the press that you sold pieces of White House china and silverware to raise money for the contras?"

Brendan and his colleagues had given me strict orders to remain silent, and no matter how provocative the questions, I did everything I could to comply. Although I chafed at this restriction, I knew there were good reasons for it. When you're facing the kind of inquisition I was, anything and everything you say in the press can, and probably will, be used against you. Unlike some of the attorneys who represented other Iran-contra defendants, my lawyers maintained a strict code of silence. They didn't talk about the case with *anybody*—and they expected the same from me.

Every day, Brendan would be given a pile of phone messages from the press, but he never returned the calls. As he came in and out of the law firm, reporters continually asked him questions. But he refused to confirm or deny anything, no matter how absurd the allegation.

"How did it go this morning, Mr. Sullivan?"

"No comment."

"Are you worried about this case?"

"No comment."

"How's the weather today?"

"No comment."

I didn't have quite as much will power, and there were a couple of times when I surrendered to overwhelming temptation. One morning, a reporter from CBS asked me how I felt about people like Maureen Reagan, who had said publicly that I should stop "hiding" behind the Fifth Amendment and start telling my story.

"I don't believe the President really wants me to abandon my individual rights under the Constitution," I said. "How many of you are willing to give up your First Amendment rights?"

Then somebody asked: "How do you feel about some of the things your erstwhile friends are saying about you?"

"On that one," I replied, "I would refer you to Psalm Seven, verse one."

"What does it say?" somebody shouted as I drove off.

"Look it up!" I yelled back. "It'll be good for you."

That night, on the "ABC Evening News," Peter Jennings actually read the verse on the air:

> O Lord my God, I take refuge in you;
>> save and deliver me from all who pursue me,
> Or they will tear me like a lion
>> and rip me to pieces with no one to rescue me.

Okay, I thought, this isn't a total disaster. At least I was able to get a verse of Scripture onto the network news.

Despite everything, I tried to retain some of my morning routine, which normally included reading at least a few verses from the Bible before I left for work. Occasionally, if I came across a line that seemed especially appropriate, I would quote it. The reporters liked to tease me about this, and sometimes I teased them back. "I try to read two things every morning," I told them. "The Bible and the *Washington Post*. That way I know what both sides are thinking."

My father had died in 1984, but my mother, living alone in upstate New York, was besieged by the press. Reporters used to ring every buzzer in her apartment building until somebody finally let them in. TV cameramen stood outside her door for hours, and there were times when she didn't dare leave. When the press couldn't get to her, they started in on her neighbors: "Do you know Mrs. North down the hall? Tell me, how often does her son come to visit? Does she have any strange habits?"

I had tried to prepare my own family for what was about to happen, but none of us could begin to imagine the full scope of it. The night I was fired, we all assembled on the living room floor where we normally played Scrabble and Trivial Pursuit. "I have been reassigned back to the Marine Corps," I said. "Although I haven't done anything wrong, there may be a lot of negative stories about me on television and in the newspaper." I didn't go into much detail, and I couldn't foresee then how brutal all this would be.

Looking back, I can see how much this whole thing has intruded on the lives of our children. In addition to the teasing, the questions, the rumors, and the wild allegations, the kids have also suffered on a more basic level. They were no longer allowed to be just Tait North, or Stuart North, or Sarah North, or Dornin North. From now on people would see them as Oliver North's kids. Even today, wherever they go, they start out either bigger or smaller in other people's eyes, depending on how those people feel about me. No matter what they accomplish on their own, it can never compete with Daddy's fame— or his notoriety. They don't deserve that, and I feel terrible about it.

Each of our children has reacted differently to these pressures. Tait, a senior in high school, a cheerleader, and head of the honor society, was furious when I was fired. She blamed the President and his whole administration. As she saw it, Ronald Reagan abandoned me after I had worked so hard for his policies, and to this day she is bitter about him. She and I have had some long talks about Iran-contra, and my role in it, and I have tried to put my own situation in a larger context. "Keep this in mind," I told her. "In many other countries, if something like this happened, your father could well have left for work one morning and you'd never have heard from him again."

Stuart, a sophomore in high school, responded with questions. I could answer some of them, but much of the information was either classified or had been declared off-limits by the lawyers. Naturally, this was hard on Stuart. Try telling your sixteen-year-old boy: "I'm sorry, but I just can't talk to you about that."

"What do you mean?" he'd say. "I'm your *son!*" He was reading all these articles in the paper, and watching news stories on TV. "Dad, what am I supposed to say when kids in class ask me questions about all the things you did?"

"Just tell them that you know your dad is a good Christian who wouldn't knowingly break the law," I told him.

Fortunately, Stuart was in a relatively protected environment at Woodbury Forest School in Orange, Virginia, where he was surrounded by supportive friends and teachers. But the long arm of the investigation reached him there, as federal agents showed up at the school to determine how Stuart's tuition bills were paid. (He was on scholarship.) Stuart knew generally what was going on, but Emmett Wright, the headmaster, made every effort to shield him from it.

Sarah, who was ten, probably suffered the most. She developed a rash on the back of her hands from nervously rubbing them together. She was hounded at school—not only by her classmates, but even by a couple of the teachers. She once asked one of her teachers what to do with a paper she had written. "Why don't you shred it?" the teacher replied. "If you don't know how, just ask your father. He's an expert at it."

But most of her teachers were far more supportive. One of them gave Betsy a pair of notes that she had confiscated from Sarah and one of her friends in class. Sarah's note breaks my heart: "Dennis says, 'Your dad's going to jail,'" she wrote. "And I was like, 'No, he's not.' I wish my dad was *normal.* You know what I mean?" But even in this there was a ray of sunshine. The response from her friend Cindy read, "No he won't. God won't let that happen."

Five-year-old Dornin, fortunately, was too young to fully grasp the content of what was being said and written about her father. We had established a family rule about not watching the news, but sometimes Dornin would see my face on television. She'd run up to Betsy and say, "Mommy, Daddy's on television. Again!"

"Cover your ears, child," Betsy would say, "and turn that thing off."

The avalanche of publicity brought the two younger girls much closer together. But even with a new and far less demanding job, I was rarely around to spend much time with them. I would arrive at Marine headquarters around seven-fifteen. At four in the afternoon, I'd drive over to Williams & Connolly to spend the next six to eight hours with the lawyers. It was like working two jobs.

Had Betsy not been a strong, devout, God-fearing woman, I shudder to think what would have happened to our family. But somehow she managed to keep us relatively sane, which was itself a full-time job. Every morning, for example, she would go through the *Post* and perform surgery on it, cutting out every article about Daddy and his legal problems so the kids wouldn't see them.

During those difficult months, Betsy and I went through a wide range of emotions. She was extremely supportive, but there were moments when the strain got to us both. "What have you done to my children?" she blurted out one night.

"Wait a minute," I said. "*Your* children?"

Obviously, the conversation didn't end there. Some of the stories in the press were just ludicrous. That Fawn Hall and I had planned to run off together to a desert island. That a private jet had stood by all through 1986, waiting to take me wherever I wanted to go on a moment's notice. That I was involved with drug-running for the contras. That I was behind an assassination attempt on Eden Pastora. That I was a compulsive liar. That I was, above all, a loose cannon on the gundeck of state.

A number of leaks clearly came from the White House. Once it became obvious that my lawyers wouldn't allow me to respond to any allegation, no matter how absurd, it seemed that a few individuals worked overtime in an attempt to divert attention away from the White House and other administration officials who had been involved in, or at least aware of, my activities. Story after story detailed operations I had supposedly conducted all on my own. "Anonymous sources" made a concerted effort to portray me as an unreliable renegade, and the press lapped it up, never stopping to ask how I could possibly have done all this on my own. Even now, many Americans believe that I sold arms to the Iranians *by myself*, and that no one in the U.S. government knew what I was doing in Central America! I believe that many of these stories originated with Don Regan's staff. He had apparently put out the word that my credibility was to be destroyed, and that I was to be depicted as some kind of deceitful wild man. (That way, nobody would believe me if I implicated the President.) Strangely, I didn't hear any of these accusations before I was fired. In fact, some of these same anonymous sources used to come up to me and tell me what a great job I was doing.

Many of the negative stories about me were based on true events, but were twisted to cast them in a nefarious light. I had indeed been supporting the resistance and meeting with Iranians, and had even used traveler's checks from the contra account in supermarkets, tire stores, and to buy leotards for my daughters at Parklane Hosiery. Because of this, it was implied that I had violated the Arms Export Control Act, broken neutrality laws, stolen money, and carried on an affair with Fawn Hall. There were also stories about my hospitalization in Bethesda, including one report that I had been found running around naked—waving a gun!

Almost all of these articles and news stories were attributed to unnamed or anonymous sources—mostly government insiders with their own axes to grind. But the media dutifully and uncritically carried them. There was a real mob mentality, and some people said things about me that they later came to regret. A couple of them even apologized.

Certainly I had made mistakes. But I had been a good staff officer. I was loyal to the President and his policies, and I bitterly resented allegations that I wasn't. I had worked my tail off at the NSC, and had kept my superiors informed every step of the way.

For me, the most offensive accusation was that I supposedly saw myself as being above the law, or that I "shredded the Constitution." That was terribly hurtful, because it was contrary to the way I was raised and educated, not to mention everything I had learned at Annapolis and as a Marine. Each time I was promoted, I had taken an oath to support and defend the Constitution of the United States. I meant those words, and I obeyed them. This tiger didn't change his stripes.

Perhaps the most disturbing story of all appeared on February 20, 1987, when it was suggested in the *Washington Post* that I had passed top-secret intelligence data to the Iranians without the permission of my superiors: "If he was acting entirely on his own," the article said, "North may have violated federal espionage laws, which for military personnel convicted of spying in peacetime carry the death penalty."

In reality, every bit of information we gave to the Iranians was prepared specifically for that purpose by the CIA and passed to the Iranians with the knowledge and approval of senior government officials. But that didn't seem to make much difference. On a Saturday morning, two days after the article appeared, Sarah and I got into the pickup truck and drove out to get some firewood. "Colonel North," one of the reporters shouted. "How do you feel about the article in the *Post* that said you might get the death penalty for treason?"

"If there's going to be an execution," I replied, "we ought to hold it in Yankee Stadium. That way we can sell tickets and send the proceeds to the contras."

As I was spouting off out the window, I couldn't see the shock and the tears on Sarah's face. It wasn't until we were halfway up the hill that I noticed she was crying.

I pulled over, put my arm around her, and said, "Don't worry, honey. It's going to be all right."

"Daddy," she said, "they *can't* give you the death penalty. It's unconstitutional."

Some of the worst stories came from the congressional investigators and the Office of the Independent Counsel, where scores of attorneys and their agents had begun probing every aspect of my life. The investigators were especially interested in my financial situation, and they left no stone unturned. They even sent agents out to California to interview a friend of Stuart's who had helped us paint our fence. I had written him a check for the whopping sum of thirty dollars. His father called me one night and said, "Boy, it's nice to know you've got friends in Washington who care enough to come all the way out here to talk about you." Our tax dollars at work.

The congressional investigators and special prosecutors went after every single business and individual to whom I had written a check. They even interviewed our baby-sitter.

One Saturday afternoon, I drove down to the gas station to fill up the pickup truck. When the owner spotted me, he came out and said, "Well, your buddies were here this week."

"What do you mean?"

"You know, the G-men. They took my business records, my tax records, everything."

The same thing happened at the little sawmill where I used to buy slab wood for our wood stove, and again at the local hardware store. They went after our plumber and the electrician. They even sent agents down to Kentucky, because our tax return had included several hundred dollars from the estate of Betsy's father.

Nothing was off-limits. They actually tried to interview a pastor about our past contributions at church. "I'm not totally familiar with the law," he told them, "but isn't there some provision for a pastoral privilege?" The agents left without answers.

Even if your neighbors like you, and ours were great, enough visits from enough investigators inevitably throw a little sand into the gears. It makes people wonder: if they're *that* interested in this guy, maybe there *is* something wrong with him. I might react the same way: when a federal agent knocks on your door and flips out his badge, it makes an impact. (It's *supposed* to.) We've all seen it on TV:

the Feds are the good guys, right? And so, inevitably, people begin to ruminate: You know, he *was* gone a lot. He *was* a little secretive. Maybe there *is* something wrong....

Before the investigations were over, every one of our friends and neighbors was either interviewed or subpoenaed by congressional investigators, or the Office of the Independent Counsel, or both. I'm surprised they didn't bump into each other as they went around asking questions. Do the Norths ever fight? Do they go away on trips? Do they live beyond their means? Betsy's sister was asked, "How much does it cost to feed the horses, dogs, and cats when the Norths are away?" Later, they went after Betsy—fingerprints, mug shots, handwriting sample, grand jury, the whole bit. It was just awful.

It was a very strange situation, with the government I had worked for these many years now using its full bureaucratic firepower against me. The IRS called: they wanted to send three agents to my house for "three or four days" to conduct a "full field audit." I had better things to do, but I was about to say, "Sure, come on over. I've got nothing to hide."

By then, however, I knew enough to check with Brendan, who just about had a cow. "Not on your life," he said. "You're not letting anybody from any agency of the government on your property, and you're not giving them anything. Tell them to call me."

The congressional inquisitors and special prosecutors weren't the only ones after me. Early in 1987, the FBI learned that certain Libyans in the United States were collecting information on my location, travel routes, and work habits with the intention of making an attack or an assassination attempt on me and/or my family. But when the FBI called Brendan, they weren't nearly so forthcoming. I was with him at the time, and the conversation went something like this:

FBI: We have information that leads us to believe that your client, Colonel North, may be in some jeopardy.
Sullivan: You're telling *me*?
FBI: This has nothing to do with the Congress or the Independent Counsel. We have some information about the possibility that someone may be trying to kill him.
Sullivan: And who might that be?

FBI: I can't give you that information.

Sullivan: Then why are you calling me?

FBI: Because Colonel North ought to have some protection.

Sullivan: I agree. Can I count on you to provide it?

FBI: We're not in the business of providing protection. All we can do is notify you.

Sullivan: Exactly what is the threat?

FBI: I'm sorry, that's all I can tell you.

Sullivan: That's really great. What are we supposed to do?

FBI: I would suggest that you contact the Department of Defense. Your client is in the military, and they have people who can deal with this sort of problem.

Sullivan: Can you tell *them* about this?

FBI: Yes, if they've got the right clearances.

Sullivan: Okay, let me get this straight. North is the target of an attempt to kill him. You can't tell us when or where, or who it is— or anything more about it. And we're supposed to get hold of somebody I don't know at the Pentagon who might be able to get more information from you?

FBI: You've got it.

Well, by the end of the afternoon, Brendan had tracked down the right people at the Naval Investigative Service. We soon learned that certain members of a group called the People's Committee for Libyan Students (PCLS), based in Virginia, were planning their first annual commemoration of the American antiterrorist bombing raid on Libya in April 1986. After my involvement in that operation, I had been threatened with death by Abu Nidal, one of the world's most dangerous terrorists. But it seemed that Abu Nidal wasn't moving fast enough for Colonel Q., because now some of his own boys were trying to speed up the timetable.

That evening, the Naval Investigative Service (NIS) assigned a small protective detail at our house that they coordinated with the Fairfax County Police Department, the state police, and the Loudoun County Sheriff's office. Nobody said so directly, but I had the feeling that they hoped to catch these guys in the act. (I would have tried the same thing in my old counterterrorist job.)

One morning, shortly after the security detail was posted, I planned to stop by Tait's school on my way to work. As we left the house, the agent who was riding with me jotted down the license numbers of the cars parked along our street, most of which belonged to reporters. While I was at the school, a report came back that one of the cars parked in front of our house had apparently been stolen. The agent with me was immediately concerned, because he had noticed that the woman driving that car appeared to be of Arab descent. He quickly alerted the local police. "Quick," he said to me, "out the back door. We've got to get you out of here."

"Where are we going?" I asked.

"To Marine Corps headquarters. You'll be safe there."

"No, we're not," I said. "If there's a problem at home, that's where we're going."

From the car, I used his portable phone to call Betsy, who was home alone. There was no answer.

We raced back to the house. The red car was gone, but there were two police cars in the driveway—and a third one parked on the street. Betsy was in the kitchen, and a very apologetic police officer was standing out front. After I had left, Betsy had gone out to the barn to feed the horses. She was out there with her coat thrown over her nightgown when the officers showed up. When they saw someone moving in the barn, they did what any police officer in that situation would have done. They drew their guns and shouted, "You there! Freeze!"

I went nuts. "That's it!" I told the agents. "You guys please leave. Call off the helicopters, the dogs, the police cruisers. It's not your fault. I'm just grateful that nobody sneezed when that gun was pointed at my wife. But that's it, gentlemen. Good-bye."

The mysterious red car turned out to be driven by a reporter from a newspaper in Philadelphia. It belonged to her boyfriend, and it hadn't been stolen after all. Somebody had copied down the license number wrong, which shows that you don't have to work at the NSC to make that kind of mistake.

When I finally got to work, there was a note on my desk telling me to report immediately to General Tom Morgan, assistant commandant of the Marine Corps.

"What happened this morning?" he asked.

I told him the story.

The general reminded me that this protection had been put in place by the government, and that nobody had any interest in having a Marine assassinated. He agreed that there had to be some changes made, and he told me that this could best be done with our family quietly out of the area until the improved security arrangements were in place. We were to report to Camp Lejeune within twenty-four hours, where we would be sequestered for a few days. This wasn't a suggestion or a request. It was an order.

It could have been worse. Someone further up the line in the Pentagon actually suggested that I should be issued permanent-change-of-station orders to a secure military facility in the Aleutian Islands off the coast of Alaska! Brendan thought it might be difficult to defend a client four thousand miles away. General Morgan agreed, and the orders were never cut.

The next morning we loaded up the car and drove down to North Carolina with a security escort. As soon as we left, agents from the NIS moved into our house and began installing sophisticated security and surveillance systems. Later, I was indicted for having accepted a $13,000 security system in 1986. At that price, it couldn't have been all that good. The federal government spent close to a million dollars protecting my family and me from February 1987 until October of that year, when pressure from angry congressmen forced the Department of Defense to cut off the security.

At Camp Lejeune we were sequestered in a beach house on a remote corner of the base. Unfortunately, late winter in North Carolina is not the best time to enjoy the beach. I read stories to Sarah and Dornin, and we played board games for hours. (Stuart remained at school, and Tait stayed with a friend so she wouldn't miss classes.) We had some good times, but I felt like a caged lion.

After the NIS had secured our house in Great Falls, we returned to a totally new situation. We were now guarded by up to thirty armed security men in three eight-hour shifts. And I do mean *men*. I'm a little old-fashioned when it comes to accepting women in traditional male jobs, but as a man with a wife and three lovely daughters, it seemed to me that our security team wasn't particularly well balanced. I know how young men think, and when Tait got in the car, some of these guys were watching her instead of the road. It was also getting just a little ridiculous: Betsy and the girls would all go shopping, and they'd be followed by five husky young men with bulging pockets, all of whom looked to be about seven feet tall.

"Can you send some female agents?" I asked General Morgan. A few days later, five very attractive women showed up to join the security team. Stuart was overjoyed. Unfortunately, the male agents became even *more* diverted. But something good came of it: two members of our security team who met on the job later got married.

Having guards around me all day took some getting used to. I liked these people. They were professionals, good at their job, and I appreciated the safety they provided for Betsy and the children. They were also extremely considerate—or so I thought. If I had to drive to the grocery store for a gallon of milk, or to the laundry to pick up the dry cleaning, one of the agents would always volunteer to do it for me. "Please, Colonel, don't trouble yourself. You stay here. I'll take care of it." It made me uncomfortable, but these guys were on their feet and out the door in no time.

At first I assumed that these were simply favors, perhaps inspired by a "servant's heart," as the Christian phrase describes it. Being new to the security routine, it took a while before it finally dawned on me that something else was going on here. It wasn't just that nobody on our security team wanted anything to happen to me; it was that they *especially* didn't want anything to happen to me *on their watch*. After all, if you're in the security business it doesn't look all that great on your résumé when you're forced to mention that the last guy you were protecting is unable to provide a recommendation because he was gunned down while picking up his dry cleaning.

Looking back on it, I can only laugh at my reaction to all the early publicity in the months after I was fired. Kid, you ain't seen nothing yet! Once the hearings began, everything that happened until then seemed trivial. It was one thing to be a household name, but after I appeared on television all day for six days, I became a household *face*. The July 9 issue of the *Washington Post* contained twenty-three pictures of me. Suddenly there were Oliver North T-shirts, buttons, and bumper stickers. There were even Oliver North dolls. Someone told me later on that after the dolls stopped selling, the manufacturer took the same mold, stuck on a new head, and replaced the Marine uniform with a fancy Italian suit. Voilà—the Mikhail Gorbachev doll. Say it ain't so!

There were Oliver North look-alike contests. In *People* magazine a celebrity dentist in Beverly Hills explained what was wrong with my teeth. On television, a plastic surgeon to the stars explained how my broken nose could be straightened and my ears pinned back so that I wouldn't look like Howdy Doody. (The shocking part about it was that my kids had no idea who Howdy Doody was.) There were cardboard cutouts, videotapes, and hundreds of editorial cartoons. There were even Ollieburgers, made of—what else?—shredded beef covered with shredded lettuce and shredded cheese. There must have been a million jokes about shredding. At least *Advertising Age* was a little more original when they suggested that I'd make a good pitch man for—warning, bad pun follows—contra-ceptives.

Newsweek, which never said anything nice about me, nonetheless ran a billboard ad showing me at the hearings, with the caption "Few things in life are as feisty as *Newsweek*." A company that made frames for eyeglasses ran an ad depicting me "wearing" their glasses, with the caption, "I've been framed." And a British bank ran a full-page ad in a London newspaper, with a photo of me and the caption, "With a few notable exceptions, no one can transfer your money round the world more efficiently than us."

The circus atmosphere eventually died down, but the memory lingers on. To this day, I'm still recognized wherever I go.

"You look an awful lot like Oliver North," people will say.

"You know," I reply, "people tell me that all the time."

Sometimes I actually get away with it. But usually they'll say, "You really *are* Oliver North, aren't you?" When I hear that, I reach for my pen.

People often have a preconceived idea of what I should look like, and they're not shy about telling me. "I expected you'd be taller," they'll say. Or a complete stranger will come up to me and say, "You've put on a little weight, Colonel." (The fact that it's usually true doesn't make me feel any better.)

At first I naïvely thought I could avoid being recognized. When our family went to Disney World, I wore a huge pair of sunglasses and an oversized hat. I even kept my head down so people wouldn't see my face. It worked, too—for about ten minutes. We were coming out of Space Mountain when a woman waiting in line called out, "Look, honey, it's Ollie North. Hey, Ollie, what's with that funny hat and the stupid glasses?" I spent the next forty minutes signing autographs while Betsy and the kids went on to the next ride.

In the summer of 1990, after sailing in an ocean race with Brendan, I showed up in Bermuda with a beard and long hair, happy in my imagined anonymity. But as soon as I walked into the hotel, somebody called out, "There's Oliver North. Nice beard, Ollie!"

One time, when I wanted to slip into Williams & Connolly without being identified by anticontra demonstrators outside the building, I donned an old gray wig that had once belonged to Betsy's mother. With a leather jacket and old jeans, I looked like an elderly Berrigan brother. Even my own lawyers didn't recognize me. When I bounded into Barry Simon's office, he jumped up and yelled, "How did *you* get in here?"

The biggest consequence of being recognized is that everything takes much longer than it used to. Whether it's leaving church, getting a haircut, or watching Stuart play football, people are always coming over to me, shaking my hand, taking pictures, asking for autographs. It got to the point where Betsy started asking me not to show up at certain events she was going to because it took us so long to leave.

Sometimes, when we're out together, Betsy has to remind me to be nice to all the people who come up to me. Somebody will ask for my autograph when I'm in the middle of a conversation. "I'm sorry," I'll tell them, "but I don't have anything to write on." Then Betsy kicks me hard on the ankle. "Wait a minute, I might have a card right here in my pocket."

"I realize how tiring it must be," she'll tell me later. "But the people who ask for your autograph have no idea that you've already been stopped fifteen times in the past hour." And of course she's right. Without the kindness, generosity, and prayers of so many Americans, we would never have been able to mount a defense. There's just no way we could have done this alone.

To my surprise, almost everybody who comes up to me is supportive and kind. I'm aware, of course, that lots of Americans disapprove of everything I did—or at least everything they *think* I did. But since the day I was fired, with the exception of congressmen and prosecutors, not more than half a dozen Americans have been unkind enough to say anything nasty or critical to my face. About the only time I encounter any hostility is when I'm out making a speech, especially at a political event. But even when people don't approve, they're usually polite.

Sometimes, on the street or in an airport, they'll say, "I watched your show," as though the hearings were some kind of soap opera or variety show. Or "I watched your trial," although the trial, which took place almost two years after the hearings, was never on television. But I can understand that, because the hearings certainly *looked* like a trial. I've even had people come up to say, "I read your book," although until now I had never written one.

When the news media showed up at our house every morning, they were able to capture—totally against our will—little vignettes of ordinary family life at our home in suburban Virginia: leaving for work, cutting the grass, or going out to buy a Christmas tree. People who saw these scenes on television started to think of us as a TV family and came to feel as if they knew us. It's *still* an odd feeling to have a perfect stranger come up and ask me about Betsy, or one of our kids, by name. They still ask me if Betsy still has the blue-and-white polka-dot dress she wore for one day at the hearings. People we have never met before invite us to stay at their houses. Maybe I'd feel differently if I were a rock star or a politician. While I certainly appreciate the support, I have never become comfortable with all the attention.

It happens at church, too, and a few people actually started attending our church because they wanted to talk to me. Several years back, I wasn't very sympathetic when President Reagan announced that he and Nancy had stopped going to church because their presence was simply too disruptive to the service. Today, after seeing the disruption even at my level, I can appreciate why he said that.

I miss having a free and totally spontaneous conversation with people I don't know. I used to enjoy talking to my seatmate on an airplane, or trading stories with the father standing next to me at a horse show where our daughters are participating. But these days, people usually ask questions or make comments about my activities, and when they don't, it's only because they're going out of their way to treat me as "normal."

To this day, our family receives a good deal of mail from people we have never met, who send us anniversary cards, birthday cards, and especially Christmas cards. Some of these cards are signed, simply, "an ordinary American," or with some other anonymous phrase. But most are signed by name, and each December, Betsy and I sort through thousands of cards in an attempt to figure out which ones come from people we actually know. Several correspondents have sent me photographs of the house in Philmont where I grew up, or of my father's wool factory. People send us cookies and cakes, which our security team tries to keep us from eating.

Let me add, however, that fame is not without certain advantages. One of the great benefits of this whole fiasco is that it put me back in touch with many of the men I served with in Vietnam. They write me letters, and some of them show up at my speeches. They have been steadfast in their support, and they knew that most of what they were reading in the papers and hearing on television just wasn't true.

It's great to see these guys again, but it's sobering, too. The last time we were together, well over twenty years ago, they were nineteen and I was twenty-five. Since then, all of us have grown fatter, balder, and older. They don't look quite as sharp as they did, and I hate to think how I must appear to them. Still, it's great to see them again, and to meet their families. We catch up as best we can, but we rarely talk about the war.

Another advantage to being known is that whenever I feel strongly about a particular subject, I can usually get myself heard. I have spoken out on a number of issues, but one of those I feel strongest about is the need to limit the number of terms that a member of Congress can serve. Most members of the House and Senate come to Washington with good intentions. They don't intend to abuse their trust, or to pillage the public treasury. But very quickly they become professional politicians whose overriding concern is getting reelected again and again and again. The President's tenure is limited; I think we should have a similar limit for Congress.

Yet another benefit of fame is that, ironically, all of this public exposure has actually strengthened my connection with my family. There have been some very difficult times, but we have emerged from that experience closer than ever. I'm home for dinner more often, and I spend more time with our children—which makes me realize how many special times I missed with our two older ones.

Finally, there's a certain financial advantage to fame. I'm not referring to my speaking fees, most of which go to cover my enormous legal and security bills. I have in mind something far more modest: these days, when I write a small check, there's at least some chance that the person I give it to may decide to keep it as a souvenir. This has messed up my checking account more than once, but I can live with that.

The first time it happened, I thought back to an anecdote about General Moshe Dayan that I once heard from Ami Nir. The story may well be apocryphal, but I'll tell it anyway in honor of Ami. Dayan was a well-known collector of antiquities, and he loved to poke around in little Arab shops in Israel. If he saw an artifact he needed for his collection that was selling for, say, a hundred Israeli pounds, he would always pay for it by check.

But the merchant wouldn't cash Dayan's check. Instead, he'd frame it and put it on display, with a note: "Check signed by Moshe Dayan. Two hundred pounds."

Before long, Dayan's check would be bought by an American tourist. As Nir explained it, everybody was a winner from this transaction. Dayan got the artifact for free. The Arab shopkeeper made twice what he expected. And some dentist from Milwaukee would be able to display Moshe Dayan's autograph on the wall of his den.

16

Circus Maximus

It was the noise that took me by surprise. After watching the Iran-contra hearings on television for seven weeks before my own testimony began, I thought I knew what to expect. But when I finally arrived at the Senate Caucus Room, the scene that greeted me was a lot more raucous than the calm and orderly image portrayed on TV.

Directly in front of me, in the narrow space between the witness table and my congressional inquisitors, well over a dozen photographers and cameramen were snapping and shooting like crazy. After so many months of the press hanging around "Scapegoat Central," as some of them referred to our house, I was amazed that anyone still wanted to take my picture. But on that first morning, the clicking and whirring of motor-driven cameras continued nonstop for what seemed like half an hour. Eventually the photographers settled down, but every time I shifted in my chair or scratched my ear, it was like stirring up a nest of insects. There were times when the commotion was so loud that I had trouble hearing the questions.

Just beyond the photographers, on an elevated, double-tiered dais, sat the twenty-six members of the Iran-Contra Committee and their innumerable staff. Peering down at me, they were closer than they appeared to be on television. This sea of faces was in constant motion, with senators, congressmen, and staffers walking in and out, whispering to each other, shuffling papers, and passing notes.

Directly behind me, seated at several long tables, were scores of reporters and commentators, like a crowd of jackals waiting for the flesh to come flying their way. They kept up a constant chatter, buzzing about everything from baseball and the weather to their opinions of my latest answer. Behind *them* were four rows of chairs for Executive Branch officials as well as the handful of American citizens in whose name all of this was ostensibly being done.

From watching the earlier witnesses, I had expected that the hearing room would resemble a theater, with everybody paying rapt attention and looking in the same direction. But this was more like the crowd at a sporting event. The only thing missing were the hot dog vendors and souvenir stands as you entered the stadium—although I was told that all of that and more could be found right outside the building on Constitution Avenue.

Circus Maximus. The hearing room, which looked so much larger on television, reminded me of a miniature Colosseum when the lions were about to be released. The committee members sat there proudly on their high platforms, like corpulent and powerful Roman potentates. They looked down their noses at the solitary gladiator while the crowd awaited the ritual slaying.

A lot of political blood had been spilled in this room. Back in 1912, the hearings on the sinking of the *Titanic* had taken place beneath these very chandeliers. Teapot Dome, the Army-McCarthy Hearings, Watergate—these walls had heard it all. Twelve months earlier, if anyone had suggested that I, too, would end up testifying here, I would have asked him what planet he was visiting from.

As I entered the arena on the morning of Tuesday, July 7, 1987, I had a fleeting thought: Who *are* these people, and what am I doing here? Taking my place at the witness table on that first morning, I was acutely aware that my mother was watching on television, that Betsy was watching at home, and that our kids would probably be seeing this, too—at least on the evening news and in the papers. (Other than that, it didn't even occur to me—on that first morning, at least—that millions of others might well be watching, too.) I was grateful that our family had just enjoyed a relaxing Fourth of July together: we had all gone sailing with Brendan Sullivan and his family, which was a lot more fun that sitting in his conference room and wading through documents. But little did I realize that our lives would never again be the same.

Even today, wherever I go, I meet people who "know" me from watching the hearings on TV. They're often surprised to find that I'm a "real" person—a fairly casual guy who loves a good laugh, and who turns out to be very different from that serious and confrontational Marine they saw on television. After six days of testimony, most people assumed that this must be my normal disposition.

Actually, I'm not like that at all. But this was a special situation. For months I had heard little but lies, distortions and innuendos about myself and my activities. No wonder I was angry.

I was well aware that some of the committee members were already convinced that I was the villain, or, as *Newsweek* put it in a colorful summary of the conventional wisdom, "the Rambo of diplomacy, a runaway swashbuckler who had run his own private foreign policy from the White House basement."

But if they believed the worst about me, that was fine, because I wasn't too crazy about some of them, either. To me, many senators, congressmen, and even staffers were people of privilege who had shamelessly abandoned the Nicaraguan resistance and left the contras on the battlefield, exposed and vulnerable to a powerful and well-armed enemy. And now they wanted to humiliate me for doing what *they* should have done!

But our differences were broader than that. Many of these people had done little in life but run for political office. They were supposed to be public servants, but far too many, in my view, were simply running reelection machines. They had turned Congress into a retirement home for professional politicians.

Unfortunately, some of my attitude seeped through in my answers. Toward the end of the hearings, one of the members said that I obviously held Congress in contempt. I don't. I have great respect for Congress as an institution, and I certainly acknowledge its right to gather information in a fair and honest manner.

But that's not what happened during the hearings. Few members came into that room with an open mind, and few questions were asked simply to elicit information. Despite all the pretense, this was not an open forum in search of the truth.

This was politics. Viewed in a larger perspective, these hearings were one more battle in a two-hundred-year-old constitutional struggle between the Legislative and Executive branches over the control of America's foreign policy. Congressional hearings are a constitutionally sanctioned way for Congress to try to nail the presidency, and even to humiliate a particular President. But to force the public testimony of witnesses who were also facing a special prosecutor created a whole new dimension. Taken together, the hearings and the special prosecutor became a way for the two branches of government—legislative and executive—to avoid resolving the broader issues of who would determine our foreign policy. By the summer of 1987, the White House was willing to give up just about anyone or anything that would permit the upper echelons of the administration to survive. By allowing the actions of those who had served the administration to be criminalized, the administration itself was able to back away from the real issues involved. This was fine with Congress, and a gift for the press.

In the hearings, as in the media, the same question kept coming up in a variety of forms: what did the President know, and when did he know it? But even this was a sham, for the committee members already knew the answers. Shortly before my public testimony began, Brendan had agreed that before I testified publicly, the committee could ask me one question in private. Not surprisingly, their most burning question was whether I had told the President about the "diversion." I explained that while I had never discussed it with President Reagan, I had always assumed that he was aware of what I was doing, and that he had, through my superiors, approved it.

The committee's infatuation with the "diversion" continued throughout the hearings. It served to distract attention from many other things that the President and his administration had done to support the contras during the Boland prohibitions. And it kept all the attention focused on me—which appeared to be just what the committee *and* the administration wanted. It was a very cozy relationship that persisted throughout—and it left John Poindexter and me out in the cold.

From the Tower Commission through the hearings, and later, the trials, the administration's approach was to give the investigators just about everything they asked for. The White House turned over tens of thousands of pages of my notes, records, and files to the committee and to the prosecutors, but wouldn't provide any of it to my attorneys. And there was a disturbing willingness on the part of the administration, the Congress, and the special prosecutor's office to spell out the intimate details of secret operations undertaken by our government while the entire world press was looking on. It didn't seem to matter that lives were at risk. Both the committee and the special prosecutor developed a charade of assigning numbers and letters to various countries and individuals, but this was merely an open invitation for the press to step in and clear up the ambiguities.

One possible victim of this process was General Gustavo Alvarez, the former commander of the Honduran armed forces who had been helpful to our government in supporting the contras. In January 1989, he was assassinated near Tegucigalpa. His direct connection to our government was certainly known by some of his own people. But until his support for American measures to aid the resistance was made public, he had been relatively safe.

Alvarez wasn't the only casualty. Several other individuals in foreign governments were hounded, harassed, and even purged because their numbers came up. Benjamin Piza, the public security minister in Costa Rica, was threatened with both violence *and* legal action because he had helped us build a secret airfield. In Israel, Ami Nir, who had risked his life in going to Tehran with us, was fired from his job in the prime minister's office. General Rafael Bustillo, the head of the Salvadoran air force, was humiliated by the special prosecutors, who had him grabbed and dragged before a grand jury when he arrived in the United States for medical treatment.

I was alarmed by the committee's willingness to reveal secrets. My inquisitors knew full well that on several occasions I had been sent to Central America to talk with heads of state and other senior government officials about support for the contras. I had promised these individuals that we would protect both their identities and the fact of their support. They didn't fully trust the United States to keep secrets, but we continually assured them that they could count on us.

The hearings made a mockery of these promises. What happened was tantamount to taking the secret archives of the NSC and dumping them out in the street.

*   *   *

People often ask if I was afraid during the hearings. I was certainly angry, disgusted, embarrassed, and occasionally contentious, but fear didn't enter into it. The one time in my life when I had experienced real fear was in Vietnam, which may explain why I didn't feel it in the Senate Caucus Room. Once you've been shot at and hit in combat, everything else tends to pale by comparison. What was the worst these people could do to me? As far as I could see, none of them had any hand grenades. I wasn't counting on enjoying my days in that room, but I fully expected to survive the experience.

The opening question came from John Nields, the arrogant, long-haired chief counsel for the House committee members:

> *Nields:* Colonel North, were you involved in the use of the proceeds of sales of weapons to Iran for the purpose of assisting the contras in Nicaragua?
> [The answer, of course, was "yes." But first there was a prearranged ritual to be played out:]
> *North:* On advice of counsel, I respectfully decline to answer the question based on my constitutional Fifth Amendment rights.

A buzz of anxiety shot through the room, which I took to mean: wait a minute—does this mean that after seven months of silence, and the entire country watching on television, this guy isn't going to *talk*?

Months earlier, I had almost gagged when my lawyers had told me I'd have to take the Fifth Amendment. "What are you talking about?" I said. "The Fifth Amendment is for *criminals*. It's for cowards. It's tantamount to pleading guilty! I've seen mafia types take the Fifth on television. I've got nothing to hide. I'll go in there and tell them everything. I'm *proud* of what I did."

"I know you are," Brendan calmly replied. "But that's not what you're going to do."

"Listen," he said, when I continued to object. "If you and I were in a plane that crashed in a jungle behind enemy lines, and we were fortunate enough to survive, I'd rely on you to get us out of there alive. Well, today you're in a different kind of jungle, and you've got to rely on me. You may not like everything I tell you to do, but as long as I'm your lawyer, that's the way it's going to be."

I *still* don't feel comfortable about taking the Fifth Amendment, but as usual, Brendan was right. From the very beginning, he and his legal team were looking ahead to the possibility of a criminal trial. They wanted to make sure that if Congress compelled me to testify, none of my answers could be used against me in court if I was later charged with a crime—as indeed I was. This arrangement is known as "use immunity." To put it into effect, I had to begin by publicly and formally claiming my constitutional protections against self-incrimination.

Senator Inouye, chairman of the Senate select committee, then spelled out the terms: that I was here because of subpoenas issued by the Senate and House committees, that I was being compelled to testify, and that "no evidence or other information obtained under the oath or any information directly or indirectly derived from such evidence may be used against you in any criminal proceeding."

I probably should have known better, but I believed him. Later, during my trial, the very first witness for the prosecution was Lee Hamilton, the cochairman of the Joint Iran-Contra Committee. But all that was yet to come. Now that the formalities were completed, the hearings could proceed.

The Fifth Amendment wasn't the only issue where I disagreed with my lawyers. We also had a brief but spirited argument over whether I should wear my uniform to the hearings. I was against it. I was a very unpopular person on Capitol Hill, and if I was dressed as a Marine, it wasn't hard for me to imagine that Congress might decide to "modify" the Corps' budget request.

My lawyers saw it differently. "You're still a Marine," they said. "You spend every day at the Marine headquarters, wearing a uniform. You ought to wear it to the hearings."

When I persisted, Brendan urged me to ask General Kelley, the commandant, for his opinion. "When I go up to testify," the general told me, "I always wear the uniform. All my Marines do, and you should, too."

That settled it. Here, too, Brendan turned out to be right. I had thought that the hearings were essentially political, and to a large extent, they were. But they were also about something even bigger.

Television.

Later on, people would come up to congratulate me, or to applaud my lawyers, for "putting the hearings on television." In some respect, the TV coverage worked in my favor, and it certainly helped me raise money for my defense. On the other hand, it also made it much easier for the special prosecutor's office to use my immunized testimony against me because so many people had heard it and seen it. But regardless of whether it helped or hurt, it wasn't my decision. This was the committee's call, not ours.

From the beginning, Brendan took the position that because of the special prosecutor's investigation, and the possibility of criminal charges, I shouldn't have to testify before Congress at all. Although he fully recognized that Congress could force me to appear, he told them in a twenty-seven-page letter that they had no statutory authority to make me testify more than once. "You have a choice," he told the committee. "You can question Colonel North in a closed session, or you can do it in public. It's up to you."

The Joint Iran-Contra Committee chose to have me testify in front of the cameras—a decision they surely came to regret.* But from their point of view it made sense. Because I had given no prior testimony, and hadn't granted a single interview to the press, there was, to say the least, a great deal of public interest in what I was going to say. For the committee members, the prospect of appearing before tens of millions of people on network television was apparently irresistible. They all remembered Watergate, when several relatively unknown politicians rose to national prominence, including Howard Baker, Lowell Weicker, Peter Rodino, Sam Ervin, and, of course, Daniel K. Inouye. You couldn't buy that kind of publicity, which was why the competition to serve on the House and Senate Iran-contra committees had been so fierce.

By March, when these two committees were merged into one panel for joint hearings, twenty-six members had already been appointed. But while almost everybody in Congress agreed that the joint committee was far too large, not a single member volunteered to step down.

Their goal, of course, was "face time"—a chance to pontificate before the cameras. The committee members didn't really want to ask

---

*Nearly three-quarters of the nation saw at least part of my testimony on television. According to a *New York Times*–CBS survey at the end of the first week of my testimony, 43 percent of the public gave me a favorable rating. In a similar survey back in March, only 6 percent rated me favorably. (*U.S. News & World Report*, July 20, 1987, p. 19.)

the questions; they preferred to make speeches. And so they left the detailed questions to their two "designated hitters"—John Nields and Arthur Liman.

As chairman, Senator Inouye retained a major role. But he ruled against us at every turn, and millions of Americans concluded that he was unfair. The hearings didn't help his career, either. He was later defeated for Senate majority leader by Senator George Mitchell, who at least appeared to be far more reasonable.

Nields and Liman did not have an easy time of it. With the other witnesses, they had a script to follow. They or their staff had spent days in depositions, interviews, and private hearings, going through questions and producing a transcript. Brendan wouldn't allow that in my case. As a trial lawyer, he knew there was nothing more powerful in the hands of a cross-examiner than prior testimony taken under oath. My lawyers wanted me to go in there with a clean slate. Without their usual road map to show them the way, Nields and Liman were forced to think on their feet and to improvise.

For weeks before I testified, Brendan and his team had tried to prepare me for what the hearings would be like. Nearly every afternoon after work, I would drive from Marine headquarters in Arlington to Williams & Connolly in downtown Washington for the pleasure of spending the evening and half the night being grilled.

Typically, the lawyers would show me the text of one of the documents that had been referred to that day in the hearings: "Tell us about this memo."

"I sent that to McFarlane shortly before the trip to Tehran. Apparently I made a few typing errors. Is that the problem?"

"Come on, Ollie, don't be a wise guy. You have a natural tendency to joke around, but don't do that during the hearings. They will expect you to be apologetic and serious. At least be serious."

But the lawyers never asked me to apologize, and I had no intention of doing so. "You don't have to be defensive," Brendan said. "The way you explain things to us, minus the wisecracks—that's how you should talk to the committee. Just tell the truth."

It's hard for me to describe how close I feel to my lawyers, and especially to Brendan. I have spent so much time with Brendan and his team that they have come to know me better than anybody else except Betsy. As we worked together month after month, we developed an intensely personal relationship.

For them, this wasn't business as usual, and I ran up well over a million dollars before I could pay them anything. But it was clear from the start that my lawyers weren't in this for the money. They believed with a passion that what was happening to me was wrong, and there were times when they were even more outraged than I was. I came to admire and appreciate them so much that I almost stopped telling lawyer jokes.

Brendan's team of five was up against more than eighty lawyers and agents on the special prosecutor's staff, and over a hundred staff members and lawyers attached to the congressional committees. But each member of the Sullivan team brought a special gift to the party. They reminded me of a crack military unit, where each member has his own MOS—military occupational specialty.

Brendan, the field marshal, is a master of legal tactics and an expert at cross-examination. Later, at my trial, even the judge and the prosecutors conceded that he did a brilliant job with some of the witnesses. Brendan's face reveals nothing. I have watched him sit through the most difficult moments of the hearings and the trial without changing his expression. (He is considerably younger than he looks; he was only forty-five at the time of the hearings—just two years older than I.) Although I trusted him completely, he still checked every decision with me, and always allowed me to voice my opinions and occasional disagreements. Once or twice he even listened to me.

Barry Simon, who has worked closely with Brendan for years, is an expert on the law. He is also the smartest man I've ever met. (Barry is partly bald, and it wouldn't surprise me if he had burned off some of his hair by thinking so hard.) He's a former chemistry major who graduated from Harvard Law School, where he was president of the *Law Review*. While Brendan reminds me of an inscrutable elder statesman, Barry is far more direct and confrontational. He has a phenomenal memory, and I wouldn't dare contradict him unless I was actually holding a document in my hand that proved I was right—and sometimes not even then. It didn't take long before he knew more about Iran-contra than I did.

Nicole Seligman is a brilliant negotiator. She was also the youngest member of the defense team, and at one point was actually mistaken for my daughter. Nicole is a master of the art of the possible; where others see only problems, she sees possibilities and finds solutions. She is blessed with an unusually clear and logical mind, and a terrific sense of humor. She's also a fine writer—which may have something to do with her previous career as an editor on the Asian edition of the *Wall Street Journal.*

John Cline joined the team after I was indicted in 1988, and brought in a remarkable talent for research. Barry would cite (from memory, of course) half a dozen cases that might apply, and John would research them. He'd write a draft of the motion or the brief under discussion, and send it on to Barry for a quick review. Barry would send it back to John, who would revise it again and deliver it to Brendan. Brendan would make a few last-minute changes, and would send it to John, then back again to Brendan for a final review before a courier delivered it to the courthouse. They never missed a deadline.

Terry O'Donnell, the fifth member of the team, was an expert on the inner workings of government. He had served in the Ford administration, and he understood the intricacies and the legal aspects of covert operations. He also appreciated the mentality of many of the government officials we had to deal with in the bureaucracy. When the FBI alerted Brendan to the Libyan threat, it was Terry who found the right office to call in the Pentagon.

The case made tremendous demands on all of the lawyers, and on their families, and on the two paralegals and three overworked secretaries who struggled along with the rest of us. One young man, Chris Capozzi, gave up a year of law school to stay on the case.

I learned a great deal from my lawyers, and some of their advice is indelibly etched in my memory. During my very first meeting with Brendan, he said, "We have a few rules here that you're going to get to know and love. The most important ones are these: Always tell the truth. Don't create anything, and don't destroy anything. Don't confirm or deny anything to the media, and don't talk to the press or anybody else. And that means *anybody* else—with the possible exception of Betsy."

He continued: "If one of your former colleagues contacts you, here's what you should tell them: 'First, tell the truth. Don't lie to anybody about anything—even if you think it will help me. Second, don't create anything and don't destroy anything. Third, get yourself a lawyer. If you don't know a lawyer, call Brendan Sullivan and he'll recommend one.'"

"Make absolutely sure your answers are truthful," Brendan told me early on. "You haven't broken any laws yet. Don't start now. Nobody will go to jail for what they did in this affair. But they might for what they do now. People could be indicted for perjury as the result of their testimony. Tell the truth—even about things you may have done wrong in the past. Call us crazy, but we have a little policy here at Williams & Connolly: we don't like to see any clients end up in jail."

Anyone who saw my testimony on television will recall that Brendan was at my side throughout the proceedings, sitting next to me at the witness table, or, as he called it, the bicycle built for two. One difference between a hearing and a trial is that at a hearing, the witness is allowed to consult with his lawyer at any point, which led to a number of quick, whispered conversations between us. The subject of these whisperings, I learned later, inspired all kinds of guessing games—and a few jokes, too. "If you keep giving him the answers," quipped one comedian, "how will he ever learn?"

On the afternoon of my first day of testimony, Brendan received an urgent message from a colleague back at the office. This lawyer's mother, who was partially deaf, had called her son to say that when Brendan covered the microphone and started whispering to me, it was possible to read his lips. From then on, Brendan held up his hand whenever we spoke.

Sometimes he reminded me to slow down. Once he pointed out that I had answered only the first half of a two-part question. Occasionally he suggested that I had not fully responded to a question, and should expand my answer. He pointed out a few traps. Once or twice, when he could see I was losing my temper, he actually told me a joke. But my favorite interruption was the time he leaned over and said, "Hi. It's been a while since you and I have had a chat, so I thought I'd just say hello. Look serious. If you smile now, I'll kick you so hard your ankle will bleed."

This was no idle threat. As we sat there at the witness table, our faces were scrutinized by a hundred cameras. But because the table was covered by a long red cloth, nobody could see our feet. Every time I said something dumb or sarcastic, Brendan would kick me—hard.

"I came here to tell you the truth," I told Nields that first morning. "The good, the bad, and the ugly."

Ouch!

And later:

Nields: Where are those memoranda?
North: Which memoranda?
Nields: The memoranda that you sent up to Admiral Poindexter seeking the President's approval.
North: Well…I think I shredded most of that. Did I get 'em all?

Ouch!

And a few minutes later:

Nields: Sir, do you remember the question?
North: My memory has been shredded.

Ouch!

I was far too insolent that first morning, and by the time we broke for lunch my ankle was killing me.

The hearings must have been terribly frustrating for Brendan. As a trial lawyer, he's used to making arguments before a judge and a jury. But during the hearings his visible role was reduced to occasional whisperings and periodic objections when the committee's unfairness became too flagrant—all of which were overruled by Inouye.

Late in the afternoon of the third day, things came to a head when Arthur Liman asked me a hypothetical question.

Sullivan: Those kinds of questions, Mr. Chairman, are wholly inappropriate, not just because of rules of evidence, not because you couldn't say it in a court, but because it's just dreamland. It's speculation…. Come on, let's have, Mr. Chairman —
Inouye: I'm certain counsel —
Sullivan:—plain fairness, plain fairness. That's all we're asking.
Inouye: May I speak, sir? May I speak?

Sullivan: Yes, sir.

Inouye: I'm certain counsel realizes that this is not a court of law.

Sullivan: I—believe me, I know *that*.

Inouye: And I'm certain you realize that the rules of evidence do not apply in this inquiry.

Sullivan: That I know as well. I'm just asking for fairness—fairness. I know the rules don't apply. I know the Congress doesn't recognize attorney-client privilege, a husband-and-wife privilege, priest-penitent privilege. I know those things are all out the window —

Inouye: We have attempted to be as fair as we can.

Sullivan:—and we rely on just fairness, Mr. Chairman. Fairness.

Inouye: Let the witness object, if he wishes to.

Sullivan: Well sir, I'm not a potted plant. I'm here as the lawyer. That's my job.

Who could have guessed that a throwaway line about foliage would capture the imagination of the American public? That afternoon, we returned to the law firm to find dozens of potted plants. By the next day, there were potted plants everywhere—in the lobby, in the corridors, and especially in Brendan's office, which now resembled a terrarium.

This botanical generosity represented just a fraction of an unimaginable outpouring of public support. At Williams & Connolly, the phones were ringing off the hook. On the building across the street, occupied by a staid old bank, the occupants of an upper story posted a scoreboard that changed each day. By the end of my testimony, it read, OLLIE 6, CONGRESS 0. In our neighborhood in Great Falls, my neighbors hung banners and flags from the trees on the road that ran past our homes.

During the hearings and shortly afterward I received over a million pieces of mail from people who had been watching on television. Some of the envelopes were simply addressed to: Oliver North, American Hero. They reached me anyway. Eventually, all of the mail ended up at Williams & Connolly, where it filled the mailroom and overflowed into the basement. The firm's regular mail was buried in the avalanche, and some of it wasn't found for weeks.

Edward Bennett Williams, who had established the law firm that bears his name, asked me if the security team could process the mail a little faster so that the place could resume some semblance of normalcy. But by then there was far too much for one bomb-sniffing dog to go through. To speed things up, the security guys arranged to bring in a few dogs from other agencies, including the Metropolitan Police, and the Bureau of Alcohol, Tobacco, and Firearms. But nobody thought to stagger their schedules, and when four huge German shepherds arrived within a few minutes of each other, there was one hellacious dog fight in the basement of Williams & Connolly. And I thought the *hearings* were noisy.

Many letters included donations for my defense fund, which my former classmates at Annapolis had established right after I was fired. Some correspondents enclosed a single dollar, with a note saying, "I want to help, but this is all I can afford." A few older people even signed over their Social Security checks, which we tried to return. The support was simply overwhelming, both logistically and emotionally.

A surprising amount of mail came in from people who described themselves as liberals. As one of them put it, "I may not like everything you stand for, but what you said at the hearings made a lot of sense. And it's obvious that the big guys have thrown you off the boat." As if to confirm that sentiment, actor Lee Majors sent me the jacket he had worn in his TV show, "The Fall Guy."

Then there were the telegrams—hundreds, thousands, and eventually tens of thousands after Western Union advertised a discounted price and set up a special toll-free number. Almost all of them were favorable:

NEXT MALE CHILD WILL BE NAMED OLIVER.

GOD LOVE YOU. MONEY TO FOLLOW.

CONGRATULATIONS BUT QUIT QUOTING THE CONSTITUTION AND THE LAW. IT IS CONFUSING THE COMMITTEE.

I CONGRATULATE YOU ON YOUR DECORUM IN THE FACE OF THOSE ILL-BRED HYENAS PUTTING YOU THROUGH THIS HELL.

YOUR'RE DOING WONDERFULLY. CHIN UP. KISS YOUR WIFE, CHILDREN. PET YOUR DOG. I'M 81. FRIENDS HERE BELIEVE YOU.

I CROWN YOU SIR OLIVER, SLAYER OF TOADS.

CONGRATULATIONS ON TAKING CAPITOL HILL. HOLD POSITIONS UNTIL RELIEVED. AMERICAN PEOPLE ON THE WAY. SEMPER FI.

My biggest supporter was Betsy. She sat behind me during the questioning, and with me during the breaks. Sometimes we held hands and prayed together. She would rub the back of my neck to help me relax, and would lighten things up with a smile or a joke. Betsy knows me so well that she could spot the occasional moment where I was groping for the right word so I could avoid using profanity on national television.

For the first two days of my testimony she had watched the hearings at home. We had some idea of what the sessions would be like, and Brendan and I agreed that there was no need for Betsy to suffer through this long and demeaning process. But on the second day, when I finally got home well after midnight from my daily posthearing stint at Williams & Connolly, Betsy was waiting up for me. She had saved some dinner, although I had already eaten at the law firm, where Brendan had ordered in yet another Domino's pizza.

"This isn't right," she said. "I should be in there with you."

"Do you really want to go?"

"I do. My place is with you. I wouldn't want anyone to think I don't support you."

It was two in the morning, but I called Brendan at home. "Can Betsy come with me tomorrow?

"Sure, if she wants to. Now get some rest."

But there wasn't much time for sleep. We had to get up at five to make it to the law firm in time for the brief morning meeting before we drove over to the hearings. Betsy got the children ready for day camp, fixed their lunches, arranged for them to go to a neighbor's in the afternoon, and reviewed their revised schedules with the security team.

I was running on adrenaline, but by the time we got to the Caucus Room, Betsy was exhausted. And for some inexplicable reason, unless you were sitting on the dais you weren't allowed to have coffee. At one point during the afternoon I noticed the cameras zooming in over my shoulder, but I couldn't figure out why. Was there a fly crawling on my ear? Only later did I learn that their target was Betsy—who had fallen fast asleep.

When we returned to Brendan's office, the networks were still showing scenes from the hearings. Betsy was mortified. She began to apologize to Brendan, but he assured her it was no problem. "In fact," he said, "when you come tomorrow, I want you to fall asleep again. It's the best thing you could have done. It shows that you're so confident in your husband that you don't even have to pay attention to all of this garbage."

During breaks in the hearings, the witnesses and their lawyers were allowed to take refuge in a small hideaway office across the hall from the Caucus Room that belonged to Senator Edward Kennedy's staff. There were French doors that opened up on a balcony, where somebody had set up a chaise longue and some deck chairs. During the lunch break on that third day, Brendan urged Betsy and me to step out on the balcony and wave to the crowd of supporters gathered on the street below. I didn't feel comfortable doing that, but Brendan literally pushed us out the door, saying, "These people came down here to see you and encourage you. They'll never get into the hearings. Let them know you appreciate their support."

Until that moment I had no real sense of what was going on outside the building. But as soon as we stepped out onto the balcony, a tremendous roar went up. I had expected to see a few dozen people, but there were *thousands*, and many of them were carrying huge banners supporting me. It was overwhelming, and I was too choked up to say a word. What a dramatic contrast to what was going on inside.

This extraordinary reception did not go unnoticed by the Senate authorities. The next morning, when our little group arrived in the holding room, we noticed that the doors leading to the balcony had been bolted shut with headless screws.

The visible signs of support weren't limited to the streets. As we walked down the long corridors of the Russell Senate Office Building on our way to and from the Caucus Room, staffers and secretaries got up from their televisions and stood in the doorways with applause and words of encouragement and support: "Keep it up. Hang in there. Great job!"

On the third day, one of the congressional staffers started something that quickly became a daily lunchtime ritual. There would be a knock on the door of the holding room, and I would be asked to go back across the hall into the now-empty hearing room to pose for photographs with staffers, pages, and even some of their family mem-

bers. The line grew to include the Senate and House security personnel, the Capitol Hill police, and few committee staffers. Even the
Sergeant-at-Arms, an Inouye appointee who was anything but friendly, insisted on bringing me to his office to meet his staff and sign autographs.

But none of these sentiments penetrated the walls of the hearing
room, where the atmosphere remained tense. As we expected, Nields
asked me about the testimony of several previous witnesses. Albert
Hakim had told the committee that he had set up a death benefit
account called "Button" in case I didn't return from my trip to
Tehran. ("Button," Albert explained, was short for "Bellybutton"—as
if that cleared things up.) Albert had once assured me that he would
make sure Betsy and the kids would be all right in case anything happened to me. "Don't worry," he had said. "I'll take care of them."

At his request, I asked Betsy to go to Philadelphia to meet with
Hakim's lawyer. There was no mention of money, or bank accounts,
and no funds were ever transferred to our possession. The lawyer
merely wanted to know how many children we had and how old they
were. Later, after I returned from Tehran, Albert's lawyer called Betsy
a second time; she didn't return the call. But it wasn't until the hearings that I had ever heard about a fund being set up, or the names
"Button" or "Bellybutton."

Another topic that came up was the now-famous security system at
our house. On the evening of April 25, 1986, eleven days after the
American antiterrorist raid on Libya, I received a call from the FBI's
counterterrorism office. The news was not good: in Lebanon, a
spokesman for the Abu Nidal organization had announced that several
American targets, including me, had been marked for assassination.
The announcement had been recorded on videotape.

My first response was that it would be best if this announcement
did not appear on television in Europe or the United States. Terrorist
organizations often commit acts of violence simply to get attention,
and to broadcast this threat would be to play into their hands. It could
also attract the attention of unstable individuals who might see this as
an opportunity for notoriety. During the next few days, Admiral
Poindexter, White House press secretary Larry Speakes, and I made

an effort to get the American networks not to run this tape on their news broadcasts.

When nothing happened for about a week, I assumed we were out of the woods. But then Betsy called me at the office to say she had just seen the videotape of the threat on the "CBS Evening News," which she had been watching with the children. They were not amused.

Bob Earl called down to the Sit Room and arranged to have the broadcast replayed so that I could see it. There, on the screen, was Abu Bakr, a spokesman for the Fatah Revolutionary Council. My fellow targets were General Jack Singlaub, Edward Luttwak, a Washington-based consultant on international affairs, and the Heritage Foundation, a Washington think tank. None of them had been involved with planning the attack on Libya, but curiously, all had in one way or another been publicly linked in the media to Central America and/or the contras.

Now, there are death threats and there are death threats. Abu Nidal has been called the world's most dangerous terrorist—and for good reason. He is responsible for the deaths of hundreds of innocent people. Some terrorist groups, like the Red Brigades in Italy, try to avoid killing women and children. But Abu Nidal's gang delights in it.

Among other atrocities, Abu Nidal had planned the Christmas 1985 massacres at the Rome and Vienna airports in which more than a dozen people were killed and over a hundred wounded by terrorists carrying hand grenades and assault rifles. One of their victims was an eleven-year-old American girl named Natasha Simpson.

I was deeply concerned about the safety of Betsy and our children. In addition to all my usual travel to Europe and Central America, I was planning to leave for what could have been a *very* long visit to Tehran. One of General Simhoni's officers at the Israeli embassy called to remind me that they were all too familiar with Abu Nidal's group, and that this was not a threat to be taken lightly. They confirmed FBI reports that Abu Nidal had operatives in the United States, and they urged me to take steps to protect myself and my family.

At the suggestion of the FBI, I contacted the Secret Service, my local police, and the Pentagon. The Fairfax County Police sent out an officer who did a site survey, and who briefed our family on the precautions we should take. They promised to increase their patrols in our neighborhood, and suggested that we install a security system immediately.

I knew that the Secret Service provided security for several White House officials including Admiral Poindexter and Bud McFarlane. I discussed the matter with the admiral and with Rod McDaniel, executive secretary of the NSC. But there wasn't much they could do: I was simply too junior to qualify for government protection.

I then called several private security companies, but nobody could come to our house before I was scheduled to depart for Tehran. At one of our planning sessions for the Tehran trip, General Secord asked me what I had done in response to the death threat. When I explained that I was having trouble getting any kind of immediate protection for my family, he told me not to worry, that he had a friend who might be able to help. A few days later he introduced me to Glenn Robinette, a former CIA employee who owned a security company. Robinette came out to the house, did a quick survey, and said he could install a system right away. And he did.

Glenn Robinette never sent me a bill, and I didn't ask him for one. In the chaos that surrounded our preparations for the trip to Tehran, I just didn't sit down and discuss the financial arrangements with Dick Secord.

I didn't think much more about it until just before I was fired. Realizing that I had never paid for the security system, I called Glenn Robinette. He was off in Central America, and when he finally called me back in December, I asked for a bill. In response, he sent me two back-dated bills.

And here I did a really stupid thing. In direct violation of Brendan's rule of "don't create anything," I continued the charade by sending two phony, back-dated letters responding to Robinette's back-dated bills. What I should have done, of course, was to tell Brendan what had happened. But I thought I knew better.

I should have shouted it from the rooftops: *"Dick Secord helped me get a security system to protect my family because there was a serious death threat and nobody in our government would help."*

Which was, in effect, what I told the committee:

North: I admit to making a serious, serious, judgment error in what I then did to paper it over and I'm willing to sit here and admit to that. But I'm also suggesting to you gentlemen that if it was General Secord who paid the bill...first of all, "Thank you, General

Secord." And second of all, you guys ought to write him a check because the government should have done it to begin with.

While some of the committee members found it convenient to play dumb, I was convinced that certain members of Congress had known a lot more than they let on about my involvement with the contras while I was at the NSC. This was especially true of the House and Senate intelligence committees, who received regular intelligence reports from the region. They knew full well that the administration in general, and I in particular, had been helping the contras. They might not have known exactly *how*, but they certainly knew about it—which was why they had asked such detailed questions in their letters to McFarlane in 1985, and to Poindexter in 1986. Not all the members of the intelligence committees knew all the facts, but there weren't many people in Washington with an interest in the Nicaraguan situation who didn't know, at least in general, that Oliver North was up to his ears in aiding the contras.

But during the hearings, Nields and Liman questioned me about my contacts with Congress during this period on the assumption that no one in Congress had the faintest idea of what I had been doing. Not surprisingly, Nields focused on my August 1986 meeting with the intelligence committee in the Sit Room:

Nields: And this was you personally talking to them?
North: It was on instructions of the national security adviser. I was instructed to meet with Chairman Hamilton and, I believe, many of the members of the Committee.
Nields: And they were interested in finding out the answers to the questions raised by the Resolution of Inquiry —
North: Exactly.
Nields:—your fund-raising activities—
North: Precisely.
Nields:—military support for the contras —
North: That's right...
Nields: The beginning of this memorandum that appears to be a description of what you said during that meeting, it says "from Boland Amendment on, North explains strictures to contras." Is that true? Did you explain the strictures to the contras?

North: I explained to them that there was no U.S. government money until more was appropriated, yes.

Nields: And it says "never violated stricture. Gave advice on Human Rights Civic Action Program."

North: I did do that.

Nields: But I take it you did considerably more, which you did not tell the committee about.

North: I have admitted that here before you today.... I will tell you right now, counsel, and all the members here gathered that I misled the Congress.

Nields: At that meeting?

North: At that meeting.

Nields: Face-to-face?

North: Face-to-face.

Nields: You made false statements to them about your activities in support of the contras?

North: I did. Furthermore, I did so with the purpose of hopefully avoiding the very kind of thing that we have before us now and avoiding a shutoff of help to the Nicaraguan resistance and avoiding an elimination of the resistance facilities in three Central American countries —

Nields: We —

North:—wherein we had promised those heads of state. On specific orders to me, I had gone down there and assured them of our absolute and total discretion.

Nields: We do live in a democracy, don't we?

North: We do, sir. Thank God.

Nields: In which it is the people, not one Marine lieutenant colonel, that gets to decide the important policy decisions for the nation.

North: Yes.

Nields: And, part of the democratic process —

North: And, I would point out that part of that answer is that this Marine lieutenant colonel was not making all of those decisions on his own. As I indicated in my testimony yesterday, Mr. Nields, I sought approval for everything I did.

There was no changing his mind. Nields, Liman, and most of the committee were intent on showing that one renegade lieutenant colonel had done all this on his own. I knew from the outset that the hearings were going to be anything but fair, and I suppose I shouldn't have expected otherwise. After all, it was Congress that set the agenda and made the rules. It was Congress that called the witnesses and decided on the questions. It was Congress that chose not to investigate itself for its fickle, vacillating, and unpredictable policy toward the Nicaraguan resistance.

The whole process, as I pointed out in my "opening statement,"* was like a baseball game in which one of the teams was also the umpire. It was Congress that called the balls and strikes, and decided who was safe and who was out. And it was Congress that added up the score and in the end, inevitably, declared itself the winner.

As if to prove my point, the committee did several things during my testimony that were just outrageous. During part of his questioning, Arthur Liman displayed a huge blowup of the text of one of the Boland Amendments, making it look as if this had been a separate, one-page document. In reality, the various Boland Amendments had been buried in government appropriations bills that ran well over a thousand pages each. But this display, which included the President's signature, gave the distinct impression that the President had read it over and said, "Oh, gosh, here's the Boland Amendment. Quick— give me a pen so I can sign it."

I wasn't the only one who felt this way. Congressman Henry Hyde of Illinois took the floor to object to this portrayal. It is "deceptive," he said, and he apologized for the way it was displayed. "If I tried this in a municipal court in Chicago," he said, "phonying up an exhibit to make a point that was half true—I'd be held in contempt."

Hyde then made a remarkable statement about the hypocrisy of the hearings. Referring to the Congress, he said:

Now, if *we* don't like a law, Colonel, and you guys ought to learn this as the NSC and then the administration, you just exempt yourself. You see, we exempt ourselves from OSHA, the Occupational Safety and Health Act. We exempt ourselves from the Ethics in Government Act; no special prosecutors are going after us. We have our own committee of our own brethren that'll take care of that. We are exempt from equal opportunity, equal employment

---

*Which—talk about fair—I wasn't allowed to give until the third day of my testimony.

opportunity; none of that because we're political people. The Budget Act; waive it. Pass it, kid the people, and waive it. Every time something comes up that's in excess of the budget, pay no attention to it....

Now, if we can't ignore the law or exempt ourselves from it, we play games with the process. Do you know how we got our pay raise?...you know what we did in the House? We waited, under the guidance of the stage director over there, the Speaker, until thirty days had elapsed, until it was vested, it could not be unvested and then we got a vote on it. We waited until it was locked in, and then we voted. And we could all tell our constituents, "I didn't vote for that pay raise." That's the way we do things. So there's much to be learned from watching us.

It was about then that the committee began to self-destruct. Brendan and I sat there in astonishment as the members turned on each other and their lawyers. Instead of focusing their undivided anger at me, they began to debate each other. During their internal squabble, Brendan leaned over to me and quoted the famous tag line of those Sergeant Preston radio shows we had both listened to as kids: "Well, King, this case is closed." Believe me, it's hard not to smile when your lawyer says something like that.

The Boland Amendment wasn't the only ill-advised exhibit. Although it was widely known that my family was at risk from terrorists who had threatened to kill me, a large blowup of a letter I had written was placed before the cameras, complete with our home address. Thanks, fellas.

There was also a farcical flap over the slide shows I had presented to various groups in Washington. Because this was the subject of some controversy, several of the committee members thought it would be appropriate for me to give this same briefing, complete with the slides, for the committee. The slide show soon became the subject of a raging debate by members of the committee, many of whom just couldn't tolerate the prospect of my being allowed to say a favorable word on behalf of the contras. And so it was claimed that for "security" reasons the lights could not be dimmed for the slides to be seen.

This was plainly ridiculous. The place was crawling with police and security agents. During the hearings, the Senate Caucus room was one of the best-protected rooms in the world.

In an inspired example of lunacy, the committee came up with a compromise: instead of showing the slides and giving the briefing, *I would hold each slide up in the air and discuss it.* This was absurd, and everybody knew it. But it was better than nothing.

I held up a slide of a Soviet HIND helicopter, and described its lethal power. I held up a slide of a textbook from a school in Nicaragua, showing how children learn arithmetic by adding up hand grenades and machine guns. I held up a slide showing several Miskito Indians, and explained how they had been driven out of their ancestral homelands. I held up a slide of the leadership of the FDN: of the sixteen men in that photograph, eleven were former Sandinistas.

The "slide show" and the two documents were only the tip of the unfairness iceberg. The whole proceeding was grossly unfair, which was one reason the American people responded as they did. But even the blatant unfairness that was captured by the cameras couldn't depict the full measure of the tilt. I can't recall a single instance in which Senator Inouye granted or sustained *any* of Brendan Sullivan's objections.

The unfairness continued right through to the very end, when it surfaced in Senator Inouye's shocking closing statement. Referring to the Uniform Code of Military Justice, which applies to all men and women in the armed services, Senator Inouye reminded his audience that the orders of a superior officer must be obeyed by subordinate members—so long as those orders are lawful.

This was certainly true. But then Inouye stepped over the line of decency and actually compared my responses to those of Nazi war criminals!

Inouye: The Uniform Code makes it abundantly clear that it must be the lawful orders of a superior officer. In fact, it says, members of the military have an obligation to disobey unlawful orders. This principle was considered so important, that we—we, the government of the United States, proposed that it be internationally applied, in the Nuremberg Trials. And so, in the Nuremberg Trials, we said that the fact that the defendant had —
Sullivan: Mr. Chairman. May I please register an objection —
Inouye: May I continue my statement?
Sullivan: I find this offensive! I find you engaging in a personal attack on Colonel North, and you're far removed from the issues of this case. To make reference to the Nuremberg Trials, I find

personally and professionally distasteful, and I can no longer sit here and listen to this.

Inouye: You will have to sit there, if you want to listen.

Sullivan: Mr. Chairman, please don't conclude these hearings on this unfair note.... You may ask questions, but you may not attack him personally. This has gone too far.

Indeed it had. It's true that the Nuremberg Trials marked the most famous use of the "authorization" defense. But even if the reference to Nuremberg hadn't been disgusting and inappropriate, there was an enormous difference between then and now. Those defendants had been ordered to kill people. I had been ordered to protect them.

17

A Smoking Gun in the Closet

"Oyez, Oyez, Oyez. This honorable court will now come to order. The United States of America versus Oliver L. North. Judge Gerhard A. Gesell presiding."

That's how it started each morning, day after day, week after week, during my trial. That phrase sickened me: The United States v. Oliver North. Why not the Congressional Police v. Oliver North? Or Independent Counsel v. Executive Branch? Either one would have been more accurate.*

I have heard it said that a trial is like war, and for lawyers that analogy must ring true. But it's not that way for the defendant. In combat, after all, you're allowed to shoot back. But in this battle Brendan and his team did all the shooting for me. They performed brilliantly, but I found it agonizing not to be able to respond.

Each night, the defense team would regroup, replenish, and rearm as they prepared for the next day's clash. As soon as the daily transcript arrived, one member of the legal team would review it for holes in the enemy's line. Another would pore over the previous statements

---

*I wasn't the only one who felt that way. As two of the three Appeals Court judges wrote later in reversing my convictions, "We do not countenance political trials in this country, and this matter is not styled *Independent Counsel* v. *Executive Branch* or even *Congress* v. *Executive Branch*."

of tomorrow's witness. A third lawyer would sift through the thousands of documents that were being introduced as exhibits in the case, while a fourth would focus on the documents and witnesses we planned to use as a rebuttal to the prosecution's arguments.

In theory, at least, the defendant is presumed innocent. But it sure didn't feel that way while the prosecution was making its case. As I had to be reminded again and again, in order to convict me of breaking the law the prosecution had to demonstrate criminal intent. "This isn't like breaking the speed limit," the lawyers explained. "They'll need to show that you were thinking and acting like a person *intending* to break the law."

Betsy tried to come to court every day, but that wasn't always possible. She was a volunteer teacher's aide in Dornin's and Sarah's classrooms, and she was also determined to keep our family life as close to normal as possible. On days when she could get there, she was accompanied by Brian Cox, the assistant pastor at our church, or by a friend. (Brian came so often that Brendan arranged for the kitchen at Williams & Connolly to prepare a sandwich for him, too.) When Betsy couldn't make it, Brian or one of the men from our family Bible study group would be there, and during the lunch break we would set aside a few minutes for a quiet prayer.

For Betsy the trial was a horror show. She was getting very little sleep, and outside of court we saw almost nothing of each other. In addition to attending the trial and wondering whether her husband and the father of her children would be sent to jail, she still had to manage the house and take care of the children. If the prosecutors had their way, at the end of this process she would have no husband, no income, and millions of dollars in debts.

People tried to help. Some of our neighbors and the members of our Bible study group pitched in to prepare casserole dishes that Betsy could heat up when she got home. But it was terribly difficult to maintain any semblance of normalcy for the children.

Not surprisingly, they were confused by the news reports of the trial. Although my story had already come out in great detail during the hearings, the media were now presenting each charge and every bit of evidence as though it were being heard for the first time. I remember when Congressman Lee Hamilton, the first prosecution witness to testify at the trial, "revealed" that in August 1986 I had met with members of the House Intelligence Committee in the White House Sit Room, and that he thought my answers were misleading. All this had been discussed in detail during the hearings, but here again it resulted in page-one coverage and lead billing on the evening network news.

During Brendan's cross-examination, Hamilton had to admit that no one had ever before been charged with lying to Congress in such a forum, that no transcript existed of the Sit Room meeting, and that I had not testified under oath. But these points rarely came out in the news. Neither did the fact that Hamilton had sat through my entire congressional testimony. When they had forced me to testify, I had been assured that nothing I said in the hearings could be used against me in a criminal prosecution. But here was the chair of the House Iran-Contra Committee, testifying against me at my trial.

After reading a newspaper account of Hamilton's testimony, our son, Stuart, called me from school late one night to ask if all this meant that I hadn't told the truth during the congressional hearings. No, I explained, this charge had nothing to do with the hearings. But Stuart wasn't the only one who was confused on this point. To this day, I hear from people who assumed I was on trial for having lied to Congress during the hearings.

One reason for the confusion may be that the special prosecutors had their own spin doctors who presided over regular briefings for the press. For most public prosecutors—U.S. Attorneys, district attorneys, and so on—a public affairs staff would be thought of as an unwarranted and inappropriate extravagance. But the special prosecutor answers to no one. At every break, and before and after each day of testimony, the special prosecutor's public affairs officer or one of his deputies would huddle outside the courtroom with members of the press to "clarify" prior or upcoming testimony and evidence. Brendan, still adhering to his no-comment rule, preferred to argue the case in front of the jury.

In addition to being longer than the hearings, the trial was far more tedious. As my lawyers already knew but I had yet to learn, a real trial is very different from the courtroom scenes on "Perry Mason" or "L.A. Law," which invariably depict the most sensational or dramatic scenes. There *are* fascinating moments in trials, but they're generally overshadowed by the drudgery of paperwork, procedure, and repetitive testimony. The congressional hearings were no picnic, but at least my part was over in six days.

And during the hearings, I was able to respond to questions and comments as soon as they were made. When other witnesses came in to testify, I could watch them on television or on videotape with Brendan in his conference room, where I could tell him exactly what I thought of each answer.

In the trial, by contrast, I had to sit there mute and impassive, day after day, as the prosecutors tried to get each witness to say terrible things about me. Just about all I could do was take notes. "North is scribbling away like a medieval monk," one reporter observed. With the exception of the jury, which had to sit through it all without uttering a word, just about everybody else had a specific task. The lawyers on both sides were busy examining and cross-examining the witnesses. The court stenographers had to type the thousands of words necessary to prepare the transcript, which ran to more than eighty-five hundred pages. The bailiffs and marshals walked around keeping order, and occasionally waking up a nodding juror. Even the judge could interrupt, ask questions, and make rulings. With so little to do, I often felt like a spectator.

For the prosecutors I felt only disdain. They had sought this job in a politically charged case that would give them enormous visibility. Unlike other public prosecutors, who are required to take cases as they come in, these guys were more like a lynch mob in pin-striped suits.

And so I especially enjoyed it when many of their own witnesses embarrassed them by saying kind things about me. Adolfo Calero was summoned by the prosecution to help make the case against me for supporting the resistance, and for setting up the operational account from which, it was alleged, I had stolen forty-four hundred dollars in traveler's checks.

During Brendan's cross-examination of Calero, he asked:

Sullivan: Would you try to tell the ladies and gentlemen of the jury as best you can who is this guy Colonel North? What did he do for you?

Calero: Well, for us he became a sort of a savior, I mean. We felt—as I said, we felt abandoned, we felt that we couldn't feed our people and that we had no way of getting support any place and then all of a sudden we were introduced to this man with whom we became more and more familiar as time went on….Our men, even though they were Nicaraguans and were not Americans, seemed to be as important for him as Americans, and he worried about us and felt like us. So we developed a very—a tremendously human relationship….We are tremendously grateful to him, and as I said before Congress, the Nicaraguan people have a tremendous appreciation for this man—so much so…that we're going to erect a monument for him once we free Nicaragua.

I don't know what the special prosecutors had been expecting from Adolfo, but I doubt they had counted on their witness wanting to put up a statue in honor of the defendant!

Later, Brendan came around to the issue of the traveler's checks:

Sullivan: Do you trust him?
Calero: Absolutely. I would say that I trust Colonel North with my life. I mean, that's the biggest thing I have.
Sullivan: The prosecution in this case says that Colonel North stole $4,400 of your traveler's checks. Do you believe that that is conceivable?
Calero: No.

And still later:

Sullivan: Did anybody in the United States government indicate to you that North was not acting properly?
Calero: Never. I mean as I said before, and I was showing in the picture [taken in 1985 in the White House], it was Colonel North who took us to the President.

Calero wasn't the only prosecution witness whose testimony must have disappointed my persecutors. Chi Chi Quintero described my "devotion to duty" and called it "a work of art." Dick Gadd called me a "national hero." Joseph Coors, whom Casey had sent to my office when Coors offered to help the resistance, told the court that I was, in his view, "a tremendously wonderful patriotic American." When Coors finished his testimony, he walked over to the defense table, gave Brendan a pat on the back, and shook my hand. The prosecutors cringed.

Had the prosecutors been less politically and personally motivated, they might have anticipated these problems. But then, these weren't regular U.S. Attorneys from the Justice Department. They had *asked* to be hired by the Office of the Independent Counsel, this strange entity created by the Congress for the sole purpose of going after members of the executive branch.*

In the regular criminal justice system, a prosecutor is normally presented with a crime—a robbed bank, a murder, whatever. His task is to find the perpetrator and bring him to justice. But in a strange perversion of that process, a special prosecutor has a much different task. First an individual from the executive branch is identified and chosen as a suspect; then the special prosecutor tries to identify a crime that this person may have perpetrated. The whole process is eerily reminiscent of that cynical line from the early days of the Soviet KGB: "First, bring us the man. We'll find the crime."

In theory the special prosecutor is accountable to the Attorney General, who can fire him only for cause. In practice, however, it's as if Congress had its own Justice Department. The Independent Counsel is independent, all right: independent of financial restraints, independent of time limitations, and independent of any obligation to show results within a given period of time. The Office of the Independent Counsel has become a pervasive and powerful machine, a legalistic tank that can roll over and flatten its victims beneath its unlimited size, time, and money. It's hard to calculate just how much of the taxpayers' money the OIC has spent on this case, but as I write these

---

*The position of special prosecutor was created in 1978, when Congress passed the Ethics in Government Act. Since 1982 the special prosecutor has been known as the independent counsel, but the original term strikes me as more accurate. In December 1986, Lawrence Walsh was appointed to the position by a special panel of judges. The Attorney General had asked for an investigation into the use of residuals from the Iran arms sales. But at the request of Congress, this narrow inquiry was quickly expanded to include just about everything short of fishing without a license.

words in the summer of 1991 the total is probably more than forty million dollars—and climbing.*

When the congressional hearings began, the special prosecutor was already in the midst of his own investigation of the individuals involved in Iran-contra. The first victim was Spitz Channell, and the pressure brought to bear on this poor man was intense. By April 1987, the special prosecutor had apparently convinced him that unless he pled guilty to a convoluted charge of conspiring to defraud the IRS through the National Endowment for the Preservation of Liberty (NEPL), a tax-exempt organization, he would face a jail sentence for personal income-tax violations.

On April 29, Channell appeared before a judge in a federal courthouse.

"You are charged with conspiracy in this case," the judge said, "and of course it requires two or more persons to have a conspiracy. Are you prepared to state the names of any of those with whom you conspired?"

"Yes, Your Honor."

"Would you please do so?"

"Yes. Colonel North, an official of the National Security Council."

Brendan called me with the news of this ridiculous charge, but it wasn't quite the shock that the prosecutors had intended when they scripted this little dialogue. We were well aware of Channell's vulnerabilities, including his inability to pay the mounting expenses of his defense—something the prosecutors certainly counted on. And so Spitz Channell became the first of several defendants who, faced with an overwhelming debt and the destruction of their reputations and future careers, would plead to a lesser offense rather than continue fighting the

---

*The Iran-contra special prosecutor constitutes the largest and most unaccountable prosecutorial staff ever assembled in the United States, and has included more than fifty lawyers, seventy-five investigators, and scores of support personnel. It is the only government office in America that is subject to no oversight and no budgetary restraints. Lawyers hired by the special prosecutor have been paid at the top of the federal pay scale—now in excess of $100,000 a year—including new attorneys right out of law school. At one point, Special Prosecutor Walsh had a press office about as large as that of the Attorney General of the United States. It's like a whole separate law firm being financed by the American taxpayers, who are powerless to limit it or stop it. The taxpayers are also footing the bill for Mr. Walsh's living quarters in the Watergate, his chauffeur-driven car, his air fare for his frequent trips to and from his home in Oklahoma, and some of the most expensive office space in Washington.

monster. Although I made a different choice, I can't say I blame them.

My next few months had been taken up with preparations for the hearings, followed by tons of legal paperwork on both sides. In March 1988, Brendan called me at Marine headquarters and asked me to come to his office. "You'd better leave work early today," he said. "There have been some developments."

By now I knew that this phrase did not signal good news. When I arrived at Williams & Connolly, Brendan sat me down and explained that the special prosecutor had decided to indict four of us—Admiral Poindexter, General Secord, Albert Hakim, and myself—on a variety of counts.*

This was my worst moment in the entire case, and one of the worst in my life. An indictment may sound like the end of the process, but it's really just the beginning. Although I should have known better, I just couldn't comprehend how the same government that Admiral Poindexter and I had served for so many years could have given birth to this creature, the Office of the Independent Counsel, which was ruining our lives. We had all hoped for months that it wouldn't come to this, and that fairness and justice would eventually win out. But the criminal investigation, like the hearings, was ultimately about politics.

I had already decided that if I was indicted, I would retire from the Marine Corps. Brendan had made it clear all along that he would do everything within the law to defend me—and that this could well include a subpoena to the President of the United States, as well as any other senior government official whose testimony might be necessary.

That left me no choice. Simply put, I had no intention of being the first serving officer in American history to cause the Commander-in-Chief to appear at a trial of a military officer. I had spent my entire adult life in an institution where the chain of command was an essen-

---

*The indictments were returned by a federal grand jury on March 16, 1988. In all, there were twenty-three counts, including conspiracy to defraud the United States, obstruction of justice, false statements, theft of government property, wire fraud, making false statements to Congress and the Attorney General, and destruction and removal of documents. Sixteen of the counts applied to me. By the time my trial began, these had been pared down to twelve.

On June 8, 1988, Judge Gesell ruled that Poindexter, Hakim, Secord, and I would all be tried separately, so that in defending ourselves we could each make use of immunized testimony that the other three had given to Congress. Secord and Hakim later pleaded guilty to reduced charges. Admiral Poindexter went to trial and was sentenced to six months in prison.

tial discipline, and this was a precedent I didn't want any part of. Not only was it degrading to the presidency, but it could erode or weaken the entire concept of the chain of command.*

And so I reluctantly announced my retirement. I cried that night, and so did Betsy, because she knew how much being a Marine had meant to me. It had been my identity every day for close to twenty years, and I had expected it would continue to be true for another ten or fifteen. I got up every morning as a Marine, and came home every night as a Marine. It was hard to imagine being anything else.

General Kelley was no longer the commandant, and when word went out that I was leaving the Marine Corps, I could almost hear the collective sigh of relief from some of the higher-ups. My retirement was fast and abrupt; twenty-four hours after I submitted the paperwork, it was approved. Normally it takes weeks to get an appointment for a retirement physical, but I heard from the dispensary the very next morning: "Colonel North, we received your request. We have an opening this afternoon."

Today, I realize that it's not the Marine Corps that I miss. It's being with Marines. I loved getting up in the morning and going off to work with a group of men who were all headed in the same direction. It was a very structured life, but it offered enormous responsibilities and a full measure of adventure. I miss the camaraderie. I miss the hours of hard work in the company of tough, talented, and motivated men. I miss drinking black coffee in the middle of the night. And I miss being part of that society of risk-takers.

Now, for the first time in my life, I didn't have anywhere to go in the morning. The day after my retirement, I woke up as usual at five-thirty, shaved, got dressed—and drove to the offices of Williams & Connolly, where I spent a lot of time over the next few months. While it wasn't exactly like going to Marine headquarters, it wasn't altogether different, either. The lawyers worked like Marines, swore like Marines, and regarded their enemies with about as much compassion. Only instead of using rifles and grenades to defeat their opponents, they apparently intended to work them to death.

---

*As things turned out, the President fought having to appear, and the judge refused to compel him to do so.

But soon the lawyers, too, had to shift to a different battleground. Shortly after the indictments, everyone who was working on my case had to leave the Williams & Connolly building and move to a special suite of offices on Connecticut Avenue. Because the lawyers on both sides and the defendants would have to review tens of thousands of highly classified documents related to the cases, we were all required to work out of a Sensitive Compartmented Information Facility. The SCIF, as it was known, was a suite of offices that were protected by sophisticated monitoring and alarm systems, and shifts of armed guards around the clock.

The SCIF had to be seen to be believed. We all were supposed to wear identification badges. Document control clerks and classified information guards kept track of every document that came in or out. The windows were always closed, and in order to prevent electronic and visual eavesdropping from surrounding buildings, the blinds were always drawn. Although the SCIF occupied most of the fourth floor of a modern office building, it had all the charm of a subway tunnel. We began to refer to ourselves as SCIF rats because we never got to see daylight. The walls were typical government gray, and we decorated them with memorabilia sent in by supporters all over the world: African masks, dolls from the Orient, photographs, and flags. Chris Capozzi, the paralegal in charge of collating and cataloging the documents, took an excerpt from one of my Marine Fitness Report duty station requests and printed it up on a big chart as a reminder of where I would rather be: "assigned to a forward-deployed unit at the edge of the empire, preferably in harm's way."

While this wasn't the edge of the empire, I was certainly in harm's way.

Even so, we had a few laughs. Barry Simon worked out a way to protect our defense strategy by having all our witnesses sign into the SCIF as "Mr. Visitor." And from the start the lawyers tried to keep things on an upbeat note. They even threw a SCIF opening party, where Admiral Poindexter and I were invited to cut the ribbon. The lawyers brought in champagne and—what else? a cake in the shape of a key.

Then we moved in. For more than a year, we ate nearly every lunch and dinner in the SCIF. We ordered in so many Domino's pizzas and Chinese takeout deliveries that Brendan finally arranged for a caterer to deliver a home-style meal one night a week.

We spent hours poring over the tons of material that the prosecutors delivered to the SCIF, including some of the documents I had worked on or written during my five and a half years at the NSC. It took us weeks to go through it all, in part because there was so much of it, but mostly because it was all so thoroughly mixed together.

I had maintained my office files by subject and, within a subject file, by date. And so, for example, all my files on Palestinian terrorist organizations were in one drawer of a safe, arranged in chronological order. But the files delivered to us in the SCIF were so jumbled up that they seemed to have been run through a blender. A 1985 document on the military situation in Afghanistan would be followed by a 1983 analysis of the Sandinista economy.

After several weeks of collating, sorting, and cataloging, I could see that we still didn't have it all. Many documents that I specifically remembered were still missing, along with tape recordings of meetings I had held with the Iranians. "There's more," I kept telling the lawyers. "I *know* there's more."

And indeed there was. Thanks to Barry Simon's tenacity and his constant haranguing, the prosecutors (after months of denial) suddenly found what we had been asking for. They had been working for more than eighteen months, but had apparently forgotten about this stuff. At last, we were allowed to go over to the OEOB. When we entered the room where my files were stored, we found *eighty cartons* of material that had been removed from my office. Astonishingly, no lawyer from the special prosecutor's office had bothered to review this material! Random documents were marked, and some boxes were identified as having been reviewed months earlier by FBI agents. But none of the highly paid lawyers from the enormous prosecution staff had taken the time to look through my files.

Barry, Nicole, John, and I sat there for days, wading through my files and jotting down the control numbers of documents we needed. Here were the tapes and transcripts I had been describing to my lawyers. Here, too, were the so-called Honduras documents, which showed how widespread the administration's support for the contras had been during the period covered by Boland. If I had shredded even half as much as people said, all of this material would have been long gone.

Meanwhile, time was running out. We found these boxes in July 1988, and the trial was scheduled to begin on September 20. The eighty boxes of documents were clearly grounds for a postponement—what lawyers call a continuance. We desperately needed time to review all these documents, and either get them declassified or receive permission from the judge to use them at the trial.

I had another concern about the schedule: if my trial began in late September, it was almost certain to hurt the Republicans in the presidential elections. The Democrats had already made *that* clear: on the opening night of their national convention, two of the principal speakers invoked Iran-contra. The publicity of a trial would only add fuel to that fire. Because the prosecution gets to state its case before the other side can respond, the defense might be forced to remain silent until after Election Day. "A trial at the height of the campaign," Brendan wrote to the judge, "transforms this case even more into an election-year issue at the expense of North's right to a fair and impartial trial."

On August 5, in light of the eighty boxes of new material, Judge Gesell agreed to postpone the trial. It finally began on February 21, 1989.

Those eighty boxes of documents proved to be invaluable to my defense. Among other benefits, they gave us critically needed ammunition to counter one of the special prosecutor's key witnesses: Bud McFarlane.

I have already discussed Bud McFarlane's appearance as a prosecution witness at my trial, where he was even more obtuse than usual. "You don't lie," he told the court at one point. "You put your interpretation on what the truth is." Huh? And when the chief prosecutor asked McFarlane whether his 1985 letter to Congressman Hamilton had been true, Bud replied in classic McFarlanese: "As written, no. In context, I think so, but it's wrong to write it, I agree. I'm wrong."

It was painful to sit there and watch as a man for whom I had once had enormous affection and respect was torn apart. The prosecutors, who had made Bud one of their star witnesses against me, couldn't resist attacking this unfortunate, broken man. They derided him for the letters he wrote at the time of his suicide attempt in early 1987, and even the judge joined the offensive as Bud made further efforts to distance himself from me—and from what he had asked me to do.

Although Bud had already pled guilty to several misdemeanor charges of misleading Congress in 1985 and 1986, and had even been sentenced, he still wouldn't admit that he had tried to cover up his knowledge and approval for what I had done to support the Nicaraguan resistance. Instead, he blew up at the prosecutor. It was after one such explosion on the witness stand that Judge Gesell referred to him as "an intensely unreliable witness."

Bud's testimony hurt me personally, and it hurt my case, too. His testimony about what he knew in 1985 was painful to hear. Brendan's task was to make clear that McFarlane had known about and authorized my actions. He started out by walking Bud through the written record, each step of which was designed to show the jury that Bud had not only known what I was doing, but had approved it, too. Then he had Bud sum up what I had been doing for the resistance—and why.

Sullivan: You had asked, indeed you had directed, that Colonel North keep the freedom fighters alive body and soul, correct?
McFarlane: Yes.
Sullivan: And you transmitted to him the direct order of the President of the United States in 1984 to keep them alive body and soul, correct?
McFarlane: Correct.
Sullivan: And you not only told him it was your order and your directive, but you told him that it was the President's order and the President's directive that he do what he could to keep them alive body and soul, correct?
McFarlane: Yes.
Sullivan: And during the period 1984 and 1985, up until the end of 1986, the Congress of the United States was not providing military money to the freedom fighters, were they?
McFarlane: No.
Sullivan: And the fact is that the mission of keeping them alive was accomplished by Colonel North and others during that period of time, isn't that true?
McFarlane: Yes.

Sullivan: They stayed alive during the years when Congress had abandoned them, didn't they?

McFarlane: Yes.

And a few minutes later:

Sullivan: Now, Mr. McFarlane, was the President angry when the Boland Amendment precluded the United States from fulfilling its commitment to the freedom fighters?

McFarlane: Yes.

Sullivan: Did he express that anger to you?

McFarlane: Yes.

Sullivan: And did you in turn express the President's anger to Colonel North?

McFarlane: Yes.

Sullivan: And what was the reason for the anger? Was it because the United States had broken a promise to these people and had abandoned them?

McFarlane: Yes, in part.

Sullivan: What was the other part?

McFarlane: The President saw the behavior of the Congress, the cutting off of support to be not only breaking faith with people who we encouraged to risk their lives, but he saw an inconsistency between the Congress that could say yes, let's support freedom fighters in Afghanistan 12,000 miles away but let's don't do it right here in our own neighborhood. It didn't track. It was inconsistent.

And still later:

Sullivan: Mr. McFarlane, you received literally hundreds of memoranda from Colonel North over the course of the time you worked with him, didn't you?

McFarlane: Yes.

Sullivan: I dare say that he might have written more memoranda that any staff officer you had, is that correct?

McFarlane: It's likely, yes.

Sullivan: And I take it that when you carry out your responsibili-

ties as the head of the NSC, that when you get matters of importance, you do read them, or have other staff officers look at them
and apprise you of what's in them, correct?

McFarlane: Yes.

Sullivan: And it is also true, isn't it, that Colonel North, based
upon your experience with him over the years, made extraordinary
efforts to keep you advised on the work that he was doing in carrying out his assignment, isn't that correct?

McFarlane: Yes. Generally, yes.

Sullivan: And wouldn't it be fair to say that from your vantage
point it may be that Colonel North gave you too much paper
rather than too little?

McFarlane: Oh, I wanted to be informed.

For me, the entire trial came down to two fundamental issues.
The first was that everything I had done was known about and
approved by those I had worked for. Even without the testimony of
President Reagan or Admiral Poindexter (who had not been granted
immunity to testify at my trial), Brendan was able to make this point
during his cross-examination of McFarlane. The other major theme
was that I hadn't acted with criminal intent. In other words, I had no
intention of breaking any laws. In fact, those of us involved in helping
the resistance went to great lengths to avoid violating the Boland
Amendment or any other statute.

On this question of criminal intent, the prosecutors based much
of their argument on the testimony of Spitz Channell. During the
trial, Channell told a story that he had related several times before:
that in September 1985, he had chartered a plane to bring me to Dallas, Texas, for a dinner with Bunker Hunt, the well-known oil man
and silver magnate. Channell hoped that Hunt would make another
contribution to NEPL on behalf of the contras, and he had brought
me down to describe the situation in Central America and the needs
of the resistance. After dinner at the Petroleum Club, Hunt, Channell,
and I had chatted while Channell's assistant went to find a cab to take
me back to the airport.

But in describing this scene at my trial, Channell added an
extraordinary new wrinkle: a conversation between Bunker Hunt and

me, which, he now said, "just stuck in my mind." As Channell described it, Hunt had asked me, "What are you going to do? Do you mind getting in trouble for this?" To which I had supposedly responded, "No, I don't care if I have to go to jail for this, and I don't care if I have to lie to Congress about this."

Brendan had consistently told me not to show any reaction to other people's testimony, no matter how bizarre it was. But when Channell told this story, I just couldn't help myself, and I looked up at him in astonishment. The conversation he had just described clearly implied that I thought what I was doing might be criminal. Had it actually occurred, I would have been in real trouble.

But this conversation never happened. I knew it, Channell knew it, and Sullivan knew it. If the prosecutors didn't know it, for several reasons, they surely should have.

In any event, they certainly appeared delighted to have this new version from Channell as "evidence" of my criminal intent. For the past two years, the poor guy had been living with the prospect of jail hanging over his head. *But his actual sentence would not be determined until the prosecution evaluated the degree of his cooperation.*

When Channell came up with this new anecdote, Brendan saw it not as a problem, but an opportunity. In Brendan's view, if the prosecutors were willing to put on such testimony in order to "get" his client, he would expose the lie.

Why did Brendan believe so strongly that Channell was lying? For one thing, the prosecution had not listed Bunker Hunt as one of their witnesses, which presumably meant that Hunt couldn't corroborate Channell's story. But then, Channell couldn't even corroborate his *own* story. He had spent scores of hours in hearings, interviews, depositions, and in front of the grand jury, but not until much later, when the "deal" he would get depended on his testimony, did he mention this alleged conversation between Hunt and me about lying to Congress or going to jail.

Unfortunately, Brendan couldn't simply jump up and point out the inconsistencies in Channell's stories. He had to wait for the cross-examination, when he would have the opportunity to show why Channell's testimony was unreliable. During the break, the lawyers tore through the box containing the transcripts of Channell's previous testimony and quickly pulled out the pages that would show how this poor, intimidated man, threatened with jail, had finally succumbed to the pressure. As we walked back in, Brendan turned to me and said, "We've got 'em."

What followed was Sullivan at his finest. He started out by gently leading Channell back through the testimony he had just given. In the process, he pressed Channell on whether or not he had intended to commit a crime. No, Channell said, he hadn't. The prosecution had basically convinced him to plead guilty to what had never before been criminal: conspiracy to use a tax-exempt organization to support the Nicaraguan resistance.

Then Brendan reminded Channell of his many previous versions of the Bunker Hunt meeting, which had included no mention of this alleged conversation with Bunker Hunt. As Sullivan began reviewing Channell's previous testimony about that evening in Dallas four years before, he confronted Channell with the fact that his testimony had changed dramatically. After Brendan pointed out several inconsistencies in Channell's testimony, the judge intervened:

The Court: And how do you explain that you told the jury that this [conversation between Hunt and North] stuck in your mind and you had no doubt about it?
Channell: Because it has, and it was very interesting how long—
The Court: You've now got three versions already.
Channell: It has —
The Court: What stuck in your mind when you told the jury it stuck in your mind?
Channell: That Colonel North said what he did relating to these two questions, and it just stuck.

And now Brendan moved in for the kill:

Sullivan: What it points out, sir, is it is hard to remember what was said. It's hard.
Channell: Well, I understand that.
Sullivan: And this is important. And sometimes when you have such an urge to cooperate, there is a little danger that you might put words in somebody's mouth that really don't belong [there]?

Is that fair to say?

Channell: Well, I'm sure there is that temptation, of course.

A moment later, after chastising poor Channell again, the judge turned to the jury and said, "My instructions are the same to you, ladies and gentlemen of the jury, as to each and every statement that has been pointed out. You may consider them in connection with your appraisal of the credibility of this witness."

In effect, the judge himself was advising the jury that Spitz Channell's testimony could not be trusted. We could only hope that the jury would be able to do what the judge had instructed. But the effect on the prosecution was visible. For them it was like a punch in the stomach—not a knockout, but enough to badly damage their argument about criminal intent.

By the time I finally took the stand it was almost anticlimactic. For me, this was "Hearings II—The Sequel." Only now, instead of looking up at congressmen, senators, and their aides, I was facing the special prosecutors. Judge Gesell was on my left, and the jury members sat in the jury box on my right.

Betsy was sitting in the first row behind the rail. Whenever I looked over at her she would smile, and each time we came back from a break she said, "I'm praying for you. It will be all right."

The courtroom looks different from the witness stand than it does from the defense table, and I was struck by the contrast in bedside manner between the chief prosecutor and Brendan. My antagonist tended to strut about and posture in front of the jury, much like the courtroom lawyers in the movies and on television. Brendan was more subdued and less affected as he leaned on the podium below the judge's bench.

During my cross-examination, the prosecutor would begin each session with "Good morning" or "Good afternoon." But I just couldn't bring myself to wish him the same. I really *didn't* want him to have a good morning or a good afternoon, and only a moment earlier I had taken an oath to tell the truth.

For some observers, the most dramatic point in a trial occurs when the defendant takes the stand. For me, however, the climax occurred during the closing arguments. The prosecutor closes first, as he tries to show that he has already proven beyond a reasonable doubt that the defendant is guilty. Then comes the defense counsel, who tries to demonstrate just the opposite.

These prosecutors claimed that they made no use of my testimony at the hearings, and that they hadn't watched it or even read about it. But oddly enough, the trial ended on the same sordid note as the hearings. In the Senate Caucus Room, Senator Inouye had ended his final remarks by comparing me to the Nazi war criminals at Nuremberg. At the trial, the chief prosecutor invoked the name of Hitler to describe what I had done. I'm not entirely sure what to make of these comments, but they certainly went far beyond the bounds of reason and civility. They remind me of the old Soviet mentality, where anyone opposed to any element of the state's domestic or foreign policy was immediately branded a "fascist."

Brendan was outraged by the prosecutor's effort to link me in the jurors' minds with Adolf Hitler, and I remember wondering what my father, who had gone to war to fight the Nazis, would have thought of that reference. "These people will stop at nothing," Brendan said.

Listening to Brendan's close was like watching a master carpenter putting the final touches on a beautiful house that he had been working on for months. Addressing the twelve individuals who would be deciding my fate, he carefully summarized all that they had seen and heard during the trial. He described my Marine Corps career, and my work on sensitive projects at the White House. He reminded the jury that there was ample proof that the people I had worked for had approved what I had done. Although I hadn't been able to articulate it well, Brendan was able to capture and describe my feelings of being abandoned by former colleagues and higher-ups.

He recalled the terrorist threats to my family, and pointed out how the lives of others had depended on what I had or hadn't done. He pointed out that criminal intent had never entered my mind. And in the end, he urged these twelve citizens to consider carefully whether or not they could convict me beyond any reasonable doubt.

By the time he was finished I was utterly drained. I remember almost nothing of the prosecutor's rebuttal, the judge's instructions to the jury, or the flurry of final motions that are so essential to a defendant. Now it was just a matter of waiting for the verdict.

With the understanding that we would return to court the moment a verdict was in, the judge had granted Brendan's request that we be allowed to wait at the law firm. That was a big relief, although it also meant that reporters and camera teams took up day-long watches at the courthouse, outside the Williams & Connolly building, and in front of our home. Brian Cox and the men from our Bible study group came by several times for lunch and prayer, and Betsy joined us when she could. Each afternoon, when the jury recessed for the day, I was able to go home and have dinner with the family.

The jury deliberated for more than eleven days. Early on the afternoon of May 14, Judge Gesell's clerk called Brendan to say, "We have a verdict." I was on my way out to meet Betsy for lunch at the nearby Army & Navy Club when one of the security agents gave me the news. Brendan had Betsy paged, and a few minutes later she joined us in Brendan's office.

As the reporters yelled out questions, we piled into the waiting van for the now-familiar trip to the courthouse. On the way over, Brendan said, "Remember, if it doesn't go our way on all counts, there will be an appeal."

As we entered the courthouse, Betsy spotted David Harper, our pastor, trying to make his way through the horde of reporters. She prevailed on Jerry Dimenna, the head of our security team, to get David into the courtroom. Once we were inside, Betsy and I stood together holding hands, and David said a quiet prayer with us. Then, glancing over at the defense table, David asked me to bring over the well-worn Bible I had brought with me to court each day.

This Bible had been around. Morton Blackwell in the White House Public Liaison Office had given it to me shortly after I arrived at the NSC, and I had carried it with me ever since. I took it with me everywhere—including Tehran.

Before I returned to my seat, David opened the Bible to Psalm Ninety-one and handed it to me. As we waited for the jury to come in, I sat there and read:

> Surely He will save you from the fowler's snare
>   and from the deadly pestilence.
> He will cover you with His feathers,
>   and under His wings you will find refuge;
>   His faithfulness will be your shield and rampart.

Meanwhile, in the hallway outside the courtroom, all order broke down as the crowd of reporters tried to surge through the metal detectors and security that the federal marshals had set up for this trial.

It was shortly before two-thirty when the jury came in. I looked at their faces, but it was impossible to know what they had decided or what they had been through. The foreperson handed the verdict form to the bailiff, who gave it to the judge.

The room was silent while the judge read the jury's decision. After what seemed like a long delay, he started to read in a steady monotone, like the roll of a drum on some faraway parade field:

"As to count one, the verdict is not guilty," (Thank you, Lord) "both of the substantive count and aiding and abetting."

"As to count two, the verdict is not guilty," (Thank you, Lord) "of the substantive count and of aiding and abetting.

"On count three the verdict is not guilty" (Thank you) "as to the substantive count and not guilty" (Thank you) "as to aiding and abetting.

"As to count four the verdict is not guilty" (Thank you) "as to the substantive count and not guilty" (Thank you) "as to aiding and abetting.

"As to count five the verdict is not guilty." (Thank you.)

"As to count six, the verdict is not guilty" (Thank you) "of the substantive count, guilty" (Oh God, *why?*) "of aiding and abetting."

Later on, I was told that these words from the judge had been punctuated by a gasp from somewhere in the court. If so, I didn't hear it, and it did nothing to slow the judge's steady rhythm:

"As to count seven, the verdict is not guilty" (Thank you) "of the substantive count, and not guilty" (Thank you) "of aiding and abetting."

"As to count eight, the verdict is not guilty." (Thank you.)

"As to count nine, the verdict is guilty." (Oh God, not another one!)

"As to count ten, the verdict is guilty." (Lord, no more, please!)

"As to count eleven, the verdict is not guilty." (Thank you, Lord.)

"As to count twelve, the verdict is not guilty." (Thank you, Lord.)

The judge's reading of the verdict lasted little more than a minute.

It seemed like hours. I was stunned, elated, crushed, and happy all at once.

The judge had said "not guilty" thirteen times and "guilty" three times. But there were only twelve counts, and for a moment I couldn't remember which ones were which. While I sat there trying to figure it out, a stampede of reporters raced for the door while Judge Gesell and the lawyers calmly took care of the final procedural obligations.

By the time they finished and the courtroom was quiet again, I had figured out what the three remaining charges were: helping to obstruct Congress, something about destroying, altering, or removing documents, and accepting the security system. And then it was over.

As the judge walked out, the courtroom again became chaotic. I walked over to Betsy and hugged her. I embraced David Harper, and shook hands with Brendan, Nicole, Barry, Terry, and John. Congressman Henry Hyde gave me a bear hug and turned to reassure Betsy.

The prosecutors left their minions behind to pack up their papers, and rushed out to the dozens of waiting microphones. As I returned to the table to retrieve my briefcase, Brendan came up behind me and gave me a pat on the back. "Let's go," he said. "It's not over yet. We're going to fight this until you are free of it *all*. Remember, you walked into this courtroom with sixteen counts against you. You went to trial on twelve, and now we're down to three. We're headed in the right direction. Come on, let's get on with the appeal. And by the way, are you having fun yet?"

On the way back to Williams & Connolly, Brendan had decided that when we arrived, he and I would each give a brief statement as a way of dealing with the horde of reporters who would be camped outside the office. Both our comments turned out to be prescient. Brendan ended his statement by saying, "You can be assured that we will never abandon Colonel North and his family in this legal battle." And they didn't.

I said, "We now face many months, perhaps years, fighting these remaining charges. [Little did I know!] Nevertheless, we are absolutely confident of the final outcome. As a Marine, I was taught to fight, and fight hard, for as long as it takes to prevail. We will continue this battle, and with the support and prayers of the American people, I will be fully vindicated."

I didn't know it at the time, but vindication would be long in coming. Brendan had already announced that there would be an appeal, and throughout the case the lawyers had carefully noted each legal issue that might later prove relevant.

One particularly sensitive point had to do with the jury. During the trial, we had all heard murmurings that I was being judged by other than a jury of my peers. Some people argued that Sullivan should have made an issue of the fact that I was a white, male, college graduate who had served in the military, had traveled extensively, and had worked in the upper echelons of government; that my background was radically different from that of the all-black, mostly female jury.

At the time, I didn't give this much thought. But a year later, in the summer of 1990, a member of the jury that convicted me was interviewed on television, and what she said came as a shock: "What were people going to think on the outside if we found him not guilty? Okay, what were they going to think of us being as blacks, finding a white man not guilty? They're really going to think that we're stupid."

I was stunned. Justice is supposed to be blind; the color of a person's skin should not determine their guilt or innocence. To this day, I don't quite know what to make of the juror's statement, which goes against everything I have ever learned and believed.

Patience was never my strong suit, but mine would be sorely tested over the next seven weeks as the judge collected information to use in determining my sentence. While we waited, Stuart graduated from high school and I tried to resume a more normal family life while working with Brendan to prepare a presentencing report, which would outline all the reasons why the judge shouldn't send me to jail.

I was assigned a probation officer, Ralph Ardito, whose task was to act as my warden during this period and to make a recommendation to the judge as to my sentence. At first I was wary of him; I assumed he was another member of the prosecution that had been arrayed against me for so long. But I soon learned that Ardito was a real professional. He was charged with a difficult task, and he carried it out with great compassion and sensitivity.

As the day of sentencing approached, Brendan's office was besieged with calls and offers of help. People I had known well and men I had served with sent letters to the judge, asking for leniency. Some of the most moving letters were from Marines I had served with in Vietnam, most of whom I hadn't seen in twenty years.

On the Fourth of July, the day before the sentencing, our family enjoyed a quiet picnic with a group of our neighbors. Afterwards, we went to watch the fireworks at the Great Falls firehouse. It was a wonderful day: we swam, played, and talked until after sunset. I didn't want it to end.

The next morning, I got up even earlier than usual and read from the Bible. As Betsy and I drove into Washington, we didn't know whether or not we would be riding home together after court. As always, the reporters and cameras followed us every step of the way. The Lone Ranger had Tonto, his faithful Indian companion. I had the press.

As we walked toward Courtroom Six, one of the reporters ran along beside me.

"You look awfully calm for a man on his way in to be sentenced," he said.

"That's because I know where I'm going," I replied. I was thinking in terms of a far larger context.

He looked astonished. "You do? How many years are you going to get?" he asked.

"Eternity," I replied. He looked totally confused. He obviously had in mind a very different kind of sentence.

And so did the special prosecutor. He pleaded with the judge to send me to prison. And he wasn't alone, either. The *New York Times* editorialized in favor of a lengthy prison term. And people wonder why I don't like the press.

The sentencing hearing was as much of an emotional roller coaster as the day the verdict was announced. Hearing somebody argue in a court of law that you deserve to go to prison is an awful experience. But there was also Brendan's eloquent plea for the judge's compassion. Drawing heavily from letters he had received, interviews he had conducted, and everything he had learned about me, Brendan took almost a full hour to explain to the judge why I should remain free. He began with my military career and moved on to more contemporary events:

In December 1986 he was named the primary target in the named request for an independent counsel. He became the target of the longest, largest, independent counsel and grand jury investigation in the history of our country....

Throughout the two and a half year period [since the firing] he and his family have been subjected to the greatest and the most intrusive media interest perhaps of any citizen except a sitting President. The media generated literally tens of thousands of articles and op-ed pieces to which he cannot respond.... For months at a time the press camped outside his home and followed him to work and to the store and to church and to the city dump. At no time has he given an interview about the case, respecting counsel's advice that that's not the proper way in litigation. He and his family have also been plagued by the unauthorized books that purport to tell in intimate detail the story of his and his wife's life, his children's lives. They've been subjected to an offensive fictionalized TV mini-series without authority, without interviews, without permission. Just like he's some commodity that people use....

North has been likened to Adolf Hitler, the worst criminal and mass murderer who ever lived....

His family has felt the extraordinary impact. The assassination threat has not abated. It's been exacerbated by the worldwide publicity caused by one branch of our government.

Colonel North didn't ask to become known throughout America. He was thrust upon the TV of every person in the country.

The threat eats away at a person like a cancer. It's always there. It's always haunting. You don't know whether it will never happen or something will happen next month.

Maybe most of all, the thing that I've heard no one say is, what is his loss as a result of all of this? It's loss of peace of mind. We all go out to the car and we go to work and we don't think for a minute that we'll be assaulted on the way, much less killed. The loss of peace of mind—what a burden. It's an extraordinary punishment which he'll carry with him today and into the foreseeable future, which should be weighed when the court determines today what the appropriate sentence is.

What must it be like to wonder about these things? To wonder whether some group that doesn't think logically wants to even the score with America by getting Ollie North, or just some deranged person who wants to get on the front page of the newspaper by attacking North.

He's suffered enough. His family has suffered enough. He's been punished enough. A prison term on top of that would be fundamentally too harsh, wrong. It's a time for forgiveness. It's a time to say it's over."

And it almost was. The judge handed down a three-year suspended sentence, fined me a hundred and fifty thousand dollars, and assigned me to two years of probation and twelve hundred hours of community service in an inner-city drug-prevention program.

There were several points in Brendan's remarks when I had to choke back tears as I listened to him describe my life. Even so, Brendan didn't use everything. He didn't mention the call I had received late one night from Billy Graham, or the supportive letters from former President Nixon. Nor did he mention three laudatory letters I had received from President Reagan while I was working at the NSC—which he hadn't known about. They turned up two years after the trial, when we were moving to a new house. When I brought them in to show Brendan, he went bonkers.

By far the most interesting piece of evidence that Brendan didn't use was what we called the "smoking gun in the closet" tape. (The title comes from a deliciously mixed metaphor that appears in the first line of the transcript.) This tape was supposed to be nothing more than a routinely recorded telephone conversation between employees in two different Manhattan offices of New York's Citibank on June 17, 1987, about three weeks before I testified at the congressional hearings. But in a coincidence that is almost too bizarre to believe, leaking through the conversation between the two bank employees was a second dialogue between two men on the subject of the Iran-contra hearings. From their discussion, it's clear that one of these men had already appeared before the congressional committee.

The bank gave the tape to the FBI, and the following summer, Barry Simon found it in a pile of potential evidence that was finally provided to us by the prosecution. Although most of the conversation between the two men was remarkably clear, we were never able to determine who they were. But there was no doubt as to what they were discussing:

A: Yeah, there's a smoking gun in the closet. Reagan knows.

B: Listen...

A: I told the committee. There was no, I told the committee there was, I had nothing to do with those papers. Ollie North knows about it. Reagan knows...Reagan knows about it—

B: Listen, he ain't testifying.

A:—and the...and the other—the other people involved do know about that.

B: [Unintelligible.]

A: Well, you have to go to the Committee.

B: [Unintelligible]...the Committee.

A: You have to go to the Committee, not me.

B: Listen...

A: Somebody's got to bring this up.

B: [Unintelligible.]

A: I think somebody ought to go, somebody's got to be responsible for this.

B: [Unintelligible.]

A: Reagan...Reagan knows. Reagan has all the memos.

B: He's got all the memos? I thought he tore all that stuff up.

A: No. He's got all the memos, and there are copies.

B: Didn't you burn that stuff?

A: No.

B: Oh, jeez. I warned you about that.

A: Nobody...no...

B: It's going to hit the papers like crazy.

A: Nobody told me to.

B: [Unintelligible.]

A: [Unintelligible.] No.

B: What about your secretary? She couldn't get the stuff copied?

A: Not all of it.

B: [Unintelligible] about Reagan [unintelligible.]

A: Well...I'm getting out of this thing, and if somebody comes to me, I'm blowing the cover.

B: I'll tell you, if I go down, I'm taking you with me.

A: Well, me too.

B: You and your...secretary...[unintelligible.]

A: I'd better call you back. I think we're tapped.
B: I think so.
A: All right. 'Bye.

When he first heard the tape during preparations for the trial, Barry was flabbergasted. "Listen to this!" he called out, and we all gathered in the SCIF conference room to hear it. Barry played it over and over to see if I could possibly identify the voices. Two of my lawyers wondered whether one of the men was Don Regan, but that struck me as unlikely: it just didn't sound like him. Regan would have come across as more arrogant, whereas these men were clearly anxious. My own guess was that one of the participants was Ed Hickey, the President's military aide, who has since passed away. Hickey was interviewed around this time by the committee, and he had been involved, along with me, in a hostage rescue attempt by the Drug Enforcement Agency that was funded with profits from the Iran arms sale.

But that's just a guess. Whoever these men were, it was clear that somebody was in possession of important documents, some of which had been destroyed. But what? And how, exactly, did all this fit into the Iran-contra story?

When I was unable to identify the voices, my attorneys took the tape to the White House. On July 28, 1988, Brendan and Barry went to the White House to meet with Arthur B. Culvahouse, the President's counsel, and one of his aides to seek access to documents and to ask for an interview with the President. They took the tape along.

As Barry described it later, Culvahouse blanched when he heard the tape, and his aide appeared visibly shaken. Both men denied any knowledge of it, and as far as they knew, no other government agency had been asked about it either. And yet the special prosecutors had received this tape months earlier.

Well, said Brendan, would you help us get to the bottom of this and let us interview the President about it?

Culvahouse told Brendan he'd think about it. Two months later the answer came back: no.

Apparently the special prosecutor's zeal in pursuing John Poindexter and me did not extend to finding out who was on that tape, or what documents they were discussing. Nobody at the White House, the FBI, or the special prosecutor's office was interested in helping us. And it's safe to assume that nobody on the congressional committee heard this tape, either. If they had, it surely would have leaked.

Without being able to identify the voices, we were not able to use the tape in court. The special prosecutor might never have given it to us except that he was required to do so under the rules of evidence. But neither they, the FBI, nor the White House ever revealed its existence.

18

Looking Back

According to the conventional wisdom, Iran-contra occurred because a small group of misfits and renegades, working out of the White House basement, rose above the law and carried out their own foreign policy, whereupon their superiors where shocked—*shocked*—to learn what they had done.

It makes for a good story, but that's not what happened. As I see it, the causes of Iran-contra lie in several directions, with plenty of blame to go around.

I have already described my own mistakes, regrets, and lapses in judgment. But I never saw myself as being above the law, nor did I ever intend to do anything illegal. The argument over the meaning and constitutional legitimacy of the Boland Amendments will continue for years, but I have always believed, and still do, that these amendments did not bar the National Security Council from supporting the contras. Even the most stringent of the Boland Amendments contained clear and substantial loopholes which we used to ensure that the Nicaraguan resistance would not be abandoned.

From 1984 on, I did my best to keep faith with two groups whom I cared about deeply, and whose fate President Reagan had put at the top of his agenda: our hostages in Lebanon and the contras. While I worked frantically on behalf of both groups, I can see now that I was also motivated by my own pride and ambition. No matter how difficult or demanding the job was, I was sure I could handle it. I knew that if these missions were successful, only a very small handful of people would ever know what I had achieved. Paradoxically, I took pride in that, too.

I still have conflicting feelings about the Iran initiative. It ended in failure, but that's not to say it wasn't worth trying. Had we succeeded, not only would all the hostages have come home, but we would have opened a new relationship with a country that is still important to our national security.

But we didn't succeed. Not only were we unable to establish a connection to the moderates in Iran, but we also undermined a valid and well-established policy of not making concessions to terrorists. Although we didn't deal directly with the terrorists in Beirut, the perception that we did was so widespread that it almost didn't matter. And while we did rescue three of the hostages, two other Americans were seized. Moreover, our contacts with Iran ultimately caused great political damage and embarrassment to the United States, and especially to President Reagan.

While I recognize the liabilities of the Iran initiative, I continue to feel that saving a life—or trying to—is even more important than preserving a policy. Earlier, we condemned several European governments for making that same choice with regard to *their* hostages in Beirut, but in the end we did the same thing. However unwise our actions may have been in retrospect, I'm glad that I live in a country where the protection of human life can still outweigh the grand designs of government.

Our Nicaraguan initiative was more straightforward, and for me, at least, presented no great moral quandary. Until Congress decided to resume its funding for the contras, we succeeded in fulfilling the mission assigned by the President: to keep the resistance alive, body and soul. Our goal was not military but political: to enable the contras to exert the kind of pressure on the Sandinistas that could ultimately lead to a free and democratic Nicaragua. Early in 1990, our efforts were vindicated when a coalition of anti-Sandinista groups, led by Violeta Chamorro, scored a decisive electoral victory over Daniel Ortega and the Sandinistas.

"Set your watches," Mrs. Chamorro had told her audiences. "Set them to the same hour as Poland, Bulgaria, and Czechoslovakia. Set them to the same hour as Chile, because this is the time of democracy and freedom."

These were lofty sentiments, but almost nobody in the United States thought she could win. And despite everything I knew and believed, I didn't either. I had begun to accept the views of the media experts who pontificated at length about the inevitable Ortega triumph.

But I underestimated the power of the secret ballot. That divine spark of liberty that exists in all of us made the difference in Nicaragua, just as it did in Berlin, Poland, Romania, and so many other places. Although I believed fervently in Ronald Reagan's messages of freedom and democracy that we had broadcast to the world, and had even helped draft some of them, I obviously missed the full magnitude of their impact.

With this global shift toward liberty, Ronald Reagan's presidency should have ended on a great victorious crescendo. But the aftermath of the Iran and contra initiatives distorted the real impact of his presidency. Brendan Sullivan had forecast this outcome when he wrote to President Reagan, urging him to pardon me, Admiral Poindexter, Joe Fernandez, and others involved in these initiatives. Brendan's letter was signed by the lawyers representing the government officials indicted in the controversy and hand-carried to the President. This letter, reprinted for the first time in the Appendix, was never acknowledged.

Brendan's assessment was correct—the controversy continues to this day. But while some of the blame goes to me, not all of it can be ascribed to those of us who carried out these policies.

Congress, too, bears some responsibility for what happened. Its vacillating support for the contras not only endangered their lives, but also broke faith with our nation's commitments.

As we've seen, both the special prosecutor and the hearings became ways for Congress to criminalize legitimate policy differences between coequal branches of government. But why were those differences so great to begin with? And aren't there *always* policy differences between the executive and legislative branches?

Yes—but rarely to the extent we saw during the Reagan years.

What happened in Washington in the 1980s was the result of changes in both the legislative and executive branches during the preceding two or three decades. Ever since Lyndon Johnson's landslide victory over Barry Goldwater, which was followed four years later by the highly contentious 1968 Democratic National Convention in Chicago, the leadership of the Democratic Party has been moving steadily to the left. These days, when the reelection of Capitol Hill incumbents is now virtually guaranteed, House members and senators have become more beholden to their party's leadership than to the voters they ostensibly represent. This helps to explain why many have drifted so far from the center of the political spectrum.

As Congress was inching to the left, the American body politic reacted in 1980 by electing a true conservative to the White House. But unlike the slow and gradual permutation on Capitol Hill, the shift in ideology when Ronald Reagan came to the White House was both enormous and abrupt. Suddenly, the traditional adversarial relationship between the President and Congress became more intense than it had in many years. And Nicaragua became the battlefield.

More than any of his recent predecessors, President Reagan came into office with clear philosophical goals. He favored less government and lower taxes, and he believed that private enterprise should replace the public sector in providing opportunities for the American people.

And in case his domestic vision wasn't shocking enough for the Democratic majority in Congress, Reagan wanted these same principles to be reflected in our *foreign* policy, too. He insisted that American foreign policy should exhibit the revolutionary and antityrannical ideals of our forefathers. In practical terms, this meant that the United States would go beyond mere "containment" and would actively support anti-Communist resistance movements in Angola, Cambodia, Afghanistan, and Nicaragua. The Reagan doctrine not only traumatized the Congress; it also stunned large sectors of Washington's permanent bureaucracy.

This was, after all, a sea change in our international posture. Since 1945, Communism had prevailed just about everywhere it had tried its hand. But Ronald Reagan and Bill Casey insisted that if we could help an indigenous anti-Communist resistance movement inflict a single major defeat, the entire Communist house of cards would come tumbling down. After the invasion of Afghanistan, the Soviet empire was stretched so thin that Moscow simply couldn't afford to continue supporting all its proxies.

For the congressional Democrats, the first two years of the Reagan administration were an unmitigated disaster. After a long string of defeats on domestic policy issues, they focused their attention on Central America—one of the few areas where the President was vulnerable. Pointing to our long and shameful history of backing Latin American regimes with abysmal human rights records, they portrayed our policy of backing the contras as simply more of the same. Here they had some success, which culminated in the various Boland Amendments, each of which whittled away at our support for the Nicaraguan resistance.

Despite all my disagreements with the congressional Democrats, I find it hard to believe that most of them really wanted to see a Communist toehold on the mainland of our hemisphere. But they were willing to try almost anything in their fight against Ronald Reagan. In the process, they put the final nail in the coffin of Sam Rayburn's famous dictum that politics stops at the water's edge.

President Reagan, too, must accept some of the blame for what happened. Ironically, his greatest strength was also his primary weakness. He always focused on the big picture, and he knew exactly what direction he wanted to go. But in the process he neglected the details. He knew where he wanted to end up, and he didn't much care how he got there.

Later, when the whole thing blew up in his face, President Reagan claimed to accept responsibility for Iran-contra. But his professions rang hollow as he evaded real responsibility for what had happened by claiming that he just didn't know. It was a weak defense, and it reflected badly on him and his presidency.

Some commentators have tried to argue that Iran-contra occurred because the executive branch carried out both of these operations in secret. But some secrecy is essential in foreign policy. The problem isn't secrecy; it's how to protect actions that cannot be publicly disclosed without cutting Congress out of the loop.

After all, the Constitution reserves for Congress the right to advise and consent. As I see it, the Founding Fathers intended to follow the biblical precept that in the counsel of many there is wisdom. But the current system of five large committees (including two intelligence committees) in the House and Senate, each with dozens of staffers, overseeing American foreign policy is simply too unwieldy. Protecting secrets has become more difficult than ever, which discourages the executive branch from revealing important information. We have gone from the counsel of many to the counsel of *too* many.

There is an alternative. We know from other operations, such as the Manhattan Project during World War II, and the subsequent building of our nuclear arsenal, that Congress *can* keep secrets if the relevant committees are small enough. In the case of intelligence operations, we would be better off with a *very* small joint committee of perhaps five members, consisting of, say, three House members and two from the Senate, with both parties represented. This body would have an equally small professional staff.

Another lesson to be learned from Iran-contra is that the team of advisers around the President would more effectively serve him and the nation if it included members of Congress. In the past, presidents usually found a way to work with congressional leaders from both parties, but in the adversarial atmosphere of Washington in the 1980s, that just wasn't possible.

And what of America's role in the larger world? The Communist threat has subsided, but we still don't live in a world of our own making. The resurgence of regional and ethnic nationalism everywhere from the Balkans to Quebec presents a host of new foreign policy challenges. While the broad threat of international terrorism seems to have diminished, at least for the moment, there are still leaders like Muammar Qaddafi and Saddam Hussein who offer havens and support for its perpetrators. And although his days are undoubtedly numbered, Fidel Castro continues to advocate the export of revolutionary Marxism.

The world must also grapple with the rise of radical Islamic fundamentalism, which is unalterably opposed to the values of individual liberty, religious freedom, and democracy that we cherish. With the twentieth century drawing to a close, Islamic fundamentalism poses serious threats to a number of nations: Saudi Arabia, Egypt, the Philippines, Indonesia, Pakistan, and even India. As one of the Iranian officials reminded us during our visit to Tehran, "The Ayatollah's picture is in all of these places, and we didn't mail it there."

Although the world we live in is now much smaller, this doesn't diminish the role the United States will have to play. But we must abandon our old tendency to support the status quo. In the past, this willingness to "deal with the devil I know" has only encouraged the very revolutions we hoped to avoid. For years we tolerated and supported repressive, right-wing, extremist regimes in places like Cuba, Nicaragua, Panama, Vietnam, and the Philippines, merely because they were anti-Communist. Some of the leaders who were advocates of change in these countries, including Fidel Castro and Ho Chi Minh, had come to us first but were rebuffed. We shouldn't have been surprised that they turned to the Soviet Union for help.

With our history and our ideals, the United States should never have allowed revolution and change to become the exclusive domain of the left. The ideals of our own revolution—freedom, tolerance, and individual liberty—were inspiring two centuries ago. They still are.

Postscript

Brendan and his team kept up the battle after the trial—right to the end of this long ordeal. On July 20, 1990, a three-judge panel of the U.S. Court of Appeals reversed one of the three outstanding counts against me and vacated the other two. If the special prosecutor still wanted to convict me, he would have to show the judge that none of my immunized congressional testimony had been used against me by the grand jury that indicted me, or by the trial jury that later convicted me.

The special prosecutor chose to appeal this decision by asking the entire appeals court to reverse its own three-judge panel. On November 27, 1990, the Court of Appeals again decided in my favor by upholding the panel's decision. As a result of the *en banc* ruling, the Marine Corps restored my pension and I recovered something even more precious: my right to vote.

I had hoped the story would end here, but it was not to be. Lawrence Walsh, the special prosecutor, decided to take his appeal to the Supreme Court. On May 28, 1991, the Supreme Court reaffirmed the two earlier appeals court decisions by announcing that it would not hear the special prosecutor's appeal.

Although Walsh had assured Brendan that he would drop the case if he lost in the Supreme Court, he changed his mind. Instead, he apparently intended to start all over again. On September 11, 1991, only six weeks before this book was due to go on sale, we returned to court for an extraordinary session. The first—and only—witness was Bud McFarlane. The prosecution had obviously expected Bud to explain that his testimony at my trial had been unaffected by my congressional testimony. But the more the prosecutor pressed McFarlane on this point, the more Bud insisted that he had been immersed in watching my appearance at the hearings: "This was very explosive testimony," he said. "Tens of millions of Americans were blown away by it.... In watching four days of riveting testimony by a man who was like a son to me, how could I *not* have been affected?"

Clearly stunned by Bud's emotional outburst, the prosecutors finally conceded that their case had collapsed.

It ended very much as it had begun. On November 23, 1986, when Ed Meese and his assistants had shown me the "diversion" memo that marked the start of my legal problems, the Washington Redskins had been playing the Dallas Cowboys at RFK Stadium. The ending of my case took place under remarkably similar circumstances. On Sunday, September 15, 1991, I was listening to a Redskins game against the Phoenix Cardinals when Brendan called me at home with the wonderful news that Lawrence Walsh had decided to drop all the charges. It was finally over.

The following morning, my family and my lawyers accompanied me to court for my last day as a defendant. The long ordeal that had begun nearly five years earlier in the Attorney General's office came to an abrupt but welcome end in less than ten minutes. Judge Gesell signed a two-line order granting the prosecutor's motion to dismiss and said, simply, "This terminates the case."

From the very beginning, Brendan had insisted that my compelled testimony to Congress made it impossible for the prosecution to proceed. And now, five years after it all began, Walsh finally admitted that Brendan was right.

As I left the courthouse, Betsy, Sarah, and Dornin joined me on the steps. As usual, reporters were waiting. But this time I spoke to them:

"For nearly five years, my family and I have been under fire. Throughout this time we have been blessed to be supported by the finest attorneys in America, and by the generosity and prayers of the

American people, and that is what has sustained us through this ordeal. Without this support and encouragement, we could not have prevailed."

And I meant it, with all my heart.

As for the other members of our cast:

Elliott Abrams, who had chaired the small, secret interagency group that had reviewed the activities of the Nicaraguan resistance, left government in 1988 to become a consultant. As this book was going to press, questions were again raised about his knowledge of my activities in support of the contras..

Charles Allen, with whom I had worked on counterterrorism, is still at the CIA. But rather than being rewarded for his hard work, he was passed over for promotion because he was too candid with his superiors with regard to the Iran initiative.

The Australian is apparently still a government official in Tehran.

Congressman Michael Barnes was defeated in his bid for a U.S. Senate seat in 1986.

Enrique Bermudez, the military commander of the Nicaraguan freedom fighters from 1981 to 1988, was murdered in Managua in the spring of 1991.

Congressman Edward Boland retired in 1988 after serving for thirty-six years in the House of Representatives.

George Bush was elected President of the United States.

Adolfo Calero continued to serve as head of the United Nicaraguan Opposition after I was fired. Later, he helped organize the resistance coalition that nominated Violeta Chamorro as the opposition candidate for president. He's returning to Nicaragua.

William Casey died of cancer and pneumonia on May 6, 1987, during the second day of the congressional hearings.

George Cave was asked to participate in one final meeting with the Second Channel after I was fired. He continues to serve as a consultant to the CIA.

Carl (Spitz) Channell was working to establish a new conservative political action committee in Washington when he was struck by a car on March 15, 1990. He died on May 7, 1990.

Duane (Dewey) Clarridge was forced to retire from the CIA in 1988 and now works for General Dynamics. In the summer of 1991, the special prosecutor named him as a target of the Iran-contra investigation.

Joe Fernandez, who served as a CIA clandestine services officer for twenty-one years, and whose last post was chief of station in Costa Rica, was indicted twice by the special prosecutor before all charges against him were dropped. He is today my business partner in Guardian Technologies International, Inc., the company we founded in 1989 to manufacture protective armor for law-enforcement officers and the military.

Alan Fiers, chief of the Central American Task Force, retired from the CIA in 1989. In the summer of 1991, faced with the prospect of indictment, he pleaded guilty to misdemeanor charges and agreed to cooperate with the special prosecutor's investigation.

Robert Gates, who served as deputy director of intelligence of the CIA, and then as deputy director of the CIA itself under Bill Casey, was nominated to become CIA director in 1988. His nomination was withdrawn in the face of congressional opposition, whereupon he was named deputy national security adviser to President Bush. In the summer of 1991, he was again nominated to become director of the CIA, which once again resulted in political controversy.

Clair George retired from the CIA in 1988, where he had been deputy director for operations. In September 1991, he was indicted by the special prosecutor, who alleged that he had withheld information from Congress about my activities.

Manucher Ghorbanifar provided separate and extensive interviews to both the special prosecutor and the congressional investigators. Gorba continues to live in Europe, where he maintains several residences.

Albert Hakim pled guilty to a misdemeanor charge brought against him by the special prosecutor. He has since returned to California, where he has established another international trading company.

Fawn Hall lives in California. She is regularly required by the special prosecutor to return to Washington to testify.

Lee Hamilton completed his six-year tenure as chairman of the House Intelligence Committee. He remains a member of the Democratic congressional leadership.

Eugene Hasenfus was released by the Sandinistas at the end of 1986. When he returned to the United States, he unsuccessfully brought suit against Dick Secord and several other individuals involved in supporting the Nicaraguan resistance.

David Jacobsen returned to California, where he wrote a memoir of his ordeal as a hostage in Beirut.

Michael Ledeen continues to serve as a consultant in Washington, and has written a book about the Iran-contra affair.

Robert (Bud) McFarlane, who had pled guilty to several misde-meanor charges, was sentenced to probation and community service and is now a consultant in Washington. He was the only witness to be called in September 1991, during the final proceedings brought against me by the special prosecutor.

Admiral Art Moreau, the real hero of the *Achille Lauro* incident, became the NATO naval commander in Naples, Italy. He died of a heart attack in 1989.

The Nephew still resides in Iran, and travels on occasion to Europe.

Abu Nidal is reportedly living in luxury in Libya.

Ami Nir left his government position, and was killed in a plane crash in Mexico in 1988. In the summer of 1991, his widow's home was broken into by thieves who made off with Nir's secret files on the Iran initiative.

Manuel Noriega surrendered to American authorities in 1990. He now resides in Miami as a guest of the U.S. government.

Daniel Ortega was defeated in the election of 1990. He remains head of the Sandinista party in Managua.

Admiral John Poindexter was convicted in 1990 on six counts, and his case is on appeal. He serves as a consultant to several Washington companies.

Ronald Reagan returned to California and wrote his memoirs.

General Richard Secord is in business in Virginia, and is writing his memoirs.

Brendan Sullivan and his legal team continue to protect the constitutional rights of those they defend.

Lawrence Walsh, the vigilante who rode into town in 1986 as the special prosecutor, remains at large.

APPENDIX

THE WHITE HOUSE

WASHINGTON

November 4, 1985

Dear Ollie:

I have been told that on the door of your office
is a passage by Thomas Merton which reads "We
must be content to live without watching
ourselves live, to work without expecting an
immediate reward, to love without instantaneous
satisfaction and to exist without special
recognition." In today's modern world many
would challenge Merton's statement and ask why
we must be content to live this way?

Ollie, you and other great Americans throughout
our nation's proud history have fully understood
why some must live this way--it is because our
nation was built by men who dedicated their
lives to building our country for the sake of
their children and countrymen, without taking
the time to worry about receiving recognition
for their efforts.

To fully acknowledge your contributions to our
country would be extremely difficult even for
those who know you well, because your own
standards of conduct and performance are higher
than those which others apply. You are a man
who has devoted your life in the most unselfish
manner to building our nation. As a heroic
soldier in the field, as a military planner and
as an aide to me on some of the most important
issues of our time, you have proven yourself to
be an outstanding American patriot. Please let
this letter serve to speak to how much the

2

American people and I appreciate the patriotism
and sacrifice of you and your family. I am
proud to have LtCol Oliver North, United States
Marine Corps, on my team.

Sincerely,

Ronald Reagan

LtCol Oliver North
Deputy Director for
 Political-Military Affairs
National Security Council
Washington, D.C. 20506

ex. NORTH T. Knickers
11-27-85

Dear Oliver,

As I head off to Maine for Thanksgiving I just want to wish you a Happy one with the hope you get some well deserved rest.

One of the many things I have to be thankful for is the way in which you have performed, under fire, in tough situations. Your dedication and tireless work with the hostage thing and with Central America really gives me cause for great pride in you and Thanks — Get some Turkey

Gg Bush

en route to Kennebunkport
11-27-85

Dear Ollie,

As I head off to Maine for Thanksgiving I just want to wish
you a happy one with the hope that you will get some well
deserved rest.

One of the many things I have to be thankful for is the way in
which you have performed, under fire, in tough situations.
Your dedication and tireless work with the hostage thing and
with Central America really give me cause for great pride in
you and thanks—get some turkey.

George Bush

422 / OLIVER L. NORTH

The Honorable Ronald Reagan
President of The United States
The White House
1600 Pennsylvania Avenue
Washington, D. C. 20500

    Re: Request That You Use Your Power to Grant Reprieves
          and Pardons as Provided in Article II, Section 2 of
          the United States Constitution

Dear Mr. President:

      Executive clemency by pardon is requested by three
former government officials: Admiral John Poindexter, USN
(Ret.), LtCol Oliver North, USMC (Ret.) and Joseph Fernandez, CIA
Operations Officer (Ret.) before a trial begins. These men have
devoted their entire adult lives to the service of their country,
but tragically, despite their good faith, they have been indicted
for carrying out foreign policy objectives of The United States.

      The decision to grant or deny this request is entirely
within your discretion; it is not a decision encumbered by legal
technicalities, or issues about whether you have the power to act
or not. In matters of clemency there are no such issues. You
have unlimited power which comes directly from Article II,
Section 2 of the Constitution. For once, there are no judicial
decisions limiting your authority to grant Executive Clemency; no
requirement for legal opinions, no Congressional limitations or
notification requirements, and no obligation to confer with
Executive Branch Agencies or Departments. The decision is yours
alone to make as Head of State. It is a decision made after
reflection and prayer; a decision predicated on your sense of
what is right and what is not; a decision which takes into
account the interest of the nation as well as compassion for the

The Honorable Ronald Reagan
Page 2
November 10, 1988

individuals and their families who have become embroiled in this
controversy and suffered so much.*/

1. The National Interest Is Best Served by
   Exercising the Power of Executive Clemency

We believe that it is in the national interest to
put an end to the Iran-Contra controversy after two years of
intense scrutiny. The matter has been fully and repeatedly
investigated. It has been probed by numerous governmental groups
including the Tower Commission, a joint committee of Congress,
and several Inspectors General. Tens of thousands of man hours,
and tens of millions of dollars have been devoted to these
inquiries since November 1986. Enough is enough! The trials of
several individuals targeted by the Independent Counsel serve no
purpose except to prolong the agony for the country and the
people involved.

The nation cries out for an end to this matter.
Since LtCol North's testimony at the Congressional hearings in
the Summer of 1987, millions of Americans have made known their
views through polls and petitions that a Presidential pardon
should be granted. Never before in the history of our country
has there been such a spontaneous outpouring of support and
sympathy from the American people as that which followed the
televised hearings. Many in Congress were against the
President's policies, but the American people understood and
sympathized with the President's goals.

The victory of George Bush is significant because he
was elected by Reagan supporters who want a continuation of your
policies. It turned out that Iran-Contra was not an issue on which
the Democrats could win the Presidency -- although they tried to
make it the cornerstone of their convention and a major campaign
issue. Clearly, the American people did not disapprove of your

---

*/   Retired Major General Richard V. Secord and naturalized
      citizen Albert Hakim have also been indicted in this
      matter. This letter consolidates the pardon request of the
      three government officials. It is our opinion, however,
      that if a pardon is granted, it should include General
      Secord and Mr. Hakim.

The Honorable Ronald Reagan
Page 3
November 10, 1988

support for the Nicaraguan freedom fighters, or your efforts to save American citizens held hostage, or your goal of opening a dialogue with Iran. Had they disapproved, as the Democrats hoped, George Bush could not have been elected.

The Administration of George Bush should be free to build on the Reagan legacy of peace through strength and economic prosperity; it should not be preoccupied with protracted trials of former officials which will consume months and perhaps years. The new administration should not have its energies diverted from the accomplishment of its own objectives.

Between 1980 and 1988, Congress attempted to usurp the powers of the Presidency. In opposing your aggressive support of our national security interests, the Congress was willing to call the administration a lawbreaker. But because you are the most popular President of our generation, Congress was unable to inflict real harm on you or on the Presidency. Instead the attack has focused on others. The goal of your political adversaries was to dismantle the Reagan legacy; and the indictment of Admiral Poindexter, LtCol North and Mr. Fernandez was but one of the boldest actions in a continuing confrontation. But Americans have a keen sense of fairness. They see the prosecution of a few individuals as unjust, and they understand the controversy is kept alive by anti-Reagan forces who have always been on the other side of the political fence.

Further damage to our national security could likely occur if trials are permitted to go forward. During their government service Admiral Poindexter, LtCol North and Mr. Fernandez fought to protect the National Security and worked hard to guard the secrets of the nation. Now they find themselves in the bizarre position of being unable to defend themselves without revealing many of those same secrets in open court. Even the Independent Counsel has had to concede that the case deals with some of the nation's most tightly held top secret, codeword matters which, if disclosed, would cause severe harm to the national security.

The concern about protecting classified material is so great that defense lawyers were required to move out of their law offices into another building with a specially constructed Sensitive Compartmented Information Facility ("SCIF"), protected

The Honorable Ronald Reagan
Page 4
November 10, 1988

round-the-clock by armed guards and monitored by additional
government security specialists. The "SCIF" contains hundreds of
thousands of documents with the highest compartmented classifications. Court records indicate that exposure of some of these
secrets could result in loss of life. The nature of a trial is
such that some of this information is bound to become known. We
were witness to the foolhardy attempt at the Congressional hearings
to designate countries by letters of the alphabet, believing that
such a code would give them the protection they deserved. While
Congressional probers referred to "Country A" and "Country B," it
was not long before the press published the actual names.

The exercise of your pardon power would eliminate the
possibility of further harm to our national security interests and
would accommodate the desire of millions of Americans to put this
matter behind us for the good of the country.

> 2. A Trial of Admiral Poindexter, LtCol North and
>   Mr. Fernandez Would be a Terrible Injustice

The proceeding pending in the District of Columbia is
nothing more than a political trial. It is paid for by a
Democratically-controlled Congress, conceived by a special force of
volunteer prosecutors, supported by the Administration's
adversaries, and fanned by the media. The chance of obtaining a
fair trial is seriously in doubt. Never before has anyone been
compelled to testify on national television and later been
prosecuted for conduct which was the subject of that testimony.
Admiral Poindexter testified for five days and LtCol North for six
days. Mr. Fernandez testified for more than two days in executive
session. They were interrogated by numerous Committee lawyers,
Congressmen and Senators. The Congress assured the widest
dissemination of the testimony by conducting televised hearings
over our strongest objections and in the process "tainted" all of
the prosecution's witnesses and, undoubtedly, the potential jurors
as well. Moreover, any jury in the District of Columbia (a
Democratic Party stronghold) will undoubtedly be hostile to a
Republican Administration. These former government officials
should not be abandoned to a protracted fight in a criminal
courtroom where the jurors start off with a strong bias against the
Reagan Administration and its policies.

The Honorable Ronald Reagan
Page 5
November 10, 1988

        These men are fighting for their freedom against an
Independent Counsel who has assembled the largest and most costly
prosecutorial force in the history of our country. It consists of
more than 30 lawyers, 50 investigators, scores of staff members,
with offices in New York, Oklahoma and Washington. It is the only
entity in the United States Government which has an unlimited
budget. It has spent significantly more than 10 million dollars of
taxpayers' money to date. The goal of this prosecutorial army is
to convict and imprison Admiral Poindexter, LtCol North and CIA
Operations Officer Joseph Fernandez. Needless to say, these men
receive not one single penny of government money to defend
themselves against this adversary.

        You are known to be a President of strength and of
courage; a President who does what he believes is right. The
American people elected you to guide this country for eight
years. They look to you now to prevent injustice. These men
should not be singled out for prosecution and subjected to a
political trial aimed at destroying them.

        As President, you demonstrated extraordinary concern for
Americans held hostage and those victimized by terrorists. The
fact that you cared about the anguish of those citizens and their
families endeared you to the people of this country. Admiral
Poindexter, LtCol North and Mr. Fernandez are no less prisoners,
held captive here in Washington. Congressional hearings, investigations, and pretrial proceedings have already consumed two years
of their lives. They have become pawns in a dispute between the
Congress and the Presidency over the control of the foreign policy
of the United States. Please end this matter now -- before they
are subjected to further abuse for doing their duty as they saw it.

        3. Fairness, Equity and Compassion Warrant a
            Pardon Before Trial

        The devastating personal and economic impact on these
men and their families cries out for a pardon to terminate the
proceedings.

        A. Impact on Families. Admiral Poindexter has been
married for thirty years and has five children, ages seventeen to
twenty-eight. LtCol North has been married for twenty years and
has four children, ages seven to nineteen. Joseph Fernandez has

The Honorable Ronald Reagan
Page 6
November 10, 1988

been married for twenty-five years and has seven children, ages
five to twenty-two. The impact on their families has been
devastating over the last two years. What must it be like for
children to see their father vilified and attacked on the front
page of the newspaper and on television news shows night after
night, accused of criminal wrongdoing thousands of times? Perhaps
some of the older children can understand the nature of this
dispute which brings their fathers into the criminal courtroom, but
certainly the younger ones cannot. Several of these children have
observed their fathers under siege for a substantial period of
their lives. The wives and children of these men have been
permanently scarred by this experience. No courtroom victory years
away can make amends. Not even an acquittal can eliminate the pain
they have had to endure; pain which will only be exacerbated by the
lengthy and highly publicized trials they face. We are confident
that you understand the torment to which they have been
subjected. Only your intervention will allow them and their
families to resume normal lives.

          B. The Impact on Careers. Admiral Poindexter served
with distinction in the United States Navy for thirty-three
years. Among his awards was the Legion of Merit. He worked at the
National Security Council and The White House for five and one-half
years, tirelessly carrying out the goals of your Presidency. As a
Naval officer, he was suggested for appointment as Commander, Sixth
Fleet and was considered a likely future candidate for Chief of
Naval Operations. The termination of his career fifteen years
before mandatory retirement was a tragic by-product of this case.

          LtCol North's service at the National Security Council
during the period August 1981 to November 1986 was characterized by
selfless devotion to his country, to your administration, and by
the expenditure of limitless energy to achieve the policy goals you
established. His devotion to duty and willingness to sacrifice all
in accomplishing an assigned mission has become an American
legend. He is a decorated Vietnam war hero having received the
Silver Star, the Bronze Star, two Purple Hearts, and numerous other
awards. His career goal has always been to simply serve his
country by being the very best Marine Corps officer. Though he was
considered a likely candidate for promotion to full Colonel and
then to General, he was forced into early retirement by the
indictment.

The Honorable Ronald Reagan
Page 7
November 10, 1988

        Joseph Fernandez is a twenty-year veteran of CIA.
Throughout his career, Mr. Fernandez served in numerous overseas
assignments where he endured the hardship of working undercover to
facilitate the policies of the United States. Most recently, he
served as CIA's Chief of Station in Costa Rica where he struggled
against great odds to carry out the policies of this Administration
in Central America. After leaving Costa Rica, Mr. Fernandez would
have attended the prestigious Senior Seminar at the Foreign Service
Institute in preparation for further assignments at the highest
levels of CIA, both overseas and at CIA Headquarters. Instead, he,
too, was forced into retirement.*/

        All of these men served selflessly, often at risk of
their lives. Their careers were ones of family hardship, long
separations and frequent moves -- all for the benefit of this
country. The termination of their service by indictment and early
retirement is a travesty that will ultimately affect the morale and
steadfastness of others in the service exposed to rigorous
demands. Your pardon will not only help these three men and their
families who have suffered so much, it will restore the morale and
esprit of their brothers-in-arms.

        C. The Economic Impact. None of these men can find
normal employment so long as criminal charges remain pending. They
are simply unavailable to work because of the enormous amount of
time and energy that must be devoted to the preparation of their
defense. LtCol North has accepted speaking engagements in an
effort to help defray the cost of legal services and other
extraordinary expenses. Admiral Poindexter has taken a part-time
job and Mr. Fernandez is still seeking work. All have had to put
their lives and futures on "hold." Without a pardon, they will
have to spend the next years of their lives in the fight against
this unjust prosecution.

        As a result of the criminal litigation, they have
incurred costs beyond what they could ever hope to pay
themselves. They have had to deal with this devastation to their
lives and to their families' economic security without any help

---

*/   The indictment of Mr. Fernandez was recently dismissed in
      the District of Columbia without prejudice. The Independent
      Counsel stated that he will reindict the case in Virginia.

The Honorable Ronald Reagan
Page 8
November 10, 1988

from the government they served for so many years. Simple fairness
justifies your intervention by a pardon to stop this process before
further damage is done to them and their loved ones.

D. Safety and Security of LtCol North's Family. In
April 1986, LtCol North's life was threatened by the Abu Nidal
terrorist organization, but the government offered no assistance or
protection. A year later, in 1987, LtCol North and his family were
protected by a large contingent of Naval Investigative Service
(NIS) agents because of additional foreign terrorist threats to his
life which were uncovered by the FBI. His televised testimony in
the summer of 1987 created unsought worldwide visibility and
instant recognition which increased the dangers to him and his
family. His photograph was even distributed on the cover of
Pravda. Despite known dangers, the Congress televised LtCol
North's home address for the world to see during the hearings in
complete disregard for the safety of his family.

Political pressure from some in Congress, shocked by
North's popularity after the hearings, resulted in the government
protection being withdrawn. In place of more than a score of
government security specialists, LtCol North now must depend on the
charity of the American people to provide protection. Even modest
security of this sort is extremely expensive but the government
provides no help.

The continued visibility caused by a lengthy trial
increases the risk of harm to him and his family. They should not
have to endure those risks, and he should not have to live in fear
that his family could be harmed.

Conclusion

A pardon at this time, prior to trial, is fair,
reasonable, and in the interest of the nation. The country has had
enough of the Iran-Contra matter. It is particularly unfair to
permit a legion of prosecutors to single out these former
officials. Each one of them embarked upon a life of service to his
country knowing that he could be called on to sacrifice his life.
But not one of them could have anticipated this kind of
nightmarish, unending turmoil and disruption to normal life, to
families and to careers. It is too much to ask of even the most

The Honorable Ronald Reagan
Page 9
November 10, 1988

devoted soldier and public servant. This matter should be ended,
not only for these men but for the good of the country.

As your eight-year Presidency comes to a close, your
impact on this great Country is clear. You will always be
remembered for renewing our economic prosperity, for supporting
freedom and democracy throughout the world, and for achieving peace
through strength. You have shown understanding and compassion for
people yet, time and time again, demonstrated remarkable
strength. People know you as a President who does what he believes
is <u>right</u>.

A pardon of these patriots would put an end to the
Iran-Contra matter after two years of turmoil, would protect the
national security, and would permit them and their families to
resume a normal life. Put this matter to rest for the nation's
sake so that we can build on the foundation of peace and prosperity
you have given to all Americans.

Respectfully yours,

WILLIAMS & CONNOLLY

Brendan V. Sullivan, Jr.
Counsel for LtCol Oliver L. North, USMC (Ret.)

FULBRIGHT & JAWORSKI

Richard W. Beckler
Counsel for Admiral John Poindexter, USN (Ret.)

SEYFARTH, SHAW, FAIRWEATHER & GERALDSON

Thomas E. Wilson
Counsel for Joseph Fernandez, CIA Operations
Officer (Ret.)

INDEX